THE WEB PROGRAMMER'S
DESK REFERENCE

THE WEB PROGRAMMER'S DESK REFERENCE

A Complete Cross-Reference to HTML, CSS, and JavaScript

by Lázaro Issi Cohen
and Joseph Issi Cohen

NO STARCH PRESS

San Francisco

Printed on recycled paper in the United States of America

<1 2 3 4 5 6 7 8 9 10 – 07 06 05 04>

No Starch Press and the No Starch Press logo are registered trademarks of No Starch Press, Inc. Other product and company names mentioned herein may be the trademarks of their respective owners. Rather than use a trademark symbol with every occurrence of a trademarked name, we are using the names only in an editorial fashion and to the benefit of the trademark owner, with no intention of infringement of the trademark.

Publisher: William Pollock
Managing Editor: Karol Jurado
Cover and Interior Design: Octopod Studios
Developmental Editor: Hillel Heinstein
Technical Reviewer: Jonathan Hara
Copyeditor: Andy Carroll
Compositor: Riley Hoffman
Proofreader: Stephanie Provines

For information on book distributors or translations, please contact No Starch Press, Inc. directly:

No Starch Press, Inc.
555 De Haro Street, Suite 250, San Francisco, CA 94107
phone: 415-863-9900; fax: 415-863-9950; info@nostarch.com; http://www.nostarch.com

The information in this book is distributed on an "As Is" basis, without warranty. While every precaution has been taken in the preparation of this work, neither the author nor No Starch Press, Inc. shall have any liability to any person or entity with respect to any loss or damage caused or alleged to be caused directly or indirectly by the information contained in it.

Library of Congress Cataloguing-in-Publication Data

```
Issi, Lázaro.
  The web programmer's desk reference : a complete cross-reference to HTML, CSS, and JavaScript /
Lázaro Issi and Joseph Cohen.
      p. cm.
  ISBN 1-59327-011-9
 1. Web sites--Design. 2.  Internet programming. 3.  HTML (Document markup language).
I. Cohen, Joseph (Joseph David), 1969- II. Title.
  TK5105.888.I572 2004
  006.7'6--dc22
                                                              2003017497
```

DEDICATION

I dedicate this book to my wonderful wife of 45 years, Rica, who has been an inspiration and my shining light all these years, and to our nine grandchildren.

Lázaro Issi Cohen

Words cannot express the gratitude I have for my wife, Karen, and our three children, for their sacrifice to make this book happen. Karen's support and understanding have allowed me to pursue the writing of this book despite the long nights and weekends that it has entailed.

Joseph Issi Cohen

BRIEF CONTENTS

CONTENTS IN DETAIL

INTRODUCTION

PART I: FUNDAMENTALS

1
CASCADING STYLE SHEETS

2
OBJECT-ORIENTED PROGRAMMING:
THE DOM AND THE NODE TREE

3
EVENTS AND EVENT HANDLERS

4
JAVASCRIPT CORE LANGUAGE
AND FUNDAMENTALS

PART II: REFERENCES

5

HTML ELEMENTS

6

HTML ATTRIBUTES

7

EVENT HANDLERS

8
CSS ATTRIBUTES AND JAVASCRIPT STYLE PROPERTIES

9
MICROSOFT INTERNET EXPLORER BEHAVIORS

10
MICROSOFT FILTERS AND TRANSITIONS

11
JAVASCRIPT PROPERTIES

12
JAVASCRIPT METHODS

13
JAVASCRIPT COLLECTIONS

14
JAVASCRIPT OBJECTS

15
HTML+TIME MICROSOFT TECHNOLOGY

INDEX OF HTML, CSS, AND JAVASCRIPT LISTINGS
1069

ACKNOWLEDGMENTS

First, I would like to thank Lázaro for asking me to collaborate with him on this book. He has been my father, teacher, and mentor, and it has been an honor for me to work with him. Lázaro and my mother always emphasized education, instilled in me a strong work ethic, and supported me in the pursuit of my goals and dreams.

I would like to give special thanks to Hillel Heinstein, editor at No Starch Press, for his impeccable work ethic, patience, and dedication. Hillel has truly been an inspiration to me and has been instrumental in getting this book done.

I would also like to thank Bill Pollock, president of No Starch Press, for giving Lázaro and me the opportunity to make this book a reality. And a very warm and grateful thank-you to the rest of the No Starch Press staff: Leigh Sacks, Karol Jurado, Alex Benson, John Mark Walker, and Riley Hoffman.

Thanks to copyeditor Andy Carroll for his meticulous attention to every period, comma, punctuation mark, and style; and to Jonathan Hara, whose technical expertise helped fine-tune, correct, and improve many of the examples. Special thanks to software developer Gidon Shuly, who helped conduct the research necessary to gather all the information that has gone into this book.

There are also many people who have contributed to my professional growth, and I want to recognize them. They are Ron Frey, Andrew Conrad, Yaron Hankin, Mark Kane, Edik Magardomian, Cheynoa Schroeder, Ron Revilla, and Thuy Van Le from Autoland, Inc.; Larry Friend, Bob Hogan, Julie Liedalh and William Joe from Baker Commodities; Scott Loffman from Loffman General; Dave Mateer,

Ben Kershberg, and Nelli Kiritzov from American Honda Motor Corporation; Marti Vego, Orin Kohon, and Ana Melon from Career Options; Agnes Gunzler from Adelante Vocational School; Jawahara Saudali from Waterside; Robert Ghajar from Howrey Law Firm; Henry Misrahi from PubliTrade SA; and Laurent Cohen from Complices Jeans.

There cannot be enough said about the woman in my life who has given me so much inspiration, laughter, and happiness. My beloved wife, Karen, you are my Rock and my Strength. Thank you for your support and dedication, and for our three children. You are truly the love of my life.

Lastly, I would like to thank you, the reader, for giving this book its purpose. I hope you keep it on your desk, and refer to it often.

Joseph Issi Cohen

INTRODUCTION

Background

Lázaro Issi Cohen is a modern-day renaissance man. During the early years of his career, he taught high school–level physics and mathematics. In 1972, his photograph of the sound wave produced by a tuning fork won a prize, and in 1973 he wrote a book on crystallography and physics. He was one of the first in Spain to command Cobol, and published five books on the subject during the 1970s. Then, in the 1980s, he became an artist, producing one-man shows in Madrid in 1994 and 1998. Yet he never abandoned his passion for computers, writing some of the best technical books published in Spain, including recent works like *La Biblia de Flash 5, La Biblia de JavaScript, La Biblia de Flash MX, La Biblia de Flash MX 2004, La Biblia de Dreamweaver Ultradev 4*, and *Programacion con ActionScript para Flash MX*.

Lázaro is also my father. My first experience with computers came on my 13th birthday, when Lázaro and my mother gave me a brand-new Commodore Vic-20 with a one-year subscription to *Compute Magazine*. I fell in love with my Commodore from the first moment. My curiosity led me to experiment with the BASIC language, and I managed to write my own mini computer games.

But my passion remained a hobby until I was fresh out of college, when I began working as a career counselor for injured workers. After six months on the job, I realized that computers could play a vital role in making the efforts of the counselors more productive, so I went back to my programming roots and wrote my first Visual Basic application. I called it the Counselor Assistant.

Shortly, every counselor was using my program, and it increased productivity enough that the company no longer needed to hire outside clerical services. I had produced my first mission-critical application.

In 1995, my wife Karen and I moved for a year to Spain, where Lázaro lives. During that year, the Internet started to take off like wildfire and I became enchanted with the emerging capabilities of HTML.

As people began creating websites using HTML, they also became frustrated by its limitations. First, it was dull; once a page was loaded into the client's browser, the page didn't do anything but sit there, waiting for the user to request a different page or to submit some sort of information. Second, it wasn't visually interesting; it was difficult to control the positioning of HTML elements, and there was only so much you could do to spruce them up. Slowly, web developers and designers began to need, develop, and use new and better tools. The result was DHTML (Dynamic HTML), the combination of HTML, CSS (cascading style sheets), and JavaScript.

With JavaScript, static and dull HTML pages came to life. All of a sudden, boring HTML content could respond to user actions, creating immediate changes on the screen. No longer did web pages have to be submitted to servers for changes to take effect, and the result was an interactive web experience.

CSS provided the final piece. With CSS, you can customize the appearance of every HTML element in countless ways, and you can precisely control the organization of those elements on the page. For example, form input and submit elements no longer all need to be the same shape and style, and you can position elements without resorting to complicated tables with innumerable rows and columns. Furthermore, combining CSS with JavaScript, you can dynamically apply styles, making content on the page change its appearance, or appear or disappear entirely, according to user actions.

When I first returned from Spain, my initial consulting assignments required that I program in Visual Basic. In 1996, companies did not view the Web as a serious tool. However, with the emergence of Microsoft's ASP (Active Server Pages) technology, other server-side web technologies like CGI, and DHTML, all that changed. The business world finally began to realize the power of the Web. For instance, whereas applications written in Visual Basic or C++ required compilation and a new executable to be reinstalled on every single machine that wanted to use an updated version, updates to web applications were immediately accessible to anyone with access to the Internet or corporate intranet. Furthermore, because web applications depended solely on a web browser rather than a particular operating system, they had the added convenience of being cross-platform compatible. As the benefits of using web applications became clear, my consulting assignments gradually required more and more ASP and DHTML and less and less Visual Basic.

As a result, my year in Spain was the beginning of a career transformation for me. Since then, I have been fortunate to consult for many companies, including American Honda Motor Corporation, Warner Brothers, PacificCare, Autoland, and Baker Commodities. In the process, I helped create some interesting web applications, using a variety of development tools. Through it all, I have never lost my initial excitement for HTML, CSS, and JavaScript.

So, when during one of his visits to California in the fall of 2003, Lázaro asked me to help him embark on a very ambitious project, I did not hesitate. The result of our collaboration is the book you are holding now.

The Purpose of This Book

During the many years that I have been developing DHTML applications, I have never had the good fortune of having a single, complete reference book that allowed me to quickly look up how the numerous parts of HTML, CSS, and JavaScript work, and how they work together. *The Web Programmer's Desk Reference* is the interconnected DHTML reference book I always wanted.

This book was written specifically for web programmers. The Internet is a great resource of information for web programmers, but I have repeatedly found that locating exactly what I'm looking for can be more difficult and time-consuming than necessary. This book gathers all the information you need into one convenient place. Rather than having to search the Web for answers, you'll have them at your fingertips, on top of your desk.

What Is in This Book

This book consists of two parts. Part I includes the first four chapters, which serve as an introduction to the basics of HTML, CSS, and JavaScript. If you're an experienced web programmer, you'll very likely know much or all of the information in this first part. If not, the information in these chapters will help you become more familiar with these languages.

Part II is the core part of the book, the reference part, and consists of Chapters 5 through 15. Each chapter is dedicated to a topic, including HTML elements and attributes; events; CSS attributes and JavaScript style properties; Microsoft behaviors, filters, and transistions; JavaScript properties, methods, collections, and objects; and the Microsoft HTML+TIME technology. The reference items in each of these chapters are listed alphabetically, and practically every reference item comes with a Netscape and Internet Explorer browser compatibility listing, a brief description of how the item works, a syntax listing that shows you generally how to use the item, a list of possible values the item can take (where applicable), an example that shows you how the item can be used in practice, and lists that cross-reference all related items.

How to Use This Book

You can use this book in many different ways.

If you want to become a web programming guru, you can read it cover to cover. In this way, you'll come across web programming elements and techniques that you never knew existed, and you'll learn how to use them.

You can also use this book to look up elements that you're a bit rusty on. Perhaps you know what element it is that you want to use, but you've forgotten how to spell it, or you remember how to spell it but you've forgotten its syntax, or you remember its syntax but you've forgotten exactly which object it belongs to. Using this book, you can look up anything you need and figure out just how to implement it.

But you can also use this book as a cross-reference of HTML, CSS, and JavaScript. Let's say that you want to create a blue button with an interesting border, rather than the boring old gray three-dimensional button. You saw a similar one on some website months ago, but you can't remember the site's URL, and you have no idea how to get your button to look like that. To figure it out, you would begin by looking up the <button> element in Chapter 5. Looking at its syntax listing, you begin with the following code:

```
<button attributes events> . . . </button>
```

Next, you search through the list of styles appearing under the "<button> CSS Attributes and JavaScript Style Properties" heading for something that sounds like it might do the trick. The third style in the list is background-color, and about one-third of the way down the list you find border-style. Now, jumping quickly to Chapter 8, you look up background-color and find that you can use either a standard web color name, or a hexadecimal color in #RRGGBB format.

Because you read through the introduction to CSS in Chapter 1, or because you already knew how to apply CSS inline styles when you bought this book, you expand your code to the following:

```
<button style="background-color:blue;">Blue Button</button>
```

Now, you flip through Chapter 8 until you reach border-style, which points you to border-bottom-style for a list of all possible border style values. After some experimenting, you settle on the solid style value, and your code is now finished:

```
<button style="border-style:solid; background-color:blue;">Solid Blue Button</button>
```

Finding information in this book is that easy.

Testing Environment

This book contains over one thousand examples. The examples designed for reference items that are compatible with Internet Explorer were tested in Internet Explorer 6.0. For those reference items that are compatible with both Internet Explorer and Netscape Navigator, small changes may need to be made to some of the examples to get them to work in Netscape. The examples designed for reference items that are only compatible with Netscape Navigator were tested in Netscape Navigator 7.1.

Updates

Computer languages are dynamic in nature, and some of the references in this book may change. Any errata information for this book will be posted on its website at http://deskref.softsmartinc.com/. The website will also provide you with a forum for posting feedback.

Code Conventions

All HTML, CSS, and JavaScript code in the book is printed in a fixed width font to make it easier to recognize. You will also notice that parts of the syntax listings of most reference items are italicized. The italicized parts indicate code that cannot be used as is, but must be replaced with an actual element, attribute, event, property, method, collection, object, or value.

I

FUNDAMENTALS

In today's highly competitive web environment, where websites compete for our attention and the Internet has become a very important part of our economy, companies are forced to use ever more pizzazz to attract visitors. A few years ago, a website containing plain vanilla HTML was enough to attract visitors and possibly increase the business of its webmaster. However, today we have come to expect more from our favorite websites.

No longer is HTML able to handle on its own the demands of visitors who expect attractive, functional, interactive, responsive sites. These requirements are among the reasons why the World Wide Web Consortium (WC3) developed technologies such as cascading style sheets (CSS) and JavaScript. CSS permits greater control over the appearance and positioning of web page elements, and JavaScript allows for more dynamic control over web page content without having to wait for server responses. The result of the interaction between CSS, JavaScript, and HTML has been termed dynamic HTML (DHTML).

The four chapters in Part I of this book introduce the fundamentals of DHTML technologies, including CSS, the Document Object Model (DOM), and JavaScript. To fully understand the material in this section, however, you should already have some familiarity with the basics of HTML, DHTML, and JavaScript.

In Chapter 1 you will find a concise explanation of cascading style sheets. Chapter 2 provides a brief overview of object-oriented programming and how this affects the node tree structure in JavaScript. Chapter 3 deals with events and event handlers, and Chapter 4 will provide you with the basics on JavaScript.

Part I of this book will provide you with a foundation for the reference section in Part II.

1

CASCADING STYLE SHEETS

Once you add HTML elements to a page, positioning and formatting take center stage. At first, CSS consisted of two parts: CSS1 and CSSP. CSS1 was used for defining style rules in a style sheet, and CSSP was used to position elements on a page. However, the W3C consortium later decided to combine both parts into one, known as CSS2, and this book follows the recommendations of the CSS2 standard. CSS2 provides control over two important functions:

The style used to format the contents of a tag   With CSS, the formatting of a tag can be defined independently of its content. For example, the <table> tag tells the browser that a table has to be placed on the page. However, the formatting and style of the <table> tag can be defined separately in a style sheet. This makes CSS scripting simple and concise.

The positioning and dimensions of elements on a page   CSS will also allow you to set the size of an element, such as a <table> tag, as well as its precise location on a web page.

Style Sheets

Style sheets contain style rules that govern the formatting and positioning of specific elements on a page. Style sheets can be placed in different locations:

External   The style sheet is located in a text document separate from the web pagedocument.

Internal   The style sheet is defined in the <head> section of the page source code. (This is also known as an *embedded* style sheet.)

Inline   Using the style attribute, the style sheet is defined inside the <html> tag that is being formatted.

External Style Sheets

Style sheets can reside on the server as a text or JavaScript document linked to from the web page document. For example, a style sheet document called myStyleSheet.css, stored in the same directory as the page, would be referenced in the <head> section of the page as follows:

```
<head>
<link rel="stylesheet" type="text/css" href="myStyleSheet.css">
</head>
```

Do not confuse the <link> element with the <a> element; the <link> element must be specified in the <head> section of the page and requires the rel, type, and href attributes. rel identifies the type of document, "stylesheet" in the preceding example; type identifies the type of content in the linked document, "text/css" in the example; and href identifies the location of the document.

This method can be used to link large style sheets, or when several HTML documents will be using the same style sheet. If the size of the style sheet is small and is not used by multiple HTML documents, the style sheet rules can be included inside the <head> section of the page, as is explained in the next section.

Using the @import Rule to Connect with External Style Sheets

The @import at-rule allows the page to import a CSS document inside the <style> element tag without requiring the use of the <link> element in the <head> section of the page. The @import at-rule uses the URL of the document in place of the <link> element's href attribute. Here's an example:

```
<style type="text/css">
@import url(myStyleSheet.css)
</style>
```

As you can see in this example, you can use the `@import` functionality in place of `<link>` when referencing an external style sheet. However, there are no distinct advantages in using one or the other.

NOTE *All rules that start with the @ symbol are known as "at-rules." Another useful at-rule is `@font-face`, which allows you to download and use fonts in the page that the browser does not already have installed. Only TrueType fonts in an .eot type file format can be downloaded using this method.*

Internal Style Sheets

If a style sheet contains only a few lines of code, then it can be inserted directly in the `<head>` section of the page using the `<style>` element tag. Although the `<style>` element tag can be placed in the `<body>` section of the page as well, it is a better practice to include it in the `<head>` section. For example,

```
<head>
<style type="text/css">
p {color:red; font-size:3; font-family:Verdana}
h1 {color:blue}
/* more style rules can go here */
</style>
</head>
```

The preceding example contains two rules — one applicable to the `<p>` element, and one applicable to the `<h1>` element. Style sheet rules are preceded by the type of element to which they are applied (`<p>`, `<h1>`, and so on), and they are enclosed in brackets {}.

Don't confuse the style attribute with the `<style>` element. While the `<style>` element can contain several rules applied to several tags and must have a closing `<style>` tag, the style attribute is defined *inside* an element's tag using an inline style sheet.

Inline Style Sheets

You can define a single style rule inside an element's tag by setting the element's style attribute. For example,

```
<p style="font-family:Verdana; font-size:3; color:red"> . . . </p>
```

This example has a single rule that sets three style attributes for the `<p>` element being defined: the font is set to Verdana, the font size is set to 3, and the font color is set to red.

Style Sheet Summary

You can use style sheets in an HTML document in four ways:

- Use the <link> element inside the <head> section.
- Use the @import at-rule in the <style> element tag defined inside the <head> section of the document.
- Insert a <style> element tag inside the <head> section of the document.
- Insert the style attribute within an HTML tag.

Declarations

The combination of an attribute like text-size with its corresponding value, say 14pt, is known as a *declaration*. When defining a style rule, you must separate multiple declarations with semicolons. For example,

```
{ text-color:red; font-size:12pt }
```

This example contains two declarations; one sets the text color to red, and the other sets the font size to 12pt.

Selectors

Selectors allow you to apply rules to elements wherever they are used on the page. You can use selectors only when using external or internal style sheets.

There are simple selectors, like h1, and there are contextual selectors, which consist of several simple selectors, like h1 h2. The syntax is as follows:

```
element1 {style rule} // simple selector
element1 element2 {style rule} // contextual selector
```

Here is an example using the <h1> and <p> elements:

```
h1 {style rule}
h1 p {style rule}
```

Simple Selectors

A *simple selector* defines a style rule for a single element type (such as <h1>, <b>, or <p>), and the rule is applied to all elements of that particular type. For example,

```
p { color:red }
```

This rule specifies that the color of the text inside *all* <p> elements be red.

Contextual Selectors

Contextual selectors allow you to define the same style rule for multiple element types. Combining elements containing the same rule avoids repeating the same code for different elements. For example,

```
h1 em ul { color:red }
```

This rule specifies that the color of all text inside <h1>, <em>, and <ul> tags should be red. Each simple selector is separated by a blank space, thus forming the contextual selector. The preceding example is equivalent to the following three lines of code:

```
h1 { color:red }
em { color:red }
ul { color:red }
```

Using the class Attribute as a Selector

There is yet another way to apply a selector to various elements that do not share the same tag. You can define a rule with a class selector that can then be used by the class attribute available to all elements. Each separate class you define must have a unique name.

In the style sheet, the name of the class needs to have a period in front of it so that the browser recognizes it as a class. For example,

```
.wide { color: red }
```

In this example, all the elements that have a class attribute with a value of wide will contain the color red.

In the following example, the <p> element tag references the wide class:

```
<p class="wide">contents</p>   // the word "contents" will be red.
```

It is also possible to define different styles for different element types that have class attributes sharing the same value. For example, to give <p> elements of a particular class the color of blue, while giving all other elements of the same class a color of red, you could use the following code:

```
.colored {color: red}
p.colored {color: blue}
```

In the preceding example, all <p> (paragraph) tags that have the class attribute of colored will turn blue, and all other elements using this class will turn red. All <p> elements that do not contain a class attribute with a value of colored will not be affected by either class declaration.

NOTE   *Only one class can be specified per selector.*

Using the id Attribute as a Selector

Sometimes you may find it necessary to apply a style rule to a single element on the page, and not to all instances of the same element type. Simple and contextual selectors apply style rules to all elements of the same tag, whereas ID selectors apply style rules to a specific element on the page uniquely identified by the id attribute. The id attribute is supported by all HTML tags.

To uniquely identify one particular element in a style sheet, add the (#) symbol in front of the element's id attribute value. In the following example, the text color will be blue for all <h1> elements, with the exception of the <h1> element whose id attribute has a value of special, which will contain red text.

```
h1 { color:blue }
#special { color:red }
```

The following HTML example references the preceding style rule:

```
<h1 id="special">Header 1</h1> // Header 1 is red
<h1>Header 1</h1>  // Header 1 is blue
```

Summary of Using Selectors

You can apply internal and external style sheets to the page in the following ways:

- Simple selectors allow you to apply a style rule to a particular tag. All elements of that tag will be formatted according to the same style rule.

- Contextual selectors allow you to apply a style to multiple elements with different tags. All elements of the specified tags will be formatted with the same style rule.

- With the class attribute, you can also apply a style rule to various elements on a page. In this case, the style name has to start with a period (.).

- Class selectors can also be element-type specific. You can apply a class selector to a particular element type, causing the formatting rules to apply only when elements of that type reference the class. In this case, the class name has to be preceded by the element name, followed by a period (.).

- The id attribute allows you to apply a style rule to an instance of an element type. In this case, the style name has to start with the # symbol.

Attribute Selectors in CSS2

The CSS2 specification adds selectors that don't correspond with HTML specifications. These include *pseudo-classes* and *pseudo-elements*. Pseudo-elements are used to address subparts of an element, whereas pseudo-classes allow style sheets to differentiate between an element's various states.

As of this writing, the pseudo-class selector is only applicable to the <a> element. Pseudo-element selectors currently provide typographical effects, such as formatting of the first line in a paragraph or the first letter of a line.

Anchor Pseudo-Classes

Anchor pseudo-classes allow you to apply style rules to the `<a>` element depending on its current status: `link`, `visited`, `hover`, or `active`. You can define the styles of the anchor element using pseudo-classes, as follows:

```
a:link { color: red }      /* unvisited link */
a:visited { color: blue } /* visited links */
a:active { color: lime }  /* link clicked but button not released */
a:hover { color: aqua }   /* mouse pointer hovering over the tag */
```

In the preceding example, the `<a>` elements on the page would appear red when not visited, blue when clicked once, lime when active (meaning that a link has been clicked but the mouse button hasn't yet been released), and aqua when the mouse pointer is hovering over them.

At present, anchor pseudo-classes affect only `<a>` elements. Therefore, the element type can be omitted from the selector. For example, the following two lines of code accomplish the same thing:

```
a:link { color: red }
:link { color: red }
```

Pseudo-classes can also be used in contextual selectors. For example, the following style rule will be applied to all `<img>` elements and to `<a>` elements not yet visited:

```
a:link img { border: solid blue }
```

Typographical Pseudo-Elements

Using pseudo-elements, you can assign typographical effects to the first line or first letter of a `<p>` element.

The First-Line Pseudo-Element

The `first-line` pseudo-element selector is used to apply special styles to the first line of all `<p>` elements. This allows you to format the first line differently from the rest of the lines in a paragraph. In the following example, the first line of each paragraph would appear blue and in small caps:

```
<style type="text/css">
  p:first-line { font-variant: small-caps; color:blue }
</style>
<p>The first line of an article in a magazine.</p>
```

The following style properties can be applied to a `first-line` element: `font`, `color`, `background`, `word-spacing`, `letter-spacing`, `text-decoration`, `vertical-align`, `text-transform`, `line-height`, and `clear`. (For more information, see Chapter 8.)

The First-Letter Pseudo-Element

The first-letter pseudo-element is used for common typographical effects such as causing the first letter of the text within an element to appear in uppercase *(initial caps)* or to appear much larger *(drop caps)* than the text in the rest of the paragraph. For example,

```
<style type="text/css">
    p { font-size: 12pt; line-height: 12pt }
    p:first-letter { font-size: 24pt; float: left }
</style>
```

In this example, the font size of normal paragraph text is 12 pt, whereas that of the first letter of the paragraph is 24 pt. The float attribute is added to make room for the first letter because of its increased size.

The following properties can be applied to a first-letter element: font, color, background, text-decoration, vertical-align, text-transform, line-height, margin properties, padding, border, float, and clear.

Pseudo-Elements in Selectors

Contextual selectors are compatible with pseudo-elements, provided that the latter come at the end of the selector. For example,

```
body p:first-letter { color: blue }
```

In this example, the <body> and <p> elements share the same pseudo-element attribute, meaning that the first letter of the <body> and <p> elements will be colored blue.

Pseudo-elements can also be combined with classes to accomplish the same thing. The syntax, ElementName.ClassName:pseudo-elementName, is used as follows:

```
p.initial:first-letter { color: red }
<p class="initial">First paragraph</p> <!--the first letter is red.-->
```

The !important Attribute

The !important attribute adds more weight to a style rule declaration, meaning that it places the style rule at a higher level of precedence than other style rules that affect the same element (the precedence order of style rules is discussed in the next section). For example,

```
h1 { color:black !important; background:white !important }
p  { font-size:12pt !important; font-style: italic }
```

In this example, the first three declarations have increased weight, while the last declaration has normal weight.

Precedence

An element can potentially have various styles applied to it at the same time, and the different styles may have property values that conflict. *Precedence* defines the order in which styles are applied to elements on a page. The precedence for the various style rules is as follows:

1. `<body>` element style rules. If no style is present, then the browser applies the default rules here.
2. Styles defined through the use of simple and contextual selectors.
3. Class rules.
4. `!important` styles.
5. Styles defined through the use of a selector ID.
6. Styles applied "inline" with the `style` attribute.

This precedence order means that any style rule from a higher order (meaning those with a larger number in the list) will overwrite any conflicting rules with a lower order of precedence. Styles from order 2 overwrite those from order 1, order 3 overwrites order 2 and order 1, order 4 overwrites order 3, order 2, and order 1, and so on.

In the following example, the color of the `<p>` element would be red, not blue, because an inline style (order 6) has precedence over a style defined through the use of a selector ID (order 5).

```
<style type="text/css">
  #myId { color: blue }
</style>
<p id="myId" style="color:red">
```

Style Attributes and Properties

CSS attributes can be referenced in JavaScript code through the use of JavaScript properties. Table 1-1 on the next page contains a list of many commonly used CSS attributes and their corresponding JavaScript properties.

CSS syntax is *not* case sensitive, while JavaScript syntax *is* case sensitive. You can refer to the `border` attribute in CSS as `Border`, `BORDER`, or any combination of upper- and lowercase letters. However, in JavaScript there is only one way to write it correctly: `border` in lowercase. For more information on any of these CSS attributes and JavaScript style properties, see Chapter 8.

Table 1-1: Style Attributes and Properties

Box Attributes and Properties	
CSS syntax (not case sensitive)	**JavaScript syntax (case sensitive)**
border	border
border-bottom	borderBottom
border-bottom-color	borderBottomColor
border-bottom-style	borderBottomStyle
border-bottom-width	borderBottomWidth
border-color	borderColor
border-left	borderLeft
border-left-color	borderLeftColor
border-left-style	borderLeftStyle
border-left-width	borderLeftWidth
border-right	borderRight
border-right-color	borderRightColor
border-right-style	borderRightStyle
border-right-width	borderRightWidth
border-style	borderStyle
border-top	borderTop
border-top-color	borderTopColor
border-top-style	borderTopStyle
border-top-width	borderTopWidth
border-width	borderWidth
clear	clear
float	floatStyle
margin	margin
margin-bottom	marginBottom
margin-left	marginLeft
margin-right	marginRight
margin-top	marginTop
padding	padding
padding-bottom	paddingBottom
padding-left	paddingLeft
padding-right	paddingRight
padding-top	paddingTop

Color and Background Attributes and Properties	
CSS syntax (not case sensitive)	**JavaScript syntax (case sensitive)**
background	background
background-attachment	backgroundAttachment
background-color	backgroundColor

Color and Background Attributes and Properties

CSS syntax (not case sensitive)	JavaScript syntax (case sensitive)
background-image	backgroundImage
background-position	backgroundPosition
background-repeat	backgroundRepeat
color	color

Classification Attributes and Properties

CSS syntax (not case sensitive)	JavaScript syntax (case sensitive)
display	display
list-style-type	listStyleType
list-style-image	listStyleImage
list-style-position	listStylePosition
list-style	listStyle
white-space	whiteSpace

Font Attributes and Properties

CSS syntax (not case sensitive)	JavaScript syntax (case sensitive)
font	font
font-family	fontFamily
font-size	fontSize
font-style	fontStyle
font-variant	fontVariant
font-weight	fontWeight

Text Attributes and Properties

CSS syntax (not case sensitive)	JavaScript syntax (case sensitive)
letter-spacing	letterSpacing
line-break	lineBreak
line-height	lineHeight
text-align	textAlign
text-decoration	textDecoration
text-indent	textIndent
text-justify	textJustify
text-transform	textTransform
vertical-align	verticalAlign

Positioning Elements on the Page

Before CSSP, elements could only be positioned on a page using nested tables, the results of which were sometimes erratic, complicated, and too dependent on the targeted browser technology.

CSSP and CSS2 allow for much more precise positioning of elements. CSS2 allows us to position elements on the page in not just two, but three dimensions. The third dimension on the page is handled by the Z coordinate, and it allows us to stack and overlap elements.

The introduction of the Z coordinate has allowed for the concept of layers, and each element positioned using CSS2 is assumed to be in a layer. You can think of each layer as a content holder that exists in its own transparent plane above the base document in the window. Each layer is like a sticky note on a page; the content, position, and other properties of each layer are independent of the base document and of any other layer defined within the document. This layering allows for elements to be overlapped and to occupy an exact position on the page.

Microsoft and Netscape have taken the recommendations of the W3C one step further by transforming layers into scriptable objects, whose properties can change in response to user actions. This allows elements to be moved, hidden or shown, and dragged and dropped.

The Rectangular Container of Block Elements

Each block element on a page exists inside an invisible rectangular container. Block elements stand alone in the page, and each (whether it is a <p>, <div>, <ol>, or <table>) contains a line break before its opening tag and after its closing tag. In contrast, inline elements (such as <strong>, <b>, or <u>) do not have line breaks before opening tags and after closing tags. Each inline element belongs to a corresponding block element.

In DHTML, you can render rectangular containers with different styles and values by defining them in the style sheet, as shown in Figure 1-1.

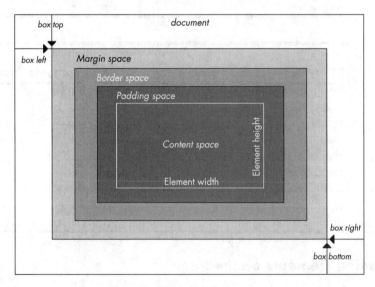

Figure 1-1: The rectangular container of block elements

NOTE   *For style sheet rules to work, you must use closing HTML tags with block elements.*

Cartesian Positioning

Each container rectangle is situated in the document using Cartesian positioning, meaning that its upper-left corner has a position relative to the upper-left corner of the page, whose coordinates are (0,0).

For example, if a block of text has the location (200,300), we know that the upper-left corner of the invisible rectangle containing the text is 200 pixels from the left border of the page and 300 pixels from the top of the page. This defines the exact position of the block element on the page.

The z-index

The z-index attribute determines the third dimension for positioning a layered element. The value of the z-index is an arbitrary integer that determines the front-to-back order of the elements on a page. Elements with a higher z-index are placed in front of elements with a lower z-index.

For example, to position the text "This is an image" in front of an image, the z-index value of the text would have to be greater than that of the image, say 25 for the text and 2 for the image. The numbers don't have to be consecutive; the only consideration is that one be greater than the other.

Nesting

In DHTML philosophy, elements are nested on the page. The base document is called the *top parent* element, and contains all other page elements. Any nested element, called a *child element,* can be a parent element too if other elements are nested within it.

Consider the following code:

```
<body>
<table>
<tr>
<td>text content</td>
</tr>
</table>
```

In this example, all the following points are true:

- The <body> element is the parent of the <table> element.
- The <table> element is the child of the <body> element and also the parent of the <tr> element.
- The <tr> element is a child of the <table> element and parent of the <td> element.
- The <td> element is a child of the <tr> element.

In this family tree, the font color is inherited from the <body> down to the <td> element. If you establish the text color as blue in the <body> tag, all text in the nested elements will be rendered blue.

Inheritance

The process by which child elements carry some of the properties of their parent elements is known as *inheritance*, though not all properties are inherited.

One effective way to create a default style for the entire page is to apply a style rule to the <body> element, which contains all other elements. In the following example, all elements within the <body> element's opening and closing tags will inherit its styles:

```
body { color:black; background:url(texture.gif) }
```

Visibility and "dragability" are examples of properties that a child element inherits from its parent (although you can override this automatic inheritance by setting the visibility property value in the child element). If a parent element can be dragged, then all its child elements are dragged along with it.

The z-index is another attribute that child elements inherit from their parents. For example, suppose that <p> is a child element of the <body> element and is also the parent element of <c1>, <c2>, and <c3>. If the <body> element has a z-index of 20, <p> will have a z-index of 20 inherited from the <body> element, and <c1>, <c2>, and <c3> will have a z-index of 20 inherited from the <p> element. On the other hand, the three children inside the <p> element must *also* have a separate z-index with respect to each other. In this case, <c1> could have a z-index of 2, <c2> a z-index of 5, and <c3> a z-index of 10. This means each child of the <p> element can have one z-index with respect to all other children of the <p> element, while at the same time inheriting the z-index of the <p> element with respect to all elements outside of their parent.

Positioning attributes are also affected by inheritance when relative positioning (default) is used. Child elements are positioned relative to their parent and not to the coordinates of the page. For example, if a parent element is located at (500,800) and a child element is positioned 100 pixels below it and 50 pixels to the right of it, the child element's coordinates would be defined as (50,100) and rendered as (550,900).

Positioning Elements Following W3C Recommendations

If an element *can* be positioned, CSS2 recommends that you include the position attribute in its style rule, whatever its value may be. For example,

```
<p style="position:absolute;">text</p>
```

The <div> element was introduced in version 4 of Internet Explorer and Netscape Navigator to create and position layers on a page. With the <div> element, you can define a layer's position, width, and height independently of its container rectangle. For example,

```
<div style="position:absolute; width:246px; height:132px;">text</div>
```

The following example shows how you can use absolute positioning to nest a `<div>` element inside of another `<div>` element, giving greater control over the position, width, and height of each:

```
<div id="Layer1" style="position:absolute; width:388px; height:299px; z-
index:1">This is the parent div element
   <div id="Layer2" style="position:absolute; visibility:inherit; width:246px;
height:132px; z-index:1">This is a child div element</div>
</div><!-- closing tag for the parent div element -->
```

To accomplish the same effect, you can use the `<span>` element within the `<div>` element, as follows:

```
<div id="Layer1" style="position:absolute; width:388px; height:299px; z-index:1">
This is the parent div element
   <span id="Layer2" style="position:absolute; visibility:inherit; width:246px;
height:132px; z-index:1"> This is a child span element </span>
</div><!-- closing tag for the parent div element -->
```

Position Values

With CSS, layers can be positioned on the page in three ways: static (which is the default), absolute, and relative.

Static Positioning

static is the default value for positioning an element, but it prevents an element from being repositioned later using a script. Moreover, static position values force elements to keep their location as assigned by HTML natural positioning, which is not very precise.

In the following example, the text will be rendered before the image, following the dictates of HTML natural positioning:

```
<p style="position:static">Some text</p>
<img src="someImage.gif">
```

In the following example, the image will be rendered before the text:

```
<img src="someImage.gif">
<p style="position:static">Some text</p>
```

Because static is the default position value, you can cause the natural HTML order to be used simply by leaving the position property unspecified in the `<div>` element. For example, the following two lines of code are equivalent:

```
<div style="position:static; color:red"></div>
<div style="color:red"></div>
```

If you don't want elements to appear in their natural HTML order, or if you want to add a dynamic dimension to a page, it is important to use relative or absolute positioning. Relative and absolute positioning are compatible with scripting, and only through scripting can you make changes and movements in a page.

Absolute Positioning

Absolute positioning is not only scriptable; by using it you can precisely situate an element on a page. The element can then be repositioned using scripting, without affecting other elements on the same page. Absolute positioning refers to the positioning of an element with respect to its parent element, and not with respect to the overall page unless the parent element is the document element. Don't be confused by the connotations of the word "absolute."

In Netscape browsers, only <div> elements and all other elements contained within <div> elements can be absolute positioned. For example, the image in the following code would have an absolute position:

```
<div style="position:absolute; left:100; top:50">
<img src="someImage.gif">
</div>
```

Internet Explorer allows you to apply absolute positioning to individual elements as well. Therefore, the preceding example could be coded for Internet Explorer as follows:

```
<img src="someImage.gif" style="postion:absolute; left:100; top:50">
```

If you want to design a single page for both browsers, the best way to go is to situate absolute-positioned elements inside a <div> element.

Relative Positioning

Relative positioning allows HTML to position elements according to their natural order in the page. In this sense, relative positioning is similar to static positioning. The difference between the two, however, is that relative positioning can be scriptable, whereas static positioning cannot.

Relative positioning is compatible with both Netscape Navigator and Internet Explorer, but can be used with the <span> or <div> tags only. Relative positioning allows you to change the location of elements in the page through a scripting change. As an element moves across the page, the other elements on the page are forced to make room for its new position. For example,

```
<div style="postion:relative; left=100; top=100">
```

This <div> element is situated at (100,100), but through a script command, you can situate it at (200,150) by changing the values of its left and top properties. You could trigger this command, for example, when the user clicks a button.

Static and relative positioning follow HTML positioning rules, while absolute positioning follows DHTML rules. You can move an element with absolute positioning across the page without affecting the position of the other elements on the page. Moving a relative-positioned element pushes other elements in the page to make room for it. On the other hand, you cannot move a static-positioned element at all.

Other Positioning Attributes

Other than the position attribute, the most common positioning attributes that you can add to the style attribute are as follows:

left and top   These two attributes specify the amount of space between the left and top edges of an element and the upper-left corner of its parent element. The left and top attributes are used to position the element's container rectangle (including padding, borders, and margins), and their values are most commonly represented in pixels, though you can use any of the units of measurement described in the next section. The values are applied to the position of the element as either absolute or relative, and they are not inheritable. Here is an example of how they are used:

```
<div style="position:relative; left=50; top=100"></div>
```

width and height   These attributes represent the width and height of the absolute or relative positioned element. They are used to define the physical dimensions of the element, and refer to the size of the content, exclusive of the element's padding, borders, and margin. Width and height are most commonly represented in pixels, but you can use any of the units of measure described in the next section. These attribute values are not inheritable.

z-index   This attribute specifies the stacking order of the layers in the page. Its value is represented by an integer, positive or negative. Elements with a lower z-index value are positioned behind elements with a higher z-index value.

visibility   This attribute determines whether the layer is visible or not. The value of this attribute can be set, or changed, at run time using a script. If the visibility attribute's value is visible, the layer and its contents will be visible; if the value is hidden, the layer and its content will be hidden; and if the value is inherit, the layer and its content will inherit the visibility value of its parent layer, if one exists. This attribute value is inheritable.

Units of Measurement Used in Attributes

The left, top, height, and width attributes have values that can be represented using several units of measurement.

The following units are commonly used for rendering pages that are displayed on the screen:

px Value in pixels. This is the most common unit used in web design. The precision of this measurement is subject to the monitor configuration of the user's computer. Example: 15px.

em This unit is based on the height of the element's font. When applicable, it is used with text content only. Example: 2.3em.

ex This unit is based on the height of the letter *x* of the element's font. When applicable, it is used with text content only. Example: 2ex.

The following absolute distance units are commonly used for rendering pages that are going to be sent to a printer for output:

in Distance in inches. Example: 2.50in.

cm Distance in centimeters. Example: 2.55cm.

mm Distance in millimeters. Example: 55mm.

pt Distance in points. A point is 1/72 of an inch. Example: 14 pt.

pc Distance in picas. One pica is equal to 12 points. Example: 2.3pc.

2

OBJECT-ORIENTED PROGRAMMING: THE DOM AND THE NODE TREE

The Document Object Model (DOM) allows HTML elements and their attributes to be manipulated using JavaScript code. There are two ways to program the elements in a document using JavaScript code: through the name of the element and through the node tree. These two methods are not mutually exclusive; they can coexist in the same script.

Introduction to Objects

What are objects? Basically, *objects* are scriptable, or programmable, elements that have properties, events, and methods. JavaScript considers all web page elements, the monitor's viewable screen area, and the browser window as programmable objects. This means that through code you can manipulate the properties of these objects, execute their methods, and trap their events.

Objects have properties, which can also be objects themselves. Imagine the human body as an example of an object. If you think in hierarchical terms, the human body object has a torso property, which in turn has a heart property, and the heart has chambers. All of these body parts are properties, and they are all related through a logical hierarchy to the main body object.

In the same way, any element in an object-oriented programming language, such as JavaScript, can be an object. All of these objects are related through a hierarchical system just as body parts are. For instance, the browser window is an object that contains several document objects, which in turn have form objects, which in turn have other objects, and so on. As you can see, the hierarchy can become quite lengthy.

Because of its object-oriented roots, JavaScript allows objects, their properties, and their events to be manipulated by scripts. And because most web browsers support JavaScript, it is the scripting language of choice for the client side of web page design (see Chapter 4 for an introduction to JavaScript).

The Period Operator (.)

The period operator (.) in JavaScript allows you to access the properties and methods of an object. Consider the human body example mentioned earlier. The humanBody object has a torso, which in turn has a heart, which in turn has a ventricle. If these were part of a real object hierarchy, they would be represented as follows:

```
humanBody + "." + torso + "." + heart + "." + ventricle
humanBody.torso.heart.ventricle
```

As you can see, the first period allows you to access the torso object inside the humanBody object. The second period allows you to access the heart object inside the torso object. And the third period allows you to access the ventricle object inside the heart object. This example has a hierarchy that is three levels deep. The period operator allows access to each object in the hierarchy, as well as to its properties and methods.

As another example, you could represent a portion of the human body extending from the torso down to the fingernail of the index finger of the right arm, as follows:

```
humanBody.torso.rightArm.rightHand.indexFinger.fingerNail
```

Browsers and Objects

As already mentioned, anything within the boundaries of the monitor's screen can be a programmable object, including the viewable screen area, the browser window, and the page inside the browser window. However, you can only program an object that is recognized by the browser. And not all browsers recognize exactly the same objects.

The collection of objects that a particular browser recognizes and supports is known as the *Document Object Model (DOM)*. The DOM also consists of the relations between these objects, their properties, and their methods. When you program for a particular browser, you must take into account the browser's DOM in order to code correctly.

Fortunately, the differences between the DOMs belonging to Internet Explorer, Netscape Navigator, and the World Wide Web Consortium (W3C, the international organization for Internet standardization) are not very great. This allows us to come up with a common set of programmable objects, or a common DOM. If you use this common DOM, you will end up developing JavaScript code that is compatible with most browsers. The common DOM is the focus of this book, and references to the DOM in this book are to the common DOM.

The window object is the parent object of all other objects in the DOM. You can think of the window object as the browser itself (be it Internet Explorer or Netscape Navigator). The window object, in turn, can contain a document object with a <head> and <body> section, or a <frameset> element. Each frame in a <frameset> element can contain a document object or another <frameset> element.

You can use window.self to refer to the current active document in the window object. When the window object contains a frameset that has nested framesets inside of it, you can use window.self to refer to the document in the current active frame, window.parent to refer to the document in the parent frame of the current frame, and window.top to refer to the document in the topmost frame in the current window or frame. The syntax is as follows:

```
window.self    //refers to the current active frame
window.parent //refers to the parent of the active frame
window.top     //refers to the topmost frame
```

If the particular document that you are trying to program for is located inside a specific frame, you can also refer to it by the frame name, as follows:

```
window.frameName
```

Every window object and <frame> element contains a document object, which contains all other objects in the page. The document object is the focal point from which all other objects in a web page are referenced. By programming the document object's properties and methods with JavaScript, you can create web page content on the client side at run time.

Properties

Object properties are essentially the adjectives that define and make up an object. For instance, suppose that a car object has two main properties, make and model. These two properties of the car object define what the car is.

For example, suppose John has a Ford Mustang. Represented using the object model, he has a car object with a make property value of Ford and a model property value of Mustang. If John were to get a new Volvo C70, you would set his car object to have a make property of Volvo and a model property of C70. Setting property values allows you to change the adjectives of the object.

With a simple property value setting, you can instruct JavaScript to display or hide a border around a frame. For example,

```
window.document.frame[0].frameBorder = "yes"
```

In this example, the window object has a document object, which in turn has a frame array, or collection. The frame array element with an index of 0 (the first <frame> element in the array) has a frameBorder property whose value has been set to yes. This means that a border will be displayed around the specified frame.

Properties can be *read-only*, or they can be *read and write*. The values of read-only properties can only be retrieved at run time, not changed. The values of read and write properties can be changed and retrieved at run time. An example of a read and write property is frameBorder, shown in the previous example. An example of a read-only property is appName, which retrieves the name of the browser:

```
var myAppName = navigator.appName
```

In this example, the value in the appName property of the navigator object is stored in the myAppName variable.

Methods

Whereas properties are the adjectives of objects, methods are the verbs of the objects, enabling them to perform actions. For example, if the wheel of a car is blue, the wheel's color property has a value of blue, as shown here:

```
car.wheel.color = "blue"
```

On the other hand, the wheel of a car can also be steered, which means that it has a method of steer().

```
car.wheel.steer()
```

Methods always end with parentheses, which differentiates them from properties.

Collections

A *collection* is an array of objects that are *not* related through the object hierarchy. In a human family, parents and their children are hierarchically related, but the siblings are not because they are at the same level in the hierarchy.

For example, John and Mary are married and they have four children: Charles, Brigitte, Olly, and Rose. The following syntax could be used to refer to the children of John and Mary:

```
John.Charles
John.Olly
Mary.Brigitte
Mary.Rose
```

However, the following hierarchical chains are incorrect:

```
John.Charles.Brigitte
Mary.Brigitte.Rose
```

While Charles, Brigitte, Olly, and Rose all belong to John *and* to Mary, Brigitte doesn't belong to Charles, and Rose doesn't belong to Brigitte. Because all the brothers and sisters are at the same level in the hierarchical order, they form a collction, or array, of siblings.

Each object in an array is known as an *element* of that array. To access the elements of an array programmatically, you must keep in mind the array syntax and the index of the element in the array. The index of an array element is determined by its position, starting with zero. For example,

```
window.document.images[0]
```

This example retrieves a reference to the first image in the images collection. image[0] specifies the first image, image[1] specifies the second image, and so on. Collections are discussed further in Chapter 4.

Nodes

Nodes provide another way of programming the HTML elements in a document. There are two types of nodes: *element nodes* and *text nodes*. An *element node* contains the element and the text inside the element's tags, whereas a *text node* contains nothing but text.

Consider, for example, the following code:

```
<p>This is a paragraph</p>
```

In this code, there are two nodes: <p>This is a paragraph</p> is a node that contains another node, the text This is a paragraph.

Here is another example:

```
<p><b>This is a phrase</b></p>
```

This example has three nodes: <p><b>This is a phrase</b></p> is a node that contains the node <b>This is a phrase</b>, which in turn contains a node, the text This is a phrase.

Table 2-1 on the next page contains a list of the different types of HTML nodes as defined by the W3C.

Table 2-1: Types of Nodes in the HTML Tree

Node ID	Node type	Node name	Node description
1	Element	Tag name	Any HTML element
2	Attribute	Attribute name	Any HTML attribute
3	Text	#text	Text that appears between the opening and closing tags of an HTML element
8	Comment	#comment	A comment
9	Document	#document	The HTML document
10	Document type	Document type name	The type of DTD document that is specified in the < !DOCTYPE> tag

A node that contains another node is the *parent* of the latter, and a node that is contained in another is the *child* of the latter. Child nodes that share the same parent are known as *siblings*. All nodes in the page have a parent node except for the document node, which only has child nodes. Whereas in the DOM the topmost object in the hierarchy is the window object, the topmost object in the node tree is the document object. The document node can contain other nodes, such as the < !DOCTYPE> and <html> nodes. In turn, the <html> node can contain other nodes, such as the <head> and <body> nodes, which in turn can also contain other nodes.

In contrast to the DOM, which allows you to program each document element without referring to any other elements, the node tree provides a way of programming HTML elements based on the relationship between elements. Let's look at how you would program the following elements, using both the DOM and the node tree:

```
<div id="myDiv">first sample text
<p id="myParag">second sample text</p>
</div>
```

Using the DOM, you can program the <div> element directly, as follows:

```
window.document.myDiv
```

Using the node tree, you can program the <p> element as a child node of the <div> element, or the <div> element as a parent of the <p> element:

```
window.document.myDiv.firstChild
window.document.myParag.parentNode
```

To access the node tree using JavaScript, you can use the nodeName, nodeValue, nodeType, parentNode, firstChild, lastChild, previousSibling, and nextSibling properties; the createElement(), createTextNode(), removeChild(), and replaceChild(*new, old*) methods; and the childNodes and attributes collections. For more information on these properties, refer to Chapter 11; for more information on the methods, refer to Chapter 12; and for more information on the collections, refer to Chapter 13.

3

EVENTS AND EVENT HANDLERS

Events occur when the system, or the user, interacts with a web page. Actions by a web user that will trigger events include clicking the mouse button and dragging an object. An event is triggered by a browser when a document is loaded in a window. Events can also be triggered using JavaScript code.

You can assign a JavaScript function or an object's method to an event, so that the code in the function or method is executed once the event is triggered. This process is called *event handling*.

Event Handlers

Event handlers allow a JavaScript function to be associated with an event through a JavaScript declaration using the following syntax:

```
onevent = function() { // JavaScript code }
```

As can be seen from the preceding syntax, event handlers are named by appending the word "on" to the beginning of the event name ("on" + event name). The event handler name is then assigned to the event handler function or method that will be executed when the event is triggered. So you have the event, the event handler, and the event handler function.

For example,

```
onclick = myFunction() {alert("hello world")}
```

In this example, click is the event, onclick is the event handler, and myFunction() is the action the event handler function will take once the event occurs. The click event will occur whenever a user clicks an object. However, the onclick event handler is not invoked unless the click event is associated with a function or method to be executed, as it is in the preceding example.

Event handlers do not belong to events; they belong to the objects where events are triggered. This means that an event can be captured by more than one object, depending on where the event occurs. For example, a click event can occur both on the web page and on a button in the page. Event handlers are used by objects, like a web page or a button, to capture the event and take some corresponding action.

For a complete list of event handlers, see Chapter 7.

Event Handlers Inside an HTML Tag

An event can be bound to an HTML element through the addition of an attribute inside the element tag. For some action to occur when the user clicks a button element, the onClick event handler has to be associated with the button. Similarly, to execute a script after a document loads, you must assign the onLoad event handler to the <body> element. These examples are illustrated in the following code:

```
<input type="button" onClick="alert('This is an alert window')">
<body onLoad="doSomething()">
```

Although HTML syntax is not case sensitive, it is customary to capitalize the first letter of the event name in the event handler (for example, "on" + Click = onClick). When the event handler is used outside of an HTML tag, as in JavaScript, it is written in lowercase because JavaScript is case sensitive (for example, HTML: onClick, JavaScript: onclick).

Event Handlers Inside the <script> Tag

Another way to manipulate events involves use of the <script> tag. In this case, the event handler has to be bound inside the <script> tag, like this:

```
<script language="JavaScript" event="onclick" for="elementName">
// event handler commands.
```

```
</script>
<element id="elementName"> content </element>
```

Event handlers inside the <script> tag do not require a function declaration. You simply put the event-handling code between the <script> element's opening and closing tags.

Event Handler Return Values

There are times when the commands in an event handler script cannot be executed, like when dealing with a non-scriptable browser (such as older browsers that don't support JavaScript, or a browser that has scripting turned off), or when a form cannot be submitted for some other reason. To handle these cases so that the browser does not pop an error message, it is necessary to return a value, true or false, either at the end of the function being used by the event handler or as a new declaration following the association of an event handler with its function.

Here's an example:

```
<a href="myDocument.html" onClick="dosomething(); return false"> . . . </a>
```

In this example, the return value comes inside the event handler attribute and outside of the function call. It is separated by a semicolon from the function call to indicate that it is a new JavaScript declaration.

Event Handlers as Object Properties

In scripts, an event can be assigned to an object as a property of that object. The period operator syntax (see Chapter 2) is used to define the relationship between objects and their event properties.

For example, suppose a <button> element named buttonName has the following place in the document object hierarchy:

```
document.formName.buttonName.onclick = doSomenthing;
```

As in this example, you must write the event handler name using lowercase letters because JavaScript syntax is case sensitive. Note also that the function name is *not* followed by parentheses. Although parentheses are usually required after a function name, we do not add parentheses when a function is being associated with a property.

The following example sets the function msg() as the action the onClick event handler will take when the myButton element is clicked:

```
<script language="JavaScript">
document.myForm.myButton.onclick = msg;
function msg() {
alert("The message");
```

```
}
</script>
<form name="myForm">
    <input type="button" value="Click me" name="myButton">
</form>
```

Capturing Event Information

When the system or a user triggers an event, you can *capture* the event using an event handler.

Prior to the release of Internet Explorer 4 and Netscape Navigator 4, events could only be captured as an attribute of an HTML element (see the "Event Handlers Inside an HTML Tag" section earlier in this chapter). For example,

```
<a onClick="function()"></a>
```

In this example, the onClick event handler is an attribute of the <a> element. This older methodology for capturing events is flawed, in that the HTML attribute, onClick, does not provide any information about the event other than that the event took place. When the user would click a button on a page, the Click event of that button would be triggered, causing the onClick event handler in the tag to be invoked. However, the location of where the click occurred and the identity the button that was clicked would be unknown.

After version 4.0 of Internet Explorer and Netscape Navigator, events became programmable objects with properties that carry relevant information about the event. Now a Click event is accompanied with information relating to the coordinates of the point where the click took place, and identifying which mouse button was used to generate the event.

In the following example you can see this improvement at work:

```
<script language="JavaScript">
function theButton() {
var x = event.button;  //event object has a button property
//this property indicates which mouse button was pressed.
if (x == 1) {y = "Left button was pressed."}
if (x == 2) {y = "Right button was pressed."}
if (x == 3) {y = "Both right and left buttons were pressed."}
if (x == 4) {y = "Middle button was pressed."}
if (x == 5) {y = "Both middle and left buttons were pressed."}
if (x == 6) {y = "Both middle and right buttons were pressed."}
if (x == 7) {y = "All three buttons were pressed."}
alert(y);  //pop-up message indicating which button was pressed.
}
</script>
<a id="myL" href="http://www.microsoft.com/" target=_blank
onMousedown="theButton()">Microsoft home page</a>
```

In this example, when the user clicks the `<a>` tag, the event handler `onMousedown` will execute `theButton()` function. The `theButton()` function then indicates via a pop-up message which button the user clicked.

Event Propagation

Another new concept added to event models is that of *event propagation*. Prior to Internet Explorer 4 and Netscape Navigator 4, an event was triggered only if an event handler was present; if the handler was not present, the event was lost, as if it never occurred. *Event propagation* refers to the way an event reaches its target, and to what happens to the event after the event handler function completes execution.

Every event has an object that is the target for user actions. The target of an event is sometimes obvious, such as with a `Click` event, where the button is the target of the mouse-related event. However, the targets of browser-generated events are not so obvious, as with the `Load` event, which is triggered once a web page is fully loaded.

Internet Explorer Event Propagation

The propagation model used in Internet Explorer versions 4.0 and up is known as *event bubbling*. In this model, the event bubbles from the target object of the event all the way up through the node tree hierarchy until it reaches the window object. For instance, if you click a button on a page, the `Click` event goes through the following objects in the node tree: button, `form`, `body`, `html`, `document`, and `window`, in that order. This means that you can set an event handler to any one of the objects in the node tree through which the event propagates.

To test this behavior, you can create a page with multiple event handlers and observe which events are triggered and in what order, as in the following example:

```
<html onClick="showSource('HTML', event)">
<head>
<script language="JavaScript">
function showSource(elem, myEvent) {
  var msg = "The click event, fired at " + myEvent.srcElement.tagName + " element,
is now at the " + elem + " level."
  alert(msg)
}
function starting() { document.onclick = docLevel}
function docLevel() { showSource("DOCUMENT", event)}
</script>
</head>
<body onLoad="starting()" onClick="showSource('BODY', event)">
Click the button, or on any part of this page.
<form onClick="showSource('FORM', event)">
<p><button onClick="showSource('BUTTON', event)">myButton</button></p>
</form></body></html>
```

In this example, when the user clicks on the `myButton` button, it causes a chain reaction of event handling that will cause the `showSource` function to be executed for the `button` object, then for the `form` object, then for the `body` object, then for the `document` object, and finally for the `html` object.

By default, events will propagate through the node tree hierarchy unless you turn bubbling off using the `cancelBubble` property. All event objects in Internet Explorer have a `cancelBubble` property, which, if set to true, will turn off bubbling. For example,

```
<html><head>
<script language="JavaScript">
function fn1() {
   if (window.event.altKey) {
      window.event.cancelBubble = true;
} else {
      window.event.cancelBubble = false;
}}
</script></head>
<body bgcolor="#FFFFFF" text="#000000">
Press and release the Alt key before clicking the image link to cancel the event.
The cursor default over a link is a hand, but pressing the Alt key changes it to a
regular arrow. The code restores the link after each click.
<a id="L1" href="http://www.nostarch.com" target=_blank>
<img src="yourimage.jpg" onClick="fn1()"></a>
</body></html>
```

Netscape Event Capture and Propagation

Netscape Navigator 4 was the first browser to introduce event handlers and the concept of *event capture*. However, because of the popularity of Internet Explorer, versions 6 and up of Netscape Navigator now use event bubbling as the method of event propagation.

Event capture was a model of event propagation that went in the opposite direction of bubbling. With event capture, event propagation starts with the highest level object in the node tree, the `window`, and propagates all the way down to the object targeted by the event. The event-capture mechanism is not compatible with Internet Explorer browsers.

4

JAVASCRIPT CORE LANGUAGE AND FUNDAMENTALS

JavaScript is a scripting version of the object-oriented language Java. The core of the language is embedded in most browsers, including Internet Explorer and Netscape Navigator. This core contains all the tools of the language, including the objects, and the properties and methods of those objects. The core language allows browsers to interpret any JavaScript code present in an HTML page.

JavaScript is responsible for the "D" (for "dynamic") in DHTML. It allows for dynamic interaction between the user and the page, and it can change content in HTML pages without having to go to the server. However, although JavaScript has great control over the browser and the HTML content therein, it has its limitations as well.

Versions of JavaScript

Like all programming languages, JavaScript is continuously being developed and enhanced. In version 1, now essentially obsolete, it was an attractive scripting language because of its promise rather than the functionality it actually provided. Later, version 1.1 was more robust and added more capabilities, such as the handling of arrays. More advanced versions have since been released, adding more functionality and promise. The current version is 1.5, although it has yet to be incorporated in all browsers.

In order to execute JavaScript code, a browser must have the appropriate JavaScript language core embedded in it. For instance, Internet Explorer 3.0 is not capable of recognizing functionality added in version 1.2 of JavaScript because that browser's core language set is based on JavaScript version 1.0. Table 4-1 lists the various versions of JavaScript that are compatible with Internet Explorer and Netscape Navigator.

Table 4-1: JavaScript Versions Supported in Different Browser Versions

Browser version	Netscape	Internet Explorer
2	JavaScript 1.0	n/a
3	JavaScript 1.1	JavaScript 1.0
4	JavaScript 1.3	JavaScript 1.2
5	n/a	JavaScript 1.3
6	JavaScript 1.5	JavaScript 1.5
7	JavaScript 1.5	n/a

What Can JavaScript Do for You?

JavaScript allows you to do all of the following:

- Maximize interactivity between the user and the page.
- Validate data at the browser level, without requiring a round trip to the server.
- Create a shopping cart at the browser level.
- Handle a relatively small amount of data.
- Handle applets and plug-ins inside multiple HTML frames.
- Preprocess information before it is submitted to the server.

Of course, it is equally important that you are aware of JavaScript's limitations. The limitations listed next are due to security and privacy concerns, not because it is impossible to incorporate this functionality in future JavaScript versions. JavaScript cannot do any of the following:

- Establish or change browser options without the user's permission.
- Execute an application in the browser's computer.
- Read or write documents in the browser's computer.

- Write documents on the server.
- Read the server's directory.
- Capture information from the server.
- Send email from the user's email address.

Client-Side JavaScript

When the language interpreter, or core, is embedded inside a browser, it is known as *client-side* JavaScript, meaning that JavaScript is executed in the browser. However, Microsoft has not only implemented JavaScript (using the European Computer Manufacturers Association (ECMA) standard) in its browser technology, it has also made use of JavaScript in the realm of ASP (Active Server Pages). When JavaScript is embedded in a server, it is known as *server-side* JavaScript.

NOTE *ECMA is an international standardization organization in charge of defining JavaScript standards.*

The examples and explanations in this book all refer to client-side JavaScript. JavaScript is not the only scripting language embedded in browsers, but it is the most common one, without a doubt. In Internet Explorer, Microsoft also makes use of VBScript, which is a limited scripting version of Visual Basic. However, one of VBScript's shortcomings is that it is not recognized by competing browsers, such as Netscape Navigator. Additionally, VBScript does not come as a valid scripting language for Internet Explorer right out of the box, and a default Internet Explorer setting must be changed to enable its recognition of VBScript. These reasons make VBScript more challenging to use as a programming language of choice.

Including JavaScript Code in an HTML Page

One of the great advantages of JavaScript is that its code can be resolved right on an HTML page, meaning that browsers do not have to ask questions of the server in order to interpret each declaration. This saves the server a great deal of time and resources, as well as Internet bandwidth.

The <script> tag is used to embed JavaScript code in a page. However, because scripts can be written in languages other than JavaScript, such as Microsoft's VBScript, you must specify the language attribute in the <script> tag, as follows:

```
<script language="JavaScript">
//JavaScript code goes here
</script>
```

Although this tag tells browsers that JavaScript code has been included in the page, some older versions of browsers are not capable of handling JavaScript. Additionally, some users may choose to disable JavaScript in their browser.

These two scenarios can cause the code placed between the <script> and </script> tags to be misinterpreted and displayed on the web page as text. When JavaScript is not interpreted correctly, the code will not be executed, and the user will not understand why there are weird "code-like" characters on the page.

To avoid this problem, you can place the JavaScript code between HTML comment tags. This approach will not prevent browsers that support JavaScript from interpreting the code correctly, while browsers that do not support JavaScript ignore anything that is between the HTML comment tags. For example,

```
<script language="JavaScript">
<!-- begin concealing JavaScript from browsers not supporting it
//JavaScript code goes here.
//--> end concealing JavaScript from browsers not supporting it
</script>
```

Many beginners confuse the order in which the <script> and comment tags are placed. To avoid confusion, remember that you must place the <script> tag first, to tell the browser that JavaScript code is going to be embedded, followed by the HTML comment tags.

The closing HTML comment tag, -->, is preceded by the two slashes (//), which the browser knows identify JavaScript comments. This is necessary so that the browser does not get confused and erroneously try to interpret the HTML closing tag as JavaScript code.

The <script> tag can be included either in the <head> section or the <body> section of the page. However, where you decide to place the <script> tag can have some ramifications on the page. If the JavaScript code is small and it deals with a specific element on the page, you may find it more convenient to include the code close to the relevant element, within the <body> section. If, on the other hand, the code needs to be executed at the time the document is loaded, you are better off including it in the <head> section, as in the following example:

```
<html>
<head>
<title>My first script</title>
<script language="JavaScript">
<!--
document.write("Hello, World!")
//-->
</script></head><body></body></html>
```

JavaScript and HTML Case Sensitivity

JavaScript code can be embedded inside the <head> section of an HTML page, but it can also be mixed in with HTML commands. However, because JavaScript and HTML share some command names, and because JavaScript is case sensitive and HTML is not, you must pay close attention when mixing HTML commands with

JavaScript code. In JavaScript, lowercase and uppercase matter. All the words used in the code — reserved words, special identifiers, names, and functions — must be coded keeping in mind the correct case.

For example, onclick is a keyword that is used in both JavaScript and HTML. In HTML it can be written in uppercase, lowercase, or in any combination of both: onClick, OnClick, onclick, and ONCLICK are all acceptable in HTML. In contrast, JavaScript code requires that this command be written in lowercase: onclick.

JavaScript Declarations

In JavaScript, each line of code is considered a *declaration*. To create a new declaration, you must introduce either a carriage return (by pressing ENTER) or a semicolon after the previous line of code. Although a semicolon is not required after each declaration, it is considered best practice to follow all JavaScript declarations with a semicolon. For example,

```
X = 100
Y = 100; //two declarations separated by a carriage return
X = 100; y = 200; //two declarations separated by a semicolon
```

NOTE *When you comment a block of code that wraps into more than one line, the browser will continue to interpret the block as one line of code as long as you do not include a carriage return between the lines.*

Using JavaScript Declarations Inside HTML

Using declarations, the JavaScript protocol enables code to be inserted within an HTML tag. Within the HTML tag, each declaration must end with a semicolon, as follows:

```
javascript: declaration1; declaration2; . . . declarationN;
```

In this manner, short code snippets or function calls (more about functions in the "Functions" section of this chapter) can be associated with an attribute of an HTML element.

One area where JavaScript can be used inside an HTML tag is in the href attribute of the <a> element tag. For example, suppose you have already declared the act() function in the <script> section of the page, and you wish to execute the function when the user clicks a link. You would accomplish this as follows:

```
<a href="javascript:act();"> . . . </a>
```

To insert a short code snippet in the href attribute, each separate JavaScript declaration needs to be separated by a semicolon:

```
<a href="javascript: var x = "hello"; alert(x);"> . . . </a>
```

Variables

Variables are placeholders — bits of information physically stored in the computer's memory that can contain different values at different times. Variables are defined by their *identifiers*, or *variable names*, and, as such, must follow the rules for naming identifiers. The following are all valid variable names: x, y, and my_variable.

The rules for naming identifiers require that the first character be an uppercase or lowercase letter, a dollar sign ($), or an underscore character (_). An identifier cannot start with a number. Any character other than the first can be a letter, number, dollar sign, or underscore character. You may not use spaces when naming an identifier.

Types of Variables

There are two types of variables: *global* and *private*. *Global variables* are available to all JavaScript code in the page and are kept in memory as long as the page is running. Global variables must be declared using the JavaScript reserved word var. For example,

```
var x = "Hello World";  //global variable is declared
function helloWorld(){
alert(x);  //contents of x are displayed in a message box
}
```

Private variables, on the other hand, live only inside the function where they are defined (functions will be discussed in the "Functions" section of this chapter). When the application completes execution of the function, private variables are removed from memory. When declaring private variables, the var reserved word is not required, although most programmers still use it for clarity. For example,

```
function helloWorld(){
var x = "Hello World"; //variable is declared
alert(x); //contents of x are displayed in a message box
}
```

JavaScript Reserved Words

As is the case in other programming languages, JavaScript has a number of reserved words that already have significance at the interpreter level. Consequently, you may only use reserved words for their predefined use (such as var, which declares a variable for use), not as identifiers in the code. Table 4-2 contains an alphabetical list of all the JavaScript reserved words.

Table 4-2: JavaScript Reserved Words

abstract	else	instanceof	switch
boolean	enum	int	synchronized
break	export	interface	this
byte	extends	long	throw
case	false	native	throws
catch	final	new	transient
char	finally	null	true
class	float	package	try
const	for	private	typeof
continue	function	protected	var
debugger	goto	public	void
default	if	return	volatile
delete	implements	short	while
do	import	static	with
double	in	super	

Working with Data

Variables, as well as all other language components, are always dealing with data. The most common data types that JavaScript handles are strings, numbers, and Booleans.

String Data

String data can include any character or sequence of characters, including numbers. In JavaScript, string data is denoted by its being enclosed in double or single quotes. The following are all examples of valid strings: "250", '025a', "same", and 'same_language_version_1.2'.

The following shows how to use strings in code:

```
var x; //declare a variable to hold the string
x = 'hello world'; //set the string to the variable
document.write(x) //send the string in the variable to the document
```

Occasionally, the string itself will contain a single or double quote, as this string does: this is my "first" message. At first, one might try to write this in JavaScript as the following:

```
"this is my "first" message"
```

However, browsers will interpret the preceding line as two different strings of text that are separated by an unrecognized word. The first of the recognized strings will be "this is my ", including a space after the word my. The second of the strings will be " message", including a space before the word message. Finally, the word that JavaScript will not understand is first.

The solution to the problem of strings with embedded double quotes is to replace the double quotes with single quotes, as follows:

```
"this is my 'first' message"
```

Or, if you are using single quotes to enclose the string, use double quotes for the internal part:

```
'this is my "first" message'
```

However, what if the string has more than one word enclosed in quotes? There are two scenarios. First, if the words between quotes are not nested between another set of quotes, follow the previous example. For example, the string this is my "first" message using "JavaScript" would be written as

```
"this is my 'first' message using 'JavaScript'"
```

The other scenario is where the words quoted in the string are nested between another set of quotes. In that case, you must alternate single quote strings and double quote strings, like this:

```
"........'........".........."........'.........."
```

The rule for nesting quotes requires that when a string begins with double quotes, and then contains a single quote inside of the double quotes, the single quote must be closed before the double quote can be closed. This is similar to the rules applied to nesting HTML tags:

```
<p><b><i> . . . </i></b></p>
```

Another way you can handle nested quotes is to use *quote escapes.* JavaScript allows you to introduce special characters in a string through the use of a backslash (\), also known as an escape sequence (Table 4-3 contains a complete list of the JavaScript escape sequences). Quote escapes use a backslash followed by the double quote (\") to replace each double quote encountered in the string. For example, the string this is my "first" message using "JavaScript" can be coded as follows:

```
"this is my \"first\" message using \"JavaScript\""
```

Table 4-3: JavaScript Escape Sequences in Strings

Escape sequence	Description
\"	Used in place of double quotes (")
\'	Used in place of single quote (')
\\	Used in place of a backslash (\)
\b	Used in place of a backspace
\t	Used in place of a tab
\n	Used in place of a carriage return and a line feed
\r	Used in place of a carriage return only

Escape sequences are used in JavaScript exclusively, and should not be confused with HTML special characters. For example, in JavaScript a carriage return and line feed are achieved using the \n escape sequence, whereas in HTML the <br> or <p> tags are used to achieve the same thing.

Concatenating String Data

Just as numbers can be added, strings can be *concatenated,* meaning that two or more strings can be combined into one longer string. The following code concatenates three strings: "Hi, ", "Reader", and "!".

```
var name = "Reader"
var message = "Hi, " + name + "!"
alert(message);
```

This will produce the resulting string "Hi, reader!". Here, the plus sign (+) is used to concatenate the three strings.

In JavaScript, the plus sign (+) can both concatenate strings and sum numbers. When concatenating strings, it is important to remember to add spaces between words. This is often overlooked in coding and can lead to some embarrassing results.

Numbers

JavaScript has two types of numbers: *integers* and *floats*. Integers have no decimal component, whereas float numbers have a decimal component and an integer component. For example,

```
5 + 6 = 11 //results in an integer
5 + 6.2 = 11.2 //results in a float number
5.8 + 6.2 = 12 //results in an integer
```

Numbers that are used in arithmetical operations are written in JavaScript the same way they are written in most other common languages, without quotes. The only special rule in JavaScript is that a number cannot start with a zero, except for the zero value (which is represented by a 0), or when representing a decimal value that is less than 1. All the following are examples of valid numbers: 25, 3, 0, 12.25, 0.25, 10000000. However, 00000001 is not a valid number in JavaScript.

NOTE *Use integers whenever possible to increase code efficiency.*

Working with Numbers

In JavaScript, you work with numbers using mathematical computations. The most common computations involve the basic *arithmetic operators*, like addition (+), subtraction (-), multiplication (*), and division (/).

Operators save countless lines of code because they replace longer phrases or words that mean the same thing. Many actions can take place in a single declaration, thanks to operators. For instance, "5 plus 4 minus 2" is represented in code as "5 + 4 – 2", making it more compact.

Table 4-4 contains a complete listing of the JavaScript arithmetic operators.

Table 4-4: JavaScript Arithmetic Operators

Operator	Name	Description
+	Plus	Can be applied to numbers and strings; with numbers it sums, and with strings it concatenates
-	Minus	Applies only to numbers
*	Multiply	Applies only to numbers
/	Divide	Applies only to numbers
%	Modulo	Returns the remainder of division of two values; for example, 10%4 = 2
++	Increment	Increments the value of a number or variable by one; for example, 4++ = 5
--	Decrement	Decrements the value of a number or variable by one; for example, 4– = 3
+	Positive value	Converts a numeric string to a corresponding positive number
-	Negative value	Converts a numeric string to a corresponding negative number

The rule of mathematical precedence must be strictly followed when using these operators in complex formulas. The rule dictates that computations in parentheses are performed first, multiplication and division are performed next, and addition and subtraction are performed last.

For example,

```
x = (100 * 2) + 100 / (2 + 3)
```

In the preceding mathematical operation, JavaScript will first compute the values inside the parentheses, as follows:

```
x = (200) + 100 / (5)
```

Then, JavaScript will perform the multiplication and division operations, resulting in the following:

```
x = (200) + 20
```

Finally, addition and subtraction are performed last, as follows:

```
x = 220
```

Converting a Number to a String

You can convert a number to a string using the toString() function. This is useful when you need to concatenate a number and a string. Here are some examples:

```
12345.toString(); //result is "12345"
var dollars = 568
dollars.toString(); //result is "568"
alert("The amount owed is " + dollars.toString());
//display a message box that shows "The amount owed is 568"
alert("The amount owed is " + dollars); //implicit conversion
```

In the last declaration above, when you try to concatenate a string and a number together, the toString() function will be implicitly invoked, and the number will be converted to a string automatically.

Converting a String Literal to a Number

The functions that convert a string to a number are parseInt() and parseFloat(). This is the syntax for those two functions:

```
parseInt(string); //returns an integer
parseFloat(string); //returns an integer or a float
```

Both of these functions turn a string into a number, but parseInt() only returns the integer portion of the string, whereas parseFloat() returns the integer and decimal portions. For example,

```
parseInt("56"); //result = 56
parseInt("56.32"); //result = 56, works with the integer only
parseFloat("56.32"); //result = 56.32, returns the decimal portion
parseFloat("56"); //result = 56
parseFloat("Aries"); //result = NaN (Not a Number)
```

The parseInt() and parseFloat() functions begin to evaluate a string from its first character. If the first character is not a number, then the functions will return NaN (not a number), no matter what follows in the string. However, if the string begins with a number, the function will continue to evaluate the string until either no more characters remain or a nonnumeric character is encountered.

Booleans

Boolean data can take one of only two possible values: true or false. This type of data is necessary in conditional code, such as if statements (discussed in the "Conditional Structures: If, If . . . Else, If . . . Else If" section later in this chapter). For example, the altKey property of the event object is a Boolean value. In the following example it returns true if the ALT key is held down, and false if it is not held down:

```
<script language="JavaScript">
function B1() {
var m = event.altKey;
if (m == false) {
alert("The Alt key is not pressed")
} else if(m == true) {
alert("The Alt key is pressed")
}}
</script>
```

Null Values

In addition to string, numeric, and Boolean values, a JavaScript variable can also contain a null value, meaning that the variable has no value at all. Zero is not the same as null, because the number 0 is a value. If a variable is set to null during program execution, it means that at that point it has no value.

The null value can be put to practical use, as JavaScript has functionality that allows you to test whether a variable contains a null value.

```
<script language=javascript>
var m = document.all.myTable.caption;
if (m==null) { alert('this table has no caption') }
</script>
<table id="myTable">
</table>
```

Because the myTable table has no caption, the document.all.myTable.caption property has a null value.

Undefined Values

While not a value, *undefined* is another variable state that you may encounter at some point. JavaScript uses this expression in place of a value when one of the following scenarios is encountered:

- A variable does not exist, or has not been defined, but yet is referenced in the code.
- A variable that has no value is referenced in code.
- A property is associated with an object, but the object does not contain that property (objects are discussed in the "Objects" section later in the chapter).

Assignment Operators

To incorporate variables with number, string, and Boolean data, you must use *assignment operators*. In a formula using an assignment operator, the expressions to the left and right of the operator are both called *operands*. For example, in the assignment x = 1, both x and 1 are operands, and = is the operator. Table 4-5 provides a complete list of JavaScript assignment operators:

Table 4-5: JavaScript Assignment Operators

Operator	Description
=	Assigns the value of the right operand to the left operand
+=	Adds the left and right operands (x += y is the same as x = x + y)
-=	Subtracts the right operand from the left (x -= y is the same as x = x - y)
*=	Multiplies the left and right operands (x *= y is the same as x = x * y)
/=	Divides the left operand by the right (x /= y is the same as x = x / y)
%=	Takes the remainder of the operands (x %= y is the same as x = x % y)

Assignment operators assign the value on the right side of the operator to the expression on the left side. For example,

```
x = 100; //x is assigned the value of 100
```

Comparative Operators

Comparative operators are used to perform data comparisons between numeric, string, and Boolean values. The result of a comparative operation is always a Boolean value, either true or false. Table 4-6 lists the JavaScript comparative operators.

Table 4-6: JavaScript Comparative Operators

Operator	Description
==	Asks whether the left operand is equal to the right operand
!=	Asks whether the left operand is different from the right operand
===	Similar to ==, but for an expression using === to resolve as true, the left and right operands must be equal and of the same data type
!==	Similar to =!, but for an expression using !== to resolve as false, the left and right operands must be equal and of the same data type
>	Asks whether the left operand is greater than the right operand
<	Asks whether the left operand is less than the right operand
>=	Asks whether the left operand is greater than or equal to the right operand
<=	Asks whether the left operand is less than or equal to the right operand

The equal sign (=) is an assignment operator, and it is not one of the comparative operator types. To illustrate the difference, the expression x=5 assigns a value of five to the variable x, whereas the expression x==5 would determine whether or not the value of the variable x is in fact 5. The following are all examples of the use of comparative operators:

```
10 == 10 //true
9 < 10 //true
9 > 10 //false
11 != 10 //true
5.99 <= 5.98 //false
"Carlos" == "carlos" //false, JavaScript is case sensitive
"Carlos" === "Carlos" //true
```

The === and !== operators were introduced in JavaScript version 1.2 for a good reason. JavaScript interprets these operators differently from the more commonly used == and != operators.

The difference between === and == becomes apparent when comparing two variables that have the same value, but one is a string and the other is a number. For example:

```
a = "125"
b = 125
a == b //returns true, although "125" is a string and 125 is a number
a === b //returns false because a is a string and b is a number
```

Logical Operators

Logical operators (aka *Boolean operators*) are used to make logical comparisons between variables or between strings. The three logical operators are listed in Table 4-7.

Table 4-7: JavaScript Logical Operators

Operator	Description
&&	Logical AND
||	Logical OR
!	Logical NOT

Here is an example of the logical NOT operator at work:

```
!true //result is false, because not true = false
```

Logical operators can also be combined with other operators in a single expression. For example, you can use logical operators when testing more than one condition, as in the following example:

```
(8 > 3)||(5 < 2) //result is true, at least one condition is true.
```

In the preceding example, there are two tests. The first test, 8 > 3, is true, and the second test, 5 < 2, is false. The result of the entire expression, (8 > 3)||(5 < 2), is true, because when using the logical OR operator, only one of the tests must be true for the result to be true.

Here is an example using the logical AND operator:

```
(8 < 3)&&(5 < 2) //result is false, both conditions must be true.
```

In this example, the first test returns true, but the second test is false. Because we are using the logical AND operator, both tests must return true for the result of the entire expression to be true, and since one test is false, the result is false.

Table 4-8 illustrates the rules for determining the Boolean result when two conditions are combined into a single expression using a logical operator.

Table 4-8: Combining Logical Operators

First expression	Operator	Second expression	Result
True	&&	True	True
True	&&	False	False
False	&&	False	False
False	&&	True	False
True	||	True	True
True	||	False	True
False	||	False	False
False	||	True	True

Conditional Structures: If, If . . . Else, If . . . Else If

Conditional structures are among the most important in all programming languages, not just in JavaScript, because they allow you to plan different responses for the two or more possible outcomes of a program's execution.

Simple Conditional Structures

Simple conditional structures can handle only two possible outcomes. If the conditional structure's conditional statement, or condition, is true, then its commands are executed; if its condition is false, then the code inside the conditional structure is not executed.

This is the syntax of simple conditional structures:

```
if (condition) commands;
```

This syntax does not require the use of opening and closing brackets, {}, because the conditional statement and the commands are executed in one line of code. However, the following syntax does require opening and closing brackets because the code is not contained on a single line:

```
if (condition) {
    //commands to be executed if condition is true
}
```

The following is an example of a simple conditional structure using brackets:

```
If (myAge < 18){
    //condition is met, meaning myAge is less than 18
    alert("You are not of voting age!");
}
```

Complex Conditional Structures

Complex conditional structures include the use of the else statement, which allows you to include commands that will be executed if the condition is not met. So if the if statement's condition is true, the commands inside the if structure are executed; otherwise, the commands inside the else structure are executed.

This is the syntax:

```
if (condition) {
    //commands to be executed if condition is true
} else {
    //commands to be executed if condition is not true
}
```

The following is an example of a complex conditional structure:

```
if (myAge < 18) {
    //condition is met, meaning myAge is less than 18
    alert("You are not of voting age!");
} else {
    //condition is not met, meaning myAge is greater than 18
    alert("you can register to vote!");
}
```

Nested Conditional Structures

Nested conditional structures can handle more than two possible outcomes in the code execution. If the if statement of a nested conditional structure is true, the program executes the commands inside the if structure. If the if condition is false, the else if conditions are tested in the order in which they appear — nested conditional structures allow for multiple else if conditions. When multiple else if conditions are present, the first else if condition to test true causes program execution to continue with the corresponding commands. However, if none of the else if conditions are met, the commands inside the else structure are executed.

This is the syntax for a nested conditional structure:

```
if (condition) {
    //commands to be executed if condition is true
} else if (alternate condition 1){
    //commands to be executed if 1st alternate condition is true
} else if (alternate condition 2){
    //commands to be executed if 2nd alternate condition is true
} else {
    //commands to be executed if none of the conditions are true
}
```

The following is an example of a nested conditional structure:

```
If (myAge < 10) {
    //age is less than 10
    alert("You can only watch G rated movies!");
} else if (myAge < 13) {
    //age is greater than or equal to 10 but less than 13
    alert("You can watch PG rated movies with a parent!");
} else if (myAge < 18) {
    //age is greater than or equal to 13 but less than 18
    alert("You can watch R rated movies with a parent!");
} else {
    //age is greater than 18 or equal to
    alert("You can watch R rated movies without a parent!");
}
```

Conditional Expressions

Conditional expressions perform the same function as conditional structures, but they are more compact and can be easier to read. However, you can only use conditional expressions in place of simple conditional structures or complex conditional structures (nested conditional structures cannot be replaced by conditional expressions).

Suppose that you wish to verify the value of the variable myVar and then change its value according to whether a particular condition is met. The following example shows how to do this using conditional structure syntax:

```
if (myVar == 0) {
myVar = 5
} else {
myVar = 8
}
```

In this example, if myVar is equal to 0, it is assigned a value of 5; otherwise myVar is assigned a value of 8.

By using a conditional expression, the preceding `if else` statement could be written using the following syntax:

```
Variable = (condition) ? value1 : value2
```

This means the previous example could be written like this:

```
myVar = (0) ? 5 : 8
```

Consider another case. If a shopping cart contains more than ten items, it should be classified as an "excellent" sale, and if the cart contains fewer than ten items, it should be classified as a "normal" sale. The following code translates this situation into conditional expression syntax:

```
var items = 9 //variable is declared
var cart = (items > 10) ? "excellent" : "normal"
```

The preceding code sets the value of the cart variable to normal because the value of the items variable is not greater than 10.

Switch Statement

The `switch` structure is like a conditional `if else` structure with many possible outcomes. This is quite useful in cases where many `if` statements are necessary and they can all be replaced with one `switch` statement. Furthermore, compared to `if else` statements, the `switch` statement has the added advantage that it can be exited at any time using the `break` command.

This is the switch statement syntax:

```
switch (expression) {
case condition1;
    //commands to be executed if condition 1 is true
    break //optional
case condition2;
    //commands to be executed if condition 2 is true
    break // optional
case condition3;
    //commands to be executed if condition 3 is true
    break //optional.
default;
    //commands to be executed if none of the conditions are true
}
```

The `switch` function evaluates the `expression` supplied to it and executes the commands as the conditions are met within the loop. This means that if `condition1` and `condition2` are both true, the commands within both conditions would be executed, which is why it is sometimes necessary to use the `break` command to exit the structure. Finally, if no other condition in the loop is met, the commands within the `default` option are executed.

Here is an example:

```
Var myName = "Larry";
Switch(myName){
case "Larry";
   alert("hello Larry!"); break;
case "Scott";
   alert("hello Scotty!"); break;
}
```

Loops

Loops enable the repeated execution of a set of commands until a particular condition is met, at which point the program flow exits the loop. There are five types of loops: for loops, for in loops, switch loops, while loops, and do while loops.

for Loop

The for method of looping allows for a set of commands to be executed a predefined number of times. The syntax is as follows:

```
for ([expression]; [condition]; [looping expression]) {
   //commands to be executed in the loop
}
```

In this syntax, the [expression] represents a numerical value that will change with each loop cycle; the [condition] represents the conditional statement, which, when false, will cause the loop to terminate; and the [looping expression] represents the way you want the [expression] to change each time the loop finishes executing the commands.

An example will help illustrate this:

```
for (var i = 8; i >= 15; i++) {
   //commands to be executed in the loop
}
```

In this example, variable i is the [expression] and is assigned an initial value of 8. The [condition] that once met will cause the loop to terminate is that the variable i be greater than or equal to 15. The [looping expression] is to increment the value of the variable i by 1 at the end of each cycle of the loop.

The commands to be executed during each cycle in the loop follow the for loop expression:

```
for (var i = 8; i >= 15; i++) {
   alert("the value of i is " + i);
   //display message box with the value of i
}
```

break

In some cases, it is necessary to exit the loop once a predefined condition in the command section is met, rather than when the condition in the loop statement is met. To exit the loop in this way, the break command is used. Exiting a loop once a condition in the command section is met means that subsequent commands in the loop are not executed and that subsequent cycles in the loop are not executed either.

Suppose you have a web page that contains a series of radio buttons, and if one of the option buttons is checked, you want to alert the user regarding the option selected. The following code demonstrates how this operation can be coded in JavaScript:

```
function theButton() {
for (var i = 0; i < selOption.length; i++) {
if (selOption[i].checked) {
alert("You chose! " + selOption[i].value + ".")
break
}}}
<select id="selOption">
  <input type="radio" name="selOption" value="first option">
  <input type="radio" name="selOption" value="second option">
  <input type="radio" name="selOption" value="third option">
</select>
```

In the preceding example, the break command allows the loop to exit as soon as the selected option is identified. Once the selected option has been found, there is no need for the loop to continue checking other options, because there can be only one option selected at a time. The break command is useful in saving the program flow from having to complete the loop.

continue

The continue command is useful when circumstances determine that execution of the commands in the loop is not required. Whereas the break command exits the loop entirely, the continue command exits just the current cycle in the loop, but allows the loop to continue with subsequent cycles.

For example,

```
for (var i = 0; i <= 20; i++) {
   if (i == 7) {continue} //skip commands if the value of i is 7
   //commands to be executed if i is not 7
}
```

In this loop, the commands will be executed for all the values of the variable i between 0 and 20, except for the loop cycle during which i has a value of 7. To also skip execution of the commands in the loop for i values 3 and 13, we simply need to modify the conditional statement, (if i == 7), to include the other values as well:

```
for (var i = 0; i <= 20; i++) {
   if (i == 7 || i == 3 || i == 13) {continue}
   //commands to be executed if i is not 7, 3 or 13
}
```

for ... in

The for in looping mechanism allows you to cycle through all the properties of an object. This is the syntax:

```
for (var variableName in object) {
   //commands to be executed for each instance of the object
}
```

For example,

```
<script language="JavaScript">
function showProperties(window, "window") {
var results = "" //initialize variable
for (var i in window) {
results += "window" + "." + i + "=" + window[i] + "<br>"}
alert(results)
}
</script>
```

while Loop

while loops are slightly different than for loops in that for loops have a predetermined number of loop cycles, whereas while loops do not. In a while loop, the code cycles through the loop commands indefinitely until the predetermined condition in the while statement is met.

This is the while loop syntax:

```
while (condition) {
   //commands to be executed in the while loop
}
```

A while loop requires that the execution of its commands somehow modify the elements in the conditional expression so that at some point the outcome of that expression becomes false, allowing the code to exit from the loop. Otherwise, the loop will continue executing the commands forever, resulting in an *endless loop*. The following example illustrates this danger:

```
var x = 0; //initial value of x.
var y = 5; //initial value of y.
while (x < 10){ //continues execution as long as x is less than 10
   y = y + x; //increment the value of y by the value of x
```

```
    x = x - 1; //decrease the value of x by 1
} //x will never get to 10, so this will run forever
```

In the preceding example, the x variable is part of the condition, x < 10, and once its value reaches 10, the loop will stop cycling. However, because the value of x is decreased by 1 each loop cycle, the condition will never be met, and the loop will run forever. A loop that runs forever is known as an endless loop and it can cause the browser and maybe the operating system to freeze.

do while Loop

The do while loop is another form of the while loop. However, it differs from the while loop in that do while checks whether a condition remains true at the end of each cycle of execution, rather than checking a condition at the beginning. This guarantees that the loop will be executed at least once.

The syntax of the do while loop is as follows:

```
do {
    //commands to be executed in the loop
}
while (condition)
```

Functions

Functions (and object methods, which are also discussed in the "Assigning a Function to an Object" section of this chapter) are the "verbs" of the JavaScript language, meaning that they execute actions. Many JavaScript functions are predefined, and JavaScript already knows what needs to be done when they are invoked. However, JavaScript is flexible in that it also allows new functions to be created and defined.

When a new function is declared, the following syntax is used:

```
function my_func(parameter1, parameter2 . . . ) {
    //commands to be executed in the function
    return value; //optional
}
```

In this syntax statement, the reserved keyword, function, indicates to the browser that a function is being declared. This keyword is followed by the name of the function, in this case my_func, which must follow all the rules for naming identifiers (discussed in the "Variables" section earlier in this chapter). The function name is then followed by parentheses, and the function parameters (also known as arguments), if there are any, are included within the parentheses. You must separate each parameter from the next with a comma. You can think of parameters as variables that already contain a set of values that are passed to the function for processing.

Following the parentheses, an opening bracket ({) indicates the beginning of the code, or commands, associated with the function. Following the code that defines the actions of the function, an optional return value can assign a result to the function, which in some cases can be used elsewhere in the code of the page.

After the function's commands and return value comes the closing bracket (}), which signals the end of the function. It is imperative that the code that defines the actions of the function be enclosed between opening and closing brackets.

Once a new function has been defined in this manner, it can be invoked using the function name followed by parentheses, as in my_func(). If the function contains parameters, you must include the parameter values inside the parentheses when calling the function.

```
Function myName(myName, myAge){
    Alert("My Name is " + myName + ", I am " + myAge + "years old");
}
myName("Jonathan", 18); //calls myName function
```

Be careful, however, that the data types of the parameter values passed to the function match the data types of the parameters in the function declaration. JavaScript 1.3 and previous versions have no means of validating data types. Therefore, to check the parameter data type, you can use the typeof operator, which determines the type of data stored in a variable. For example,

```
if (typeof myVariable == "number")  {
    //commands
}
```

The result of a typeof operation can be number, string, Boolean, object, or undefined. This operator is most commonly used in conditional if statements.

NOTE *Functions are inefficient when used in loops because the function is invoked and recompiled by the browser during each cycle of the loop. The use of functions inside loops can also produce errors.*

The Parameters of a Function

The *parameters* (or *arguments*) of a function are treated as objects that are part of an array called the arguments array. The fact that a function's arguments are part of an array means that when you invoke a function, you do not necessarily have to pass the same number of arguments to it as were defined within the function declaration. In fact, you can put any number of arguments inside a function invocation. JavaScript will accommodate the function to the number of arguments supplied when the function is invoked.

The following example shows how to retrieve the largest number in a series by passing all of the numbers in the series to a function with no arguments defined in its declaration:

```
var myGreaterValue = returnLargest(10, 100, 2, 5, 1500, 4, 56, 10000)
function returnLargest() {
   var m = Number.NEGATIVE_INFINITY; //Smallest possible number
   for (var i = 0;  i < arguments.length;  i++) {
   //Loop through all the elements of the arguments array
      if (arguments[i] > m) {
      //If the value of the element arguments[i] is greater than m
         m = arguments[i];
         //Reset the value of m equal to the value of arguments[i]
      }
   return m; //return the value of m once the loop finishes
   }
}
```

You can obtain the number of array parameters by using the length property of the array. The preceding function loops through the list of parameters and stores the largest of them in variable m. Before the function completes execution, it returns the value of m.

When some outcome of the execution of a function needs to be known outside of the function, the function code must use the return keyword to provide the required result. The syntax is as follows:

```
function my_function() {
   return expression;
}
```

In the previous parameter example, the return value is m, which corresponds to the number 10000, the largest of the numeric parameters passed to the function.

The Void Operator

Giving a function a return value with the return keyword can produce undesirable results in some browsers when the function is called inside an HTML tag.

Earlier in this chapter, we looked at how a function can be assigned to the href attribute of the <a> element. Now, let's define the act() function with a return value of true:

```
function act() {
   return true;
}
```

The following link inside the <body> section of a web page is used to invoke the function:

```
<a href="javascript:act();">......</a>
```

Because the function returns the value true, and because the function is called from within a link tag, the browser may cause the current page in the browser window to be discarded, and if multiple browser windows are open, the browser window containing the page may close as well. However, you can avoid this by including the void keyword in front of the function call, thereby eliminating the undesirable result:

```
<a href="void javascript:act()">
```

The void operator allows a function to be executed while ignoring the return value. The void keyword is subject to the order of precedence of all JavaScript operators, as will be covered later in this chapter in Table 4-9. It is important to have this table handy, as it may help avoid many programming headaches when using the void operator. For example, when the function declaration contains an operator that has precedence over the void operator, you should include the entire declaration between parentheses, like this:

```
<a href="void (javascript:act())">
```

If you use the parentheses in the wrong place or you make too much use of them, you may find problems with the code.

Literal Functions

Literal functions allow you to create a function that will be executed only one time. JavaScript version 1.2 allows a function to be both created and executed in the same line of code, with the function returning a value to a specified variable. In this case, the function does not have a name, and this is why it is called a *literal* function.

Here's an example:

```
var myFunction = function(x) { return x*x }
//opening and closing brackets{} need to be used
```

The return value is passed to the myFunction variable, and this value can be used throughout the allowed scope.

Nested Functions

In the first two versions of JavaScript (1.0 and 1.1), a function declaration could neither be nested inside another function declaration, nor inside a structure like a for or if statement. Version 1.2 enabled a function declaration to be nested within another function, though not within a loop.

Suppose you wanted to calculate the length of the hypotenuse of a right triangle, which is equal to the square root of the sum of the squares of the other two sides of the triangle. The nested functions would be written as follows:

```
function hypotenuse(a, b) {
    function square(x) {
        return x*x;
    }
    return Math.sqrt(square(a) + square(b));
}
```

The hypotenuse function contains two parameters, a and b, which represent the lengths of the other two sides of the triangle. This function extracts the square root of the sum of the squares of the two lengths by sending the lengths of the sides, a and b, to the nested square function. The square function takes the parameter x, and returns the value of x squared to the hypotenuse function. The square function is only available to be called from inside the hypotenuse function, and it is both created and destroyed there.

Function Constructors

Functions can also be declared using what is called a *function constructor*. The advantage of declaring a function in this way is that the function is assigned to a variable and can be managed with greater ease. The new keyword is used in such a declaration.

Take, for example, the following function using ordinary function declaration syntax:

```
var x = 5; var y = 2;
function myFunction (x, y) {return x*y;}
alert (myFunction(x, y)); //displays a message box with the result
```

The preceding function can also be declared using a function constructor, and the following code is equivalent to the previous example:

```
var x = 5; var y = 2;
var myFunction = new function("x", "y", "return x*y;")
alert (myFunction);  //displays a message box with the result
```

No brackets, {}, are used in the declaration of a function constructor. The variable extracts the return value of the function, and the variable can then be used in other calculations or declarations. Support for function constructors was not added until JavaScript version 1.1.

Objects

Many objects and properties are already predefined in the JavaScript language. However, you can also create your own objects in JavaScript.

In the following sections, we will look at how you can create your own objects. Later, we will review some of the predefined JavaScript objects that you will likely be using.

Creating Your Own Objects

Any object that is either predefined in JavaScript, or that your code creates for the first time, is known as an *object prototype*, or *class*. Classes are found in all object-oriented programming languages, such as C, C++, and Java. JavaScript also makes use of classes, although it calls them object prototypes.

Object prototypes contain definitions of their properties and methods. For example, the following code creates the car object prototype and names the parameters that will need to be used in constructing each instance of the car object:

```
function car(m, c, pt) {
this.model = m //create a property called model and assign it m
this.color = c //create a property called color and assign it c
this.plate = pt //create a property called plate and assign it pt
}
```

The car object prototype requires three parameters whose values are assigned to three corresponding properties of the object. These properties are created using the this object, which references the current object, in this case the car object prototype (the properties could also have been created by replacing the this keyword with car).

To be useful, however, object prototypes must be instantiated into a usable object by using the new constructor keyword and by supplying the parameter values that will become the property values of the new object. For example, you can use the following declarations to create two instances of a car object:

```
var car1 = new car("Acura", "green", "0458BGN")
var car2 = new car("Polo", "blue", "1572KPL")
```

The preceding code does not include parameters for the cars' makers because the car object prototype that we created is missing maker as one of its properties. However, it is possible to modify an existing class by using the prototype property. Using the prototype property allows properties to be added to object prototypes at run time. For example, the following declaration tells JavaScript that the car class should now include a new property called maker:

```
car.prototype.maker = true;
```

The property value can then be set by using standard JavaScript coding conventions. Either of the following lines of code would work:

```
this.maker = "Chevrolet";
car.maker = "Chevrolet";
```

Given this ability to modify object prototypes in the JavaScript of a web page, predefined objects are not untouchable. However, adding properties using this method will only affect object prototypes for the duration of the page's execution. Moreover, object prototypes created in one page will not be usable in other pages.

Assigning a Function to an Object

Functions can be assigned to an object and its properties, thus becoming methods of the object. Take, for instance, the following function:

```
function myFunction(parameter) {
    //commands to be executed in the function
}
```

Assuming that this function is declared in the <head> section of a page, you could reference the function in a method of the car object by using the following syntax:

```
car.myMethod() = myFunction
```

Note that in this declaration the function parentheses are not included with the name of the function being referenced. This is because the method is being assigned to the function and is not being executed.

At this point, you could invoke the function using the standard way of calling methods, as follows:

```
car.myMethod(parameterValue);
```

In this example, the parameterValue parameter is passed to the myFunction function, which is then executed.

The with Operator

The with operator is especially helpful in shortening the code of a set of commands when many of the commands make reference to the same object. However, the with operator can be used to shorten any object reference. The syntax is as follows:

```
with (object) {
    //commands to be executed on the object
}
```

The following is an example in which a function displays the color, maker, and model of the car object described earlier, but without using the with operator:

```
function showCar(car) { //instance of car object is a parameter
    alert(car.color); //display message box with the color
    alert(car.maker); //display message box with the maker
    alert(car.model); //display message box with the model
}
```

The preceding example could be written as follows using the with operator:

```
function showCar(car) {
    with (car) { //no need to use "car" to use the properties
        alert(color);  //display message box with the color
        alert(maker); //display message box with the maker
        alert(model); //display message box with the model
    }
}
```

Operator Precedence

Given that the with operator is the second-to-last of the operators covered in this chapter (the instanceof operator will be covered momentarily), it is a good time to introduce the subject of operator precedence.

The order in which JavaScript executes operators can be quite complicated, and it is definitely more complex than the standard mathematical operator precedence that you may be familiar with. You will find Table 4-9 to be a handy reference in identifying how mathematical expressions involving more than one operator are executed.

Table 4-9: JavaScript Operator Order of Precedence

Operator	Description
( )	The innermost parenthetical is acted upon before the outermost parenthetical
[ ]	Indices of an Array element
.	Call to a function or method
!	Logical NOT
-	Negative
++, --	Increment and decrement
typeOf, void	Check variable types
delete	Eliminate an element from an Array
*, /, %, +, -	Multiplication, division, modulo, addition, and subtraction
<, <=, >, >=	Less than, less than or equal to, greater than, and greater than or equal to
==, !=	Is equal to, and is not equal to
&&, ||, !	Logical AND, OR, and NOT
?	Conditional expression
=, =+, -=, *=, %=, /=, <<=, >>=	Assignment operators
,	Comma operator for delimiting the properties of an object

The following example will help illustrate how operator precedence works:

```
95 + 10 > 100 && 100 - 5 < 100 //returns true
```

In this example, the + and - operations are performed first, the > and < operations are performed next, and the && operation is performed last. The result of the first set of operators, the arithmetic + and −, is as follows:

```
105 > 100 && 95 < 100 //returns true
```

The result of the second set of operators, the comparative > and <, is as follows:

```
true && true //returns true
```

Finally, the logical && operation results in true.

JavaScript Predefined Objects

Among the predefined objects in JavaScript, the Array, String, Math, Number, Boolean, and Date objects are important. These predefined objects provide you with a great starting point because they free you from having to write code to re-create the basic functionality that they provide. Before we look at them, though, we need to look at the instanceof operator.

The instanceof Operator

The instanceof operator is used to ascertain what type of object prototype, or class, a particular object is an instance of. The following declaration creates an instance of an Array class:

```
var x = new Array();
```

Now, using the instanceof operator, we can prove that both of the following statements are true:

```
x instanceof Array; //returns true
Array instanceof Object  //returns true
```

The first expression is true because x is a new instance of the Array class, and the second expression is true because the Array object is in turn an instance of the Object class.

The Array Object

Arrays are objects that contain a collection of variables or other objects. Arrays offer a simple way of storing and manipulating elements in a list.

Suppose we want to store the members of a family (Vanessa, Pete, John, Mary, and Adele) in an array:

```
var family = new Array();  //an instance of the Array object
family[0] = "Vanessa";
family[1] = "Pete";
```

```
family[2] = "John";
family[3] = "Mary";
family[4] = "Adele";
```

Because arrays are objects, they are instantiated using the constructor of the array class, `new Array()`. The constructor creates an instance of an array, and assigns the array to a variable named `family`. Once defined, an array's elements can be accessed by using the name of the array in combination with the numeric *index* of a particular element in the array.

The first element of an array has an index of [0], and each successive element in the array has an index value one integer greater than the previous element. In the previous example, `family[2]` refers to John. John is the third element of the array, so his index value is [2].

Creating an Empty Array

Just as a variable can be created without assigning a value to it, an array can be created without specifying its number of elements. The following code, also used in the previous example, creates an empty array:

```
var myArray = new Array();
```

Empty arrays are usually created when the number of elements that they will contain is unknown at the time of creation. If, on the other hand, the number of elements of an array is known, say four, then the array is declared with the number of elements included in its parentheses, as follows:

```
var myArray = new Array(4);
```

Once the array has been created, you can define the values of the array elements. Here's an example:

```
var myArray = new Array(4);
myArray[0] = 3.5;
myArray[1] = "This is a string";
myArray[2] = false;
myArray[3] = {x:2, y:5} //a style sheet stored in an array
```

This example illustrates two important points about arrays. First, be aware that because the first element in all arrays has an index of 0, the index of the last element in the preceding array is 3, not 4. And second, a single array can contain elements having different types of data, including dates, numbers, strings, objects, or even other arrays.

Literal Arrays

Introduced in version 1.2 of JavaScript, *literal arrays* are created without the use of the `new` constructor keyword. You can use this method when creating an array with only a few elements. For example,

```
var myArray = [3.5, "This is a string", false, {x:2, y:5}]
```

The syntax for creating literal arrays saves space, as you can see by comparing this code with the code in the previous section, which creates the same array using the new constructor keyword.

Removing an Element from an Array

Any time you create an array, the browser stores references to the array elements using memory space. Therefore, eliminating the content of an array element by setting its value to null does not eliminate the element itself, because the element's memory space remains.

However, the delete operator, introduced in version 4 of Netscape Navigator and Internet Explorer, allows for array elements to be completely removed. Using the delete operator will eliminate both the contents of the array element and the space allocated to the element in memory. Consider the following example:

```
var myArray = new Array()
myArray[0] = "Seville"
myArray[1] = "Madrid"
myArray[2] = "Barcelona"
myArray[3] = "Valence"
alert(myArray.length); //4 elements in the array
delete myArray[2]
alert(myArray.length); //4 elements still in the array
```

The delete operator removes the third element of the array, "Barcelona". The result is the following array:

```
myArray[0] = "Seville"
myArray[1] = "Madrid"
myArray[3] = "Valence"
```

Notice that although array element [2] has been removed and is no longer available in memory, the index values of all subsequent array elements remain the same. The same is true for the length property of the array; before and after the removal of the third element, the length of myArray is 4. For a list of the Array object's properties and methods, see Chapter 14.

Predefined Arrays

Arrays are also used by browsers to store the elements of a web page. One global array stores all the elements in a page, and other arrays store elements grouped by their element type, such as images, forms, frames, buttons, and links.

```
document.elements[] //Array containing all elements on the page.
document.images[] //Array containing all image elements.
document.forms[]
```

```
document.frames[]
document.buttons[]
document.links[]
```

For example, if a web page has five forms, the browser will store all of them in an array. Using the Document Object Model (discussed in Chapter 2), you can reference each form either using its name or its index in the document's forms array. The index of each form is determined by the order in which it appears in the document, with forms defined earlier in the page having a lower index value. The declaration, document.forms[0], represents the first form element in the page.

NOTE *It is important to remember that all the elements of an array are also objects, with methods, properties, and events of their own.*

The String Object

The String object is another object prototype of JavaScript. An instance of the String object can be created in the following two ways, with a constructor and without:

```
var myString = new String("string's characters")
var myString = "string's characters";
```

You can access the String object's properties and methods just like any other object's properties and methods, with the following syntax:

```
myString.property;
myString.method();
```

The following example illustrates use of the length property, which calculates the number of characters in a string, and the use of the toUpperCase() method, which converts all the letters of a string to uppercase:

```
"This is a message".length //returns 17
"This is a message".toUpperCase() //results in "THIS IS A MESSAGE"
```

As in the previous examples, a string, followed by the period operator (.), followed by the name of the property or method, will allow you to access each property and method of the String object. For a list of the String object's properties and methods, see Chapter 14.

The Math Object

You can perform all mathematical operations with the operators mentioned earlier in this chapter. However, mathematical operations that use special constants (such as pi) and trigonometric functions can be very difficult to implement with the standard mathematical operators. You can use the Math object in these special circumstances and in other cases where applicable.

The properties of the `Math` object return the values of the constants they represent. You can use these properties inside standard mathematical operations. For example, to calculate the longitude of the circumference of diameter d, you can do the following:

```
longCircumf = d * Math.PI;
```

For a list of the `Math` object's properties and methods, see Chapter 14.

The Number Object

The `Number` object is not commonly used; however, this object contains properties and methods that you will at times find useful. An instance of the `Number` object is declared, and its properties and methods are used, just like other JavaScript objects:

```
var num = new Number(number);
num.properties;
num.method(param);
```

Some of the methods of the `Number` object are illustrated in the following examples:

```
123456.toExponential(6) = 1.23456e+5
var n = 123.456789;
n.toFixed(3); = 123.456
n.toPrecision(5); = 123.45
```

For a list of the `Number` object's properties and methods, see Chapter 14.

The Boolean Object

You can create a `Boolean` object using the standard constructor, as follows:

```
var bo = new Boolean(param);
```

The parameter param can either be a number (0 for false, and any other number for true), or it can be one of the Boolean values true or false. The `Boolean` object provides a different way of using Boolean type variables, but it offers no distinct advantages because it does not have any properties or methods.

The Date Object

If you wish to add a clock, multimedia object, or counter to a page, you must use the `Date` object. The `Date` object has no properties, but it has many methods. For a list of the `Date` object's methods, see Chapter 14.

All methods retrieve and set times in GMT (Greenwich Mean Time) unless otherwise noted. Computers internally handle dates and time in the GMT format, and the time zone used by the `Date` object is GMT. The UTC (Universal

Time Coordinate) time, on the other hand, provides a value that depends on the local user's time zone. When the time zone of the user must be taken into account, you should use UTC times.

You can create an instance of the Date object as you can with any other object:

```
var myDate = new Date(date); //value is null if no date is supplied
```

The following example creates a Date object containing a birth date, which is then manipulated with the getDay() method to find the day of the week on which a baby was born:

```
var myBirth = new Date("February 3, 2003"); //use a valid date format.
r = myBirth.getDay(); //This date is a Tuesday, therefore r = 2.
```

Performing Date and Time Calculations

The standard timekeeping unit of all computers throughout the world is milliseconds, and most computers start counting as of 1/1/1970 00:00:00. All date calculations should be done in milliseconds, which is also the way JavaScript handles dates. To obtain a time in milliseconds, use the getTime() function, like this:

```
var myDate = new Date(); //creates an instance of the Date object.
var now = myDate.getTime(); //get the time in milliseconds
```

Now, to perform calculations with dates already in milliseconds, all times must also be converted to milliseconds. You can achieve this by creating variables whose values represent different quantities of time in milliseconds:

```
var minute = 60 * 1000
//1000 ms in a second, 60 seconds in a minute.
var hour = minute * 60
var day = hour * 24
var week = day * 7
```

Once you have established these values, performing the mathematical calculation is much easier. For example, now you can calculate a date that is one week prior to the current date:

```
var myDate = new Date(); //instantiate a date object called myDate
var dateMillis = myDate.getTime(); //Gets date in milliseconds
dateMillis = dateMillis - week; //subtract a week from the date
myDate.setTime(dateMillis);
```

The last declaration in the preceding example sets the myDate object with the new date and time.

▌▌

REFERENCES

This part of the book provides a comprehensive reference of DHTML. The anchor point for this part of the book is Chapter 5, which contains an alphabetical reference of all HTML elements currently supported by Netscape Navigator and Microsoft Internet Explorer. Each HTML element listed in Chapter 5 is accompanied by alphabetical listings of its HTML attributes, event handlers, CSS and JavaScript style properties, Microsoft behaviors, Microsoft filters, JavaScript properties, JavaScript methods, JavaScript collections, and JavaScript objects.

To get more information on any of the items in any of the lists above, you can jump directly to the reference chapters of interest and look up the items alphabetically. The remainder of the reference chapters are organized as follows:

HTML attributes (Chapter 6), event handlers (Chapter 7), CSS attributes and JavaScript style properties (Chapter 8), Microsoft behaviors (Chapter 9), Microsoft filters (Chapter 10), JavaScript properties (Chapter 11), JavaScript methods (Chapter 12), JavaScript collections (Chapter 13), and JavaScript objects (Chapter 14).

For example, if you look up the <a> element in Chapter 5, search its HTML attributes list, and decide that you want more information on the href attribute, you would jump to Chapter 6 and look up the href attribute alphabetically.

Chapter 15 provides a reference to the HTML+TIME Microsoft technology, and is organized like no other chapter in this book. All of the HTML elements, HTML attributes, events, JavaScript properties, JavaScript methods, JavaScript collections, and JavaScript objects that pertain to the HTML+TIME technology are grouped together in Chapter 15, rather than being distributed throughout Chapters 5, 6, 7, 11, 12, 13, and 14, respectively. The simple reason for this is that for the most part HTML+TIME has its own elements, attributes, events, properties, methods, collections, and objects, which are not compatible with anything outside of this Microsoft technology. Therefore, if you are looking for reference material on HTML+TIME, you must look in Chapter 15.

Each chapter contains an introduction explaining the material covered in the chapter, as well as any particular conventions used in presenting the material. For each DHTML element in each of the reference chapters, you will find browser compatibility information with Netscape Navigator and Internet Explorer, a description of what the DHTML element does, syntax information, and, in most cases, an example. Additionally, each DHTML element comes with an applies-to list that cross-references all of the other HTML elements and JavaScript objects that work with the element at hand. This is very important because it will allow you to see how each piece of DHTML functionality relates to each other piece of DHTML functionality.

5

HTML ELEMENTS

This chapter provides an alphabetical list of all HTML elements, along with a description, the syntax, and an example for each. In order to comply with the new XHTML standard, this book uses lowercase letters in the code for all HTML elements and attributes.

In this chapter, you can see all of the HTML attributes, event handlers, CSS attributes and JavaScript style properties, Microsoft behaviors and filters, and JavaScript properties, methods, collections, and objects that relate to each HTML element, all organized into comma-delimited lists. In the heading for each of these lists, you will see a number inside parentheses that corresponds to the chapter in which the material is covered in greater depth. For example, the heading for the list of HTML attributes belonging to the <body> element looks like this:

<body> HTML Attributes (6)

To find further information on any of the attributes in this list, you can turn to Chapter 6 and look up the attribute alphabetically. The heading for the list of JavaScript properties pertaining to the <body> element looks like this:

body. JavaScript Properties (11)

The period (.) following body denotes that JavaScript properties are accessed using the body object and the period operator. To find further information on any of the properties in this list, you can turn to Chapter 11 and look up the property alphabetically.

The examples in this chapter are meant to provide you with a concise, self-contained illustration of how each element works. All examples in this chapter were tested extensively using Internet Explorer 6.0 for Windows. For the most part, these examples should work right out of the box. However, some examples in this chapter make reference to outside files (graphic files, Flash movie files, sound files, and so on). To make these examples work properly, you need to supply the file being referenced and place it in the same directory where you placed the example HTML file.

There are two other details related to the content of this chapter that you should be aware of. First, not all sections of this chapter contain lists — in these cases, the "missing" information does not pertain to the element in that section. For example, Microsoft filters do not pertain to many of the elements in this chapter, so they are not mentioned in those sections.

Second, it is important to note that the lists related to CSS attributes and JavaScript style properties contain property names that are written using CSS syntax. To convert CSS syntax (which is not case sensitive) to JavaScript syntax (which is case sensitive), simply remove the dashes and capitalize the first letter of all words other than the first word. For example, the CSS attribute text-underline-position would be written in JavaScript as textUnderlinePosition.

`<a> ... </a>`

Compatibility: NN4, NN6, NN7, IE4, IE5, IE5.5, IE6

This element is at the heart of the hyperlink structure of the Web. It represents a point in the page on which a reader can click to "jump" to another region of the same page, another page entirely, or a specific region of another page. Both text and images can be included within this element. When text exists between the opening and closing tags, the text forms the label of the hyperlink or anchor.

This element is referred to as a *hyperlink* when its destination is another document, and it is referred to as an *anchor* when its destination is a location within the same (or another) document.

Syntax for the hyperlink version:

```
<a href="http://www.example.com" attributes events>label</a>
```

Syntax for the anchor version:

```
<a href="#anchorName" attributes events>label</a>
```

Example of a hyperlink and an anchor:

```
<html><head><title>A element example</title></head>
<body bgcolor="#FFFFFF" text="#000000">
<a name="top"></a>
```

```
<h2>Used as a hyperlink:</h2>
  <p><a href="http://www.w3.org/" target="_blank">World Wide Web Organization</a></
p>
<h2>Used as an anchor:</h2>
  <p><a href="#par3">Go to paragraph #3 in this page</a></p>
  <p><a href=" yourdocument.html#sty">Go to the yourdocument.htm page, sty
location</a></p>
  .......................
  <p align="left">Paragraph #2</p>
  .......................
  <p align="left"><a name="par3">Paragraph #3</a></p>
  ....................
  <p align="left"><a href="#top">Top</a></p>
</body></html>
```

`<a>` HTML Attributes (6)

accesskey, begin, charset, class, contenteditable, coords, datafld, datasrc, dir,
disabled, end, hidefocus, href, hreflang, id, lang, language, methods, name, rel,
rev, shape, style, syncmaster, systemBitrate, systemCaptions, systemLanguage,
systemOverdubOrSubtitle, tabindex, target, timecontainer, title, type,
unselectable, urn

`<a>` Event Handlers (7)

onActivate, onAfterUpdate, onBeforeActivate, onBeforeCopy, onBeforeCut,
onBeforeDeactivate, onBeforeEditFocus, onBeforePaste, onBeforeUpdate, onBlur,
onClick, onContextMenu, onControlSelect, onCopy, onCut, onDblClick, onDeactivate,
onDrag, onDragEnd, onDragEnter, onDragLeave, onDragOver, onDragStart, onDrop,
onErrorUpdate, onFocus, onFocusIn, onFocusOut, onHelp, onKeyDown, onKeyPress,
onKeyUp, onLoseCapture, onMouseDown, onMouseEnter, onMouseLeave, onMouseMove,
onMouseOut, onMouseOver, onMouseUp, onMouseWheel, onMove, onMoveEnd, onMoveStart,
onPaste, onPropertyChange, onReadyStateChange, onResize, onResizeEnd,
onResizeStart, onSelectStart, onTimeError

`<a>` CSS Attributes and JavaScript Style Properties (8)

The names are in CSS syntax. See the introduction to this chapter for the
JavaScript syntax rules. Names noted with an asterisk (*) are JavaScript
properties only.

!important, :active, :hover, :link, :visited, accelerator, background, background-
attachment, background-color, background-image, background-position, background-
position-x, background-position-y, background-repeat, behavior, border, border-
bottom, border-bottom-color, border-bottom-style, border-bottom-width, border-
color, border-left, border-left-color, border-left-style, border-left-width,
border-right, border-right-color, border-right-style, border-right-width, border-
style, border-top, border-top-color, border-top-style, border-top-width, border-
width, bottom, clear, clip, color, cursor, direction, display, filter, float, font,
font-family, font-size, font-style, font-variant, font-weight, hasLayout(*),
height, layout-flow, layout-grid, layout-grid-mode, left, letter-spacing, line-
height, margin, margin-bottom, margin-left, margin-right, margin-top, overflow,

overflow-x, overflow-y, padding, padding-bottom, padding-left, padding-right, padding-top, pixelBottom(*), pixelHeight(*), pixelLeft(*), pixelRight(*), pixelTop(*), pixelWidth(*), posBottom(*), posHeight(*), position, posLeft(*), posRight(*), posTop(*), posWidth(*), right, styleFloat(*), text-autospace, text-decoration, text-overflow, text-transform, text-underline-position, textDecorationBlink(*), textDecorationLineThrough(*), textDecorationNone(*), textDecorationOverline(*), textDecorationUnderline(*), top, unicode-bidi, visibility, width, word-spacing, word-wrap, writing-mode, z-index, zoom

`<a>` Microsoft Behaviors (9)

anchorClick, clientCaps, download, homePage, httpFolder, saveFavorite, saveHistory, saveSnapshot, time, time2, userData

`<a>` Microsoft Filters (10)

Alpha, Barn, BasicImage, BlendTrans, Blinds, Blur, CheckerBoard, Chroma, Compositor, DropShadow, Emboss, Engrave, Fade, FlipH, FlipV, Glow, GradientWipe, Gray, ICMFilter, Inset, Invert, Iris, Light, MaskFilter, Matrix, MotionBlur, Pixelate, RadialWipe, RandomBars, RandomDissolve, RevealTrans, Shadow, Slide, Spiral, Stretch, Strips, Wave, Wheel, Xray, Zigzag

a. JavaScript Properties (11)

accessKey, canHaveChildren, canHaveHTML, charset, className, clientHeight, clientLeft, clientTop, clientWidth, contentEditable, coords, cursor, dataFld, datasrc, dir, disabled, end, firstChild, hash, hasLayout, hideFocus, host, hostname, href, hreflang, id, innerHTML, innerText, isContentEditable, isDisabled, isMultiLine, isTextEdit, lang, language, lastChild, Methods, name, nameProp, nextSibling, nodeName, nodeType, nodeValue, offsetHeight, offsetLeft, offsetParent, offsetTop, offsetWidth, outerHTML, outerText, ownerDocument, parentElement, parentNode, parentTextEdit, pathname, port, previousSibling, protocol, readyState, recordNumber, rel, rev, scopeName, scrollHeight, scrollLeft, scrollTop, scrollWidth, search, shape, sourceIndex, tabIndex, tagName, tagUrn, target, text, title, type, uniqueID, urn

a. JavaScript Methods (12)

addBehavior, appendChild, applyElement, attachEvent, blur, clearAttributes, click, cloneNode, componentFromPoint, contains, detachEvent, dragDrop, fireEvent, focus, getAdjacentText, getAttribute, getAttributeNode, getBoundingClientRect, getClientRects, getElementsByTagName, getExpression, hasChildNodes, insertAdjacentElement, insertAdjacentHTML, insertAdjacentText, insertBefore, mergeAttributes, normalize, releaseCapture, removeAttribute, removeAttributeNode, removeBehavior, removeChild, removeExpression, removeNode, replaceAdjacentText, replaceChild, replaceNode, scrollIntoView, setActive, setAttribute, setAttributeNode, setCapture, setExpression, swapNode

a. JavaScript Collections (13)

all, attributes, behaviorUrns, childNodes, children

a. JavaScript Objects (14)

currentStyle, runtimeStyle, style

\<acronym> ... \</acronym>

Compatibility: NN6, NN7, IE4, IE5, IE5.5, IE6

This element is used to display a message or abbreviation. The value of the
\<acronym> element's title attribute specifies the message that will be displayed
in a small box (a tooltip) while the mouse hovers over some text.

Syntax:

```
<acronym attributes events>abbreviation</acronym>
```

Example:

```
<html><head><title>acronym element example</title></head>
<body bgcolor="#FFFFFF" text="#000000">
<p align="center">acronym element</p>
<acronym title="Hyper Text Markup Language">HTML</acronym>
</body></html>
```

\<acronym> HTML Attributes (6)

accesskey, begin, class, contenteditable, dir, disabled, end, hidefocus, id, lang,
language, style, syncmaster, systemBitrate, systemCaptions, systemLanguage,
systemOverdubOrSubtitle, tabindex, timecontainer, title, unselectable

\<acronym> Event Handlers (7)

onActivate, onBeforeDeactivate, onBeforeEditFocus, onBlur, onClick,
onControlSelect, onDblClick, onDeactivate, onDrag, onDragEnd, onDragEnter,
onDragLeave, onDragOver, onDragStart, onDrop, onFocus, onHelp, onKeyDown,
onKeyPress, onKeyUp, onMouseDown, onMouseEnter, onMouseLeave, onMouseMove,
onMouseOut, onMouseOver, onMouseUp, onMove, onMoveEnd, onMoveStart,
onReadyStateChange, onResize, onResizeEnd, onResizeStart, onSelectStart,
onTimeError

\<acronym> CSS Attributes and JavaScript Style Properties (8)

The names are in CSS syntax. See the introduction to this chapter for the
JavaScript syntax rules. Names noted with an asterisk (*) are JavaScript
properties only.

accelerator, background-position-x, background-position-y, behavior, border,
border-bottom, border-bottom-color, border-bottom-style, border-bottom-width,
border-color, border-left, border-left-color, border-left-style, border-left-width,
border-right, border-right-color, border-right-style, border-right-width, border-
style, border-top, border-top-color, border-top-style, border-top-width, border-

width, direction, display, filter, hasLayout(*), height, layout-flow, layout-grid, layout-grid-mode, margin, margin-bottom, margin-left, margin-right, margin-top, overflow, overflow-x, overflow-y, padding, padding-bottom, padding-left, padding-right, padding-top, pixelBottom(*), pixelHeight(*), pixelLeft(*), pixelRight(*), pixelTop(*), pixelWidth(*), posBottom(*), posHeight(*), posLeft(*), posRight(*), posTop(*), posWidth(*), text-autospace, text-overflow, text-underline-position, unicode-bidi, white-space, width, word-wrap, writing-mode, zoom

<acronym> Microsoft Behaviors (9)

clientCaps, download, homePage, httpFolder, saveFavorite, saveHistory, saveSnapshot, time, time2, userData

<acronym> Microsoft Filters (10)

Alpha, Barn, BasicImage, BlendTrans, Blinds, Blur, CheckerBoard, Chroma, Compositor, DropShadow, Emboss, Engrave, Fade, FlipH, FlipV, Glow, GradientWipe, Gray, ICMFilter, Inset, Invert, Iris, Light, MaskFilter, Matrix, MotionBlur, Pixelate, RadialWipe, RandomBars, RandomDissolve, RevealTrans, Shadow, Slide, Spiral, Stretch, Strips, Wave, Wheel, Xray, Zigzag

acronym. JavaScript Properties (11)

accessKey, canHaveChildren, canHaveHTML, className, clientHeight, clientWidth, contentEditable, dir, disabled, end, firstChild, hasLayout, hideFocus, id, innerHTML, innerText, isContentEditable, isDisabled, isMultiLine, isTextEdit, lang, language, lastChild, nextSibling, nodeName, nodeType, nodeValue, offsetHeight, offsetLeft, offsetParent, offsetTop, offsetWidth, outerHTML, outerText, ownerDocument, parentElement, parentNode, parentTextEdit, previousSibling, readyState, scopeName, scrollHeight, scrollLeft, scrollTop, scrollWidth, sourceIndex, tabIndex, tagName, tagUrn, title, uniqueID

acronym. JavaScript Methods (12)

addBehavior, appendChild, applyElement, attachEvent, blur, clearAttributes, cloneNode, componentFromPoint, detachEvent, fireEvent, focus, getAdjacentText, getAttribute, getAttributeNode, getBoundingClientRect, getClientRects, getElementsByTagName, getExpression, hasChildNodes, insertAdjacentElement, insertBefore, mergeAttributes, normalize, removeAttribute, removeAttributeNode, removeBehavior, removeChild, removeExpression, removeNode, replaceAdjacentText, replaceChild, replaceNode, setActive, setAttribute, setAttributeNode, setExpression, swapNode

acronym. JavaScript Collections (13)

all, attributes, behaviorUrns, childNodes, children

acronym. JavaScript Objects (14)

currentStyle, runtimeStyle, style

`<address>` ... `</address>`

Compatibility: NN4, NN6, NN7, IE4, IE5, IE5.5, IE6

This element is usually rendered in italics and is used for displaying information about the author of the web content. This element is intended for placement in the top or bottom of the page.

Syntax:

```
<address attributes events>string</address>
```

Example:

```
<html><head><title>address element example</title></head>
<body bgcolor="#ffffff" text="#000000">
<address style="color:blue">Lázaro Issi Cohen.</address>
<address style="color:red">Los Angeles, CA 91606.</address>
</body></html>
```

`<address>` HTML Attributes (6)

```
accesskey, begin, class, contenteditable, dir, disabled, end, hidefocus, id, lang,
language, style, syncmaster, systemBitrate, systemCaptions, systemLanguage,
systemOverdubOrSubtitle, tabindex, timecontainer, title, unselectable
```

`<address>` Event Handlers (7)

```
onActivate, onBeforeActivate, onBeforeCopy, onBeforeCut, onBeforeDeactivate,
onBeforeEditFocus, onBeforePaste, onBlur, onClick, onContextMenu, onControlSelect,
onCopy, onCut, onDblClick, onDeactivate, onDrag, onDragEnd, onDragEnter,
onDragLeave, onDragOver, onDragStart, onDrop, onFocus, onFocusIn, onFocusOut,
onHelp, onKeyDown, onKeyPress, onKeyUp, onLoseCapture, onMouseDown, onMouseEnter,
onMouseLeave, onMouseMove, onMouseOut, onMouseOver, onMouseUp, onMouseWheel,
onMove, onMoveEnd, onMoveStart, onPaste, onPropertyChange, onReadyStateChange,
onResize, onResizeEnd, onResizeStart, onSelectStart, onTimeError
```

`<address>` CSS Attributes and JavaScript Style Properties (8)

The names are in CSS syntax. See the introduction to this chapter for the JavaScript syntax rules. Names noted with an asterisk (*) are JavaScript properties only.

```
!important, :first-letter, :first-line, accelerator, background, background-
attachment, background-color, background-image, background-position, background-
position-x, background-position-y, background-repeat, behavior, bottom, clear,
clip, color, cursor, direction, display, filter, float, font, font-family, font-
size, font-style, font-variant, font-weight, hasLayout(*), height, layout-flow,
layout-grid, layout-grid-mode, left, letter-spacing, line-break, line-height,
overflow, overflow-x, overflow-y, padding, padding-bottom, padding-left, padding-
right, padding-top, page-break-before, pixelBottom(*), pixelHeight(*),
pixelLeft(*), pixelRight(*), pixelTop(*), pixelWidth(*), posBottom(*),
```

posHeight(*), position, posLeft(*), posRight(*), posTop(*), posWidth(*), right, styleFloat(*), text-align-last, text-autospace, text-decoration, text-justify, text-kashida-space, text-overflow, text-transform, text-underline-position, textDecorationBlink(*), textDecorationLineThrough(*), textDecorationNone(*), textDecorationOverline(*), textDecorationUnderline(*), top, unicode-bidi, visibility, white-space, width, word-break, word-spacing, word-wrap, writing-mode, z-index, zoom

<address> Microsoft Behaviors (9)

clientCaps, download, homePage, httpFolder, saveFavorite, saveHistory, saveSnapshot, time, time2, userData

<address> Microsoft Filters (10)

Alpha, Barn, BasicImage, BlendTrans, Blinds, Blur, CheckerBoard, Chroma, Compositor, DropShadow, Emboss, Engrave, Fade, FlipH, FlipV, Glow, GradientWipe, Gray, ICMFilter, Inset, Invert, Iris, Light, MaskFilter, Matrix, MotionBlur, Pixelate, RadialWipe, RandomBars, RandomDissolve, RevealTrans, Shadow, Slide, Spiral, Stretch, Strips, Wave, Wheel, Xray, Zigzag

address. JavaScript Properties (11)

accessKey, blockDirection, canHaveChildren, canHaveHTML, className, clientHeight, clientLeft, clientTop, clientWidth, contentEditable, cursor, dir, disabled, end, firstChild, hasLayout, hideFocus, id, innerHTML, innerText, isContentEditable, isDisabled, isMultiLine, isTextEdit, lang, language, lastChild, nextSibling, nodeName, nodeType, nodeValue, offsetHeight, offsetLeft, offsetParent, offsetTop, offsetWidth, outerHTML, outerText, ownerDocument, parentElement, parentNode, parentTextEdit, previousSibling, readyState, scopeName, scrollHeight, scrollLeft, scrollTop, scrollWidth, sourceIndex, tabIndex, tagName, tagUrn, title, uniqueID

address JavaScript Methods (12)

addBehavior, appendChild, applyElement, attachEvent, blur, clearAttributes, click, cloneNode, componentFromPoint, contains, detachEvent, fireEvent, focus, getAdjacentText, getAttribute, getAttributeNode, getBoundingClientRect, getClientRects, getElementsByTagName, getExpression, hasChildNodes, insertAdjacentElement, insertAdjacentHTML, insertAdjacentText, insertBefore, mergeAttributes, normalize, releaseCapture, removeAttribute, removeAttributeNode, removeBehavior, removeChild, removeExpression, removeNode, replaceAdjacentText, replaceChild, replaceNode, scrollIntoView, setActive, setAttribute, setAttributeNode, setCapture, setExpression, swapNode

address. JavaScript Collections (13)

all, attributes, behaviorUrns, childNodes, children

address. JavaScript Objects (14)

currentStyle, runtimeStyle, style

<applet> ... </applet>

Compatibility: NN4, NN6, NN7, IE4, IE5, IE5.5, IE6

This element is used to invoke a Java application. In order to run applets, you have to install the JAVA 2 plug-in in your machine. Then the applet's code is transferred to your system and is executed by the browser's Java virtual machine (JVM). Download the JAVA 2 plug-in from http://wp.netscape.com/plugins/jvm.html. Use of this element has been deprecated in favor of the <object> element.

Syntax:

```
<applet attributes events> . . . </applet>
```

Example:

```
<html><head><title>applet element example</title></head>
<body bgcolor="#FFFFFF" text="#000000">
<applet code="aipwave.class" width="350" height="260">
<param name="regcode"   value="99999999">
<param name="loading"   value="1">
<param name="image"     value="aipwave.jpg">
<param name="border"    value="0">
<param name="delay"     value="50">
<param name="url"       value="none">
<param name="maxscalex" value="2.5">
<param name="frames"    value="10">
</applet></body></html>
```

<applet> HTML Attributes (6)

accesskey, align, alt, archive, class, code, codebase, datafld, datasrc, height, hidefocus, hspace, id, lang, language, name, src, style, tabindex, title, unselectable, vspace, width

<applet> Event Handlers (7)

onActivate, onAfterUpdate, onBeforeActivate, onBeforeCut, onBeforeDeactivate, onBeforeEditFocus, onBeforePaste, onBeforeUpdate, onBlur, onCellChange, onClick, onContextMenu, onControlSelect, onCut, onDataAvailable, onDatasetChanged, onDatasetComplete, onDblClick, onDeactivate, onFocus, onFocusIn, onFocusOut, onHelp, onKeyDown, onKeyPress, onKeyUp, onLoad, onLoseCapture, onMouseDown, onMouseEnter, onMouseLeave, onMouseMove, onMouseOut, onMouseOver, onMouseUp, onMouseWheel, onMove, onMoveEnd, onMoveStart, onPaste, onPropertyChange, onReadyStateChange, onResize, onResizeEnd, onResizeStart, onRowEnter, onRowExit, onRowsDelete, onRowsInserted, onScroll

\<applet\> CSS Attributes and JavaScript Style Properties (8)

The names are in CSS syntax. See the introduction to this chapter for the JavaScript syntax rules. Names noted with an asterisk (*) are JavaScript properties only.

accelerator, background-position-x, background-position-y, behavior, bottom, clear, clip, color, cursor, display, float, font-size, hasLayout(*), height, layout-grid, layout-grid-mode, left, overflow, overflow-x, overflow-y, padding, padding-bottom, padding-left, padding-right, padding-top, pixelBottom(*), pixelHeight(*), pixelLeft(*), pixelRight(*), pixelTop(*), pixelWidth(*), posBottom(*), posHeight(*), position, posLeft(*), posRight(*), posTop(*), posWidth(*), right, scrollbar-3dlight-color, scrollbar-arrow-color, scrollbar-base-color, scrollbar-darkshadow-color, scrollbar-face-color, scrollbar-highlight-color, scrollbar-shadow-color, scrollbar-track-color, styleFloat(*), text-autospace, text-underline-position, top, visibility, width, word-wrap, z-index, zoom

\<applet\> Microsoft Behaviors (9)

clientCaps, download, homePage

applet. JavaScript Properties (11)

accessKey, align, alt, altHTML, archive, canHaveHTML, className, clientHeight, clientLeft, clientTop, clientWidth, code, codeBase, cursor, dataFld, datasrc, dir, firstChild, hasLayout, height, hideFocus, hspace, id, innerHTML, isContentEditable, isDisabled, isMultiLine, isTextEdit, lang, language, lastChild, name, nextSibling, nodeName, nodeType, nodeValue, object, offsetHeight, offsetLeft, offsetParent, offsetTop, offsetWidth, outerHTML, outerText, ownerDocument, parentElement, parentNode, parentTextEdit, previousSibling, readyState, scopeName, scrollHeight, scrollLeft, scrollTop, scrollWidth, sourceIndex, src, tabIndex, tagName, tagUrn, title, uniqueID, vspace, width

applet. JavaScript Methods (12)

addBehavior, appendChild, applyElement, attachEvent, blur, clearAttributes, click, cloneNode, componentFromPoint, contains, detachEvent, fireEvent, focus, getAdjacentText, getAttribute, getAttributeNode, getBoundingClientRect, getClientRects, getElementsByTagName, hasChildNodes, insertAdjacentElement, insertBefore, mergeAttributes, namedRecordset, normalize, releaseCapture, removeAttribute, removeAttributeNode, removeBehavior, removeChild, removeExpression, replaceAdjacentText, replaceChild, scrollIntoView, setActive, setAttribute, setAttributeNode, setCapture, setExpression, swapNode

applet. JavaScript Collections (13)

all, attributes, behaviorUrns, childNodes, children

applet. JavaScript Objects (14)

currentStyle, runtimeStyle, style

<area> ... </area>

Compatibility: NN4, NN6, NN7, IE4, IE5, IE5.5, IE6

This element is used to define the clickable area on a graphic or image. The clickable area is defined using the shape (a rectangle, square, or other geometric shape) and the coords (coordinates that are used to define the size and positioning of the clickable area inside the image or graphic) attributes. This element is used in conjunction with the <map> element, which in turn is referenced by the usemap attribute of the <img> element; therefore, this element defines a clickable area in an <img> element.

Example:

```
<html><head><title>area element example</title></head>
<body bgcolor="#FFFFFF" text="#000000">
<img src="yourimage.gif" alt="" width="200" height="100" usemap="#myMap">
<map name="myMap">
<area shape="rect" coords="0, 0, 100, 50" href="http://www.w3c.com">
<area shape="rect" coords="100, 0, 200, 50" href="http://www.microsoft.com">
<area shape="rect" coords="0, 50, 100, 100" href="http://www.msn.com">
<area shape="rect" coords="100, 50, 200, 100" href="http://www.yahoo.com">
</map></body></html>
```

<area> HTML Attributes (6)

accesskey, alt, begin, class, coords, dir, end, hidefocus, href, id, lang, language, nohref, shape, style, syncmaster, systemBitrate, systemCaptions, systemLanguage, systemOverdubOrSubtitle, tabindex, target, timecontainer, title, unselectable

<area> Event Handlers (7)

onActivate, onBeforeActivate, onBeforeCopy, onBeforeCut, onBeforeDeactivate, onBeforeEditFocus, onBeforePaste, onBlur, onClick, onContextMenu, onControlSelect, onCopy, onCut, onDblClick, onDeactivate, onDrag, onDragEnd, onDragEnter, onDragLeave, onDragOver, onDragStart, onDrop, onFocus, onFocusIn, onFocusOut, onHelp, onKeyDown, onKeyPress, onKeyUp, onLoseCapture, onMouseDown, onMouseEnter, onMouseLeave, onMouseMove, onMouseOut, onMouseOver, onMouseUp, onMouseWheel, onMove, onMoveEnd, onMoveStart, onPaste, onPropertyChange, onReadyStateChange, onResizeEnd, onResizeStart, onSelectStart, onTimeError

<area> CSS Attributes and JavaScript Style Properties (8)

behavior

<area> Microsoft Behaviors (9)

clientCaps, download, homePage, httpFolder, saveFavorite, saveHistory,
saveSnapshot, time, time2, userData

area. JavaScript Properties (11)

accessKey, alt, canHaveHTML, className, clientHeight, clientWidth, coords, dir,
disabled, end, firstChild, hash, hideFocus, host, hostname, href, id, innerHTML,
isContentEditable, isDisabled, isMultiLine, isTextEdit, lang, language, lastChild,
nextSibling, nodeName, nodeType, nodeValue, noHref, offsetHeight, offsetLeft,
offsetParent, offsetTop, offsetWidth, outerHTML, outerText, ownerDocument,
parentElement, parentNode, parentTextEdit, pathname, port, previousSibling,
protocol, readyState, scopeName, scrollHeight, scrollLeft, scrollTop, scrollWidth,
search, shape, sourceIndex, tabIndex, tagName, tagUrn, target, title, uniqueID

area. JavaScript Methods (12)

addBehavior, appendChild, applyElement, attachEvent, blur, clearAttributes, click,
cloneNode, componentFromPoint, contains, detachEvent, dragDrop, fireEvent, focus,
getAdjacentText, getAttribute, getAttributeNode, getBoundingClientRect,
getClientRects, getElementsByTagName, getExpression, hasChildNodes,
insertAdjacentElement, insertAdjacentHTML, insertAdjacentText, insertBefore,
mergeAttributes, normalize, releaseCapture, removeAttribute, removeAttributeNode,
removeBehavior, removeChild, removeExpression, replaceAdjacentText, replaceChild,
scrollIntoView, setActive, setAttribute, setAttributeNode, setCapture,
setExpression, swapNode

area. JavaScript Collections (13)

all, attributes, behaviorUrns, childNodes, children

<b> ... </b>

Compatibility: NN4, NN6, NN7, IE4, IE5, IE5.5, IE6

This element causes the text between its opening and closing tags to be
emphasized in boldface.

   Syntax:

```
<b attributes events> . . . </b>
```

   Example:

```
<html><head><title>b element example</title></head>
<body bgcolor="#FFFFFF" text="#000000">
This formulation is <b>new</b> and <b>improved</b>
</body></html>
```

<b> HTML Attributes (6)

accesskey, begin, class, contenteditable, dir, disabled, end, hidefocus, id, lang, language, style, syncmaster, systemBitrate, systemCaptions, systemLanguage, systemOverdubOrSubtitle, tabindex, timecontainer, title, unselectable

<b> Event Handlers (7)

onActivate, onBeforeActivate, onBeforeCopy, onBeforeCut, onBeforeDeactivate, onBeforeEditFocus, onBeforePaste, onBlur, onClick, onContextMenu, onControlSelect, onCopy, onCut, onDblClick, onDeactivate, onDrag, onDragEnd, onDragEnter, onDragLeave, onDragOver, onDragStart, onDrop, onFocus, onFocusIn, onFocusOut, onHelp, onKeyDown, onKeyPress, onKeyUp, onLoseCapture, onMouseDown, onMouseEnter, onMouseLeave, onMouseMove, onMouseOut, onMouseOver, onMouseUp, onMouseWheel, onMove, onMoveEnd, onMoveStart, onPaste, onPropertyChange, onReadyStateChange, onResize, onResizeEnd, onResizeStart, onSelectStart, onTimeError

<b> CSS Attributes and JavaScript Style Properties (8)

The names are in CSS syntax. See the introduction to this chapter for the JavaScript syntax rules. Names noted with an asterisk (*) are JavaScript properties only.

!important, accelerator, background, background-attachment, background-color, background-image, background-position, background-position-x, background-position-y, background-repeat, behavior, border, border-bottom, border-bottom-color, border-bottom-style, border-bottom-width, border-color, border-left, border-left-color, border-left-style, border-left-width, border-right, border-right-color, border-right-style, border-right-width, border-style, border-top, border-top-color, border-top-style, border-top-width, border-width, bottom, clear, clip, color, cursor, direction, display, filter, float, font, font-family, font-size, font-style, font-variant, font-weight, hasLayout(*), height, layout-flow, layout-grid, layout-grid-mode, left, letter-spacing, line-height, margin, margin-bottom, margin-left, margin-right, margin-top, overflow, overflow-x, overflow-y, padding, padding-bottom, padding-left, padding-right, padding-top, pixelBottom(*), pixelHeight(*), pixelLeft(*), pixelRight(*), pixelTop(*), pixelWidth(*), posBottom(*), posHeight(*), position, posLeft(*), posRight(*), posTop(*), posWidth(*), right, styleFloat(*), text-autospace, text-decoration, text-transform, text-underline-position, textDecorationBlink(*), textDecorationLineThrough(*), textDecorationNone(*), textDecorationOverline(*), textDecorationUnderline(*), top, unicode-bidi, visibility, width, word-spacing, word-wrap, writing-mode, z-index, zoom

<b> Microsoft Behaviors (9)

clientCaps, download, homePage, httpFolder, saveFavorite, saveHistory, saveSnapshot, time, time2, userData

<b> Microsoft Filters (10)

Alpha, Barn, BasicImage, BlendTrans, Blinds, Blur, CheckerBoard, Chroma, Compositor, DropShadow, Emboss, Engrave, Fade, FlipH, FlipV, Glow, GradientWipe, Gray, ICMFilter, Inset, Invert, Iris, Light, MaskFilter, Matrix, MotionBlur,

Pixelate, RadialWipe, RandomBars, RandomDissolve, RevealTrans, Shadow, Slide, Spiral, Stretch, Strips, Wave, Wheel, Xray, Zigzag

b. JavaScript Properties (11)

accessKey, canHaveChildren, canHaveHTML, className, clientHeight, clientLeft, clientTop, clientWidth, contentEditable, cursor, dir, disabled, end, firstChild, hasLayout, hideFocus, id, innerHTML, innerText, isContentEditable, isDisabled, isMultiLine, isTextEdit, lang, language, lastChild, nextSibling, nodeName, nodeType, nodeValue, offsetHeight, offsetLeft, offsetParent, offsetTop, offsetWidth, outerHTML, outerText, ownerDocument, parentElement, parentNode, parentTextEdit, previousSibling, readyState, scopeName, scrollHeight, scrollLeft, scrollTop, scrollWidth, sourceIndex, tabIndex, tagName, tagUrn, title, uniqueID

b. JavaScript Methods (12)

addBehavior, appendChild, applyElement, attachEvent, blur, clearAttributes, click, cloneNode, componentFromPoint, contains, detachEvent, fireEvent, focus, getAdjacentText, getAttribute, getAttributeNode, getBoundingClientRect, getClientRects, getElementsByTagName, getExpression, hasChildNodes, insertAdjacentElement, insertAdjacentHTML, insertAdjacentText, insertBefore, mergeAttributes, normalize, releaseCapture, removeAttribute, removeAttributeNode, removeBehavior, removeChild, removeExpression, removeNode, replaceAdjacentText, replaceChild, replaceNode, scrollIntoView, setActive, setAttribute, setAttributeNode, setCapture, setExpression, swapNode

b. JavaScript Collections (13)

all, attributes, behaviorUrns, childNodes, children

b. JavaScript Objects (14)

currentStyle, runtimeStyle, style

<base>

Compatibility: NN4, NN6, NN7, IE4, IE5, IE5.5, IE6

This element establishes a base URL for the website. This allows you to direct every link in the page to a specific site, and thereafter the <a> element only has to refer to the specific page inside the site. This element can also be useful in forcing all page links to be opened in a new window by setting the target attribute to _blank. This element is inserted within the <head> element and therefore is not visible on the page.

Syntax:

<base attributes events>

Example:

```
<html><head><title>base element example:</title>
<base href="http://www.advocar.com/" target="_blank">
</head>
<body bgcolor="#FFFFFF" text="#000000">
<p><a href="NewCars/VehicleSelect.asp">Click here</a> to go to the new car
section.</p>
</body></html>
```

<base> HTML Attributes (6)

href, id, target

<base> Event Handlers (7)

onLayoutComplete, onMouseEnter, onMouseLeave, onReadyStateChange

<base> CSS Attributes and JavaScript Style Properties (8)

The names are in CSS syntax. See the introduction to this chapter for the JavaScript syntax rules. Names noted with an asterisk (*) are JavaScript properties only.

background-position-x, background-position-y, behavior, layout-grid, layout-grid-mode, pixelBottom(*), pixelHeight(*), pixelLeft(*), pixelRight(*), pixelTop(*), pixelWidth(*), posBottom(*), posHeight(*), posLeft(*), posRight(*), posTop(*), posWidth(*), text-autospace, text-underline-position

<base> Microsoft Behaviors (9)

clientCaps, download, homePage

base. JavaScript Properties (11)

canHaveHTML, className, clientHeight, clientWidth, dir, firstChild, href, id, innerHTML, isContentEditable, isDisabled, isMultiLine, isTextEdit, lang, lastChild, nextSibling, nodeName, nodeType, nodeValue, offsetHeight, offsetLeft, offsetParent, offsetTop, offsetWidth, ownerDocument, parentElement, parentNode, parentTextEdit, previousSibling, readyState, scopeName, scrollHeight, scrollLeft, scrollTop, scrollWidth, sourceIndex, tagName, tagUrn, target, title, uniqueID

base. JavaScript Methods (12)

addBehavior, appendChild, applyElement, attachEvent, clearAttributes, cloneNode, componentFromPoint, contains, detachEvent, fireEvent, getAdjacentText, getAttribute, getAttributeNode, getBoundingClientRect, getClientRects, getElementsByTagName, hasChildNodes, insertAdjacentElement, insertBefore, mergeAttributes, normalize, removeAttribute, removeAttributeNode, removeBehavior, removeChild, replaceAdjacentText, replaceChild, setAttribute, setAttributeNode, swapNode

base. JavaScript Collections (13)

all, attributes, behaviorUrns, childNodes, children

<basefont>

Compatibility: NN4, IE4, IE5, IE5.5, IE6

This element is used to establish a default font face, size, and style for the text on an entire web page. However, you can still set the font of a portion of text inside the page using the <font> element. Additionally, the font size of <font> elements used throughout the page is set relative to the font size of the <basefont> element. This element has been deprecated, and you can achieve the same or better results using CSS (see Chapter 1 for information on CSS).

Syntax:

```
<basefont attributes events>
```

Example:

```
<html><head><title>basefont element example</title>
<basefont face="Times, serif" size=5>
</head>
<body bgcolor="#FFFFFF" text="#000000">
<p>This text will appear in the Times font.<font face="Courier, serif" size=5
color="blue"> However, this text will appear in a blue Courier font.</font>
</body></html>
```

<basefont> HTML Attributes (6)

color, face, id, size

<basefont> Event Handlers (7)

onLayoutComplete, onMouseEnter, onMouseLeave, onReadyStateChange

<basefont> CSS Attributes and JavaScript Style Properties (8)

The names are in CSS syntax. See the introduction to this chapter for the JavaScript syntax rules. Names noted with an asterisk (*) are JavaScript properties only.

background-position-x, background-position-y, behavior, font-family, layout-grid, layout-grid-mode, pixelBottom(*), pixelHeight(*), pixelLeft(*), pixelRight(*), pixelTop(*), pixelWidth(*), posBottom(*), posHeight(*), posLeft(*), posRight(*), posTop(*), posWidth(*), text-autospace, text-underline-position, white-space

<basefont> Microsoft Behaviors (9)

clientCaps, download, homePage

basefont. JavaScript Properties (11)

canHaveHTML, className, clientHeight, clientWidth, color, dir, disabled, face, firstChild, id, innerHTML, isContentEditable, isDisabled, isMultiLine, isTextEdit, lang, lastChild, nextSibling, nodeName, nodeType, nodeValue, offsetHeight, offsetLeft, offsetParent, offsetTop, offsetWidth, ownerDocument, parentElement, parentNode, parentTextEdit, previousSibling, readyState, scopeName, scrollHeight, scrollLeft, scrollTop, scrollWidth, size, sourceIndex, tagName, tagUrn, title, uniqueID

basefont. JavaScript Methods (12)

addBehavior, appendChild, applyElement, attachEvent, clearAttributes, cloneNode, componentFromPoint, contains, detachEvent, dragDrop, fireEvent, getAdjacentText, getAttribute, getAttributeNode, getBoundingClientRect, getClientRects, getElementsByTagName, hasChildNodes, insertAdjacentElement, insertAdjacentHTML, insertAdjacentText, insertBefore, mergeAttributes, normalize, removeAttribute, removeAttributeNode, removeBehavior, removeChild, replaceAdjacentText, replaceChild, setAttribute, setAttributeNode, swapNode

basefont. JavaScript Collections (13)

all, attributes, behaviorUrns, childNodes, children

<bdo> ... </bdo>

Compatibility: IE5, IE5.5, IE6

The value of the dir attribute of this element determines the reading direction of text (either from left to right or from right to left).

Syntax:

```
<bdo attributes events> . . . </bdo>
```

Example:

```
<html><head><title>bdo element example</title></head>
<body bgcolor="#FFFFFF" text="#000000">
<bdo dir="ltr">This text is read from left to right</bdo><br>
```

```
<bdo dir="rtl">tfel ot thgir morf daer si txet sihT</bdo>
</body></html>
```

<bdo> HTML Attributes (6)

accesskey, class, contenteditable, dir, disabled, hidefocus, id, lang, language,
style, tabindex, title, unselectable

<bdo> Event Handlers (7)

onActivate, onAfterUpdate, onBeforeActivate, onBeforeCopy, onBeforeCut,
onBeforeDeactivate, onBeforeEditFocus, onBeforePaste, onBeforeUpdate, onBlur,
onCellChange, onClick, onContextMenu, onControlSelect, onCopy, onCut, onDblClick,
onDeactivate, onDrag, onDragEnd, onDragEnter, onDragLeave, onDragOver, onDragStart,
onDrop, onErrorUpdate, onFilterChange, onFocus, onFocusIn, onFocusOut, onHelp,
onKeyDown, onKeyPress, onKeyUp, onLoseCapture, onMouseDown, onMouseEnter,
onMouseLeave, onMouseMove, onMouseOut, onMouseOver, onMouseUp, onMouseWheel,
onMove, onMoveEnd, onMoveStart, onPaste, onPropertyChange, onReadyStateChange,
onResizeEnd, onResizeStart, onScroll, onSelectStart

<bdo> CSS Attributes and JavaScript Style Properties (8)

The names are in CSS syntax. See the introduction to this chapter for the
JavaScript syntax rules. Names noted with an asterisk (*) are JavaScript
properties only.

accelerator, border, border-bottom, border-bottom-color, border-bottom-style,
border-bottom-width, border-color, border-left, border-left-color, border-left-
style, border-left-width, border-right, border-right-color, border-right-style,
border-right-width, border-style, border-top, border-top-color, border-top-style,
border-top-width, border-width, clip, direction, display, filter, hasLayout(*),
height, layout-grid, layout-grid-mode, margin, margin-bottom, margin-left, margin-
right, margin-top, overflow, overflow-x, overflow-y, padding, padding-bottom,
padding-left, padding-right, padding-top, position, scrollbar-3dlight-color,
scrollbar-arrow-color, scrollbar-base-color, scrollbar-darkshadow-color, scrollbar-
face-color, scrollbar-highlight-color, scrollbar-shadow-color, scrollbar-track-
color, text-autospace, text-overflow, text-underline-position, unicode-bidi, white-
space, width, word-wrap, zoom

<bdo> Microsoft Behaviors (9)

clientCaps, download, homePage

<bdo> Microsoft Filters (10)

Alpha, Barn, BasicImage, BlendTrans, Blinds, Blur, CheckerBoard, Chroma,
Compositor, DropShadow, Emboss, Engrave, Fade, FlipH, FlipV, Glow, GradientWipe,
Gray, ICMFilter, Inset, Invert, Iris, Light, MaskFilter, Matrix, MotionBlur,
Pixelate, RadialWipe, RandomBars, RandomDissolve, RevealTrans, Shadow, Slide,
Spiral, Stretch, Strips, Wave, Wheel, Xray, Zigzag

bdo. JavaScript Properties (11)

accessKey, canHaveChildren, canHaveHTML, className, clientHeight, clientLeft, clientTop, clientWidth, contentEditable, dir, disabled, firstChild, hasLayout, hideFocus, id, innerHTML, innerText, isContentEditable, isDisabled, isMultiLine, isTextEdit, lang, language, lastChild, nextSibling, nodeName, nodeType, nodeValue, offsetHeight, offsetLeft, offsetParent, offsetTop, offsetWidth, outerHTML, outerText, ownerDocument, parentElement, parentNode, parentTextEdit, previousSibling, readyState, scopeName, scrollHeight, scrollLeft, scrollTop, scrollWidth, sourceIndex, tabIndex, tagName, tagUrn, title

bdo. JavaScript Methods (12)

appendChild, applyElement, blur, clearAttributes, cloneNode, componentFromPoint, fireEvent, focus, getAdjacentText, getAttribute, getAttributeNode, getElementsByTagName, getExpression, hasChildNodes, insertAdjacentElement, insertBefore, mergeAttributes, normalize, removeAttribute, removeAttributeNode, removeChild, removeExpression, removeNode, replaceAdjacentText, replaceChild, replaceNode, setActive, setAttribute, setAttributeNode, setExpression, swapNode

bdo. JavaScript Collections (13)

all, attributes, behaviorUrns, childNodes, children, filters

bdo. JavaScript Objects (14)

currentStyle

<bgsound>

Compatibility: IE4, IE5, IE5.5, IE6

This element causes a sound to be played in the background while the user visits the page. <bgsound> is only allowed inside the <head> element. The sound file specified in its src attribute can be in the .wav, .au, or .mid formats.

Syntax:

<bgsound *attributes events*>

Example:

```
<html><head><title>bgsound element example</title><bgsound src="yoursoundfile.wav"
loop="3">
<script language="javascript">
function stopS() {
document.all.tags("bgsound")[0].volume = -10000;
}
function restartS() {
document.all.tags("bgsound")[0].volume = 0;
```

```
    }
    </script>
    </head>
    <body bgcolor="#FFFFFF" text="#000000">
    <p>You are listening to the yoursoundfile.wav sound file.
    </p>
    <button type="button" onClick="stopS()">Stop the music</button><br>
    <button type="button" onClick="restartS()">Restart the music</button>
    </body></html>
```

`<bgsound>` HTML Attributes (6)

balance, id, loop, src, volume

`<bgsound>` Event Handlers (7)

onLayoutComplete, onMouseEnter, onMouseLeave, onReadyStateChange

`<bgsound>` CSS Attributes and JavaScript Style Properties (8)

behavior, text-autospace, text-underline-position

`<bgsound>` Microsoft Behaviors (9)

clientCaps, download, homePage

bgsound. JavaScript Properties (11)

balance, canHaveHTML, disabled, id, isContentEditable, isDisabled, isMultiLine,
loop, nextSibling, nodeName, nodeType, nodeValue, outerHTML, outerText,
parentElement, parentNode, parentTextEdit, previousSibling, readyState, scopeName,
sourceIndex, src, tagName, tagUrn, uniqueID, volume

bgsound. JavaScript Methods (12)

addBehavior, applyElement, attachEvent, clearAttributes, cloneNode,
componentFromPoint, detachEvent, dragDrop, fireEvent, getAttribute,
getAttributeNode, getElementsByTagName, insertAdjacentElement, mergeAttributes,
normalize, removeAttribute, removeAttributeNode, removeBehavior, setAttribute,
setAttributeNode, swapNode

bgsound. JavaScript Collections (13)

all, attributes, behaviorUrns

<big> ... </big>

Compatibility: NN4, NN6, NN7, IE4, IE5, IE5.5, IE6

This element causes text between the opening and closing tags to be displayed using a font size value one greater (in HTML's 1–7 scale) than the current font size on the page.

Syntax:

```
<big attributes events> . . . </big>
```

Example:

```
<html><head><title>big element example</title></head>
<body bgcolor="#FFFFFF" text="#000000">
<p align="center">If you nest <big><big>big</big> elements</big>, the <big>effects
on the <big>nested</big> elements are cumulative.</big>
</body></html>
```

<big> HTML Attributes (6)

accesskey, begin, class, contenteditable, dir, disabled, end, hidefocus, id, lang, language, style, syncmaster, systemBitrate, systemCaptions, systemLanguage, systemOverdubOrSubtitle, tabindex, timecontainer, title, unselectable

<big> Event Handlers (7)

onActivate, onBeforeActivate, onBeforeCopy, onBeforeCut, onBeforeDeactivate, onBeforeEditFocus, onBeforePaste, onBlur, onClick, onContextMenu, onControlSelect, onCopy, onCut, onDblClick, onDeactivate, onDrag, onDragEnd, onDragEnter, onDragLeave, onDragOver, onDragStart, onDrop, onFocus, onFocusIn, onFocusOut, onHelp, onKeyDown, onKeyPress, onKeyUp, onLoseCapture, onMouseDown, onMouseEnter, onMouseLeave, onMouseMove, onMouseOut, onMouseOver, onMouseUp, onMouseWheel, onMove, onMoveEnd, onMoveStart, onPaste, onPropertyChange, onReadyStateChange, onResize, onResizeEnd, onResizeStart, onSelectStart, onTimeError

<big> CSS Attributes and JavaScript Style Properties (8)

The names are in CSS syntax. See the introduction to this chapter for the JavaScript syntax rules. Names noted with an asterisk (*) are JavaScript properties only.

!important, accelerator, background, background-attachment, background-color, background-image, background-position, background-position-x, background-position-y, background-repeat, behavior, border, border-bottom, border-bottom-color, border-bottom-style, border-bottom-width, border-color, border-left, border-left-color, border-left-style, border-left-width, border-right, border-right-color, border-right-style, border-right-width, border-style, border-top, border-top-color, border-top-style, border-top-width, border-width, bottom, clear, clip, color, cursor, direction, display, filter, float, font, font-family, font-size, font-style, font-variant, font-weight, hasLayout(*), height, layout-flow, layout-grid, layout-grid-mode, left, letter-spacing, line-height, margin, margin-bottom, margin-left, margin-right, margin-top, overflow, overflow-x, overflow-y, padding, padding-bottom, padding-left, padding-right, padding-top, pixelBottom(*), pixelHeight(*), pixelLeft(*), pixelRight(*), pixelTop(*), pixelWidth(*), posBottom(*), posHeight(*), position, posLeft(*), posRight(*), posTop(*), posWidth(*), right, styleFloat(*), text-autospace, text-decoration, text-overflow, text-transform, text-underline-position, textDecorationBlink(*), textDecorationLineThrough(*), textDecorationNone(*), textDecorationOverline(*), textDecorationUnderline(*), top, unicode-bidi, visibility, white-space, width, word-spacing, word-wrap, writing-mode, z-index, zoom

\<big\> Microsoft Behaviors (9)

clientCaps, download, homePage, httpFolder, saveFavorite, saveHistory, saveSnapshot, time, time2, userData

\<big\> Microsoft Filters (10)

Alpha, Barn, BasicImage, BlendTrans, Blinds, Blur, CheckerBoard, Chroma, Compositor, DropShadow, Emboss, Engrave, Fade, FlipH, FlipV, Glow, GradientWipe, Gray, ICMFilter, Inset, Invert, Iris, Light, MaskFilter, Matrix, MotionBlur, Pixelate, RadialWipe, RandomBars, RandomDissolve, RevealTrans, Shadow, Slide, Spiral, Stretch, Strips, Wave, Wheel, Xray, Zigzag

big. JavaScript Properties (11)

accessKey, canHaveChildren, canHaveHTML, className, clientHeight, clientLeft, clientTop, clientWidth, contentEditable, cursor, dir, disabled, end, firstChild, hasLayout, hideFocus, id, innerHTML, innerText, isContentEditable, isDisabled, isMultiLine, isTextEdit, lang, language, lastChild, nextSibling, nodeName, nodeType, nodeValue, offsetHeight, offsetLeft, offsetParent, offsetTop, offsetWidth, outerHTML, outerText, ownerDocument, parentElement, parentNode, parentTextEdit, previousSibling, readyState, scopeName, scrollHeight, scrollLeft, scrollTop, scrollWidth, sourceIndex, tabIndex, tagName, tagUrn, title, uniqueID

big. JavaScript Methods (12)

addBehavior, appendChild, applyElement, attachEvent, blur, clearAttributes, click, cloneNode, componentFromPoint, contains, detachEvent, fireEvent, focus, getAdjacentText, getAttribute, getAttributeNode, getBoundingClientRect, getClientRects, getElementsByTagName, getExpression, hasChildNodes, insertAdjacentElement, insertAdjacentHTML, insertAdjacentText, insertBefore, mergeAttributes, normalize, releaseCapture, removeAttribute, removeAttributeNode, removeBehavior, removeChild, removeExpression, removeNode, replaceAdjacentText, replaceChild, replaceNode, scrollIntoView, setActive, setAttribute, setAttributeNode, setCapture, setExpression, swapNode

big. JavaScript Collections (13)

all, attributes, behaviorUrns, childNodes, children

big. JavaScript Objects (14)

currentStyle, runtimeStyle, style

<blockquote> ... </blockquote>

Compatibility: NN4, NN6, NN7, IE4, IE5, IE5.5, IE6

This element causes the text between its opening and closing tags to be indented by 40 pixels. This element is used for displaying long quotations, whereas its sister element, <q>, is used for shorter inline quotations.

Syntax:

<blockquote *attributes events*> . . . </blockquote>

Example:

```
<html><head><title>blockquote element example</title></head>
<body bgcolor="#FFFFFF" text="#000000">
<p>The blockquote content is indented by 40 pixels. You can shrink the size of the
browser to better see the effects of this example.</p>
<blockquote cite="http://www.advocar.com/Help/HowItWorks.asp">For over thirty
years, Advocar has been helping people like you to</blockquote>
</body></html>
```

<blockquote> HTML Attributes (6)

accesskey, begin, cite, class, contenteditable, dir, disabled, end, hidefocus, id, lang, language, style, syncmaster, systemBitrate, systemCaptions, systemLanguage, systemOverdubOrSubtitle, tabindex, timecontainer, title, unselectable

<blockquote> Event Handlers (7)

onActivate, onBeforeActivate, onBeforeCopy, onBeforeCut, onBeforeDeactivate, onBeforeEditFocus, onBeforePaste, onBlur, onClick, onContextMenu, onControlSelect, onCopy, onCut, onDblClick, onDeactivate, onDrag, onDragEnd, onDragEnter, onDragLeave, onDragOver, onDragStart, onDrop, onFocus, onFocusIn, onFocusOut, onHelp, onKeyDown, onKeyPress, onKeyUp, onLoseCapture, onMouseDown, onMouseEnter, onMouseLeave, onMouseMove, onMouseOut, onMouseOver, onMouseUp, onMouseWheel, onMove, onMoveEnd, onMoveStart, onPaste, onPropertyChange, onReadyStateChange, onResize, onResizeEnd, onResizeStart, onSelectStart, onTimeError

<blockquote> CSS Attributes and JavaScript Style Properties (8)

The names are in CSS syntax. See the introduction to this chapter for the JavaScript syntax rules. Names noted with an asterisk (*) are JavaScript properties only.

!important, :first-letter, :first-line, accelerator, background, background-attachment, background-color, background-image, background-position, background-position-x, background-position-y, background-repeat, behavior, border, border-bottom, border-bottom-color, border-bottom-style, border-bottom-width, border-color, border-left, border-left-color, border-left-style, border-left-width, border-right, border-right-color, border-right-style, border-right-width, border-style, border-top, border-top-color, border-top-style, border-top-width, border-width, bottom, clear, clip, color, cursor, direction, display, filter, float, font, font-family, font-size, font-style, font-variant, font-weight, hasLayout(*), height, layout-flow, layout-grid, layout-grid-char, layout-grid-line, layout-grid-mode, layout-grid-type, left, letter-spacing, line-break, line-height, margin, margin-bottom, margin-left, margin-right, margin-top, overflow, overflow-x, overflow-y, padding, padding-bottom, padding-left, padding-right, padding-top, page-break-after, page-break-before, pixelBottom(*), pixelHeight(*), pixelLeft(*), pixelRight(*), pixelTop(*), pixelWidth(*), posBottom(*), posHeight(*), position, posLeft(*), posRight(*), posTop(*), posWidth(*), right, styleFloat(*), text-align, text-align-last, text-autospace, text-decoration, text-indent, text-justify, text-kashida-space, text-overflow, text-transform, text-underline-position, textDecorationBlink(*), textDecorationLineThrough(*), textDecorationNone(*), textDecorationOverline(*), textDecorationUnderline(*), top, unicode-bidi, visibility, white-space, width, word-break, word-spacing, word-wrap, writing-mode, z-index, zoom

<blockquote> Microsoft Behaviors (9)

clientCaps, download, homePage, httpFolder, saveFavorite, saveHistory, saveSnapshot, time, time2, userData

<blockquote> Microsoft Filters (10)

Alpha, Barn, BasicImage, BlendTrans, Blinds, Blur, CheckerBoard, Chroma, Compositor, DropShadow, Emboss, Engrave, Fade, FlipH, FlipV, Glow, GradientWipe, Gray, ICMFilter, Inset, Invert, Iris, Light, MaskFilter, Matrix, MotionBlur, Pixelate, RadialWipe, RandomBars, RandomDissolve, RevealTrans, Shadow, Slide, Spiral, Stretch, Strips, Wave, Wheel, Xray, Zigzag

blockquote. JavaScript Properties (11)

accessKey, blockDirection, canHaveChildren, canHaveHTML, cite, className, clientHeight, clientLeft, clientTop, clientWidth, contentEditable, cursor, dir, disabled, end, firstChild, hasLayout, hideFocus, id, innerHTML, innerText, isContentEditable, isDisabled, isMultiLine, isTextEdit, lang, language, lastChild, nextSibling, nodeName, nodeType, nodeValue, offsetHeight, offsetLeft, offsetParent, offsetTop, offsetWidth, outerHTML, outerText, ownerDocument, parentElement, parentNode, parentTextEdit, previousSibling, readyState, scopeName, scrollHeight, scrollLeft, scrollTop, scrollWidth, sourceIndex, tabIndex, tagName, tagUrn, title, uniqueID

blockquote. JavaScript Methods (12)

addBehavior, appendChild, applyElement, attachEvent, blur, clearAttributes, click, cloneNode, componentFromPoint, contains, detachEvent, fireEvent, focus, getAdjacentText, getAttribute, getAttributeNode, getBoundingClientRect, getClientRects, getElementsByTagName, getExpression, hasChildNodes, insertAdjacentElement, insertAdjacentHTML, insertAdjacentText, insertBefore, mergeAttributes, normalize, releaseCapture, removeAttribute, removeAttributeNode,

removeBehavior, removeChild, removeExpression, removeNode, replaceAdjacentText, replaceChild, replaceNode, scrollIntoView, setActive, setAttribute, setAttributeNode, setCapture, setExpression, swapNode

blockquote. JavaScript Collections (13)

all, attributes, behaviorUrns, childNodes, children

blockquote. JavaScript Objects (14)

currentStyle, runtimeStyle, style

<body> ... </body>

Compatibility: NN4, NN6, NN7, IE4, IE5, IE5.5, IE6

This element defines the place on the screen where all text, graphics, and other web page content are displayed.

Syntax:

```
<body attributes events> . . . </body>
```

Example:

```
<html><head><title>body element example</title></head>
<body bgcolor="#FFFFFF" text="#000000" bgproperties="fixed"
background="yourbackgroundfile.jpg" bottommargin="150">
<p>Web page content will scroll independently from the background image because the
bgproperties property equals "fixed".</p>
</body></html>
```

<body> HTML Attributes (6)

accesskey, alink, background, bgcolor, bgproperties, bottommargin, class, contenteditable, dir, disabled, hidefocus, id, lang, language, leftmargin, link, nowrap, rightmargin, scroll, style, t:timestartrule, tabindex, text, title, topmargin, unselectable, vlink

<body> Event Handlers (7)

onActivate, onAfterPrint, onBeforeActivate, onBeforeCut, onBeforeDeactivate, onBeforeEditFocus, onBeforePaste, onBeforePrint, onBeforeUnload, onClick, onContextMenu, onControlSelect, onCut, onDblClick, onDeactivate, onDrag, onDragEnd, onDragEnter, onDragLeave, onDragOver, onDragStart, onDrop, onFilterChange, onFocus, onFocusIn, onFocusOut, onHelp, onKeyDown, onKeyPress, onKeyUp, onLoad, onLoseCapture, onMouseDown, onMouseEnter, onMouseLeave, onMouseMove, onMouseOut, onMouseOver, onMouseUp, onMouseWheel, onMove, onMoveEnd, onMoveStart, onPaste, onPropertyChange, onReadyStateChange, onResizeEnd, onResizeStart, onScroll, onSelect, onSelectStart, onUnload

\<body\> CSS Attributes and JavaScript Style Properties (8)

The names are in CSS syntax. See the introduction to this chapter for the JavaScript syntax rules. Names noted with an asterisk (*) are JavaScript properties only.

!important, :first-letter, :first-line, accelerator, background, background-attachment, background-color, background-image, background-position, background-position-x, background-position-y, background-repeat, behavior, border, border-bottom, border-bottom-color, border-bottom-style, border-bottom-width, border-color, border-left, border-left-color, border-left-style, border-left-width, border-right, border-right-color, border-right-style, border-right-width, border-style, border-top, border-top-color, border-top-style, border-top-width, border-width, color, cursor, direction, display, filter, font, font-family, font-size, font-style, font-variant, font-weight, hasLayout(*), layout-grid, layout-grid-char, layout-grid-line, layout-grid-mode, layout-grid-type, letter-spacing, line-break, line-height, margin, margin-bottom, margin-left, margin-right, margin-top, overflow, overflow-x, overflow-y, padding, padding-bottom, padding-left, padding-right, padding-top, page-break-after, page-break-before, pixelBottom(*), pixelHeight(*), pixelLeft(*), pixelRight(*), pixelTop(*), pixelWidth(*), posBottom(*), posHeight(*), posLeft(*), posRight(*), posTop(*), posWidth(*), scrollbar-3dlight-color, scrollbar-arrow-color, scrollbar-base-color, scrollbar-darkshadow-color, scrollbar-face-color, scrollbar-highlight-color, scrollbar-shadow-color, scrollbar-track-color, text-align, text-align-last, text-autospace, text-decoration, text-indent, text-justify, text-kashida-space, text-overflow, text-transform, text-underline-position, textDecorationBlink(*), textDecorationLineThrough(*), textDecorationNone(*), textDecorationOverline(*), textDecorationUnderline(*), unicode-bidi, visibility, white-space, word-break, word-spacing, word-wrap, zoom

---

\<body\> Microsoft Behaviors (9)

---

clientCaps, download, homePage, httpFolder

\<body\> Microsoft Filters (10)

Alpha, Barn, BasicImage, BlendTrans, Blinds, Blur, CheckerBoard, Chroma, Compositor, Emboss, Engrave, Fade, FlipH, FlipV, Glow, GradientWipe, Gray, ICMFilter, Inset, Invert, Iris, Light, MaskFilter, Matrix, MotionBlur, Pixelate, RadialWipe, RandomBars, RandomDissolve, RevealTrans, Shadow, Slide, Spiral, Stretch, Strips, Wave, Wheel, Xray, Zigzag

---

body. JavaScript Properties (11)

---

accessKey, aLink, background, bgColor, bgProperties, blockDirection, bottomMargin, canHaveChildren, canHaveHTML, className, clientHeight, clientLeft, clientTop, clientWidth, contentEditable, cursor, dir, disabled, firstChild, hasLayout, hideFocus, id, innerHTML, innerText, isContentEditable, isDisabled, isMultiLine, isTextEdit, lang, language, lastChild, leftMargin, link, nextSibling, nodeName, nodeType, nodeValue, noWrap, offsetHeight, offsetLeft, offsetParent, offsetTop, offsetWidth, ownerDocument, parentElement, parentNode, parentTextEdit, previousSibling, readyState, rightMargin, scopeName, scroll, scrollHeight, scrollLeft, scrollTop, scrollWidth, sourceIndex, tabIndex, tagName, tagUrn, text, title, topMargin, uniqueID, vLink

body. JavaScript Methods (12)

addBehavior, appendChild, applyElement, attachEvent, blur, clearAttributes, click, cloneNode, componentFromPoint, contains, createControlRange, createTextRange, detachEvent, doScroll, dragDrop, fireEvent, focus, getAdjacentText, getAttribute, getAttributeNode, getBoundingClientRect, getClientRects, getElementsByTagName, getExpression, hasChildNodes, insertAdjacentElement, insertAdjacentHTML, insertAdjacentText, insertBefore, mergeAttributes, normalize, releaseCapture, removeAttribute, removeAttributeNode, removeBehavior, removeChild, removeExpression, removeNode, replaceAdjacentText, replaceChild, replaceNode, setActive, setAttribute, setAttributeNode, setCapture, setExpression, swapNode

body. JavaScript Collections (13)

all, attributes, behaviorUrns, childNodes, children, filters, timeAll, timeChildren

body. JavaScript Objects (14)

currentStyle, runtimeStyle, style

Compatibility: NN4, NN6, NN7, IE4, IE5, IE5.5, IE6

This element adds a new line to the web page.
  Syntax:

```
<br attributes events>
```

  Example:

```
<html><head><title>br element example</title></head>
<body bgcolor="#FFFFFF" text="#000000">
<p>The p element occupies more vertical space than the br element.<br> The br<br>
element adds a new line to the page.</p>
</body></html>
```


 HTML Attributes (6)

class, clear, id, style, title

 Event Handlers (7)

onLayoutComplete, onLoseCapture, onReadyStateChange, onSelectStart

 CSS Attributes and JavaScript Style Properties (8)

display

 Microsoft Behaviors (9)

clientCaps, download, homePage

br. JavaScript Properties (11)

canHaveHTML, className, clear, clientHeight, clientWidth, dir, disabled, firstChild, id, innerHTML, isContentEditable, isDisabled, isMultiLine, isTextEdit, lang, lastChild, nextSibling, nodeName, nodeType, nodeValue, offsetHeight, offsetLeft, offsetParent, offsetTop, offsetWidth, outerHTML, outerText, ownerDocument, parentElement, parentNode, parentTextEdit, previousSibling, readyState, scopeName, scrollHeight, scrollLeft, scrollTop, scrollWidth, sourceIndex, tagName, tagUrn, title, uniqueID

br. JavaScript Methods (12)

addBehavior, appendChild, applyElement, attachEvent, clearAttributes, cloneNode, componentFromPoint, detachEvent, dragDrop, fireEvent, getAdjacentText, getAttribute, getAttributeNode, getElementsByTagName, getExpression, hasChildNodes, insertAdjacentElement, insertBefore, mergeAttributes, normalize, releaseCapture, removeAttribute, removeAttributeNode, removeBehavior, removeChild, removeExpression, replaceAdjacentText, replaceChild, scrollIntoView, setAttribute, setAttributeNode, setCapture, setExpression, swapNode

br. JavaScript Collections (13)

attributes, behaviorUrns, childNodes

br. JavaScript Objects (14)

currentStyle, runtimeStyle, style

<button> ... </button>

Compatibility: NN6, NN7, IE4, IE5, IE5.5, IE6

This element performs a similar function to the <input type="submit"> and <input type="button"> elements, except that it provides richer rendering capabilities.

Syntax:

```
<button attributes events> . . . </button>
```

Example:

```
<html><head><title>button element example</title></head>
<body bgcolor="#FFFFFF" text="#000000">
<center><button type="button" id="myButton" style="font-weight:bold;
color:darkblue; background:cyan; border-color:blue; font-family:Verdana;">This is
the button's label</button>
</center></body></html>
```

<button> HTML Attributes (6)

accesskey, begin, class, contenteditable, datafld, dataformatas, datasrc, dir, disabled, end, hidefocus, id, lang, language, name, style, syncmaster, systemBitrate, systemCaptions, systemLanguage, systemOverdubOrSubtitle, tabindex, timecontainer, title, type, unselectable, value

<button> Event Handlers (7)

onActivate, onAfterUpdate, onBeforeActivate, onBeforeCut, onBeforeDeactivate, onBeforeEditFocus, onBeforePaste, onBeforeUpdate, onBlur, onClick, onContextMenu, onControlSelect, onCut, onDblClick, onDeactivate, onDrag, onDragEnd, onDragEnter, onDragLeave, onDragOver, onDragStart, onDrop, onErrorUpdate, onFilterChange, onFocus, onFocusIn, onFocusOut, onHelp, onKeyDown, onKeyPress, onKeyUp, onLoseCapture, onMouseDown, onMouseEnter, onMouseLeave, onMouseMove, onMouseOut, onMouseOver, onMouseUp, onMouseWheel, onMove, onMoveEnd, onMoveStart, onPaste, onPropertyChange, onReadyStateChange, onResize, onResizeEnd, onResizeStart, onSelectStart, onTimeError

<button> CSS Attributes and JavaScript Style Properties (8)

The names are in CSS syntax. See the introduction to this chapter for the JavaScript syntax rules. Names noted with an asterisk (*) are JavaScript properties only.

background, background-attachment, background-color, background-image, background-position, background-position-x, background-position-y, background-repeat, behavior, border, border-bottom, border-bottom-color, border-bottom-style, border-bottom-width, border-color, border-left, border-left-color, border-left-style, border-left-width, border-right, border-right-color, border-right-style, border-right-width, border-style, border-top, border-top-color, border-top-style, border-top-width, border-width, bottom, clear, clip, color, direction, display, filter, float, font, font-family, font-size, font-style, font-variant, font-weight, hasLayout(*), height, layout-flow, layout-grid, layout-grid-mode, left, letter-spacing, line-height, margin, margin-bottom, margin-left, margin-right, margin-top, padding, padding-bottom, padding-left, padding-right, padding-top, page-break-after, pixelBottom(*), pixelHeight(*), pixelLeft(*), pixelRight(*), pixelTop(*), pixelWidth(*), posBottom(*), posHeight(*), position, posLeft(*), posRight(*), posTop(*), posWidth(*), right, styleFloat(*), text-autospace, text-decoration, text-indent, text-overflow, text-transform, text-underline-position, textDecorationBlink(*), textDecorationLineThrough(*), textDecorationNone(*), textDecorationOverline(*), textDecorationUnderline(*), top, unicode-bidi, visibility, width, word-spacing, word-wrap, writing-mode, z-index, zoom

\<button\> Microsoft Behaviors (9)

clientCaps, download, homePage, httpFolder, saveFavorite, saveHistory, saveSnapshot, time, time2, userData

\<button\> Microsoft Filters (10)

Alpha, Barn, BasicImage, BlendTrans, Blinds, Blur, CheckerBoard, Chroma, Compositor, DropShadow, Emboss, Engrave, Fade, FlipH, FlipV, Glow, GradientWipe, Gray, ICMFilter, Inset, Invert, Iris, Light, MaskFilter, Matrix, MotionBlur, Pixelate, RadialWipe, RandomBars, RandomDissolve, RevealTrans, Shadow, Slide, Spiral, Stretch, Strips, Wave, Wheel, Xray, Zigzag

button. JavaScript Properties (11)

accessKey, canHaveChildren, canHaveHTML, className, clientHeight, clientLeft, clientTop, clientWidth, contentEditable, dataFld, dataFormatAs, datasrc, dir, disabled, end, firstChild, form, hasLayout, hideFocus, id, innerHTML, innerText, isContentEditable, isDisabled, isMultiLine, isTextEdit, lang, language, lastChild, name, nextSibling, nodeName, nodeType, nodeValue, offsetHeight, offsetLeft, offsetParent, offsetTop, offsetWidth, outerHTML, outerText, ownerDocument, parentElement, parentNode, parentTextEdit, previousSibling, readyState, recordNumber, scopeName, scrollHeight, scrollLeft, scrollTop, scrollWidth, sourceIndex, tabIndex, tagName, tagUrn, title, type, uniqueID, value

button. JavaScript Methods (12)

addBehavior, appendChild, applyElement, attachEvent, blur, clearAttributes, click, cloneNode, componentFromPoint, contains, createTextRange, detachEvent, dragDrop, fireEvent, focus, getAdjacentText, getAttribute, getAttributeNode, getBoundingClientRect, getClientRects, getElementsByTagName, getExpression, hasChildNodes, insertAdjacentElement, insertAdjacentHTML, insertAdjacentText, insertBefore, mergeAttributes, normalize, releaseCapture, removeAttribute, removeAttributeNode, removeBehavior, removeChild, removeExpression, removeNode, replaceAdjacentText, replaceChild, replaceNode, scrollIntoView, setActive, setAttribute, setAttributeNode, setCapture, setExpression, swapNode

button. JavaScript Collections (13)

all, attributes, behaviorUrns, childNodes, children, filters

button. JavaScript Objects (14)

currentStyle, runtimeStyle, style

\<caption> ... \</caption>

Compatibility: NN4, NN6, NN7, IE4, IE5, IE5.5, IE6

This element allows a short description to be added to a table. It may *only* be placed immediately after an opening \<table> tag.
    Syntax:

\<caption *attributes events*> . . . \</caption>

    Example:

```
<html><head><title>caption element example</title></head>
<body><center>
<table id="myT" width="200" border="8" cellspacing="5" cellpadding="5"
align="center">
<caption id="myC" valign="bottom" style="color:red">Table 2-5. This is the caption
for this table.</caption>
<tr><td>Cell 1</td><td>Cell 2</td></tr>
<tr><td>Cell 3</td><td>Cell 4</td></tr>
</table></center></body></html>
```

\<caption> HTML Attributes (6)

accesskey, align, begin, class, dir, disabled, end, hidefocus, id, lang, language, style, syncmaster, systemBitrate, systemCaptions, systemLanguage, systemOverdubOrSubtitle, tabindex, timecontainer, title, unselectable, valign

\<caption> Event Handlers (7)

onActivate, onAfterUpdate, onBeforeActivate, onBeforeCopy, onBeforeCut, onBeforeDeactivate, onBeforePaste, onBeforeUpdate, onBlur, onChange, onClick, onContextMenu, onControlSelect, onCopy, onCut, onDblClick, onDeactivate, onDrag, onDragEnd, onDragEnter, onDragLeave, onDragOver, onDragStart, onDrop, onFocus, onFocusIn, onFocusOut, onHelp, onKeyDown, onKeyPress, onKeyUp, onLoseCapture, onMouseDown, onMouseEnter, onMouseLeave, onMouseMove, onMouseOut, onMouseOver, onMouseUp, onMouseWheel, onMove, onMoveEnd, onMoveStart, onPaste, onPropertyChange, onReadyStateChange, onResizeEnd, onResizeStart, onSelectStart, onTimeError

\<caption> CSS Attributes and JavaScript Style Properties (8)

The names are in CSS syntax. See the introduction to this chapter for the JavaScript syntax rules. Names noted with an asterisk (*) are JavaScript properties only.

!important, background, background-attachment, background-color, background-image, background-position, background-position-x, background-position-y, background-repeat, behavior, border, border-bottom, border-bottom-color, border-bottom-style, border-bottom-width, border-color, border-left, border-left-color, border-left-style, border-left-width, border-right, border-right-color, border-right-style, border-right-width, border-style, border-top, border-top-color, border-top-style, border-top-width, border-width, clear, color, cursor, direction, display, filter, font, font-family, font-size, font-style, font-variant, font-weight, hasLayout(*), height, layout-flow, layout-grid, layout-grid-mode, letter-spacing, line-height, margin, margin-bottom, margin-left, margin-right, margin-top, padding, padding-bottom, padding-left, padding-right, padding-top, page-break-after, page-break-before, pixelBottom(*), pixelHeight(*), pixelLeft(*), pixelRight(*), pixelTop(*), pixelWidth(*), posBottom(*), posHeight(*), posLeft(*), posRight(*), posTop(*), posWidth(*), text-autospace, text-decoration, text-overflow, text-transform, text-underline-position, textDecorationBlink(*), textDecorationLineThrough(*), textDecorationNone(*), textDecorationOverline(*), textDecorationUnderline(*), unicode-bidi, visibility, width, word-spacing, writing-mode, z-index, zoom

\<caption\> Microsoft Behaviors (9)

clientCaps, download, homePage, httpFolder, saveFavorite, saveHistory, time, time2, userData

\<caption\> Microsoft Filters (10)

Alpha, Barn, BasicImage, BlendTrans, Blinds, Blur, CheckerBoard, Chroma, Compositor, DropShadow, Emboss, Engrave, Fade, FlipH, FlipV, Glow, GradientWipe, Gray, ICMFilter, Inset, Invert, Iris, Light, MaskFilter, Matrix, MotionBlur, Pixelate, RadialWipe, RandomBars, RandomDissolve, RevealTrans, Shadow, Slide, Spiral, Stretch, Strips, Wave, Wheel, Xray, Zigzag

caption. JavaScript Properties (11)

accessKey, align, canHaveChildren, canHaveHTML, className, clientHeight, clientLeft, clientTop, clientWidth, cursor, dir, disabled, end, firstChild, hasLayout, hideFocus, id, innerHTML, innerText, isContentEditable, isDisabled, isMultiLine, isTextEdit, lang, language, lastChild, nextSibling, nodeName, nodeType, nodeValue, offsetHeight, offsetLeft, offsetParent, offsetTop, offsetWidth, outerHTML, ownerDocument, parentElement, parentNode, parentTextEdit, previousSibling, readyState, scopeName, scrollHeight, scrollLeft, scrollTop, scrollWidth, sourceIndex, tabIndex, tagName, tagUrn, title, uniqueID, vAlign

caption. JavaScript Methods (12)

addBehavior, appendChild, applyElement, attachEvent, blur, clearAttributes, click, cloneNode, componentFromPoint, contains, detachEvent, dragDrop, fireEvent, focus, getAdjacentText, getAttribute, getAttributeNode, getBoundingClientRect, getClientRects, getElementsByTagName, getExpression, hasChildNodes, insertAdjacentElement, insertAdjacentHTML, insertAdjacentText, insertBefore, mergeAttributes, normalize, releaseCapture, removeAttribute, removeAttributeNode,

removeBehavior, removeChild, removeExpression, removeNode, replaceAdjacentText, replaceChild, replaceNode, scrollIntoView, setActive, setAttribute, setAttributeNode, setCapture, setExpression, swapNode

caption. JavaScript Collections (13)

all, attributes, behaviorUrns, childNodes, children

caption. JavaScript Objects (14)

currentStyle, runtimeStyle, style

<center> ... </center>

Compatibility: NN4, NN6, NN7, IE4, IE5, IE5.5, IE6

This element causes the content to be centered between the margins of a page, table, or other object. This element has been deprecated in HTML 4.0 in favor of using CSS or the align attribute (see Chapter 1 for information on CSS). Nonetheless, this element is still supported by most browsers.

Syntax:

```
<center attributes events> . . . </center>
```

Example:

```
<html><head><title>center element example</title></head>
<body bgcolor="#FFFFFF" text="#000000">
<center><table width="400" border="8" cellspacing="5" cellpadding="5"
align="center"><caption valign="bottom" style="color:blue">This table is centered
within the margins of the page.</caption>
<tr><td>Text 1, not centered</td><td><center>Text 2, centered</center></td></tr>
<tr><td><center>Text 3, centered</center></td><td>Text 4, not centered</td></tr>
</table></center></body></html>
```

<center> HTML Attributes (6)

accesskey, begin, class, contenteditable, dir, disabled, end, hidefocus, id, lang, language, style, syncmaster, systemBitrate, systemCaptions, systemLanguage, systemOverdubOrSubtitle, tabindex, timecontainer, title, unselectable

<center> Event Handlers (7)

onActivate, onBeforeActivate, onBeforeCopy, onBeforeCut, onBeforeDeactivate, onBeforeEditFocus, onBeforePaste, onBlur, onClick, onContextMenu, onControlSelect, onCopy, onCut, onDblClick, onDeactivate, onDrag, onDragEnd, onDragEnter, onDragLeave, onDragOver, onDragStart, onDrop, onFocus, onFocusIn, onFocusOut, onHelp, onKeyDown, onKeyPress, onKeyUp, onLoseCapture, onMouseDown, onMouseEnter, onMouseLeave, onMouseMove, onMouseOut, onMouseOver, onMouseUp, onMouseWheel, onMove, onMoveEnd, onMoveStart, onPaste, onPropertyChange, onReadyStateChange, onResize, onResizeEnd, onResizeStart, onSelectStart, onTimeError

<center> CSS Attributes and JavaScript Style Properties (8)

The names are in CSS syntax. See the introduction to this chapter for the JavaScript syntax rules. Names noted with an asterisk (*) are JavaScript properties only.

!important, :first-letter, :first-line, accelerator, background, background-attachment, background-color, background-image, background-position, background-position-x, background-position-y, background-repeat, behavior, border, border-bottom, border-bottom-color, border-bottom-style, border-bottom-width, border-color, border-left, border-left-color, border-left-style, border-left-width, border-right, border-right-color, border-right-style, border-right-width, border-style, border-top, border-top-color, border-top-style, border-top-width, border-width, bottom, clear, clip, color, cursor, direction, display, filter, float, font, font-family, font-size, font-style, font-variant, font-weight, hasLayout(*), height, layout-flow, layout-grid, layout-grid-char, layout-grid-line, layout-grid-mode, layout-grid-type, left, letter-spacing, line-break, line-height, margin, margin-bottom, margin-left, margin-right, margin-top, overflow, overflow-x, overflow-y, padding, padding-bottom, padding-left, padding-right, padding-top, page-break-after, page-break-before, pixelBottom(*), pixelHeight(*), pixelLeft(*), pixelRight(*), pixelTop(*), pixelWidth(*), posBottom(*), posHeight(*), position, posLeft(*), posRight(*), posTop(*), posWidth(*), right, styleFloat(*), text-align, text-align-last, text-autospace, text-decoration, text-indent, text-justify, text-kashida-space, text-overflow, text-transform, text-underline-position, textDecorationBlink(*), textDecorationLineThrough(*), textDecorationNone(*), textDecorationOverline(*), textDecorationUnderline(*), top, unicode-bidi, visibility, white-space, width, word-break, word-spacing, word-wrap, writing-mode, z-index, zoom

<center> Microsoft Behaviors (9)

clientCaps, download, homePage, httpFolder, saveFavorite, saveHistory, saveSnapshot, time, time2, userData

<center> Microsoft Filters (10)

Alpha, Barn, BasicImage, BlendTrans, Blinds, Blur, CheckerBoard, Chroma, Compositor, DropShadow, Emboss, Engrave, Fade, FlipH, FlipV, Glow, GradientWipe, Gray, ICMFilter, Inset, Invert, Iris, Light, MaskFilter, Matrix, MotionBlur, Pixelate, RadialWipe, RandomBars, RandomDissolve, RevealTrans, Shadow, Slide, Spiral, Stretch, Strips, Wave, Wheel, Xray, Zigzag

center. JavaScript Properties (11)

accessKey, blockDirection, canHaveChildren, canHaveHTML, className, clientHeight, clientLeft, clientTop, clientWidth, contentEditable, cursor, dir, disabled, end, firstChild, hasLayout, hideFocus, id, innerHTML, innerText, isContentEditable, isDisabled, isMultiLine, isTextEdit, lang, language, lastChild, nextSibling, nodeName, nodeType, nodeValue, offsetHeight, offsetLeft, offsetParent, offsetTop, offsetWidth, outerHTML, outerText, ownerDocument, parentElement, parentNode, parentTextEdit, previousSibling, readyState, scopeName, scrollHeight, scrollLeft, scrollTop, scrollWidth, sourceIndex, tabIndex, tagName, tagUrn, uniqueID

center. JavaScript Methods (12)

addBehavior, appendChild, applyElement, attachEvent, blur, clearAttributes, click, cloneNode, componentFromPoint, contains, detachEvent, fireEvent, focus, getAdjacentText, getAttribute, getAttributeNode, getBoundingClientRect, getClientRects, getElementsByTagName, getExpression, hasChildNodes, insertAdjacentElement, insertAdjacentHTML, insertAdjacentText, insertBefore, mergeAttributes, normalize, releaseCapture, removeAttribute, removeAttributeNode, removeBehavior, removeChild, removeExpression, removeNode, replaceAdjacentText, replaceChild, replaceNode, scrollIntoView, setActive, setAttribute, setAttributeNode, setCapture, setExpression, swapNode

center. JavaScript Collections (13)

all, attributes, behaviorUrns, childNodes, children

center. JavaScript Objects (14)

currentStyle, runtimeStyle, style

<cite> ... </cite>

Compatibility: NN4, NN6, NN7, IE4, IE5, IE5.5, IE6

This element is used to indicate a citation by causing text between its opening and closing tags to be rendered in italics.

Syntax:

```
<cite attributes events> . . . </cite>
```

Example:

```
<html><head><title>cite element example</title></head>
<body bgcolor="#FFFFFF" text="#000000">
<p>. . . One by one the trucks struggled up the steep road . . .<br>
  (Robert Ludlum, <cite>The Gemini Contenders</cite>)</p>
</body></html>
```

<cite> HTML Attributes (6)

accesskey, begin, class, contenteditable, dir, disabled, end, hidefocus, id, lang, language, style, syncmaster, systemBitrate, systemCaptions, systemLanguage, systemOverdubOrSubtitle, tabindex, timecontainer, title, unselectable

<cite> Event Handlers (7)

onActivate, onBeforeActivate, onBeforeCopy, onBeforeCut, onBeforeDeactivate,
onBeforeEditFocus, onBeforePaste, onBlur, onClick, onContextMenu, onControlSelect,
onCopy, onCut, onDblClick, onDeactivate, onDrag, onDragEnd, onDragEnter,
onDragLeave, onDragOver, onDragStart, onDrop, onFocus, onFocusIn, onFocusOut,
onHelp, onKeyDown, onKeyPress, onKeyUp, onLoseCapture, onMouseDown, onMouseEnter,
onMouseLeave, onMouseMove, onMouseOut, onMouseOver, onMouseUp, onMouseWheel,
onMove, onMoveEnd, onMoveStart, onPaste, onPropertyChange, onReadyStateChange,
onResize, onResizeEnd, onResizeStart, onSelectStart, onTimeError

<cite> CSS Attributes and JavaScript Style Properties (8)

The names are in CSS syntax. See the introduction to this chapter for the
JavaScript syntax rules. Names noted with an asterisk (*) are JavaScript
properties only.

!important, accelerator, background, background-attachment, background-color,
background-image, background-position, background-position-x, background-position-
y, background-repeat, behavior, border, border-bottom, border-bottom-color, border-
bottom-style, border-bottom-width, border-color, border-left, border-left-color,
border-left-style, border-left-width, border-right, border-right-color, border-
right-style, border-right-width, border-style, border-top, border-top-color,
border-top-style, border-top-width, border-width, bottom, clear, clip, color,
cursor, direction, display, filter, float, font, font-family, font-size, font-
style, font-variant, font-weight, hasLayout(*), height, layout-flow, layout-grid,
layout-grid-mode, left, letter-spacing, line-height, margin, margin-bottom, margin-
left, margin-right, margin-top, overflow, overflow-x, overflow-y, padding, padding-
bottom, padding-left, padding-right, padding-top, pixelBottom(*), pixelHeight(*),
pixelLeft(*), pixelRight(*), pixelTop(*), pixelWidth(*), posBottom(*),
posHeight(*), position, posLeft(*), posRight(*), posTop(*), posWidth(*), right,
styleFloat(*), text-autospace, text-decoration, text-overflow, text-transform,
text-underline-position, textDecorationBlink(*), textDecorationLineThrough(*),
textDecorationNone(*), textDecorationOverline(*), textDecorationUnderline(*), top,
unicode-bidi, visibility, white-space, width, word-spacing, word-wrap, writing-
mode, z-index, zoom

<cite> Microsoft Behaviors (9)

clientCaps, download, homePage, httpFolder, saveFavorite, saveHistory,
saveSnapshot, time, time2, userData

<cite> Microsoft Filters (10)

Alpha, Barn, BasicImage, BlendTrans, Blinds, Blur, CheckerBoard, Chroma,
Compositor, DropShadow, Emboss, Engrave, Fade, FlipH, FlipV, Glow, GradientWipe,
Gray, ICMFilter, Inset, Invert, Iris, Light, MaskFilter, Matrix, MotionBlur,
Pixelate, RadialWipe, RandomBars, RandomDissolve, RevealTrans, Shadow, Slide,
Spiral, Stretch, Strips, Wave, Wheel, Xray, Zigzag

cite. JavaScript Properties (11)

accessKey, canHaveChildren, canHaveHTML, className, clientHeight, clientLeft, clientTop, clientWidth, contentEditable, cursor, dir, disabled, end, firstChild, hasLayout, hideFocus, id, innerHTML, innerText, isContentEditable, isDisabled, isMultiLine, isTextEdit, lang, language, lastChild, nextSibling, nodeName, nodeType, nodeValue, offsetHeight, offsetLeft, offsetParent, offsetTop, offsetWidth, outerHTML, outerText, ownerDocument, parentElement, parentNode, parentTextEdit, previousSibling, readyState, scopeName, scrollHeight, scrollLeft, scrollTop, scrollWidth, sourceIndex, tabIndex, tagName, tagUrn, title, uniqueID

cite. JavaScript Methods (12)

addBehavior, appendChild, applyElement, attachEvent, blur, clearAttributes, click, cloneNode, componentFromPoint, contains, detachEvent, fireEvent, focus, getAdjacentText, getAttribute, getAttributeNode, getBoundingClientRect, getClientRects, getElementsByTagName, getExpression, hasChildNodes, insertAdjacentElement, insertAdjacentHTML, insertAdjacentText, insertBefore, mergeAttributes, normalize, releaseCapture, removeAttribute, removeAttributeNode, removeBehavior, removeChild, removeExpression, removeNode, replaceAdjacentText, replaceChild, replaceNode, scrollIntoView, setActive, setAttribute, setAttributeNode, setCapture, setExpression, swapNode

cite. JavaScript Collections (13)

all, attributes, behaviorUrns, childNodes, children

cite. JavaScript Objects (14)

currentStyle, runtimeStyle, style

<code> ... </code>

Compatibility: NN4, NN6, NN7, IE4, IE5, IE5.5, IE6

This element causes text to be displayed in a monospaced font and is usually applied to code samples.

Syntax:

```
<code attributes events> . . . </code>
```

Example:

```
<html><head><title>code element example</title></head>
<body bgcolor="#FFFFFF" text="#000000">
<p>You can apply the <font size="5"><code style="font-
weight:normal">systemLanguage</code></font> attribute to nearly any element.</p>
</body></html>
```

`<code>` HTML Attributes (6)

begin, class, contenteditable, dir, disabled, end, id, lang, language, style, syncmaster, systemBitrate, systemCaptions, systemLanguage, systemOverdubOrSubtitle, timecontainer, title, unselectable

`<code>` Event Handlers (7)

onBeforeActivate, onBeforeCopy, onBeforeCut, onBeforeEditFocus, onBeforePaste, onClick, onContextMenu, onCopy, onCut, onDblClick, onDrag, onDragEnd, onDragEnter, onDragLeave, onDragOver, onDragStart, onDrop, onFocusIn, onFocusOut, onHelp, onKeyDown, onKeyPress, onKeyUp, onLoseCapture, onMouseDown, onMouseEnter, onMouseLeave, onMouseMove, onMouseOut, onMouseOver, onMouseUp, onMouseWheel, onPaste, onPropertyChange, onReadyStateChange, onResize, onSelectStart, onTimeError

`<code>` CSS Attributes and JavaScript Style Properties (8)

The names are in CSS syntax. See the introduction to this chapter for the JavaScript syntax rules. Names noted with an asterisk (*) are JavaScript properties only.

!important, accelerator, background, background-attachment, background-color, background-image, background-position, background-position-x, background-position-y, background-repeat, behavior, border, border-bottom, border-bottom-color, border-bottom-style, border-bottom-width, border-color, border-left, border-left-color, border-left-style, border-left-width, border-right, border-right-color, border-right-style, border-right-width, border-style, border-top, border-top-color, border-top-style, border-top-width, border-width, bottom, clear, clip, color, cursor, direction, display, filter, float, font, font-family, font-size, font-style, font-variant, font-weight, hasLayout(*), height, layout-flow, layout-grid, layout-grid-mode, left, letter-spacing, line-height, margin, margin-bottom, margin-left, margin-right, margin-top, overflow, overflow-x, overflow-y, padding, padding-bottom, padding-left, padding-right, padding-top, pixelBottom(*), pixelHeight(*), pixelLeft(*), pixelRight(*), pixelTop(*), pixelWidth(*), posBottom(*), posHeight(*), position, posLeft(*), posRight(*), posTop(*), posWidth(*), right, styleFloat(*), text-autospace, text-decoration, text-overflow, text-transform, text-underline-position, textDecorationBlink(*), textDecorationLineThrough(*), textDecorationNone(*), textDecorationOverline(*), textDecorationUnderline(*), top, unicode-bidi, visibility, white-space, width, word-spacing, word-wrap, writing-mode, z-index, zoom

`<code>` Microsoft Behaviors (9)

clientCaps, download, homePage, httpFolder, saveFavorite, saveHistory, saveSnapshot, time, time2, userData

`<code>` Microsoft Filters (10)

Alpha, Barn, BasicImage, BlendTrans, Blinds, Blur, CheckerBoard, Chroma, Compositor, DropShadow, Emboss, Engrave, Fade, FlipH, FlipV, Glow, GradientWipe, Gray, ICMFilter, Inset, Invert, Iris, Light, MaskFilter, Matrix, MotionBlur,

Pixelate, RadialWipe, RandomBars, RandomDissolve, RevealTrans, Shadow, Slide, Spiral, Stretch, Strips, Wave, Wheel, Xray, Zigzag

code. JavaScript Properties (11)

canHaveChildren, canHaveHTML, className, clientHeight, clientLeft, clientTop, clientWidth, contentEditable, cursor, dir, disabled, end, firstChild, hasLayout, id, innerHTML, innerText, isContentEditable, isDisabled, isMultiLine, isTextEdit, lang, language, lastChild, nextSibling, nodeName, nodeType, nodeValue, offsetHeight, offsetLeft, offsetParent, offsetTop, offsetWidth, outerHTML, outerText, ownerDocument, parentElement, parentNode, parentTextEdit, previousSibling, readyState, scopeName, scrollHeight, scrollLeft, scrollTop, scrollWidth, sourceIndex, tagName, tagUrn, title, uniqueID

code. JavaScript Methods (12)

addBehavior, appendChild, applyElement, attachEvent, clearAttributes, click, cloneNode, componentFromPoint, contains, detachEvent, fireEvent, getAdjacentText, getAttribute, getAttributeNode, getBoundingClientRect, getClientRects, getElementsByTagName, getExpression, hasChildNodes, insertAdjacentElement, insertAdjacentHTML, insertAdjacentText, insertBefore, mergeAttributes, normalize, releaseCapture, removeAttribute, removeAttributeNode, removeBehavior, removeChild, removeExpression, removeNode, replaceAdjacentText, replaceChild, replaceNode, scrollIntoView, setAttribute, setAttributeNode, setCapture, setExpression, swapNode

code. JavaScript Collections (13)

all, attributes, behaviorUrns, childNodes, children

code. JavaScript Objects (14)

currentStyle, runtimeStyle, style

<col>

Compatibility: NN6, NN7, IE4, IE5, IE5.5, IE6

This element specifies the properties of a column in a <table>.
Syntax:

```
<col attributes events>
```

Example:

```
<html><head><title>col element example</title></head>
<body bgcolor="#FFFFFF" text="#000000">
<table width="500" border="8" cellspacing="5" cellpadding="5" align="center">
<col style="color:maroon">
<col style="color:red">
```

```
<tr><td>col 1: maroon</td>
<td>col 2: red</td>
<tr><td>col 1: maroon</td>
<td>col 2: red</td></tr>
</table></body></html>
```

<col> HTML Attributes (6)

align, bgcolor, ch, choff, class, dir, id, lang, span, style, title, valign, width

<col> Event Handlers (7)

onLayoutComplete, onReadyStateChange

<col> CSS Attributes and JavaScript Style Properties (8)

The names are in CSS syntax. See the introduction to this chapter for the JavaScript syntax rules. Names noted with an asterisk (*) are JavaScript properties only.

!important, background, background-attachment, background-color, background-image, background-position, background-position-x, background-position-y, background-repeat, behavior, clear, color, cursor, direction, display, font, font-family, font-size, font-style, font-variant, font-weight, layout-grid, layout-grid-mode, letter-spacing, line-height, overflow, padding, padding-bottom, padding-left, padding-right, padding-top, pixelBottom(*), pixelHeight(*), pixelLeft(*), pixelRight(*), pixelTop(*), pixelWidth(*), posBottom(*), posHeight(*), posLeft(*), posRight(*), posTop(*), posWidth(*), text-autospace, text-decoration, text-transform, text-underline-position, textDecorationBlink(*), textDecorationLineThrough(*), textDecorationNone(*), textDecorationOverline(*), textDecorationUnderline(*), unicode-bidi, vertical-align, visibility, word-spacing, z-index, zoom

<col> Microsoft Behaviors (9)

clientCaps, download, homePage

col. JavaScript Properties (11)

align, canHaveChildren, canHaveHTML, ch, chOff, className, clientHeight, clientLeft, clientTop, clientWidth, cursor, dir, disabled, firstChild, id, innerHTML, isContentEditable, isDisabled, isMultiLine, isTextEdit, lang, lastChild, nextSibling, nodeName, nodeType, nodeValue, offsetHeight, offsetLeft, offsetParent, offsetTop, offsetWidth, outerHTML, ownerDocument, parentElement, parentNode, parentTextEdit, previousSibling, readyState, scopeName, scrollHeight, scrollLeft, scrollTop, scrollWidth, sourceIndex, span, tagName, tagUrn, title, uniqueID, vAlign, width

col. JavaScript Methods (12)

addBehavior, appendChild, applyElement, attachEvent, clearAttributes, cloneNode, componentFromPoint, contains, detachEvent, dragDrop, fireEvent, getAdjacentText, getAttribute, getAttributeNode, getBoundingClientRect, getClientRects, getElementsByTagName, getExpression, hasChildNodes, insertAdjacentElement, insertBefore, mergeAttributes, normalize, removeAttribute, removeAttributeNode, removeBehavior, removeChild, removeExpression, removeNode, replaceAdjacentText, replaceChild, replaceNode, scrollIntoView, setAttribute, setAttributeNode, setExpression, swapNode

col. JavaScript Collections (13)

all, attributes, behaviorUrns, childNodes, children

col. JavaScript Objects (14)

currentStyle, runtimeStyle, style

<colgroup> ... </colgroup>

Compatibility: NN6, NN7, IE4, IE5, IE5.5, IE6

This element groups table columns together and allows the columns in the group to share properties and style settings.

Syntax:

<colgroup *attributes events*> . . . </colgroup>

Example:

```
<html><head><title>colgroup element example</title></head>
<body bgcolor="#FFFFFF" text="#000000">
<table width="500" border="8" cellspacing="5" cellpadding="5" align="center">
<colgroup span="2" style="color:blue;"></colgroup>
<colgroup style="color:red;"></colgroup>
<tr><td>col: 1, group: 1</td>
<td>col: 2, group: 1</td>
<td>col: 3, group: 2</td></tr>
<tr><td>col: 1, group: 1</td>
<td>col: 2, group: 1</td>
<td>col: 3, group: 2</td></tr>
<tr><td>col: 1, group: 1</td>
<td>col: 2, group: 1</td>
<td>col: 3, group: 2</td></tr>
</table></body></html>
```

\<colgroup> HTML Attributes (6)

align, bgcolor, ch, choff, class, dir, id, lang, span, style, valign, width

\<colgroup> Event Handlers (7)

onReadyStateChange

\<colgroup> CSS Attributes and JavaScript Style Properties (8)

The names are in CSS syntax. See the introduction to this chapter for the
JavaScript syntax rules. Names noted with an asterisk (*) are JavaScript
properties only.

!important, background, background-attachment, background-color, background-image,
background-position, background-position-x, background-position-y, background-
repeat, behavior, clear, color, cursor, direction, display, font, font-family,
font-size, font-style, font-variant, font-weight, layout-grid, layout-grid-mode,
letter-spacing, line-height, overflow, padding, padding-bottom, padding-left,
padding-right, padding-top, pixelBottom(*), pixelHeight(*), pixelLeft(*),
pixelRight(*), pixelTop(*), pixelWidth(*), posBottom(*), posHeight(*), posLeft(*),
posRight(*), posTop(*), posWidth(*), text-autospace, text-decoration, text-
transform, text-underline-position, textDecorationBlink(*),
textDecorationLineThrough(*), textDecorationNone(*), textDecorationOverline(*),
textDecorationUnderline(*), unicode-bidi, visibility, word-spacing, z-index, zoom

\<colgroup> Microsoft Behaviors (9)

clientCaps, download, homePage

colgroup. JavaScript Properties (11)

align, canHaveChildren, canHaveHTML, ch, chOff, className, clientHeight,
clientLeft, clientTop, clientWidth, cursor, dir, firstChild, id, innerHTML,
isContentEditable, isDisabled, isMultiLine, isTextEdit, lang, lastChild,
nextSibling, nodeName, nodeType, nodeValue, offsetHeight, offsetLeft, offsetParent,
offsetTop, offsetWidth, outerHTML, ownerDocument, parentElement, parentNode,
parentTextEdit, previousSibling, readyState, scopeName, scrollHeight, scrollLeft,
scrollTop, scrollWidth, sourceIndex, span, tagName, tagUrn, title, uniqueID,
vAlign, width

colgroup. JavaScript Methods (12)

addBehavior, appendChild, applyElement, attachEvent, clearAttributes, cloneNode,
componentFromPoint, contains, detachEvent, fireEvent, getAdjacentText,
getAttribute, getAttributeNode, getBoundingClientRect, getClientRects,
getElementsByTagName, getExpression, hasChildNodes, insertAdjacentElement,
insertBefore, mergeAttributes, normalize, removeAttribute, removeAttributeNode,
removeBehavior, removeChild, removeExpression, removeNode, replaceAdjacentText,
replaceChild, replaceNode, scrollIntoView, setAttribute, setAttributeNode,
setExpression, swapNode

colgroup. JavaScript Collections (13)

all, attributes, behaviorUrns, childNodes, children

colgroup. JavaScript Objects (14)

currentStyle, runtimeStyle, style

<comment> ... </comment>

Compatibility: IE4, IE5, IE5.5, IE6

This element causes the text between its tags not to be displayed. The function of this element is the same as its sibling tag, <!-- . . . -->.

Syntax:

<comment *attributes events*> . . . </comment>

Example:

```
<html><head><title>comment element example</title></head>
<body bgcolor="#FFFFFF" text="#000000">
<comment>This is a comment.</comment>
<p>This text is displayed on the page</p>
</body></html>
```

<comment> HTML Attributes (6)

data, id, lang

<comment> Event Handlers (7)

onPropertyChange, onReadyStateChange

<comment> CSS Attributes and JavaScript Style Properties (8)

The names are in CSS syntax. See the introduction to this chapter for the JavaScript syntax rules. Names noted with an asterisk (*) are JavaScript properties only.

background-position-x, background-position-y, behavior, pixelBottom(*), pixelHeight(*), pixelLeft(*), pixelRight(*), pixelTop(*), pixelWidth(*), posBottom(*), posHeight(*), posLeft(*), posRight(*), posTop(*), posWidth(*), text-autospace, text-underline-position

<comment> Microsoft Behaviors (9)

clientCaps, download, homePage

comment. JavaScript Properties (11)

canHaveChildren, canHaveHTML, data, disabled, firstChild, id, isContentEditable,
isDisabled, isMultiLine, isTextEdit, lang, lastChild, length, nextSibling,
nodeName, nodeType, nodeValue, offsetParent, outerText, ownerDocument,
parentElement, parentNode, parentTextEdit, previousSibling, readyState, scopeName,
sourceIndex, tagName, tagUrn, text, uniqueID

comment. JavaScript Methods (12)

addBehavior, appendChild, appendData, applyElement, attachEvent, clearAttributes,
cloneNode, componentFromPoint, deleteData, detachEvent, dragDrop, fireEvent,
getAdjacentText, getAttribute, getAttributeNode, getBoundingClientRect,
getClientRects, hasChildNodes, insertAdjacentElement, insertAdjacentHTML,
insertAdjacentText, insertBefore, insertData, mergeAttributes, normalize,
removeAttribute, removeAttributeNode, removeBehavior, removeChild, removeNode,
replaceAdjacentText, replaceChild, replaceData, replaceNode, scrollIntoView,
setAttribute, setAttributeNode, substringData, swapNode

comment. JavaScript Collections (13)

attributes, behaviorUrns, childNodes

<custom> ... </custom>

Compatibility: IE5, IE5.5, IE6

This element creates a user-defined element. This Microsoft technology allows
custom elements to be created and used in the page.

The syntax in HTML must adhere to the following rules:

1. A namespace must be created in the HTML tag, using the xmlns attribute to
    define it, as follows:

```
<html xmlns:myElement>
```

2. A style sheet defining the elements must be included in the <head> section of
    the document, under the @media wrapper, as follows:

```
<style>
@media all {
    myElement\:one { color: red }
    myElement\:two { font-family: Verdana }
    myElement\:three { text-decoration: none }
}
</style>
```

3. Once the elements are defined, they can be recalled in the page using the
    namespace and the element name:

```
<myElement:one> . . . </myElement:one>
<myElement:two> . . . </myElement:two>
<myElement:three> . . . </myElement:three>
```

Example:

```
<html xmlns:usertag><head>
<style>
@media all {
    usertag\:italic { font-style: italic; }
    usertag\:bold { font-weight: bold; }
    usertag\:normal { font-style: normal; }
}
</style></head>
<body bgcolor="#FFFFFF" text="#000000">
<usertag:italic>This text will be formated in italic using the usertag:italic
custom element</usertag:italic><br>
<usertag:bold>This text will be formated in bold using the usertag:bold custom
element</usertag:bold><br>
<usertag:normal>This text will be formated normally using the usertag:normal custom
element</usertag:normal></body></html>
```

<custom> HTML Attributes (6)

accesskey, class, contenteditable, dir, disabled, hidefocus, id, lang, language,
style, tabindex, title, unselectable

<custom> Event Handlers (7)

onActivate, onAfterUpdate, onBeforeActivate, onBeforeCopy, onBeforeCut,
onBeforeDeactivate, onBeforeEditFocus, onBeforePaste, onBeforeUpdate, onBlur,
onClick, onContextMenu, onControlSelect, onCopy, onCut, onDblClick, onDeactivate,
onDrag, onDragEnd, onDragEnter, onDragLeave, onDragOver, onDragStart, onDrop,
onErrorUpdate, onFilterChange, onFocus, onFocusIn, onFocusOut, onHelp, onKeyDown,
onKeyPress, onKeyUp, onLoseCapture, onMouseDown, onMouseEnter, onMouseLeave,
onMouseMove, onMouseOut, onMouseOver, onMouseUp, onMouseWheel, onMove, onMoveEnd,
onMoveStart, onPaste, onPropertyChange, onReadyStateChange, onResize, onResizeEnd,
onResizeStart, onScroll, onSelectStart

<custom> CSS Attributes and JavaScript Style Properties (8)

The names are in CSS syntax. See the introduction to this chapter for the
JavaScript syntax rules. Names noted with an asterisk (*) are JavaScript
properties only.

accelerator, background, background-attachment, background-color, background-image,
background-position, background-position-x, background-position-y, background-
repeat, behavior, border, border-bottom, border-bottom-color, border-bottom-style,
border-bottom-width, border-color, border-left, border-left-color, border-left-

style, border-left-width, border-right, border-right-color, border-right-style, border-right-width, border-style, border-top, border-top-color, border-top-style, border-top-width, border-width, bottom, clear, clip, color, cursor, direction, display, filter, float, font, font-family, font-size, font-style, font-variant, font-weight, hasLayout(*), height, layout-flow, layout-grid, layout-grid-mode, left, letter-spacing, line-height, margin, margin-bottom, margin-left, margin-right, margin-top, overflow, overflow-x, overflow-y, padding, padding-bottom, padding-left, padding-right, padding-top, pixelBottom(*), pixelHeight(*), pixelLeft(*), pixelRight(*), pixelTop(*), pixelWidth(*), posBottom(*), posHeight(*), position, posLeft(*), posRight(*), posTop(*), posWidth(*), scrollbar-3dlight-color, scrollbar-arrow-color, scrollbar-base-color, scrollbar-darkshadow-color, scrollbar-face-color, scrollbar-highlight-color, scrollbar-shadow-color, scrollbar-track-color, styleFloat(*), text-align-last, text-autospace, text-decoration, text-kashida-space, text-overflow, text-transform, text-underline-position, textDecorationBlink(*), textDecorationLineThrough(*), textDecorationNone(*), textDecorationOverline(*), textDecorationUnderline(*), top, unicode-bidi, vertical-align, visibility, white-space, width, word-spacing, word-wrap, writing-mode, z-index, zoom

<custom> Microsoft Filters (10)

Alpha, Barn, BasicImage, BlendTrans, Blinds, Blur, CheckerBoard, Chroma, Compositor, DropShadow, Emboss, Engrave, Fade, FlipH, FlipV, Glow, GradientWipe, Gray, ICMFilter, Inset, Invert, Iris, Light, MaskFilter, Matrix, MotionBlur, Pixelate, RadialWipe, RandomBars, RandomDissolve, RevealTrans, Shadow, Slide, Spiral, Stretch, Strips, Wave, Wheel, Xray, Zigzag

custom. JavaScript Properties (11)

accessKey, blockDirection, canHaveChildren, canHaveHTML, className, clientHeight, clientLeft, clientTop, clientWidth, contentEditable, cursor, dir, disabled, hasLayout, hideFocus, id, innerHTML, innerText, isContentEditable, isDisabled, isMultiLine, isTextEdit, lang, language, offsetHeight, offsetLeft, offsetParent, offsetTop, offsetWidth, outerHTML, outerText, parentElement, parentTextEdit, readyState, scopeName, scrollHeight, scrollLeft, scrollTop, scrollWidth, sourceIndex, tabIndex, tagName, tagUrn, title

custom. JavaScript Methods (12)

addBehavior, applyElement, attachEvent, blur, clearAttributes, click, componentFromPoint, contains, detachEvent, doScroll, fireEvent, focus, getAdjacentText, getAttribute, getAttributeNode, getBoundingClientRect, getClientRects, getElementsByTagName, getExpression, insertAdjacentHTML, insertAdjacentText, mergeAttributes, normalize, releaseCapture, removeAttribute, removeAttributeNode, removeBehavior, removeExpression, replaceAdjacentText, scrollIntoView, setActive, setAttribute, setAttributeNode, setCapture, setExpression

custom. JavaScript Collections (13)

all, behaviorUrns, children, filters

custom. JavaScript Objects (14)

currentStyle, document, runtimeStyle, style

<dd> ... </dd>

Compatibility: NN4, NN6, NN7, IE4, IE5, IE5.5, IE6

This element is known as the *definition description,* and it is used in conjunction with the <dl> and <dt> elements. The <dl> element is a *definition list* that you can use to contain multiple *definition terms,* <dt>, along with *definition descriptions,* <dd>. These elements provide a standardized method for displaying terms and definitions in HTML (such as in a glossary).

Syntax:

```
<dd attributes events> . . . </dd>
```

Example:

```
<html><head><title>dd element example</title></head>
<body bgcolor="#FFFFFF" text="#000000">
<dl>
<dt>&lt;TABLE&gt;</dt>
<dd>an html element.</dd>
<dt>border-color</dt>
<dd>a style sheet property.</dd>
<dt>innerText</dt>
<dd>a JavaScript property.</dd>
<dt>cloneNode()</dt>
<dd>a JavaScript method.</dd>
</dl></body></html>
```

<dd> HTML Attributes (6)

accesskey, begin, class, contenteditable, dir, disabled, end, hidefocus, id, lang, language, nowrap, style, syncmaster, systemBitrate, systemCaptions, systemLanguage, systemOverdubOrSubtitle, tabindex, timecontainer, title, unselectable

<dd> Event Handlers (7)

onActivate, onBeforeActivate, onBeforeCopy, onBeforeCut, onBeforeDeactivate, onBeforeEditFocus, onBeforePaste, onBlur, onClick, onContextMenu, onControlSelect, onCopy, onCut, onDblClick, onDeactivate, onDrag, onDragEnd, onDragEnter, onDragLeave, onDragOver, onDragStart, onDrop, onFocus, onFocusIn, onFocusOut, onHelp, onKeyDown, onKeyPress, onKeyUp, onLayoutComplete, onLoseCapture, onMouseDown, onMouseEnter, onMouseLeave, onMouseMove, onMouseOut, onMouseOver, onMouseUp, onMouseWheel, onMove, onMoveEnd, onMoveStart, onPaste, onPropertyChange, onReadyStateChange, onResize, onResizeEnd, onResizeStart, onSelectStart, onTimeError

\<dd> CSS Attributes and JavaScript Style Properties (8)

The names are in CSS syntax. See the introduction to this chapter for the JavaScript syntax rules. Names noted with an asterisk (*) are JavaScript properties only.

!important, :first-letter, :first-line, accelerator, background, background-attachment, background-color, background-image, background-position, background-position-x, background-position-y, background-repeat, behavior, border, border-bottom, border-bottom-color, border-bottom-style, border-bottom-width, border-color, border-left, border-left-color, border-left-style, border-left-width, border-right, border-right-color, border-right-style, border-right-width, border-style, border-top, border-top-color, border-top-style, border-top-width, border-width, bottom, clear, clip, color, cursor, direction, display, filter, float, font, font-family, font-size, font-style, font-variant, font-weight, hasLayout(*), height, layout-flow, layout-grid, layout-grid-char, layout-grid-line, layout-grid-mode, layout-grid-type, left, letter-spacing, line-break, line-height, margin, margin-bottom, margin-left, margin-right, margin-top, overflow, overflow-x, overflow-y, padding, padding-bottom, padding-left, padding-right, padding-top, page-break-after, page-break-before, pixelBottom(*), pixelHeight(*), pixelLeft(*), pixelRight(*), pixelTop(*), pixelWidth(*), posBottom(*), posHeight(*), position, posLeft(*), posRight(*), posTop(*), posWidth(*), right, styleFloat(*), text-align, text-align-last, text-autospace, text-decoration, text-indent, text-justify, text-kashida-space, text-overflow, text-transform, text-underline-position, textDecorationBlink(*), textDecorationLineThrough(*), textDecorationNone(*), textDecorationOverline(*), textDecorationUnderline(*), top, unicode-bidi, visibility, white-space, width, word-break, word-spacing, word-wrap, writing-mode, z-index, zoom

\<dd> Microsoft Behaviors (9)

clientCaps, download, homePage, httpFolder, saveFavorite, saveHistory, saveSnapshot, time, time2, userData

\<dd> Microsoft Filters (10)

Alpha, Barn, BasicImage, BlendTrans, Blinds, Blur, CheckerBoard, Chroma, Compositor, DropShadow, Emboss, Engrave, Fade, FlipH, FlipV, Glow, GradientWipe, Gray, ICMFilter, Inset, Invert, Iris, Light, MaskFilter, Matrix, MotionBlur, Pixelate, RadialWipe, RandomBars, RandomDissolve, RevealTrans, Shadow, Slide, Spiral, Stretch, Strips, Wave, Wheel, Xray, Zigzag

dd. JavaScript Properties (11)

accessKey, blockDirection, canHaveChildren, canHaveHTML, className, clientHeight, clientLeft, clientTop, clientWidth, contentEditable, cursor, dir, disabled, end, firstChild, hasLayout, hideFocus, id, innerHTML, innerText, isContentEditable, isDisabled, isMultiLine, isTextEdit, lang, language, lastChild, nextSibling, nodeName, nodeType, nodeValue, noWrap, offsetHeight, offsetLeft, offsetParent, offsetTop, offsetWidth, outerHTML, outerText, ownerDocument, parentElement, parentNode, parentTextEdit, previousSibling, readyState, scopeName, scrollHeight, scrollLeft, scrollTop, scrollWidth, sourceIndex, tabIndex, tagName, tagUrn, title, uniqueID

dd. JavaScript Methods (12)

addBehavior, appendChild, applyElement, attachEvent, blur, clearAttributes, click, cloneNode, componentFromPoint, contains, detachEvent, dragDrop, fireEvent, focus, getAdjacentText, getAttribute, getAttributeNode, getBoundingClientRect, getClientRects, getElementsByTagName, getExpression, hasChildNodes, insertAdjacentElement, insertAdjacentHTML, insertAdjacentText, insertBefore, mergeAttributes, normalize, releaseCapture, removeAttribute, removeAttributeNode, removeBehavior, removeChild, removeExpression, removeNode, replaceAdjacentText, replaceChild, replaceNode, scrollIntoView, setActive, setAttribute, setAttributeNode, setCapture, setExpression, swapNode

dd. JavaScript Collections (13)

all, attributes, behaviorUrns, childNodes, children

dd. JavaScript Objects (14)

currentStyle, runtimeStyle, style

<del> ... </del>

Compatibility: NN6, NN7, IE4, IE5, IE5.5, IE6

This element is used to highlight text that is removed from a document by displaying it with a line drawn though.

Syntax:

```
<del attributes events> . . . </del>
```

Example:

```
<html><head><title>del element example</title></head>
<body bgcolor="#FFFFFF" text="#000000">
<p>The following text has been <span style="color: red;"><del>deleted</del></span></p>
</body></html>
```

<del> HTML Attributes (6)

accesskey, begin, cite, class, contenteditable, datetime, dir, disabled, end, id, lang, language, style, syncmaster, systemBitrate, systemCaptions, systemLanguage, systemOverdubOrSubtitle, tabindex, timecontainer, title, unselectable

<del> Event Handlers (7)

onBeforeEditFocus, onBlur, onClick, onDblClick, onDrag, onDragEnd, onDragEnter, onDragLeave, onDragOver, onDragStart, onDrop, onFocus, onHelp, onKeyDown, onKeyPress, onKeyUp, onMouseDown, onMouseMove, onMouseOut, onMouseOver, onMouseUp, onReadyStateChange, onSelectStart, onTimeError

<del> CSS Attributes and JavaScript Style Properties (8)

The names are in CSS syntax. See the introduction to this chapter for the JavaScript syntax rules. Names noted with an asterisk (*) are JavaScript properties only.

accelerator, background-position-x, background-position-y, behavior, border, border-bottom, border-bottom-color, border-bottom-style, border-bottom-width, border-color, border-left, border-left-color, border-left-style, border-left-width, border-right, border-right-color, border-right-style, border-right-width, border-style, border-top, border-top-color, border-top-style, border-top-width, border-width, direction, display, filter, hasLayout(*), height, layout-flow, layout-grid, layout-grid-mode, margin, margin-bottom, margin-left, margin-right, margin-top, overflow, overflow-x, overflow-y, padding, padding-bottom, padding-left, padding-right, padding-top, pixelBottom(*), pixelHeight(*), pixelLeft(*), pixelRight(*), pixelTop(*), pixelWidth(*), posBottom(*), posHeight(*), posLeft(*), posRight(*), posTop(*), posWidth(*), text-autospace, text-overflow, text-underline-position, unicode-bidi, width, word-wrap, writing-mode, zoom

<del> Microsoft Behaviors (9)

clientCaps, download, homePage, httpFolder, saveFavorite, saveHistory, saveSnapshot, time, time2, userData

<del> Microsoft Filters (10)

Alpha, Barn, BasicImage, BlendTrans, Blinds, Blur, CheckerBoard, Chroma, Compositor, DropShadow, Emboss, Engrave, Fade, FlipH, FlipV, Glow, GradientWipe, Gray, ICMFilter, Inset, Invert, Iris, Light, MaskFilter, Matrix, MotionBlur, Pixelate, RadialWipe, RandomBars, RandomDissolve, RevealTrans, Shadow, Slide, Spiral, Stretch, Strips, Wave, Wheel, Xray, Zigzag

del. JavaScript Properties (11)

accessKey, canHaveChildren, canHaveHTML, cite, className, clientHeight, clientWidth, contentEditable, dateTime, dir, disabled, end, firstChild, hasLayout, id, innerHTML, innerText, isContentEditable, isDisabled, isMultiLine, isTextEdit, lang, language, lastChild, nextSibling, nodeName, nodeType, nodeValue, offsetHeight, offsetLeft, offsetParent, offsetTop, offsetWidth, outerHTML, outerText, ownerDocument, parentElement, parentNode, parentTextEdit, previousSibling, readyState, scopeName, scrollHeight, scrollLeft, scrollTop, scrollWidth, sourceIndex, tabIndex, tagName, tagUrn, title, uniqueID

del. JavaScript Methods (12)

addBehavior, appendChild, applyElement, attachEvent, blur, clearAttributes, cloneNode, componentFromPoint, detachEvent, fireEvent, focus, getAdjacentText, getAttribute, getAttributeNode, getBoundingClientRect, getClientRects, getElementsByTagName, getExpression, hasChildNodes, insertAdjacentElement, insertBefore, mergeAttributes, normalize, removeAttribute, removeAttributeNode, removeBehavior, removeChild, removeExpression, removeNode, replaceAdjacentText, replaceChild, replaceNode, setAttribute, setAttributeNode, setExpression, swapNode

del. JavaScript Collections (13)

all, attributes, behaviorUrns, childNodes, children

del. JavaScript Objects (14)

currentStyle, runtimeStyle, style

<dfn> ... </dfn>

Compatibility: NN6, NN7, IE4, IE5, IE5.5, IE6

This element causes its enclosed text to appear in an italic format, and it is often used to display term definitions. For instance, you can use this element to contain an acronym with its definition.

Syntax:

```
<dfn attributes events> . . . </dfn>
```

Example:

```
<html><head><title>dfn element example</title></head>
<body bgcolor="#FFFFFF" text="#000000">
<p><acronym>W3C</acronym> stands for <dfn>World Wide Web Consortium.</dfn></p>
</body></html>
```

<dfn> HTML Attributes (6)

accesskey, class, contenteditable, dir, disabled, hidefocus, id, lang, language, style, tabindex, title, unselectable

<dfn> Event Handlers (7)

onActivate, onBeforeActivate, onBeforeCopy, onBeforeCut, onBeforeDeactivate, onBeforeEditFocus, onBeforePaste, onBlur, onClick, onContextMenu, onControlSelect, onCopy, onCut, onDblClick, onDeactivate, onDrag, onDragEnd, onDragEnter, onDragLeave, onDragOver, onDragStart, onDrop, onFocus, onFocusIn, onFocusOut, onHelp, onKeyDown, onKeyPress, onKeyUp, onLoseCapture, onMouseDown, onMouseEnter, onMouseLeave, onMouseMove, onMouseOut, onMouseOver, onMouseUp, onMouseWheel, onMove, onMoveEnd, onMoveStart, onPaste, onPropertyChange, onReadyStateChange, onResize, onResizeEnd, onResizeStart, onSelectStart

<dfn> CSS Attributes and JavaScript Style Properties (8)

The names are in CSS syntax. See the introduction to this chapter for the JavaScript syntax rules. Names noted with an asterisk (*) are JavaScript properties only.

!important, accelerator, background, background-attachment, background-color, background-image, background-position, background-position-x, background-position-y, background-repeat, behavior, border, border-bottom, border-bottom-color, border-bottom-style, border-bottom-width, border-color, border-left, border-left-color, border-left-style, border-left-width, border-right, border-right-color, border-right-style, border-right-width, border-style, border-top, border-top-color, border-top-style, border-top-width, border-width, bottom, clear, clip, color, cursor, direction, display, filter, float, font, font-family, font-size, font-style, font-variant, font-weight, hasLayout(*), height, layout-flow, layout-grid, layout-grid-mode, left, letter-spacing, line-height, margin, margin-bottom, margin-left, margin-right, margin-top, overflow, overflow-x, overflow-y, padding, padding-bottom, padding-left, padding-right, padding-top, pixelBottom(*), pixelHeight(*), pixelLeft(*), pixelRight(*), pixelTop(*), pixelWidth(*), posBottom(*), posHeight(*), position, posLeft(*), posRight(*), posTop(*), posWidth(*), right, styleFloat(*), text-autospace, text-decoration, text-indent, text-overflow, text-transform, text-underline-position, textDecorationBlink(*), textDecorationLineThrough(*), textDecorationNone(*), textDecorationOverline(*), textDecorationUnderline(*), top, unicode-bidi, visibility, width, word-spacing, word-wrap, writing-mode, z-index, zoom

\<dfn> Microsoft Behaviors (9)

clientCaps, download, homePage, httpFolder, saveFavorite, saveHistory, saveSnapshot, userData

\<dfn> Microsoft Filters (10)

Alpha, Barn, BasicImage, BlendTrans, Blinds, Blur, CheckerBoard, Chroma, Compositor, DropShadow, Emboss, Engrave, Fade, FlipH, FlipV, Glow, GradientWipe, Gray, ICMFilter, Inset, Invert, Iris, Light, MaskFilter, Matrix, MotionBlur, Pixelate, RadialWipe, RandomBars, RandomDissolve, RevealTrans, Shadow, Slide, Spiral, Stretch, Strips, Wave, Wheel, Xray, Zigzag

dfn. JavaScript Properties (11)

accessKey, canHaveChildren, canHaveHTML, cite, className, clientHeight, clientLeft, clientTop, clientWidth, contentEditable, cursor, dir, disabled, firstChild, hasLayout, hideFocus, id, innerHTML, innerText, isContentEditable, isDisabled, isMultiLine, isTextEdit, lang, language, lastChild, nextSibling, nodeName, nodeType, nodeValue, offsetHeight, offsetLeft, offsetParent, offsetTop, offsetWidth, outerHTML, outerText, ownerDocument, parentElement, parentNode, parentTextEdit, previousSibling, readyState, scopeName, scrollHeight, scrollLeft, scrollTop, scrollWidth, sourceIndex, tabIndex, tagName, tagUrn, title, uniqueID

dfn. JavaScript Methods (12)

addBehavior, appendChild, applyElement, attachEvent, blur, clearAttributes, click, cloneNode, componentFromPoint, contains, detachEvent, fireEvent, focus, getAdjacentText, getAttribute, getAttributeNode, getBoundingClientRect, getClientRects, getElementsByTagName, getExpression, hasChildNodes, insertAdjacentElement, insertAdjacentHTML, insertAdjacentText, insertBefore, mergeAttributes, normalize, releaseCapture, removeAttribute, removeAttributeNode, removeBehavior, removeChild, removeExpression, removeNode, replaceAdjacentText, replaceChild, replaceNode, scrollIntoView, setActive, setAttribute, setAttributeNode, setCapture, setExpression, swapNode

dfn. JavaScript Collections (13)

all, attributes, behaviorUrns, childNodes, children

dfn. JavaScript Objects (14)

currentStyle, runtimeStyle, style

<dir> ... </dir>

Compatibility: NN4, NN6, NN7, IE4, IE5, IE5.5, IE6

This element can be used to display a bulleted list. HTML 4.0 favors use of the <ul> element in place of the <dir> element, although the <dir> element is still supported.

   Syntax:

<dir *attributes events*> . . . </dir>

   Example:

```
<html><head><title>dir element example</title></head>
<body bgcolor="#FFFFFF" text="#000000">
<dir>
   <li>Books</li>
   <li>Posters</li>
   <li>Electronics</li>
   <li>Toys</li>
   <li>Games</li>
   <li>Magazines</li>
   <li>DVDs</li>
   <li>VHS</li>
</dir></body></html>
```

<dir> HTML Attributes (6)

accesskey, begin, class, compact, contenteditable, dir, disabled, end, hidefocus, id, lang, language, style, syncmaster, systemBitrate, systemCaptions, systemLanguage, systemOverdubOrSubtitle, tabindex, timecontainer, title, unselectable

<dir> Event Handlers (7)

onActivate, onBeforeActivate, onBeforeCopy, onBeforeCut, onBeforeDeactivate, onBeforeEditFocus, onBeforePaste, onBlur, onClick, onContextMenu, onControlSelect, onCopy, onCut, onDblClick, onDeactivate, onDrag, onDragEnd, onDragEnter, onDragLeave, onDragOver, onDragStart, onDrop, onFocus, onFocusIn, onFocusOut, onHelp, onKeyDown, onKeyPress, onKeyUp, onLoseCapture, onMouseDown, onMouseEnter, onMouseLeave, onMouseMove, onMouseOut, onMouseOver, onMouseUp, onMouseWheel, onMove, onMoveEnd, onMoveStart, onPaste, onPropertyChange, onReadyStateChange, onResize, onResizeEnd, onResizeStart, onSelectStart, onTimeError

`<dir>` CSS Attributes and JavaScript Style Properties (8)

The names are in CSS syntax. See the introduction to this chapter for the JavaScript syntax rules. Names noted with an asterisk (*) are JavaScript properties only.

!important, accelerator, background, background-attachment, background-color, background-image, background-position, background-position-x, background-position-y, background-repeat, behavior, border, border-bottom, border-bottom-color, border-bottom-style, border-bottom-width, border-color, border-left, border-left-color, border-left-style, border-left-width, border-right, border-right-color, border-right-style, border-right-width, border-style, border-top, border-top-color, border-top-style, border-top-width, border-width, bottom, clear, clip, color, cursor, direction, display, filter, float, font, font-family, font-size, font-style, font-variant, font-weight, hasLayout(*), height, layout-flow, layout-grid, layout-grid-char, layout-grid-line, layout-grid-mode, layout-grid-type, left, letter-spacing, line-break, line-height, margin, margin-bottom, margin-left, margin-right, margin-top, overflow, overflow-x, overflow-y, padding, padding-bottom, padding-left, padding-right, padding-top, page-break-after, pixelBottom(*), pixelHeight(*), pixelLeft(*), pixelRight(*), pixelTop(*), pixelWidth(*), posBottom(*), posHeight(*), position, posLeft(*), posRight(*), posTop(*), posWidth(*), right, styleFloat(*), text-align, text-autospace, text-decoration, text-indent, text-justify, text-overflow, text-transform, text-underline-position, textDecorationBlink(*), textDecorationLineThrough(*), textDecorationNone(*), textDecorationOverline(*), textDecorationUnderline(*), top, unicode-bidi, visibility, white-space, width, word-break, word-spacing, word-wrap, writing-mode, z-index, zoom

`<dir>` Microsoft Behaviors (9)

clientCaps, download, homePage, httpFolder, saveFavorite, saveHistory, saveSnapshot, time, time2, userData

`<dir>` Microsoft Filters (10)

Alpha, Barn, BasicImage, BlendTrans, Blinds, Blur, CheckerBoard, Chroma, Compositor, DropShadow, Emboss, Engrave, Fade, FlipH, FlipV, Glow, GradientWipe, Gray, ICMFilter, Inset, Invert, Iris, Light, MaskFilter, Matrix, MotionBlur, Pixelate, RadialWipe, RandomBars, RandomDissolve, RevealTrans, Shadow, Slide, Spiral, Stretch, Strips, Wave, Wheel, Xray, Zigzag

dir. JavaScript Properties (11)

accessKey, canHaveChildren, canHaveHTML, className, clientHeight, clientLeft, clientTop, clientWidth, compact, contentEditable, cursor, dir, disabled, end, firstChild, hasLayout, hideFocus, id, innerHTML, innerText, isContentEditable, isDisabled, isMultiLine, isTextEdit, lang, language, lastChild, nextSibling, nodeName, nodeType, nodeValue, offsetHeight, offsetLeft, offsetParent, offsetTop, offsetWidth, outerHTML, outerText, ownerDocument, parentElement, parentNode, parentTextEdit, previousSibling, readyState, scopeName, scrollHeight, scrollLeft, scrollTop, scrollWidth, sourceIndex, tabIndex, tagName, tagUrn, title, uniqueID

dir. JavaScript Methods (12)

addBehavior, appendChild, applyElement, attachEvent, blur, clearAttributes, click, cloneNode, componentFromPoint, contains, detachEvent, fireEvent, focus, getAdjacentText, getAttribute, getAttributeNode, getBoundingClientRect, getClientRects, getElementsByTagName, getExpression, hasChildNodes, insertAdjacentElement, insertAdjacentHTML, insertAdjacentText, insertBefore, mergeAttributes, normalize, releaseCapture, removeAttribute, removeAttributeNode, removeBehavior, removeChild, removeExpression, removeNode, replaceAdjacentText, replaceChild, replaceNode, scrollIntoView, setActive, setAttribute, setAttributeNode, setCapture, setExpression, swapNode

dir. JavaScript Collections (13)

all, attributes, behaviorUrns, childNodes, children

dir. JavaScript Objects (14)

currentStyle, runtimeStyle, style

<div> ... </div>

Compatibility: NN4, NN6, NN7, IE4, IE5, IE5.5, IE6

The <div> element stands for *division*, and as the name indicates, it is used to segregate a group of elements from the other elements on the page. Using its id attribute and an inline style attribute with top, left, and Z-index values allows this element to double as a layer (making the <layer> element obsolete for versions of NN4+ and IE). The <div> element causes a line space to be placed before and after the contents between its opening and closing tags.

NOTE *Earlier versions of Netscape do not support the use of event handlers for the <div> element, so the <layer> and <ilayer> elements would still be required to maintain compatibility with those browsers when using event handlers.*

Syntax:

```
<div attributes events> . . . </div>
```

Example:

```
<html><head><title>div element example</title></head>
<body bgcolor="#FFFFFF" text="#000000">
<div id="Layer1" style="position:absolute; visibility:visible; left:166px;
top:312px; width:300px; height:294px; background-color:#FFFFCC; layer-background-
color:#FFFFCC; border:1px none #000000; z-index:1">
  <p><img src="somegraphic.jpg" alt="" width="300" height="225"></p>
  <p align="center">This div element contains an image plus a center aligned
text.</p>
</div>
```

```
<div id="Layer2" style="position:absolute; visibility:visible; left:499px;
top:338px; width:315px; height:174px; background-color:#CCFFCC; layer-background-
color:#CCFFCC; border:1px none #000000; z-index:2">
  <p>This div element contains only text.</p>
  <p>The style of the text is rendered independently from
     the div's own style.</p>
  <p>Color has been added to both div element backgrounds.</p>
</div></body></html>
```

`<div>` HTML Attributes (6)

accesskey, align, begin, class, contenteditable, datafld, dataformatas, datasrc,
dir, disabled, end, hidefocus, id, lang, language, nowrap, style, syncmaster,
systemBitrate, systemCaptions, systemLanguage, systemOverdubOrSubtitle, tabindex,
timecontainer, title, unselectable

`<div>` Event Handlers (7)

onActivate, onAfterUpdate, onBeforeActivate, onBeforeCopy, onBeforeCut,
onBeforeDeactivate, onBeforeEditFocus, onBeforePaste, onBeforeUpdate, onBlur,
onClick, onContextMenu, onControlSelect, onCopy, onCut, onDblClick, onDeactivate,
onDrag, onDragEnd, onDragEnter, onDragLeave, onDragOver, onDragStart, onDrop,
onErrorUpdate, onFilterChange, onFocus, onFocusIn, onFocusOut, onHelp, onKeyDown,
onKeyPress, onKeyUp, onLayoutComplete, onLoseCapture, onMouseDown, onMouseEnter,
onMouseLeave, onMouseMove, onMouseOut, onMouseOver, onMouseUp, onMouseWheel,
onMove, onMoveEnd, onMoveStart, onPaste, onPropertyChange, onReadyStateChange,
onResize, onResizeEnd, onResizeStart, onScroll, onSelectStart, onTimeError

`<div>` CSS Attributes and JavaScript Style Properties (8)

The names are in CSS syntax. See the introduction to this chapter for the
JavaScript syntax rules. Names noted with an asterisk (*) are JavaScript
properties only.

!important, :first-letter, :first-line, accelerator, background, background-
attachment, background-color, background-image, background-position, background-
position-x, background-position-y, background-repeat, behavior, border, border-
bottom, border-bottom-color, border-bottom-style, border-bottom-width, border-
color, border-left, border-left-color, border-left-style, border-left-width,
border-right, border-right-color, border-right-style, border-right-width, border-
style, border-top, border-top-color, border-top-style, border-top-width, border-
width, bottom, clear, clip, color, cursor, direction, display, filter, float, font,
font-family, font-size, font-style, font-variant, font-weight, hasLayout(*),
height, layout-flow, layout-grid, layout-grid-char, layout-grid-line, layout-grid-
mode, layout-grid-type, left, letter-spacing, line-break, line-height, margin,
margin-bottom, margin-left, margin-right, margin-top, overflow, overflow-x,
overflow-y, padding, padding-bottom, padding-left, padding-right, padding-top,
page-break-after, page-break-before, pixelBottom(*), pixelHeight(*), pixelLeft(*),
pixelRight(*), pixelTop(*), pixelWidth(*), posBottom(*), posHeight(*), position,
posLeft(*), posRight(*), posTop(*), posWidth(*), right, scrollbar-3dlight-color,
scrollbar-arrow-color, scrollbar-base-color, scrollbar-darkshadow-color, scrollbar-
face-color, scrollbar-highlight-color, scrollbar-shadow-color, scrollbar-track-
color, styleFloat(*), text-align, text-align-last, text-autospace, text-decoration,

text-indent, text-justify, text-kashida-space, text-overflow, text-transform, text-underline-position, textDecorationBlink(*), textDecorationLineThrough(*), textDecorationNone(*), textDecorationOverline(*), textDecorationUnderline(*), top, unicode-bidi, visibility, white-space, width, word-break, word-spacing, word-wrap, writing-mode, z-index, zoom

<div> Microsoft Behaviors (9)

clientCaps, download, homePage, httpFolder, saveFavorite, saveHistory, saveSnapshot, time, time2, userData

<div> Microsoft Filters (10)

Alpha, Barn, BasicImage, BlendTrans, Blinds, Blur, CheckerBoard, Chroma, Compositor, DropShadow, Emboss, Engrave, Fade, FlipH, FlipV, Glow, GradientWipe, Gray, ICMFilter, Inset, Invert, Iris, Light, MaskFilter, Matrix, MotionBlur, Pixelate, RadialWipe, RandomBars, RandomDissolve, RevealTrans, Shadow, Slide, Spiral, Stretch, Strips, Wave, Wheel, Xray, Zigzag

div. JavaScript Properties (11)

accessKey, align, blockDirection, canHaveChildren, canHaveHTML, className, clientHeight, clientLeft, clientTop, clientWidth, contentEditable, cursor, dataFld, dataFormatAs, datasrc, dir, disabled, end, firstChild, hasLayout, hideFocus, id, innerHTML, innerText, isContentEditable, isDisabled, isMultiLine, isTextEdit, lang, language, lastChild, nextSibling, nodeName, nodeType, nodeValue, noWrap, offsetHeight, offsetLeft, offsetParent, offsetTop, offsetWidth, outerHTML, outerText, ownerDocument, parentElement, parentNode, parentTextEdit, previousSibling, readyState, recordNumber, scopeName, scrollHeight, scrollLeft, scrollTop, scrollWidth, sourceIndex, tabIndex, tagName, tagUrn, title, uniqueID

div. JavaScript Methods (12)

addBehavior, appendChild, applyElement, attachEvent, blur, clearAttributes, click, cloneNode, componentFromPoint, contains, detachEvent, doScroll, dragDrop, fireEvent, getAdjacentText, getAttribute, getAttributeNode, getBoundingClientRect, getClientRects, getElementsByTagName, getExpression, hasChildNodes, insertAdjacentElement, insertAdjacentHTML, insertAdjacentText, insertBefore, mergeAttributes, normalize, releaseCapture, removeAttribute, removeAttributeNode, removeBehavior, removeChild, removeExpression, removeNode, replaceAdjacentText, replaceChild, replaceNode, scrollIntoView, setActive, setAttribute, setAttributeNode, setCapture, setExpression, swapNode

div. JavaScript Collections (13)

all, attributes, behaviorUrns, childNodes, children, filters

div. JavaScript Objects (14)

currentStyle, runtimeStyle, style

<dl> ... </dl>

Compatibility: NN4, NN6, NN7, IE4, IE5, IE5.5, IE6

This element is known as the *definition list*, and it is used in conjunction with the <dt> and <dd> elements. You can use the <dl> element to contain multiple *definition terms*, <dt>, along with *definition descriptions*, <dd>. These elements provide a standardized method for displaying terms and definitions in HTML (such as in a glossary).

Syntax:

```
<dl attributes events> . . . </dl>
```

Example:

```
<html><head><title>dl element example</title></head>
<body bgcolor="#FFFFFF" text="#000000">
<dl>
<dt>&lt;TABLE&gt;</dt>
<dd>an html element.</dd>
<dt>border-color</dt>
<dd>a style sheet property.</dd>
<dt>innerText</dt>
<dd>a JavaScript property.</dd>
<dt>cloneNode()</dt>
<dd>a JavaScript method.</dd>
</dl></body></html>
```

<dl> HTML Attributes (6)

accesskey, begin, class, compact, contenteditable, dir, disabled, end, hidefocus, id, lang, language, style, syncmaster, systemBitrate, systemCaptions, systemLanguage, systemOverdubOrSubtitle, tabindex, timecontainer, title, unselectable

<dl> Event Handlers (7)

onActivate, onBeforeActivate, onBeforeCopy, onBeforeCut, onBeforeDeactivate, onBeforeEditFocus, onBeforePaste, onBlur, onClick, onContextMenu, onControlSelect, onCopy, onCut, onDblClick, onDeactivate, onDrag, onDragEnd, onDragEnter, onDragLeave, onDragOver, onDragStart, onDrop, onFocus, onFocusIn, onFocusOut, onHelp, onKeyDown, onKeyPress, onKeyUp, onLayoutComplete, onLoseCapture, onMouseDown, onMouseEnter, onMouseLeave, onMouseMove, onMouseOut, onMouseOver, onMouseUp, onMouseWheel, onMove, onMoveEnd, onMoveStart, onPaste, onPropertyChange, onReadyStateChange, onResize, onResizeEnd, onResizeStart, onSelectStart, onTimeError

◁dl▷ CSS Attributes and JavaScript Style Properties (8)

The names are in CSS syntax. See the introduction to this chapter for the JavaScript syntax rules. Names noted with an asterisk (*) are JavaScript properties only.

```
!important, :first-letter, :first-line, accelerator, background, background-
attachment, background-color, background-image, background-position, background-
position-x, background-position-y, background-repeat, behavior, border, border-
bottom, border-bottom-color, border-bottom-style, border-bottom-width, border-color,
border-left, border-left-color, border-left-style, border-left-width, border-right,
border-right-color, border-right-style, border-right-width, border-style, border-
top, border-top-color, border-top-style, border-top-width, border-width, bottom,
clear, clip, color, cursor, direction, display, filter, float, font, font-family,
font-size, font-style, font-variant, font-weight, hasLayout(*), height, layout-flow,
layout-grid, layout-grid-char, layout-grid-line, layout-grid-mode, layout-grid-type,
left, letter-spacing, line-break, line-height, margin, margin-bottom, margin-left,
margin-right, margin-top, overflow, overflow-x, overflow-y, padding, padding-bottom,
padding-left, padding-right, padding-top, page-break-after, page-break-before,
pixelBottom(*), pixelHeight(*), pixelLeft(*), pixelRight(*), pixelTop(*),
pixelWidth(*), posBottom(*), posHeight(*), position, posLeft(*), posRight(*),
posTop(*), posWidth(*), right, styleFloat(*), text-align, text-align-last, text-
autospace, text-decoration, text-indent, text-justify, text-kashida-space, text-
overflow, text-transform, text-underline-position, textDecorationBlink(*),
textDecorationLineThrough(*), textDecorationNone(*), textDecorationOverline(*),
textDecorationUnderline(*), top, unicode-bidi, visibility, white-space, width, word-
break, word-spacing, word-wrap, writing-mode, z-index, zoom
```

◁dl▷ Microsoft Behaviors (9)

```
clientCaps, download, homePage, httpFolder, saveFavorite, saveHistory,
saveSnapshot, time, time2, userData
```

◁dl▷ Microsoft Filters (10)

```
Alpha, Barn, BasicImage, BlendTrans, Blinds, Blur, CheckerBoard, Chroma,
Compositor, DropShadow, Emboss, Engrave, Fade, FlipH, FlipV, Glow, GradientWipe,
Gray, ICMFilter, Inset, Invert, Iris, Light, MaskFilter, Matrix, MotionBlur,
Pixelate, RadialWipe, RandomBars, RandomDissolve, RevealTrans, Shadow, Slide,
Spiral, Stretch, Strips, Wave, Wheel, Xray, Zigzag
```

dl. JavaScript Properties (11)

```
accessKey, blockDirection, canHaveChildren, canHaveHTML, className, clientHeight,
clientLeft, clientTop, clientWidth, compact, contentEditable, cursor, dir,
disabled, end, firstChild, hasLayout, hideFocus, id, innerHTML, isContentEditable,
isDisabled, isMultiLine, isTextEdit, lang, language, lastChild, nextSibling,
nodeName, nodeType, nodeValue, offsetHeight, offsetLeft, offsetParent, offsetTop,
offsetWidth, outerHTML, outerText, ownerDocument, parentElement, parentNode,
parentTextEdit, previousSibling, readyState, scopeName, scrollHeight, scrollLeft,
scrollTop, scrollWidth, sourceIndex, tabIndex, tagName, tagUrn, title, uniqueID
```

dl. JavaScript Methods (12)

addBehavior, appendChild, applyElement, attachEvent, blur, clearAttributes, click, cloneNode, componentFromPoint, contains, detachEvent, fireEvent, focus, getAdjacentText, getAttribute, getAttributeNode, getBoundingClientRect, getClientRects, getElementsByTagName, getExpression, hasChildNodes, insertAdjacentElement, insertAdjacentHTML, insertAdjacentText, insertBefore, mergeAttributes, normalize, releaseCapture, removeAttribute, removeAttributeNode, removeBehavior, removeChild, removeExpression, removeNode, replaceAdjacentText, replaceChild, replaceNode, scrollIntoView, setActive, setAttribute, setAttributeNode, setCapture, setExpression, swapNode

dl. JavaScript Collections (13)

all, attributes, behaviorUrns, childNodes, children

dl. JavaScript Objects (14)

currentStyle, runtimeStyle, style

<!DOCTYPE>

Compatibility: NN4, NN6, NN7, IE4, IE5, IE5.5, IE6

This element specifies which document type definition (DTD) should be applied to the document. It must appear before the HTML tag.

Syntax:

```
<!DOCTYPE TopElement Availability "-//Organization//Type LanguageVersion
Definition//LanguageCountry">
```

Correct syntax requires that the attribute values be specified without attribute names, as in the following examples:

```
<!DOCTYPE HTML PUBLIC "-//W3C//DTD HTML 4.0//EN">
```

<!DOCTYPE> Specific Attributes Ordered by Syntax

Top Element

Compatibility: NN4, NN6, NN7, IE4, IE5, IE5.5, IE6

This attribute specifies the markup language used in the document. The default value is HTML.

Availability

Compatibility: NN4, NN6, NN7, IE4, IE5, IE5.5, IE6

This attribute specifies whether the DTD is publicly accessible or is available as a system resource.

Values:

PUBLIC	Indicates the DTD is publicly accessible; this is the default value
SYSTEM	Indicates a local DTD file or a URL that points to a DTD file

Organization

Compatibility: NN4, NN6, NN7, IE4, IE5, IE5.5, IE6

This attribute specifies the organization responsible for the creation and maintenance of the DTD being used.

Values: W3C or IETF.

Type

Compatibility: NN4, NN6, NN7, IE4, IE5, IE5.5, IE6

This attribute specifies the type of object used in the page. The default value is DTD.

Language Version

Compatibility: NN4, NN6, NN7, IE4, IE5, IE5.5, IE6

This attribute specifies the version of the markup language used for the document. The default value is HTML 4.0.

Definition

Compatibility: NN4, NN6, NN7, IE4, IE5, IE5.5, IE6

This attribute defines the document type. If no value is specified, the document can make use of any of the types.

Values:

frameset	For frameset documents
strict	Supports mainly style sheets
transitional	Does not contain frameset elements

Language Country

Compatibility: NN4, NN6, NN7, IE4, IE5, IE5.5, IE6

This attribute specifies the language used in the document (Spanish, English, and so on). Table 6-1, in the hreflang section of Chapter 6, contains a list of possible values for this attribute.

<dt> ... </dt>

Compatibility: NN4, NN6, NN7, IE4, IE5, IE5.5, IE6

This element is known as the *definition term*, and it is used in conjunction with the <dl> and <dd> elements. The <dl> element is a *definition list* that you can use to contain multiple *definition terms*, <dt>, along with *definition descriptions*, <dd>. These elements provide a standardized method for displaying terms and definitions in HTML (such as in a glossary).

Syntax:

```
<dt attributes events> . . . </dt>
```

Example:

```
<html><head><title>dt element example</title></head>
<body bgcolor="#FFFFFF" text="#000000">
<dl>
<dt>&lt;TABLE&gt;</dt>
<dd>an html element.</dd>
<dt>border-color</dt>
<dd>a style sheet property.</dd>
<dt>innerText</dt>
<dd>a JavaScript property.</dd>
<dt>cloneNode()</dt>
<dd>a JavaScript method.</dd>
</dl></body></html>
```

<dt> HTML Attributes (6)

```
accesskey, begin, class, contenteditable, dir, disabled, end, hidefocus, id, lang,
language, nowrap, style, syncmaster, systemBitrate, systemCaptions, systemLanguage,
systemOverdubOrSubtitle, tabindex, timecontainer, title, unselectable
```

<dt> Event Handlers (7)

```
onActivate, onBeforeActivate, onBeforeCopy, onBeforeCut, onBeforeDeactivate,
onBeforeEditFocus, onBeforePaste, onBlur, onClick, onContextMenu, onControlSelect,
onCopy, onCut, onDblClick, onDeactivate, onDrag, onDragEnd, onDragEnter,
onDragLeave, onDragOver, onDragStart, onDrop, onFocus, onFocusIn, onFocusOut,
onHelp, onKeyDown, onKeyPress, onKeyUp, onLayoutComplete, onLoseCapture,
onMouseDown, onMouseEnter, onMouseLeave, onMouseMove, onMouseOut, onMouseOver,
onMouseUp, onMouseWheel, onMove, onMoveEnd, onMoveStart, onPaste, onPropertyChange,
onReadyStateChange, onResize, onResizeEnd, onResizeStart, onSelectStart,
onTimeError
```

<dt> CSS Attributes and JavaScript Style Properties (8)

The names are in CSS syntax. See the introduction to this chapter for the
JavaScript syntax rules. Names noted with an asterisk (*) are JavaScript
properties only.

```
!important, :first-letter, :first-line, accelerator, background, background-
attachment, background-color, background-image, background-position, background-
position-x, background-position-y, background-repeat, behavior, border, border-
bottom, border-bottom-color, border-bottom-style, border-bottom-width, border-
color, border-left, border-left-color, border-left-style, border-left-width,
border-right, border-right-color, border-right-style, border-right-width,
border-style, border-top, border-top-color, border-top-style, border-top-width,
```

border-width, clear, clip, color, cursor, direction, display, filter, float, font, font-family, font-size, font-style, font-variant, font-weight, hasLayout(*), height, layout-flow, layout-grid, layout-grid-char, layout-grid-line, layout-grid-mode, layout-grid-type, left, letter-spacing, line-break, line-height, margin, margin-bottom, margin-left, margin-right, margin-top, overflow, overflow-x, overflow-y, padding, padding-bottom, padding-left, padding-right, padding-top, page-break-after, page-break-before, pixelBottom(*), pixelHeight(*), pixelLeft(*), pixelRight(*), pixelTop(*), pixelWidth(*), posBottom(*), posHeight(*), position, posLeft(*), posRight(*), posTop(*), posWidth(*), styleFloat(*), text-align, text-align-last, text-autospace, text-decoration, text-indent, text-justify, text-kashida-space, text-overflow, text-transform, text-underline-position, textDecorationBlink(*), textDecorationLineThrough(*), textDecorationNone(*), textDecorationOverline(*), textDecorationUnderline(*), top, unicode-bidi, visibility, white-space, width, word-break, word-spacing, word-wrap, writing-mode, z-index, zoom

<dt> Microsoft Behaviors (9)

clientCaps, download, homePage, httpFolder, saveFavorite, saveHistory, saveSnapshot, time, time2, userData

<dt> Microsoft Filters (10)

Alpha, Barn, BasicImage, BlendTrans, Blinds, Blur, CheckerBoard, Chroma, Compositor, DropShadow, Emboss, Engrave, Fade, FlipH, FlipV, Glow, GradientWipe, Gray, ICMFilter, Inset, Invert, Iris, Light, MaskFilter, Matrix, MotionBlur, Pixelate, RadialWipe, RandomBars, RandomDissolve, RevealTrans, Shadow, Slide, Spiral, Stretch, Strips, Wave, Wheel, Xray, Zigzag

dt. JavaScript Properties (11)

accessKey, blockDirection, canHaveChildren, canHaveHTML, className, clientHeight, clientLeft, clientTop, clientWidth, contentEditable, cursor, dir, disabled, end, firstChild, hasLayout, hideFocus, id, innerHTML, isContentEditable, isDisabled, isMultiLine, isTextEdit, lang, language, lastChild, nextSibling, nodeName, nodeType, nodeValue, noWrap, offsetHeight, offsetLeft, offsetParent, offsetTop, offsetWidth, outerHTML, outerText, ownerDocument, parentElement, parentNode, parentTextEdit, previousSibling, readyState, scopeName, scrollHeight, scrollLeft, scrollTop, scrollWidth, sourceIndex, tabIndex, tagName, tagUrn, title, uniqueID

dt. JavaScript Methods (12)

addBehavior, appendChild, applyElement, attachEvent, blur, clearAttributes, click, cloneNode, componentFromPoint, contains, detachEvent, dragDrop, fireEvent, focus, getAdjacentText, getAttribute, getAttributeNode, getBoundingClientRect, getClientRects, getElementsByTagName, getExpression, hasChildNodes, insertAdjacentElement, insertAdjacentHTML, insertAdjacentText, insertBefore, mergeAttributes, normalize, releaseCapture, removeAttribute, removeAttributeNode, removeBehavior, removeChild, removeExpression, removeNode, replaceAdjacentText, replaceChild, replaceNode, scrollIntoView, setActive, setAttribute, setAttributeNode, setCapture, setExpression, swapNode

dt. JavaScript Collections (13)

all, attributes, behaviorUrns, childNodes, children

dt. JavaScript Objects (14)

currentStyle, runtimeStyle, style

<em> ... </em>

Compatibility: NN4, NN6, NN7, IE4, IE5, IE5.5, IE6

This element causes text to be rendered in italics, and it can thus give *emphasis* to particular words or phrases. You can also use the <i> element to achieve the same formatting results; however, using this element is preferred because it allows the browser to distinguish between emphasized text and other text that may be drawn in italics.

Syntax:

```
<em attributes events> . . . </em>
```

Example:

```
<html><head><title>em element example</title></head>
<body bgcolor="#FFFFFF" text="#000000">
<p align="center"> The words to <em>emphasize</em> are placed inside the <em>em</em> element.</p>
</body></html>
```

<em> HTML Attributes (6)

accesskey, begin, class, contenteditable, dir, disabled, end, hidefocus, id, lang, language, style, syncmaster, systemBitrate, systemCaptions, systemLanguage, systemOverdubOrSubtitle, tabindex, timecontainer, title, unselectable

<em> Event Handlers (7)

onActivate, onBeforeActivate, onBeforeCopy, onBeforeCut, onBeforeDeactivate, onBeforeEditFocus, onBeforePaste, onBlur, onClick, onContextMenu, onControlSelect, onCopy, onCut, onDblClick, onDeactivate, onDrag, onDragEnd, onDragEnter, onDragLeave, onDragOver, onDragStart, onDrop, onFocus, onFocusIn, onFocusOut, onHelp, onKeyDown, onKeyPress, onKeyUp, onLoseCapture, onMouseDown, onMouseEnter, onMouseLeave, onMouseMove, onMouseOut, onMouseOver, onMouseUp, onMouseWheel, onMove, onMoveEnd, onMoveStart, onPaste, onPropertyChange, onReadyStateChange, onResize, onResizeEnd, onResizeStart, onSelectStart, onTimeError

<em> CSS Attributes and JavaScript Style Properties (8)

The names are in CSS syntax. See the introduction to this chapter for the JavaScript syntax rules. Names noted with an asterisk (*) are JavaScript properties only.

!important, accelerator, background, background-attachment, background-color, background-image, background-position, background-position-x, background-position-y, background-repeat, behavior, border, border-bottom, border-bottom-color, border-bottom-style, border-bottom-width, border-color, border-left, border-left-color, border-left-style, border-left-width, border-right, border-right-color, border-right-style, border-right-width, border-style, border-top, border-top-color, border-top-style, border-top-width, border-width, clear, clip, color, cursor, direction, display, filter, float, font, font-family, font-size, font-style, font-variant, font-weight, hasLayout(*), height, layout-flow, layout-grid, layout-grid-mode, left, letter-spacing, line-height, margin, margin-bottom, margin-left, margin-right, margin-top, overflow, overflow-x, overflow-y, padding, padding-bottom, padding-left, padding-right, padding-top, pixelBottom(*), pixelHeight(*), pixelLeft(*), pixelRight(*), pixelTop(*), pixelWidth(*), posBottom(*), posHeight(*), position, posLeft(*), posRight(*), posTop(*), posWidth(*), styleFloat(*), text-autospace, text-decoration, text-overflow, text-transform, text-underline-position, textDecorationBlink(*), textDecorationLineThrough(*), textDecorationNone(*), textDecorationOverline(*), textDecorationUnderline(*), top, unicode-bidi, visibility, white-space, width, word-spacing, word-wrap, writing-mode, z-index, zoom

---

<em> Microsoft Behaviors (9)

---

clientCaps, download, homePage, httpFolder, saveFavorite, saveHistory, saveSnapshot, time, time2, userData

---

<em> Microsoft Filters (10)

Alpha, Barn, BasicImage, BlendTrans, Blinds, Blur, CheckerBoard, Chroma, Compositor, DropShadow, Emboss, Engrave, Fade, FlipH, FlipV, Glow, GradientWipe, Gray, ICMFilter, Inset, Invert, Iris, Light, MaskFilter, Matrix, MotionBlur, Pixelate, RadialWipe, RandomBars, RandomDissolve, RevealTrans, Shadow, Slide, Spiral, Stretch, Strips, Wave, Wheel, Xray, Zigzag

---

em. JavaScript Properties (11)

---

accessKey, canHaveChildren, canHaveHTML, className, clientHeight, clientLeft, clientTop, clientWidth, contentEditable, cursor, dir, disabled, end, firstChild, hasLayout, hideFocus, id, innerHTML, innerText, isContentEditable, isDisabled, isMultiLine, isTextEdit, lang, language, lastChild, nextSibling, nodeName, nodeType, nodeValue, offsetHeight, offsetLeft, offsetParent, offsetTop, offsetWidth, outerHTML, outerText, ownerDocument, parentElement, parentNode, parentTextEdit, previousSibling, readyState, scopeName, scrollHeight, scrollLeft, scrollTop, scrollWidth, sourceIndex, tabIndex, tagName, tagUrn, title, uniqueID

---

em. JavaScript Methods (12)

addBehavior, appendChild, applyElement, attachEvent, blur, clearAttributes, click, cloneNode, componentFromPoint, contains, detachEvent, fireEvent, focus, getAdjacentText, getAttribute, getAttributeNode, getBoundingClientRect, getClientRects, getElementsByTagName, getExpression, hasChildNodes, insertAdjacentElement, insertAdjacentHTML, insertAdjacentText, insertBefore, mergeAttributes, normalize, releaseCapture, removeAttribute, removeAttributeNode, removeBehavior, removeChild, removeExpression, removeNode, replaceAdjacentText, replaceChild, replaceNode, scrollIntoView, setActive, setAttribute, setAttributeNode, setCapture, setExpression, swapNode

em. JavaScript Collections (13)

all, attributes, behaviorUrns, childNodes, children

em. JavaScript Objects (14)

currentStyle, runtimeStyle, style

<embed> ... </embed>

Compatibility: NN4, NN6, NN7, IE4, IE5, IE5.5, IE6

This element was created by Netscape to load sound files or other file types not supported by the browser, such as Flash movies.

Syntax:

```
<embed attributes events></embed>
```

Example:

```
<html><head><title>embed element example</title></head>
<body bgcolor="#FFFFFF" text="#000000">
<object classid="clsid:D27CDB6E-AE6D-11cf-96B8-444553540000" codebase="http://
download.macromedia.com/pub/shockwave/cabs/flash/swflash.cab#version=5,0,0,0"
width="320" height="400">
    <param name=movie value="anyflashmovie.swf">
    <!--Flash movie must be in the same directory as html file-->
    <param name="quality" value="high">
    <embed src="3dflashcube.swf" quality="high" pluginspage="http://
www.macromedia.com/shockwave/download/index.cgi?P1_Prod_Version=ShockwaveFlash"
type="application/x-shockwave-flash" width="320" height="400">
</embed></object>
</body></html>
```

NOTE *The preceding example requires that you have a Flash movie called* anyflashmovie.swf *located in the same directory where the HTML file containing this code is located.*

<embed> HTML Attributes (6)

accesskey, align, border, class, dir, frameborder, height, hidden, hidefocus, hspace, id, lang, language, name, pluginspage, src, style, title, type, units, unselectable, width

<embed> Event Handlers (7)

onActivate, onBeforeActivate, onBeforeCut, onBeforeDeactivate, onBeforePaste, onBlur, onClick, onContextMenu, onControlSelect, onCut, onDblClick, onDeactivate, onFocus, onFocusIn, onFocusOut, onHelp, onLoad, onLoseCapture, onMouseDown, onMouseEnter, onMouseLeave, onMouseMove, onMouseOut, onMouseOver, onMouseUp, onMouseWheel, onMove, onMoveEnd, onMoveStart, onPaste, onPropertyChange, onReadyStateChange, onResize, onResizeEnd, onResizeStart, onScroll

<embed> CSS Attributes and JavaScript Style Properties (8)

The names are in CSS syntax. See the introduction to this chapter for the JavaScript syntax rules. Names noted with an asterisk (*) are JavaScript properties only.

accelerator, background-position-x, background-position-y, behavior, border, border-bottom, border-bottom-color, border-bottom-style, border-bottom-width, border-color, border-left, border-left-color, border-left-style, border-left-width, border-right, border-right-color, border-right-style, border-right-width, border-style, border-top, border-top-color, border-top-style, border-top-width, border-width, clear, clip, cursor, direction, display, float, hasLayout(*), height, layout-grid, layout-grid-mode, left, margin, margin-bottom, margin-left, margin-right, margin-top, overflow, overflow-x, overflow-y, padding, padding-bottom, padding-left, padding-right, padding-top, pixelBottom(*), pixelHeight(*), pixelLeft(*), pixelRight(*), pixelTop(*), pixelWidth(*), posBottom(*), posHeight(*), position, posLeft(*), posRight(*), posTop(*), posWidth(*), scrollbar-3dlight-color, scrollbar-arrow-color, scrollbar-base-color, scrollbar-darkshadow-color, scrollbar-face-color, scrollbar-highlight-color, scrollbar-shadow-color, scrollbar-track-color, styleFloat(*), text-autospace, text-underline-position, top, unicode-bidi, visibility, word-wrap, zoom

<embed> Microsoft Behaviors (9)

clientCaps, download, homePage

embed. JavaScript Properties (11)

accessKey, align, canHaveHTML, className, clientHeight, clientLeft, clientTop, clientWidth, cursor, dir, disabled, firstChild, hasLayout, height, hidden, hideFocus, id, isContentEditable, isDisabled, isMultiLine, isTextEdit, lang, language, lastChild, name, nextSibling, nodeName, nodeType, nodeValue, offsetHeight, offsetLeft, offsetParent, offsetTop, offsetWidth, outerHTML, outerText, ownerDocument, palette, parentElement, parentNode, parentTextEdit, pluginspage, previousSibling, readyState, scopeName, scrollHeight, scrollLeft, scrollTop, scrollWidth, sourceIndex, src, tagName, tagUrn, title, uniqueID, units, width

embed. JavaScript Methods (12)

addBehavior, applyElement, attachEvent, blur, clearAttributes, click, cloneNode, componentFromPoint, contains, detachEvent, dragDrop, fireEvent, focus, getAdjacentText, getAttribute, getAttributeNode, getBoundingClientRect, getClientRects, getElementsByTagName, hasChildNodes, insertAdjacentElement, mergeAttributes, normalize, releaseCapture, removeAttribute, removeAttributeNode, removeBehavior, removeExpression, replaceAdjacentText, scrollIntoView, setActive, setAttribute, setAttributeNode, setCapture, setExpression, swapNode

embed. JavaScript Collections (13)

all, attributes, behaviorUrns, childNodes, children

embed. JavaScript Objects (14)

currentStyle, runtimeStyle, style

<fieldset> ... </fieldset>

Compatibility: NN6, NN7, IE4, IE5, IE5.5, IE6

This element groups <form> elements together by drawing a rectangle around all elements within its opening and closing tags.

Syntax:

<fieldset *attributes events*> . . . </fieldset>

Example:

```
<html><head><title>fieldset element example</title></head>
<body bgcolor="#FFFFFF" text="#000000">
<form name="form1" method="post" action="">
<p><fieldset>
<input type="text" name="textfield" value="First text field in first fieldset"
size="60"><br>
<input type="text" name="textfield2" value="Second text field in first fieldset"
size="50">
</fieldset></p></form>
<form name="form2" method="post" action="">
<p><fieldset>
<input type="text" name="textfield3" value="First text field in second fieldset"
size="65"><br>
<input type="text" name="textfield4" value="Second text field in second fieldset"
size="45"><br>
<input type="text" name="textfield5" value="Third text field in second fieldset"
size="55">
</fieldset></p></form>
</body></html>
```

`<fieldset>` HTML Attributes (6)

accesskey, align, begin, class, contenteditable, datafld, dir, disabled, end,
hidefocus, id, lang, language, style, syncmaster, systemBitrate, systemCaptions,
systemLanguage, systemOverdubOrSubtitle, tabindex, timecontainer, title,
unselectable

`<fieldset>` Event Handlers (7)

onActivate, onBeforeActivate, onBeforeCopy, onBeforeCut, onBeforeDeactivate,
onBeforeEditFocus, onBeforePaste, onBlur, onClick, onContextMenu, onControlSelect,
onCopy, onCut, onDblClick, onDeactivate, onDrag, onDragEnd, onDragEnter,
onDragLeave, onDragOver, onDragStart, onDrop, onFilterChange, onFocus, onFocusIn,
onFocusOut, onHelp, onKeyDown, onKeyPress, onKeyUp, onLoseCapture, onMouseDown,
onMouseEnter, onMouseLeave, onMouseMove, onMouseOut, onMouseOver, onMouseUp,
onMouseWheel, onMove, onMoveEnd, onMoveStart, onPaste, onPropertyChange,
onReadyStateChange, onResize, onResizeEnd, onResizeStart, onSelectStart,
onTimeError

`<fieldset>` CSS Attributes and JavaScript Style Properties (8)

The names are in CSS syntax. See the introduction to this chapter for the
JavaScript syntax rules. Names noted with an asterisk (*) are JavaScript
properties only.

:first-letter, :first-line, accelerator, background, background-attachment,
background-color, background-image, background-position, background-position-x,
background-position-y, background-repeat, behavior, border, border-bottom, border-
bottom-color, border-bottom-style, border-bottom-width, border-color, border-left,
border-left-color, border-left-style, border-left-width, border-right, border-
right-color, border-right-style, border-right-width, border-style, border-top,
border-top-color, border-top-style, border-top-width, border-width, bottom, clear,
clip, color, cursor, direction, display, filter, float, font, font-family, font-
size, font-style, font-variant, font-weight, hasLayout(*), height, layout-flow,
layout-grid, layout-grid-char, layout-grid-line, layout-grid-mode, layout-grid-
type, left, letter-spacing, line-break, line-height, margin, margin-bottom, margin-
left, margin-right, margin-top, overflow, overflow-x, overflow-y, padding, padding-
bottom, padding-left, padding-right, padding-top, page-break-after, page-break-
before, pixelBottom(*), pixelHeight(*), pixelLeft(*), pixelRight(*), pixelTop(*),
pixelWidth(*), posBottom(*), posHeight(*), position, posLeft(*), posRight(*),
posTop(*), posWidth(*), right, styleFloat(*), text-align, text-align-last, text-
autospace, text-decoration, text-indent, text-justify, text-kashida-space, text-
overflow, text-transform, text-underline-position, textDecorationBlink(*),
textDecorationLineThrough(*), textDecorationNone(*), textDecorationOverline(*),
textDecorationUnderline(*), top, unicode-bidi, visibility, white-space, width,
word-break, word-spacing, word-wrap, writing-mode, z-index, zoom

`<fieldset>` Microsoft Behaviors (9)

clientCaps, download, homePage, time, time2

\<fieldset> Microsoft Filters (10)

Alpha, Barn, BasicImage, BlendTrans, Blinds, Blur, CheckerBoard, Chroma,
Compositor, DropShadow, Emboss, Engrave, Fade, FlipH, FlipV, Glow, GradientWipe,
Gray, ICMFilter, Inset, Invert, Iris, Light, MaskFilter, Matrix, MotionBlur,
Pixelate, RadialWipe, RandomBars, RandomDissolve, RevealTrans, Shadow, Slide,
Spiral, Stretch, Strips, Wave, Wheel, Xray, Zigzag

fieldset. JavaScript Properties (11)

accessKey, align, blockDirection, canHaveChildren, canHaveHTML, className,
clientHeight, clientLeft, clientTop, clientWidth, contentEditable, cursor, dataFld,
dir, disabled, end, firstChild, form, hasLayout, hideFocus, id, innerHTML,
innerText, isContentEditable, isDisabled, isMultiLine, isTextEdit, lang, language,
lastChild, nextSibling, nodeName, nodeType, nodeValue, offsetHeight, offsetLeft,
offsetParent, offsetTop, offsetWidth, outerHTML, outerText, ownerDocument,
parentElement, parentNode, parentTextEdit, previousSibling, readyState, scopeName,
scrollHeight, scrollLeft, scrollTop, scrollWidth, sourceIndex, tabIndex, tagName,
tagUrn, title, uniqueID

fieldset. JavaScript Methods (12)

addBehavior, appendChild, applyElement, attachEvent, blur, clearAttributes, click,
cloneNode, componentFromPoint, contains, detachEvent, fireEvent, focus,
getAdjacentText, getAttribute, getAttributeNode, getBoundingClientRect,
getClientRects, getElementsByTagName, getExpression, hasChildNodes,
insertAdjacentElement, insertAdjacentHTML, insertAdjacentText, insertBefore,
mergeAttributes, normalize, releaseCapture, removeAttribute, removeAttributeNode,
removeBehavior, removeChild, removeExpression, removeNode, replaceAdjacentText,
replaceChild, replaceNode, scrollIntoView, setActive, setAttribute,
setAttributeNode, setCapture, setExpression, swapNode

fieldset. JavaScript Collections (13)

all, attributes, behaviorUrns, childNodes, children, filters

fieldset. JavaScript Objects (14)

currentStyle, runtimeStyle, style

\<font> ... \</font>

Compatibility: NN4, NN6, NN7, IE4, IE5, IE5.5, IE6

This element specifies the font and text properties to be applied to the text
between its opening and closing tags. This element has been deprecated, and
with CSS you can obtain the same or better results (see Chapter 1 for information on CSS).

Syntax:

```
<font attributes events> . . . </font>
```

Example:

```
<html><head><title>font element example</title></head>
<body bgcolor="#FFFFFF" text="#000000">
<font face="Verdana, Arial, Helvetica, sans-serif" size="3" color="#006699">This
element is an inline element.</font><br>
<font face="Times New Roman, Times, serif" size="4" color="#CC3366"><i>This font
will appear in Times.</i></font><br>
<font face="Courier New, Courier, mono" size="2" color="#0000FF">This font will
appear in Courier New.</font>
</body></html>
```

\<font> HTML Attributes (6)

accesskey, begin, class, color, contenteditable, dir, disabled, end, face,
hidefocus, id, lang, language, point-size, size, style, syncmaster, systemBitrate,
systemCaptions, systemLanguage, systemOverdubOrSubtitle, tabindex, timecontainer,
title, unselectable, weight

\<font> Event Handlers (7)

onActivate, onBeforeActivate, onBeforeCut, onBeforeDeactivate, onBeforeEditFocus,
onBeforePaste, onBlur, onClick, onContextMenu, onControlSelect, onCut, onDblClick,
onDeactivate, onDrag, onDragEnd, onDragEnter, onDragLeave, onDragOver, onDragStart,
onDrop, onFocus, onFocusIn, onFocusOut, onHelp, onKeyDown, onKeyPress, onKeyUp,
onLayoutComplete, onLoseCapture, onMouseDown, onMouseEnter, onMouseLeave,
onMouseMove, onMouseOut, onMouseOver, onMouseUp, onMouseWheel, onMove, onMoveEnd,
onMoveStart, onPaste, onPropertyChange, onReadyStateChange, onResizeEnd,
onResizeStart, onSelectStart, onTimeError

\<font> CSS Attributes and JavaScript Style Properties (8)

The names are in CSS syntax. See the introduction to this chapter for the
JavaScript syntax rules. Names noted with an asterisk (*) are JavaScript
properties only.

accelerator, background-position-x, background-position-y, behavior, border,
border-bottom, border-bottom-color, border-bottom-style, border-bottom-width,
border-color, border-left, border-left-color, border-left-style, border-left-width,
border-right, border-right-color, border-right-style, border-right-width, border-
style, border-top, border-top-color, border-top-style, border-top-width, border-
width, bottom, direction, display, filter, hasLayout(*), height, layout-flow,
layout-grid, layout-grid-mode, left, margin, margin-bottom, margin-left, margin-
right, margin-top, overflow, overflow-x, overflow-y, padding, padding-bottom,
padding-left, padding-right, padding-top, pixelBottom(*), pixelHeight(*),
pixelLeft(*), pixelRight(*), pixelTop(*), pixelWidth(*), posBottom(*),

posHeight(*), position, posLeft(*), posRight(*), posTop(*), posWidth(*), right, text-autospace, text-overflow, text-underline-position, top, unicode-bidi, white-space, width, word-wrap, writing-mode, zoom

\<font\> Microsoft Behaviors (9)

clientCaps, download, homePage, httpFolder, saveFavorite, saveHistory, saveSnapshot, time, time2, userData

\<font\> Microsoft Filters (10)

Alpha, Barn, BasicImage, BlendTrans, Blinds, Blur, CheckerBoard, Chroma, Compositor, DropShadow, Emboss, Engrave, Fade, FlipH, FlipV, Glow, GradientWipe, Gray, ICMFilter, Inset, Invert, Iris, Light, MaskFilter, Matrix, MotionBlur, Pixelate, RadialWipe, RandomBars, RandomDissolve, RevealTrans, Shadow, Slide, Spiral, Stretch, Strips, Wave, Wheel, Xray, Zigzag

font. JavaScript Properties (11)

accessKey, canHaveChildren, canHaveHTML, className, color, contentEditable, dir, disabled, end, face, firstChild, hasLayout, hideFocus, id, innerHTML, innerText, isContentEditable, isDisabled, isMultiLine, isTextEdit, lang, language, lastChild, nextSibling, nodeName, nodeType, nodeValue, offsetHeight, offsetLeft, offsetParent, offsetTop, offsetWidth, outerHTML, outerText, ownerDocument, parentElement, parentNode, parentTextEdit, previousSibling, readyState, scopeName, size, sourceIndex, tabIndex, tagName, tagUrn, title, uniqueID

font. JavaScript Methods (12)

addBehavior, appendChild, applyElement, attachEvent, blur, clearAttributes, click, cloneNode, componentFromPoint, contains, detachEvent, dragDrop, fireEvent, focus, getAdjacentText, getAttribute, getAttributeNode, getBoundingClientRect, getClientRects, getElementsByTagName, getExpression, hasChildNodes, insertAdjacentElement, insertAdjacentHTML, insertAdjacentText, insertBefore, mergeAttributes, normalize, releaseCapture, removeAttribute, removeAttributeNode, removeBehavior, removeChild, removeExpression, removeNode, replaceAdjacentText, replaceChild, replaceNode, scrollIntoView, setActive, setAttribute, setAttributeNode, setCapture, setExpression, swapNode

font. JavaScript Collections (13)

all, attributes, behaviorUrns, childNodes, children

font. JavaScript Objects (14)

currentStyle, runtimeStyle, style

\<form\> ... \</form\>

Compatibility: NN4, NN6, NN7, IE4, IE5, IE5.5, IE6

This element creates a form that a user can complete and submit to send information to a server for further processing. All input elements between the form element's opening and closing tags are submitted when the form is submitted.

Syntax:

```
<form attributes events> . . . </form>
```

Example:

```
<html><head><title>form element example</title></head>
<body bgcolor="#FFFFFF" text="#000000">
<form name="form2" method="post" action="yourhtmlpage.htm">
<input type="text" name="textfield2" value="This is a text field" size="30"><br>
<input type="checkbox" name="checkbox2" value="checkbox">A checkbox.<br>
<input type="radio" name="radiobutton" value="radiobutton">A radio button.<br>
<select name="select2">
    <option>List item 1</option>
    <option>List item 2</option>
    <option>List item 3</option>
    <option>List item 4</option>
    <option>List item 5</option>
</select>A select list.<br>
<input type="button" name="myButton2" value="Submit">A submit button.
</form></body></html>
```

\<form> HTML Attributes (6)

acceptcharset, action, autocomplete, begin, class, contenteditable, dir, disabled, enctype, end, hidefocus, id, lang, language, method, name, style, syncmaster, systemBitrate, systemCaptions, systemLanguage, systemOverdubOrSubtitle, tabindex, target, timecontainer, title, unselectable

\<form> Event Handlers (7)

onActivate, onBeforeActivate, onBeforeCopy, onBeforeCut, onBeforeDeactivate, onBeforeEditFocus, onBeforePaste, onBlur, onClick, onContextMenu, onControlSelect, onCopy, onCut, onDblClick, onDeactivate, onDrag, onDragEnd, onDragEnter, onDragLeave, onDragOver, onDragStart, onDrop, onFocus, onFocusIn, onFocusOut, onHelp, onKeyDown, onKeyPress, onKeyUp, onLoseCapture, onMouseDown, onMouseEnter, onMouseLeave, onMouseMove, onMouseOut, onMouseOver, onMouseUp, onMouseWheel, onMove, onMoveEnd, onMoveStart, onPaste, onPropertyChange, onReadyStateChange, onResize, onResizeEnd, onResizeStart, onSelectStart, onSubmit, onTimeError

\<form> CSS Attributes and JavaScript Style Properties (8)

The names are in CSS syntax. See the introduction to this chapter for the JavaScript syntax rules. Names noted with an asterisk (*) are JavaScript properties only.

!important, :first-letter, :first-line, accelerator, background, background-attachment, background-color, background-image, background-position, background-position-x, background-position-y, background-repeat, behavior, border, border-bottom, border-bottom-color, border-bottom-style, border-bottom-width, border-color, border-left, border-left-color, border-left-style, border-left-width, border-right, border-right-color, border-right-style, border-right-width, border-style, border-top, border-top-color, border-top-style, border-top-width, border-width, bottom, clear, clip, color, cursor, direction, display, filter, float, font, font-family, font-size, font-style, font-variant, font-weight, hasLayout(*), height, layout-flow, layout-grid, layout-grid-char, layout-grid-line, layout-grid-mode, layout-grid-type, left, letter-spacing, line-break, line-height, margin, margin-bottom, margin-left, margin-right, margin-top, overflow, overflow-x, overflow-y, padding, padding-bottom, padding-left, padding-right, padding-top, page-break-after, page-break-before, pixelBottom(*), pixelHeight(*), pixelLeft(*), pixelRight(*), pixelTop(*), pixelWidth(*), posBottom(*), posHeight(*), position, posLeft(*), posRight(*), posTop(*), posWidth(*), right, styleFloat(*), text-align, text-align-last, text-autospace, text-decoration, text-indent, text-justify, text-kashida-space, text-overflow, text-transform, text-underline-position, textDecorationBlink(*), textDecorationLineThrough(*), textDecorationNone(*), textDecorationOverline(*), textDecorationUnderline(*), top, unicode-bidi, visibility, white-space, width, word-break, word-spacing, word-wrap, writing-mode, z-index, zoom

\<form\> Microsoft Behaviors (9)

clientCaps, download, homePage, httpFolder, saveFavorite, saveHistory, saveSnapshot, time, time2, userData

\<form\> Microsoft Filters (10)

Alpha, Barn, BasicImage, BlendTrans, Blinds, Blur, CheckerBoard, Chroma, Compositor, DropShadow, Emboss, Engrave, Fade, FlipH, FlipV, Glow, GradientWipe, Gray, ICMFilter, Inset, Invert, Iris, Light, MaskFilter, Matrix, MotionBlur, Pixelate, RadialWipe, RandomBars, RandomDissolve, RevealTrans, Shadow, Slide, Spiral, Stretch, Strips, Wave, Wheel, Xray, Zigzag

form. JavaScript Properties (11)

acceptCharset, action, autocomplete, blockDirection, canHaveChildren, canHaveHTML, className, clientHeight, clientLeft, clientTop, clientWidth, contentEditable, cursor, dir, disabled, encoding, enctype, end, firstChild, hasLayout, hideFocus, id, innerHTML, innerText, isContentEditable, isDisabled, isMultiLine, isTextEdit, lang, language, lastChild, length, method, name, nextSibling, nodeName, nodeType, nodeValue, offsetHeight, offsetLeft, offsetParent, offsetTop, offsetWidth, outerHTML, outerText, ownerDocument, parentElement, parentNode, parentTextEdit, previousSibling, readyState, scopeName, scrollHeight, scrollLeft, scrollTop, scrollWidth, sourceIndex, tabIndex, tagName, tagUrn, target, title, uniqueID

form. JavaScript Methods (12)

addBehavior, appendChild, applyElement, attachEvent, blur, clearAttributes, click, cloneNode, componentFromPoint, contains, detachEvent, dragDrop, fireEvent, focus, getAdjacentText, getAttribute, getAttributeNode, getBoundingClientRect,

getClientRects, getElementsByTagName, getExpression, hasChildNodes,
insertAdjacentElement, insertAdjacentHTML, insertAdjacentText, insertBefore,
item, mergeAttributes, namedItem, normalize, releaseCapture, removeAttribute,
removeAttributeNode, removeBehavior, removeChild, removeExpression, removeNode,
replaceAdjacentText, replaceChild, replaceNode, reset, scrollIntoView, setActive,
setAttribute, setAttributeNode, setCapture, setExpression, submit, swapNode, urns

form. JavaScript Collections (13)

all, attributes, behaviorUrns, childNodes, children, elements

form. JavaScript Objects (14)

currentStyle, runtimeStyle, style

<frame>

Compatibility: NN4, NN6, NN7, IE4, IE5, IE5.5, IE6

This element creates a single frame within the <frameset> element. By using a
frameset, this element divides the browser window into multiple windows, with
each frame creating an additional window, and it also controls how each window
is populated. The <frameset> tag replaces the <body> tag.

Syntax:

<frame *attributes events*>

Example:

```
<frameset rows="33%, 33%, *" cols="33%, 33%, *">
    <frame name="frame_1" src="frame(1).html">
    <frame name="frame_2" src="frame(2).html">
    <frame name="frame_3" src="frame(3).html">
    <frame name="frame_4" src="frame(4).html">
    <frame name="frame_5" src="frame(5).html">
    <frame name="frame_6" src="frame(6).html">
    <frame name="frame_7" src="frame(7).html">
    <frame name="frame_8" src="frame(8).html">
    <frame name="frame_9" src="frame(9).html">
    </frameset>
<noframes>Your system doesn't support frames.</noframes>
```

<frame> HTML Attributes (6)

allowtransparency, application, bordercolor, class, datafld, datasrc, frameborder,
height, hidefocus, id, lang, language, marginheight, marginwidth, name, noresize,
scrolling, security, src, style, tabindex, title, unselectable, width

\<frame\> Event Handlers (7)

onActivate, onAfterUpdate, onBeforeDeactivate, onBeforeUpdate, onBlur, onClick, onControlSelect, onDblClick, onDeactivate, onErrorUpdate, onFocus, onLoad, onMove, onMoveEnd, onMoveStart, onResize, onResizeEnd, onResizeStart

\<frame\> CSS Attributes and JavaScript Style Properties (8)

The names are in CSS syntax. See the introduction to this chapter for the JavaScript syntax rules. Names noted with an asterisk (*) are JavaScript properties only.

background-position-x, background-position-y, behavior, border, border-bottom, border-bottom-color, border-bottom-style, border-bottom-width, border-color, border-left, border-left-color, border-left-style, border-left-width, border-right, border-right-color, border-right-style, border-right-width, border-style, border-top, border-top-color, border-top-style, border-top-width, border-width, display, filter, height, layout-grid, layout-grid-mode, padding, padding-bottom, padding-left, padding-right, padding-top, pixelBottom(*), pixelHeight(*), pixelLeft(*), pixelRight(*), pixelTop(*), pixelWidth(*), posBottom(*), posHeight(*), posLeft(*), posRight(*), posTop(*), posWidth(*), text-autospace, zoom

\<frame\> Microsoft Behaviors (9)

clientCaps, download, homePage

\<frame\> Microsoft Filters (10)

Alpha, Barn, BasicImage, BlendTrans, Blinds, Blur, CheckerBoard, Chroma, Compositor, DropShadow, Emboss, Engrave, Fade, FlipH, FlipV, Glow, GradientWipe, Gray, ICMFilter, Inset, Invert, Iris, Light, MaskFilter, Matrix, MotionBlur, Pixelate, RadialWipe, RandomBars, RandomDissolve, RevealTrans, Shadow, Slide, Spiral, Stretch, Strips, Wave, Wheel, Xray, Zigzag

frame. JavaScript Properties (11)

allowTransparency, borderColor, canHaveHTML, className, clientHeight, clientWidth, contentWindow, dataFld, datasrc, dir, disabled, firstChild, frameBorder, height, hideFocus, id, innerHTML, isContentEditable, isDisabled, isMultiLine, isTextEdit, lang, language, lastChild, longDesc, name, nextSibling, nodeName, nodeType, nodeValue, noResize, offsetHeight, offsetLeft, offsetParent, offsetTop, offsetWidth, ownerDocument, parentElement, parentNode, parentTextEdit, previousSibling, readyState, recordNumber, scopeName, scrollHeight, scrollLeft, scrollTop, scrollWidth, self, sourceIndex, src, tabIndex, tagName, tagUrn, title, uniqueID, width

frame. JavaScript Methods (12)

addBehavior, appendChild, applyElement, attachEvent, blur, clearAttributes, cloneNode, componentFromPoint, contains, detachEvent, dragDrop, fireEvent, focus, getAdjacentText, getAttribute, getAttributeNode, getElementsByTagName, hasChildNodes, insertAdjacentElement, insertBefore, mergeAttributes, normalize,

removeAttribute, removeAttributeNode, removeBehavior, removeChild,
replaceAdjacentText, replaceChild, setActive, setAttribute, setAttributeNode,
swapNode

frame. JavaScript Collections (13)

all, attributes, behaviorUrns, childNodes, children

frame. JavaScript Objects (14)

runtimeStyle, style

<frameset> ... </frameset>

Compatibility: NN4, NN6, NN7, IE4, IE5, IE5.5, IE6

This element is used in conjunction with the <frame> element to display multiple
web page documents simultaneously in a single browser window. The <frameset>
tag replaces the <body> tag.

Syntax:

```
<frameset attributes events> . . . </frameset>
```

Example:

```
<frameset rows="33%, 33%, *" cols="33%, 33%, *">
   <frame name="frame_1" src="frame(1).html">
   <frame name="frame_2" src="frame(2).html">
   <frame name="frame_3" src="frame(3).html">
   <frame name="frame_4" src="frame(4).html">
   <frame name="frame_5" src="frame(5).html">
   <frame name="frame_6" src="frame(6).html">
   <frame name="frame_7" src="frame(7).html">
   <frame name="frame_8" src="frame(8).html">
   <frame name="frame_9" src="frame(9).html">
</frameset>
<noframes>Your system doesn't support frames.</noframes>
```

<frameset> HTML Attributes (6)

border, bordercolor, class, cols, frameborder, framespacing, hidefocus, id, lang,
language, name, rows, style, tabindex, title, unselectable, width

<frameset> Event Handlers (7)

onActivate, onAfterPrint, onAfterUpdate, onBeforeDeactivate, onBeforePrint,
onBeforeUnload, onBeforeUpdate, onBlur, onControlSelect, onDeactivate, onFocus,
onLoad, onMove, onMoveEnd, onMoveStart, onResizeEnd, onResizeStart, onUnload

\<frameset> CSS Attributes and JavaScript Style Properties (8)

The names are in CSS syntax. See the introduction to this chapter for the JavaScript syntax rules. Names noted with an asterisk (*) are JavaScript properties only.

---

background-position-x, background-position-y, behavior, border-bottom, border-left, border-right, border-top, filter, height, layout-grid, layout-grid-mode, pixelBottom(*), pixelHeight(*), pixelLeft(*), pixelRight(*), pixelTop(*), pixelWidth(*), posBottom(*), posHeight(*), posLeft(*), posRight(*), posTop(*), posWidth(*), text-underline-position, zoom

---

\<frameset> Microsoft Behaviors (9)

---

clientCaps, download, homePage

\<frameset> Microsoft Filters (10)

Barn, BasicImage, Blinds, Blur, CheckerBoard, Compositor, Emboss, Engrave, Fade, GradientWipe, ICMFilter, Inset, Iris, Matrix, Pixelate, RadialWipe, RandomBars, RandomDissolve, Slide, Spiral, Stretch, Strips, Wheel, Zigzag

---

frameset. JavaScript Properties (11)

---

border, borderColor, canHaveChildren, canHaveHTML, className, clientHeight, clientWidth, cols, dir, firstChild, frameBorder, frameSpacing, hideFocus, id, innerHTML, isContentEditable, isDisabled, isMultiLine, isTextEdit, lang, language, lastChild, name, nextSibling, nodeName, nodeType, nodeValue, offsetHeight, offsetLeft, offsetParent, offsetTop, offsetWidth, outerHTML, ownerDocument, parentElement, parentNode, parentTextEdit, previousSibling, readyState, rows, scopeName, scrollHeight, scrollLeft, scrollTop, scrollWidth, sourceIndex, tabIndex, tagName, tagUrn, title, uniqueID, width

---

frameset. JavaScript Methods (12)

---

addBehavior, appendChild, applyElement, attachEvent, blur, clearAttributes, cloneNode, componentFromPoint, contains, detachEvent, fireEvent, focus, getAdjacentText, getAttribute, getAttributeNode, getElementsByTagName, hasChildNodes, insertAdjacentElement, insertAdjacentHTML, insertAdjacentText, insertBefore, mergeAttributes, normalize, removeAttribute, removeAttributeNode, removeBehavior, removeChild, removeNode, replaceAdjacentText, replaceChild, replaceNode, setActive, setAttribute, setAttributeNode, swapNode

---

frameset. JavaScript Collections (13)

---

all, attributes, behaviorUrns, childNodes, children

---

frameset. JavaScript Objects (14)

---

runtimeStyle, style

<head> ... </head>

Compatibility: NN4, NN6, NN7, IE4, IE5, IE5.5, IE6

As the name suggests, this element creates the header section of an HTML document. In this section, you can define the title of the document, establish links to CSS style sheets, reference JavaScript code, and so on.

Syntax:

```
<head attributes events> . . . </head>
```

Example:

```
<html><head>
<title>head element example</title>
<link rel="stylesheet" type="text/css" href="yourstylesheet.css"
<script language="javascript">
<!-- alert("Hello World"); -->
</script></head>
<body>This is the content of the page</body>
</html>
```

<head> HTML Attributes (6)

class, dir, id, lang, profile

<head> Event Handlers (7)

onLayoutComplete, onReadyStateChange

<head> CSS Attributes and JavaScript Style Properties (8)

The names are in CSS syntax. See the introduction to this chapter for the JavaScript syntax rules. Names noted with an asterisk (*) are JavaScript properties only.

background-position-x, background-position-y, behavior, layout-grid, layout-grid-mode, pixelBottom(*), pixelHeight(*), pixelLeft(*), pixelRight(*), pixelTop(*), pixelWidth(*), posBottom(*), posHeight(*), posLeft(*), posRight(*), posTop(*), posWidth(*), text-autospace, text-underline-position, zoom

<head> Microsoft Behaviors (9)

clientCaps, download, homePage

head. JavaScript Properties (11)

align, canHaveChildren, canHaveHTML, className, clientHeight, clientWidth, dir, disabled, firstChild, id, innerHTML, isContentEditable, isDisabled, isMultiLine, isTextEdit, lang, lastChild, nextSibling, nodeName, nodeType, nodeValue, offsetHeight, offsetLeft, offsetParent, offsetTop, offsetWidth, ownerDocument, parentElement, parentNode, parentTextEdit, previousSibling, profile, readyState, scopeName, scrollHeight, scrollLeft, scrollTop, scrollWidth, sourceIndex, tagName, tagUrn, title, uniqueID

head. JavaScript Methods (12)

addBehavior, appendChild, applyElement, attachEvent, clearAttributes, cloneNode, componentFromPoint, contains, detachEvent, dragDrop, fireEvent, getAdjacentText, getAttribute, getAttributeNode, getElementsByTagName, hasChildNodes, insertAdjacentElement, insertBefore, mergeAttributes, normalize, removeAttribute, removeAttributeNode, removeBehavior, removeChild, removeNode, replaceAdjacentText, replaceChild, replaceNode, setAttribute, setAttributeNode, swapNode

head. JavaScript Collections (13)

all, attributes, behaviorUrns, childNodes, children

<h*N*> ... </h*N*>

Compatibility: NN4, NN6, NN7, IE4, IE5, IE5.5, IE6

This element sets the font size for text between its opening and closing tags. The letter *N* in the syntax and example below represents the size of the font relative to the base font of the document. To display text in a size equal to the base font, omit *N*, using the <h> tag. The value of *N* can be from 1 to 6. The size of the font has an inverse relationship with the number, so 1 is the largest font, and 6 is the smallest font.

Syntax:

<h*N* attributes events> . . . </h*N*>

Example:

```
<html><head><title>h3 element example</title></head>
<body bgcolor="#FFFFFF" text="#000000">
<h3 id="myH">This is a #3 heading</h3>
</body></html>
```

<h*N*> HTML Attributes (6)

accesskey, align, begin, class, contenteditable, dir, disabled, end, hidefocus, id, lang, language, style, syncmaster, systemBitrate, systemCaptions, systemLanguage, systemOverdubOrSubtitle, tabindex, timecontainer, title, unselectable

<h*N*> Event Handlers (7)

onActivate, onBeforeActivate, onBeforeCopy, onBeforeCut, onBeforeDeactivate, onBeforeEditFocus, onBeforePaste, onBlur, onClick, onContextMenu, onControlSelect, onCopy, onCut, onDblClick, onDeactivate, onDrag, onDragEnd, onDragEnter, onDragLeave, onDragOver, onDragStart, onDrop, onFocus, onFocusIn, onFocusOut, onHelp, onKeyDown, onKeyPress, onKeyUp, onLoseCapture, onMouseDown, onMouseEnter, onMouseLeave, onMouseMove, onMouseOut, onMouseOver, onMouseUp, onMouseWheel, onMove, onMoveEnd, onMoveStart, onPaste, onPropertyChange, onReadyStateChange, onResize, onResizeEnd, onResizeStart, onSelectStart, onTimeError

<h*N*> CSS Attributes and JavaScript Style Properties (8)

The names are in CSS syntax. See the introduction to this chapter for the JavaScript syntax rules. Names noted with an asterisk (*) are JavaScript properties only.

!important, :first-letter, :first-line, accelerator, background, background-attachment, background-color, background-image, background-position, background-position-x, background-position-y, background-repeat, behavior, border, border-bottom, border-bottom-color, border-bottom-style, border-bottom-width, border-color, border-left, border-left-color, border-left-style, border-left-width, border-right, border-right-color, border-right-style, border-right-width, border-style, border-top, border-top-color, border-top-style, border-top-width, border-width, bottom, clear, clip, color, cursor, direction, display, filter, float, font, font-family, font-size, font-style, font-variant, font-weight, hasLayout(*), height, layout-flow, layout-grid, layout-grid-char, layout-grid-line, layout-grid-mode, layout-grid-type, left, letter-spacing, line-break, line-height, margin, margin-bottom, margin-left, margin-right, margin-top, overflow, overflow-x, overflow-y, padding, padding-bottom, padding-left, padding-right, padding-top, page-break-after, page-break-before, pixelBottom(*), pixelHeight(*), pixelLeft(*), pixelRight(*), pixelTop(*), pixelWidth(*), posBottom(*), posHeight(*), position, posLeft(*), posRight(*), posTop(*), posWidth(*), right, styleFloat(*), text-align, text-align-last, text-autospace, text-decoration, text-indent, text-justify, text-kashida-space, text-overflow, text-transform, text-underline-position, textDecorationBlink(*), textDecorationLineThrough(*), textDecorationNone(*), textDecorationOverline(*), textDecorationUnderline(*), top, unicode-bidi, visibility, white-space, width, word-break, word-spacing, word-wrap, writing-mode, zoom

<h*N*> Microsoft Behaviors (9)

clientCaps, download, homePage, httpFolder, saveFavorite, saveHistory, saveSnapshot, time, time2, userData

<h*N*> Microsoft Filters (10)

Alpha, Barn, BasicImage, BlendTrans, Blinds, Blur, CheckerBoard, Chroma, Compositor, DropShadow, Emboss, Engrave, Fade, FlipH, FlipV, Glow, GradientWipe, Gray, ICMFilter, Inset, Invert, Iris, Light, MaskFilter, Matrix, MotionBlur, Pixelate, RadialWipe, RandomBars, RandomDissolve, RevealTrans, Shadow, Slide, Spiral, Stretch, Strips, Wave, Wheel, Xray, Zigzag

h*N*. JavaScript Properties (11)

accessKey, align, blockDirection, canHaveChildren, canHaveHTML, className, clientHeight, clientLeft, clientTop, clientWidth, contentEditable, cursor, dir, disabled, end, firstChild, hasLayout, hideFocus, id, innerHTML, innerText, isContentEditable, isDisabled, isMultiLine, isTextEdit, lang, language, lastChild, nextSibling, nodeName, nodeType, nodeValue, offsetHeight, offsetLeft, offsetParent, offsetTop, offsetWidth, outerHTML, outerText, ownerDocument, parentElement, parentNode, parentTextEdit, previousSibling, readyState, scopeName, scrollHeight, scrollLeft, scrollTop, scrollWidth, sourceIndex, tabIndex, tagName, tagUrn, title, uniqueID

hN. JavaScript Methods (12)

addBehavior, appendChild, applyElement, attachEvent, blur, clearAttributes, click, cloneNode, componentFromPoint, contains, detachEvent, fireEvent, focus, getAdjacentText, getAttribute, getAttributeNode, getBoundingClientRect, getClientRects, getElementsByTagName, getExpression, hasChildNodes, insertAdjacentElement, insertAdjacentHTML, insertAdjacentText, insertBefore, mergeAttributes, normalize, releaseCapture, removeAttribute, removeAttributeNode, removeBehavior, removeChild, removeExpression, removeNode, replaceAdjacentText, replaceChild, replaceNode, scrollIntoView, setActive, setAttribute, setAttributeNode, setCapture, setExpression, swapNode

hN. JavaScript Collections (13)

all, attributes, behaviorUrns, childNodes, children

hN. JavaScript Objects (14)

currentStyle, runtimeStyle, style

<hr>

Compatibility: NN4, NN6, NN7, IE4, IE5, IE5.5, IE6

This element creates a horizontal rule going across the page. The default setting causes the line to be shaded, giving it a 3D appearance.

Syntax:

```
<hr attributes events>
```

Example:

```
<html><head><title>hr element example</title></head>
<body>
paragraph#1
<hr id="firstRule" noshade color="blue">
paragraph#2
<hr id="firstRule" color="blue">
</body></html>
```

`<hr>` HTML Attributes (6)

accesskey, align, begin, class, color, dir, end, hidefocus, id, lang, language, noshade, size, style, syncmaster, systemBitrate, systemCaptions, systemLanguage, systemOverdubOrSubtitle, tabindex, timecontainer, title, unselectable, width

`<hr>` Event Handlers (7)

onActivate, onBeforeActivate, onBeforeCut, onBeforeDeactivate, onBeforePaste, onBlur, onClick, onContextMenu, onControlSelect, onCopy, onCut, onDblClick, onDeactivate, onDrag, onDragEnd, onDragEnter, onDragLeave, onDragOver, onDragStart, onDrop, onFocus, onFocusIn, onFocusOut, onHelp, onKeyDown, onKeyPress, onKeyUp, onLayoutComplete, onLoseCapture, onMouseDown, onMouseEnter, onMouseLeave, onMouseMove, onMouseOut, onMouseOver, onMouseUp, onMouseWheel, onMove, onMoveEnd, onMoveStart, onPaste, onPropertyChange, onReadyStateChange, onResize, onResizeEnd, onResizeStart, onSelectStart, onTimeError

`<hr>` CSS Attributes and JavaScript Style Properties (8)

The names are in CSS syntax. See the introduction to this chapter for the JavaScript syntax rules. Names noted with an asterisk (*) are JavaScript properties only.

background-position-x, background-position-y, behavior, border-bottom-color, border-bottom-style, border-bottom-width, border-color, border-left-color, border-left-style, border-left-width, border-right-color, border-right-style, border-right-width, border-style, border-top-color, border-top-style, border-top-width, border-width, bottom, clear, clip, cursor, display, float, height, layout-flow, layout-grid, layout-grid-char, layout-grid-line, layout-grid-mode, layout-grid-type, left, line-break, margin, margin-bottom, margin-left, margin-right, margin-top, padding, padding-bottom, padding-left, padding-right, padding-top, pixelBottom(*), pixelHeight(*), pixelLeft(*), pixelRight(*), pixelTop(*), pixelWidth(*), posBottom(*), posHeight(*), position, posLeft(*), posRight(*), posTop(*), posWidth(*), right, styleFloat(*), text-align, text-align-last, text-autospace, text-indent, text-justify, text-kashida-space, text-underline-position, top, visibility, white-space, width, word-break, word-wrap, writing-mode, zoom

`<hr>` Microsoft Behaviors (9)

clientCaps, download, homePage, httpFolder, saveFavorite, saveHistory, saveSnapshot, time, time2, userData

`<hr>` Microsoft Filters (10)

FlipH, FlipV

hr. JavaScript Properties (11)

accessKey, align, canHaveHTML, className, clientHeight, clientWidth, color, cursor, dir, disabled, end, firstChild, hideFocus, id, innerHTML, isContentEditable, isDisabled, isMultiLine, isTextEdit, lang, language, lastChild, nextSibling, nodeName, nodeType, nodeValue, noShade, offsetHeight, offsetLeft, offsetParent, offsetTop, offsetWidth, outerHTML, outerText, ownerDocument, parentElement, parentNode, parentTextEdit, previousSibling, readyState, scopeName, scrollHeight, scrollLeft, scrollTop, scrollWidth, size, sourceIndex, tabIndex, tagName, tagUrn, title, uniqueID, width

hr. JavaScript Methods (12)

addBehavior, appendChild, applyElement, attachEvent, blur, clearAttributes, click, cloneNode, componentFromPoint, contains, detachEvent, dragDrop, fireEvent, focus, getAdjacentText, getAttribute, getAttributeNode, getElementsByTagName, getExpression, hasChildNodes, insertAdjacentElement, insertAdjacentHTML, insertAdjacentText, insertBefore, mergeAttributes, normalize, releaseCapture, removeAttribute, removeAttributeNode, removeBehavior, removeChild, removeExpression, replaceAdjacentText, replaceChild, scrollIntoView, setActive, setAttribute, setAttributeNode, setCapture, setExpression, swapNode

hr. JavaScript Collections (13)

all, attributes, behaviorUrns, childNodes, children

hr. JavaScript Objects (14)

currentStyle, runtimeStyle, style

<html> ... </html>

Compatibility: NN4, NN6, NN7, IE4, IE5, IE5.5, IE6

This element identifies the page as an HTML document. It has two main sections, <head> and <body>, which are also covered in this chapter.

Syntax:

<html *attributes events*> . . . </html>

<html> HTML Attributes (6)

class, dir, id, lang, scroll, version, xmlns

<html> Event Handlers (7)

onLayoutComplete, onMouseEnter, onMouseLeave, onReadyStateChange

<html> CSS Attributes and JavaScript Style Properties (8)

The names are in CSS syntax. See the introduction to this chapter for the JavaScript syntax rules. Names noted with an asterisk (*) are JavaScript properties only.

```
!important, background, background-attachment, background-color, background-image,
background-position, background-repeat, behavior, color, cursor, display, font,
font-family, font-size, font-style, font-variant, font-weight, letter-spacing,
line-height, overflow, overflow-x, overflow-y, text-autospace, text-decoration,
text-transform, text-underline-position, textDecorationBlink(*),
textDecorationLineThrough(*), textDecorationNone(*), textDecorationOverline(*),
textDecorationUnderline(*), visibility, word-spacing, word-wrap
```

<html> Microsoft Behaviors (9)

```
clientCaps, download, homePage
```

html. JavaScript Properties (11)

```
canHaveChildren, canHaveHTML, className, clientHeight, clientLeft, clientTop,
clientWidth, cursor, dir, disabled, firstChild, id, innerHTML, innerText,
isContentEditable, isDisabled, isMultiLine, isTextEdit, lang, lastChild,
nextSibling, nodeName, nodeType, nodeValue, offsetHeight, offsetLeft, offsetParent,
offsetTop, offsetWidth, outerHTML, outerText, ownerDocument, parentElement,
parentNode, parentTextEdit, previousSibling, readyState, scopeName, scroll,
scrollHeight, scrollLeft, scrollTop, scrollWidth, sourceIndex, tagName, tagUrn,
title, uniqueID, version
```

html. JavaScript Methods (12)

```
addBehavior, appendChild, applyElement, attachEvent, clearAttributes, cloneNode,
componentFromPoint, contains, detachEvent, dragDrop, fireEvent, getAdjacentText,
getAttribute, getAttributeNode, getElementsByTagName, hasChildNodes,
insertAdjacentElement, insertBefore, mergeAttributes, normalize, removeAttribute,
removeAttributeNode, removeBehavior, removeChild, removeNode, replaceAdjacentText,
replaceChild, replaceNode, setAttribute, setAttributeNode, swapNode
```

html. JavaScript Collections (13)

```
all, attributes, behaviorUrns, childNodes, children
```

html. JavaScript Objects (14)

```
currentStyle, runtimeStyle, style
```

<i> ... </i>

Compatibility: NN4, NN6, NN7, IE4, IE5, IE5.5, IE6

This element causes enclosed text to be displayed in an italic font, if one is available.

Syntax:

```
<i attributes events> . . . </i>
```

Example:

```
<html><head><title>i element example</title></head>
<body bgcolor="#FFFFFF" text="#000000">
<p align="center"><font size="4">This formulation is <i>new</i> and <i>improved</i>.</font></p>
</body></html>
```

<i> HTML Attributes (6)

accesskey, begin, class, contenteditable, dir, disabled, end, hidefocus, id, lang, language, style, syncmaster, systemBitrate, systemCaptions, systemLanguage, systemOverdubOrSubtitle, tabindex, timecontainer, title, unselectable

<i> Event Handlers (7)

onActivate, onBeforeActivate, onBeforeCopy, onBeforeCut, onBeforeDeactivate, onBeforeEditFocus, onBeforePaste, onBlur, onClick, onContextMenu, onControlSelect, onCopy, onCut, onDblClick, onDeactivate, onDrag, onDragEnd, onDragEnter, onDragLeave, onDragOver, onDragStart, onDrop, onFocus, onFocusIn, onFocusOut, onHelp, onKeyDown, onKeyPress, onKeyUp, onLoseCapture, onMouseDown, onMouseEnter, onMouseLeave, onMouseMove, onMouseOut, onMouseOver, onMouseUp, onMouseWheel, onMove, onMoveEnd, onMoveStart, onPaste, onPropertyChange, onReadyStateChange, onResize, onResizeEnd, onResizeStart, onSelectStart, onTimeError

<i> CSS Attributes and JavaScript Style Properties (8)

The names are in CSS syntax. See the introduction to this chapter for the JavaScript syntax rules. Names noted with an asterisk (*) are JavaScript properties only.

!important, accelerator, background, background-attachment, background-color, background-image, background-position, background-position-x, background-position-y, background-repeat, behavior, border, border-bottom, border-bottom-color, border-bottom-style, border-bottom-width, border-color, border-left, border-left-color, border-left-style, border-left-width, border-right, border-right-color, border-right-style, border-right-width, border-style, border-top, border-top-color, border-top-style, border-top-width, border-width, bottom, clear, clip, color, cursor, direction, display, filter, float, font, font-family, font-size, font-style, font-variant, font-weight, hasLayout(*), height, layout-flow, layout-grid, layout-grid-mode, left, letter-spacing, line-height, margin, margin-bottom, margin-left, margin-right, margin-top, overflow, overflow-x, overflow-y, padding, padding-bottom, padding-left, padding-right, padding-top, pixelBottom(*), pixelHeight(*), pixelLeft(*), pixelRight(*), pixelTop(*), pixelWidth(*), posBottom(*), posHeight(*), position, posLeft(*), posRight(*), posTop(*), posWidth(*), right, styleFloat(*), text-autospace, text-decoration, text-overflow, text-transform, text-underline-position, textDecorationBlink(*), textDecorationLineThrough(*), textDecorationNone(*), textDecorationOverline(*), textDecorationUnderline(*), top, unicode-bidi, visibility, white-space, width, word-spacing, word-wrap, writing-mode, z-index, zoom

<i> Microsoft Behaviors (9)

clientCaps, download, homePage, httpFolder, saveFavorite, saveHistory, saveSnapshot, time, time2, userData

<i> Microsoft Filters (10)

Alpha, Barn, BasicImage, BlendTrans, Blinds, Blur, CheckerBoard, Chroma, Compositor, DropShadow, Emboss, Engrave, Fade, FlipH, FlipV, Glow, GradientWipe, Gray, ICMFilter, Inset, Invert, Iris, Light, MaskFilter, Matrix, MotionBlur, Pixelate, RadialWipe, RandomBars, RandomDissolve, RevealTrans, Shadow, Slide, Spiral, Stretch, Strips, Wave, Wheel, Xray, Zigzag

i. JavaScript Properties (11)

accessKey, canHaveChildren, canHaveHTML, className, clientHeight, clientLeft, clientTop, clientWidth, contentEditable, cursor, dir, disabled, end, firstChild, hasLayout, hideFocus, id, innerHTML, innerText, isContentEditable, isDisabled, isMultiLine, isTextEdit, lang, language, lastChild, nextSibling, nodeName, nodeType, nodeValue, offsetHeight, offsetLeft, offsetParent, offsetTop, offsetWidth, outerHTML, outerText, ownerDocument, parentElement, parentNode, parentTextEdit, previousSibling, readyState, scopeName, scrollHeight, scrollLeft, scrollTop, scrollWidth, sourceIndex, tabIndex, tagName, tagUrn, title, uniqueID

i. JavaScript Methods (12)

addBehavior, appendChild, applyElement, attachEvent, blur, clearAttributes, click, cloneNode, componentFromPoint, contains, detachEvent, fireEvent, focus, getAdjacentText, getAttribute, getAttributeNode, getBoundingClientRect, getClientRects, getElementsByTagName, getExpression, hasChildNodes, insertAdjacentElement, insertAdjacentHTML, insertAdjacentText, insertBefore, mergeAttributes, normalize, releaseCapture, removeAttribute, removeAttributeNode, removeBehavior, removeChild, removeExpression, removeNode, replaceAdjacentText, replaceChild, replaceNode, scrollIntoView, setActive, setAttribute, setAttributeNode, setCapture, setExpression, swapNode

i. JavaScript Collections (13)

all, attributes, behaviorUrns, childNodes, children

i. JavaScript Objects (14)

currentStyle, runtimeStyle, style

<iframe> ... </iframe>

Compatibility: NN6, NN7, IE4, IE5, IE5.5, IE6

This element was created by Microsoft as a frame that can be placed anywhere inside a document. Unlike the <frame> element, it is inserted into a normal HTML page that has a <body> tag.

Syntax:

```
<iframe attributes events> . . . </iframe>
```

Example:

```
<html><head><title>iframe element example</title></head>
<body bgcolor="#FFFFFF" text="#000000">
<p align="center"><iframe id="myIframe" frameborder="1" scrolling="yes"
src="yourframe.html" width="600" height="400"></iframe></p>
</body></html>
```

<iframe> HTML Attributes (6)

align, allowtransparency, application, begin, border, class, datafld, datasrc, end, frameborder, height, hidefocus, hspace, id, lang, language, marginheight, marginwidth, name, scrolling, security, src, style, syncmaster, systemBitrate, systemCaptions, systemLanguage, systemOverdubOrSubtitle, tabindex, timecontainer, title, unselectable, vspace, width

<iframe> Event Handlers (7)

onActivate, onAfterUpdate, onBeforeDeactivate, onBeforeUpdate, onBlur, onControlSelect, onDeactivate, onErrorUpdate, onFocus, onLoad, onMove, onMoveEnd, onMoveStart, onReadyStateChange, onResizeEnd, onResizeStart, onTimeError

<iframe> CSS Attributes and JavaScript Style Properties (8)

The names are in CSS syntax. See the introduction to this chapter for the JavaScript syntax rules. Names noted with an asterisk (*) are JavaScript properties only.

accelerator, background-attachment, background-color, background-position-x, background-position-y, behavior, border-bottom, border-bottom-color, border-bottom-style, border-bottom-width, border-color, border-left, border-left-color, border-left-style, border-left-width, border-right, border-right-color, border-right-style, border-right-width, border-style, border-top, border-top-color, border-top-style, border-top-width, border-width, bottom, clear, clip, cursor, display, filter, float, height, layout-grid, layout-grid-mode, left, margin, margin-bottom, margin-left, margin-right, margin-top, overflow-x, overflow-y, pixelBottom(*), pixelHeight(*), pixelLeft(*), pixelRight(*), pixelTop(*), pixelWidth(*), posBottom(*), posHeight(*), position, posLeft(*), posRight(*), posTop(*), posWidth(*), right, styleFloat(*), text-autospace, top, visibility, z-index, zoom

\<iframe\> Microsoft Behaviors (9)

clientCaps, download, homePage, time, time2

\<iframe\> Microsoft Filters (10)

Alpha, Barn, BasicImage, BlendTrans, Blinds, Blur, CheckerBoard, Chroma, Compositor, DropShadow, Emboss, Engrave, Fade, FlipH, FlipV, Glow, GradientWipe, Gray, ICMFilter, Inset, Invert, Iris, Light, MaskFilter, Matrix, MotionBlur, Pixelate, RadialWipe, RandomBars, RandomDissolve, RevealTrans, Shadow, Slide, Spiral, Stretch, Strips, Wave, Wheel, Xray, Zigzag

iframe. JavaScript Properties (11)

align, allowTransparency, border, canHaveChildren, canHaveHTML, className, clientHeight, clientWidth, contentWindow, cursor, dataFld, datasrc, dir, disabled, end, firstChild, frameBorder, height, hideFocus, hspace, id, innerHTML, innerText, isContentEditable, isDisabled, isMultiLine, isTextEdit, lang, language, lastChild, longDesc, name, nextSibling, nodeName, nodeType, nodeValue, offsetHeight, offsetLeft, offsetParent, offsetTop, offsetWidth, outerHTML, outerText, ownerDocument, parentElement, parentNode, parentTextEdit, previousSibling, readyState, recordNumber, scopeName, scrollHeight, scrollLeft, scrollTop, scrollWidth, sourceIndex, src, tabIndex, tagName, tagUrn, title, uniqueID, vspace, width

iframe. JavaScript Methods (12)

addBehavior, appendChild, applyElement, attachEvent, blur, clearAttributes, cloneNode, componentFromPoint, contains, detachEvent, dragDrop, fireEvent, focus, getAdjacentText, getAttribute, getAttributeNode, getElementsByTagName, getExpression, hasChildNodes, insertAdjacentElement, insertAdjacentHTML, insertAdjacentText, insertBefore, mergeAttributes, normalize, removeAttribute, removeAttributeNode, removeBehavior, removeChild, removeExpression, removeNode, replaceAdjacentText, replaceChild, replaceNode, scrollIntoView, setActive, setAttribute, setAttributeNode, setExpression, swapNode

iframe. JavaScript Collections (13)

all, attributes, behaviorUrns, childNodes, children

iframe. JavaScript Objects (14)

runtimeStyle, style

\<img\>

Compatibility: NN4, NN6, NN7, IE4, IE5, IE5.5, IE6

This element controls how a picture or a video clip is displayed on a web page.

Syntax:

```
<img attributes events>
```

Example:

```
<html><head><title>img element example</title></head>
<body bgcolor="#FFFFFF" text="#000000">
<img src="Yosemite.jpg" alt="The Capitan Rock in Yosemite" width="300"
height="225">
</body></html>
```

<img> HTML Attributes (6)

accesskey, align, alt, begin, border, class, datafld, datasrc, dir, dynsrc, end, galleryimg, height, hidefocus, hspace, id, ismap, lang, language, loop, lowsrc, name, src, start, style, syncmaster, systemBitrate, systemCaptions, systemLanguage, systemOverdubOrSubtitle, tabindex, timecontainer, title, unselectable, usemap, vspace, width

<img> Event Handlers (7)

onAbort, onActivate, onAfterUpdate, onBeforeActivate, onBeforeCopy, onBeforeCut, onBeforeDeactivate, onBeforePaste, onBeforeUpdate, onBlur, onClick, onContextMenu, onControlSelect, onCopy, onCut, onDblClick, onDeactivate, onDrag, onDragEnd, onDragEnter, onDragLeave, onDragOver, onDragStart, onDrop, onError, onErrorUpdate, onFilterChange, onFocus, onFocusIn, onFocusOut, onHelp, onLoad, onLoseCapture, onMouseDown, onMouseEnter, onMouseLeave, onMouseMove, onMouseOut, onMouseOver, onMouseUp, onMouseWheel, onMove, onMoveEnd, onMoveStart, onPaste, onPropertyChange, onReadyStateChange, onResize, onResizeEnd, onResizeStart, onSelectStart, onTimeError

<img> CSS Attributes and JavaScript Style Properties (8)

The names are in CSS syntax. See the introduction to this chapter for the JavaScript syntax rules. Names noted with an asterisk (*) are JavaScript properties only.

!important, background, background-attachment, background-color, background-image, background-position, background-position-x, background-position-y, background-repeat, behavior, border, border-bottom, border-bottom-color, border-bottom-style, border-bottom-width, border-color, border-left, border-left-color, border-left-style, border-left-width, border-right, border-right-color, border-right-style, border-right-width, border-style, border-top, border-top-color, border-top-style, border-top-width, border-width, bottom, clear, clip, cursor, direction, display, filter, float, font, font-family, font-style, font-variant, font-weight, hasLayout(*), height, layout-grid, layout-grid-mode, left, letter-spacing, line-height, margin, margin-bottom, margin-left, margin-right, margin-top, padding, padding-bottom, padding-left, padding-right, padding-top, pixelBottom(*), pixelHeight(*), pixelLeft(*), pixelRight(*), pixelTop(*), pixelWidth(*), posBottom(*), posHeight(*), position, posLeft(*), posRight(*), posTop(*), posWidth(*), right, styleFloat(*), text-autospace, text-underline-position, top, unicode-bidi, vertical-align, visibility, word-spacing, word-wrap, zoom

\<img\> Microsoft Behaviors (9)

clientCaps, download, homePage, httpFolder, saveFavorite, saveHistory, saveSnapshot, time, time2, userData

\<img\> Microsoft Filters (10)

Alpha, Barn, BasicImage, BlendTrans, Blinds, Blur, CheckerBoard, Chroma, Compositor, DropShadow, Emboss, Engrave, Fade, FlipH, FlipV, Glow, GradientWipe, Gray, ICMFilter, Inset, Invert, Iris, Light, MaskFilter, Matrix, MotionBlur, Pixelate, RadialWipe, RandomBars, RandomDissolve, RevealTrans, Shadow, Slide, Spiral, Stretch, Strips, Wave, Wheel, Xray, Zigzag

img. JavaScript Properties (11)

accessKey, align, alt, border, canHaveHTML, className, clientHeight, clientLeft, clientTop, clientWidth, complete, cursor, dataFld, datasrc, dir, disabled, dynsrc, end, fileCreatedDate, fileModifiedDate, fileSize, fileUpdatedDate, firstChild, galleryImg, hasLayout, height, hideFocus, hspace, id, innerHTML, isContentEditable, isDisabled, isMap, isMultiLine, isTextEdit, lang, language, lastChild, longDesc, loop, lowsrc, name, nameProp, nextSibling, nodeName, nodeType, nodeValue, offsetHeight, offsetLeft, offsetParent, offsetTop, offsetWidth, outerHTML, outerText, ownerDocument, parentElement, parentNode, parentTextEdit, previousSibling, protocol, readyState, recordNumber, scopeName, scrollHeight, scrollLeft, scrollTop, scrollWidth, sourceIndex, src, start, tabIndex, tagName, tagUrn, title, uniqueID, useMap, vspace, width

img. JavaScript Methods (12)

addBehavior, appendChild, applyElement, attachEvent, blur, clearAttributes, click, cloneNode, componentFromPoint, contains, detachEvent, dragDrop, fireEvent, focus, getAdjacentText, getAttribute, getAttributeNode, getBoundingClientRect, getClientRects, getElementsByTagName, getExpression, hasChildNodes, insertAdjacentElement, insertAdjacentHTML, insertAdjacentText, insertBefore, mergeAttributes, normalize, releaseCapture, removeAttribute, removeAttributeNode, removeBehavior, removeChild, removeExpression, replaceAdjacentText, replaceChild, scrollIntoView, setActive, setAttribute, setAttributeNode, setCapture, setExpression, swapNode

img. JavaScript Collections (13)

all, attributes, behaviorUrns, childNodes, children, filters

img. JavaScript Objects (14)

currentStyle, runtimeStyle, style

<input>

Compatibility: NN4, NN6, NN7, IE4, IE5, IE5.5, IE6

This element allows a web page to receive information input by the user and to send the information to a server for processing. All <input> elements must be placed within the <form> element's opening and closing tags.

The <input> element's type attribute is its most important attribute because its value determines which of the many input controls will be displayed on the page. These are the possible type attribute values:

Button	Creates a button on the page.
Checkbox	Creates a checkbox.
File	Creates a text box with a file browse button. The text box allows a user to select a file to upload to the server for processing.
Hidden	Stores information that is not visible on the web page. However, this information can be viewed in the source HTML code.
Image	Creates an image that will submit the contents of its form to the server when it is clicked.
Password	Creates a text box that displays an asterisk (or other placeholder character) in place of each character that a user enters.
Radio	Creates a radio button on the page. The radio button is useful for presenting users with a handful of choices. You must create a new radio button for each choice presented to the user. Each radio button must have the same value for its name attribute.
Reset	Creates a button on the page. This button will reset the original values of the form.
Submit	Creates a button on the page. This button will submit the contents of the form to the server for processing.
Text	Creates a text box.

Syntax:

```
<input attributes events>
```

Example:

```
<html><head><title>input element example</title></head>
<body bgcolor="#FFFFFF" text="#000000">
<form name="form2" method="post" action="">
<p>This is a form with several input elements.</p>
<input type="text" name="textfield2" value="This is a text field" size="30"><br>
<input type="checkbox" name="checkbox2" value="checkbox">
A checkbox.<br>
<input type="radio" name="radiobutton" value="radiobutton1">
<input type="radio" name="radiobutton" value="radiobutton2">
A set of radio buttons.<br>
```

```
<input type="button" name="myButton2" value="Submit">
A submit button.<br>
<input type="button" name="myButton2" value="Reset">
A reset button.<br><br>
<input type="image" border="0" name="imageField" src="Yosemite.jpg" width="300"
height="225" alt="An input image">
</form></body></html>
```

<input> HTML Attributes (6)

The following table lists which attributes are available for the different input types.

Attribute	Input alone	Button	Check box	File	Hidden	Image	Password	Radio	Reset	Submit	Text
accept	x										
accesskey		x	x	x		x	x	x	x	x	x
align	x					x					
alt	x					x					
atomicselection		x	x	x	x	x	x	x	x	x	x
autocomplete							x				x
begin		x	x	x	x	x	x	x	x	x	x
checked			x					x			
class		x	x	x	x	x	x	x	x	x	x
contenteditable		x					x	x	x	x	x
datafld		x	x		x	x	x	x			x
dataformatas		x									
datasrc		x	x		x	x	x	x			x
dir		x	x	x		x	x	x	x	x	x
disabled		x	x	x		x	x	x	x	x	x
dynsrc	x					x					
end		x	x	x	x	x	x	x	x	x	x
hidefocus		x	x	x	x	x	x	x	x	x	x
hspace	x					x					
id		x	x	x	x	x	x	x	x	x	x
ismap						x					
lang		x	x	x	x	x	x	x	x	x	x
language		x	x	x	x	x	x	x	x	x	x
loop	x			x		x					
lowsrc	x					x					
maxlength							x				x
name		x	x	x	x	x	x	x	x	x	x
readonly							x				x
size		x	x	x		x	x	x	x	x	x
src						x					

Attribute	Input alone	Button	Check box	File	Hidden	Image	Password	Radio	Reset	Submit	Text
start	X					X					
style		X	X	X	X	X	X	X	X	X	X
syncMaster		X	X	X	X	X	X	X	X	X	X
systemBitrate		X	X	X	X	X	X	X	X	X	X
systemCaptions		X	X	X	X	X	X	X	X	X	X
systemLanguage		X	X	X	X	X	X	X	X	X	X
systemOverdubOrsubtitle		X	X	X	X	X	X	X	X	X	X
tabindex		X	X	X		X	X	X	X	X	X
timecontainer		X	X	X	X	X	X	X	X	X	X
title		X	X	X		X	X	X	X	X	X
type	X										
unselectable		X	X	X	X	X	X	X	X	X	X
usemap	X										
value	X	X	X		X						X
vcard_name							X				X
vspace	X					X					
width		X	X	X		X	X	X	X	X	X

<input> Event Handlers (7)

The following table lists which events are available for the different input types.

Event handler	Button	Checkbox	File	Hidden	Image	Password	Radio	Reset	Submit	Text
onActivate	X	X	X	X	X	X	X	X	X	X
onAfterUpdate		X		X		X	X			X
onBeforeActivate	X	X	X		X	X	X	X	X	X
onBeforeCut	X	X	X		X	X	X	X	X	X
onBeforeDeactivate	X	X	X	X	X	X	X	X	X	X
onBeforeEditFocus	X	X	X	X	X	X	X	X	X	X
onBeforePaste	X	X	X		X	X	X	X	X	X
onBeforeUpdate		X		X		X	X			X
onBlur	X	X	X		X	X	X	X	X	X
onChange										X
onClick	X	X	X		X	X	X	X	X	X
onContextMenu	X	X	X		X	X	X	X	X	X
onControlSelect	X	X	X	X	X	X	X	X	X	X
onCut	X	X	X		X	X	X	X	X	X
onDblClick	X	X	X		X	X	X	X	X	X
onDeactivate	X	X	X	X	X	X	X	X	X	X
onDrag	X	X	X		X	X	X	X	X	X
onDragEnd	X	X	X		X	X	X	X	X	X

Event handler	Button	Checkbox	File	Hidden	Image	Password	Radio	Reset	Submit	Text
onDragEnter	X	X	X		X	X	X	X	X	X
onDragLeave	X	X	X		X	X	X	X	X	X
onDragOver	X	X	X		X	X	X	X	X	X
onDragStart	X	X	X		X	X	X	X	X	X
onDrop	X	X	X		X	X	X	X	X	X
onErrorUpdate		X		X		X	X			X
onFilterChange	X	X	X		X	X	X	X	X	X
onFocus	X	X	X	X	X	X	X	X	X	X
onFocusIn	X	X	X		X	X	X	X	X	X
onFocusOut	X	X	X		X	X	X	X	X	X
onHelp	X	X	X		X	X	X	X	X	X
onKeyDown	X	X	X		X	X	X	X	X	X
onKeyPress	X	X	X		X	X	X	X	X	X
onKeyUp	X	X	X		X	X	X	X	X	X
onLoseCapture	X	X	X	X	X	X	X	X	X	X
onMouseDown	X	X	X		X	X	X	X	X	X
onMouseEnter	X	X	X		X	X	X	X	X	X
onMouseLeave	X	X	X		X	X	X	X	X	X
onMouseMove	X	X	X		X	X	X	X	X	X
onMouseOut	X	X	X		X	X	X	X	X	X
onMouseOver	X	X	X		X	X	X	X	X	X
onMouseDown	X	X	X		X	X	X	X	X	X
onMouseEnter	X	X	X		X	X	X	X	X	X
onMouseLeave	X	X	X		X	X	X	X	X	X
onMouseMove	X	X	X		X	X	X	X	X	X
onMouseOut	X	X	X		X	X	X	X	X	X
onMouseOver	X	X	X		X	X	X	X	X	X
onMouseUp	X	X	X		X	X	X	X	X	X
onMouseWheel	X	X	X		X	X	X	X	X	X
onMove	X	X	X	X	X	X	X	X	X	X
onMoveEnd	X	X	X	X	X	X	X	X	X	X
onMoveStart	X	X	X	X	X	X	X	X	X	X
onPaste	X	X	X		X	X	X	X	X	X
onPropertyChange	X	X	X	X	X	X	X	X	X	X
onReadyStateChange	X	X	X	X	X	X	X	X	X	X
onResize	X		X		X	X		X	X	X
onResizeEnd	X	X	X	X	X	X	X	X	X	X
onResizeStart	X	X	X	X	X	X	X	X	X	X
onSelect										X
onSelectStart	X	X	X		X	X	X	X	X	X
onTimeError	X	X	X	X	X	X	X	X	X	X

<input> CSS Attributes and JavaScript Style Properties (8)

The following table lists which CSS attributes or JavaScript style properties are available for the different input types. The names are in CSS syntax. See the introduction to this chapter for the JavaScript syntax rules. Names noted with an asterisk (*) are JavaScript properties only.

Styles	Input alone	Button	Check box	File	Hidden	Image	Password	Radio	Reset	Submit	Text
!important		x	x	x	x	x	x	x	x	x	x
background		x	x	x		x	x	x	x	x	x
background-attachment		x	x	x		x	x	x	x	x	x
background-color		x	x	x		x	x	x	x	x	x
background-image		x	x	x		x	x	x	x	x	x
background-position		x	x	x		x	x	x	x	x	x
background-position-x		x	x	x		x	x	x	x	x	x
background-position-y		x	x	x		x	x	x	x	x	x
background-repeat		x	x	x		x	x	x	x	x	x
behavior		x	x	x	x	x	x	x	x	x	x
border		x	x	x		x	x	x	x	x	x
border-bottom		x	x	x		x	x	x	x	x	x
border-bottom-color		x	x	x		x	x	x	x	x	x
border-bottom-style		x	x	x		x	x	x	x	x	x
border-bottom-width		x	x	x		x	x	x	x	x	x
border-color		x	x	x		x	x	x	x	x	x
border-left		x	x	x		x	x	x	x	x	x
border-left-color		x	x	x		x	x	x	x	x	x
border-left-style		x	x	x		x	x	x	x	x	x
border-left-width		x	x	x		x	x	x	x	x	x
border-right		x	x	x		x	x	x	x	x	x
border-right-color		x	x	x		x	x	x	x	x	x
border-right-style		x	x	x		x	x	x	x	x	x
border-right-width		x	x	x		x	x	x	x	x	x
border-style		x	x	x		x	x	x	x	x	x
border-top		x	x	x		x	x	x	x	x	x
border-top-color		x	x	x		x	x	x	x	x	x
border-top-style		x	x	x		x	x	x	x	x	x
border-top-width		x	x	x		x	x	x	x	x	x
border-width		x	x	x		x	x	x	x	x	x
bottom		x	x	x		x	x	x	x	x	x
clear		x	x	x		x	x	x	x	x	x
clip		x	x	x		x	x	x	x	x	x
color		x	x	x		x	x	x	x	x	x

Styles	Input alone	Button	Check box	File	Hidden	Image	Password	Radio	Reset	Submit	Text
cursor		X	X	X		X	X	X	X	X	X
direction		X	X	X		X	X	X	X	X	X
display		X	X	X		X	X	X	X	X	X
filter		X	X	X		X	X	X	X	X	X
float		X	X	X		X	X	X	X	X	X
font		X	X	X		X	X	X	X	X	X
font-family		X	X	X		X	X	X	X	X	X
font-size		X		X		X	X				X
font-style		X	X	X		X	X	X	X	X	X
font-variant		X	X	X		X	X	X	X	X	X
font-weight		X	X	X		X	X	X	X	X	X
hasLayout(*)					X	X	X	X	X	X	X
height		X	X	X		X	X	X	X	X	X
ime-mode											X
layout-flow	X	X	X	X	X	X	X	X	X	X	X
layout-grid		X	X	X		X	X	X	X	X	X
layout-grid-mode		X	X	X		X	X	X	X	X	X
left		X	X	X		X	X	X	X	X	X
letter-spacing		X	X	X		X	X	X	X	X	X
line-height		X	X	X		X	X	X	X	X	X
margin		X	X	X		X	X	X	X	X	X
margin-bottom		X	X	X		X	X	X	X	X	X
margin-left		X	X	X		X	X	X	X	X	X
margin-right		X	X	X		X	X	X	X	X	X
margin-top		X	X	X		X	X	X	X	X	X
overflow		X	X	X		X	X	X	X	X	X
overflow-x		X	X	X		X	X	X	X	X	X
overflow-y		X	X	X		X	X	X	X	X	X
padding		X	X	X		X	X	X	X	X	X
padding-bottom		X	X	X		X	X	X	X	X	X
padding-left		X	X	X		X	X	X	X	X	X
padding-right		X	X	X		X	X	X	X	X	X
padding-top		X	X	X		X	X	X	X	X	X
pixelBottom(*)		X	X	X		X	X	X	X	X	X
pixelHeight(*)		X	X	X		X	X	X	X	X	X
pixelLeft(*)		X	X	X		X	X	X	X	X	X
pixelRight(*)		X	X	X		X	X	X	X	X	X
pixelTop(*)		X	X	X		X	X	X	X	X	X
pixelWidth(*)		X	X	X		X	X	X	X	X	X
posBottom(*)		X	X	X		X	X	X	X	X	X
posHeight(*)		X	X	X		X	X	X	X	X	X

Styles	Input alone	Button	Check box	File	Hidden	Image	Password	Radio	Reset	Submit	Text
position		X	X	X		X	X	X	X	X	X
posLeft(*)		X	X	X		X	X	X	X	X	X
posRight(*)		X	X	X		X	X	X	X	X	X
posTop(*)		X	X	X		X	X	X	X	X	X
posWidth(*)		X	X	X		X	X	X	X	X	X
right		X	X	X		X	X	X	X	X	X
styleFloat(*)		X	X	X		X	X	X	X	X	X
text-align							X				X
text-autospace		X	X	X	X	X	X	X	X	X	X
text-decoration		X		X			X	X	X	X	X
textDecorationBlink(*)		X	X	X		X	X	X	X	X	X
textDecorationLine Through(*)		X	X	X		X	X	X	X	X	X
textDecorationNone(*)		X	X	X		X	X	X	X	X	X
textDecorationOver line(*)		X	X	X		X	X	X	X	X	X
textDecorationUnder line(*)		X	X	X		X	X	X	X	X	X
text-overflow		X	X	X		X	X	X	X	X	X
text-transform		X	X	X		X	X	X	X	X	X
text-underline-position	X	X	X	X	X	X	X	X	X	X	X
top		X	X	X		X	X	X	X	X	X
unicode-bidi		X	X	X		X	X	X	X	X	X
visibility		X	X	X		X	X	X	X	X	X
word-spacing		X	X	X		X	X	X	X	X	X
word-wrap	X	X	X	X	X	X	X	X	X	X	X
writing-mode	X	X		X			X		X	X	X
z-index		X	X	X		X	X	X	X	X	X
zoom	X	X	X	X	X	X	X	X	X	X	X

\<input\> Microsoft Behaviors (9)

The following table lists which behaviors are available for the different input types.

Behaviors	Input alone	Button	Check box	File	Hidden	Image	Password	Radio	Reset	Submit	Text
clientCaps		X	X	X	X	X	X	X	X	X	X
colorPick											X
download		X	X	X	X	X	X	X	X	X	X
homePage		X	X	X	X	X	X	X	X	X	X
httpFolder		X	X	X	X	X	X	X	X	X	X
mask	X										
saveFavorite		X	X	X	X	X	X	X	X	X	X

Behaviors	Input alone	Button	Check box	File	Hidden	Image	Password	Radio	Reset	Submit	Text
saveHistory		X	X	X	X	X	X	X	X	X	X
saveSnapshot		X	X	X	X	X		X	X	X	X
time1		X	X	X	X	X	X	X	X	X	X
time2		X	X	X	X	X	X	X	X	X	X
userData		X	X	X	X	X	X	X	X	X	X

<input> Microsoft Filters (10)

All are supported by the following input controls: button, checkbox, file, image, password, radio, reset, submit, and text. Filters are *not* supported for the hidden input type or for input elements without a type attribute value.

input. JavaScript Properties (11)

The following table lists which JavaScript properties are available for the different input types.

Property	Input alone	Button	Check box	File	Hidden	Image	Password	Radio	Reset	Submit	Text
accept	X										
accessKey		X	X	X		X	X	X	X	X	X
align	X					X					
alt	X					X					
autocomplete							X				X
begin		X	X	X	X	X	X	X	X	X	X
canHaveChildren		X	X	X		X	X	X	X	X	X
canHaveHTML		X	X	X	X	X	X	X	X	X	X
checked			X					X			
className		X	X	X	X	X	X	X	X	X	X
clientHeight		X	X	X		X	X	X	X	X	X
clientLeft		X	X	X		X	X	X	X	X	X
clientTop		X	X	X		X	X	X	X	X	X
clientWidth		X	X	X		X	X	X	X	X	X
complete	X					X					
contentEditable		X				X	X	X	X	X	X
cursor		X	X	X	X	X	X	X	X	X	X
dataFld		X	X		X	X	X	X			X
dataFormatAs		X									
dataSrc		X	X		X	X	X	X			X
defaultChecked			X					X			
defaultValue		X	X	X	X	X	X	X	X	X	X
dir		X	X	X		X	X	X	X	X	X
disabled		X	X	X		X	X	X	X	X	X
dynsrc	X					X					

Property	Input alone	Button	Check box	File	Hidden	Image	Password	Radio	Reset	Submit	Text
end		X	X	X	X	X	X	X	X	X	X
firstChild		X	X	X		X	X	X	X	X	X
form		X	X	X	X	X	X	X	X	X	X
hasMedia		X	X	X	X	X	X	X	X	X	X
hasLayout					X	X	X	X	X	X	X
hideFocus		X	X	X	X	X	X	X	X	X	X
hspace	X					X					
id		X	X	X	X	X	X	X	X	X	X
indeterminate			X								
isContentEditable		X	X	X	X	X	X	X	X	X	X
isDisabled		X	X	X	X	X	X	X	X	X	X
isMultiLine		X	X	X	X	X	X	X	X	X	X
isTextEdit		X	X	X	X	X	X	X	X	X	X
lang		X	X	X	X	X	X	X	X	X	X
language		X	X	X	X	X	X	X	X	X	X
lastChild		X	X	X		X	X	X	X	X	X
loop	X					X					
lowsrc	X					X					
maxLength							X				X
name		X	X	X	X	X	X	X	X	X	X
nextSibling		X	X	X	X	X	X	X	X	X	X
nodeName		X	X	X	X	X	X	X	X	X	X
nodeType		X	X	X	X	X	X	X	X	X	X
nodeValue		X	X	X	X	X	X	X	X	X	X
offsetHeight		X	X	X		X	X	X	X	X	X
offsetLeft		X	X	X		X	X	X	X	X	X
offsetParent		X	X	X	X	X	X	X	X	X	X
offsetTop		X	X	X		X	X	X	X	X	X
offsetWidth		X	X	X		X	X	X	X	X	X
onOffBehavior		X	X	X		X	X	X	X	X	X
outerHTML		X	X	X	X	X	X	X	X	X	X
outerText		X	X	X	X	X	X	X	X	X	X
ownerDocument		X	X	X		X	X	X	X	X	X
parentElement		X	X	X	X	X	X	X	X	X	X
parentNode		X	X	X	X	X	X	X	X	X	X
parentTextEdit		X	X	X	X	X	X	X	X	X	X
previousSibling	X	X	X	X	X	X	X	X	X	X	X
readOnly							X				X
readyState		X	X	X	X	X	X	X	X	X	X
recordNumber			X		X		X	X			X
scopeName		X	X	X	X	X	X	X	X	X	X

Property	Input alone	Button	Check box	File	Hidden	Image	Password	Radio	Reset	Submit	Text
scrollHeight	X	X	X	X		X	X	X	X	X	X
scrollLeft	X	X	X	X		X	X	X	X	X	X
scrollTop	X	X	X	X		X	X	X	X	X	X
scrollWidth	X	X	X	X		X	X	X	X	X	X
size		X	X	X		X	X	X	X	X	X
sourceIndex		X	X	X	X	X	X	X	X	X	X
src						X					
status			X					X			
start	X					X					
syncMaster		X	X	X	X	X	X	X	X	X	X
tabIndex		X	X	X		X	X	X	X	X	X
tagName	X	X	X	X	X	X	X	X	X	X	X
tagUrn		X	X	X	X	X	X	X	X	X	X
timeContainer		X	X	X	X	X	X	X	X	X	X
title	X	X	X	X		X	X	X	X	X	X
uniqueID		X	X	X	X	X	X	X	X	X	X
usemap	X										
value	X	X	X	X	X		X	X	X	X	X
vcard_name							X				X
vspace	X					X					
width		X	X	X		X	X	X	X	X	X

input. JavaScript Methods (12)

The following table lists which JavaScript methods are available for the different input types.

Method	Button	Check box	File	Hidden	Image	Password	Radio	Reset	Submit	Text
addBehavior	X	X	X	X	X	X	X	X	X	X
appendChild	X	X	X		X	X	X	X	X	X
applyElement	X	X	X	X	X	X	X	X	X	X
attachEvent	X	X	X	X	X	X	X	X	X	X
blur	X	X	X		X	X	X	X	X	X
clearAttributes	X	X	X	X	X	X	X	X	X	X
click	X	X	X		X	X	X	X	X	X
cloneNode	X	X	X	X	X	X	X	X	X	X
componentFromPoint	X	X	X	X	X	X	X	X	X	X
contains	X	X	X		X	X	X	X	X	X
createTextRange	X			X		X		X	X	X
detachEvent	X	X	X	X	X	X	X	X	X	X
dragDrop	X	X	X		X	X	X	X	X	X

Method	Button	Check box	File	Hidden	Image	Password	Radio	Reset	Submit	Text
fireEvent	x	x	x	x	x	x	x	x	x	x
focus	x	x	x		x	x	x	x	x	x
getAdjacentText	x	x	x	x	x	x	x	x	x	x
getAttribute	x	x	x	x	x	x	x	x	x	x
getAttributeNode	x	x	x	x	x	x	x	x	x	x
getBoundingClientRect	x	x	x		x	x	x	x	x	x
getClientRects	x	x	x		x	x	x	x	x	x
getExpression	x	x	x	x	x	x	x	x	x	x
hasChildNodes	x	x	x		x	x	x	x	x	x
insertAdjacentElement	x	x	x	x	x	x	x	x	x	x
insertAdjacentHTML	x	x	x	x	x	x	x	x	x	x
insertAdjacentText	x	x	x	x	x	x	x	x	x	x
insertBefore	x	x	x		x	x	x	x	x	x
mergeAttributes	x	x	x	x	x	x	x	x	x	x
normalize	x	x	x	x	x	x	x	x	x	x
releaseCapture	x	x	x	x	x	x	x	x	x	x
removeAttribute	x	x	x	x	x	x	x	x	x	x
removeAttributeNode	x	x	x	x	x	x	x	x	x	x
removeBehavior	x	x	x	x	x	x	x	x	x	x
removeChild	x	x	x	x	x	x	x	x	x	x
removeExpression	x	x	x	x	x	x	x	x	x	x
removeNode	x	x	x		x	x	x	x	x	x
replaceAdjacentText	x	x	x	x	x	x	x	x	x	x
replaceChild	x	x	x	x	x	x	x	x	x	x
replaceNode	x	x	x		x	x	x	x	x	x
scrollIntoView	x	x	x		x	x	x	x	x	x
select	x	x	x		x	x	x	x	x	x
setActive	x	x	x	x	x	x	x	x	x	x
setAttribute	x	x	x	x	x	x	x	x	x	x
setAttributeNode	x	x	x	x	x	x	x	x	x	x
setCapture	x	x	x	x	x	x	x	x	x	x
setExpression	x	x	x	x	x	x	x	x	x	x
swapNode	x	x	x	x	x	x	x	x	x	x

input. JavaScript Collections (13)

The following table lists which JavaScript collections are available for the different input types.

Collection	Button	Check box	File	Hidden	Image	Password	Radio	Reset	Submit	Text
attributes	x	x	x	x	x	x	x	x	x	x
behaviorUrns	x	x	x	x	x	x	x	x	x	x
filters	x	x	x		x	x	x	x	x	x

input. JavaScript Objects (14)

The following table lists which JavaScript objects are available for the different input types.

Object	Button	Check box	File	Hidden	Image	Password	Radio	Reset	Submit	Text
currentStyle	x	x	x		x	x	x	x	x	x
runtimeStyle	x	x	x	x	x	x	x	x	x	x
style	x	x	x	x	x	x	x	x	x	x

<ins> ... </ins>

Compatibility: NN6, NN7, IE4, IE5, IE5.5, IE6

This element is used to mark the text between its opening and closing tags as having been inserted into the document. In doing so, the text is rendered with an underline. This tag is similar to <u> in the way it renders text, but future browser enhancements may differentiate this element from the <u> element.

Syntax:

```
<ins attributes events> . . . </ins>
```

Example:

```
<html><head><title>ins element example</title></head>
<body bgcolor="#FFFFFF" text="#000000">
<p><ins>This text has been inserted in the document.</ins></p>
</body></html>
```

<ins> HTML Attributes (6)

```
accesskey, begin, cite, class, contenteditable, datetime, dir, disabled, end,
hidefocus, id, lang, language, style, syncmaster, systemBitrate, systemCaptions,
systemLanguage, systemOverdubOrSubtitle, tabindex, timecontainer, title,
unselectable
```

\<ins\> Event Handlers (7)

onActivate, onBeforeDeactivate, onBeforeEditFocus, onBlur, onClick, onControlSelect, onDblClick, onDeactivate, onFocus, onHelp, onKeyDown, onKeyPress, onKeyUp, onMouseDown, onMouseMove, onMouseOut, onMouseOver, onMouseUp, onMove, onMoveEnd, onMoveStart, onReadyStateChange, onResize, onResizeEnd, onResizeStart, onTimeError

\<ins\> CSS Attributes and JavaScript Style Properties (8)

The names are in CSS syntax. See the introduction to this chapter for the JavaScript syntax rules. Names noted with an asterisk (*) are JavaScript properties only.

accelerator, background-position-x, background-position-y, behavior, border, border-bottom, border-bottom-color, border-bottom-style, border-bottom-width, border-color, border-left, border-left-color, border-left-style, border-left-width, border-right, border-right-color, border-right-style, border-right-width, border-style, border-top, border-top-color, border-top-style, border-top-width, border-width, direction, display, filter, hasLayout(*), height, layout-flow, layout-grid, layout-grid-mode, margin, margin-bottom, margin-left, margin-right, margin-top, overflow, overflow-x, overflow-y, padding, padding-bottom, padding-left, padding-right, padding-top, pixelBottom(*), pixelHeight(*), pixelLeft(*), pixelRight(*), pixelTop(*), pixelWidth(*), posBottom(*), posHeight(*), posLeft(*), posRight(*), posTop(*), posWidth(*), text-autospace, text-overflow, text-underline-position, unicode-bidi, white-space, width, word-wrap, writing-mode, zoom

\<ins\> Microsoft Behaviors (9)

clientCaps, download, homePage, time, time2

\<ins\> Microsoft Filters (10)

Alpha, Barn, BasicImage, BlendTrans, Blinds, Blur, CheckerBoard, Chroma, Compositor, DropShadow, Emboss, Engrave, Fade, FlipH, FlipV, Glow, GradientWipe, Gray, ICMFilter, Inset, Invert, Iris, Light, MaskFilter, Matrix, MotionBlur, Pixelate, RadialWipe, RandomBars, RandomDissolve, RevealTrans, Shadow, Slide, Spiral, Stretch, Strips, Wave, Wheel, Xray, Zigzag

ins. JavaScript Properties (11)

accessKey, canHaveChildren, canHaveHTML, cite, className, clientHeight, clientWidth, contentEditable, dateTime, dir, disabled, end, firstChild, hasLayout, hideFocus, id, innerHTML, innerText, isContentEditable, isDisabled, isMultiLine, isTextEdit, lang, language, lastChild, nextSibling, nodeName, nodeType, nodeValue, offsetHeight, offsetLeft, offsetParent, offsetTop, offsetWidth, outerHTML, outerText, ownerDocument, parentElement, parentNode, parentTextEdit, previousSibling, readyState, scopeName, scrollHeight, scrollLeft, scrollTop, scrollWidth, sourceIndex, tabIndex, tagName, tagUrn, title, uniqueID

ins. JavaScript Methods (12)

addBehavior, appendChild, applyElement, attachEvent, blur, clearAttributes,
cloneNode, componentFromPoint, detachEvent, fireEvent, focus, getAdjacentText,
getAttribute, getAttributeNode, getBoundingClientRect, getClientRects,
getElementsByTagName, getExpression, hasChildNodes, insertAdjacentElement,
insertBefore, mergeAttributes, normalize, removeAttribute, removeAttributeNode,
removeBehavior, removeChild, removeExpression, removeNode, replaceAdjacentText,
replaceChild, replaceNode, setActive, setAttribute, setAttributeNode,
setExpression, swapNode

ins. JavaScript Collections (13)

all, attributes, behaviorUrns, childNodes, children

ins. JavaScript Objects (14)

currentStyle, runtimeStyle, style

<isindex>

Compatibility: NN4, NN6, NN7, IE4, IE5, IE5.5, IE6

This element creates a text input field between two <hr> elements, and using
the prompt attribute prompts the user for information. This element can be
included inside a form and be passed to the server the same way an input
control is passed to the server. This element has been deprecated in favor of
the <input type="text"> element.

Syntax:

<isindex *attributes events*>

Example:

```
<html><head><title>isindex element example</title></head>
<body bgcolor="#FFFFFF" text="#000000">
<isindex prompt="Please enter your name and surname . . . ">
</body></html>
```

<isindex> HTML Attributes (6)

accesskey, action, class, contenteditable, dir, disabled, hidefocus, id, lang,
language, prompt, style, tabindex, title, unselectable

\<isindex\> Event Handlers (7)

onActivate, onBeforeDeactivate, onBeforeEditFocus, onBlur, onControlSelect, onDeactivate, onFocus, onMove, onMoveEnd, onMoveStart, onReadyStateChange, onResize, onResizeEnd, onResizeStart

\<isindex\> CSS Attributes and JavaScript Style Properties (8)

The names are in CSS syntax. See the introduction to this chapter for the JavaScript syntax rules. Names noted with an asterisk (*) are JavaScript properties only.

background, background-attachment, background-color, background-image, background-position, background-repeat, behavior, border, border-bottom, border-bottom-color, border-bottom-style, border-bottom-width, border-color, border-left, border-left-color, border-left-style, border-left-width, border-right, border-right-color, border-right-style, border-right-width, border-style, border-top, border-top-color, border-top-style, border-top-width, bottom, clear, clip, color, float, font, font-family, font-size, font-style, font-variant, font-weight, hasLayout(*), layout-flow, left, letter-spacing, line-height, margin, margin-bottom, margin-left, margin-right, margin-top, page-break-after, page-break-before, position, right, styleFloat(*), text-align-last, text-autospace, text-decoration, text-indent, text-kashida-space, text-overflow, text-transform, text-underline-position, textDecorationBlink(*), textDecorationLineThrough(*), textDecorationNone(*), textDecorationOverline(*), textDecorationUnderline(*), top, visibility, white-space, word-spacing, word-wrap, writing-mode, z-index, zoom

\<isindex\> Microsoft Behaviors (9)

clientCaps, download, homePage

isindex. JavaScript Properties (11)

accessKey, action, blockDirection, canHaveHTML, className, clientHeight, clientLeft, clientTop, clientWidth, contentEditable, dir, disabled, firstChild, form, hasLayout, hideFocus, id, innerHTML, isContentEditable, isDisabled, isMultiLine, lang, language, lastChild, nextSibling, nodeName, nodeType, nodeValue, offsetHeight, offsetLeft, offsetParent, offsetTop, offsetWidth, ownerDocument, parentElement, parentNode, previousSibling, readyState, scopeName, scrollHeight, scrollLeft, scrollTop, scrollWidth, tabIndex, tagName, tagUrn, title

isindex. JavaScript Methods (12)

addBehavior, appendChild, blur, cloneNode, componentFromPoint, dragDrop, fireEvent, focus, getAttribute, getAttributeNode, getBoundingClientRect, getClientRects, getElementsByTagName, hasChildNodes, insertBefore, normalize, removeAttribute, removeAttributeNode, removeBehavior, removeChild, replaceChild, setActive, setAttribute, setAttributeNode

attributes, behaviorUrns, childNodes

isindex. JavaScript Objects (14)

currentStyle

<kbd> ... </kbd>

Compatibility: NN4, NN6, NN7, IE4, IE5, IE5.5, IE6

This element displays text between its opening and closing tags in a fixed-size or monospaced font. This element is similar to the <code> element in that it allows you to alter the font to some other fixed-size or monospaced font, although the <code> element limits you to the system's default fixed-sized font.

Syntax:

```
<kbd attributes events> . . . </kbd>
```

Example:

```
<html><head><title>kbd element example</title></head>
<body bgcolor="#FFFFFF" text="#000000">
<p align="center">You can apply the <font size="5"><kbd style="font-
weight:normal">systemLanguage</kbd></font> attribute to nearly any element.</p>
</body></html>
```

<kbd> HTML Attributes (6)

accesskey, begin, class, contenteditable, dir, disabled, end, hidefocus, id, lang, language, style, syncmaster, systemBitrate, systemCaptions, systemLanguage, systemOverdubOrSubtitle, tabindex, timecontainer, title, unselectable

<kbd> Event Handlers (7)

onActivate, onBeforeActivate, onBeforeCut, onBeforeDeactivate, onBeforeEditFocus, onBeforePaste, onBlur, onClick, onContextMenu, onControlSelect, onCut, onDblClick, onDeactivate, onDrag, onDragEnd, onDragEnter, onDragLeave, onDragOver, onDragStart, onDrop, onFocus, onFocusIn, onFocusOut, onHelp, onKeyDown, onKeyPress, onKeyUp, onLoseCapture, onMouseDown, onMouseEnter, onMouseLeave, onMouseMove, onMouseOut, onMouseOver, onMouseUp, onMouseWheel, onMove, onMoveEnd, onMoveStart, onPaste, onPropertyChange, onReadyStateChange, onResize, onResizeEnd, onResizeStart, onSelectStart, onTimeError

<kbd> CSS Attributes and JavaScript Style Properties (8)

The names are in CSS syntax. See the introduction to this chapter for the JavaScript syntax rules. Names noted with an asterisk (*) are JavaScript properties only.

```
!important, accelerator, background, background-attachment, background-color,
background-image, background-position, background-position-x, background-position-
y, background-repeat, behavior, border, border-bottom, border-bottom-color, border-
bottom-style, border-bottom-width, border-color, border-left, border-left-color,
border-left-style, border-left-width, border-right, border-right-color, border-
right-style, border-right-width, border-style, border-top, border-top-color,
border-top-style, border-top-width, border-width, bottom, clear, clip, color,
cursor, direction, display, filter, float, font, font-family, font-size, font-
style, font-variant, font-weight, hasLayout(*), height, layout-flow, layout-grid,
layout-grid-mode, left, letter-spacing, line-height, margin, margin-bottom, margin-
left, margin-right, margin-top, overflow, overflow-x, overflow-y, padding, padding-
bottom, padding-left, padding-right, padding-top, pixelBottom(*), pixelHeight(*),
pixelLeft(*), pixelRight(*), pixelTop(*), pixelWidth(*), posBottom(*),
posHeight(*), position, posLeft(*), posRight(*), posTop(*), posWidth(*), right,
styleFloat(*), text-autospace, text-decoration, text-overflow, text-transform,
text-underline-position, textDecorationBlink(*), textDecorationLineThrough(*),
textDecorationNone(*), textDecorationOverline(*), textDecorationUnderline(*), top,
unicode-bidi, visibility, white-space, width, word-spacing, word-wrap, writing-
mode, z-index, zoom
```

<kbd> Microsoft Behaviors (9)

```
clientCaps, download, homePage, httpFolder, saveFavorite, saveHistory,
saveSnapshot, time, time2, userData
```

<kbd> Microsoft Filters (10)

```
Alpha, Barn, BasicImage, BlendTrans, Blinds, Blur, CheckerBoard, Chroma,
Compositor, DropShadow, Emboss, Engrave, Fade, FlipH, FlipV, Glow, GradientWipe,
Gray, ICMFilter, Inset, Invert, Iris, Light, MaskFilter, Matrix, MotionBlur,
Pixelate, RadialWipe, RandomBars, RandomDissolve, RevealTrans, Shadow, Slide,
Spiral, Stretch, Strips, Wave, Wheel, Xray, Zigzag
```

kbd. JavaScript Properties (11)

```
accessKey, canHaveChildren, canHaveHTML, className, clientHeight, clientLeft,
clientTop, clientWidth, contentEditable, cursor, dir, disabled, end, firstChild,
hasLayout, hideFocus, id, innerHTML, innerText, isContentEditable, isDisabled,
isMultiLine, isTextEdit, lang, language, lastChild, nextSibling, nodeName,
nodeType, nodeValue, offsetHeight, offsetLeft, offsetParent, offsetTop,
offsetWidth, outerHTML, outerText, ownerDocument, parentElement, parentNode,
parentTextEdit, previousSibling, readyState, scopeName, scrollHeight, scrollLeft,
scrollTop, scrollWidth, sourceIndex, tabIndex, tagName, tagUrn, title, uniqueID
```

kbd. JavaScript Methods (12)

addBehavior, appendChild, applyElement, attachEvent, blur, clearAttributes, click, cloneNode, componentFromPoint, contains, detachEvent, fireEvent, focus, getAdjacentText, getAttribute, getAttributeNode, getBoundingClientRect, getClientRects, getElementsByTagName, getExpression, hasChildNodes, insertAdjacentElement, insertAdjacentHTML, insertAdjacentText, insertBefore, mergeAttributes, normalize, releaseCapture, removeAttribute, removeAttributeNode, removeBehavior, removeChild, removeExpression, removeNode, replaceAdjacentText, replaceChild, replaceNode, scrollIntoView, setActive, setAttribute, setAttributeNode, setCapture, setExpression, swapNode

kbd. JavaScript Collections (13)

all, attributes, behaviorUrns, childNodes, children

kbd. JavaScript Objects (14)

currentStyle, runtimeStyle, style

<keygen> ... </keygen>

Compatibility: NN4

This element generates a key, which is maintained by a web-based certificate management system. Note that, this element has been rendered obsolete because of newer encryption technologies available to Netscape Navigator and Internet Explorer.

Syntax:

```
<keygen attributes events></keygen>
```

Example:

```
<html><head><title>keygen element example</title></head>
<body>
<keygen name="encOrder" challenge="45879214">My text</keygen>
</body></html>
```

<keygen> HTML Specific Attributes

CHALLENGE

Compatibility: NN4

This attribute specifies the challenge string to be packaged with the public key for use in the verification of the form submission.

Syntax:

```
<keygen challenge="value"></keygen>
```

NAME

Compatibility: NN4

This attribute specifies the name portion of the name-value pair. The name is a way to identify the element in the document.

Syntax:

```
<keygen name="value"></keygen>
```

<label> ... </label>

Compatibility: NN6, NN7, IE4, IE5, IE5.5, IE6

This element creates a label and associates it with another element on the page. The element to which the label is linked must contain the id attribute. When giving the accesskey attribute of the <label> element a value, pressing ALT and the access key simultaneously will set the focus on the linked element.

Syntax:

```
<label attributes events> . . . </label>
```

Example:

```
<html><head><title>label element example</title></head>
<body bgcolor="#ffffff">
<p>If you click on the italic text that follows or press
<label for="tb" accesskey="a"><i>Alt+A you will set focus on the text box</i></
label>
<input id="tb" type="text" value="textbox" size="20"></p>
</body></html>
```

<label> HTML Attributes (6)

accesskey, class, contenteditable, datafld, dataformatas, datasrc, dir, disabled, for, hidefocus, id, lang, language, style, tabindex, title, unselectable

<label> Event Handlers (7)

onActivate, onAfterUpdate, onBeforeActivate, onBeforeCopy, onBeforeCut, onBeforeDeactivate, onBeforeEditFocus, onBeforePaste, onBeforeUpdate, onBlur, onClick, onContextMenu, onControlSelect, onCut, onDblClick, onDeactivate, onDrag, onDragEnd, onDragEnter, onDragLeave, onDragOver, onDragStart, onDrop, onErrorUpdate, onFocus, onFocusIn, onFocusOut, onHelp, onKeyDown, onKeyPress, onKeyUp, onLoseCapture, onMouseDown, onMouseEnter, onMouseLeave, onMouseMove, onMouseOut, onMouseOver, onMouseUp, onMouseWheel, onMove, onMoveEnd, onMoveStart, onPaste, onPropertyChange, onReadyStateChange, onResize, onResizeEnd, onResizeStart, onSelectStart

<label> CSS Attributes and JavaScript Style Properties (8)

The names are in CSS syntax. See the introduction to this chapter for the JavaScript syntax rules. Names noted with an asterisk (*) are JavaScript properties only.

!important, accelerator, background, background-attachment, background-color, background-image, background-position, background-position-x, background-position-y, background-repeat, behavior, border, border-bottom, border-bottom-color, border-bottom-style, border-bottom-width, border-color, border-left, border-left-color, border-left-style, border-left-width, border-right, border-right-color, border-right-style, border-right-width, border-style, border-top, border-top-color, border-top-style, border-top-width, border-width, bottom, clear, clip, color, cursor, direction, display, filter, float, font, font-family, font-size, font-style, font-variant, font-weight, hasLayout(*), height, layout-flow, layout-grid, layout-grid-mode, left, letter-spacing, line-height, margin, margin-bottom, margin-left, margin-right, margin-top, overflow, overflow-x, overflow-y, padding, padding-bottom, padding-left, padding-right, padding-top, pixelBottom(*), pixelHeight(*), pixelLeft(*), pixelRight(*), pixelTop(*), pixelWidth(*), posBottom(*), posHeight(*), position, posLeft(*), posRight(*), posTop(*), posWidth(*), right, styleFloat(*), text-autospace, text-decoration, text-overflow, text-transform, text-underline-position, textDecorationBlink(*), textDecorationLineThrough(*), textDecorationNone(*), textDecorationOverline(*), textDecorationUnderline(*), top, unicode-bidi, visibility, white-space, width, word-spacing, word-wrap, writing-mode, z-index, zoom

<label> Microsoft Behaviors (9)

clientCaps, download, homePage, httpFolder, saveFavorite, saveHistory, saveSnapshot, userData

<label> Microsoft Filters (10)

Alpha, Barn, BasicImage, BlendTrans, Blinds, Blur, CheckerBoard, Chroma, Compositor, DropShadow, Emboss, Engrave, Fade, FlipH, FlipV, Glow, GradientWipe, Gray, ICMFilter, Inset, Invert, Iris, Light, MaskFilter, Matrix, MotionBlur, Pixelate, RadialWipe, RandomBars, RandomDissolve, RevealTrans, Shadow, Slide, Spiral, Stretch, Strips, Wave, Wheel, Xray, Zigzag

label. JavaScript Properties (11)

accessKey, canHaveChildren, canHaveHTML, className, clientHeight, clientLeft, clientTop, clientWidth, contentEditable, cursor, dataFld, dataFormatAs, datasrc, dir, disabled, firstChild, form, hasLayout, hideFocus, htmlFor, id, innerHTML, innerText, isContentEditable, isDisabled, isMultiLine, isTextEdit, lang, language, lastChild, nextSibling, nodeName, nodeType, nodeValue, offsetHeight, offsetLeft, offsetParent, offsetTop, offsetWidth, outerHTML, outerText, ownerDocument, parentElement, parentNode, parentTextEdit, previousSibling, readyState, recordNumber, scopeName, scrollHeight, scrollLeft, scrollTop, scrollWidth, sourceIndex, tabIndex, tagName, tagUrn, title, uniqueID

label. JavaScript Methods (12)

addBehavior, appendChild, applyElement, attachEvent, blur, clearAttributes, click, cloneNode, componentFromPoint, contains, detachEvent, dragDrop, fireEvent, focus, getAdjacentText, getAttribute, getAttributeNode, getBoundingClientRect, getClientRects, getElementsByTagName, getExpression, hasChildNodes, insertAdjacentElement, insertAdjacentHTML, insertAdjacentText, insertBefore, mergeAttributes, normalize, releaseCapture, removeAttribute, removeAttributeNode, removeBehavior, removeChild, removeExpression, removeNode, replaceAdjacentText, replaceChild, replaceNode, scrollIntoView, setActive, setAttribute, setAttributeNode, setCapture, setExpression, swapNode

label. JavaScript Collections (13)

all, attributes, behaviorUrns, childNodes, children

label. JavaScript Objects (14)

currentStyle, runtimeStyle, style

<legend> ... </legend>

Compatibility: NN6, NN7, IE4, IE5, IE5.5, IE6

This element inserts a descriptive caption in the container box of a <fieldset> element. You use this element to define the group of fields contained between the <fieldset> element's opening and closing tags. This element must be the first element between the opening and closing tags of the <fieldset> element.

Syntax:

```
<legend attributes events> . . . </legend>
```

Example:

```
<html><head><title>legend element example</title></head>
<body bgcolor="#FFFFFF" text="#000000">
<form name="form1" method="post" action="">
<p><fieldset align="center"> <legend>Credit Card Information:</legend>
<input type="text" name="textfield" value="Name" size="60"><br>
<input type="text" name="textfield2" value="Exp. date" size="50"><br>
<input type="text" name="textfield3" value="Type" size="65"><br>
<input type="text" name="textfield4" value="Number" size="45">
</fieldset></p>
</form></body></html>
```

`<legend>` HTML Attributes (6)

accesskey, align, begin, class, contenteditable, dataformatas, dir, disabled, end, hidefocus, id, lang, language, style, syncmaster, systemBitrate, systemCaptions, systemLanguage, systemOverdubOrSubtitle, tabindex, timecontainer, title, unselectable

`<legend>` Event Handlers (7)

onActivate, onAfterUpdate, onBeforeActivate, onBeforeCopy, onBeforeCut, onBeforeDeactivate, onBeforeEditFocus, onBeforePaste, onBeforeUpdate, onBlur, onClick, onContextMenu, onControlSelect, onCopy, onCut, onDblClick, onDeactivate, onDragStart, onErrorUpdate, onFocus, onFocusIn, onFocusOut, onHelp, onKeyDown, onKeyPress, onKeyUp, onLoseCapture, onMouseDown, onMouseEnter, onMouseLeave, onMouseMove, onMouseOut, onMouseOver, onMouseUp, onMouseWheel, onMove, onMoveEnd, onMoveStart, onPaste, onPropertyChange, onReadyStateChange, onResize, onResizeEnd, onResizeStart, onTimeError

`<legend>` CSS Attributes and JavaScript Style Properties (8)

The names are in CSS syntax. See the introduction to this chapter for the JavaScript syntax rules. Names noted with an asterisk (*) are JavaScript properties only.

!important, :first-letter, :first-line, accelerator, background, background-attachment, background-color, background-image, background-position, background-position-x, background-position-y, background-repeat, behavior, bottom, clear, clip, color, cursor, direction, display, filter, float, font, font-family, font-size, font-style, font-variant, font-weight, hasLayout(*), height, layout-flow, layout-grid, layout-grid-mode, left, letter-spacing, line-break, line-height, overflow, overflow-x, overflow-y, padding, padding-bottom, padding-left, padding-right, padding-top, pixelBottom(*), pixelHeight(*), pixelLeft(*), pixelRight(*), pixelTop(*), pixelWidth(*), posBottom(*), posHeight(*), position, posLeft(*), posRight(*), posTop(*), posWidth(*), right, styleFloat(*), text-autospace, text-decoration, text-justify, text-overflow, text-transform, text-underline-position, textDecorationBlink(*), textDecorationLineThrough(*), textDecorationNone(*), textDecorationOverline(*), textDecorationUnderline(*), top, unicode-bidi, visibility, white-space, width, word-break, word-spacing, word-wrap, writing-mode, z-index, zoom

`<legend>` Microsoft Behaviors (9)

clientCaps, download, homePage, time, time2

`<legend>` Microsoft Filters (10)

Alpha, Barn, BasicImage, BlendTrans, Blinds, Blur, CheckerBoard, Chroma, Compositor, DropShadow, Emboss, Engrave, Fade, FlipH, FlipV, Glow, GradientWipe, Gray, ICMFilter, Inset, Invert, Iris, Light, MaskFilter, Matrix, MotionBlur, Pixelate, RadialWipe, RandomBars, RandomDissolve, RevealTrans, Shadow, Slide, Spiral, Stretch, Strips, Wave, Wheel, Xray, Zigzag

legend. JavaScript Properties (11)

accessKey, align, canHaveChildren, canHaveHTML, className, clientHeight, clientLeft, clientTop, clientWidth, contentEditable, cursor, dataFormatAs, dir, disabled, end, firstChild, form, hasLayout, hideFocus, id, innerHTML, innerText, isContentEditable, isDisabled, isMultiLine, isTextEdit, lang, language, lastChild, nextSibling, nodeName, nodeType, nodeValue, offsetHeight, offsetLeft, offsetParent, offsetTop, offsetWidth, outerHTML, outerText, ownerDocument, parentElement, parentNode, parentTextEdit, previousSibling, readyState, recordNumber, scopeName, scrollHeight, scrollLeft, scrollTop, scrollWidth, tabIndex, tagName, tagUrn, title, uniqueID

legend. JavaScript Methods (12)

addBehavior, appendChild, applyElement, attachEvent, blur, clearAttributes, click, cloneNode, componentFromPoint, contains, detachEvent, dragDrop, fireEvent, focus, getAdjacentText, getAttribute, getAttributeNode, getBoundingClientRect, getClientRects, getElementsByTagName, getExpression, hasChildNodes, insertAdjacentElement, insertAdjacentHTML, insertAdjacentText, insertBefore, mergeAttributes, normalize, releaseCapture, removeAttribute, removeAttributeNode, removeBehavior, removeChild, removeExpression, removeNode, replaceAdjacentText, replaceChild, replaceNode, scrollIntoView, setActive, setAttribute, setAttributeNode, setCapture, setExpression, swapNode

legend. JavaScript Collections (13)

all, attributes, behaviorUrns, childNodes, children

legend. JavaScript Objects (14)

currentStyle, runtimeStyle, style

\<li> ... \</li>

Compatibility: NN4, NN6, NN7, IE4, IE5, IE5.5, IE6

This element creates one item in an ordered list, <ol>, or unordered list, <ul>.
   Syntax:

```
<li attributes events> . . . </li>
```

   Example:

```
<html><head><title>li element example</title></head>
<body bgcolor="#FFFFFF" text="#000000">
  <ul type="square">
    <li>first item</li>
    <li>second item</li>
    <li>third item</li>
```

```
    <li>fourth item</li>
    <li>fifth item</li>
  </ul>
</body></html>
```

<li> HTML Attributes (6)

accesskey, begin, class, contenteditable, dir, disabled, end, hidefocus, id, lang, language, style, syncmaster, systemBitrate, systemCaptions, systemLanguage, systemOverdubOrSubtitle, tabindex, timecontainer, title, type, unselectable, value

<li> Event Handlers (7)

onActivate, onBeforeActivate, onBeforeCopy, onBeforeCut, onBeforeDeactivate, onBeforeEditFocus, onBeforePaste, onBlur, onClick, onContextMenu, onControlSelect, onCopy, onCut, onDblClick, onDeactivate, onDrag, onDragEnd, onDragEnter, onDragLeave, onDragOver, onDragStart, onDrop, onFocus, onFocusIn, onFocusOut, onHelp, onKeyDown, onKeyPress, onKeyUp, onLayoutComplete, onLoseCapture, onMouseDown, onMouseEnter, onMouseLeave, onMouseMove, onMouseOut, onMouseOver, onMouseUp, onMouseWheel, onMove, onMoveEnd, onMoveStart, onPaste, onPropertyChange, onReadyStateChange, onResize, onResizeEnd, onResizeStart, onSelectStart, onTimeError

<li> CSS Attributes and JavaScript Style Properties (8)

The names are in CSS syntax. See the introduction to this chapter for the JavaScript syntax rules. Names noted with an asterisk (*) are JavaScript properties only.

!important, :first-letter, :first-line, accelerator, background, background-attachment, background-color, background-image, background-position, background-position-x, background-position-y, background-repeat, behavior, border, border-bottom, border-bottom-color, border-bottom-style, border-bottom-width, border-color, border-left, border-left-color, border-left-style, border-left-width, border-right, border-right-color, border-right-style, border-right-width, border-style, border-top, border-top-color, border-top-style, border-top-width, border-width, bottom, clear, clip, color, cursor, direction, display, filter, float, font, font-family, font-size, font-style, font-variant, font-weight, hasLayout(*), height, layout-flow, layout-grid, layout-grid-char, layout-grid-line, layout-grid-mode, layout-grid-type, left, letter-spacing, line-break, line-height, list-style, list-style-image, list-style-position, list-style-type, margin, margin-bottom, margin-left, margin-right, margin-top, overflow, overflow-x, overflow-y, padding, padding-bottom, padding-left, padding-right, padding-top, page-break-after, page-break-before, pixelBottom(*), pixelHeight(*), pixelLeft(*), pixelRight(*), pixelTop(*), pixelWidth(*), posBottom(*), posHeight(*), position, posLeft(*), posRight(*), posTop(*), posWidth(*), right, styleFloat(*), text-align, text-align-last, text-autospace, text-decoration, text-indent, text-justify, text-kashida-space, text-overflow, text-transform, text-underline-position, textDecorationBlink(*), textDecorationLineThrough(*), textDecorationNone(*), textDecorationOverline(*), textDecorationUnderline(*), top, unicode-bidi, visibility, white-space, width, word-break, word-spacing, word-wrap, writing-mode, z-index, zoom

<li> Microsoft Behaviors (9)

clientCaps, download, homePage, httpFolder, saveFavorite, saveHistory, saveSnapshot, time, time2, userData

<li> Microsoft Filters (10)

Alpha, Barn, BasicImage, BlendTrans, Blinds, Blur, CheckerBoard, Chroma, Compositor, DropShadow, Emboss, Engrave, Fade, FlipH, FlipV, Glow, GradientWipe, Gray, ICMFilter, Inset, Invert, Iris, Light, MaskFilter, Matrix, MotionBlur, Pixelate, RadialWipe, RandomBars, RandomDissolve, RevealTrans, Shadow, Slide, Spiral, Stretch, Strips, Wave, Wheel, Xray, Zigzag

li. JavaScript Properties (11)

accessKey, blockDirection, canHaveChildren, canHaveHTML, className, clientHeight, clientLeft, clientTop, clientWidth, contentEditable, cursor, dir, disabled, end, firstChild, hasLayout, hideFocus, id, innerHTML, innerText, isContentEditable, isDisabled, isMultiLine, isTextEdit, lang, language, lastChild, nextSibling, nodeName, nodeType, nodeValue, offsetHeight, offsetLeft, offsetParent, offsetTop, offsetWidth, outerHTML, outerText, ownerDocument, parentElement, parentNode, parentTextEdit, previousSibling, readyState, scopeName, scrollHeight, scrollLeft, scrollTop, scrollWidth, sourceIndex, tabIndex, tagName, tagUrn, title, type, uniqueID, value

li. JavaScript Methods (12)

addBehavior, appendChild, applyElement, attachEvent, blur, clearAttributes, click, cloneNode, componentFromPoint, contains, detachEvent, dragDrop, fireEvent, focus, getAdjacentText, getAttribute, getAttributeNode, getBoundingClientRect, getClientRects, getElementsByTagName, getExpression, hasChildNodes, insertAdjacentElement, insertAdjacentHTML, insertAdjacentText, insertBefore, mergeAttributes, normalize, releaseCapture, removeAttribute, removeAttributeNode, removeBehavior, removeChild, removeExpression, removeNode, replaceAdjacentText, replaceChild, replaceNode, scrollIntoView, setActive, setAttribute, setAttributeNode, setCapture, setExpression, swapNode

li. JavaScript Collections (13)

all, attributes, behaviorUrns, childNodes, children

li. JavaScript Objects (14)

currentStyle, runtimeStyle, style

<link>

Compatibility: NN4, NN6, NN7, IE4, IE5, IE5.5, IE6

This element defines the relationship between the current page and external documents. It is commonly used to allow external style sheets to be accessed from the document, and it is usually placed in the <head> section of the page.

Syntax:

```
<link attributes events>
```

Example:

```
<html><head><title>link element example</title>
<link rel="stylesheet" href="myStyleSheet.css" type="text/css"></head>
<body>This text will have the font specified in myStyleSheet </body></html>
```

<link> HTML Attributes (6)

charset, dir, href, hreflang, id, lang, media, name, rel, rev, style, target, title, type

<link> Event Handlers (7)

onLoad, onReadyStateChange

<link> CSS Attributes and JavaScript Style Properties (8)

The names are in CSS syntax. See the introduction to this chapter for the JavaScript syntax rules. Names noted with an asterisk (*) are JavaScript properties only.

background-position-x, background-position-y, behavior, pixelBottom(*), pixelHeight(*), pixelLeft(*), pixelRight(*), pixelTop(*), pixelWidth(*), posBottom(*), posHeight(*), posLeft(*), posRight(*), posTop(*), posWidth(*), text-autospace, text-underline-position

<link> Microsoft Behaviors (9)

clientCaps, download, homePage

link. JavaScript Properties (11)

canHaveHTML, charset, className, clientHeight, clientWidth, dir, disabled, firstChild, href, hreflang, id, innerHTML, isContentEditable, isDisabled, isMultiLine, isTextEdit, lang, lastChild, media, name, nextSibling, nodeName, nodeType, nodeValue, offsetHeight, offsetLeft, offsetParent, offsetTop, offsetWidth, ownerDocument, parentElement, parentNode, parentTextEdit, previousSibling, readyState, rel, rev, scopeName, scrollHeight, scrollLeft, scrollTop, scrollWidth, sourceIndex, tagName, tagUrn, target, title, type, uniqueID

link. JavaScript Methods (12)

addBehavior, appendChild, applyElement, attachEvent, clearAttributes, cloneNode, componentFromPoint, contains, detachEvent, fireEvent, getAdjacentText, getAttribute, getAttributeNode, getBoundingClientRect, getClientRects, getElementsByTagName, hasChildNodes, insertAdjacentElement, insertBefore, mergeAttributes, normalize, removeAttribute, removeAttributeNode, removeBehavior, removeChild, replaceAdjacentText, replaceChild, setAttribute, setAttributeNode, swapNode

link. JavaScript Collections (13)

all, attributes, behaviorUrns, childNodes, children

<listing> ... </listing>

Compatibility: NN4, IE4, IE5

This element displays text in a fixed-width font. However, the <pre> element performs the same functionality and is preferred over this element.

Syntax:

<listing *attributes events*> . . . </listing>

Example:

```
<html><head><title>listing element example</title></head>
<body bgcolor="#FFFFFF" text="#000000">
<font size="4"><listing style="font-weight:normal">
  first line<br>
  second line<br>
  third line<br>
  fourth line<br>
</listing></font>
</body></html>
```

<listing> HTML Attributes (6)

accesskey, begin, class, contenteditable, dir, disabled, end, hidefocus, id, lang, language, style, syncmaster, systemBitrate, systemCaptions, systemLanguage, systemOverdubOrSubtitle, tabindex, timecontainer, title, unselectable

<listing> Event Handlers (7)

onActivate, onBeforeActivate, onBeforeCopy, onBeforeCut, onBeforeDeactivate, onBeforeEditFocus, onBeforePaste, onBlur, onClick, onContextMenu, onControlSelect, onCopy, onCut, onDblClick, onDeactivate, onDrag, onDragEnd, onDragEnter, onDragLeave, onDragOver, onDragStart, onDrop, onFocus, onFocusIn, onFocusOut, onHelp, onKeyDown, onKeyPress, onKeyUp, onLoseCapture, onMouseDown, onMouseEnter, onMouseLeave, onMouseMove, onMouseOut, onMouseOver, onMouseUp, onMouseWheel, onMove, onMoveEnd, onMoveStart, onPaste, onPropertyChange, onReadyStateChange, onResize, onResizeEnd, onResizeStart, onSelectStart, onTimeError

\<listing\> CSS Attributes and JavaScript Style Properties (8)

The names are in CSS syntax. See the introduction to this chapter for the JavaScript syntax rules. Names noted with an asterisk (*) are JavaScript properties only.

!important, :first-letter, :first-line, accelerator, background, background-attachment, background-color, background-image, background-position, background-position-x, background-position-y, background-repeat, behavior, border, border-bottom, border-bottom-color, border-bottom-style, border-bottom-width, border-color, border-left, border-left-color, border-left-style, border-left-width, border-right, border-right-color, border-right-style, border-right-width, border-style, border-top, border-top-color, border-top-style, border-top-width, border-width, bottom, clear, clip, color, cursor, direction, display, float, font, font-family, font-size, font-style, font-variant, font-weight, hasLayout(*), height, layout-grid, layout-grid-char, layout-grid-line, layout-grid-mode, layout-grid-type, left, letter-spacing, line-break, line-height, margin, margin-bottom, margin-left, margin-right, margin-top, overflow, overflow-x, overflow-y, padding, padding-bottom, padding-left, padding-right, padding-top, page-break-after, page-break-before, pixelBottom(*), pixelHeight(*), pixelLeft(*), pixelRight(*), pixelTop(*), pixelWidth(*), posBottom(*), posHeight(*), position, posLeft(*), posRight(*), posTop(*), posWidth(*), right, styleFloat(*), text-align, text-align-last, text-autospace, text-decoration, text-indent, text-justify, text-kashida-space, text-overflow, text-transform, text-underline-position, textDecorationBlink(*), textDecorationLineThrough(*), textDecorationNone(*), textDecorationOverline(*), textDecorationUnderline(*), top, unicode-bidi, visibility, white-space, width, word-break, word-spacing, word-wrap, z-index, zoom

---

\<listing\> Microsoft Behaviors (9)

---

clientCaps, download, homePage, httpFolder, saveFavorite, saveHistory, saveSnapshot, time, time2, userData

---

listing. JavaScript Properties (11)

---

accessKey, blockDirection, canHaveChildren, canHaveHTML, className, clientHeight, clientLeft, clientTop, clientWidth, contentEditable, cursor, dir, disabled, end, firstChild, hasLayout, hideFocus, id, innerHTML, innerText, isContentEditable, isDisabled, isMultiLine, isTextEdit, lang, language, lastChild, nextSibling, nodeName, nodeType, nodeValue, offsetHeight, offsetLeft, offsetParent, offsetTop, offsetWidth, outerHTML, outerText, ownerDocument, parentElement, parentNode, parentTextEdit, previousSibling, readyState, scopeName, scrollHeight, scrollLeft, scrollTop, scrollWidth, sourceIndex, tabIndex, tagName, tagUrn, title, uniqueID

---

listing. JavaScript Methods (12)

---

addBehavior, appendChild, applyElement, attachEvent, blur, clearAttributes, click, cloneNode, componentFromPoint, contains, detachEvent, fireEvent, focus, getAdjacentText, getAttribute, getAttributeNode, getBoundingClientRect, getClientRects, getElementsByTagName, getExpression, hasChildNodes, insertAdjacentElement, insertAdjacentHTML, insertAdjacentText, insertBefore, mergeAttributes, normalize, releaseCapture, removeAttribute, removeAttributeNode,

removeBehavior, removeChild, removeExpression, removeNode, replaceAdjacentText, replaceChild, replaceNode, scrollIntoView, setActive, setAttribute, setAttributeNode, setCapture, setExpression, swapNode

listing. JavaScript Collections (13)

all, attributes, behaviorUrns, childNodes, children

listing. JavaScript Objects (14)

currentStyle, runtimeStyle, style

<map> ... </map>

Compatibility: NN4, NN6, NN7, IE4, IE5, IE5.5, IE6

This element is used to specify the coordinates of an image map in the page. You must use this element in conjunction with the <img> element (to define the image to use) and the <area> element (to define the area inside the image that is clickable and linked to another web page).

Syntax:

```
<map attributes events> . . . </map>
```

Example:

```
<html><head><title>map element example</title></head>
<body bgcolor="#FFFFFF" text="#000000">
<img src="area1.gif" alt="" width=200 height=100 usemap="#myMap">
<map name="myMap">
<area shape="rect" coords="0, 0, 100, 50" href="http://www.w3c.com">
<area shape="rect" coords="100, 0, 200, 50" href="http://www.microsoft.com">
<area shape="rect" coords="0, 50, 100, 100" href="http://www.msn.com">
<area shape="rect" coords="100, 50, 200, 100" href="http://www.yahoo.com">
</map></body></html>
```

<map> HTML Attributes (6)

class, dir, id, lang, language, name, style, title

<map> Event Handlers (7)

onAfterUpdate, onBeforeActivate, onBeforeCut, onBeforePaste, onBeforeUpdate, onBlur, onClick, onCut, onDblClick, onDrag, onDragEnd, onDragEnter, onDragLeave, onDragOver, onDragStart, onDrop, onErrorUpdate, onFocus, onFocusIn, onFocusOut, onHelp, onKeyDown, onKeyPress, onKeyUp, onLoseCapture, onMouseDown, onMouseEnter, onMouseLeave, onMouseMove, onMouseOut, onMouseOver, onMouseUp, onMouseWheel, onPaste, onPropertyChange, onReadyStateChange, onScroll, onSelectStart

\<map\> CSS Attributes and JavaScript Style Properties (8)

behavior

\<map\> Microsoft Behaviors (9)

clientCaps, download, homePage, httpFolder, saveFavorite, saveHistory, saveSnapshot, userData

map. JavaScript Properties (11)

canHaveChildren, canHaveHTML, className, clientHeight, clientWidth, dir, disabled, firstChild, id, innerHTML, innerText, isContentEditable, isDisabled, isMultiLine, isTextEdit, lang, language, lastChild, name, nextSibling, nodeName, nodeType, nodeValue, offsetHeight, offsetLeft, offsetParent, offsetTop, offsetWidth, outerHTML, outerText, ownerDocument, parentElement, parentNode, parentTextEdit, previousSibling, readyState, scopeName, scrollHeight, scrollLeft, scrollTop, scrollWidth, sourceIndex, tagName, tagUrn, title, uniqueID

map. JavaScript Methods (12)

addBehavior, appendChild, applyElement, attachEvent, clearAttributes, click, cloneNode, componentFromPoint, contains, detachEvent, dragDrop, fireEvent, getAdjacentText, getAttribute, getAttributeNode, getBoundingClientRect, getClientRects, getElementsByTagName, hasChildNodes, insertAdjacentElement, insertAdjacentHTML, insertAdjacentText, insertBefore, mergeAttributes, normalize, releaseCapture, removeAttribute, removeAttributeNode, removeBehavior, removeChild, removeNode, replaceAdjacentText, replaceChild, replaceNode, scrollIntoView, setAttribute, setAttributeNode, setCapture, swapNode

map. JavaScript Collections (13)

all, areas, attributes, behaviorUrns, childNodes, children

\<marquee\> ... \</marquee\>

Compatibility: IE4, IE5, IE5.5, IE6

This element creates scrolling text on the page.
Syntax:

\<marquee *attributes events*\> . . . \</marquee\>

Example:

```
<html><head><title>marquee element example</title></head>
<body bgcolor="#FFFFFF" text="#000000">
<center><marquee behavior="slide" direction="left" width="400" bgcolor="blue"
```

```
loop="5" style="color:white">Make sure you place your order today to take advantage
of our great saving.</marquee></center>
</body></html>
```

\<marquee\> HTML Attributes (6)

```
accesskey, begin, behavior, bgcolor, class, contenteditable, datafld, dataformatas,
datasrc, dir, direction, disabled, end, height, hidefocus, hspace, id, lang,
language, loop, scrollamount, scrolldelay, style, syncmaster, systemBitrate,
systemCaptions, systemLanguage, systemOverdubOrSubtitle, tabindex, timecontainer,
title, truespeed, unselectable, vspace, width
```

\<marquee\> Event Handlers (7)

```
onActivate, onAfterUpdate, onBeforeActivate, onBeforeCut, onBeforeDeactivate,
onBeforeEditFocus, onBeforePaste, onBeforeUpdate, onBlur, onBounce, onClick,
onContextMenu, onControlSelect, onCut, onDblClick, onDeactivate, onDrag, onDragEnd,
onDragEnter, onDragLeave, onDragOver, onDragStart, onDrop, onErrorUpdate,
onFilterChange, onFinish, onFocus, onFocusIn, onFocusOut, onHelp, onKeyDown,
onKeyPress, onKeyUp, onLoseCapture, onMouseDown, onMouseEnter, onMouseLeave,
onMouseMove, onMouseOut, onMouseOver, onMouseUp, onMouseWheel, onMove, onMoveEnd,
onMoveStart, onPaste, onPropertyChange, onReadyStateChange, onResize, onResizeEnd,
onResizeStart, onScroll, onSelectStart, onStart, onTimeError
```

\<marquee\> CSS Attributes and JavaScript Style Properties (8)

The names are in CSS syntax. See the introduction to this chapter for the
JavaScript syntax rules. Names noted with an asterisk (*) are JavaScript
properties only.

```
!important, :first-letter, :first-line, background, background-attachment,
background-color, background-image, background-position, background-position-x,
background-position-y, background-repeat, behavior, border, border-bottom, border-
bottom-color, border-bottom-style, border-bottom-width, border-color, border-left,
border-left-color, border-left-style, border-left-width, border-right, border-
right-color, border-right-style, border-right-width, border-style, border-top,
border-top-color, border-top-style, border-top-width, border-width, bottom, clear,
clip, color, cursor, display, filter, float, font, font-family, font-size, font-
style, font-variant, font-weight, hasLayout(*), height, layout-flow, layout-grid,
layout-grid-char, layout-grid-line, layout-grid-mode, layout-grid-type, left,
letter-spacing, line-break, line-height, margin, margin-bottom, margin-left,
margin-right, margin-top, padding, padding-bottom, padding-left, padding-right,
padding-top, page-break-after, pixelBottom(*), pixelHeight(*), pixelLeft(*),
pixelRight(*), pixelTop(*), pixelWidth(*), posBottom(*), posHeight(*), position,
posLeft(*), posRight(*), posTop(*), posWidth(*), right, styleFloat(*), text-align,
text-autospace, text-decoration, text-indent, text-justify, text-overflow, text-
transform, text-underline-position, textDecorationBlink(*),
textDecorationLineThrough(*), textDecorationNone(*), textDecorationOverline(*),
textDecorationUnderline(*), top, unicode-bidi, visibility, word-break, word-
spacing, writing-mode, z-index, zoom
```

\<marquee> Microsoft Behaviors (9)

clientCaps, download, homePage, httpFolder, saveFavorite, saveHistory, saveSnapshot, time, time2, userData

\<marquee> Microsoft Filters (10)

Alpha, Barn, BasicImage, BlendTrans, Blinds, Blur, CheckerBoard, Chroma, Compositor, DropShadow, Emboss, Engrave, Fade, FlipH, FlipV, Glow, GradientWipe, Gray, ICMFilter, Inset, Invert, Iris, Light, MaskFilter, Matrix, MotionBlur, Pixelate, RadialWipe, RandomBars, RandomDissolve, RevealTrans, Shadow, Slide, Spiral, Stretch, Strips, Wave, Wheel, Xray, Zigzag

marquee. JavaScript Properties (11)

accessKey, behavior, bgColor, canHaveChildren, canHaveHTML, className, clientHeight, clientLeft, clientTop, clientWidth, contentEditable, cursor, dataFld, dataFormatAs, datasrc, dir, direction, disabled, end, firstChild, hasLayout, height, hideFocus, hspace, id, innerHTML, innerText, isContentEditable, isDisabled, isMultiLine, isTextEdit, lang, language, lastChild, loop, nextSibling, nodeName, nodeType, nodeValue, offsetHeight, offsetLeft, offsetParent, offsetTop, offsetWidth, outerHTML, outerText, ownerDocument, parentElement, parentNode, parentTextEdit, previousSibling, readyState, recordNumber, scopeName, scrollAmount, scrollDelay, scrollHeight, scrollLeft, scrollTop, sourceIndex, tabIndex, tagName, tagUrn, title, trueSpeed, uniqueID, vspace, width

marquee. JavaScript Methods (12)

addBehavior, appendChild, applyElement, attachEvent, blur, clearAttributes, click, cloneNode, componentFromPoint, contains, detachEvent, dragDrop, fireEvent, focus, getAdjacentText, getAttribute, getAttributeNode, getBoundingClientRect, getClientRects, getElementsByTagName, getExpression, hasChildNodes, insertAdjacentElement, insertAdjacentHTML, insertAdjacentText, insertBefore, mergeAttributes, normalize, releaseCapture, removeAttribute, removeAttributeNode, removeBehavior, removeChild, removeExpression, removeNode, replaceAdjacentText, replaceChild, replaceNode, scrollIntoView, setActive, setAttribute, setAttributeNode, setCapture, setExpression, start, stop, swapNode

marquee. JavaScript Collections (13)

all, attributes, behaviorUrns, childNodes, children, filters

marquee. JavaScript Objects (14)

currentStyle, runtimeStyle, style

`<menu>` ... `</menu>`

Compatibility: NN4, NN6, NN7, IE4, IE5, IE5.5, IE6

This element creates a list of items. However, this element has been deprecated in favor of the `<ul>` element.

Syntax:

```
<menu attributes events> . . . </menu>
```

Example:

```
<html><head><title>menu element example</title></head>
<body bgcolor="#FFFFFF" text="#000000">
  <menu type="square">
    <li>first item</li>
    <li>second item</li>
    <li>third item</li>
    <li>fourth item</li>
    <li>fifth item</li>
  </menu>
</body></html>
```

`<menu>` HTML Attributes (6)

accesskey, begin, class, compact, contenteditable, dir, disabled, end, hidefocus, id, lang, style, syncmaster, systemBitrate, systemCaptions, systemLanguage, systemOverdubOrSubtitle, tabindex, timecontainer, title, unselectable

`<menu>` Event Handlers (7)

onActivate, onBeforeActivate, onBeforeCopy, onBeforeCut, onBeforeDeactivate, onBeforeEditFocus, onBeforePaste, onBlur, onClick, onContextMenu, onControlSelect, onCopy, onCut, onDblClick, onDeactivate, onDrag, onDragEnd, onDragEnter, onDragLeave, onDragOver, onDragStart, onDrop, onFocus, onFocusIn, onFocusOut, onHelp, onKeyDown, onKeyPress, onKeyUp, onLoseCapture, onMouseDown, onMouseEnter, onMouseLeave, onMouseMove, onMouseOut, onMouseOver, onMouseUp, onMouseWheel, onMove, onMoveEnd, onMoveStart, onPaste, onPropertyChange, onReadyStateChange, onResize, onResizeEnd, onResizeStart, onSelectStart, onTimeError

`<menu>` CSS Attributes and JavaScript Style Properties (8)

The names are in CSS syntax. See the introduction to this chapter for the JavaScript syntax rules. Names noted with an asterisk (*) are JavaScript properties only.

!important, :first-letter, :first-line, accelerator, background, background-attachment, background-color, background-image, background-position, background-position-x, background-position-y, background-repeat, behavior, border, border-bottom, border-bottom-color, border-bottom-style, border-bottom-width, border-color, border-left, border-left-color, border-left-style, border-left-width, border-right, border-right-color, border-right-style, border-right-width, border-style, border-top, border-top-color, border-top-style, border-top-width, border-width, bottom, clear, clip, color, cursor, direction, display, filter, float, font, font-family, font-size, font-style, font-variant, font-weight, hasLayout(*), height, layout-flow, layout-grid, layout-grid-char, layout-grid-line, layout-grid-mode, layout-grid-type, left, letter-spacing, line-break, line-height, margin, margin-bottom, margin-left, margin-right, margin-top, overflow, overflow-x, overflow-y, padding, padding-bottom, padding-left, padding-right, padding-top, page-break-after, page-break-before, pixelBottom(*), pixelHeight(*), pixelLeft(*), pixelRight(*), pixelTop(*), pixelWidth(*), posBottom(*), posHeight(*), position, posLeft(*), posRight(*), posTop(*), posWidth(*), right, styleFloat(*), text-align, text-align-last, text-autospace, text-decoration, text-indent, text-justify, text-kashida-space, text-overflow, text-transform, text-underline-position, textDecorationBlink(*), textDecorationLineThrough(*), textDecorationNone(*), textDecorationOverline(*), textDecorationUnderline(*), top, unicode-bidi, visibility, white-space, width, word-break, word-spacing, word-wrap, writing-mode, z-index, zoom

\<menu> Microsoft Behaviors (9)

clientCaps, download, homePage, httpFolder, saveFavorite, saveHistory, saveSnapshot, time, time2, userData

\<menu> Microsoft Filters (10)

Alpha, Barn, BasicImage, BlendTrans, Blinds, Blur, CheckerBoard, Chroma, Compositor, DropShadow, Emboss, Engrave, Fade, FlipH, FlipV, Glow, GradientWipe, Gray, ICMFilter, Inset, Invert, Iris, Light, MaskFilter, Matrix, MotionBlur, Pixelate, RadialWipe, RandomBars, RandomDissolve, RevealTrans, Shadow, Slide, Spiral, Stretch, Strips, Wave, Wheel, Xray, Zigzag

menu. JavaScript Properties (11)

accessKey, blockDirection, canHaveChildren, canHaveHTML, className, clientHeight, clientLeft, clientTop, clientWidth, compact, contentEditable, cursor, dir, disabled, end, firstChild, hasLayout, hideFocus, id, innerHTML, innerText, isContentEditable, isDisabled, isMultiLine, isTextEdit, lang, lastChild, nextSibling, nodeName, nodeType, nodeValue, offsetHeight, offsetLeft, offsetParent, offsetTop, offsetWidth, outerHTML, outerText, ownerDocument, parentElement, parentNode, parentTextEdit, previousSibling, readyState, scopeName, scrollHeight, scrollLeft, scrollTop, scrollWidth, sourceIndex, tabIndex, tagName, tagUrn, title, uniqueID

menu. JavaScript Methods (12)

addBehavior, appendChild, applyElement, attachEvent, blur, clearAttributes, click, cloneNode, componentFromPoint, contains, detachEvent, fireEvent, focus, getAdjacentText, getAttribute, getAttributeNode, getBoundingClientRect, getClientRects, getElementsByTagName, getExpression, hasChildNodes, insertAdjacentElement, insertAdjacentHTML, insertAdjacentText, insertBefore, mergeAttributes, normalize, releaseCapture, removeAttribute, removeAttributeNode, removeBehavior, removeChild, removeExpression, removeNode, replaceAdjacentText, replaceChild, replaceNode, scrollIntoView, setActive, setAttribute, setAttributeNode, setCapture, setExpression, swapNode

menu. JavaScript Collections (13)

all, attributes, behaviorUrns, childNodes, children

menu. JavaScript Objects (14)

currentStyle, runtimeStyle, style

<meta>

Compatibility: NN4, NN6, NN7, IE4, IE5, IE5.5, IE6

Every HTML page contains special HTTP header information. This information is used by the browser (be it Netscape Navigator or Internet Explorer) in the client computer or by the server computer to perform a variety of tasks, or to pass additional information back and forth.

The <meta> element allows you to include additional HTTP header information about the document. This element is placed in the <head> section of the document.

Syntax:

<meta *attributes events*>

<meta> HTML Specific Attributes

content

Compatibility: NN4, NN6, NN7, IE4, IE5, IE5.5, IE6

This attribute is used in conjunction with either the http-equiv (HTTP headers) attribute or the name attribute. The value that you define in this attribute will be used to set either the http-equiv value or the value of the variable defined in the name attribute.

Syntax:

<meta http-equiv="headername" content="value_assigned to the header">

http-equiv

Compatibility: NN4, NN6, NN7, IE4, IE5, IE5.5, IE6

<meta> tags containing an http-equiv attribute produce the same results as HTTP headers. They can be used to provide additional instructions to the server, to complement the HTTP headers, or to provide additional functionality to the browsers. Some of the most common http-equiv values are: content-language, content-script-type, content-style-type, content-type, default-style, expires, refresh, set-cookie, and window-target.

Syntax:

```
<meta http-equiv="value" content=". . .">
```

content-language

This header specifies the language of the document.
Example:

```
<meta http-equiv="content-language" content="en-US">
```

content-script-type

This header specifies the default scripting language that the browser should use for the loaded page.
Example:

```
<meta http-equiv="content-script-type" content="text/javascript">
```

content-style-type

This header sets the default style sheet language used in the document.
Example:

```
<meta http-equiv="content-style-type" content="text/css">
```

content-type

This header specifies the type of media that is sent between the browser and server. You can also extend the content-type to other character sets by including a charset declaration in the content-type value.
Example:

```
<meta http-equiv="content-type" content="text/html; charset=ISO646-US">
```

default-style

This header sets the default style sheet used document.
Example:

```
<meta http-equiv="default-style" content="stylesheet">
```

expires

This header sets the expiration date and time of the document.
Example:

```
<meta http-equiv="expires" content="WED, 20 Jan 1999 15:20:30 GMT">
```

refresh

This header specifies how frequently a page should be reloaded. Additionally, an alternate URL can be used when reloading the page.

Example:

```
<meta http-equiv="refresh" content="3">
<meta http-equiv="refresh" content="3;url=http://www.advocar.com">
```

set-cookie

This header sets a cookie (only in Netscape Navigator).

Example:

```
<meta http-equiv="set-cookie"
content="cookievalue=xxx;expires=Friday, 31-Jan-03 12:59:59 GMT; path=/">
```

window-target

This header allows you to specify a window or frame as the target for the current page. By specifying "_top" as the target, you can make sure that the linked page is not displayed within another frameset.

Example:

```
<meta http-equiv="window-target" content="_top">
```

name

Compatibility: NN4, NN6, NN7, IE4, IE5, IE5.5, IE6

This attribute is used to include other types of non-header information (such as the author, a description of the document, copyright information, keywords, and so on) in the document. Search engines usually look for the following names: author, copyright, description, and keywords. Other possible names are generator, progid, robots, and template.

Syntax:

```
<meta name="value" content=". . .">
```

author

Identifies the author of the document.

Example:

```
<meta name="author" content="Lázaro Issi Cohen">
```

copyright

An unqualified copyright statement.

description

This describes the document in the browser window. This is used by some search engines to provide a document description to the users performing searches.

Example:

```
<meta name="description" content="High Tech books.">
```

generator

Identifies the name and version number of the publishing or development tool used in creating the document.
Example:

```
<meta name="generator" content="Dreamweaver4.0">
```

keywords

A comma-separated list of keywords used by search engines to index the document.
Example:

```
<meta name="keywords" content="art, oils, landscape">
```

progid

The program ID of the document's editor.
Example:

```
<meta name="progid" content="word.document">
```

robots

This header instructs web robots how to act on the page. Web robots are commonly used by search engines such as Altavista and Google.
Example:

```
<meta name="robots" content="noindex">
```

template

The name and location of the template used to create or modify the document.
Example:

```
<meta name="template" content="C:\Program Files\Microsoft Office\Office\html.dot">
```

scheme

Compatibility: NN6, NN7, IE6

This header allows the browser to correctly interpret data formats used in different regions of the world. The following two examples imply MM-DD-YYYY and DD-MM-YYYY formats, respectively:

```
<meta scheme="USA" name="date" content="10-08-2003">
<meta scheme="Europe" name="date" content="10-08-2003">
```

The following is a W3C example for an item cataloged according to the Dewey Decimal System.

```
<meta scheme="dds" name="description" content="04.251 Supercomputers systems design">
```

Other <meta> Tags

Apple <meta> Tags   Author-Corporate, Author-Personal, Publisher-Email, Identifier-URL, Identifier, Coverage, Bookmark.

Eastman Kodak <meta> Tags   EKBU, EKdocType, EKdocOwner, EKdocTech, EKreviewDate, EKArea.

IBM <meta> Tags   ABSTRACT, CC, ALIAS, OWNER.

Microsoft <meta> Tags   Page-Enter, Page-Exit, Site-Enter, Site-Exit (filters and transitions).

Example:

```
<meta http-equiv="Page-Enter" content="revealTrans(Duration=4.0,Transition=3)">
```

<meta> Event Handlers (7)

```
onLayoutComplete
```

<meta> CSS Attributes and JavaScript Style Properties (8)

The names are in CSS syntax. See the introduction to this chapter for the JavaScript syntax rules. Names noted with an asterisk (*) are JavaScript properties only.

```
background-position-x, background-position-y, layout-grid, layout-grid-mode,
pixelBottom(*), pixelHeight(*), pixelLeft(*), pixelRight(*), pixelTop(*),
pixelWidth(*), posBottom(*), posHeight(*), posLeft(*), posRight(*), posTop(*),
posWidth(*)
```

meta. JavaScript Properties (11)

```
charset, className, clientHeight, clientLeft, clientTop, clientWidth, content, dir,
firstChild, httpEquiv, innerHTML, isTextEdit, lang, lastChild, name, nextSibling,
nodeName, nodeType, nodeValue, offsetHeight, offsetLeft, offsetParent, offsetTop,
offsetWidth, ownerDocument, parentNode, parentTextEdit, previousSibling, scheme,
scrollHeight, scrollLeft, scrollTop, scrollWidth, tagName, title
```

meta. JavaScript Methods (12)

```
appendChild, cloneNode, contains, dragDrop, getAttribute, getAttributeNode,
getElementsByTagName, hasChildNodes, insertBefore, normalize, removeAttribute,
removeAttributeNode, removeChild, replaceChild, setAttribute, setAttributeNode
```

meta. JavaScript Collections (13)

---

attributes, childNodes

\<nobr\> ... \</nobr\>

Compatibility: NN4, NN6, NN7, IE4, IE5, IE5.5, IE6

This element causes text between its opening and closing tags to be displayed without any line breaks.

Syntax:

\<nobr *attributes events*\> . . . \</nobr\>

Example:

```
<html><head><title>nobr element example</title></head>
<body bgcolor="#FFFFFF" text="#000000">
<nobr>It was the night of March 10. The children were
    asleep across the hall; the last of the winter winds blew in gusts outside
    the windows of their bedroom.</nobr>
</body></html>
```

\<nobr\> HTML Attributes (6)

---

class, contenteditable, dir, disabled, height, id, lang, language, unselectable

---

\<nobr\> Event Handlers (7)

---

onBeforeActivate, onBeforeCopy, onBeforeCut, onBeforeEditFocus, onBeforePaste, onClick, onContextMenu, onCopy, onCut, onDblClick, onDrag, onDragEnd, onDragEnter, onDragLeave, onDragOver, onDragStart, onDrop, onFocusIn, onFocusOut, onHelp, onKeyDown, onKeyPress, onKeyUp, onLoseCapture, onMouseEnter, onMouseLeave, onMouseMove, onMouseOver, onMouseUp, onMouseWheel, onPaste, onPropertyChange, onReadyStateChange, onSelectStart

---

\<nobr\> CSS Attributes and JavaScript Style Properties (8)

The names are in CSS syntax. See the introduction to this chapter for the JavaScript syntax rules. Names noted with an asterisk (*) are JavaScript properties only.

---

background, background-color, background-image, background-position-x, background-position-y, background-repeat, behavior, border, border-bottom, border-bottom-color, border-bottom-style, border-bottom-width, border-color, border-left, border-left-color, border-left-style, border-left-width, border-right, border-right-color, border-right-style, border-right-width, border-style, border-top, border-top-color, border-top-style, border-top-width, border-width, color, direction, display, filter, font, hasLayout(*), height, layout-grid, layout-grid-mode, margin, margin-bottom, margin-left, margin-right, margin-top, padding, padding-bottom, padding-left, padding-right, padding-top, pixelBottom(*), pixelHeight(*), pixelLeft(*), pixelRight(*), pixelTop(*), pixelWidth(*), posBottom(*), posHeight(*), posLeft(*), posRight(*), posTop(*), posWidth(*), text-autospace, text-overflow, text-underline-position, unicode-bidi, visibility, width, word-wrap, zoom

\<nobr\> Microsoft Behaviors (9)

clientCaps, download, homePage

\<nobr\> Microsoft Filters (10)

Alpha, Barn, BasicImage, BlendTrans, Blinds, Blur, CheckerBoard, Chroma, Compositor, DropShadow, Emboss, Engrave, Fade, FlipH, FlipV, Glow, GradientWipe, Gray, ICMFilter, Inset, Invert, Iris, Light, MaskFilter, Matrix, MotionBlur, Pixelate, RadialWipe, RandomBars, RandomDissolve, RevealTrans, Shadow, Slide, Spiral, Stretch, Strips, Wave, Wheel, Xray, Zigzag

nobr. JavaScript Properties (11)

canHaveHTML, className, clientHeight, clientLeft, clientTop, clientWidth, contentEditable, dir, disabled, hasLayout, height, id, innerHTML, innerText, isContentEditable, isDisabled, isMultiLine, isTextEdit, lang, language, offsetHeight, offsetLeft, offsetParent, offsetTop, offsetWidth, outerHTML, outerText, parentElement, parentTextEdit, readyState, scopeName, scrollHeight, scrollLeft, scrollTop, scrollWidth, sourceIndex, tagName, tagUrn, uniqueID

nobr. JavaScript Methods (12)

addBehavior, attachEvent, click, componentFromPoint, contains, detachEvent, fireEvent, getAttribute, getAttributeNode, getBoundingClientRect, getClientRects, getExpression, insertAdjacentHTML, insertAdjacentText, normalize, releaseCapture, removeAttribute, removeAttributeNode, removeBehavior, removeExpression, scrollIntoView, setAttribute, setAttributeNode, setCapture, setExpression

nobr. JavaScript Collections (13)

behaviorUrns

nobr. JavaScript Objects (14)

currentStyle, runtimeStyle, style

\<noembed\> ... \</noembed\>

Compatibility: NN4

This element typically contains a message for browsers that do not support \<embed\> elements. It does not have any attributes.

Syntax:

```
<noembed> . . . </noembed>
```

Example:

```
<html><head><title>noembed element example</title></head>
<body bgcolor="#FFFFFF" text="#000000">
<noembed>If this text appears, your browser does not support the embed element</
noembed>
</body></html>
```

<noframes> ... </noframes>

Compatibility: NN4, NN6, NN7, IE4, IE5, IE5.5, IE6

This element is used to deliver HTML content to those browsers that do not support frames or to those that have frames turned off.

Syntax:

```
<noframes attributes events> . . . </noframes>
```

Example:

```
<frameset rows="33%, 33%, *" cols="33%, 33%, *">
    <frame name="frame_1" src="frame(1).html">
    <frame name="frame_2" src="frame(2).html">
    <frame name="frame_3" src="frame(3).html">
    <frame name="frame_4" src="frame(4).html">
    <frame name="frame_5" src="frame(5).html">
    <frame name="frame_6" src="frame(6).html">
    <frame name="frame_7" src="frame(7).html">
    <frame name="frame_8" src="frame(8).html">
    <frame name="frame_9" src="frame(9).html">
    </frameset>
<noframes>Your system doesn't support frames.</noframes>
```

<noframes> HTML Attributes (6)

```
dir, id, lang, style, title
```

<noframes> Event Handlers (7)

```
onClick, onDblClick, onKeyDown, onKeyPress, onKeyUp, onLoseCapture, onMouseMove,
onMouseOut, onMouseOver, onMouseUp, onReadyStateChange
```

<noframes> CSS Attributes and JavaScript Style Properties (8)

The names are in CSS syntax. See the introduction to this chapter for the JavaScript syntax rules.

```
behavior, text-autospace, text-underline-position, zoom
```

<noframes> Microsoft Behaviors (9)

```
clientCaps, download, homePage
```

noframes. JavaScript Properties (11)

```
align, canHaveHTML, className, clientHeight, clientWidth, dir, firstChild, id,
innerHTML, isContentEditable, isDisabled, isMultiLine, lang, lastChild,
nextSibling, nodeName, nodeType, nodeValue, offsetHeight, offsetLeft, offsetParent,
offsetTop, offsetWidth, ownerDocument, parentElement, parentNode, previousSibling,
readyState, scopeName, scrollHeight, scrollLeft, scrollTop, scrollWidth, tagName,
tagUrn, title
```

noframes. JavaScript Methods (12)

```
addBehavior, appendChild, cloneNode, componentFromPoint, fireEvent, getAttribute,
getAttributeNode, getElementsByTagName, hasChildNodes, insertBefore, normalize,
removeAttribute, removeAttributeNode, removeBehavior, removeChild, replaceChild,
setAttribute, setAttributeNode
```

noframes. JavaScript Collections (13)

```
attributes, behaviorUrns, childNodes
```

<noscript> ... </noscript>

Compatibility: NN4, NN6, NN7, IE4, IE5, IE5.5, IE6

This element causes browsers to display content between its opening and closing tags as HTML, both in cases where the browser does not support JavaScript, and where the JavaScript functionality has been turned off. If JavaScript is supported, the content between <noscript> and </noscript> is not displayed on the page.

Syntax:

```
<noscript attributes events> . . . </noscript>
```

Example:

```
<script language="JavaScript">
<!--
function name() {
commands
```

```
    }
//-->
</script>
<noscript>Your browser doesn't support script codes.</noscript>
```

<noscript> HTML Attributes (6)

id

<noscript> Event Handlers (7)

onClick, onDblClick, onKeyDown, onKeyPress, onKeyUp, onMouseMove, onMouseOut,
onMouseOver, onMouseUp, onReadyStateChange

<noscript> CSS Attributes and JavaScript Style Properties (8)

The names are in CSS syntax. See the introduction to this chapter for the
JavaScript syntax rules.

behavior, text-autospace, text-underline-position, zoom

<noscript> Microsoft Behaviors (9)

clientCaps, download, homePage

noscript. JavaScript Properties (11)

align, canHaveHTML, className, clientHeight, clientWidth, dir, firstChild, id,
innerHTML, isContentEditable, isDisabled, isMultiLine, lang, lastChild,
nextSibling, nodeName, nodeType, nodeValue, offsetHeight, offsetLeft, offsetParent,
offsetTop, offsetWidth, ownerDocument, parentElement, parentNode, previousSibling,
readyState, scopeName, scrollHeight, scrollLeft, scrollTop, scrollWidth, tagName,
tagUrn, title

noscript. JavaScript Methods (12)

addBehavior, appendChild, cloneNode, componentFromPoint, fireEvent, getAttribute,
getAttributeNode, getElementsByTagName, hasChildNodes, insertBefore, normalize,
removeAttribute, removeAttributeNode, removeBehavior, removeChild, replaceChild,
setAttribute, setAttributeNode

noscript. JavaScript Collections (13)

attributes, behaviorUrns, childNodes

<object> ... </object>

Compatibility: NN4, NN6, NN7, IE4, IE5, IE5.5, IE6

This element allows an object to be inserted in the page. It can be used for a variety of purposes, including as an alternate to the <img> element, and it provides an effective way to deal with new media while maintaining backward compatibility. This element also gives you control over the data and code in the created object.

The text between the element's opening and closing tags is displayed in the event that the object cannot be loaded.

Syntax:

```
<object attributes events> . . . </object>
```

Example:

```
<html><head><title>object element example</title></head>
<body bgcolor="#FFFFFF" text="#000000">
  <object data="area1.gif" shapes>
  <a target="main" shape="rect" coords="0, 0, 100, 50" href="http://www.w3c.com"></a>
  <a target="main" shape="rect" coords="100, 0, 200, 50" href="http://
www.microsoft.com"></a>
  <a target="main" shape="rect" coords="0, 50, 100, 100" href="http://
www.msn.com"></a>
  <a target="main" shape="rect" coords="100, 50, 200, 100" href="http://
www.yahoo.com"></a></object><br>
    <object classid="clsid:22D6F312-B0F6-11D0-94AB-0080C74C7E95">
    <span style="color:red">Object failed to load</span>
</object>
</body></html>
```

<object> HTML Attributes (6)

accesskey, align, alt, archive, border, class, classid, code, codebase, codetype, contenteditable, data, declare, dir, height, hidefocus, hspace, id, lang, language, name, standby, style, tabindex, title, type, unselectable, usemap, vspace, width

<object> Event Handlers (7)

onActivate, onAfterUpdate, onBeforeDeactivate, onBeforeEditFocus, onBeforeUpdate, onBlur, onCellChange, onClick, onControlSelect, onDataAvailable, onDatasetChanged, onDatasetComplete, onDblClick, onDeactivate, onDrag, onDragEnd, onDragEnter, onDragLeave, onDragOver, onDragStart, onDrop, onError, onErrorUpdate, onFocus, onHelp, onKeyDown, onKeyPress, onKeyUp, onLoad, onLoseCapture, onMouseDown, onMouseMove, onMouseOut, onMouseOver, onMouseUp, onMove, onMoveEnd, onMoveStart, onPropertyChange, onReadyStateChange, onResize, onResizeEnd, onResizeStart, onRowEnter, onRowExit, onRowsDelete, onRowsInserted, onScroll, onSelectStart

<object> CSS Attributes and JavaScript Style Properties (8)

The names are in CSS syntax. See the introduction to this chapter for the JavaScript syntax rules. Names noted with an asterisk (*) are JavaScript properties only.

background-position-x, background-position-y, behavior, border, border-bottom, border-bottom-color, border-bottom-style, border-bottom-width, border-color, border-left, border-left-color, border-left-style, border-left-width, border-right, border-right-color, border-right-style, border-right-width, border-style, border-top, border-top-color, border-top-style, border-top-width, border-width, bottom, clear, clip, cursor, direction, display, float, hasLayout(*), height, layout-grid, layout-grid-mode, left, margin, margin-bottom, margin-left, margin-right, margin-top, padding, padding-bottom, padding-left, padding-right, padding-top, pixelBottom(*), pixelHeight(*), pixelLeft(*), pixelRight(*), pixelTop(*), pixelWidth(*), posBottom(*), posHeight(*), position, posLeft(*), posRight(*), posTop(*), posWidth(*), right, scrollbar-3dlight-color, scrollbar-arrow-color, scrollbar-base-color, scrollbar-darkshadow-color, scrollbar-face-color, scrollbar-highlight-color, scrollbar-shadow-color, scrollbar-track-color, styleFloat(*), text-autospace, text-underline-position, top, unicode-bidi, visibility, word-wrap, zoom

\<object> Microsoft Behaviors (9)

clientCaps, download, homePage, httpFolder, saveFavorite, saveHistory, saveSnapshot, userData

\<object> Microsoft Filters (10)

Alpha, Barn, BasicImage, BlendTrans, Blinds, Blur, CheckerBoard, Chroma, Compositor, DropShadow, Emboss, Engrave, Fade, FlipH, FlipV, Glow, GradientWipe, Gray, ICMFilter, Inset, Invert, Iris, Light, MaskFilter, Matrix, MotionBlur, Pixelate, RadialWipe, RandomBars, RandomDissolve, RevealTrans, Shadow, Slide, Spiral, Stretch, Strips, Wave, Wheel, Xray, Zigzag

object. JavaScript Properties (11)

accessKey, align, alt, altHTML, archive, BaseHref, border, canHaveChildren, canHaveHTML, classid, className, clientHeight, clientLeft, clientTop, clientWidth, code, codeBase, codeType, cursor, data, declare, dir, disabled, fieldDelim, firstChild, form, hasLayout, height, hideFocus, hspace, id, innerHTML, isContentEditable, isDisabled, isMultiLine, isTextEdit, lang, language, lastChild, name, nextSibling, nodeName, nodeType, nodeValue, object, offsetHeight, offsetLeft, offsetParent, offsetTop, offsetWidth, outerHTML, outerText, ownerDocument, parentElement, parentNode, parentTextEdit, previousSibling, readyState, recordset, scopeName, scrollHeight, scrollLeft, scrollTop, scrollWidth, sourceIndex, standby, tabIndex, tagName, tagUrn, title, type, uniqueID, useMap, vspace, width

object. JavaScript Methods (12)

addBehavior, appendChild, applyElement, attachEvent, blur, clearAttributes, click, cloneNode, componentFromPoint, detachEvent, dragDrop, fireEvent, focus, getAdjacentText, getAttribute, getAttributeNode, getBoundingClientRect, getClientRects, getElementsByTagName, getExpression, hasChildNodes, insertAdjacentElement, insertBefore, mergeAttributes, namedRecordset, normalize, releaseCapture, removeAttribute, removeAttributeNode, removeBehavior, removeChild, removeExpression, removeNode, replaceAdjacentText, replaceChild, replaceNode, scrollIntoView, setActive, setAttribute, setAttributeNode, setCapture, setExpression, swapNode

object. JavaScript Collections (13)

all, attributes, behaviorUrns, childNodes

object. JavaScript Objects (14)

currentStyle, runtimeStyle, style

<ol> ... </ol>

Compatibility: NN4, NN6, NN7, IE4, IE5, IE5.5, IE6

This element creates an indented numbered (ordered) list. This element is used in conjunction with the <li> element, which creates each item in the list.

Syntax:

<ol *attributes events*> . . . </ol>

Example:

```
<html><head><title>ol element example</title></head>
<body bgcolor="#FFFFFF" text="#000000">
  <ol type="I">
    <li>first item</li>
    <li>second item</li>
    <li>third item</li>
    <li>fourth item</li>
    <li>fifth item</li>
  </ol>
</body></html>
```

<ol> HTML Attributes (6)

accesskey, begin, class, compact, contenteditable, dir, disabled, end, hidefocus, id, lang, language, start, style, syncmaster, systemBitrate, systemCaptions, systemLanguage, systemOverdubOrSubtitle, tabindex, timecontainer, title, type, unselectable

<ol> Event Handlers (7)

onActivate, onBeforeActivate, onBeforeCopy, onBeforeCut, onBeforeDeactivate, onBeforeEditFocus, onBeforePaste, onBlur, onClick, onContextMenu, onControlSelect, onCopy, onCut, onDblClick, onDeactivate, onDrag, onDragEnd, onDragEnter, onDragLeave, onDragOver, onDragStart, onDrop, onFocus, onFocusIn, onFocusOut, onHelp, onKeyDown, onKeyPress, onKeyUp, onLayoutComplete, onLoseCapture, onMouseDown, onMouseEnter, onMouseLeave, onMouseMove, onMouseOut, onMouseOver, onMouseUp, onMouseWheel, onMove, onMoveEnd, onMoveStart, onPaste, onPropertyChange, onReadyStateChange, onResize, onResizeEnd, onResizeStart, onSelectStart, onTimeError

`<ol>` CSS Attributes and JavaScript Style Properties (8)

The names are in CSS syntax. See the introduction to this chapter for the JavaScript syntax rules. Names noted with an asterisk (*) are JavaScript properties only.

```
!important, accelerator, background, background-attachment, background-color,
background-image, background-position, background-position-x, background-position-
y, background-repeat, behavior, border, border-bottom, border-bottom-color, border-
bottom-style, border-bottom-width, border-color, border-left, border-left-color,
border-left-style, border-left-width, border-right, border-right-color, border-
right-style, border-right-width, border-style, border-top, border-top-color,
border-top-style, border-top-width, border-width, bottom, clear, clip, color,
cursor, direction, display, filter, float, font, font-family, font-size, font-
style, font-variant, font-weight, hasLayout(*), height, layout-flow, layout-grid,
layout-grid-char, layout-grid-line, layout-grid-mode, layout-grid-type, left,
letter-spacing, line-break, line-height, list-style, list-style-image, list-style-
position, list-style-type, margin, margin-bottom, margin-left, margin-right,
margin-top, overflow, overflow-x, overflow-y, padding, padding-bottom, padding-
left, padding-right, padding-top, page-break-after, page-break-before,
pixelBottom(*), pixelHeight(*), pixelLeft(*), pixelRight(*), pixelTop(*),
pixelWidth(*), posBottom(*), posHeight(*), position, posLeft(*), posRight(*),
posTop(*), posWidth(*), right, styleFloat(*), text-align, text-align-last, text-
autospace, text-decoration, text-indent, text-justify, text-kashida-space, text-
overflow, text-transform, text-underline-position, textDecorationBlink(*),
textDecorationLineThrough(*), textDecorationNone(*), textDecorationOverline(*),
textDecorationUnderline(*), top, unicode-bidi, visibility, white-space, width,
word-break, word-spacing, word-wrap, writing-mode, z-index, zoom
```

`<ol>` Microsoft Behaviors (9)

```
clientCaps, download, homePage, httpFolder, saveFavorite, saveHistory,
saveSnapshot, time, time2, userData
```

`<ol>` Microsoft Filters (10)

```
Alpha, Barn, BasicImage, BlendTrans, Blinds, Blur, CheckerBoard, Chroma,
Compositor, DropShadow, Emboss, Engrave, Fade, FlipH, FlipV, Glow, GradientWipe,
Gray, ICMFilter, Inset, Invert, Iris, Light, MaskFilter, Matrix, MotionBlur,
Pixelate, RadialWipe, RandomBars, RandomDissolve, RevealTrans, Shadow, Slide,
Spiral, Stretch, Strips, Wave, Wheel, Xray, Zigzag
```

ol. JavaScript Properties (11)

```
accessKey, blockDirection, canHaveChildren, canHaveHTML, className, clientHeight,
clientLeft, clientTop, clientWidth, compact, contentEditable, cursor, dir,
disabled, end, firstChild, hasLayout, hideFocus, id, innerHTML, innerText,
isContentEditable, isDisabled, isMultiLine, isTextEdit, lang, language, lastChild,
nextSibling, nodeName, nodeType, nodeValue, offsetHeight, offsetLeft, offsetParent,
offsetTop, offsetWidth, outerHTML, outerText, ownerDocument, parentElement,
parentNode, parentTextEdit, previousSibling, readyState, scopeName, scrollHeight,
scrollLeft, scrollTop, scrollWidth, sourceIndex, start, tabIndex, tagName, tagUrn,
title, type, uniqueID
```

ol. JavaScript Methods (12)

addBehavior, appendChild, applyElement, attachEvent, blur, clearAttributes, click, cloneNode, componentFromPoint, contains, detachEvent, dragDrop, fireEvent, focus, getAdjacentText, getAttribute, getAttributeNode, getBoundingClientRect, getClientRects, getElementsByTagName, getExpression, hasChildNodes, insertAdjacentElement, insertAdjacentHTML, insertAdjacentText, insertBefore, mergeAttributes, normalize, releaseCapture, removeAttribute, removeAttributeNode, removeBehavior, removeChild, removeExpression, removeNode, replaceAdjacentText, replaceChild, replaceNode, scrollIntoView, setActive, setAttribute, setAttributeNode, setCapture, setExpression, swapNode

ol. JavaScript Collections (13)

all, attributes, behaviorUrns, childNodes, children

ol. JavaScript Objects (14)

currentStyle, runtimeStyle, style

<optgroup> ... </optgroup>

Compatibility: NN6, NN7, IE6

This element allows multiple options within a <select> element list to be grouped together. Note that option groups cannot be nested within other option groups.

Syntax:

```
<optgroup attributes events> . . . </optgroup>
```

Example:

```
<html><head><title>optgroup element example</title></head>
<body bgcolor="#FFFFFF" text="#000000">
  <form name="form2" method="post" action="">
    <p><span class="example">
    <select name="select1">
      <optgroup label="First Group">
        <option>First item in first group </option>
        <option>Second item in first group </option>
        <option>Third item in first group </option>
      </optgroup>
      <optgroup label="Second Group">
        <option>First item in second group </option>
        <option>Second item in second group </option>
        <option>Third item in second group </option>
      </optgroup>
    </select>
    </span></p>
```

```
  </form>
</body></html>
```

<optgroup> HTML Attributes (6)

disabled, label

<optgroup> Event Handlers (7)

onBlur, onChange, onClick, onDblClick, onFocus, onKeyDown, onKeyPress, onKeyUp, onMouseDown, onMouseMove, onMouseOut, onMouseOver, onMouseUp

optgroup. JavaScript Properties (11)

className, clientHeight, clientWidth, dir, firstChild, id, innerHTML, label, lang, lastChild, nextSibling, nodeName, nodeType, nodeValue, offsetHeight, offsetLeft, offsetParent, offsetTop, offsetWidth, ownerDocument, parentNode, previousSibling, scrollHeight, scrollLeft, scrollTop, scrollWidth, tagName, title

optgroup. JavaScript Methods (12)

appendChild, cloneNode, getAttribute, getAttributeNode, getElementsByTagName, hasChildNodes, insertBefore, normalize, removeAttribute, removeAttributeNode, removeChild, replaceChild, setAttribute, setAttributeNode

optgroup. JavaScript Collections (13)

attributes, childNodes

<option> ... </option>

Compatibility: NN4, NN6, NN7, IE4, IE5, IE5.5, IE6

This element is used to create a list item in a <select> element list.

Syntax:

```
<option attributes events> . . . </option>
```

Example:

```
<html><head><title>option element example</title></head>
<body bgcolor="#FFFFFF" text="#000000">
  <form name="form2" method="post" action="">
    <p><span class="example">
    <select name="select1">
      <optgroup label="First Group">
        <option>First item in first group </option>
        <option>Second item in first group </option>
```

```
        <option>Third item in first group </option>
      </optgroup>
    <optgroup label="Second Group">
        <option>First item in second group </option>
        <option>Second item in second group </option>
        <option>Third item in second group </option>
    </optgroup>
    </select>
    </span></p>
  </form>
</body></html>
```

<option> HTML Attributes (6)

begin, class, dir, disabled, end, id, label, lang, language, selected, syncmaster,
systemBitrate, systemCaptions, systemLanguage, systemOverdubOrSubtitle,
timecontainer, value

<option> Event Handlers (7)

onBlur, onChange, onClick, onDblClick, onDrag, onDragEnd, onDragEnter, onDragLeave,
onDragOver, onDragStart, onDrop, onFocus, onKeyDown, onKeyPress, onKeyUp,
onLayoutComplete, onLoseCapture, onMouseDown, onMouseMove, onMouseOut, onMouseOver,
onPropertyChange, onReadyStateChange, onSelectStart, onTimeError

<option> CSS Attributes and JavaScript Style Properties (8)

The names are in CSS syntax. See the introduction to this chapter for the
JavaScript syntax rules. Names noted with an asterisk (*) are JavaScript
properties only.

background-attachment, background-color, background-position-x, background-
position-y, behavior, clear, color, direction, hasLayout(*), height, layout-flow,
layout-grid, layout-grid-mode, pixelBottom(*), pixelHeight(*), pixelLeft(*),
pixelRight(*), pixelTop(*), pixelWidth(*), posBottom(*), posHeight(*), posLeft(*),
posRight(*), posTop(*), posWidth(*), text-autospace, text-underline-position,
unicode-bidi, width, word-wrap, writing-mode, zoom

<option> Microsoft Behaviors (9)

clientCaps, download, homePage, httpFolder, saveFavorite, saveHistory, time, time2,
userData

option. JavaScript Properties (11)

canHaveChildren, canHaveHTML, className, clientHeight, clientLeft, clientTop,
clientWidth, defaultSelected, dir, disabled, end, firstChild, form, hasLayout, id,
index, innerHTML, innerText, isContentEditable, isDisabled, isMultiLine,
isTextEdit, label, lang, language, lastChild, nextSibling, nodeName, nodeType,

nodeValue, offsetHeight, offsetLeft, offsetParent, offsetTop, offsetWidth,
ownerDocument, parentElement, parentNode, parentTextEdit, previousSibling,
readyState, scopeName, scrollHeight, scrollLeft, scrollTop, scrollWidth, selected,
tagName, tagUrn, text, title, uniqueID, value

option. JavaScript Methods (12)

addBehavior, appendChild, applyElement, attachEvent, clearAttributes, click,
cloneNode, componentFromPoint, contains, detachEvent, dragDrop, fireEvent,
getAdjacentText, getAttribute, getAttributeNode, getBoundingClientRect,
getClientRects, getElementsByTagName, getExpression, hasChildNodes,
insertAdjacentElement, insertAdjacentHTML, insertAdjacentText, insertBefore,
mergeAttributes, normalize, releaseCapture, removeAttribute, removeAttributeNode,
removeBehavior, removeChild, removeExpression, removeNode, replaceAdjacentText,
replaceChild, replaceNode, setAttribute, setAttributeNode, setCapture,
setExpression, swapNode

option. JavaScript Collections (13)

all, attributes, behaviorUrns, childNodes, children

option. JavaScript Objects (14)

currentStyle, runtimeStyle, style

<p> ... </p>

Compatibility: NN4, NN6, NN7, IE4, IE5, IE5.5, IE6

This element creates a paragraph. A closing tag is only required if a style sheet is
used with this element.

Syntax:

```
<p attributes events> . . . </p>
```

Example:

```
<html><head><title>p element example</title></head>
<body bgcolor="#FFFFFF" text="#000000">
<p align="center">This is the first paragraph.</p>
<p align="center">This is the second paragraph.</p>
<p align="center">This is the third paragraph.</p>
</body></html>
```

<p> HTML Attributes (6)

accesskey, align, begin, class, contenteditable, dir, disabled, end, hidefocus, id,
lang, language, style, syncmaster, systemBitrate, systemCaptions, systemLanguage,
systemOverdubOrSubtitle, tabindex, timecontainer, title, unselectable

\<p\> Event Handlers (7)

---

onActivate, onBeforeActivate, onBeforeCopy, onBeforeCut, onBeforeDeactivate, onBeforeEditFocus, onBeforePaste, onBlur, onClick, onContextMenu, onControlSelect, onCopy, onCut, onDblClick, onDeactivate, onDrag, onDragEnd, onDragEnter, onDragLeave, onDragOver, onDragStart, onDrop, onFocus, onFocusIn, onFocusOut, onHelp, onKeyDown, onKeyPress, onKeyUp, onLayoutComplete, onLoseCapture, onMouseDown, onMouseEnter, onMouseLeave, onMouseMove, onMouseOut, onMouseOver, onMouseUp, onMouseWheel, onMove, onMoveEnd, onMoveStart, onPaste, onPropertyChange, onReadyStateChange, onResize, onResizeEnd, onResizeStart, onSelectStart, onTimeError

---

\<p\> CSS Attributes and JavaScript Style Properties (8)

The names are in CSS syntax. See the introduction to this chapter for the JavaScript syntax rules. Names noted with an asterisk (*) are JavaScript properties only.

!important, :first-letter, :first-line, accelerator, background, background-attachment, background-color, background-image, background-position, background-position-x, background-position-y, background-repeat, behavior, border, border-bottom, border-bottom-color, border-bottom-style, border-bottom-width, border-color, border-left, border-left-color, border-left-style, border-left-width, border-right, border-right-color, border-right-style, border-right-width, border-style, border-top, border-top-color, border-top-style, border-top-width, border-width, bottom, clear, clip, color, cursor, direction, display, filter, float, font, font-family, font-size, font-style, font-variant, font-weight, hasLayout(*), height, layout-flow, layout-grid, layout-grid-char, layout-grid-line, layout-grid-mode, layout-grid-type, left, letter-spacing, line-break, line-height, margin, margin-bottom, margin-left, margin-right, margin-top, overflow, overflow-x, overflow-y, padding, padding-bottom, padding-left, padding-right, padding-top, page-break-after, page-break-before, pixelBottom(*), pixelHeight(*), pixelLeft(*), pixelRight(*), pixelTop(*), pixelWidth(*), posBottom(*), posHeight(*), position, posLeft(*), posRight(*), posTop(*), posWidth(*), right, styleFloat(*), text-align, text-align-last, text-autospace, text-decoration, text-indent, text-justify, text-kashida-space, text-overflow, text-transform, text-underline-position, textDecorationBlink(*), textDecorationLineThrough(*), textDecorationNone(*), textDecorationOverline(*), textDecorationUnderline(*), top, unicode-bidi, visibility, white-space, width, word-break, word-spacing, word-wrap, writing-mode, z-index, zoom

---

\<p\> Microsoft Behaviors (9)

---

clientCaps, download, homePage, httpFolder, saveFavorite, saveHistory, saveSnapshot, time, time2, userData

---

\<p\> Microsoft Filters (10)

Alpha, Barn, BasicImage, BlendTrans, Blinds, Blur, CheckerBoard, Chroma, Compositor, DropShadow, Emboss, Engrave, Fade, FlipH, FlipV, Glow, GradientWipe, Gray, ICMFilter, Inset, Invert, Iris, Light, MaskFilter, Matrix, MotionBlur, Pixelate, RadialWipe, RandomBars, RandomDissolve, RevealTrans, Shadow, Slide, Spiral, Stretch, Strips, Wave, Wheel, Xray, Zigzag

---

p. JavaScript Properties (11)

accessKey, align, blockDirection, canHaveChildren, canHaveHTML, className, clientHeight, clientLeft, clientTop, clientWidth, contentEditable, cursor, dir, disabled, end, firstChild, hasLayout, hideFocus, id, innerHTML, innerText, isContentEditable, isDisabled, isMultiLine, isTextEdit, lang, language, lastChild, nextSibling, nodeName, nodeType, nodeValue, offsetHeight, offsetLeft, offsetParent, offsetTop, offsetWidth, outerHTML, outerText, ownerDocument, parentElement, parentNode, parentTextEdit, previousSibling, readyState, scopeName, scrollHeight, scrollLeft, scrollTop, scrollWidth, sourceIndex, tabIndex, tagName, tagUrn, title, uniqueID

p. JavaScript Methods (12)

addBehavior, appendChild, applyElement, attachEvent, blur, clearAttributes, click, cloneNode, componentFromPoint, contains, detachEvent, dragDrop, fireEvent, focus, getAdjacentText, getAttribute, getAttributeNode, getBoundingClientRect, getClientRects, getElementsByTagName, getExpression, hasChildNodes, insertAdjacentElement, insertAdjacentHTML, insertAdjacentText, insertBefore, mergeAttributes, normalize, releaseCapture, removeAttribute, removeAttributeNode, removeBehavior, removeChild, removeExpression, removeNode, replaceAdjacentText, replaceChild, replaceNode, scrollIntoView, setActive, setAttribute, setAttributeNode, setCapture, setExpression, swapNode

p. JavaScript Collections (13)

all, attributes, behaviorUrns, childNodes, children

p. JavaScript Objects (14)

currentStyle, runtimeStyle, style

<param>

Compatibility: NN4, NN6, NN7, IE4, IE5, IE5.5, IE6

This element is used to establish the starting property values of the <applet>, <embed>, and <object> elements.

Syntax:

<param *attributes*>

Example:

```
<html><head><title>param element example</title></head>
<body bgcolor="#FFFFFF" text="#000000">
<center><object classid="clsid:D27CDB6E-AE6D-11cf-96B8-444553540000"
codebase="http://download.macromedia.com/pub/shockwave/cabs/flash/
swflash.cab#version=5,0,0,0" width="320" height="400">
    <param name="movie" value="anyflashmovie.swf">
```

```
<!--flash movie must be in the same directory as html file-->
    <param name="quality" value="high">
    <embed src="anyflashmovie.swf" quality="high" pluginspage="http://
www.macromedia.com/shockwave/download/index.cgi?P1_Prod_Version=ShockwaveFlash"
type="application/x-shockwave-flash" width="320" height="400">
</embed></object></center>
</body></html>
```

NOTE *The preceding example requires that you have a Flash movie called* anyflashmovie.swf *located in the same directory where the HTML file containing this code is located.*

<param> HTML Attributes (6)

datafld, dataformatas, datasrc, id, name, type, value, valuetype

param. JavaScript Properties (11)

className, clientHeight, clientWidth, dir, firstChild, id, innerHTML, lang,
lastChild, name, nextSibling, nodeName, nodeType, nodeValue, offsetHeight,
offsetLeft, offsetParent, offsetTop, offsetWidth, ownerDocument, parentNode,
previousSibling, scrollHeight, scrollLeft, scrollTop, scrollWidth, tagName, title,
type, value, valuetype

param. JavaScript Methods (12)

appendChild, cloneNode, getAttribute, getAttributeNode, getElementsByTagName,
hasChildNodes, insertBefore, normalize, removeAttribute, removeAttributeNode,
removeChild, replaceChild, setAttribute, setAttributeNode

param. JavaScript Collections (13)

attributes, childNodes

<plaintext> ... </plaintext>

Compatibility: NN4, IE4, IE5

This element displays text in a monospaced, or fixed-size, font. Any elements
included between the opening and closing tags will be displayed as plain text
(meaning that formatting will be ignored, and the tags will be displayed along
with the text). The <pre> element has similar rendering capabilities and is pre-
ferred over this element.

Syntax:

```
<plaintext attributes events> . . . </plaintext>
```

Example:

```
<html><head><title>plaintext element example</title></head>
<body bgcolor="#FFFFFF" text="#000000">
<p><plaintext>This <b>text</b> will not appear in bold.</plaintext></p></body></
html>
```

<plaintext> Event Handlers (7)

onActivate, onBeforeCopy, onBeforeCut, onBeforeDeactivate, onBeforePaste, onBlur,
onClick, onContextMenu, onControlSelect, onCopy, onCut, onDblClick, onDeactivate,
onDrag, onDragEnd, onDragEnter, onDragLeave, onDragOver, onDragStart, onDrop,
onFocus, onHelp, onKeyDown, onKeyPress, onKeyUp, onLoseCapture, onMouseDown,
onMouseEnter, onMouseLeave, onMouseMove, onMouseOut, onMouseOver, onMouseUp,
onPaste, onPropertyChange, onReadyStateChange, onResize, onResizeEnd,
onResizeStart, onSelectStart

plaintext. JavaScript Properties (11)

accessKey, align, blockDirection, canHaveChildren, canHaveHTML, clientHeight,
clientLeft, clientTop, clientWidth, contentEditable, cursor, dir, disabled,
firstChild, hasLayout, hideFocus, id, innerText, isDisabled, isMultiLine,
isTextEdit, lang, language, lastChild, nextSibling, nodeName, nodeType, nodeValue,
offsetHeight, offsetLeft, offsetParent, offsetTop, offsetWidth, outerHTML,
outerText, parentElement, parentNode, parentTextEdit, previousSibling, readyState,
scopeName, scrollHeight, scrollLeft, scrollTop, scrollWidth, tabIndex, tagName,
tagUrn, uniqueID

plaintext. JavaScript Methods (12)

addBehavior, appendChild, applyElement, attachEvent, blur, clearAttributes, click,
cloneNode, componentFromPoint, contains, detachEvent, fireEvent, focus,
getAdjacentText, getAttribute, getAttributeNode, getElementsByTagName,
hasChildNodes, insertAdjacentElement, insertAdjacentHTML, insertBefore,
mergeAttributes, normalize, releaseCapture, removeAttribute, removeAttributeNode,
removeBehavior, removeChild, removeNode, replaceAdjacentText, replaceChild,
replaceNode, scrollIntoView, setActive, setAttribute, setAttributeNode, setCapture,
swapNode

<pre> ... </pre>

Compatibility: NN4, NN6, NN7, IE4, IE5, IE5.5, IE6

This element renders a block of text in a fixed-width or monospaced font.
   Syntax:

```
<pre attributes events> . . . </pre>
```

Example:

```
<html><head><title>pre element example</title></head>
<body bgcolor="#FFFFFF" text="#000000">
<pre>No nonbreaking spaces ( ) are
necessary in a pre element.</pre>
</body></html>
```

<pre> HTML Attributes (6)

accesskey, begin, cols, class, contenteditable, dir, disabled, end, hidefocus, id, lang, language, style, syncmaster, systemBitrate, systemCaptions, systemLanguage, systemOverdubOrSubtitle, tabindex, timecontainer, title, unselectable, width, wrap

<pre> Event Handlers (7)

onActivate, onBeforeActivate, onBeforeCopy, onBeforeCut, onBeforeDeactivate, onBeforeEditFocus, onBeforePaste, onBlur, onClick, onContextMenu, onControlSelect, onCopy, onCut, onDblClick, onDeactivate, onDrag, onDragEnd, onDragEnter, onDragLeave, onDragOver, onDragStart, onDrop, onFocus, onFocusIn, onFocusOut, onHelp, onKeyDown, onKeyPress, onKeyUp, onLoseCapture, onMouseDown, onMouseEnter, onMouseLeave, onMouseMove, onMouseOut, onMouseOver, onMouseUp, onMouseWheel, onMove, onMoveEnd, onMoveStart, onPaste, onPropertyChange, onReadyStateChange, onResize, onResizeEnd, onResizeStart, onSelectStart, onTimeError

<pre> CSS Attributes and JavaScript Style Properties (8)

The names are in CSS syntax. See the introduction to this chapter for the JavaScript syntax rules. Names noted with an asterisk (*) are JavaScript properties only.

!important, :first-letter, :first-line, accelerator, background, background-attachment, background-color, background-image, background-position, background-position-x, background-position-y, background-repeat, behavior, border, border-bottom, border-bottom-color, border-bottom-style, border-bottom-width, border-color, border-left, border-left-color, border-left-style, border-left-width, border-right, border-right-color, border-right-style, border-right-width, border-style, border-top, border-top-color, border-top-style, border-top-width, border-width, bottom, clear, clip, color, cursor, direction, display, filter, float, font, font-family, font-size, font-style, font-variant, font-weight, hasLayout(*), height, layout-flow, layout-grid, layout-grid-char, layout-grid-line, layout-grid-mode, layout-grid-type, left, letter-spacing, line-break, line-height, margin, margin-bottom, margin-left, margin-right, margin-top, overflow, overflow-x, overflow-y, padding, padding-bottom, padding-left, padding-right, padding-top, page-break-after, page-break-before, pixelBottom(*), pixelHeight(*), pixelLeft(*), pixelRight(*), pixelTop(*), pixelWidth(*), posBottom(*), posHeight(*), position, posLeft(*), posRight(*), posTop(*), posWidth(*), right, styleFloat(*), text-align, text-align-last, text-autospace, text-decoration, text-indent, text-justify, text-kashida-space, text-overflow, text-transform, text-underline-position, textDecorationBlink(*), textDecorationLineThrough(*), textDecorationNone(*), textDecorationOverline(*), textDecorationUnderline(*), top, unicode-bidi, visibility, white-space, width, word-break, word-spacing, word-wrap, writing-mode, z-index, zoom

<pre> Microsoft Behaviors (9)

clientCaps, download, homePage, httpFolder, saveFavorite, saveHistory, saveSnapshot, time, time2, userData

<pre> Microsoft Filters (10)

Alpha, Barn, BasicImage, BlendTrans, Blinds, Blur, CheckerBoard, Chroma, Compositor, DropShadow, Emboss, Engrave, Fade, FlipH, FlipV, Glow, GradientWipe, Gray, ICMFilter, Inset, Invert, Iris, Light, MaskFilter, Matrix, MotionBlur, Pixelate, RadialWipe, RandomBars, RandomDissolve, RevealTrans, Shadow, Slide, Spiral, Stretch, Strips, Wave, Wheel, Xray, Zigzag

pre. JavaScript Properties (11)

accessKey, blockDirection, canHaveChildren, canHaveHTML, className, clientHeight, clientLeft, clientTop, clientWidth, contentEditable, cursor, dir, disabled, end, firstChild, hasLayout, hideFocus, id, innerHTML, innerText, isContentEditable, isDisabled, isMultiLine, isTextEdit, lang, language, lastChild, nextSibling, nodeName, nodeType, nodeValue, offsetHeight, offsetLeft, offsetParent, offsetTop, offsetWidth, outerHTML, outerText, ownerDocument, parentElement, parentNode, parentTextEdit, previousSibling, readyState, scopeName, scrollHeight, scrollLeft, scrollTop, scrollWidth, sourceIndex, tabIndex, tagName, tagUrn, title, uniqueID, width, wrap

pre. JavaScript Methods (12)

addBehavior, appendChild, applyElement, attachEvent, blur, clearAttributes, click, cloneNode, componentFromPoint, contains, detachEvent, fireEvent, focus, getAdjacentText, getAttribute, getAttributeNode, getBoundingClientRect, getClientRects, getElementsByTagName, getExpression, hasChildNodes, insertAdjacentElement, insertAdjacentHTML, insertAdjacentText, insertBefore, mergeAttributes, normalize, releaseCapture, removeAttribute, removeAttributeNode, removeBehavior, removeChild, removeExpression, removeNode, replaceAdjacentText, replaceChild, replaceNode, scrollIntoView, setActive, setAttribute, setAttributeNode, setCapture, setExpression, swapNode

pre. JavaScript Collections (13)

all, attributes, behaviorUrns, childNodes, children

pre. JavaScript Objects (14)

currentStyle, runtimeStyle, style

<q> ... </q>

Compatibility: NN6, NN7, IE4, IE5, IE5.5, IE6

This element causes text to be marked by the browser as a quotation. This element works like the <blockquote> element, except that the text contained between its opening and closing tags is not indented 40 pixels, as is the case with <blockquote>. The <blockquote> element is more appropriate for long quotations because it indents the text.

Syntax:

```
<q attributes events> . . . </q>
```

Example:

```
<html><head><title>q element example</title></head>
<body bgcolor="#FFFFFF" text="#000000">
<q><p>The q content is <big>not</big> rendered as a 40-pixel indented
block.</p></q>
</body></html>
```

<q> HTML Attributes (6)

accesskey, begin, cite, class, contenteditable, dir, disabled, end, hidefocus, id, lang, language, style, syncmaster, systemBitrate, systemCaptions, systemLanguage, systemOverdubOrSubtitle, tabindex, timecontainer, title, unselectable

<q> Event Handlers (7)

onActivate, onBeforeDeactivate, onBeforeEditFocus, onBlur, onClick, onControlSelect, onDblClick, onDeactivate, onDrag, onDragEnd, onDragEnter, onDragLeave, onDragOver, onDragStart, onDrop, onFocus, onHelp, onKeyDown, onKeyPress, onKeyUp, onMouseDown, onMouseMove, onMouseOut, onMouseOver, onMouseUp, onMove, onMoveEnd, onMoveStart, onReadyStateChange, onResizeEnd, onResizeStart, onSelectStart, onTimeError

<q> CSS Attributes and JavaScript Style Properties (8)

The names are in CSS syntax. See the introduction to this chapter for the JavaScript syntax rules. Names noted with an asterisk (*) are JavaScript properties only.

accelerator, background-position-x, background-position-y, behavior, border, border-bottom, border-bottom-color, border-bottom-style, border-bottom-width, border-color, border-left, border-left-color, border-left-style, border-left-width, border-right, border-right-color, border-right-style, border-right-width, border-style, border-top, border-top-color, border-top-style, border-top-width, border-width, direction, display, filter, hasLayout(*), height, layout-flow, layout-grid, layout-grid-mode, margin, margin-bottom, margin-left, margin-right, margin-top, overflow, overflow-x, overflow-y, padding, padding-bottom, padding-left, padding-right, padding-top, pixelBottom(*), pixelHeight(*), pixelLeft(*), pixelRight(*), pixelTop(*), pixelWidth(*), posBottom(*), posHeight(*), posLeft(*), posRight(*), posTop(*), posWidth(*), text-autospace, text-overflow, text-underline-position, unicode-bidi, white-space, width, word-wrap, writing-mode, zoom

`<q>` Microsoft Behaviors (9)

clientCaps, download, homePage, httpFolder, saveFavorite, saveHistory, saveSnapshot, time, time2, userData

`<q>` Microsoft Filters (10)

Alpha, Barn, BasicImage, BlendTrans, Blinds, Blur, CheckerBoard, Chroma, Compositor, DropShadow, Emboss, Engrave, Fade, FlipH, FlipV, Glow, GradientWipe, Gray, ICMFilter, Inset, Invert, Iris, Light, MaskFilter, Matrix, MotionBlur, Pixelate, RadialWipe, RandomBars, RandomDissolve, RevealTrans, Shadow, Slide, Spiral, Stretch, Strips, Wave, Wheel, Xray, Zigzag

q. JavaScript Properties (11)

accessKey, canHaveChildren, canHaveHTML, cite, className, clientHeight, clientWidth, contentEditable, dir, disabled, end, firstChild, hasLayout, hideFocus, id, innerHTML, innerText, isContentEditable, isDisabled, isMultiLine, isTextEdit, lang, language, lastChild, nextSibling, nodeName, nodeType, nodeValue, offsetHeight, offsetLeft, offsetParent, offsetTop, offsetWidth, outerHTML, outerText, ownerDocument, parentElement, parentNode, parentTextEdit, previousSibling, readyState, scopeName, scrollHeight, scrollLeft, scrollTop, scrollWidth, sourceIndex, tabIndex, tagName, tagUrn, title, uniqueID

q. JavaScript Methods (12)

addBehavior, appendChild, applyElement, attachEvent, blur, clearAttributes, cloneNode, componentFromPoint, detachEvent, fireEvent, focus, getAdjacentText, getAttribute, getAttributeNode, getBoundingClientRect, getClientRects, getElementsByTagName, getExpression, hasChildNodes, insertAdjacentElement, insertBefore, mergeAttributes, normalize, removeAttribute, removeAttributeNode, removeBehavior, removeChild, removeExpression, removeNode, replaceAdjacentText, replaceChild, replaceNode, setActive, setAttribute, setAttributeNode, setExpression, swapNode

q. JavaScript Collections (13)

all, attributes, behaviorUrns, childNodes, children

q. JavaScript Objects (14)

currentStyle, runtimeStyle, style

`<rt>`

Compatibility: IE5, IE5.5, IE6

This element is used with the `<ruby>` element. The text following `<rt>` appears as a note to the base text displayed by the `<ruby>` element.

Syntax:

```
<ruby> base text <rt attributes events> ruby text </ruby>
```

Example:

```
<html><head><title>ruby element example</title></head>
<body bgcolor="#FFFFFF" text="#000000">
<ruby><span style="font-family:Verdana; font-size:14pt">This is the base text.</
span><rt><span style="font-family:Times New Roman; font-size: 8pt; color:red">This
is the ruby text</span></ruby>
</body></html>
```

\<rt\> HTML Attributes (6)

accesskey, class, contenteditable, dir, disabled, hidefocus, id, lang, language, name, style, tabindex, title, unselectable

\<rt\> Event Handlers (7)

onActivate, onAfterUpdate, onBeforeActivate, onBeforeCut, onBeforeDeactivate, onBeforeEditFocus, onBeforePaste, onBeforeUpdate, onBlur, onClick, onContextMenu, onControlSelect, onCut, onDblClick, onDeactivate, onDragStart, onErrorUpdate, onFilterChange, onFocus, onFocusIn, onFocusOut, onHelp, onKeyDown, onKeyPress, onKeyUp, onMouseDown, onMouseEnter, onMouseLeave, onMouseMove, onMouseOut, onMouseOver, onMouseUp, onMouseWheel, onMove, onMoveEnd, onMoveStart, onPaste, onReadyStateChange, onResizeEnd, onResizeStart, onSelectStart

\<rt\> CSS Attributes and JavaScript Style Properties (8)

The names are in CSS syntax. See the introduction to this chapter for the JavaScript syntax rules. Names noted with an asterisk (*) are JavaScript properties only.

accelerator, background-position-x, background-position-y, behavior, cursor, direction, display, filter, float, height, layout-grid, layout-grid-mode, overflow, overflow-x, overflow-y, padding, padding-bottom, padding-left, padding-right, padding-top, pixelBottom(*), pixelHeight(*), pixelLeft(*), pixelRight(*), pixelTop(*), pixelWidth(*), posBottom(*), posHeight(*), posLeft(*), posRight(*), posTop(*), posWidth(*), styleFloat(*), text-autospace, text-overflow, text-underline-position, unicode-bidi, width, word-wrap, writing-mode, zoom

\<rt\> Microsoft Behaviors (9)

clientCaps, download, homePage

\<rt\> Microsoft Filters (10)

Alpha, Barn, BasicImage, BlendTrans, Blinds, Blur, CheckerBoard, Chroma, Compositor, DropShadow, Emboss, Engrave, Fade, FlipH, FlipV, Glow, GradientWipe, Gray, ICMFilter, Inset, Invert, Iris, Light, MaskFilter, Matrix, MotionBlur,

Pixelate, RadialWipe, RandomBars, RandomDissolve, RevealTrans, Shadow, Slide, Spiral, Stretch, Strips, Wave, Wheel, Xray, Zigzag

rt. JavaScript Properties (11)

accessKey, canHaveHTML, className, contentEditable, cursor, dir, disabled, hideFocus, id, innerHTML, innerText, isContentEditable, isDisabled, isMultiLine, lang, language, name, offsetHeight, offsetLeft, offsetParent, offsetTop, offsetWidth, outerHTML, outerText, parentElement, readyState, scopeName, tabIndex, tagName, tagUrn, title

rt. JavaScript Methods (12)

addBehavior, blur, componentFromPoint, fireEvent, focus, getAttributeNode, getExpression, normalize, removeAttributeNode, removeBehavior, removeExpression, setActive, setAttributeNode, setExpression

rt. JavaScript Collections (13)

behaviorUrns, children, filters

<ruby> ... </ruby>

Compatibility: IE5, IE5.5, IE6

This element is useful in defining text (known as base text) that is accompanied by a notation above or below the text. It is used in conjunction with the <rt> element, with the text specified before <rt> considered the base text, and the text following <rt> considered the notation. The <span> element can be used to set the formatting of each part of the element.

Syntax:

```
<ruby attributes events> base text <rt> ruby text </ruby>
```

Example:

```
<html><head><title>ruby element example</title></head>
<body bgcolor="#FFFFFF" text="#000000">
<ruby><span style="font-family:Verdana; font-size:14pt">This is the base text.</
span><rt><span style="font-family:Times New Roman; font-size: 8pt; color:red">This
is the ruby text</span></ruby>
</body></html>
```

<ruby> HTML Attributes (6)

accesskey, class, contenteditable, dir, disabled, hidefocus, id, lang, language, name, style, tabindex, title, unselectable

<ruby> Event Handlers (7)

onActivate, onAfterUpdate, onBeforeActivate, onBeforeCut, onBeforeDeactivate,
onBeforeEditFocus, onBeforePaste, onBeforeUpdate, onBlur, onClick, onContextMenu,
onControlSelect, onCut, onDblClick, onDeactivate, onDragStart, onErrorUpdate,
onFilterChange, onFocus, onFocusIn, onFocusOut, onHelp, onKeyDown, onKeyPress,
onKeyUp, onMouseDown, onMouseEnter, onMouseLeave, onMouseMove, onMouseOut,
onMouseOver, onMouseUp, onMouseWheel, onMove, onMoveEnd, onMoveStart, onPaste,
onReadyStateChange, onResizeEnd, onResizeStart, onSelectStart

<ruby> CSS Attributes and JavaScript Style Properties (8)

The names are in CSS syntax. See the introduction to this chapter for the
JavaScript syntax rules. Names noted with an asterisk (*) are JavaScript
properties only.

accelerator, background-position-x, background-position-y, behavior, clip, cursor,
direction, display, filter, float, height, layout-flow, layout-grid, layout-grid-
mode, overflow, overflow-x, overflow-y, padding, padding-bottom, padding-left,
padding-right, padding-top, pixelBottom(*), pixelHeight(*), pixelLeft(*),
pixelRight(*), pixelTop(*), pixelWidth(*), posBottom(*), posHeight(*), position,
posLeft(*), posRight(*), posTop(*), posWidth(*), ruby-align, ruby-overhang, ruby-
position, styleFloat(*), text-autospace, text-overflow, text-underline-position,
unicode-bidi, width, word-wrap, writing-mode, zoom

<ruby> Microsoft Behaviors (9)

clientCaps, download, homePage

<ruby> Microsoft Filters (10)

Alpha, Barn, BasicImage, BlendTrans, Blinds, Blur, CheckerBoard, Chroma,
Compositor, DropShadow, Emboss, Engrave, Fade, FlipH, FlipV, Glow, GradientWipe,
Gray, ICMFilter, Inset, Invert, Iris, Light, MaskFilter, Matrix, MotionBlur,
Pixelate, RadialWipe, RandomBars, RandomDissolve, RevealTrans, Shadow, Slide,
Spiral, Stretch, Strips, Wave, Wheel, Xray, Zigzag

ruby. JavaScript Properties (11)

accessKey, canHaveHTML, className, contentEditable, cursor, dir, disabled,
hideFocus, id, innerHTML, innerText, isContentEditable, isDisabled, isMultiLine,
lang, language, name, offsetHeight, offsetLeft, offsetParent, offsetTop,
offsetWidth, outerHTML, outerText, parentElement, readyState, scopeName, tabIndex,
tagName, tagUrn, title

ruby. JavaScript Methods (12)

addBehavior, blur, componentFromPoint, fireEvent, focus, getAttributeNode,
getExpression, normalize, removeAttributeNode, removeBehavior, removeExpression,
setActive, setAttributeNode, setExpression

ruby. JavaScript Collections (13)

behaviorUrns, children, filters

`<s> ... </s>`

Compatibility: NN4, NN6, NN7, IE4, IE5, IE5.5, IE6

This element causes text between its opening and closing tags to be displayed with a strike-out line through it. This element has been deprecated in favor of using CSS (see Chapter 1).

Syntax:

```
<s attributes events> . . . </s>
```

Example:

```
<html><head><title>s element example</title></head>
<body bgcolor="#FFFFFF" text="#000000">
<p><s>This is the text that has been crossed out.</s></p>
</body></html>
```

`<s>` HTML Attributes (6)

accesskey, begin, class, contenteditable, dir, disabled, end, hidefocus, id, lang, language, style, syncmaster, systemBitrate, systemCaptions, systemLanguage, systemOverdubOrSubtitle, tabindex, timecontainer, title, unselectable

`<s>` Event Handlers (7)

onActivate, onBeforeActivate, onBeforeCopy, onBeforeCut, onBeforeDeactivate, onBeforeEditFocus, onBeforePaste, onBlur, onClick, onContextMenu, onControlSelect, onCopy, onCut, onDblClick, onDeactivate, onDrag, onDragEnd, onDragEnter, onDragLeave, onDragOver, onDragStart, onDrop, onFocus, onFocusIn, onFocusOut, onHelp, onKeyDown, onKeyPress, onKeyUp, onLoseCapture, onMouseDown, onMouseEnter, onMouseLeave, onMouseMove, onMouseOut, onMouseOver, onMouseUp, onMouseWheel, onMove, onMoveEnd, onMoveStart, onPaste, onPropertyChange, onReadyStateChange, onResize, onResizeEnd, onResizeStart, onSelectStart, onTimeError

`<s>` CSS Attributes and JavaScript Style Properties (8)

The names are in CSS syntax. See the introduction to this chapter for the JavaScript syntax rules. Names noted with an asterisk (*) are JavaScript properties only.

!important, accelerator, background, background-attachment, background-color, background-image, background-position, background-position-x, background-position-y, background-repeat, behavior, border, border-bottom, border-bottom-color, border-bottom-style, border-bottom-width, border-color, border-left, border-left-color, border-left-style, border-left-width, border-right, border-right-color, border-right-style, border-right-width, border-style, border-top, border-top-color, border-top-style, border-top-width, border-width, bottom, clear, clip, color, cursor, direction, display, filter, float, font, font-family, font-size, font-style, font-variant, font-weight, hasLayout(*), height, layout-flow, layout-grid, layout-grid-mode, left, letter-spacing, line-height, margin, margin-bottom, margin-left, margin-right, margin-top, overflow, overflow-x, overflow-y, padding, padding-bottom, padding-left, padding-right, padding-top, pixelBottom(*), pixelHeight(*), pixelLeft(*), pixelRight(*), pixelTop(*), pixelWidth(*), posBottom(*), posHeight(*), position, posLeft(*), posRight(*), posTop(*), posWidth(*), right, styleFloat(*), text-autospace, text-decoration, text-overflow, text-transform, text-underline-position, textDecorationBlink(*), textDecorationLineThrough(*), textDecorationNone(*), textDecorationOverline(*), textDecorationUnderline(*), top, unicode-bidi, visibility, white-space, width, word-spacing, word-wrap, writing-mode, z-index, zoom

<s> Microsoft Behaviors (9)

clientCaps, download, homePage, httpFolder, saveFavorite, saveHistory, saveSnapshot, time, time2, userData

<s> Microsoft Filters (10)

Alpha, Barn, BasicImage, BlendTrans, Blinds, Blur, CheckerBoard, Chroma, Compositor, DropShadow, Emboss, Engrave, Fade, FlipH, FlipV, Glow, GradientWipe, Gray, ICMFilter, Inset, Invert, Iris, Light, MaskFilter, Matrix, MotionBlur, Pixelate, RadialWipe, RandomBars, RandomDissolve, RevealTrans, Shadow, Slide, Spiral, Stretch, Strips, Wave, Wheel, Xray, Zigzag

s. JavaScript Properties (11)

accessKey, canHaveChildren, canHaveHTML, className, clientHeight, clientLeft, clientTop, clientWidth, contentEditable, cursor, dir, disabled, end, firstChild, hasLayout, hideFocus, id, innerHTML, innerText, isContentEditable, isDisabled, isMultiLine, isTextEdit, lang, language, lastChild, nextSibling, nodeName, nodeType, nodeValue, offsetHeight, offsetLeft, offsetParent, offsetTop, offsetWidth, outerHTML, outerText, ownerDocument, parentElement, parentNode, parentTextEdit, previousSibling, readyState, scopeName, scrollHeight, scrollLeft, scrollTop, scrollWidth, sourceIndex, tabIndex, tagName, tagUrn, title, uniqueID

s. JavaScript Methods (12)

addBehavior, appendChild, applyElement, attachEvent, blur, clearAttributes, click, cloneNode, componentFromPoint, contains, detachEvent, fireEvent, focus, getAdjacentText, getAttribute, getAttributeNode, getBoundingClientRect, getClientRects, getElementsByTagName, getExpression, hasChildNodes, insertAdjacentElement, insertAdjacentHTML, insertAdjacentText, insertBefore, mergeAttributes, normalize, releaseCapture, removeAttribute, removeAttributeNode, removeBehavior, removeChild, removeExpression, removeNode, replaceAdjacentText, replaceChild, replaceNode, scrollIntoView, setActive, setAttribute, setAttributeNode, setCapture, setExpression, swapNode

s. JavaScript Collections (13)

all, attributes, behaviorUrns, childNodes, children

s. JavaScript Objects (14)

currentStyle, runtimeStyle, style

\<samp\> ... \</samp\>

Compatibility: NN4, NN6, NN7, IE4, IE5, IE5.5, IE6

This element causes text to be displayed in a monospaced or fixed-width font. It is typically used to display code samples.

Syntax:

\<samp *attributes events*\> . . . \</samp\>

Example:

```
<html><head><title>samp element example</title></head>
<body bgcolor="#FFFFFF" text="#000000">
<p>You can apply the <font size="5"><samp style="font-
weight:normal">systemLanguage</samp></font> attribute to nearly any element.</p>
</body></html>
```

\<samp\> HTML Attributes (6)

accesskey, begin, class, contenteditable, dir, disabled, end, hidefocus, id, lang, language, style, syncmaster, systemBitrate, systemCaptions, systemLanguage, systemOverdubOrSubtitle, tabindex, timecontainer, title, unselectable

\<samp\> Event Handlers (7)

onActivate, onBeforeActivate, onBeforeCopy, onBeforeCut, onBeforeDeactivate, onBeforeEditFocus, onBeforePaste, onBlur, onClick, onContextMenu, onControlSelect, onCopy, onCut, onDblClick, onDeactivate, onDrag, onDragEnd, onDragEnter, onDragLeave, onDragOver, onDragStart, onDrop, onFocus, onFocusIn, onFocusOut, onHelp, onKeyDown, onKeyPress, onKeyUp, onLoseCapture, onMouseDown, onMouseEnter, onMouseLeave, onMouseMove, onMouseOut, onMouseOver, onMouseUp, onMouseWheel, onMove, onMoveEnd, onMoveStart, onPaste, onPropertyChange, onReadyStateChange, onResize, onResizeEnd, onResizeStart, onSelectionChange, onSelectStart, onTimeError

\<samp\> CSS Attributes and JavaScript Style Properties (8)

The names are in CSS syntax. See the introduction to this chapter for the JavaScript syntax rules. Names noted with an asterisk (*) are JavaScript properties only.

!important, accelerator, background, background-attachment, background-color,
background-image, background-position, background-position-x, background-position-y,
background-repeat, behavior, border, border-bottom, border-bottom-color, border-
bottom-style, border-bottom-width, border-color, border-left, border-left-color,
border-left-style, border-left-width, border-right, border-right-color, border-
right-style, border-right-width, border-style, border-top, border-top-color, border-
top-style, border-top-width, border-width, bottom, clear, clip, color, cursor,
direction, display, filter, float, font, font-family, font-size, font-style, font-
variant, font-weight, hasLayout(*), height, layout-flow, layout-grid, layout-grid-
mode, left, letter-spacing, line-height, margin, margin-bottom, margin-left, margin-
right, margin-top, overflow, overflow-x, overflow-y, padding, padding-bottom,
padding-left, padding-right, padding-top, pixelBottom(*), pixelHeight(*),
pixelLeft(*), pixelRight(*), pixelTop(*), pixelWidth(*), posBottom(*), posHeight(*),
position, posLeft(*), posRight(*), posTop(*), posWidth(*), right, styleFloat(*),
text-autospace, text-decoration, text-overflow, text-transform, text-underline-
position, textDecorationBlink(*), textDecorationLineThrough(*),
textDecorationNone(*), textDecorationOverline(*), textDecorationUnderline(*), top,
unicode-bidi, visibility, width, word-spacing, word-wrap, writing-mode, z-index, zoom

<samp> Microsoft Behaviors (9)

clientCaps, download, homePage, httpFolder, saveFavorite, saveHistory,
saveSnapshot, time, time2, userData

<samp> Microsoft Filters (10)

Alpha, Barn, BasicImage, BlendTrans, Blinds, Blur, CheckerBoard, Chroma,
Compositor, DropShadow, Emboss, Engrave, Fade, FlipH, FlipV, Glow, GradientWipe,
Gray, ICMFilter, Inset, Invert, Iris, Light, MaskFilter, Matrix, MotionBlur,
Pixelate, RadialWipe, RandomBars, RandomDissolve, RevealTrans, Shadow, Slide,
Spiral, Stretch, Strips, Wave, Wheel, Xray, Zigzag

samp. JavaScript Properties (11)

accessKey, canHaveChildren, canHaveHTML, className, clientHeight, clientLeft,
clientTop, clientWidth, contentEditable, cursor, dir, disabled, end, firstChild,
hasLayout, hideFocus, id, innerHTML, innerText, isContentEditable, isDisabled,
isMultiLine, isTextEdit, lang, language, lastChild, nextSibling, nodeName,
nodeType, nodeValue, offsetHeight, offsetLeft, offsetParent, offsetTop,
offsetWidth, outerHTML, outerText, ownerDocument, parentElement, parentNode,
parentTextEdit, previousSibling, readyState, scopeName, scrollHeight, scrollLeft,
scrollTop, scrollWidth, sourceIndex, tabIndex, tagName, tagUrn, title, uniqueID

samp. JavaScript Methods (12)

addBehavior, appendChild, applyElement, attachEvent, blur, clearAttributes, click,
cloneNode, componentFromPoint, contains, detachEvent, fireEvent, focus,
getAdjacentText, getAttribute, getAttributeNode, getBoundingClientRect,
getClientRects, getElementsByTagName, getExpression, hasChildNodes,
insertAdjacentElement, insertAdjacentHTML, insertAdjacentText, insertBefore,
mergeAttributes, normalize, releaseCapture, removeAttribute, removeAttributeNode,

removeBehavior, removeChild, removeExpression, removeNode, replaceAdjacentText, replaceChild, replaceNode, scrollIntoView, setActive, setAttribute, setAttributeNode, setCapture, setExpression, swapNode

samp. JavaScript Collections (13)

all, attributes, behaviorUrns, childNodes, children

samp. JavaScript Objects (14)

currentStyle, runtimeStyle, style

<script> ... </script>

Compatibility: NN4, NN6, NN7, IE4, IE5, IE5.5, IE6

This element contains the scripts that will be executed in the page, and it can occur in either the <head> or the <body> section of the page.

Syntax:

```
<script attributes events> . . . </script>
```

Example:

```
<html><head><title>script element example</title>
<script language="javascript" src="yourlinkedjavascriptfile.js"></script>
<script id="script1" language="javascript">
<!--
script code declarations
//-->
</script>
</head>
<body bgcolor="#FFFFFF" text="#000000">
<script id="script2" language="javascript">
<!--
script code declarations
//-->
</script>
</body></html>
```

<script> HTML Attributes (6)

charset, defer, event, for, id, lang, language, src, type

<script> Event Handlers (7)

onLoad, onPropertyChange, onReadyStateChange

<script> CSS Attributes and JavaScript Style Properties (8)

The names are in CSS syntax. See the introduction to this chapter for the JavaScript syntax rules. Names noted with an asterisk (*) are JavaScript properties only.

```
background-position-x, background-position-y, behavior, layout-grid, layout-grid-
mode, pixelBottom(*), pixelHeight(*), pixelLeft(*), pixelRight(*), pixelTop(*),
pixelWidth(*), posBottom(*), posHeight(*), posLeft(*), posRight(*), posTop(*),
posWidth(*), text-autospace, text-underline-position
```

<script> Microsoft Behaviors (9)

```
clientCaps, download, homePage, saveSnapshot
```

script. JavaScript Properties (11)

```
canHaveHTML, charset, className, clientHeight, clientLeft, clientTop, clientWidth,
defer, dir, disabled, event, firstChild, htmlFor, id, innerHTML, innerText,
isContentEditable, isDisabled, isMultiLine, isTextEdit, lang, language, lastChild,
nextSibling, nodeName, nodeType, nodeValue, offsetHeight, offsetLeft, offsetParent,
offsetTop, offsetWidth, ownerDocument, parentElement, parentNode, parentTextEdit,
previousSibling, readyState, scopeName, scrollHeight, scrollLeft, scrollTop,
scrollWidth, sourceIndex, src, tagName, tagUrn, text, title, type, uniqueID
```

script. JavaScript Methods (12)

```
addBehavior, appendChild, applyElement, attachEvent, clearAttributes, cloneNode,
componentFromPoint, contains, detachEvent, dragDrop, fireEvent, getAdjacentText,
getAttribute, getAttributeNode, getElementsByTagName, hasChildNodes,
insertAdjacentElement, insertBefore, mergeAttributes, normalize, removeAttribute,
removeAttributeNode, removeBehavior, removeChild, replaceAdjacentText,
replaceChild, setAttribute, setAttributeNode, swapNode
```

script. JavaScript Collections (13)

```
all, attributes, behaviorUrns, childNodes, children
```

<select> ... </select>

Compatibility: NN4, NN6, NN7, IE4, IE5, IE5.5, IE6

This attribute creates a drop-down or pick list. The options displayed on the list are created by using the <option> element.
 Syntax:

```
<select attributes events> . . . </select>
```

Example:

```
<html><head><title>select element example</title></head>
<body bgcolor="#FFFFFF" text="#000000">
  <form name="form2" method="post" action="">
    <p><span class="example">
    <select name="select1">
      <optgroup label="First Group">
        <option>First item in first group </option>
        <option>Second item in first group </option>
        <option>Third item in first group </option>
      </optgroup>
      <optgroup label="Second Group">
        <option>First item in second group </option>
        <option>Second item in second group </option>
        <option>Third item in second group </option>
      </optgroup>
    </select>
    </span></p>
  </form>
</body></html>
```

<select> HTML Attributes (6)

accesskey, align, class, datafld, datasrc, dir, disabled, hidefocus, id, lang, language, multiple, name, size, style, tabindex, title, unselectable, value

<select> Event Handlers (7)

onActivate, onAfterUpdate, onBeforeActivate, onBeforeCut, onBeforeDeactivate, onBeforeEditFocus, onBeforePaste, onBeforeUpdate, onBlur, onChange, onClick, onContextMenu, onControlSelect, onCut, onDblClick, onDeactivate, onDrag, onDragEnd, onDragEnter, onDragLeave, onDragOver, onDragStart, onDrop, onErrorUpdate, onFocus, onFocusIn, onFocusOut, onHelp, onKeyDown, onKeyPress, onKeyUp, onLoseCapture, onMouseDown, onMouseEnter, onMouseLeave, onMouseMove, onMouseOut, onMouseOver, onMouseUp, onMouseWheel, onMove, onMoveEnd, onMoveStart, onPaste, onPropertyChange, onReadyStateChange, onResize, onResizeEnd, onResizeStart, onSelectStart

<select> CSS Attributes and JavaScript Style Properties (8)

The names are in CSS syntax. See the introduction to this chapter for the JavaScript syntax rules. Names noted with an asterisk (*) are JavaScript properties only.

!important, accelerator, background-color, behavior, bottom, clear, clip, color, direction, display, float, font, font-family, font-size, font-style, font-weight, hasLayout(*), height, layout-flow, layout-grid, layout-grid-mode, left, letter-spacing, line-height, padding, padding-bottom, padding-left, padding-right, padding-top, pixelBottom(*), pixelHeight(*), pixelLeft(*), pixelRight(*), pixelTop(*), pixelWidth(*), posBottom(*), posHeight(*), position, posLeft(*), posRight(*), posTop(*), posWidth(*), right, styleFloat(*), text-autospace, text-decoration, text-transform, text-underline-position, textDecorationBlink(*), textDecorationLineThrough(*), textDecorationNone(*), textDecorationOverline(*), textDecorationUnderline(*), top, unicode-bidi, visibility, width, word-spacing, word-wrap, zoom

<select> Microsoft Behaviors (9)

clientCaps, download, homePage, httpFolder, saveFavorite, saveHistory, saveSnapshot, time, userData

select. JavaScript Properties (11)

accessKey, align, canHaveChildren, canHaveHTML, className, clientHeight, clientLeft, clientTop, clientWidth, dataFld, datasrc, dir, disabled, firstChild, form, hasLayout, hideFocus, id, innerHTML, innerText, isContentEditable, isDisabled, isMultiLine, isTextEdit, lang, language, lastChild, length, multiple, name, nextSibling, nodeName, nodeType, nodeValue, offsetHeight, offsetLeft, offsetParent, offsetTop, offsetWidth, outerHTML, outerText, ownerDocument, parentElement, parentNode, parentTextEdit, previousSibling, readyState, recordNumber, scopeName, scrollHeight, scrollLeft, scrollTop, scrollWidth, selectedIndex, size, sourceIndex, tabIndex, tagName, tagUrn, type, uniqueID, value

select. JavaScript Methods (12)

add, addBehavior, appendChild, applyElement, attachEvent, blur, clearAttributes, click, cloneNode, componentFromPoint, contains, detachEvent, dragDrop, fireEvent, focus, getAdjacentText, getAttribute, getAttributeNode, getBoundingClientRect, getClientRects, getElementsByTagName, getExpression, hasChildNodes, insertAdjacentElement, insertAdjacentHTML, insertAdjacentText, insertBefore, mergeAttributes, namedItem, normalize, releaseCapture, remove, removeAttribute, removeAttributeNode, removeBehavior, removeChild, removeExpression, removeNode, replaceAdjacentText, replaceChild, replaceNode, scrollIntoView, setActive, setAttribute, setAttributeNode, setCapture, setExpression, swapNode, urns

select. JavaScript Collections (13)

all, attributes, behaviorUrns, childNodes, children, options

select. JavaScript Objects (14)

currentStyle, runtimeStyle, style

<small> ... </small>

Compatibility: NN4, NN6, NN7, IE4, IE5, IE5.5, IE6

This element causes text between its opening and closing tags to be displayed in a smaller font.

Syntax:

```
<small attributes events> . . . </small>
```

Example:

```
<html><head><title>small element example</title></head>
<body bgcolor="#FFFFFF" text="#000000">
<p align="center">If you nest <small><small>small</small> elements</small>, the
<small>effects on the <small>nested</small> elements are cumulative.</small>
</body></html>
```

`<small>` HTML Attributes (6)

accesskey, begin, class, contenteditable, dir, disabled, end, hidefocus, id, lang,
language, style, syncmaster, systemBitrate, systemCaptions, systemLanguage,
systemOverdubOrSubtitle, tabindex, timecontainer, title, unselectable

`<small>` Event Handlers (7)

onActivate, onBeforeActivate, onBeforeCopy, onBeforeCut, onBeforeDeactivate,
onBeforeEditFocus, onBeforePaste, onBlur, onClick, onContextMenu, onControlSelect,
onCopy, onCut, onDblClick, onDeactivate, onDrag, onDragEnd, onDragEnter,
onDragLeave, onDragOver, onDragStart, onDrop, onFocus, onFocusIn, onFocusOut,
onHelp, onKeyDown, onKeyPress, onKeyUp, onLoseCapture, onMouseDown, onMouseEnter,
onMouseLeave, onMouseMove, onMouseOut, onMouseOver, onMouseUp, onMouseWheel,
onMove, onMoveEnd, onMoveStart, onPaste, onPropertyChange, onReadyStateChange,
onResize, onResizeEnd, onResizeStart, onSelectStart, onTimeError

`<small>` CSS Attributes and JavaScript Style Properties (8)

The names are in CSS syntax. See the introduction to this chapter for the
JavaScript syntax rules. Names noted with an asterisk (*) are JavaScript
properties only.

!important, accelerator, background, background-attachment, background-color,
background-image, background-position, background-position-x, background-position-
y, background-repeat, behavior, border, border-bottom, border-bottom-color, border-
bottom-style, border-bottom-width, border-color, border-left, border-left-color,
border-left-style, border-left-width, border-right, border-right-color, border-
right-style, border-right-width, border-style, border-top, border-top-color,
border-top-style, border-top-width, border-width, bottom, clear, clip, color,
cursor, direction, display, filter, float, font, font-family, font-size, font-
style, font-variant, font-weight, hasLayout(*), height, layout-flow, layout-grid,
layout-grid-mode, left, letter-spacing, line-height, margin, margin-bottom, margin-
left, margin-right, margin-top, overflow, overflow-x, overflow-y, padding, padding-
bottom, padding-left, padding-right, padding-top, pixelBottom(*), pixelHeight(*),
pixelLeft(*), pixelRight(*), pixelTop(*), pixelWidth(*), posBottom(*),
posHeight(*), position, posLeft(*), posRight(*), posTop(*), posWidth(*), right,
styleFloat(*), text-autospace, text-decoration, text-overflow, text-transform,

text-underline-position, textDecorationBlink(*), textDecorationLineThrough(*), textDecorationNone(*), textDecorationOverline(*), textDecorationUnderline(*), top, unicode-bidi, visibility, white-space, width, word-spacing, word-wrap, writing-mode, z-index, zoom

<small> Microsoft Behaviors (9)

clientCaps, download, homePage, httpFolder, saveFavorite, saveHistory, saveSnapshot, time, time2, userData

<small> Microsoft Filters (10)

Alpha, Barn, BasicImage, BlendTrans, Blinds, Blur, CheckerBoard, Chroma, Compositor, DropShadow, Emboss, Engrave, Fade, FlipH, FlipV, Glow, GradientWipe, Gray, ICMFilter, Inset, Invert, Iris, Light, MaskFilter, Matrix, MotionBlur, Pixelate, RadialWipe, RandomBars, RandomDissolve, RevealTrans, Shadow, Slide, Spiral, Stretch, Strips, Wave, Wheel, Xray, Zigzag

small. JavaScript Properties (11)

accessKey, canHaveChildren, canHaveHTML, className, clientHeight, clientLeft, clientTop, clientWidth, contentEditable, cursor, dir, disabled, end, firstChild, hasLayout, hideFocus, id, innerHTML, innerText, isContentEditable, isDisabled, isMultiLine, isTextEdit, lang, language, lastChild, nextSibling, nodeName, nodeType, nodeValue, offsetHeight, offsetLeft, offsetParent, offsetTop, offsetWidth, outerHTML, outerText, ownerDocument, parentElement, parentNode, parentTextEdit, previousSibling, readyState, scopeName, scrollHeight, scrollLeft, scrollTop, scrollWidth, sourceIndex, tabIndex, tagName, tagUrn, title, uniqueID

small. JavaScript Methods (12)

addBehavior, appendChild, applyElement, attachEvent, blur, clearAttributes, click, cloneNode, componentFromPoint, contains, detachEvent, fireEvent, focus, getAdjacentText, getAttribute, getAttributeNode, getBoundingClientRect, getClientRects, getElementsByTagName, getExpression, hasChildNodes, insertAdjacentElement, insertAdjacentHTML, insertAdjacentText, insertBefore, mergeAttributes, normalize, releaseCapture, removeAttribute, removeAttributeNode, removeBehavior, removeChild, removeExpression, removeNode, replaceAdjacentText, replaceChild, replaceNode, scrollIntoView, setActive, setAttribute, setAttributeNode, setCapture, setExpression, swapNode

small. JavaScript Collections (13)

all, attributes, behaviorUrns, childNodes, children

small. JavaScript Objects (14)

currentStyle, runtimeStyle, style

<spacer>

Compatibility: NN4

This element provides better control over the spacing of content. It creates blank space without forcing you to use spaces ( ), too many <p> tags, or transparent images.

Syntax:

```
<spacer attributes> . . . </spacer>
```

Example:

```
<html><head><title>spacer element example</title></head>
<body bgcolor="#FFFFFF" text="#000000">
<p>This is the first line of a paragraph.<spacer type="vertical" size=200>and this
text completes the paragraph after a two line gap.</p>
</body></html>
```

<spacer> HTML Attributes (6)

align, height, size, type, width

<span> ... </span>

Compatibility: NN4, NN6, NN7, IE4, IE5, IE5.5, IE6

This element is used to apply style sheet properties only to the text between its opening and closing tags.

Syntax:

```
<span attributes events> . . . </span>
```

Example:

```
<html><head><title>span element example</title></head>
<body bgcolor="#FFFFFF" text="#000000">
<p align="center">This <span style="color:#FF0000; font-size:10pt; text-
transform:uppercase;">paragraph</span> has text of <span style="color:blue; font-
size:18pt; text-transform:uppercase;">three </span> different <span
style="color:blue; font-size:14pt; text-decoration:underline;"> styles </span>.</p>
</body></html>
```

<span> HTML Attributes (6)

accesskey, begin, class, contenteditable, datafld, dataformatas, datasrc, dir, end,
hidefocus, id, lang, language, style, syncmaster, systemBitrate, systemCaptions,
systemLanguage, systemOverdubOrSubtitle, tabindex, timecontainer, title,
unselectable

<span> Event Handlers (7)

---

onActivate, onAfterUpdate, onBeforeActivate, onBeforeCopy, onBeforeCut,
onBeforeDeactivate, onBeforeEditFocus, onBeforePaste, onBeforeUpdate, onBlur,
onClick, onContextMenu, onControlSelect, onCopy, onCut, onDblClick, onDeactivate,
onDrag, onDragEnd, onDragEnter, onDragLeave, onDragOver, onDragStart, onDrop,
onErrorUpdate, onFilterChange, onFocus, onFocusIn, onFocusOut, onHelp, onKeyDown,
onKeyPress, onKeyUp, onLoseCapture, onMouseDown, onMouseEnter, onMouseLeave,
onMouseMove, onMouseOut, onMouseOver, onMouseUp, onMouseWheel, onMove, onMoveEnd,
onMoveStart, onPaste, onPropertyChange, onReadyStateChange, onResize, onResizeEnd,
onResizeStart, onSelectStart, onTimeError

<span> CSS Attributes and JavaScript Style Properties (8)

The names are in CSS syntax. See the introduction to this chapter for the
JavaScript syntax rules. Names noted with an asterisk (*) are JavaScript
properties only.

!important, accelerator, background, background-attachment, background-color,
background-image, background-position, background-position-x, background-position-
y, background-repeat, behavior, border, border-bottom, border-bottom-color, border-
bottom-style, border-bottom-width, border-color, border-left, border-left-color,
border-left-style, border-left-width, border-right, border-right-color, border-
right-style, border-right-width, border-style, border-top, border-top-color,
border-top-style, border-top-width, border-width, bottom, clear, clip, color,
cursor, direction, display, filter, float, font, font-family, font-size, font-
style, font-variant, font-weight, hasLayout(*), height, layout-flow, layout-grid,
layout-grid-mode, left, letter-spacing, line-height, margin, margin-bottom, margin-
left, margin-right, margin-top, overflow, overflow-x, overflow-y, padding, padding-
bottom, padding-left, padding-right, padding-top, pixelBottom(*), pixelHeight(*),
pixelLeft(*), pixelRight(*), pixelTop(*), pixelWidth(*), posBottom(*),
posHeight(*), position, posLeft(*), posRight(*), posTop(*), posWidth(*), right,
styleFloat(*), text-autospace, text-decoration, text-overflow, text-transform,
text-underline-position, textDecorationBlink(*), textDecorationLineThrough(*),
textDecorationNone(*), textDecorationOverline(*), textDecorationUnderline(*), top,
unicode-bidi, vertical-align, visibility, white-space, width, word-spacing, word-
wrap, writing-mode, z-index, zoom

<span> Microsoft Behaviors (9)

---

clientCaps, download, homePage, httpFolder, saveFavorite, saveHistory,
saveSnapshot, time, time2, userData

<span> Microsoft Filters (10)

Alpha, Barn, BasicImage, BlendTrans, Blinds, Blur, CheckerBoard, Chroma,
Compositor, DropShadow, Emboss, Engrave, Fade, FlipH, FlipV, Glow, GradientWipe,
Gray, ICMFilter, Inset, Invert, Iris, Light, MaskFilter, Matrix, MotionBlur,
Pixelate, RadialWipe, RandomBars, RandomDissolve, RevealTrans, Shadow, Slide,
Spiral, Stretch, Strips, Wave, Wheel, Xray, Zigzag

---

span. JavaScript Properties (11)

accessKey, canHaveChildren, canHaveHTML, className, clientHeight, clientLeft, clientTop, clientWidth, contentEditable, cursor, dataFld, dataFormatAs, datasrc, dir, disabled, end, firstChild, hasLayout, hideFocus, id, innerHTML, innerText, isContentEditable, isDisabled, isMultiLine, isTextEdit, lang, language, lastChild, nextSibling, nodeName, nodeType, nodeValue, offsetHeight, offsetLeft, offsetParent, offsetTop, offsetWidth, outerHTML, outerText, ownerDocument, parentElement, parentNode, parentTextEdit, previousSibling, readyState, recordNumber, scopeName, scrollHeight, scrollLeft, scrollTop, scrollWidth, sourceIndex, tabIndex, tagName, tagUrn, title, uniqueID

span. JavaScript Methods (12)

addBehavior, appendChild, applyElement, attachEvent, blur, clearAttributes, click, cloneNode, componentFromPoint, contains, detachEvent, doScroll, dragDrop, fireEvent, focus, getAdjacentText, getAttribute, getAttributeNode, getBoundingClientRect, getClientRects, getElementsByTagName, getExpression, hasChildNodes, insertAdjacentElement, insertAdjacentHTML, insertAdjacentText, insertBefore, mergeAttributes, normalize, releaseCapture, removeAttribute, removeAttributeNode, removeBehavior, removeChild, removeExpression, removeNode, replaceAdjacentText, replaceChild, replaceNode, scrollIntoView, setActive, setAttribute, setAttributeNode, setCapture, setExpression, swapNode

span. JavaScript Collections (13)

all, attributes, behaviorUrns, childNodes, children, filters

span. JavaScript Objects (14)

currentStyle, runtimeStyle, style

<strike> ... </strike>

Compatibility: NN4, NN6, NN7, IE4, IE5, IE5.5, IE6

This element causes the text between its opening and closing tags to appear with a strike-out line through it. This element has been deprecated in favor of using CSS (see Chapter 1).

Syntax:

```
<strike attributes events> . . . </strike>
```

Example:

```
<html><head><title>strike element example</title></head>
<body bgcolor="#FFFFFF" text="#000000">
<p><strike>This is the text that has been crossed out</strike></p>
</body></html>
```

<strike> HTML Attributes (6)

accesskey, begin, class, contenteditable, dir, disabled, end, hidefocus, id, lang, language, style, syncmaster, systemBitrate, systemCaptions, systemLanguage, systemOverdubOrSubtitle, tabindex, timecontainer, title, unselectable

<strike> Event Handlers (7)

onActivate, onBeforeActivate, onBeforeCopy, onBeforeCut, onBeforeDeactivate, onBeforeEditFocus, onBeforePaste, onBlur, onClick, onContextMenu, onControlSelect, onCopy, onCut, onDblClick, onDeactivate, onDrag, onDragEnd, onDragEnter, onDragLeave, onDragOver, onDragStart, onDrop, onFocus, onFocusIn, onFocusOut, onHelp, onKeyDown, onKeyPress, onKeyUp, onLoseCapture, onMouseDown, onMouseEnter, onMouseLeave, onMouseMove, onMouseOut, onMouseOver, onMouseUp, onMouseWheel, onMove, onMoveEnd, onMoveStart, onPaste, onPropertyChange, onReadyStateChange, onResize, onResizeEnd, onResizeStart, onSelectStart, onTimeError

<strike> CSS Attributes and JavaScript Style Properties (8)

The names are in CSS syntax. See the introduction to this chapter for the JavaScript syntax rules. Names noted with an asterisk (*) are JavaScript properties only.

!important, accelerator, background, background-attachment, background-color, background-image, background-position, background-position-x, background-position-y, background-repeat, behavior, border, border-bottom, border-bottom-color, border-bottom-style, border-bottom-width, border-color, border-left, border-left-color, border-left-style, border-left-width, border-right, border-right-color, border-right-style, border-right-width, border-style, border-top, border-top-color, border-top-style, border-top-width, border-width, bottom, clear, clip, color, cursor, direction, display, filter, float, font, font-family, font-size, font-style, font-variant, font-weight, hasLayout(*), height, layout-flow, layout-grid, layout-grid-mode, left, letter-spacing, line-height, margin, margin-bottom, margin-left, margin-right, margin-top, overflow, overflow-x, overflow-y, padding, padding-bottom, padding-left, padding-right, padding-top, pixelBottom(*), pixelHeight(*), pixelLeft(*), pixelRight(*), pixelTop(*), pixelWidth(*), posBottom(*), posHeight(*), position, posLeft(*), posRight(*), posTop(*), posWidth(*), right, styleFloat(*), text-autospace, text-decoration, text-overflow, text-transform, text-underline-position, textDecorationBlink(*), textDecorationLineThrough(*), textDecorationNone(*), textDecorationOverline(*), textDecorationUnderline(*), top, unicode-bidi, visibility, white-space, width, word-spacing, word-wrap, writing-mode, z-index, zoom

<strike> Microsoft Behaviors (9)

clientCaps, download, homePage, httpFolder, saveFavorite, saveHistory, saveSnapshot, time, time2, userData

<strike> Microsoft Filters (10)

Alpha, Barn, BasicImage, BlendTrans, Blinds, Blur, CheckerBoard, Chroma, Compositor, DropShadow, Emboss, Engrave, Fade, FlipH, FlipV, Glow, GradientWipe, Gray, ICMFilter, Inset, Invert, Iris, Light, MaskFilter, Matrix, MotionBlur,

Pixelate, RadialWipe, RandomBars, RandomDissolve, RevealTrans, Shadow, Slide, Spiral, Stretch, Strips, Wave, Wheel, Xray, Zigzag

strike. JavaScript Properties (11)

accessKey, canHaveChildren, canHaveHTML, className, clientHeight, clientLeft, clientTop, clientWidth, contentEditable, cursor, dir, disabled, end, firstChild, hasLayout, hideFocus, id, innerHTML, innerText, isContentEditable, isDisabled, isMultiLine, isTextEdit, lang, language, lastChild, nextSibling, nodeName, nodeType, nodeValue, offsetHeight, offsetLeft, offsetParent, offsetTop, offsetWidth, outerHTML, outerText, ownerDocument, parentElement, parentNode, parentTextEdit, previousSibling, readyState, scopeName, scrollHeight, scrollLeft, scrollTop, scrollWidth, sourceIndex, tabIndex, tagName, tagUrn, title, uniqueID

strike. JavaScript Methods (12)

addBehavior, appendChild, applyElement, attachEvent, blur, clearAttributes, click, cloneNode, componentFromPoint, contains, detachEvent, fireEvent, focus, getAdjacentText, getAttribute, getAttributeNode, getBoundingClientRect, getClientRects, getElementsByTagName, getExpression, hasChildNodes, insertAdjacentElement, insertAdjacentHTML, insertAdjacentText, insertBefore, mergeAttributes, normalize, releaseCapture, removeAttribute, removeAttributeNode, removeBehavior, removeChild, removeExpression, removeNode, replaceAdjacentText, replaceChild, replaceNode, scrollIntoView, setActive, setAttribute, setAttributeNode, setCapture, setExpression, swapNode

strike. JavaScript Collections (13)

all, attributes, behaviorUrns, childNodes, children

strike. JavaScript Objects (14)

currentStyle, runtimeStyle, style

\<strong\> ... \</strong\>

Compatibility: NN4, NN6, NN7, IE4, IE5, IE5.5, IE6

This element causes text between its opening and closing tags to appear in boldface.

Syntax:

```
<strong attributes events> . . . </strong>
```

Example:

```
<html><head><title>strong element example</title></head>
<body bgcolor="#FFFFFF" text="#000000">
<p align="center">This <strong>paragraph</strong>
```

has text rendered in normal and <strong>bold</strong> face.</p>
</body></html>

<strong> HTML Attributes (6)

accesskey, begin, class, contenteditable, dir, disabled, end, hidefocus, id, lang, language, style, syncmaster, systemBitrate, systemCaptions, systemLanguage, systemOverdubOrSubtitle, tabindex, timecontainer, title, unselectable

---

<strong> Event Handlers (7)

onActivate, onBeforeActivate, onBeforeCopy, onBeforeCut, onBeforeDeactivate, onBeforeEditFocus, onBeforePaste, onBlur, onClick, onContextMenu, onControlSelect, onCopy, onCut, onDblClick, onDeactivate, onDrag, onDragEnd, onDragEnter, onDragLeave, onDragOver, onDragStart, onDrop, onFocus, onFocusIn, onFocusOut, onHelp, onKeyDown, onKeyPress, onKeyUp, onLoseCapture, onMouseDown, onMouseEnter, onMouseLeave, onMouseMove, onMouseOut, onMouseOver, onMouseUp, onMouseWheel, onMove, onMoveEnd, onMoveStart, onPaste, onPropertyChange, onReadyStateChange, onResize, onResizeEnd, onResizeStart, onSelectStart, onTimeError

---

<strong> CSS Attributes and JavaScript Style Properties (8)

The names are in CSS syntax. See the introduction to this chapter for the JavaScript syntax rules. Names noted with an asterisk (*) are JavaScript properties only.

!important, accelerator, background, background-attachment, background-color, background-image, background-position, background-position-x, background-position-y, background-repeat, behavior, border, border-bottom, border-bottom-color, border-bottom-style, border-bottom-width, border-color, border-left, border-left-color, border-left-style, border-left-width, border-right, border-right-color, border-right-style, border-right-width, border-style, border-top, border-top-color, border-top-style, border-top-width, border-width, bottom, clear, clip, color, cursor, direction, display, filter, float, font, font-family, font-size, font-style, font-variant, font-weight, hasLayout(*), height, layout-flow, layout-grid, layout-grid-mode, left, letter-spacing, line-height, margin, margin-bottom, margin-left, margin-right, margin-top, overflow, overflow-x, overflow-y, padding, padding-bottom, padding-left, padding-right, padding-top, pixelBottom(*), pixelHeight(*), pixelLeft(*), pixelRight(*), pixelTop(*), pixelWidth(*), posBottom(*), posHeight(*), position, posLeft(*), posRight(*), posTop(*), posWidth(*), right, styleFloat(*), text-autospace, text-decoration, text-overflow, text-transform, text-underline-position, textDecorationBlink(*), textDecorationLineThrough(*), textDecorationNone(*), textDecorationOverline(*), textDecorationUnderline(*), top, unicode-bidi, visibility, white-space, width, word-spacing, word-wrap, writing-mode, z-index, zoom

---

<strong> Microsoft Behaviors (9)

---

clientCaps, download, homePage, httpFolder, saveFavorite, saveHistory, saveSnapshot, time, time2, userData

<strong> Microsoft Filters (10)

Alpha, Barn, BasicImage, BlendTrans, Blinds, Blur, CheckerBoard, Chroma,
Compositor, DropShadow, Emboss, Engrave, Fade, FlipH, FlipV, Glow, GradientWipe,
Gray, ICMFilter, Inset, Invert, Iris, Light, MaskFilter, Matrix, MotionBlur,
Pixelate, RadialWipe, RandomBars, RandomDissolve, RevealTrans, Shadow, Slide,
Spiral, Stretch, Strips, Wave, Wheel, Xray, Zigzag

strong. JavaScript Properties (11)

accessKey, canHaveChildren, canHaveHTML, className, clientHeight, clientLeft,
clientTop, clientWidth, contentEditable, cursor, dir, disabled, end, firstChild,
hasLayout, hideFocus, id, innerHTML, innerText, isContentEditable, isDisabled,
isMultiLine, isTextEdit, lang, language, lastChild, nextSibling, nodeName,
nodeType, nodeValue, offsetHeight, offsetLeft, offsetParent, offsetTop,
offsetWidth, outerHTML, outerText, ownerDocument, parentElement, parentNode,
parentTextEdit, previousSibling, readyState, scopeName, scrollHeight, scrollLeft,
scrollTop, scrollWidth, sourceIndex, tabIndex, tagName, tagUrn, title, uniqueID

strong. JavaScript Methods (12)

addBehavior, appendChild, applyElement, attachEvent, blur, clearAttributes,
click, cloneNode, componentFromPoint, contains, detachEvent, fireEvent, focus,
getAdjacentText, getAttribute, getAttributeNode, getBoundingClientRect,
getClientRects, getElementsByTagName, getExpression, hasChildNodes,
insertAdjacentElement, insertAdjacentHTML, insertAdjacentText, insertBefore,
mergeAttributes, normalize, releaseCapture, removeAttribute, removeAttributeNode,
removeBehavior, removeChild, removeExpression, removeNode, replaceAdjacentText,
replaceChild, replaceNode, scrollIntoView, setActive, setAttribute,
setAttributeNode, setCapture, setExpression, swapNode

strong. JavaScript Collections (13)

all, attributes, behaviorUrns, childNodes, children

strong. JavaScript Objects (14)

currentStyle, runtimeStyle, style

<style> ... </style>

Compatibility: NN4, NN6, NN7, IE4, IE5, IE5.5, IE6

This element allows a style sheet to be specified for the page. It should appear
within the <head> section of a document, though Internet Explorer 4.0 and later
allow multiple style blocks to be defined.

    Syntax:

<style *attributes events*> . . . </style>

Example:

```
<html><title>style element example</title><head>
<style>
body {  background-color: black; color: white; }
</style>
</head>
<body>The body cotains a black background and white letters.</body>
</html>
```

<style> HTML Attributes (6)

dir, id, lang, media, title, type

<style> Event Handlers (7)

onError, onReadyStateChange

style. JavaScript Properties (11)

className, clientHeight, clientWidth, cursor, dir, disabled, firstChild, id,
innerHTML, lang, lastChild, media, nextSibling, nodeName, nodeType, nodeValue,
offsetHeight, offsetLeft, offsetParent, offsetTop, offsetWidth, ownerDocument,
parentNode, previousSibling, scrollHeight, scrollLeft, scrollTop, scrollWidth,
tagName, type

style. JavaScript Methods (12)

addBehavior, appendChild, cloneNode, dragDrop, getAttribute, getAttributeNode,
getElementsByTagName, hasChildNodes, insertBefore, removeBehavior, removeChild,
removeNode, replaceChild, setAttribute, setAttributeNode

style. JavaScript Collections (13)

attributes, behaviorUrns, childNodes

<sub> ... </sub>

Compatibility: NN4, NN6, NN7, IE4, IE5, IE5.5, IE6

This element causes text between its opening and closing tags to appear in subscript format and in a smaller font than other text on the page.

Syntax:

```
<sub attributes events> . . . </sub>
```

Example:

```
<html><head><title>sub element example</title></head>
<body bgcolor="#FFFFFF" text="#000000">
<p align="center">H<sub>2</sub>O is the chemical formula for regular water.</p>
</body></html>
```

<sub> HTML Attributes (6)

accesskey, begin, class, contenteditable, dir, disabled, end, hidefocus, id, lang, language, style, syncmaster, systemBitrate, systemCaptions, systemLanguage, systemOverdubOrSubtitle, tabindex, timecontainer, title, unselectable

<sub> Event Handlers (7)

onActivate, onBeforeActivate, onBeforeCopy, onBeforeCut, onBeforeDeactivate, onBeforeEditFocus, onBeforePaste, onBlur, onClick, onContextMenu, onControlSelect, onCopy, onCut, onDblClick, onDeactivate, onDrag, onDragEnd, onDragEnter, onDragLeave, onDragOver, onDragStart, onDrop, onFocus, onFocusIn, onFocusOut, onHelp, onKeyDown, onKeyPress, onKeyUp, onLoseCapture, onMouseDown, onMouseEnter, onMouseLeave, onMouseMove, onMouseOut, onMouseOver, onMouseUp, onMouseWheel, onMove, onMoveEnd, onMoveStart, onPaste, onPropertyChange, onReadyStateChange, onResize, onResizeEnd, onResizeStart, onSelectStart, onTimeError

<sub> CSS Attributes and JavaScript Style Properties (8)

The names are in CSS syntax. See the introduction to this chapter for the JavaScript syntax rules. Names noted with an asterisk (*) are JavaScript properties only.

!important, accelerator, background, background-attachment, background-color, background-image, background-position, background-position-x, background-position-y, background-repeat, behavior, border, border-bottom, border-bottom-color, border-bottom-style, border-bottom-width, border-color, border-left, border-left-color, border-left-style, border-left-width, border-right, border-right-color, border-right-style, border-right-width, border-style, border-top, border-top-color, border-top-style, border-top-width, border-width, bottom, clear, clip, color, cursor, direction, display, filter, float, font, font-family, font-size, font-style, font-variant, font-weight, hasLayout(*), height, layout-flow, layout-grid, layout-grid-mode, left, letter-spacing, line-height, margin, margin-bottom, margin-left, margin-right, margin-top, overflow, overflow-x, overflow-y, padding, padding-bottom, padding-left, padding-right, padding-top, pixelBottom(*), pixelHeight(*), pixelLeft(*), pixelRight(*), pixelTop(*), pixelWidth(*), posBottom(*), posHeight(*), position, posLeft(*), posRight(*), posTop(*), posWidth(*), right, styleFloat(*), text-autospace, text-decoration, text-overflow, text-transform, text-underline-position, textDecorationBlink(*), textDecorationLineThrough(*), textDecorationNone(*), textDecorationOverline(*), textDecorationUnderline(*), top, unicode-bidi, visibility, white-space, width, word-spacing, word-wrap, writing-mode, z-index, zoom

\<sub> Microsoft Behaviors (9)

clientCaps, download, homePage, httpFolder, saveFavorite, saveHistory, saveSnapshot, time, time2, userData

\<sub> Microsoft Filters (10)

Alpha, Barn, BasicImage, BlendTrans, Blinds, Blur, CheckerBoard, Chroma, Compositor, DropShadow, Emboss, Engrave, Fade, FlipH, FlipV, Glow, GradientWipe, Gray, ICMFilter, Inset, Invert, Iris, Light, MaskFilter, Matrix, MotionBlur, Pixelate, RadialWipe, RandomBars, RandomDissolve, RevealTrans, Shadow, Slide, Spiral, Stretch, Strips, Wave, Wheel, Xray, Zigzag

sub. JavaScript Properties (11)

accessKey, canHaveChildren, canHaveHTML, className, clientHeight, clientLeft, clientTop, clientWidth, contentEditable, cursor, dir, disabled, end, firstChild, hasLayout, hideFocus, id, innerHTML, innerText, isContentEditable, isDisabled, isMultiLine, isTextEdit, lang, language, lastChild, nextSibling, nodeName, nodeType, nodeValue, offsetHeight, offsetLeft, offsetParent, offsetTop, offsetWidth, outerHTML, outerText, ownerDocument, parentElement, parentNode, parentTextEdit, previousSibling, readyState, scopeName, scrollHeight, scrollLeft, scrollTop, scrollWidth, sourceIndex, tabIndex, tagName, tagUrn, title, uniqueID

sub. JavaScript Methods (12)

addBehavior, appendChild, applyElement, attachEvent, blur, clearAttributes, click, cloneNode, componentFromPoint, contains, detachEvent, fireEvent, focus, getAdjacentText, getAttribute, getAttributeNode, getBoundingClientRect, getClientRects, getElementsByTagName, getExpression, hasChildNodes, insertAdjacentElement, insertAdjacentHTML, insertAdjacentText, insertBefore, mergeAttributes, normalize, releaseCapture, removeAttribute, removeAttributeNode, removeBehavior, removeChild, removeExpression, removeNode, replaceAdjacentText, replaceChild, replaceNode, scrollIntoView, setActive, setAttribute, setAttributeNode, setCapture, setExpression, swapNode

sub. JavaScript Collections (13)

all, attributes, behaviorUrns, childNodes, children

sub. JavaScript Objects (14)

currentStyle, runtimeStyle, style

\^{... \}

Compatibility: NN4, NN6, NN7, IE4, IE5, IE5.5, IE6

This element renders the enclosed text in superscript format and in smaller font.

Syntax:

```
<sup attributes events> . . . </sup>
```

Example:

```
<html><head><title>sup element example</title></head>
<body bgcolor="#FFFFFF" text="#000000">
<p align="center" class="explanations">HTML+TIME is a noteworthy
Microsoft<sup>&reg;</sup> technology.</p>
</body></html>
```

\<sup\> HTML Attributes (6)

accesskey, begin, class, contenteditable, dir, disabled, end, hidefocus, id, lang, language, style, syncmaster, systemBitrate, systemCaptions, systemLanguage, systemOverdubOrSubtitle, tabindex, timecontainer, title, unselectable

\<sup\> Event Handlers (7)

onActivate, onBeforeActivate, onBeforeCopy, onBeforeCut, onBeforeDeactivate, onBeforeEditFocus, onBeforePaste, onBlur, onClick, onContextMenu, onControlSelect, onCopy, onCut, onDblClick, onDeactivate, onDrag, onDragEnd, onDragEnter, onDragLeave, onDragOver, onDragStart, onDrop, onFocus, onFocusIn, onFocusOut, onHelp, onKeyDown, onKeyPress, onKeyUp, onLoseCapture, onMouseDown, onMouseEnter, onMouseLeave, onMouseMove, onMouseOut, onMouseOver, onMouseUp, onMouseWheel, onMove, onMoveEnd, onMoveStart, onPaste, onPropertyChange, onReadyStateChange, onResize, onResizeEnd, onResizeStart, onSelectStart, onTimeError

\<sup\> CSS Attributes and JavaScript Style Properties (8)

The names are in CSS syntax. See the introduction to this chapter for the JavaScript syntax rules. Names noted with an asterisk (*) are JavaScript properties only.

!important, accelerator, background, background-attachment, background-color, background-image, background-position, background-position-x, background-position-y, background-repeat, behavior, border, border-bottom, border-bottom-color, border-bottom-style, border-bottom-width, border-color, border-left, border-left-color, border-left-style, border-left-width, border-right, border-right-color, border-right-style, border-right-width, border-style, border-top, border-top-color, border-top-style, border-top-width, border-width, bottom, clear, clip, color, cursor, direction, display, filter, float, font, font-family, font-size, font-style, font-variant, font-weight, hasLayout(*), height, layout-flow, layout-grid, layout-grid-mode, left, letter-spacing, line-height, margin, margin-bottom, margin-left, margin-right, margin-top, overflow, overflow-x, overflow-y, padding, padding-bottom, padding-left, padding-right, padding-top, pixelBottom(*), pixelHeight(*), pixelLeft(*), pixelRight(*), pixelTop(*), pixelWidth(*), posBottom(*), posHeight(*), position, posLeft(*), posRight(*), posTop(*), posWidth(*), right, styleFloat(*), text-autospace, text-decoration, text-overflow, text-transform, text-underline-position, textDecorationBlink(*), textDecorationLineThrough(*), textDecorationNone(*), textDecorationOverline(*), textDecorationUnderline(*), top, unicode-bidi, visibility, white-space, width, word-spacing, word-wrap, writing-mode, z-index, zoom

<sup> Microsoft Behaviors (9)

clientCaps, download, homePage, httpFolder, saveFavorite, saveHistory, saveSnapshot, time, time2, userData

<sup> Microsoft Filters (10)

Alpha, Barn, BasicImage, BlendTrans, Blinds, Blur, CheckerBoard, Chroma, Compositor, DropShadow, Emboss, Engrave, Fade, FlipH, FlipV, Glow, GradientWipe, Gray, ICMFilter, Inset, Invert, Iris, Light, MaskFilter, Matrix, MotionBlur, Pixelate, RadialWipe, RandomBars, RandomDissolve, RevealTrans, Shadow, Slide, Spiral, Stretch, Strips, Wave, Wheel, Xray, Zigzag

sup. JavaScript Properties (11)

accessKey, canHaveChildren, canHaveHTML, className, clientHeight, clientLeft, clientTop, clientWidth, contentEditable, cursor, dir, disabled, end, firstChild, hasLayout, hideFocus, id, innerHTML, innerText, isContentEditable, isDisabled, isMultiLine, isTextEdit, lang, language, lastChild, nextSibling, nodeName, nodeType, nodeValue, offsetHeight, offsetLeft, offsetParent, offsetTop, offsetWidth, outerHTML, outerText, ownerDocument, parentElement, parentNode, parentTextEdit, previousSibling, readyState, scopeName, scrollHeight, scrollLeft, scrollTop, scrollWidth, sourceIndex, tabIndex, tagName, tagUrn, title, uniqueID

sup. JavaScript Methods (12)

addBehavior, appendChild, applyElement, attachEvent, blur, clearAttributes, click, cloneNode, componentFromPoint, contains, detachEvent, fireEvent, focus, getAdjacentText, getAttribute, getAttributeNode, getBoundingClientRect, getClientRects, getElementsByTagName, getExpression, hasChildNodes, insertAdjacentElement, insertAdjacentHTML, insertAdjacentText, insertBefore, mergeAttributes, normalize, releaseCapture, removeAttribute, removeAttributeNode, removeBehavior, removeChild, removeExpression, removeNode, replaceAdjacentText, replaceChild, replaceNode, scrollIntoView, setActive, setAttribute, setAttributeNode, setCapture, setExpression, swapNode

sup. JavaScript Collections (13)

all, attributes, behaviorUrns, childNodes, children

sup. JavaScript Objects (14)

currentStyle, runtimeStyle, style

\<table> ... \</table>

Compatibility: NN4, NN6, NN7, IE4, IE5, IE5.5, IE6

This element creates a table on the page that can contain rows and columns. The
\<tr> element creates rows in the table, and the \<td> element creates the cells in
each table row.

Syntax:

```
<table attributes events> . . . </table>
```

Example:

```
<html><head><title>col element example</title></head>
<body bgcolor="#FFFFFF" text="#000000">
<table width="500" border="8" cellspacing="5" cellpadding="5" align="center">
<col style="color:maroon">
<col style="color:red">
<tr><td>col 1: maroon</td>
<td>col 2: red</td>
<tr><td>col 1: maroon</td>
<td>col 2: red</td></tr>
</table></body></html>
```

\<table> HTML Attributes (6)

accesskey, align, background, begin, bgcolor, border, bordercolor, bordercolordark,
bordercolorlight, cellpadding, cellspacing, class, cols, datapagesize, datasrc,
dir, end, frame, height, hidefocus, id, lang, language, rules, style, summary,
syncmaster, systemBitrate, systemCaptions, systemLanguage, systemOverdubOrSubtitle,
tabindex, timecontainer, title, unselectable, width

\<table> Event Handlers (7)

onActivate, onAfterUpdate, onBeforeActivate, onBeforeCut, onBeforeDeactivate,
onBeforeEditFocus, onBeforePaste, onBeforeUpdate, onBlur, onClick, onContextMenu,
onControlSelect, onCut, onDblClick, onDeactivate, onDrag, onDragEnd, onDragEnter,
onDragLeave, onDragOver, onDragStart, onDrop, onFilterChange, onFocus, onFocusIn,
onFocusOut, onHelp, onKeyDown, onKeyPress, onKeyUp, onLoseCapture, onMouseDown,
onMouseEnter, onMouseLeave, onMouseMove, onMouseOut, onMouseOver, onMouseUp,
onMouseWheel, onMove, onMoveEnd, onMoveStart, onPaste, onPropertyChange,
onReadyStateChange, onResize, onResizeEnd, onResizeStart, onScroll, onSelectStart,
onTimeError

\<table> CSS Attributes and JavaScript Style Properties (8)

The names are in CSS syntax. See the introduction to this chapter for the
JavaScript syntax rules. Names noted with an asterisk (*) are JavaScript
properties only.

!important, accelerator, background, background-attachment, background-color, background-image, background-position, background-position-x, background-position-y, background-repeat, behavior, border, border-bottom, border-bottom-color, border-bottom-style, border-bottom-width, border-collapse, border-color, border-left, border-left-color, border-left-style, border-left-width, border-right, border-right-color, border-right-style, border-right-width, border-style, border-top, border-top-color, border-top-style, border-top-width, border-width, bottom, clear, clip, color, cursor, direction, display, filter, float, font, font-family, font-size, font-style, font-variant, font-weight, hasLayout(*), height, layout-grid, layout-grid-char, layout-grid-line, layout-grid-mode, layout-grid-type, left, letter-spacing, line-break, line-height, margin, margin-bottom, margin-left, margin-right, margin-top, padding, page-break-after, page-break-before, pixelBottom(*), pixelHeight(*), pixelLeft(*), pixelRight(*), pixelTop(*), pixelWidth(*), posBottom(*), posHeight(*), position, posLeft(*), posRight(*), posTop(*), posWidth(*), right, styleFloat(*), table-layout, text-align, text-autospace, text-decoration, text-indent, text-justify, text-transform, text-underline-position, textDecorationBlink(*), textDecorationLineThrough(*), textDecorationNone(*), textDecorationOverline(*), textDecorationUnderline(*), top, unicode-bidi, visibility, word-break, word-spacing, z-index, zoom

<table> Microsoft Behaviors (9)

clientCaps, download, homePage, httpFolder, saveFavorite, saveHistory, saveSnapshot, time, time2, userData

<table> Microsoft Filters (10)

Alpha, Barn, BasicImage, BlendTrans, Blinds, Blur, CheckerBoard, Chroma, Compositor, DropShadow, Emboss, Engrave, Fade, FlipH, FlipV, Glow, GradientWipe, Gray, ICMFilter, Inset, Invert, Iris, Light, MaskFilter, Matrix, MotionBlur, Pixelate, RadialWipe, RandomBars, RandomDissolve, RevealTrans, Shadow, Slide, Spiral, Stretch, Strips, Wave, Wheel, Xray, Zigzag

table. JavaScript Properties (11)

accessKey, align, background, bgColor, border, borderColor, borderColorDark, borderColorLight, canHaveChildren, canHaveHTML, caption, cellPadding, cellSpacing, className, clientHeight, clientLeft, clientTop, clientWidth, cols, cursor, dataPageSize, datasrc, dir, disabled, end, firstChild, frame, hasLayout, height, hideFocus, id, innerHTML, innerText, isContentEditable, isDisabled, isMultiLine, isTextEdit, lang, language, lastChild, nextSibling, nodeName, nodeType, nodeValue, offsetHeight, offsetLeft, offsetParent, offsetTop, offsetWidth, outerHTML, outerText, ownerDocument, parentElement, parentNode, parentTextEdit, previousSibling, readyState, rules, scopeName, scrollHeight, scrollLeft, scrollTop, scrollWidth, sourceIndex, summary, tabIndex, tagName, tagUrn, tFoot, tHead, title, uniqueID, width

table. JavaScript Methods (12)

addBehavior, appendChild, applyElement, attachEvent, blur, clearAttributes, click, cloneNode, componentFromPoint, contains, createCaption, createTFoot, createTHead, deleteCaption, deleteRow, deleteTFoot, deleteTHead, detachEvent, dragDrop, fireEvent, firstPage, focus, getAdjacentText, getAttribute, getAttributeNode, getBoundingClientRect, getClientRects, getElementsByTagName, getExpression, hasChildNodes, insertAdjacentElement, insertBefore, insertRow, lastPage, mergeAttributes, moveRow, nextPage, normalize, previousPage, refresh, releaseCapture, removeAttribute, removeAttributeNode, removeBehavior, removeChild, removeExpression, removeNode, replaceAdjacentText, replaceChild, replaceNode, scrollIntoView, setActive, setAttribute, setAttributeNode, setCapture, setExpression, swapNode

table. JavaScript Collections (13)

all, attributes, behaviorUrns, cells, childNodes, children, filters, rows, tBodies

table. JavaScript Objects (14)

currentStyle, runtimeStyle, style

<tbody> ... </tbody>

Compatibility: NN4, NN6, NN7, IE4, IE5, IE5.5, IE6

The <table> element can be sectioned into three horizontal parts: <thead>, <tbody>, and <tfoot>. <thead> contains the rows at the head of the <table>; <tbody> contains the rows in the body of the <table>; and <tfoot> contains the rows at the foot of the table.

Although you can accomplish similar results with additional table rows, using the <thead>, <tbody>, and <tfoot> elements with the <table> element indicates to the browser the breakdown of the sections and allows you to apply different styles to the heading, body, and footer.

Syntax:

```
<tbody attributes events> . . . </tbody>
```

Example:

```
<html><head><title>tbody element example</title></head>
<body bgcolor="#FFFFFF" text="#000000">
<table width="500" border="8" cellspacing="5" cellpadding="5" align="center">
<thead style="color:blue" align="center">
   <td>This cell is in the thead rows group.</td>
   <td>This cell is in the thead rows group.</td>
   <td>This cell is in the thead rows group.</td>
</thead>
<tbody>
<tr>
   <td>This cell is in the tbody rows group.</td>
   <td>This cell is in the tbody rows group.</td>
   <td>This cell is in the tbody rows group.</td>
</tr>
```

```
<tr>
   <td>This cell is in the tbody rows group.</td>
   <td>This cell is in the tbody rows group.</td>
   <td>This cell is in the tbody rows group.</td>
</tr>
</tbody>
<tfoot style="color:red" align="right">
   <td>This cell is in the tfoot rows group.</td>
   <td>This cell is in the tfoot rows group.</td>
   <td>This cell is in the tfoot rows group.</td>
</tfoot>
</table>
</body></html>
```

\<tbody\> HTML Attributes (6)

```
accesskey, align, begin, bgcolor, ch, choff, class, dir, end, hidefocus, id, lang,
language, style, syncmaster, systemBitrate, systemCaptions, systemLanguage,
systemOverdubOrSubtitle, tabindex, timecontainer, title, unselectable, valign
```

\<tbody\> Event Handlers (7)

```
onActivate, onBeforeActivate, onBeforeCut, onBeforeDeactivate, onBeforePaste,
onBlur, onClick, onContextMenu, onControlSelect, onCut, onDblClick, onDeactivate,
onDrag, onDragEnd, onDragEnter, onDragLeave, onDragOver, onDragStart, onDrop,
onFocus, onFocusIn, onFocusOut, onHelp, onKeyDown, onKeyPress, onKeyUp,
onLoseCapture, onMouseDown, onMouseEnter, onMouseLeave, onMouseMove, onMouseOut,
onMouseOver, onMouseUp, onMouseWheel, onMove, onMoveEnd, onMoveStart, onPaste,
onPropertyChange, onReadyStateChange, onResizeEnd, onResizeStart, onSelectStart,
onTimeError
```

\<tbody\> CSS Attributes and JavaScript Style Properties (8)

The names are in CSS syntax. See the introduction to this chapter for the
JavaScript syntax rules. Names noted with an asterisk (*) are JavaScript
properties only.

```
!important, background, background-attachment, background-color, background-image,
background-position, background-position-x, background-position-y, background-
repeat, behavior, clear, color, cursor, direction, display, font, font-family,
font-size, font-style, font-variant, font-weight, layout-grid, layout-grid-mode,
letter-spacing, line-height, page-break-after, page-break-before, pixelBottom(*),
pixelHeight(*), pixelLeft(*), pixelRight(*), pixelTop(*), pixelWidth(*),
posBottom(*), posHeight(*), posLeft(*), posRight(*), posTop(*), posWidth(*), text-
autospace, text-decoration, text-transform, text-underline-position,
textDecorationBlink(*), textDecorationLineThrough(*), textDecorationNone(*),
textDecorationOverline(*), textDecorationUnderline(*), unicode-bidi, vertical-
align, visibility, word-spacing, z-index, zoom
```

<tbody> Microsoft Behaviors (9)

clientCaps, download, homePage, time, time2

tbody. JavaScript Properties (11)

accessKey, align, bgColor, canHaveChildren, canHaveHTML, ch, chOff, className, clientHeight, clientLeft, clientTop, clientWidth, cursor, dir, end, firstChild, hideFocus, id, innerHTML, innerText, isContentEditable, isDisabled, isMultiLine, isTextEdit, lang, language, lastChild, nextSibling, nodeName, nodeType, nodeValue, offsetHeight, offsetLeft, offsetParent, offsetTop, offsetWidth, outerHTML, outerText, ownerDocument, parentElement, parentNode, parentTextEdit, previousSibling, readyState, scopeName, scrollHeight, scrollLeft, scrollTop, scrollWidth, sourceIndex, tabIndex, tagName, tagUrn, title, uniqueID, vAlign

tbody. JavaScript Methods (12)

addBehavior, appendChild, applyElement, attachEvent, blur, clearAttributes, click, cloneNode, componentFromPoint, contains, deleteRow, deleteTFoot, deleteTHead, detachEvent, fireEvent, focus, getAdjacentText, getAttribute, getAttributeNode, getBoundingClientRect, getClientRects, getElementsByTagName, getExpression, hasChildNodes, insertAdjacentElement, insertBefore, insertRow, mergeAttributes, moveRow, normalize, releaseCapture, removeAttribute, removeAttributeNode, removeBehavior, removeChild, removeExpression, removeNode, replaceAdjacentText, replaceChild, replaceNode, scrollIntoView, setActive, setAttribute, setAttributeNode, setCapture, setExpression, swapNode

tbody. JavaScript Collections (13)

all, attributes, behaviorUrns, childNodes, children, rows

tbody. JavaScript Objects (14)

currentStyle, runtimeStyle, style

<td> ... </td>

Compatibility: NN4, NN6, NN7, IE4, IE5, IE5.5, IE6

This element creates a cell in a table. This element is used in conjunction with the <table> and <tr> elements. For each table row, <tr>, you can have one or more table details, <td>, or cells.

Syntax:

<td attributes events> . . . </td>

Example:

```
<html><head><title>td element example</title></head>
<body bgcolor="#FFFFFF" text="#000000">
  <table width="200" border="8" cellspacing="5" cellpadding="5" align="center">
    <tr align="center"><td>Cell 1</td><td>Cell 2</td></tr>
    <tr align="center"><td>Cell 3</td><td>Cell 4</td></tr>
  </table>
</body></html>
```

\<td> HTML Attributes (6)

abbr, accesskey, align, axis, background, begin, bgcolor, bordercolor, ch, choff, class, colspan, dir, end, headers, height, hidefocus, id, lang, language, nowrap, rowspan, scope, style, syncmaster, systemBitrate, systemCaptions, systemLanguage, systemOverdubOrSubtitle, tabindex, timecontainer, title, unselectable, valign, width

\<td> Event Handlers (7)

onActivate, onAfterUpdate, onBeforeActivate, onBeforeCopy, onBeforeCut, onBeforeDeactivate, onBeforeEditFocus, onBeforePaste, onBeforeUpdate, onBlur, onClick, onContextMenu, onControlSelect, onCopy, onCut, onDblClick, onDeactivate, onDrag, onDragEnd, onDragEnter, onDragLeave, onDragOver, onDragStart, onDrop, onFilterChange, onFocus, onFocusIn, onFocusOut, onHelp, onKeyDown, onKeyPress, onKeyUp, onLoseCapture, onMouseDown, onMouseEnter, onMouseLeave, onMouseMove, onMouseOut, onMouseOver, onMouseUp, onMouseWheel, onMove, onMoveEnd, onMoveStart, onPaste, onPropertyChange, onReadyStateChange, onResize, onResizeEnd, onResizeStart, onScroll, onSelectStart, onTimeError

\<td> CSS Attributes and JavaScript Style Properties (8)

The names are in CSS syntax. See the introduction to this chapter for the JavaScript syntax rules. Names noted with an asterisk (*) are JavaScript properties only.

!important, background, background-attachment, background-color, background-image, background-position, background-position-x, background-position-y, background-repeat, behavior, border, border-bottom, border-bottom-color, border-bottom-style, border-bottom-width, border-color, border-left, border-left-color, border-left-style, border-left-width, border-right, border-right-color, border-right-style, border-right-width, border-style, border-top, border-top-color, border-top-style, border-top-width, border-width, clear, clip, color, cursor, direction, display, filter, font, font-family, font-size, font-style, font-variant, font-weight, hasLayout(*), height, layout-flow, layout-grid, layout-grid-char, layout-grid-line, layout-grid-mode, layout-grid-type, letter-spacing, line-break, line-height, margin, margin-bottom, margin-left, margin-right, margin-top, min-height, padding, padding-bottom, padding-left, padding-right, padding-top, page-break-before, pixelBottom(*), pixelHeight(*), pixelLeft(*), pixelRight(*), pixelTop(*), pixelWidth(*), posBottom(*), posHeight(*), position, posLeft(*), posRight(*), posTop(*), posWidth(*), text-align, text-autospace, text-decoration, text-indent, text-justify, text-transform, text-underline-position, textDecorationBlink(*), textDecorationLineThrough(*), textDecorationNone(*), textDecorationOverline(*), textDecorationUnderline(*), unicode-bidi, vertical-align, visibility, word-break, word-spacing, word-wrap, writing-mode, z-index, zoom

`<td>` Microsoft Behaviors (9)

clientCaps, download, homePage, time, time2

`<td>` Microsoft Filters (10)

Alpha, Barn, BasicImage, BlendTrans, Blinds, Blur, CheckerBoard, Chroma, Compositor, DropShadow, Emboss, Engrave, Fade, FlipH, FlipV, Glow, GradientWipe, Gray, ICMFilter, Inset, Invert, Iris, Light, MaskFilter, Matrix, MotionBlur, Pixelate, RadialWipe, RandomBars, RandomDissolve, RevealTrans, Shadow, Slide, Spiral, Stretch, Strips, Wave, Wheel, Xray, Zigzag

td. JavaScript Properties (11)

abbr, accessKey, align, axis, background, bgColor, border, borderColor, borderColorDark, borderColorLight, canHaveChildren, canHaveHTML, cellIndex, ch, chOff, className, clientHeight, clientLeft, clientTop, clientWidth, colSpan, cursor, dir, disabled, end, firstChild, hasLayout, headers, height, hideFocus, id, innerHTML, innerText, isContentEditable, isDisabled, isMultiLine, isTextEdit, lang, language, lastChild, nextSibling, nodeName, nodeType, nodeValue, noWrap, offsetHeight, offsetLeft, offsetParent, offsetTop, offsetWidth, outerHTML, outerText, ownerDocument, parentElement, parentNode, parentTextEdit, previousSibling, readyState, rowSpan, scope, scopeName, scrollHeight, scrollLeft, scrollTop, scrollWidth, sourceIndex, tabIndex, tagName, tagUrn, title, uniqueID, vAlign, width

td. JavaScript Methods (12)

addBehavior, appendChild, applyElement, attachEvent, blur, clearAttributes, click, cloneNode, componentFromPoint, contains, detachEvent, dragDrop, fireEvent, focus, getAdjacentText, getAttribute, getAttributeNode, getBoundingClientRect, getClientRects, getElementsByTagName, getExpression, hasChildNodes, insertAdjacentElement, insertAdjacentHTML, insertAdjacentText, insertBefore, mergeAttributes, normalize, releaseCapture, removeAttribute, removeAttributeNode, removeBehavior, removeChild, removeExpression, removeNode, replaceAdjacentText, replaceChild, replaceNode, scrollIntoView, setActive, setAttribute, setAttributeNode, setCapture, setExpression, swapNode

td. JavaScript Collections (13)

all, attributes, behaviorUrns, childNodes, children, filters

td. JavaScript Objects (14)

currentStyle, runtimeStyle, style

\<textarea\> ... \</textarea\>

Compatibility: NN4, NN6, NN7, IE4, IE5, IE5.5, IE6

This element creates a multiline text entry control. Text enclosed between its opening and closing tags is displayed in the text field when the form is first displayed. This element is usually used in conjunction with the \<form\> element.

Syntax:

```
<textarea attributes events> . . . </textarea>
```

Example:

```
<html><head><title>textarea element example</title></head>
<body bgcolor="#FFFFFF" text="#000000">
<form name="form1" method="post" action="">
    <p><fieldset align="center">
    <textarea name="textfield1" cols="40" rows="2" wrap="hard">Please, use this
area to type your name and surname</textarea><br>
    </fieldset></p>
</form>
<form name="form2" method="post" action="">
    <p><fieldset>
    <input type="text" name="textfield3" value="Street address" size="65"><br>
    <input type="text" name="textfield4" value="City" size="45"><br>
    <input type="text" name="textfield5" value="Zip Code" size="55">
    </fieldset></p>
</form>
</body></html>
```

\<textarea\> HTML Attributes (6)

accesskey, begin, class, cols, contenteditable, datafld, datasrc, dir, disabled, end, hidefocus, id, lang, language, name, readonly, rows, style, syncmaster, systemBitrate, systemCaptions, systemLanguage, systemOverdubOrSubtitle, tabindex, timecontainer, title, unselectable, wrap

\<textarea\> Event Handlers (7)

onActivate, onAfterUpdate, onBeforeActivate, onBeforeCopy, onBeforeCut, onBeforeDeactivate, onBeforeEditFocus, onBeforePaste, onBeforeUpdate, onBlur, onChange, onClick, onContextMenu, onControlSelect, onCut, onDblClick, onDeactivate, onDrag, onDragEnd, onDragEnter, onDragLeave, onDragOver, onDragStart, onDrop, onErrorUpdate, onFilterChange, onFocus, onFocusIn, onFocusOut, onHelp, onKeyDown, onKeyPress, onKeyUp, onLoseCapture, onMouseDown, onMouseEnter, onMouseLeave, onMouseMove, onMouseOut, onMouseOver, onMouseUp, onMouseWheel, onMove, onMoveEnd, onMoveStart, onPaste, onPropertyChange, onReadyStateChange, onResize, onResizeEnd, onResizeStart, onScroll, onSelect, onSelectStart, onTimeError

<textarea> CSS Attributes and JavaScript Style Properties (8)

The names are in CSS syntax. See the introduction to this chapter for the JavaScript syntax rules. Names noted with an asterisk (*) are JavaScript properties only.

!important, accelerator, background, background-attachment, background-color, background-image, background-position, background-position-x, background-position-y, background-repeat, behavior, border, border-bottom, border-bottom-color, border-bottom-style, border-bottom-width, border-color, border-left, border-left-color, border-left-style, border-left-width, border-right, border-right-color, border-right-style, border-right-width, border-style, border-top, border-top-color, border-top-style, border-top-width, border-width, bottom, clear, clip, color, cursor, direction, display, filter, float, font, font-family, font-size, font-style, font-variant, font-weight, hasLayout(*), height, ime-mode, layout-flow, layout-grid, layout-grid-mode, left, letter-spacing, line-height, margin, margin-bottom, margin-left, margin-right, margin-top, overflow, overflow-x, overflow-y, padding, padding-bottom, padding-left, padding-right, padding-top, pixelBottom(*), pixelHeight(*), pixelLeft(*), pixelRight(*), pixelTop(*), pixelWidth(*), posBottom(*), posHeight(*), position, posLeft(*), posRight(*), posTop(*), posWidth(*), right, scrollbar-3dlight-color, scrollbar-arrow-color, scrollbar-base-color, scrollbar-darkshadow-color, scrollbar-face-color, scrollbar-highlight-color, scrollbar-shadow-color, scrollbar-track-color, styleFloat(*), text-align, text-align-last, text-autospace, text-decoration, text-overflow, text-transform, text-underline-position, textDecorationBlink(*), textDecorationLineThrough(*), textDecorationNone(*), textDecorationOverline(*), textDecorationUnderline(*), top, unicode-bidi, visibility, width, word-spacing, word-wrap, writing-mode, z-index, zoom

---

<textarea> Microsoft Behaviors (9)

---

clientCaps, download, homePage, httpFolder, saveFavorite, saveHistory, saveSnapshot, time, time2, userData

---

<textarea> Microsoft Filters (10)

Alpha, Barn, BasicImage, BlendTrans, Blinds, Blur, CheckerBoard, Chroma, Compositor, DropShadow, Emboss, Engrave, Fade, FlipH, FlipV, Glow, GradientWipe, Gray, ICMFilter, Inset, Invert, Iris, Light, MaskFilter, Matrix, MotionBlur, Pixelate, RadialWipe, RandomBars, RandomDissolve, RevealTrans, Shadow, Slide, Spiral, Stretch, Strips, Wave, Wheel, Xray, Zigzag

---

textarea. JavaScript Properties (11)

---

accessKey, canHaveChildren, canHaveHTML, className, clientHeight, clientLeft, clientTop, clientWidth, cols, contentEditable, cursor, dataFld, datasrc, defaultValue, dir, disabled, end, firstChild, form, hasLayout, hideFocus, id, innerHTML, innerText, isContentEditable, isDisabled, isMultiLine, isTextEdit, lang, language, lastChild, name, nextSibling, nodeName, nodeType, nodeValue, offsetHeight, offsetLeft, offsetParent, offsetTop, offsetWidth, outerHTML, outerText, ownerDocument, parentElement, parentNode, parentTextEdit, previousSibling, readOnly, readyState, recordNumber, rows, scopeName, scrollHeight, scrollLeft, scrollTop, scrollWidth, sourceIndex, status, tabIndex, tagName, tagUrn, title, type, uniqueID, value, wrap

textarea. JavaScript Methods (12)

addBehavior, appendChild, applyElement, attachEvent, blur, clearAttributes, click, cloneNode, componentFromPoint, contains, createTextRange, detachEvent, doScroll, dragDrop, fireEvent, focus, getAdjacentText, getAttribute, getAttributeNode, getBoundingClientRect, getClientRects, getElementsByTagName, getExpression, hasChildNodes, insertAdjacentElement, insertAdjacentHTML, insertAdjacentText, insertBefore, mergeAttributes, normalize, releaseCapture, removeAttribute, removeAttributeNode, removeBehavior, removeChild, removeExpression, removeNode, replaceAdjacentText, replaceChild, replaceNode, scrollIntoView, select, setActive, setAttribute, setAttributeNode, setCapture, setExpression, swapNode

textarea. JavaScript Collections (13)

all, attributes, behaviorUrns, childNodes, children, filters

textarea. JavaScript Objects (14)

currentStyle, runtimeStyle, style

<tfoot> ... </tfoot>, <thead> ... </thead>

Compatibility: NN6, NN7, IE4, IE5, IE5.5, IE6

All <table> elements can be divided into three parts: <thead>, <tbody>, and <tfoot>. <thead> contains the rows in the table header, <tbody> contains the rows in the table body, and <tfoot> contains the rows in the table footer.

Although you can accomplish similar results with additional table rows, using the <thead>, <tbody>, and <tfoot> elements with the <table> element indicates to the browser the breakdown of the sections and allows you to apply different styles to the heading, body, and footer.

Syntax for <tfoot>:

```
<tfoot attributes events> . . . </tfoot>
```

Syntax for <thead>:

```
<thead attributes events> . . . </thead>
```

Example:

```
<html><head><title>tfoot, thead element examples</title></head>
<body bgcolor="#FFFFFF" text="#000000">
<table width="500" border="8" cellspacing="5" cellpadding="5" align="center">
<thead style="color:blue" align="center">
```

```
  <td>This cell is in the thead rows group.</td>
  <td>This cell is in the thead rows group.</td>
  <td>This cell is in the thead rows group.</td>
</thead>
<tbody>
<tr>
  <td>This cell is in the tbody rows group.</td>
  <td>This cell is in the tbody rows group.</td>
  <td>This cell is in the tbody rows group.</td>
</tr>
<tr>
  <td>This cell is in the tbody rows group.</td>
  <td>This cell is in the tbody rows group.</td>
  <td>This cell is in the tbody rows group.</td>
</tr>
</tbody>
<tfoot style="color:red" align="right">
  <td>This cell is in the tfoot rows group.</td>
  <td>This cell is in the tfoot rows group.</td>
  <td>This cell is in the tfoot rows group.</td>
</tfoot>
</table>
</body></html>
```

\<tfoot\> and \<thead\> HTML Attributes (6)

accesskey, align, begin, bgcolor, ch, choff, class, dir, end, hidefocus, id, lang, language, style, syncmaster, systemBitrate, systemCaptions, systemLanguage, systemOverdubOrSubtitle, tabindex, timecontainer, title, unselectable, valign

\<tfoot\> and \<thead\> Event Handlers (7)

onActivate, onBeforeActivate, onBeforeCut, onBeforeDeactivate, onBeforePaste, onBlur, onClick, onContextMenu, onControlSelect, onCut, onDblClick, onDeactivate, onDragEnter, onDragStart, onFocus, onFocusIn, onFocusOut, onHelp, onKeyDown, onKeyPress, onKeyUp, onLoseCapture, onMouseDown, onMouseEnter, onMouseLeave, onMouseMove, onMouseOut, onMouseOver, onMouseUp, onMouseWheel, onMove, onMoveEnd, onMoveStart, onPaste, onPropertyChange, onReadyStateChange, onResizeEnd, onResizeStart, onSelectStart, onTimeError

\<tfoot\> and \<thead\> CSS Attributes and JavaScript Style Properties (8)

The names are in CSS syntax. See the introduction to this chapter for the JavaScript syntax rules. Names noted with an asterisk (*) are JavaScript properties only.

!important, background, background-attachment, background-color, background-image, background-position, background-position-x, background-position-y, background-repeat, behavior, clear, color, cursor, direction, display, font, font-family, font-size, font-style, font-variant, font-weight, layout-grid, layout-grid-mode, letter-spacing, line-height, page-break-after, page-break-before, pixelBottom(*), pixelHeight(*), pixelLeft(*), pixelRight(*), pixelTop(*), pixelWidth(*), posBottom(*), posHeight(*), posLeft(*), posRight(*), posTop(*), posWidth(*), text-autospace, text-decoration, text-transform, text-underline-position, textDecorationBlink(*), textDecorationLineThrough(*), textDecorationNone(*), textDecorationOverline(*), textDecorationUnderline(*), unicode-bidi, vertical-align, visibility, word-spacing, z-index, zoom

<tfoot> and <thead> Microsoft Behaviors (9)

clientCaps, download, homePage, time, time2

tfoot. and thead. JavaScript Properties (11)

accessKey, align, bgColor, canHaveChildren, canHaveHTML, ch, chOff, className, clientHeight, clientLeft, clientTop, clientWidth, cursor, dir, end, firstChild, hideFocus, id, innerHTML, innerText, isContentEditable, isDisabled, isMultiLine, isTextEdit, lang, language, lastChild, nextSibling, nodeName, nodeType, nodeValue, offsetHeight, offsetLeft, offsetParent, offsetTop, offsetWidth, outerHTML, outerText, ownerDocument, parentElement, parentNode, parentTextEdit, previousSibling, readyState, scopeName, scrollHeight, scrollLeft, scrollTop, scrollWidth, sourceIndex, tabIndex, tagName, tagUrn, title, uniqueID, vAlign

tfoot. and thead. JavaScript Methods (12)

addBehavior, appendChild, applyElement, attachEvent, blur, clearAttributes, click, cloneNode, componentFromPoint, contains, deleteRow, detachEvent, fireEvent, focus, getAdjacentText, getAttribute, getAttributeNode, getBoundingClientRect, getClientRects, getElementsByTagName, getExpression, hasChildNodes, insertAdjacentElement, insertBefore, insertRow, mergeAttributes, moveRow, normalize, releaseCapture, removeAttribute, removeAttributeNode, removeBehavior, removeChild, removeExpression, removeNode, replaceAdjacentText, replaceChild, replaceNode, scrollIntoView, setActive, setAttribute, setAttributeNode, setCapture, setExpression, swapNode

tfoot. and thead. JavaScript Collections (13)

all, attributes, behaviorUrns, childNodes, children, rows

tfoot. and thead. JavaScript Objects (14)

currentStyle, runtimeStyle, style

<th> ... </th>

Compatibility: NN4, NN6, NN7, IE4, IE5, IE5.5, IE6

This element creates a single cell as a table heading. This cell must have a colspan attribute, whose value is equal to the number of cells in subsequent table rows. The text in this element appears in bold and is aligned to the center by default.

Syntax:

```
<th attributes events> . . . </th>
```

Example:

```
<html><head><title>th element example</title></head>
<body bgcolor="#FFFFFF" text="#000000">
<table border="1">
  <tr><th colspan="3">Bold and centered text</th></tr>
  <tr><td>first column</td><td>second column</td><td>third column</td></tr>
  <tr><td> </td><td>  </td><td>  </td></tr>
</table>
</body></html>
```

`<th>` HTML Attributes (6)

abbr, accesskey, align, axis, background, begin, bgcolor, bordercolor, ch, choff, class, colspan, dir, end, headers, height, hidefocus, id, lang, language, nowrap, rowspan, scope, style, syncmaster, systemBitrate, systemCaptions, systemLanguage, systemOverdubOrSubtitle, tabindex, timecontainer, title, valign, width

`<th>` Event Handlers (7)

onActivate, onBeforeActivate, onBeforeCopy, onBeforeCut, onBeforeDeactivate, onBeforePaste, onBlur, onClick, onContextMenu, onControlSelect, onCopy, onCut, onDblClick, onDeactivate, onDragEnter, onDragStart, onFilterChange, onFocus, onFocusIn, onFocusOut, onHelp, onKeyDown, onKeyPress, onKeyUp, onLoseCapture, onMouseDown, onMouseEnter, onMouseLeave, onMouseMove, onMouseOut, onMouseOver, onMouseUp, onMouseWheel, onMove, onMoveEnd, onMoveStart, onPaste, onPropertyChange, onReadyStateChange, onResizeEnd, onResizeStart, onScroll, onSelectStart, onTimeError

`<th>` CSS Attributes and JavaScript Style Properties (8)

The names are in CSS syntax. See the introduction to this chapter for the JavaScript syntax rules. Names noted with an asterisk (*) are JavaScript properties only.

!important, background, background-attachment, background-color, background-image, background-position, background-position-x, background-position-y, background-repeat, behavior, border, border-bottom, border-bottom-color, border-bottom-style, border-bottom-width, border-color, border-left, border-left-color, border-left-style, border-left-width, border-right, border-right-color, border-right-style, border-right-width, border-style, border-top, border-top-color, border-top-style, border-top-width, border-width, clear, clip, color, cursor, direction, display, filter, font, font-family, font-size, font-style, font-variant, font-weight, hasLayout(*), height, layout-flow, layout-grid, layout-grid-char, layout-grid-line, layout-grid-mode, layout-grid-type, letter-spacing, line-break, line-height, margin, margin-bottom, margin-left, margin-right, margin-top, min-height, padding, padding-bottom, padding-left, padding-right, padding-top, page-break-after, page-break-before, pixelBottom(*), pixelHeight(*), pixelLeft(*), pixelRight(*), pixelTop(*), pixelWidth(*), posBottom(*), posHeight(*), position, posLeft(*), posRight(*), posTop(*), posWidth(*), text-align, text-autospace, text-decoration, text-indent, text-justify, text-transform, text-underline-position, textDecorationBlink(*), textDecorationLineThrough(*), textDecorationNone(*), textDecorationOverline(*), textDecorationUnderline(*), unicode-bidi, vertical-align, visibility, word-break, word-spacing, word-wrap, writing-mode, z-index, zoom

<th> Microsoft Behaviors (9)

clientCaps, download, homePage, time, time2

<th> Microsoft Filters (10)

Alpha, Barn, BasicImage, BlendTrans, Blinds, Blur, CheckerBoard, Chroma, Compositor, DropShadow, Emboss, Engrave, Fade, FlipH, FlipV, Glow, GradientWipe, Gray, ICMFilter, Inset, Invert, Iris, Light, MaskFilter, Matrix, MotionBlur, Pixelate, RadialWipe, RandomBars, RandomDissolve, RevealTrans, Slide, Spiral, Stretch, Strips, Wave, Wheel, Xray, Zigzag

th. JavaScript Properties (11)

abbr, accessKey, align, axis, background, bgColor, borderColor, borderColorDark, borderColorLight, canHaveChildren, canHaveHTML, cellIndex, ch, chOff, className, clientHeight, clientLeft, clientTop, clientWidth, colSpan, cursor, dir, end, firstChild, hasLayout, headers, height, hideFocus, id, innerHTML, innerText, isContentEditable, isDisabled, isMultiLine, isTextEdit, lang, language, lastChild, nextSibling, nodeName, nodeType, nodeValue, noWrap, offsetHeight, offsetLeft, offsetParent, offsetTop, offsetWidth, outerHTML, outerText, ownerDocument, parentElement, parentNode, parentTextEdit, previousSibling, readyState, rowSpan, scope, scopeName, scrollHeight, scrollLeft, scrollTop, scrollWidth, sourceIndex, tabIndex, tagName, tagUrn, title, uniqueID, vAlign, width

th. JavaScript Methods (12)

addBehavior, appendChild, applyElement, attachEvent, blur, clearAttributes, click, cloneNode, componentFromPoint, contains, detachEvent, fireEvent, focus, getAdjacentText, getAttribute, getAttributeNode, getBoundingClientRect, getClientRects, getElementsByTagName, getExpression, hasChildNodes, insertAdjacentElement, insertAdjacentHTML, insertAdjacentText, insertBefore, mergeAttributes, normalize, releaseCapture, removeAttribute, removeAttributeNode, removeBehavior, removeChild, removeExpression, removeNode, replaceAdjacentText, replaceChild, replaceNode, scrollIntoView, setActive, setAttribute, setAttributeNode, setCapture, setExpression, swapNode

th. JavaScript Collections (13)

all, attributes, behaviorUrns, childNodes, filters

th. JavaScript Objects (14)

```
currentStyle, runtimeStyle, style
```

<title> ... </title>

Compatibility: NN4, NN6, NN7, IE4, IE5, IE5.5, IE6

This element defines the title of a document. The <title> element must be located inside the <head> element.

Syntax:

```
<title attributes events> . . . </title>
```

Example:

```
<html><head><title>title element example</title></head>
<body bgcolor="#FFFFFF" text="#000000">body content
</body></html>
```

<title> HTML Attributes (6)

```
dir, id, lang
```

<title> Event Handlers (7)

```
onLayoutComplete, onReadyStateChange
```

<title> CSS Attributes and JavaScript Style Properties (8)

The names are in CSS syntax. See the introduction to this chapter for the JavaScript syntax rules. Names noted with an asterisk (*) are JavaScript properties only.

```
background-position-x, background-position-y, behavior, pixelBottom(*),
pixelHeight(*), pixelLeft(*), pixelRight(*), pixelTop(*), pixelWidth(*),
posBottom(*), posHeight(*), posLeft(*), posRight(*), posTop(*), posWidth(*),
text-autospace, text-underline-position
```

<title> Microsoft Behaviors (9)

```
clientCaps, download, homePage
```

title. JavaScript Properties (11)

```
canHaveHTML, className, clientHeight, clientWidth, dir, disabled, firstChild, id,
innerHTML, innerText, isContentEditable, isDisabled, isMultiLine, isTextEdit, lang,
lastChild, nextSibling, nodeName, nodeType, nodeValue, offsetHeight, offsetLeft,
```

offsetParent, offsetTop, offsetWidth, ownerDocument, parentElement, parentNode,
parentTextEdit, previousSibling, readyState, scopeName, scrollHeight, scrollLeft,
scrollTop, scrollWidth, sourceIndex, tagName, tagUrn, text, title, uniqueID

title. JavaScript Methods (12)

addBehavior, appendChild, applyElement, attachEvent, clearAttributes, cloneNode,
componentFromPoint, contains, detachEvent, dragDrop, fireEvent, getAdjacentText,
getAttribute, getAttributeNode, getElementsByTagName, hasChildNodes,
insertAdjacentElement, insertBefore, mergeAttributes, normalize, removeAttribute,
removeAttributeNode, removeBehavior, removeChild, replaceAdjacentText,
replaceChild, setAttribute, setAttributeNode, swapNode

title. JavaScript Collections (13)

all, attributes, behaviorUrns, childNodes, children

<tr> ... </tr>

Compatibility: NN4, NN6, NN7, IE4, IE5, IE5.5, IE6

This element creates a single row inside a <table> element. In turn, the cells in
each row are created by the <td> element.

Syntax:

```
<tr attributes events> . . . </tr>
```

Example:

```
<html><head><title>tr element example</title></head>
<body bgcolor="#FFFFFF" text="#000000">
  <table width="200" border="8" cellspacing="5" cellpadding="5" align="center">
    <tr align="center"><td>Cell 1</td><td>Cell 2</td></tr>
    <tr align="center"><td>Cell 3</td><td>Cell 4</td></tr>
  </table>
</body></html>
```

<tr> HTML Attributes (6)

accesskey, align, begin, bgcolor, bordercolor, ch, choff, class, dir, end, height,
hidefocus, id, lang, language, style, syncmaster, systemBitrate, systemCaptions,
systemLanguage, systemOverdubOrSubtitle, tabindex, timecontainer, title, valign,
width

<tr> Event Handlers (7)

onActivate, onAfterUpdate, onBeforeActivate, onBeforeCopy, onBeforeCut,
onBeforeDeactivate, onBeforeEditFocus, onBeforePaste, onBeforeUpdate, onBlur
onClick, onContextMenu, onControlSelect, onCopy, onCut, onDblClick, onDeactivate,

onDrag, onDragEnd, onDragEnter, onDragLeave, onDragOver, onDragStart, onDrop, onFilterChange, onFocus, onFocusIn, onFocusOut, onHelp, onKeyDown, onKeyPress, onKeyUp, onLoseCapture, onMouseDown, onMouseEnter, onMouseLeave, onMouseMove, onMouseOut, onMouseOver, onMouseUp, onMouseWheel, onMove, onMoveEnd, onMoveStart, onPaste, onPropertyChange, onReadyStateChange, onResize, onResizeEnd, onResizeStart, onSelectStart, onTimeError

\<tr\> CSS Attributes and JavaScript Style Properties (8)

The names are in CSS syntax. See the introduction to this chapter for the JavaScript syntax rules. Names noted with an asterisk (*) are JavaScript properties only.

!important, background, background-attachment, background-color, background-image, background-position, background-position-x, background-position-y, background-repeat, behavior, clear, clip, color, cursor, direction, display, font, font-family, font-size, font-style, font-variant, font-weight, height, layout-grid, layout-grid-char, layout-grid-line, layout-grid-mode, layout-grid-type, letter-spacing, line-break, line-height, min-height, page-break-after, page-break-before, pixelBottom(*), pixelHeight(*), pixelLeft(*), pixelRight(*), pixelTop(*), pixelWidth(*), posBottom(*), posHeight(*), position, posLeft(*), posRight(*), posTop(*), posWidth(*), text-align, text-autospace, text-decoration, text-indent, text-justify, text-transform, text-underline-position, textDecorationBlink(*), textDecorationLineThrough(*), textDecorationNone(*), textDecorationOverline(*), textDecorationUnderline(*), unicode-bidi, vertical-align, visibility, word-break, word-spacing, z-index, zoom

\<tr\> Microsoft Behaviors (9)

clientCaps, download, homePage, time, time2

tr. JavaScript Properties (11)

accessKey, align, bgColor, borderColor, borderColorDark, borderColorLight, canHaveChildren, canHaveHTML, ch, chOff, className, clientHeight, clientLeft, clientTop, clientWidth, cursor, dir, disabled, end, firstChild, height, hideFocus, id, innerHTML, innerText, isContentEditable, isDisabled, isMultiLine, isTextEdit, lang, language, lastChild, nextSibling, nodeName, nodeType, nodeValue, offsetHeight, offsetLeft, offsetParent, offsetTop, offsetWidth, outerHTML, outerText, ownerDocument, parentElement, parentNode, parentTextEdit, previousSibling, readyState, rowIndex, scopeName, scrollHeight, scrollLeft, scrollTop, scrollWidth, sectionRowIndex, sourceIndex, tabIndex, tagName, tagUrn, title, uniqueID, vAlign, width

tr. JavaScript Methods (12)

addBehavior, appendChild, applyElement, attachEvent, blur, clearAttributes, click, cloneNode, componentFromPoint, contains, deleteCell, detachEvent, dragDrop, fireEvent, focus, getAdjacentText, getAttribute, getAttributeNode, getBoundingClientRect, getClientRects, getElementsByTagName, getExpression, hasChildNodes, insertAdjacentElement, insertBefore, insertCell, mergeAttributes, normalize, releaseCapture, removeAttribute, removeAttributeNode, removeBehavior, removeChild, removeExpression, removeNode, replaceAdjacentText, replaceChild, replaceNode, scrollIntoView, setActive, setAttribute, setAttributeNode, setCapture, setExpression, swapNode

tr. JavaScript Collections (13)

all, attributes, behaviorUrns, cells, childNodes, children

tr. JavaScript Objects (14)

currentStyle, runtimeStyle, style

<tt> ... </tt>

Compatibility: NN4, NN6, NN7, IE4, IE5, IE5.5, IE6

This element causes text between its opening and closing tags to be rendered in a monospaced, fixed-sized font.

Syntax:

<tt *attributes events*> . . . </tt>

Example:

```
<html><head><title>tt element example</title></head>
<body bgcolor="#FFFFFF" text="#000000">
<tt>This text is rendered using a monospaced font</tt>
</body></html>
```

<tt> HTML Attributes (6)

accesskey, begin, class, contenteditable, dir, disabled, end, hidefocus, id, lang, language, style, syncmaster, systemBitrate, systemCaptions, systemLanguage, systemOverdubOrSubtitle, tabindex, timecontainer, title, unselectable

<tt> Event Handlers (7)

onActivate, onBeforeActivate, onBeforeCopy, onBeforeCut, onBeforeDeactivate, onBeforeEditFocus, onBeforePaste, onBlur, onClick, onContextMenu, onControlSelect, onCopy, onCut, onDblClick, onDeactivate, onDrag, onDragEnd, onDragEnter, onDragLeave, onDragOver, onDragStart, onDrop, onFocus, onFocusIn, onFocusOut, onHelp, onKeyDown, onKeyPress, onKeyUp, onLoseCapture, onMouseDown, onMouseEnter, onMouseLeave, onMouseMove, onMouseOut, onMouseOver, onMouseUp, onMouseWheel, onMove, onMoveEnd, onMoveStart, onPaste, onPropertyChange, onReadyStateChange, onResize, onResizeEnd, onResizeStart, onSelectStart, onTimeError

<tt> CSS Attributes and JavaScript Style Properties (8)

The names are in CSS syntax. See the introduction to this chapter for the JavaScript syntax rules. Names noted with an asterisk (*) are JavaScript properties only.

!important, accelerator, background, background-attachment, background-color, background-image, background-position, background-position-x, background-position-y, background-repeat, behavior, border, border-bottom, border-bottom-color, border-bottom-style, border-bottom-width, border-color, border-left, border-left-color, border-left-style, border-left-width, border-right, border-right-color, border-right-style, border-right-width, border-style, border-top, border-top-color, border-top-style, border-top-width, border-width, bottom, clear, clip, color, cursor, direction, display, filter, float, font, font-family, font-size, font-style, font-variant, font-weight, hasLayout(*), height, layout-flow, layout-grid, layout-grid-mode, left, letter-spacing, line-height, margin, margin-bottom, margin-left, margin-right, margin-top, overflow, overflow-x, overflow-y, padding, padding-bottom, padding-left, padding-right, padding-top, pixelBottom(*), pixelHeight(*), pixelLeft(*), pixelRight(*), pixelTop(*), pixelWidth(*), posBottom(*), posHeight(*), position, posLeft(*), posRight(*), posTop(*), posWidth(*), right, styleFloat(*), text-autospace, text-decoration, text-overflow, text-transform, text-underline-position, textDecorationBlink(*), textDecorationLineThrough(*), textDecorationNone(*), textDecorationOverline(*), textDecorationUnderline(*), top, unicode-bidi, visibility, white-space, width, word-spacing, word-wrap, writing-mode, z-index, zoom

<tt> Microsoft Behaviors (9)

clientCaps, download, homePage, httpFolder, saveFavorite, saveHistory, saveSnapshot, time, time2, userData

<tt> Microsoft Filters (10)

Alpha, Barn, BasicImage, BlendTrans, Blinds, Blur, CheckerBoard, Chroma, Compositor, DropShadow, Emboss, Engrave, Fade, FlipH, FlipV, Glow, GradientWipe, Gray, ICMFilter, Inset, Invert, Iris, Light, MaskFilter, Matrix, MotionBlur, Pixelate, RadialWipe, RandomBars, RandomDissolve, RevealTrans, Shadow, Slide, Spiral, Stretch, Strips, Wave, Wheel, Xray, Zigzag

tt. JavaScript Properties (11)

accessKey, canHaveChildren, canHaveHTML, className, clientHeight, clientLeft, clientTop, clientWidth, contentEditable, cursor, dir, disabled, end, firstChild, hasLayout, hideFocus, id, innerHTML, innerText, isContentEditable, isDisabled, isMultiLine, isTextEdit, lang, language, lastChild, nextSibling, nodeName, nodeType, nodeValue, offsetHeight, offsetLeft, offsetParent, offsetTop, offsetWidth, outerHTML, outerText, ownerDocument, parentElement, parentNode, parentTextEdit, previousSibling, readyState, scopeName, scrollHeight, scrollLeft, scrollTop, scrollWidth, sourceIndex, tabIndex, tagName, tagUrn, title, uniqueID

tt. JavaScript Methods (12)

addBehavior, appendChild, applyElement, attachEvent, blur, clearAttributes, click, cloneNode, componentFromPoint, contains, detachEvent, fireEvent, focus, getAdjacentText, getAttribute, getAttributeNode, getBoundingClientRect, getClientRects, getElementsByTagName, getExpression, hasChildNodes, insertAdjacentElement, insertAdjacentHTML, insertAdjacentText, insertBefore, mergeAttributes, normalize, releaseCapture, removeAttribute, removeAttributeNode, removeBehavior, removeChild, removeExpression, removeNode, replaceAdjacentText, replaceChild, replaceNode, scrollIntoView, setActive, setAttribute, setAttributeNode, setCapture, setExpression, swapNode

tt. JavaScript Collections (13)

all, attributes, behaviorUrns, childNodes, children

tt. JavaScript Objects (14)

currentStyle, runtimeStyle, style

<u> ... </u>

Compatibility: NN4, NN6, NN7, IE4, IE5, IE5.5, IE6

This element causes the text between its opening and closing tags to be underlined. This element has been deprecated in favor of using CSS (see Chapter 1).

Syntax:

```
<u attributes events> . . . </u>
```

Example:

```
<html><head><title>u element example</title></head>
<body bgcolor="#FFFFFF" text="#000000">
<p>This formulation is <u>new</u> and <u>improved</u>.</p>
</body></html>
```

<u> HTML Attributes (6)

accesskey, begin, class, contenteditable, dir, disabled, end, hidefocus, id, lang, language, style, syncmaster, systemBitrate, systemCaptions, systemLanguage, systemOverdubOrSubtitle, tabindex, timecontainer, title, unselectable

<u> Event Handlers (7)

onActivate, onBeforeActivate, onBeforeCopy, onBeforeCut, onBeforeDeactivate, onBeforeEditFocus, onBeforePaste, onBlur, onClick, onContextMenu, onControlSelect, onCopy, onCut, onDblClick, onDeactivate, onDrag, onDragEnd, onDragEnter, onDragLeave, onDragOver, onDragStart, onDrop, onFocus, onFocusIn, onFocusOut, onHelp, onKeyDown, onKeyPress, onKeyUp, onLoseCapture, onMouseDown, onMouseEnter, onMouseLeave, onMouseMove, onMouseOut, onMouseOver, onMouseUp, onMouseWheel, onMove, onMoveEnd, onMoveStart, onPaste, onPropertyChange, onReadyStateChange, onResize, onResizeEnd, onResizeStart, onSelectStart, onTimeError

\<u\> CSS Attributes and JavaScript Style Properties (8)

The names are in CSS syntax. See the introduction to this chapter for the JavaScript syntax rules. Names noted with an asterisk (*) are JavaScript properties only.

!important, accelerator, background, background-attachment, background-color, background-image, background-position, background-position-x, background-position-y, background-repeat, behavior, border, border-bottom, border-bottom-color, border-bottom-style, border-bottom-width, border-color, border-left, border-left-color, border-left-style, border-left-width, border-right, border-right-color, border-right-style, border-right-width, border-style, border-top, border-top-color, border-top-style, border-top-width, border-width, bottom, clear, clip, color, cursor, direction, display, filter, float, font, font-family, font-size, font-style, font-variant, font-weight, hasLayout(*), height, layout-flow, layout-grid, layout-grid-mode, left, letter-spacing, line-height, margin, margin-bottom, margin-left, margin-right, margin-top, overflow, overflow-x, overflow-y, padding, padding-bottom, padding-left, padding-right, padding-top, pixelBottom(*), pixelHeight(*), pixelLeft(*), pixelRight(*), pixelTop(*), pixelWidth(*), posBottom(*), posHeight(*), position, posLeft(*), posRight(*), posTop(*), posWidth(*), right, styleFloat(*), text-autospace, text-decoration, text-overflow, text-transform, text-underline-position, textDecorationBlink(*), textDecorationLineThrough(*), textDecorationNone(*), textDecorationOverline(*), textDecorationUnderline(*), top, unicode-bidi, visibility, white-space, width, word-spacing, word-wrap, writing-mode, z-index, zoom

\<u\> Microsoft Behaviors (9)

clientCaps, download, homePage, httpFolder, saveFavorite, saveHistory, saveSnapshot, time, time2, userData

\<u\> Microsoft Filters (10)

Alpha, Barn, BasicImage, BlendTrans, Blinds, Blur, CheckerBoard, Chroma, Compositor, DropShadow, Emboss, Engrave, Fade, FlipH, FlipV, Glow, GradientWipe, Gray, ICMFilter, Inset, Invert, Iris, Light, MaskFilter, Matrix, MotionBlur, Pixelate, RadialWipe, RandomBars, RandomDissolve, RevealTrans, Shadow, Slide, Spiral, Stretch, Strips, Wave, Wheel, Xray, Zigzag

u. JavaScript Properties (11)

accessKey, canHaveChildren, canHaveHTML, className, clientHeight, clientLeft, clientTop, clientWidth, contentEditable, cursor, dir, disabled, end, firstChild, hasLayout, hideFocus, id, innerHTML, innerText, isContentEditable, isDisabled, isMultiLine, isTextEdit, lang, language, lastChild, nextSibling, nodeName, nodeType, nodeValue, offsetHeight, offsetLeft, offsetParent, offsetTop, offsetWidth, outerHTML, outerText, ownerDocument, parentElement, parentNode, parentTextEdit, previousSibling, readyState, scopeName, scrollHeight, scrollLeft, scrollTop, scrollWidth, sourceIndex, tabIndex, tagName, tagUrn, title, uniqueID

v. JavaScript Methods (12)

addBehavior, appendChild, applyElement, attachEvent, blur, clearAttributes, click, cloneNode, componentFromPoint, contains, detachEvent, fireEvent, focus, getAdjacentText, getAttribute, getAttributeNode, getBoundingClientRect, getClientRects, getElementsByTagName, getExpression, hasChildNodes, insertAdjacentElement, insertAdjacentHTML, insertAdjacentText, insertBefore, mergeAttributes, normalize, releaseCapture, removeAttribute, removeAttributeNode, removeBehavior, removeChild, removeExpression, removeNode, replaceAdjacentText, replaceChild, replaceNode, scrollIntoView, setActive, setAttribute, setAttributeNode, setCapture, setExpression, swapNode

v. JavaScript Collections (13)

all, attributes, behaviorUrns, childNodes, children

v. JavaScript Objects (14)

currentStyle, runtimeStyle, style

<ul> ... </ul>

Compatibility: NN4, NN6, NN7, IE4, IE5, IE5.5, IE6

This element creates an unordered (bulleted) list. Each item in the list is, in turn, created by the <li> element.

Syntax:

```
<ul attributes events> . . . </ul>
```

Example:

```
<html><head><title>ul element example</title></head>
<body bgcolor="#FFFFFF" text="#000000">
  <ul type="disc">
    <li>Africa</li>
    <li>Antarctica</li>
    <li>Asia</li>
    <li>America</li>
    <li>Europe</li>
  </ul>
</body></html>
```

`<ul>` HTML Attributes (6)

accesskey, begin, class, compact, contenteditable, dir, disabled, end, hidefocus, id, lang, language, style, syncmaster, systemBitrate, systemCaptions, systemLanguage, systemOverdubOrSubtitle, tabindex, timecontainer, title, type, unselectable

`<ul>` Event Handlers (7)

onActivate, onBeforeActivate, onBeforeCopy, onBeforeCut, onBeforeDeactivate, onBeforeEditFocus, onBeforePaste, onBlur, onClick, onContextMenu, onControlSelect, onCopy, onCut, onDblClick, onDeactivate, onDrag, onDragEnd, onDragEnter, onDragLeave, onDragOver, onDragStart, onDrop, onFocus, onFocusIn, onFocusOut, onHelp, onKeyDown, onKeyPress, onKeyUp, onLayoutComplete, onLoseCapture, onMouseDown, onMouseEnter, onMouseLeave, onMouseMove, onMouseOut, onMouseOver, onMouseUp, onMouseWheel, onMove, onMoveEnd, onMoveStart, onPaste, onPropertyChange, onReadyStateChange, onResize, onResizeEnd, onResizeStart, onSelectStart, onTimeError

`<ul>` CSS Attributes and JavaScript Style Properties (8)

The names are in CSS syntax. See the introduction to this chapter for the JavaScript syntax rules. Names noted with an asterisk (*) are JavaScript properties only.

!important, accelerator, background, background-attachment, background-color, background-image, background-position, background-position-x, background-position-y, background-repeat, behavior, border, border-bottom, border-bottom-color, border-bottom-style, border-bottom-width, border-color, border-left, border-left-color, border-left-style, border-left-width, border-right, border-right-color, border-right-style, border-right-width, border-style, border-top, border-top-color, border-top-style, border-top-width, border-width, bottom, clear, clip, color, cursor, direction, display, filter, float, font, font-family, font-size, font-style, font-variant, font-weight, hasLayout(*), height, layout-flow, layout-grid, layout-grid-char, layout-grid-line, layout-grid-mode, layout-grid-type, left, letter-spacing, line-break, line-height, list-style, list-style-image, list-style-position, list-style-type, margin, margin-bottom, margin-left, margin-right, margin-top, overflow, overflow-x, overflow-y, padding, padding-bottom, padding-left, padding-right, padding-top, page-break-after, page-break-before, pixelBottom(*), pixelHeight(*), pixelLeft(*), pixelRight(*), pixelTop(*), pixelWidth(*), posBottom(*), posHeight(*), position, posLeft(*), posRight(*), posTop(*), posWidth(*), right, styleFloat(*), text-align, text-align-last, text-autospace, text-decoration, text-indent, text-justify, text-kashida-space, text-overflow, text-transform, text-underline-position, textDecorationBlink(*), textDecorationLineThrough(*), textDecorationNone(*), textDecorationOverline(*), textDecorationUnderline(*), top, unicode-bidi, visibility, white-space, width, word-break, word-spacing, word-wrap, writing-mode, z-index, zoom

`<ul>` Microsoft Behaviors (9)

clientCaps, download, homePage, httpFolder, saveFavorite, saveHistory, saveSnapshot, time, time2, userData

`<ul>` Microsoft Filters (10)

Alpha, Barn, BasicImage, BlendTrans, Blinds, Blur, CheckerBoard, Chroma,
Compositor, DropShadow, Emboss, Engrave, Fade, FlipH, FlipV, Glow, GradientWipe,
Gray, ICMFilter, Inset, Invert, Iris, Light, MaskFilter, Matrix, MotionBlur,
Pixelate, RadialWipe, RandomBars, RandomDissolve, RevealTrans, Shadow, Slide,
Spiral, Stretch, Strips, Wave, Wheel, Xray, Zigzag

ul. JavaScript Properties (11)

accessKey, blockDirection, canHaveChildren, canHaveHTML, className, clientHeight,
clientLeft, clientTop, clientWidth, compact, contentEditable, cursor, dir,
disabled, end, firstChild, hasLayout, hideFocus, id, innerHTML, innerText,
isContentEditable, isDisabled, isMultiLine, isTextEdit, lang, language, lastChild,
nextSibling, nodeName, nodeType, nodeValue, offsetHeight, offsetLeft, offsetParent,
offsetTop, offsetWidth, outerHTML, outerText, ownerDocument, parentElement,
parentNode, parentTextEdit, previousSibling, readyState, scopeName, scrollHeight,
scrollLeft, scrollTop, scrollWidth, sourceIndex, tabIndex, tagName, tagUrn, title,
type, uniqueID

ul. JavaScript Methods (12)

addBehavior, appendChild, applyElement, attachEvent, blur, clearAttributes, click,
cloneNode, componentFromPoint, contains, detachEvent, dragDrop, fireEvent, focus,
getAdjacentText, getAttribute, getAttributeNode, getBoundingClientRect,
getClientRects, getElementsByTagName, getExpression, hasChildNodes,
insertAdjacentElement, insertAdjacentHTML, insertAdjacentText, insertBefore,
mergeAttributes, normalize, releaseCapture, removeAttribute, removeAttributeNode,
removeBehavior, removeChild, removeExpression, removeNode, replaceAdjacentText,
replaceChild, replaceNode, scrollIntoView, setActive, setAttribute,
setAttributeNode, setCapture, setExpression, swapNode

ul. JavaScript Collections (13)

all, attributes, behaviorUrns, childNodes, children

ul. JavaScript Objects (14)

currentStyle, runtimeStyle, style

`<var>` ... `</var>`

Compatibility: NN4, NN6, NN7, IE4, IE5, IE5.5, IE6

This element usually causes text to be rendered in italics. It is used to format programming variable names that appear in a web page.

Syntax:

`<var attributes events>` . . . `</var>`

Example:

```
<html><head><title>var element example</title></head>
<body bgcolor="#FFFFFF" text="#000000">
<var>myField</var>
</body></html>
```

\<var\> HTML Attributes (6)

accesskey, begin, class, contenteditable, dir, disabled, end, hidefocus, id, lang, language, style, syncmaster, systemBitrate, systemCaptions, systemLanguage, systemOverdubOrSubtitle, tabindex, timecontainer, title, unselectable

\<var\> Event Handlers (7)

onActivate, onBeforeActivate, onBeforeCut, onBeforeDeactivate, onBeforeEditFocus, onBeforePaste, onBlur, onClick, onContextMenu, onControlSelect, onCut, onDblClick, onDeactivate, onDrag, onDragEnd, onDragEnter, onDragLeave, onDragOver, onDragStart, onDrop, onFocus, onFocusIn, onFocusOut, onHelp, onKeyDown, onKeyPress, onKeyUp, onLoseCapture, onMouseDown, onMouseEnter, onMouseLeave, onMouseMove, onMouseOut, onMouseOver, onMouseUp, onMouseWheel, onMove, onMoveEnd, onMoveStart, onPaste, onPropertyChange, onReadyStateChange, onResize, onResizeEnd, onResizeStart, onSelectStart, onTimeError

\<var\> CSS Attributes and JavaScript Style Properties (8)

The names are in CSS syntax. See the introduction to this chapter for the JavaScript syntax rules. Names noted with an asterisk (*) are JavaScript properties only.

!important, accelerator, background, background-attachment, background-color, background-image, background-position, background-position-x, background-position-y, background-repeat, behavior, border, border-bottom, border-bottom-color, border-bottom-style, border-bottom-width, border-color, border-left, border-left-color, border-left-style, border-left-width, border-right, border-right-color, border-right-style, border-right-width, border-style, border-top, border-top-color, border-top-style, border-top-width, border-width, bottom, clear, clip, color, cursor, direction, display, filter, float, font, font-family, font-size, font-style, font-variant, font-weight, hasLayout(*), height, layout-flow, layout-grid, layout-grid-mode, left, letter-spacing, line-height, margin, margin-bottom, margin-left, margin-right, margin-top, overflow, overflow-x, overflow-y, padding, padding-bottom, padding-left, padding-right, padding-top, pixelBottom(*), pixelHeight(*), pixelLeft(*), pixelRight(*), pixelTop(*), pixelWidth(*), posBottom(*), posHeight(*), position, posLeft(*), posRight(*), posTop(*), posWidth(*), right, styleFloat(*), text-autospace, text-decoration, text-overflow, text-transform, text-underline-position, textDecorationBlink(*), textDecorationLineThrough(*), textDecorationNone(*), textDecorationOverline(*), textDecorationUnderline(*), top, unicode-bidi, visibility, width, word-spacing, word-wrap, writing-mode, z-index, zoom

`<var>` Microsoft Behaviors (9)

clientCaps, download, homePage, httpFolder, saveFavorite, saveHistory, saveSnapshot, time, time2, userData

`<var>` Microsoft Filters (10)

Alpha, Barn, BasicImage, BlendTrans, Blinds, Blur, CheckerBoard, Chroma, Compositor, DropShadow, Emboss, Engrave, Fade, FlipH, FlipV, Glow, GradientWipe, Gray, ICMFilter, Inset, Invert, Iris, Light, MaskFilter, Matrix, MotionBlur, Pixelate, RadialWipe, RandomBars, RandomDissolve, RevealTrans, Shadow, Slide, Spiral, Stretch, Strips, Wave, Wheel, Xray, Zigzag

`var.` JavaScript Properties (11)

accessKey, canHaveChildren, canHaveHTML, className, clientHeight, clientLeft, clientTop, clientWidth, contentEditable, cursor, dir, disabled, end, firstChild, hasLayout, hideFocus, id, innerHTML, innerText, isContentEditable, isDisabled, isMultiLine, isTextEdit, lang, language, lastChild, nextSibling, nodeName, nodeType, nodeValue, offsetHeight, offsetLeft, offsetParent, offsetTop, offsetWidth, outerHTML, outerText, ownerDocument, parentElement, parentNode, parentTextEdit, previousSibling, readyState, scopeName, scrollHeight, scrollLeft, scrollTop, scrollWidth, sourceIndex, tabIndex, tagName, tagUrn, title, uniqueID

`var.` JavaScript Methods (12)

addBehavior, appendChild, applyElement, attachEvent, blur, clearAttributes, click, cloneNode, componentFromPoint, contains, detachEvent, fireEvent, focus, getAdjacentText, getAttribute, getAttributeNode, getBoundingClientRect, getClientRects, getElementsByTagName, getExpression, hasChildNodes, insertAdjacentElement, insertAdjacentHTML, insertAdjacentText, insertBefore, mergeAttributes, normalize, releaseCapture, removeAttribute, removeAttributeNode, removeBehavior, removeChild, removeExpression, removeNode, replaceAdjacentText, replaceChild, replaceNode, scrollIntoView, setActive, setAttribute, setAttributeNode, setCapture, setExpression, swapNode

`var.` JavaScript Collections (13)

all, attributes, behaviorUrns, childNodes, children

`var.` JavaScript Objects (14)

currentStyle, runtimeStyle, style

`<wbr>`

Compatibility: IE4, IE5, IE5.5, IE6

This element is used within the <nobr> element, which causes the text between its opening and closing tags to appear without a line break, regardless of the size of the window. However, introducing the <wbr> element within the <nobr> tags will create a spot where a line-break point can be introduced. This will cause the text to be broken into a new line if the window gets to be small enough.

Syntax:

```
<wbr attributes events> . . . </wbr>
```

Example:

```
<html><head><title>wbr element example</title></head>
<body bgcolor="#ffffff" text="#000000">
<nobr>This line of text will not be broken because the nobr element is being used.</nobr><br><br>
<nobr>When you use the wbr element <wbr> it will introduce a line break as in this example.</nobr>
</body></html>
```

<wbr> HTML Attributes (6)

id

<wbr> CSS Attributes and JavaScript Style Properties (8)

behavior

<wbr> Microsoft Behaviors (9)

clientCaps, download, homePage

wbr. JavaScript Properties (11)

canHaveHTML, id, isContentEditable, isDisabled, isMultiLine, outerHTML, outerText, parentElement, scopeName, tagUrn

wbr. JavaScript Methods (12)

addBehavior, componentFromPoint, fireEvent, getAttribute, getAttributeNode, normalize, removeAttribute, removeAttributeNode, removeBehavior, scrollIntoView, setAttribute, setAttributeNode

wbr. JavaScript Collections (13)

behaviorUrns

wbr. JavaScript Objects (14)

currentStyle

<xml> ... </xml>

Compatibility: IE5, IE5.5, IE6

This element defines an XML dataset inside the page. Text contained within the opening and closing tags of this element is not rendered on the page. However, it is useful for storing information in the page source code that will be useful to the web page server.

Syntax:

```
<xml attributes events> . . . </xml>
```

Example:

```
<html>
<xml id="myOwnData">
  <myData>
    <firstname>Gidon</firstname>
    <lastname>Shuly</lastname>
    <age>10</age>
</myData>
</xml></html>
```

<xml> HTML Attributes (6)

id, src

<xml> Event Handlers (7)

onDataAvailable, onDatasetChanged, onDatasetComplete, onReadyStateChange, onRowEnter, onRowExit, onRowsDelete, onRowsInserted

<xml> CSS Attributes and JavaScript Style Properties (8)

The names are in CSS syntax. See the introduction to this chapter for the JavaScript syntax rules.

behavior, text-autospace, text-underline-position

<xml> Microsoft Behaviors (9)

clientCaps, download, homePage

xml. JavaScript Properties (11)

canHaveHTML, id, isContentEditable, isDisabled, isMultiLine, parentElement, readyState, recordset, scopeName, src, tagUrn, XMLdocument

xml. JavaScript Methods (12)

addBehavior, componentFromPoint, fireEvent, getAttributeNode, namedRecordset, normalize, removeAttributeNode, removeBehavior, setAttributeNode

xml. JavaScript Collections (13)

behaviorUrns

<xmp> ... </xmp>

Compatibility: NN4, NN6, NN7, IE4, IE5

This element renders a block of text in a monospaced font, or a fixed-sized font such as Courier, and is used to render HTML and JavaScript code. However, HTML 4.0 favors use of the <pre> and <samp> elements.

Syntax:

```
<xmp attributes events> . . . </xmp>
```

Example:

```
<html><head><title>xmp element example</title></head>
<body bgcolor="#FFFFFF" text="#000000">
<xmp>This text is rendered in a monospaced font.</xmp>
</body></html>
```

<xmp> HTML Attributes (6)

accesskey, begin, class, contenteditable, dir, disabled, end, hidefocus, id, lang, language, style, syncmaster, systemBitrate, systemCaptions, systemLanguage, systemOverdubOrSubtitle, tabindex, timecontainer, title, unselectable

<xmp> Event Handlers (7)

onActivate, onBeforeActivate, onBeforeCut, onBeforeDeactivate, onBeforeEditFocus, onBeforePaste, onBlur, onClick, onContextMenu, onControlSelect, onCut, onDblClick, onDeactivate, onDrag, onDragEnd, onDragEnter, onDragLeave, onDragOver, onDragStart, onDrop, onFocus, onFocusIn, onFocusOut, onHelp, onKeyDown, onKeyPress, onKeyUp, onLoseCapture, onMouseDown, onMouseEnter, onMouseLeave, onMouseMove, onMouseOut, onMouseOver, onMouseUp, onMouseWheel, onMove, onMoveEnd, onMoveStart, onPaste, onPropertyChange, onReadyStateChange, onResize, onResizeEnd, onResizeStart, onSelectStart, onTimeError

`<xmp>` CSS Attributes and JavaScript Style Properties (8)

The names are in CSS syntax. See the introduction to this chapter for the JavaScript syntax rules. Names noted with an asterisk (*) are JavaScript properties only.

!important, :first-letter, :first-line, accelerator, background, background-attachment, background-color, background-image, background-position, background-position-x, background-position-y, background-repeat, behavior, border, border-bottom, border-bottom-color, border-bottom-style, border-bottom-width, border-color, border-left, border-left-color, border-left-style, border-left-width, border-right, border-right-color, border-right-style, border-right-width, border-style, border-top, border-top-color, border-top-style, border-top-width, border-width, bottom, clear, clip, color, cursor, direction, display, filter, float, font, font-family, font-size, font-style, font-variant, font-weight, hasLayout(*), height, layout-grid, layout-grid-char, layout-grid-line, layout-grid-mode, layout-grid-type, left, letter-spacing, line-break, line-height, margin, margin-bottom, margin-left, margin-right, margin-top, overflow, overflow-x, overflow-y, padding, padding-bottom, padding-left, padding-right, padding-top, page-break-after, page-break-before, pixelBottom(*), pixelHeight(*), pixelLeft(*), pixelRight(*), pixelTop(*), pixelWidth(*), posBottom(*), posHeight(*), position, posLeft(*), posRight(*), posTop(*), posWidth(*), right, styleFloat(*), text-align, text-align-last, text-autospace, text-decoration, text-indent, text-justify, text-kashida-space, text-overflow, text-transform, text-underline-position, textDecorationBlink(*), textDecorationLineThrough(*), textDecorationNone(*), textDecorationOverline(*), textDecorationUnderline(*), top, unicode-bidi, visibility, white-space, width, word-break, word-spacing, word-wrap, z-index, zoom

---

`<xmp>` Microsoft Behaviors (9)

---

clientCaps, download, homePage, httpFolder, saveFavorite, saveHistory, saveSnapshot, time, time2, userData

---

`<xmp>` Microsoft Filters (10)

Alpha, Barn, BasicImage, BlendTrans, Blinds, Blur, CheckerBoard, Chroma, Compositor, DropShadow, Emboss, Engrave, Fade, FlipH, FlipV, Glow, GradientWipe, Gray, ICMFilter, Inset, Invert, Iris, Light, MaskFilter, Matrix, MotionBlur, Pixelate, RadialWipe, RandomBars, RandomDissolve, RevealTrans, Shadow, Slide, Spiral, Stretch, Strips, Wave, Wheel, Xray, Zigzag

---

`xmp.` JavaScript Properties (11)

---

accessKey, blockDirection, canHaveChildren, canHaveHTML, className, clientHeight, clientLeft, clientTop, clientWidth, contentEditable, cursor, dir, disabled, end, firstChild, hasLayout, hideFocus, id, innerText, isContentEditable, isDisabled, isMultiLine, isTextEdit, lang, language, lastChild, nextSibling, nodeName, nodeType, nodeValue, offsetHeight, offsetLeft, offsetParent, offsetTop, offsetWidth, outerHTML, outerText, ownerDocument, parentElement, parentNode, parentTextEdit, previousSibling, readyState, scopeName, scrollHeight, scrollLeft, scrollTop, scrollWidth, sourceIndex, tabIndex, tagName, tagUrn, title, uniqueID

---

xmp. JavaScript Methods (12)

addBehavior, appendChild, applyElement, attachEvent, blur, clearAttributes, click, cloneNode, componentFromPoint, contains, detachEvent, fireEvent, focus, getAdjacentText, getAttribute, getAttributeNode, getBoundingClientRect, getClientRects, getElementsByTagName, hasChildNodes, insertAdjacentElement, insertAdjacentHTML, insertBefore, mergeAttributes, normalize, releaseCapture, removeAttribute, removeAttributeNode, removeBehavior, removeChild, removeNode, replaceAdjacentText, replaceChild, replaceNode, scrollIntoView, setActive, setAttribute, setAttributeNode, setCapture, swapNode

xmp. JavaScript Collections (13)

all, attributes, behaviorUrns, childNodes, children

xmp. JavaScript Objects (14)

currentStyle, runtimeStyle, style

6

HTML ATTRIBUTES

In a nutshell, HTML attributes are the "adjectives" of HTML elements. Through the use of attributes, you can establish how an element will behave and how it will appear.

This chapter contains a comprehensive list of attributes that belong, or apply, to the HTML elements covered in Chapter 5. The attributes in this chapter contain browser compatibility information, a brief description, acceptable values (where applicable), syntax information, a functional example (in most cases), and a list of HTML elements that the attribute can be used with.

abbr

Compatibility: NN6, NN7, IE6

This attribute establishes the abbreviated text for the cell, and can be used by the browser to replace the cell contents.

Syntax:

```
<element abbr="value"> . . . </element>
```

Example:

```
<table border="1">
<tr><td abbr="C1"> Cell 1 content </td></tr>
<tr><td abbr="C2"> Cell 2 content </td>
<td abbr="C3"> Cell 3 content </td></tr>
</table>
```

Applies to:

```
<td>, <th>
```

accept

Compatibility: NN6, NN7, IE6

This attribute provides a comma-separated list of the MIME content types that the server will be able to process correctly.

Syntax:

```
<input accept="value">
```

Example:

```
<input type="text" size=50 accept="image/gif,text/html" value='The content type
that this field accepts is "image/gif,text/html"'>
```

Applies to:

```
<input>
```

acceptcharset

Compatibility: NN6, NN7, IE5, IE5.5, IE6

This attribute provides a comma-separated list of the nonstandard character sets that can be used with the form and can be accepted by the server.

Syntax:

```
<form acceptcharset="value"> . . . </form>
```

Example:

```
<form name="form1" method="post" action="" acceptcharset="UTF-8">
<input type="text" size=80 accept="image/gif" value="If you type a character that
is not in the list of character sets used in the form, then the UTF-8 character set
will be used">
</form>
```

Applies to:

```
<form>
```

accesskey

Compatibility: NN6, NN7, IE4, IE5, IE5.5, IE6

This attribute permits the user to interact with page elements using the keyboard. Pressing ALT and the keyboard character invokes the element.
 Syntax:

```
<element accesskey="value"> . . . </element>
```

Example:

```
<input type="Button" accesskey="M" value="Press Alt + M to bring this button into
focus">
```

Applies to:

```
<a>, <acronym>, <address>, <applet>, <area>, <b>, <bdo>, <big>, <blockquote>,
<body>, <button>, <caption>, <center>, <cite>, <custom>, <dd>, <del>, <dfn>, <dir>,
<div>, <dl>, <dt>, <em>, <embed>, <fieldset>, <font>, <hn>, <hr>, <i>, <img>,
<input type="button">, <input type="checkbox">, <input type="file">, <input
type="image">, <input type="password">, <input type="radio">, <input type="reset">,
<input type="submit">, <input type="text">, <ins>, <isindex>, <kbd>, <label>,
<legend>, <li>, <listing>, <marquee>, <menu>, <object>, <ol>, <p>, <pre>, <q>,
<rt>, <ruby>, <s>, <samp>, <select>, <small>, <span>, <strike>, <strong>, <sub>,
<sup>, <table>, <tbody>, <td>, <textarea>, <tfoot>, <th>, <thead>, <tr>, <tt>, <u>,
<ul>, <var>, <xmp>
```

action

Compatibility: NN4, NN6, NN7, IE4, IE5, IE5.5, IE6

This attribute specifies the URL that will receive the form content for processing. If no URL is specified, the base URL of the form is used.
 Syntax:

```
<element action="value"> . . . </element>
```

Example:

```
<form action="http://www.somedomain.com" method="post">
   Enter the car maker of your choice:
   <select name="Car">
      <option value="Honda">Honda
      <option value="Chevrolet">Chevrolet
      <option value="Buick" selected>Buick
```

```
    </select>
    <input type=submit onClick="return false">
</form>
```

Applies to:

```
<form>, <isindex>
```

align (1)

Compatibility: NN4, NN6, NN7, IE4, IE5, IE5.5, IE6

This attribute specifies how the element is aligned with adjacent text.
Syntax:

```
<element align="value"> . . . </element>
```

Possible values:

absbottom	Aligns the bottom of the element with the bottom of the adjacent text.
absmiddle	Aligns the middle of the element with the middle of the adjacent text.
baseline	Aligns the bottom of the element with the baseline of the adjacent text.
bottom	Has the same effect as baseline.
left	Aligns the element to the left of the adjacent text. This is the default value.
middle	Aligns the middle of an element with the baseline of the text.
right	Aligns the element to the right of the adjacent text.

Example:

```
<img id="myImage" src="yourimage.jpg" alt="" width="74" height="99" align="baseline">
```

Applies to:

```
<applet>, <col>, <colgroup>, <embed>, <fieldset>, <img>, <input>, <input
type="image">, <object>, <select>, <spacer>, <tbody>, <tfoot>, <thead>
```

align (2)

Compatibility: NN6, NN7, IE4, IE5, IE5.5, IE6

This attribute specifies the alignment of text within the element. Possible values
include bottom, top, left, center, and right.
Syntax:

```
<element align="value"> . . . </element>
```

Example:

```
<table id="myTable" width="560" border="8" cellspacing="5" cellpadding="5">
<caption align="bottom">This is the caption text for the table</caption>
<tr><td>Cell 1</td><td>Cell 2</td></tr><tr><td>Cell 3</td><td>Cell 4</td></tr></table>
```

Applies to:

```
<caption>, <legend>
```

align (3)

Compatibility: NN4 (<div>, <td>, <th>, <tr> only), NN6, NN7, IE4, IE5, IE5.5, IE6

This attribute specifies the alignment of text or other content within the elements that contain them. Possible values include left, center, right, justify, and indent.

Syntax:

```
<element align="value"> . . . </element>
```

Example:

```
<div align="justify"  style="position:absolute; left:77px; top:299px; width:354px;
height:122px; background-color:#CCCCFF;  z-index:5"><span>This block of text
represents the content of the div element.</span></div>
```

Applies to:

```
<div>, <hn>, <hr>, <p>, <td>, <th>, <tr>
```

align (4)

Compatibility: NN6, NN7, IE4, IE5, IE5.5, IE6

This attribute specifies the horizontal alignment of the <table> and <iframe> elements within their respective container elements. Possible values include left, right, and center.

Syntax:

```
<element align="value"> . . . </element>
```

Example:

```
<table border="1" align="center"><tr><td>Cell 1 content</td><td>Cell 2 content
</td><td>Cell 3 content</td></tr></table>
```

Applies to:

```
<iframe>, <table>
```

alink

Compatibility: NN6, NN7, IE4, IE5, IE5.5, IE6

This attribute specifies the color that each link inside the `<body>` element will take when it has the focus. Its value is either a color name (some browsers do not support color names) or a hexadecimal color value using the "#RRGGBB" method.
   Syntax:

```
<body alink="value"> . . . </body>
```

   Example:

```
<body bgcolor="#FFFFFF" text="#000000" alink="red">
<p><a href="http://www.advocar.com/" target=_blank>Advocar Network</a></p>
</body>
```

   Applies to:

```
<body>
```

allowtransparency

Compatibility: IE5.5, IE6

This attribute establishes the transparency of frames. It is a Boolean attribute, taking the values true and false (the default).
   Syntax:

```
<element allowtransparency="value"> . . . </element>
```

   Example:

```
<iframe src="http://www.advocar.com" allowTransparency="true" style="width:40%;
background-color:transparent"></iframe>
<iframe src="http://www.advocar.com" style="width: 40%; background-color: green"></
iframe>
<iframe src="http://www.advocar.com" allowTransparency="false" style='width:40%;
background-color:white'></iframe>
<iframe src="http://www.advocar.com" allowTransparency =
"true" style="width:40%; background-color:lightgreen"></iframe>
```

   Applies to:

```
<frame>, <iframe>
```

alt

Compatibility: NN4 (<img> only), NN6, NN7, IE4, IE5, IE5.5, IE6

This attribute allows elements, such as embedded objects or images, to have an alternate description. In the event that a browser has images or objects turned off, it will display the value of this attribute instead.

Syntax:

```
<element alt="value"> . . . </element>
```

Example:

```
<input type="image" alt="This is a Picasso cubist painting" border="0"
src="yourimage.jpg" width="99" height="79">
```

Applies to:

```
<applet>, <area>, <img>, <input>, <input type="image">, <object>
```

application

Compatibility: IE5, IE5.5, IE6

This attribute indicates whether or not the element points to an HTA application, which, if true, would exempt it from the browser security model. It is a Boolean attribute, taking the values yes and no (the default).

Syntax:

```
<element application="value"> . . . </element>
```

Example:

```
<iframe application="yes" src="yourpage.html" style="width:40%;"></iframe>
<iframe application="no" src="yourpage.html" style="width: 40%;"> </iframe>
```

Applies to:

```
<frame>, <iframe>
```

archive

Compatibility: NN6, NN7, IE6

This attribute is used to specify a list of URIs that contain archive information that is relevant to the object loaded in the <object> and <applet> elements.

Syntax:

```
<element archive="value"> . . . </element>
```

Example:

```
<object archive="http://www.macromedia.com/shockwave/downloads/index.html"
classid="clsid:D27CDB6E-AE6D-11cf-96B8-444553540000"
codebase="http://download.macromedia.com/pub/shockwave/cabs/flash/
swflash.cab#version=5,0,0,0" width="250" height="230">
    <param name=movie value="yourshockwavemovie.swf">
    <param name=quality value=high>
<embed src="Puzzle.swf"quality=high pluginspage="http://www.macromedia.com/
shockwave/download/index.cgi?P1_Prod_Version=ShockwaveFlash" type="application/x-
shockwave-flash" width="250" height="230"></embed>
</object>
```

Applies to:

```
<applet>, <object>
```

autocomplete

Compatibility: IE5, IE5.5, IE6

The setting of this attribute can help users quickly enter information into a form. autocomplete stores and recalls data entered into the text and password <input> elements, allowing the user to complete the entry without having to type the entire value. autocomplete is a Boolean attribute, taking values on and off (the default).

Syntax:

```
<element autocomplete="value">
```

Example:

```
<form name="form1" method="post" action="">
<input type="text" size=30 name="text1" autocomplete="on">
<input type="submit" value="Submit">
</form>
```

Applies to:

```
<form>, <input type="password">, <input type="text">
```

axis

Compatibility: NN6, NN7, IE6

This attribute allows you to categorize <td> and <th> elements.

Syntax:

```
<element axis="value"> . . . </element>
```

Example:

```
<table border="1" summary="Billable time report">
<caption>Billable time report</caption>
<tr>
  <th> </th>
  <th id="head1" axis="hours">Travel Time</th>
  <th id="head2" axis="hours">Consulting Hours</th>
</tr>
<tr>
  <th id="a6" axis="employee">Joseph</th>
      <th> </th><th> </th><th> </th>
</tr>
<tr>
<td id="a7" axis="date">January 1, 2004</td>
  <td headers="head1 head2">7.50</td>
  <td headers="head1 head2">2.00</td>
  <td> </td>
</tr>
<td id="a7" axis="date">January 2, 2004</td>
  <td headers="head1 head2">9.50</td>
  <td headers="head1 head2">1.70</td>
  <td> </td>
</tr>
<td id="a7" axis="date">January 3, 2004</td>
  <td headers="head1 head2">7.00</td>
  <td headers="head1 head2">1.00</td>
  <td> </td>
</tr>
<tr bgcolor="#CCCCCC">
  <td>Total</td><td>24.00</td>
  <td>4.70</td><td>28.70</td>
</tr>
</table>
```

Applies to:

```
<td>, <th>
```

background

Compatibility: NN4, NN6, NN7, IE4, IE5, IE5.5, IE6

This attribute specifies the URL of an image to display in the background of an element.

Syntax:

```
<element background="value"> . . . </element>
```

Example:

```
<body id="myBody" bgcolor="#FFFFFF" text="#000000" bgproperties="fixed"
background="yourbackgroundimage.gif">
</body>
```

Applies to:

```
<body>, <table>, <td>, <th>
```

balance

Compatibility: IE4, IE5, IE5.5, IE6

This attribute establishes the way in which the volume of the background sound is distributed between the left and right speakers. The value of this attribute is a number between -10000 (only the left speaker emits sound) and +10000 (only the right speaker emits sound).

Syntax:

```
<bgsound balance="value">
```

Example:

```
<head>
<bgsound src="yourmoviefile.wav" balance=0 loop=3>
</head>
<body bgcolor="white" text="#000000">
</body>
```

Applies to:

```
<bgsound>
```

begin

Compatibility: IE5.5, IE6

This attribute belongs to the HTML+TIME technology introduced by Microsoft. See Chapter 15 for more information.

Applies to:

```
<a>, <acronym>, <address>, <area>, <b>, <big>, <blockquote>, <button>, <caption>,
<center>, <cite>, <code>, <dd>, <del>, <dir>, <div>, <dl>, <dt>, <em>, <fieldset>,
<font>, <form>, <hn>, <hr>, <i>, <iframe>, <img>, <input type="button">, <input
type="checkbox">, <input type="file">, <input type="hidden">, <input type="image">,
<input type="password">, <input type="radio">, <input type="reset">, <input
type="submit">, <input type="text">, <ins>, <kbd>, <legend>, <li>, <listing>,
<marquee>, <menu>, <ol>, <option>, <p>, <pre>, <q>, <s>, <samp>, <small>, <span>,
<strike>, <strong>, <sub>, <sup>, <table>, <tbody>, <td>, <textarea>, <tfoot>,
<th>, <thead>, <tr>, <tt>, <u>, <ul>, <var>, <xmp>
```

behavior

Compatibility: IE4, IE5, IE5.5, IE6

This attribute specifies how content will scroll in the `<marquee>` element.
Syntax:

```
<marquee behavior="value"> . . . </marquee>
```

Possible values:

alternate	The content moves back and forth between the borders.
scroll	The content loops through. This is the default value.
slide	The content moves to the end and stops.

Example:

```
<marquee behavior="slide" bgcolor="#99ffff">Come and see our new car models.</marquee>
```

Applies to:

```
<marquee>
```

bgcolor

Compatibility: NN4, NN6, NN7, IE4, IE5, IE5.5, IE6

This attribute establishes the background color of an element. Its value is either a color name (some browsers do not support color names) or a hexadecimal color value using the "#RRGGBB" method.
Syntax:

```
<element bgcolor="value"> . . . </element>
```

Example:

```
<body bgcolor="#ccffcc" text="#000000">
<table bgcolor="white">
<col span="2" bgcolor="blue">
<col bgcolor="green">
<tr><td></td></tr></table></body>
```

Applies to:

```
<body>, <col>, <colgroup>, <marquee>, <table>, <tbody>, <td>, <tfoot>, <th>,
<thead>, <tr>
```

bgproperties

Compatibility: IE4, IE5, IE5.5, IE6

This attribute sets the scroll properties of the background image. If its value is empty (that is, if the attribute is not included in the code, or if it is given a value of ""), the background image is scrollable; if its value is fixed, the background image is *not* scrollable.

Syntax:

```
<body bgproperties="value"> . . . </body>
```

Example:

```
<html><head>
<style>.body1 { background-image:url("YourImage.gif"); }
.body2 { background-image:none;!important }
</style>
<script>
function myB1() {
location.reload();}
</script>
</head>
<body id="myBody" bgcolor="#FFFFFF" text="#000000" bgproperties="fixed"
background="YourImage.gif" onclick="this.className='body2'">
<input type="button" name="B1" value="Add background image" onClick="myB1()">
<input type="button" name="B2" value="Remove background image"></body></html>
```

Applies to:

```
<body>
```

border

Compatibility: NN4 (<embed>, <frameset>, <table> only), NN6, NN7, IE4, IE5, IE5.5, IE6

This attribute establishes the thickness in pixels of the border around an element.

Syntax:

```
<element border="value"> . . . </element>
```

Example:

```
<table width="542" border="10"><tr><td>@@@@@@@@</td></tr></table>
```

Applies to:

```
<embed>, <frameset>, <iframe>, <img>, <object>, <table>
```

bordercolor

Compatibility: NN4 (<frame> only), NN6, NN7, IE4, IE5, IE5.5, IE6

This attribute specifies the color of the border of the element. Its value is either a color name (some browsers do not support color names) or a hexadecimal color value using the "#RRGGBB" method.

Syntax:

```
<element bordercolor="value"> . . . </element>
```

Example:

```
<table width="542" border="10" bordercolor="red">
<tr><td>@@@@@@</td></tr></table>
```

Applies to:

```
<frame>, <frameset>, <table>, <td>, <th>, <tr>
```

bordercolordark

Compatibility: IE4, IE5, IE5.5, IE6

A three-dimensional border requires two shades of the same color to give the appearance of 3D. This attribute defines the darker shade of the border color. Its value is either a color name (some browsers do not support color names) or a hexadecimal color value using the "#RRGGBB" method.

Syntax:

```
<table bordercolordark="value"> . . . </table>
```

Example:

```
<table width="542" border="10" bordercolordark="red"
bordercolorlight="salmon"><tr><td>@@@@@@@</td></tr></table>
```

Applies to:

```
<table>
```

bordercolorlight

Compatibility: IE4, IE5, IE5.5, IE6

A three-dimensional border requires two shades of the same color to give the appearance of 3D. This attribute defines the lighter shade of the border color. Its value is either a color name (some browsers do not support color names) or a hexadecimal color value using the "#RRGGBB" method.

Syntax:

```
<table bordercolorlight="value"> . . . </table>
```

Example:

```
<table width="542" border="10" bordercolordark="red"
bordercolorlight="salmon"><tr><td>@@@@@@</td></tr></table>
```

Applies to:

```
<table>
```

bottommargin

Compatibility: IE4, IE5, IE5.5, IE6

This attribute sets the height in pixels of the bottom margin of the page. Its default value is 15.

Syntax:

```
<body bottommargin="value"> . . . </body>
```

Example:

```
<body bottommargin="20"><p>Some text in the paragraph</p></body>
```

Applies to:

```
<body>
```

cellpadding

Compatibility: NN4, NN6, NN7, IE4, IE5, IE5.5, IE6

This attribute establishes the width of the empty space between a cell's border and its content. Its value can be either an integer that specifies the amount of space in pixels or a percentage of the total cell size to use as space.

Syntax:

```
<table cellpadding="value"> . . . </table>
```

Example:

```
<table width="542" border="10" bordercolor="red" cellpadding="15">
    <tr><th height="79" colspan="2">This table has:<br>
        border = 10; cellpadding="15"; bordercolor="red"</th>
    </tr>
    <tr><td>Cell 1 content</td>
    <td>Cell 2 content</td>
    </tr>
</table>
```

Applies to:

<table>

cellspacing

Compatibility: NN4, NN6, NN7, IE4, IE5, IE5.5, IE6

This attribute establishes the width of the empty space between cells in a table. Its value can be either an integer that specifies the amount of space in pixels or a percentage of the total cell size to use as space.

Syntax:

```
<table cellspacing="value"> . . . </table>
```

Example:

```
<table width="542" border="10" bordercolor="red" cellSpacing="15">
   <tr><th height="79" colspan="2">This table has:<br>
      border = 10; cellSpacing="15"; bordercolor="red"</th>
   </tr>
   <tr><td height="79">Cell 1 content</td>
     <td height="79">Cell 2 content</td>
   </tr>
</table>
```

Applies to:

<table>

ch

Compatibility: NN6, NN7, IE6

This attribute replaces the char attribute proposed by the W3C, which has not found support from the main browsers. The value of ch is a character that specifies the alignment of subsequent text. This is usually used when displaying monetary values.

Syntax:

```
<element ch="value"> . . . </element>
```

Example:

```
<table><tr><td id="myTd" ch=",">1245,Pts.</td></tr></table>
```

Applies to:

<col>, <colgroup>, <tbody>, <td>, <tfoot>, <th>, <thead>, <tr>

checked

Compatibility: NN4, NN6, NN7, IE4, IE5, IE5.5, IE6

This attribute determines whether a checkbox or radio button is selected or not. If this attribute is specified, the checkbox or radio button is selected; if it is not specified, then it is not selected.

Syntax:

```
<input checked>
```

Example:

```
<form>
<p>Type of media you wish to purchase:<br>
<input type="checkbox" value="checkbox" checked>CD
<input type="checkbox" value="checkbox">DVD </p>
<p>Credit Card:</p>
<input type="radio" value="radiobutton" checked>VISA
<input type="radio" value="radiobutton">MASTERCARD
<input type="radio" value="radiobutton">DISCOVER
<input type="radio" value="radiobutton">AMERICAN EXPRESS
</form>
```

Applies to:

```
<input type="checkbox">, <input type="radio">
```

choff

Compatibility: NN6, NN7, IE6

This attribute replaces the charoff attribute proposed by the W3C, which has not found support from any of the main browsers. The value of choff is a decimal number that specifies an offset from the beginning of the table cell. This attribute is used in conjunction with the dir attribute, which specifies the direction of the offset.

Syntax:

```
<element choff="value"> . . . </element>
```

Example:

```
<td choff=5 dir="rtl">004578</td>
```

Applies to:

```
<col>, <colgroup>, <tbody>, <td>, <tfoot>, <th>, <thead>, <tr>
```

cite

Compatibility: NN6, NN7, IE6

This attribute is intended to provide a URL where reference information related to a borrowed quotation is located.

Syntax:

```
<element cite="value"> . . . </element>
```

Example:

```
<q cite="http://www.macromedia.com">ActionScript is Macromedia's programming
language for Flash MX, the popular authoring tool for creating rich Internet
applications and animations for the Web.</q>
```

Applies to:

```
<blockquote>, <del>, <ins>, <q>
```

class

Compatibility: NN4, NN6, NN7, IE4, IE5, IE5.5, IE6

This attribute determines the style that will be applied to an element. Internet Explorer 5.0 added the ability to apply multiple styles in a class attribute. If there is a conflict between multiple styles that define the same attribute, the last style applied takes precedence.

The styles to which the class attribute refers can be defined either within the style attribute of an element, in a custom style sheet, or in a <style> element tag.

Syntax:

```
<element class="className"> . . . </element>
<element class="class1 class2 class3 . . ."> . . . </element>
```

Example:

```
<head>
<style>.myclass { font-family:times new roman; font-weight:bold; font-size:16px;
color:red; } </style>
</head>
<body bgcolor="#FFFFFF" text="#000000">
<p class="myclass">"This text is being rendered applying a class attribute
value."</p></body>
```

Applies to:

```
<a>, <acronym>, <address>, <applet>, <area>, <b>, <bdo>, <big>, <blockquote>,
<body>, <br>, <button>, <caption>, <center>, <cite>, <code>, <col>, <colgroup>,
<custom>, <dd>, <del>, <dfn>, <dir>, <div>, <dl>, <dt>, <em>, <embed>, <fieldset>,
```

`<font>`, `<form>`, `<frame>`, `<frameset>`, `<head>`, `<hn>`, `<hr>`, `<html>`, `<i>`, `<iframe>`, `<img>`, `<input type="button">`, `<input type="checkbox">`, `<input type="file">`, `<input type="hidden">`, `<input type="image">`, `<input type="password">`, `<input type="radio">`, `<input type="reset">`, `<input type="submit">`, `<input type="text">`, `<ins>`, `<isindex>`, `<kbd>`, `<label>`, `<legend>`, `<li>`, `<listing>`, `<map>`, `<marquee>`, `<menu>`, `<nobr>`, `<object>`, `<ol>`, `<option>`, `<p>`, `<pre>`, `<q>`, `<rt>`, `<ruby>`, `<s>`, `<samp>`, `<select>`, `<small>`, `<span>`, `<strike>`, `<strong>`, `<sub>`, `<sup>`, `<table>`, `<tbody>`, `<td>`, `<textarea>`, `<tfoot>`, `<th>`, `<thead>`, `<tr>`, `<tt>`, `<u>`, `<ul>`, `<var>`, `<xmp>`

classid

Compatibility: IE4, IE5, IE5.5, IE6

This attribute is used to determine the class identifier for an `<object>` element. It can be a URL string or a globally unique identifier (GUID) value. A GUID is a 32-bit value that is associated with an object prototype or class, such as a Flash movie player. When using a GUID value, the string clsid: must precede the GUID.

NOTE *The format of this value for registered Microsoft ActiveX controls is:* "clsid:XXX-XXXX-XXXX-XXXX-XX". *The syntax for a Flash 5 movie is:* classid="clsid:D27CDB6E-AE6D-11cf-96B8-444553540000".

Syntax:

```
<object classid="value"> . . . </object>
```

Example:

```
<object classid="clsid:D27CDB6E-AE6D-11cf-96B8-444553540000"
codebase="http://download.macromedia.com/pub/shockwave/cabs/flash/
swflash.cab#version=5,0,0,0"
width="250" height="230">
    <param name=movie value="yourflashmoviefile.swf">
    <param name=quality value=high>
    <embed src="yourflashmoviefile.swf" quality=high
pluginspage="http://www.macromedia.com/shockwave/download/
index.cgi?P1_Prod_Version=ShockwaveFlash"
type="application/x-shockwave-flash" width="250" height="230">
    </embed>
</object>
```

Applies to:

```
<object>
```

clear

Compatibility: NN4, NN6, NN7, IE4, IE5, IE5.5, IE6

Determines how the browser will create space around the area of a `<br>` element.

Syntax:

```
<br clear="value">
```

Possible values:

all	Text is moved directly below all floating objects.
left	Text is moved below all floating objects on the left side.
right	Text is moved below all floating objects on the right side.
no value	Floating text can be rendered on all sides.

Example:

```
<img src="yourimagefile.jpg" alt="This is a float-left image" width="71"
height="99"
style="float:left">Here is the br element with a clear attribute value of left<br
clear="left">
<img src="yourimagefile.jpg" alt="This is a float-left image" width="79"
height="99"
style="float:left">
Here is the br element<img src="yourimagefile.jpg" alt="This is a float-left image"
width="99" height="80" style="float:left">
```

Applies to:

```
<br>
```

code

Compatibility: NN6, NN7, IE4, IE5, IE5.5, IE6

This attribute specifies the URL of the compiled Java class file.

Syntax:

```
<element code="value"> . . . </element>
```

Example:

```
<applet id="myjavaclass" code=yourjava.class width=350 height=260>
<param name="param1"    value="1">
<param name="param2"    value="2">
</applet>
```

Applies to:

```
<applet>, <object>
```

codebase

Compatibility: NN6, NN7, IE4, IE5, IE5.5, IE6

This attribute specifies the URL of an applet or an object. If this attribute is not specified, then the base URL for the applet or object is the same as for the current document.

Syntax:

```
<element codebase="value"> . . . </element>
```

Example:

```
<object classid="clsid:D27CDB6E-AE6D-11cf-96B8-444553540000"
codebase="http://download.macromedia.com/pub/shockwave/cabs/flash/
swflash.cab#version=5,0,0,0"
width="250" height="230" codetype="application/x-shockwave-flash">
    <param name="movie" value="yourflashmovie.swf">
    <param name="quality" value="high">
<embed src="yourflashmovie.swf" quality="high" pluginspage="http://
www.macromedia.com/shockwave/download/index.cgi?P1_Prod_Version=ShockwaveFlash"
type="application/x-shockwave-flash" width="250" height="230"></embed>
</object>
```

Applies to:

```
<applet>, <object>
```

codetype

Compatibility: NN6, NN7, IE4, IE5, IE5.5, IE6

This attribute is used in conjunction with the classid attribute to specify the type of data that is expected by the <object> element. Possible values are audio/basic, image/gif, image/png, text/css, text/html, text/javascript, text/vbscript, and video/mpeg.

Syntax:

```
<object codetype="value"> . . . </object>
```

Example: See example for the codebase attribute.
Applies to:

```
<object>
```

color

Compatibility: NN4, NN6, NN7, IE4, IE5, IE5.5, IE6

This attribute is used to set the color of the text, but its use is no longer favored in HTML 4.0 because the same or better formatting results can be achieved using style sheets (see Chapter 1). Its value is either a color name (some browsers do not support color names) or a hexadecimal color value using the "#RRGGBB" method.

Syntax:

```
<element color="value"> . . . </element>
```

Example:

```
<p><font face="Verdana" color="#ff0000">Text</font></p>
```

Applies to:

```
<basefont>, <font>, <hr>
```

cols (1)

Compatibility: NN4, NN6, NN7, IE4, IE5, IE5.5, IE6

This attribute establishes the number of columns and the size of the columns in a frameset. Each column value is separated by a comma.

Syntax:

```
<frameset cols="value"> . . . </frameset>
```

Possible values:

integer	Specifies the width in pixels.
integer%	Specifies the percent of the total width of the frameset.
integer*	Specifies the width of the frame as a relative value. Once space is allocated for all frames with cols attribute values that take the integer or integer% forms, the remaining space in the frameset is divided equally among all frames with cols attribute values that take the integer* form.

Example:

```
<html><head></head>
<frameset rows="50,*" frameborder="yes" border="20px" framespacing="5">
<frame name="topFrame" scrolling="NO" noresize src="firstPage.html">
<frameset cols="20%,*" border="15px" framespacing="0">
<frame name="topFrame" noresize scrolling="NO" src="secondPage.html">
<frame name="mainFrame" src="thirdPage.html">        </frameset></frameset>
<noframes><body bgcolor="#FFFFFF" text="#000000"></body></noframes></html>
```

Applies to:

```
<frameset>
```

cols (2)

Compatibility: NN4, NN6, NN7, IE4, IE5, IE5.5, IE6

This attribute is used to specify the maximum number of characters that can fit on a single line of a <pre> or <textarea> element. This effectively causes the element to turn on word wrapping when the text in the element exceeds the maximum number of characters specified. In the case of the <textarea> element, the width of the element will be set to the number of cols specified.

Syntax:

```
<element cols="value"> . . . </element>
```

Example:

```
<textarea cols="10" rows="10">This is a sample text containing more than the 10
characters specified. Thus, the text will wrap automatically. Additionally, the
textarea's height will contain 10 rows.</textarea>
```

Applies to:

```
<pre> (NN4 only), <textarea>
```

cols (3)

Compatibility: NN4, NN6, NN7, IE4, IE5, IE5.5, IE6

This attribute establishes the number of columns in a table. Specifying this attribute causes the table to be rendered faster.

Syntax:

```
<table cols="value"> . . . </table>
```

Example:

```
<table border="4" cols="4">
<tr><td>Row 1, Column 1</td><td>Row 1, Column 2</td><td>Row 1, Column 3</td><td>Row
1, Column 4</tr>
<tr><td>Row 2, Column 1</td><td>Row 2, Column 2</td><td>Row 2, Column 3</td><td>Row
2, Column 4</tr>
</table>
```

Applies to:

```
<table>
```

colspan

Compatibility: NN4, NN6, NN7, IE4, IE5, IE5.5, IE6

This attribute determines how many columns in a table a particular cell spans.

Syntax:

```
<element colspan="value"> . . . </element>
```

Example:

```
<table bgcolor="white" width="593" border="1">
    <tr><th colspan="3" align="center" bgcolor="blue" style="color:white;">First
Header (3 cells spanned)</th>
    <th height="79" bgcolor="green" style="color:white;"width="150">Second Header</
th></tr>
    <tr>
      <td height="79">Cell 1 content</td>
      <td height="79">Cell 2 content</td>
      <td height="79">Cell 3 content</td>
      <td height="79">Cell 4 content</td>
    </tr>
</table>
```

Applies to:

```
<td>, <th>
```

compact

Compatibility: NN6, NN7, IE4, IE5, IE5.5, IE6

This attribute reduces the white space between each item in a list or menu. It is a Boolean attribute, taking the values true (extra space is removed) and false (default).

Syntax:

```
<element compact="value"> . . . </element>
```

Example:

```
<dl compact>
<dt>Compacted Definition List</dt>
<dt>1.</dt>
<dd>Definition 1.</dd>
<dt>2.</dt>
<dd>Definition 2.</dd></dl>
```

Applies to:

```
<dir> (IE6), <dl>, <menu> (IE6), <ol>, <ul>
```

contenteditable

Compatibility: IE5.5, IE6

This attribute determines whether an element can be edited or not. This is most applicable for input elements.

Syntax:

```
<element contenteditable="value" > . . . </element>
```

Possible values:

inherit	This indicates that the setting should be determined by the element's parent object. This is the default value.
false	The contents of the element cannot be modified.
true	The contents of the element can be modified.

Example:

```
<p contenteditable=true>My favorite river is "Mississippi", but you can overwrite
any part of this text with your own favorite river.</p>
```

Applies to:

`<a>`, `<acronym>`, `<address>`, `<b>`, `<bdo>`, `<big>`, `<blockquote>`, `<body>`, `<button>`, `<center>`, `<cite>`, `<code>`, `<custom>`, `<dd>`, `<del>`, `<dfn>`, `<dir>`, `<div>`, `<dl>`, `<dt>`, `<em>`, `<fieldset>`, `<font>`, `<form>`, `<hn>`, `<i>`, `<input type="button">`, `<input type="password">`, `<input type="radio">`, `<input type="reset">`, `<input type="submit">`, `<input type="text">`, `<ins>`, `<isindex>`, `<kbd>`, `<label>`, `<legend>`, `<li>`, `<listing>`, `<marquee>`, `<menu>`, `<nobr>`, `<object>`, `<ol>`, `<p>`, `<pre>`, `<q>`, `<rt>`, `<ruby>`, `<s>`, `<samp>`, `<small>`, `<span>`, `<strike>`, `<strong>`, `<sub>`, `<sup>`, `<textarea>`, `<tt>`, `<u>`, `<ul>`, `<var>`, `<xmp>`

coords

Compatibility: NN4, NN6, NN7, IE4, IE5, IE5.5, IE6

This attribute determines the coordinates of an `<a>` or `<area>` element. It is used in conjunction with the shape attribute. The shape attribute determines the shape of the object, and the coords attribute determines the size of the shape specified.

Syntax for a circle shape, where x and y are coordinates for the center of the circle, and r represents the radius:

```
<element shape="circ" coords="x, y, r"> . . . </element>
```

Syntax for a rectangle shape, where x1 and y1 represent the top-left corner coordinates, and x2 and y2 represent the bottom-right corner coordinates:

```
<element shape="rect" coords="x1, y1, x2, y2"> . . . </element>
```

Syntax for a polygon shape, where each x and y pair represents the coordinates of a vertex in the polygon:

```
<element shape="poly" coords="x1, y1, x2, y2, . . . xn, yn"> . . . </element>
```

NOTE *The point of origin for each coordinate is the upper-left corner of the document (or the parent element) known as the point of reference (0,0). The x coordinate increases toward the right, and the y coordinate increases toward the bottom.*

Example:

```
<img src="yourimage.gif" alt="" width=300 height=100 usemap="#myMap">
    <map name="myMap">
      <area shape="rect" coords="0, 0, 100, 50" href="http://www.w3c.com">
      <area shape="rect" coords="100, 0, 200, 50" href="http://www.microsoft.com">
      <area shape="rect" coords="200, 0, 300, 50" href="http://www.advocar.com">
      <area shape="rect" coords="0, 50, 100, 100" href="http://www.msn.com">
      <area shape="rect" coords="100, 50, 200, 100" href="http://www.yahoo.com">
      <area shape="rect" coords="200, 50, 300, 100" href="http://
www.softsmartinc.com">
    </map>
```

Applies to:

```
<a> (IE6 only), <area>
```

data

Compatibility: NN4, NN6, NN7, IE4, IE5, IE5.5, IE6

This attribute establishes the URL that references the data of the `<comment>` or `<object>` elements.

Syntax:

```
<element data="value"> . . . </element>
```

Example:

```
<object classid="clsid:D27CDB6E-AE6D-11cf-96B8-444553540000"
data="http://download.macromedia.com/pub/shockwave/cabs/flash/
swflash.cab#version=5,0,0,0"
width="480" height="240">
    <param name="movie" value="yourflashmovie.swf">
    <param name="quality" value="high">
    <embed src="yourflashmovie.swf" quality="high"
pluginspage="http://www.macromedia.com/shockwave/download/
index.cgi?P1_Prod_Version=ShockwaveFlash"
width="480" height="240"></embed>
</object>
```

Applies to:

```
<comment> (IE6 only), <object>
```

datafld

Compatibility: IE4, IE5, IE5.5, IE6

This attribute determines which field in the datasrc the element should be bound to. datafld acts as an intermediary between the page and the datasrc, which must be attached to the page as an object.

Syntax:

```
<element datafld="value" > . . . </element>
```

Example:

```
<a datasrc="#myDataSource" datafld="column1" dataformatas="html"
target="_blank">Example of datafld attribute</a>
<object id="myDataSource" classid="clsid:333C7BC4-460F-11D0-BC04-0080C7055A83">
<param name="DataURL" value="YourDatafldDatasrc.txt">
<param name="FieldDelim" value="\">
<param name="RowDelim" value="\">
</object>
```

Applies to:

```
<a>, <applet>, <button>, <div>, <fieldset>, <frame>, <iframe>, <img>, <input
type="button">, <input type="checkbox">, <input type="hidden">, <input
type="image">, <input type="password">, <input type="radio">, <input type="text">,
<label>, <marquee>, <param>, <select>, <span>, <textarea>
```

dataformatas

Compatibility: IE4, IE5, IE5.5, IE6

This attribute establishes how the data in an element is to be displayed. Possible values include text, html, and localized-text (the data is displayed using the locale setting of the browser's computer).

Syntax:

```
<element dataformatas="value"> . . . </element>
```

Example: See example for the datafld attribute.
Applies to:

```
<button>, <div>, <input type="button">, <label>, <legend>, <marquee>, <param>,
<span>
```

datapagesize

Compatibility: IE4, IE5, IE5.5, IE6

This attribute establishes the number of records from a data source to be displayed in a table. This is helpful when there are more rows of data records than can be displayed in one table. You can define the number of records to display as a "page."

Syntax:

```
<table datapagesize="value"> . . . </table>
```

Example:

```
<table bgcolor="#00ffff" border=1 datasrc="#carMaker" datapagesize="10">
<tr><td><input type=textbox size=30 value="This is the first record"
datafld="car_model"></td></tr>
<tr><td><input type=textbox size=30 value="This is the second record"
datafld="car_price"></td></tr></table>
<object id="myDT" classid="clsid:333C7BC4-460F-11D0-BC04-0080C7055A83">
<param name="DataURL" value="carMaker.txt">
<param name="FieldDelim" value="\">
<param name="RowDelim" value="\"></object>
```

Applies to:

```
<table>
```

datasrc

Compatibility: IE4, IE5, IE5.5, IE6

This attribute specifies the data source for binding data to elements on the page.

Syntax:

```
<element datasrc="value" > . . . </element>
```

Example: See example for the datafld attribute.
Applies to:

```
<a>, <applet>, <button>, <div>, <frame>, <iframe>, <img>, <input type="button">,
<input type="checkbox">, <input type="hidden">, <input type="image">, <input
type="password">, <input type="radio">, <input type="text">, <label>, <marquee>,
<param>, <select>, <span>, <table>, <textarea>
```

datetime

Compatibility: NN6, NN7, IE6

This attribute specifies the date and time at which the text in a <del> or <ins> element was deleted.

Syntax:

```
<element datetime="value"> . . . </element>
```

Example:

```
<del datetime="2003-04-15T14:50:30Z">This is a text that has been deleted from the
document at 04/15/2003 14:50:30.</del>
```

Applies to:

```
<del>, <ins>
```

declare

Compatibility: NN6, NN7, IE6

This attribute determines whether an object definition is a simple declaration or something more. declare is a Boolean attribute, taking values yes or true (indicating that the object is only a declaration) and no or false (meaning that the object is more than a declaration).

Syntax:

```
<object declare="value"> . . . </object>
```

Example:

```
<object classid="clsid:D27CDB6E-AE6D-11cf-96B8-444553540000" declare=false
codebase="http://download.macromedia.com/pub/shockwave/cabs/flash/
swflash.cab#version=5,0,0,0"
width="480" height="240">
    <param name="movie" value="flashmoviefile.swf">
    <param name="quality" value="high">
</object>
```

Applies to:

```
<object>
```

defer

Compatibility: NN6, NN7, IE4, IE5, IE5.5, IE6

This attribute determines whether the script specified in the <script> element is executed while the page is loading or if it is deferred until after the page loads. This is a Boolean attribute, taking the values false (default) and true.

Syntax:

```
<script defer="value"> . . . </script>
```

Example (to better see the effect, copy the code into a large HTML document):

```
<script language="javascript" defer="true">
document.write('<p>The script has been deferred and the browser is placed on hold</p>')
</script>
```

Applies to:

```
<script>
```

dir

Compatibility: NN6, NN7, IE5, IE5.5, IE6

This attribute determines the direction in which elements on the page are read. The default value is ltr, which causes content to be read from left to right. When you set this attribute value to rtl, it causes content to be read from right to left.

Syntax:

```
<element dir="value" > . . . </element>
```

Example:

```
<a dir="rtl" href="http://www.advocar.com" target="_blank">LEFT TO RIGHT FROM READ
IS TEXT THIS</a>
```

Applies to:

```
<a>, <acronym>, <address>, <area>, <b>, <bdo>, <big>, <blockquote>, <body>,
<button>, <caption>, <center>, <cite>, <code>, <col>, <colgroup>, <custom>, <dd>,
<del>, <dfn>, <dir>, <div>, <dl>, <dt>, <em>, <embed>, <fieldset>, <font>, <form>,
<head>, <hn>, <hr>, <html>, <i>, <img>, <input type="button">, <input
type="checkbox">, <input type="file">, <input type="image">, <input
type="password">, <input type="radio">, <input type="reset">, <input
type="submit">, <input type="text">, <ins>, <isindex>, <kbd>, <label>, <legend>,
<li>, <link>, <listing>, <map>, <marquee>, <menu>, <nobr>, <noframes>, <object>,
<ol>, <option>, <p>, <pre>, <q>, <rt>, <ruby>, <s>, <samp>, <select>, <small>,
<span>, <strike>, <strong>, <style>, <sub>, <sup>, <table>, <tbody>, <td>,
<textarea>, <tfoot>, <th>, <thead>, <title>, <tr>, <tt>, <u>, <ul>, <var>, <xmp>
```

direction

Compatibility: IE4, IE5, IE5.5, IE6

This attribute specifies the scrolling direction of the text in a <marquee> element. Possible values include down, left, right, and up.

Syntax:

```
<marquee direction="value"> . . . </marquee>
```

Example:

```
<marquee id="myM" direction="right" behavior="slide" bgcolor="cyan">
This is a marquee with a direction = right.</marquee>
```

Applies to:

```
<marquee>
```

disabled

Compatibility: IE4, IE5, IE5.5, IE6

This attribute determines the enabled state of an element. disabled is a Boolean attribute, taking the values false (the default) and true.

Syntax:

```
<element disabled="value" > . . . </element>
```

Example:

```
<input type="button" value="This button is enabled">
<input disabled=true type="button" value="This button is disabled">
```

Applies to:

```
<a>, <acronym>, <address>, <b>, <bdo>, <big>, <blockquote>, <body>, <button>,
<caption>, <center>, <cite>, <code>, <custom>, <dd>, <del>, <dfn>, <dir>, <div>,
<dl>, <dt>, <em>, <fieldset>, <font>, <form>, <hn>, <i>, <input type="button">,
<input type="checkbox">, <input type="file">, <input type="image">, <input
type="password">, <input type="radio">, <input type="reset">, <input
type="submit">, <input type="text">, <ins>, <isindex>, <kbd>, <label>, <legend>,
<li>, <listing>, <marquee>, <menu>, <nobr>, <ol>, <optgroup>, <option>, <p>, <pre>,
<q>, <rt>, <ruby>, <s>, <samp>, <select>, <small>, <strike>, <strong>, <sub>,
<sup>, <textarea>, <tt>, <u>, <ul>, <var>, <xmp>
```

dynsrc

Compatibility: IE4, IE5, IE5.5, IE6

This attribute specifies the URL of a video clip that is to be displayed on the page.

Syntax:

```
<element dynsrc="value"> . . . </element>
```

Example:

```
<img start="mouseover" dynsrc="yourvideoclip.avi" alt="">
```

Applies to:

```
<img>, <input>, <input type="image">
```

enctype / encoding

Compatibility: NN4, NN6, NN7, IE4, IE5, IE5.5, IE6

This attribute specifies the MIME encoding type used to submit the form to the server when the method attribute is set to post. The default value is application/x-www-form-urlencoded.

Syntax:

```
<form enctype="value"> . . . </form>
```

Example:

```
<body bgcolor="#FFFFFF" text="#000000" onUnload="document.forms[0].reset()">
<form name="form1" method="post" action="" encoding="text/plain">
<p>My Password: <input type="password" name="textfield" value="15151515"
size="20"><input type="button" name="Submit" value="Submit"></p>
</form>
</body>
```

Applies to:

```
<form>
```

end

Compatibility: IE5.5, IE6

This attribute belongs to the HTML+TIME technology introduced by Microsoft. See Chapter 15 for more information.

Applies to:

```
<a>, <acronym>, <address>, <area>, <b>, <big>, <blockquote>, <button>, <caption>,
<center>, <cite>, <code>, <dd>, <del>, <dir>, <div>, <dl>, <dt>, <em>, <fieldset>,
<font>, <form>, <hn>, <hr>, <i>, <iframe>, <img>, <input type="button">, <input
type="checkbox">, <input type="file">, <input type="hidden">, <input type="image">,
<input type="password">, <input type="radio">, <input type="reset">, <input
type="submit">, <input type="text">, <ins>, <kbd>, <legend>, <li>, <listing>,
<marquee>, <menu>, <ol>, <option>, <p>, <pre>, <q>, <s>, <samp>, <small>, <span>,
<strike>, <strong>, <sub>, <sup>, <table>, <tbody>, <td>, <textarea>, <tfoot>,
<th>, <thead>, <tr>, <tt>, <u>, <ul>, <var>, <xmp>
```

event

Compatibility: NN6, NN7, IE4, IE5, IE5.5, IE6

This attribute specifies the event, which, once triggered, will cause the script code to be executed.

Syntax:

```
<script event="value"> . . . </script>
```

Example:

```
<body bgcolor="#FFFFFF" text="#000000">
<script language="JavaScript" for="myButton" event="onclick()">
    alert('button was clicked!')
</script>
<input type="Button" id="myButton" value="Click here to trigger event">
</body>
```

Applies to:

```
<script>
```

face

Compatibility: NN4, NN6, NN7, IE4, IE5, IE5.5, IE6

This attribute was used to set the typeface (font face) applied to text between the opening and closing tags of an element. However, HTML 4.0 no longer favors use of this attribute, given that CSS and the style attribute can achieve the same or better results.

The value of the face attribute is a comma-separated list of fonts. The fonts in the list are used in their order of appearance, provided that the browser has access to one or more of them.

Syntax:

```
<element face="value"> . . . </element>
```

Example:

```
<p><font face="Verdana, Arial, Helvetica, sans-serif" size="2">
This text is rendered with a "Verdana" font family.</font></p>
```

Applies to:

```
<basefont>, <font>
```

for

Compatibility: IE4, IE5, IE5.5, IE6

This attribute associates an element with another element in the same document. The value of this attribute must match the value of the id attribute of the associated element.

Syntax:

```
<element for="value"> . . . </element>
```

Example:

```
<label for="myCheckbox" accesskey="L">Press Alt+L to set the focus to the
checkbox</label>
<input type="checkbox" id="myCheckbox">
```

Applies to:

```
<label>, <script>
```

frame

Compatibility: NN6, NN7, IE4, IE5, IE5.5, IE6

This attribute determines what portion of a table's border frame is displayed. Possible values include void (default), above, below, border, box, hsides, lhs, rhs, and vsides.

Syntax:

```
<table frame="value"> . . . </table>
```

Example:

```
<table id="myT2" border="" frame="">
<thead><tr><td>Header</td><td>Header</td><td>Header</td>
<td>Header</td><td>Header</td><td>Header</td></tr></thead>
<tr><td>Cell</td><td>Cell</td><td>Cell</td><td>Cell</td><td>Cell</td>
<td>Cell</td><tr>
<tr><td>Cell</td><td>Cell</td><td>Cell</td><td>Cell</td><td>Cell</td>
<td>Cell</td><tr>
<tr><td>Cell</td><td>Cell</td><td>Cell</td><td>Cell</td><td>Cell</td>
<td>Cell</td><tr>
<tr><td>Cell</td><td>Cell</td><td>Cell</td><td>Cell</td><td>Cell</td>
<td>Cell</td><tr>
<tfoot><tr><td>Footer</td><td>Footer</td><td>Footer</td>
<td>Footer</td><td>Footer</td><td>Footer</td></tr></tfoot>
</table><br>
<button onclick="myT2.frame='void'">VOID</button>
  <button onclick="myT2.frame='above'">ABOVE</button>
  <button onclick="myT2.frame='below'">BELOW</button>
  <button onclick="myT2.frame='border'">BORDER</button>
  <button onclick="myT2.frame='hsides'">HSIDES</button>
  <button onclick="myT2.frame='lhs'">LHS</button>
  <button onclick="myT2.frame='rhs'">RHS</button>
  <button onclick="myT2.frame='vsides'">VSIDES</button>
  <button onclick="myT2.frame='box'">BOX</button>
```

Applies to:

`<table>`

---

frameborder

Compatibility: NN4, NN6, NN7, IE4, IE5, IE5.5, IE6

This attribute indicates to the browser whether a border should be displayed around a frame or frameset. Possible values include 0 or no (no border is displayed), and 1 or yes (the default — a border is displayed).

Syntax:

```
<element frameborder="value"> . . . </element>
```

Example:

```
<frameset rows="*" cols="125,*" frameborder="yes" border="20px" framespacing="5">
    <frame name="leftFrame" scrolling="NO" noresize src="fr1b.html">
    <frameset rows="200,*" border="15px" framespacing="0">
        <frame name="topFrame" noresize scrolling="NO" src="fr2b.html">
        <frame name="mainFrame" src="fr3b.html">
    </frameset>
</frameset>
```

Applies to:

`<embed>`, `<frame>`, `<frameset>`, `<iframe>`

---

framespacing

Compatibility: IE4, IE5, IE5.5, IE6

This attribute is used to create additional space in pixels between the frames of a frameset.

Syntax:

```
<frameset framespacing="value"> . . . </frameset>
```

Example: See example for the frameborder attribute.
Applies to:

`<frameset>`

---

galleryimg

Compatibility: IE6

This attribute determines whether a toolbar is displayed when the user hovers the mouse cursor over an image created with the `<img>` element. The toolbar is displayed without requiring the use of the right mouse button, and it has four choices: save, print, email, and open the MyPictures folder in Windows. galleryimg is a Boolean attribute, taking the values true or yes (the default), and false or no.

To eliminate the appearance of the toolbar for all `<img>` elements, use the following command in the `<head>` section of the page:

```
<meta http-equiv="imagetoolbar" content="no">
```

Syntax:

```
<img galleryimg="value">
```

Example:

```
<img src="yourimagefile.jpg" galleryimg="no">
```

Applies to:

```
<img>
```

headers

Compatibility: NN6, NN7, IE6

This attribute specifies a list of `<th>` elements in the table that provide header information and formatting for the affected `<td>` element. The value of this attribute can be the id attribute of a single `<th>` or a space-separated list of `<th>` elements. This attribute is useful in associating a cell to a column header based on the id attribute instead of the position or order in which it appears in the HTML code.

Syntax:

```
<element headers="value"> . . . </element>
```

Example:

```
<table width="450" border="3" bordercolor="#FF0000">
<tr>
<th id="hdr1">Item Number</th>
<th id="hdr2">Item Name</th>
<th id="hdr3">Item Description</th>
</tr>
<tr>
<td headers="hdr2">JS CD-ROM</td>
<td headers="hdr1">28030</td>
```

```
<td headers="hdr3">Tutorial</td>
</tr>
</table>
```

Applies to:

```
<td>, <th>
```

height

Compatibility: NN4 (<embed>, <img>, <table> only), NN6, NN7, IE4, IE5, IE5.5, IE6

This attribute establishes the height of an element in pixels.

   Syntax:

```
<element height="value"> . . . </element>
```

   Example:

```
<table width="450" border="3" cellspacing="5" cellpadding="10"
bordercolor="#FF0000" height="200">
<tr><th colspan="3" height="80">Header</th></tr>
<tr><td height="100">Cell 1</td></tr>
</table>
```

   Applies to:

```
<applet>, <embed>, <frame>, <iframe>, <img>, <marquee>, <nobr>, <object>, <spacer>,
<table>, <td>, <th>, <tr>
```

hidden

Compatibility: NN4, NN6, NN7, IE4, IE5, IE5.5, IE6

This attribute causes the console to be hidden. It is a Boolean attribute, taking
the values true and false.

   Syntax:

```
<embed hidden="value"></embed>
```

   Example:

```
<embed src="yourmacromediadocument.swf" quality=high
pluginspage="http://www.macromedia.com/shockwave/download/
index.cgi?P1_Prod_Version=ShockwaveFlash"
width="480" height="240" hidden=true></embed>
```

   Applies to:

```
<embed>
```

Compatibility: IE5.5, IE6

This attribute determines whether an element's state of focus is made visible to the viewer or not. This attribute only affects how the element is displayed when it has the focus. It is a Boolean attribute, taking the values true and false (the default).

Syntax:

```
<element hidefocus="value"> . . . </element>
```

Example:

```
<a hidefocus="true" href="http://www.w3c.org/">World Wide Web Consortium</a>
```

Applies to:

```
<a>, <acronym>, <address>, <applet>, <area>, <b>, <bdo>, <big>, <blockquote>,
<body>, <button>, <caption>, <center>, <cite>, <custom>, <dd>, <dfn>, <dir>, <div>,
<dl>, <dt>, <em>, <embed>, <fieldset>, <font>, <form>, <frame>, <frameset>, <hn>,
<hr>, <i>, <iframe>, <img>, <input type="button">, <input type="checkbox">, <input
type="file">, <input type="hidden">, <input type="image">, <input type="password">,
<input type="radio">, <input type="reset">, <input type="submit">, <input
type="text">, <ins>, <isindex>, <kbd>, <label>, <legend>, <li>, <listing>,
<marquee>, <menu>, <object>, <ol>, <p>, <pre>, <q>, <rt>, <ruby>, <s>, <samp>,
<select>, <small>, <span>, <strike>, <strong>, <sub>, <sup>, <table>, <tbody>,
<td>, <textarea>, <tfoot>, <th>, <thead>, <tr>, <tt>, <u>, <ul>, <var>, <xmp>
```

href

Compatibility: NN4, NN6, NN7, IE4, IE5, IE5.5, IE6

The href attribute establishes the destination URL or anchor point of the <a>, <area>, <base>, and <link> elements.

Syntax:

```
<element href="value"> . . . </element>
```

Possible values:

URL	Specifies the location of the requested file.
#name	Specifies the target anchor "#name" in the target page, be it the same page or a different one.
Filename	Specifies the name of a file in a network or local hard drive.
Other protocols	You can use any of the following protocols in your href value:
	afs:// AFS file access.
	cid:// Content identifiers for MIME body part.
	file:// Specifies the address of a file from the locally accessible drive.
	ftp:// Uses Internet File Transfer Protocol (FTP) to retrieve a file.

http://	The most commonly used access method. It requires a program running on the destination computer that understands and responds to this protocol.
https://	An access method designed to provide some level of security of transmission.
mailto://	Opens an email program.
mid://	The message identifier for email.
news://	Usenet newsgroup.
x-exec://	Executable program.

Example:

```
<a href="#jumpto">Scroll down to the bottom paragraph</a>
<br><br><br><br><br><br><br><br><br><br><br><br><br><br>
<br><br><br><br><br><br><br><br><br><br><br><br><br><br>
<p id="jumpto">This is the last paragraph on the page</p>
<br><br><br><br><br><br><br><br><br><br><br><br><br><br>
```

Applies to:

```
<a>, <area>, <base>, <link> (not NN4)
```

hreflang

Compatibility: NN6, NN7, IE6

Establishes the base language of the page specified in the href attribute and can only be used when href is specified. The most common language codes are listed in Table 6-1.

Syntax:

```
<element hreflang="value"> . . . </element>
```

Example:

```
<a href="http://www.advocar.com" hreflang="en-us">
```

Applies to:

```
<a>, <link>
```

Table 6-1: Common Language Codes

Code	Language	Code	Language
ca	Catalan	is	Icelandic
cs	Czech	it	Italian
da	Danish	ja	Japanese
nl	Dutch	ko	Korean

Table 6-1: Common Language Codes, continued

Code	Language	Code	Language
en	English	lv	Latvian
en-us	English (USA)	lt	Lithuanian
en-gb	English (G.B.)	no	Norwegian
fi	Finnish	pl	Polish
fr	French	pt	Portuguese
fr-be	French (Belgium)	ro	Romanian
de	German	ru	Russian
de-at	German (Austria)	es	Spanish
el	Greek	es-ar	Spanish (Argentina)
he	Hebrew	sv	Swedish
hi	Hindi	sv-fi	Swedish (Finland)
hu	Hungarian	tr	Turkish

hspace

Compatibility: NN4 (<embed>, <table> only), NN6, NN7, IE4, IE5, IE5.5, IE6

This attribute specifies the amount of space in pixels to be placed on the left and right sides of an element.

Syntax:

```
<element hspace="value"> . . . </element>
```

Example:

```
<table border="1"><tr><td><img src="yourimagefile.jpg" alt="" width="300"
height="225" hspace="100"></td></tr></table>
```

Applies to:

```
<applet>, <embed>, <iframe>, <img>, <input>, <input type="image">, <marquee>,
<object>
```

id

Compatibility: NN4, NN6, NN7, IE4, IE5, IE5.5, IE6

This attribute defines the name that can be used to reference the element throughout the HTML and JavaScript code. It is preferable to use the id attribute in addition to the name attribute, given that the name attribute is not available to all the HTML elements, whereas the id attribute is.

Syntax:

```
<element ID="value"> . . . </element>
```

Example: See example for the href attribute.

Applies to:

`<a>`, `<acronym>`, `<address>`, `<applet>`, `<area>`, `<b>`, `<base>`, `<basefont>`, `<bdo>`, `<bgsound>`, `<big>`, `<blockquote>`, `<body>`, `<br>`, `<button>`, `<caption>`, `<center>`, `<cite>`, `<code>`, `<col>`, `<colgroup>`, `<comment>`, `<custom>`, `<dd>`, `<del>`, `<dfn>`, `<dir>`, `<div>`, `<dl>`, `<dt>`, `<em>`, `<embed>`, `<fieldset>`, `<font>`, `<form>`, `<frame>`, `<frameset>`, `<head>`, `<hn>`, `<hr>`, `<html>`, `<i>`, `<iframe>`, `<img>`, `<input type="button">`, `<input type="checkbox">`, `<input type="file">`, `<input type="hidden">`, `<input type="image">`, `<input type="password">`, `<input type="radio">`, `<input type="reset">`, `<input type="submit">`, `<input type="text">`, `<ins>`, `<isindex>`, `<kbd>`, `<label>`, `<legend>`, `<li>`, `<link>`, `<listing>`, `<map>`, `<marquee>`, `<menu>`, `<nobr>`, `<noframes>`, `<noscript>`, `<object>`, `<ol>`, `<option>`, `<p>`, `<param>`, `<pre>`, `<q>`, `<rt>`, `<ruby>`, `<s>`, `<samp>`, `<script>`, `<select>`, `<small>`, `<span>`, `<strike>`, `<strong>`, `<style>`, `<sub>`, `<sup>`, `<table>`, `<tbody>`, `<td>`, `<textarea>`, `<tfoot>`, `<th>`, `<thead>`, `<title>`, `<tr>`, `<tt>`, `<u>`, `<ul>`, `<var>`, `<wbr>`, `<xml>`, `<xmp>`

---

ismap

Compatibility: NN4, NN6, NN7, IE4, IE5, IE5.5, IE6

This attribute is used to establish whether or not the image referenced in the `<img>` element is a server-side image map. It is a Boolean attribute, taking the values true and false.

Syntax:

```
<img ismap="value">
```

Example:

```
<head>
<script language="JavaScript">
function A6() {
var x = document.getElementById("myimage").isMap;
if (x == true) {
alert("Yes");
}}
</script>
</head>
<body bgcolor="#FFFFFF" text="#000000">
<img id="myimage" src="yourimage.gif" alt="" width=300 height=100 usemap="#myMap"
ismap="false">
    <map name="myMap">
      <area shape="rect" coords="0, 0, 100, 50" href=http://www.w3c.org>
      <area shape="rect" coords="100, 0, 200, 50" href="http://www.microsoft.com">
      <area shape="rect" coords="200, 0, 300, 50" href="http://www.advocar.com">
      <area shape="rect" coords="0, 50, 100, 100" href="http://www.msn.com">
      <area shape="rect" coords="100, 50, 200, 100" href="http://www.yahoo.com">
      <area shape="rect" coords="200, 50, 300, 100" href="http://
www.softsmartinc.com">
    </map>
```

```
<input type="button" name="B6" value="Is this image a server-side map?"
onClick="A6()">
</body>
```

Applies to:

```
<img>
```

label (1)

Compatibility: NN6, NN7, IE6

This attribute specifies the text that will appear at the head of all select-list
options within an `<optgroup>` element.

Syntax:

```
<optgroup label="value"> . . . </optgroup>
```

Example:

```
<form name="form1" method="post" action="">
    <select name="select1">
      <optgroup label="first group">
      <option>first item in first group </option>
      <option>second item in first group </option>
      <option>third item in first group </option>
      </optgroup> <optgroup label="second group">
      <option>first item in second group </option>
      <option>second item in second group </option>
      <option>third item in second group </option>
      </optgroup>
    </select>
</form>
```

Applies to:

```
<optgroup>
```

label (2)

Compatibility: NN6, NN7, IE6

This attribute specifies a text string that can be associated to the `<option>`
element. There is no specific functionality associated with this attribute, but
you could use it to store a value that gives more significance to your option —
for example, a unique ID or a long description.

Syntax:

```
<option label="value"> . . . </option>
```

Example:

```
<form name="form1" method="post" action="">
    <select name="select">
      <option label="testing1">first item</option>
      <option label="testing2">second item</option>
      <option label="testing3">third item</option>
    </select>
</form>
```

Applies to:

```
<option>
```

lang

Compatibility: NN4, NN6, NN7, IE4, IE5, IE5.5, IE6

This attribute determines what language will be used in displaying the document. The browser will use this information to determine how quotes, numbers, and the like are displayed. See Table 6-1 in the hreflang section for a list of possible values.

Syntax:

```
<element lang="value"> . . . </element>
```

Example:

```
<p lang="es">Este es un número escrito en español: 12,38 </p>
<p lang="fr">Celui-ci est un nombre écrit en français  : 0,52</p>
```

Applies to:

```
<a>, <acronym>, <address>, <applet>, <area>, <b>, <bdo>, <big>, <blockquote>,
<body>, <button>, <caption>, <center>, <cite>, <code>, <col>, <colgroup>,
<comment>, <custom>, <dd>, <del>, <dfn>, <dir>, <div>, <dl>, <dt>, <em>, <embed>,
<fieldset>, <font>, <form>, <frame>, <frameset>, <head>, <hn>, <hr>, <html>, <i>,
<iframe>, <img>, <input type="button">, <input type="checkbox">, <input
type="file">, <input type="hidden">, <input type="image">, <input type="password">,
<input type="radio">, <input type="reset">, <input type="submit">, <input
type="text">, <ins>, <isindex>, <kbd>, <label>, <legend>, <li>, <link>, <listing>,
<map>, <marquee>, <menu>, <nobr>, <noframes>, <object>, <ol>, <option>, <p>, <pre>,
<q>, <rt>, <ruby>, <s>, <samp>, <script>, <select>, <small>, <span>, <strike>,
<strong>, <style>, <sub>, <sup>, <table>, <tbody>, <td>, <textarea>, <tfoot>, <th>,
<thead>, <title>, <tr>, <tt>, <u>, <ul>, <var>, <xmp>
```

language

Compatibility: NN4, NN6, NN7, IE4, IE5, IE5.5, IE6

This attribute specifies the programming language in which a client- or server-side script is written. Possible values include Jscript, javascript, vbs or vbscript, XML, and other browser-supported languages.

Syntax:

```
<element language="value"> . . . </element>
```

Example:

```
<script language="JavaScript"> … </script>
```

Applies to:

```
<a>, <acronym>, <address>, <applet>, <area>, <b>, <bdo>, <big>, <blockquote>,
<body>, <button>, <caption>, <center>, <cite>, <code>, <custom>, <dd>, <del>,
<dfn>, <dir>, <div>, <dl>, <dt>, <em>, <embed>, <fieldset>, <font>, <form>,
<frame>, <frameset>, <hn>, <hr>, <i>, <iframe>, <img>, <input type="button">,
<input type="checkbox">, <input type="file">, <input type="hidden">, <input
type="image">, <input type="password">, <input type="radio">, <input type="reset">,
<input type="submit">, <input type="text">, <ins>, <isindex>, <kbd>, <label>,
<legend>, <li>, <listing>, <map>, <marquee>, <nobr>, <object>, <ol>, <option>, <p>,
<pre>, <q>, <rt>, <ruby>, <s>, <samp>, <script>, <select>, <small>, <span>,
<strike>, <strong>, <sub>, <sup>, <table>, <tbody>, <td>, <textarea>, <tfoot>,
<th>, <thead>, <tr>, <tt>, <u>, <ul>, <var>, <xmp>
```

leftmargin

Compatibility: IE4, IE5, IE5.5, IE6

This attribute establishes the distance, in pixels, that the page will be indented from the left margin of the browser window. The default value is 10.

Syntax:

```
<body leftmargin="value"> . . . </body>
```

Example:

```
<html><body bgcolor="#FFFFFF" text="#000000" leftmargin="100">The document has a
left margin of 100px</body></html>
```

Applies to:

```
<body>
```

link

Compatibility: NN4, NN6, NN7, IE4, IE5, IE5.5, IE6

This attribute sets the color of all links in an HTML document. Its value is either a color name (some browsers do not support color names) or a hexadecimal color value using the "#RRGGBB" method.

Syntax:

```
<body link="value"> . . . </body>
```

Example:

```
<body link="#ff0000" bgcolor="#FFFFFF" text="#000000">
<a href="">Some interesting web page</a></body>
```

Applies to:

```
<body>
```

loop

Compatibility: IE4, IE5, IE5.5, IE6

This attribute allows the video clip, sound clip, or marquee to be repeated a specified number of times. A value of -1 means that the element continuously repeats while the page is active; a value of 0 means that the element loops only one time; and any other positive integer indicates the number of times the loop should be repeated.

Syntax:

```
<element loop="value"> . . . </element>
```

Example:

```
<marquee bgcolor="#99ffff" loop="-1">Come and see our new car models.</marquee>
```

Applies to:

```
<bgsound>, <img>, <input>, <input type="image">, <marquee>
```

lowsrc

Compatibility: NN7, IE4, IE5, IE5.5, IE6

This attribute provides the URL of the location of a low-resolution image that resides in the `<img>` or `<input>` elements. This image is displayed while the real image is being downloaded.

Syntax:

```
<element lowsrc="value">
```

Example:

```
<img lowsrc="yourimage_lowresolution.jpg" src="yourimage.jpg"
alt="" width="71" height="99">
<input type="image" lowsrc="yourimage_lowres.jpg" src="yourimage.jpg">
```

Applies to:

```
<img>, <input>, <input type="image">
```

marginheight

Compatibility: NN4, NN6, NN7, IE4, IE5, IE5.5, IE6

This attribute establishes the size, in pixels, of the top and bottom margins of a frame.

Syntax:

```
<element marginheight="value"> . . . </element>
```

Example:

```
<frameset rows="50,*" frameborder="yes" border="20px" framespacing="5" cols="*">
  <frame name="topFrame" scrolling="NO" noresize src="topframe.html">
  <frameset cols="25%,*" border="15px" framespacing="0">
    <frame name="leftFrame" marginheight="100" marginwidth="15" noresize
scrolling="NO" src="leftframe.html">
    <frame name="mainFrame" src="mainframe.html">
  </frameset>
</frameset>
```

Applies to:

```
<frame>, <iframe>
```

marginwidth

Compatibility: NN4, NN6, NN7, IE4, IE5, IE5.5, IE6

This attribute establishes the amount of space, in pixels, to place at the left and right margins of a frame.

Syntax:

```
<element marginwidth="value"> . . . </element>
```

Example: See example for the marginheight attribute.

Applies to:

```
<frame>, <iframe>
```

maxlength

Compatibility: NN4, NN6, NN7, IE4, IE5, IE5.5, IE6

This attribute specifies the maximum number of characters that the user can enter in a text or password control. If this attribute is not specified, then there will be no limit on the maximum length allowed.

Syntax:

```
<input maxlength="value">
```

Example:

```
<input type="password" name="text1" maxlength="10">
```

Applies to:

```
<input type="password">, <input type="text">
```

media

Compatibility: NN6, NN7, IE4, IE5, IE5.5, IE6

This attribute is used to set the media type. The possible values include screen (if the element is intended to be displayed on the user's computer screen), print (if it is meant to be displayed as a screen preview or in printed form), and all to include all media types.

Syntax:

```
<element media="value">
```

Example:

```
<link rel="stylesheet" href="yourfile.css" type="text/css" media="screen">This is a
link</link>
```

Applies to:

```
<link>, <style> (not IE4)
```

method

Compatibility: NN4, NN6, NN7, IE4, IE5, IE5.5, IE6

This attribute defines the manner in which form data is sent to the server. Possible values are get and post.

The get method appends the form input elements and their data to the underlying URL. This can be useful when dealing with small amounts of data, but the URL length is limited to 2,048 bytes. The post method sends the data via an HTTP post transaction, and there is no limit to the amount of data that can be sent to the HTTP server using this method.

Syntax:

```
<form method="value"> . . . </form>
```

Example:

```
<form name="form1" method="post" action="">
<input type="text" cols=50 size=50 value="This is one element of the form.">
```

Applies to:

```
<form>
```

methods

Compatibility: NN6, NN7, IE4, IE5, IE5.5, IE6

Establishes a comma-separated list of HTTP methods supported by the element. This attribute is only applicable to the `<a>` element.

Syntax:

```
<a methods="value"> . . . </a>
```

Example:

```
<a methods="get, post" href="http://www.w3c.org/">World Wide Web Consortium</a>
```

Applies to:

```
<a>
```

multiple

Compatibility: NN4, NN6, NN7, IE4, IE5, IE5.5, IE6

This attribute specifies whether multiple `<option>` elements can be simultaneously selected inside a `<select>` element. The user can select multiple options by simultaneously clicking on options in the list and pressing the SHIFT key or CONTROL key.

Syntax:

```
<select multiple> . . . </select>
```

Example:

```
<body bgcolor="#FFFFFF" text="#000000" onUnload="document.forms[0].reset()">
<form name="form1" method="post" action="">
<select name="Chapters" multiple>
<option>Chapter 1</option>
<option>Chapter 2</option>
<option>Chapter 3</option>
<option>Chapter 4</option>
<option>Chapter 5</option>
<option>Chapter 6</option>
</select></form></body>
```

Applies to:

```
<select>
```

name

Compatibility: NN4, NN6, NN7, IE4, IE5, IE5.5, IE6

This attribute establishes the name of an element or establishes the target within a page or a frame of a separate <a> element. HTML 4.0 favors use of the id attribute instead, though support still exists for the name attribute. This attribute is also used to identify the elements that are sent to the server using the post method.

Syntax:

```
<element name="value"> . . . </element>
```

Example:

```
<a href="#bottom">Go to the bottom of this page</a>
<br><br><br><br><br><br><br><br><br><br><br><br><br><br><br><br>
<br><br><br><br><br><br><br><br><br><br><br><br><br><br><br><br>
<p name="bottom"></p>
```

Applies to:

```
<a>, <applet>, <button>, <embed>, <form>, <frame>, <frameset>, <iframe>, <img>,
<input type="button">, <input type="checkbox">, <input type="file">, <input
type="hidden">, <input type="image">, <input type="password">, <input
type="radio">, <input type="reset">, <input type="submit">, <input type="text">,
<link>, <map>, <object>, <param>, <rt>, <ruby>, <select>, <textarea>
```

nohref

Compatibility: NN4, NN6, NN7, IE4, IE5, IE5.5, IE6

This attribute indicates that the <area> element specified within the <map> element does not contain a link. It is a Boolean attribute, taking the values true and false.

Syntax:

```
<area nohref="value"> . . . </area>
```

Example:

```
<img src="yourimage.gif" alt="" width=300 height=100 usemap="#myMap"><map
name="myMap">
<area shape="rect" coords="0, 0, 100, 50" nohref="true" onClick="alert('not active
region')">
<area shape="rect" coords="100, 0, 200, 50" nohref="true" onClick="alert('not
active region')">
<area shape="rect" coords="200, 0, 300, 50" href="http://www.advocar.com" >
<area shape="rect" coords="0, 50, 100, 100" href="http://www.msn.com" alt="The MSN
home page">
<area shape="rect" coords="100, 50, 200, 100" href="http://www.yahoo.com" alt="The
Yahoo home page">
<area shape="rect" coords="200, 50, 300, 100" href="http://www.softsmartinc.com">
</map>
```

Applies to:

```
<area>
```

noresize

Compatibility: NN4, NN6, NN7, IE4, IE5, IE5.5, IE6

This attribute, when used, ensures that the specified frame is not resizable.
   Syntax:

```
<frame noresize>
```

Example:

```
<frameset rows="50,*" frameborder="yes" border="20px" framespacing="5" cols="*">
<frame id="topF" name="topFrame" scrolling="NO" noresize src="fr2c.html">
<frameset cols="25%,*" border="15px" framespacing="0">
<frame name="leftFrame" marginheight="15" noresize scrolling="NO" src="fr1h.html">
<frame name="mainFrame" src="fr3h.html">  </frameset></frameset>
```

Applies to:

```
<frame>
```

noshade

Compatibility: NN6, NN7, IE4, IE5, IE5.5, IE6

This attribute causes an <hr> rule to appear as a solid bar with no shading.

Syntax:

```
<hr noshade>
```

Example:

```
<html><head></head><body bgcolor="#FFFFFF" text="#000000">
<hr>
<hr noshade>
</body></html>
```

Applies to:

```
<hr>
```

nowrap

Compatibility: IE4, IE5, IE5.5, IE6

This attribute produces a result similar to the <pre> element, which determines whether or not the browser automatically performs word wrapping. The HTML 4.0 standard favors using style sheet rules over using this attribute. nowrap is a Boolean attribute, taking the values true and false.

Syntax:

```
<element nowrap="value"> . . . </element>
```

Example:

```
<div id="Layer1">Attribute nowrap is not present in this div element's tag. If this
line is not wrapped please make the browser window smaller.</div>
<div id="Layer2" nowrap="true">Attribute nowrap is present in this div element's
tag.</div>
```

Applies to:

```
<body>, <dd>, <div>, <dt>, <td>, <th>
```

pluginspage

Compatibility: NN4, NN6, NN7, IE4, IE5, IE5.5, IE6

This attribute specifies the URL of a page that contains the instructions for installing a plug-in.

Syntax:

```
<embed pluginspage="value"></embed>
```

Example:

```
<embed src="yourflashmovie.swf" quality=high
pluginspage="http://www.macromedia.com/shockwave/download/
index.cgi?P1_Prod_Version=ShockwaveFlash"
type="application/x-shockwave-flash" width="243" height="194"></embed>
```

Applies to:

```
<embed>
```

point-size

Compatibility: NN4

This attribute indicates the point size (1–7) of a font.
Syntax:

```
<font point-size="value"> . . . </font>
```

Example:

```
<font point-size="3" face="Verdana">Sample text</font>
```

Applies to:

```
<font>
```

profile

Compatibility: NN6, NN7, IE6

This attribute indicates the URI (Uniform Resource Identifier) of one or more metadata profiles, separated by a space. User agents may use the value in this property to perform some specific task. A *user agent* is any application that can interpret HTML documents. Internet Explorer and Netscape Navigator are examples of user agents.
Syntax:

```
<head profile="value"> . . . </head>
```

Example:

```
<head profile="profiles.htm">
<meta name="author" content="Lázaro Issi Cohen">
<meta name="copyright" content="Reference book">
<meta name="keywords" content="html,reference,JavaScript,css">
<meta name="date" content="1 Aug 2003 12:30:00 EST">
</head>
```

Applies to:

<head>

prompt

Compatibility: NN4, NN6, NN7, IE4

This attribute provides a prompt string for the <isindex> input field. However, <isindex> has been deprecated in favor of the <input type="text"> element.

Syntax:

<isindex prompt>

Applies to:

<isindex>

readonly

Compatibility: NN6, NN7, IE4, IE5, IE5.5, IE6

This attribute determines whether the content of an element is read-only or not.

Syntax:

<*element* readonly> . . . </*element*>

Example:

<input type="text" name="tfd" value="This text field is not editable" readonly size="30">

Applies to:

<input type="password">, <input type="text">, <textarea>

rel

Compatibility: NN4, NN6, NN7, IE4, IE5, IE5.5, IE6

This attribute describes the relationship of the document specified by the value of the href attribute to the current document. The browser will make use of this information to determine how to treat the referenced link specified in href.

Possible values include alternate (specifying a substitute document), appendix, bookmark, chapter, contents (identifying a table of contents), copyright, glossary, help, index, next (indicating the next in a sequence of documents), offline, prev (indicating the previous in a sequence of documents), section, shortcut icon, start (indicating the first in a sequence of documents), stylesheet, and subsection.

Syntax:

```
<element rel="value"> . . . </element>
```

Example:

```
<a id="myL" href="examples.css" rel="stylesheet" target="_blank">
The style sheet attached to this document</a>
```

Applies to:

```
<a>, <link>
```

rev

Compatibility: NN6, NN7, IE4, IE5, IE5.5, IE6

Establishes the reverse of the rel attribute. rev describes the relationship of the current document to the document specified by the value of the href attribute. For a list of possible values, see the rel attribute.

Syntax:

```
<element rev="value"> . . . </element>
```

Example:

```
<a id="myL" lang="it" href="A.html" rev="index" target="_blank">The index page for
this document</a>
```

Applies to:

```
<a>, <link>
```

rightmargin

Compatibility: IE4, IE5, IE5.5, IE6

This attribute establishes the amount of space in pixels that the page will be indented from the right margin of the browser window. The default value is 10.

Syntax:

```
<body rightmargin="value"> . . . </body>
```

Example:

```
<body bgcolor="white" text="#000000" bottommargin="100" rightmargin="150">Content
on the page</body>
```

Applies to:

<body>

rows (1)

Compatibility: NN4, NN6, NN7, IE4, IE5, IE5.5, IE6

This attribute establishes the number of rows and the size of the rows in a frameset. Each row value is separated by a comma.

Syntax:

```
<frameset rows="value"> . . . </frameset>
```

Possible values:

integer	Specifies the height in pixels.
integer%	Specifies the percent of the total height of the frameset.
integer*	Specifies the height of the frame as a relative value. Once space is allocated for all frames with rows attribute values that take the integer or integer% forms, the remaining space in the frameset is divided equally among all frames with rows attribute values that take the integer* form.

Example: See example for the cols (3) attribute.
Applies to:

<frameset>

rows (2)

Compatibility: NN4, NN6, NN7, IE4, IE5, IE5.5, IE6

This attribute establishes the height of the element in terms of rows. The value is indicated by an integer.

Syntax:

```
<textarea rows="value"> . . . </textarea>
```

Example: See example for the cols (2) attribute.
Applies to:

<textarea>

rowspan

Compatibility: NN4, NN6, NN7, IE4, IE5, IE5.5, IE6

The integer value of this attribute determines how many table rows a cell spans.

Syntax:

```
<element rowspan="value"> . . . </element>
```

Example:

```
<table border="1">
    <tr>
        <th height="79" rowspan="2">Cell 1</th>
        <th height="79">Cell 2</th>
        <th height="79" rowspan="3">Cell 3</th>
        <th height="79">Cell 4</th>
        <th height="79">Cell 5</th>
    </tr>
    <tr>
        <th height="79" rowspan="3">Cell 7</th>
        <th height="79" rowspan="2">Cell 9</th>
        <th height="79">Cell 10</th>
    </tr>
    <tr>
        <th height="79">Cell 6</th>
        <th height="79">Cell 11</th>
    </tr>
    <tr>
        <th height="79">Cell 12</th>
        <th height="79">Cell 8</th>
        <th height="79">Cell 13</th>
        <th height="79">Cell 14</th>
    </tr>
</table>
```

Applies to:

```
<td>, <th>
```

rules

Compatibility: NN6, NN7, IE4, IE5, IE5.5, IE6

This attribute controls which portions of a table's borders are displayed. Possible values include all, cols, group (displays only group borders), none, and rows.

Syntax:

```
<table rules="value"> . . . </table>
```

Example:

```
<body><table id="myTable" border="" rules="">
<thead><tr><td>Header</td><td>Header</td><td>Header</td><td>Header</td><td>Header</td><td>Header</td></tr></thead>
```

```
<tr><td>Cell</td><td>Cell</td><td>Cell</td><td>Cell</td><td>Cell</td><td>Cell</
td></tr><tr><td>Cell</td><td>Cell</td><td>Cell</td><td>Cell</td><td>Cell
</td><td>Cell</td></tr><tr><td>Cell</td><td>Cell</td><td>Cell</td><td>Cell</
td><td>Cell</td><td>Cell</td></tr><tr><td>Cell</td><td>Cell</td><td>Cell</
td><td>Cell</td><td>Cell</td><td>Cell</td></tr>
<tfoot><tr><td>Footer</td><td>Footer</td><td>Footer</td><td>Footer</td><td>Footer</
td><td>Footer</td></tr></tfoot>
</table><br>
<button onclick="myTable.rules='none'">none</button>
<button onclick="myTable.rules='all'">all</button>
<button onclick="myTable.rules='cols'">cols</button>
<button onclick="myTable.rules='groups'">groups</button>
<button onclick="myTable.rules='rows'">rows</button>
</body>
```

Applies to:

```
<table>
```

scope

Compatibility: NN6, NN7, IE6

This attribute specifies the group of cells in a table to which header information on the current cell refers. If its value is row or rowgroup, the cell provides header information for the current row. If its value is col or colgroup, the cell provides header information for the current column. This attribute may be used in place of the headers attribute discussed earlier in this chapter.

Syntax:

```
<element scope="value"> . . . </element>
```

Example:

```
<table id="myT2" rules="" border="1">
  <tr>
      <th scope="colgroup">Header 1</th>
      <th scope="colgroup">Header 2</th>
      <th scope="colgroup">Header 3</th>
      <th scope="colgroup">Header 4</th>
      <th scope="colgroup">Header 5</th>
      <th scope="colgroup">Header 6</th>
  </tr>
  <tr>
      <th scope="rowgroup">Row 1</th>
      <td>Cell</td><td>Cell</td><td>Cell</td>
      <td scope="col">Cell info 1</td>
      <td>Cell</td>
  </tr>
  <tr>
  <th scope="rowgroup">Row 2</th>
```

```
<td>Cell</td><td>Cell</td><td>Cell</td><td>Cell</td><td>Cell</td>
    </tr>
    <tr><th scope="rowgroup">Row 3</th>
<td>Cell</td><td>Cell</td><td>Cell</td><td>Cell</td><td>Cell</td>
    </tr>
    <tr>
      <th scope="rowgroup">Row 4</th>
      <td scope="row">Cell info 2</td>
      <td>Cell</td><td>Cell</td><td>Cell</td><td>Cell</td>
    </tr>
  </table>
```

Applies to:

`<td>`, `<th>`

scroll

Compatibility: IE4, IE5, IE5.5, IE6

This attribute controls whether or not the scroll bars appear on the page. It is a Boolean attribute, taking the values true (the default), no, and auto (scroll bars are shown when the page content exceeds the visible area).

Syntax:

```
<element scroll="value"> . . . </element>
```

Example:

```
<body id="myBody" bgcolor="white" text="#000000">
<button onclick="myBody.scroll='yes'">Scroll bars do appear</button>
<button onclick="myBody.scroll='no'">Scroll bars do not appear</button>
<button onclick="myBody.scroll='auto'">Scroll = auto</button></body>
```

Applies to:

`<body>`, `<html>` (IE6 only)

scrollamount

Compatibility: IE4, IE5, IE5.5, IE6

Text in a `<marquee>` element appears to be moving because it is displayed, hidden, and then redisplayed in a different location. This attribute establishes how many pixels (the default is 6) the text is displaced between the time it is hidden and later made to reappear.

Syntax:

```
<marquee scrollamount="value"> . . . </marquee>
```

Example:

```
<marquee behavior="slide" bgcolor="#99ffff" scrollamount="15">
    This marquee has a scrollamount value of 15.
</marquee>
```

Applies to:

```
<marquee>
```

scrolldelay

Compatibility: IE4, IE5, IE5.5, IE6

This attribute determines the velocity at which the text appears to move inside a <marquee> element. Its value specifies the delay in milliseconds (the default is 85) before the text is made to reappear each time.

Syntax:

```
<marquee scrolldelay="value"> . . . </marquee>
```

Example:

```
<marquee behavior="slide" scrolldelay="150" bgcolor="#99ffff">This marquee has a
scrolldelay value of 150.</marquee>
```

Applies to:

```
<marquee>
```

scrolling

Compatibility: NN4, NN6, NN7, IE4, IE5, IE5.5, IE6

This attribute specifies whether a frame should have a scroll bar or not. Possible values are yes, no, and auto (the default; the browser decides whether scroll bars are necessary).

Syntax:

```
<element scrolling="value"> . . . </element>
```

Example:

```
<iframe scrolling="yes" name="myFI" src="iF1.html" style="width:30%"></iframe>
```

Applies to:

```
<frame>, <iframe>
```

security

Compatibility: IE6

This attribute establishes whether the source file has security restrictions. If its value is restricted, security settings are applied to the source file.

Syntax:

```
<element security="value"> . . . </element>
```

Example:

```
<iframe id="IF1" security="restricted" name="myFI" src="iFr1.html"
style="width:30%">
```

Applies to:

```
<frame>, <iframe>
```

selected

Compatibility: NN4, NN6, NN7, IE4, IE5, IE5.5, IE6

This attribute establishes the chosen option in a drop-down or select list.

Syntax:

```
<option selected> . . . </option>
```

Example:

```
<select><option>First Option</option><option>Second Option</option><option
selected>Third Option</option></select>
```

Applies to:

```
<option>
```

shape

Compatibility: NN4, NN6, NN7, IE4, IE5, IE5.5, IE6

Establishes the shape of an <a> or <area> element. This attribute must be used in conjunction with the coords attribute. The shape attribute determines the shape of the element, while the coords attribute is used to define its size. Possible values of the shape attribute are circ, circle, rect, rectangle, poly, and polygon.

Syntax where x and y are coordinates for the center of the circle, and r represents the radius:

```
<element shape="circle" coords="x, y, r"> . . . </element>
```

Syntax where x1 and y1 represent the top-left corner coordinates of a rectangle, and x2 and y2 represent the bottom-right corner coordinates:

```
<element shape="rectangle" coords="x1, y1, x2, y2"> . . . </element>
```

Syntax where each x and y pair represents the coordinates of a vertex in a polygon:

```
<element shape="polygon" coords="x1, y1, x2, y2, . . . xn, yn"> . . . </element>
```

NOTE   *The point of origin in the document is (0,0). X increases toward the right and Y increases toward the bottom.*

Example:

```
<img src="area1.gif" alt="" width=200 height=100 usemap="#myMap">
   <map name="myMap">
      <area shape="rect" coords="0, 0, 100, 50" href=http://www.w3c.org>
      <area shape="rect" coords="100, 0, 200, 50" href=http://www.microsoft.com>
      <area shape="rect" coords="0, 50, 100, 100" href=http://www.msn.com>
      <area shape="rect" coords="100, 50, 200, 100" href=http://www.yahoo.com>
   </map>
```

Applies to:

```
<a> (IE6 only), <area>
```

size

Compatibility: NN4, NN6, NN7, IE4, IE5, IE5.5, IE6

This attribute determines the size of the font in an element block. However, later versions of Internet Explorer no longer favor use of this attribute.

In the case of the <input> element, the size attribute represents the width of the element in characters. In the case of the <select> element, the size causes a list with the specified number of rows to be displayed.

Syntax:

```
<element size="value"> . . . </element>
```

Example:

```
<font size="14">Text</font>
<hr size=15 color="red">
<input type="text" size="100">
<select size="10"><option>option 1</option><option>option 2</option>
<option>option 3</option><option>option 4</option>
<option>option 5</option><option>option 6</option>
<option>option 7</option><option>option 8</option></select>
```

Applies to:

`<basefont>` (not NN4), `<font>` (not NN4), `<hr>`, `<input type="button">`, `<input type="checkbox">`, `<input type="file">`, `<input type="image">`, `<input type="password">`, `<input type="radio">`, `<input type="reset">`, `<input type="submit">`, `<input type="text">`, `<select>`, `<spacer>`

---

span

Compatibility: NN6, NN7, IE4, IE5, IE5.5, IE6

This attribute establishes the number of columns in a group. Its default value is 1.
   Syntax:

```
<element span="value">
```

   Example:

```
<table border="3" cellspacing="5" cellpadding="5">
  <colgroup>
  <col span="3" align="left" style="color:red; font-weight:bold">
  <col span="1" align="center" style="color:green">
  <col span="2" align="right" style="color:blue">
  <tr><td>Column 1</td><td>Column 2</td><td>Column 3</td>
<td>Column 4</td><td>Column 5</td><td>Column 6</td></tr>
  <tr><td>Cell 1</td><td>Cell 2</td><td>Cell 3</td>
<td>Cell 4</td><td>Cell 5</td><td>Cell 6</td></tr>
</table>
```

   Applies to:

`<col>`, `<colgroup>`

---

src (1)

Compatibility: NN4, NN6, NN7, IE4, IE5, IE5.5, IE6

This attribute specifies a URL to be loaded by the element.
   Syntax:

```
<element src="value"> . . . </element>
```

   Example:

```
<img src="yourimagefile.jpg" alt="" width="71" height="92">
```

   Applies to:

`<applet>`, `<bgsound>`, `<embed>`, `<frame>`, `<iframe>`, `<img>`, `<input type="image">`, `<xml>`

src (2)

Compatibility: NN4, NN6, NN7, IE4, IE5, IE5.5, IE6

This attribute is used with the `<script>` element and specifies the URL of an external JavaScript file that contains the script. The file specified in this attribute must contain the appropriate suffix for JavaScript files (.js).

Syntax:

```
<script src="value"> . . . </script>
```

Example:

```
<head><script language="JavaScript1.2" src="myJSfile.js">
</script></head>
```

Applies to:

```
<script>
```

standby

Compatibility: NN6, NN7, IE6

This attribute allows you to specify a short text string that the browser can show while the object that is being referenced is loading.

Syntax:

```
<object standby="value"> . . . </object>
```

Example:

```
<object standby="You can play this puzzle"
classid="clsid:D27CDB6E-AE6D-11cf-96B8-444553540000"
codebase=http://download.macromedia.com/pub/shockwave/cabs/flash/
swflash.cab#version=5,0,0,0 width="250" height="230">
     <param name=movie value="Puzzle.swf">
     <param name=quality value=high>
</object>
```

Applies to:

```
<object>
```

start (1)

Compatibility: IE4, IE5, IE5.5, IE6

This attribute specifies when a video clip should start playing. Possible values are fileopen (the video starts playing when the file is completely downloaded) and mouseover (the video starts playing when the user moves the mouse cursor over the animation).

Syntax:

```
<element start="value">
```

Example:

```
<img start="mouseover" dynsrc="yourmovie.avi" alt="">
```

Applies to:

```
<img>, <input>, <input type="image">
```

start (2)

Compatibility: NN4, NN6, NN7, IE4, IE5, IE5.5, IE6

This attribute specifies the starting number in an ordered list, <ol>.

Syntax:

```
<ol start="value"> . . . </ol>
```

Example:

```
<ol start="12">
  <li>Item 1</li>
  <li>Item 2</li>
  <li>Item 3</li>
  <li>Item 4</li>
  <li>Item 5</li>
</ol>
```

Applies to:

```
<ol>
```

style

Compatibility: NN4, NN6, NN7, IE4, IE5, IE5.5, IE6

This attribute allows style rules to be applied inline to an element.

Syntax:

```
<element style="value"> . . . </element>
```

Example:

```
<a href="http://www.w3c.com" target="_blank" style="font-family:verdana;
color:green; font-size:14pt;">World Wide Web</a>
```

Applies to:

```
<a>, <acronym>, <address>, <applet>, <area>, <b>, <bdo>, <big>, <blockquote>,
<body>, <br>, <button>, <caption>, <center>, <cite>, <code>, <col>, <colgroup>,
<custom>, <dd>, <del>, <dfn>, <dir>, <div>, <dl>, <dt>, <em>, <embed>, <fieldset>,
<font>, <form>, <frame>, <frameset>, <hn>, <hr>, <i>, <iframe>, <img>, <input
type="button">, <input type="checkbox">, <input type="file">, <input
type="hidden">, <input type="image">, <input type="password">, <input
type="radio">, <input type="reset">, <input type="submit">, <input type="text">,
<ins>, <isindex>, <kbd>, <label>, <legend>, <li>, <link>, <listing>, <map>,
<marquee>, <menu>, <noframes>, <object>, <ol>, <p>, <pre>, <q>, <rt>, <ruby>, <s>,
<samp>, <select>, <small>, <span>, <strike>, <strong>, <sub>, <sup>, <table>,
<tbody>, <td>, <textarea>, <tfoot>, <th>, <thead>, <tr>, <tt>, <u>, <ul>, <var>,
<xmp>
```

summary

Compatibility: NN6, NN7, IE6

This attribute specifies a brief description of a table and can be used to provide something to render for nonvisual media.

Syntax:

```
<table summary="value"> . . . </table>
```

Example:

```
<table summary="US cities with population of over 1,000,000 people"> . . . </table>
```

Applies to:

```
<table>
```

syncmaster

Compatibility: IE5.5, IE6

This attribute belongs to the HTML+TIME technology introduced by Microsoft. See Chapter 15 for more information.

Applies to:

```
<a>, <acronym>, <address>, <area>, <b>, <big>, <blockquote>, <button>, <caption>,
<center>, <cite>, <code>, <dd>, <del>, <dir>, <div>, <dl>, <dt>, <em>, <fieldset>,
<font>, <form>, <hn>, <hr>, <i>, <iframe>, <img>, <input type="button">, <input
type="checkbox">, <input type="file">, <input type="hidden">, <input type="image">,
<input type="password">, <input type="radio">, <input type="reset">, <input
```

type="submit">, <input type="text">, <ins>, <kbd>, <legend>, <li>, <listing>, <marquee>, <menu>, <ol>, <option>, <p>, <pre>, <q>, <s>, <samp>, <small>, <span>, <strike>, <strong>, <sub>, <sup>, <table>, <tbody>, <td>, <textarea>, <tfoot>, <th>, <thead>, <tr>, <tt>, <u>, <ul>, <var>, <xmp>

systemBitrate

Compatibility: IE5.5, IE6

This attribute belongs to the HTML+TIME technology introduced by Microsoft. See Chapter 15 for more information.

    Applies to:

<a>, <acronym>, <address>, <area>, <b>, <big>, <blockquote>, <button>, <caption>, <center>, <cite>, <code>, <dd>, <del>, <dir>, <div>, <dl>, <dt>, <em>, <fieldset>, <font>, <form>, <hn>, <hr>, <i>, <iframe>, <img>, <input type="button">, <input type="checkbox">, <input type="file">, <input type="hidden">, <input type="image">, <input type="password">, <input type="radio">, <input type="reset">, <input type="submit">, <input type="text">, <ins>, <kbd>, <legend>, <li>, <listing>, <marquee>, <menu>, <ol>, <option>, <p>, <pre>, <q>, <s>, <samp>, <small>, <span>, <strike>, <strong>, <sub>, <sup>, <table>, <tbody>, <td>, <textarea>, <tfoot>, <th>, <thead>, <tr>, <tt>, <u>, <ul>, <var>, <xmp>

systemCaptions

Compatibility: IE5.5, IE6

This attribute belongs to the HTML+TIME technology introduced by Microsoft. See Chapter 15 for more information.

    Applies to:

<a>, <acronym>, <address>, <area>, <b>, <big>, <blockquote>, <button>, <caption>, <center>, <cite>, <code>, <dd>, <del>, <dir>, <div>, <dl>, <dt>, <em>, <fieldset>, <font>, <form>, <hn>, <hr>, <i>, <iframe>, <img>, <input type="button">, <input type="checkbox">, <input type="file">, <input type="hidden">, <input type="image">, <input type="password">, <input type="radio">, <input type="reset">, <input type="submit">, <input type="text">, <ins>, <kbd>, <legend>, <li>, <listing>, <marquee>, <menu>, <ol>, <option>, <p>, <pre>, <q>, <s>, <samp>, <small>, <span>, <strike>, <strong>, <sub>, <sup>, <table>, <tbody>, <td>, <textarea>, <tfoot>, <th>, <thead>, <tr>, <tt>, <u>, <ul>, <var>, <xmp>

systemLanguage

Compatibility: IE5.5, IE6

This attribute belongs to the HTML+TIME technology introduced by Microsoft. See Chapter 15 for more information.

    Applies to:

<a>, <acronym>, <address>, <area>, <b>, <big>, <blockquote>, <button>, <caption>, <center>, <cite>, <code>, <dd>, <del>, <dir>, <div>, <dl>, <dt>, <em>, <fieldset>, <font>, <form>, <hn>, <hr>, <i>, <iframe>, <img>, <input type="button">, <input type="checkbox">, <input type="file">, <input type="hidden">, <input type="image">,

```
<input type="password">, <input type="radio">, <input type="reset">, <input
type="submit">, <input type="text">, <ins>, <kbd>, <legend>, <li>, <listing>,
<marquee>, <menu>, <ol>, <option>, <p>, <pre>, <q>, <s>, <samp>, <small>, <span>,
<strike>, <strong>, <sub>, <sup>, <table>, <tbody>, <td>, <textarea>, <tfoot>,
<th>, <thead>, <tr>, <tt>, <u>, <ul>, <var>, <xmp>
```

systemOverdubOrSubtitle

Compatibility: IE5.5, IE6

This attribute belongs to the HTML+TIME technology introduced by Microsoft.
See Chapter 15 for more information.

Applies to:

```
<a>, <acronym>, <address>, <area>, <b>, <big>, <blockquote>, <button>, <caption>,
<center>, <cite>, <code>, <dd>, <del>, <dir>, <div>, <dl>, <dt>, <em>, <fieldset>,
<font>, <form>, <hn>, <hr>, <i>, <iframe>, <img>, <input type="button">, <input
type="checkbox">, <input type="file">, <input type="hidden">, <input type="image">,
<input type="password">, <input type="radio">, <input type="reset">, <input
type="submit">, <input type="text">, <ins>, <kbd>, <legend>, <li>, <listing>,
<marquee>, <menu>, <ol>, <option>, <p>, <pre>, <q>, <s>, <samp>, <small>, <span>,
<strike>, <strong>, <sub>, <sup>, <table>, <tbody>, <td>, <textarea>, <tfoot>,
<th>, <thead>, <tr>, <tt>, <u>, <ul>, <var>, <xmp>
```

tabindex

Compatibility: NN6, NN7, IE4, IE5, IE5.5, IE6

This attribute assigns an index value to an element that defines its position in the
tab order.

Syntax:

```
<element tabindex="value"> . . . </element>
```

Example:

```
First Name: <input type="text" tabindex="1">
Last Name: <input type="text" tabindex="2">
Address: <input type="text" tabindex="3">
Suite/Apt: <input type="text" tabindex="4">
City, State and Zip Code: <input type="text" tabindex="5">,
<input type="text" tabindex="6"> <input type="text" tabindex="7">
```

Applies to:

```
<a>, <acronym>, <address>, <applet>, <area>, <b>, <bdo>, <big>, <blockquote>,
<body>, <button>, <caption>, <center>, <cite>, <custom>, <dd>, <del>, <dfn>, <dir>,
<div>, <dl>, <dt>, <em>, <fieldset>, <font>, <form>, <frame>, <frameset>, <hn>,
<hr>, <i>, <iframe>, <img>, <input type="button">, <input type="checkbox">, <input
type="file">, <input type="image">, <input type="password">, <input type="radio">,
<input type="reset">, <input type="submit">, <input type="text">, <ins>, <isindex>,
```

`<kbd>`, `<label>`, `<legend>`, `<li>`, `<listing>`, `<marquee>`, `<menu>`, `<object>`, `<ol>`, `<p>`, `<pre>`, `<q>`, `<rt>`, `<ruby>`, `<s>`, `<samp>`, `<select>`, `<small>`, `<span>`, `<strike>`, `<strong>`, `<sub>`, `<sup>`, `<table>`, `<tbody>`, `<td>`, `<textarea>`, `<tfoot>`, `<th>`, `<thead>`, `<tr>`, `<tt>`, `<u>`, `<ul>`, `<var>`, `<xmp>`

target

Compatibility: NN4, NN6, NN7, IE4, IE5, IE5.5, IE6

This attribute specifies the window or frame in which the linked document will be loaded. If there is no frame or window that matches the specified target, a new window is opened for the link.

Syntax:

```
<element target="value"> . . . </element>
```

Possible values:

name	Document is loaded into the window or frame with the specified name (IE4+ only).
_blank	Document is loaded in a new window.
_media	Document is loaded in the HTML content area of the Media Bar (IE6 only).
_parent	Document is loaded in the parent window.
_search	Document is loaded in the browser search pane (IE5+ only).
_self	Document is loaded in the same window.
_top	Document is loaded in the topmost window for the site.

Example:

```
<a href="http://www.w3c.org" target="_blank">W3C Consortium (blank)</a><br>
<a href="http://www.microsoft.com" target="_parent">Microsoft home page (parent)</a><br>
<a href="http://www.yahoo.com" target="_self">Yahoo home page (self)</a><br>
<a href="http://www.amazon.com" target="_top">Amazon home page (top)</a>
```

Applies to:

`<a>`, `<area>`, `<base>`, `<form>`, `<link>`

text

Compatibility: NN4, NN6, NN7, IE4, IE5, IE5.5, IE6

This attribute sets the color of all text in the `<body>` section of the document. Its value is either a color name (some browsers do not support color names) or a hexadecimal color value using the "#RRGGBB" method.

Syntax:

```
<body text="value"> . . . </body>
```

Example:

```
<body id="myBody" bgcolor="#FFFFFF" text="#bbbbbb">
```

Applies to:

```
<body>
```

timecontainer

Compatibility: IE5.5, IE6

This attribute belongs to the HTML+TIME technology introduced by Microsoft. See Chapter 15 for more information.

Applies to:

```
<a>, <acronym>, <address>, <area>, <b>, <big>, <blockquote>, <button>, <caption>,
<center>, <cite>, <code>, <dd>, <del>, <dir>, <div>, <dl>, <dt>, <em>, <fieldset>,
<font>, <form>, <hn>, <hr>, <i>, <iframe>, <img>, <input type="button">, <input
type="checkbox">, <input type="file">, <input type="hidden">, <input type="image">,
<input type="password">, <input type="radio">, <input type="reset">, <input
type="submit">, <input type="text">, <ins>, <kbd>, <legend>, <li>, <listing>,
<marquee>, <menu>, <ol>, <option>, <p>, <pre>, <q>, <s>, <samp>, <small>, <span>,
<strike>, <strong>, <sub>, <sup>, <table>, <tbody>, <td>, <textarea>, <tfoot>,
<th>, <thead>, <tr>, <tt>, <u>, <ul>, <var>, <xmp>
```

timestartrule

Compatibility: IE5.5, IE6

This attribute belongs to the HTML+TIME technology introduced by Microsoft. See Chapter 15 for more information.

Applies to:

```
<a>, <acronym>, <address>, <applet>, <area>, <b>, <big>, <blockquote>, <body>,
<button>, <caption>, <center>, <cite>, <code>, <dd>, <del>, <dir>, <div>, <dl>,
<dt>, <em>, <fieldset>, <fig>, <font>, <form>, <hn>, <hr>, <i>, <img>, <input
type="button">, <input type="checkbox">, <input type="file">, <input
type="hidden">, <input type="image">, <input type="password">, <input
type="radio">, <input type="reset">, <input type="submit">, <input type="text">,
<ins>, <kbd>, <li>, <listing>, <marquee>, <menu>, <ol>, <option>, <p>, <pre>, <q>,
<rt>, <ruby>, <s>, <samp>, <select>, <small>, <span>, <strike>, <strong>, <sub>,
<sup>, <table>, <tbody>, <td>, <textarea>, <tfoot>, <th>, <thead>, <tr>, <tt>, <u>,
<ul>, <var>, <xmp>
```

title

Compatibility: NN4, NN6, NN7, IE4, IE5, IE5.5, IE6

This attribute causes a margin note on a tooltip to be displayed when the mouse cursor hovers over the element. If it is left blank, no tooltip is displayed.

Syntax:

```
<element title="value"> . . . </element>
```

Example:

```
<a id="myL" title="The Advocar home page" href="http://www.advocar.com/"
target=_blank>Hover the mouse over this link to unveil the destination document</a>
```

Applies to:

```
<a>, <acronym>, <address>, <applet>, <area>, <b>, <bdo>, <big>, <blockquote>,
<body>, <br>, <button>, <caption>, <center>, <cite>, <code>, <col>, <custom>, <dd>,
<del>, <dfn>, <dir>, <div>, <dl>, <dt>, <em>, <embed>, <fieldset>, <font>, <form>,
<frame>, <frameset>, <hn>, <hr>, <i>, <iframe>, <img>, <input type="button">,
<input type="checkbox">, <input type="file">, <input type="image">, <input
type="password">, <input type="radio">, <input type="reset">, <input
type="submit">, <input type="text">, <ins>, <isindex>, <kbd>, <label>, <legend>,
<li>, <link>, <listing>, <map>, <marquee>, <menu>, <noframes>, <object>, <ol>, <p>,
<pre>, <q>, <rt>, <ruby>, <s>, <samp>, <select>, <small>, <span>, <strike>,
<strong>, <style>, <sub>, <sup>, <table>, <tbody>, <td>, <textarea>, <tfoot>, <th>,
<thead>, <tr>, <tt>, <u>, <ul>, <var>, <xmp>
```

topmargin

Compatibility: IE4, IE5, IE5.5, IE6

This attribute sets the height of the top margin for the page in pixels. The default value is 15.

Syntax:

```
<body topmargin="value"> . . . </body>
```

Example:

```
<body id="myBody" bgcolor="white" text="#000000" topmargin="100px">
```

Applies to:

```
<body>
```

truespeed

Compatibility: IE4, IE5, IE5.5, IE6

This attribute applies to the <marquee> element only. The scrolldelay attribute will usually ignore any value that is under 60 milliseconds. However, specifying the truespeed attribute will override the scrolldelay 60-millisecond limitation.

Syntax:

```
<marquee truespeed> . . . </marquee>
```

Example:

```
<marquee behavior="slide" bgcolor="cyan" scrolldelay="20" truespeed>
This marquee has a scrolldelay value of 20. Truespeed.</marquee>
```

Applies to:

```
<marquee>
```

type (1)

Compatibility: NN4, NN6, NN7, IE4, IE5, IE5.5, IE6

This attribute establishes the style of the list items in an ordered list, <ol>, or unordered list, <ul>.

Syntax:

```
<element type="value"> . . . </element>
```

Possible values:

1	Each item in an ordered list is displayed with numbers; this is the default value
a	Each item in an ordered list is displayed with lowercase letters
A	Each item in an ordered list is displayed with uppercase letters
i	Each item in an ordered list is displayed with lowercase roman numerals
I	Each item in an ordered list is displayed with uppercase roman numerals
disc	Each item in an unordered list is displayed with a solid disc or bullet
circle	Each item in an unordered list is displayed with a hollow circle
square	Each item in an unordered list is displayed with a solid square

Example:

```
<ol type="1">
<li>Item 1</li>
<li>Item 2</li>
</ol>
```

Applies to:

```
<li>, <ol>, <ul>
```

type (2)

Compatibility: NN6, NN7, IE4, IE5, IE5.5, IE6

This attribute specifies the Internet media (MIME) type of data that is referenced by the associated data attribute.

Syntax:

```
<element type="value"> . . . </element>
```

Example:

```
<object classid="clsid:D27CDB6E-AE6D-11cf-96B8-444553540000"
codebase="http://download.macromedia.com/pub/shockwave/cabs/flash/
swflash.cab#version=5,0,0,0" width="243" height="194">
<param name=movie DATA="yourfile.swf" valuetype="ref" type="video/*">
<param name="quality" value="high">
</object>
```

Applies to:

```
<link>, <object>, <script>
```

type (3)

Compatibility: NN6, NN7, IE6

Establishes the MIME content type of the document specified by the value of the href attribute.

Syntax:

```
<a type="value"> . . . </a>
```

Example:

```
<a type="text/html" href=www.someServer.com/somePage.html id="myLink">Open the new
page in this same window</a>
```

Applies to:

```
<a>
```

type (4)

Compatibility: NN4

This attribute specifies the MIME content type of the embed object.

Syntax:

```
<embed type="value"></embed>
```

Example:

```
<embed type="application/x-shockwave-flash"></embed>
```

Applies to:

<embed>

type (5)

Compatibility: NN6, NN7, IE6

When the valueType attribute of the <param> element is set to a value of ref, the type attribute is used to specify the content type of the resource designated by the value attribute. Possible values include text/html, image/png, image/gif, video/mpeg, audio/basic, text/tcl, text/javascript, and text/vbscript.

Syntax:

```
<param type="value">
```

Example:

```
<object classid="clsid:D27CDB6E-AE6D-11cf-96B8-444553540000"
codebase="http://download.macromedia.com/pub/shockwave/cabs/flash/
swflash.cab#version=5,0,0,0" width="243" height="194">
<param name="movie" value="yourfile.swf" valuetype="ref" type="video/*">
<param name="quality" value="high"></object>
```

Applies to:

<param>

type (6)

Compatibility: NN4, NN6, NN7, IE4, IE5, IE5.5, IE6

This attribute allows the default style sheet language of the document to be overridden. This attribute does not have a default value and is, therefore, required in order to specify the style content type of the style sheet language. Possible values are text/css (the most common value), text/html, image/png, image/gif, video/mpeg, text/css, and audio/basic.

Syntax:

```
<style type="value"> . . . </style>
```

Example:

```
<style id="myS" type="CSS2">
</style>
```

Applies to:

<style>

type (7)

Compatibility: NN4, NN6, NN7, IE4, IE5, IE5.5, IE6

This attribute determines the functionality of the <input> element. Please refer to Table 6-2 for a list of input elements.

Syntax:

```
<input type="value">
```

Example:

```
<input type="button" id="myButton" onclick="alert('hello!');" value="Button Text>
```

Applies to:

```
<input>
```

Table 6-2: Input Types and Possible Values

Element	Possible values
input type="button"	Any string
input type="checkbox"	Only the value of a selected checkbox is returned to the server
input type="file"	A file name
input type="hidden"	Any string
input type="image"	Any filename
input type="password"	Any string
input type="radio"	Only the value of the selected radio button is returned to the server
input type="reset"	Any string; default value is reset
input type="submit"	Any string; the default value is submit
input type="text"	Any string

type (8)

Compatibility: NN6, NN7, IE4, IE5, IE5.5, IE6

This attribute determines the functionality of the <button> element.

Syntax:

```
<button type="value"> . . . </button>
```

Possible values:

button	Creates a command button that can execute any command when clicked. This is the default value.
reset	Creates a button that resets the page when clicked.
submit	Creates a button that submits the page to the server when clicked.

Example:

```
<button id="myButton" type="button" onclick="alert('hello!');">Button Text</button>
```

Applies to:

```
<button>
```

type (9)

Compatibility: NN4

This attribute determines how the `<spacer>` element is rendered on the page. Possible values include `block` (a spacer element is rendered based on its height and width), `horizontal` (this value inserts horizontal spaces as specified by the size attribute), and `vertical` (this value inserts vertical spaces as specified by the size attribute).

Syntax:

```
<spacer type="value"> . . . </spacer>
```

Example:

```
<p>text before<spacer type="horizontal" size="10">text after</p>
```

Applies to:

```
<spacer>
```

units

Compatibility: NN4, NN6, NN7, IE4, IE5, IE5.5, IE6

This attribute defines the units in which the height and width attributes will be measured. Possible values are `em` (height and width are relative to the height and width of the element's font) and `px` (the default, which stands for pixels).

Syntax:

```
<embed units="value"></embed>
```

Example:

```
<embed id="myE" src="yourflashmovie.swf" quality="high"
pluginspage="http://www.macromedia.com/shockwave/download/
index.cgi?P1_Prod_Version=ShockwaveFlash"
type="application/x-shockwave-flash" width="243" height="194" units="px"></embed>
```

Applies to:

<embed>

unselectable

Compatibility: IE5.5, IE6

This attribute specifies whether or not an element can be selected. Possible values are on and off (the default).

Syntax:

```
<element unselectable="value"> . . . </element>
```

Example:

```
<p unselectable="on">You cannot select this text because it has been marked as
unselectable.</p>
<p unselectable="off">This text can be selected and transferred to the clipboard.</p>
```

Applies to:

```
<a>, <acronym>, <address>, <applet>, <area>, <b>, <bdo>, <big>, <blockquote>,
<body>, <button>, <caption>, <center>, <cite>, <code>, <custom>, <dd>, <del>,
<dfn>, <dir>, <div>, <dl>, <dt>, <em>, <embed>, <fieldset>, <font>, <form>,
<frame>, <frameset>, <hn>, <hr>, <i>, <iframe>, <img>, <input type="button">,
<input type="checkbox">, <input type="file">, <input type="hidden">, <input
type="image">, <input type="password">, <input type="radio">, <input type="reset">,
<input type="submit">, <input type="text">, <ins>, <isindex>, <kbd>, <label>,
<legend>, <li>, <listing>, <marquee>, <menu>, <nobr>, <object>, <ol>, <p>, <pre>,
<q>, <rt>, <ruby>, <s>, <samp>, <select>, <small>, <span>, <strike>, <strong>,
<sub>, <sup>, <table>, <tbody>, <td>, <textarea>, <tfoot>, <thead>, <tt>, <u>,
<ul>, <var>, <xmp>
```

urn

Compatibility: IE4, IE5, IE5.5, IE6

This attribute establishes a Uniform Resource Name (URN) for a target document. URN is one way to locate a document on the internet, the other way being by its URL. To locate a document using its URN, the URN must be registered within one of the approved namespaces listed in the IANA registry (see http://www.iana.org/assignments/urn-namespaces).

Syntax:

```
<a urn="value"> . . . </a>
```

Example:

```
<a urn="mace:shibboleth" href="http://middleware.internet2.edu/urn-mace/urn-mace-
shibboleth.html">Mace \ Shibboleth</a>
```

Applies to:

```
<a>
```

usemap

Compatibility: NN4 (<img> only), NN6, NN7, IE4 (<img> only), IE5 (<img> only), IE5.5 (<img> only), IE6

This attribute establishes the client-side image map to use for the element. The value of this attribute must either be the URL of an image map, or a "#" followed by the id attribute value of a <map> element on the same page.

Syntax:

```
<element usemap="value">
```

Example:

```
<map name="myMap">
<area shape="rect" coords="0, 0, 100, 50" href=http://www.w3c.com>
<area shape="rect" coords="100, 0, 200, 50" href="http://www.microsoft.com">
<area shape="rect" coords="200, 0, 300, 50" href="http://www.advocar.com">
<area shape="rect" coords="0, 50, 100, 100" href="http://www.msn.com">
<area shape="rect" coords="100, 50, 200, 100" href="http://www.yahoo.com">
<area shape="rect" coords="200, 50, 300, 100" href="http://www.softsmartinc.com">
</map>
<img src="yourimage.gif" alt="" width=300 height=100 usemap="#myMap">
```

Applies to:

```
<img>, <input>, <object>
```

valign

Compatibility: NN4 (<td>, <th>, <tr> only), NN6, NN7, IE4, IE5, IE5.5, IE6

This attribute defines the vertical alignment of text within the table cell or other element. Possible values are top, middle (the default), absmiddle, bottom, and baseline.

Syntax:

```
<element valign="value"> . . . </element>
```

Example:

```
<table width="200" border="8">
<caption valign="bottom" style="color:red;">Table 2-5. This is the caption for this table.</caption>
<tr><td>Cell 1</td><td>Cell 2</td></tr><tr><td>Cell 3</td><td>Cell 4</td></tr>
</table>
```

Applies to:

<caption>, <col>, <colgroup>, <tbody>, <td>, <tfoot>, <th>, <thead>, <tr>

value (1)

Compatibility: NN4, NN6, NN7, IE4, IE5, IE5.5, IE6

This attribute establishes the value of control elements. See Table 6-2 in the type (7) attribute section for the possible values for this attribute.

Syntax:

```
<element value="value"> . . . </element>
```

Example:

```
<form id="myForm">
<input type="button" value='type = "button"' onClick="alert('This element value is: '+this.value)">
<input type="reset" value='input type = "reset"' onClick="alert('This element value is: '+this.value)">
<input type="submit" value='input type = "submit"' onClick="alert('This element value is: '+this.value)">
<input type="checkbox" value="checkbox">
</form>
```

Applies to:

<button>, <input>, <input type="button">, <input type="checkbox">, <input type="hidden">, <input type="password">, <input type="radio">, <input type="reset">, <input type="submit">, <input type="text">, <li>, <option>, <select>

value (2)

Compatibility: NN4, NN6, NN7, IE4, IE5, IE5.5, IE6

This attribute is required when the <param> element is used. The value attribute specifies the value of the property specified in the name attribute. HTML does not make use of this value, but instead passes it straight to the object whose property is being set.

Syntax:

```
<param value="value">
```

Example:

```
<object classid="clsid:D27CDB6E-AE6D-11cf-96B8-444553540000"
codebase="http://download.macromedia.com/pub/shockwave/cabs/flash/
swflash.cab#version=5,0,0,0"
width="243" height="194">
    <param name="movie" value="yourflashmovie.swf" valuetype="ref" type="video/*">
```

```
    <param name="quality" value="high">
    <embed src="yourflashmovie.swf" quality="high" pluginspage="http://
www.macromedia.com/shockwave/download/index.cgi?P1_Prod_Version=ShockwaveFlash"
type="application/x-shockwave-flash" width="243"
    height="194"></embed>
</object>
```

Applies to:

```
<param>
```

valuetype

Compatibility: NN6, NN7, IE6

This attribute is used in conjunction with the value attribute of the `<param>`
element. It is used to define the type of the value attribute.

Syntax:

```
<param valuetype="value">
```

Possible values:

data	value is a string. This is the default value.
ref	value is a valid Uniform Resource Identifier (URI).
object	value is the value of an id attribute of an element or object on the page.

Example: See example for the value (2) attribute.
Applies to:

```
<param>
```

vcard_name

Compatibility: IE5, IE5.5, IE6

This attribute establishes the vCard value of the element to be used with
the autocomplete list provided by the browser. The vCard contains standard
information about the user. See Table 6-3 for possible values.

Syntax:

```
<input type="password" vcard_name="value">
```

Example:

```
<html><body><form name="myForm">
Customer Name: <input type="text" name="CustomerName" vcard_name="vCard.DisplayName">
Address: <input type="text" name="CustomerAddress" vcard_name="
vCard.Home.StreetAddress ">
```

```
City: <input type="text" name="CustomerCity" vcard_name=" vCard.Home.City ">
State: <input type="text" name="CustomerState" vcard_name=" vCard.Home.State ">
Zip Code: <input type="text" name="CustomerZipcode" vcard_name=" vCard.Home. Zipcode ">
</form></body></html>
```

Applies to:

```
<input type="password">, <input type="text">
```

Table 6-3: Possible vcard_name Values

vCard.Business.City	vCard.Department	vCard.Home.StreetAddress
vCard.Business.Country	vCard.DisplayName	vCard.Home.Zipcode
vCard.Business.Fax	vCard.Email	vCard.Homepage
vCard.Business.Phone	vCard.FirstName	vCard.JobTitle
vCard.Business.State	vCard.Gender	vCard.LastName
vCard.Business.StreetAddress	vCard.Home.City	vCard.MiddleName
vCard.Business.URLBusiness	vCard.Home.Country	vCard.Notes
vCard.Business.Zipcode	vCard.Home.Fax	vCard.Office
vCard.Cellular	vCard.Home.Phone	vCard.Page
vCard.Company	vCard.Home.State	

version

Compatibility: NN6, NN7, IE6

This attribute indicates the version of HTML that is used in the page.
Syntax:

```
<html version="value"> . . . </html>
```

Example:

```
<html version="4.0">
<!doctype html public "-//w3c//dtd html 4.0//en">
<head>
<meta http-equiv="Content-Type" content="text/html; charset=iso-8859-1">
</head>
```

Applies to:

```
<html>
```

vlink

Compatibility: NN4, NN6, NN7, IE4, IE5, IE5.5, IE6

This attribute sets the color of links in the document that have already been
visited. Its value is either a color name (some browsers do not support color
names) or a hexadecimal color value using the "#RRGGBB" method.

Syntax:

```
<body vlink="value"> . . . </body>
```

Example:

```
<body bgcolor="white" text="#000000" bottommargin="100" vlink="green">
```

Applies to:

```
<body>
```

volume

Compatibility: IE4, IE5, IE5.5, IE6

This attribute indicates the volume at which the sound clip will be played. Its value is an integer from -10,000 to 0. A larger value plays the sound clip louder (for example, -500 is louder than -10,000).

Syntax:

```
<bgsound volume="value">
```

Example:

```
<head><bgsound src="yoursoundfile.wav" balance="0" loop="1" volume="-500"></head>
```

Applies to:

```
<bgsound>
```

vspace

Compatibility: NN4 (<embed>, <table> only), NN6, NN7, IE4, IE5, IE5.5, IE6

This attribute establishes the size, in pixels, of the vertical margins of an element. hspace and vspace combined specify the empty space around an element.

Syntax:

```
<element vspace="value"> . . . </element>
```

Example:

```
<img vspace="50" src="yourimage.jpg" alt="" width="99" height="75">
```

Applies to:

```
<applet>, <iframe>, <img>, <input>, <input type="image">, <marquee>, <object>
```

weight

Compatibility: NN4

This attribute indicates the weight, or "boldness," of a font. Its value is an integer from 100 (least bold) to 900 (most bold), and it can only take multiples of 100.

Syntax:

```
<font weight="value"> . . . </font>
```

Example:

```
<font face="Verdana" weight="300">Text</font>
```

Applies to:

```
<font>
```

width

Compatibility: NN4 (<embed>, <img>, <spacer>, <table> only), NN6, NN7, IE4, IE5, IE5.5, IE6

This attribute determines the width of an element.

Syntax:

```
<element width="value"> . . . </element>
```

Possible values:

integer	Specifies the width of an element in pixels
integer%	Specifies the percentage of the total width of the parent element

Example:

```
<pre width="500" style="font-size:14pt;">This text is embedded between pre tags.</pre>
```

Applies to:

```
<applet>, <col>, <colgroup>, <embed>, <frame>, <frameset>, <hr>, <iframe>, <img>,
<input type="button">, <input type="checkbox">, <input type="file">, <input
type="image">, <input type="password">, <input type="radio">, <input type="reset">,
<input type="submit">, <input type="text">, <marquee>, <object>, <pre>, <spacer>,
<table>, <td>, <th>, <tr>
```

wrap

Compatibility: NN4, NN6, NN7, IE4, IE5, IE5.5, IE6

This attribute determines how text will be wrapped in an element.

Syntax:

```
<element wrap="value"> . . . </element>
```

Possible values:

soft	Causes text to word-wrap if it extends past the width of its container element; this is the default value
hard	Causes text to word-wrap, but the wrapping is created with carriage-return and line-feed characters
off	Turns word wrapping off

Example:

```
<textarea wrap="soft" rows="4">The SUSPECT: Even as a teenager, arrested for
possession of drug paraphernalia and stolen credit cards, his arrogance showed
through in a defiant smiling mug shot</textarea>
<textarea wrap="off"  rows="4">The SUSPECT: Even as a teenager, arrested for
possession of drug paraphernalia and stolen credit cards, his arrogance showed
through in a defiant smiling mug shot</textarea>
```

Applies to:

```
<pre> (IE5.5+ only), <textarea>
```

xmlns

Compatibility: IE5, IE5.5, IE6

This attribute declares a namespace for creating unique custom tags in the HTML document. When more than one namespace is required, repeat the xmlns declaration for each additional namespace, and separate each declaration with a space.

Syntax:

```
<html xmlns:value> . . . </html>
```

Example:

```
<html xmlns:t ="urn:schemas-microsoft-com:time">
<?import namespace="t" implementation="#default#time2">
<head>
<style>
.time { behavior: url(#default#time2); }
</style>
</head>
<body bgcolor="#FFFFFF" text="#000000">
<div id="myObject" class="time" style="position:absolute; top:300px; left:50px;
width:200px; height:100px; background-color:lightblue; text-align:center;">
Moving object with changing color animation</div>
```

```
<t:animatecolor targetElement="myObject" attributeName="backgroundColor"
to="yellow"
start="1" dur="5"
fill="hold" to="cyan" start="1" dur="5" fill="hold">
<t:animatemotion
targetElement="myObject" to="400,0" dur="5" fill="hold">
</body>
</html>
```

Applies to:

```
<html>
```

7

EVENT HANDLERS

This chapter contains a comprehensive listing of all the events that are compatible with the elements shown in Chapter 5. Each one of the events contains a brief description, a functional example (in most cases), a list of properties that belong to the underlying object of the event, and a list of HTML elements and JavaScript objects that can be used with the event (< and > angle brackets surround the applicable HTML elements, whereas JavaScript object names appear normally).

As mentioned in Chapter 3, each time an event is fired, an instance of the event object is created and is given a set of property values. Therefore, for each event handler in this chapter, you will see a list of properties that are affected by the event. For more information on any of these properties, look up the property name in Chapter 11.

For more information on event handler syntax, and on how event handlers and their underlying objects are used, please refer to Chapter 3.

onAbort

Compatibility: NN4, NN6, NN7, IE4, IE5, IE5.5, IE6

This event fires when the loading of an image is stopped by the user before completion. To trigger the abort event you must do one of the following: click the browser's stop button, navigate to another page, or click another link on the page if available.

Example:

```
<head><script language="JavaScript">
function B1() {
alert("The loading action has been aborted\nTry later")
}
</script></head>
<body bgcolor="#FFFFFF" text="#000000">
<img src="yourimage.jpg" onabort="B1()">
</body>
```

Properties:

```
altKey, altLeft, ctrlLeft, returnValue, shiftLeft, srcElement, type
```

Applies to:

```
<img>
```

onActivate

Compatibility: IE5.5, IE6

This event fires when the object has received focus in a document that has the focus.

Example:

```
<head><script language="JavaScript">
function B1() {
window.open("http://www.w3.org/", "", "width=700, height=600, resizable,
scrollbars")
}
</script></head>
<body bgcolor="#FFFFFF" text="#000000">
<label for="myL" accesskey="L">Press Alt+L to invoke the link </label>
<a id="myL" href="http://www.w3.org/" target=_blank onActivate="B1()">World Wide
Web Consortium</a>
</body>
```

Properties:

altKey, altLeft, clientX, clientY, ctrlLeft, offsetX, offsetY, returnValue, screenX, screenY, shiftLeft, srcElement, type, x, y

Applies to:

`<a>`, `<acronym>`, `<address>`, `<applet>`, `<area>`, `<b>`, `<bdo>`, `<big>`, `<blockquote>`, `<body>`, `<button>`, `<caption>`, `<center>`, `<cite>`, `<custom>`, `<dd>`, `<dfn>`, `<dir>`, `<div>`, `<dl>`, document, `<dt>`, `<em>`, `<embed>`, `<fieldset>`, `<font>`, `<form>`, `<frame>`, `<frameset>`, `<hn>`, `<hr>`, `<i>`, `<iframe>`, `<img>`, `<input type="button">`, `<input type="checkbox">`, `<input type="file">`, `<input type="hidden">`, `<input type="image">`, `<input type="password">`, `<input type="radio">`, `<input type="reset">`, `<input type="submit">`, `<input type="text">`, `<ins>`, `<isindex>`, `<kbd>`, `<label>`, `<legend>`, `<li>`, `<listing>`, `<marquee>`, `<menu>`, `<object>`, `<ol>`, `<p>`, `<pre>`, `<q>`, `<rt>`, `<ruby>`, `<s>`, `<samp>`, `<select>`, `<small>`, `<span>`, `<strike>`, `<strong>`, `<sub>`, `<sup>`, `<table>`, `<tbody>`, `<td>`, `<textarea>`, `<tfoot>`, `<th>`, `<thead>`, `<tr>`, `<tt>`, `<u>`, `<ul>`, `<var>`, window, `<xmp>`

onAfterPrint

Compatibility: IE5, IE5.5, IE6

This event fires when the document prints or previews for printing.

Example:

```
<head><script language="JavaScript">
function B1() {
window.print();
}
</script></head>
<body bgcolor="#FFFFFF" text="#000000" onafterprint="alert('the printing of this
page is complete')">
<p>Some body Content to print.</p>
<input type="button" value="Print" onclick="B1()">
</body>
```

Properties:

altKey, altLeft, button, cancelBubble, clientX, clientY, ctrlKey, ctrlLeft, offsetX, offsetY, returnValue, screenX, screenY, shiftKey, shiftLeft, srcElement, type, x, y

Applies to:

`<body>`, `<frameset>`, window

onAfterUpdate

Compatibility: IE4, IE5, IE5.5, IE6

This event fires when a databound object's data has been successfully updated. This event fires only if the onbeforeupdate event has already fired.

The datasrc and datafld attributes must be set for the element to which the onAfterUpdate event handler is applied, and the value of the datasrc attribute must reference an object in the page.

Example:

```html
<html>
<head><title>Recordset Events</title>
<script language="javascript">
function rowEnter(){
myTable.rows[myData.recordset.AbsolutePosition].style.backgroundColor = 'yellow';
}
function add(){myData.recordset.AddNew();}
function del(){if (myData.recordset.RecordCount > 0) myData.recordset.Delete();}
</script>
<script for="myTable" event="onreadystatechange">
if (this.readyState == 'complete')
{
this.rows(myData.recordset.AbsolutePosition).style.backgroundColor = 'yellow';
myData.onrowenter = rowEnter;
}
</script>
<script for="myData" event="onrowexit">
for (var i = 1; i <= myData.recordset.RecordCount; i++) {
    myTable.rows[i].style.backgroundColor = '';
}
</script>
<script for="tableList" event="onclick">
myData.recordset.AbsolutePosition = this.recordNumber;
window.event.cancelBubble = true;
</script>
<script for="myData" event="ondatasetcomplete">
alert('data set complete');
</script>
<script for="myData" event="ondatasetchanged">
alert('data set changed');
</script>
<script for="myData" event="ondataavailable">
alert('data set available');
</script>
<script for="myData" event="oncellchange">
alert('Cell Changed');
</script>
<script for="firstname" event="onbeforeupdate">
alert('Data is about to change');
</script>
```

```
<script for="firstname" event="onafterupdate">
alert('Data has changed');
</script>
<script for="birth" event="onerrorupdate">
alert('Error Updating');
</script>
<script for="myData" event="onrowsinserted">
alert('Inserted');
</script>
<script for="myData" event="onrowsdelete">
alert('Deleted');
</script>
</head>
<body>

<input id=cmdAdd type="button" value="add record" onclick="add();">
<input id=cmdDelete type="button" value="delete" onclick="del();">

<object classid="clsid:333C7BC4-460F-11D0-BC04-0080C7055A83" id="myData">
    <param name="DataURL" value="myfile.csv">
    <param name="UseHeader" value="True">
    <param name="TextQualifier" value="'">
</object>

<table>
<tr><td>First Name</td><td><input id=firstname type=text datasrc=#myData
datafld=firstname></td></tr>
<tr><td>Last Name</td><td><input id=lastname type=text datasrc=#myData
datafld=lastname></td></tr>
<tr><td>Year Born</td><td><input id=birth type=text datasrc=#myData
datafld=birth></td></tr>
</table>

<table id=myTable datasrc=#myData>
<thead>
<tr style="font-weight:bold">
    <td>First</td><td>Last</td><td>Age</td>
</tr>
</thead>
<tbody>
<tr id="tableList">
    <td><span datafld="firstname"></span></td>
    <td><span datafld="lastname"></span></td>
    <td><span datafld="birth"></span></td>
</tr>
</tbody>
</table>
</body>
</html>
```

Contents of myfile.csv:

```
firstname:string,lastname:string,birth:int
John,Smith,2003
Manny,Ramirez,1956
Troy,Belling,1956
```

Properties:

```
altKey, altLeft, cancelBubble, ctrlLeft, shiftLeft, srcElement, type
```

Applies to:

```
<a>, <applet>, <bdo>, <button>, <caption>, <custom>, <div>, <frame>, <frameset>,
<iframe>, <img>, <input type="checkbox">, <input type="hidden">, <input
type="password">, <input type="radio">, <input type="text">, <label>, <legend>,
<map>, <marquee>, <object>, <rt>, <ruby>, <select>, <span>, <table>, <td>,
<textarea>, <tr>
```

onBeforeActivate

Compatibility: IE6

This event fires immediately before the object receives focus in a document that has the focus.

Example:

```
<p>Press tab to bring the following link into focus.</p>
<a href="http://www.w3c.org/" target=_blank
onbeforeactivate="alert('This link is on the verge of being activated')">World Wide
Web Consortium</a>
```

Properties:

```
altKey, altLeft, cancelBubble, clientX, clientY, ctrlKey, ctrlLeft, fromElement,
offsetX, offsetY, screenX, screenY, shiftKey, shiftLeft, srcElement, type,
wheelDelta, x, y
```

Applies to:

```
<a>, <address>, <applet>, <area>, <b>, <bdo>, <big>, <blockquote>, <body>,
<button>, <caption>, <center>, <cite>, <code>, <custom>, <dd>, <dfn>, <dir>, <div>,
<dl>, document, <dt>, <em>, <embed>, <fieldset>, <font>, <form>, <hn>, <hr>, <i>,
<img>, <input type="button">, <input type="checkbox">, <input type="file">, <input
type="image">, <input type="password">, <input type="radio">, <input type="reset">,
<input type="submit">, <input type="text">, <kbd>, <label>, <legend>, <li>,
<listing>, <map>, <marquee>, <menu>, <nobr>, <ol>, <p>, <pre>, <rt>, <ruby>, <s>,
<samp>, <select>, <small>, <span>, <strike>, <strong>, <sub>, <sup>, <table>,
<tbody>, <td>, <textarea>, <tfoot>, <th>, <thead>, <tr>, <tt>, <u>, <ul>, <var>,
<xmp>
```

onBeforeCopy

Compatibility: IE5, IE5.5, IE6

This event fires before the selection in the document is copied to the clipboard.
Example:

```
<p onbeforecopy="alert('The text is on the verge of being copied to the
clipboard')">Copy this text to the system clipboard by pressing Ctrl+C.</p>
```

Properties:

altKey, altLeft, cancelBubble, clientX, clientY, ctrlKey, ctrlLeft, dataTransfer,
offsetX, offsetY, returnValue, screenX, screenY, shiftKey, shiftLeft, srcElement,
type, x, y

Applies to:

<a>, <address>, <area>, <b>, <bdo>, <big>, <blockquote>, <caption>, <center>,
<cite>, <code>, <custom>, <dd>, <dfn>, <dir>, <div>, <dl>, <dt>, <em>, <fieldset>,
<form>, <hn>, <i>, <img>, <label>, <legend>, <li>, <listing>, <menu>, <nobr>, <ol>,
<p>, <pre>, <s>, <samp>, <small>, <span>, <strike>, <strong>, <sub>, <sup>, <td>,
<textarea>, <th>, <tr>, <tt>, <u>, <ul>

onBeforeCut

Compatibility: IE5, IE5.5, IE6

This event fires before the selection in the document is cut and copied to the
clipboard.
Example:

```
<p class="explanations" contenteditable="true"
onbeforecut="alert('The text is on the verge of being copied to the clipboard')">
Cut this text and copy it to the system clipboard by pressing Ctrl+X.</p>
```

Properties:

altKey, altLeft, cancelBubble, clientX, clientY, ctrlKey, ctrlLeft, dataTransfer,
offsetX, offsetY, returnValue, screenX, screenY, shiftKey, shiftLeft, srcElement,
type, x, y

Applies to:

<a>, <address>, <applet>, <area>, <b>, <bdo>, <big>, <blockquote>, <body>,
<button>, <caption>, <center>, <cite>, <code>, <custom>, <dd>, <dfn>, <dir>, <div>,
<dl>, document, <dt>, <em>, <embed>, <fieldset>, <font>, <form>, <hn>, <hr>, <i>,
<img>, <input type="button">, <input type="checkbox">, <input type="file">, <input
type="image">, <input type="password">, <input type="radio">, <input type="reset">,
<input type="submit">, <input type="text">, <kbd>, <label>, <legend>, <li>,
<listing>, <map>, <marquee>, <menu>, <nobr>, <ol>, <p>, <pre>, <rt>, <ruby>, <s>,

```
<samp>, <select>, <small>, <span>, <strike>, <strong>, <sub>, <sup>, <table>,
<tbody>, <td>, <textarea>, <tfoot>, <th>, <thead>, <tr>, <tt>, <u>, <ul>, <var>,
<xmp>
```

onBeforeDeactivate

Compatibility: IE5.5, IE6

This event fires immediately before the current active object loses focus to another object in the document.

Example:

```
<p>Press tab to bring the following link into focus.</p>
<a id="myL" href="http://www.w3c.org/" target=_blank
onbeforedeactivate="alert('This link is on the verge of losing focus')">World Wide
Web Consortium</a>
```

Properties:

```
altKey, altLeft, cancelBubble, ctrlLeft, offsetX, offsetY, returnValue, screenX,
screenY, shiftLeft, srcElement, toElement, type, x, y
```

Applies to:

```
<a>, <acronym>, <address>, <applet>, <area>, <b>, <bdo>, <big>, <blockquote>,
<body>, <button>, <caption>, <center>, <cite>, <custom>, <dd>, <dfn>, <dir>, <div>,
<dl>, document, <dt>, <em>, <embed>, <fieldset>, <font>, <form>, <frame>,
<frameset>, <hn>, <hr>, <i>, <iframe>, <img>, <input type="button">, <input
type="checkbox">, <input type="file">, <input type="hidden">, <input type="image">,
<input type="password">, <input type="radio">, <input type="reset">, <input
type="submit">, <input type="text">, <ins>, <isindex>, <kbd>, <label>, <legend>,
<li>, <listing>, <marquee>, <menu>, <object>, <ol>, <p>, <pre>, <q>, <rt>, <ruby>,
<s>, <samp>, <select>, <small>, <span>, <strike>, <strong>, <sub>, <sup>, <table>,
<tbody>, <td>, <textarea>, <tfoot>, <th>, <thead>, <tr>, <tt>, <u>, <ul>, <var>,
window, <xmp>
```

onBeforeEditFocus

Compatibility: IE5, IE5.5, IE6

This event fires before an element enters edit mode. To put an element in edit mode, you must set its contenteditable attribute value to true. (This can have unexpected results. For instance, the <a> element will not act as a link if this property is set to true.)

Example:

```
<p contenteditable="true" onbeforeeditfocus="alert('The text is prepared for
editing')">Click in this text to bring it into focus. Type some text after
accepting the alert window.</p>
```

Properties:

altKey, altLeft, cancelBubble, clientX, clientY, ctrlLeft, returnValue, screenX, screenY, shiftLeft, srcElement, type, x, y

Applies to:

<a>, <acronym>, <address>, <applet>, <area>, <b>, <bdo>, <big>, <blockquote>, <body>, <button>, <center>, <cite>, <code>, <custom>, <dd>, defaults, <del>, <dfn>, <dir>, <div>, <dl>, document, <dt>, <em>, <fieldset>, <font>, <form>, <hn>, <i>, <input type="button">, <input type="checkbox">, <input type="file">, <input type="hidden">, <input type="image">, <input type="password">, <input type="radio">, <input type="reset">, <input type="submit">, <input type="text">, <ins>, <isindex>, <kbd>, <label>, <legend>, <li>, <listing>, <marquee>, <menu>, <nobr>, <object>, <ol>, <p>, <pre>, <q>, <rt>, <ruby>, <s>, <samp>, <select>, <small>, <span>, <strike>, <strong>, <sub>, <sup>, <table>, <td>, <textarea>, <tr>, <tt>, <u>, <ul>, <var>, <xmp>

onBeforePaste

Compatibility: IE5, IE5.5, IE6

This event fires before the clipboard contents are pasted in the document.
Example:

```
<p>Copy this text and paste it into the textarea element below.</p>
<textarea cols="60" onbeforepaste="alert('The text is on the verge of being
pasted')"></textarea>
```

Properties:

altKey, altLeft, cancelBubble, clientX, clientY, ctrlKey, ctrlLeft, dataTransfer, offsetX, offsetY, returnValue, screenX, screenY, shiftKey, shiftLeft, srcElement, type, x, y

Applies to:

<a>, <address>, <applet>, <area>, <b>, <bdo>, <big>, <blockquote>, <body>, <button>, <caption>, <center>, <cite>, <code>, <custom>, <dd>, <dfn>, <dir>, <div>, <dl>, document, <dt>, <em>, <embed>, <fieldset>, <font>, <form>, <hn>, <hr>, <i>, <img>, <input type="button">, <input type="checkbox">, <input type="file">, <input type="image">, <input type="password">, <input type="radio">, <input type="reset">, <input type="submit">, <input type="text">, <kbd>, <label>, <legend>, <li>, <listing>, <map>, <marquee>, <menu>, <nobr>, <ol>, <p>, <pre>, <rt>, <ruby>, <s>, <samp>, <select>, <small>, <span>, <strike>, <strong>, <sub>, <sup>, <table>, <tbody>, <td>, <textarea>, <tfoot>, <th>, <thead>, <tr>, <tt>, <u>, <ul>, <var>, <xmp>

onBeforePrint

Compatibility: IE5, IE5.5, IE6

This event fires before the document prints.

Example:

```
<head><script language="JavaScript">
function B1() {
window.print();
}
</script></head>
<body bgcolor="#FFFFFF" text="#000000" onbeforeprint="alert('This page is about to
be printed')">
<p>Some body Content to print.</p>
<input type="button" value="Print" onclick="B1()">
</body>
```

Properties:

altKey, altLeft, button, cancelBubble, clientX, clientY, ctrlKey, ctrlLeft, returnValue, screenX, screenY, shiftKey, shiftLeft, srcElement, type, x, y

Applies to:

<body>, <frameset>, window

onBeforeUnload

Compatibility: IE4, IE5, IE5.5, IE6

This event fires immediately before the document is unloaded. The document is unloaded when the user navigates to a different URL or attempts to close the browser window.

Example:

```
<head><script language="JavaScript">
function B1() { self.close() }
function B2() {
window.open("http://www.w3.org/", "", "width=300, height=200, left=200, noresize,
top=200")
}
</script></head>
<body bgcolor="#FFFFFF" text="#000000" onbeforeunload="B2()">
<input type="button" value="Unload the document" onclick="B1()">
</body>
```

Properties:

altKey, altLeft, clientX, clientY, ctrlKey, ctrlLeft, returnValue, shiftKey, shiftLeft, type

Applies to:

<body>, <frameset>, window

onBeforeUpdate

Compatibility: IE4, IE5, IE5.5, IE6

This event fires before a databound object is updated. The `datasrc` and `datafld` attributes must be set for the element to which the `onBeforeUpdate` event handler is applied. The value of the `datasrc` attribute must reference an object in the page.

Example: See the `onAfterUpdate` event.

Properties:

```
altKey, altLeft, cancelBubble, clientX, clientY, ctrlLeft, offsetX, offsetY,
returnValue, screenX, screenY, shiftLeft, srcElement, type, x, y
```

Applies to:

```
<a>, <applet>, <bdo>, <button>, <caption>, <custom>, <div>, <frame>, <frameset>,
<iframe>, <img>, <input type="checkbox">, <input type="hidden">, <input
type="password">, <input type="radio">, <input type="text">, <label>, <legend>,
<map>, <marquee>, <object>, <rt>, <ruby>, <select>, <span>, <table>, <td>,
<textarea>, <tr>
```

onBlur

Compatibility: NN4, NN6, NN7, IE4, IE5, IE5.5, IE6

This event fires when the element loses focus.

Example:

```
<head><script language="JavaScript">
function B1() {

window.open("http://www.w3c.org", "", "");
}
</script></head>
<body bgcolor="#FFFFFF" text="#000000">
Press the Tab key to set focus on the link below.<br>
<a id="myL" href="http://www.w3c.org/" target=_blank onBlur="B1()">World Wide Web
Consortium</a><br>
Now press the Tab key again to move focus to another element, causing the onblur
event to fire, and opening the W3C home page in a new window.
</body>
```

Properties:

```
altKey, altLeft, clientX, clientY, ctrlLeft, offsetX, offsetY, screenX, screenY,
shiftLeft, srcElement, type, x, y
```

Applies to:

```
<a>, <acronym>, <address>, <applet>, <area>, <b>, <bdo>, <big>, <blockquote>,
<button>, <caption>, <center>, <cite>, <custom>, <dd>, <del>, <dfn>, <dir>, <div>,
<dl>, <dt>, <em>, <embed>, <fieldset>, <font>, <form>, <frame>, <frameset>, <hn>,
```

```
<hr>, <i>, <iframe>, <img>, <input type="button">, <input type="checkbox">, <input
type="file">, <input type="image">, <input type="password">, <input type="radio">,
<input type="reset">, <input type="submit">, <input type="text">, <ins>, <isindex>,
<kbd>, <label>, <legend>, <li>, <listing>, <map>, <marquee>, <menu>, <object>,
<ol>, <optgroup>, <option>, <p>, <pre>, <q>, <rt>, <ruby>, <s>, <samp>, <select>,
<small>, <span>, <strike>, <strong>, <sub>, <sup>, <table>, <tbody>, <td>,
<textarea>, <tfoot>, <th>, <thead>, <tr>, <tt>, <u>, <ul>, <var>, window, <xmp>
```

onBounce

Compatibility: IE4, IE5, IE5.5, IE6

This event applies to the <marquee> element when its behavior attribute value is set
to alternate. It fires when the content of the marquee reaches either its right or
its left edge.

Example:

```
<head><script language="JavaScript">
function B1() {
alert("The marquee content reached one of its edges")
}
</script></head>
<body bgcolor="#FFFFFF" text="#000000">
<marquee id="myM" width=500 behavior="alternate" onbounce="B1()"
bgcolor="#99ffff">Come and see our new car models.</marquee>
</body>
```

Properties:

```
altKey, altLeft, clientX, clientY, ctrlLeft, offsetX, offsetY, returnValue,
screenX, screenY, shiftLeft, srcElement, type, x, y
```

Applies to:

```
<marquee>
```

onCellChange

Compatibility: IE5, IE5.5, IE6

This event fires when the source data displayed in a databound object changes.
Example: See the onAfterUpdate event.
Properties:

```
altKey, altLeft, cancelBubble, clientX, clientY, ctrlLeft, dataFld, offsetX,
offsetY, qualifier, recordset, returnValue, screenX, screenY, shiftLeft,
srcElement, type, x, y
```

Applies to:

```
<applet>, <bdo>, <object>
```

onChange

Compatibility: NN4, NN6, NN7, IE4, IE5, IE5.5, IE6

This event fires when the content of a form element is changed.

Example:

```
<head><script language="JavaScript">
function B2(colors) {
var col = (colors.options[colors.selectedIndex].value);
if (col) { document.bgColor = col; }
alert("The background color has changed to "+col)
}
</script></head>
<body>
<select name="colors" onChange="B2(this)">
   <option value="white" selected>White</option>
   <option value="cyan">Cyan</option>
   <option value="ivory">Ivory</option>
   <option id="myO" value="blue">Blue</option>
   <option value="red">Red</option>
   <option value="lightblue">Lightblue</option>
   <option value="beige">Beige</option>
</select>
</body>
```

Properties:

```
altKey, altLeft, button, clientX, clientY, ctrlLeft, offsetX, offsetY, returnValue,
screenX, screenY, shiftKey, shiftLeft, srcElement, type, x, y
```

Applies to:

```
<caption>, <input type="text">, <optgroup>, <option>, <select>, <textarea>
```

onClick

Compatibility: NN4, NN6, NN7, IE4, IE5, IE5.5, IE6

This event fires when the user clicks an element with the left mouse button.

Example:

```
<input type="text" name="textfield" onclick="alert('You clicked an input text
field')" value="Click me">
```

Properties:

```
altKey, altLeft, cancelBubble, clientX, clientY, ctrlKey, ctrlLeft, offsetX,
offsetY, returnValue, screenX, screenY, shiftKey, shiftLeft, srcElement, type, x, y
```

Applies to:

`<a>`, `<acronym>`, `<address>`, `<applet>`, `<area>`, `<b>`, `<bdo>`, `<big>`, `<blockquote>`, `<body>`, `<button>`, `<caption>`, `<center>`, `<cite>`, `<code>`, `<custom>`, `<dd>`, `<del>`, `<dfn>`, `<dir>`, `<div>`, document, `<dt>`, `<em>`, `<embed>`, `<fieldset>`, `<font>`, `<form>`, `<frame>`, `<hn>`, `<hr>`, `<i>`, `<img>`, `<input type="button">`, `<input type="checkbox">`, `<input type="file">`, `<input type="image">`, `<input type="password">`, `<input type="radio">`, `<input type="reset">`, `<input type="submit">`, `<input type="text">`, `<ins>`, `<kbd>`, `<label>`, `<legend>`, `<li>`, `<listing>`, `<map>`, `<marquee>`, `<menu>`, `<nobr>`, `<noframes>`, `<noscript>`, `<object>`, `<ol>`, `<optgroup>`, `<option>`, `<p>`, `<pre>`, `<q>`, `<rt>`, `<ruby>`, `<s>`, `<samp>`, `<select>`, `<small>`, `<span>`, `<strike>`, `<strong>`, `<sub>`, `<sup>`, `<table>`, `<tbody>`, `<td>`, `<textarea>`, `<tfoot>`, `<th>`, `<thead>`, `<tr>`, `<tt>`, `<u>`, `<ul>`, `<var>`, `<xmp>`

---

onContextMenu

Compatibility: NN6, NN7, IE4, IE5, IE5.5, IE6

This event fires when the user opens the context menu by clicking the right mouse button.

Example:

```
<head><script language="JavaScript">
function B2() {
alert("This image is copyrighted")
}
</script></head>
<body bgcolor="#FFFFFF" text="#000000" oncontextmenu="B2()">
<p>Right click in the image.</p>
<img oncontextmenu="B2()" src="yourimagefile.jpg" alt="" width="99" height="76">
</body>
```

If you want to prevent the user from opening the context menu, add the following code to the `<body>` element above:

```
oncontextmenu="B2(); return false;"
```

Properties:

---

altKey, altLeft, cancelBubble, clientX, clientY, ctrlKey, ctrlLeft, offsetX, offsetY, returnValue, screenX, screenY, shiftKey, shiftLeft, srcElement, type, x, y

---

Applies to:

`<a>`, `<address>`, `<applet>`, `<area>`, `<b>`, `<bdo>`, `<big>`, `<blockquote>`, `<body>`, `<button>`, `<caption>`, `<center>`, `<cite>`, `<code>`, `<custom>`, `<dd>`, `<dfn>`, `<dir>`, `<div>`, `<dl>`, document, `<dt>`, `<em>`, `<embed>`, `<fieldset>`, `<font>`, `<form>`, `<hn>`, `<hr>`, `<i>`, `<img>`, `<input type="button">`, `<input type="checkbox">`, `<input type="file">`, `<input type="image">`, `<input type="password">`, `<input type="radio">`, `<input type="reset">`, `<input type="submit">`, `<input type="text">`, `<kbd>`, `<label>`, `<legend>`, `<li>`,

`<listing>`, `<marquee>`, `<menu>`, `<nobr>`, `<ol>`, `<p>`, `<pre>`, `<rt>`, `<ruby>`, `<s>`, `<samp>`, `<select>`, `<small>`, `<span>`, `<strike>`, `<strong>`, `<sub>`, `<sup>`, `<table>`, `<tbody>`, `<td>`, `<textarea>`, `<tfoot>`, `<th>`, `<thead>`, `<tr>`, `<tt>`, `<u>`, `<ul>`, `<var>`, `<xmp>`

onControlSelect

Compatibility: IE5.5, IE6

This event fires when the user selects the element. The contenteditable attribute value must be set to true in the `<container>` element.

Example:

```
<div contenteditable=true>You can edit the following controls.
Once you click one of them and it gets the focus, the oncontrolselect event will
fire:
<input type=text value="This is a text box"
oncontrolselect="alert('oncontrolselect for the text box fires!')">
<button oncontrolselect="alert('oncontrolselect for the button fires!')">This is a
button</button>
</div>
```

Properties:

```
altKey, altLeft, ctrlLeft, offsetX, offsetY, returnValue, screenX, screenY,
shiftLeft, srcElement, type, x, y
```

Applies to:

```
<a>, <acronym>, <address>, <applet>, <area>, <b>, <bdo>, <big>, <blockquote>,
<body>, <button>, <caption>, <center>, <cite>, <custom>, <dd>, <dfn>, <dir>, <div>,
<dl>, document, <dt>, <em>, <embed>, <fieldset>, <font>, <form>, <frame>,
<frameset>, <hn>, <hr>, <i>, <iframe>, <img>, <input type="button">, <input
type="checkbox">, <input type="file">, <input type="hidden">, <input type="image">,
<input type="password">, <input type="radio">, <input type="reset">, <input
type="submit">, <input type="text">, <ins>, <isindex>, <kbd>, <label>, <legend>,
<li>, <listing>, <marquee>, <menu>, <object>, <ol>, <p>, <pre>, <q>, <rt>, <ruby>,
<s>, <samp>, <select>, <small>, <span>, <strike>, <strong>, <sub>, <sup>, <table>,
<tbody>, <td>, <textarea>, <tfoot>, <th>, <thead>, <tr>, <tt>, <u>, <ul>, <var>,
window, <xmp>
```

onCopy

Compatibility: IE5, IE5.5, IE6

This event fires when the user copies the selection in the document to the clipboard.

Example:

```
<p oncopy="alert('The text is copied to the clipboard')">
Copy this text to the system clipboard.</p>
```

Properties:

altKey, altLeft, cancelBubble, clientX, clientY, ctrlKey, ctrlLeft, dataFld, dataTransfer, offsetX, offsetY, returnValue, screenX, screenY, shiftKey, shiftLeft, srcElement, type, x, y

Applies to:

<a>, <address>, <area>, <b>, <bdo>, <big>, <blockquote>, <caption>, <center>, <cite>, <code>, <custom>, <dd>, <dfn>, <dir>, <div>, <dl>, <dt>, <em>, <fieldset>, <form>, <hn>, <hr>, <i>, <img>, <legend>, <li>, <listing>, <menu>, <nobr>, <ol>, <p>, <pre>, <s>, <samp>, <small>, <span>, <strike>, <strong>, <sub>, <sup>, <td>, <th>, <tr>, <tt>, <u>, <ul>

onCut

Compatibility: IE5, IE5.5, IE6

This event fires when user cuts the selection from the document and adds it to the clipboard. To cut a selection from the document, the selection must be editable.

Example:

```
<p contenteditable="true" oncut="alert('The text is cut and copied to the clipboard')">Cut and copy this text to the system clipboard by pressing Ctrl+X.</p>
```

Properties:

altKey, altLeft, cancelBubble, clientX, clientY, ctrlKey, ctrlLeft, dataTransfer, offsetX, offsetY, returnValue, screenX, screenY, shiftKey, shiftLeft, srcElement, type, x, y

Applies to:

<a>, <address>, <applet>, <area>, <b>, <bdo>, <big>, <blockquote>, <body>, <button>, <caption>, <center>, <cite>, <code>, <custom>, <dd>, <dfn>, <dir>, <div>, <dl>, document, <dt>, <em>, <embed>, <fieldset>, <font>, <form>, <hn>, <hr>, <i>, <img>, <input type="button">, <input type="checkbox">, <input type="file">, <input type="image">, <input type="password">, <input type="radio">, <input type="reset">, <input type="submit">, <input type="text">, <kbd>, <label>, <legend>, <li>, <listing>, <map>, <marquee>, <menu>, <nobr>, <ol>, <p>, <pre>, <rt>, <ruby>, <s>, <samp>, <select>, <small>, <span>, <strike>, <strong>, <sub>, <sup>, <table>, <tbody>, <td>, <textarea>, <tfoot>, <th>, <thead>, <tr>, <tt>, <u>, <ul>, <var>, <xmp>

onDataAvailable

Compatibility: IE4, IE5, IE5.5, IE6

This event fires when a databound object receives the data from the data source specified by the datasrc attribute. The datasrc and datafld attributes must be set for the element to which the onDataAvailable event handler applies, and the value of the datasrc attribute must reference an object in the page.

Example: See the onAfterUpdate event.

Properties:

---

altKey, altLeft, cancelBubble, clientX, clientY, ctrlLeft, shiftLeft, srcElement, type

---

Applies to:

<applet>, <object>, <xml>

---

onDatasetChanged

Compatibility: IE4, IE5, IE5.5, IE6

This event fires when a databound object's data set changes. The datasrc and datafld attributes must be set for the element to which the onDatasetChanged event handler applies, and the value of the datasrc attribute must reference an object in the page.

Example: See the onAfterUpdate event.

Properties:

---

altKey, altLeft, cancelBubble, ctrlLeft, qualifier, reason, recordset, shiftLeft, srcElement, type

---

Applies to:

<applet>, <object>, <xml>

---

onDatasetComplete

Compatibility: IE4, IE5, IE5.5, IE6

This event fires when a databound object can access all the data in the data source specified by the datasrc attribute. The datasrc and datafld attributes must be set for the element to which the onDatasetComplete event handler applies, and the value of the datasrc attribute must reference an object in the page.

Example: See the onAfterUpdate event.

Properties:

---

altKey, altLeft, cancelBubble, ctrlLeft, qualifier, reason, recordset, shiftLeft, srcElement, type

---

Applies to:

<applet>, <object>, <xml>

---

onDblClick

Compatibility: NN4, NN6, NN7, IE4, IE5, IE5.5, IE6

This event fires when the user double-clicks an element.

Example:

```
<body bgcolor="#FFFFFF" text="#000000" bottommargin=150 ondblclick="alert('Thank
you!')">
<p>Double-click anywhere in the page.</p>
</body>
```

Properties:

altKey, altLeft, cancelBubble, clientX, clientY, ctrlKey, ctrlLeft, offsetX,
offsetY, returnValue, screenX, screenY, shiftKey, shiftLeft, srcElement, type, x, y

Applies to:

<a>, <acronym>, <address>, <applet>, <area>, <b>, <bdo>, <big>, <blockquote>,
<body>, <button>, <caption>, <center>, <cite>, <code>, <custom>, <dd>, <del>,
<dfn>, <dir>, <div>, <dl>, document, <dt>, <em>, <embed>, <fieldset>, <font>,
<form>, <frame>, <hn>, <hr>, <i>, <img>, <input type="button">, <input
type="checkbox">, <input type="file">, <input type="image">, <input
type="password">, <input type="radio">, <input type="reset">, <input
type="submit">, <input type="text">, <ins>, <kbd>, <label>, <legend>, <li>,
<listing>, <map>, <marquee>, <menu>, <nobr>, <noframes>, <noscript>, <object>,
<ol>, <optgroup>, <option>, <p>, <pre>, <q>, <rt>, <ruby>, <s>, <samp>, <select>,
<small>, <span>, <strike>, <strong>, <sub>, <sup>, <table>, <tbody>, <td>,
<textarea>, <tfoot>, <th>, <thead>, <tr>, <tt>, <u>, <ul>, <var>, <xmp>

onDeactivate

Compatibility: IE5.5, IE6

This event fires when the current object in the page loses focus because the user
activates another object.

Example:

```
<p class="explanations">Press tab to bring the following link in and out of
focus.</p>
<a tabindex="3" id="myL" href="http://www.w3c.org/" target=_blank
ondeactivate="alert('The link has been deactivated')">World Wide Web Consortium</a>
```

Properties:

altKey, altLeft, ctrlLeft, offsetX, offsetY, qualifier, returnValue, screenX,
screenY, shiftLeft, srcElement, toElement, type, x, y

Applies to:

<a>, <acronym>, <address>, <applet>, <area>, <b>, <bdo>, <big>, <blockquote>, <body>, <button>, <caption>, <center>, <cite>, <custom>, <dd>, <dfn>, <dir>, <div>, <dl>, document, <dt>, <em>, <embed>, <fieldset>, <font>, <form>, <frame>, <frameset>, <hn>, <hr>, <i>, <iframe>, <img>, <input type="button">, <input type="checkbox">, <input type="file">, <input type="hidden">, <input type="image">, <input type="password">, <input type="radio">, <input type="reset">, <input type="submit">, <input type="text">, <ins>, <isindex>, <kbd>, <label>, <legend>, <li>, <listing>, <marquee>, <menu>, <object>, <ol>, <p>, <pre>, <q>, <rt>, <ruby>, <s>, <samp>, <select>, <small>, <span>, <strike>, <strong>, <sub>, <sup>, <table>, <tbody>, <td>, <textarea>, <tfoot>, <th>, <thead>, <tr>, <tt>, <u>, <ul>, <var>, window, <xmp>

onDrag

Compatibility: IE5, IE5.5, IE6

This event fires continuously while an object is being dragged. For this event to fire, the object must support drag-and-drop.

Example:

```
<html>
<head>
<script language="JavaScript">
<!--
function B1() {
  msg = 'on' + event.type + ' event fired by  ' + '"' + event.srcElement.id + '"';
  alert(msg+"\nPress Enter twice to close this window")
}
-->
</script>
</head>
<body bgcolor="#FFFFFF" text="#000000" bottommargin=150>
  <p>Source object:
<input id="sourceObject" size=50 value="The text to Drag" ondrag="B1()">
<!-- Try replacing the ondrag event with ondragenter, ondragleave, ondragover,
ondragstart or ondrop -->
<br>
  </p>
  <p>Drop selected text into the following text field.</p>
  Target object:
<input id="targetObject" size=50 value="Drag destination element">
</body>
</html>
```

Properties:

altKey, altLeft, cancelBubble, clientX, clientY, ctrlKey, ctrlLeft, dataTransfer, offsetX, offsetY, returnValue, screenX, screenY, srcElement, type, x, y

Applies to:

<a>, <acronym>, <address>, <area>, <b>, <bdo>, <big>, <blockquote>, <body>,
<button>, <caption>, <center>, <cite>, <code>, <custom>, <dd>, <del>, <dfn>, <dir>,
<div>, <dl>, document, <dt>, <em>, <fieldset>, <font>, <form>, <hn>, <hr>, <i>,
<img>, <input type="button">, <input type="checkbox">, <input type="file">, <input
type="image">, <input type="password">, <input type="radio">, <input type="reset">,
<input type="submit">, <input type="text">, <kbd>, <label>, <li>, <listing>, <map>,
<marquee>, <menu>, <nobr>, <object>, <ol>, <option>, <p>, <pre>, <q>, <s>, <samp>,
<select>, <small>, <span>, <strike>, <strong>, <sub>, <sup>, <table>, <tbody>,
<td>, <textarea>, <tr>, <tt>, <u>, <ul>, <var>, <xmp>

onDragEnd

Compatibility: IE5, IE5.5, IE6

This event fires when the user releases a drag-and-drop operation. For this event
to fire, the object must support drag-and-drop.

Example: See the onDrag event.

Properties:

altKey, altLeft, cancelBubble, clientX, clientY, ctrlKey, ctrlLeft, dataTransfer,
offsetX, offsetY, returnValue, screenX, screenY, shiftLeft, srcElement, type, x, y

Applies to:

<a>, <acronym>, <address>, <area>, <b>, <bdo>, <big>, <blockquote>, <body>,
<button>, <caption>, <center>, <cite>, <code>, <custom>, <dd>, <del>, <dfn>, <dir>,
<div>, <dl>, document, <dt>, <em>, <fieldset>, <font>, <form>, <hn>, <hr>, <i>,
<img>, <input type="button">, <input type="checkbox">, <input type="file">, <input
type="image">, <input type="password">, <input type="radio">, <input type="reset">,
<input type="submit">, <input type="text">, <kbd>, <label>, <li>, <listing>, <map>,
<marquee>, <menu>, <nobr>, <object>, <ol>, <option>, <p>, <pre>, <q>, <s>, <samp>,
<select>, <small>, <span>, <strike>, <strong>, <sub>, <sup>, <table>, <tbody>,
<td>, <textarea>, <tr>, <tt>, <u>, <ul>, <var>, <xmp>

onDragEnter

Compatibility: IE5, IE5.5, IE6

This event fires when the user enters the target area in a drag-and-drop
operation. For this event to fire, the object must support drag-and-drop.

Example: See the onDrag event.

Properties:

altKey, altLeft, cancelBubble, clientX, clientY, ctrlKey, ctrlLeft, dataTransfer,
offsetX, offsetY, returnValue, screenX, screenY, shiftLeft, srcElement, type, x, y

Applies to:

<a>, <acronym>, <address>, <area>, <b>, <bdo>, <big>, <blockquote>, <body>,
<button>, <caption>, <center>, <cite>, <code>, <custom>, <dd>, <del>, <dfn>, <dir>,
<div>, <dl>, document, <dt>, <em>, <fieldset>, <font>, <form>, <hn>, <hr>, <i>,
<img>, <input type="button">, <input type="checkbox">, <input type="file">, <input
type="image">, <input type="password">, <input type="radio">, <input type="reset">,
<input type="submit">, <input type="text">, <kbd>, <label>, <li>, <listing>, <map>,
<marquee>, <menu>, <nobr>, <object>, <ol>, <option>, <p>, <pre>, <q>, <s>, <samp>,
<select>, <small>, <span>, <strike>, <strong>, <sub>, <sup>, <table>, <tbody>,
<td>, <textarea>, <tfoot>, <th>, <thead>, <tr>, <tt>, <u>, <ul>, <var>, <xmp>

onDragLeave

Compatibility: IE5, IE5.5, IE6

This event fires when the user leaves the target area in a drag-and-drop
operation. For this event to fire, the object must support drag-and-drop.

Example: See the onDrag event.

Properties:

altKey, altLeft, cancelBubble, clientX, clientY, ctrlKey, ctrlLeft, dataTransfer,
offsetX, offsetY, returnValue, screenX, screenY, shiftLeft, srcElement, type, x, y

Applies to:

<a>, <acronym>, <address>, <area>, <b>, <bdo>, <big>, <blockquote>, <body>,
<button>, <caption>, <center>, <cite>, <code>, <custom>, <dd>, <del>, <dfn>, <dir>,
<div>, <dl>, document, <dt>, <em>, <fieldset>, <font>, <form>, <hn>, <hr>, <i>,
<img>, <input type="button">, <input type="checkbox">, <input type="file">, <input
type="image">, <input type="password">, <input type="radio">, <input type="reset">,
<input type="submit">, <input type="text">, <kbd>, <label>, <li>, <listing>, <map>,
<marquee>, <menu>, <nobr>, <object>, <ol>, <option>, <p>, <pre>, <q>, <s>, <samp>,
<select>, <small>, <span>, <strike>, <strong>, <sub>, <sup>, <table>, <tbody>,
<td>, <textarea>, <tr>, <tt>, <u>, <ul>, <var>, <xmp>

onDragOver

Compatibility: NN6, NN7, IE5, IE5.5, IE6

This event fires continuously while the cursor is on the target area in a drag-and-
drop operation. For this event to fire, the object must support drag-and-drop.

Example: See the onDrag event.

Properties:

altKey, altLeft, cancelBubble, clientX, clientY, ctrlKey, ctrlLeft, dataTransfer,
offsetX, offsetY, returnValue, screenX, screenY, shiftLeft, srcElement, type, x, y

Applies to:

`<a>`, `<acronym>`, `<address>`, `<area>`, `<b>`, `<bdo>`, `<big>`, `<blockquote>`, `<body>`,
`<button>`, `<caption>`, `<center>`, `<cite>`, `<code>`, `<custom>`, `<dd>`, `<del>`, `<dfn>`, `<dir>`,
`<div>`, `<dl>`, document, `<dt>`, `<em>`, `<fieldset>`, `<font>`, `<form>`, `<hn>`, `<hr>`, `<i>`,
`<img>`, `<input type="button">`, `<input type="checkbox">`, `<input type="file">`, `<input
type="image">`, `<input type="password">`, `<input type="radio">`, `<input type="reset">`,
`<input type="submit">`, `<input type="text">`, `<kbd>`, `<label>`, `<li>`, `<listing>`, `<map>`,
`<marquee>`, `<menu>`, `<nobr>`, `<object>`, `<ol>`, `<option>`, `<p>`, `<pre>`, `<q>`, `<s>`, `<samp>`,
`<select>`, `<small>`, `<span>`, `<strike>`, `<strong>`, `<sub>`, `<sup>`, `<table>`, `<tbody>`,
`<td>`, `<textarea>`, `<tr>`, `<tt>`, `<u>`, `<ul>`, `<var>`, `<xmp>`

---

onDragStart

Compatibility: NN6, NN7, IE4, IE5, IE5.5, IE6

This event fires when the user starts a drag-and-drop operation on a selection in
the document. For this event to fire, the object must support drag-and-drop.

Example: See the onDrag event.

Properties:

---

altKey, altLeft, cancelBubble, clientX, clientY, ctrlKey, ctrlLeft, dataTransfer,
offsetX, offsetY, returnValue, screenX, screenY, shiftLeft, srcElement, type, x, y

---

Applies to:

`<a>`, `<acronym>`, `<address>`, `<area>`, `<b>`, `<bdo>`, `<big>`, `<blockquote>`, `<body>`,
`<button>`, `<caption>`, `<center>`, `<cite>`, `<code>`, `<custom>`, `<dd>`, `<del>`, `<dfn>`, `<dir>`,
`<div>`, `<dl>`, document, `<dt>`, `<em>`, `<fieldset>`, `<font>`, `<form>`, `<hn>`, `<hr>`, `<i>`,
`<img>`, `<input type="button">`, `<input type="checkbox">`, `<input type="file">`, `<input
type="image">`, `<input type="password">`, `<input type="radio">`, `<input type="reset">`,
`<input type="submit">`, `<input type="text">`, `<kbd>`, `<label>`, `<legend>`, `<li>`,
`<listing>`, `<map>`, `<marquee>`, `<menu>`, `<nobr>`, `<object>`, `<ol>`, `<option>`, `<p>`, `<pre>`,
`<q>`, `<rt>`, `<ruby>`, `<s>`, `<samp>`, `<select>`, `<small>`, `<span>`, `<strike>`, `<strong>`,
`<sub>`, `<sup>`, `<table>`, `<tbody>`, `<td>`, `<textarea>`, `<tfoot>`, `<th>`, `<thead>`, `<tr>`,
`<tt>`, `<u>`, `<ul>`, `<var>`, `<xmp>`

---

onDrop

Compatibility: IE5, IE5.5, IE6

This event fires when the user releases the mouse button on the target area in a
drag-and-drop operation. For this event to fire, the object must support drag-
and-drop.

Example: See the onDrag event.

Properties:

---

altKey, altLeft, cancelBubble, clientX, clientY, ctrlKey, ctrlLeft, dataTransfer,
offsetX, offsetY, returnValue, screenX, screenY, shiftLeft, srcElement, type, x, y

---

Applies to:

```
<a>, <acronym>, <address>, <area>, <b>, <bdo>, <big>, <blockquote>, <body>,
<button>, <caption>, <center>, <cite>, <code>, <custom>, <dd>, <del>, <dfn>, <dir>,
<div>, <dl>, document, <dt>, <em>, <fieldset>, <font>, <form>, <hn>, <hr>, <i>,
<img>, <input type="button">, <input type="checkbox">, <input type="file">, <input
type="image">, <input type="password">, <input type="radio">, <input type="reset">,
<input type="submit">, <input type="text">, <kbd>, <label>, <li>, <listing>, <map>,
<marquee>, <menu>, <nobr>, <object>, <ol>, <option>, <p>, <pre>, <q>, <s>, <samp>,
<select>, <small>, <span>, <strike>, <strong>, <sub>, <sup>, <table>, <tbody>,
<td>, <textarea>, <tr>, <tt>, <u>, <ul>, <var>, <xmp>
```

onError

Compatibility: NN4, NN6, NN7, IE4, IE5, IE5.5, IE6

This event fires when an object-loading operation fails. This may occur for any number of reasons, such as referencing an object that has not been instantiated, calling a function that does not exist, or referencing a variable that was not declared.

Example:

```
<head><script language="JavaScript">
window.onerror = alert("One of the scripts in this page has errors")
</script></head>
```

Properties:

```
altKey, altLeft, ctrlLeft, returnValue, shiftLeft, type
```

Applies to:

```
<img>, <object>, <style>, window
```

onErrorUpdate

Compatibility: IE4, IE5, IE5.5, IE6

This event fires if an error occurs while updating data in a databound object.
    Example: See the onAfterUpdate event.
    Properties:

```
altKey, altLeft, cancelBubble, ctrlLeft, shiftLeft, srcElement, type
```

Applies to:

```
<a>, <bdo>, <button>, <custom>, <div>, <frame>, <iframe>, <img>, <input
type="checkbox">, <input type="hidden">, <input type="password">, <input
type="radio">, <input type="text">, <label>, <legend>, <map>, <marquee>, <object>,
<rt>, <ruby>, <select>, <span>, <textarea>
```

Compatibility: IE4, IE5, IE5.5, IE6

This event fires when the state of a filter changes. For transition filters, this event also fires when a transition is completed.

Example:

```
<head><script language="JavaScript">
function B1() {
Layer1.filters[0].Apply();
if (Layer1.style.visibility == "visible") {
   Layer1.style.visibility = "hidden";
   Layer1.filters.revealTrans.transition=2;
   document.all.myB1.value = "Play Transition Circle Out"
   } else {
       Layer1.style.visibility = "visible";
       Layer1.filters[0].transition=3;
       document.all.myB1.value = "Play Transition Circle In"
   }
   Layer1.filters[0].Play();
}
</script></head>
<body onLoad="B1()">
<div id="Layer1" style="position:absolute; visibility:visible;
Filter:revealTrans(duration=2, transition=3); left:92px; top:257px; width:100px;
height:75px; background-color:#FFFF99; layer-background-color:#FFFF99; z-index:2;
border: 1px none #000000" onfilterchange="alert('The filter has completed
transition')">
<img src="yourimagefile.jpg" alt="" width="99" height="75">
</div>
<div id="Layer2" style="position:absolute; visibility:visible;
left:90px; top:245px; width:103; height:103; background-color:#FFFF99; layer-
background-color:#FFFF99; border:1px none #000000; z-index:1"></div>
<input type="button" id="myB1" onClick="B1()" value="Play Transition Circle In">
</body>
```

Properties:

```
altKey, altLeft, cancelBubble, ctrlLeft, shiftLeft, srcElement, srcFilter, type
```

Applies to:

```
<bdo>, <body>, <button>, <custom>, <div>, <fieldset>, <img>, <input type="button">,
<input type="checkbox">, <input type="file">, <input type="image">, <input
type="password">, <input type="radio">, <input type="reset">, <input
type="submit">, <input type="text">, <marquee>, <rt>, <ruby>, <span>, <table>,
<td>, <textarea>, <th>, <tr>
```

onFinish

Compatibility: IE4, IE5, IE5.5, IE6

This event fires when a looping is completed for a `<marquee>` element.
Example:

```
<marquee loop="2" width=250 onfinish="alert('Car sale is over!')"
bgcolor="#99ffff">The car sale ends in November.</marquee>
```

Properties:

altKey, altLeft, clientX, clientY, ctrlLeft, offsetX, offsetY, returnValue,
screenX, screenY, shiftLeft, srcElement, type, x, y

Applies to:

`<marquee>`

onFocus

Compatibility: NN4, NN6, NN7, IE4, IE5, IE5.5, IE6

This event fires when the element on the page receives focus.
Example:

```
<head><script language="JavaScript">
function B1() {
//blur() method is necessary to avoid W3C infinite openings.
document.getElementById("myL").blur();
alert("<A> element has received focus. When you accept, the W3C home page will be
displayed in a new window");
window.open("http://www.w3c.org", "", "");
}
</script></head>
<body bgcolor="#FFFFFF" text="#000000">
<a id="myL" href="http://www.w3c.org/" target=_blank onFocus="B1()"> World Wide Web
Consortium</a></body>
```

Properties:

altKey, altLeft, clientX, clientY, ctrlLeft, offsetX, offsetY, returnValue,
screenX, screenY, shiftLeft, srcElement, type, x, y

Applies to:

`<a>`, `<acronym>`, `<address>`, `<applet>`, `<area>`, `<b>`, `<bdo>`, `<big>`, `<blockquote>`,
`<body>`, `<button>`, `<caption>`, `<center>`, `<cite>`, `<custom>`, `<dd>`, `<del>`, `<dfn>`, `<dir>`,
`<div>`, `<dl>`, `<dt>`, `<em>`, `<embed>`, `<fieldset>`, `<font>`, `<form>`, `<frame>`, `<frameset>`,
`<hn>`, `<hr>`, `<i>`, `<iframe>`, `<img>`, `<input type="button">`, `<input type="checkbox">`,
`<input type="file">`, `<input type="hidden">`, `<input type="image">`, `<input
type="password">`, `<input type="radio">`, `<input type="reset">`, `<input
type="submit">`, `<input type="text">`, `<ins>`, `<isindex>`, `<kbd>`, `<label>`, `<legend>`,
`<li>`, `<listing>`, `<map>`, `<marquee>`, `<menu>`, `<object>`, `<ol>`, `<optgroup>`, `<option>`,

`<p>`, `<pre>`, `<q>`, `<rt>`, `<ruby>`, `<s>`, `<samp>`, `<select>`, `<small>`, `<span>`, `<strike>`, `<strong>`, `<sub>`, `<sup>`, `<table>`, `<tbody>`, `<td>`, `<textarea>`, `<tfoot>`, `<th>`, `<thead>`, `<tr>`, `<tt>`, `<u>`, `<ul>`, `<var>`, window, `<xmp>`

onFocusIn

Compatibility: IE6

This event fires just before the focus is set on an element.

Example:

```
<head><script language="JavaScript">
function B1() {
//blur() method is necessary to avoid W3C infinite openings.
document.getElementById("myL").blur();
alert("<A> element has received focus. When you accept, the W3C home page will be
displayed in a new window");
window.open("http://www.w3.org", "", "");
}
function B2() {
alert("<a> element will receive focus upon accepting this message")
}
</script></head>
<body bgcolor="#FFFFFF" text="#000000">
<a id="myL" href="http://www.w3.org/" target=_blank onFocus="B1()"
onfocusin="B2()">World Wide Web Consortium</a></body>
```

Properties:

altKey, altLeft, cancelBubble, clientX, clientY, ctrlKey, ctrlLeft, offsetX, offsetY, screenX, screenY, shiftKey, shiftLeft, srcElement, type, wheelDelta, x, y

Applies to:

`<a>`, `<address>`, `<applet>`, `<area>`, `<b>`, `<bdo>`, `<big>`, `<blockquote>`, `<body>`, `<button>`, `<caption>`, `<center>`, `<cite>`, `<code>`, `<custom>`, `<dd>`, `<dfn>`, `<dir>`, `<div>`, `<dl>`, document, `<dt>`, `<em>`, `<embed>`, `<fieldset>`, `<font>`, `<form>`, `<hn>`, `<hr>`, `<i>`, `<img>`, `<input type="button">`, `<input type="checkbox">`, `<input type="file">`, `<input type="image">`, `<input type="password">`, `<input type="radio">`, `<input type="reset">`, `<input type="submit">`, `<input type="text">`, `<kbd>`, `<label>`, `<legend>`, `<li>`, `<listing>`, `<map>`, `<marquee>`, `<menu>`, `<nobr>`, `<ol>`, `<p>`, `<pre>`, `<rt>`, `<ruby>`, `<s>`, `<samp>`, `<select>`, `<small>`, `<span>`, `<strike>`, `<strong>`, `<sub>`, `<sup>`, `<table>`, `<tbody>`, `<td>`, `<textarea>`, `<tfoot>`, `<th>`, `<thead>`, `<tr>`, `<tt>`, `<u>`, `<ul>`, `<var>`, `<xmp>`

onFocusOut

Compatibility: IE6

This event fires immediately after focus leaves an element.

Example:

```
<head><script language="JavaScript">
function B1() {
//blur() method is necessary to avoid W3C infinite openings.
document.getElementById("myL").blur();
alert("<a> element has received focus. When you accept, the W3C home page will be
displayed in a new window");
window.open("http://www.w3c.org", "", "");
}
function B2() {
alert("<a> element lost focus")
}
</script></head>
<body bgcolor="#FFFFFF" text="#000000">
<a id="myL" href="http://www.w3c.org/" target=_blank onFocus="B1()"
onfocusout="B2()">World Wide Web Organization</a></body>
```

Properties:

altKey, altLeft, cancelBubble, clientX, clientY, ctrlKey, ctrlLeft, offsetX, offsetY, screenX, screenY, shiftKey, shiftLeft, srcElement, type, wheelDelta, x, y

Applies to:

<a>, <address>, <applet>, <area>, <b>, <bdo>, <big>, <blockquote>, <body>, <button>, <caption>, <center>, <cite>, <code>, <custom>, <dd>, <dfn>, <dir>, <div>, <dl>, document, <dt>, <em>, <embed>, <fieldset>, <font>, <form>, <hn>, <hr>, <i>, <img>, <input type="button">, <input type="checkbox">, <input type="file">, <input type="image">, <input type="password">, <input type="radio">, <input type="reset">, <input type="submit">, <input type="text">, <kbd>, <label>, <legend>, <li>, <listing>, <map>, <marquee>, <menu>, <nobr>, <ol>, <p>, <pre>, <rt>, <ruby>, <s>, <samp>, <select>, <small>, <span>, <strike>, <strong>, <sub>, <sup>, <table>, <tbody>, <td>, <textarea>, <tfoot>, <th>, <thead>, <tr>, <tt>, <u>, <ul>, <var>, <xmp>

onHelp

Compatibility: IE4, IE5, IE5.5, IE6

This event fires when the user presses the F1 key.

Example:

```
<body bgcolor="#FFFFFF" text="#000000" onHelp="alert('The user is looking for
help')">
```

Properties:

altKey, altLeft, cancelBubble, clientX, clientY, ctrlKey, ctrlLeft, offsetX, offsetY, returnValue, screenX, screenY, shiftKey, shiftLeft, srcElement, type, x, y

Applies to:

<a>, <acronym>, <address>, <applet>, <area>, <b>, <bdo>, <big>, <blockquote>,
<body>, <button>, <caption>, <center>, <cite>, <code>, <custom>, <dd>, <del>,
<dfn>, <dir>, <div>, <dl>, document, <dt>, <em>, <embed>, <fieldset>, <font>,
<form>, <hn>, <hr>, <i>, <img>, <input type="button">, <input type="checkbox">,
<input type="file">, <input type="image">, <input type="password">, <input
type="radio">, <input type="reset">, <input type="submit">, <input type="text">,
<ins>, <kbd>, <label>, <legend>, <li>, <listing>, <map>, <marquee>, <menu>, <nobr>,
<object>, <ol>, <p>, <pre>, <q>, <rt>, <ruby>, <s>, <samp>, <select>, <small>,
<span>, <strike>, <strong>, <sub>, <sup>, <table>, <tbody>, <td>, <textarea>,
<tfoot>, <th>, <thead>, <tr>, <tt>, <u>, <ul>, <var>, window, <xmp>

---

onKeyDown

Compatibility: NN4, NN6, NN7, IE4, IE5, IE5.5, IE6

This event fires when the user presses any keyboard key.

Example:

```
<html>
<head>
<script language="JavaScript">
function B1() {
msg = 'on' + event.type + ' event fired by  ' + '"' + event.srcElement.id + '"';
alert(msg)
}
</script></head>
<body id="myBody" onkeydown="B1()">
<!-- Try replacing onkeydown with onkeypress or onkeyup-->
<p>Press any key to fire the event</p>
</body></html>
```

Properties:

---

altKey, altLeft, cancelBubble, clientX, clientY, ctrlKey, ctrlLeft, keyCode,
offsetX, offsetY, repeat, returnValue, screenX, screenY, shiftKey, shiftLeft,
srcElement, type, x, y

Applies to:

<a>, <acronym>, <address>, <applet>, <area>, <b>, <bdo>, <big>, <blockquote>,
<body>, <button>, <caption>, <center>, <cite>, <code>, <custom>, <dd>, <del>,
<dfn>, <dir>, <div>, <dl>, document, <dt>, <em>, <fieldset>, <font>, <form>, <hn>,
<hr>, <i>, <input type="button">, <input type="checkbox">, <input type="file">,
<input type="image">, <input type="password">, <input type="radio">, <input
type="reset">, <input type="submit">, <input type="text">, <ins>, <kbd>, <label>,
<legend>, <li>, <listing>, <map>, <marquee>, <menu>, <nobr>, <noframes>,
<noscript>, <object>, <ol>, <optgroup>, <option>, <p>, <pre>, <q>, <rt>, <ruby>,
<s>, <samp>, <select>, <small>, <span>, <strike>, <strong>, <sub>, <sup>, <table>,
<tbody>, <td>, <textarea>, <tfoot>, <th>, <thead>, <tr>, <tt>, <u>, <ul>, <var>,
<xmp>

---

onKeyPress

Compatibility: NN4, NN6, NN7, IE4, IE5, IE5.5, IE6

This event fires when the user presses any key on the keyboard.

Example: See the onKeyDown example and replace the onkeydown event in the <body> tag with onkeypress.

Properties:

```
altKey, altLeft, cancelBubble, clientX, clientY, ctrlKey, ctrlLeft, keyCode,
offsetX, offsetY, returnValue, screenX, screenY, shiftKey, shiftLeft, srcElement,
type, x, y
```

Applies to:

```
<a>, <acronym>, <address>, <applet>, <area>, <b>, <bdo>, <big>, <blockquote>,
<body>, <button>, <caption>, <center>, <cite>, <code>, <custom>, <dd>, <del>,
<dfn>, <dir>, <div>, <dl>, document, <dt>, <em>, <fieldset>, <font>, <form>, <hn>,
<hr>, <i>, <input type="button">, <input type="checkbox">, <input type="file">,
<input type="image">, <input type="password">, <input type="radio">, <input
type="reset">, <input type="submit">, <input type="text">, <ins>, <kbd>, <label>,
<legend>, <li>, <listing>, <map>, <marquee>, <menu>, <nobr>, <noframes>,
<noscript>, <object>, <ol>, <optgroup>, <option>, <p>, <pre>, <q>, <rt>, <ruby>,
<s>, <samp>, <select>, <small>, <span>, <strike>, <strong>, <sub>, <sup>, <table>,
<tbody>, <td>, <textarea>, <tfoot>, <th>, <thead>, <tr>, <tt>, <u>, <ul>, <var>,
<xmp>
```

onKeyUp

Compatibility: NN4, NN6, NN7, IE4, IE5, IE5.5, IE6

This event fires when the user releases any key on the keyboard.

Example: See the onKeyDown example and replace the onkeydown event in the <body> tag with onkeyup.

Properties:

```
altKey, altLeft, cancelBubble, clientX, clientY, ctrlKey, ctrlLeft, keyCode,
offsetX, offsetY, repeat, returnValue, screenX, screenY, shiftKey, shiftLeft,
srcElement, type, x, y
```

Applies to:

```
<a>, <acronym>, <address>, <applet>, <area>, <b>, <bdo>, <big>, <blockquote>,
<body>, <button>, <caption>, <center>, <cite>, <code>, <custom>, <dd>, <del>,
<dfn>, <dir>, <div>, <dl>, document, <dt>, <em>, <fieldset>, <font>, <form>, <hn>,
<hr>, <i>, <input type="button">, <input type="checkbox">, <input type="file">,
<input type="image">, <input type="password">, <input type="radio">, <input
type="reset">, <input type="submit">, <input type="text">, <ins>, <kbd>, <label>,
<legend>, <li>, <listing>, <map>, <marquee>, <menu>, <nobr>, <noframes>,
<noscript>, <object>, <ol>, <optgroup>, <option>, <p>, <pre>, <q>, <rt>, <ruby>,
<s>, <samp>, <select>, <small>, <span>, <strike>, <strong>, <sub>, <sup>, <table>,
<tbody>, <td>, <textarea>, <tfoot>, <th>, <thead>, <tr>, <tt>, <u>, <ul>, <var>,
<xmp>
```

onLayoutComplete

Compatibility: NN6, NN7, IE4, IE5, IE5.5, IE6

This event fires when a print or print preview command completes execution.
Example:

```
<html><head>
<script language="JavaScript">
function B1() {window.print();}
</script>
</head>
<body bgcolor="#FFFFFF" text="#000000">
<p>Some body content to print</p>
<input type="button" value="Print" onclick="B1()"
onlayoutcomplete='alert("The preview layout process is finished")'>
</body></html>
```

Properties:

```
altKey, altLeft, contentOverflow, ctrlLeft, shiftLeft
```

Applies to:

```
<base>, <basefont>, <bgsound>, <br>, <col>, <dd>, <div>, <dl>, <dt>, <font>,
<head>, <hr>, <html>, <li>, <meta>, <ol>, <option>, <p>, <title>, <ul>
```

onLoad

Compatibility: NN4, NN6, NN7, IE4, IE5, IE5.5, IE6

This event fires immediately after a document, frameset, or image is fully loaded.
Example:

```
<body onLoad="alert('The document is fully loaded')"><img src="yourimage.jpg"></body>
```

Properties:

```
altKey, altLeft, clientX, clientY, ctrlLeft, offsetX, offsetY, screenX, screenY,
shiftLeft, type, x, y
```

Applies to:

```
<applet>, <body>, <embed>, <frame>, <frameset>, <iframe>, <img>, <link>, <object>,
<script>, window
```

onLoseCapture

Compatibility: IE5, IE5.5, IE6

This event fires when an element that is currently trapping mouse events loses that ability.

Example:

```
<head><script language="JavaScript">
</script></head>
<body onload="captureMode.setCapture()" onclick="captureMode.releaseCapture()">
<div id="captureMode" onlosecapture="alert('Mouse capture terminated.')">
<p>Mouse capture is currently turned on. To terminate mouse capture mode, click
this page!</p>
</div></body>
```

Properties:

altKey, altLeft, clientX, clientY, ctrlKey, ctrlLeft, offsetX, offsetY, screenX, screenY, shiftKey, shiftLeft, srcElement, type, x, y

Applies to:

\<a\>, \<address\>, \<applet\>, \<area\>, \<b\>, \<bdo\>, \<big\>, \<blockquote\>, \<body\>, \<br\>, \<button\>, \<caption\>, \<center\>, \<cite\>, \<code\>, \<custom\>, \<dd\>, \<dfn\>, \<dir\>, \<div\>, \<dl\>, \<dt\>, \<em\>, \<embed\>, \<fieldset\>, \<font\>, \<form\>, \<hn\>, \<hr\>, \<i\>, \<img\>, \<input type="button"\>, \<input type="checkbox"\>, \<input type="file"\>, \<input type="hidden"\>, \<input type="image"\>, \<input type="password"\>, \<input type="radio"\>, \<input type="reset"\>, \<input type="submit"\>, \<input type="text"\>, \<kbd\>, \<label\>, \<legend\>, \<li\>, \<listing\>, \<map\>, \<marquee\>, \<menu\>, \<nobr\>, \<noframes\>, \<object\>, \<ol\>, \<option\>, \<p\>, \<pre\>, \<s\>, \<samp\>, \<select\>, \<small\>, \<span\>, \<strike\>, \<strong\>, \<sub\>, \<sup\>, \<table\>, \<tbody\>, \<td\>, \<textarea\>, \<tfoot\>, \<th\>, \<thead\>, \<tr\>, \<tt\>, \<u\>, \<ul\>, \<var\>, \<xmp\>

onMouseDown

Compatibility: NN4, NN6, NN7, IE4, IE5, IE5.5, IE6

This event fires when the user presses either mouse button on an object.

Example:

```
<head><script language="JavaScript">
</script></head>
<body bgcolor="#FFFFFF" text="#000000">
<input type="button" value="Click here" onmousedown="alert('You just pressed down
on a mouse button')">
</body>
```

Properties:

altKey, altLeft, button, cancelBubble, clientX, clientY, ctrlKey, ctrlLeft, offsetX, offsetY, returnValue, screenX, screenY, shiftKey, shiftLeft, srcElement, type, x, y

Applies to:

<a>, <acronym>, <address>, <applet>, <area>, <b>, <bdo>, <big>, <blockquote>,
<body>, <button>, <caption>, <center>, <cite>, <code>, <custom>, <dd>, <del>,
<dfn>, <dir>, <div>, <dl>, document, <dt>, <em>, <embed>, <fieldset>, <font>,
<form>, <hn>, <hr>, <i>, <img>, <input type="button">, <input type="checkbox">,
<input type="file">, <input type="image">, <input type="password">, <input
type="radio">, <input type="reset">, <input type="submit">, <input type="text">,
<ins>, <kbd>, <label>, <legend>, <li>, <listing>, <map>, <marquee>, <menu>,
<object>, <ol>, <optgroup>, <option>, <p>, <pre>, <q>, <rt>, <ruby>, <s>, <samp>,
<select>, <small>, <span>, <strike>, <strong>, <sub>, <sup>, <table>, <tbody>,
<td>, <textarea>, <tfoot>, <th>, <thead>, <tr>, <tt>, <u>, <ul>, <var>, <xmp>

onMouseEnter

Compatibility: IE5.5, IE6

This event fires when the user causes the mouse pointer to enter an object's area.
Example:

```
<head><script language="JavaScript">
function B1() {
alert('The '+event.type+' event fired')
}
</script></head>
<body bgcolor="#FFFFFF" text="#000000">
<div id="myDiv" onmouseenter="B1()">
<!-- Try replacing onmouseenter with onmouseleave, onmouseover, onmousemove,
onmouseout, or onmouseup -->
Move the mouse over this div element area.
</div></body>
```

Properties:

altKey, altLeft, button, cancelBubble, clientX, clientY, ctrlKey, ctrlLeft,
fromElement, offsetX, offsetY, returnValue, screenX, screenY, shiftKey, shiftLeft,
srcElement, toElement, type, x, y

Applies to:

<a>, <acronym>, <address>, <applet>, <area>, <b>, <base>, <basefont>, <bdo>,
<bgsound>, <big>, <blockquote>, <body>, <button>, <caption>, <center>, <cite>,
<code>, <custom>, <dd>, <dfn>, <dir>, <div>, <dl>, <dt>, <em>, <embed>, <fieldset>,
<font>, <form>, <hn>, <hr>, <html>, <i>, <img>, <input type="button">, <input
type="checkbox">, <input type="file">, <input type="image">, <input
type="password">, <input type="radio">, <input type="reset">, <input
type="submit">, <input type="text">, <kbd>, <label>, <legend>, <li>, <listing>,
<map>, <marquee>, <menu>, <nobr>, <ol>, <p>, <pre>, <rt>, <ruby>, <s>, <samp>,
<select>, <small>, <span>, <strike>, <strong>, <sub>, <sup>, <table>, <tbody>,
<td>, <textarea>, <tfoot>, <th>, <thead>, <tr>, <tt>, <u>, <ul>, <var>, <xmp>

onMouseLeave

Compatibility: IE5.5, IE6

This event fires when the user causes the mouse pointer to leave an object's area.

Example: See the onMouseEnter example, and in the <div> tag replace the onmouseenter event with onmouseleave.

Properties:

```
altKey, altLeft, button, cancelBubble, clientX, clientY, ctrlKey, ctrlLeft,
fromElement, offsetX, offsetY, returnValue, screenX, screenY, shiftKey, shiftLeft,
srcElement, toElement, type, x, y
```

Applies to:

```
<a>, <acronym>, <address>, <applet>, <area>, <b>, <base>, <basefont>, <bdo>,
<bgsound>, <big>, <blockquote>, <body>, <button>, <caption>, <center>, <cite>,
<code>, <custom>, <dd>, <dfn>, <dir>, <div>, <dl>, <dt>, <em>, <embed>, <fieldset>,
<font>, <form>, <hn>, <hr>, <html>, <i>, <img>, <input type="button">, <input
type="checkbox">, <input type="file">, <input type="image">, <input
type="password">, <input type="radio">, <input type="reset">, <input
type="submit">, <input type="text">, <kbd>, <label>, <legend>, <li>, <listing>,
<map>, <marquee>, <menu>, <nobr>, <ol>, <p>, <pre>, <rt>, <ruby>, <s>, <samp>,
<select>, <small>, <span>, <strike>, <strong>, <sub>, <sup>, <table>, <tbody>,
<td>, <textarea>, <tfoot>, <th>, <thead>, <tr>, <tt>, <u>, <ul>, <var>, <xmp>
```

onMouseMove

Compatibility: NN4, NN6, NN7, IE4, IE5, IE5.5, IE6

This event fires when the user moves the mouse pointer while it resides inside the object's area.

Example: See the onMouseEnter example, and in the <div> element replace the onmouseenter event with onmousemove.

Properties:

```
altKey, altLeft, cancelBubble, clientX, clientY, ctrlKey, ctrlLeft, offsetX,
offsetY, screenX, screenY, shiftKey, shiftLeft, srcElement, toElement, type, x, y
```

Applies to:

```
<a>, <acronym>, <address>, <applet>, <area>, <b>, <bdo>, <big>, <blockquote>,
<body>, <button>, <caption>, <center>, <cite>, <code>, <custom>, <dd>, <del>,
<dfn>, <dir>, <div>, <dl>, document, <dt>, <em>, <embed>, <fieldset>, <font>,
<form>, <hn>, <hr>, <i>, <img>, <input type="button">, <input type="checkbox">,
<input type="file">, <input type="image">, <input type="password">, <input
type="radio">, <input type="reset">, <input type="submit">, <input type="text">,
<ins>, <kbd>, <label>, <legend>, <li>, <listing>, <map>, <marquee>, <menu>, <nobr>,
<noframes>, <noscript>, <object>, <ol>, <optgroup>, <option>, <p>, <pre>, <q>,
<rt>, <ruby>, <s>, <samp>, <select>, <small>, <span>, <strike>, <strong>, <sub>,
<sup>, <table>, <tbody>, <td>, <textarea>, <tfoot>, <th>, <thead>, <tr>, <tt>, <u>,
<ul>, <var>, <xmp>
```

onMouseOut

Compatibility: NN4, NN6, NN7, IE4, IE5, IE5.5, IE6

This event fires when the user moves the mouse pointer outside of an object's area.

Example: See the onMouseEnter example, and in the <div> tag replace the onmouseenter event with onmouseout.

Properties:

altKey, altLeft, button, cancelBubble, clientX, clientY, ctrlKey, ctrlLeft, fromElement, offsetX, offsetY, screenX, screenY, shiftKey, shiftLeft, srcElement, toElement, type, x, y

Applies to:

<a>, <acronym>, <address>, <applet>, <area>, <b>, <bdo>, <big>, <blockquote>, <body>, <button>, <caption>, <center>, <cite>, <code>, <custom>, <dd>, <del>, <dfn>, <dir>, <div>, <dl>, document, <dt>, <em>, <embed>, <fieldset>, <font>, <form>, <hn>, <hr>, <i>, <img>, <input type="button">, <input type="checkbox">, <input type="file">, <input type="image">, <input type="password">, <input type="radio">, <input type="reset">, <input type="submit">, <input type="text">, <ins>, <kbd>, <label>, <legend>, <li>, <listing>, <map>, <marquee>, <menu>, <noframes>, <noscript>, <object>, <ol>, <optgroup>, <option>, <p>, <pre>, <q>, <rt>, <ruby>, <s>, <samp>, <select>, <small>, <span>, <strike>, <strong>, <sub>, <sup>, <table>, <tbody>, <td>, <textarea>, <tfoot>, <th>, <thead>, <tr>, <tt>, <u>, <ul>, <var>, <xmp>

onMouseOver

Compatibility: NN4, NN6, NN7, IE4, IE5, IE5.5, IE6

This event fires when the user moves the mouse pointer over an object's area.

Example: See the onMouseEnter example, and in the <div> tag replace the onmouseenter event with onmouseover.

Properties:

altKey, altLeft, button, cancelBubble, clientX, clientY, ctrlKey, ctrlLeft, fromElement, offsetX, offsetY, returnValue, screenX, screenY, shiftKey, shiftLeft, srcElement, toElement, type, x, y

Applies to:

<a>, <acronym>, <address>, <applet>, <area>, <b>, <bdo>, <big>, <blockquote>, <body>, <button>, <caption>, <center>, <cite>, <code>, <custom>, <dd>, <del>, <dfn>, <dir>, <div>, <dl>, document, <dt>, <em>, <embed>, <fieldset>, <font>, <form>, <hn>, <hr>, <i>, <img>, <input type="button">, <input type="checkbox">, <input type="file">, <input type="image">, <input type="password">, <input type="radio">, <input type="reset">, <input type="submit">, <input type="text">, <ins>, <kbd>, <label>, <legend>, <li>, <listing>, <map>, <marquee>, <menu>, <nobr>,

`<noframes>`, `<noscript>`, `<object>`, `<ol>`, `<optgroup>`, `<option>`, `<p>`, `<pre>`, `<q>`, `<rt>`, `<ruby>`, `<s>`, `<samp>`, `<select>`, `<small>`, `<span>`, `<strike>`, `<strong>`, `<sub>`, `<sup>`, `<table>`, `<tbody>`, `<td>`, `<textarea>`, `<tfoot>`, `<th>`, `<thead>`, `<tr>`, `<tt>`, `<u>`, `<ul>`, `<var>`, `<xmp>`

onMouseUp

Compatibility: NN4, NN6, NN7, IE4, IE5, IE5.5, IE6

This event fires when the user releases the mouse button while the pointer is hovering over an object's area.

Example: See the onMouseEnter example, and in the `<div>` tag replace the onmouseenter event with onmouseup.

Properties:

altKey, altLeft, button, cancelBubble, clientX, clientY, ctrlKey, ctrlLeft, offsetX, offsetY, returnValue, screenX, screenY, shiftKey, shiftLeft, srcElement, type, x, y

Applies to:

`<a>`, `<acronym>`, `<address>`, `<applet>`, `<area>`, `<b>`, `<bdo>`, `<big>`, `<blockquote>`, `<body>`, `<button>`, `<caption>`, `<center>`, `<cite>`, `<code>`, `<custom>`, `<dd>`, `<del>`, `<dfn>`, `<dir>`, `<div>`, `<dl>`, document, `<dt>`, `<em>`, `<embed>`, `<fieldset>`, `<font>`, `<form>`, `<hn>`, `<hr>`, `<i>`, `<img>`, `<input type="button">`, `<input type="checkbox">`, `<input type="file">`, `<input type="image">`, `<input type="password">`, `<input type="radio">`, `<input type="reset">`, `<input type="submit">`, `<input type="text">`, `<ins>`, `<kbd>`, `<label>`, `<legend>`, `<li>`, `<listing>`, `<map>`, `<marquee>`, `<menu>`, `<nobr>`, `<noframes>`, `<noscript>`, `<object>`, `<ol>`, `<optgroup>`, `<p>`, `<pre>`, `<q>`, `<rt>`, `<ruby>`, `<s>`, `<samp>`, `<select>`, `<small>`, `<span>`, `<strike>`, `<strong>`, `<sub>`, `<sup>`, `<table>`, `<tbody>`, `<td>`, `<textarea>`, `<tfoot>`, `<th>`, `<thead>`, `<tr>`, `<tt>`, `<u>`, `<ul>`, `<var>`, `<xmp>`

onMouseWheel

Compatibility: IE6

This event fires when the mouse wheel button is rotated. This event is the only one that exposes the wheelDelta object property. wheelDelta returns a positive value when the wheel button has rotated away from the user, and a negative value when the wheel button has rotated toward the user.

Example:

```
<html><body>
<p>Move the pointer on top of the image and then move the mouse wheel up or down.</p>
<img id="yourimage" src="yourimage.gif" onmousewheel="alert('Wheel Delta: ' +
event.wheelDelta);">
</body></html>
```

Properties:

---

altKey, altLeft, cancelBubble, clientX, clientY, ctrlKey, ctrlLeft, offsetX, offsetY, screenX, screenY, shiftKey, shiftLeft, srcElement, type, wheelDelta, x, y

---

Applies to:

<a>, <address>, <applet>, <area>, <b>, <bdo>, <big>, <blockquote>, <body>, <button>, <caption>, <center>, <cite>, <code>, <custom>, <dd>, <dfn>, <dir>, <div>, <dl>, document, <dt>, <em>, <embed>, <fieldset>, <font>, <form>, <hn>, <hr>, <i>, <img>, <input type="button">, <input type="checkbox">, <input type="file">, <input type="image">, <input type="password">, <input type="radio">, <input type="reset">, <input type="submit">, <input type="text">, <kbd>, <label>, <legend>, <li>, <listing>, <map>, <marquee>, <menu>, <nobr>, <ol>, <p>, <pre>, <rt>, <ruby>, <s>, <samp>, <select>, <small>, <span>, <strike>, <strong>, <sub>, <sup>, <table>, <tbody>, <td>, <textarea>, <tfoot>, <th>, <thead>, <tr>, <tt>, <u>, <ul>, <var>, <xmp>

---

onMove

Compatibility: NN4, NN6, NN7, IE5.5, IE6

This event fires when an object that supports drag-and-drop is moved.

Example:

```
<html>
<head>
<script language="JavaScript">
<!--
// Turn on 2-D positioning
document.execCommand("2D-position",false,true);
function B1() {
window.onmove = alert("The div element has been dragged");
}
-->
</script>
</head>
<body bgcolor="#FFFFFF" text="#000000" bottommargin=150 onmove="B1()">
<!-- Try replacing onmove with onmoveend or onmovestart -->
<div contenteditable="true">
<div style="width:300px;height:75px; color:yellow; background-color:black;
position:absolute; left: 50px; top: 150px">Select and Drag me with the mouse.</div>
</div>
</body>
</html>
```

Properties:

---

altKey, altLeft, cancelBubble, clientX, clientY, ctrlKey, ctrlLeft, offsetX, offsetY, returnValue, screenX, screenY, shiftKey, shiftLeft, srcElement, type, x, y

---

Applies to:

<a>, <acronym>, <address>, <applet>, <area>, <b>, <bdo>, <big>, <blockquote>, <body>, <button>, <caption>, <center>, <cite>, <custom>, <dd>, <dfn>, <dir>, <div>, <dl>, document, <dt>, <em>, <embed>, <fieldset>, <font>, <form>, <frame>, <frameset>, <hn>, <hr>, <i>, <iframe>, <img>, <input type="button">, <input type="checkbox">, <input type="file">, <input type="hidden">, <input type="image">, <input type="password">, <input type="radio">, <input type="reset">, <input type="submit">, <input type="text">, <ins>, <isindex>, <kbd>, <label>, <legend>, <li>, <listing>, <marquee>, <menu>, <object>, <ol>, <p>, <pre>, <q>, <rt>, <ruby>, <s>, <samp>, <select>, <small>, <span>, <strike>, <strong>, <sub>, <sup>, <table>, <tbody>, <td>, <textarea>, <tfoot>, <th>, <thead>, <tr>, <tt>, <u>, <ul>, <var>, window, <xmp>

onMoveEnd

Compatibility: IE5.5, IE6

This event fires when an object that supports drag-and-drop stops moving.

Example: See the onMove example, and in the <body> tag replace the onmove event with onmoveend.

Properties:

altKey, altLeft, cancelBubble, clientX, clientY, ctrlKey, ctrlLeft, offsetX, offsetY, returnValue, screenX, screenY, shiftKey, shiftLeft, srcElement, type, x, y

Applies to:

<a>, <acronym>, <address>, <applet>, <area>, <b>, <bdo>, <big>, <blockquote>, <body>, <button>, <caption>, <center>, <cite>, <custom>, <dd>, <dfn>, <dir>, <div>, <dl>, document, <dt>, <em>, <embed>, <fieldset>, <font>, <form>, <frame>, <frameset>, <hn>, <hr>, <i>, <iframe>, <img>, <input type="button">, <input type="checkbox">, <input type="file">, <input type="hidden">, <input type="image">, <input type="password">, <input type="radio">, <input type="reset">, <input type="submit">, <input type="text">, <ins>, <isindex>, <kbd>, <label>, <legend>, <li>, <listing>, <marquee>, <menu>, <object>, <ol>, <p>, <pre>, <q>, <rt>, <ruby>, <s>, <samp>, <select>, <small>, <span>, <strike>, <strong>, <sub>, <sup>, <table>, <tbody>, <td>, <textarea>, <tfoot>, <th>, <thead>, <tr>, <tt>, <u>, <ul>, <var>, window, <xmp>

onMoveStart

Compatibility: IE5.5, IE6

This event fires when an object that supports drag-and-drop starts moving.

Example: See the onMove example, and in the <body> tag replace the onmove event with onmovestart.

Properties:

altKey, altLeft, cancelBubble, clientX, clientY, ctrlKey, ctrlLeft, offsetX, offsetY, returnValue, screenX, screenY, shiftKey, shiftLeft, srcElement, type, x, y

Applies to:

```
<a>, <acronym>, <address>, <applet>, <area>, <b>, <bdo>, <big>, <blockquote>,
<body>, <button>, <caption>, <center>, <cite>, <custom>, <dd>, <dfn>, <dir>, <div>,
<dl>, document, <dt>, <em>, <embed>, <fieldset>, <font>, <form>, <frame>,
<frameset>, <hn>, <hr>, <i>, <iframe>, <img>, <input type="button">, <input
type="checkbox">, <input type="file">, <input type="hidden">, <input type="image">,
<input type="password">, <input type="radio">, <input type="reset">, <input
type="submit">, <input type="text">, <ins>, <isindex>, <kbd>, <label>, <legend>,
<li>, <listing>, <marquee>, <menu>, <object>, <ol>, <p>, <pre>, <q>, <rt>, <ruby>,
<s>, <samp>, <select>, <small>, <span>, <strike>, <strong>, <sub>, <sup>, <table>,
<tbody>, <td>, <textarea>, <tfoot>, <th>, <thead>, <tr>, <tt>, <u>, <ul>, <var>,
window, <xmp>
```

onPaste

Compatibility: IE5, IE5.5, IE6

This event fires when the user pastes data from the clipboard into the document.
Example:

```
<p>Copy and paste this text into the textarea element below by pressing Ctrl+V.</p>
<textarea cols=60 onpaste="alert('The text is being pasted')">
</textarea>
```

Properties:

```
altKey, altLeft, cancelBubble, clientX, clientY, ctrlKey, ctrlLeft, dataTransfer,
offsetX, offsetY, returnValue, screenX, screenY, shiftKey, shiftLeft, srcElement,
type, x, y
```

Applies to:

```
<a>, <address>, <applet>, <area>, <b>, <bdo>, <big>, <blockquote>, <body>,
<button>, <caption>, <center>, <cite>, <code>, <custom>, <dd>, <dfn>, <dir>, <div>,
<dl>, document, <dt>, <em>, <embed>, <fieldset>, <font>, <form>, <hn>, <hr>, <i>,
<img>, <input type="button">, <input type="checkbox">, <input type="file">, <input
type="image">, <input type="password">, <input type="radio">, <input type="reset">,
<input type="submit">, <input type="text">, <kbd>, <label>, <legend>, <li>,
<listing>, <map>, <marquee>, <menu>, <nobr>, <ol>, <p>, <pre>, <rt>, <ruby>, <s>,
<samp>, <select>, <small>, <span>, <strike>, <strong>, <sub>, <sup>, <table>,
<tbody>, <td>, <textarea>, <tfoot>, <th>, <thead>, <tr>, <tt>, <u>, <ul>, <var>,
<xmp>
```

onPropertyChange

Compatibility: IE5, IE5.5, IE6

This event fires when an object's property changes.

Example:

```
<html>
<head>
<script language="JavaScript">
<!--
function styleProp() {
    if (myDiv.style.backgroundColor == "gray"){myDiv.style.backgroundColor = "red";
return;}
    if (myDiv.style.backgroundColor == "red"){myDiv.style.backgroundColor = "blue";
return;}
    if (myDiv.style.backgroundColor == "blue"){myDiv.style.backgroundColor =
"green"; return;}
    if (myDiv.style.backgroundColor == "green"){myDiv.style.backgroundColor =
"orange"; return;}
    if (myDiv.style.backgroundColor == "orange"){myDiv.style.backgroundColor =
"gray"; return;}
}
function final() {
alert("backgroundColor property has changed value!");
}
-->
</script>
</head>
<body bgcolor="#FFFFFF" text="#000000" bottommargin=150>
<div id="myDiv" style="width:500; height:200; cursor:hand; color: white;
background-color:gray" onclick="styleProp()" onpropertychange="final();">Click here
to change the background color of this box.</div>
</body>
</html>
```

Properties:

altKey, altLeft, ctrlLeft, propertyName, shiftLeft, srcElement, type

Applies to:

<a>, <address>, <applet>, <area>, <b>, <bdo>, <big>, <blockquote>, <body>, <button>, <caption>, <center>, <cite>, <code>, <comment>, <custom>, <dd>, <dfn>, <dir>, <div>, <dl>, document, <dt>, <em>, <embed>, <fieldset>, <font>, <form>, <hn>, <hr>, <i>, <img>, <input type="button">, <input type="checkbox">, <input type="file">, <input type="hidden">, <input type="image">, <input type="password">, <input type="radio">, <input type="reset">, <input type="submit">, <input type="text">, <kbd>, <label>, <legend>, <li>, <listing>, <map>, <marquee>, <menu>, <nobr>, <object>, <ol>, <option>, <p>, <pre>, <s>, <samp>, <script>, <select>, <small>, <span>, <strike>, <strong>, <sub>, <sup>, <table>, <tbody>, <td>, <textarea>, <tfoot>, <th>, <thead>, <tr>, <tt>, <u>, <ul>, <var>, <xmp>

Compatibility: IE5, IE5.5, IE6

This event fires when the state of an object changes. This event is useful in determining when elements that load images or data have finished loading them.

Example:

```
<html><head>
<script language="JavaScript">
document.onreadystatechange=fnrs;
function fnrs () {
if (document.readyState=="complete") {
   alert('The document ready state is "complete"')
}}
</script></head>
<body>
<p>Body content</p>
</body></html>
```

Properties:

```
altKey, altLeft, ctrlLeft, shiftLeft, srcElement, type
```

Applies to:

```
<a>, <acronym>, <address>, <applet>, <area>, <b>, <base>, <basefont>, <bdo>,
<bgsound>, <big>, <blockquote>, <body>, <br>, <button>, <caption>, <center>,
<cite>, <code>, <col>, <colgroup>, <comment>, <custom>, <dd>, <del>, <dfn>, <dir>,
<div>, <dl>, document, <dt>, <em>, <embed>, <fieldset>, <font>, <form>, <head>,
<hn>, <hr>, <html>, <i>, <iframe>, <img>, <input type="button">, <input
type="checkbox">, <input type="file">, <input type="hidden">, <input type="image">,
<input type="password">, <input type="radio">, <input type="reset">, <input
type="submit">, <input type="text">, <ins>, <isindex>, <kbd>, <label>, <legend>,
<li>, <link>, <listing>, <map>, <marquee>, <menu>, namespace, <nobr>, <noframes>,
<noscript>, <object>, <ol>, <option>, <p>, <pre>, <q>, <rt>, <ruby>, <s>, <samp>,
<script>, <select>, <small>, <span>, <strike>, <strong>, <style>, <sub>, <sup>,
<table>, <tbody>, <td>, <textarea>, <tfoot>, <th>, <thead>, <title>, <tr>, <tt>,
<u>, <ul>, <var>, <xml>, <xmp>
```

onReset

Compatibility: NN4, NN6, NN7, IE4, IE5, IE5.5, IE6

This event fires when the form is reset.

Example:

```
<p>Input some text in the text field below.</p>
<form name="form1" method="post" action="" onreset="alert('The form is being
reset')">
<input type="text" value=""><input type="reset" value="Reset">
</form>
```

Properties:

altKey, altLeft, ctrlLeft, returnValue, shiftLeft, srcElement, type

Applies to:

<form>

onResize

Compatibility: NN4, NN6, NN7, IE4, IE5, IE5.5, IE6

This event fires when the user resizes an object.

Example:

```
<head><script language="JavaScript">
function B1() {alert('The '+event.type+' event fired')}
</script></head>
<body bgcolor="#FFFFFF" text="#000000">
<a id="myL" href="" contenteditable=true onresize="B1()">
<!-- Try replacing onresize with onresizeend or onresizestart-->
<img src="yourimagefile.jpg" alt="" width="79" height="99"></a>
</body>
```

Properties:

altKey, altLeft, clientX, clientY, ctrlKey, ctrlLeft, offsetX, offsetY, returnValue, screenX, screenY, shiftKey, shiftLeft, srcElement, type, x, y

Applies to:

<a>, <acronym>, <address>, <applet>, <b>, <big>, <blockquote>, <button>, <center>, <cite>, <code>, <custom>, <dd>, <dfn>, <dir>, <div>, <dl>, <dt>, <em>, <embed>, <fieldset>, <form>, <frame>, <hn>, <hr>, <i>, <img>, <input type="button">, <input type="file">, <input type="image">, <input type="password">, <input type="reset">, <input type="submit">, <input type="text">, <ins>, <isindex>, <kbd>, <label>, <legend>, <li>, <listing>, <marquee>, <menu>, <object>, <ol>, <p>, <pre>, <s>, <samp>, <select>, <small>, <span>, <strike>, <strong>, <sub>, <sup>, <table>, <td>, <textarea>, <tr>, <tt>, <u>, <ul>, <var>, window, <xmp>

onResizeEnd

Compatibility: IE5.5, IE6

This event fires when the user completes resizing an object.

Example: See the onResize example, and in the <a> tag replace the onresize event with onresizeend.

Properties:

altKey, altLeft, button, cancelBubble, clientX, clientY, ctrlKey, ctrlLeft, fromElement, offsetX, offsetY, returnValue, screenX, screenY, shiftKey, shiftLeft, srcElement, toElement, type, x, y

Applies to:

<a>, <acronym>, <address>, <applet>, <area>, <b>, <bdo>, <big>, <blockquote>, <body>, <button>, <caption>, <center>, <cite>, <custom>, <dd>, <dfn>, <dir>, <div>, <dl>, document, <dt>, <em>, <embed>, <fieldset>, <font>, <form>, <frame>, <frameset>, <hn>, <hr>, <i>, <iframe>, <img>, <input type="button">, <input type="checkbox">, <input type="file">, <input type="hidden">, <input type="image">, <input type="password">, <input type="radio">, <input type="reset">, <input type="submit">, <input type="text">, <ins>, <isindex>, <kbd>, <label>, <legend>, <li>, <listing>, <marquee>, <menu>, <object>, <ol>, <p>, <pre>, <q>, <rt>, <ruby>, <s>, <samp>, <select>, <small>, <span>, <strike>, <strong>, <sub>, <sup>, <table>, <tbody>, <td>, <textarea>, <tfoot>, <th>, <thead>, <tr>, <tt>, <u>, <ul>, <var>, window, <xmp>

onResizeStart

Compatibility: IE5.5, IE6

This event fires when the user starts resizing an object.

Example: See the onResize example, and in the <a> tag replace the onresize event with onresizestart.

Properties:

altKey, altLeft, button, cancelBubble, clientX, clientY, ctrlKey, ctrlLeft, fromElement, offsetX, offsetY, returnValue, screenX, screenY, shiftKey, shiftLeft, srcElement, toElement, type, x, y

Applies to:

<a>, <acronym>, <address>, <applet>, <area>, <b>, <bdo>, <big>, <blockquote>, <body>, <button>, <caption>, <center>, <cite>, <custom>, <dd>, <dfn>, <dir>, <div>, <dl>, document, <dt>, <em>, <embed>, <fieldset>, <font>, <form>, <frame>, <frameset>, <hn>, <hr>, <i>, <iframe>, <img>, <input type="button">, <input type="checkbox">, <input type="file">, <input type="hidden">, <input type="image">, <input type="password">, <input type="radio">, <input type="reset">, <input type="submit">, <input type="text">, <ins>, <isindex>, <kbd>, <label>, <legend>, <li>, <listing>, <marquee>, <menu>, <object>, <ol>, <p>, <pre>, <q>, <rt>, <ruby>, <s>, <samp>, <select>, <small>, <span>, <strike>, <strong>, <sub>, <sup>, <table>, <tbody>, <td>, <textarea>, <tfoot>, <th>, <thead>, <tr>, <tt>, <u>, <ul>, <var>, window, <xmp>

onRowEnter

Compatibility: IE4, IE5, IE5.5, IE6

This event fires when a new row of data is selected in a databound object. The datasrc and datafld attributes must be set for the element to which the onRowEnter event handler is applied, and the value of the datasrc attribute must reference an object in the page.

Example: See the onAfterUpdate event.

Properties:

altKey, altLeft, ctrlLeft, qualifier, recordset, returnValue, shiftLeft,
srcElement, type

Applies to:

<applet>, <object>, <xml>

onRowExit

Compatibility: IE4, IE5, IE5.5, IE6

This event fires when the current row of data in a databound object is exited.
The datasrc and datafld attributes must be set for the element to which the
onRowExit event handler is applied, and the value of the datasrc attribute must
reference an object in the page.
   Example: See the onAfterUpdate event.
   Properties:

altKey, altLeft, ctrlLeft, qualifier, recordset, returnValue, shiftLeft,
srcElement, type

Applies to:

<applet>, <object>, <xml>

onRowsDelete

Compatibility: IE4, IE5, IE5.5, IE6

This event fires when a row is deleted from the recordset of a databound object.
The datasrc and datafld attributes must be set for the element to which the
onRowsDelete event handler is applied, and the value of the datasrc attribute must
reference an object in the page.
   Example: See the onAfterUpdate event.
   Properties:

altKey, altLeft, cancelBubble, ctrlLeft, reason, recordset, shiftLeft, srcElement,
type

Applies to:

<applet>, <object>, <xml>

onRowsInserted

Compatibility: IE4, IE5, IE5.5, IE6

This event fires when a row is inserted into the recordset of a databound object. The datasrc and datafld attributes must be set for the element to which the onRowsInserted event handler is applied, and the value of the datasrc attribute must reference an object in the page.

Example: See the onAfterUpdate event.

Properties:

altKey, altLeft, cancelBubble, ctrlLeft, qualifier, reason, recordset, shiftLeft, srcElement, type

Applies to:

<applet>, <object>, <xml>

onScroll

Compatibility: NN6, NN7, IE4, IE5, IE5.5, IE6

This event fires when the user moves the scroll bar of an object.

Example:

```
<body onscroll="alert('The user is scrolling the document')">
<br><br><br><br><br><br><br><br><br><br><br><br><br><br><br><br>
Reduce the size of your browser window until a scroll bar appears
</body>
```

Properties:

altKey, altLeft, clientX, clientY, ctrlLeft, offsetX, offsetY, screenX, screenY, shiftLeft, srcElement, type, x, y

Applies to:

<applet>, <bdo>, <body>, <custom>, <div>, <embed>, <map>, <marquee>, <object>, <table>, <td>, <textarea>, <th>, window

onSelect

Compatibility: NN4, NN6, NN7, IE4, IE5, IE5.5, IE6

This event fires when the user highlights a portion of text in an element.

Example:

```
<body onselect="alert('The user is selecting some body object')">Try to select a
portion of this text</body>
```

Properties:

altKey, altLeft, ctrlLeft, clientX, clientY, offsetX, offsetY, returnValue, screenX, screenY, srcElement, type, x, y

Applies to:

```
<body>, <input type="text">, <textarea>
```

onSelectionChange

Compatibility: IE5.5, IE6

This event fires when a document's selection state is changed, meaning that a section of the document has been selected (highlighted) or unselected. This event is also triggered by the <samp> element.

Example:

```
<head>
<script language="JavaScript" for=document event=onselectionchange>
alert('The selection has changed');
</script>
</head>
<body bgcolor="#FFFFFF" text="#000000">
<p>Copy this text into the textarea element below.</p>
<textarea cols=30 contenteditable=true>Click here</textarea>
</body>
```

Properties:

```
altKey, altLeft, ctrlLeft, offsetX, offsetY, returnValue, shiftLeft, srcElement,
screenX, screenY, type, x, y
```

Applies to:

```
document, <samp>
```

onSelectStart

Compatibility: IE4, IE5, IE5.5, IE6

This event fires when an element or its contents are selected (highlighted using the mouse pointer). For this event to fire, the value of the <body> tag's contenteditable attribute must be set to true.

Example:

```
<head>
<script language="JavaScript">
function B1() {
alert("The W3C home page will open only after this alert window is closed");
window.open("http://www.w3c.org","","")
}
</script></head>
```

```
<body bgcolor="#FFFFFF" text="#000000" contenteditable=true>
<a style="text-decoration:underline" href="http://www.w3c.org"
onselectstart="B1()">World Wide Web Consortium</a></body>
```

Properties:

altKey, altLeft, cancelBubble, clientX, clientY, ctrlLeft, offsetX, offsetY,
returnValue, screenX, screenY, shiftLeft, srcElement, type, x, y

Applies to:

`<a>`, `<acronym>`, `<address>`, `<area>`, `<b>`, `<bdo>`, `<big>`, `<blockquote>`, `<body>`, `<br>`,
`<button>`, `<caption>`, `<center>`, `<cite>`, `<code>`, `<custom>`, `<dd>`, `<del>`, `<dfn>`, `<dir>`,
`<div>`, `<dl>`, `<dt>`, `<em>`, `<fieldset>`, `<font>`, `<form>`, `<hn>`, `<hr>`, `<i>`, `<img>`, `<input
type="button">`, `<input type="checkbox">`, `<input type="file">`, `<input type="image">`,
`<input type="password">`, `<input type="radio">`, `<input type="reset">`, `<input
type="submit">`, `<input type="text">`, `<kbd>`, `<label>`, `<li>`, `<listing>`, `<map>`,
`<marquee>`, `<menu>`, `<nobr>`, `<object>`, `<ol>`, `<option>`, `<p>`, `<pre>`, `<q>`, `<rt>`, `<ruby>`,
`<s>`, `<samp>`, `<select>`, `<small>`, `<span>`, `<strike>`, `<strong>`, `<sub>`, `<sup>`, `<table>`,
`<tbody>`, `<td>`, `<textarea>`, `<tfoot>`, `<th>`, `<thead>`, `<tr>`, `<tt>`, `<u>`, `<ul>`, `<var>`,
`<xmp>`

onStart

Compatibility: IE4, IE5, IE5.5, IE6

This event fires each time a loop of the `<marquee>` element starts.

Example:

```
<marquee width=300 onstart="alert('New loop is about to start')"
bgcolor="#99ffff">Come and see our car models.</marquee>
```

Properties:

altKey, altLeft, clientX, clientY, ctrlLeft, type, offsetX, offsetY, screenX,
screenY, shiftLeft, srcElement, x, y

Applies to:

`<marquee>`

onStop

Compatibility: IE5, IE5.5, IE6

This event fires when the user clicks the stop button in the browser window or
when the user leaves the web page by going to another page.

Example:

```
<head><script language="JavaScript">
document.onstop = B1
function B1() {
```

```
alert("You pressed the browser stop button, or you are about to exit this page");
}
</script></head>
<body bgcolor="#FFFFFF" text="#000000"></body>
```

NOTE *The body content should be filled with images so that there will be enough time to stop the page from fully loading.*

Properties:

```
altKey, altLeft, ctrlLeft, shiftLeft, type
```

Applies to:

```
document
```

onSubmit

Compatibility: NN4, NN6, NN7, IE4, IE5, IE5.5, IE6

This event fires when the user submits a form. Use this capability to validate data on the client side to prevent invalid data from being submitted to the server.

NOTE *This event fires only in response to the clicking of a Submit button and not in response to the* form.submit() *method.*

Example:

```
<form name="form1" method="post" action="" onsubmit="alert('The form is being
submitted')">
<input type="text" name="textfield">
<input type="submit" value="Submit">
</form>
```

Properties:

```
altKey, altLeft, ctrlKey, ctrlLeft, returnValue, shiftLeft, srcElement, type
```

Applies to:

```
<form>
```

onTimeError

Compatibility: IE5.5, IE6

This event fires when a specific time error occurs.

Example:

```
<html xmlns:t = "urn:schemas-microsoft-com:time">
<head></head>
```

```
<body text=#000000 bottomMargin=150 bgColor=#ffffff
ontimeerror="alert('An HTML+TIME error has ocurred')">
<?import namespace=t urn="urn:schemas-microsoft-com:time"
implementation="#default#time2"/>
<t:excl id=t1 onend="alert('The animation ended')" onbegin="alert('Beginning
animation!')" begin="indefinite" dur="5" repeatCount="3">
<t:animatemotion id=a1 targetElement="myDiv" to="250,0" autoReverse="true"
begin="1" dur="2"></t:animatemotion>
</t:excl>
<div class=time id=myDiv style="border:1px solid black; font-size: large; left:
25px; width: 250px; font-family: verdana; position: relative; top: 15px; height:
75px; background-color: yellow; text-align: center">Animated div element.</div>
<p> </p>
<button onclick=t1.beginElement();>Start animation</button>
<button onclick=t1.endElement();>Stop animation</button>
</body></html>
```

Properties:

srcElement, type

Applies to:

<a>, <acronym>, <address>, <area>, <b>, <big>, <blockquote>, <button>, <caption>,
<center>, <cite>, <code>, <dd>, <del>, <dir>, <div>, <dl>, <dt>, <em>, <fieldset>,
<font>, <form>, <hn>, <hr>, <i>, <iframe>, <img>, <input type="button">, <input
type="checkbox">, <input type="file">, <input type="hidden">, <input type="image">,
<input type="password">, <input type="radio">, <input type="reset">, <input
type="submit">, <input type="text">, <ins>, <kbd>, <legend>, <li>, <listing>,
<marquee>, <menu>, <ol>, <option>, <p>, <pre>, <q>, <s>, <samp>, selection,
<small>, <span>, <strike>, <strong>, <sub>, <sup>, <table>, <tbody>, <td>,
<textarea>, <tfoot>, <th>, <thead>, <tr>, <tt>, <u>, <ul>, <var>, <xmp>

onUnload

Compatibility: NN4, NN6, NN7, IE4, IE5, IE5.5, IE6

This event fires immediately before the document begins to unload. The
document will unload when the user clicks the close button in the browser
window, or when the user goes to a different page.

Example:

```
<body onunload="alert('Exiting the page!')">
```

Properties:

altKey, altLeft, ctrlLeft, shiftLeft, type

Applies to:

<body>, <frameset>, window

8

CSS ATTRIBUTES AND JAVASCRIPT STYLE PROPERTIES

This chapter contains a comprehensive listing of all the CSS attributes and JavaScript style properties listed in Chapter 5. As in Chapter 5, the style property names are listed using CSS syntax. To convert CSS syntax (which is not case sensitive) to JavaScript syntax (which is case sensitive), simply remove the dashes and capitalize the first letter of all words other than the first word. For example, the CSS attribute `text-underline-position` would be written in JavaScript as `textUnderlinePosition`.

Unless otherwise noted, all style properties appearing in this chapter are read and write properties. Also, nearly all of the style properties in this chapter are compatible with both CSS and JavaScript syntax. For style properties that are only compatible with JavaScript, the style property names are followed by an asterisk inside parentheses: (*).

Each of the style properties in this chapter contains a brief description, a listing of acceptable syntaxes, a functional example (in most cases), and a list of HTML elements and JavaScript objects that can be used with the style property (< and > angle brackets surround the applicable HTML elements, whereas JavaScript object names appear normally).

For more information regarding style sheets, see Chapter 1.

!important

Compatibility: NN6, NN7, IE4, IE5, IE5.5, IE6

This style property adds more importance to a declaration. In the following example, the first three declarations have increased importance, while the last declaration has normal weight.

Example:

```
h1 { color: black !important; background: white !important }
p  { font-size: 12pt !important; font-style: italic }
```

Applies to:

```
<a>, <address>, <b>, <big>, <blockquote>, <body>, <caption>, <center>, <cite>,
<code>, <col>, <colgroup>, <dd>, <dfn>, <dir>, <div>, <dl>, <dt>, <em>, <form>,
<hn>, <html>, <i>, <img>, <input>, <input type="button">, <input type="checkbox">,
<input type="file">, <input type="hidden">, <input type="image">, <input
type="password">, <input type="radio">, <input type="reset">, <input
type="submit">, <input type="text">, <kbd>, <label>, <legend>, <li>, <listing>,
<marquee>, <menu>, <ol>, <p>, <pre>, <s>, <samp>, <select>, <small>, <span>,
<strike>, <strong>, <sub>, <sup>, <table>, <tbody>, <td>, <textarea>, <tfoot>,
<th>, <thead>, <tr>, <tt>, <u>, <ul>, <var>, <xmp>
```

:active

Compatibility: NN6, NN7, IE4, IE5, IE5.5, IE6

This anchor pseudo-class sets the style of the <a> element when it has the focus.

Example:

```
<html><head>
<style>
a:active { font-weight:bold; color:red }
</style>
</head><body>
<p>Press tab key to bring the link into focus.</p>
<a href="http://www.nostarch.com" target="_blank">This is the No Starch Press Home
Page link</a>
</body></html>
```

Applies to:

```
<a>
```

:first-letter

Compatibility: NN6, NN7, IE5.5, IE6

This pseudo-element is used to apply special styles to the first letter of a text block element.

Example:

```
<html><head>
<style>
p:first-letter { font-size:150%; color:red; }
</style>
</head>
<body>
<p>This is a sample text.</p>
</body></html>
```

Applies to:

```
<address>, <blockquote>, <body>, <center>, <dd>, <div>, <dl>, <dt>, <fieldset>,
<form>, <hn>, <legend>, <li>, <listing>, <marquee>, <menu>, <p>, <pre>, <xmp>
```

:first-line

Compatibility: NN6, NN7, IE5.5, IE6

This pseudo-element is used to apply special styles to the first line of a text block element.

Example:

```
<html><head>
<style>
p:first-line { font-size:200%; color:red; }
</style>
</head><body>
<p>This is the first line of a sample text.<br>
This is the second line.</p>
</body></html>
```

Applies to:

```
<address>, <blockquote>, <body>, <center>, <dd>, <div>, <dl>, <dt>, <fieldset>,
<form>, <hn>, <legend>, <li>, <listing>, <marquee>, <menu>, <p>, <pre>, <xmp>
```

:hover

Compatibility: NN6, NN7, IE4, IE5, IE5.5, IE6

This anchor pseudo-class sets the style of the <a> element when the user moves the mouse pointer over it.

Example:

```
<html><head>
<style>
a:hover { font-weight:bold; color:red }
</style>
</head>
<body>
<p>Move the mouse over the following link.</p>
<a href="http://www.nostarch.com" target="_blank">This is the No Starch Press home
page link</a>
</body></html>
```

Applies to:

```
<a>
```

:link

Compatibility: NN6, NN7, IE4, IE5, IE5.5, IE6

This anchor pseudo-class sets the style of the `<a>` element before the URL specified in its href attribute has been visited.

Example:

```
<html><head>
<style>
a:link { font-weight:bold; color:red }
</style>
</head>
<body>
<a href="http://www.nostarch.com" target="_blank">This is the No Starch Press home
page link</a>
</body></html>
```

Applies to:

```
<a>
```

:visited

Compatibility: NN6, NN7, IE4, IE5, IE5.5, IE6

This anchor pseudo-class sets the style of the `<a>` element after the user has already visited the URL specified in its href attribute.

Example:

```
<html><head>
<style>
a:visited { font-size:75%; color:gray }
</style>
```

```
</head>
<body>
<a href="http://www.nostarch.com" target="_blank">This is the No Starch Press home
page link</a>
</body></html>
```

Applies to:

```
<a>
```

@charset

Compatibility: IE5, IE5.5, IE6

This at-rule establishes the character set that will be used by an external style sheet. An external style sheet will usually use the default character set from the browser; @charset allows you to establish a character set that will be compatible with your document. For more information on character sets, refer to http://www.iana.org/assignments/character-sets.

Example:

```
<html><head>
<style>@charset "iso-8859-1"</style>
</head>
<body bgcolor="#FFFFFF" text="#000000"><p>This is a block of text.</p></body></html>
```

Applies to: n/a.

@font-face

Compatibility: IE5, IE5.5, IE6

This at-rule establishes a font that is downloaded to the browser for use in the page. Once the font has been defined, it is downloaded and kept in RAM for as long as the page is active in the browser, and it can be used anywhere on the page using a style sheet or in the style attribute.

Example:

```
<head>
<style type="text/css">
@font-face { font-family: Lucida; font-style: normal; font-weight: normal; src:
url("fontFile.eot")
</style></head>
<body><p style="font-family: Lucida"> Paragraph text </p></body>
</html>
```

Applies to: n/a.

@import

Compatibility: IE4, IE5, IE5.5, IE6

This at-rule allows the page to import an external style sheet inside the `<style>` tag without requiring use of the `<link>` tag.

Example:

```
<html><head>
<link rel="stylesheet" href="examples.css" type="text/css">
<style type="text/css">
 @import url("examples.css");
</style>
</head>
<body bgcolor="#FFFFFF" text="#000000"><p>All text blocks in this page are rendered
using the "examples.css" imported style sheet.</p>
</body></html>
```

Applies to: n/a.

@media

Compatibility: IE5, IE5.5, IE6

This at-rule establishes a set of style rules that apply to output that is sent to the various media types.

Syntax:

```
@media value { style sheet rules }
```

Values:

screen	Output is meant for the computer screen
print	Output is meant for the printer
all	Output is meant for any device

Example:

```
<html><head>
<style type="text/css">
@media print {    body { font-family: Verdana; font-size: 14pt; }
</style>
</head>
<body bgcolor="#FFFFFF" text="#000000"><p>(body content)</p>
</body></html>
```

Applies to: n/a.

@page

Compatibility: IE5.5, IE6

This at-rule establishes the style rules that determine the dimensions, orientation, and margins of the various pages that are to be printed. These rules will only work with customized print templates; they will not work with Internet

Explorer's default print templates. For information on print templates, refer to http://msdn.microsoft.com/workshop/browser/hosting/printpreview/ reference/reference.asp.

Syntax:

```
@page value { style sheet rules }
```

Values:

:first	Applies to the first page of the collection of pages
:left	Applies to the pages positioned on the left side
:right	Applies to the pages positioned on the right side

```
<html><head>
<style type="text/css">
@page:first { font-family:Times New Roman; font-size:18pt; color:blue; }
@page:left { font-family: Verdana; font-size: 14pt; }
@page:right { font-family: Verdana; font-size: 14pt; }
</style>
</head>
<body bgcolor="#FFFFFF" text="#000000"><p>(body content)</p>
</body></html>
```

Applies to: n/a.

accelerator

Compatibility: IE5, IE5.5, IE6

This style property is a Boolean (true or false) that determines whether or not the element can be activated by pressing a combination of the ALT key and the accelerator, or shortcut key. Therefore, the element containing this style property must also have an accesskey attribute value indicating the shortcut key.

Syntax:

```
element { accelerator: value }
elementID.style.accelerator = "value"
document.all.elementID.style.accelerator = "value"
```

Example:

```
<html><head></head>
<body bgcolor="#FFFFFF"
text="#000000">
<p style="accelerator:true">Press Alt+N to bring the control into focus.</p>
<input id="myN" type="text" size="30" accesskey="N" value="Access N">
</body></html>
```

Applies to:

<a>, <acronym>, <address>, <applet>, <b>, <bdo>, <big>, <blockquote>, <body>,
<center>, <cite>, <code>, currentStyle, <custom>, <dd>, defaults, <del>, <dfn>,
<dir>, <div>, <dl>, <dt>, <em>, <embed>, <fieldset>, <font>, <form>, <hn>, <i>,
<iframe>, <ins>, <kbd>, <label>, <legend>, <li>, <listing>, <menu>, <ol>, <p>,
<pre>, <q>, <rt>, <ruby>, runtimeStyle, <s>, <samp>, <select>, <small>, <span>,
<strike>, <strong>, style, <sub>, <sup>, <table>, <textarea>, <tt>, <u>, <ul>,
<var>, <xmp>

---

background

Compatibility: NN4, NN6, NN7, IE4, IE5, IE5.5, IE6

This style property is a shorthand for setting the values of five different background properties at once: background-color, background-image, background-attachment, background-position, and background-repeat.

Syntax:

```
element { background: values }
elementID.style.background = "values"
document.all.elementID.style.background = "values" // IE only
```

Values: See the values of the background-attachment, background-color, background-image, background-position, and background-repeat style properties. The five property values are separated by a space, and the order in which they appear is irrelevant.

Example:

```
<html><head>
</head><body bgcolor="#FFFFFF" text="#000000">
<div style="background:blue url(yourbackgroundimage.jpg) repeat top left; width:200;
border:3; height:150; font-size:14"></div><br><br><br><br><br><br><br><br><br>
<div style="background-color:red; background-attachment:fixed; background-
image:url(yourbackgroundimage.jpg); background-repeat:repeat; background-position-
x:top; background-position-y:left; width:200; border:3; height:150; font-size:14"></div>
</body></html>
```

Applies to:

<a>, <address>, <b>, <big>, <blockquote>, <body>, <button>, <caption>, <center>,
<cite>, <code>, <col>, <colgroup>, <custom>, <dd>, defaults, <dfn>, <dir>, <div>,
<dl>, <dt>, <em>, <fieldset>, <form>, <hn>, <html>, <i>, <img>, <input
type="button">, <input type="checkbox">, <input type="file">, <input type="image">,
<input type="password">, <input type="radio">, <input type="reset">, <input
type="submit">, <input type="text">, <isindex>, <kbd>, <label>, <legend>, <li>,
<listing>, <marquee>, <menu>, <nobr>, <ol>, <p>, <pre>, runtimeStyle, <s>, <samp>,
<small>, <span>, <strike>, <strong>, style, <sub>, <sup>, <table>, <tbody>, <td>,
<textarea>, <tfoot>, <th>, <thead>, <tr>, <tt>, <u>, <ul>, <var>, <xmp>

---

background-attachment

Compatibility: NN6, NN7, IE4, IE5, IE5.5, IE6

This style property defines whether the background image remains fixed or scrolls with the content.

Syntax:

```
element { background-attachment: value }
elementID.style.backgroundAttachment = "value"
document.all.elementID.style.backgroundAttachment = "value" // IE only
```

Values: fixed (keeps the image stationary), scroll (image scrolls with the object).

Example: See the background style example.

Applies to:

```
<a>, <address>, <b>, <big>, <blockquote>, <body>, <button>, <caption>, <center>,
<cite>, <code>, <col>, <colgroup>, currentStyle, <custom>, <dd>, defaults, <dfn>,
<dir>, <div>, <dl>, <dt>, <em>, <fieldset>, <form>, <hn>, <html>, <i>, <iframe>,
<img>, <input type="button">, <input type="checkbox">, <input type="file">, <input
type="image">, <input type="password">, <input type="radio">, <input type="reset">,
<input type="submit">, <input type="text">, <isindex>, <kbd>, <label>, <legend>,
<li>, <listing>, <marquee>, <menu>, <ol>, <option>, <p>, <pre>, runtimeStyle, <s>,
<samp>, <small>, <span>, <strike>, <strong>, style, <sub>, <sup>, <table>, <tbody>,
<td>, <textarea>, <tfoot>, <th>, <thead>, <tr>, <tt>, <u>, <ul>, <var>, <xmp>
```

background-color

Compatibility: NN6, NN7, IE4, IE5, IE5.5, IE6

This style property defines the background color of the element.

Syntax:

```
element { background-color: value }
elementID.style.backgroundColor = "value"
document.all.elementID.style.backgroundColor = "value" // IE only
```

Values: color name, hexadecimal number (#RRGGBB), or transparent (the default, which makes the underlying colors shine through).

Example: See the background style example.

Applies to:

```
<a>, <address>, <b>, <big>, <blockquote>, <body>, <button>, <caption>, <center>,
<cite>, <code>, <col>, <colgroup>, currentStyle, <custom>, <dd>, defaults, <dfn>,
<dir>, <div>, <dl>, <dt>, <em>, <fieldset>, <form>, <hn>, <html>, <i>, <iframe>,
<img>, <input type="button">, <input type="checkbox">, <input type="file">, <input
type="image">, <input type="password">, <input type="radio">, <input type="reset">,
<input type="submit">, <input type="text">, <isindex>, <kbd>, <label>, <legend>,
<li>, <listing>, <marquee>, <menu>, <nobr>, <ol>, <option>, <p>, <pre>,
```

runtimeStyle, `<s>`, `<samp>`, `<select>`, `<small>`, `<span>`, `<strike>`, `<strong>`, style, `<sub>`, `<sup>`, `<table>`, `<tbody>`, `<td>`, `<textarea>`, `<tfoot>`, `<th>`, `<thead>`, `<tr>`, `<tt>`, `<u>`, `<ul>`, `<var>`, `<xmp>`

background-image

Compatibility: NN4, NN6, NN7, IE4, IE5, IE5.5, IE6

This style property defines the URL of the background image of the element.

Syntax:

```
element { background-image: value }
elementID.style.backgroundImage = "value"
document.all.elementID.style.backgroundImage = "value" // IE only
```

Values:

url(*pathname*)	The *pathname* is the absolute or relative URL of the image file
none	The default, which causes the underlying background to show through

Example: See the background style example.

Applies to:

`<a>`, `<address>`, `<b>`, `<big>`, `<blockquote>`, `<body>`, `<button>`, `<caption>`, `<center>`, `<cite>`, `<code>`, `<col>`, `<colgroup>`, currentStyle, `<custom>`, `<dd>`, defaults, `<dfn>`, `<dir>`, `<div>`, `<dl>`, `<dt>`, `<em>`, `<fieldset>`, `<form>`, `<hn>`, `<html>`, `<i>`, `<img>`, `<input type="button">`, `<input type="checkbox">`, `<input type="file">`, `<input type="image">`, `<input type="password">`, `<input type="radio">`, `<input type="reset">`, `<input type="submit">`, `<input type="text">`, `<isindex>`, `<kbd>`, `<label>`, `<legend>`, `<li>`, `<listing>`, `<marquee>`, `<menu>`, `<nobr>`, `<ol>`, `<p>`, `<pre>`, runtimeStyle, `<s>`, `<samp>`, `<small>`, `<span>`, `<strike>`, `<strong>`, style, `<sub>`, `<sup>`, `<table>`, `<tbody>`, `<td>`, `<textarea>`, `<tfoot>`, `<th>`, `<thead>`, `<tr>`, `<tt>`, `<u>`, `<ul>`, `<var>`, `<xmp>`

background-position

Compatibility: NN6, NN7, IE4, IE5, IE5.5, IE6

This style property defines the left and top coordinates of the background image.

If two values are provided, separated by a space, the first value will set the horizontal position, and the second value will set the vertical position. If one value is provided, only the horizontal position is set, and the vertical position will be set to 50 percent of the page height.

Syntax:

```
element { background-position: value }
elementID.style.backgroundPosition = "value"
document.all.elementID.style.backgroundPosition = "value" // IE only
```

Values:

length	A floating-point number followed by a unit designator
percentage	An integer followed by a percent sign; the percent is based on the height and width of the element
constant	left, center, or right for the horizontal alignment and top, center, or bottom for the vertical alignment

Example: See the background style example.
Applies to:

```
<a>, <address>, <b>, <big>, <blockquote>, <body>, <button>, <caption>, <center>,
<cite>, <code>, <col>, <colgroup>, <custom>, <dd>, defaults, <dfn>, <dir>, <div>,
<dl>, <dt>, <em>, <fieldset>, <form>, <hn>, <html>, <i>, <img>, <input
type="button">, <input type="checkbox">, <input type="file">, <input type="image">,
<input type="password">, <input type="radio">, <input type="reset">, <input
type="submit">, <input type="text">, <isindex>, <kbd>, <label>, <legend>, <li>,
<listing>, <marquee>, <menu>, <ol>, <p>, <pre>, runtimeStyle, <s>, <samp>, <small>,
<span>, <strike>, <strong>, style, <sub>, <sup>, <table>, <tbody>, <td>,
<textarea>, <tfoot>, <th>, <thead>, <tr>, <tt>, <u>, <ul>, <var>, <xmp>
```

background-position-x

Compatibility: IE4, IE5, IE5.5, IE6

This style property defines the horizontal coordinate (the left position) of the element.

Syntax:

```
element { background-position-x: value }
elementID.style.backgroundPositionX = "value"
document.all.elementID.style.backgroundPositionX = "value"
```

Values: Same as for the background-position style property.
Example: See the background style example.
Applies to: Same as for the background-position style property.

background-position-y

Compatibility: IE4, IE5, IE5.5, IE6

This style property defines the vertical coordinate (the top position) of the element.

Syntax:

```
element { background-position-y: value }
elementID.style.backgroundPositionY = "value"
document.all.elementID.style.backgroundPositionY = "value"
```

Values: Same as for the background-position style property.

Example: See the background style example.

Applies to: Same as for the background-position style property.

background-repeat

Compatibility: NN6, NN7, IE4, IE5, IE5.5, IE6

This style property defines if and how the background image is repeated (tiled) on the page.

Syntax:

```
element {background-repeat: value }
elementID.style.backgroundRepeat = "value"
document.all.elementID.style.backgroundRepeat = "value" // IE only
```

Values:

repeat	The image is repeated both horizontally and vertically
no-repeat	The image is not repeated; only one copy of the image is drawn
repeat-x	The image is only repeated horizontally
repeat-y	The image is only repeated vertically

Example:

```
<head>
<style>
#myL {background-color:#ffccff; background-image:url("yourimage.jpg");
     height:100; background-repeat:repeat; }
</style>
</head>
<body bgcolor="#FFFFFF" text="#000000">
<div id="myL" style="width:236"></div>
</body></html>
```

Applies to:

`<a>`, `<address>`, `<b>`, `<big>`, `<blockquote>`, `<body>`, `<button>`, `<caption>`, `<center>`, `<cite>`, `<code>`, `<col>`, `<colgroup>`, currentStyle, `<custom>`, `<dd>`, defaults, `<dfn>`, `<dir>`, `<div>`, `<dl>`, `<dt>`, `<em>`, `<fieldset>`, `<form>`, `<hn>`, `<html>`, `<i>`, `<img>`, `<input type="button">`, `<input type="checkbox">`, `<input type="file">`, `<input type="image">`, `<input type="password">`, `<input type="radio">`, `<input type="reset">`, `<input type="submit">`, `<input type="text">`, `<isindex>`, `<kbd>`, `<label>`, `<legend>`, `<li>`, `<listing>`, `<marquee>`, `<menu>`, `<nobr>`, `<ol>`, `<p>`, `<pre>`, runtimeStyle, `<s>`, `<samp>`, `<small>`, `<span>`, `<strike>`, `<strong>`, style, `<sub>`, `<sup>`, `<table>`, `<tbody>`, `<td>`, `<textarea>`, `<tfoot>`, `<th>`, `<thead>`, `<tr>`, `<tt>`, `<u>`, `<ul>`, `<var>`, `<xmp>`

behavior

Compatibility: IE5, IE5.5, IE6

This style property defines the location of a behavior attached to an element. To specify multiple behaviors, separate each behavior with a space.

Syntax:

```
element { behavior: value }
elementID.style.behavior = "value"
document.all.elementID.style.behavior = "value"
```

Values:

url(*HTCpathname*)	The *pathname* can be an absolute or relative location
url(*#objectName*)	The behavior is defined in an <object> element embedded in the page
url(#default#*behaviorName*)	The URL identifies an IE default behavior by its name

Example:

```
<html xmlns:ie>
<head>
<style>@media all { IE\:homePage {behavior:url(#default#homepage)}}
</style>
</head><body bgcolor="#FFFFFF" text="#000000">
<ie:homepage id="HP" /><p><id="myL" a href="" onclick="goHomePage()">Navigate to
your home page</a></p>
</body></html>
```

Applies to:

<a>, <acronym>, <address>, <applet>, <area>, <b>, <base>, <basefont>, <bgsound>, <big>, <blockquote>, <body>, <button>, <caption>, <center>, <cite>, <code>, <col>, <colgroup>, <comment>, currentStyle, <custom>, <dd>, defaults, <del>, <dfn>, <dir>, <div>, <dl>, <dt>, <em>, <embed>, <fieldset>, <font>, <form>, <frame>, <frameset>, <head>, <hn>, <hr>, <html>, <i>, <iframe>, <img>, <input type="button">, <input type="checkbox">, <input type="file">, <input type="hidden">, <input type="image">, <input type="password">, <input type="radio">, <input type="reset">, <input type="submit">, <input type="text">, <ins>, <isindex>, <kbd>, <label>, <legend>, <li>, <link>, <listing>, <map>, <marquee>, <menu>, nextID, <nobr>, <noframes>, <noscript>, <object>, <ol>, <option>, <p>, <pre>, <q>, <rt>, <ruby>, runtimeStyle, <s>, <samp>, <script>, <select>, <small>, <span>, <strike>, <strong>, style, <sub>, <sup>, <table>, <tbody>, <td>, <textarea>, <tfoot>, <th>, <thead>, <title>, <tr>, <tt>, <u>, <ul>, <var>, <wbr>, <xml>, <xmp>

border

Compatibility: NN6, NN7, IE4, IE5, IE5.5, IE6

This style property is a shorthand property that defines three different border properties of the element: border-color, border-width, and border-style. The three property values are separated by blank spaces, and the order in which they are specified is irrelevant.

Syntax:

```
element { border: values }
elementID.style.border = "values"
document.all.elementID.style.border = "values" // IE only
```

Values: Same as for the border-color, border-width, and border-style style properties.

Example:

```
<html><head>
<style>
.style1 { border:3px solid blue;  font-family:verdana; font-weight:bold}
.style2 { border:"none";  font-family:verdana; font-weight:bold }
</style>
</head><body bgcolor="#FFFFFF" text="#000000">
<div id="myL" style="width:230; height:100; background-color:beige"
onmouseover="this.className='style1'"
onmouseout="this.className='style2'">This is a div element.</div>
</body></html>
```

Applies to:

```
<a>, <acronym>, <b>, <bdo>, <big>, <blockquote>, <body>, <button>, <caption>,
<center>, <cite>, <code>, <custom>, <dd>, defaults, <del>, <dfn>, <dir>, <div>,
<dl>, <dt>, <em>, <embed>, <fieldset>, <font>, <form>, <frame>, <hn>, <i>, <img>,
<input type="button">, <input type="checkbox">, <input type="file">, <input
type="image">, <input type="password">, <input type="radio">, <input type="reset">,
<input type="submit">, <input type="text">, <ins>, <isindex>, <kbd>, <label>, <li>,
<listing>, <marquee>, <menu>, <nobr>, <object>, <ol>, <p>, <pre>, <q>,
runtimeStyle, <s>, <samp>, <small>, <span>, <strike>, <strong>, style, <sub>,
<sup>, <table>, <td>, <textarea>, <th>, <tt>, <u>, <ul>, <var>, <xmp>
```

border-bottom, border-left, border-right, border-top

Compatibility: NN6, NN7, IE4, IE5, IE5.5, IE6

These style properties are shorthand properties that each define three different border properties of the element: color, width, and style. The syntax and example below apply to border-bottom, and define the values of the border-bottom-color, border-bottom-width, and border-bottom-style style properties. You can use border-left, border-right, and border-top in place of border-bottom in the syntax and the examples below.

Syntax:

```
element { border-bottom: values }
elementID.style.borderBottom = "values"
document.all.elementID.style.borderBottom = "values" // IE only
```

Values: Same as for the border-bottom-color, border-bottom-width, and border-bottom-style style properties.

Example:

```
<html><head>
<style>
.style1 { border:5px solid #cccccc;  border-bottom:5px solid red; font-
family:verdana; font-weight:bold}
.style2 { border:"none";  font-family:verdana; font-weight:bold }
</style>
</head><body bgcolor="#FFFFFF" text="#000000">
<div id="myL" style="width:230; height:100; background-color:beige"
onmouseover="this.className='style1'"
onmouseout="this.className='style2'">This is a div element.</div>
</body></html>
```

Applies to: Same as for the border style property.

border-bottom-color, border-left-color, border-right-color, border-top-color

Compatibility: NN6, NN7, IE4, IE5, IE5.5, IE6

These style properties define the color of the bottom, left, right, and top sides of the border.
   Syntax:

```
element { border-bottom-color: value }
elementID.style.borderTopColor = "value"
document.all.elementID.style.borderLeftColor = "value" // IE only
```

Values: Color name or hexadecimal value (#RRGGBB).
   Example:

```
<html><head>
<style>
.style1 { border:5px solid #cccccc;  border-bottom-color:red; font-family:verdana;
font-weight:bold}
.style2 { border:"none";  font-family:verdana; font-weight:bold }
</style>
</head><body bgcolor="#FFFFFF" text="#000000">
<div id="myL" style="width:230; height:100; background-color:beige"
onmouseover="this.className='style1'"
onmouseout="this.className='style2'">This is a div element.</div>
</body></html>
```

Applies to: Same as for the border style property.

border-bottom-style, border-left-style, border-right-style, border-top-style

Compatibility: NN6, NN7, IE4, IE5, IE5.5, IE6

These style properties define the styles for the bottom, left, right, and top sides of the border.

Syntax:

```
element { border-bottom-style: value }
elementID.style.borderTopStyle = "value"
document.all.elementID.style.borderRightStyle = "value" // IE only
```

Values:

none	Default value; no border is drawn
dashed	Dashed line
dotted	Dotted line
double	Double line (minimum size is 3px wide)
groove	3D groove
inset	3D inset
outset	3D outset
ridge	3D ridge
solid	Solid line

Example: See the example in `border-bottom-color`, and replace style1 with the following style:

```
.style1 { border:5px solid #cccccc;  border-bottom-style:dashed; font-family:verdana; font-weight:bold}
```

Applies to: Same as for the border style property.

border-bottom-width, border-left-width, border-right-width, border-top-width

Compatibility: NN6, NN7, IE4, IE5, IE5.5, IE6

These style properties define the width of the bottom, left, right, and top sides of the border.

Syntax:

```
element {border-bottom-width: value }
elementID.style.borderTopWidth = "value"
document.all.elementID.style.borderRightWidth = "value" // IE only
```

Values:

medium	Default value
thin	Thinner border than medium
thick	Thicker border than medium
length	A floating point number followed by a unit designator

Example: See the example in `border-bottom-color` and replace style1 with the following style:

```
.style1 { border:5px solid #cccccc;  border-bottom-width:6px; font-family:verdana;
font-weight:bold}
```

Applies to: Same as for the border style property.

border-collapse

Compatibility: NN6, NN7, IE5, IE5.5, IE6

This style property defines whether or not the borders of adjacent table elements
(cells, rows, and columns) are rendered with spacing.

Syntax:

```
element { border-collapse: value }
elementID.style.borderCollapse = "value"
document.all.elementID.style.borderCollapse = "value" // IE only
```

Values: collapse (no space between borders), separate (the default; borders
are rendered separately).

Example:

```
<table id="myEle" border="1" style="border-collapse:collapse">
<tr><td>column 1</td><td>column 2</td><td>column 3</td></tr>
<tr><td>cell 1</td><td>cell 2</td><td>cell 3</td></tr>
<tr><td>cell 1</td><td>cell 2</td><td>cell 3</td></tr>
</table>
<button onclick="myEle.style.borderCollapse='separate'">separate</button>
<button onclick="myEle.style.borderCollapse='collapse'">collapse</button>
```

Applies to: Same as for the border style property.

border-color

Compatibility: NN4, NN6, NN7, IE4, IE5, IE5.5, IE6

This style property defines multiple border colors.

Syntax:

```
element { border-color: value }
elementID.style.borderColor = "value"
document.all.elementID.style.borderColor = "value" // IE only
```

Values: Color names (delimited by a space) for one to four rectangle sides
(IE only). Supply one value (the same color for all sides), two values (top and
bottom sides use the first value, left and right use the second value), three values
(top uses the first, right and left use the second, bottom uses the third value), or
four values (top, right, bottom, and left, in that order).

Example: See the border-bottom-color example and replace style1 with the
following:

```
.style1 { border:5px solid #cccccc;  border-color:red; font-family:verdana; font-
weight:bold}
```

Applies to: Same as for the border style property.

border-style

Compatibility: NN4, NN6, NN7, IE4, IE5, IE5.5, IE6

This style property defines the style for all sides of the border.
Syntax:

```
element { border-style: value }
elementID.style.borderStyle = "value"
document.all.elementID.style.borderStyle = "value" // IE only
```

Values: Same as for the `border-bottom-style` style property.
Example: See the `border-bottom-color` example and replace `style1` with the
following:

```
.style1 { border:5px solid #cccccc;  border-style:dashed; font-family:verdana;
font-weight:bold}
```

Applies to: Same as for the border style property.

border-width

Compatibility: NN4, NN6, NN7, IE4, IE5, IE5.5, IE6

This style property defines the width for all sides of the border.
Syntax:

```
element { border-width: value }
elementID.style.borderWidth = "value"
document.all.elementID.style.borderWidth = "value" // IE only
```

Values: Same as for the `border-bottom-width` style property.
Example: See the `border-bottom-color` example, and replace `style1` with the
following:

```
.style1 { border:5px solid #cccccc;  border-width:6px; font-family:verdana; font-
weight:bold}
```

Applies to: Same as for the border style property.

bottom

Compatibility: NN6, NN7, IE4, IE5, IE5.5, IE6

This style property defines the bottom position of the element relative to the
bottom edge of the next element in the page.

Syntax:

```
element { bottom: value }
elementID.style.bottom = "value"
document.all.elementID.style.bottom = "value" // IE only
```

Values: These values are strings and cannot be used for calculations.

auto	The default; regular positioning is used
length	A floating-point number followed by a unit designator
percentage	An integer followed by a percent sign, which signals a position relative to the height of the parent object

Example:

```
<html><head>
<style>
#secL { position:absolute; }
.style1 { bottom:100px!important; }
.style2 { bottom:auto!important; }
</style>
</head><body bgcolor="#FFFFFF" text="#000000">
<img id="myL" src="yourImage.jpg" width="79" height="99"
onClick="this.className='style2';return false"
onMouseOver="this.className='style1'" style="position:absolute; cursor:hand;
z-index=5">
</body></html>
```

Applies to:

```
<a>, <address>, <applet>, <b>, <big>, <blockquote>, <button>, <center>, <cite>,
<code>, currentStyle, <custom>, <dd>, defaults, <dfn>, <dir>, <div>, <dl>,
<fieldset>, <font>, <form>, <hn>, <hr>, <i>, <iframe>, <img>, <input
type="button">, <input type="checkbox">, <input type="file">, <input type="image">,
<input type="password">, <input type="radio">, <input type="reset">, <input
type="submit">, <input type="text">, <isindex>, <kbd>, <label>, <legend>, <li>,
<listing>, <marquee>, <menu>, <object>, <ol>, <p>, <pre>, runtimeStyle, <s>,
<samp>, <select>, <small>, <span>, <strike>, <strong>, style, <sub>, <sup>,
<table>, <textarea>, <tt>, <u>, <ul>, <var>, <xmp>
```

clear

Compatibility: NN4, NN6, NN7, IE4, IE5, IE5.5, IE6

This style property establishes whether the element allows other floating objects on its sides.

Syntax:

```
element { clear: value }
elementID.style.clear = "value"
document.all.elementID.style.clear = "value" // IE only
```

Values:

both	No floating objects are allowed on the left and right sides
left	The left side is kept clear
right	The right side is kept clear
none	The default; floating objects are allowed on the left and right sides

Example:

```
<html><head>
<style>#secL { position:absolute; }
.style1 { clear:left!important; }
.style2 { clear:none!important; }
</style>
</head><body bgcolor="#FFFFFF" text="#000000">
<img src="yourImage.jpg" width="71" height="99" style="float:left">
<a id="myL" href="" onClick="this.className='style2';return false"
onMouseOver="this.className='style1'">Disabled link</a>
<img src="yourImage2.jpg" alt="This is a float=right image" width="79" height="99">
</body></html>
```

Applies to:

```
<a>, <address>, <applet>, <b>, <big>, <blockquote>, <button>, <caption>, <center>,
<cite>, <code>, <col>, <colgroup>, currentStyle, <custom>, <dd>, defaults, <dfn>,
<dir>, <div>, <dl>, <dt>, <em>, <embed>, <fieldset>, <form>, <hn>, <hr>, <i>,
<iframe>, <img>, <input type="button">, <input type="checkbox">, <input
type="file">, <input type="image">, <input type="password">, <input type="radio">,
<input type="reset">, <input type="submit">, <input type="text">, <isindex>, <kbd>,
<label>, <legend>, <li>, <listing>, <marquee>, <menu>, <object>, <ol>, <option>,
<p>, <pre>, runtimeStyle, <s>, <samp>, <select>, <small>, <span>, <strike>,
<strong>, style, <sub>, <sup>, <table>, <tbody>, <td>, <textarea>, <tfoot>, <th>,
<thead>, <tr>, <tt>, <u>, <ul>, <var>, <xmp>
```

clip

Compatibility: NN4, NN6, NN7, IE4, IE5, IE5.5, IE6

This style property defines a clipping region (the area of the element outside of the clipping region is not displayed) for an element using absolute positioning. If you want to clip only one of the bottom, left, right, and top regions of an element, you can use the JavaScript properties clipBottom, clipLeft, clipRight, and clipTop.

Syntax:

```
element { clip: values }
elementID.style.clip = "values"
document.all.elementID.style.clip = "values" // IE only
```

Values:

auto	The default; the element is not clipped and is rendered complete.
rect(*top right bottom left***)**	The size of the region to clip is specified in the order shown, and each of the four values is a floating-point number followed by a unit designator (see "Units of Measurement Used in Attributes" in Chapter 1). Any of these values can be replaced by auto, leaving that side unclipped, but all four values must be present for the clipping to be accurate.

Example:

```
<img id="myImg" src="yourimage.gif" height="80" width="120" border="0"
style="position:absolute;top:200px;left:375px">
<center>
<button onclick="myImg.style.clip='rect(25px auto auto auto)'">Applying top value</
button>
<button onclick="myImg.style.clip='rect(auto 100px auto auto)'">Applying right
value</button>
<button onclick="myImg.style.clip='rect(auto auto 60px auto)'">Applying bottom
value</button>
<button onclick="myImg.style.clip='rect(auto auto auto 50px)'">Applying left
value</button>
<button style="position:absolute;top:250px;left:450px"
onclick="myImg.style.clip='rect(auto)'">Restore image</button>
```

Applies to:

```
<a>, <address>, <applet>, <b>, <bdo>, <big>, <blockquote>, <button>, <center>,
<cite>, <code>, <custom>, <dd>, defaults, <dfn>, <dir>, <div>, <dl>, <dt>, <em>,
<embed>, <fieldset>, <form>, <hn>, <hr>, <i>, <iframe>, <img>, <input
type="button">, <input type="checkbox">, <input type="file">, <input type="image">,
<input type="password">, <input type="radio">, <input type="reset">, <input
type="submit">, <input type="text">, <isindex>, <kbd>, <label>, <legend>, <li>,
<listing>, <marquee>, <menu>, <object>, <ol>, <p>, <pre>, <ruby>, runtimeStyle,
<s>, <samp>, <select>, <small>, <span>, <strike>, <strong>, style, <sub>, <sup>,
<table>, <td>, <textarea>, <th>, <tr>, <tt>, <u>, <ul>, <var>, <xmp>
```

color

Compatibility: NN4, NN6, NN7, IE4, IE5, IE5.5, IE6

This style property defines the color of the text of the element.

Syntax:

```
element { color: value }
elementID.style.color = "value"
document.all.elementID.style.color = "value" // IE only
```

Values: Color name or hexadecimal value (#RRGGBB).

Example:

```
<head><style>
.style1 { font-family:verdana; color:purple }
</style></head>
<body bgcolor="#FFFFFF" text="#000000">
<p class="style1">A color style rule has been applied to this text.</p>
</body>
```

Applies to:

`<a>`, `<address>`, `<applet>`, `<b>`, `<big>`, `<blockquote>`, `<body>`, `<button>`, `<caption>`, `<center>`, `<cite>`, `<code>`, `<col>`, `<colgroup>`, currentStyle, `<custom>`, `<dd>`, defaults, `<dfn>`, `<dir>`, `<div>`, `<dl>`, `<dt>`, `<em>`, `<fieldset>`, `<form>`, `<hn>`, `<html>`, `<i>`, `<input type="button">`, `<input type="checkbox">`, `<input type="file">`, `<input type="image">`, `<input type="password">`, `<input type="radio">`, `<input type="reset">`, `<input type="submit">`, `<input type="text">`, `<isindex>`, `<kbd>`, `<label>`, `<legend>`, `<li>`, `<listing>`, `<marquee>`, `<menu>`, `<nobr>`, `<ol>`, `<option>`, `<p>`, `<pre>`, runtimeStyle, `<s>`, `<samp>`, `<select>`, `<small>`, `<span>`, `<strike>`, `<strong>`, style, `<sub>`, `<sup>`, `<table>`, `<tbody>`, `<td>`, `<textarea>`, `<tfoot>`, `<th>`, `<thead>`, `<tr>`, `<tt>`, `<u>`, `<ul>`, `<var>`, `<xmp>`

cursor

Compatibility: NN6, NN7, IE4, IE5, IE5.5, IE6

This style property specifies the type of cursor to be displayed when the mouse pointer hovers over the element.

Syntax:

```
element { cursor: value }
elementID.style.cursor = "value"
document.all.elementID.style.cursor = "value" // IE only
```

Values:

all-scroll	(IE6+) The cursor has four arrows pointing up, down, left, and right. When this cursor is present, the user can scroll the element in any direction.
auto	The default; the browser determines the cursor to display based on the current element. The browser may set the cursor to be an arrow, hand, question mark, crosshair, or any other cursors listed here.
col-resize	(IE6+) The cursor contains left and right arrows separated by a vertical bar. When this cursor is present, the user can resize the element horizontally.
crosshair	The cursor is a crosshair.
move	Crossed arrows, indicating that you can move an object on the screen.
default	The cursor is operating system dependent, usually an arrow pointer.

hand	The cursor is a hand with the index finger pointing up, usually used when the pointer moves over a link.
help	The cursor has an arrow with a question mark. When this cursor is displayed, the user can obtain help by clicking with it.
no-drop	(IE6 only) The cursor is a hand with a small stop sign.
not-allowed	(IE6 only) The cursor is a small stop sign.
pointer	(IE6 only) Same as hand.
progress	(IE6 only) The cursor is an arrow with an hourglass next to it.
row-resize	(IE6 only) The cursor contains up and down arrows connected by a horizontal line. This indicates that the user can resize the element vertically.
text, vertical-text	(IE6 only) The cursor is an I-bar indicating that the text in the element can be edited.
url	(IE6 only) This specifies the location of the cursor file.
wait	The cursor is an hourglass or watch.
n-resize, ne-resize, nw-resize, s-resize, se-resize, sw-resize, e-resize, w-resize	The cursor is an arrow pointing to any of the eight compass directions (with "north" being the top of the screen). The user can resize the element in the direction pointed to by the cursor.

Example:

```
<div class="explanations" style="background-color:#dddddd; cursor:hand;">Move the
mouse over this element.</div>
```

Applies to:

```
<a>, <address>, <applet>, <b>, <big>, <blockquote>, <body>, <caption>, <center>,
<cite>, <code>, <col>, <colgroup>, currentStyle, <custom>, <dd>, defaults, <dfn>,
<dir>, <div>, <dl>, <dt>, <em>, <embed>, <fieldset>, <form>, <hn>, <hr>, <html>,
<i>, <iframe>, <img>, <input type="button">, <input type="checkbox">, <input
type="file">, <input type="image">, <input type="password">, <input type="radio">,
<input type="reset">, <input type="submit">, <input type="text">, <kbd>, <label>,
<legend>, <li>, <listing>, <marquee>, <menu>, <object>, <ol>, <p>, <pre>, <rt>,
<ruby>, runtimeStyle, <s>, <samp>, <small>, <span>, <strike>, <strong>, style,
<sub>, <sup>, <table>, <tbody>, <td>, <textarea>, <tfoot>, <th>, <thead>, <tr>,
<tt>, <u>, <ul>, <var>, <xmp>
```

direction

Compatibility: NN6, NN7, IE5, IE5.5, IE6

This style property defines the reading order of the element. In addition, this property can be used to specify the direction of the table column layout and the direction of the horizontal overflow.

NOTE *The property does not affect the directional flow of alphanumeric characters in documents that use the Latin alphabet; these characters will always be displayed from left to right.*

Syntax:

```
element { direction: value }
elementID.style.direction = "value"
document.all.elementID.style.direction = "value" // IE only
```

Values:

ltr	The default; left to right
rtl	Right to left
inherit	Direction is inherited from container element

Example:

```
<body>
<input type="button" onclick="myDiv.style.direction=event.srcElement.value;"
value="rtl">
    <input type="button" onclick="myDiv.style.direction=event.srcElement.value;"
value="ltr">
<div id=myDiv style="background:aqua; padding:10px;" class="explanations">The
following may be the most boring three lines of sample code that you will ever read
in your life. But you will at least understand how this style works. The following
may be the most boring three lines of sample code that you will ever read in your
life. But you will at least understand how this style works.</div>
</body>
```

Applies to:

```
<a>, <acronym>, <address>, <b>, <bdo>, <big>, <blockquote>, <body>, <button>,
<caption>, <center>, <cite>, <code>, <col>, <colgroup>, currentStyle, <custom>,
<dd>, defaults, <del>, <dfn>, <dir>, <div>, <dl>, <dt>, <em>, <embed>, <fieldset>,
<font>, <form>, <hn>, <i>, <img>, <input type="button">, <input type="checkbox">,
<input type="file">, <input type="image">, <input type="password">, <input
type="radio">, <input type="reset">, <input type="submit">, <input type="text">,
<ins>, <kbd>, <label>, <legend>, <li>, <listing>, <menu>, <nobr>, <object>, <ol>,
<option>, <p>, <pre>, <q>, <rt>, <ruby>, runtimeStyle, <s>, <samp>, <select>,
<small>, <span>, <strike>, <strong>, style, <sub>, <sup>, <table>, <tbody>, <td>,
<textarea>, <tfoot>, <th>, <thead>, <tr>, <tt>, <u>, <ul>, <var>, <xmp>
```

display

Compatibility: NN4, NN6, NN7, IE4, IE5, IE5.5, IE6

This style property defines whether or not the element is to be rendered. If the element is not rendered, it occupies no space on the page, unlike an element with a visibility property value of false, which occupies space even though it is not visible.

Syntax:

```
element { display: value }
elementID.style.display = "value"
document.all.elementID.style.display = "value" // IE only
```

Values:

block	This value causes an element to be rendered as a block element, with border features, that occupies a new line.
inline	The default; this value causes an element to generate one or more boxes without occupying a new line.
none	The element is not rendered.
compact	This value creates either a block or an inline element, depending on the content of the element.
inline-block	The element is rendered inline, but the contents of the element are rendered as a block element with border features.
list-item	(IE6+) This value causes an element to generate a principal block box and list-item inline box with border features.
table-header-group	This value displays the element as a table header group.
table-footer-group	This value displays the element as a table footer group.

Example:

```
<head>
<style>
.style1 { display:none }
</style>
<script language="JavaScript">
function fn1() {
    item1.style.display="";
    item2.style.display="none";
    item3.style.display="none";
    }
function fn2() {
    item1.style.display="none";
    item2.style.display="";
    item3.style.display="none";
    }
function fn3_1() {
    item1.style.display="none";
    item2.style.display="none";
    item3.style.display="";
    }
function fn5() {
    item1.style.display="";
    item2.style.display="";
    item3.style.display="";
    }
```

```
function fn6() {
    item1_1.style.visibility="visible";
    item2_1.style.visibility="visible";
    item3_1.style.visibility="visible";
    }
</script>
</head>
<body bgcolor="#FFFFFF" text="#000000">
<ul>
        <li onclick="className='style1'">Item 1 - Double-click me</li>
        <li onclick="className='style1'">Item 2</li>
        <li onclick="className='style1'">Item 3</li>
        <li onclick="className='style1'">Item 4</li>
        <li onclick="className='style1'">Item 5</li>
</ul>
<!--JavaScript -->
<table cellspacing=5 cellpadding=5 border=2>
<th>Vehicles</th><th>Potency</th><th>Speed</th>
<tr id="item1"><td>Cars</td>
<td id="item1_1">180 H.P.</td>
<td>High</td></tr>
<tr id="item2"><td>Cycles</td>
<td id="item2_1">250 c.c.</td>
<td>High</td></tr>
<tr id="item3"><td>Bicycles</td>
<td id="item3_1">1 H.P.</td>
<td>Slow</td></tr>
</table>
<p>
<input type=button style="width:175" onclick="fn1()" value="Show Cars">
<input type=button style="width:175" onclick="fn2()" value="Show Cycles">
<input type=button style="width:175" onclick="fn3_1()" value="Show Bicycles">
<input type=button style="width:175" onclick="fn6();fn5()" value="Reset">
</body>
```

Applies to:

<a>, <acronym>, <address>, <applet>, <b>, <bdo>, <big>, <blockquote>, <body>, <br>,
<button>, <caption>, <center>, <cite>, <code>, <col>, <colgroup>, currentStyle,
<custom>, <dd>, defaults, <del>, <dfn>, <dir>, <div>, <dl>, <dt>, <em>, <embed>,
<fieldset>, <font>, <form>, <frame>, <hn>, <hr>, <html>, <i>, <iframe>, <img>,
<input type="button">, <input type="checkbox">, <input type="file">, <input
type="image">, <input type="password">, <input type="radio">, <input type="reset">,
<input type="submit">, <input type="text">, <ins>, <kbd>, <label>, <legend>, <li>,
<listing>, <marquee>, <menu>, <nobr>, <object>, <ol>, <p>, <pre>, <q>, <rt>,
<ruby>, <s>, <samp>, <select>, <small>, <span>, <strike>, <strong>, style, <sub>,
<sup>, <table>, <tbody>, <td>, <textarea>, <tfoot>, <th>, <thead>, <tr>, <tt>, <u>,
<ul>, <var>, <xmp>

filter

Compatibility: IE5.5, IE6

This property can be used to specify the filter or collection of filters of an element. For more information, see Chapter 10.

Syntax:

```
element { filter: value }
elementID.style.filter = "value"
document.all.elementID.style.filter = "value"
```

Example:

```
<script language="JavaScript">
function fn1(elem) {
    elem.style.filter="blendTrans(duration=1)";
        elem.filters.blendTrans.Apply();
        elem.style.visibility="hidden";
        elem.filters.blendTrans.Play();
elem.filters.percent=30;
}
function fn2(elem) {
    elem.style.filter="blendTrans(duration=1)";
        elem.filters.blendTrans.Apply();
        elem.style.visibility="visible";
        elem.filters.blendTrans.Play();
elem.filters.percent=70;
}
</script>
</head>
<body bgcolor="#FFFFFF" text="#000000">
<img id="myImg" src=" yourImg.jpg">
  <button onclick="fn1(yourImg)">Cause the image to fade out</button>
  <button onclick="fn2(yourImg)">Cause the image to fade in</button>
</body>
```

Applies to:

```
<a>, <acronym>, <address>, <b>, <bdo>, <big>, <blockquote>, <body>, <button>,
<caption>, <center>, <cite>, <code>, <custom>, <dd>, <del>, <dfn>, <dir>, <div>,
<dl>, <dt>, <em>, <fieldset>, <font>, <form>, <frame>, <frameset>, <hn>, <i>,
<iframe>, <img>, <input type="button">, <input type="checkbox">, <input
type="file">, <input type="image">, <input type="password">, <input type="radio">,
<input type="reset">, <input type="submit">, <input type="text">, <ins>, <kbd>,
<label>, <legend>, <li>, <marquee>, <menu>, <nobr>, <ol>, <p>, <pre>, <q>, <rt>,
<ruby>, <s>, <samp>, <small>, <span>, <strike>, <strong>, <sub>, <sup>, <table>,
<td>, <textarea>, <th>, <tt>, <u>, <ul>, <var>, <xmp>
```

float

Compatibility: NN4, NN6, NN7, IE4, IE5, IE5.5, IE6

This CSS-only style property specifies whether the text on the page will flow to the left of an element, right of an element, or not at all. This can be used for elements that are not using absolute positioning. This CSS attribute is equivalent to the styleFloat JavaScript property.

Syntax:

```
element { float: value }
```

Values: left, right, and none.

Example:

```
<img id="myImg1" src="yourimage.gif" border="0" style="float:left">
<p style="font-family:verdana; width=200; cursor:hand">Move the mouse pointer
here</p>
<button onclick="myImg1.style.styleFloat='right'">Change float to right</button>
```

Applies to:

```
<a>, <address>, <applet>, <b>, <big>, <blockquote>, <button>, <center>, <cite>,
<code>, currentStyle, <custom>, <dd>, defaults, <dfn>, <dir>, <div>, <dl>, <dt>,
<em>, <embed>, <fieldset>, <form>, <hn>, <hr>, <i>, <iframe>, <img>, <input
type="button">, <input type="checkbox">, <input type="file">, <input type="image">,
<input type="password">, <input type="radio">, <input type="reset">, <input
type="submit">, <input type="text">, <isindex>, <kbd>, <label>, <legend>, <li>,
<listing>, <marquee>, <menu>, <object>, <ol>, <p>, <pre>, <rt>, <ruby>,
runtimeStyle, <s>, <samp>, <select>, <small>, <span>, <strike>, <strong>, style,
<sub>, <sup>, <table>, <textarea>, <tt>, <u>, <ul>, <var>, <xmp>
```

font

Compatibility: NN6, NN7, IE4, IE5, IE5.5, IE6

This style property is a shorthand property that establishes the values of one or more font style properties: font-family, font-style, font-size, font-variant, font-weight, and line-height.

Syntax:

```
element { font: values }
elementID.style.font = "value"
document.all.elementID.style.font = "values" // IE only
```

Values: See the font-family, font-style, font-size, font-variant, font-weight, and line-height style properties. Additionally, you can use the following CSS font constants for which the browser has default settings:

caption	The font used for captioned controls (buttons, drop-downs, and so on)
icon	The font used by the browser to label icons
menu	The font the browser uses for menus and drop-down lists
message-box	The font used by the browser for dialog boxes
small-caption	The font used for labeling small controls
status-bar	The font used in the window status bars

Example:

```
<div style="background:#e4e4e4; padding:10px; font:italic normal bolder 12pt
verdana">
This element has a font style attribute value of: "italic normal bolder 12pt
verdana".</div>
  <hr>
  <div style="background:#e4e4e4; padding:10px;"
onmouseover="this.style.font='italic small-caps bold 12pt serif'"
onmouseout="this.style.font='normal normal normal normal medium times new
roman'">Move the mouse pointer over this element to change the font style.</div>
```

Applies to:

```
<a>, <address>, <b>, <big>, <blockquote>, <body>, <button>, <caption>, <center>,
<cite>, <code>, <col>, <colgroup>, <custom>, <dd>, defaults, <dfn>, <dir>, <div>,
<dl>, <dt>, <em>, <fieldset>, <form>, <hn>, <html>, <i>, <img>, <input
type="button">, <input type="checkbox">, <input type="file">, <input type="image">,
<input type="password">, <input type="radio">, <input type="reset">, <input
type="submit">, <input type="text">, <isindex>, <kbd>, <label>, <legend>, <li>,
<listing>, <marquee>, <menu>, <nobr>, <ol>, <p>, <pre>, runtimeStyle, <s>, <samp>,
<select>, <small>, <span>, <strike>, <strong>, style, <sub>, <sup>, <table>,
<tbody>, <td>, <textarea>, <tfoot>, <th>, <thead>, <tr>, <tt>, <u>, <ul>, <var>,
<xmp>
```

font-family

Compatibility: NN4, NN6, NN7, IE4, IE5, IE5.5, IE6

This style property specifies which font family is to be used to render the text.
   Syntax:

```
element { font-family: value }
elementID.style.fontFamily = "value"
document.all.elementID.style.fontFamily = "value" // IE only
```

Values: Any of the available font families supported by the browser's
operating system. For example, Times, Helvetica, Zapf-Chancery, Western,
Courier, serif, sans-serif, cursive, fantasy, or monospace.
   Example:

```
<div onmouseover="this.style.fontFamily='arial'"
onmouseout="this.style.fontFamily='times'">Move the mouse pointer over this element
to change the font-family value.</div>
```

Applies to:

```
<a>, <address>, <b>, <basefont>, <big>, <blockquote>, <body>, <button>, <caption>,
<center>, <cite>, <code>, <col>, <colgroup>, currentStyle, <custom>, <dd>,
defaults, <dfn>, <dir>, <div>, <dl>, <dt>, <em>, <fieldset>, <form>, <hn>, <html>,
<i>, <img>, <input type="button">, <input type="checkbox">, <input type="file">,
<input type="image">, <input type="password">, <input type="radio">, <input
```

type="reset">, <input type="submit">, <input type="text">, <isindex>, <kbd>, <label>, <legend>, <li>, <listing>, <marquee>, <menu>, <ol>, <p>, <pre>, runtimeStyle, <s>, <samp>, <select>, <small>, <span>, <strike>, <strong>, style, <sub>, <sup>, <table>, <tbody>, <td>, <textarea>, <tfoot>, <th>, <thead>, <tr>, <tt>, <u>, <ul>, <var>, <xmp>

font-size

Compatibility: NN4, NN6, NN7, IE4, IE5, IE5.5, IE6

This style property defines the font size of the text.

Syntax:

```
element { font-size: value }
elementID.style.fontSize = "value"
document.all.elementID.style.fontSize = "value" // IE only
```

Values:

absolute	Any of the following values: xx-small, x-small, small, medium, large, x-large, and xx-large
relative	The size of the font is relative to the font size of the parent element, values are either larger or smaller
length	A floating point number followed by a unit designator
percentage	An integer followed by a percent sign, which specifies the size relative to the parent element's font size

Example:

```
<p style="font-size:14pt">This text will be rendered in 14pt size.</p>
<hr>
<div style="background:#e4e4e4; padding:10px;"
onmouseover="this.style.fontSize='16pt'"
onmouseout="this.style.fontSize='12pt'">
Move the mouse pointer over this element to change the font-size value.</div>
```

Applies to: Same as for the font-family style property.

font-style

Compatibility: NN4, NN6, NN7, IE4, IE5, IE5.5, IE6

This style property determines the font style of the text.

Syntax:

```
element { font-style: value }
elementID.style.fontStyle = "value"
document.all.elementID.style.fontStyle = "value" // IE only
```

Values: normal (the default), italic, and oblique (the last two are IE only).

Example:

```
<div onmouseover="this.style.fontStyle='italic'"
onmouseout="this.style.fontStyle='normal'">Move the mouse pointer over this element
to change the font style value.</div>
```

Applies to: Same as for the `font-family` style property.

font-variant

Compatibility: NN6, NN7, IE4, IE5, IE5.5, IE6

This style property indicates whether the text is to be rendered using small capital letters for lowercase characters.

The `font-family` specified may support normal, small-caps, or both types of glyph. The `font-variant` style property is used to request an appropriate glyph, provided that the `font-family` supports both glyph variants.

Syntax:

```
element { font-variant: value }
elementID.style.fontVariant = "value"
document.all.elementID.style.fontVariant = "value" // IE only
```

Values: `normal` and `small-caps`.

Example:

```
<div font-size:16pt"
onmouseover="this.style.fontVariant='small-caps'"
onmouseout="this.style.fontVariant='normal'">
Move the mouse pointer over this element to change the font-variant value.</div>
```

Applies to:

```
<a>, <address>, <b>, <big>, <blockquote>, <body>, <button>, <caption>, <center>,
<cite>, <code>, <col>, <colgroup>, currentStyle, <custom>, <dd>, defaults, <dfn>,
<dir>, <div>, <dl>, <dt>, <em>, <fieldset>, <form>, <hn>, <html>, <i>, <img>,
<input type="button">, <input type="checkbox">, <input type="file">, <input
type="image">, <input type="password">, <input type="radio">, <input type="reset">,
<input type="submit">, <input type="text">, <isindex>, <kbd>, <label>, <legend>,
<li>, <listing>, <marquee>, <menu>, <ol>, <p>, <pre>, runtimeStyle, <s>, <samp>,
<small>, <span>, <strike>, <strong>, style, <sub>, <sup>, <table>, <tbody>, <td>,
<textarea>, <tfoot>, <th>, <thead>, <tr>, <tt>, <u>, <ul>, <var>, <xmp>
```

font-weight

Compatibility: NN4, NN6, NN7, IE4, IE5, IE5.5, IE6

This style property defines the boldness or lightness of the font used to render the text.

Syntax:

```
element { font-weight: value }
elementID.style.fontWeight = "value"
document.all.elementID.style.fontWeight = "value" // IE only
```

Relative values: normal (the default), bold, bolder, and lighter.

Constant values: 100, 200, 300 (lighter than normal), 400 (normal), 500, 600 (bolder than normal), 700 (bold), 800, 900 (even bolder).

Example:

```
<div style="font-size:16pt "onmouseover="this.style.fontWeight='bold'"
onmouseout="this.style.fontWeight='normal'">Move the mouse pointer over this
element to change the font-weight value.</div>
```

Applies to: Same as for the font-family style property.

hasLayout (*)

Compatibility: IE5.5, IE6

This read-only JavaScript-only style property indicates whether the element has a layout.

Syntax:

```
elementID.currentStyle.hasLayout = "value"
```

Values: true and false (the default). The following style properties can cause an element to have layout: display (values: inline or block), height, float (values: left or right), position (value: absolute), width, writing-mode (value: tb-rl), and zoom.

Example:

```
<div align="left" id="myDiv1" style="width:70%; background-color:aqua"
onMouseOver="alert('hasLayout property value: '+this.currentStyle.hasLayout)">The
width of this div element is 70% of the page.</div><br>
<div align="left" id="myDiv2" style="background-color:aqua"
onMouseOver="alert('hasLayout property value: '+this.currentStyle.hasLayout)">This
div element has no layout or positioning set.</div>
```

Applies to:

```
<a>, <address>, <b>, <big>, <blockquote>, <body>, <button>, <caption>, <center>,
<cite>, <code>, <col>, <colgroup>, currentStyle, <custom>, <dd>, defaults, <dfn>,
<dir>, <div>, <dl>, <dt>, <em>, <fieldset>, <form>, <hn>, <html>, <i>, <img>,
<input type="button">, <input type="checkbox">, <input type="file">, <input
type="image">, <input type="password">, <input type="radio">, <input type="reset">,
<input type="submit">, <input type="text">, <isindex>, <kbd>, <label>, <legend>,
<li>, <listing>, <marquee>, <menu>, <ol>, <p>, <pre>, runtimeStyle, <s>, <samp>,
<select>, <small>, <span>, <strike>, <strong>, style, <sub>, <sup>, <table>,
<tbody>, <td>, <textarea>, <tfoot>, <th>, <thead>, <tr>, <tt>, <u>, <ul>, <var>,
<xmp>
```

Compatibility: NN4, NN6, NN7, IE4, IE5, IE5.5, IE6

This style property sets and retrieves the element's content height. This property does not take into consideration the size of borders, padding, or margins.

Syntax:

```
element { height: value }
elementID.style.height = "value"
document.all.elementID.style.height = "value" // IE only
```

Values:

auto	The height is set automatically
integer	Specifies a fixed height with a number followed by a unit designator
percentage	Represents the percent of the height of the element's container element with an integer followed by a percent sign

Example:

```
<p><img id="myImg" src=".yourimage.jpg" style="width:74; height:100"></p>
<input type="button" value="Reduce height" onclick="myImg.style.height=50">
<input type="button" value="Restore height" onclick="myImg.style.height=100">
```

Applies to:

```
<a>, <acronym>, <address>, <applet>, <b>, <bdo>, <big>, <blockquote>, <button>,
<caption>, <center>, <cite>, <code>, currentStyle, <custom>, <dd>, <del>, <dfn>,
<dir>, <div>, <dl>, <dt>, <em>, <embed>, <fieldset>, <font>, <form>, <frame>,
<frameset>, <hn>, <hr>, <i>, <iframe>, <img>, <input type="button">, <input
type="checkbox">, <input type="file">, <input type="image">, <input
type="password">, <input type="radio">, <input type="reset">, <input
type="submit">, <input type="text">, <ins>, <kbd>, <label>, <legend>, <li>,
<listing>, <marquee>, <menu>, <nobr>, <object>, <ol>, <option>, <p>, <pre>, <q>,
<rt>, <ruby>, runtimeStyle, <s>, <samp>, <select>, <small>, <span>, <strike>,
<strong>, style, <sub>, <sup>, <table>, <td>, <textarea>, <th>, <tr>, <tt>, <u>,
<ul>, <var>, <xmp>
```

ime-mode

Compatibility: IE5, IE5.5, IE6

This style property defines the mode of an Input Method Editor (IME), a special device for writing Chinese, Japanese, and Korean scripts.

Syntax:

```
element { ime-mode: value }
elementID.style.imeMode = "value"
document.all.elementID.style.imeMode = "value"
```

Values: auto, active, inactive, and disabled.

Example:

```
<input id="myInput" type="text" size=60 value='This input control has ime-mode
property set to "inactive"'>
<button onclick="myInput.style.imeMode='active'">Set imeMode property to active</
button>
<button onclick="myInput.style.imeMode='inactive'">Set imeMode property to
inactive</button>
```

NOTE *In order for the example to work, you must use Chinese, Japanese, or Korean writing and have a browser that can display these languages.*

Applies to:

currentStyle, <input type="text">, runtimeStyle, style, <textarea>

layout-flow

Compatibility: IE5.5, IE6

This style property specifies the flow direction of the element's content. Use of the writing-mode style property is favored over use of layout-flow.

Syntax:

```
element { layout-flow: value }
elementID.style.layoutFlow = "value"
document.all.elementID.style.layoutFlow = "value"
```

Values: horizontal (content flows from left to right) and vertical-ideographic (content flows from top to bottom, as in East Asian typography).

Example:

```
<p id="myP">This text has a regular horizontal flow</p>
<button onclick="myP.style.layoutFlow='vertical-ideographic';myP.innerText=
'This text has a vertical-ideographic flow'">Set layoutFlow to vertical-ideographic
</button>
```

Applies to:

```
<a>, <acronym>, <address>, <b>, <big>, <blockquote>, <button>, <caption>, <center>,
<cite>, <code>, currentStyle, <custom>, <dd>, <del>, <dfn>, <dir>, <div>, <dl>,
<dt>, <em>, <fieldset>, <font>, <form>, <hn>, <hr>, <i>, <input>, <input
type="button">, <input type="checkbox">, <input type="file">, <input
type="hidden">, <input type="image">, <input type="password">, <input
type="radio">, <input type="reset">, <input type="submit">, <input type="text">,
<ins>, <isindex>, <kbd>, <label>, <legend>, <li>, <marquee>, <menu>, <ol>,
<option>, <p>, <pre>, <q>, <ruby>, runtimeStyle, <s>, <samp>, <select>, <small>,
<span>, <strike>, <strong>, style, <sub>, <sup>, <td>, <textarea>, <th>, <tt>, <u>,
<ul>, <var>
```

layout-grid

Compatibility: IE5, IE5.5, IE6

This style property is a shorthand that establishes four different object-grid space-delimited style properties: layout-grid-mode, layout-grid-type, layout-grid-line, and layout-grid-char. These style properties specify the layout of text characters. One of the main uses for the layout-grid style property is to incorporate Asian languages into web documents.

Syntax:

```
element { layout-grid: values }
elementID.style.layoutGrid = "values"
document.all.elementID.style.layoutGrid = "values"
```

Values: See the values for the layout-grid-mode, layout-grid-type, layout-grid-line, and layout-grid-char style properties. The order of the style properties in the preceding list indicates the order for specifying the values of the layout-grid style property.

Example:

```
<p id=myP>This text is only a sample text.</p>
<button onclick="myP.style.layoutGrid='both fixed 16px 10px'">
Set layoutGrid to both fixed 16px 10px</button>
```

Applies to:

```
<a>, <acronym>, <address>, <applet>, <b>, <base>, <basefont>, <bdo>, <big>,
<blockquote>, <body>, <button>, <caption>, <center>, <cite>, <code>, <col>,
<colgroup>, <custom>, <dd>, defaults, <del>, <dfn>, <dir>, <div>, <dl>, <dt>, <em>,
<embed>, <fieldset>, <font>, <form>, <frame>, <frameset>, <head>, <hn>, <hr>, <i>,
<iframe>, <img>, <input type="button">, <input type="checkbox">, <input
type="file">, <input type="image">, <input type="password">, <input type="radio">,
<input type="reset">, <input type="submit">, <input type="text">, <ins>, <kbd>,
<label>, <legend>, <li>, <listing>, <marquee>, <menu>, <meta>, nextID, <nobr>,
<object>, <ol>, <option>, <p>, <pre>, <q>, <rt>, <ruby>, runtimeStyle, <s>, <samp>,
<script>, <select>, <small>, <span>, <strike>, <strong>, style, <sub>, <sup>,
<table>, <tbody>, <td>, <textarea>, <tfoot>, <th>, <thead>, <tr>, <tt>, <u>, <ul>,
<var>, <xmp>
```

layout-grid-char

Compatibility: IE5, IE5.5, IE6

This style property defines the size of the character grid used for rendering an element's text content.

Syntax:

```
element { layout-grid-char: value }
elementID.style.layoutGridChar = "value"
document.all.elementID.style.layoutGridChar = "value"
```

Values:

none	The default
auto	The grid is set according to the largest character for the font being used
length	The grid size is specified with a floating-point number followed by a unit designator
percentage	The grid size is specified with an integer followed by a percent sign representing the percentage relative to the parent object

Example:

```
<p id=myP>This is only a sample text.</p>
<button onclick="myP.style.layoutGridChar='16px'">Set layoutGridChar to 16px</button>
```

Applies to:

```
<blockquote>, <body>, <center>, currentStyle, <dd>, <dir>, <div>, <dl>, <dt>,
<fieldset>, <form>, <hn>, <hr>, <li>, <listing>, <marquee>, <menu>, <ol>, <p>,
<pre>, runtimeStyle, style, <table>, <td>, <th>, <tr>, <ul>, <xmp>
```

layout-grid-line

Compatibility: IE5, IE5.5, IE6

This style property defines the layout grid value used for rendering an element's text content.

Syntax:

```
element { layout-grid-line: value }
elementID.style.layoutGridLine = "value"
document.all.elementID.style.layoutGridLine = "value"
```

Values: Same as for the layout-grid-char style property.

Example:

```
<p style="layout-grid-line:14px">This is only a sample text.</p>
<br>
<p id="myP">This is only a sample text.</p>
<button onclick="myP.style.layoutGridLine='40px'">Set layoutGridLine to 40px</button>
```

Applies to:

```
<blockquote>, <body>, <center>, currentStyle, <dd>, <dir>, <div>, <dl>, <dt>,
<fieldset>, <form>, <hn>, <hr>, <li>, <listing>, <marquee>, <menu>, <ol>, <p>,
<pre>, runtimeStyle, style, <table>, <td>, <th>, <tr>, <ul>, <xmp>
```

layout-grid-mode

Compatibility: IE5, IE5.5, IE6

This style property defines whether the character and line grid modes are enabled.

Syntax:

```
element { layout-grid-mode: value }
elementID.style.layoutGridMode = "value"
document.all.elementID.style.layoutGridMode = "value"
```

Values: both (the default), none, line, and char.

Example:

```
<span style="layout-grid-mode:line">This is only a sample text.</span>
<br>
<span id="myS">This is only a sample text.</span>
<button onclick="myS.style.layoutGridMode='both'">Set layoutGridMode to line</button>
```

Applies to:

```
<a>, <acronym>, <address>, <applet>, <b>, <base>, <basefont>, <bdo>, <big>,
<blockquote>, <body>, <button>, <caption>, <center>, <cite>, <code>, <col>,
<colgroup>, currentStyle, <custom>, <dd>, defaults, <del>, <dfn>, <dir>, <div>,
<dl>, <dt>, <em>, <embed>, <fieldset>, <font>, <form>, <frame>, <frameset>, <head>,
<hn>, <hr>, <i>, <iframe>, <img>, <input type="button">, <input type="checkbox">,
<input type="file">, <input type="image">, <input type="password">, <input
type="radio">, <input type="reset">, <input type="submit">, <input type="text">,
<ins>, <kbd>, <label>, <legend>, <li>, <listing>, <marquee>, <menu>, <meta>,
nextID, <nobr>, <object>, <ol>, <option>, <p>, <pre>, <q>, <rt>, <ruby>,
runtimeStyle, <s>, <samp>, <script>, <select>, <small>, <span>, <strike>, <strong>,
style, <sub>, <sup>, <table>, <tbody>, <td>, <textarea>, <tfoot>, <th>, <thead>,
<tr>, <tt>, <u>, <ul>, <var>, <xmp>
```

layout-grid-type

Compatibility: IE5, IE5.5, IE6

This style property defines how the layout-grid will be used for displaying the text within the specified element.

Syntax:

```
element { layout-grid-type: value }
elementID.style.layoutGridType = "value"
document.all.elementID.style.layoutGridType = "value"
```

Values: loose (the default; for rendering Japanese and Korean characters), strict (for rendering Chinese characters), and fixed (for laying out characters in a fixed amount of space).

Example:

```
<div style="layout-grid-type:strict">This is only a sample text.</div>
<br>
<span id="myP">This is only a sample text.</span>
<button onclick="myP.style.layoutGridType='fixed'">Set layoutGridType to fixed</button>
```

Applies to: Same as for the layout-grid-char style property.

left

Compatibility: NN6, NN7, IE4, IE5, IE5.5, IE6

This style property defines the position of the left edge of an element rectangle container, taking into consideration the container's padding, border, and margin.

Syntax:

```
element { left: value }
elementID.style.left = "value"
document.all.elementID.style.left= "value" // IE only
```

Values:

auto	The default; regular HTML position.
length	A floating-point number followed by a unit designator.
percentage	An integer followed by a percent sign representing the percentage of the width of the parent element.

Example:

```
<p><img id="myImg" src=".yourimage.jpg" width=74 height=100"
style="position:relative"></p>
<input type="button" value="Set left property to 100"
onclick="myImg.style.left=100">
<input type="button" value="Set left property to 200"
onclick="myImg.style.left=200">
<input type="button" value="Restore image position" onclick="myImg.style.left=0">
```

Applies to:

```
<a>, <address>, <applet>, <b>, <big>, <blockquote>, <button>, <center>, <cite>,
<code>, currentStyle, <custom>, <dd>, defaults, <dfn>, <dir>, <div>, <dl>, <dt>,
<em>, <embed>, <fieldset>, <font>, <form>, <hn>, <hr>, <i>, <iframe>, <img>, <input
type="button">, <input type="checkbox">, <input type="file">, <input type="image">,
<input type="password">, <input type="radio">, <input type="reset">, <input
type="submit">, <input type="text">, <isindex>, <kbd>, <label>, <legend>, <li>,
<listing>, <marquee>, <menu>, <object>, <ol>, <p>, <pre>, runtimeStyle, <s>,
<samp>, <select>, <small>, <span>, <strike>, <strong>, style, <sub>, <sup>,
<table>, <textarea>, <tt>, <u>, <ul>, <var>, <xmp>
```

letter-spacing

Compatibility: NN4, NN6, NN7, IE4, IE5, IE5.5, IE6

This style property controls the amount of additional space between text characters within the element, and it is used to justify text.

Syntax:

```
element { letter-spacing: value }
elementID.style.letterSpacing = "value"
document.all.elementID.style.letterSpacing = "value" // IE only
```

Values: normal (the default; normal spacing) and length (a floating-point number followed by a unit designator).

Example:

```
<p id="myP">This is a sample text.</p>
<input type="button" value="Set letterSpacing to 0.5mm"
onclick="myP.style.letterSpacing='0.5mm'">
<input type="button" value="Set letterSpacing to 1mm"
onclick="myP.style.letterSpacing='1mm'">
<input type="button" value="Set letterSpacing to normal"
onclick="myP.style.letterSpacing='normal'">
```

Applies to:

```
<a>, <address>, <b>, <big>, <blockquote>, <body>, <button>, <caption>, <center>,
<cite>, <code>, <col>, <colgroup>, currentStyle, <custom>, <dd>, defaults, <dfn>,
<dir>, <div>, <dl>, <dt>, <em>, <fieldset>, <form>, <hn>, <html>, <i>, <img>,
<input type="button">, <input type="checkbox">, <input type="file">, <input
type="image">, <input type="password">, <input type="radio">, <input type="reset">,
<input type="submit">, <input type="text">, <isindex>, <kbd>, <label>, <legend>,
<li>, <listing>, <marquee>, <menu>, <ol>, <p>, <pre>, runtimeStyle, <s>, <samp>,
<select>, <small>, <span>, <strike>, <strong>, style, <sub>, <sup>, <table>,
<tbody>, <td>, <textarea>, <tfoot>, <th>, <thead>, <tr>, <tt>, <u>, <ul>, <var>,
<xmp>
```

line-break

Compatibility: IE5, IE5.5, IE6

This style property defines line-breaking rules for text that is rendered using Japanese language characters.

Syntax:

```
element { line-break: value }
elementID.style.lineBreak = "value"
document.all.elementID.style.lineBreak = "value"
```

Values: normal (the default) and strict (Japanese line-breaking rules are applied more strictly than normal).

Example:

```
<p id="myP">This is a long sample text. This is a long sample text. This is a long
sample text.</p>
<input type="button" value="Set lineBreak to strict"
onclick="myP.style.lineBreak='strict'">
```

Applies to:

`<address>`, `<blockquote>`, `<body>`, `<center>`, currentStyle, `<dd>`, `<dir>`, `<div>`, `<dl>`,
`<dt>`, `<fieldset>`, `<form>`, `<hn>`, `<hr>`, `<legend>`, `<li>`, `<listing>`, `<marquee>`, `<menu>`,
`<ol>`, `<p>`, `<pre>`, runtimeStyle, style, `<table>`, `<td>`, `<th>`, `<tr>`, `<ul>`, `<xmp>`

---

line-height

Compatibility: NN4, NN6, NN7, IE4, IE5, IE5.5, IE6

This style property defines the height of the container element. This value can be used to control the distance between two lines of text.

Syntax:

```
element { line-height: value }
elementID.style.lineHeight = "value"
document.all.elementID.style.lineHeight = "value" // IE only
```

Values:

normal	The default
height	A floating-point number followed by a unit designator
percentage	An integer followed by a percent sign representing the percentage of the height of the parent object

Example:

```
<p id="myP" style="background-color:#dddddd">
This is the first line if a sample text.<br>
And this is its second line.</p>
  <input type="button" value="Set lineHeight to 30px"
onclick="myP.style.lineHeight='30px'">
  <input type="button" value="Restore line height to normal"
onclick="myP.style.lineHeight='normal'">
```

Applies to:

`<a>`, `<address>`, `<b>`, `<big>`, `<blockquote>`, `<body>`, `<button>`, `<caption>`, `<center>`,
`<cite>`, `<code>`, `<col>`, `<colgroup>`, currentStyle, `<custom>`, `<dd>`, defaults, `<dfn>`,
`<dir>`, `<div>`, `<dl>`, `<dt>`, `<em>`, `<fieldset>`, `<form>`, `<hn>`, `<html>`, `<i>`, `<img>`,
`<input type="button">`, `<input type="checkbox">`, `<input type="file">`, `<input
type="image">`, `<input type="password">`, `<input type="radio">`, `<input type="reset">`,
`<input type="submit">`, `<input type="text">`, `<isindex>`, `<kbd>`, `<label>`, `<legend>`,
`<li>`, `<listing>`, `<marquee>`, `<menu>`, `<ol>`, `<p>`, `<pre>`, runtimeStyle, `<s>`, `<samp>`,
`<select>`, `<small>`, `<span>`, `<strike>`, `<strong>`, style, `<sub>`, `<sup>`, `<table>`,
`<tbody>`, `<td>`, `<textarea>`, `<tfoot>`, `<th>`, `<thead>`, `<tr>`, `<tt>`, `<u>`, `<ul>`, `<var>`,
`<xmp>`

---

list-style

Compatibility: NN6, NN7, IE4, IE5, IE5.5, IE6

This style property is a shorthand that establishes three different list-style style properties: `list-style-type`, `list-style-position`, and `list-style-image`. These three style properties define the styles to be used when rendering the marker with each list item.

Syntax:

```
element { list-style: value }
elementID.style.listStyle = "value"
document.all.elementID.style.listStyle = "value"
```

Values: See the values for the `list-style-type`, `list-style-position`, and `list-style-image` style properties. JavaScript default values are: `disc`, `outside`, and `none`. The three values are space delimited, and their order is irrelevant.

Example:

```
<html><head></head>
<body bgcolor="#FFFFFF" text="#000000">
<ul style="list-style:'circle outside none'">  <li>Item 1.</li>
<li>Item 2.</li>
<li>Item 3.</li>
<li>Item 4.</li>
<li>Item 5.</li></ul>
</body></html>
```

Applies to:

```
<li>, <ol>, runtimeStyle, style, <ul>
```

list-style-image

Compatibility: NN6, NN7, IE4, IE5, IE5.5, IE6

This style property defines an image that will be used as the list item marker.

Syntax:

```
element { list-style-image: value }
elementID.style.listStyleImage = "value"
document.all.elementID.style.listStyleImage = "value" // IE only
```

Values:

none	The default; no image is used
url(*pathname*)	The *pathname* indicates the location of the image file to use

Example:

```
<ul style="list-style-image:url(yourimage.gif)">
  <li>Item 1.</li>
  <li>Item 2.</li>
  <li>Item 3.</li>
```

```
  <li>Item 4.</li>
  <li>Item 5.</li>
</ul>
```

Applies to:

```
currentStyle, <li>, <ol>, runtimeStyle, style, <ul>
```

list-style-position

Compatibility: NN6, NN7, IE4, IE5, IE5.5, IE6

This style property defines the position of the marker of a list item relative to the area of the list item's text.

Syntax:

```
element { list-style-position: value }
elementID.style.listStylePosition = "value"
document.all.elementID.style.listStylePosition = "value" //IE only
```

Values: outside (the default) and inside.
Example:

```
<html><head></head>
<body bgcolor="#FFFFFF" text="#000000">
<p>The following list uses an inside position for the marker.</p>
<ul style="list-style-image:url(yourMarker.gif); list-style-position:inside">
<li>Item 1.</li>
<li>Item 2.</li>
<li>Item 3.</li>
<li>Item 4.</li>
<li>Item 5.</li></ul>
</body></html>
```

Applies to:

```
currentStyle, <li>, <ol>, runtimeStyle, style, <ul>
```

list-style-type

Compatibility: NN4, NN6, NN7, IE4, IE5, IE5.5, IE6

This style property defines the type of marker used by each list item of the element.

Syntax:

```
element { list-style-type: value }
elementID.style.listStyleType = "value"
document.all.elementID.style.listStyleType = "value" // IE only
```

Values: disc (<ul> default; solid circle), circle (empty circle), square, decimal (<ol> default), lower-alpha, lower-roman, upper-alpha, and upper-roman. Other values include, decimal-leading-zero, lower-greek, lower-latin (same as lower-roman), hebrew, armenian, georgian, cjk-ideographic, hiragana, katakana, hiragana-iroha, and katakana-iroba.

Example:

```
<ol id="myL" class="explanations">
  <li>Item 1.</li>
  <li>Item 2.</li>
  <li>Item 3.</li>
  <li>Item 4.</li>
  <li>Item 5.</li>
</ol>
  <input type="button" value='Set listStyleType to "circle"'
onclick="myL.style.listStyleType='circle'"><br>
  <input type="button" value='Set listStyleType to "square"'
onclick="myL.style.listStyleType='square'"><br>
  <input type="button" value='Set listStyleType to "disc"'
onclick="myL.style.listStyleType='disc'"><br>
  <input type="button" value='Set listStyleType to "lower-alpha"'
onclick="myL.style.listStyleType='lower-alpha'"><br>
  <input type="button" value='Set listStyleType to "lower-roman"'
onclick="myL.style.listStyle='lower-roman'">
```

Applies to:

```
currentStyle, <li>, <ol>, runtimeStyle, style, <ul>
```

margin

Compatibility: NN4, NN6, NN7, IE4, IE5, IE5.5, IE6

This style property is a shorthand that establishes the values of four different margin style properties: margin-top, margin-right, margin-bottom, and margin-left.

Syntax:

```
element { margin: values }
elementID.style.margin = "values"
document.all.elementID.style.margin = "values" // IE only
```

Values: See the values for the margin-top, margin-right, margin-bottom, and margin-left style properties. The values of these style properties are space delimited and must appear in the order listed here.

Example:

```
<img id="myImg" src="yourimage.gif" height="50" width="50" border="1">
<button onclick="myImg.style.margin='25 25 25 25'">25 Px Margin</button>
<button onclick="myImg.style.margin='0 0 0 0'">0 Margin</button>
```

Applies to:

<a>, <acronym>, <b>, <bdo>, <big>, <blockquote>, <body>, <button>, <caption>,
<center>, <cite>, <code>, currentStyle, <custom>, <dd>, defaults, <del>, <dfn>,
<dir>, <div>, <dl>, <dt>, <em>, <embed>, <fieldset>, <font>, <form>, <hn>, <hr>,
<i>, <iframe>, <img>, <input type="button">, <input type="checkbox">, <input
type="file">, <input type="image">, <input type="password">, <input type="radio">,
<input type="reset">, <input type="submit">, <input type="text">, <ins>, <isindex>,
<kbd>, <label>, <li>, <listing>, <marquee>, <menu>, <nobr>, <object>, <ol>, <p>,
<pre>, <q>, runtimeStyle, <s>, <samp>, <small>, <span>, <strike>, <strong>, style,
<sub>, <sup>, <table>, <td>, <textarea>, <th>, <tt>, <u>, <ul>, <var>, <xmp>

margin-bottom, margin-left, margin-right, margin-top

Compatibility: NN6, NN7, IE4, IE5, IE5.5, IE6

These style properties define the length of the bottom, left, right, and top margins of the element.

Syntax:

```
element { margin-bottom: value }
elementID.style.marginTop = "value"
document.all.elementID.style.marginRight = "value" // IE only
```

Values:

auto	The default; bottom and top margins are set equal to each other.
integer	The margin is specified by a floating-point number followed by a unit designator.
percentage	The margin is specified by an integer followed by a percent sign representing the percentage of the height of the parent element.

Example:

```
<html><head></head>
<body bgcolor="#FFFFFF" text="#000000">
<p>The following image has a left margin of 3mm.</p>
<img src="yourImage.gif" height="50" width="50" style="margin-left='3mm'">
</body></html>
```

Applies to: Same as for the margin style property.

min-height

Compatibility: NN6, NN7, IE6

This style property establishes a minimum height for the element. In Internet Explorer, if the height property of a cell or row is set in a fixed-layout table, any text that exceeds the height of the cell or row is clipped. However, setting the min-height style property to a value greater than the height property of the cell or row can accommodate overflow text.

Syntax:

```
element { min-height: value }
elementID.style.minHeight = "value"
document.all.elementID.style.minHeight = "value" // IE only
```

Values:

integer	A floating-point number followed by a unit designator
percentage	An integer followed by a percent sign representing the percentage of the container element's minimum height

Example:

```
<table border="1" style="table-layout:fixed; width:100%;">
<tr><td style="min-height:25px"> . . . </td></tr></table>
```

Applies to:

```
currentStyle, style, runtimeStyle, <td>, <th>, <tr>
```

overflow

Compatibility: NN6, NN7, IE4, IE5, IE5.5, IE6

This style property defines how to treat element content that exceeds the height and/or width of its container element. This style property is applicable to positioned elements only.

Syntax:

```
element { overflow: value }
elementID.style.overflow = "value"
document.all.elementID.style.overflow = "value" // IE only
```

Values:

visible	The default; the entire content is shown
scroll	Excess content is clipped and scroll bars are added
hidden	Excess content is clipped and not shown
auto	Excess content is clipped and scroll bars are added when necessary

Example:

```
<script language="JavaScript">
function fn1(){
    if(myBody.style.overflow=="auto"){
        myBody.style.overflow="scroll";
        myButton.value="Set overflow to hidden.";
        results.innerText="overflow is set to scroll.";
        return false;
    }
```

```
        if (myBody.style.overflow=="scroll"){
            myBody.style.overflow="hidden";
            myButton.value="Set overflow to auto";
            results.innerText="overflow is set to hidden.";
            return false;
        }
        if(myBody.style.overflow=="hidden"){
            myBody.style.overflow="auto";
            myButton.value="Set overflow to scroll";
            results.innerText="overflow is set to auto.";
            return false;
        }
}
</script>
<body id="myBody" bgcolor="#FFFFFF" text="#000000" bottommargin="150"
style="overflow:auto">
<div id="results" style="color:red">overflow is set to auto.</div><br>
  <input id=myButton type=button value="Set overflow to scroll" onclick="fn1();">
```

Applies to:

<a>, <acronym>, <address>, <applet>, <b>, <bdo>, <big>, <blockquote>, <body>,
<center>, <cite>, <code>, <col>, <colgroup>, currentStyle, <custom>, <dd>,
defaults, <del>, <dfn>, <dir>, <div>, <dl>, <dt>, <em>, <embed>, <fieldset>,
<font>, <form>, <hn>, <html>, <i>, <input type="button">, <input type="checkbox">,
<input type="file">, <input type="image">, <input type="password">, <input
type="radio">, <input type="reset">, <input type="submit">, <input type="text">,
<ins>, <kbd>, <label>, <legend>, <li>, <listing>, <menu>, <ol>, <p>, <pre>, <q>,
<rt>, <ruby>, runtimeStyle, <s>, <samp>, <small>, <span>, <strike>, <strong>,
style, <sub>, <sup>, <textarea>, <tt>, <u>, <ul>, <var>, <xmp>

---

overflow-x

Compatibility: IE4, IE5, IE5.5, IE6

This style property, applicable to positioned elements only, defines how to treat
content that exceeds the width of its container element.

Syntax:

```
element { overflow-x: value }
elementID.style.overflowX = "value"
document.all.elementID.style.overflowX = "value"
```

Values: Same as for the overflow style property.

Example:

```
<div style="overflow-x:auto; background-color:#ccccff; width:200; height:50">This
div element has an overflow-x property value of auto. The browser will display
scroll bars when necessary.</div>
  <div style="overflow-x:scroll; background-color:#ffffcc; width:200;
height:50">This div element has an overflow-x property value of scroll. The browser
will display scroll bars on the bottom side of the element.</div>
```

Applies to:

<a>, <acronym>, <address>, <applet>, <b>, <bdo>, <big>, <blockquote>, <body>, <center>, <cite>, <code>, currentStyle, <custom>, <dd>, defaults, <del>, <dfn>, <dir>, <div>, <dl>, <dt>, <em>, <embed>, <fieldset>, <font>, <form>, <hn>, <html>, <i>, <iframe>, <input type="button">, <input type="checkbox">, <input type="file">, <input type="image">, <input type="password">, <input type="radio">, <input type="reset">, <input type="submit">, <input type="text">, <ins>, <kbd>, <label>, <legend>, <li>, <listing>, <menu>, <ol>, <p>, <pre>, <q>, <rt>, <ruby>, runtimeStyle, <s>, <samp>, <small>, <span>, <strike>, <strong>, style, <sub>, <sup>, <textarea>, <tt>, <u>, <ul>, <var>, <xmp>

overflow-y

Compatibility: IE4, IE5, IE5.5, IE6

This style property, applicable to positioned elements only, defines how to treat content that exceeds the height of its container element.

Syntax:

```
element { overflow-y: value }
elementID.style.overflowY = "value"
document.all.elementID.style.overflowY = "value"
```

Values: Same as for the overflow style property.

Example:

```
<div style="overflow-y:auto; background-color:#ccccff; width:200; height:75">This
div element has an overflow-y property value of auto. The browser will display
scroll bars when necessary.</div>
   <div style="overflow-y:scroll; background-color:#ffffcc; width:200;
height:75">This div element has an overflow-y property value of scroll. The browser
will display scroll bars on the right side of the element.</div>
```

Applies to: Same as for the overflow-x property.

padding

Compatibility: NN6, NN7, IE4, IE5, IE5.5, IE6

This style property is a shorthand that establishes the values of four different space-delimited padding style properties: padding-top, padding-right, padding-bottom, and padding-left.

Syntax:

```
element { padding: values }
elementID.style.padding = "values"
document.all.elementID.style.padding = "values" // IE only
```

Values: See the values of the padding-top, padding-right, padding-bottom, and padding-left space-delimited style properties. The values of these style properties are space delimited and must appear in the order listed here.

Example:

```
<p>The image below has an all-around padding of 30px.</p>
<table border><tr><td style="padding:'30 30 30 30'">
<img src="yourImage.gif" height="50" width="50" border="1">
</td></tr></table>
```

Applies to:

```
<a>, <acronym>, <address>, <applet>, <b>, <bdo>, <big>, <blockquote>, <body>,
<button>, <caption>, <center>, <cite>, <code>, <col>, <colgroup>, currentStyle,
<custom>, <dd>, defaults, <del>, <dfn>, <dir>, <div>, <dl>, <dt>, <em>, <embed>,
<fieldset>, <font>, <form>, <frame>, <hn>, <hr>, <i>, <img>, <input type="button">,
<input type="checkbox">, <input type="file">, <input type="image">, <input
type="password">, <input type="radio">, <input type="reset">, <input
type="submit">, <input type="text">, <ins>, <kbd>, <label>, <legend>, <li>,
<listing>, <marquee>, <menu>, nextID, <nobr>, <object>, <ol>, <p>, <pre>, <q>,
<rt>, <ruby>, runtimeStyle, <s>, <samp>, <select>, <small>, <span>, <strike>,
<strong>, style, <sub>, <sup>, <table>, <td>, <textarea>, <th>, <tt>, <u>, <ul>,
<var>, <xmp>
```

padding-bottom, padding-left, padding-right, padding-top

Compatibility: NN4, NN6, NN7, IE4, IE5, IE5.5, IE6

These style properties define the size of the bottom, left, right, and top padding of an element.

Syntax:

```
element { padding-bottom: value }
elementID.style.paddingTop = "value"
document.all.elementID.style.paddingRight = "value" // IE only
```

Values:

length	A floating-point number followed by a unit designator
percentage	An integer followed by a percent sign representing the percentage of the height of the parent object

Example:

```
<table><tr><td id="myTd">
<img src="yourimage.gif" height="50" width="50" border="1">
</td></tr></table>
<button onclick="myTd.style.paddingTop=0">Set padding to 0</button>
<button onclick="myTd.style.paddingTop=20">Set padding to 20</button>
```

Applies to: Same as for the padding style property.

page-break-after, page-break-before, page-break-inside

Compatibility: NN6, NN7, IE4, IE5, IE5.5, IE6

These style properties indicate whether, when the document is sent to a printer, a page break occurs after or before the element. The `page-break-inside` property specifies that the page break occurs inside the generated box. Page breaks are not permitted inside positioned objects.

Syntax:

```
element { page-break-after: value }
elementID.style.pageBreakBefore = "value"
document.all.elementID.style.pageBreakInside = "value" // IE only
```

Values:

always	A page break is always inserted after/before the element.
auto	A page break is neither forced nor avoided before/after/inside the element.
avoid	A page break is avoided before/after/inside the element.
"" (empty string)	A page break is not inserted.
left	CSS: Forces one or two page breaks before/after the element so that the next page is formatted as a left page in a book. IE: See always.
right	CSS: Forces one or two page breaks before/after the element so that the next page is formatted as a right page in a book. IE: See always.

Example:

```
<div id="myDiv1" class="explanations" style="page-break-after:'always'; background-color:#ccccff; width:400; height:70">When you print this page, there will be a page-break after this object.</div>
```

Applies to:

```
<blockquote>, <body>, <button>, <caption>, <center>, currentStyle, <dd>, <dir>,
<div>, <dl>, <dt>, <fieldset>, <form>, <hn>, <isindex>, <li>, <listing>, <marquee>,
<menu>, <ol>, <p>, <pre>, runtimeStyle, style, <table>, <tbody>, <tfoot>, <th>,
<thead>, <tr>, <ul>, <xmp>
```

pixelBottom (*), pixelLeft (*), pixelRight (*), pixelTop (*)

Compatibility: IE4, IE5, IE5.5, IE6

These JavaScript-only style properties define the bottom, left, right, and top position in number of pixels. These properties are equivalent to the CSS-compatible bottom, left, right, and top style properties.

Syntax (replace Bottom with Left, Right, or Top):

```
elementID.style.pixelBottom = "value"
document.all.elementID.style.pixelBottom = "value"
```

Example:

```
<html><head>
<script language="JavaScript">
```

```
function fn1(){
document.all.myDiv.style.pixelTop = 500
}
</script>
</head>
<body bgcolor="#FFFFFF" text="#000000">
<div id="myDiv" style="background-color:#ccffcc; position:absolute; width:300;
cursor:hand"; onclick="fn1()">Click on this div element to send it to 500 px from
the top.</div></body></html>
```

Applies to:

```
<a>, <acronym>, <address>, <applet>, <b>, <base>, <basefont>, <big>, <blockquote>,
<body>, <button>, <caption>, <center>, <cite>, <code>, <col>, <colgroup>,
<comment>, <custom>, <dd>, defaults, <del>, <dfn>, <dir>, <div>, <dl>, <dt>, <em>,
<embed>, <fieldset>, <font>, <form>, <frame>, <frameset>, <head>, <hn>, <hr>, <i>,
<iframe>, <img>, <input type="button">, <input type="checkbox">, <input
type="file">, <input type="image">, <input type="password">, <input type="radio">,
<input type="reset">, <input type="submit">, <input type="text">, <ins>, <kbd>,
<label>, <legend>, <li>, <link>, <listing>, <marquee>, <menu>, <meta>, nextID,
<nobr>, <object>, <ol>, <option>, <p>, <pre>, <q>, <rt>, <ruby>, runtimeStyle, <s>,
<samp>, <script>, <select>, <small>, <span>, <strike>, <strong>, style, <sub>,
<sup>, <table>, <tbody>, <td>, <textarea>, <tfoot>, <th>, <thead>, <title>, <tr>,
<tt>, <u>, <ul>, <var>, <xmp>
```

pixelHeight (*), pixelWidth (*)

Compatibility: IE4, IE5, IE5.5, IE6

These JavaScript-only style properties specify the height and the width of the
element in pixels.

Syntax (replace Height with Width):

```
elementID.style.pixelHeight = "value"
document.all.elementID.style.pixelHeight = "value"
```

Example:

```
<head>
<script language="JavaScript">
function fn1(){
myDiv.style.pixelHeight = 200
}
</script>
</head>
<body bgcolor="#FFFFFF" text="#000000">
<div id="myDiv" style="background-color:#ccffcc; position:absolute; width:300;
cursor:hand"; onmouseover="fn1()" onmouseout="this.style.pixelHeight=60">Mouse over
this div element to change the value of its height property to 200.</div></body>
```

Applies to: Same as for the pixelBottom, pixelLeft, pixelRight, and pixelTop
properties.

posBottom (*), posLeft (*), posRight (*), posTop (*)

Compatibility: IE4, IE5, IE5.5, IE6

These JavaScript-only style properties define the bottom, left, right, and top position of the element in pixels (unless a different unit of measure has been designated in the `bottom`, `left`, `right`, or `top` style attributes).

Syntax (Replace `Bottom` with `Left`, `Right`, or `Top`):

```
elementID.style.posBottom = "value"
document.all.elementID.style.posBottom = "value"
```

Example:

```
<head>
<script language="JavaScript">
function fn1(){
myDiv.style.posTop = 500
}
</script>
</head>
<body bgcolor="#FFFFFF" text="#000000">
<div id="myDiv" style="background-color:#ccffcc; position:absolute; width:300;
cursor:hand"; onclick="fn1()">Click this div element to send it to 500 px from the
top.</div></body>
```

Applies to: Same as for the `pixelBottom`, `pixelLeft`, `pixelRight`, and `pixelTop` properties.

posHeight (*), posWidth (*)

Compatibility: IE4, IE5, IE5.5, IE6

These JavaScript-only style properties define the width and height of the element in pixels (unless a different unit of measure has been designated in the `bottom`, `left`, `right`, or `top` style attributes).

Syntax (replace `Height` with `Width`):

```
elementID.style.posHeight = "value"
document.all.elementID.style.posHeight = "value"
```

Example:

```
<head>
<script language="JavaScript">
function fn1(){
myDiv.style.posWidth = 200
}
</script>
</head>
<body bgcolor="#FFFFFF" text="#000000">
```

```
<div id="myDiv" style="background-color:#ccffcc; position:absolute; cursor:hand";
onmouseover="fn1()" onclick="this.style.posWidth=900">
Mouse over this div element to change the value of its width property to 200. Click
inside to restore width.</div></body>
```

Applies to: Same as for the `pixelBottom`, `pixelLeft`, `pixelRight`, and `pixelTop`
properties.

position

Compatibility: NN6, NN7, IE4, IE5, IE5.5, IE6

This style property defines the type of positioning used for the element. (See
Chapter 1 for more information regarding positioning.)
　　Syntax:

```
element { position: value }
elementID.style.position = "value"
document.all.elementID.style.position = "value" // IE only
```

　　Values:

static	The default; position is determined by the normal flow of HTML elements
absolute	Position is relative to the parent element
relative	Position is calculated according to the normal flow of the HTML elements, and then moved down by the top property and moved right by the left property

　　Example:

```
<head>
<script language="JavaScript">
function fn1(){
myDiv.style.position = "absolute";
}
</script>
</head>
<body bgcolor="#FFFFFF" text="#000000">
<br><br><br><br><br>
<div id="myDiv" style="background-color:#ccffcc; width:300; cursor:hand"
onclick="fn1()">Click this div element to establish its position as absolute.</
div></body>
```

NOTE　*The preceding example illustrates the proper syntax for the* position *style property. However,
for this property to be better illustrated, it must be part of a much more complete page.*

　　Applies to:

```
<a>, <address>, <applet>, <b>, <bdo>, <big>, <blockquote>, <button>, <center>,
<cite>, <code>, currentStyle, <custom>, <dd>, defaults, <dfn>, <dir>, <div>, <dl>,
<dt>, <em>, <embed>, <fieldset>, <font>, <form>, <hn>, <hr>, <i>, <iframe>, <img>,
<input type="button">, <input type="checkbox">, <input type="file">, <input
```

type="image">, <input type="password">, <input type="radio">, <input type="reset">, <input type="submit">, <input type="text">, <isindex>, <kbd>, <label>, <legend>, <li>, <listing>, <marquee>, <menu>, <object>, <ol>, <p>, <pre>, <ruby>, runtimeStyle, <s>, <samp>, <select>, <small>, <span>, <strike>, <strong>, style, <sub>, <sup>, <table>, <td>, <textarea>, <th>, <tr>, <tt>, <u>, <ul>, <var>, <xmp>

right

Compatibility: NN6, NN7, IE4, IE5, IE5.5, IE6

This style property defines the position of the right edge of an element container, including any padding, border, and margin, and is relative to adjacent elements. The value set is applicable to elements using absolute positioning.

Syntax:

```
element { right: value }
elementID.style.right = "value"
document.all.elementID.style.right = "value" // IE only
```

Values:

auto	The default; regular HTML position
length	A floating-point number followed by a unit designator
percentage	An integer followed by a percent sign, representing the percentage of the width of the parent element

Example:

```
<p><img id="myImg" src="yourimage.jpg" width=74 height=100"
style="position:relative"></p>
  <input type="button" value="Set right property to 100"
onclick="myImg.style.right=100">
  <input type="button" value="Set right property to 200"
onclick="myImg.style.right=200">
  <input type="button" value="Restore image position"
onclick="myImg.style.right=0">
```

Applies to:

<a>, <address>, <applet>, <b>, <big>, <blockquote>, <button>, <center>, <cite>, <code>, currentStyle, <dd>, <dfn>, <dir>, <div>, <dl>, <fieldset>, <font>, <form>, <hn>, <hr>, <i>, <iframe>, <img>, <input type="button">, <input type="checkbox">, <input type="file">, <input type="image">, <input type="password">, <input type="radio">, <input type="reset">, <input type="submit">, <input type="text">, <isindex>, <kbd>, <label>, <legend>, <li>, <listing>, <marquee>, <menu>, <object>, <ol>, <p>, <pre>, runtimeStyle, <s>, <samp>, <select>, <small>, <span>, <strike>, <strong>, style, <sub>, <sup>, <table>, <textarea>, <tt>, <u>, <ul>, <var>, <xmp>

ruby-align

Compatibility: IE5, IE5.5, IE6

This style property defines the horizontal alignment of the ruby text relative to the base text. In the example that follows, the base text is the text that immediately follows the opening ‹ruby› tag and precedes the ‹rt› tag declaration. The ruby text is the text between the ‹rt› tag and the closing ‹/ruby› tag. (See Chapter 5 for information about the ‹ruby› and the ‹rt› elements.)

Syntax:

```
element { ruby-align: value }
elementID.style.rubyAlign = "value"
document.all.elementID.style.rubyAlign = "value"
```

Values: auto (the default), left, center, right, distribute-letter (justifies), distribute-space (justifies, adding one blank space at the beginning and the end of the ruby text), and line-edge (if ruby text is next to a line edge, the side of the ruby text is aligned with the side of the base text; otherwise, it is centered).

Example:

```
<p>Click in the following div element to change the ruby alignment to the left.</p>
<div style="background-color:#ccffff; width:200; cursor:hand"
onclick="myRuby.style.rubyAlign='left'">
<ruby id="myRuby" style="ruby-align:right">
<span style="font-family:Verdana; font-size:16pt">..........base text..........</
span>
<rt><span style="font-family:Times New Roman; font-size: 14pt; color:red">ruby text
</span></rt></ruby></div>
```

Applies to:

```
currentStyle, <ruby>, runtimeStyle, style
```

ruby-overhang

Compatibility: IE5, IE5.5, IE6

This style property defines whether the ruby text overhangs the base text only or adjacent text as well. This is a relatively new feature and may not work in some browsers. In the example that follows, the base text is the text that immediately follows the opening ‹ruby› tag and precedes the ‹rt› tag declaration. The ruby text is the text between the ‹rt› tag and the closing ‹/ruby› tag. (See Chapter 5 for information about the ‹ruby› and the ‹rt› elements.)

Syntax:

```
element { ruby-overhang: value }
elementID.style.rubyOverhang = "value"
document.all.elementID.style.rubyOverhang = "value"
```

Values:

auto	The default; ruby text is positioned over (overhangs) any other text adjacent to the base text
whitespace	The ruby text is only positioned over white-space characters
none	Ruby text is positioned over text adjacent to its base text

Example:

```
<p>The following ruby text has an overhang property value of "whitespace".</p>
  <div style="background-color:#ccffff; width:200"><ruby style="ruby-
overhang:whitespace"><span style="font-family:Verdana; font-size:
16pt">..........base text..........</span><span style="font-size: 14pt"> this
text is in the same line as the base text</span><rt><span style="font-family:Times
New Roman; font-size: 14pt; color:red">ruby text</span></ruby></div>
```

Applies to:

```
currentStyle, <ruby>, runtimeStyle, style
```

ruby-position

Compatibility: IE5, IE5.5, IE6

This style property specifies whether the ruby text is displayed above the base text or on the same line as the base text. In the example that follows, the base text is the text that immediately follows the opening <ruby> tag and precedes the <rt> tag declaration. The ruby text is the text between the <rt> tag and the closing </ruby> tag. (See Chapter 5 for information about the <ruby> and the <rt> elements.)

Syntax:

```
element { ruby-position: value }
elementID.style.rubyPosition = "value"
document.all.elementID.style.rubyPosition = "value"
```

Values: above (the default) and inline.

Example:

```
<p>The following ruby text has a ruby-position property value of "inline".</p>
  <div style="background-color:#ccffff; width:400"><ruby style="ruby-
position:inline"><span style="font-family:Verdana; font-size: 16pt">..........base
text..........</span><span style="font-size: 14pt"> this text is in the same line
as the base text</span><rt><span style="font-family:Times New Roman; font-size:
14pt; color:red">ruby text</span></ruby></div>
```

Applies to:

```
currentStyle, <ruby>, runtimeStyle, style
```

Compatibility: IE5.5, IE6

These style properties define the color of the various elements that make up a scroll bar. The values of these style properties have priority when applied to the <body> element.

Syntax:

```
element { scrollbar-element-color: value }
elementID.style.scrollbarElementColor = "value"
document.all.elementID.style.scrollbarElementColor = "value"
```

Values: Color name or hexadecimal value (#RRGGBB).

scrollbar-3dlight-color

This style property defines the color settings for the top and left sides of the scroll box and arrows.

scrollbar-arrow-color

This style property defines the color settings for the arrows.

scrollbar-base-color

This style property defines the color settings for the scroll box, track, and arrows.

scrollbar-darkshadow-color

This style property defines the color settings for the dark shadow part of the scroll box and arrows.

scrollbar-face-color

This style property defines the color settings for the scroll box and arrows.

scrollbar-highlight-color

This style property defines the color settings for the top and left sides of the scroll box and arrows.

scrollbar-shadow-color

This style property defines the color settings for the bottom and right sides of the scroll box and arrows.

scrollbar-track-color

This style property defines the color settings for the track of the scroll bar.

Example:

```
<textarea cols="30" rows="5" wrap="off" style="scrollbar-arrow-color:white;
scrollbar-base-color:green; scrollbar-darkshadow-color:black; scrollbar-highlight-
color:yellow; scrollbar-shadow-color:blue"> . . . a long text </textarea>
```

Applies to:

```
<applet>, <bdo>, <body>, currentStyle, <custom>, defaults, <div>, <embed>,
<object>, runtimeStyle, style, <textarea>
```

styleFloat (*)

Compatibility: IE4, IE5, IE5.5, IE6

This JavaScript-only style property defines whether the element should float to the left, to the right, or not at all. This property may be set for elements that are not absolutely positioned.

Syntax:

```
elementID.style.styleFloat = "value"
document.all.elementID.style.styleFloat = "value"
```

Values: left, right, and none.
Example: See the float example.
Applies to:

```
<a>, <address>, <applet>, <b>, <big>, <blockquote>, <button>, <center>, <cite>,
<code>, <custom>, <dd>, <dfn>, <dir>, <div>, <dl>, <dt>, <em>, <embed>, <fieldset>,
<form>, <hn>, <hr>, <i>, <iframe>, <img>, <input type="button">, <input
type="checkbox">, <input type="file">, <input type="image">, <input
type="password">, <input type="radio">, <input type="reset">, <input
type="submit">, <input type="text">, <isindex>, <kbd>, <label>, <legend>, <li>,
<listing>, <marquee>, <menu>, <object>, <ol>, <p>, <pre>, <rt>, <ruby>, <s>,
<samp>, <select>, <small>, <span>, <strike>, <strong>, <sub>, <sup>, <table>,
<textarea>, <tt>, <u>, <ul>, <var>, <xmp>
```

table-layout

Compatibility: NN6, NN7, IE5, IE5.5, IE6

This style property determines whether or not the table layout is fixed, meaning that if the contents of a cell exceed the width of the column, the content is wrapped or clipped (if wrapping is not possible).

Syntax:

```
table { table-layout: value }
elementID.style.tableLayout = "value"
document.all.elementID.style.tableLayout = "value" // IE only
```

Values:

auto	The default; content in the column determines column width
fixed	The value of the width property determines column width

Example:

```
<table style="table-layout:fixed" width="400" border>
  <col width="150">
  <col width="300">
  <col width="200">
  <thead height="20">
    <tr><th>150px wide column</th><th>300px wide column</th><th>200px wide column</th></tr></thead>
    <tr height="20"><td>Cell 1 content</td><td>Cell 2 content</td><td>Cell 3 content</td></tr>
</table>
```

Applies to:

currentStyle, runtimeStyle, style, <table>

text-align

Compatibility: NN4, NN6, NN7, IE4, IE5, IE5.5, IE6

This style property establishes the horizontal alignment of the text.

Syntax:

```
element { text-align: value }
elementID.style.textAlign = "value"
document.all.elementID.style.textAlign = "value" // IE only
```

Values: left (the default), right, center, and justify.

Example:

```
<div id="myDiv" style="text-align:center">Sample text, aligned center. Click to
change alignment to right.</div>
<button onclick="myDiv.style.textAlign='right';">Align Right</button>
```

Applies to:

<blockquote>, <body>, <center>, currentStyle, <dd>, <dir>, <div>, <dl>, <dt>,
<fieldset>, <form>, <hn>, <hr>, <input type="password">, <input type="text">, <li>,
<listing>, <marquee>, <menu>, <ol>, <p>, <pre>, runtimeStyle, style, <table>, <td>,
<textarea>, <th>, <tr>, <ul>, <xmp>

text-align-last

Compatibility: IE5.5, IE6

This style property sets the alignment of the last line of text in the element.

Syntax:

```
element { text-align-last: value }
elementID.style.textAlignLast = "value"
document.all.elementID.style.textAlignLast = "value"
```

Values: auto (the default; text alignment is normal, or equal to the value of text-align style property), left, inherit, right, center, and justify.

Example:

```
<div onclick="this.style.textAlignLast='right'" style="text-align:justify">Sample text, aligned justify. Click to change last alignment to right.</div>
```

Applies to:

```
<address>, <blockquote>, <body>, <center>, currentStyle, <custom>, <dd>, <div>,
<dl>, <dt>, <fieldset>, <form>, <hn>, <hr>, <isindex>, <li>, <listing>, <menu>,
<ol>, <p>, <pre>, runtimeStyle, style, <textarea>, <ul>, <xmp>
```

text-autospace

Compatibility: IE5, IE5.5, IE6

This style property controls the adjustment of space between ideograph text and alphanumeric text. Ideograph characters belong to Asian writing systems.

Syntax:

```
element { text-autospace: value }
elementID.style.textAutospace = "value"
document.all.elementID.style.textAutospace = "value"
```

Values:

none	The default; no extra spaces are added.
ideograph-alpha	Adds extra spacing between ideograph and non-ideograph texts.
ideograph-numeric	Adds extra spacing between ideograph and numeric characters.
ideograph-parenthesis	Adds extra spacing between ideograph and a normal parenthesis.
ideograph-space	Enlarges the width of the space character when it is next to ideograph text.

Example:

```
<html><head></head>
<body bgcolor="#FFFFFF" text="#000000">
<div style="text-autospace:none;" >This is a sample text with text-autospace set to none</div>
</div></body></html>
```

Applies to:

```
<a>, <acronym>, <address>, <applet>, <b>, <base>, <basefont>, <bdo>, <bgsound>,
<big>, <blockquote>, <body>, <button>, <caption>, <center>, <cite>, <code>, <col>,
<colgroup>, <comment>, currentStyle, <custom>, <dd>, defaults, <del>, <dfn>, <dir>,
<div>, <dl>, <dt>, <em>, <embed>, <fieldset>, <font>, <form>, <frame>, <head>,
<hn>, <hr>, <html>, <i>, <iframe>, <img>, <input type="button">, <input
type="checkbox">, <input type="file">, <input type="hidden">, <input type="image">,
<input type="password">, <input type="radio">, <input type="reset">, <input
type="submit">, <input type="text">, <ins>, <isindex>, <kbd>, <label>, <legend>,
```

`<li>`, `<link>`, `<listing>`, `<marquee>`, `<menu>`, nextID, `<nobr>`, `<noframes>`, `<noscript>`, `<object>`, `<ol>`, `<option>`, `<p>`, `<pre>`, `<q>`, `<rt>`, `<ruby>`, runtimeStyle, `<s>`, `<samp>`, `<script>`, `<select>`, `<small>`, `<span>`, `<strike>`, `<strong>`, style, styleSheet, `<sub>`, `<sup>`, `<table>`, `<tbody>`, `<td>`, `<textarea>`, `<tfoot>`, `<th>`, `<thead>`, `<title>`, `<tr>`, `<tt>`, `<u>`, `<ul>`, `<var>`, `<xml>`, `<xmp>`

text-decoration

Compatibility: NN4, NN6, NN7, IE4, IE5, IE5.5, IE6

This style property specifies decorative additions to the text.

Syntax:

```
element { text-decoration: value }
elementID.style.textDecoration = "value"
document.all.elementID.style.textDecoration = "value" // IE only
```

Values: none (the default), blink (NN only), line-through, overline (IE only), and underline.

Example:

```
<a href="..." style="text-decoration: none"> This link uses text-decoration:none to
eliminate the standard underline.</a><hr>
<p id="myT">Text sample.</p>
  <input type="button" value="decoration:lineThrough"
onclick="myT.style.textDecoration = 'line-through'">
  <input type="button" value="decoration:overline"
onclick="myT.style.textDecoration = 'overline'">
  <input type="button" value="decoration:underline"
onclick="myT.style.textDecoration = 'underline'">
```

Applies to:

`<a>`, `<address>`, `<b>`, `<big>`, `<blockquote>`, `<body>`, `<button>`, `<caption>`, `<center>`, `<cite>`, `<code>`, `<col>`, `<colgroup>`, currentStyle, `<custom>`, `<dd>`, defaults, `<dfn>`, `<dir>`, `<div>`, `<dl>`, `<dt>`, `<em>`, `<fieldset>`, `<form>`, `<hn>`, `<html>`, `<i>`, `<input type="button">`, `<input type="file">`, `<input type="password">`, `<input type="radio">`, `<input type="reset">`, `<input type="submit">`, `<input type="text">`, `<isindex>`, `<kbd>`, `<label>`, `<legend>`, `<li>`, `<listing>`, `<marquee>`, `<menu>`, `<ol>`, `<p>`, `<pre>`, runtimeStyle, `<s>`, `<samp>`, `<select>`, `<small>`, `<span>`, `<strike>`, `<strong>`, style, `<sub>`, `<sup>`, `<table>`, `<tbody>`, `<td>`, `<textarea>`, `<tfoot>`, `<th>`, `<thead>`, `<tr>`, `<tt>`, `<u>`, `<ul>`, `<var>`, `<xmp>`

textDecoration Properties (*)

Compatibility: IE4, IE5, IE5.5, IE6

These JavaScript-only style properties specify decorative additions to the text.

Syntax:

```
elementID.style.textDecorationElement = "value"
document.all.elementID.style.textDecorationElement = "value"
```

Values: true or false.

textDecorationLineThrough (*)

This style property defines whether a line is drawn through the text.

textDecorationNone (*)

This style property determines whether decoration is added to the text.

textDecorationOverline (*)

This style property defines whether a line is drawn over the text.

textDecorationUnderline (*)

This style property defines whether a line is drawn below the text.

text-indent

Compatibility: NN4, NN6, NN7, IE4, IE5, IE5.5, IE6

This style property specifies the size of indentation of the first line of text in a text block or paragraph.

Syntax:

```
element { text-indent: value }
elementID.style.textIndent = "value"
document.all.elementID.style.textIndent = "value" // IE only
```

Values:

| length | A floating-point number followed by a unit designator |
| percentage | An integer followed by a percent sign, representing the percent width of the parent element |

Example:

```
<div style="width:200; background-color:beige; text-indent:100px">
This is a sample paragraph with an indent of 100px.
This is a sample paragraph with an indent of 100px.
This is a sample paragraph with an indent of 100px.</div>
```

Applies to:

```
<blockquote>, <body>, <button>, <center>, currentStyle, <dd>, <dfn>, <dir>, <div>,
<dl>, <dt>, <fieldset>, <form>, <hn>, <hr>, <isindex>, <li>, <listing>, <marquee>,
<menu>, <ol>, <p>, <pre>, runtimeStyle, style, <table>, <td>, <th>, <tr>, <ul>,
<xmp>
```

text-justify

Compatibility: IE5, IE5.5, IE6

This style property defines how the text in the element should be justified. In order to implement this property, the text-align style property value must be set to justify.

Syntax:

```
element { text-justify: value }
elementID.style.textJustify = "value"
document.all.elementID.style.textJustify = "value"
```

Values:

auto	The default; the browser determines the type of alignment
distribute-all-lines	Justifies all lines of text in the block, including the last line
inter-cluster	Justifies text that does not contain inter-word spacing
inter-ideograph	Justifies ideographic text
inter-word	Justifies by increasing space between words in all lines, but the last line of the paragraph is not justified
kashida	Justifies by increasing the length of the characters; applies to Arabic texts
newspaper	Justifies by increasing or decreasing space between words and letters

Example:

```
<div style="width:300px; height:30px; background-color:beige; text-align:justify;
text-justify:inter-word">
This sample paragraph is justified.
</div>
```

Applies to:

```
<address>, <blockquote>, <body>, <center>, currentStyle, <dd>, <dir>, <div>, <dl>,
<dt>, <fieldset>, <form>, <hn>, <hr>, <legend>, <li>, <listing>, <marquee>, <menu>,
<ol>, <p>, <pre>, runtimeStyle, style, <table>, <td>, <th>, <tr>, <ul>, <xmp>
```

text-kashida-space

Compatibility: IE5.5, IE6

This style property determines the relation between white-space expansion between words and the kashida expansion between characters. A kashida space elongates characters in Arabic writing.

Syntax:

```
element { text-kashida-space: value }
elementID.style.textKashidaSpace = "value"
document.all.elementID.style.textKashidaSpace = "value"
```

Values: A percentage of the kashida-space/white-space ratio: 0% means that only white space is used; 100% means that only kashida space is used.

Applies to:

<address>, <blockquote>, <body>, <center>, currentStyle, <custom>, <dd>, <div>, <dl>, <dt>, <fieldset>, <form>, <hn>, <hr>, <isindex>, <li>, <listing>, <menu>, <ol>, <p>, <pre>, runtimeStyle, style, <ul>, <xmp>

text-overflow

Compatibility: IE6

This style property determines whether ellipses (...) are displayed or whether text is clipped when the text overflows its layout area. The element's overflow style property value must be set to hidden, and its text must be wrapped in a <nobr> tag.

Syntax:

```
element { text-overflow: value }
elementID.style.textOverflow = "value"
document.all.elementID.style.textOverflow = "value"
```

Values: ellipsis and clip.

Example:

```
<div id="myT" style="width:200; background-color:beige; overflow:hidden;">
<nobr>This is a sample paragraph with an overflow value of hidden.<nobr>
</div>
  <input type="button" value='text-overflow = "ellipsis"'
onclick="myT.style.textOverflow = 'ellipsis'">
  <input type="button" value='text-overflow = "clip"'
onclick="myT.style.textOverflow = 'clip'">
```

Applies to:

<a>, <acronym>, <address>, <bdo>, <big>, <blockquote>, <body>, <button>, <caption>, <center>, <cite>, <code>, <custom>, <dd>, <del>, <dfn>, <dir>, <div>, <dl>, <dt>, <em>, <fieldset>, <font>, <form>, <hn>, <i>, <input type="button">, <input type="checkbox">, <input type="file">, <input type="image">, <input type="password">, <input type="radio">, <input type="reset">, <input type="submit">, <input type="text">, <ins>, <isindex>, <kbd>, <label>, <legend>, <li>, <listing>, <marquee>, <menu>, <nobr>, <ol>, <p>, <pre>, <q>, <rt>, <ruby>, <s>, <samp>, <small>, <span>, <strike>, <strong>, <sub>, <sup>, <textarea>, <tt>, <u>, <ul>, <var>, <xmp>

text-transform

Compatibility: NN4, NN6, NN7, IE4, IE5, IE5.5, IE6

This style property determines how text is capitalized.

Syntax:

```
element { text-transform: value }
elementID.style.textTransform = "value"
document.all.elementID.style.textTransform = "value" // IE only
```

Values: none (the default), capitalize (capitalizes the first letter of every word), uppercase, and lowercase.

Example:

```
<div id="myDiv" style="text-transform:capitalize">sample text.</div>
<button onclick="myDiv.style.textTransform = 'uppercase';">uppercase</button>
<button onclick="myDiv.style.textTransform = 'lowercase';">lowercase</button>
```

Applies to:

```
<a>, <address>, <b>, <big>, <blockquote>, <body>, <button>, <caption>, <center>,
<cite>, <code>, <col>, <colgroup>, currentStyle, <custom>, <dd>, defaults, <dfn>,
<dir>, <div>, <dl>, <dt>, <em>, <fieldset>, <form>, <hn>, <html>, <i>, <input
type="button">, <input type="checkbox">, <input type="file">, <input type="image">,
<input type="password">, <input type="radio">, <input type="reset">, <input
type="submit">, <input type="text">, <isindex>, <kbd>, <label>, <legend>, <li>,
<listing>, <marquee>, <menu>, <ol>, <p>, <pre>, runtimeStyle, <s>, <samp>,
<select>, <small>, <span>, <strike>, <strong>, style, <sub>, <sup>, <table>,
<tbody>, <td>, <textarea>, <tfoot>, <th>, <thead>, <tr>, <tt>, <u>, <ul>, <var>,
<xmp>
```

text-underline-position

Compatibility: IE5.5, IE6

This style property specifies the position of the underline decoration of the text. This style property is most commonly used with Japanese language text. For this style property to work, the text-decoration style property must be set to underline.

Syntax:

```
element { text-underline-position: value }
elementID.style.textUnderlinePosition = "value"
document.all.elementID.style.textUnderlinePosition = "value"
```

Values: above, below (IE5.5 default), auto (IE6 default), auto-pos (IE6+).

Example:

```
<div class="explanations" style="width:600; background-color:beige; text-underline-
position:above; text-decoration:underline; text-align:center">This is a sample
paragraph.<br>The text-underline-position property is set to "above"</div>
```

Applies to:

```
<a>, <acronym>, <address>, <applet>, <b>, <base>, <basefont>, <bdo>, <bgsound>,
<big>, <blockquote>, <body>, <button>, <caption>, <center>, <cite>, <code>, <col>,
<colgroup>, <comment>, currentStyle, <custom>, <dd>, <del>, <dfn>, <dir>, <div>,
<dl>, <dt>, <em>, <embed>, <fieldset>, <font>, <form>, <frameset>, <head>, <hn>,
<hr>, <html>, <i>, <img>, <input>, <input type="button">, <input type="checkbox">,
<input type="file">, <input type="hidden">, <input type="image">, <input
type="password">, <input type="radio">, <input type="reset">, <input
type="submit">, <input type="text">, <ins>, <isindex>, <kbd>, <label>, <legend>,
<li>, <link>, <listing>, <marquee>, <menu>, nextID, <nobr>, <noframes>, <noscript>,
```

`<object>`, `<ol>`, `<option>`, `<p>`, `<pre>`, `<q>`, `<rt>`, `<ruby>`, runtimeStyle, `<s>`, `<samp>`,
`<script>`, `<select>`, `<small>`, `<span>`, `<strike>`, `<strong>`, style, `<sub>`, `<sup>`,
`<table>`, `<tbody>`, `<td>`, `<textarea>`, `<tfoot>`, `<th>`, `<thead>`, `<title>`, `<tr>`, `<tt>`,
`<u>`, `<ul>`, `<var>`, `<xml>`, `<xmp>`

top

Compatibility: NN6, NN7, IE4, IE5, IE5.5, IE6

This style property defines the top position of the element relative to the top
edge of the next element in the page.

Syntax:

```
element { top: value }
elementID.style.top = "value"
document.all.elementID.style.top = "value" // IE only
```

Values:

auto	The default; regular HTML position
length	A floating-point number followed by a unit designator
percentage	An integer followed by a percent sign, representing the percent height of the parent object

Example:

```
<img id="myImg" src="yourImage.gif" width=74 height=100"
style="position:relative"></p></center>
<input type="button" value="Set top property to 100" onclick="myImg.style.top=100">
<input type="button" value="Set top property to 200" onclick="myImg.style.top=200">
<input type="button" value="Restore image position" onclick="myImg.style.top=0">
```

Applies to:

`<a>`, `<address>`, `<applet>`, `<b>`, `<big>`, `<blockquote>`, `<button>`, `<center>`, `<cite>`,
`<code>`, currentStyle, `<custom>`, `<dd>`, defaults, `<dfn>`, `<dir>`, `<div>`, `<dl>`, `<dt>`,
`<em>`, `<embed>`, `<fieldset>`, `<font>`, `<form>`, `<hn>`, `<hr>`, `<i>`, `<iframe>`, `<img>`, `<input
type="button">`, `<input type="checkbox">`, `<input type="file">`, `<input type="image">`,
`<input type="password">`, `<input type="radio">`, `<input type="reset">`, `<input
type="submit">`, `<input type="text">`, `<isindex>`, `<kbd>`, `<label>`, `<legend>`, `<li>`,
`<listing>`, `<marquee>`, `<menu>`, `<object>`, `<ol>`, `<p>`, `<pre>`, runtimeStyle, `<s>`,
`<samp>`, `<select>`, `<small>`, `<span>`, `<strike>`, `<strong>`, style, `<sub>`, `<sup>`,
`<table>`, `<textarea>`, `<tt>`, `<u>`, `<ul>`, `<var>`, `<xmp>`

unicode-bidi

Compatibility: NN6, NN7, IE5, IE5.5, IE6

This style property controls how text for languages with different reading
directions is displayed, such as when left-to-right text (such as European) is
combined with a right-to-left text (such as Hebrew or Arabic). This is known as
the bidirectional algorithm. This property is used with the direction property.

Syntax:

```
element { unicode-bidi: value }
elementID.style.unicodeBidi = "value"
document.all.elementID.style.unicodeBidi = "value" // IE only
```

Values:

normal	The default; no additional embedding level is open
embed	An additional level of embedding is open
bidi-override	The display of the text is done according to the `direction` property inside the element

Example:

```
<p style="direction:ltr; unicode-bidi:bidi-override">This is an English sample text
. . . followed by this supposed HEBREW TEXT</p>
```

Applies to:

```
<a>, <acronym>, <address>, <b>, <bdo>, <big>, <blockquote>, <body>, <button>,
<caption>, <center>, <cite>, <code>, <col>, <colgroup>, currentStyle, <custom>,
<dd>, defaults, <del>, <dfn>, <dir>, <div>, <dl>, <dt>, <em>, <embed>, <fieldset>,
<font>, <form>, <hn>, <i>, <img>, <input type="button">, <input type="checkbox">,
<input type="file">, <input type="image">, <input type="password">, <input
type="radio">, <input type="reset">, <input type="submit">, <input type="text">,
<ins>, <kbd>, <label>, <legend>, <li>, <listing>, <marquee>, <menu>, <nobr>,
<object>, <ol>, <option>, <p>, <pre>, <q>, <rt>, <ruby>, runtimeStyle, <s>, <samp>,
<select>, <small>, <span>, <strike>, <strong>, style, <sub>, <sup>, <table>,
<tbody>, <td>, <textarea>, <tfoot>, <th>, <thead>, <tr>, <tt>, <u>, <ul>, <var>, .
<xmp>
```

vertical-align

Compatibility: NN6, NN7, IE4, IE5, IE5.5, IE6

This style property determines the vertical alignment in conjunction with the valign attribute.

Syntax:

```
element { vertical-align: value }
elementID.style.verticalAlign = "value"
document.all.elementID.style.verticalAlign = "value" // IE only
```

Values: auto, baseline (the default), sub (aligns to subscript), sup (aligns to superscript), top, middle, bottom, text-top, and text-bottom.

Example:

```
<table width="70%" border="1" cellspacing="5" cellpadding="5">
  <tr height="50"><td>Cell 1 content</td><td>Cell 2 content</td></tr>
  <tr height="100" id="myT">
      <td><img src="../IMAGES/bg2.gif">Cell 3 text content</td>
      <td>Cell 4 text content</td>
```

```
    </tr>
  </table><br>
<input type="button" onclick="myT.style.verticalAlign='text-top'" value="Set
verticalAlign to text-top">
<input type="button" onclick="myT.style.verticalAlign='text-bottom'" value="Set
verticalAlign to text-bottom">
<input type="button" onclick="myT.style.verticalAlign='top'" value="Set
verticalAlign to top">
<input type="button" onclick="myT.style.verticalAlign='bottom'" value="Set
verticalAlign to bottom">
<input type="button" onclick="myT.style.verticalAlign='auto'"  value="Restore
position">
```

Applies to:

```
<col>, currentStyle, <custom>, defaults, <img>, runtimeStyle, <span>, style,
<tbody>, <td>, <tfoot>, <th>, <thead>, <tr>
```

visibility

Compatibility: NN4, NN6, NN7, IE4, IE5, IE5.5, IE6

This style property determines whether the element on the page is visible.
Syntax:

```
element { visibility: value }
elementID.style.visibility = "value"
document.all.elementID.style.visibility = "value" // IE only
```

Values:

inherit	The default
visible	
hidden	Transparent, but still affects the layout
collapse	Same as hidden, but causes the entire row or column to be removed from the display, and the space normally taken up by the row or column is made available for other content; this applies only to rows and columns, and if it is applied to other elements, it is the same as hidden

Example:

```
<p><img id="myImg" src="yourimage.jpg" top:50; width:74; height:100"></p>
  <input type="button" value="Set visibility property to hidden"
onclick="myImg.style.visibility='hidden'">
  <input type="button" value="Set visibility property to visible"
onclick="myImg.style.visibility='visible'">
```

Applies to:

```
<a>, <address>, <applet>, <b>, <big>, <blockquote>, <body>, <button>, <caption>,
<center>, <cite>, <code>, <col>, <colgroup>, currentStyle, <custom>, <dd>,
defaults, <dfn>, <dir>, <div>, <dl>, <dt>, <em>, <embed>, <fieldset>, <form>, <hn>,
```

<hr>, <html>, <i>, <iframe>, <img>, <input type="button">, <input type="checkbox">, <input type="file">, <input type="image">, <input type="password">, <input type="radio">, <input type="reset">, <input type="submit">, <input type="text">, <isindex>, <kbd>, <label>, <legend>, <li>, <listing>, <marquee>, <menu>, <nobr>, <object>, <ol>, <p>, <pre>, runtimeStyle, <s>, <samp>, <select>, <small>, <span>, <strike>, <strong>, style, <sub>, <sup>, <table>, <tbody>, <td>, <textarea>, <tfoot>, <th>, <thead>, <tr>, <tt>, <u>, <ul>, <var>, <xmp>

white-space

Compatibility: NN6, NN7, IE5.5, IE6

This style property determines how white space (line breaks, spaces, tabs) is handled. Usually HTML ignores extra white space. You can add extra space with one or more   entities, and you can add extra lines with the <br> element.

Syntax:

```
element { white-space: value }
elementID.style.whiteSpace = "value"
document.all.elementID.style.whiteSpace = "value" // IE only
```

Values:

normal	The default; no extra white space is added.
nowrap	Text wrapping is turned off, meaning that line breaks are disabled.
pre	Content wraps to the next line; this is supported in IE6 when the !DOCTYPE declaration specifies standards-compliant mode. (For example, see http://www.w3c.org/tr/rec-html40/strict.dtd.) The full !DOCTYPE declaration would be: <!DOCTYPE HTML PUBLIC "-//W3C//DTD HTML 4.0 //EN" "http://www.w3.org/TR/REC-html40/strict.dtd">.

Example:

```
<!DOCTYPE HTML PUBLIC "-//W3C//DTD HTML 4.0 //EN" "http://www.w3.org/TR/REC-html40/strict.dtd">
<div id="myDiv" style="background:beige; width:400px;">
  This   text   is   written   with   additional spaces   between   words.<br>
  This sentence has line 1
  line 2
  and line 3
  <br>
  This is a regular block of text.
</div>
<br>
<button onclick="myDiv.style.whiteSpace='normal';">Set whiteSpace property to:
normal</button>
<button onclick="myDiv.style.whiteSpace='pre';">Set whiteSpace property to:
pre</button>
```

Applies to:

<acronym>, <address>, <basefont>, <bdo>, <big>, <blockquote>, <body>, <center>, <cite>, <code>, currentStyle, <custom>, <dd>, <dir>, <div>, <dl>, <dt>, <em>, <fieldset>, <font>, <form>, <hn>, <hr>, <i>, <ins>, <isindex>, <kbd>, <label>, <legend>, <li>, <listing>, <menu>, <ol>, <p>, <pre>, <q>, <s>, <small>, <span>, <strike>, <strong>, style, <sub>, <sup>, <tt>, <u>, <ul>, <xmp>

width

Compatibility: NN4, NN6, NN7, IE4, IE5, IE5.5, IE6

This style property sets the width of the element.

Syntax:

```
element { width: value }
elementID.style.width = "value"
document.all.elementID.style.width = "value" // IE only
```

Values:

auto	The default; regular HTML position
length	A floating-point number followed by a unit designator
percentage	An integer followed by a percent sign, representing the percent width of the parent object

Example:

```
<img id="myImg" src="yourimage.jpg" width="132">
  <br><input type="button" value="Shrink image" onclick="myImg.style.width='65'">
  <input type="button" value="Restore image" onclick="myImg.style.width='132'">
```

Applies to:

<a>, <acronym>, <address>, <applet>, <b>, <bdo>, <big>, <blockquote>, <button>, <caption>, <center>, <cite>, <code>, currentStyle, <custom>, <dd>, <del>, <dfn>, <dir>, <div>, <dl>, <dt>, <em>, <fieldset>, <font>, <form>, <hn>, <hr>, <i>, <ins>, <kbd>, <label>, <legend>, <li>, <listing>, <menu>, <nobr>, <ol>, <option>, <p>, <pre>, <q>, <rt>, <ruby>, runtimeStyle, <s>, <samp>, <select>, <small>, <span>, <strike>, <strong>, style, <sub>, <sup>, <textarea>, <tt>, <u>, <ul>, <var>, <xmp>

word-break

Compatibility: IE5, IE5.5, IE6

This style property defines how line breaks are used to break up words when the edge of the element is reached. When using the word-break style property with a table, you must set the table-layout property to fixed.

Syntax:

```
element { word-break: value }
elementID.style.wordBreak = "value"
document.all.elementID.style.wordBreak = "value"
```

Values:

normal	The default; normal line breaks are used
break-all	This is normal for Asian text
keep-all	Allows line breaking for non-Asian text and does not allow line breaking for Asian text

Example:

```
<div id="myD" style="width:300px; background-color:beige;">
This is a sample paragraph. This is a sample paragraph. This is a sample paragraph.
This is a sample paragraph.</div><br>
<input type="button" value="Set wordBreak property to break-all"
onclick="myD.style.wordBreak='break-all'">
```

Applies to:

`<address>`, `<blockquote>`, `<body>`, `<center>`, currentStyle, `<dd>`, `<dir>`, `<div>`, `<dl>`, `<dt>`, `<fieldset>`, `<form>`, `<hn>`, `<hr>`, `<legend>`, `<li>`, `<listing>`, `<marquee>`, `<menu>`, `<ol>`, `<p>`, `<pre>`, runtimeStyle, style, `<table>`, `<td>`, `<th>`, `<tr>`, `<ul>`, `<xmp>`

word-spacing

Compatibility: NN6, NN7, IE6

This style property defines the use of additional spaces between words.

Syntax:

```
element { word-spacing: value }
elementID.style.wordSpacing = "value"
document.all.elementID.style.wordSpacing = "value" // IE only
```

Values:

normal	The default; no additional spaces are allowed
length	A floating-point number followed by a unit designator

Example:

```
<div id="myD" style="width:300px; background-color:beige;">
    This is a sample paragraph.</div>
  <br>
  <input type="button" value="Set wordSpacing property to 10px"
onclick="myD.style.wordSpacing='10px'">
```

```
   <input type="button" value="Set wordSpacing property to 0.5cm"
onclick="myD.style.wordSpacing='0.5cm'">
   <input type="button" value="Set wordSpacing property to normal"
onclick="myD.style.wordSpacing='normal'">
```

Applies to:

```
<a>, <address>, <b>, <big>, <blockquote>, <body>, <button>, <caption>, <center>,
<cite>, <code>, <col>, <colgroup>, currentStyle, <custom>, <dd>, <dfn>, <dir>,
<div>, <dl>, <dt>, <em>, <fieldset>, <form>, <hn>, <html>, <i>, <img>, <input
type="button">, <input type="checkbox">, <input type="file">, <input type="image">,
<input type="password">, <input type="radio">, <input type="reset">, <input
type="submit">, <input type="text">, <isindex>, <kbd>, <label>, <legend>, <li>,
<listing>, <marquee>, <menu>, <ol>, <p>, <pre>, runtimeStyle, <s>, <samp>,
<select>, <small>, <span>, <strike>, <strong>, style, <sub>, <sup>, <table>,
<tbody>, <td>, <textarea>, <tfoot>, <th>, <thead>, <tr>, <tt>, <u>, <ul>, <var>,
<xmp>
```

word-wrap

Compatibility: IE5.5, IE6

This style property defines whether words can be broken at the end of the
line. This property is applied to elements absolutely positioned or that have
a specified height or width.

Syntax:

```
element { word-wrap: value }
elementID.style.wordWrap = "value"
document.all.elementID.style.wordWrap = "value"
```

Values:

normal	The default; content does not break words
break-word	Content wraps to the next line

Example:

```
<div style="width:80pt; background-color:beige; word-wrap:break-
word;">Thisisaonelongwordparagraph,withaword-wrappropertyvalueofbreak-word.</div>
```

Applies to:

```
<a>, <acronym>, <address>, <applet>, <b>, <bdo>, <big>, <blockquote>, <body>,
<button>, <center>, <cite>, <code>, currentStyle, <custom>, <dd>, <del>, <dfn>,
<dir>, <div>, <dl>, <dt>, <em>, <embed>, <fieldset>, <font>, <form>, <hn>, <hr>,
<html>, <i>, <img>, <input>, <input type="button">, <input type="checkbox">, <input
type="file">, <input type="hidden">, <input type="image">, <input type="password">,
<input type="radio">, <input type="reset">, <input type="submit">, <input
type="text">, <ins>, <isindex>, <kbd>, <label>, <legend>, <li>, <listing>, <menu>,
```

`<nobr>`, `<object>`, `<ol>`, `<option>`, `<p>`, `<pre>`, `<q>`, `<rt>`, `<ruby>`, runtimeStyle, `<s>`, `<samp>`, `<select>`, `<small>`, `<span>`, `<strike>`, `<strong>`, style, `<sub>`, `<sup>`, `<td>`, `<textarea>`, `<th>`, `<tt>`, `<u>`, `<ul>`, `<var>`, `<xmp>`

writing-mode

Compatibility: IE5.5, IE6

This style property determines the writing direction of text.

Syntax:

```
element { writing-mode: value }
elementID.style.writingMode = "value"
document.all.elementID.style.writingMode = "value"
```

Values:

lr-tb	The default; left to right, top to bottom
tb-rl	Top to bottom, right to left; used in Asian writing

Example:

```
<div id="myD" style="width:100%; background-color:beige;">This is sample text.</div><br>
  <input type="button" value="Set writingMode property to tb-rl"
onclick="myD.style.writingMode='tb-rl'">
  <input type="button" value="Set writingMode property to lr-tb"
onclick="myD.style.writingMode='lr-tb'">
```

Applies to:

`<a>`, `<acronym>`, `<address>`, `<b>`, `<big>`, `<blockquote>`, `<button>`, `<caption>`, `<center>`, `<cite>`, `<code>`, currentStyle, `<custom>`, `<dd>`, `<del>`, `<dfn>`, `<dir>`, `<div>`, `<dl>`, `<dt>`, `<em>`, `<fieldset>`, `<font>`, `<form>`, `<hn>`, `<hr>`, `<i>`, `<input>`, `<input type="button">`, `<input type="file">`, `<input type="password">`, `<input type="reset">`, `<input type="submit">`, `<input type="text">`, `<ins>`, `<isindex>`, `<kbd>`, `<label>`, `<legend>`, `<li>`, `<marquee>`, `<menu>`, `<ol>`, `<option>`, `<p>`, `<pre>`, `<q>`, `<rt>`, `<ruby>`, runtimeStyle, `<s>`, `<samp>`, `<small>`, `<span>`, `<strike>`, `<strong>`, style, `<sub>`, `<sup>`, `<td>`, `<textarea>`, `<th>`, `<tt>`, `<u>`, `<ul>`, `<var>`

z-index

Compatibility: NN4, NN6, NN7, IE4, IE5, IE5.5, IE6

This style property specifies how positioned elements are stacked on the page.

Syntax:

```
element { z-index: value }
elementID.style.zIndex = "value"
document.all.elementID.style.zIndex = "value" // IE only
```

Values:

auto	The default; elements are displayed in the position in which they appear in the HTML source.
integer	An integer value that determines the position of the element in the stacking order. Elements that have a higher z-index value appear on top of elements that have a lower z-index value.

Example:

```
<div id="myDiv" style="position:absolute; left:168px; top:251px; width:192px;
height:66px; z-index:1; background-color:red;">This div is absolute positioned with
an z-index of 1.</div>
<div style="position:absolute; left:168px; top:251px; z-index:12; height:50;
background-color:blue;">This is a div element with a z-index of 12.</div>
<button onclick="myDiv.style.zIndex = 20;">Bring red to front</button>
```

Applies to:

```
<a>, <address>, <applet>, <b>, <big>, <blockquote>, <button>, <caption>, <center>,
<cite>, <code>, <col>, <colgroup>, currentStyle, <custom>, <dd>, defaults, <dfn>,
<dir>, <div>, <dl>, <dt>, <em>, <fieldset>, <form>, <i>, <iframe>, <input
type="button">, <input type="checkbox">, <input type="file">, <input type="image">,
<input type="password">, <input type="radio">, <input type="reset">, <input
type="submit">, <input type="text">, <isindex>, <kbd>, <label>, <legend>, <li>,
<listing>, <marquee>, <menu>, <ol>, <p>, <pre>, runtimeStyle, <s>, <samp>, <small>,
<span>, <strike>, <strong>, style, <sub>, <sup>, <table>, <tbody>, <td>,
<textarea>, <tfoot>, <th>, <thead>, <tr>, <tt>, <u>, <ul>, <var>, <xmp>
```

zoom

Compatibility: IE5.5, IE6

This style property determines how an element is zoomed to appear smaller or larger.

Syntax:

```
element { zoom: value }
elementID.style.zoom = "value"
document.all.elementID.style.zoom = "value"
```

Values:

normal	The default; normal HTML size.
number	A floating-point number specifying the zoom; 1.0 is normal size.
percentage	A percent representation of the zoom value. If greater than 100% the element is enlarged, and if less than 100% the element is reduced; 100% is normal size.

Example:

```
<div id="myDiv" style="width:100pt; background-color:beige; font-family:verdana;">
This is some sample text.</div>
<button onclick="myDiv.style.zoom='200%'">Zoom 200%</button>
<button onclick="myDiv.style.zoom='100%'">Zoom 100%</button>
```

Applies to:

<a>, <acronym>, <address>, <applet>, <b>, <bdo>, <big>, <blockquote>, <body>, <button>, <caption>, <center>, <cite>, <code>, <col>, <colgroup>, currentStyle, <custom>, <dd>, <del>, <dfn>, <dir>, <div>, <dl>, <dt>, <em>, <embed>, <fieldset>, <font>, <form>, <frame>, <frameset>, <head>, <hn>, <hr>, <i>, <iframe>, <img>, <input>, <input type="button">, <input type="checkbox">, <input type="file">, <input type="hidden">, <input type="image">, <input type="password">, <input type="radio">, <input type="reset">, <input type="submit">, <input type="text">, <ins>, <isindex>, <kbd>, <label>, <legend>, <li>, <listing>, <marquee>, <menu>, <nobr>, <noframes>, <noscript>, <object>, <ol>, <option>, <p>, <pre>, <q>, <rt>, <ruby>, runtimeStyle, <s>, <samp>, <select>, <small>, <span>, <strike>, <strong>, style, <sub>, <sup>, <table>, <tbody>, <td>, <textarea>, <tfoot>, <th>, <thead>, <tr>, <tt>, <u>, <ul>, <var>, <xmp>

Style Properties No Longer Supported

azimuth, caption-side, content, counter-increment, counter-reset, cue, cue-after, cue-before, elevation, empty-cells, font-size-adjust, font-stretch, marks, marker-offset, max-height, max-width, min-width, orphans, outline, page, pause, pause-after, pause-before, pitch, pitch-range, play-during, quotes, richness, row-span, size, speak, speak-date, speak-beader, speak-numeral, speak-punctuation, speak-time, speech-rate, stress, text-shadow, voice-family, volume, windows

9

MICROSOFT INTERNET EXPLORER BEHAVIORS

DHTML behaviors are components that contain specific web page functionality. Applying a DHTML behavior to a standard HTML element will enhance that element's default behavior in some particular way. Microsoft provides standard behaviors, but you can create your own as well. For instance, a user-defined behavior can allow the background color of an <input> element to change when the element gets the focus.

As a component of DHTML, each behavior has its own members (properties, events, and methods), and these members are added to the list of members of the HTML element to which the behavior is applied. These added properties, events, and methods can then be utilized as though they belonged to the HTML element with the behavior.

This exclusive Microsoft technology can be used in Internet Explorer 5 or later. Microsoft proposed the behavior attribute to W3C as an addition to the CSS2 language.

NOTE *The examples in this chapter require that you have Windows Personal Web Server (for older versions of Windows) or IIS (for Windows XP and Windows 2000) installed in your computer.*

Behavior Types

There are two types of behaviors: first, user-defined behaviors written and prepared using a compiled language like Microsoft Visual C++ and saved in a .htc file format, and second, Microsoft default behaviors. This chapter documents and provides examples on how to use Microsoft default behaviors. For information on user-defined behaviors please go to the following URL: http://msdn.microsoft.com/library/default.asp?url=/workshop/author/behaviors/overview.asp.

Using Behaviors

Behaviors can be attached to elements by using styles. However, the syntax depends on the type of behavior, the language being used to reference the behavior (either CSS or JavaScript), and where on the page the behavior is being referenced.

Through CSS

Using the inline HTML style attribute with the inline CSS behavior attribute:

```
<element style="behavior:url(behaviorName.htc)">  // author's behavior
<element style="behavior:url('#default#behaviorName')">  // Microsoft default
behavior
```

Multiple behaviors can only be attached to an element by using the inline HTML style attribute with the inline CSS behavior attribute. Each behavior specified must be separated by a blank space:

```
<element style="behavior:url(behaviorName1.htc) url(behaviorName2.htc) . . .">
<element style="behavior:url(#default#behaviorName1) url(#default#behaviorName2)
. . .">
```

Using the HTML <style> element with the CSS behavior attribute, applied to HTML elements, classes, and selectors, respectively:

```
<style>
    element { behavior:url(behaviorName.htc) }
    .myClass { behavior:url(behaviorName.htc) }
    .mySelector { behavior:url(behaviorName.htc) }
</style>
```

To specify a user-defined behavior using the syntax above, simply replace *behaviorName*.htc in any of the declarations above with #default#*behaviorName*.

Through JavaScript

Using the JavaScript addBehavior() method:

```
document.all.elementID.addBehavior("behaviorName.htc")
//user-defined behavior
```

or,

```
document.all.tags("myTag").addBehavior("#default#behaviorName")
//Microsoft default behavior
```

Using the JavaScript style object:

```
document.elementArray[index].style.behavior = "url('behaviorName.htc)"
//user-defined behavior
```

or,

```
document.all.elementID.style.behavior = "url('#default#behaviorName')"
// Microsoft default behavior
```

NOTE *To avoid scripting errors when using behaviors, it is important to ensure that the document is fully loaded in the browser.*

Default Microsoft Behaviors

Each behavior listed in this chapter has its own set of events, properties, and methods. Some behaviors also contain objects, which in turn have their own properties and methods. Following are general syntax conventions for using behaviors with events, properties, methods, and objects:

Syntax for properties:

```
behaviorName.propertyName;
```

Syntax for methods:

```
behaviorName.methodName();
```

Syntax for objects:

```
behaviorName.objectName.objectProperties;
behaviorName.objectName.objectMethods;
```

For events, use the same syntax described in Chapter 7.

This behavior exposes the folder attribute for the `<a>` element, which enables the browser to navigate to a folder view. If the folder attribute is not specified for the `<a>` element, then the href attribute will be used as normal.

Example:

```
<head><style>
a {behavior:url(#default#AnchorClick);}
</style></head><body>
<a href="http://www.advocar.com" folder="c:\" target="_blank">Open the contents of
your c drive in a folder view</a></body>
```

Applies to:

```
<a>
```

Properties:

folder	This read/write JavaScript property specifies the address or path of the folder or file
target	This read/write JavaScript property specifies the window or frame into which the document will open

Value: Astring (the name of the window or frame), _self (loads document into the same window in which the link is located), or _top (loads document into the topmost window).

anim

This behavior exposes the functionality of the Microsoft DirectAnimation viewer inside an HTML page. For more information on DirectAnimation please go to the following url: http://msdn.microsoft.com/archive/default.asp?url=/archive/en-us/dnarmulmed/html/msdn_directan.asp.

Example (yourimage.gif must be an animated gif file):

```
<head>
<xml:namespace prefix="anim"/>
<style>
.time { behavior: url(#time); }
anim\:DA{ behavior: url(#default#anim); }
</style>
</head>
<body>
<div align="center">
    <anim:da id="da1" style="z-index: -1; width: 200px; height: 200px"
t:rendermode = "replace">
</div>
<script language="JavaScript">
```

```
<!--
    //Assign a variable to the DA statics library
    m = da1.statics;
    //Create the DAImage, yourimage.gif is an animated gif file.
    img1 = m.ImportImage("yourimage.gif");
    //Specify the DAImage to be displayed by the ANIM:DA tag
    da1.image = img1;
//-->
</script></body>
```

Applies to: n/a.

Properties:

image	This read/write JavaScript property specifies the DirectAnimation image file to be displayed by the anim:DA element
sound	This read/write JavaScript property specifies the DirectAnimation sound file to be played by the anim:DA element
statics	This read-only JavaScript property refers to an object that contains the DAStatics class library used in DirectAnimation

Methods:

addDABehavior(*behaviorName, behaviorID*)	This method adds a DirectAnimation behavior. The added behavior starts at the same time as the original animation. The required behaviorName parameter is the name of the behavior to be added. The required behaviorID parameter is an integer value that specifies the identifier of the behavior to be added.
removeDABehavior(*behaviorID*)	This method removes a behavior previously added with addDABehavior(). The required behaviorID parameter is an integer value that specifies the identifier of the behavior to be removed.

clientCaps

This behavior provides a way for installing customized or third-party browser components and exposes a set of properties that provide information about Internet Explorer's capabilities.

clientCaps behavior properties can be accessed in custom user-defined HTML elements created using an XML island in the HTML document.

Example:

```
<html xmlns:myCl>
<head>
<style>@media all { myCl \:clientcaps {behavior:url(#default#clientCaps)} }</style>
</head>
<body>
<h1>Example of clientCaps Behavior</h1>
<myCl:clientcaps id="myObject" />
<button onclick="alert(myObject.height + 'x' + myObject.width);">Your Screen
Resolution</button>
```

```
<button onclick="alert(myObject.isComponentInstalled('{76C19B36-F0C8-11CF-87CC-
0020AFEECF20}', 'componentid'));">Is Hebrew Text Support Installed</button>
</body></html>
```

Applies to:

<a>, <acronym>, <address>, <applet>, <area>, <b>, <base>, <basefont>, <bdo>,
<bgsound>, <big>, <blockquote>, <body>, <br>, <button>, <caption>, <center>,
<cite>, <code>, <col>, <colgroup>, <comment>, <dd>, <del>, <dfn>, <dir>, <div>,
<dl>, <dt>, <em>, <embed>, <fieldset>, <font>, <form>, <frame>, <frameset>, <head>,
<hn>, <hr>, <html>, <i>, <iframe>, <img>, <input type="button">, <input
type="checkbox">, <input type="file">, <input type="hidden">, <input type="image">,
<input type="password">, <input type="radio">, <input type="reset">, <input
type="submit">, <input type="text">, <ins>, <isindex>, <kbd>, <label>, <legend>,
<li>, <link>, <listing>, <map>, <marquee>, <menu>, <nobr>, <noframes>, <noscript>,
<object>, <ol>, <option>, <p>, <pre>, <q>, <rt>, <ruby>, <s>, <samp>, <script>,
<select>, <small>, <span>, <strike>, <strong>, <sub>, <sup>, <table>, <tbody>,
<td>, <textarea>, <tfoot>, <th>, <thead>, <title>, <tr>, <tt>, <u>, <ul>, <var>,
<wbr>, <xml>, <xmp>

Properties:

availHeight	This property is equivalent to the scale height of the screen minus the height of the Windows taskbar
availWidth	This property is equivalent to the scale width of the screen minus the width of the Windows taskbar
bufferDepth	This property contains the size of the buffer dedicated to storing color information in the system
colorDepth	This property returns the color depth of the system in bits (e.g., 64-bit color)
connectionType	This property retrieves the type of Internet connection available to the system
cookieEnabled	This property indicates if cookies are enabled for the browser.
cpuClass	Returns the type of CPU being used in the system
height	This property returns the height of the screen in pixels
javaEnabled	This property indicates whether the Microsoft Virtual Machine is installed and active in the system
platform	This property indicates the operating system platform being used by the system
systemLanguage	This property indicates the system's default language
userLanguage	This property indicates the system's current user language setting
width	This property indicates the width of the screen in pixels

Methods:

addComponentRequest(*componentID, componentName, version*)	This method adds the specified third-party or custom component to the queue of components to be installed in Internet Explorer. The components are downloaded when a call is made to the doComponentRequest function. The version parameter is optional.

doComponentRequest()	This method downloads all components in the list of requested components complied using the addComponentRequest method. Return value: A Boolean indicating whether or not the download operation has been successful.
clearComponentRequest()	This method removes all components from the list of requested components complied using the addComponentRequest method.
getComponentVersion(*componentID*, *componentName*)	This method retrieves the version of the component specified by the componentID that is installed in Internet Explorer.
compareVersions(*versionNumber1*, *versionNumber2*)	This method compares the version number of two installed components and returns a value from the comparison. Return value: -1 if versionNumber1 < versionNumber2; 0 if versionNumber1 = versionNumber2; 1 if versionNumber1 > versionNumber2.
isComponentInstalled(*componentID*, *componentName*, *version*)	This method returns a Boolean value that indicates whether or not the specified component has been installed. The optional version parameter specifies the minimum version number of the component.

NOTE · *For a complete listing of* componentID *and* componentName *parameter values, refer to http://msdn.microsoft.com/workshop/author/behaviors/reference/methods/detectable.asp.*

download

This behavior allows the specified file to be downloaded from the server to the browser and notifies the browser using a callback function when the download operation is completed. The contents of the file are downloaded to the memory space of the browser and are passed in the callback function as a parameter.

Example:

```
<html xmlns:YourNamespace>
<msie:download id="myBehavior" style="behavior:url(#default#download)"/>
<script>
function downloadComplete(strFileContent){
    alert('download completed');
}
</script>
<button onclick="myBehavior.startDownload('yourimage.txt',
downloadComplete);">Download File</button>
</html>
```

Applies to:

```
<a>, <acronym>, <address>, <applet>, <area>, <b>, <base>, <basefont>, <bdo>,
<bgsound>, <big>, <blockquote>, <body>, <br>, <button>, <caption>, <center>,
<cite>, <code>, <col>, <colgroup>, <comment>, <dd>, <del>, <dfn>, <dir>, <div>,
<dl>, <dt>, <em>, <embed>, <fieldset>, <font>, <form>, <frame>, <frameset>, <head>,
```

```
<hn>, <hr>, <html>, <i>, <iframe>, <img>, <input type="button">, <input
type="checkbox">, <input type="file">, <input type="hidden">, <input type="image">,
<input type="password">, <input type="radio">, <input type="reset">, <input
type="submit">, <input type="text">, <ins>, <isindex>, <kbd>, <label>, <legend>,
<li>, <link>, <listing>, <map>, <marquee>, <menu>, <nobr>, <noframes>, <noscript>,
<object>, <ol>, <option>, <p>, <pre>, <q>, <rt>, <ruby>, <s>, <samp>, <script>,
<select>, <small>, <span>, <strike>, <strong>, <sub>, <sup>, <table>, <tbody>,
<td>, <textarea>, <tfoot>, <th>, <thead>, <title>, <tr>, <tt>, <u>, <ul>, <var>,
<wbr>, <xml>, <xmp>
```

Methods:

startDownload(*url*, *functionName*)	This method starts the download operation on the file specified by the url parameter. The required functionName parameter specifies the name of the function that has to be executed once the file is downloaded. The callback function specified by functionName must have a single parameter to receive the contents of the file downloaded to the browser.

homePage

This behavior exposes functionality that allows you to extract information about the browser's home page.

Example:

```
<html xmlns:myBehavior><head>
<style>@media all {myBehavior\:homepage {behavior:url(#default#homepage)}}</style>
</head>
<body>
<myBehavior:homepage id="myHomepage"/>
<button onclick="myHomepage.navigateHomePage();">Navigate to your browser's home
page</button>
</body></html>
```

Applies to:

```
<a>, <acronym>, <address>, <applet>, <area>, <b>, <base>, <basefont>, <bdo>,
<bgsound>, <big>, <blockquote>, <body>, <br>, <button>, <caption>, <center>,
<cite>, <code>, <col>, <colgroup>, <comment>, <dd>, <del>, <dfn>, <dir>, <div>,
<dl>, <dt>, <em>, <embed>, <fieldset>, <font>, <form>, <frame>, <frameset>, <head>,
<hn>, <hr>, <html>, <i>, <iframe>, <img>, <input type="button">, <input
type="checkbox">, <input type="file">, <input type="hidden">, <input type="image">,
<input type="password">, <input type="radio">, <input type="reset">, <input
type="submit">, <input type="text">, <ins>, <isindex>, <kbd>, <label>, <legend>,
<li>, <link>, <listing>, <map>, <marquee>, <menu>, <nobr>, <noframes>, <noscript>,
<object>, <ol>, <option>, <p>, <pre>, <q>, <rt>, <ruby>, <s>, <samp>, <script>,
<select>, <small>, <span>, <strike>, <strong>, <sub>, <sup>, <table>, <tbody>,
<td>, <textarea>, <tfoot>, <th>, <thead>, <title>, <tr>, <tt>, <u>, <ul>, <var>,
<wbr>, <xml>, <xmp>
```

Methods:

isHomePage(*url*)	This method returns a Boolean value, testing whether or not the specified url is the same as the browser's home page
navigateHomePage()	This method causes the browser to navigate to the browser's home page
setHomePage(*url*)	This method replaces the browser's home page with the specified url

httpFolder

This behavior allows the browser to navigate to a folder view in much the same way that the windows operating system navigates through folders.

Example:

```
<p id="myElement" style="behavior:url(#default#httpFolder);"/></p>
<button onclick="myElement.navigateFrame('http://www.advocar.com',
'_self');">navigate to the folder of a site</button>
```

NOTE *The example above assumes that folder browsing is enabled on the web server.*

Applies to:

```
<a>, <acronym>, <address>, <area>, <b>, <big>, <blockquote>, <body>, <button>,
<caption>, <center>, <cite>, <code>, <dd>, <del>, <dfn>, <dir>, <div>, <dl>, <dt>,
<em>, <font>, <form>, <hn>, <hr>, <i>, <img>, <input type="button">, <input
type="checkbox">, <input type="file">, <input type="hidden">, <input type="image">,
<input type="password">, <input type="radio">, <input type="reset">, <input
type="submit">, <input type="text">, <kbd>, <label>, <li>, <listing>, <map>,
<marquee>, <menu>, <object>, <ol>, <option>, <p>, <pre>, <q>, <s>, <samp>,
<select>, <small>, <span>, <strike>, <strong>, <sub>, <sup>, <table>, <textarea>,
<tt>, <u>, <ul>, <var>, <xmp>
```

Methods:

navigate(*myHttp*)	This method instructs the browser to replace the current document in the window with the path specified by the myHttp parameter and causes the browser to switch into folder view mode.
navigateFrame(*myHttp, targetFrame*)	This method replaces the document in the specified target frame with the path specified by the myHttp parameter and causes the browser to switch the target frame into folder view mode. The targetFrame parameter can be _self, _top, or the name of a window or frame.

mediaBar

The mediaBar behavior opens a media bar interface in the browser to the left of the document. The interface exposed by the mediaBar behavior gives control over the Microsoft Media Player's user interface and offers navigation options to various media sites. Additionally, it allows HTML to be loaded in the Media Bar content area. The mediaBar behavior is only compatible with IE6+.

Example:

```
<body bgcolor="#FFFFFF" text="#000000">
<div style="behavior:url(#default#mediaBar)" onShow="alert('testing');"></div>
<button onclick="window.location.href = 'yourvideo.avi'">Play Video</button>
</body>
```

NOTE *You can prepare a playlist using Visual Basic, C, C++, or XML. The simplest method is through XML. For more information on creating a playlist, refer to the following link at Microsoft's website: http://msdn.microsoft.com/library/default.asp?url=/library/en-us/wmsrvsdk/htm/usingxmltodefineplylsts.asp.*

Applies to: n/a.

Properties:

currentItem	This read-only JavaScript property returns a reference to the media item currently selected in the media bar.
disabledUI	This read/write JavaScript property has a Boolean value that specifies whether the Media Bar user interface (UI) is enabled or disabled.
enabled	This read/write JavaScript property has a Boolean value that determines if the Microsoft Media Bar player is enabled or disabled.
hasNextItem	This read-only JavaScript property has a boolean value that indicates whether the playlist collection contains media items in addition to the currentItem.
openState	This read-only JavaScript property returns the current state of the Media Bar Player. Value: An integer from 0 to 21. For a complete list and description of the possible values please refer to http://msdn.microsoft.com/workshop/author/behaviors/reference/properties/openstate.asp.
playlistInfo	This read-only JavaScript property retrieves a reference to a playlist object.
playState	This read-only JavaScript property indicates the play state of the Media Bar player. Value: An integer from 0 to 10. For a list of possible values and their meaning refer to http://msdn.microsoft.com/workshop/author/behaviors/reference/properties/playstate.asp.

Events:

onHide	This event fires immediately after the Media Bar is hidden from the page
onOpenStateChange	This event fires when the Media Bar's openState property changes
onPlayStateChange	This event fires when the Media Bar's playState property changes
onShow	This event fires when the Media Bar player is displayed on the page

Methods:

playNext()	This method instructs the browser to start playing the next media item in a playlist.
playURL(*url*, *mimeType*)	This method causes the Media Bar player to load and start playing the media specified by the url parameter. The mimeType parameter is required, and it must be a valid mime type.
stop()	This method causes the Media Bar to stop playing the current media item.

Example:

```
<a target="_media" href="test.htm">Load Media Bar</a>
```

Contents of test.htm:

```
<html>
<body>
<div style="behavior:url(#default#mediaBar)" onhide="alert('onhide event fired');"
onshow="alert('onshow event fired');" OnOpenStateChange="alert('onopenstatechange
event fired')" OnPlayStateChange="alert('onplaystatechange event fired');"
id="myMedia"></div>
<input type=button onclick="myMedia.playURL('yourvideo.avi','video/avi');"
value="Play a video file">
</body>
</html>
```

Objects:

MediaItem	This object represents a single media item in the playlist in the Media Bar. The MediaItem object has the following JavaScript properties and methods:

	attributeCount	This is a read-only property whose integer value indicates the number of attributes associated with the media item.
	duration	This is a read-only property whose integer value indicates the length in time of the current media item.
	name	This is a read-only property that retrieves the name of the media item.
	sourceURL	This property retrieves the location of the media item.
	getAttributeName(*itemno*)	This method uses the itemno parameter to retrieve the name of the attribute.
	getItemInfo(*itemno*)	This method uses the itemno parameter to return the value of the attribute.

PlaylistInfo	This object can be used to retrieve information regarding a media playlist. The PlaylistInfo object has the following JavaScript properties and methods:

	attributeCount	This read-only property returns the number of attributes used in the PlaylistInfo object.
	name	This is a read-only property that retrieves the name of the media player playlist.
	getAttributeName(*itemno*)	This method uses the itemno parameter to retrieve the name of the attribute.
	getItemInfo(*itemno*)	This method uses the itemno parameter to return the value of the attribute.

Example:

```
<a target="_media" href="test.htm">Load Media Bar</a>
```

Contents of test.htm:

```
<html>
<body>
<div style="behavior:url(#default#mediaBar)" id="myMedia"></div>
<button onclick="alert(myMedia.PlayListInfo.attributeCount);">PlayListInfo Object</
button>
<button onclick="alert(myMedia.currentItem.name);">MediaItem Object</button>
</body>
</html>
```

NOTE *The above example requires the use of a playlist. You can prepare a playlist using Visual Basic, C, C++, or XML. The simplest method is through XML. For more information on creating a playlist, please refer to the following link at Microsoft's website: http://msdn.microsoft.com/library/default.asp?url=/library/en-us/wmsrvsdk/htm/ usingxmltodefineplylsts.asp.*

saveFavorite

This behavior allows the current state of a web page, including any user input entered in its forms, to be saved when the web page is added to the Favorites menu. The page that is saved in the Favorites menu has a persistent state because it retains the page link and user input entered into the form.

Example:

```
<body bgcolor="#FFFFFF" text="#000000">
<form name="myForm" style="behavior:url(#default#savefavorite);">
<pre>
Instructions:
1) type text into the text box below
2) add this page to the favorites
3) close the browser
4) open the browser
5) go to the favorites and open the page
6) your data will be in the input box
</pre>
<input id="myInput" onsave="this.setAttribute('myText', myForm.myInput.value);"
onload="this.value=myForm.myInput.getAttribute('myText');">
</form>
</body>
```

Applies to:

```
<a>, <acronym>, <address>, <area>, <b>, <big>, <blockquote>, <button>, <caption>,
<center>, <cite>, <code>, <dd>, <del>, <dfn>, <dir>, <div>, <dl>, <dt>, <em>,
<font>, <form>, <hn>, <hr>, <i>, <img>, <input type="button">, <input
type="checkbox">, <input type="file">, <input type="hidden">, <input type="image">,
<input type="password">, <input type="radio">, <input type="reset">, <input
```

type="submit">, <input type="text">, <kbd>, <label>, <li>, <listing>, <map>, <marquee>, <menu>, <object>, <ol>, <option>, <p>, <pre>, <q>, <s>, <samp>, <select>, <small>, <span>, <strike>, <strong>, <sub>, <sup>, <table>, <textarea>, <tt>, <u>, <ul>, <var>, <xmp>

Properties:

XMLDocument(*objectName*)	This read-only JavaScript property points to a XML Document Object Model corresponding to the *objectName* parameter.

Events:

onLoad	This event fires when the page is reloaded from the favorites.
onSave	This event fires when the page is saved to the favorites or bookmarked, or when the user navigates to another page.

Methods:

getAttribute(*atrName*)	This method returns the value of the attribute specified by the *atrName* parameter. This method is used to retrieve attribute values that have been set using the setAttribute method.
removeAttribute(*atrName*)	This method removes the attribute specified by the atrName parameter from the object. This method removes an attribute that was added using the setAttribute method.
setAttribute(*atrName*, *atrValue*)	This method adds an attribute and its corresponding value to an element on the page.

saveHistory

This behavior saves the current state of a page, which includes any user input entered in its forms, in the history object of the document. The saveHistory behavior persists only for the current session.

For a list of properties, methods, and events please refer to the saveFavorite behavior in the preceding section.

Example:

```
<meta name="save" content="history">
<body bgcolor="#FFFFFF" text="#000000">
<form name="myForm">
<pre>
Instructions:
1) type text into the text box below
2) add this page to the favorites
3) click to browse to a different page and press back
5) go to the favorites and open the page
6) your data will be in the input box
</pre>
<input style="behavior:url(#default#savehistory);" id="myInput"
onsave="alert('testing'); this.setAttribute('myText', myForm.myInput.value);"
onload="this.value=myForm.myInput.getAttribute('myText');">
```

```
<br><a href="http://www.advocar.com/">Different Page</a>
</form>
</body>
```

Applies to:

```
<a>, <acronym>, <address>, <area>, <b>, <big>, <blockquote>, <button>, <caption>,
<center>, <cite>, <code>, <dd>, <del>, <dfn>, <dir>, <div>, <dl>, <dt>, <em>,
<font>, <form>, <hn>, <hr>, <i>, <img>, <input type="button">, <input
type="checkbox">, <input type="file">, <input type="hidden">, <input type="image">,
<input type="password">, <input type="radio">, <input type="reset">, <input
type="submit">, <input type="text">, <kbd>, <label>, <li>, <listing>, <map>,
<marquee>, <menu>, <object>, <ol>, <option>, <p>, <pre>, <q>, <s>, <samp>,
<select>, <small>, <span>, <strike>, <strong>, <sub>, <sup>, <table>, <textarea>,
<tt>, <u>, <ul>, <var>, <xmp>
```

saveSnapshot

This behavior allows form data to be saved when the user saves the page. Your code must contain a `<meta>` tag that identifies the type of persistence to use with this behavior.

Example:

```
<head>
<meta name="save" content="snapshot">
<style>
.mySnapshot { behavior: url(#default#savesnapshot ) }
</style></head>
<body bgcolor="#FFFFFF" text="#000000">
<pre>
Enter some text in the input below.
Save the page using "Save as . . ." on your hard disk.
Anything you enter before saving will reappear when you open the saved file.
<input type="text" class="mySnapshot" id="myText">
</body>
```

Applies to:

```
<a>, <acronym>, <address>, <area>, <b>, <big>, <blockquote>, <button>, <center>,
<cite>, <code>, <dd>, <del>, <dfn>, <dir>, <div>, <dl>, <dt>, <em>, <font>, <form>,
<hn>, <hr>, <i>, <img>, <input type="button">, <input type="checkbox">, <input
type="file">, <input type="hidden">, <input type="image">, <input type="radio">,
<input type="reset">, <input type="submit">, <input type="text">, <kbd>, <label>,
<li>, <listing>, <map>, <marquee>, <menu>, <object>, <ol>, <p>, <pre>, <q>, <s>,
<samp>, <script>, <select>, <small>, <span>, <strike>, <strong>, <sub>, <sup>,
<table>, <textarea>, <tt>, <u>, <ul>, <var>, <xmp>
```

Events:

onSave	This event fires when the page is saved, bookmarked, or abandoned. The srcElement property can be applied to this event.

This behavior allows user session information to be saved without resorting to cookies, by writing to a UserData store. The UserData store can be more useful and flexible than using cookies, but it is not as secure. Therefore, this behavior is not recommended for storing sensitive data such as credit card numbers. The saveFavorite, saveHistory, and saveSnapshot behaviors make use of this behavior.

A UserData store can be accessed only when a user is viewing a web page residing in the same directory and using the same protocol in which the data store was saved.

As is the case with cookies, there is a maximum amount of UserData storage available per individual document and per domain. See Table 9-1 for specifications.

Table 9-1: UserData Storage Limits

Storage location	Document limit (KB)	Domain limit (KB)
Local machine, trusted sites, Internet	128	1,024
Intranet	512	10,240
Restricted	64	640

Example:

```
<head>
<style>.myData {behavior: url(#default#userdata)}</style>
<script language="JavaScript">
function saveData(){
    var myPersist=myForm.myText;
    myPersist.setAttribute("myPersistText",myPersist.value);
    myPersist.save("myXML");
    myPersist.value="";
}
function  loadData(){
    var myPersist=myForm.myText;
    myPersist.load("myXML");
    myPersist.value=myPersist.getAttribute("myPersistText");
}
</script>
</head>
<body>
<pre>
1) type text into the text box
2) click the save button
3) <a href="http://www.advocar.com/">exit page</a>
4) click back button
5) click on the load button
</pre>
<form name="myForm">
<input id="myText" class="myData">
```

```
<button onclick="saveData()">Save</button>
<button onclick="loadData()">Load</button>
</form>
</body>
```

Applies to:

`<a>`, `<acronym>`, `<address>`, `<area>`, `<b>`, `<big>`, `<blockquote>`, `<button>`, `<caption>`, `<center>`, `<cite>`, `<code>`, `<dd>`, `<del>`, `<dfn>`, `<dir>`, `<div>`, `<dl>`, `<dt>`, `<em>`, `<font>`, `<form>`, `<hn>`, `<hr>`, `<i>`, `<img>`, `<input type="button">`, `<input type="checkbox">`, `<input type="file">`, `<input type="hidden">`, `<input type="image">`, `<input type="password">`, `<input type="radio">`, `<input type="reset">`, `<input type="submit">`, `<input type="text">`, `<kbd>`, `<label>`, `<li>`, `<listing>`, `<map>`, `<marquee>`, `<menu>`, `<object>`, `<ol>`, `<option>`, `<p>`, `<pre>`, `<q>`, `<s>`, `<samp>`, `<select>`, `<small>`, `<span>`, `<strike>`, `<strong>`, `<sub>`, `<sup>`, `<table>`, `<textarea>`, `<tt>`, `<u>`, `<ul>`, `<var>`, `<xmp>`

Properties:

Expires	This read/write JavaScript property specifies the date on which the persistency of the saved user data expires.
XMLDocument(*objectName***)**	This read-only JavaScript property points to an XML Document Object Model corresponding to the objectName parameter.

Methods:

load(*objectName***)**	This method loads an object from a UserData store.
getAttribute(*atrName***)**	This method returns the value of the attribute specified by the atrName parameter.
removeAttribute(*atrName***)**	This method removes the attribute specified by the atrName parameter.
setAttribute(*atrName***, ***atrValue***)**	This method sets the value of the attribute specified by the atrName parameter to atrValue.
save(*objectName***)**	This method saves an object in the UserData store.

10

MICROSOFT FILTERS AND TRANSITIONS

Microsoft filters add special effects to elements on a web page. There are two types of filters: *static filters* (also known simply as *filters*) and *transition filters* (dynamic filters, also known as *transitions*). Multiple filters and transitions can be assigned to a single HTML element by declaring each filter and transition in the filter property of the element.

While filters and transitions were introduced in Internet Explorer 4, they began to be treated differently beginning with IE5.5+. Therefore, two different CSS syntaxes are used with an element's style attribute. In IE versions 4 and 5, the following syntax is used:

```
<element style="filter:filterName(filterProperties)" >
```

In IE versions 5.5 and 6, the following syntax is used:

```
<element style="filter:prodig:
DXImageTransform.Microsoft.filterName(filterProperties)" >
```

Although you can still use the IE4 syntax when declaring filters, Microsoft recommends that the IE5.5+ syntax be used in most development relating to filters. This chapter conforms with the IE5.5+ syntax.

In both examples above, the filter properties are specified by inserting a comma-delimited list of CSS name-value pairs between the parentheses after the filterName. Many filter properties are shared by more than one filter, but other filter properties belong to individual filters.

In addition to adding filters using an HTML element's style attribute, as in the previous examples, JavaScript syntax can also be used to add a filter to an element in the following way:

```
elementID.style.filter = "prodig:
DXImageTransform.Microsoft.filterName(filterProperties)"
```

Once a filter is added, JavaScript syntax can be used to reference the filter's properties in a script. The following two ways to do this are equivalent, and you will see both of them used in this chapter:

```
elementID.filters[index].filterProperty = value
elementID.filters.item(index).filterProperty = value
```

In addition to properties, filters also have methods. Again there are two equivalent ways to reference these methods in a script:

```
elementID.filters[index].filterMethod()
elementID.filters.item(index).filterMethod()
```

As with filter properties, some filter methods are shared by more than one filter, while other methods are particular to individual filters.

NOTE   *For more information on this Microsoft technology, please refer to http://msdn.microsoft.com/library/default.asp?url=/workshop/author/filter/filters_transitions_entry.asp.*

Common Filter Properties

Filter properties allow you to control the way the filter affects the underlying object or element. As described above, you can reference a filter's properties using either CSS or JavaScript, except where otherwise noted.

All filter properties are read/write unless otherwise noted. Filter properties come in two varieties, those that are common to multiple filters and those that are common to individual filters only. The following properties are common to many filters. Properties that are specific to only one filter will be listed and explained in the appropriate filter section.

add

Compatibility: IE4, IE5, IE5.5, IE6

This property specifies whether or not the filter image is displayed in front of the original image. Value: Boolean; true or false (the default).

Filters:

```
MotionBlur, Wave
```

bands

Compatibility: IE5.5, IE6

This property specifies the number of bands the affected element is divided into during the transition effect.

Filters:

```
Blinds, Slide
```

bias

Compatibility: IE5.5, IE6

This property determines the contrast level of the color content before the filter is applied. Value: A floating-point number ranging from -1.0 to 1.0. The default value is 0.7.

Filters:

```
Emboss, Engrave
```

color

Compatibility: IE4, IE5, IE5.5, IE6

This property specifies the color applied with the filter. Value: Color name, or hexadecimal format (#AARRGGBB). The AA in this format represents the Alpha opacity hexadecimal value, the RR, GG, and BB represent the red, green and blue values, respectively.

Filters:

```
Chroma, DropShadow, Glow, MaskFilter, Shadow
```

duration

Compatibility: IE4, IE5, IE5.5, IE6

This property establishes the duration of the filter transition. Value: Length of time in seconds and milliseconds (for example, 12.25 = 12 seconds + 250 milliseconds).

Filters:

BlendTrans, RevealTrans, Barn, Blinds, Fade, GradientWipe, Inset, Iris, Pixelate, RadialWipe, RandomBars, RandomDissolve, Slide, Spiral, Stretch, Strips, Wheel, Zigzag

enabled

Compatibility: IE4, IE5, IE5.5, IE6

This property establishes whether the filter is enabled or disabled. Value: Boolean; true or false.

Filters: All except `Compositor` and `ICMFilter`.

gridSizeX

Compatibility: IE5.5, IE6

This property is used in combination with the `GridSizeY` property to divide the content of the object into a grid that will be used by the filter. This property specifies the number of columns in the grid. The default value is 16.

Filters:

Spiral, Zigzag

gridSizeY

Compatibility: IE5.5, IE6

This property is used in combination with the `GridSizeX` property to divide the content of the object into a grid that will be used by the filter. This property specifies the number of rows in the grid. The default value is 16.

Filters:

Spiral, Zigzag

orientation

Compatibility: IE5.5, IE6

This property determines the directional orientation of the filter's effect. Value: horizontal or vertical (the default).

Filters:

Barn, RandomBars

percent (*)

Compatibility: IE4, IE5, IE5.5, IE6

This JavaScript-only property enables a transition to be used to create a static filter. This property establishes the point in the duration of the transition's play when the transition stops its progress, thus displaying a static filter output. Value: A number between 0 (the default; filter has not started) and 100 (filter is finished).

In order to create a static filter using a transition, follow these steps. For an example please refer to the BlendTrans filter section.

1. Use the transition's apply method.
2. Set the transition's enabled property to true.
3. Specify the transition's percent property.

Filters:

BlendTrans, RevealTrans, Barn, Blinds, Fade, GradientWipe, Inset, Iris, Pixelate, RadialWipe, RandomBars, RandomDissolve, Slide, Spiral, Stretch, Strips, Wheel, Zigzag

---

status (*)

Compatibility: IE4, IE5, IE5.5, IE6

This read-only JavaScript-only property retrieves the status of the transition. Value: Integer; 0 (filter has stopped), 1 (filter has been applied), 2 (filter is playing).

Filters:

BlendTrans, RevealTrans, Barn, Blinds, Fade, GradientWipe, Inset, Iris, Pixelate, RadialWipe, RandomBars, RandomDissolve, Slide, Spiral, Stretch, Strips, Wheel, Zigzag

---

strength

Compatibility: IE4, IE5, IE5.5, IE6

This property specifies the length that a filter effect can extend, in pixels. Value: The distance in pixels, ranging from 0 to 255. The default value is 5.

Filters:

MotionBlur, Glow, Wave, Shadow

Common Filter Methods

Filter methods allow you to control the activation and cessation of filters. Filter methods come in two varieties, those that are common to multiple filters and those that are common to individual filters only. The following are all of the JavaScript methods common to many filters. Methods that are specific to only one filter will be listed and explained in the appropriate filter section.

apply()

Compatibility: IE4, IE5, IE5.5, IE6

This method applies the initial filter settings of an element before playing a transition.

Filters:

```
BlendTrans, RevealTrans, Barn, Blinds, Compositor, Fade, GradientWipe, Inset, Iris,
Pixelate, RadialWipe, RandomBars, RandomDissolve, Slide, Spiral, Stretch, Strips,
Wheel, Zigzag
```

play()

Compatibility: IE4, IE5, IE5.5, IE6

This method plays the transition filter.

Filters:

```
BlendTrans, RevealTrans, Barn, Blinds, Compositor, Fade, GradientWipe, Inset, Iris,
Pixelate, RadialWipe, RandomBars, RandomDissolve, Slide, Spiral, Stretch, Strips,
Wheel, Zigzag
```

stop()

Compatibility: IE4, IE5, IE5.5, IE6

This method stops the transition filter.

Filters:

```
BlendTrans, RevealTrans, Barn, Blinds, Fade, GradientWipe, Inset, Iris, Pixelate,
RadialWipe, RandomBars, RandomDissolve, Slide, Spiral, Stretch, Strips, Wheel,
Zigzag
```

Static Filters

Static filters change the way the content of an object or element is displayed. Static filters only render the final output of the object or element, whereas transition filters display the process through which the content of an object or element is revealed.

Alpha

Compatibility: IE4, IE5, IE5.5, IE6

This filter controls the opacity/transparency of the contents of the element.

Example:

```
<img id="myDiv" src="yourimage.gif">
<br>
```

```
<button onclick="myDiv.style.filter =
'progid:DXImageTransform.Microsoft.Alpha(enabled=true, opacity=50,
finishopacity=50, style=1, startx=0, finishx=0, starty=0, finishy=0)';">Apply
Filter</button>
<button onclick="myDiv.style.filter =
'progid:DXImageTransform.Microsoft.Alpha(enabled=false)';">Restore</button>
```

Applies to:

```
<a>, <acronym>, <address>, <b>, <bdo>, <big>, <blockquote>, <body>, <button>,
<caption>, <center>, <cite>, <code>, <custom>, <dd>, <del>, <dfn>, <dir>, <div>,
<dl>, <dt>, <em>, <fieldset>, <font>, <form>, <frame>, <hn>, <i>, <iframe>, <img>,
<input type="button">, <input type="checkbox">, <input type="file">, <input
type="image">, <input type="password">, <input type="radio">, <input type="reset">,
<input type="submit">, <input type="text">, <ins>, <kbd>, <label>, <legend>, <li>,
<marquee>, <menu>, <nobr>, <object>, <ol>, <p>, <pre>, <q>, <rt>, <ruby>, <s>,
<samp>, <small>, <span>, <strike>, <strong>, <sub>, <sup>, <table>, <td>,
<textarea>, <th>, <tt>, <u>, <ul>, <var>, <xmp>
```

Common properties:

```
enabled
```

Other properties:

finishOpacity	This property specifies the opacity level at the end of an alpha filter gradient. Its value must be an integer from 0 (the default; fully transparent) to 100 (fully opaque). Use of this property requires that the style property be set to 1, 2, or 3.
finishX	This property specifies the horizontal position, as a percent of the width of the object, where the filter ends. Its value must be an integer from 0 (the default) to 100. Use of this property requires that the style property be set to 1.
finishY	This property specifies the vertical position, as a percent of the height of the object, where the filter ends. Its value must be an integer from 0 (the default) to 100. Use of this property requires that the style property be set to 1.
opacity	This property specifies the opacity level at the beginning of the filter gradient. Its value must be an integer from 0 (the default; fully transparent) to 100 (fully opaque).
startX	This property specifies the horizontal position, as a percent of the width of the object, where the filter starts. Its value must be an integer from 0 (the default) to 100. Use of this property requires that the style property be set to 1.
startY	This property specifies the horizontal position, as a percent of the height of the object, where the filter starts. Its value must be an integer from 0 (the default) to 100. Default value is 0. Use of this property requires that the style property be set to 1.
style	This property specifies the shape of the filter as it is applied in the element. Value: Integer; 0 (the default; opacity is applied evenly across the element), 1 (linear gradient), 2 (radial gradient, without affecting the corners), 3 (rectangular gradient).

BasicImage

Compatibility: IE5.5, IE6

This filter controls the color processing, image rotation, and opacity of the element's content.

Example:

```
<div id="myDiv" style="position:absolute; top:40px; left:40px;
filter:progid:DXImageTransform.Microsoft.BasicImage(enabled=false;)"><img
src="yourImage.gif"></div>
<script language="javascript">
function resetImage(){
    myDiv.filters[0].enabled = true;
    myDiv.filters[0].Mask = 0;
    myDiv.filters[0].grayscale = 0;
    myDiv.filters[0].invert = 0;
    myDiv.filters[0].xray = 0;
}
</script>
<button onclick="resetImage(); myDiv.filters[0].MaskColor = 0x00ffff00;
myDiv.filters[0].Mask=1">Mask color Yellow</button>
<button onclick="resetImage(); myDiv.filters[0].grayScale = 1;">Grayscale</button>
<button onclick="resetImage(); myDiv.filters[0].xray = 1;">X Ray</button>
<button onclick="resetImage(); myDiv.filters[0].invert = 1;">Invert</button>
```

Applies to:

`<a>`, `<acronym>`, `<address>`, `<b>`, `<bdo>`, `<big>`, `<blockquote>`, `<body>`, `<button>`, `<caption>`, `<center>`, `<cite>`, `<code>`, `<custom>`, `<dd>`, `<del>`, `<dfn>`, `<dir>`, `<div>`, `<dl>`, `<dt>`, `<em>`, `<fieldset>`, `<font>`, `<form>`, `<frame>`, `<frameset>`, `<hn>`, `<i>`, `<iframe>`, `<img>`, `<input type="button">`, `<input type="checkbox">`, `<input type="file">`, `<input type="image">`, `<input type="password">`, `<input type="radio">`, `<input type="reset">`, `<input type="submit">`, `<input type="text">`, `<ins>`, `<kbd>`, `<label>`, `<legend>`, `<li>`, `<marquee>`, `<menu>`, `<nobr>`, `<object>`, `<ol>`, `<p>`, `<pre>`, `<q>`, `<rt>`, `<ruby>`, `<s>`, `<samp>`, `<small>`, `<span>`, `<strike>`, `<strong>`, `<sub>`, `<sup>`, `<table>`, `<td>`, `<textarea>`, `<th>`, `<tt>`, `<u>`, `<ul>`, `<var>`, `<xmp>`

Common properties:

enabled

Other properties:

grayScale	This property establishes whether content is displayed in a normal RGB color or in the corresponding grayscale color. Value: Boolean; 1 (display content as a grayscale) or 0 (the default; display the content as normal RGB color).
invert	This property specifies whether the content is displayed in the color complement of its original color. For instance the color complement of blue is yellow. Value: Boolean; 0 (the default; displays content in the specified RGB color value) or 1 (displays content in the complementary RGB color value).

mask	This property specifies whether the content of an element is masked with the value of the maskColor property. Value: Boolean; 0 (the default; content is not masked) or 1 (content is masked).
maskColor(*)	This JavaScript-only property establishes the color with which to mask the content of an element. Value: Hexadecimal integer in the format 0xAARRGGBB, using 32-bit format color values (AA indicates the color is in the alpha channel).
mirror	This property indicates whether the content is rendered as a mirror image. Value: Boolean; 1 (content reversed) or 0 (the default; normal display).
opacity	This property establishes the transparency/opacity level applied to the content of the element. Value: Floating-point number from 0.0 (fully transparent) to 1.0 (the default; fully opaque).
rotation	This property causes the content of the element to rotate clockwise in 90-degree increments. Value. Integer; 0 (the default; no rotation), 1 (rotates 90 degrees), 2 (rotates 180 degrees), 3 (rotates 270 degrees).
xRay	This property specifies whether the content is displayed as a grayscale negative (as is the case with film negatives in photography, where the blacks are displayed as whites, and the whites are displayed as blacks). Value: Boolean; 1 (displays content in X-ray fashion) or 0 (the default; normal).

BlendTrans

Compatibility: IE4, IE5, IE5.5, IE6

This filter allows you to gradually blend in any style that is applied to the element over a specified period of time. To do this you must make all changes between the apply() and play() methods of this filter.

Example:

```
<html>
<head>
<script language="JavaScript">
function applyFilter(elem) {
    elem.style.filter="blendTrans(duration=1)";
    elem.filters.blendTrans.Apply();
    elem.style.backgroundColor="blue";
    elem.filters.blendTrans.Play();
    elem.filters.percent=30;
}
</script>
</head>
<body bgcolor="#FFFFFF" text="#000000">
  <img id="myImg" src="yourimage.gif">
  <button onclick="applyFilter(myImg)">Fade in a blue background</button>
  <button onclick="myImg.style.backgroundColor='white';">Restore image</button>
</body>
</html>
```

Applies to:

<a>, <acronym>, <address>, <b>, <bdo>, <big>, <blockquote>, <body>, <button>,
<caption>, <center>, <cite>, <code>, <custom>, <dd>, <del>, <dfn>, <dir>, <div>,
<dl>, <dt>, <em>, <fieldset>, <font>, <form>, <frame>, <hn>, <i>, <iframe>, <img>,
<input type="button">, <input type="checkbox">, <input type="file">, <input
type="image">, <input type="password">, <input type="radio">, <input type="reset">,
<input type="submit">, <input type="text">, <ins>, <kbd>, <label>, <legend>, <li>,
<marquee>, <menu>, <nobr>, <object>, <ol>, <p>, <pre>, <q>, <rt>, <ruby>, <s>,
<samp>, <small>, <span>, <strike>, <strong>, <sub>, <sup>, <table>, <td>,
<textarea>, <th>, <tt>, <u>, <ul>, <var>, <xmp>

Common properties:

duration, enabled, percent, status

Common methods:

apply(), play(), stop()

Blur

Compatibility: IE5.5, IE6

This filter forces the content of the element to appear out of focus.

Example:

```
<html>
<head>
</script>
</head>
<body bgcolor="#FFFFFF" text="#000000">
<img src="yourimage.gif" id="myImg">
<button onclick="myImg.style.filter='blur(pixelradius=5, enabled=true)';">Apply
filter</button>
<button onclick="myImg.style.filter='blur(pixelradius=5,
enabled=false)';">Restore</button>
</body>
</html>
```

Applies to:

<a>, <acronym>, <address>, <b>, <bdo>, <big>, <blockquote>, <body>, <button>,
<caption>, <center>, <cite>, <code>, <custom>, <dd>, <del>, <dfn>, <dir>, <div>,
<dl>, <dt>, <em>, <fieldset>, <font>, <form>, <frame>, <frameset>, <hn>, <i>,
<iframe>, <img>, <input type="button">, <input type="checkbox">, <input
type="file">, <input type="image">, <input type="password">, <input type="radio">,
<input type="reset">, <input type="submit">, <input type="text">, <ins>, <kbd>,
<label>, <legend>, <li>, <marquee>, <menu>, <nobr>, <object>, <ol>, <p>, <pre>,
<q>, <rt>, <ruby>, <s>, <samp>, <small>, <span>, strike>, <strong>, <sub>, <sup>,
<table>, <td>, <textarea>, <th>, <tt>, <u>, <ul>, <var>, <xmp>

Common properties:

---

enabled

Other properties:

makeShadow	This property causes the content to appear as a shadow. Value: Boolean; true (displays the content as a shadow), false (the default; normal display).
pixelRadius	This property establishes the radius of the area blurred around each pixel. Value: Floating-point number ranging from 1.0 to 100.0 (the default value is 2).
shadowOpacity	This property specifies the level of opacity applied by the Blur filter. Value: Floating-point number ranging from 0.0 (fully transparent) to 1.0 (fully opaque); the default value is 0.75.

Chroma

Compatibility: IE4, IE5, IE5.5, IE6

This filter causes the specified color to be transparent in the element's content.
Example:

```
<html>
<head>
<script language="JavaScript">
function applyChroma(elem) {elem.style.filter="Chroma(color='blue')";}
function disableChroma(elem) {elem.style.filter="Chroma(enabled='false')";}
</script>
</head>
<body bgcolor="#FFFFFF" text="#000000">
<div id="myDiv" style="filter:
progid:DXImageTransform.Microsoft.chroma(enabled='false'); background:blue;
width:100; height:100;"></div>
<button onclick="applyChroma(myDiv);">Apply Chroma</button>
<button onclick="disableChroma(myDiv);">Disable Chroma</button>
</body>
</html>
```

Applies to:

<a>, <acronym>, <address>, <b>, <bdo>, <big>, <blockquote>, <body>, <button>, <caption>, <center>, <cite>, <code>, <custom>, <dd>, <del>, <dfn>, <dir>, <div>, <dl>, <dt>, <em>, <fieldset>, <font>, <form>, <frame>, <hn>, <i>, <iframe>, <img>, <input type="button">, <input type="checkbox">, <input type="file">, <input type="image">, <input type="password">, <input type="radio">, <input type="reset">, <input type="submit">, <input type="text">, <ins>, <kbd>, <label>, <legend>, <li>, <marquee>, <menu>, <nobr>, <object>, <ol>, <p>, <pre>, <q>, <rt>, <ruby>, <s>, <samp>, <small>, <span>, <strike>, <strong>, <sub>, <sup>, <table>, <td>, <textarea>, <th>, <tt>, <u>, <ul>, <var>, <xmp>

Common properties:

---

color, enabled

Compositor

Compatibility: IE5.5, IE6

This filter combines the color and alpha values of two superimposed elements
and produces a new result.

   Example:

```
<html>
<head>
<script language="JavaScript">
function applyFilter() {
    myDiv1.filters.item('DXImageTransform.Microsoft.Compositor').enabled = true;
    myDiv1.filters.item('DXImageTransform.Microsoft.Compositor').Function = 3;
}
function init(){
    myDiv1.style.filter =
'progid:DXImageTransform.Microsoft.Compositor(function=20);';
    myDiv1.filters.item('DXImageTransform.Microsoft.Compositor').Apply();
    myDiv1.innerHTML = myDiv2.innerHTML;
    myDiv1.filters.item('DXImageTransform.Microsoft.Compositor').Play();
}
</script>
</head>
<body onload="init();">
<p> <input type="button" value="Apply Filter" onclick="applyFilter();">
 <button
onclick="myDiv1.filters.item('DXImageTransform.Microsoft.Compositor').enabled=false
;">Restore</button> </p>
<div id="myDiv1" style="position:absolute; top:100; left:10; width:400; height:100;
background-color: red; border:solid 1px;">FIRST ELEMENT</div>
<div id="myDiv2" style="position:abosulte; top:400; display:none;">THIS DIV IS
PLACED IN FRONT OF THE FIRST ELEMENT</div>
</body>
</html>
```

NOTE   *A more comprehensive example can be found at http://msdn.microsoft.com/workshop/
samples/author/filter/Compositor.htm.*

   Applies to:

<a>, <acronym>, <address>, <b>, <bdo>, <big>, <blockquote>, <body>, <button>,
<caption>, <center>, <cite>, <code>, <custom>, <dd>, <del>, <dfn>, <dir>, <div>,
<dl>, <dt>, <em>, <fieldset>, <font>, <form>, <frame>, <frameset>, <hn>, <i>,
<iframe>, <img>, <input type="button">, <input type="checkbox">, <input
type="file">, <input type="image">, <input type="password">, <input type="radio">,

```
<input type="reset">, <input type="submit">, <input type="text">, <ins>, <kbd>,
<label>, <legend>, <li>, <marquee>, <menu>, <nobr>, <object>, <ol>, <p>, <pre>,
<q>, <rt>, <ruby>, <s>, <samp>, <small>, <span>, <strike>, <strong>, <sub>, <sup>,
<table>, <td>, <textarea>, <th>, <tt>, <u>, <ul>, <var>, <xmp>
```

Other properties:

function	This property performs a composition function with the element's content. Value: an integer from 0 – 10 or 19 – 25. For a description of the possible values, please refer to http://msdn.microsoft.com/workshop/author/filter/reference/properties/function.asp.

Common methods:

apply(), play()

DropShadow

Compatibility: IE4, IE5, IE5.5, IE6

This filter creates the effect of a drop shadow for the element affected.

Example:

```
<html><head>
<script language="JavaScript">
function applyFilter(){
    myDiv.style.filter = "progid:DXImageTransform.Microsoft.dropshadow();"
    myDiv.filters.item('DXImageTransform.Microsoft.dropshadow').OffX = 3;
    myDiv.filters.item('DXImageTransform.Microsoft.dropshadow').OffY = 3;
    myDiv.filters.item('DXImageTransform.Microsoft.dropshadow').Positive = true;
    myDiv.filters.item('DXImageTransform.Microsoft.dropshadow').Color = 'red';
    myDiv.filters.item('DXImageTransform.Microsoft.dropshadow').enabled = true;
}
</script></head>
<body>
<img id="myDiv" src="yourimage.gif"><br><br><br><br>
<button onclick="applyFilter();">Apply Filter</button>
<button
onclick="myDiv.filters.item('DXImageTransform.Microsoft.dropshadow').enabled =
false;">Restore</button>
</body>
</html>
```

Applies to:

```
<a>, <acronym>, <address>, <b>, <bdo>, <big>, <blockquote>, <button>, <caption>,
<center>, <cite>, <code>, <custom>, <dd>, <del>, <dfn>, <dir>, <div>, <dl>, <dt>,
<em>, <fieldset>, <font>, <form>, <frame>, <hn>, <i>, <iframe>, <img>, <input
type="button">, <input type="checkbox">, <input type="file">, <input type="image">,
<input type="password">, <input type="radio">, <input type="reset">, <input
```

type="submit">, <input type="text">, <ins>, <kbd>, <label>, <legend>, <li>,
<marquee>, <menu>, <nobr>, <object>, <ol>, <p>, <pre>, <q>, <rt>, <ruby>, <s>,
<samp>, <small>, <span>, <strike>, <strong>, <sub>, <sup>, <table>, <td>,
<textarea>, <th>, <tt>, <u>, <ul>, <var>, <xmp>

Common properties:

color, enabled

Other properties:

offX	This property specifies the horizontal offset by which the drop shadow moves from the element. Value: An integer that specifies the offset value in pixels. A positive value causes the drop shadow to appear to the right of the element, and a negative value causes it to appear to the left of the element. The default value is 5.
offY	This property specifies the vertical offset by which the drop shadow moves from the element. Value: An integer that specifies the offset value in pixels. A positive value causes the drop shadow to appear below the element, and a negative value causes it to appear above the element. The default value is 5.
positive	This property allows a transparent element to have a drop shadow outside of the boundaries of the element. Value: Boolean; true (the default; drop shadow appears outside of the element) or false (drop shadow is visible behind the transparent element).

Emboss

Compatibility: IE5.5, IE6

This filter causes the content of the element to appear embossed by using shades of gray.

Example:

```
<html><head>
<script language="JavaScript">
function applyFilter(){
    myDiv.style.filter = "progid:DXImageTransform.Microsoft.emboss();"
    myDiv.filters.item('DXImageTransform.Microsoft.emboss').bias = .5;
    myDiv.filters.item('DXImageTransform.Microsoft.emboss').enabled = true;
}
</script></head>
<body>
<img id="myDiv" src="yourimage.gif"><br><br><br><br>
<button onclick="applyFilter();">Apply Filter</button>
<button onclick="myDiv.filters.item('DXImageTransform.Microsoft.emboss').enabled =
false;">Restore</button>
</body>
</html>
```

Applies to:

<a>, <acronym>, <address>, <b>, <bdo>, <big>, <blockquote>, <body>, <button>, <caption>, <center>, <cite>, <code>, <custom>, <dd>, <del>, <dfn>, <dir>, <div>, <dl>, <dt>, <em>, <fieldset>, <font>, <form>, <frame>, <frameset>, <hn>, <i>, <iframe>, <img>, <input type="button">, <input type="checkbox">, <input type="file">, <input type="image">, <input type="password">, <input type="radio">, <input type="reset">, <input type="submit">, <input type="text">, <ins>, <kbd>, <label>, <legend>, <li>, <marquee>, <menu>, <nobr>, <object>, <ol>, <p>, <pre>, <q>, <rt>, <ruby>, <s>, <samp>, <small>, <span>, <strike>, <strong>, <sub>, <sup>, <table>, <td>, <textarea>, <th>, <tt>, <u>, <ul>, <var>, <xmp>

Common properties:

bias, enabled

Engrave

Compatibility: IE5.5, IE6

This filter causes the content of the object to appear engraved by using shades of gray.

Example:

```
<html><head>
<script language="JavaScript">
function applyFilter(){
    myDiv.style.filter = "progid:DXImageTransform.Microsoft.engrave();"
    myDiv.filters.item('DXImageTransform.Microsoft.engrave').bias = .5;
    myDiv.filters.item('DXImageTransform.Microsoft.engrave').enabled = true;
}
</script></head>
<body>
<img id="myDiv" src="yourimage.gif"><br><br><br><br>
<button onclick="applyFilter();">Apply Filter</button>
<button onclick="myDiv.filters.item('DXImageTransform.Microsoft.engrave').enabled =
false;">Restore</button>
</body>
</html>
```

Applies to:

<a>, <acronym>, <address>, <b>, <bdo>, <big>, <blockquote>, <body>, <button>, <caption>, <center>, <cite>, <code>, <custom>, <dd>, <del>, <dfn>, <dir>, <div>, <dl>, <dt>, <em>, <fieldset>, <font>, <form>, <frame>, <frameset>, <hn>, <i>, <iframe>, <img>, <input type="button">, <input type="checkbox">, <input type="file">, <input type="image">, <input type="password">, <input type="radio">, <input type="reset">, <input type="submit">, <input type="text">, <ins>, <kbd>, <label>, <legend>, <li>, <marquee>, <menu>, <nobr>, <object>, <ol>, <p>, <pre>, <q>, <rt>, <ruby>, <s>, <samp>, <small>, <span>, <strike>, <strong>, <sub>, <sup>, <table>, <td>, <textarea>, <th>, <tt>, <u>, <ul>, <var>, <xmp>

Common properties:

---

bias, enabled

FlipH

Compatibility: IE4, IE5, IE5.5, IE6

This filter causes the element's content to flip horizontally. However, Microsoft recommends you use the BasicImage filter with rotation=2 and mirror=1 instead of this filter.

Example:

```
<html><head>
<script language="JavaScript">
function applyFilter(){
    myDiv.style.filter = "FlipH();"
    myDiv.filters.item('FlipH').enabled = true;
}
</script></head>
<body>
<img id="myDiv" src="yourimage.gif"><br><br><br><br>
<button onclick="applyFilter();">Apply Filter</button>
<button onclick="myDiv.filters.item('flipH').enabled = false;">Restore</button>
</body>
</html>
```

Applies to:

<a>, <acronym>, <address>, <b>, <bdo>, <big>, <blockquote>, <body>, <button>, <caption>, <center>, <cite>, <code>, <custom>, <dd>, <del>, <dfn>, <dir>, <div>, <dl>, <dt>, <em>, <fieldset>, <font>, <form>, <frame>, <hn>, <hr>, <i>, <iframe>, <img>, <input type="button">, <input type="checkbox">, <input type="file">, <input type="image">, <input type="password">, <input type="radio">, <input type="reset">, <input type="submit">, <input type="text">, <ins>, <kbd>, <label>, <legend>, <li>, <marquee>, <menu>, <nobr>, <object>, <ol>, <p>, <pre>, <q>, <rt>, <ruby>, <s>, <samp>, <small>, <span>, <strike>, <strong>, <sub>, <sup>, <table>, <td>, <textarea>, <th>, <tt>, <u>, <ul>, <var>, <xmp>

Common properties:

---

enabled

FlipV

Compatibility: IE4, IE5, IE5.5, IE6

This filter causes the object's content to flip vertically.

Example: See the FlipH filter example and replace FlipH with FlipV.

Applies to:

<a>, <acronym>, <address>, <b>, <bdo>, <big>, <blockquote>, <body>, <button>, <caption>, <center>, <cite>, <code>, <custom>, <dd>, <del>, <dfn>, <dir>, <div>, <dl>, <dt>, <em>, <fieldset>, <font>, <form>, <frame>, <hn>, <hr>, <i>, <iframe>, <img>, <input type="button">, <input type="checkbox">, <input type="file">, <input type="image">, <input type="password">, <input type="radio">, <input type="reset">, <input type="submit">, <input type="text">, <ins>, <kbd>, <label>, <legend>, <li>, <marquee>, <menu>, <nobr>, <object>, <ol>, <p>, <pre>, <q>, <rt>, <ruby>, <s>, <samp>, <small>, <span>, <strike>, <strong>, <sub>, <sup>, <table>, <td>, <textarea>, <th>, <tt>, <u>, <ul>, <var>, <xmp>

Common properties:

enabled

Glow

Compatibility: IE4, IE5, IE5.5, IE6

This filter causes the content of the element to appear to be glowing.

Example:

```
<html><head>
<script language="JavaScript">
function applyFilter(){
    myDiv.style.filter = "progid:DXImageTransform.Microsoft.glow();"
    myDiv.filters.item('DXImageTransform.Microsoft.glow').color = 'red';
    myDiv.filters.item('DXImageTransform.Microsoft.glow').enabled = true;
}
</script></head>
<body>
<img id="myDiv" src="yourimage.gif"><br><br><br><br>
<button onclick="applyFilter();">Apply Filter</button>
<button onclick="myDiv.filters.item('DXImageTransform.Microsoft.glow').enabled =
false;">Restore</button>
</body>
</html>
```

Applies to:

<a>, <acronym>, <address>, <b>, <bdo>, <big>, <blockquote>, <body>, <button>, <caption>, <center>, <cite>, <code>, <custom>, <dd>, <del>, <dfn>, <dir>, <div>, <dl>, <dt>, <em>, <fieldset>, <font>, <form>, <frame>, <hn>, <i>, <iframe>, <img>, <input type="button">, <input type="checkbox">, <input type="file">, <input type="image">, <input type="password">, <input type="radio">, <input type="reset">, <input type="submit">, <input type="text">, <ins>, <kbd>, <label>, <legend>, <li>, <marquee>, <menu>, <nobr>, <object>, <ol>, <p>, <pre>, <q>, <rt>, <ruby>, <s>, <samp>, <small>, <span>, <strike>, <strong>, <sub>, <sup>, <table>, <td>, <textarea>, <th>, <tt>, <u>, <ul>, <var>, <xmp>

Common properties:

---

color, enabled, strength

Gray

Compatibility: IE4, IE5, IE5.5, IE6

This filter causes the element's content to be displayed in grayscale instead of color. However, Microsoft recommends you use the BasicImage filter with grayscale=1.

Example:

```
<html><head>
<script language="JavaScript">
function applyFilter(){
    myDiv.style.filter = "gray();"
    myDiv.filters.item('gray').enabled = true;
}
</script></head>
<body>
<img id="myDiv" src="yourimage.gif"><br><br><br><br>
<button onclick="applyFilter();">Apply Filter</button>
<button onclick="myDiv.filters.item('gray').enabled = false;">Restore</button>
</body>
</html>
```

Applies to:

<a>, <acronym>, <address>, <b>, <bdo>, <big>, <blockquote>, <body>, <button>, <caption>, <center>, <cite>, <code>, <custom>, <dd>, <del>, <dfn>, <dir>, <div>, <dl>, <dt>, <em>, <fieldset>, <font>, <form>, <frame>, <frameset>, <hn>, <i>, <iframe>, <img>, <input type="button">, <input type="checkbox">, <input type="file">, <input type="image">, <input type="password">, <input type="radio">, <input type="reset">, <input type="submit">, <input type="text">, <ins>, <kbd>, <label>, <legend>, <li>, <marquee>, <menu>, <nobr>, <object>, <ol>, <p>, <pre>, <q>, <rt>, <ruby>, <s>, <samp>, <small>, <span>, <strike>, <strong>, <sub>, <sup>, <table>, <td>, <textarea>, <th>, <tt>, <u>, <ul>, <var>, <xmp>

Common properties:

---

enabled

ICMFilter

Compatibility: IE5.5, IE6

This filter adjusts the color content of the element with a specific hardware device Image Color Management (ICM) profile. Hardware devices (such as printers) usually come with a .icm profile file, which must be present in the system. The .icm file contains information that defines how color content compares to the RGB color standard for a hardware device.

Example:

```
<img src="yourimage.gif"
style="filter:progid:DXImageTransform.Microsoft.ICMFilter(colorSpace='myColorspace.
icm'; intent='Picture')">
```

Applies to:

`<a>`, `<acronym>`, `<address>`, `<b>`, `<bdo>`, `<big>`, `<blockquote>`, `<body>`, `<button>`, `<caption>`, `<center>`, `<cite>`, `<code>`, `<custom>`, `<dd>`, `<del>`, `<dfn>`, `<dir>`, `<div>`, `<dl>`, `<dt>`, `<em>`, `<fieldset>`, `<font>`, `<form>`, `<frame>`, `<frameset>`, `<hn>`, `<i>`, `<iframe>`, `<img>`, `<input type="button">`, `<input type="checkbox">`, `<input type="file">`, `<input type="image">`, `<input type="password">`, `<input type="radio">`, `<input type="reset">`, `<input type="submit">`, `<input type="text">`, `<ins>`, `<kbd>`, `<label>`, `<legend>`, `<li>`, `<marquee>`, `<menu>`, `<nobr>`, `<object>`, `<ol>`, `<p>`, `<pre>`, `<q>`, `<rt>`, `<ruby>`, `<s>`, `<samp>`, `<small>`, `<span>`, `<strike>`, `<strong>`, `<sub>`, `<sup>`, `<table>`, `<td>`, `<textarea>`, `<th>`, `<tt>`, `<u>`, `<ul>`, `<var>`, `<xmp>`

Other properties:

colorSpace	This property either specifies the path and file name of the .icm file, or a string that identifies the colorSpace name.
intent	This property specifies the intended purpose for applying the filter to the element. The filter adjusts the color output according to the specified intent to best match the color capabilities of your monitor or printer. Value: Picture (the default; best for images and photographs), Graphic (used with solid color graphics), Proof (used for proofs; selects the closest matching color, but does not account for the white point), Match (used for proofs; selects the closest matching color, and also accounts for the white point).

NOTE *All images are composed of colored dots (points). Some of those dots don't have a color at all, which would make that dot transparent. However, transparent dots are represented as white points, so that the image can have better color contrast.*

Invert

Compatibility: IE4, IE5, IE5.5, IE6

This filter causes an image to be converted to its photographic negative.

Example:

```
<html><head>
<script language="JavaScript">
function applyFilter(){
    myDiv.style.filter = "invert();"
    myDiv.filters.item('invert').enabled = true;
}
</script></head>
<body>
<img id="myDiv" src="yourimage.gif"><br><br><br><br>
<button onclick="applyFilter();">Apply Filter</button>
<button onclick="myDiv.filters.item('invert').enabled = false;">Restore</button>
```

```
</body>
</html>
```

Applies to:

```
<a>, <acronym>, <address>, <b>, <bdo>, <big>, <blockquote>, <body>, <button>,
<caption>, <center>, <cite>, <code>, <custom>, <dd>, <del>, <dfn>, <dir>, <div>,
<dl>, <dt>, <em>, <fieldset>, <font>, <form>, <frame>, <hn>, <i>, <iframe>, <img>,
<input type="button">, <input type="checkbox">, <input type="file">, <input
type="image">, <input type="password">, <input type="radio">, <input type="reset">,
<input type="submit">, <input type="text">, <ins>, <kbd>, <label>, <legend>, <li>,
<marquee>, <menu>, <nobr>, <object>, <ol>, <p>, <pre>, <q>, <rt>, <ruby>, <s>,
<samp>, <small>, <span>, <strike>, <strong>, <sub>, <sup>, <table>, <td>,
<textarea>, <th>, <tt>, <u>, <ul>, <var>, <xmp>
```

Common properties:

```
enabled
```

Light

Compatibility: IE4, IE5, IE5.5, IE6

This filter causes an element to appear as though a bright light were illuminating it.

Example:

```
<html><head>
<script language="JavaScript">
function applyFilter(){
    myDiv.style.filter = "progid:DXImageTransform.Microsoft.light();"
    myDiv.filters.item('DXImageTransform.Microsoft.light').addAmbient(255, 255,
255, 30);
    myDiv.filters.item('DXImageTransform.Microsoft.light').enabled = true;
}
</script></head>
<body>
<img id="myDiv" src="yourimage.gif"><br><br><br><br>
<button onclick="applyFilter();">Apply Filter</button>
<button onclick="myDiv.filters.item('DXImageTransform.Microsoft.light').enabled =
false;">Restore</button>
</body>
</html>
```

Applies to:

```
<a>, <acronym>, <address>, <b>, <bdo>, <big>, <blockquote>, <body>, <button>,
<caption>, <center>, <cite>, <code>, <custom>, <dd>, <del>, <dfn>, <dir>, <div>,
<dl>, <dt>, <em>, <fieldset>, <font>, <form>, <frame>, <hn>, <i>, <iframe>, <img>,
<input type="button">, <input type="checkbox">, <input type="file">, <input
type="image">, <input type="password">, <input type="radio">, <input type="reset">,
```

```
<input type="submit">, <input type="text">, <ins>, <kbd>, <label>, <legend>, <li>,
<marquee>, <menu>, <nobr>, <object>, <ol>, <p>, <pre>, <q>, <rt>, <ruby>, <s>,
<samp>, <small>, <span>, <strike>, <strong>, <sub>, <sup>, <table>, <td>,
<textarea>, <th>, <tt>, <u>, <ul>, <var>, <xmp>
```

Common properties:

enabled

Methods:

addAmbient(*vRed, vGreen, vBlue, vStrength* **)**	This method creates a nondirectional ambient light that shines on the element. All parameters are required. vRed (specifies the red value, 0 to 255), vBlue (specifies the blue value, 0 to 255), vGreen (specifies the green value, 0 to 255), vStrength (specifies the strength of the light, 0 to 100).
addCone(*vX1, vY1, vZ1, vX2, vY2, vRed, vGreen, vBlue, vStrength, vSpread* **)**	This method adds a cone-shaped source of directional light that shines on the web page. All parameters are required. vX1, vY1, vZ1 (integers; X, Y, and Z coordinates of the light source), vX2, vY2 (X and Y coordinates of the light's target on the web page), vRed, vGreen, vBlue (specify the red, green, and blue values, 0 to 255), vStrength (specifies the strength of the light, 0 to 100), vSpread (specifies the vertical angle from the light source to the element, 0 to 90 degrees).
addPoint(*vX, vY, vZ, vRed, vGreen, vBlue, vStrength* **)**	This method adds a point of light that starts as a single point on the element and from there spreads evenly in all directions. All parameters are required. vX, vY, vZ (integers; X, Y, and Z coordinates of the light source), vRed, vGreen, vBlue (specify the red, green, and blue values, 0 to 255), vStrength (specifies the strength of the light, 0 to 100).
changeColor(*vLightNumber, vRed, vGreen, vBlue, vAbsolute* **)**	This method causes the color of the light shining on the element to change. All parameters are required. vLightNumber (integer; the ID of the light), vRed, vGreen, vBlue (integers; specify the new red, green, and blue values, 0 to 255), vAbsolute (Boolean; 0 means the color values are added to the current values in the light, and any nonzero value indicates that the light's red, green, and blue color values are replaced with the color values specified in this function).
changeStrength(*vlightNumber, vStrength, vAbsolute* **)**	This method causes the strength of the light illuminating the element on the web page to change. All parameters are required. vLightNumber (integer; the ID of the light), vStrength (specifies the strength of the light, 0 to 100), vAbsolute (Boolean; 0 means the color values are added to the current color values in the light, and any nonzero value indicates that the light's red, green, and blue color values are replaced with the color values specified in this function).
clear()	This method causes all lighting to be removed from the object using the filter.

moveLight(*vlightNumber*, *vX*, *vY*, *vZ*, *vAbsolute*)	This method causes a change in the position of the light source (for lights added using the addPoint method) or the position of the focus (for lights added using the addCone method). All parameters are required. vLightNumber (integer; the ID of the light), vX, vY, vZ (integers; X, Y, and Z coordinates of the light source), vAbsolute (Boolean; 0 value means the X, Y, and Z coordinate values are added to the current values in the light, while any nonzero value indicates that the light's current coordinate values are replaced with the coordinate values specified in the function).

NOTE *Each filter can contain up to ten lights; the* vLightNumber *refers to the light in the filter for which this method is being used.*

MaskFilter

Compatibility: IE4, IE5, IE5.5, IE6

This filter changes transparent pixels to a specified color, and makes non-transparent pixels transparent.

Example:

```
<html><head>
<script language="JavaScript">
function applyFilter(){
    myDiv.style.filter = "progid:DXImageTransform.Microsoft.maskfilter();"
    myDiv.filters.item('DXImageTransform.Microsoft.maskfilter').color='blue';
    myDiv.filters.item('DXImageTransform.Microsoft.maskfilter').enabled = true;
}
</script></head>
<body>
<img id="myDiv" src="yourimage.gif"><br><br><br><br>
<button onclick="applyFilter();">Apply Filter</button>
<button
onclick="myDiv.filters.item('DXImageTransform.Microsoft.maskfilter').enabled =
false;">Restore</button>
</body>
</html>
```

Applies to:

```
<a>, <acronym>, <address>, <b>, <bdo>, <big>, <blockquote>, <body>, <button>,
<caption>, <center>, <cite>, <code>, <custom>, <dd>, <del>, <dfn>, <dir>, <div>,
<dl>, <dt>, <em>, <fieldset>, <font>, <form>, <frame>, <hn>, <i>, <iframe>, <img>,
<input type="button">, <input type="checkbox">, <input type="file">, <input
type="image">, <input type="password">, <input type="radio">, <input type="reset">,
<input type="submit">, <input type="text">, <ins>, <kbd>, <label>, <legend>, <li>,
<marquee>, <menu>, <nobr>, <object>, <ol>, <p>, <pre>, <q>, <rt>, <ruby>, <s>,
<samp>, <small>, <span>, <strike>, <strong>, <sub>, <sup>, <table>, <td>,
<textarea>, <th>, <tt>, <u>, <ul>, <var>, <xmp>
```

Common properties:

color, enabled

Matrix

Compatibility: IE5.5, IE6

This filter uses a matrix transformation to perform some effect on an element. You can use this filter to flip horizontally, flip vertically, resize, rotate, or stretch an element's content. More complex transformations are possible but require a strong command of linear algebra. The basis of the transformation is a grid/matrix that has 2 rows and 2 columns, which are represented by the M11, M12, M21 and M22 properties.

Example:

```
<html><head>
<script language="JavaScript">
function applyFilter(){
    myDiv.style.filter = "progid:DXImageTransform.Microsoft.matrix();"
    myDiv.filters.item('DXImageTransform.Microsoft.matrix').M11=3;
    myDiv.filters.item('DXImageTransform.Microsoft.matrix').M22=3;
    myDiv.filters.item('DXImageTransform.Microsoft.matrix').M21=0;
    myDiv.filters.item('DXImageTransform.Microsoft.matrix').M12=0;
    myDiv.filters.item('DXImageTransform.Microsoft.matrix').DX=0;
    myDiv.filters.item('DXImageTransform.Microsoft.matrix').DY=0;
    myDiv.filters.item('DXImageTransform.Microsoft.matrix').FilterType='bilinear';
    myDiv.filters.item('DXImageTransform.Microsoft.matrix').SizingMethod='auto
expand';
    myDiv.filters.item('DXImageTransform.Microsoft.matrix').enabled = true;
}
</script></head>
<body>
<img id="myDiv" src="yourimage.gif"><br><br><br><br>
<button onclick="applyFilter();">Apply Filter</button>
<button onclick="myDiv.filters.item('DXImageTransform.Microsoft.matrix').enabled =
false;">Restore</button>
</body>
</html>
```

Applies to:

<a>, <acronym>, <address>, <b>, <bdo>, <big>, <blockquote>, <body>, <button>, <caption>, <center>, <cite>, <code>, <custom>, <dd>, <del>, <dfn>, <dir>, <div>, <dl>, <dt>, <em>, <fieldset>, <font>, <form>, <frame>, <frameset>, <hn>, <i>, <iframe>, <img>, <input type="button">, <input type="checkbox">, <input type="file">, <input type="image">, <input type="password">, <input type="radio">, <input type="reset">, <input type="submit">, <input type="text">, <ins>, <kbd>,

`<label>`, `<legend>`, `<li>`, `<marquee>`, `<menu>`, `<nobr>`, `<object>`, `<ol>`, `<p>`, `<pre>`, `<q>`, `<rt>`, `<ruby>`, `<s>`, `<samp>`, `<small>`, `<span>`, `<strike>`, `<strong>`, `<sub>`, `<sup>`, `<table>`, `<td>`, `<textarea>`, `<th>`, `<tt>`, `<u>`, `<ul>`, `<var>`, `<xmp>`

Common properties:

enabled

Other properties:

Dx	This property specifies the horizontal coordinate for resizing the matrix. This property is only useful when the sizingMethod property is set to clip to original. Value: A floating-point number (default value is 1.0).
Dy	This property specifies the vertical coordinate for resizing the matrix. This property is only useful when the sizingMethod property is set to clip to original. Value: A floating-point number (default value is 1.0).
filterType	This property establishes how pixels transition from their current state to their filtered state. Values: bilinear (the default; produces a smoother output) or nearest neighbor (transition effect is not as smooth, and the final resolution is achieved by transpolarization).
M11	This property specifies the first row and first column of the matrix. Value: A floating-point number (default value is 1.0).
M12	This property specifies the first row and second column of the matrix. Value: A floating-point number (default value is 0.0).
M21	This property specifies the second row and first column of the matrix. Value: A floating-point number (default value is 0.0).
M22	This property specifies the second row and second column of the matrix. Value: A floating-point number (default value is 1.0).
sizingMethod	This property specifies whether the container element is resized or clipped. Value: clip to original (the default; no resizing) or auto expand (element is resized).

MotionBlur

Compatibility: IE4, IE5, IE5.5, IE6

This filter causes the contents of the element to appear to be moving.

Example:

```
<html><head>
<script language="JavaScript">
function applyFilter(){
    myDiv.style.filter = "progid:DXImageTransform.Microsoft.motionblur();"
    myDiv.filters.item('DXImageTransform.Microsoft.motionblur').strength=30;
    myDiv.filters.item('DXImageTransform.Microsoft.motionblur').direction=45;
    myDiv.filters.item('DXImageTransform.Microsoft.motionblur').enabled = true;
}
</script></head>
<body>
<img id="myDiv" src="yourimage.gif"><br><br><br><br>
<button onclick="applyFilter();">Apply Filter</button>
```

```
<button
onclick="myDiv.filters.item('DXImageTransform.Microsoft.motionblur').enabled =
false;">Restore</button>
</body>
</html>
```

Applies to:

`<a>`, `<acronym>`, `<address>`, `<b>`, `<bdo>`, `<big>`, `<blockquote>`, `<body>`, `<button>`, `<caption>`, `<center>`, `<cite>`, `<code>`, `<custom>`, `<dd>`, `<del>`, `<dfn>`, `<dir>`, `<div>`, `<dl>`, `<dt>`, `<em>`, `<fieldset>`, `<font>`, `<form>`, `<frame>`, `<hn>`, `<i>`, `<iframe>`, `<img>`, `<input type="button">`, `<input type="checkbox">`, `<input type="file">`, `<input type="image">`, `<input type="password">`, `<input type="radio">`, `<input type="reset">`, `<input type="submit">`, `<input type="text">`, `<ins>`, `<kbd>`, `<label>`, `<legend>`, `<li>`, `<marquee>`, `<menu>`, `<nobr>`, `<object>`, `<ol>`, `<p>`, `<pre>`, `<q>`, `<rt>`, `<ruby>`, `<s>`, `<samp>`, `<small>`, `<span>`, `<strike>`, `<strong>`, `<sub>`, `<sup>`, `<table>`, `<td>`, `<textarea>`, `<th>`, `<tt>`, `<u>`, `<ul>`, `<var>`, `<xmp>`

Common properties:

`add, enabled, strength`

Other properties:

direction	This property specifies the direction of the motion applied by the filter. Value: integer (degrees from the top going clockwise) specifying direction; 0, 45, 90, 135, 180, 225, 270, 315.

RevealTrans

Compatibility: IE4, IE5, IE5.5, IE6

This filter causes new content in the element to be revealed using one of the 24 standard transition filters. The various transitions that this filter uses are identical to the transition filters described later in this chapter.

Example:

```
<html><head>
<script language="JavaScript">
function applyFilter(){
    myDiv.style.filter = "progid:DXImageTransform.Microsoft.revealtrans();"
    myDiv.filters.item('DXImageTransform.Microsoft.revealtrans').transition=3;
    myDiv.filters.item('DXImageTransform.Microsoft.revealtrans').enabled = true;

    myDiv.filters.item('DXImageTransform.Microsoft.revealtrans').apply();
    myDiv.style.backgroundColor = 'blue';
    myDiv.filters.item('DXImageTransform.Microsoft.revealtrans').play();
}
</script></head>
<body>
<img id="myDiv" src="yourimage.gif"><br><br><br><br>
```

```
<button onclick="applyFilter();">Apply Filter</button>
<button
onclick="myDiv.filters.item('DXImageTransform.Microsoft.revealtrans').enabled =
false; myDiv.style.backgroundColor='white';">Restore</button>
</body>
</html>
```

Applies to:

`<a>`, `<acronym>`, `<address>`, `<b>`, `<bdo>`, `<big>`, `<blockquote>`, `<body>`, `<button>`, `<caption>`, `<center>`, `<cite>`, `<code>`, `<custom>`, `<dd>`, `<del>`, `<dfn>`, `<dir>`, `<div>`, `<dl>`, `<dt>`, `<em>`, `<fieldset>`, `<font>`, `<form>`, `<frame>`, `<hn>`, `<i>`, `<iframe>`, `<img>`, `<input type="button">`, `<input type="checkbox">`, `<input type="file">`, `<input type="image">`, `<input type="password">`, `<input type="radio">`, `<input type="reset">`, `<input type="submit">`, `<input type="text">`, `<ins>`, `<kbd>`, `<label>`, `<legend>`, `<li>`, `<marquee>`, `<menu>`, `<nobr>`, `<object>`, `<ol>`, `<p>`, `<pre>`, `<q>`, `<rt>`, `<ruby>`, `<s>`, `<samp>`, `<small>`, `<span>`, `<strike>`, `<strong>`, `<sub>`, `<sup>`, `<table>`, `<td>`, `<textarea>`, `<th>`, `<tt>`, `<u>`, `<ul>`, `<var>`, `<xmp>`

Common properties:

`duration`, `enabled`, `percent`, `status`

Other properties:

transition	This property determines the type of transition that is used with the RevealTransition filter. Possible values are 0 through 23. For a complete description of the effect of each value, please refer to http://msdn.microsoft.com/workshop/author/filter/reference/properties/transition.asp.

Common methods:

`apply()`, `play()`, `stop()`

Shadow

Compatibility: IE4, IE5, IE5.5, IE6

This filter causes an element's content to display a shadow that shifts toward a specified direction.

Example:

```
<html><head>
<script language="JavaScript">
function applyFilter(){
    myDiv.style.filter = "progid:DXImageTransform.Microsoft.shadow();"
    myDiv.filters.item('DXImageTransform.Microsoft.shadow').direction=45;
    myDiv.filters.item('DXImageTransform.Microsoft.shadow').color='red';
    myDiv.filters.item('DXImageTransform.Microsoft.shadow').enabled = true;
}
```

```
</script></head>
<body>
<img id="myDiv" src="yourimage.gif"><br><br><br><br>
<button onclick="applyFilter();">Apply Filter</button>
<button onclick="myDiv.filters.item('DXImageTransform.Microsoft.shadow').enabled =
false;">Restore</button>
</body>
</html>
```

Applies to:

`<a>`, `<acronym>`, `<address>`, `<b>`, `<bdo>`, `<big>`, `<blockquote>`, `<body>`, `<button>`,
`<caption>`, `<center>`, `<cite>`, `<code>`, `<custom>`, `<dd>`, `<del>`, `<dfn>`, `<dir>`, `<div>`,
`<dl>`, `<dt>`, `<em>`, `<fieldset>`, `<font>`, `<form>`, `<frame>`, `<hn>`, `<i>`, `<iframe>`, `<img>`,
`<input type="button">`, `<input type="checkbox">`, `<input type="file">`, `<input
type="image">`, `<input type="password">`, `<input type="radio">`, `<input type="reset">`,
`<input type="submit">`, `<input type="text">`, `<ins>`, `<kbd>`, `<label>`, `<legend>`, `<li>`,
`<marquee>`, `<menu>`, `<nobr>`, `<object>`, `<ol>`, `<p>`, `<pre>`, `<q>`, `<rt>`, `<ruby>`, `<s>`,
`<samp>`, `<small>`, `<span>`, `<strike>`, `<strong>`, `<sub>`, `<sup>`, `<table>`, `<td>`,
`<textarea>`, `<tt>`, `<u>`, `<ul>`, `<var>`, `<xmp>`

Common properties:

`color, enabled, strength`

Other properties:

direction	This property specifies the direction of the shadow applied by the filter. Value: An integer (degrees from the top going clockwise); 0, 45, 90, 135, 180, 225, 270, 315.

Wave

Compatibility: IE4, IE5, IE5.5, IE6

This filter creates the effect of a wave in the element.

Example:

```
<html><head>
<script language="JavaScript">
function applyFilter(){
    myDiv.style.filter = "progid:DXImageTransform.Microsoft.wave();"
    myDiv.filters.item('DXImageTransform.Microsoft.wave').strength=4;
    myDiv.filters.item('DXImageTransform.Microsoft.wave').freq=3;
    myDiv.filters.item('DXImageTransform.Microsoft.wave').lightstrength=20;
    myDiv.filters.item('DXImageTransform.Microsoft.wave').add=0;
    myDiv.filters.item('DXImageTransform.Microsoft.wave').phase=90;
    myDiv.filters.item('DXImageTransform.Microsoft.wave').enabled = true;
}
</script></head>
<body>
```

```
<img id="myDiv" src="yourimage.gif"><br><br><br><br>
<button onclick="applyFilter();">Apply Filter</button>
<button onclick="myDiv.filters.item('DXImageTransform.Microsoft.wave').enabled =
false;">Restore</button>
</body>
</html>
```

Applies to:

```
<a>, <acronym>, <address>, <b>, <bdo>, <big>, <blockquote>, <body>, <button>,
<caption>, <center>, <cite>, <code>, <custom>, <dd>, <del>, <dfn>, <dir>, <div>,
<dl>, <dt>, <em>, <fieldset>, <font>, <form>, <frame>, <hn>, <i>, <iframe>, <img>,
<input type="button">, <input type="checkbox">, <input type="file">, <input
type="image">, <input type="password">, <input type="radio">, <input type="reset">,
<input type="submit">, <input type="text">, <ins>, <kbd>, <label>, <legend>, <li>,
<marquee>, <menu>, <nobr>, <object>, <ol>, <p>, <pre>, <q>, <rt>, <ruby>, <s>,
<samp>, <small>, <span>, <strike>, <strong>, <sub>, <sup>, <table>, <td>,
<textarea>, <th>, <tt>, <u>, <ul>, <var>, <xmp>
```

Common properties:

```
add, enabled, strength
```

Other properties:

freq	This property specifies the number of waves applied. Value: An integer (default value is 3).
lightStrength	This property establishes the contrast between the light at the top of each wave and the light at the bottom of each wave. Value: An integer (percentage) from 0 (least contrast) to 100 (most contrast).
phase	This property specifies the offset into the period of the first wave. Value: An integer from 0 (the default; the first wave starts from the beginning of its period) to 100 (the first wave starts from the end of its period).

XRay

Compatibility: IE5.5, IE6

This filter displays the content of the element as a grayscale negative.

Example:

```
<html><head>
<script language="JavaScript">
function applyFilter(){
    myDiv.style.filter = "xray();"
    myDiv.filters.item('xray').enabled = true;
}
</script></head>
<body>
<img id="myDiv" src="yourimage.gif"><br><br><br><br>
<button onclick="applyFilter();">Apply Filter</button>
```

```
<button onclick="myDiv.filters.item('xray').enabled = false;">Restore</button>
</body>
</html>
```

Applies to:

```
<a>, <acronym>, <address>, <b>, <bdo>, <big>, <blockquote>, <body>, <button>,
<caption>, <center>, <cite>, <code>, <custom>, <dd>, <del>, <dfn>, <dir>, <div>,
<dl>, <dt>, <em>, <fieldset>, <font>, <form>, <frame>, <hn>, <i>, <iframe>, <img>,
<input type="button">, <input type="checkbox">, <input type="file">, <input
type="image">, <input type="password">, <input type="radio">, <input type="reset">,
<input type="submit">, <input type="text">, <ins>, <kbd>, <label>, <legend>, <li>,
<marquee>, <menu>, <nobr>, <object>, <ol>, <p>, <pre>, <q>, <rt>, <ruby>, <s>,
<samp>, <small>, <span>, <strike>, <strong>, <sub>, <sup>, <table>, <td>,
<textarea>, <th>, <tt>, <u>, <ul>, <var>, <xmp>
```

Common properties:

```
enabled
```

Transition Filters

Transition filters use visual effects to reveal new content of an object or element. Whereas static filters only render the final output of the object or element, transition filters display the process through which the content of an object or element is revealed.

Barn

Compatibility: IE5.5, IE6

This filter reveals new content through the motion of a barn door opening. The effect can be rendered on the horizontal axis or the vertical axis. For this transition to work, the element's hasLayout property must be set to true. The hasLayout property is automatically set to true by the browser when the width, height, or position attribute is explicitly set within the style attribute.

Example:

```
<html><head>
<script language="JavaScript">
function applyFilter() {
trans.style.filter = 'progid:DXImageTransform.Microsoft.barn()';
    trans.filters[0].orientation = 'horizontal';
    trans.filters[0].motion = 'in';
    trans.filters[0].Apply();
        myDiv2.style.visibility="visible";
        myDiv1.style.visibility="hidden";
        trans.filters[0].Play(duration=2);
}
</script></head>
```

```
<body bgcolor="#FFFFFF" text="#000000">
<button onclick="applyFilter();">Apply Filter</button>
<button onclick="myDiv1.style.visibility='visible'; myDiv2.style.visibility =
'hidden';">Restore</button>
<div id="trans" style="position:absolute; top:50; left:50; width:240; height:180; ">
<div id="myDiv1" style="position:absolute; top:0; left:0; width:240; height: 180;
background:red;  padding:10px; font-size:15pt; border:2px solid black; font-
size:12pt; font-family:verdana; color:white">This is the first div element.</div>
<div id="myDiv2" style="visibility:hidden; position:absolute; top:0; left:0;
width:240; height: 180; color:black; background: beige;  padding:10px; font-
size:12pt; font-family:verdana; border:2px solid black;"> This is the second div
element.</div>
</body></html>
```

Applies to:

<a>, <acronym>, <address>, <b>, <bdo>, <big>, <blockquote>, <body>, <button>,
<caption>, <center>, <cite>, <code>, <custom>, <dd>, <del>, <dfn>, <dir>, <div>,
<dl>, <dt>, <em>, <fieldset>, <font>, <form>, <frame>, <frameset>, <hn>, <i>,
<iframe>, <img>, <input type="button">, <input type="checkbox">, <input
type="file">, <input type="image">, <input type="password">, <input type="radio">,
<input type="reset">, <input type="submit">, <input type="text">, <ins>, <kbd>,
<label>, <legend>, <li>, <marquee>, <menu>, <nobr>, <object>, <ol>, <p>, <pre>,
<q>, <rt>, <ruby>, <s>, <samp>, <small>, <span>, <strike>, <strong>, <sub>, <sup>,
<table>, <td>, <textarea>, <th>, <tt>, <u>, <ul>, <var>, <xmp>

Common properties:

duration, enabled, orientation, percent, status

Other properties:

motion	This property specifies whether the barn doors appear to be opening from the inside out or from the outside in. Values: out (the default; from inside to outside) or in (from outside to inside).

Common methods:

apply(), play(), stop()

Blinds

Compatibility: IE5.5, IE6

This filter gives the effect of revealing new content with a motion similar to the
way a window blind reveals the view of its window. For this transition to work, the
element's hasLayout property must be true. The hasLayout property is
automatically set to true by the browser when the width, height, or position
attribute is explicitly set within the style attribute.

Example:

```
<html><head>
<script language="JavaScript">
function applyFilter() {
trans.style.filter = 'progid:DXImageTransform.Microsoft.blinds()';
    trans.filters[0].duration = 10;
    trans.filters[0].direction = 'left';
    trans.filters[0].bands = 10;
trans.filters[0].Apply();
        myDiv2.style.visibility="visible";
        myDiv1.style.visibility="hidden";
        trans.filters[0].Play(duration=2);
}
</script></head>
<body bgcolor="#FFFFFF" text="#000000">
<button onclick="applyFilter();">Apply Filter</button>
<button onclick="myDiv1.style.visibility='visible'; myDiv2.style.visibility =
'hidden';">Restore</button>
<div id="trans" style="position:absolute; top:50; left:50; width:240; height:180; ">
<div id="myDiv1" style="position:absolute; top:0; left:0; width:240; height: 180;
background:red;  padding:10px; font-size:15pt; border:2px solid black; font-
size:12pt; font-family:verdana; color:white">This is the first div element.</div>
<div id="myDiv2" style="visibility:hidden; position:absolute; top:0; left:0;
width:240; height: 180; color:black; background: beige;  padding:10px; font-
size:12pt; font-family:verdana; border:2px solid black;"> This is the second div
element.</div>
</body></html>
```

Applies to:

`<a>`, `<acronym>`, `<address>`, `<b>`, `<bdo>`, `<big>`, `<blockquote>`, `<body>`, `<button>`, `<caption>`, `<center>`, `<cite>`, `<code>`, `<custom>`, `<dd>`, `<del>`, `<dfn>`, `<dir>`, `<div>`, `<dl>`, `<dt>`, `<em>`, `<fieldset>`, `<font>`, `<form>`, `<frame>`, `<frameset>`, `<hn>`, `<i>`, `<iframe>`, `<img>`, `<input type="button">`, `<input type="checkbox">`, `<input type="file">`, `<input type="image">`, `<input type="password">`, `<input type="radio">`, `<input type="reset">`, `<input type="submit">`, `<input type="text">`, `<ins>`, `<kbd>`, `<label>`, `<legend>`, `<li>`, `<marquee>`, `<menu>`, `<nobr>`, `<object>`, `<ol>`, `<p>`, `<pre>`, `<q>`, `<rt>`, `<ruby>`, `<s>`, `<samp>`, `<small>`, `<span>`, `<strike>`, `<strong>`, `<sub>`, `<sup>`, `<table>`, `<td>`, `<textarea>`, `<th>`, `<tt>`, `<u>`, `<ul>`, `<var>`, `<xmp>`

Common properties:

bands, duration, enabled, percent, status

Other properties:

direction	This property specifies the direction in which the motion of the blinds progresses. Values: up, down, right, or left.

Common methods:

---

apply(), play(), stop()

CheckerBoard

Compatibility: IE5.5, IE6

This transition filter gives the effect of revealing new content with a motion that progresses through a checkerboard pattern.

Example:

```
<html><head>
<script language="JavaScript">
function applyFilter() {
trans.style.filter = 'progid:DXImageTransform.Microsoft.checkerboard()';
    trans.filters[0].squaresx = 10;
    trans.filters[0].direction = 'left';
    trans.filters[0].squaresy = 10;
    trans.filters[0].Apply();
        myDiv2.style.visibility="visible";
        myDiv1.style.visibility="hidden";
        trans.filters[0].Play(duration=2);
}
</script></head>
<body bgcolor="#FFFFFF" text="#000000">
<button onclick="applyFilter();">Apply Filter</button>
<button onclick="myDiv1.style.visibility='visible'; myDiv2.style.visibility =
'hidden';">Restore</button>
<div id="trans" style="position:absolute; top:50; left:50; width:240; height:180; ">
<div id="myDiv1" style="position:absolute; top:0; left:0; width:240; height: 180;
background:red;  padding:10px; font-size:15pt; border:2px solid black; font-
size:12pt; font-family:verdana; color:white">This is the first div element.</div>
<div id="myDiv2" style="visibility:hidden; position:absolute; top:0; left:0;
width:240; height: 180; color:black; background: beige;  padding:10px; font-
size:12pt; font-family:verdana; border:2px solid black;"> This is the second div
element.</div>
</body></html>
```

Applies to:

`<a>`, `<acronym>`, `<address>`, `<b>`, `<bdo>`, `<big>`, `<blockquote>`, `<body>`, `<button>`, `<caption>`, `<center>`, `<cite>`, `<code>`, `<custom>`, `<dd>`, `<del>`, `<dfn>`, `<dir>`, `<div>`, `<dl>`, `<dt>`, `<em>`, `<fieldset>`, `<font>`, `<form>`, `<frame>`, `<frameset>`, `<hn>`, `<i>`, `<iframe>`, `<img>`, `<input type="button">`, `<input type="checkbox">`, `<input type="file">`, `<input type="image">`, `<input type="password">`, `<input type="radio">`, `<input type="reset">`, `<input type="submit">`, `<input type="text">`, `<ins>`, `<kbd>`, `<label>`, `<legend>`, `<li>`, `<marquee>`, `<menu>`, `<nobr>`, `<object>`, `<ol>`, `<p>`, `<pre>`, `<q>`, `<rt>`, `<ruby>`, `<s>`, `<samp>`, `<small>`, `<span>`, `<strike>`, `<strong>`, `<sub>`, `<sup>`, `<table>`, `<td>`, `<textarea>`, `<th>`, `<tt>`, `<u>`, `<ul>`, `<var>`, `<xmp>`

Other properties:

direction	This property specifies the direction in which the motion of the checkerboard progresses. Values: up, down, right, or left.
squaresX	This property sets the number of columns in the checkerboard. Value: An integer value that is greater than 1 (default value is 12).
squaresY	This property sets the number of rows in the checkerboard. Value: An integer value that is greater than 1 (default value is 10).

Fade

Compatibility: IE5.5, IE6

This transition filter gives the effect of revealing new content by causing the original content of the element to gradually fade out.

Example:

```
<html><head>
<script language="JavaScript">
function applyFilter() {
trans.style.filter = 'progid:DXImageTransform.Microsoft.fade()';
    trans.filters[0].duration = 10;
    trans.filters[0].Apply();
    myDiv2.style.visibility="visible";
    myDiv1.style.visibility="hidden";
    trans.filters[0].Play(duration=2);
}
</script></head>
<body bgcolor="#FFFFFF" text="#000000">
<button onclick="applyFilter();">Apply Filter</button>
<button onclick="myDiv1.style.visibility='visible'; myDiv2.style.visibility =
'hidden';">Restore</button>
<div id="trans" style="position:absolute; top:50; left:50; width:240; height:180;
">
<div id="myDiv1" style="position:absolute; top:0; left:0; width:240; height: 180;
background:red;  padding:10px; font-size:15pt; border:2px solid black; font-
size:12pt; font-family:verdana; color:white">This is the first div element.</div>
<div id="myDiv2" style="visibility:hidden; position:absolute; top:0; left:0;
width:240; height: 180; color:black; background: beige;  padding:10px; font-
size:12pt; font-family:verdana; border:2px solid black;"> This is the second div
element.</div>
</body></html>
```

Applies to:

```
<a>, <acronym>, <address>, <b>, <bdo>, <big>, <blockquote>, <body>, <button>,
<caption>, <center>, <cite>, <code>, <custom>, <dd>, <del>, <dfn>, <dir>, <div>,
<dl>, <dt>, <em>, <fieldset>, <font>, <form>, <frame>, <frameset>, <hn>, <i>,
<iframe>, <img>, <input type="button">, <input type="checkbox">, <input
type="file">, <input type="image">, <input type="password">, <input type="radio">,
```

```
<input type="reset">, <input type="submit">, <input type="text">, <ins>, <kbd>,
<label>, <legend>, <li>, <marquee>, <menu>, <nobr>, <object>, <ol>, <p>, <pre>,
<q>, <rt>, <ruby>, <s>, <samp>, <small>, <span>, <strike>, <strong>, <sub>, <sup>,
<table>, <td>, <textarea>, <th>, <tt>, <u>, <ul>, <var>, <xmp>
```

Common properties:

```
duration, enabled, percent, status
```

Other properties:

overlap	This property establishes the duration during which the transitional effect displays both new and original content simultaneously. Value: A floating-point number from 0.0 to 1.0 (default value is 1.0). For example, setting the overlap property to 0.2 and the duration property to 30 seconds will cause the original content to be displayed for 12 seconds, then both the original and the new content to be displayed for 6 seconds, and finally the new content to be displayed for 12 seconds.

Common methods:

```
apply(), play(), stop()
```

GradientWipe

Compatibility: IE5.5, IE6

This filter gives the effect of revealing new content by causing a gradient band to pass over the element.

Example:

```
<html><head>
<script language="JavaScript">
function applyFilter() {
trans.style.filter = 'progid:DXImageTransform.Microsoft.gradientwipe()';
    trans.filters[0].gradientsize = .1;
    trans.filters[0].Apply();
    myDiv2.style.visibility="visible";
    myDiv1.style.visibility="hidden";
    trans.filters[0].Play(duration=2);
}
</script></head>
<body bgcolor="#FFFFFF" text="#000000">
<button onclick="applyFilter();">Apply Filter</button>
<button onclick="myDiv1.style.visibility='visible'; myDiv2.style.visibility =
'hidden';">Restore</button>
<div id="trans" style="position:absolute; top:50; left:50; width:240; height:180;
">
<div id="myDiv1" style="position:absolute; top:0; left:0; width:240; height: 180;
background:red;  padding:10px; font-size:15pt; border:2px solid black; font-
size:12pt; font-family:verdana; color:white">This is the first div element.</div>
```

```
<div id="myDiv2" style="visibility:hidden; position:absolute; top:0; left:0;
width:240; height: 180; color:black; background: beige;  padding:10px; font-
size:12pt; font-family:verdana; border:2px solid black;"> This is the second div
element.</div>
</body></html>
```

Applies to:

`<a>`, `<acronym>`, `<address>`, `<b>`, `<bdo>`, `<big>`, `<blockquote>`, `<body>`, `<button>`,
`<caption>`, `<center>`, `<cite>`, `<code>`, `<custom>`, `<dd>`, `<del>`, `<dfn>`, `<dir>`, `<div>`,
`<dl>`, `<dt>`, `<em>`, `<fieldset>`, `<font>`, `<form>`, `<frame>`, `<frameset>`, `<hn>`, `<i>`,
`<iframe>`, `<img>`, `<input type="button">`, `<input type="checkbox">`, `<input
type="file">`, `<input type="image">`, `<input type="password">`, `<input type="radio">`,
`<input type="reset">`, `<input type="submit">`, `<input type="text">`, `<ins>`, `<kbd>`,
`<label>`, `<legend>`, `<li>`, `<marquee>`, `<menu>`, `<nobr>`, `<object>`, `<ol>`, `<p>`, `<pre>`,
`<q>`, `<rt>`, `<ruby>`, `<s>`, `<samp>`, `<small>`, `<span>`, `<strike>`, `<strong>`, `<sub>`, `<sup>`,
`<table>`, `<td>`, `<textarea>`, `<th>`, `<tt>`, `<u>`, `<ul>`, `<var>`, `<xmp>`

Common properties:

duration, enabled, percent, status

Other properties:

gradientSize	This property specifies the size of the gradient wipe band in relation to the size of the element. Value: A floating-point number from 0.0 (there is no gradient band) to 1.0 (the gradient band covers the entire element). Default value is 0.25 (25 percent).
motion	This property indicates whether the band moves from right to left or left to right (if wipeStyle is 0), or from top to bottom or bottom to top (if wipeStyle is 1). Values: forward (the default; left to right or top to bottom) or reverse (right to left or bottom to top).
wipeStyle	This property establishes whether the band moves vertically or horizontally. Values: 0 (the default; horizontally) or 1 (vertically).

Common methods:

apply(), play(), stop()

Inset

Compatibility: IE5.5, IE6

This filter gives the effect of revealing new content by creating a diagonal motion across the element's content.

Example:

```
<html><head>
<script language="JavaScript">
function applyFilter() {
trans.style.filter = 'progid:DXImageTransform.Microsoft.inset()';
    trans.filters[0].duration = 10;
```

```
        trans.filters[0].Apply();
        myDiv2.style.visibility="visible";
        myDiv1.style.visibility="hidden";
        trans.filters[0].Play(duration=2);
}
</script></head>
<body bgcolor="#FFFFFF" text="#000000">
<button onclick="applyFilter();">Apply Filter</button>
<button onclick="myDiv1.style.visibility='visible'; myDiv2.style.visibility =
'hidden';">Restore</button>
<div id="trans" style="position:absolute; top:50; left:50; width:240; height:180;
">
<div id="myDiv1" style="position:absolute; top:0; left:0; width:240; height: 180;
background:red;  padding:10px; font-size:15pt; border:2px solid black; font-
size:12pt; font-family:verdana; color:white">This is the first div element.</div>
<div id="myDiv2" style="visibility:hidden; position:absolute; top:0; left:0;
width:240; height: 180; color:black; background: beige;  padding:10px; font-
size:12pt; font-family:verdana; border:2px solid black;"> This is the second div
element.</div>
</body></html>
```

Applies to:

```
<a>, <acronym>, <address>, <b>, <bdo>, <big>, <blockquote>, <body>, <button>,
<caption>, <center>, <cite>, <code>, <custom>, <dd>, <del>, <dfn>, <dir>, <div>,
<dl>, <dt>, <em>, <fieldset>, <font>, <form>, <frame>, <frameset>, <hn>, <i>,
<iframe>, <img>, <input type="button">, <input type="checkbox">, <input
type="file">, <input type="image">, <input type="password">, <input type="radio">,
<input type="reset">, <input type="submit">, <input type="text">, <ins>, <kbd>,
<label>, <legend>, <li>, <marquee>, <menu>, <nobr>, <object>, <ol>, <p>, <pre>,
<q>, <rt>, <ruby>, <s>, <samp>, <small>, <span>, <strike>, <strong>, <sub>, <sup>,
<table>, <td>, <textarea>, <th>, <tt>, <u>, <ul>, <var>, <xmp>
```

Common properties:

```
duration, enabled, percent, status
```

Common methods:

```
apply(), play(), stop()
```

Iris

Compatibility: IE5.5, IE6

This filter gives the effect of revealing new content by using a motion that is
similar to that of the iris of an eye opening and closing.

Example:

```
<html><head>
<script language="JavaScript">
function applyFilter() {
```

```
trans.style.filter = 'progid:DXImageTransform.Microsoft.iris()';
    trans.filters[0].duration = 10;
    trans.filters[0].irisstyle = 'diamond';
    trans.filters[0].Apply();
    myDiv2.style.visibility="visible";
    myDiv1.style.visibility="hidden";
    trans.filters[0].Play(duration=2);
}
</script></head>
<body bgcolor="#FFFFFF" text="#000000">
<button onclick="applyFilter();">Apply Filter</button>
<button onclick="myDiv1.style.visibility='visible'; myDiv2.style.visibility =
'hidden';">Restore</button>
<div id="trans" style="position:absolute; top:50; left:50; width:240; height:180;
">
<div id="myDiv1" style="position:absolute; top:0; left:0; width:240; height: 180;
background:red;  padding:10px; font-size:15pt; border:2px solid black; font-
size:12pt; font-family:verdana; color:white">This is the first div element.</div>
<div id="myDiv2" style="visibility:hidden; position:absolute; top:0; left:0;
width:240; height: 180; color:black; background: beige;  padding:10px; font-
size:12pt; font-family:verdana; border:2px solid black;"> This is the second div
element.</div>
</body></html>
```

Applies to:

<a>, <acronym>, <address>, <b>, <bdo>, <big>, <blockquote>, <body>, <button>,
<caption>, <center>, <cite>, <code>, <custom>, <dd>, <del>, <dfn>, <dir>, <div>,
<dl>, <dt>, <em>, <fieldset>, <font>, <form>, <frame>, <frameset>, <hn>, <i>,
<iframe>, <img>, <input type="button">, <input type="checkbox">, <input
type="file">, <input type="image">, <input type="password">, <input type="radio">,
<input type="reset">, <input type="submit">, <input type="text">, <ins>, <kbd>,
<label>, <legend>, <li>, <marquee>, <menu>, <nobr>, <object>, <ol>, <p>, <pre>,
<q>, <rt>, <ruby>, <s>, <samp>, <small>, <span>, <strike>, <strong>, <sub>, <sup>,
<table>, <td>, <textarea>, <th>, <tt>, <u>, <ul>, <var>, <xmp>

Common properties:

duration, enabled, percent, status

Other properties:

irisStyle	This property specifies the shape of the filter. Values: diamond, circle, cross, plus, square, and star.
motion	This property determines whether the filter effect moves from the outside in or from the inside out. Values: out (the default; from inside to outside) or in (from outside to inside).

Common methods:

apply(), play(), stop()

Compatibility: IE5.5, IE6

This transition filter effect pixelates the original content and then depixelates the image to reveal the new content.

Example:

```
<html><head>
<script language="JavaScript">
function applyFilter() {
    trans.style.filter = 'progid:DXImageTransform.Microsoft.Pixelate()';
    trans.filters[0].Apply();
    myDiv2.style.visibility="visible";
    myDiv1.style.visibility="hidden";
    trans.filters[0].Play(duration=3);
}
</script></head>
<body bgcolor="#FFFFFF" text="#000000">
<button onclick="applyFilter();">Apply Filter</button>
<button onclick="myDiv1.style.visibility='visible'; myDiv2.style.visibility =
'hidden';">Restore</button>
<div id="trans" style="position:absolute; top:50; left:50; width:240; height:180;">
<div id="myDiv1" style="position:absolute; top:0; left:0; width:240; height: 180;
background:red;  padding:10px; font-size:15pt; border:2px solid black; font-
size:12pt; font-family:verdana; color:white">This is the first div element.</div>
<div id="myDiv2" style="visibility:hidden; position:absolute; top:0; left:0;
width:240; height: 180; color:black; background: beige;  padding:10px; font-
size:12pt; font-family:verdana; border:2px solid black;"> This is the second div
element.</div>
</body></html>
```

Applies to:

```
<a>, <acronym>, <address>, <b>, <bdo>, <big>, <blockquote>, <body>, <button>,
<caption>, <center>, <cite>, <code>, <custom>, <dd>, <del>, <dfn>, <dir>, <div>,
<dl>, <dt>, <em>, <fieldset>, <font>, <form>, <frame>, <frameset>, <hn>, <i>,
<iframe>, <img>, <input type="button">, <input type="checkbox">, <input
type="file">, <input type="image">, <input type="password">, <input type="radio">,
<input type="reset">, <input type="submit">, <input type="text">, <ins>, <kbd>,
<label>, <legend>, <li>, <marquee>, <menu>, <nobr>, <object>, <ol>, <p>, <pre>,
<q>, <rt>, <ruby>, <s>, <samp>, <small>, <span>, <strike>, <strong>, <sub>, <sup>,
<table>, <td>, <textarea>, <th>, <tt>, <u>, <ul>, <var>, <xmp>
```

Common properties:

```
duration, enabled, percent, status
```

Other properties:

maxSquare	This property establishes the maximum width of the pixilated squares. Value: An integer value ranging from 2 to 50 pixels (default is 50 pixels).

Common methods:

apply(), play(), stop()

RadialWipe

Compatibility: IE5.5, IE6

This filter transition gives the effect of revealing new content by creating a motion that resembles a radar screen wipe.

Example:

```
<html><head>
<script language="JavaScript">
function applyFilter() {
    trans.style.filter =
'progid:DXImageTransform.Microsoft.RadialWipe(wipestyle=clock)';
    trans.filters[0].Apply();
    myDiv2.style.visibility="visible";
    myDiv1.style.visibility="hidden";
    trans.filters[0].Play(duration=3);
}
</script></head>
<body bgcolor="#FFFFFF" text="#000000">
<button onclick="applyFilter();">Apply Filter</button>
<button onclick="myDiv1.style.visibility='visible'; myDiv2.style.visibility =
'hidden';">Restore</button>
<div id="trans" style="position:absolute; top:50; left:50; width:240; height:180;">
<div id="myDiv1" style="position:absolute; top:0; left:0; width:240; height: 180;
background:red;  padding:10px; font-size:15pt; border:2px solid black; font-
size:12pt; font-family:verdana; color:white">This is the first div element.</div>
<div id="myDiv2" style="visibility:hidden; position:absolute; top:0; left:0;
width:240; height: 180; color:black; background: beige;  padding:10px; font-
size:12pt; font-family:verdana; border:2px solid black;"> This is the second div
element.</div>
</body></html>
```

Applies to:

<a>, <acronym>, <address>, <b>, <bdo>, <big>, <blockquote>, <body>, <button>, <caption>, <center>, <cite>, <code>, <custom>, <dd>, <del>, <dfn>, <dir>, <div>, <dl>, <dt>, <em>, <fieldset>, <font>, <form>, <frame>, <frameset>, <hn>, <i>, <iframe>, <img>, <input type="button">, <input type="checkbox">, <input type="file">, <input type="image">, <input type="password">, <input type="radio">, <input type="reset">, <input type="submit">, <input type="text">, <ins>, <kbd>, <label>, <legend>, <li>, <marquee>, <menu>, <nobr>, <object>, <ol>, <p>, <pre>, <q>, <rt>, <ruby>, <s>, <samp>, <small>, <span>, <strike>, <strong>, <sub>, <sup>, <table>, <td>, <textarea>, <th>, <tt>, <u>, <ul>, <var>, <xmp>

Common properties:

duration, enabled, percent, status

Other properties:

wipeStyle	This property establishes the manner in which the band moves. Values: clock (the default; moves in a clockwise direction starting at the top), wedge (moves in both directions from the top), and radial (moves from the upper-left corner).

Common methods:

apply(), play(), stop()

RandomBars

Compatibility: IE5.5, IE6

This is a filter transition that gives the effect of revealing new content by banding together many horizontal or vertical lines (usually one pixel wide).

Example:

```html
<html><head>
<script language="JavaScript">
function applyFilter() {
    trans.style.filter = 'progid:DXImageTransform.Microsoft.randombars()';
    trans.filters[0].Apply();
    myDiv2.style.visibility="visible";
    myDiv1.style.visibility="hidden";
    trans.filters[0].Play(duration=3);
}
</script></head>
<body bgcolor="#FFFFFF" text="#000000">
<button onclick="applyFilter();">Apply Filter</button>
<button onclick="myDiv1.style.visibility='visible'; myDiv2.style.visibility =
'hidden';">Restore</button>
<div id="trans" style="position:absolute; top:50; left:50; width:240; height:180;">
<div id="myDiv1" style="position:absolute; top:0; left:0; width:240; height: 180;
background:red;  padding:10px; font-size:15pt; border:2px solid black; font-
size:12pt; font-family:verdana; color:white">This is the first div element.</div>
<div id="myDiv2" style="visibility:hidden; position:absolute; top:0; left:0;
width:240; height: 180; color:black; background: beige;  padding:10px; font-
size:12pt; font-family:verdana; border:2px solid black;"> This is the second div
element.</div>
</body></html>
```

Applies to:

`<a>`, `<acronym>`, `<address>`, `<b>`, `<bdo>`, `<big>`, `<blockquote>`, `<body>`, `<button>`, `<caption>`, `<center>`, `<cite>`, `<code>`, `<custom>`, `<dd>`, `<del>`, `<dfn>`, `<dir>`, `<div>`, `<dl>`, `<dt>`, `<em>`, `<fieldset>`, `<font>`, `<form>`, `<frame>`, `<frameset>`, `<hn>`, `<i>`, `<iframe>`, `<img>`, `<input type="button">`, `<input type="checkbox">`, `<input type="file">`, `<input type="image">`, `<input type="password">`, `<input type="radio">`, `<input type="reset">`, `<input type="submit">`, `<input type="text">`, `<ins>`, `<kbd>`,

```
<label>, <legend>, <li>, <marquee>, <menu>, <nobr>, <object>, <ol>, <p>, <pre>,
<q>, <rt>, <ruby>, <s>, <samp>, <small>, <span>, <strike>, <strong>, <sub>, <sup>,
<table>, <td>, <textarea>, <th>, <tt>, <u>, <ul>, <var>, <xmp>
```

Common properties:

```
duration, enabled, orientation, percent, status
```

Common methods:

```
apply(), play(), stop()
```

RandomDissolve

Compatibility: IE5.5, IE6

This is a filter transition that gives the effect of revealing new content by filling
the element with dots, similar to a stardust effect.

Example:

```
<html><head>
<script language="JavaScript">
function applyFilter() {
    trans.style.filter = 'progid:DXImageTransform.Microsoft.randomdissolve()';
    trans.filters[0].Apply();
    myDiv2.style.visibility="visible";
    myDiv1.style.visibility="hidden";
    trans.filters[0].Play(duration=3);
}
</script></head>
<body bgcolor="#FFFFFF" text="#000000">
<button onclick="applyFilter();">Apply Filter</button>
<button onclick="myDiv1.style.visibility='visible'; myDiv2.style.visibility =
'hidden';">Restore</button>
<div id="trans" style="position:absolute; top:50; left:50; width:240; height:180;">
<div id="myDiv1" style="position:absolute; top:0; left:0; width:240; height: 180;
background:red;  padding:10px; font-size:15pt; border:2px solid black; font-
size:12pt; font-family:verdana; color:white">This is the first div element.</div>
<div id="myDiv2" style="visibility:hidden; position:absolute; top:0; left:0;
width:240; height: 180; color:black; background: beige;  padding:10px; font-
size:12pt; font-family:verdana; border:2px solid black;"> This is the second div
element.</div>
</body></html>
```

Applies to:

```
<a>, <acronym>, <address>, <b>, <bdo>, <big>, <blockquote>, <body>, <button>,
<caption>, <center>, <cite>, <code>, <custom>, <dd>, <del>, <dfn>, <dir>, <div>,
<dl>, <dt>, <em>, <fieldset>, <font>, <form>, <frame>, <frameset>, <hn>, <i>,
<iframe>, <img>, <input type="button">, <input type="checkbox">, <input
type="file">, <input type="image">, <input type="password">, <input type="radio">,
```

```
<input type="reset">, <input type="submit">, <input type="text">, <ins>, <kbd>,
<label>, <legend>, <li>, <marquee>, <menu>, <nobr>, <object>, <ol>, <p>, <pre>,
<q>, <rt>, <ruby>, <s>, <samp>, <small>, <span>, <strike>, <strong>, <sub>, <sup>,
<table>, <td>, <textarea>, <th>, <tt>, <u>, <ul>, <var>, <xmp>
```

Common properties:

```
duration, enabled, percent, status
```

Common methods:

```
apply(), play(), stop()
```

Slide

Compatibility: IE5.5, IE6

This filter transition gives the effect of revealing new content by sliding the element's original content horizontally.

Example:

```
<html><head>
<script language="JavaScript">
function applyFilter() {
    trans.style.filter =
'progid:DXImageTransform.Microsoft.slide(slidestyle=hide)';
    trans.filters[0].Apply();
    myDiv2.style.visibility="visible";
    myDiv1.style.visibility="hidden";
    trans.filters[0].Play(duration=3);
}
</script></head>
<body bgcolor="#FFFFFF" text="#000000">
<button onclick="applyFilter();">Apply Filter</button>
<button onclick="myDiv1.style.visibility='visible'; myDiv2.style.visibility =
'hidden';">Restore</button>
<div id="trans" style="position:absolute; top:50; left:50; width:240; height:180;">
<div id="myDiv1" style="position:absolute; top:0; left:0; width:240; height: 180;
background:red;  padding:10px; font-size:15pt; border:2px solid black; font-
size:12pt; font-family:verdana; color:white">This is the first div element.</div>
<div id="myDiv2" style="visibility:hidden; position:absolute; top:0; left:0;
width:240; height: 180; color:black; background: beige;  padding:10px; font-
size:12pt; font-family:verdana; border:2px solid black;"> This is the second div
element.</div>
</body></html>
```

Applies to:

```
<a>, <acronym>, <address>, <b>, <bdo>, <big>, <blockquote>, <body>, <button>,
<caption>, <center>, <cite>, <code>, <custom>, <dd>, <del>, <dfn>, <dir>, <div>,
<dl>, <dt>, <em>, <fieldset>, <font>, <form>, <frame>, <frameset>, <hn>, <i>,
<iframe>, <img>, <input type="button">, <input type="checkbox">, <input
```

```
type="file">, <input type="image">, <input type="password">, <input type="radio">,
<input type="reset">, <input type="submit">, <input type="text">, <ins>, <kbd>,
<label>, <legend>, <li>, <marquee>, <menu>, <nobr>, <object>, <ol>, <p>, <pre>,
<q>, <rt>, <ruby>, <s>, <samp>, <small>, <span>, <strike>, <strong>, <sub>, <sup>,
<table>, <td>, <textarea>, <th>, <tt>, <u>, <ul>, <var>, <xmp>
```

Common properties:

```
bands, duration, enabled, percent, status
```

Other properties:

slideStyle	This property establishes the sliding method used by the filter. Values: hide (the default; as it slides, the band hides the original content and reveals the new content), push (the band containing new content pushes the original content out), and swap (combines the two bands).

Common methods:

```
apply(), play(), stop()
```

Spiral

Compatibility: IE5.5, IE6

This filter gives the effect of revealing new content by creating a spiral motion. This motion is very similar to that of water being flushed down the toilet.

Example:

```html
<html><head>
<script language="JavaScript">
function applyFilter() {
    trans.style.filter = 'progid:DXImageTransform.Microsoft.spiral(gridsizex=30,
gridsizey=30)';
    trans.filters[0].Apply();
    myDiv2.style.visibility="visible";
    myDiv1.style.visibility="hidden";
    trans.filters[0].Play(duration=3);
}
</script></head>
<body bgcolor="#FFFFFF" text="#000000">
<button onclick="applyFilter();">Apply Filter</button>
<button onclick="myDiv1.style.visibility='visible'; myDiv2.style.visibility =
'hidden';">Restore</button>
<div id="trans" style="position:absolute; top:50; left:50; width:240; height:180;">
<div id="myDiv1" style="position:absolute; top:0; left:0; width:240; height: 180;
background:red;  padding:10px; font-size:15pt; border:2px solid black; font-
size:12pt; font-family:verdana; color:white">This is the first div element.</div>
<div id="myDiv2" style="visibility:hidden; position:absolute; top:0; left:0;
width:240; height: 180; color:black; background: beige;  padding:10px; font-
size:12pt; font-family:verdana; border:2px solid black;"> This is the second div
element.</div>
</body></html>
```

Applies to:

<a>, <acronym>, <address>, <b>, <bdo>, <big>, <blockquote>, <body>, <button>, <caption>, <center>, <cite>, <code>, <custom>, <dd>, <del>, <dfn>, <dir>, <div>, <dl>, <dt>, <em>, <fieldset>, <font>, <form>, <frame>, <frameset>, <hn>, <i>, <iframe>, <img>, <input type="button">, <input type="checkbox">, <input type="file">, <input type="image">, <input type="password">, <input type="radio">, <input type="reset">, <input type="submit">, <input type="text">, <ins>, <kbd>, <label>, <legend>, <li>, <marquee>, <menu>, <nobr>, <object>, <ol>, <p>, <pre>, <q>, <rt>, <ruby>, <s>, <samp>, <small>, <span>, <strike>, <strong>, <sub>, <sup>, <table>, <td>, <textarea>, <th>, <tt>, <u>, <ul>, <var>, <xmp>

Common properties:

duration, enabled, gridSizeX, gridSizeY, percent, status

Common methods:

apply(), play(), stop()

Stretch

Compatibility: IE5.5, IE6

This filter gives the effect of revealing new content by causing the element's new content to be revealed using a stretching motion.

Example:

```
<html><head>
<script language="JavaScript">
function applyFilter() {
    trans.style.filter =
'progid:DXImageTransform.Microsoft.stretch(stretchstyle=hide)';
    trans.filters[0].Apply();
    myDiv2.style.visibility="visible";
    myDiv1.style.visibility="hidden";
    trans.filters[0].Play(duration=3);
}
</script></head>
<body bgcolor="#FFFFFF" text="#000000">
<button onclick="applyFilter();">Apply Filter</button>
<button onclick="myDiv1.style.visibility='visible'; myDiv2.style.visibility =
'hidden';">Restore</button>
<div id="trans" style="position:absolute; top:50; left:50; width:240; height:180;">
<div id="myDiv1" style="position:absolute; top:0; left:0; width:240; height: 180;
background:red;  padding:10px; font-size:15pt; border:2px solid black; font-
size:12pt; font-family:verdana; color:white">This is the first div element.</div>
<div id="myDiv2" style="visibility:hidden; position:absolute; top:0; left:0;
width:240; height: 180; color:black; background: beige;  padding:10px; font-
size:12pt; font-family:verdana; border:2px solid black;"> This is the second div
element.</div>
</body></html>
```

Applies to:

<a>, <acronym>, <address>, <b>, <bdo>, <big>, <blockquote>, <body>, <button>, <caption>, <center>, <cite>, <code>, <custom>, <dd>, <del>, <dfn>, <dir>, <div>, <dl>, <dt>, <em>, <fieldset>, <font>, <form>, <frame>, <frameset>, <hn>, <i>, <iframe>, <img>, <input type="button">, <input type="checkbox">, <input type="file">, <input type="image">, <input type="password">, <input type="radio">, <input type="reset">, <input type="submit">, <input type="text">, <ins>, <kbd>, <label>, <legend>, <li>, <marquee>, <menu>, <nobr>, <object>, <ol>, <p>, <pre>, <q>, <rt>, <ruby>, <s>, <samp>, <small>, <span>, <strike>, <strong>, <sub>, <sup>, <table>, <td>, <textarea>, <th>, <tt>, <u>, <ul>, <var>, <xmp>

Common properties:

duration, enabled, percent, status

Other properties:

stretchStyle	This property establishes the stretching method used by the filter. Values: hide (hides original content while new content is revealed from left to right), push (pushes original content out while revealing new content), and spin (the default; pushes original content from the center to the sides to reveal new content).

Common methods:

apply(), play(), stop()

Strips

Compatibility: IE5.5, IE6

This filter gives the effect of revealing new content by causing a jagged line to pass across the element's original content.

Example:

```
<html><head>
<script language="JavaScript">
function applyFilter() {
    trans.style.filter =
'progid:DXImageTransform.Microsoft.strips(motion=rightdown)';
    trans.filters[0].Apply();
    myDiv2.style.visibility="visible";
    myDiv1.style.visibility="hidden";
    trans.filters[0].Play(duration=3);
}
</script></head>
<body bgcolor="#FFFFFF" text="#000000">
<button onclick="applyFilter();">Apply Filter</button>
<button onclick="myDiv1.style.visibility='visible'; myDiv2.style.visibility =
'hidden';">Restore</button>
```

```
<div id="trans" style="position:absolute; top:50; left:50; width:240; height:180;">
<div id="myDiv1" style="position:absolute; top:0; left:0; width:240; height: 180;
background:red;  padding:10px; font-size:15pt; border:2px solid black; font-
size:12pt; font-family:verdana; color:white">This is the first div element.</div>
<div id="myDiv2" style="visibility:hidden; position:absolute; top:0; left:0;
width:240; height: 180; color:black; background: beige;  padding:10px; font-
size:12pt; font-family:verdana; border:2px solid black;"> This is the second div
element.</div>
</body></html>
```

Applies to:

`<a>`, `<acronym>`, `<address>`, `<b>`, `<bdo>`, `<big>`, `<blockquote>`, `<body>`, `<button>`,
`<caption>`, `<center>`, `<cite>`, `<code>`, `<custom>`, `<dd>`, `<del>`, `<dfn>`, `<dir>`, `<div>`,
`<dl>`, `<dt>`, `<em>`, `<fieldset>`, `<font>`, `<form>`, `<frame>`, `<frameset>`, `<hn>`, `<i>`,
`<iframe>`, `<img>`, `<input type="button">`, `<input type="checkbox">`, `<input
type="file">`, `<input type="image">`, `<input type="password">`, `<input type="radio">`,
`<input type="reset">`, `<input type="submit">`, `<input type="text">`, `<ins>`, `<kbd>`,
`<label>`, `<legend>`, `<li>`, `<marquee>`, `<menu>`, `<nobr>`, `<object>`, `<ol>`, `<p>`, `<pre>`,
`<q>`, `<rt>`, `<ruby>`, `<s>`, `<samp>`, `<small>`, `<span>`, `<strike>`, `<strong>`, `<sub>`, `<sup>`,
`<table>`, `<td>`, `<textarea>`, `<th>`, `<tt>`, `<u>`, `<ul>`, `<var>`, `<xmp>`

Common properties:

`duration, enabled, percent, status`

Other properties:

motion	This property indicates the direction of the filter. Values: `leftdown` (the default; starts from the upper-right and ends at the lower-left), `leftup` (starts from the lower-right and ends at the upper-left), `rightdown` (starts from the upper-left and ends at the lower-right), and `rightup` (starts from the lower-left and ends at the upper-right).

Common methods:

`apply(), play(), stop()`

Wheel

Compatibility: IE5.5, IE6

This transition filter gives the effect of revealing new content through a rotating wheel motion.

Example:

```
<html><head>
<script language="JavaScript">
function applyFilter() {
    trans.style.filter = 'progid:DXImageTransform.Microsoft.wheel(spokes=12)';
    trans.filters[0].Apply();
```

```
        myDiv2.style.visibility="visible";
        myDiv1.style.visibility="hidden";
        trans.filters[0].Play(duration=3);
}
</script></head>
<body bgcolor="#FFFFFF" text="#000000">
<button onclick="applyFilter();">Apply Filter</button>
<button onclick="myDiv1.style.visibility='visible'; myDiv2.style.visibility =
'hidden';">Restore</button>
<div id="trans" style="position:absolute; top:50; left:50; width:240; height:180;">
<div id="myDiv1" style="position:absolute; top:0; left:0; width:240; height: 180;
background:red;  padding:10px; font-size:15pt; border:2px solid black; font-
size:12pt; font-family:verdana; color:white">This is the first div element.</div>
<div id="myDiv2" style="visibility:hidden; position:absolute; top:0; left:0;
width:240; height: 180; color:black; background: beige;  padding:10px; font-
size:12pt; font-family:verdana; border:2px solid black;"> This is the second div
element.</div>
</body></html>
```

Applies to:

```
<a>, <acronym>, <address>, <b>, <bdo>, <big>, <blockquote>, <body>, <button>,
<caption>, <center>, <cite>, <code>, <custom>, <dd>, <del>, <dfn>, <dir>, <div>,
<dl>, <dt>, <em>, <fieldset>, <font>, <form>, <frame>, <frameset>, <hn>, <i>,
<iframe>, <img>, <input type="button">, <input type="checkbox">, <input
type="file">, <input type="image">, <input type="password">, <input type="radio">,
<input type="reset">, <input type="submit">, <input type="text">, <ins>, <kbd>,
<label>, <legend>, <li>, <marquee>, <menu>, <nobr>, <object>, <ol>, <p>, <pre>,
<q>, <rt>, <ruby>, <s>, <samp>, <small>, <span>, <strike>, <strong>, <sub>, <sup>,
<table>, <td>, <textarea>, <th>, <tt>, <u>, <ul>, <var>, <xmp>
```

Common properties:

```
duration, enabled, percent, status
```

Other properties:

spokes	This property specifies the number of spokes the wheel motion has during the filtering effect. Value: An integer value ranging from 2 to 20 (default value is 4).

Common methods:

```
apply(), play(), stop()
```

ZigZag

Compatibility: IE5.5, IE6

This filter gives the effect of revealing new content by creating a zigzag motion
from top to bottom.

Example:

```
<html><head>
<script language="JavaScript">
function applyFilter() {
    trans.style.filter = 'progid:DXImageTransform.Microsoft.zigzag(gridsizex=30,
gridsizey=30)';
    trans.filters[0].Apply();
    myDiv2.style.visibility="visible";
    myDiv1.style.visibility="hidden";
    trans.filters[0].Play(duration=3);
}
</script></head>
<body bgcolor="#FFFFFF" text="#000000">
<button onclick="applyFilter();">Apply Filter</button>
<button onclick="myDiv1.style.visibility='visible'; myDiv2.style.visibility =
'hidden';">Restore</button>
<div id="trans" style="position:absolute; top:50; left:50; width:240; height:180;">
<div id="myDiv1" style="position:absolute; top:0; left:0; width:240; height: 180;
background:red;  padding:10px; font-size:15pt; border:2px solid black; font-
size:12pt; font-family:verdana; color:white">This is the first div element.</div>
<div id="myDiv2" style="visibility:hidden; position:absolute; top:0; left:0;
width:240; height: 180; color:black; background: beige;  padding:10px; font-
size:12pt; font-family:verdana; border:2px solid black;"> This is the second div
element.</div>
</body></html>
```

Applies to:

<a>, <acronym>, <address>, <b>, <bdo>, <big>, <blockquote>, <body>, <button>,
<caption>, <center>, <cite>, <code>, <custom>, <dd>, <del>, <dfn>, <dir>, <div>,
<dl>, <dt>, <em>, <fieldset>, <font>, <form>, <frame>, <frameset>, <hn>, <i>,
<iframe>, <img>, <input type="button">, <input type="checkbox">, <input
type="file">, <input type="image">, <input type="password">, <input type="radio">,
<input type="reset">, <input type="submit">, <input type="text">, <ins>, <kbd>,
<label>, <legend>, <li>, <marquee>, <menu>, <nobr>, <object>, <ol>, <p>, <pre>,
<q>, <rt>, <ruby>, <s>, <samp>, <small>, <span>, <strike>, <strong>, <sub>, <sup>,
<table>, <td>, <textarea>, <th>, <tt>, <u>, <ul>, <var>, <xmp>

Common properties:

duration, enabled, gridSizeX, gridSizeY, percent, status

Common methods:

apply(), play(), stop()

11

JAVASCRIPT PROPERTIES

This chapter provides a comprehensive list of JavaScript properties. Each property contains compatibility information, a brief description, its syntax, an example, and an applies-to list of HTML elements, JavaScript collections, and JavaScript objects that make use of this property.

In order to distinguish between the HTML elements, JavaScript collections, and JavaScript objects that appear in the applies-to lists, the following conventions have been used:

- Angle bracket tags (< and >) surround the names of HTML elements (for example, <html>).

- An asterisk follows the names of JavaScript collections (areas*).

- The names of JavaScript objects appear without adornment (window).

NOTE *See Chapter 4 for an introduction to JavaScript properties.*

Compatibility: NN6, NN7, IE6

Read and write property. Specifies an abbreviated text for the element. It can be used by alternate means of rendering content, such as speech synthesis or Braille.

Syntax:

```
document.getElementById("elementID").abbr = value
document.all.elementID.abbr = value // IE only
```

Example:

```
<html><head><script language="JavaScript">
function goAbbr() {document.all.myTH.abbr = "Abbreviation";}
</script></head>
<body onLoad="goAbbr();">
<table width="428" border="1" cellspacing="5" cellpadding="5"
bordercolor="#0000FF">
    <th id="myTH" colspan="2">This is the table heading </th>
    <tr><td> Cell 1 content </td><td> Cell 2 content </td></tr>
    <tr><td> Cell 3 content </td><td> Cell 4 content </td></tr>
</table>
</body></html>
```

Applies to:

```
<td>, <th>
```

Compatibility: NN6, NN7, IE6

Read and write property. Specifies the comma-separated list of MIME content types that the element can accept. Values: text/html, image/png, image/gif, video/mpeg, audio/basic, text/tcl, text/javascript, and text/vbscript.

Syntax:

```
document.getElementById("inputID").accept = value
document.all.inputID.accept = value // IE only
```

Example:

```
<html><head><script language="JavaScript">
function goAccept() { document.all.myB.accept = "image/gif"; }
</script></head>
<body bgcolor="#FFFFFF" text="#000000" onLoad="goAccept();">
<input type="text" name="textfield" size="50" accept="image/gif"
```

```
value='The content type of this field is "text/html"'>
<input type="button" id="myB" value='The content type for this button is "image/
gif"'>
</body></html>
```

Applies to:

```
<input>
```

acceptCharset

Compatibility: NN6, NN7, IE5, IE5.5, IE6

Read and write property. Specifies a comma- or space-separated list of character sets that the server receiving form input must support. The UTF-8 character set will be used if the server does not support the character set sent by the document.

Syntax:

```
document.getElementById("formID").acceptCharset = value
document.all.formID.acceptCharset = value // IE only
```

Example:

```
<html><head><script language="JavaScript">
function goAcceptCharset() {alert(document.all.myForm.acceptCharset);}
</script></head>
<body onLoad="goAcceptCharset();">
<form id="myForm" method="post" action="" acceptcharset="UTF-8">
<!--input elements go here-->
</form>
</body></html>
```

Applies to:

```
<form>
```

accessKey

Compatibility: NN6, NN7, IE4, IE5, IE5.5, IE6

Read and write property. Specifies the one-character accelerator key for the element. Pressing the ALT key and the accelerator key simultaneously brings the element into focus.

Syntax:

```
document.getElementById("elementID").accessKey = value
document.all.elementID.accessKey = value // IE only
```

Example:

```
<html>
<body bgcolor="#FFFFFF" text="#000000">
<input type="text" size="40" id="myButton" accesskey="M" value="Press Alt + M to
bring me into focus">
<button onclick="myButton.accessKey='N';">Change Access Key to N</button>
</body></html>
```

Applies to:

`<a>`, `<acronym>`, `<address>`, `<applet>`, `<area>`, `<b>`, `<bdo>`, `<big>`, `<blockquote>`, `<body>`, `<button>`, `<caption>`, `<center>`, `<cite>`, `<custom>`, `<dd>`, `<del>`, `<dfn>`, `<dir>`, `<div>`, `<dl>`, `<dt>`, `<em>`, `<embed>`, `<fieldset>`, `<font>`, `<hn>`, `<hr>`, `<i>`, `<img>`, `<input type="button">`, `<input type="checkbox">`, `<input type="file">`, `<input type="image">`, `<input type="password">`, `<input type="radio">`, `<input type="reset">`, `<input type="submit">`, `<input type="text">`, `<ins>`, `<isindex>`, `<kbd>`, `<label>`, `<legend>`, `<li>`, `<listing>`, `<marquee>`, `<menu>`, `<object>`, `<ol>`, `<p>`, `<plaintext>`, `<pre>`, `<q>`, `<rt>`, `<ruby>`, `<s>`, `<samp>`, `<select>`, `<small>`, `<span>`, `<strike>`, `<strong>`, `<sub>`, `<sup>`, `<table>`, `<tbody>`, `<td>`, `<textarea>`, `<tfoot>`, `<th>`, `<thead>`, `<tr>`, `<tt>`, `<u>`, `<ul>`, `<var>`, `<xmp>`

action

Compatibility: NN4, NN6, NN7, IE4, IE5, IE5.5, IE6

Read and write property. Specifies the URL to which the form content is submitted.

Syntax:

```
document.getElementById("elementID").action = value
document.all.elementID.action = value // IE only
```

Example:

```
<html><head><script>
function sending() {
document.all.myForm.action = 'yourprocessingpage.asp';
document.all.myForm.submit();
}
</script></head>
<body bgcolor="#FFFFFF" text="#000000">
<form id="myForm">
Full Name: <input type="text" name="fullname" value="">
<button onclick="sending();">Submit</button>
</form>
</body></html>
```

Applies to:

<form>, <isindex>

activeElement

Compatibility: IE4, IE5, IE5.5, IE6

Read-only property. Retrieves the element that has focus in the document, provided that the document is fully loaded.

Syntax:

```
document.activeElement
```

Example:

```
<body bgcolor="#FFFFFF" text="#000000" onLoad="myB1.focus();">
<input type="Button" id="myB1" value="Element 1" onClick="B1();">
<script language="JavaScript">
function B1() {
var m = document.activeElement.value;
alert('The active element is '+m);
}
</script></body>
```

Applies to:

```
document
```

align (1)

Compatibility: NN4, NN6, NN7, IE4, IE5, IE5.5, IE6

Read and write property. Controls both horizontal and vertical alignment with adjacent text. Values: absbottom (aligns the bottom of the object with the bottom of the lowest item in the current line), absmiddle (aligns the bottom of the object with the middle of the text in the current line), baseline (aligns the bottom of the object with the baseline of the text in the current line), bottom (equivalent to baseline), left (aligns to the left), middle (aligns to the center), right (aligns to the right), texttop (aligns the top of the object with the top of the tallest text in the current line), and top (the same as texttop).

Syntax:

```
document.getElementById("elementID").align = value
document.all.elementID.align = value // IE only
```

Example:

```
<html><head>
<script language="JavaScript">
function B1() {document.all.myImage.align = "middle";}</script></head>
<body>
<img id="myImage" src="yourimage.jpg" width="74" height="99">
Sample Text<button onclick="B1();">Align Middle</button>
</body></html>
```

Applies to:

```
<applet>, <embed>, <fieldset>, <img>, <input>, <input type="image">, <object>,
<select>
```

align (2)

Compatibility: NN6, NN7, IE4, IE5, IE5.5, IE6

Read and write property. Controls the alignment of the element. Values: bottom, left, center, right, and top.

Syntax:

```
document.getElementById("elementID").align = value
document.all.elementID.align = value // IE only
```

Example:

```
<html><head>
<script language="JavaScript">
function B1() {document.all.myC.align = event.srcElement.id;}
</script></head>
<body bgcolor="#FFFFFF" text="#000000">
<table id="myTable" width="560" border="8" cellspacing="5" cellpadding="5">
<caption id="myC">This is the caption text for the table</caption>
<tr><td>Cell 1</td><td>Cell 2</td></tr><tr><td>Cell 3</td><td>Cell 4 </td></tr>
</table><br>
<input type="Button" id="bottom" value='align "bottom"' onClick="B1();">
<input type="Button" id="left" value='align "left"' onClick="B1();">
<input type="Button" id="right" value='align "right"' onClick="B1();">
<input type="Button" id="top" value='align "top"' onClick="B1();">
</body></html>
```

Applies to:

```
<caption>, <legend>
```

align (3)

Compatibility: NN4, NN6, NN7, IE4, IE5, IE5.5, IE6

Read and write property. Specifies the alignment of the object within the page or container element. Values: left, center, indent (only for the <p> element), right, and justify (only for the <div>, <hN>, and <p> elements).

Syntax:

```
document.getElementById("elementID").align = value
document.all.elementID.align = value // IE only
```

Example:

```
<html><head><script language="JavaScript">
function B1() {document.all.myDiv.align = "center";}
function B2() {document.all.myDiv.align = "justify";}
function B3() {document.all.myDiv.align = "left";}
function B4() {document.all.myDiv.align = "right";}
</script></head>
<body><div id="myDiv" style="position:absolute; visibility:visible; left:77px;
top:299px; width:354px; height:122px; background-color:red; border:1px none
#000000"><span>This block of text represents the content of the div element.</
span></div>
<input type="Button" value="Center" onClick="B1();">
<input type="Button" value="Justify" onClick="B2();">
<input type="Button" value="Left" onClick="B3();">
<input type="Button" value="Right" onClick="B4();">
</body></html>
```

Applies to:

```
<col>, <colgroup>, <div>, <hn>, <hr>, <p>, <tbody>, <td>, <tfoot>, <th>, <thead>, <tr>
```

align (4)

Compatibility: NN6, NN7, IE4, IE5, IE5.5, IE6

Read and write property. Specifies the horizontal alignment of the element, rather than of its contents. Values: left, center (the default), and right.

Syntax:

```
document.getElementById("elementID").align = value
document.all.elementID.align = value // IE only
```

Example:

```
<html><head><script>
function B1() {
```

```
document.all.myTable.align = event.srcElement.id;
}
</script></head>
<body bgcolor="#FFFFFF" text="#000000" style="width:650;">
<table id="myTable" width="560" border="8" cellspacing="5" cellpadding="5">
    <tr><td>Cell 1</td><td>Cell 2</td></tr>
    <tr><td>Cell 3</td><td>Cell 4</td></tr>
</table><br>
<input type="Button" id="center" value='align "center"' onClick="B1();">
<input type="Button" id="left" value='align "left"' onClick="B1();">
<input type="Button" id="right" value='align "right"' onClick="B1();">
</body></html>
```

Applies to:

```
<iframe>, <table>
```

aLink

Compatibility: NN6, NN7, IE4, IE5, IE5.5, IE6

Read and write property. Establishes the color of all active links on the page.
Value: Web color name or hexadecimal value in #RRGGBB format.

Syntax:

```
document.body.aLink = value
document.getElementById("bodyID").aLink = value
document.all.bodyID.aLink = value // IE only
```

Example:

```
<body bgcolor="#FFFFFF" text="#000000" onLoad="goColor();">
<script>function goColor() {document.body.aLink = "red";}</script>
<a href="http://www.advocar.com/">Advocar Link (click to turn red)</a>
</body>
```

Applies to:

```
<body>
```

alinkColor

Compatibility: NN4, NN6, NN7, IE4, IE5, IE5.5, IE6

Read and write property. Establishes the color of all active links in the document.
This property differs from the aLink property in that it applies to the document
object, whereas the aLink property applies to the <body> element. Value: Web
color name or hexadecimal value in #RRGGBB format.

Syntax:

```
document.alinkColor = value
```

Example:

```
<body bgcolor="#FFFFFF" text="#000000" onLoad="goColor();">
<script>function goColor() {document.alinkColor = "red";}</script>
<a href="http://www.advocar.com/">Advocar Link</a>
</body>
```

Applies to:

```
document
```

allowTransparency

Compatibility: IE5.5, IE6

Read and write property. Establishes whether or not the element is transparent. Values: true or false (the default).

Syntax:

```
document.all.elementID.allowTransparency = value
```

Example:

```
<html><head><script>
function B1() {
document.all.frame1.allowTransparency = "false";
document.all.frame1.style.backgroundColor = "white";
document.all.frame2.allowTransparency = "true";
document.all.frame2.style.backgroundColor = "lightgreen";
}
</script></head>
<body onLoad="B1();">
<iframe id="frame1" src="test2.htm" allowTransparency="true" style="width:200;">
</iframe>
<iframe id="frame2" src="test2.htm" style="width:200;"> </iframe>
</body></html>
```

Contents of test2.htm:

```
<body style="background-color:transparent;">
This is some text in a transparent html document
</body>
```

Applies to:

`<frame>`, `<iframe>`

---

alt

Compatibility: NN4 (`<img>` only), NN6, NN7, IE4, IE5, IE5.5, IE6

Read and write property. Specifies an alternative text to display for the element, either in place of the element when it cannot be displayed, or in a tooltip box that appears when the mouse hovers over the element.

Syntax:

```
document.getElementById("elementID").alt = value
document.all.elementID.alt = value // IE only
```

Example:

```
<img id="guernica" onmouseover="B1();" src="yourimage.jpg">
<script>
function B1() {
document.all.guernica.alt = 'The "Guernica". The most renowned Picasso painting!';}
</script>
```

Applies to:

`<applet>` (NN6, IE6 only), `<area>`, `<img>`, `<input>`, `<input type="image">`, `<object>` (NN6, IE6 only)

---

altHTML

Compatibility: IE4, IE5, IE5.5, IE6

Read and write property. Provides HTML content to render if the element doesn't load.

Syntax:

```
document.all.elementID.altHTML = value
```

Example:

```
<object id="myO" classid="clsid:D27CDB6E-AE6D-11cf-96B8-444553540000"
codebase="http://download.macromedia.com/pub/shockwave/cabs/flash/
swflash.cab#version=5,0,0,0"
width="243" height="194">
    <param id="myP1" name="movie" value="yourflashmovie.swf" valuetype="ref"
type="video/*">
    <param id="myP2" value="high" name="quality">
<script language="JavaScript">
```

```
document.all.myO.altHTML = "Alternative text";
</script>
</object>
```

Applies to:

`<applet>`, `<object>`

altKey

Compatibility: IE4, IE5, IE5.5, IE6

Read-only property. Indicates whether or not the ALT key is being held down.
Values: true or false.

Syntax:

```
window.event.altKey
```

Example:

```
<html><head><script language="JavaScript">
function B1() {
var m = event.altKey;
if (m == false) {
alert("The Alt Key is not pressed");
document.all.myB.value = "Click here while pressing the Alt key";
} else if(m == true) {
alert("The Alt Key is pressed");
document.all.myB.value = "Click here";
}}
</script></head>
<body bgcolor="#FFFFFF" text="#000000">
<input id="myB" type="button" value="Click here" onClick="B1();">
</body></html>
```

Applies to:

event

altLeft

Compatibility: IE5.5, IE6

Read-only property. Indicates whether or not the left ALT key is being held down.
Syntax:

```
window.event.altLeft
```

Example: See the altKey property example.

Applies to:

event

appCodeName

Compatibility: NN4, NN6, NN7, IE4, IE5, IE5.5, IE6

Read-only property. Returns the code name of the browser. The value returned for most browsers is Mozilla.

Syntax:

objectName.appCodeName

Example:

```
<html><head><script language="JavaScript">
function B1() {alert(navigator.appCodeName);}
</script></head>
<body bgcolor="#FFFFFF" text="#000000">
<input type="button" value="Browser Code Name" onClick="B1();">
</body></html>
```

Applies to:

clientInformation, navigator

appMinorVersion

Compatibility: IE4, IE5, IE5.5, IE6

Read-only property. Returns the browser's minor version (sub-version).

Syntax:

objectName.appMinorVersion

Example:

```
<html><head><script language="JavaScript">
function B1() {alert(navigator.appMinorVersion);}
</script></head>
<body bgcolor="#FFFFFF" text="#000000">
<input type="button" value="Minor Version" onClick="B1();">
</body></html>
```

Applies to:

clientInformation, navigator

appName

Compatibility: NN4, NN6, NN7, IE4, IE5, IE5.5, IE6

Read-only property. Returns the complete name of the browser.
Syntax:

```
objectName.appName
```

Example:

```
<html><head><script language="JavaScript">
function B1() {alert(navigator.appName);}
</script></head>
<body bgcolor="#FFFFFF" text="#000000">
<input type="button" value="Browser Name" onClick="B1();">
</body></html>
```

Applies to:

```
clientInformation, navigator
```

appVersion

Compatibility: NN4, NN6, NN7, IE4, IE5, IE5.5, IE6

Read-only property. Returns the browser's platform and version information.
The format of the returned value is: `browserVersion (platform; additional
information; . . . ; additional information)`.
Syntax:

```
objectName.appVersion
```

Example:

```
<html><head><script language="JavaScript">
function B1() {alert(navigator.appVersion);}
</script></head>
<body><input type="button" value="Version" onClick="B1()">
</body></html>
```

Applies to:

```
clientInformation, navigator
```

archive

Compatibility: NN6, NN7, IE6

Read and write property. Specifies the URL of a ZIP file that contains Java code needed by the element.

Syntax:

```
document.getElementById("elementID").archive = value
document.all.elementID.archive = value // IE only
```

Example:

```
<applet code="aipwave.class" width="350" height="260" archive="archive.ZIP">
</applet>
<script language="JavaScript">
document.all.myA.archive = "archive.ZIP";
</script>
```

Applies to:

```
<applet>, <object>
```

autocomplete

Compatibility: IE5, IE5.5, IE6

Read and write property. Allows the browser to supply hints to the user for filling out form controls. Values: on or off.

Syntax:

```
document.all.elementID.autocomplete = value
```

Example:

```
<html><head><script>
function goAC() {
document.all.myName.autocomplete = "on";
}
</script></head>
<body bgcolor="#FFFFFF" text="#000000" onLoad="goAC();">
<form name="form1" method="post" action="">
<pre>
1. Type your name in the text field.
2. Press "Submit" button.
3. Type the first letter of your name in the text field.
</pre>
<input type="text" size=30 name="text2" id="myName">
<input type="submit" value="Submit">
</form>
</body></html>
```

Applies to:

```
<form>, <input type="password">, <input type="text">
```

availHeight

Compatibility: NN6, NN7, IE4, IE5, IE5.5, IE6

Read-only property. Returns the height in pixels of the working area of the computer screen. The working area of the screen does not include the taskbar.
   Syntax:

```
screen.availHeight
```

Example:

```
<button onClick=" alert(screen.availHeight);">Available Height</button>
<button onClick="alert(screen.availWidth);">Available Width</button>
```

Applies to:

```
screen
```

availLeft

Compatibility: NN6, NN7

Read-only property. Returns the first pixel on the left of the screen that is not part of the taskbar area.
   Syntax:

```
screen.availLeft
```

Example:

```
<button onclick="alert(screen.availLeft);">AvailLeft</button>
```

Applies to:

```
screen
```

availTop

Compatibility: NN6, NN7

Read-only property. Returns the first pixel on the top of the screen that is not part of the taskbar area.

Syntax:

```
screen.availTop
```

Example:

```
<button onclick="alert(screen.availTop);">AvailTop</button>
```

Applies to:

```
screen
```

---

availWidth

Compatibility: NN6, NN7, IE4, IE5, IE5.5, IE6

Read-only property. Returns the width in pixels of the working area of the computer screen. The working area of the screen does not include the taskbar.
   Syntax:

```
screen.availWidth
```

Example: See the availHeight property example.
Applies to:

```
screen
```

---

axis

Compatibility: NN6, NN7, IE6

Read and write property. Allows you to categorize <td> and <th> elements.
Value: Any string.
   Syntax:

```
document.getElementById("elementID").axis = value
document.all.elementID.axis = value // IE only
```

Example:

```
<table border="1" summary="Billable time report">
<caption>Billable time report</caption>
<tr>
  <th> </th>
  <th id="head1" axis="hours">Travel Time</th>
  <th id="head2" axis="hours">Consulting Hours</th>
</tr>
<tr>
  <th id="a6" axis="employee">Joseph</th>
```

```
<th> </th><th> </th><th> </th>
</tr>
<tr>
  <td id="a7" axis="date">January 1, 2004</td>
  <td headers="head1 head2">7.50</td>
  <td headers="head1 head2">2.00</td>
  <td> </td>
</tr>
<td id="a7" axis="date">January 2, 2004</td>
  <td headers="head1 head2">9.50</td>
  <td headers="head1 head2">1.70</td>
  <td> </td>
</tr>
<td id="a7" axis="date">January 3, 2004</td>
  <td headers="head1 head2">7.00</td>
  <td headers="head1 head2">1.00</td>
  <td> </td>
</tr>
<tr bgcolor="#CCCCCC">
  <td>Total</td><td>24.00</td>
  <td>4.70</td><td>28.70</td>
</tr>
</table>
<button onclick="alert(head1.axis);">Get the axis for heading 1</button>
```

Applies to:

`<td>`, `<th>`

background

Compatibility: NN6 (`<body>` only), NN7 (`<body>` only), IE4, IE5, IE5.5, IE6

Read and write property. Specifies the URL of an image file that will be used as the background for the element. The background image will appear in front of any background color.

Syntax:

```
document.getElementById("elementID").background = value
document.all.elementID.background = value // IE only
```

Example:

```
<html><head><script>
function B2() {
document.all.C1.background = "yourimage.gif";
}
function B4() {
document.all.C1.background = "";
```

```
}
</script></head>
<body bgcolor="white" text="white">
<table><tr>
    <td id="C1" height="79" bgcolor="green">Cell 1 content</td>
    <td height="79">Cell 2 content</td>
    <td height="79">Cell 3 content</td>
</tr></table>
<input type="button" name="button2" value="Add background image to Cell 1"
onClick="B2();">
<input type="button" name="button3" value="Remove background image"
onClick="B4();">
</body></html>
```

Applies to:

```
<body>, <table>, <td>, <th>
```

balance

Compatibility: IE4, IE5, IE5.5, IE6

Read and write property. Controls how the volume of the background sound of a page is split between the left and right system speakers. Value: A number from -10000 (all sound goes through the left speaker) to +10000 (all sound goes through the right speaker).

Syntax:

```
document.all.bgsoundID.balance = value
```

Example:

```
<head>
<bgsound id="mySound" src="sound.mp3" balance="0" loop="1">
<script>
function B1() {
document.all.mySound.src = "sound.mp3";
document.all.mySound.balance = -10000;
document.all.mySound.volume = -3000;
}
</script></head>
<body bgcolor="white" text="#000000" onLoad="B1();">
<input type="button" value="balance = -10000" onClick="B1();">
</body>
```

Applies to:

```
<bgsound>
```

BaseHref

Compatibility: IE4, IE5, IE5.5, IE6

Read-only property. Returns either the full URL of the current document or the value set by the <base> element's href attribute.

Syntax:

```
document.all.objectID.BaseHref
```

Example:

```
<object id="myO" classid="clsid:D27CDB6E-AE6D-11cf-96B8-444553540000"
codebase="http://download.macromedia.com/pub/shockwave/cabs/flash/
swflash.cab#version=5,0,0,0"
width="243" height="194">
    <param id="myP1" name=movie value="yourflashmovie.swf" valuetype="ref"
type="video/*">
    <param id="myP2" value=high name=quality>
</object>
<script language="JavaScript">
function B1() {var m = document.all.myO.BaseHref; alert(m);}
</script>
<input type="button" value="The current document's full URL" onClick="B1();">
```

Applies to:

```
<object>
```

behavior

Compatibility: IE4, IE5, IE5.5, IE6

Read and write property. Controls the scrolling of the text within the <marquee> element. Values: scroll (the default; text scrolls off the end and starts over), alternate (text scrolls back and forth), and slide (the text scrolls once to the end and stops).

Syntax:

```
document.all.marqueeID.behavior = value
```

Example:

```
<html><head><script language="JavaScript">
function M1(){document.all.myM.behavior = "alternate";}
function M2(){document.all.myM.behavior = "slide";}
</script></head>
<body bgcolor="#FFFFFF" text="#000000">
<marquee id="myM">Come and see our new car models.</marquee>
<input type="button" value="behavior = alternate" onClick="M1();">
```

```
<input type="button" value="behavior = slide" onClick="M2();">
</body></html>
```

Applies to:

```
<marquee>
```

bgColor

Compatibility: NN4 (`<body>` only), NN6, NN7, IE4, IE5, IE5.5, IE6

Read and write property. Specifies the background color. Value: Web color name or hexadecimal color value in #RRGGBB format.
Syntax:

```
document.getElementById("elementID").bgColor = value
document.all.elementID.bgColor = value // IE only
document.bgcolor = value
```

Example:

```
<html><head><script>
function B2() {document.all.C1.bgColor = "red";}
function B4() {document.all.C1.bgColor = "";}
</script></head>
<body bgcolor="#ccffcc" text="#000000">
<table><tr><td id="C1" height="79">Cell 1 content</td><td height="79">Cell 2
content</td></tr></table>
<input type="button" value="Add background color to Cell 1" onClick="B2();">
<input type="button" value="Remove background colors" onClick="B4();">
</body></html>
```

Applies to:

```
<body>, document, <marquee>, <table>, <tbody>, <td>, <tfoot>, <th>, <thead>, <tr>
```

bgProperties

Compatibility: IE4, IE5, IE5.5, IE6

Read and write property. Controls the attachment of a background image to the body content of the document. Values: An empty string (the default; the image scrolls with the body content) or fixed (the image stays fixed when the body content scrolls).
Syntax:

```
document.all.bodyID.bgProperties = value
```

Example:

```
<html><head><script>
function B1() {document.all.myBody.bgProperties = "fixed";}
</script></head>
<body background="yourImage.gif" onclick="B1();" id="myBody">
</body></html>
```

Applies to:

```
<body>
```

blockDirection

Compatibility: IE5, IE5.5, IE6

Read-only property. Indicates the direction of text flow in an element. Values: ltr (flows from left to right) or rtl (flows from right to left).
Syntax:

```
document.all.elementID.blockDirection
```

Example:

```
<p id="myP1" blockDirection="rtl" onClick="B1();">Click in this text that must be
read from right to left.</p>
<script language="JavaScript">
function B1() {var m = document.all.myP1.blockDirection; alert(m);}
</script>
```

Applies to:

```
<address>, <blockquote>, <body>, <center>, currentStyle, <custom>, <dd>, defaults,
<div>, <dl>, <dt>, <fieldset>, <form>, <hn>, <isindex>, <li>, <listing>, <menu>,
<ol>, <p>, <plaintext>, <pre>, <ul>, <xmp>
```

border

Compatibility: NN6 (not <table>), NN7, IE4, IE5, IE5.5, IE6

Read and write property. Specifies the width in pixels of the element's border.
Syntax:

```
document.getElementById("elementID").border = value
document.all.elementID.border = value // IE only
```

Example:

```
<img id="myI" src="yourimage.gif">
<button onclick="myI.border = 15;">Add a border</button>
<button onclick="myI.border = 0;">Remove border</button>
```

Applies to:

```
<frameset>, <iframe>, <img>, <object>, <table>, <td>
```

borderColor

Compatibility: IE4, IE5, IE5.5, IE6

Read and write property. Specifies the color of the element's border. Value: Web color name or hexadecimal value in #RRGGBB format.

Syntax:

```
document.all.elementID.borderColor = value
```

Example:

```
<table border="10" id="myT2"><tr><td>Contents of the cell</td></tr></table>
<button onclick="myT2.borderColor='mediumblue';">Add color to the border</button>
<button onclick="myT2.borderColorDark='blue';">Border color dark</button>
<button onclick="myT2.borderColorLight='skyblue';">Border color light</button>
```

Applies to:

```
<frame>, <frameset>, <table>, <td>, <th>, <tr>
```

borderColorDark

Compatibility: IE4, IE5, IE5.5, IE6

Read and write property. Specifies the color of the two dark sides of the border, creating the effect of a 3D border. Value: Web color name or hexadecimal value in #RRGGBB format.

Syntax:

```
document.all.elementID.borderColorDark = value
```

Example: See the borderColor property example.
Applies to:

```
<table>, <td>, <th>, <tr>
```

borderColorLight

Compatibility: IE4, IE5, IE5.5, IE6

Read and write property. Specifies the color of the two light sides of the border, creating the effect of a 3D border. Value: Web color name or hexadecimal value in #RRGGBB format.

Syntax:

```
document.all.elementID.borderColorLight = value
```

Example: See the borderColor property example.
Applies to:

```
<table>, <td>, <th>, <tr>
```

bottom

Compatibility: IE5, IE5.5, IE6

Read and write property. Establishes the value in pixels of the bottom coordinate of the container rectangle surrounding the element's content.

Syntax:

```
TextRectangleName.bottom = value
```

Example:

```
<p id="myP" style="background-color:black; color:white; width:200;">
This is some sample text.</p>
<button onclick="alert(myP.getBoundingClientRect().bottom);">Bottom</button>
<button onclick="alert(myP.getBoundingClientRect().top);">Top</button>
<button onclick="alert(myP.getBoundingClientRect().left);">Left</button>
<button onclick="alert(myP.getBoundingClientRect().right);">Right</button>
```

Applies to:

```
TextRectangle
```

bottomMargin

Compatibility: IE4, IE5, IE5.5, IE6

Read and write property. Specifies the height in pixels of the bottom margin of the `<body>` element. The default value is 15.

Syntax:

```
document.all.bodyID.bottomMargin = value
```

Example:

```
<body id="myBody">
<button onclick="alert(document.body.bottomMargin);">Bottom Margin</button></body>
<button onclick="alert(document.body.topMargin);">Top Margin</button></body>
<button onclick="alert(document.body.leftMargin);">Left Margin</button></body>
<button onclick="alert(document.body.rightMargin);">Right Margin</button>
</body>
```

Applies to:

```
<body>
```

boundingHeight, boundingWidth

Compatibility: IE4, IE5, IE5.5, IE6

Read-only properties. Retrieve the height and width in pixels of the bounding rectangle of the element.

Syntax:

```
TextRangeName.boundingHeight
TextRangeName.boundingWidth
```

Example:

```
<textarea id="myText" cols="70" rows="2" onclick="B1(this);">
Sample text for the document</textarea>
<button onclick="B1()">Bounding Height</button>
<button onclick="B2()">Bounding Width</button>
<button onclick="B3()">Bounding Left</button>
<button onclick="B4()">Bounding Top</button>
<script language="JavaScript">
function B1() {var m = myText.createTextRange(); alert(m.boundingHeight);}
function B2() {var m = myText.createTextRange(); alert(m.boundingWidth);}
function B3() {var m = myText.createTextRange(); alert(m.boundingLeft);}
function B4() {var m = myText.createTextRange(); alert(m.boundingTop);}
</script>
```

Applies to:

```
TextRange
```

boundingLeft, boundingTop

Compatibility: IE4, IE5, IE5.5, IE6

Read-only properties. Retrieve the size in pixels of the left and top padding between the element's container rectangle and the actual object that contains the content.

Syntax:

```
TextRangeName.boundingLeft
TextRangeName.boundingTop
```

Example: See the boundingWidth, boundingHeight example.
Applies to:

```
TextRange
```

browserLanguage

Compatibility: IE4, IE5, IE5.5, IE6

Read-only property. Returns the language code of the browser language.
Syntax:

```
objectName.browserLanguage
```

Example:

```
<script language="JavaScript">
var m = navigator.browserLanguage;
alert("The language of your browser is "+'"'+m+'"')
</script>
```

Applies to:

```
clientInformation, navigator
```

bufferDepth

Compatibility: IE4, IE5, IE5.5, IE6

Read and write property. Controls the color depth of the screen buffer, specified in bits per pixel. Values: 0 (the default; no buffering occurs), -1 (buffering occurs at screen depth; this is the optimum value), 1, 4, 8, 15, 16, 24, 32 (buffering occurs at the specified color depth).
Syntax:

```
screen.bufferDepth = value
```

Example:

```
<html><head><script language="JavaScript">
function B1() {
```

```
if (navigator.appName.indexOf("Microsoft") != -1) {
var m = screen.bufferDepth;
alert("The buffering for this screen is "+m);
} else {alert("Netscape: no default for buffering depth");
}}
function B2() {
screen.bufferDepth = -1;
var m = screen.bufferDepth;
alert("The buffering depth for this screen has been changed to "+m);
}
</script>
</head>
<body bgcolor="#FFFFFF" text="#000000">
<input type="button" value="No Buffering" onClick="B1();">
<input type="button" value="Same as Color Depth" onClick="B2();">
</body></html>
```

Applies to:

```
screen
```

button

Compatibility: IE4, IE5, IE5.5, IE6

Read and write property. Specifies the mouse button pressed by the user. Values: 0 (the default; no button is pressed), 1 (left button is pressed), 2 (right button is pressed), 3 (left and right buttons are pressed), 4 (middle button is pressed), 5 (left and middle buttons are pressed), 6 (right and middle buttons are pressed), and 7 (all three buttons are pressed).

Syntax:

```
window.event.button = value
```

Example:

```
<script language="JavaScript">
function B1() {
var m = window.event.button;
if (m == 1) {
alert("The left button has been pressed");
} else if (m == 2) {
alert("The right button has been pressed");
}}
</script>
<div style="width:200; height:200; background-color:blue; color:white;"
onmousedown="B1();">
Press on mouse while on top of this blue box.</div>
```

Applies to:

event

cancelBubble

Compatibility: IE4, IE5, IE5.5, IE6

Read and write property. Specifies whether or not the current event stops bubbling through the document hierarchy. Values: true or false (the default).
    Syntax:

```
window.event.cancelBubble = value
```

Example:

```
<html><head>
<script language="JavaScript">
function B1() {
if (window.event.shiftKey){window.event.cancelBubble = true;}
alert(window.event.cancelBubble);}
</script></head>
<body bgcolor="#FFFFFF" text="#000000">
<button onclick="B1();">Click here while pressing the Shift key</button>
</body></html>
```

Applies to:

event

canHaveChildren

Compatibility: IE5, IE5.5, IE6

Read-only property. Indicates whether or not the element can have children.
    Syntax:

```
document.all.elementID.canHaveChildren
```

Example:

```
<html><head><script language="JavaScript">
function C2() {
for (var i = 0; i < document.all.length; i++) {
if (document.all[i].canHaveChildren) {
document.all[i].style.color = "blue";
}}
alert("Elements have not been colored!");}
</script></head>
```

```
<body bgcolor="#FFFFFF" text="#000000">
<input type="button" value="Color in blue only the elements that can have children"
onClick="C2();">
<input type="checkbox" checked>The checkbox label
<input type="text" name="text1" value="Some textbox here.">
<table cellpadding="10" border="2">
<tr><th width="80">Header 1</th><th width="80">Header 2</th><th width="80">Header
3</th>
<tr><td>Cell 1<td>Cell 2<td>Cell 3</tr>
<tr><td>Cell 4<td>Cell 5<td>Cell 6</tr>
</table>
</body></html>
```

Applies to:

```
<a>, <acronym>, <address>, <b>, <bdo>, <big>, <blockquote>, <body>, <button>,
<caption>, <center>, <cite>, <code>, <col>, <colgroup>, <comment>, <custom>, <dd>,
<del>, <dfn>, <dir>, <div>, <dl>, <dt>, <em>, <fieldset>, <font>, <form>,
<frameset>, <head>, <hn>, <html>, <i>, <iframe>, <input type="button">, <input
type="checkbox">, <input type="file">, <input type="image">, <input
type="password">, <input type="radio">, <input type="reset">, <input
type="submit">, <input type="text">, <ins>, <kbd>, <label>, <legend>, <li>,
<listing>, <map>, <marquee>, <menu>, <object>, <ol>, <option>, <p>, <plaintext>,
<pre>, <q>, <s>, <samp>, <select>, <small>, <span>, <strike>, <strong>, <sub>,
<sup>, <table>, <tbody>, <td>, <textarea>, <tfoot>, <th>, <thead>, <tr>, <tt>, <u>,
<ul>, <var>, <xmp>
```

canHaveHTML

Compatibility: IE5.5, IE6

Read-only property. Indicates whether or not the element can contain HTML
content. Most elements allow HTML content between their opening and closing
tags, but some elements like <br> do not.

Syntax:

```
document.all.elementID.canHaveHTML
```

Example:

```
<body id="myBody">
<button onclick="alert(myBody.canHaveHTML);">Can BODY Have HTML</button>
<input type="text" id="myText" value="This cannot have children!"
style="width:200;">
<button onclick="alert(myText.canHaveHTML);">Can INPUT Have HTML</button>
</body>
```

Applies to:

<a>, <acronym>, <address>, <applet>, <area>, <b>, <base>, <basefont>, <bdo>, <bgsound>, <big>, <blockquote>, <body>, <br>, <button>, <caption>, <center>, <cite>, <code>, <col>, <colgroup>, <comment>, <custom>, <dd>, defaults, <del>, <dfn>, <dir>, <div>, <dl>, <dt>, <em>, <embed>, <fieldset>, <font>, <form>, <frame>, <frameset>, <head>, <hn>, <hr>, <html>, <i>, <iframe>, <img>, <input type="button">, <input type="checkbox">, <input type="file">, <input type="hidden">, <input type="image">, <input type="password">, <input type="radio">, <input type="reset">, <input type="submit">, <input type="text">, <ins>, <isindex>, <kbd>, <label>, <legend>, <li>, <link>, <listing>, <map>, <marquee>, <menu>, <nobr>, <noframes>, <noscript>, <object>, <ol>, <option>, <p>, <plaintext>, <pre>, <q>, <rt>, <ruby>, <s>, <samp>, <script>, <select>, <small>, <span>, <strike>, <strong>, styleSheet, <sub>, <sup>, <table>, <tbody>, <td>, <textarea>, <tfoot>, <th>, <thead>, <title>, <tr>, <tt>, <u>, <ul>, <var>, <wbr>, <xml>, <xmp>

caption

Compatibility: NN6, NN7, IE4, IE5, IE5.5, IE6

Read and write property (NN), and read-only (IE) property. Establishes the caption for the table.

Syntax:

```
document.getElementById("tableID").caption = value
document.all.tableID.caption // IE only
```

Example:

```
<body id="myBody">
<table id="myTable" width="600" caption="This is the Caption" border="1">
<tr><td>Cell 1</td><td>Cell 2</td><td>Cell 3</td></tr>
<tr><td>Cell 1</td><td>Cell 2</td><td>Cell 3</td></tr>
<tr><td>Cell 1</td><td>Cell 2</td><td>Cell 3</td></tr>
</table>
<button onclick="alert(document.all.myTable.caption);">Table Caption</button>
</body>
```

Applies to:

<table>

cellIndex

Compatibility: NN6, NN7, IE4, IE5, IE5.5, IE6

Read-only property. Returns the zero-based index of the cell in its row.

Syntax:

```
document.getElementById("elementID").cellIndex
document.all.elementID.cellIndex // IE only
```

Example:

```
<body>Click in any cell to view the cellIndex value.
<table width="400" border="2" cellspacing="5" cellpadding="10" id="myTable"
cols="3">
    <tr>
      <th id="th1" onclick="B1(this);">Header 1</th>
      <th id="th2" onclick="B1(this);">Header 2</th>
      <th id="th3" onclick="B1(this);">Header 3</th>
    </tr>
    <tr>
      <td id="td1" onclick="B1(this);">Cell 1</td>
      <td id="td2" onclick="B1(this);">Cell 2</td>
      <td id="td3" onclick="B1(this);">Cell 3</td>
    </tr>
</table><br>
<button onclick="alert(myTable.cellPadding);">Cell Padding</button>
<button onclick="alert(myTable.cellSpacing);">Cell Spacing</button>
<button onclick="alert(myTable.cols);">cols</button>
<script language="JavaScript">
function B1(elem) {alert("Cell Index :"+ elem.cellIndex);}
</script>
</body>
```

Applies to:

```
<td>, <th>
```

cellPadding

Compatibility: NN4, NN6, NN7, IE4, IE5, IE5.5, IE6

Read and write property. Specifies the amount of padding between the border of the cell and its content. Value: An integer (the amount of padding in pixels), or integer% (the percent of space between the wall of the cell and its content).

Syntax:

```
document.getElementById("tableID").cellPadding = value
document.all.tableID.cellPadding = value // IE only
```

Example: See the cellIndex property example.
Applies to:

```
<table>
```

cellSpacing

Compatibility: NN4, NN6, NN7, IE4, IE5, IE5.5, IE6

Read and write property. Specifies the amount of space between adjacent cells.
Value: An integer (the amount of padding in pixels), or integer% (the percent
of space between the wall of the cell plus the padding and its content).
Syntax:

```
document.getElementById("tableID").cellSpacing = value
document.all.tableID.cellSpacing = value // IE only
```

Example: See the cellIndex property example.
Applies to:

```
<table>
```

charset

Compatibility: NN6, NN7, IE4, IE5, IE5.5, IE6

Read and write property. Specifies the character set of the element or object.
Syntax:

```
document.getElementById("elementID").charset = value
document.all.elementID.charset = value // IE only
```

Example:

```
<button onclick="alert(document.charset);">Character Encoding for Document</button>
```

Applies to:

```
<a> (IE6, NN6, NN7 only), document (not NN6, NN7), <link>, <meta>, <script> (IE6,
NN6, NN7 only)
```

checked

Compatibility: NN4, NN6, NN7, IE4, IE5, IE5.5, IE6

Read and write property. Specifies whether or not a checkbox or radio button is
checked. Values: true or false.
Syntax:

```
document.getElementById("inputID").checked = value
document.all.inputID.checked = value // IE only
```

Example:

```
<form>
<script>
```

```
function C3() {document.all.R1.checked = true;}
function C4() {document.all.R2.checked = true;}
function C5() {document.all.R3.checked = true;}
function C6() {document.all.R4.checked = true;}
</script>
<input id="R1" type="radio" name="radiobutton" value="radiobutton">VISA
<input id="R2" type="radio" name="radiobutton" value="radiobutton">MASTERCARD
<input id="R3" type="radio" name="radiobutton" value="radiobutton">DISCOVER
<input id="R4" type="radio" name="radiobutton" value="radiobutton">AMERICAN
EXPRESS<br>
<input type="button" value="VISA checked" onClick="C3();">
<input type="button" value="MASTERCARD checked" onClick="C4();">
<input type="button" value="DISCOVER checked" onClick="C5();">
<input type="button" value="AMERICAN EXPRESS checked" onClick="C6();">
</form>
```

Applies to:

```
<input type="checkbox">, <input type="radio">
```

cite

Compatibility: NN6, NN7, IE6

Read and write property. Specifies the URL of the source of the quotation.
Syntax:

```
document.getElementById("elementID").cite = value
document.all.elementID.cite = value // IE only
```

Example:

```
<q id="myQ" cite="http://www.advocar.com/">Welcome to hassle-free auto buying. Our
experienced consultants have helped more than 200,000 people find and finance the
car of their dreams. Shouldn't you be next?</q><br>
<input type="button" value="Value of Cite Property" onclick="alert(myQ.cite);">
```

Applies to:

```
<blockquote>, <del>, <dfn>, <ins>, <q>
```

classid

Compatibility: IE4, IE5, IE5.5, IE6

Read and write property. Specifies the class identifier for the component to
be used in rendering the object. Value: A string with the following format:
"clsid:XXXXXXXX-XXXX-XXXX-XXXX-XXXXXXXXXXXX".

Syntax:

```
document.all.objectID.classid = value
```

Example:

```
<script>
function activate() {
document.all.myO.classid = "clsid:D27CDB6E-AE6D-11cf-96B8-444553540000";
}
</script>
<object id="myO"
codebase="http://download.macromedia.com/pub/shockwave/cabs/flash/
swflash.cab#version=5,0,0,0"
width="250" height="230">
    <param name=movie value="yourflashmovie.swf">
    <param name=quality value=high>
</object><br>
<button onclick="activate();">Activate</button>
```

Applies to:

```
<object>
```

className

Compatibility: NN6, NN7, IE4, IE5, IE5.5, IE6

Read and write property. Specifies the CSS class or selector that applies to the element.

Syntax:

```
document.getElementById("elementID").className = value
document.all.elementID.className = value // IE only
```

Example:

```
<html><head><script language="JavaScript">
function Q1() {document.getElementById("myP").className = "myC"}
</script>
<style>
.myC { font-family:verdana, arial; font-weight:bold; font-size:16px; }
</style></head>
<body bgcolor="#FFFFFF" text="#000000">
<p id="myP" style="text-decoration:underline; cursor:hand;"
onclick="Q1()">Render this text using the myC class</p>
</body></html>
```

Applies to:

`<a>`, `<acronym>`, `<address>`, `<applet>`, `<area>`, `<b>`, `<base>`, `<basefont>`, `<bdo>`, `<big>`, `<blockquote>`, `<body>`, `<br>`, `<button>`, `<caption>`, `<center>`, `<cite>`, `<code>`, `<col>`, `<colgroup>`, `<custom>`, `<dd>`, `<del>`, `<dfn>`, `<dir>`, `<div>`, `<dl>`, `<dt>`, `<em>`, `<embed>`, `<fieldset>`, `<font>`, `<form>`, `<frame>`, `<frameset>`, `<head>`, `<hn>`, `<hr>`, `<html>`, `<i>`, `<iframe>`, `<img>`, `<input type="button">`, `<input type="checkbox">`, `<input type="file">`, `<input type="hidden">`, `<input type="image">`, `<input type="password">`, `<input type="radio">`, `<input type="reset">`, `<input type="submit">`, `<input type="text">`, `<ins>`, `<isindex>`, `<kbd>`, `<label>`, `<legend>`, `<li>`, `<link>`, `<listing>`, `<map>`, `<marquee>`, `<menu>`, `<meta>`, `<nobr>`, `<noframes>`, `<noscript>`, `<object>`, `<ol>`, `<optgroup>`, `<option>`, `<p>`, `<param>`, `<pre>`, `<q>`, `<rt>`, `<ruby>`, `<s>`, `<samp>`, `<script>`, `<select>`, `<small>`, `<span>`, `<strike>`, `<strong>`, `<style>`, `<sub>`, `<sup>`, `<table>`, `<tbody>`, `<td>`, `<textarea>`, `<tfoot>`, `<th>`, `<thead>`, `<title>`, `<tr>`, `<tt>`, `<u>`, `<ul>`, `<var>`, `<xmp>`

---

clear

Compatibility: NN4, NN6, NN7, IE4, IE5, IE5.5, IE6

Read and write property. Specifies if and how other elements may be positioned around a `<br>` element. Values: all (clears all sides), left (clears the left side), right (clears the right side), and none (all sides allow floating objects).

Syntax:

```
document.getElementById("brID").clear = value
document.all.brID.clear = value // IE only
```

Example:

```
<html><head><script language="JavaScript">
function s1() {document.getElementById("myB").clear = 'all';}
function s2() {document.getElementById("myB").clear = 'left';}
function s3() {document.getElementById("myB").clear = 'right';}
function s4() {document.getElementById("myB").clear = "none";}
</script></head>
<body bgcolor="#FFFFFF" text="#000000">
<img src="yourimage.gif" alt="This is a float=left image"
width="99" height="80" style="float:left">
<br id="myB">
<p align="left">Here is the <br> element</p>
<input type="button" value="Clear all" onClick="s1();">
<input type="button" value="Clear left" onClick="s2();">
<input type="button" value="Clear right" onClick="s3();">
<input type="button" value="Clear none" onClick="s4();">
</body></html>
```

Applies to:

`<br>`

Compatibility: NN6, NN7, IE4, IE5, IE5.5, IE6

Read-only properties. Retrieve the height and width in pixels of the content and padding of an element.

Syntax:

```
document.getElementById("elementID").clientHeight
document.getElementById("elementID").clientWidth
document.all.elementID.clientHeight // IE only
document.all.elementID.clientWidth // IE only
```

Example:

```
<div id="myDiv" style="position:absolute; left:150; top:100; width:400; height:200;
background-color:blue;"></div>
<button onclick="alert(myDiv.clientHeight);">clientHeight</button> 
<button onclick="alert(myDiv.clientWidth);">clientWidth</button> 
<button onclick="alert(myDiv.clientLeft);">clientLeft</button> 
<button onclick="alert(myDiv.clientTop);">clientTop</button><br><br>
```

Applies to:

```
<a>, <acronym>, <address>, <applet>, <area>, <b>, <base>, <basefont>, <bdo>, <big>,
<blockquote>, <body>, <br>, <button>, <caption>, <center>, <cite>, <code>, <col>,
<colgroup>, <custom>, <dd>, <del>, <dfn>, <dir>, <div>, <dl>, <dt>, <em>, <embed>,
<fieldset>, <form>, <frame>, <frameset>, <head>, <hn>, <hr>, <html>, <i>, <iframe>,
<img>, <input type="button">, <input type="checkbox">, <input type="file">, <input
type="image">, <input type="password">, <input type="radio">, <input type="reset">,
<input type="submit">, <input type="text">, <ins>, <isindex>, <kbd>, <label>,
<legend>, <li>, <link>, <listing>, <map>, <marquee>, <menu>, <meta>, <nobr>,
<noframes>, <noscript>, <object>, <ol>, <optgroup>, <option>, <p>, <param>,
<plaintext>, <pre>, <q>, <s>, <samp>, <script>, <select>, <small>, <span>,
<strike>, <strong>, <style>, <sub>, <sup>, <table>, <tbody>, <td>, <textarea>,
<tfoot>, <th>, <thead>, <title>, <tr>, <tt>, <u>, <ul>, <var>, <xmp>
```

clientLeft, clientTop

Compatibility: IE4, IE5, IE5.5, IE6

Read-only properties. Retrieve the distance between the offsetLeft property and the left side of the client area of a positioned element, or between the offsetTop property and the top side of the client area of a positioned element.

Syntax:

```
document.all.elementID.clientLeft
document.all.elementID.clientTop
```

Example: See the clientHeight, clientWidth property example.

Applies to:

`<a>`, `<address>`, `<applet>`, `<b>`, `<bdo>`, `<big>`, `<blockquote>`, `<body>`, `<button>`, `<caption>`, `<center>`, `<cite>`, `<code>`, `<col>`, `<colgroup>`, `<custom>`, `<dd>`, `<dfn>`, `<dir>`, `<div>`, `<dl>`, `<dt>`, `<em>`, `<embed>`, `<fieldset>`, `<form>`, `<hn>`, `<html>`, `<i>`, `<img>`, `<input type="button">`, `<input type="checkbox">`, `<input type="file">`, `<input type="image">`, `<input type="password">`, `<input type="radio">`, `<input type="reset">`, `<input type="submit">`, `<input type="text">`, `<isindex>`, `<kbd>`, `<label>`, `<legend>`, `<li>`, `<listing>`, `<marquee>`, `<menu>`, `<meta>`, `<nobr>`, `<object>`, `<ol>`, `<option>`, `<p>`, `<plaintext>`, `<pre>`, `<s>`, `<samp>`, `<script>`, `<select>`, `<small>`, `<span>`, `<strike>`, `<strong>`, `<sub>`, `<sup>`, `<table>`, `<tbody>`, `<td>`, `<textarea>`, `<tfoot>`, `<th>`, `<thead>`, `<tr>`, `<tt>`, `<u>`, `<ul>`, `<var>`, `<xmp>`

---

clientX, clientY

Compatibility: IE4, IE5, IE5.5, IE6

Read and write properties. Establish the X and Y coordinates of the mouse pointer's position in pixels, taking into account both the visible document area of the browser's window and the scroll bars.

Syntax:

```
window.event.clientX = value
window.event.clientY = value
```

Example:

```
<script language="JavaScript">
function C1() {
    myX.value = window.event.clientX;
    myY.value = window.event.clientY;
}
</script>
<body onmousemove="C1();">
X Coordinate: <input type="text" value="" id="myX" style="border:none;"><br>
Y Coordinate: <input type="text" value="" id="myY" style="border:none;">
</body>
```

Applies to:

---

event

---

clipBottom, dipLeft, clipRight, clipTop

Compatibility: IE5, IE5.5, IE6

Read-only properties. Return the bottom, left, right, and top coordinates of an element's clipping region. Values: auto (the default; bottom side is not clipped) or a floating-point number followed by a unit designator: cm, mm, in, pt, pc, px, em, or ex (pixels are used if no unit designator is specified).

Syntax:

```
document.all.currentStyle.clipBottom
document.all.currentStyle.clipLeft
document.all.currentStyle.clipRight
document.all.currentStyle.clipTop
```

Example:

```
<html><head>
<style>#myI {position:absolute; top:224px; left:75px; clip:rect(0,300,225,0)}</
style>
<script language="JavaScript">
function R() {document.all.myI.style.clip = "rect(0,300,225,0)"}
function C1() {document.all.myI.style.clip = "rect(0,300, 50,0)";}
function C2() {document.all.myI.style.clip = "rect(0,50,225,0)";}
function C3() {document.all.myI.style.clip = "rect(50,300,225,0)";}
function C4() {document.all.myI.style.clip = "rect(0,300,225,50)";}
</script></head>
<body bgcolor="#FFFFFF" bottommargin="100">
<img src="yourimage.gif" id="myI">
<input type="button" value="Restore" onClick="R();">
<input type="button" value="Clip bottom 50" onClick="C1(50);">
<input type="button" value="Clip right 50" onClick="C2(50);">
<input type="button" value="Clip top 50" onClick="C3(50);">
<input type="button" value="Clip left 50" onClick="C4(50);">
</body></html>
```

Applies to:

```
currentStyle
```

closed

Compatibility: NN4, NN6, NN7, IE4, IE5, IE5.5, IE6

Read-only property. Indicates whether or not the window is closed.

Syntax:

```
window.closed
windowName.closed // IE only
```

Example:

```
<button onclick="alert(window.closed);">closed Property Value</button>
```

Applies to:

```
window
```

code

Compatibility: NN4, NN6, NN7, IE4, IE5, IE5.5, IE6

Read and write property. Returns the URL of the Java class file that is to begin loading the object.

Syntax:

```
document.getElementById("elementID").code = value
document.all.elementID.code = value // IE only
```

Example:

```
<script language="javascript">
document.getElementById("myA").code = "aipwave.class";
</script>
<applet id="myA" code="aipwave.class" width="350" height="260">
<param name=regcode    value="99999999">
<param name=loading    value="1">
<param name=image      value="yourimage.jpg">
<param name=border     value="0">
<param name=delay      value="50">
<param name=url        value="none">
<param name=maxscalex value="2.5">
<param name=frames     value="10">
</applet>
```

Applies to:

```
<applet>, <object>
```

codeBase

Compatibility: NN6, NN7, IE4, IE5, IE5.5, IE6

Read and write property. Establishes the full URL (cannot be local) of the component file that is to begin loading the object.

Syntax:

```
document.getElementById("elementID").codeBase = value
document.all.elementID.codeBase = value // IE only
```

Example:

```
<html><head>
<script language="JavaScript">
function activate() {
document.all.myO.codebase="http://download.macromedia.com/pub/shockwave/cabs/flash/
swflash.cab#version=5,0,0,0";
```

```
}
</script></head>
<body bgcolor="#FFFFFF" text="#000000">
<object id="myO" width="250" height="230">
<param name="movie" value="Puzzle.swf">
<param name="quality" value="high">
<embed src="yourshockwavemovie.swf" quality=highpluginspage=http://
www.macromedia.com/shockwave/download/index.cgi?P1_Prod_Version=ShockwaveFlash
type="application/x-shockwave-flash" width="250" height="230">
</embed>
</object>
</body></html>
```

Applies to:

`<applet>`, `<object>`

codeType

Compatibility: NN6, NN7, IE4, IE5, IE5.5, IE6

Read and write property. Returns the MIME type of the object that is defined by
the code attribute value.

Syntax:

```
document.getElementById("objectID").codeType = value
document.all.objectID.codeType = value // IE only
```

Example:

```
<html><head>
<script language="javascript">
function cT() {
var m = document.getElementById("myO").codeType;
alert("The value of codeType property is:\n"+m);
}
</script></head>
<body bgcolor="#FFFFFF" text="#000000">
<object codebase="http://download.macromedia.com/pub/shockwave/cabs/flash/
swflash.cab#version=5,0,0,0" width="250" height="230" >
    <param name="movie" value="yourshockwavefile.swf">
    <param name="quality" value="high">
    <embed id="myO" src="yourshockwavefile.swf" quality="high" pluginspage="http://
www.macromedia.com/shockwave/download/index.cgi?P1_Prod_Version=ShockwaveFlash"
width="250" height="230" codeType="application/x-shockwave-flash">
</embed> </object></p>
<input type="button" value="Click here" onClick="cT();">
</body></html>
```

Applies to:

<object>

color

Compatibility: NN4, NN6, NN7, IE4, IE5, IE5.5, IE6

Read and write property. Specifies the color to be rendered with the element. Value: Web color name or hexadecimal value in #RRGGBB format.

Syntax:

```
document.getElementById("elementID").color = value
document.all.elementID.color = value // IE only
```

Example:

```
<script language="JavaScript">
function B1() {document.getElementById("myF").color = "green";}
function B2() {document.getElementById("myF").color = "maroon";}
</script>
<p><font face="Verdana" id="myF"><b>Sample text.</b></font></p>
<button onClick="B1();">Make Text Green</button>
<button onClick="B2();">Make Text Maroon</button>
```

Applies to:

<basefont>, <font>, <hr>

colorDepth

Compatibility: NN4, NN6, NN7, IE4, IE5, IE5.5, IE6

Read-only property. Returns the color depth of the screen. Values: An integer representing the number of bits per pixel: 1, 4, 8, 15, 16, 24, or 32.

Syntax:

```
screen.colorDepth
```

Example:

```
<html><head>
<script language="JavaScript">
function B1() {
var m = screen.colorDepth;
alert("The color depth of the screen is "+m+" bits per pixel");
}
</script></head>
<body bgcolor="#FFFFFF" ondblclick="B1();"></body></html>
```

Applies to:

screen

cols (1)

Compatibility: NN4, NN6, NN7, IE4, IE5, IE5.5, IE6

Read and write property. Specifies a comma-delimited list of the widths of the frames in a frameset. Values: Integer (width in pixels), integer% (percentage of total available width), or integer* (the width as a relative value).

Syntax:

```
document.getElementById("framesetID").cols = value
document.all.framesetID.cols = value // IE only
```

Example:

```
<frameset onmouseover="alert(this.cols);" cols="20%,*" border="15px"
framespacing="0">
  <frame name="topFrame" noresize scrolling="NO" src="myTest.htm">
  <frame name="mainFrame" src="myTest.htm">
</frameset>
```

Applies to:

```
<frameset>
```

cols (2)

Compatibility: NN4, NN6, NN7, IE4, IE5, IE5.5, IE6

Read and write property. Specifies the number of columns in a table. Specifying this property can help the browser render the table faster, even though this property does not affect the actual number of columns that are displayed.

Syntax:

```
document.getElementById("tableID").cols = value
document.all.tableID.cols = value // IE only
```

Example: See the cellIndex property example.
Applies to:

```
<table>
```

cols (3)

Compatibility: NN4, NN6, NN7, IE4, IE5, IE5.5, IE6

Read and write property. Specifies the width in characters of a <textarea> element.

Syntax:

```
document.getElementById("textareaID").cols = value
document.all.textareaID.cols = value // IE only
```

Example:

```
<textarea id="myText" rows="3" cols="15" onclick="ab();"></textarea><br>
<button onclick="myText.cols=100;">Set width of Textarea to 100</button>
<button onclick="myText.rows=20;">Set height of Textarea to 100</button>
```

Applies to:

```
<textarea>
```

colSpan

Compatibility: NN4, NN6, NN7, IE4, IE5, IE5.5, IE6

Read and write property. Specifies the number of columns in a table that a <td> or <th> element will span.

Syntax:

```
document.getElementById("elementID").colSpan = value
document.all.elementID.colSpan = value // IE only
```

Example:

```
<script language="JavaScript">
function B1() {document.all.myTh.colSpan = "3";}
function B2() {document.all.myTd1.colSpan = "3";}
function B3() {document.all.myTd2.colSpan = "2";}
function B4() {
document.all.myTh.colSpan = "1";
document.all.myTd1.colSpan = "1";
document.all.myTd2.colSpan = "1";
}
</script>
<table bgcolor="white" border="3">
<tr><th align="center" bgcolor="blue" style="color:white;">First Header</th>
<th id="myTh" bgcolor="green" style="color:white;"width="140">Second Header</th>
<th align="center" bgcolor="red" style="color:white;" width="140">Third Header</th>
<th align="center" bgcolor="gray" style="color:white;"width="140">Fourth Header</th></tr>
<tr><td id="myTd1">Cell 1 content</td><td>Cell 2 content</td><td id="myTd2">Cell 3 content</td><td>Cell 4 content</td></tr>
</table>
```

```
<input type="button" name="S1" value="Span Second Header" onClick="B1();">
<input type="button" name="S2" value="Span Cell 1" onClick="B2();">
<input type="button" name="S3" value="Span Cell 3" onClick="B3();">
<input type="button" name="S4" value="Restore" onClick="B4();">
```

Applies to:

`<td>`, `<th>`

compact

Compatibility: NN6, NN7, IE4, IE5, IE5.5, IE6

Read and write property. Specifies whether or not to remove extra spaces between a list element's items.

Syntax:

```
document.getElementById("elementID").compact = value
document.all.elementID.compact = value // IE only
```

Example:

```
<dl id="myDL">
<dt>Definition List:</dt>
<dt>1.</dt><dd>Definition 1.</dd>
<dt>2.</dt><dd>Definition 2.</dd>
<dt>3.</dt><dd>Definition 3.</dd>
</dl>
<button onclick="myDL.compact=true;">Compact</button>
<button onclick="myDL.compact=false;">De-Compact</button>
```

Applies to:

`<dir>` (IE6 only), `<dl>`, `<menu>` (IE6 only), `<ol>`, `<ul>`

compatMode

Compatibility: IE6

Read-only property. Indicates whether or not standards-compliant mode is included in the `<!DOCTYPE>` tag.

Syntax:

```
document.compatMode
```

Values:

CSS1Compat	Standards-compliant mode is included. Internet Explorer renders the document in compliance with the CSS1 language standards.
back-compat	Standards-compliant mode is not included. Document is rendered in a manner that is consistent with previous versions of Internet Explorer.

Example:

```
<!DOCTYPE HTML PUBLIC "-//W3C//DTD HTML 4.0 Transitional//EN" "http://www.w3c.org/
TR/html4/loose.dtd">
<html>
<head><script language="JavaScript">
function B1() {alert(document.compatMode);}
</script></head>
<body><button onclick ="B1();">CompatMode</button>
</body></html>
```

Applies to:

document

complete

Compatibility: NN4, NN6, NN7, IE4, IE5, IE5.5, IE6

Read-only property. Indicates whether or not the element is completely loaded.
   Syntax:

```
document.getElementById("elementID").complete
document.all.elementID.complete // IE only
```

Example:

```
<img id="myI" src="yourimage.gif" alt="">
<script language="JavaScript">
var m = document.getElementById("myI").complete;
if (m == true) {
alert("The image is fully loaded");
} else {alert("The image is not completely loaded")}</script>
```

Applies to:

`<img>`, `<input>`, `<input type="image">`

constructor

Compatibility: NN6, NN7, IE5, IE5.5, IE6

Read-only property. This is a string that contains the function call that was
made in order to create the object. This property returns the same string as
the toSource() method.
   Syntax:

```
objectName.constructor
```

Example:

```
<script language="javascript">
function myFunction(){
    var array = new Array('Testing1', 'Testing2');
    alert(array.constructor);
}
</script>
<button onclick="myFunction();">Array Constructor</button>
```

Applies to:

```
Array, Boolean, Date, Math, Number, Object, String
```

content

Compatibility: NN6, NN7, IE4, IE5, IE5.5, IE6

Read and write property. Specifies the value of the content attribute associated with the http-equiv or name attributes of the <meta> element.

Syntax:

```
document.getElementById("metaID").content = value
document.all.metaID.content = value // IE only
```

Example:

```
<head><meta id="myM" http-equiv="Content-Type">
<script language="JavaScript">
document.getElementById("myM").content = "text/html; charset=iso-8859-1"</script>
</head>
```

Applies to:

```
<meta>
```

contentEditable

Compatibility: IE5.5, IE6

Read and write property. Specifies whether or not the content of the selected element can be modified. Values: true or false.

Syntax:

```
document.all.elementID.contentEditable = value
```

Example:

```
<script language="JavaScript">
function E1() {
myP.innerText = "Try to edit this text by overwriting any part of it.";
document.all.myP.contentEditable = "true";
}
function E2() {
myP.innerText = "Try again.";
document.all.myP.contentEditable = "false";
}
function E3(){alert(document.all.myP.isContentEditable);}
</script>
<p id="myP">Try to edit this text by overwriting any part of it.</p>
<button onclick="E1();">Make the text editable</button>
<button onclick="E2();">Make the text non-editable</button>
<button onclick="E3();">isContentEditable</button>
```

Applies to:

```
<a>, <acronym>, <address>, <b>, <bdo>, <big>, <blockquote>, <body>, <button>,
<center>, <cite>, <code>, <custom>, <dd>, defaults, <del>, <dfn>, <dir>, <div>,
<dl>, <dt>, <em>, <fieldset>, <font>, <form>, <hn>, <i>, <input type="button">,
<input type="password">, <input type="radio">, <input type="reset">, <input
type="submit">, <input type="text">, <ins>, <isindex>, <kbd>, <label>, <legend>,
<li>, <listing>, <marquee>, <menu>, <nobr>, <ol>, <p>, <plaintext>, <pre>, <q>,
<rt>, <ruby>, <s>, <samp>, <small>, <span>, <strike>, <strong>, <sub>, <sup>,
<textarea>, <tt>, <u>, <ul>, <var>, <xmp>
```

contentOverflow

Compatibility: IE5.5, IE6

Read-only property. Indicates whether or not the document content overflows the boundaries of the customized print or print preview templates.

Syntax:

```
window.event.contentOverflow
```

Example:

```
<script language="JavaScript">
function B1() {
alert("contentOverflow: "+ event.contentOverflow);}
</script>
<body bgcolor="#FFFFFF" bottommargin=100 onLoad="B1()"></body>
```

Applies to:

```
event
```

contentWindow

Compatibility: NN6, NN7, IE5.5, IE6

Read-only property. Returns a reference to the window object for a <frame> or <iframe> element.

Syntax:

```
document.getElementById("elementID").contentWindow
document.all.elementID.contentWindow // IE only
```

Example:

```
<script language="JavaScript">
function myLocation() {alert(document.all.myFrame.contentWindow.location);}
</script>
<iframe id="myFrame" src="yourdocument1.html" style="width:200;"></iframe><br>
<button onclick="myLocation();">Location of Frame</button>
```

Applies to:

```
<frame>, <iframe>
```

cookie

Compatibility: NN4, NN6, NN7, IE4, IE5, IE5.5, IE6

Read and write property. Specifies the value of a cookie. A cookie can contain all of the following name-value pairs: expires=(date), domain=(domain name), path=(usually the current directory), and secure (only secure environments can access the cookie).

Syntax:

```
document.cookie = value
```

Example:

```
<script language="JavaScript">
myDate = new Date('12/22/2005 12:00 AM');
document.cookie = 'firstName=Joseph; expires=' + myDate.toString + ';';
</script>
<button onclick="alert(document.cookie);">See Document Cookie</button>
```

Applies to:

```
document
```

cookieEnabled

Compatibility: NN6, NN7, IE4, IE5, IE5.5, IE6

Read-only property. Indicates whether or not cookies are enabled in the browser. Values: true or false.

Syntax:

```
objectName.cookieEnabled
```

Example:

```
<button onClick="alert(navigator.cookieEnabled);">Are Cookies Enabled</button>
```

Applies to:

```
clientInformation, navigator
```

coords

Compatibility: NN4, NN6, NN7, IE4, IE5, IE5.5, IE6

Read and write property. Specifies the coordinates of the clickable region of the element.

Syntax:

```
document.getElementById("elementID").coords = value
document.all.elementID.coords = value // IE only
```

Values depend on the shape attribute's value:

shape = circ or circle	x, y (coordinates of the center), r (radius).
shape = rect or rectangle	x1, y1 (coordinates of the upper-left corner), x2, y2 (coordinates of the lower-right corner).
shape = poly or polygon	x1, y1, x2, y2, x3, y3, . . . (pairs of coordinates for each vertex of the polygon.

Example:

```
<html><head>
<script language="JavaScript">
function A1() {document.all.area1.coords = "0, 0, 100, 50";}
function A2() {
document.all.area2.coords = "100, 0, 200, 50";
document.all.area2.noHref = 'true'}
function A3() {document.all.area3.coords = "0, 50, 100, 100";}
function A4() {document.all.area4.coords = "100, 50, 200, 100";}
function A5() {
document.getElementById("area1").coords = "0, 0, 0, 0";
```

```
document.getElementById("area2").coords = "0, 0, 0, 0";
document.getElementById("area3").coords = "0, 0, 0, 0";
document.getElementById("area4").coords = "0, 0, 0, 0";}
</script></head>
<body>
<img src="yourimage.gif" id="myImg" alt="" width="200" height="100"
usemap="#myMap2">
<map name="myMap2">
<area id="area1" shape="rect" href="http://www.w3c.org" alt="The W3C home page"
onClick="return false">
<area id="area2" shape="rect" href="http://www.microsoft.com" nohref="true"
alt="The Microsoft home page" onClick="return false">
<area id="area3" shape="rect" href="http://www.msn.com" alt="The MSN home page"
onClick="return false">
<area id="area4" shape="rect" href="http://www.advocar.com" alt="The Advocar home
page" onClick="return false">
</map><br>
<input type="button" value="Make area 1 active" onClick="A1();">
<input type="button" value="Make area 2 active" onClick="A2();">
<input type="button" value="Make area 3 active" onClick="A3();">
<input type="button" value="Make area 4 active" onClick="A4();">
<button onclick="A5();">Restore areas to inactive</button>
<button onclick="alert(myImg.isMap);">IS MAP</button>
<button onclick="alert(area2.noHref);">noHref for Area 2</button>
</body></html>
```

Applies to:

```
<a> (IE6, NN6, and NN7 only), <area>
```

Count

Compatibility: IE5.5, IE6

Read-only property. Returns the number of block-format elements.

Syntax:

dialogHelperName.*collectionName*.Count

Example:

```
<object id="myDhelper" classid="clsid:3050f819-98b5-11cf-bb82-00aa00bdce0b">
</object>
<button onclick="alert(myDhelper.blockFormats.Count);">Number of Block Formats
</button>
```

Applies to:

blockFormats*, fonts*

cpuClass

Compatibility: IE4, IE5, IE5.5, IE6

Read-only property. Indicates the type of client machine processor. Values: x86 (Intel), 68K (Motorola), Alpha (Digital), PPC (Motorola), or Other.

Syntax:

```
objectName.cpuClass
```

Example:

```
<html><head>
<script language="JavaScript">
function B1() {
var m = navigator.cpuClass;
if (m == "x86") {n = "Intel processor";
} else if (m == "68K") {n = "Motorola processor";
} else if (m == "Alpha") {n = "Digital processor"
} else if (m == "PPC") {n = "Motorola processor";
} else {n = "Unknown processor";
}alert("The CPU of this machine is "+'"'+m+'"'+'\n'+n);
}
</script>
<body><input type="button" value="Click here" onClick="B1();"></body>
```

Applies to:

```
clientInformation, navigator
```

cssRules

Compatibility: NN6, NN7

Read-only property. Returns an array of style sheet rules. The corresponding IE property is rules.

Syntax:

```
document.styleSheet[index].cssRules
```

Example:

```
<html><head>
<style>#Layer1 { font-family:Verdana; color:blue }</style>
<script language="JavaScript">
function B1() {var n = document.styleSheets[0].cssRules;alert(n);}
</script></head>
<body>
```

```
<div id="Layer1" style="position:absolute; left:213px; top:106px; width:264px;
height:147px; z-index:1; background-color: #FFFF99; layer-background-color:
#FFFF99; border: 1px solid #000000;">div element content.</div>
<button onClick="B1();">Click here</button>
</body></html>
```

Applies to:

styleSheet

cssText

Compatibility: NN6, NN7, IE5, IE5.5, IE6

Read and write property. Establishes an array of style sheet rules.
Syntax:

objectName.cssText = value

Example:

```
<script language="JavaScript">
function B1() {
document.all.myP1.style.cssText = "color:green; font-family:verdana; font-
weight:bold; font-size:16";
}
</script>
<p id="myP1">This text will be affected by an array of style rules.</p>
<input type="button" value="Click to apply the style rules" onClick="B1();">
```

Applies to:

runtimeStyle, style, styleSheet

ctrlKey

Compatibility: IE4, IE5, IE5.5, IE6

Read-only property. Indicates whether or not the CTRL key was pressed. Values:
true or false.
Syntax:

window.event.ctrlKey

Example:

```
<input type="button" value="Click this button while pressing either Ctrl key"
onClick="alert(event.ctrlKey);">
```

Applies to:

event

ctrlLeft

Compatibility: IE5.5, IE6

Read-only property. Indicates whether or not the left CTRL key was pressed. The ctrlLeft property is currently supported only by Windows NT, 2000, and XP). Values: true or false.

Syntax:

```
window.event.ctrlLeft
```

Example:

```
<input type="button" value="Click this button while pressing the left Ctrl key"
onClick="alert(event.ctrlLeft);">
```

Applies to:

event

cursor

Compatibility: IE4, IE5, IE5.5, IE6

Read and write property. Specifies the type of cursor to display when hovering over the element. Cursor types compatible with all versions of IE include: auto, crosshair, default, hand, help, move, pointer, text, wait, and arrow-resize. The following cursor types are compatible with IE6 only: progress, not-allowed, no-drop, vertical-text, all-scroll, col-resize, row-resize, and url(uri).

Syntax:

```
document.all.elementID.cursor = value
```

Example:

```
<script language="JavaScript">
function C1() {document.all.Layer1.style.cursor = "hand";}
function C2() {document.all.Layer1.style.cursor = "help";}
function C3() {document.all.Layer1.style.cursor = "wait";}
</script>
<div id="Layer1" style="position:absolute; visibility:visible; left:43px;
top:233px; width:216px; height:61px; background-color:#66FFFF; layer-background-
color:#66FFFF; border:1px none #000000; z-index:1">Move the mouse over this div
element.</div>
```

```
<button onclick="C1();">Replace cursor for "hand"</button>
<button onclick="C2();">Replace cursor for "help"</button>
<button onclick="C3();">Replace cursor for "wait"</button>
```

Applies to:

```
<a>, <address>, <applet>, <b>, <big>, <blockquote>, <body>, <caption>, <center>,
<cite>, <code>, <col>, <colgroup>, <custom>, <dd>, <dfn>, <dir>, <div>, <dl>, <dt>,
<em>, <embed>, <fieldset>, <form>, <hN>, <hr>, <html>, <i>, <iframe>, <img>, <input
type="button">, <input type="checkbox">, <input type="file">, <input
type="hidden">, <input type="image">, <input type="password">, <input
type="radio">, <input type="reset">, <input type="submit">, <input type="text">,
<kbd>, <label>, <legend>, <li>, <listing>, <marquee>, <menu>, <object>, <ol>, <p>,
<plaintext>, <pre>, <rt>, <ruby>, <s>, <samp>, <small>, <span>, <strike>, <strong>,
<style>, <sub>, <sup>, <table>, <tbody>, <td>, <textarea>, <tfoot>, <th>, <thead>,
<tr>, <tt>, <u>, <ul>, <var>, <xmp>
```

data (1)

Compatibility: NN4, NN6, NN7, IE4, IE5, IE5.5, IE6

Read and write property. Specifies the URL of the data.
Syntax:

```
document.getElementById("elementID").data = value
document.all.elementID.data = value // IE only
```

Example:

```
<script>
function cT() {
document.all.myO.data =
'http://download.macromedia.com/pub/shockwave/cabs/flash/
swflash.cab#version=5,0,0,0" width="250" height="230"';
}
</script>
<object id="myO" classid="clsid:D27CDB6E-AE6D-11cf-96B8-444553540000">
    <param name="movie" value="yourshockwavemovie.swf">
    <param name="quality" value="high">
</object>
```

Applies to:

```
<comment> (IE6 only), <object>
```

data (2)

Compatibility: IE5, IE5.5, IE6

Read and write property. Specifies the string content in the text node.

Syntax:

```
textNodeName.data = value
```

Example:

```
<script language="javascript">
function B1(){
var myText = document.createTextNode();
myText.data="Data Property for textNode";
alert(myText.data);}
</script>
<button onclick="B1();">View Node Value</button>
```

Applies to:

```
TextNode
```

dataFld (1)

Compatibility: IE4, IE5, IE5.5, IE6

Read and write property. Establishes the field from the data source (dataSrc) that is bound to the element. To create a data source, you must make use of the <object> element.

Syntax:

```
document.all.elementID.dataFld = value
```

Example:

```
<html><head><script language="javascript">
function rowEnter(){
myTable.rows[myData.recordset.AbsolutePosition].style.backgroundColor = 'yellow';}
function add(){myData.recordset.AddNew();}
function del(){if (myData.recordset.RecordCount > 0) myData.recordset.Delete();}
</script>
<script for="myTable" event="onreadystatechange">
if (this.readyState == 'complete'){
this.rows(myData.recordset.AbsolutePosition).style.backgroundColor = 'yellow';
myData.onrowenter = rowEnter;}
</script>
<script for="myData" event="onrowexit">
for (var i = 1; i <= myData.recordset.RecordCount; i++){
myTable.rows[i].style.backgroundColor = '';}
</script>
<script for="tableList" event="onclick">
myData.recordset.AbsolutePosition = this.recordNumber;
```

```
window.event.cancelBubble = true;
</script>
<script for="myData" event="oncellchange">alert(event.dataFld);</script>
</head>
<body>
<button onclick="add();">Add Record</button>
<button onclick="del();">Delete</button>
<button onclick="alert(firstname.dataFld);">dataFld</button>
<button onclick="alert(myDiv.dataFormatAs);">dataFormatAs</button>
<button onclick="alert(myTable.dataPageSize);">dataPage</button>
<button onclick="alert(myTable.dataSrc);">dataSrc</button>
<div datasrc="#myData" id="myDiv" dataformatas="text"></div>
<object classid="clsid:333C7BC4-460F-11D0-BC04-0080C7055A83" id="myData">
    <param name="DataURL" value="myfile.csv">
    <param name="UseHeader" value="True">
    <param name="TextQualifier" value="'">
</object><br><br>
First Name: <input id="firstname" type="text" datasrc="#myData"
datafld="firstname"><br>
Last Name: <input id="lastname" type="text" datasrc="#myData"
datafld="lastname"><br>
Income: <input id="income" type="text" datasrc="#myData" datafld="income"><br>
<table id="myTable" datasrc="#myData" datapagesize="10">
<thead><tr style="font-weight:bold"><td>First Name</td><td>Last Name</
td><td>Income</td></tr></thead><tbody>
<tr id="tableList">
    <td><span datafld="firstname"></span></td>
    <td><span datafld="lastname"></span></td>
    <td><span datafld="income"></span></td>
</tr></tbody></table>
</body></html>
```

Contents of myfile.csv:

```
firstname:STRING,lastname:STRING,income:INT
John,Smith,200387
Manny,Ramirez,195687
Troy,Belling,195006
```

Applies to:

```
<a>, <applet>, <button>, <div>, <fieldset>, <frame>, <iframe>, <img>, <input
type="button">, <input type="checkbox">, <input type="hidden">, <input
type="image">, <input type="password">, <input type="radio">, <input type="text">,
<label>, <marquee>, <select>, <span>, <textarea>
```

dataFld (2)

Compatibility: IE5, IE5.5, IE6

Read and write property. Specifies the data column in a recordset that is affected by the onCellChange event.

Syntax:

```
window.event.dataFld = value
```

Example: See the dataFld (1) property example.
Applies to:

```
event
```

dataFormatAs

Compatibility: IE4, IE5, IE5.5, IE6

Read and write property. Specifies how to render the data coming from a data source. Values: text (the default), html, and localized-text (uses local machine settings).

Syntax:

```
document.all.elementID.dataFormatAs = value
```

Example: See the dataFld (1) property example.
Applies to:

```
<button>, <div>, <input type="button">, <label>, <legend>, <marquee>, <span>
```

dataPageSize

Compatibility: IE4, IE5, IE5.5, IE6

Read and write property. Specifies the number of records shown in a table at any given time. This is helpful when the data source has more rows than can be displayed in the table at one time.

Syntax:

```
document.all.tableID.dataPageSize = value
```

Example: See the dataFld (1) property example.
Applies to:

```
<table>
```

dataSrc

Compatibility: IE4, IE5, IE5.5, IE6

Read and write property. Specifies the data object to which the element is bound. The data source must be attached to the page as an object.

Syntax:

```
document.all.elementID.dataSrc = value
```

Example: See the dataFld (1) property example.

Applies to:

```
<a>, <applet>, <button>, <div>, <frame>, <iframe>, <img>, <input type="button">,
<input type="checkbox">, <input type="hidden">, <input type="image">, <input
type="password">, <input type="radio">, <input type="text">, <label>, <marquee>,
<select>, <span>, <table>, <textarea>
```

dateTime

Compatibility: NN6, NN7, IE6

Read and write property. Specifies a new date and time for the element. Values: YYYY-MM-DDThh:mm:ssTZD (standard time format) or YYYY-MM-DDZ±hh:mm:ssTZD (UTC time format).

Syntax:

```
document.getElementById("elementID").dateTime = value
document.all.elementID.dateTime = value // IE only
```

Example:

```
<script language="JavaScript">
function B1() {
document.all.myDel.dateTime = "2003-04-15T14:50:30Z";
alert(document.all.myDel.dateTime);
}
</script>
<del id="myDel">This text has been deleted.</del>
<input type="button" onClick="B1();" value="Display date and time of the above text
deletion">
```

Applies to:

```
<del>, <ins>
```

declare

Compatibility: NN6, NN7, IE6

Read and write property. Specifies whether or not to simply declare the element without loading or running it. Values: true or false.

Syntax:

```
document.getElementById("objectID").declare = value
document.all.objectID.declare = value // IE only
```

Example:

```
<script>function cT() {document.all.myO.declare = true;}</script>
<object id="myO"
codebase="http://download.macromedia.com/pub/shockwave/cabs/flash/
swflash.cab#version=5,0,0,0"
width="250" height="230">
    <param name="movie" value="Puzzle.swf">
    <param name="quality" value="high">
</object>
```

Applies to:

```
<object>
```

defaultCharset

Compatibility: IE4, IE5, IE5.5, IE6

Read-only property. Returns the character set used by the browser.

Syntax:

```
document.defaultCharset
```

Example:

```
<button onclick="alert(document.defaultCharset);">Default Charset</button>
```

Applies to:

```
document
```

defaultChecked

Compatibility: NN4, NN6, NN7, IE4, IE5, IE5.5, IE6

Read and write property. Specifies the checked state of an element when the page is loaded. Values: true or false.

Syntax:

```
document.getElementById("inputID").defaultChecked = value
document.all.inputID.defaultChecked = value // IE only
```

Example:

```
<script language="JavaScript">
function C1() {
if (myR1.defaultChecked) {alert("Radio 1 is checked");}
if (myR2.defaultChecked) {alert("Radio 2 is checked");}
```

```
if (myC.defaultChecked) {alert("Checkbox is checked");}
}
</script>
<input id="myR1" type="radio" checked value="radiobutton">Radio 1<br>
<input id="myR2" type="radio" value="radiobutton">Radio 2<br>
<input id="myC" type="checkbox" value="checkbox" checked>Checkbox</p>
<input type="button" value='Click here' onclick="C1();">
```

Applies to:

```
<input type="checkbox">, <input type="radio">
```

defaultSelected

Compatibility: NN6, NN7, IE4, IE5, IE5.5, IE6

Read and write property. Specifies the selected state of an element when the page is loaded. Values: true or false.

Syntax:

```
document.getElementById("optionID").defaultSelected = value
document.all.optionID.defaultSelected = value // IE only
```

Example:

```
<form id="myF"><select name="select">
    <option value="1">Item 1</option>
    <option value="2">Item 2</option>
    <option id="o3" value="3">Default selected Option</option>
<script language="JavaScript">
document.getElementById("o3").defaultSelected = true;
var n = document.getElementById("o3").innerText;
function C1() {
alert('Default selected Option label:\n'+'"'+n+'"');
document.getElementById("myF").reset();
}
</script>
    <option value="4">Item 4</option>
    <option value="5">Item 5</option>
</select></form>
<input type="button" value='Click here' onclick="C1();">
```

Applies to:

```
<option>
```

defaultStatus

Compatibility: NN4, NN6, NN7, IE4, IE5, IE5.5, IE6

Read and write property. Specifies the status bar message.
   Syntax:

```
window.defaultStatus = value
```

   Example:

```
<body bgcolor="#FFFFFF" text="#000000" bottommargin=150"
onLoad="window.defaultStatus='This is the status bar message'">
```

   Applies to:

```
window
```

defaultValue

Compatibility: NN4, NN6, NN7, IE4, IE5, IE5.5, IE6

Read-only property. Returns the content of the element when the page is loaded.
   Syntax:

```
document.getElementById("elementID").defaultValue
document.all.elementID.defaultValue // IE only
```

   Example:

```
<script language="JavaScript">
function C1() {
var m = document.getElementById("myB").defaultValue;
alert("The value of this element is: "+'"'+m+'"');
}
</script>
<input id="myB" type="button" value='Click here' onclick="C1();">
```

   Applies to:

```
<input type="button">, <input type="checkbox">, <input type="file">, <input
type="hidden">, <input type="image">, <input type="password">, <input
type="radio">, <input type="reset">, <input type="submit">, <input type="text">,
<textarea>
```

defer

Compatibility: NN6, NN7, IE4, IE5, IE5.5, IE6

Read and write property. Specifies whether or not a script's execution is
deferred. This property is helpful because deferring script execution can
improve the download performance of a page. Values: true or false.

Syntax:

```
document.getElementById("scriptID").defer = value
document.all.scriptID.defer = value // IE only
```

Example:

```
<script language="javascript" defer="true">
function B4() {document.all.myS.defer = false;}
</script>
<script id="myS" language="javascript">
<input type="button" value=" onClick="B4();">
</script>
```

Applies to:

```
<script>
```

description

Compatibility: NN6, NN7

Read-only property. Specifies a descriptive name for the MIME type.
Syntax:

```
navigator.objectName[index].description
```

Example:

```
<button onclick="alert(navigator.mimeTypes[0].description);">mime</button>
<button onclick="alert(navigator.mimeTypes[0].suffixes);">suffixes</button>
<button onclick="alert(navigator.mimeTypes[0].type);">Type</button>
```

Applies to:

```
mimeType, plugin
```

designMode

Compatibility: NN6, NN7, IE5, IE5.5, IE6

Read and write property. Specifies whether or not the document content can be modified. Values: on (can be modified), off or inherited (the default; cannot be modified).
Syntax:

```
document.designMode = value
```

Example:

```
<button onclick="alert(document.designMode);">Design Mode Status</button>
```

Applies to:

```
document
```

deviceXDPI

Compatibility: IE6

Read-only property. Returns the dpi (dots per inch) for the height of the screen.
Syntax:

```
screen.deviceXDPI
```

Example:

```
<button onclick="alert(screen.deviceXDPI);">device XDPI</button>
<button onclick="alert(screen.deviceYDPI);">device YDPI</button>
```

Applies to:

```
screen
```

deviceYDPI

Compatibility: IE6

Read-only property. Returns the dpi (dots per inch) for the width of the screen.
Syntax:

```
screen.deviceYDPI
```

Example: See the deviceXDPI property example.
Applies to:

```
screen
```

dialogArguments

Compatibility: IE4, IE5, IE5.5, IE6

Read-only property. Returns an array of the parameters passed to the
showModalDialog() or showModelessDialog() method used to create a dialog window.
Syntax:

```
window.dialogArguments
```

Example:

```
<script language="JavaScript">
<script language="JavaScript">
function openWindow() {
    var myArguments = new Object();
    myArguments.param1 = document.all.myColor.value;
    window.showModalDialog("dw.htm", myArguments, '');
}
</script>
<select id="myColor">
<option value="red">Red</option>
<option value="green">Green</option>
<option value="blue">Blue</option>
<option value="yellow">Yellow</option>
</select>
<button onclick="openWindow();">Open Window</button>
```

Contents of dw.htm:

```
<script language="JavaScript">
function loadForm(){
myBody.style.backgroundColor = window.dialogArguments.param1;
myBody.style.color = 'black';
myBody.style.fontSize = '14pt';
window.dialogHeight = '300px';
window.dialogLeft = '500px';
window.dialogTop = '300px';
window.dialogWidth = '500px';
}
</script>
<body id="myBody" onload="loadForm();"><br>
This window has the color specified in the previous window<br><br>
<button onclick="window.close();">Close This Window</button>
</body>
```

Applies to:

```
window
```

dialogHeight, dialogWidth

Compatibility: IE4, IE5, IE5.5, IE6

Read and write properties. Specify the height and width of the dialog window created by the showModalDialog() or showModelessDialog() method. Value: A floating-point number followed by a unit designator (the default unit is em for IE4 and px for IE5+).

Syntax:

```
window.dialogWidth = value
window.dialogHeight = value
```

Example: See the dialogArguments property example.
Applies to:

```
window
```

dialogLeft, dialogTop

Compatibility: IE4, IE5, IE5.5, IE6

Read and write properties. Specify the left and top coordinates of the dialog window created by the showModalDialog() or showModelessDialog() method. Value: A floating-point number followed by a unit designator (the default unit is em for IE4 and px for IE5+).
Syntax:

```
window.dialogLeft = value
window.dialogTop = value
```

Example: See the dialogArguments property example.
Applies to:

```
window
```

dir

Compatibility: NN6, NN7, IE5, IE5.5, IE6

Read and write property. Specifies the reading order of the text within the element. The property does not affect alphanumeric characters in Latin documents. Values: ltr (left to right) or rtl (right to left).
Syntax:

```
document.getElementById("elementID").dir = value
document.all.elementID.dir = value // IE only
```

Example:

```
<script language="JavaScript">
function D1() {document.all.myP.dir = "rtl";}</script>
<p id="myP" onload="D1();">ARABIC OR HEBREW IN TEXT THIS</p>
```

Applies to:

```
<a>, <acronym>, <address>, <applet>, <area>, <b>, <base>, <basefont>, <bdo>, <big>,
<blockquote>, <body>, <br>, <button>, <caption>, <center>, <cite>, <code>, <col>,
```

<colgroup>, <custom>, <dd>, <del>, <dfn>, <dir>, <div>, <dl>, document, <dt>, <em>,
<embed>, <fieldset>, <font>, <form>, <frame>, <frameset>, <head>, <hn>, <hr>,
<html>, <i>, <iframe>, <img>, <input type="button">, <input type="checkbox">,
<input type="file">, <input type="image">, <input type="password">, <input
type="radio">, <input type="reset">, <input type="submit">, <input type="text">,
<ins>, <isindex>, <kbd>, <label>, <legend>, <li>, <link>, <listing>, <map>,
<marquee>, <menu>, <meta>, <nobr>, <noframes>, <noscript>, <object>, <ol>,
<optgroup>, <option>, <p>, <param>, <plaintext>, <pre>, <q>, <rt>, <ruby>, <s>,
<samp>, <script>, <select>, <small>, <span>, <strike>, <strong>, <style>, <sub>,
<sup>, <table>, <tbody>, <td>, <textarea>, <tfoot>, <th>, <thead>, <title>, <tr>,
<tt>, <u>, <ul>, <var>, <xmp>

direction

Compatibility: IE4, IE5, IE5.5, IE6

Read and write property. Specifies the scrolling direction of the text within
a <marquee> element. Values: left (the default), right, down, or up.

Syntax:

```
document.all.marqueeID.direction = value
```

Example:

```
<script language="JavaScript">
function M1(){document.all.myM.direction = "up";}
function M2(){document.all.myM.direction = "left";}
function M3(){document.all.myM.direction = "right";}
function M4(){document.all.myM.direction = "down";}
</script>
<marquee id="myM" bgcolor="cyan">SCROLLING MARQUEE</marquee>
<button onclick="M1();">Up</button>
<button onclick="M2();">Left</button>
<button onclick="M3();">Right</button>
<button onclick="M4();">Down</button>
```

Applies to:

```
<marquee>
```

disabled

Compatibility: IE4, IE5, IE5.5, IE6

Read and write property. Specifies whether or not the element is disabled.
Values: true or false (the default).

Syntax:

```
document.all.elementID.disabled = value
```

Example:

```
<script>
function B1() {document.all.B1.disabled = true;}
function B2() {document.all.B1.disabled = false;}
</script>
<input id="B1" type="button" value="Disable" onClick="B1();">
<input type="button" value="Enable" onClick="B2();">
```

Applies to:

```
<a>, <acronym>, <address>, <area>, <b>, <basefont>, <bdo>, <basefont>, <bgsound>,
<big>, <blockquote>, <body>, <br>, <button>, <caption>, <center>, <cite>, <code>,
<col>, <comment>, <custom>, <dd>, defaults, <del>, <dfn>, <dir>, <div>, <dl>, <dt>,
<em>, <embed>, <fieldset>, <font>, <form>, <frame>, <head>, <hn>, <hr>, <html>,
<i>, <iframe>, <img>, <input type="button">, <input type="checkbox">, <input
type="file">, <input type="image">, <input type="password">, <input type="radio">,
<input type="reset">, <input type="submit">, <input type="text">, <ins>, <isindex>,
<kbd>, <label>, <legend>, <li>, <link>, <listing>, <map>, <marquee>, <menu>,
<nobr>, <object>, <ol>, <optgroup> (IE6), <option>, <p>, <plaintext>, <pre>, <q>,
<rt>, <ruby>, <s>, <samp>, <script>, <select>, <small>, <span>, <strike>, <strong>,
<style>, styleSheet, <sub>, <sup>, <table>, <td>, <textarea>, <title>, <tr>, <tt>,
<u>, <ul>, <var>, <xmp>
```

doctype

Compatibility: NN6, NN7, IE6

Read-only property. Returns the document type for the current page. For HTML documents, the return value is null.

Syntax:

```
document.doctype
```

Example:

```
<!doctype html public "-//w3c//dtd html 4.0//en-us">
<html><head><script language="JavaScript">
function B1() {alert(document.doctype); }
</script></head><body>
<input type="button" onClick="B1();" value="doctype">
</body></html>
```

Applies to:

```
document
```

documentElement

Compatibility: NN6, NN7, IE5, IE5.5, IE6

Read-only property. Returns the HTML element that contains all the content of the document.

Syntax:

```
document.documentElement
```

Example:

```
<button onClick="alert(document.documentElement.nodeName);">Root Node</button>
```

Applies to:

```
document
```

domain

Compatibility: NN4, NN6, NN7, IE4, IE5, IE5.5, IE6

Read and write property. Specifies the security domain name of the document.

Syntax:

```
document.domain = value
```

Example:

```
<script language="JavaScript">
function D1() {
var m = document.domain;
if (m) {alert(m);} else {alert("No security domain");}}
</script>
<input type="button" onClick="D1();" value="Domain Name">
```

Applies to:

```
document
```

dropEffect

Compatibility: IE5, IE5.5, IE6

Read and write property. Specifies both the drag-and-drop operation and the type of cursor to be used. This property must be accompanied by the effectAllowed property. Values: copy, link, move, or none.

Syntax:

```
window.event.dataTransfer.dropEffect = value
```

Example:

```
<html><head>
<script language="JavaScript">
function transferDrop() {
```

```
window.event.srcElement.innerText = window.event.dataTransfer.getData("text");
window.event.returnValue = false;
}
function transferDrag() {
window.event.dataTransfer.dropEffect = 'move';
window.event.returnValue = false;
}
</script></head>
<body bgcolor="#FFFFFF" text="#000000" bottommargin="150">
<p id="mySource" ondragstart="window.event.dataTransfer.effectAllowed =
'move';">Highlight text in this paragraph and drag
it to the text area bellow</p>
<textarea id="myTarget" ondrop="transferDrop();"
ondragover="window.event.returnValue = false;" ondragenter="transferDrag();">
</textarea>
```

Applies to:

```
dataTransfer
```

dynsrc

Compatibility: IE4, IE5, IE5.5, IE6

Read and write property. Specifies the URL of a video clip.

Syntax:

```
document.all.elementID.dynsrc = value
```

Example:

```
<script language="JavaScript">
function setSource() {document.all.myImage.dynsrc = "yourvideo.avi";}
</script>
<img id="myImage" start="mouseover" alt="" width="200" height="200">
<button onclick="setSource();">Set Source</button>
```

Applies to:

```
<img>, <input>, <input type="image">
```

E

Compatibility: NN4, NN6, NN7, IE4, IE5, IE5.5, IE6

Read-only property. A mathematical constant that returns the natural log base.

Syntax:

```
Math.E
```

Example:

```
<button onclick="alert(Math.E);">Math.E</button>
```

Applies to:

```
Math
```

effectAllowed

Compatibility: IE5, IE5.5, IE6

Read and write property. Specifies the data transfer operation. This property must be accompanied by the `dropEffect` property. Values: `copy` (allows the copy operation on the selection), `link` (allows the selection to be linked with the drop target), `move` (allows the selection to be moved to the drop target), `copyLink` (allows the copy or link operation, depending on the target settings), `copyMove` (allows the copy or move operation, depending on the target settings), `linkMove` (allows the link or move operation, depending on the target settings), `all` (allows all drop effects), `none` (no drop effect is allowed and the `no-drop` cursor is shown), and `uninitialized` (the default; the `effectAllowed` property has not been initialized yet).

Syntax:

```
window.event.dataTransfer.effectAllowed = value
```

Example: See the `dropEffect` property example.
Applies to:

```
dataTransfer
```

encoding

Compatibility: NN4, NN6, NN7, IE4, IE5, IE5.5, IE6

Read and write property. Specifies the MIME content type code, alerting the server that the data submitted is in a MIME type. Default value: `application/x-www-form-urlencoded`.

Syntax:

```
document.getElementById("formID").encoding = value
document.all.formID.encoding = value // IE only
document.encoding = value
```

Example:

```
<form id="fm" method="post">
<button onclick="alert(document.all.fm.encoding);">encoding</button>
```

```
<button onclick="alert(document.all.fm.enctype);">enctype</button>
</form>
```

Applies to:

```
document, <form>
```

enctype

Compatibility: NN6, NN7, IE6

Read and write property. Provides the same functionality as the encoding property.
Syntax:

```
document.getElementById("formID").enctype = value
document.all.formID.enctype = value // IE only
```

Example: See the encoding property example.
Applies to:

```
<form>
```

event

Compatibility: NN6, NN7, IE4, IE5, IE5.5, IE6

Read and write property. Specifies the name of the event that will trigger
execution of the script.
Syntax:

```
document.getElementById("scriptID").event = value
document.all.scriptID.event = value // IE only
```

Example:

```
<script id="myScript" for="myButton" event="onclick()">
alert(myScript.event);</script>
<button id="myButton">Event for This Script</button>
```

Applies to:

```
<script>
```

expando

Compatibility: IE4, IE5, IE5.5, IE6

Read and write property. Specifies whether or not custom properties can be
added to the object. Values: true (the default) or false.

Syntax:

```
objectName.expando = value
```

The following example illustrates how to create a custom counter property:

```
document.expando = true; // instruct the browser to "expand" the properties array
document.counter = 0; // introduce a new property
```

Example:

```
<p id="myElement">Sample text, try to select part of it</p>
<script language="JavaScript">
function E1() {
myElement.setAttribute("unselectable", "off",  0);
document.expando = true;}
function E2() {
myElement.setAttribute("unselectable", "on",  0);
document.expando = true;}
</script>
<button onclick="E2();">Unselectable</button>
<button onclick="E1();">Selectable</button>
```

Applies to:

```
attribute (IE6 only), document
```

face

Compatibility: NN6, NN7, IE4, IE5, IE5.5, IE6

Read and write property. Specifies a comma-delimited list of the font-family names used to render the element's content.
Syntax:

```
document.getElementById("elementID").face = value
document.all.elementID.face = value // IE only
```

Example:

```
<font id="myElement">Sample Text</font><br>
<button onclick="myElement.face='courier';">Courier Font</button>
<button onclick="myElement.face='arial';">Arial Font</button>
```

Applies to:

```
<basefont>, <font>
```

fgColor

Compatibility: NN4, NN6, NN7, IE4, IE5, IE5.5, IE6

Read and write property. Specifies the color used to render the text in the document. Value: Web color name or hexadecimal value in #RRGGBB format.

Syntax:

```
document.fgColor = value
document.body.fgColor = value // NN6, IE
```

Example:

```
<body>Sample Text<br>
<button onclick="document.fgColor='red';">Red</button>
<button onclick="document.fgColor='blue';">Blue</button>
</body>
```

Applies to:

```
document
```

fieldDelim

Compatibility: IE4, IE5, IE5.5, IE6

Read and write property. Specifies the character used to separate fields or table columns. Value: Any alphanumeric character (default is a comma), or any encoding for a nonprintable character, such as # for the # symbol).

The TDC (Tabular Data Control, a Microsoft ActiveX control) object allows an HTML page to display data from delimited text files either as part of tables or one row at a time. Using the <object> element, you can embed the TDC control inside a page.

Syntax:

```
objectName.fieldDelim = value
```

Example: See the dataFld (1) property example.
Applies to:

```
<object>
```

fileCreatedDate

Compatibility: IE4, IE5, IE5.5, IE6

Read-only property. Returns the date the file was created.

Syntax:

```
document.all.imgID.fileCreatedDate
document.fileCreatedDate
```

Example:

```
<img id="myImage" src="yourimage.gif"><br>
<button onclick="alert(document.fileCreatedDate);">Document Created On</button>
<button onclick="alert(myImage.fileModifiedDate);">Image Modified On</button>
<button onclick="alert(myImage.fileSize);">Image Size</button>
<button onclick="alert(myImage.fileUpdatedDate);">Image Updated on</button>
<button onclick="alert(document.lastModified);">Document Modified On</button>
```

Applies to:

```
document, <img>
```

fileModifiedDate

Compatibility: IE4, IE5, IE5.5, IE6

Read-only property. Returns the date the file was last modified.
    Syntax:

```
document.all.imgID.fileModifiedDate
document.fileModifiedDate
```

Example: See the fileCreatedDate property example.
Applies to:

```
document, <img>
```

filename

Compatibility: NN6, NN7

Read-only property. Specifies the filename of the plug-in module in Netscape browsers.
    Syntax:

```
navigator.plugins[index].filename
```

Example:

```
<button onclick="alert(navigator.plugins.length);">Length</button>
<button onclick="alert(navigator.plugins[0].description);">mimetype</button>
```

```
<button onclick="alert(navigator. plugins[0].filename);">suffixes</button>
<button onclick="alert(navigator.plugins[0].name);">Type</button>
```

Applies to:

plugin

fileSize

Compatibility: IE4, IE5, IE5.5, IE6

Read-only property. Returns the size of the file in bytes.
Syntax:

```
document.all.imgID.fileSize
document.fileSize
```

Example: See the fileCreatedDate property example.
Applies to:

document, <img>

fileUpdatedDate

Compatibility: IE4, IE5, IE5.5, IE6

Read-only property. Returns the date the file was last updated.
Syntax:

```
document.all.imgID.fileUpdatedDate
```

Example: See the fileCreatedDate property example.
Applies to:

<img>

firstChild

Compatibility: NN6, NN7, IE5, IE5.5, IE6

Read-only property. Returns the first child element in the childNodes collection of
the parent element.
Syntax:

```
document.getElementById("elementID").firstChild
document.all.elementID.firstChild // IE only
```

Example:

```
<script language="JavaScript">
function newElem(myT) {
    var newI = document.createElement("LI")
    newI.innerHTML = myT
    return newI}
function R1(form) {
    var newI = newElem(form.enter.value);
    var fLi = document.getElementById("myL").firstChild;
    document.getElementById("myL").replaceChild(newI, fLi);}
function R2(form) {
    var newI = newElem(form.enter.value);
    var fLi = document.getElementById("myL").lastChild;
    document.getElementById("myL").replaceChild(newI, fLi);}
</script>
<form>
<input type="text" name="enter" size="50">
<button onClick="R1(this.form);"> Replace first item</button>
<button onClick="R2(this.form);"> Replace last item</button>
<ul id="myL"><li>First List Item</li><li>Second List Item</li></ul>
</form>
```

Applies to:

```
<a>, <acronym>, <address>, <applet>, <area>, attribute, <b>, <base>, <basefont>,
<bdo>, <big>, <blockquote>, <body>, <br>, <button>, <caption>, <center>, <cite>,
<code>, <col>, <colgroup>, <comment>, <dd>, <del>, <dfn>, <dir>, <div>, <dl>, <dt>,
<em>, <embed>, <fieldset>, <font>, <form>, <frame>, <frameset>, <head>, <hn>, <hr>,
<html>, <i>, <iframe>, <img>, <input type="button">, <input type="checkbox">,
<input type="file">, <input type="image">, <input type="password">, <input
type="radio">, <input type="reset">, <input type="submit">, <input type="text">,
<ins>, <isindex>, <kbd>, <label>, <legend>, <li>, <link>, <listing>, <map>,
<marquee>, <menu>, <meta>, <noframes>, <noscript>, <object>, <ol>, <optgroup>,
<option>, <p>, <param>, <plaintext>, <pre>, <q>, <s>, <samp>, <script>, <select>,
<small>, <span>, <strike>, <strong>, <style>, <sub>, <sup>, <table>, <tbody>, <td>,
<textarea>, <tfoot>, <th>, <thead>, <title>, <tr>, <tt>, <u>, <ul>, <var>, <xmp>
```

fontSmoothingEnabled

Compatibility: IE4, IE5, IE5.5, IE6

Read-only property. Returns a value indicating whether or not the system has font smoothing enabled. Values: true or false.

Syntax:

```
screen.fontSmoothingEnabled
```

Example:

```
<script language="JavaScript">
function B1() {alert(screen.fontSmoothingEnabled);}
</script>
<button onclick="B1();">Font Smoothing Enabled</button>
```

Applies to:

screen

form

Compatibility: NN4, NN6, NN7, IE4, IE5, IE5.5, IE6

Read-only property. Returns a reference to the <form> element that contains the control. Value: An object or null (if the container element is not a <form>).

Syntax:

```
document.getElementById("elementID").form
document.all.elementID.form // IE only
```

Example:

```
<script language="JavaScript">
function B1(form) {
    var elem = document.getElementById("myB1").form.id;
    alert(elem);
    return true;
}
</script>
<form id="myF"><input id="myB1" type="button" value="Click for the ID of this
control's form" onClick="B1(this.form);"></form>
```

Applies to:

<button>, <fieldset> (IE6), <input type="button">, <input type="checkbox">, <input
type="file">, <input type="hidden">, <input type="image">, <input type="password">,
<input type="radio">, <input type="reset">, <input type="submit">, <input
type="text">, <isindex> (IE6), <label> (IE6, NN6, and NN7), <legend> (IE6),
<object>, <option>, <select>, <textarea>

frame

Compatibility: NN4, NN6, NN7, IE4, IE5, IE5.5, IE6

Read and write property. Specifies how the border of the table should be rendered. Values: void, above, below, border, box, hsides, lhs, rhs, and vsides.

Syntax:

```
document.getElementById("tableID").frame = value
document.all.tableID.frame = value // IE only
```

Example:

```
<script>
function B1() {document.getElementById("myT2").frame = "void";}
function B2() {document.getElementById("myT2").frame = "above";}
function B3() {document.getElementById("myT2").frame = "below";}
function B4() {document.getElementById("myT2").frame = "border";}
function B5() {document.getElementById("myT2").frame = "box";}
function B6() {document.getElementById("myT2").frame = "hsides";}
function B7() {document.getElementById("myT2").frame = "lhs";}
function B8() {document.getElementById("myT2").frame = "rhs";}
function B9() {document.getElementById("myT2").frame = "vsides";}
</script>
<table id="myT2" width="542" bordercolor="blue" cellspacing="5" cellpadding="5">
<tr><td id="C1">Cell 1</td><td>Cell 2</td><td>Cell 3</td></tr>
<tr><td id="C1">Cell 4</td><td>Cell 5</td><td>Cell 6</td></tr>
</table>
<input type="button" value='Frame = "above"' onClick="B2();">
<input type="button" value='Frame = "below"' onClick="B3();">
<input type="button" value='Frame = "border"' onClick="B4();">
<input type="button" value='Frame = "box"' onClick="B5();">
<input type="button" value='Frame = "hsides"' onClick="B6();">
<input type="button" value='Frame = "lhw"' onClick="B7();">
<input type="button" value='Frame = "rhs"' onClick="B8();">
<input type="button" value='Frame = "vsides"' onClick="B9();">
<input type="button" value='Frame = "void"' onClick="B1();">
```

Applies to:

```
<table>
```

frameBorder

Compatibility: NN6, NN7, IE4, IE5, IE5.5, IE6

Read and write property. Specifies whether or not the border of the element should be displayed. Values: 1 or yes (the default; border is displayed), 0 or no (no border is displayed).

Syntax:

```
document.getElementById("elementID").frameBorder = value
document.all.elementID.frameBorder = value // IE only
```

Example:

```
<iframe id="myFrame" src="test2.htm" width="300" frameborder="no"
framespacing="5"></iframe><br>
<button onclick="alert(document.all.myFrame.frameBorder);">Frame Border</button>
<button onclick="alert(document.all.myFrame.frameSpacing);">Frame Spacing</button>
```

Applies to:

```
<frame> (IE4, IE5, IE5.5, and IE6 only), <frameset>, <iframe>
```

frameElement

Compatibility: NN7, IE5.5, IE6

Read-only property. When the window is contained within a <frame> or <iframe> element, this property returns a reference to the container element.

Syntax:

```
window.frameElement
```

Example:

```
<html><head>
</head><body text="#000000" bgcolor="#FFFFFF">
<iframe id="IF1" src="yourPage1.html" style="width:40%"></iframe>
</body></html>
```

Contents of yourPage1.html:

```
<html><head>
<script language="JavaScript">
function F1() {
var m = window.frameElement;
m.src = "yourPage2.html"; // the replacement page
}
</script></head>
<body bgcolor="white">
<input type="button" value="Replace the iframe content" onclick="F1();">
</body></html>
```

Applies to:

```
window
```

frameSpacing

Compatibility: IE4, IE5, IE5.5, IE6

Read and write property. Specifies the spacing in pixels between frames of a frameset. Default value is 2.

Syntax:

```
window.framesetID.frameSpacing = value
```

Example:

```
<frameset id="myFrameset" onload="alert(window.myFrameset.frameSpacing);"
rows="200,*" border="15px" framespacing="2">
<frame name="topFrame" noresize scrolling="NO" src="fr2b.html">
<frame name="mainFrame" src="fr3b.html">
</frameset>
```

Applies to:

```
<frameset>
```

fromElement

Compatibility: IE4, IE5, IE5.5, IE6

Read-only property. Returns the last element that the cursor hovered over before triggering the event.

Syntax:

```
window.event.fromElement
```

Example:

```
<html><head><script>
function alertMe() {alert(event.fromElement.innerText);}
</script></head>
<body><table border="1">
<table>
<tr><td onmouseover="alertMe();">CELL 1</td></tr>
<tr><td onmouseover="alertMe();">CELL 2</td></tr>
<tr><td onmouseover="alertMe();">CELL 3</td></tr>
</table>
</body></html>
```

Applies to:

```
event
```

galleryImg

Compatibility: IE6

Read and write property. Specifies whether or not the My Pictures toolbar is visible when the cursor hovers over the image. Values: yes or true (the default; toolbar is enabled), no or false (toolbar is not enabled).

Syntax:

```
document.all.imgID.galleryImg = value
```

Example:

```
<script>
function B1() {document.all.myImage.galleryImg = "yes";}
</script>
<input type="Button" id="b1" value='Turn Galleryimg "on"' onClick="B1();">
<img id="myImage" src="yourimage.jpg" alt="" width="74" height="99">
```

Applies to:

```
<img>
```

hash

Compatibility: NN4, NN6, NN7, IE4, IE5, IE5.5, IE6

Read and write property. Specifies the hash part of the element's URL (the part that follows a # sign).

Syntax:

```
document.getElementById("elementID").hash = value
document.all.elementID.hash = value // IE only
location.hash = value
```

Example:

```
<script language="JavaScript">
function B1() {alert(document.getElementById("myA").hash);}
</script>
<a tabindex="2" id="myA" href="test.htm#sty" target="_blank">
anchor element</a>
<button onclick="B1();">Hash Value</button>
```

Applies to:

```
<a>, <area>, location
```

hasLayout

Compatibility: IE5.5, IE6

Read-only property. Indicates whether or not the element has layout. In order for an object to have layout, all of the following properties must have a value (either a default value or a value explicitly declared): display, height, float, position, width, writing-mode, and zoom. Values: true or false (the default).

Syntax:

```
document.all.elementID.currentStyle.hasLayout
```

Example:

```
<div id="myDiv" style="width:500; height:200; background-color:red;">
<button onclick="alert(document.all.myDiv.currentStyle.hasLayout);">Haslayout
</button>
```

Applies to:

```
<a>, <acronym>, <address>, <applet>, <b>, <bdo>, <big>, <blockquote>, <body>,
<button>, <caption>, <center>, <cite>, <code>, currentStyle, <custom>, <dd>, <del>,
<dfn>, <dir>, <div>, <dl>, <dt>, <em>, <embed>, <fieldset>, <font>, <form>, <hn>,
<i>, <img>, <input type="hidden">, <input type="image">, <input type="password">,
<input type="radio">, <input type="reset">, <input type="submit">, <input
type="text">, <ins>, <isindex>, <kbd>, <label>, <legend>, <li>, <listing>,
<marquee>, <menu>, <nobr>, <object>, <ol>, <option>, <p>, <plaintext>, <pre>, <q>,
<s>, <samp>, <select>, <small>, <span>, <strike>, <strong>, <sub>, <sup>, <table>,
<td>, <textarea>, <th>, <tt>, <u>, <ul>, <var>, <xmp>
```

headers

Compatibility: NN6, NN7, IE6

Read and write property. Specifies a list of space-separated header cell identifiers. This property is useful for browsers that provide nonvisual means of rendering content, like speech or Braille.

Syntax:

```
document.getElementById("elementID").headers = value
document.all.elementID.headers = value // IE only
```

Example:

```
<script>
function B1() {
document.getElementById("td1").headers = "hdr1";
document.getElementById("td2").headers = "hdr2";
document.getElementById("td3").headers = "hdr3";
}
</script>
<table width="450" border="3" cellspacing="5" cellpadding="10"
bordercolor="#FF0000">
<tr>
```

```
<th id="hdr1">Item Number</th>
<th id="hdr2">Item Name</th>
<th id="hdr3">Item Description</th>
</tr>
<tr>
<td id="td1">28030</td>
<td id="td2">CD-ROM</td>
<td id="td3">Tutorial</td>
</tr>
</table>
<input type="Button" id="b1" value='Turn Headers "on"' onClick="B1();">
```

Applies to:

`<td>`, `<th>`

height (1)

Compatibility: NN4, NN6, NN7, IE4, IE5, IE5.5, IE6

Read and write property. Establishes the height of the element. Value: An integer (specifying the height in pixels) or integer% (a string specifying a percentage of the parent element height).

Syntax:

```
document.getElementById("elementID").height = value
document.all.elementID.height = value // IE only
```

Example:

```
<script>
function B1() {document.all.myImage.height = "150";}
</script>
<img id="myImage" src="yourimage.jpg" alt="">
<button onclick="B1();">Change Height to 150</button>
```

Applies to:

`<applet>`, `<embed>`, `<frame>`, `<iframe>`, `<img>`, `<marquee>`, `<nobr>`, `<object>`, `<table>`, `<td>`, `<th>`, `<tr>`

height (2)

Compatibility: NN4, NN6, NN7, IE4, IE5, IE5.5, IE6

Read-only property. Returns the height of the object in pixels.

Syntax:

```
objectName.height
```

Example:

```
<button onclick="alert(screen.height);">Screen Height</button>
```

Applies to:

```
document (NN6 and NN7 only), event (NN6 and NN7 only), screen
```

hidden

Compatibility: IE4, IE5, IE5.5, IE6

Read and write property. Establishes whether or not the <embed> element is visible.
Values: true or false (the default).
 Syntax:

```
document.all.embedID.hidden = value
```

Example:

```
<embed id="myE" src="yourswf.swf" width="150" height="150"></embed>
<script language="JavaScript">
function B1() {document.all.myE.hidden = true;}
</script>
<input type="Button" value='Make it hidden' onClick="B1();">
```

Applies to:

```
<embed>
```

hideFocus

Compatibility: IE5.5, IE6

Read and write property. A dotted rectangle is usually displayed around an
element when it has focus. This property specifies whether or not to hide that
rectangle. Values: true or false (the default).
 Syntax:

```
document.all.elementID.hideFocus = value
```

Example:

```
<script>
function hFocus() {
document.all.myA.hideFocus = "true";
alert("The A element lost focus.\nPress tab key to verify");}
</script>
<a tabindex="2" id="myA" href="http://www.advocar.com">Advocar home page</a>
<button onclick="hFocus();">Hide Focus</button>
```

Applies to:

<a>, <acronym>, <address>, <applet>, <area>, <b>, <bdo>, <big>, <blockquote>, <body>, <button>, <caption>, <center>, <cite>, <custom>, <dd>, <dfn>, <dir>, <div>, <dl>, <dt>, <em>, <embed>, <fieldset>, <font>, <form>, <frame>, <frameset>, <hn>, <hr>, <i>, <iframe>, <img>, <input type="button">, <input type="checkbox">, <input type="file">, <input type="hidden">, <input type="image">, <input type="password">, <input type="radio">, <input type="reset">, <input type="submit">, <input type="text">, <ins>, <isindex>, <kbd>, <label>, <legend>, <li>, <listing>, <marquee>, <menu>, <object>, <ol>, <p>, <plaintext>, <pre>, <q>, <rt>, <ruby>, <s>, <samp>, <select>, <small>, <span>, <strike>, <strong>, <sub>, <sup>, <table>, <tbody>, <td>, <textarea>, <tfoot>, <th>, <thead>, <tr>, <tt>, <u>, <ul>, <var>, <xmp>

host

Compatibility: NN4, NN6, NN7, IE4, IE5, IE5.5, IE6

Read and write property. Specifies the domain name and port number of the URL.

Syntax:

```
document.getElementById("elementID").host = value
document.all.elementID.host = value // IE only
location.host = value
```

Example:

```
<script language="JavaScript">
function B1() {alert(document.getElementById("myA").host);}
</script>
<a id="myA" href="http://www.advocar.com" target="_blank">Advocar Home Page</a>
<button onclick="B1();">Host Value</button>
<button onclick="alert(document.all.myA.hostname);">Host Name</button>
```

Applies to:

<a>, <area>, location

hostname

Compatibility: NN4, NN6, NN7, IE4, IE5, IE5.5, IE6

Read and write property. Specifies the domain name of the URL.
Syntax:

```
document.getElementById("elementID").hostname = value
document.all.elementID.hostname = value // IE only
location.hostname = value
```

Example: See the host property example.

Applies to:

`<a>`, `<area>`, location

href

Compatibility: NN4, NN6, NN7, IE4, IE5, IE5.5, IE6

Read and write property. For the `<a>`, `<area>`, and `<link>` elements, this property specifies the anchor point of the URL. For the `<base>` element, it establishes a default URL upon which all relative links will be based. For the location object, it specifies the entire URL. For the styleSheet object, it specifies the URL of the linked style sheet.

Syntax:

```
document.getElementById("elementID").href = value
document.all.elementID.href = value // IE only
```

Example:

```
<html><head>
<base id="myBase">
<script language="JavaScript">
function B1() {document.all.myBase.href= "http://www.advocar.com";}
</script>
<link rel="stylesheet" type="text/css" href="/stylesheets/advocar_a.css">
</head>
<body bgcolor="#FFFFFF" text="#000000">
Clicking this <a id="myAnchor" href="/home.asp" hreflang="en">Advocar site</a> link
will not work until you set the base.href property by clicking the "Change the base
URL" button<br><br>
<button onclick="B1();">Change the base URL</button>
<button onclick="alert(myAnchor.href);">Anchor</button>
<button onclick="alert(location.href);">Location</button>
<button onclick="alert(document.styleSheets(0).href);">style sheet</button>
<button onclick="alert(myAnchor.hreflang);">Language</button>
</body></html>
```

Applies to:

`<a>`, `<area>`, `<base>`, `<link>`, location, styleSheet

hreflang

Compatibility: NN6, NN7, IE6

Read and write property. Advises the browser about the written language code of the element's href destination.

Syntax:

```
document.getElementById("elementID").hreflang = value
document.all.elementID.hreflang = value // IE only
```

Example: See the href property example.
Applies to:

```
<a>, <link>
```

hspace

Compatibility: NN4, NN6, NN7, IE4, IE5, IE5.5, IE6

Read and write property. Establishes the number of pixels of space on the left and right sides of the element.

Syntax:

```
document.getElementById("elementID").hspace = value
document.all.elementID.hspace = value // IE only
```

Example:

```
<script language="JavaScript">
function B1() {
if (document.all.myButton.value == "Allow an hspace of 200px and vspace of 10px") {
document.getElementById("myImg").hspace = 200;
document.getElementById("myImg").vspace = 10;
document.all.myButton.value = "Restore";
} else {
document.getElementById("myImg").hspace = 0;
document.getElementById("myImg").vspace = 0;
document.all.myButton.value = "Allow an hspace of 200px and vspace of 10px";
}}
</script>
<img id="myImg" src="yourimage.jpg" alt="" width="99" height="64">
<input id="myButton" type="button" value="Allow an hspace of 200px and vspace of
10px" onclick="B1();">
```

Applies to:

```
<applet> (not NN4), <iframe>, <img>, <input>, <input type="image">, <marquee>,
<object> (not NN4)
```

htmlFor

Compatibility: NN6, NN7, IE4, IE5, IE5.5, IE6

Read and write property. Specifies the id of the element to which a particular <label> or <script> element is assigned. This property is equivalent to the for attribute. When using this property with the <script> element, you must also specify the event property for the <script>.

Syntax:

```
document.getElementById("labelID").htmlFor = value
document.all.labelID.htmlFor = value // IE only
```

Example:

```
<script language="JavaScript">
function goFocus() {alert(document.all.myL.htmlFor);}
</script>
<script id="myScript" for="myButton2" event="onclick">
alert(myScript.htmlFor);</script>
<p><label id="myL" for="myButton"></label></p>
<button id="myButton" onclick="goFocus();">HTML for Label</button>
<button id="myButton2">HTML for Script</button>
```

Applies to:

<label>, <script>

htmlText

Compatibility: IE4, IE5, IE5.5, IE6

Read-only property. Returns the HTML content of the object.

Syntax:

```
textRangeName.htmlText
```

Example:

```
<html><head>
<script language="JScript">
function me() {
var b = document.all.tags("input");
alert(b[0].createTextRange().htmlText);}
</script></head>
<body topmargin="50" leftmargin="100" bgcolor="#FFFFFF">
<input type="button" value="Click here" onclick="me();">
</body></html>
```

Applies to:

TextRange

Compatibility: NN6, NN7, IE4, IE5, IE5.5, IE6

Read and write property. Specifies the binding of <meta> content to an HTTP response header. Controls the action of browsers and may be used to refine the information provided by the actual headers. See the http-equiv attribute values in the <meta> tag description in Chapter 5 for more information.

Syntax:

```
document.getElementById("metaID").httpEquiv = value
document.all.metaID.httpEquiv = value // IE only
```

Example:

```
<html><meta id="myM">
<head>
<script language="JavaScript">
function b1() {
  document.all.myM.httpEquiv = "refresh";
  document.all.myM.content = 3;
}
</script></head>
<body bgcolor="#FFFFFF" text="#000000">
<input type="button" value="Refresh this page every 3 seconds." onClick="b1();">
</body></html>
```

Applies to:

```
<meta>
```

id

Compatibility: NN4, NN6, NN7, IE4, IE5, IE5.5, IE6

Read and write property. Specifies the identifier of the element.

Syntax:

```
document.getElementById("elementID").id = value
document.all.elementID.id = value // IE only
```

Example:

```
<script language="JavaScript">
function getID(elem) {
  var id = elem.id;
  alert("This element's id attribute is set to \"" + id + "\".");
}
</script>
```

```
<p>Click in the following image to display the id attribute's value.</p>
<img id="myImg" src="yourimage.jpg" alt="" width="99" height="78"
onclick="getID(this);">
```

Applies to:

`<a>`, `<acronym>`, `<address>`, `<applet>`, `<area>`, `<b>`, `<base>`, `<basefont>`, `<bdo>`, `<bgsound>`, `<big>`, `<blockquote>`, `<body>`, `<br>`, `<button>`, `<caption>`, `<center>`, `<cite>`, `<code>`, `<col>`, `<colgroup>`, `<comment>`, `<custom>`, `<dd>`, `<del>`, `<dfn>`, `<dir>`, `<div>`, `<dl>`, `<dt>`, `<em>`, `<embed>`, `<fieldset>`, `<font>`, `<form>`, `<frame>`, `<frameset>`, `<head>`, `<hn>`, `<hr>`, `<html>`, `<i>`, `<iframe>`, `<img>`, `<input type="button">`, `<input type="checkbox">`, `<input type="file">`, `<input type="hidden">`, `<input type="image">`, `<input type="password">`, `<input type="radio">`, `<input type="reset">`, `<input type="submit">`, `<input type="text">`, `<ins>`, `<isindex>`, `<kbd>`, `<label>`, `<legend>`, `<li>`, `<link>`, `<listing>`, `<map>`, `<marquee>`, `<menu>`, `<nobr>`, `<noframes>`, `<noscript>`, `<object>`, `<ol>`, `<optgroup>`, `<option>`, `<p>`, `<param>`, `<plaintext>`, `<pre>`, `<q>`, `<rt>`, `<ruby>`, `<s>`, `<samp>`, `<script>`, `<select>`, `<small>`, `<span>`, `<strike>`, `<strong>`, `<style>`, styleSheet, `<sub>`, `<sup>`, `<table>`, `<tbody>`, `<td>`, `<textarea>`, `<tfoot>`, `<th>`, `<thead>`, `<title>`, `<tr>`, `<tt>`, `<u>`, `<ul>`, `<var>`, `<wbr>`, `<xml>`, `<xmp>`

indeterminate

Compatibility: IE4, IE5, IE5.5, IE6

Read and write property. Specifies whether or not the state of a checkbox is dimmed. Values: true or false (the default).

Syntax:

```
document.all.checkboxID.indeterminate = value
```

Example:

```
<input type="checkbox" id="myC1" value="checkbox" checked>
Indeterminate = true.
<input type="button" value="Checkbox state" onClick="b1();">
<script language="JavaScript">
document.all.myC1.indeterminate = true;
function b1() {
  var m = document.all.myC1.indeterminate;
  alert("Indeterminate: "+m);
}
</script>
```

Applies to:

`<input type="checkbox">`

index

Compatibility: NN6, NN7, IE4, IE5, IE5.5, IE6

Read and write property. Specifies the index number of an `<option>` element in a `<select>` list box.

Syntax:

```
document.getElementById("optionID").index = value
document.all.optionID.index = value // IE only
```

Example:

```
<select id="myS" size=5>
    <option id="o1">Washington</option>
    <option id="o2">London</option>
    <option id="o3">Madrid</option>
    <option id="o4">Roma</option>
    <option id="o5">Lisbon</option>
</select>
<input type="button" value="Washington" onClick="b1(o1);">
<input type="button" value="London" onClick="b1(o2);">
<input type="button" value="Madrid" onClick="b1(o3);">
<input type="button" value="Roma" onClick="b1(o4);">
<input type="button" value="Lisbon" onClick="b1(o5);">
<script language="JavaScript">
function b1(elem) {alert("Index: "+ elem.index);}
</script>
```

Applies to:

```
<option>
```

innerHTML

Compatibility: NN6, NN7, IE4, IE5, IE5.5, IE6

Read and write property. Specifies the HTML between the opening and closing tags of an element.

Syntax:

```
document.getElementById("elementID").innerHTML = value
document.all.elementID.innerHTML = value // IE only
```

Example:

```
<p id="myP">Sample Text inside a <b>p</b> element</p>
<button onclick="alert(myP.innerHTML);">InnerHTML</button>
<button onclick="alert(myP.innerText);">InnerText</button>
```

Applies to:

```
<a>, <acronym>, <address>, <applet>, <area>, <b>, <base>, <basefont>, <bdo>, <big>,
<blockquote>, <body>, <br>, <button>, <caption>, <center>, <cite>, <code>, <col>,
```

```
<colgroup>, <custom>, <dd>, <del>, <dfn>, <dir>, <div>, <dl>, <dt>, <em>,
<fieldset>, <font>, <form>, <frame>, <frameset>, <head>, <hn>, <hr>, <html>, <i>,
<iframe>, <img>, <ins>, <isindex>, <kbd>, <label>, <legend>, <li>, <link>,
<listing>, <map>, <marquee>, <menu>, <meta>, <nobr>, <noframes>, <noscript>,
<object>, <ol>, <optgroup>, <option>, <p>, <param>, <pre>, <q>, <rt>, <ruby>, <s>,
<samp>, <script>, <select>, <small>, <span>, <strike>, <strong>, <style>, <sub>,
<sup>, <table>, <tbody>, <td>, <textarea>, <tfoot>, <th>, <thead>, <title>, <tr>,
<tt>, <u>, <ul>, <var>
```

innerText

Compatibility: IE4, IE5, IE5.5, IE6

Read and write property. Specifies the text between the opening and closing tags
of an element.

Syntax:

```
document.all.elementID.innerText = value
```

Example: See the innerHTML property example.

Applies to:

```
<a>, <acronym>, <address>, <b>, <bdo>, <big>, <blockquote>, <body>, <button>,
<caption>, <center>, <cite>, <code>, <custom>, <dd>, <del>, <dfn>, <dir>, <div>,
<em>, <fieldset>, <font>, <form>, <hn>, <html>, <i>, <iframe>, <ins>, <kbd>,
<label>, <legend>, <li>, <listing>, <map>, <marquee>, <menu>, <nobr>, <ol>,
<option>, <p>, <plaintext>, <pre>, <q>, <rt>, <ruby>, <s>, <samp>, <script>,
<select>, <small>, <span>, <strike>, <strong>, <sub>, <sup>, <table>, <tbody>, <td>,
<textarea>, <tfoot>, <th>, <thead>, <title>, <tr>, <tt>, <u>, <ul>, <var>, <xmp>
```

isContentEditable

Compatibility: IE5.5, IE6

Read-only property. Indicates whether or not the content of an element can be
edited by the user. Values: true or false.

Syntax:

```
document.all.elementID.isContentEditable
```

Example: See the contentEditable property example.

Applies to:

```
<a>, <acronym>, <address>, <applet>, <area>, <b>, <base>, <basefont>, <bdo>,
<bgsound>, <big>, <blockquote>, <body>, <br>, <button>, <caption>, <center>,
<cite>, <code>, <col>, <colgroup>, <comment>, <custom>, <dd>, <del>, <dfn>, <dir>,
<div>, <dl>, <dt>, <em>, <embed>, <fieldset>, <font>, <form>, <frame>, <frameset>,
<head>, <hn>, <hr>, <html>, <i>, <iframe>, <img>, <input type="button">, <input
type="checkbox">, <input type="file">, <input type="hidden">, <input type="image">,
<input type="password">, <input type="radio">, <input type="reset">, <input
type="submit">, <input type="text">, <ins>, <isindex>, <kbd>, <label>, <legend>,
<li>, <link>, <listing>, <map>, <marquee>, <menu>, <nobr>, <noframes>, <noscript>,
```

`<object>`, `<ol>`, `<option>`, `<p>`, `<pre>`, `<q>`, `<rt>`, `<ruby>`, `<s>`, `<samp>`, `<script>`, `<select>`, `<small>`, `<span>`, `<strike>`, `<strong>`, styleSheet, `<sub>`, `<sup>`, `<table>`, `<tbody>`, `<td>`, `<textarea>`, `<tfoot>`, `<th>`, `<thead>`, `<title>`, `<tr>`, `<tt>`, `<u>`, `<ul>`, `<var>`, `<wbr>`, `<xml>`, `<xmp>`

isDisabled

Compatibility: IE5.5, IE6

Read-only property. Indicates whether or not the element is disabled. Values: true or false.

Syntax:

```
document.all.elementID.isDisabled
```

Example:

```
<button onclick="this.disabled='true'; alert(this.isDisabled);">Disable Me</button>
```

Applies to:

`<a>`, `<acronym>`, `<address>`, `<applet>`, `<area>`, `<b>`, `<base>`, `<basefont>`, `<bdo>`, `<bgsound>`, `<big>`, `<blockquote>`, `<body>`, `<br>`, `<button>`, `<caption>`, `<center>`, `<cite>`, `<code>`, `<col>`, `<colgroup>`, `<comment>`, `<custom>`, `<dd>`, `<del>`, `<dfn>`, `<dir>`, `<div>`, `<dl>`, `<dt>`, `<em>`, `<embed>`, `<fieldset>`, `<font>`, `<form>`, `<frame>`, `<frameset>`, `<head>`, `<hn>`, `<hr>`, `<html>`, `<i>`, `<iframe>`, `<img>`, `<input type="button">`, `<input type="checkbox">`, `<input type="file">`, `<input type="hidden">`, `<input type="image">`, `<input type="password">`, `<input type="radio">`, `<input type="reset">`, `<input type="submit">`, `<input type="text">`, `<ins>`, `<isindex>`, `<kbd>`, `<label>`, `<legend>`, `<li>`, `<link>`, `<listing>`, `<map>`, `<marquee>`, `<menu>`, `<nobr>`, `<noframes>`, `<noscript>`, `<object>`, `<ol>`, `<option>`, `<p>`, `<plaintext>`, `<pre>`, `<q>`, `<rt>`, `<ruby>`, `<s>`, `<samp>`, `<script>`, `<select>`, `<small>`, `<span>`, `<strike>`, `<strong>`, styleSheet, `<sub>`, `<sup>`, `<table>`, `<tbody>`, `<td>`, `<textarea>`, `<tfoot>`, `<th>`, `<thead>`, `<title>`, `<tr>`, `<tt>`, `<u>`, `<ul>`, `<var>`, `<wbr>`, `<xml>`, `<xmp>`

isMap

Compatibility: NN4, NN6, NN7, IE4, IE5, IE5.5, IE6

Read and write property. Specifies whether or not the image should act as a server-side map. Values: true or false.

Syntax:

```
document.getElementById("imgID").isMap = value
document.all.imgID.isMap = value // IE only
```

Example: See the coords property example.
Applies to:

`<img>`

isMultiline

Compatibility: IE5.5, IE6

Read-only property. Indicates whether or not the element can display more than one line of text. Values: true or false.

Syntax:

```
document.all.elementID.isMultiline
```

Example:

```
<textarea id="myText" cols="200" rows="20"></textarea>
<button onclick="alert(myText.isMultiLine);">Is Textarea Multiline</button>
```

Applies to:

```
<a>, <acronym>, <address>, <applet>, <area>, <b>, <base>, <basefont>, <bdo>,
<bgsound>, <big>, <blockquote>, <body>, <br>, <button>, <caption>, <center>,
<cite>, <code>, <col>, <colgroup>, <comment>, <custom>, <dd>, defaults, <del>,
<dfn>, <dir>, <div>, <dl>, <dt>, <em>, <embed>, <fieldset>, <font>, <form>,
<frame>, <frameset>, <head>, <hn>, <hr>, <html>, <i>, <iframe>, <img>, <input
type="button">, <input type="checkbox">, <input type="file">, <input
type="hidden">, <input type="image">, <input type="password">, <input
type="radio">, <input type="reset">, <input type="submit">, <input type="text">,
<ins>, <isindex>, <kbd>, <label>, <legend>, <li>, <link>, <listing>, <map>,
<marquee>, <menu>, <nobr>, <noframes>, <noscript>, <object>, <ol>, <option>, <p>,
<plaintext>, <pre>, <q>, <rt>, <ruby>, <s>, <samp>, <script>, <select>, <small>,
<span>, <strike>, <strong>, styleSheet, <sub>, <sup>, <table>, <tbody>, <td>,
<textarea>, <tfoot>, <th>, <thead>, <title>, <tr>, <tt>, <u>, <ul>, <var>, <wbr>,
<xml>, <xmp>
```

isOpen

Compatibility: IE5.5, IE6

Read-only property. Indicates whether or not a pop-up window is open. Values: true or false. The pop-up window must be visible in order to return a true value.

Syntax:

```
popup.isOpen
```

Example:

```
<script language="JavaScript">
function B1() {
var m = window.createPopup();
var n = m.document.body;
n.style.border="solid 2px black";
n.innerHTML = "<font face='verdana'>This is the pop-up window content</font>";
m.show(350, 270, 200, 50, document.body);
```

```
if (m.isOpen == true) {setTimeout("C1()", 2000);}
}
function C1() {alert("The pop-up window is Open");}
</script>
<input type="button" value="Open pop-up window" onclick="B1();">
```

Applies to:

popup

isTextEdit

Compatibility: IE4, IE5, IE5.5, IE6

Read-only property. Indicates whether or not the element allows a TextRange object to be created to modify its content. Values: true or false.

Syntax:

```
document.all.elementID.isTextEdit
```

Example:

```
<script language="JavaScript">
function B1(elem) {elem ? alert("Yes") : alert("No");}
</script>
<input type="text" id="myInput" value="Input element">
<textarea id="myTxtArea">Textarea element</textarea>
<p id="myP">P element</p><br>
<button onclick="B1(myInput.isTextEdit);">Input</button>
<button onclick="B1(myTxtArea.isTextEdit);">TextArea</button>
<button onclick="B1(myP.isTextEdit);">Paragraph</button>
```

Applies to:

`<a>`, `<acronym>`, `<address>`, `<applet>`, `<area>`, `<b>`, `<base>`, `<basefont>`, `<bdo>`, `<big>`, `<blockquote>`, `<body>`, `<br>`, `<button>`, `<caption>`, `<center>`, `<cite>`, `<code>`, `<col>`, `<colgroup>`, `<comment>`, `<custom>`, `<dd>`, `<del>`, `<dfn>`, `<dir>`, `<div>`, `<dl>`, `<dt>`, `<em>`, `<embed>`, `<fieldset>`, `<font>`, `<form>`, `<frame>`, `<frameset>`, `<head>`, `<hn>`, `<hr>`, `<html>`, `<i>`, `<iframe>`, `<img>`, `<input type="button">`, `<input type="checkbox">`, `<input type="file">`, `<input type="hidden">`, `<input type="image">`, `<input type="password">`, `<input type="radio">`, `<input type="reset">`, `<input type="submit">`, `<input type="text">`, `<ins>`, `<kbd>`, `<label>`, `<legend>`, `<li>`, `<link>`, `<listing>`, `<map>`, `<marquee>`, `<menu>`, `<meta>`, `<nobr>`, `<object>`, `<ol>`, `<option>`, `<p>`, `<plaintext>`, `<pre>`, `<q>`, `<s>`, `<samp>`, `<script>`, `<select>`, `<small>`, `<span>`, `<strike>`, `<strong>`, `<sub>`, `<sup>`, `<table>`, `<tbody>`, `<td>`, `<textarea>`, `<tfoot>`, `<th>`, `<thead>`, `<title>`, `<tr>`, `<tt>`, `<u>`, `<ul>`, `<var>`, `<xmp>`

keyCode

Compatibility: IE4, IE5, IE5.5, IE6

Read-only property. Returns the key code number of the keyboard key pressed. The property is used with the onKeyDown, onKeyUp, and onKeyPress events.

With the onKeyPress event, the return value is in Unicode. This code distinguishes between uppercase and lowercase characters. With the onKeyDown and onKeyUp events, the return value code is a character code. This means the value is the same whether the character is in uppercase or in lowercase.

Syntax:

```
window.event.keyCode
```

Example:

```
<script language="JavaScript">
function B1() {x = event.keyCode; alert("Unicode Value: "+x);}
function B2() {x = event.keyCode; alert("Keyboard Value: "+x);}
</script>
<p>Press Any Key While The Browser is in Focus</p>
<body onKeyDown="B2();" onKeyPress="B1();"></body>
```

Applies to:

```
event
```

label

Compatibility: NN6, NN7, IE6

Read and write property. For the <optgroup> element, it establishes the label that helps group list items in a <select> element. For the <option> element, this property is simply used to record additional information regarding the element.

Syntax:

```
document.getElementById("elementID").label = value
document.all.elementID.label = value // IE only
```

Example:

```
<form name="form2" method="post" action="">
<select name="select1">
<optgroup id="optg1">
    <option id="opt1_1">first item in first group </option>
    <option>second item in first group </option>
    <option>third item in first group </option>
</optgroup>
<optgroup id="optg2">
    <option>first item in second group </option>
    <option id="opt2_2">second item in second group </option>
    <option>third item in second group </option>
</optgroup>
```

```
<script language="JavaScript">
document.getElementById("optg1").label = "first group";
document.getElementById("optg2").label = "second group";
</script>
</select>
</form>
```

Applies to:

`<option>`

lang

Compatibility: NN4, NN6, NN7, IE4, IE5, IE5.5, IE6

Read and write property. Establishes the written language to use with the element's text. Do not confuse the lang property with the language property.

Syntax:

```
document.getElementById("elementID").lang = value
document.all.elementID.lang = value // IE only
```

Example:

```
<p id="myPfr">Celui-ci est un nombre &eacute;crit en fran&ccedil;ais: 0,52</p>
<script language="JavaScript">
document.getElementById("myPfr").lang = "fr";
</script>
```

Applies to:

`<a>`, `<acronym>`, `<address>`, `<applet>`, `<area>`, `<b>`, `<base>`, `<basefont>`, `<bdo>`, `<big>`, `<blockquote>`, `<body>`, `<br>`, `<button>`, `<caption>`, `<center>`, `<cite>`, `<code>`, `<col>`, `<colgroup>`, `<comment>`, `<custom>`, `<dd>`, `<del>`, `<dfn>`, `<dir>`, `<div>`, `<dl>`, `<dt>`, `<em>`, `<embed>`, `<fieldset>`, `<font>`, `<form>`, `<frame>`, `<frameset>`, `<head>`, `<hn>`, `<hr>`, `<html>`, `<i>`, `<iframe>`, `<img>`, `<input type="button">`, `<input type="checkbox">`, `<input type="file">`, `<input type="hidden">`, `<input type="image">`, `<input type="password">`, `<input type="radio">`, `<input type="reset">`, `<input type="submit">`, `<input type="text">`, `<ins>`, `<isindex>`, `<kbd>`, `<label>`, `<legend>`, `<li>`, `<link>`, `<listing>`, `<map>`, `<marquee>`, `<menu>`, `<meta>`, `<nobr>`, `<noframes>`, `<noscript>`, `<object>`, `<ol>`, `<optgroup>`, `<option>`, `<p>`, `<param>`, `<plaintext>`, `<pre>`, `<q>`, `<rt>`, `<ruby>`, `<s>`, `<samp>`, `<script>`, `<select>`, `<small>`, `<span>`, `<strike>`, `<strong>`, `<style>`, `<sub>`, `<sup>`, `<table>`, `<tbody>`, `<td>`, `<textarea>`, `<tfoot>`, `<th>`, `<thead>`, `<title>`, `<tr>`, `<tt>`, `<u>`, `<ul>`, `<var>`, `<xmp>`

language (1)

Compatibility: IE4, IE5, IE5.5, IE6

Read and write property. Establishes the scripting language for the inline script or `<script>` element. Values: JScript, javascript, vbs, vbscript, or XML.

Syntax:

---

document.all.*elementID*.language = *value*

Example:

```
<script id="myS" language="JavaScript">
function A1() {alert(document.all.myS.language);}
</script>
<input type="button" value="Scripting Language" onClick="A1();">
```

Applies to:

```
<a>, <acronym>, <address>, <applet>, <area>, <b>, <bdo>, <big>, <blockquote>,
<body>, <button>, <caption>, <center>, <cite>, <code>, <custom>, <dd>, <del>,
<dfn>, <dir>, <div>, <dl>, <dt>, <em>, <embed>, <fieldset>, <font>, <form>,
<frame>, <frameset>, <hn>, <hr>, <i>, <iframe>, <img>, <input type="button">,
<input type="checkbox">, <input type="file">, <input type="hidden">, <input
type="image">, <input type="password">, <input type="radio">, <input type="reset">,
<input type="submit">, <input type="text">, <ins>, <isindex>, <kbd>, <label>,
<legend>, <li>, <listing>, <map>, <marquee>, <nobr>, <object>, <ol>, <option>, <p>,
<plaintext>, <pre>, <q>, <rt>, <ruby>, <s>, <samp>, <script>, <select>, <small>,
<span>, <strike>, <strong>, <sub>, <sup>, <table>, <tbody>, <td>, <textarea>,
<tfoot>, <th>, <thead>, <tr>, <tt>, <u>, <ul>, <var>, <xmp>
```

---

language (2)

Compatibility: NN6, NN7

Read-only property. Returns the system's default language.

Syntax:

---

objectName.language

Example:

```
<button onclick="alert(navigator.language);">Language</button>
```

Applies to:

---

navigator

---

lastChild

Compatibility: NN6, NN7, IE5, IE5.5, IE6

Read-only property. Returns the last child in the `childNodes` collection of the parent element.

Syntax:

```
document.getElementById("elementID").lastChild
document.all.elementID.lastChild // IE only
```

Example: See the firstChild property example.
Applies to:

`<a>`, `<acronym>`, `<address>`, `<applet>`, `<area>`, attribute, `<b>`, `<base>`, `<basefont>`, `<bdo>`, `<big>`, `<blockquote>`, `<body>`, `<br>`, `<button>`, `<caption>`, `<center>`, `<cite>`, `<code>`, `<col>`, `<colgroup>`, `<comment>`, `<dd>`, `<del>`, `<dfn>`, `<dir>`, `<div>`, `<dl>`, `<dt>`, `<em>`, `<embed>`, `<fieldset>`, `<font>`, `<form>`, `<frame>`, `<frameset>`, `<head>`, `<hn>`, `<hr>`, `<html>`, `<i>`, `<iframe>`, `<img>`, `<input type="button">`, `<input type="checkbox">`, `<input type="file">`, `<input type="image">`, `<input type="password">`, `<input type="radio">`, `<input type="reset">`, `<input type="submit">`, `<input type="text">`, `<ins>`, `<isindex>`, `<kbd>`, `<label>`, `<legend>`, `<li>`, `<link>`, `<listing>`, `<map>`, `<marquee>`, `<menu>`, `<meta>`, `<noframes>`, `<noscript>`, `<object>`, `<ol>`, `<optgroup>`, `<option>`, `<p>`, `<param>`, `<plaintext>`, `<pre>`, `<q>`, `<s>`, `<samp>`, `<script>`, `<select>`, `<small>`, `<span>`, `<strike>`, `<strong>`, `<style>`, `<sub>`, `<sup>`, `<table>`, `<tbody>`, `<td>`, `<textarea>`, `<tfoot>`, `<th>`, `<thead>`, `<title>`, `<tr>`, `<tt>`, `<u>`, `<ul>`, `<var>`, `<xmp>`

lastModified

Compatibility: NN4, NN6, NN7, IE4, IE5, IE5.5, IE6

Read-only property. Returns the last-modified date of the document. This property is very similar to the fileUpdatedDate property, differing only in the objects to which they apply.
Syntax:

```
document.lastModified
```

Example: See the fileCreatedDate property example.
Applies to:

document

layerX

Compatibility: NN6, NN7

Read-only property. Establishes either the X coordinate of the cursor's position in pixels or the width of the object that triggered the onResize event.
Syntax:

```
window.event.layerX
eventName.layerX
```

Example:

```
<script>
function B1(myEvent) {
```

```
        document.getElementById("myX").innerHTML = myEvent.layerX;
        document.getElementById("myY").innerHTML = myEvent.layerY;
}
document.onmousemove = B1;
</script>
<p><b>Layer X Coordinate:</b> <span id="myX">0</span></p>
<p><b>Layer Y Coordinate:</b> <span id="myY">0</span></p>
<button onclick="alert(event.type);">Event Type</button>
```

Applies to:

event

layerY

Compatibility: NN6, NN7

Read-only property. Establishes either the Y coordinate of the cursor's position in pixels, or the height of the object that triggered the onResize event.

Syntax:

```
event.layerY
eventName.layerY
```

Example: See the layerX property example.
Applies to:

event

left

Compatibility: IE5, IE5.5, IE6

Read and write property. Specifies the left coordinate of the container rectangle of the element.

Syntax:

```
textRectangleName.left = value
```

Example: See the bottom property example.
Applies to:

TextRectangle

leftMargin

Compatibility: IE4, IE5, IE5.5, IE6

Read and write property. Specifies the left margin in pixels of the <body> element. Default value is 10.

Syntax:

---

document.all.*bodyID*.leftMargin = *value*

Example: See the bottomMargin property example.
Applies to:

<body>

---

length (1)

Compatibility: NN4, NN6, NN7, IE4, IE5, IE5.5, IE6

Read-only property. For collections, this property specifies the number of items within a collection. For the <select> element, it returns the number of options in the select list. For the window object, it returns the number of frames in the window. For the <form> object, it returns the number of <input> elements in the form whose type attribute value is not image.

Syntax:

```
document.collectionName.length
objectName.length
document.all.elementID.length
```

Example:

```html
<html>
<body bgcolor="#FFFFFF" text="#000000">
<form name="form1" method="post" action="">
<input type="text" name="textfield">
</form>
<form name="form2" method="post" action="">
<input type="button" value="Only a sample button" onclick="return false">
</form>
<form name="form3" method="post" action="">
<input type="checkbox" name="checkbox" value="checkbox">
</form>
<button onclick="B1()">Click here</button>
<script language="JavaScript">
function B1() {
var m = document.forms.length;
alert("There are "+m+" forms in this document")
}
</script>
</body></html>
```

Applies to:

---

all*, anchors*, applets*, areas*, Array, attributes*, behaviorUrns*, boundElements*, cells*, childNodes*, children*, controlRange*, elements*, embeds*,

filters*, \<form>, forms*, frames*, images*, imports*, links*, mimeTypes*,
namespaces*, options*, pages*, plugins*, rows*, rules*, scripts*, \<select>,
styleSheets*, tBodies*, window

length (2)

Compatibility: NN4, NN6, NN7, IE4, IE5, IE5.5, IE6

Read-only property. Returns the number of stored URLs in the history object.
Syntax:

```
history.length
```

Example:

```
<button onclick="alert(window.history.length);">History Length</button>
```

Applies to:

```
history
```

length (3)

Compatibility: NN4, NN6, NN7, IE4, IE5, IE5.5, IE6

Read-only property. Returns the number of characters in the object.
Syntax:

```
stringName.length
textNodeName.length // IE only
```

Example:

```
<html><body>
<p id="myP">How many characters in this sample text?</p>
<button onclick="B1();">Click me to find out</button>
<script language="JavaScript">
function B1() {
var m = "How many characters in this sample text?".length;
alert(m);
}
</script>
</body></html>
```

Applies to:

```
<comment>, TextNode (IE5 only), String
```

link

Compatibility: NN6, NN7, IE4, IE5, IE5.5, IE6

Read and write property. Establishes the color used for `<a>` elements that appear within the `<body>` element's opening and closing tags. Value: Web color name or hexadecimal value in #RRGGBB format.

Syntax:

```
document.body.link = value
```

Example:

```
<body onload="document.body.link = 'blue';">
<script language="JavaScript">
function B1() {document.linkColor = "green";}
</script>
<a href="">Advocar Web page</a>
<input type="button" value="Change the link color to green" onClick="B1();">
</body>
```

Applies to:

```
<body>
```

linkColor

Compatibility: NN4, NN6, NN7, IE4, IE5, IE5.5, IE6

Read and write property. Establishes the color of the document's links. This property is very similar to the `link` property, but the `link` property applies to the `<body>` element, whereas this property applies to the `document` object. Value: Web color name or hexadecimal value in #RRGGBB format.

Syntax:

```
document.linkColor = value
```

Example: See the `link` property example.
Applies to:

```
document
```

LN10

Compatibility: NN4, NN6, NN7, IE4, IE5, IE5.5, IE6

Read-only property. A mathematical constant that returns the natural log for the number 10.

Syntax:

```
Math.LN10
```

Example:

```
<button onclick="alert(Math.LN2);">Math.LN2</button>
```

Applies to:

```
Math
```

LN2

Compatibility: NN4, NN6, NN7, IE4, IE5, IE5.5, IE6

Read-only property. A mathematical constant that returns the natural log for the number 2.
Syntax:

```
Math.LN2
```

Example:

```
<button onclick="alert(Math.LN10);">Math.LN10</button>
```

Applies to:

```
Math
```

LOG10E

Compatibility: NN4, NN6, NN7, IE4, IE5, IE5.5, IE6

Read-only property. A mathematical constant that returns the natural log for the E property in base-10.
Syntax:

```
Math.LOG10E
```

Example:

```
<button onclick="alert(Math.LOG10E);">Math.Log10E</button>
```

Applies to:

```
Math
```

LOG2E

Compatibility: NN4, NN6, NN7, IE4, IE5, IE5.5, IE6

Read-only property. A mathematical constant that returns the natural log for the E property in base-2.

Syntax:

```
Math.LOG2E
```

Example:

```
<button onclick="alert(Math.LOG2E);">Math.Log2E</button>
```

Applies to:

```
Math
```

logicalXDPI

Compatibility: IE6

Read-only property. Returns the horizontal dpi (dots per inch) of the screen.

Syntax:

```
screen.logicalXDPI
```

Example:

```
<script language="JavaScript">
function B1() {
var m = screen.logicalXDPI;
var n = screen.logicalYDPI;
alert("Screen XDPI =\n"+m);
alert("Screen YDPI =\n"+n);
}
</script>
<input type="button" value="Click me" onclick="B1();">
```

Applies to:

```
screen
```

logicalYDPI

Compatibility: IE6.

Read-only property. Returns the vertical dpi (dots per inch) of the screen.

Syntax:

```
screen.logicalYDPI
```

Example: See the `logicalXDPI` example.
Applies to:

```
screen
```

longDesc

Compatibility: NN6, NN7, IE6

Read and write property. Specifies the URL of a file that contains a long description of the element.
Syntax:

```
document.getElementById("elementID").longDesc = value
document.all.elementID.longDesc = value // IE only
```

Example:

```
<img id="myImg" src="yourimage.gif" longdesc="Advocar's Logo">
<button onclick="alert(myImg.longDesc);">Long Desc</button>
```

Applies to:

```
<frame>, <iframe>, <img>
```

loop

Compatibility: IE4, IE5, IE5.5, IE6

Read and write property. Specifies the number of times the object will loop. For the `<marquee>` element, a value of 0 or -1 (the default) will cause the element to loop indefinitely. For the `<bgsound>`, `<img>`, `<input>`, and `<image>` elements, a value of 0 will cause the element to loop once, and a value of -1 will cause it to loop indefinitely (the default value is 1).
Syntax:

```
document.all.elementID.loop = value
```

Example:

```
<bgsound id="myBgS" src="yourmusic.wav" loop="1">
<script language="JavaScript">
function B1() {document.all.myBgS.loop = 2;}
</script>
<input type="button" value="Set the loop value to 2" onClick="B1();">
```

Applies to:

<bgsound>, <img>, <input>, <input type="image">, <marquee>

lowsrc

Compatibility: NN4, NN6, NN7, IE4, IE5, IE5.5, IE6

Read and write property. Specifies the URL of a lower-resolution image, or some other quick-loading placeholder, to be displayed while the bigger image is loaded.

Syntax:

```
document.getElementById("elementID").lowsrc = value
document.all.elementID.lowsrc = value // IE only
```

Example:

```
<script language="JavaScript">
document.all.myLsrc.lowsrc = "yourimage.jpg";
</script>
<img id="myLsrc" src="yourlowresimage.jpg" width="99" height="76">
```

Applies to:

<img>, <input>, <input type="image">

MAX_VALUE

Compatibility: NN4, NN6, NN7, IE4, IE5, IE5.5, IE6

Read-only property. A mathematical constant that returns the largest number the system can represent that is less than infinity.

Syntax:

```
Number.MAX_VALUE
```

Example:

```
<button onclick="alert(Number.MAX_VALUE);">MAX_VALUE</button>
<button onclick="alert(Number.MIN_VALUE);">MIN_VALUE</button>
<button onclick="alert(Number.NEGATIVE_INFINITY);">NEGATIVE_INFINITY</button>
<button onclick="alert(Number.POSITIVE_INFINITY);">POSITIVE_INFINITY</button>
```

Applies to:

```
Number
```

maxLength

Compatibility: NN6, NN7, IE4, IE5, IE5.5, IE6

Read and write property. Specifies the maximum number of characters that can be typed into the text field.

Syntax:

```
document.getElementById("inputID").maxLength = value
document.all.inputID.maxLength = value // IE only
```

Example:

```
<input type="password" id="myText">
<script language="JavaScript">
document.getElementById("myText").maxLength = 10;
</script>
```

Applies to:

```
<input type="password">, <input type="text">
```

media

Compatibility: NN6, NN7, IE4, IE5, IE5.5, IE6

Read and write property. Specifies the output device for the object. Values: screen, print, or all (the default).

Syntax:

```
document.getElementById("elementID").media = value
document.all.elementID.media = value // IE only
document.styleSheets[index].media = value
```

Example:

```
<script language="JavaScript">
function B1() {document.all.myL.media = "print";}
</script>
<a id="myL" href="" onClick="return false" media="screen">Some link</a>
<input type="button" id="myB" onClick="B1();" value='Change the output media to
"print"'>
```

Applies to:

```
<link>, <style>, styleSheet
```

menuArguments

Compatibility: IE4, IE5, IE5.5, IE6

Read-only property. Returns a reference to the window object when called from a context menu.

Syntax:

```
window.external.menuArguments
```

Example:

```
<script language = "JavaScript">
var yourWindow = window.external.menuArguments;
var theDocument = yourWindow.document;
</script>
```

Applies to:

```
external
```

method

Compatibility: NN4, NN6, NN7, IE4, IE5, IE5.5, IE6

Read and write property. Specifies the mode of transferring the <form> data to the server. Values: get (appends the data to the URL; the maximum amount of data is 2,084 bytes), or post (sends the data through an HTTP post transaction; no limit on the amount of data).

Syntax:

```
document.getElementById("formID").method = value
document.all.formID.method = value // IE only
```

Example:

```
<script language=javascript>
function M1() {document.getElementById("myForm").method = "post";}
</script>
<form name="myForm" method="get" action="">
<textarea rows="3" cols="200"></textarea>
</form>
<input type="button" value='Change the mode of transferring the data to "post"'
onclick="M1();">
```

Applies to:

```
<form>
```

Methods

Compatibility: IE4, IE5, IE5.5, IE6

Read and write property. Defines a comma-separated list of the HTTP methods to use for accessing the destination document.

Syntax:

```
document.all.aID.Methods = value
```

Example:

```
<script language="JavaScript">
function B1() {document.all.myL.Methods = "post";}</script>
<a id="myL" href="http://www.microsoft.com/">Microsoft Home Page</a>
<input type="button" value='Change mode to "post"' onclick="B1();">
```

Applies to:

```
<a>
```

MIN_VALUE

Compatibility: NN4, NN6, NN7, IE4, IE5, IE5.5, IE6

Read-only property. A mathematical constant that returns the smallest number the system can represent that is greater than negative infinity.

Syntax:

```
Number.MIN_VALUE
```

Example: See the MAX_VALUE property example.
Applies to:

```
Number
```

multiple

Compatibility: NN4, NN6, NN7, IE4, IE5, IE5.5, IE6

Read and write property. Specifies whether or not multiple <option> elements can be simultaneously selected in a <select> list element. Values: true or false.

Syntax:

```
document.getElementById("selectID").multiple = value
document.all.selectID.multiple = value // IE only
```

Example:

```
Choose your Ice Creams<br>
<select name="mySelect" rows="10">
<option>Chocolate</option><option>Vanilla</option>
<option>Chocolate Chip</option>
<option>Chocolate Almonds</option>
</select>
<button onclick="mySelect.multiple=true;">Multiple</button>
<button onclick="mySelect.multiple=false;">Single</button>
```

Applies to:

`<select>`

name (1)

Compatibility: NN4, NN6, NN7, IE4, IE5, IE5.5, IE6

Read and write property. Specifies the name of the object or element.

Syntax:

```
document.getElementById("elementID").name
document.all.elementID.name // IE only
document.tags("html").xmlns.name // namespace object
window.name
```

Example:

```
<script language="JavaScript">
document.getElementById("yourAnchor").name = "par3";
</script>
<a href="#par3">Go to paragraph # 3 in this page</a>
<a id="yourAnchor"></a>
```

Applies to:

`<a>`, `<applet>`, attribute, `<button>`, `<embed>`, `<form>`, `<frame>`, `<frameset>`, `<iframe>`, `<img>`, `<input type="button">`, `<input type="checkbox">`, `<input type="file">`, `<input type="hidden">`, `<input type="image">`, `<input type="password">`, `<input type="radio">`, `<input type="reset">`, `<input type="submit">`, `<input type="text">`, `<link>`, `<map>`, `<meta>`, namespace, `<object>`, `<param>`, plugin, `<rt>`, `<ruby>`, `<select>`, `<textarea>`, window

name (2)

Compatibility: NN4, NN6, NN7, IE4, IE5, IE5.5, IE6

Read and write property. You can assign any arbitrary value to the name property of a <meta> element, but the fixed values are Description, Generator, Keywords, ProgID, Robots, and Template.

Syntax:

```
document.getElementById("metaID").name = value
document.all.metaID.name = value // IE only
```

Example:

```
<script language="JavaScript">
document.tags("head").meta.name = "Description";
</script>
```

Applies to:

```
<meta>
```

nameProp

Compatibility: IE5, IE5.5, IE6

Read-only property. Returns the name of the file specified in the href or src property of the element.

Syntax:

```
document.all.elementID.nameProp
```

Example:

```
<script language="JavaScript">
function B1() {alert(document.getElementById("myA").nameProp);}
</script>
<a id="myA" href="http://www.advocar.com/" target=_blank>Advocar Home Page</a>
<button onclick="B1();">Advocar Home Page nameProp</button>
```

Applies to:

```
<a>, <img>
```

NEGATIVE_INFINITY

Compatibility: NN4, NN6, NN7, IE4, IE5, IE5.5, IE6

Read-only property. A mathematical constant that returns negative infinity.

Syntax:

```
Number.NEGATIVE_INFINITY
```

Example: See the MAX_VALUE property example.

Applies to:

Number

---

nextPage

Compatibility: IE5.5, IE6

Read-only property. Only applicable when the browser uses a print template behavior, and it returns the position of the next page. Values: left or right. If no @page rule has been specified, the return value is an empty string.

Syntax:

```
window.event.nextPage
```

Example:

```
<html><head>
<script language="JavaScript">
function H1() {
var m = event.nextPage;
alert("If no at-rule page was specified, the value is an empty string:
\n"+'"'+m+'"');}
</script></head>
<body bgcolor="#FFFFFF" text="#000000" bottommargin="150">
<input type="Button" id="myB" value="Click here" onClick="H1();">
</body></html>
```

Applies to:

---

event

---

nextSibling

Compatibility: NN6, NN7, IE5, IE5.5, IE6

Read-only property. Returns a reference to the next child of the parent element. All the children elements of a single parent element are referred to as siblings.

Syntax:

```
document.getElementById("elementID").nextSibling
document.all.elementID.nextSibling // IE only
```

Example:

```
<script language="JavaScript">
function B1() {
  var m = document.getElementById("myNodeOne").nextSibling;
```

```
  m ? alert("Yes") : alert("No");}
function B2() {alert(document.all.myNodeOne.nodeName);}
function B3() {alert(document.all.myNodeOne.nodeType);}
function B4() {alert(document.all.myNodeOne.childNodes(0).nodeValue);}
function B5() {
  var m = document.getElementById("myNodeOne").previousSibling;
  m ? alert("Yes") : alert("No");}
</script>
<p>This PARAGRAPH has two nodes, <b id="myNodeOne">Node One</b>, and <b
id="myNodeTwo">Node Two</b>.</p>
<button onclick="B1();">Node One has a Next Sibling</button>
<button onclick="B5();">Node One has a Previous Sibling</button>
<button onclick="B2();">Node One Name</button>
<button onclick="B3();">Node One Type</button>
<button onclick="B4();">Node One Value</button>
```

Applies to:

<a>, <acronym>, <address>, <applet>, <area>, attribute, <b>, <base>, <basefont>,
<bdo>, <bgsound>, <big>, <blockquote>, <body>, <br>, <button>, <caption>, <center>,
<cite>, <code>, <col>, <colgroup>, <comment>, <dd>, <del>, <dfn>, <dir>, <div>,
<dl>, <dt>, <em>, <embed>, <fieldset>, <font>, <form>, <frame>, <frameset>, <head>,
<hn>, <hr>, <html>, <i>, <iframe>, <img>, <input type="button">, <input
type="checkbox">, <input type="file">, <input type="hidden">, <input type="image">,
<input type="password">, <input type="radio">, <input type="reset">, <input
type="submit">, <input type="text">, <ins>, <isindex>, <kbd>, <label>, <legend>,
<li>, <link>, <listing>, <map>, <marquee>, <menu>, <meta>, <noframes>, <noscript>,
<object>, <ol>, <optgroup>, <option>, <p>, <param>, <plaintext>, <pre>, <q>, <s>,
<samp>, <script>, <select>, <small>, <span>, <strike>, <strong>, <style>, <sub>,
<sup>, <table>, <tbody>, <td>, <textarea>, TextNode, <tfoot>, <th>, <thead>,
<title>, <tr>, <tt>, <u>, <ul>, <var>, <xmp>

nodeName

Compatibility: NN6, NN7, IE5, IE5.5, IE6

Read-only property. Returns the name of the node. Values: The tag name for
a regular node, the attribute name for an attribute node, or #text for the text
content of an element (text node).

Syntax:

```
document.getElementById("elementID").nodeName
document.all.elementID.nodeName // IE only
```

Example: See the nextSibling property example.
Applies to:

<a>, <acronym>, <address>, <applet>, <area>, attribute, <b>, <base>, <basefont>,
<bdo>, <bgsound>, <big>, <blockquote>, <body>, <br>, <button>, <caption>, <center>,
<cite>, <code>, <col>, <colgroup>, <comment>, <dd>, <del>, <dfn>, <dir>, <div>,
<dl>, <dt>, <em>, <embed>, <fieldset>, <font>, <form>, <frame>, <frameset>, <head>,
<hn>, <hr>, <html>, <i>, <iframe>, <img>, <input type="button">, <input

type="checkbox">, <input type="file">, <input type="hidden">, <input type="image">, <input type="password">, <input type="radio">, <input type="reset">, <input type="submit">, <input type="text">, <ins>, <isindex>, <kbd>, <label>, <legend>, <li>, <link>, <listing>, <map>, <marquee>, <menu>, <meta>, <noframes>, <noscript>, <object>, <ol>, <optgroup>, <option>, <p>, <param>, <plaintext>, <pre>, <q>, <s>, <samp>, <script>, <select>, <small>, <span>, <strike>, <strong>, <style>, <sub>, <sup>, <table>, <tbody>, <td>, <textarea>, TextNode, <tfoot>, <th>, <thead>, <title>, <tr>, <tt>, <u>, <ul>, <var>, <xmp>

nodeType

Compatibility: NN6, NN7, IE5, IE5.5, IE6

Read-only property. Returns the type of the node. Values: 1 for element node, 3 for text node. IE6 returns 2 for an attribute node. NN6+ supports other values as well: 8 for a comment node and 9 for a document node.

Syntax:

```
document.getElementById("elementID").nodeType
document.all.elementID.nodeType // IE only
```

Example: See the nextSibling property example.
Applies to:

<a>, <acronym>, <address>, <applet>, <area>, attribute, <b>, <base>, <basefont>, <bdo>, <bgsound>, <big>, <blockquote>, <body>, <br>, <button>, <caption>, <center>, <cite>, <code>, <col>, <colgroup>, <comment>, <dd>, <del>, <dfn>, <dir>, <div>, <dl>, <dt>, <em>, <embed>, <fieldset>, <font>, <form>, <frame>, <frameset>, <head>, <hn>, <hr>, <html>, <i>, <iframe>, <img>, <input type="button">, <input type="checkbox">, <input type="file">, <input type="hidden">, <input type="image">, <input type="password">, <input type="radio">, <input type="reset">, <input type="submit">, <input type="text">, <ins>, <isindex>, <kbd>, <label>, <legend>, <li>, <link>, <listing>, <map>, <marquee>, <menu>, <meta>, <noframes>, <noscript>, <object>, <ol>, <optgroup>, <option>, <p>, <param>, <plaintext>, <pre>, <q>, <s>, <samp>, <script>, <select>, <small>, <span>, <strike>, <strong>, <style>, <sub>, <sup>, <table>, <tbody>, <td>, <textarea>, TextNode, <tfoot>, <th>, <thead>, <title>, <tr>, <tt>, <u>, <ul>, <var>, <xmp>

nodeValue

Compatibility: NN6, NN7, IE5, IE5.5, IE6

Read-only property. Returns the value of the node. For a text node, the value is the text string. For an attribute node, the value is the attribute's value. For an element node, the value is null.

Syntax:

```
document.getElementById("elementID").nodeValue
document.all.elementID.nodeValue // IE only
```

Example: See the nextSibling property example.

Applies to:

<a>, <acronym>, <address>, <applet>, <area>, attribute, <b>, <base>, <basefont>, <bdo>, <bgsound>, <big>, <blockquote>, <body>, <br>, <button>, <caption>, <center>, <cite>, <code>, <col>, <colgroup>, <comment>, <dd>, <del>, <dfn>, <dir>, <div>, <dl>, <dt>, <em>, <embed>, <fieldset>, <font>, <form>, <frame>, <frameset>, <head>, <hn>, <hr>, <html>, <i>, <iframe>, <img>, <input type="button">, <input type="checkbox">, <input type="file">, <input type="hidden">, <input type="image">, <input type="password">, <input type="radio">, <input type="reset">, <input type="submit">, <input type="text">, <ins>, <isindex>, <kbd>, <label>, <legend>, <li>, <link>, <listing>, <map>, <marquee>, <menu>, <meta>, <noframes>, <noscript>, <object>, <ol>, <optgroup>, <option>, <p>, <param>, <plaintext>, <pre>, <q>, <s>, <samp>, <script>, <select>, <small>, <span>, <strike>, <strong>, <style>, <sub>, <sup>, <table>, <tbody>, <td>, <textarea>, textNode, <tfoot>, <th>, <thead>, <title>, <tr>, <tt>, <u>, <ul>, <var>, <xmp>

noHref

Compatibility: NN4, NN6, NN7, IE4, IE5, IE5.5, IE6

Read and write property. Defines whether or not clicking a region within an <area> element will have no effect. Values: true or false (the default).

Syntax:

```
document.getElementById("areaID").noHref = value
document.all.areaID.noHref = value // IE only
```

Example: See the coords property example.

Applies to:

<area>

noResize

Compatibility: NN4, NN6, NN7, IE4, IE5, IE5.5, IE6

Read and write property. Determines whether the user is not allowed to resize the frame. Values: true or false (the default).

Syntax:

```
document.getElementById("frameID").noResize = value
document.all.frameID.noResize = value // IE only
```

Example:

```
<html>
<frameset rows="50,*" frameborder="yes" border="20px" framespacing="5" cols="*">
<frame id="topF" name="topFrame" scrolling="NO" src="page1.html">
<script language="javascript">
document.getElementById("topF").noResize = true;
</script>
```

```
<frameset cols="25%,*" border="15px" framespacing="0">
<frame name="leftFrame" marginheight="15" noresize scrolling="NO" src="page2.html">
<frame name="mainFrame" src="page3.html">
</frameset></frameset>
</html>
```

Applies to:

```
<frame>
```

noShade

Compatibility: NN6, NN7, IE4, IE5, IE5.5, IE6

Read and write property. Specifies whether or not the `<hr>` element is rendered without a shade. Values: true or false (the default).

Syntax:

```
document.getElementById("hrID").noShade = value
document.all.hrID.noShade = value // IE only
```

Example:

```
<script language="JavaScript">
function B1() {document.getElementById("myH").noShade = false}
</script>
<hr id="myH" noshade="true" size="3">
<input type="button" value="Add a shade" onClick="B1();">
```

Applies to:

```
<hr>
```

noWrap

Compatibility: NN6 and NN7 (`<td>` and `<th>` only), IE4, IE5, IE5.5, IE6

Read and write property. Establishes whether or not the browser will avoid performing word wrap when the content of an element exceeds its allotted space. Values: true or false (the default).

NOTE   *For the* `<td>` *element, the* width *property overrides* noWrap. *For the* `<th>` *element, the* noWrap *property overrides* width.

Syntax:

```
document.body.noWrap = value
document.getElementById("elementID").noWrap = value
document.all.elementID.noWrap = value // IE only
```

Example:

```
<script language="JavaScript">
function B1() {document.getElementById("myL").noWrap = true;}
function B2() {document.getElementById("myL").noWrap = false;}
</script>
<div id="myL" style="position:absolute; width=50px;">Attribute nowrap is not
present in this div element's tag.</div><br><br>
<input type="button" value="Add noWrap = true" onclick="B1();">
<input type="button" value="Restore noWrap = false" onclick="B2();">
```

Applies to:

```
<body>, <dd>, <div>, <dt>, <td>, <th>
```

object

Compatibility: NN6, NN7, IE4, IE5, IE5.5, IE6

Read-only property. Returns the object contained by the element.
Syntax:

```
document.getElementById("elementID").object
document.all.elementID.object // IE only
```

Example:

```
<object id="myO" classid="clsid:D27CDB6E-AE6D-11cf-96B8-444553540000"
codebase="http://download.macromedia.com/pub/shockwave/cabs/flash/
swflash.cab#version=5,0,0,0"
width="250" height="230">
   <param name="movie" value="yourshockwavefile.swf">
   <param name="quality" value="high">
</object>
<script language="JavaScript">
  function O1() {
  var m = document.getElementById("myO").object;
  alert(m);
  }
</script>
<input type="Button" id="myB" value='Get "myO" object property value'
onClick="O1();">
```

Applies to:

```
<applet>, <object>
```

offScreenBuffering

Compatibility: IE4, IE5, IE5.5, IE6

Read and write property. Specifies whether or not a document's elements are buffered off-screen before being presented on the visible screen. Internet Explorer initially renders a page in a chunk of memory (a buffer) before drawing its content on the screen. Values: true , false, or auto (the default).

Syntax:

```
window.offScreenBuffering = value
```

Example:

```
<script language="JavaScript">
function B1() {
window.offScreenBuffering = false;
var m = window.offScreenBuffering;
alert("The value of offScreenBuffering for this window is: \n"+m);}
</script>
<input type="Button" value='Turn "off" the offScreenBuffering of this window'
onClick="B1();">
```

Applies to:

```
window
```

offsetHeight, offsetWidth

Compatibility: NN6, NN7, IE4, IE5, IE5.5, IE6

Read-only properties. Return the height and width in pixels of any block-level or inline element.

Syntax:

```
document.getElementById("elementID").offsetHeight
document.all.elementID.offsetHeight // IE only
document.getElementById("elementID").offsetWidth
document.all.elementID.offsetWidth // IE only
```

Example:

```
<div id="myDiv" style="position:absolute; left:150; top:100; width:400; height:200;
background-color:blue;"></div>
<button onclick="alert(myDiv.offsetHeight);">offsetHeight</button>
<button onclick="alert(myDiv.offsetWidth);">offsetWidth</button>
<button onclick="alert(myDiv.offsetLeft);">offsetLeft</button>
<button onclick="alert(myDiv.offsetTop);">offsetTop</button>
```

Applies to:

<a>, <acronym>, <address>, <applet>, <area>, <b>, <base>, <basefont>, <bdo>, <big>, <blockquote>, <body>, <br>, <button>, <caption>, <center>, <cite>, <code>, <col>, <colgroup>, <custom>, <dd>, <del>, <dfn>, <dir>, <div>, <dl>, <dt>, <em>, <embed>, <fieldset>, <font>, <form>, <frame>, <frameset>, <head>, <hn>, <hr>, <html>, <i>, <iframe>, <img>, <input type="button">, <input type="checkbox">, <input type="file">, <input type="image">, <input type="password">, <input type="radio">, <input type="reset">, <input type="submit">, <input type="text">, <ins>, <isindex>, <kbd>, <label>, <legend>, <li>, <link>, <listing>, <map>, <marquee>, <menu>, <meta>, <nobr>, <noframes>, <noscript>, <object>, <ol>, <optgroup>, <option>, <p>, <param>, <plaintext>, <pre>, <q>, <rt>, <ruby>, <s>, <samp>, <script>, <select>, <small>, <span>, <strike>, <strong>, <style>, <sub>, <sup>, <table>, <tbody>, <td>, <textarea>, <tfoot>, <th>, <thead>, <title>, <tr>, <tt>, <u>, <ul>, <var>, <xmp>

offsetLeft, offsetTop

Compatibility: NN6, NN7, IE4, IE5, IE5.5, IE6

Read-only properties. Return the horizontal and vertical coordinates in pixels of the upper-left corner of any block-level or inline element.

Syntax:

```
document.getElementById("elementID").offsetLeft
document.all.elementID.offsetLeft // IE only
document.getElementById("elementID").offsetTop
document.all.elementID.offsetTop // IE only
```

Example: See the offsetHeight, offsetWidth property example.

Applies to:

<a>, <acronym>, <address>, <applet>, <area>, <b>, <base>, <basefont>, <bdo>, <big>, <blockquote>, <body>, <br>, <button>, <caption>, <center>, <cite>, <code>, <col>, <colgroup>, <custom>, <dd>, <del>, <dfn>, <dir>, <div>, <dl>, <dt>, <em>, <embed>, <fieldset>, <font>, <form>, <frame>, <frameset>, <head>, <hn>, <hr>, <html>, <i>, <iframe>, <img>, <input type="button">, <input type="checkbox">, <input type="file">, <input type="image">, <input type="password">, <input type="radio">, <input type="reset">, <input type="submit">, <input type="text">, <ins>, <isindex>, <kbd>, <label>, <legend>, <li>, <link>, <listing>, <map>, <marquee>, <menu>, <meta>, <nobr>, <noframes>, <noscript>, <object>, <ol>, <optgroup>, <option>, <p>, <param>, <plaintext>, <pre>, <q>, <rt>, <ruby>, <s>, <samp>, <script>, <select>, <small>, <span>, <strike>, <strong>, <style>, <sub>, <sup>, <table>, <tbody>, <td>, <textarea>, textRange, <tfoot>, <th>, <thead>, <title>, <tr>, <tt>, <u>, <ul>, <var>, <xmp>

offsetParent

Compatibility: NN6, NN7, IE4, IE5, IE5.5, IE6

Read-only property. Returns a reference to the parent element, which controls the offsetTop and offsetLeft properties of the child element.

Syntax:

```
document.getElementById("elementID").offsetParent
document.all.elementID.offsetParent // IE only
```

Example:

```
<script language="JavaScript">
function B1() {alert(document.all.myText.offsetParent.tagName);}
</script>
<textarea id="myText"></textarea>
<button onclick="B1();">Offset Parent</button>
```

Applies to:

```
<a>, <acronym>, <address>, <applet>, <area>, <b>, <base>, <basefont>, <bdo>, <big>,
<blockquote>, <body>, <br>, <button>, <caption>, <center>, <cite>, <code>, <col>,
<colgroup>, <comment>, <custom>, <dd>, <del>, <dfn>, <dir>, <div>, <dl>, <dt>,
<em>, <embed>, <fieldset>, <font>, <form>, <frame>, <frameset>, <head>, <hn>, <hr>,
<html>, <i>, <iframe>, <img>, <input type="button">, <input type="checkbox">,
<input type="file">, <input type="hidden">, <input type="image">, <input
type="password">, <input type="radio">, <input type="reset">, <input
type="submit">, <input type="text">, <ins>, <isindex>, <kbd>, <label>, <legend>,
<li>, <link>, <listing>, <map>, <marquee>, <menu>, <meta>, <nobr>, <noframes>,
<noscript>, <object>, <ol>, <optgroup>, <option>, <p>, <param>, <plaintext>, <pre>,
<q>, <rt>, <ruby>, <s>, <samp>, <script>, <select>, <small>, <span>, <strike>,
<strong>, <style>, <sub>, <sup>, <table>, <tbody>, <td>, <textarea>, <tfoot>, <th>,
<thead>, <title>, <tr>, <tt>, <u>, <ul>, <var>, <xmp>
```

offsetX, offsetY

Compatibility: IE4, IE5, IE5.5, IE6

Read-only properties. Return the X and Y coordinates of the mouse position in pixels relative to the element that triggered the event.

Syntax:

```
window.event.offsetX
window.event.offsetY
```

Example:

```
<script language="JavaScript">
function C1() {
myX.innerHTML = window.event.offsetX;
myY.innerHTML = window.event.offsetY;
mySX.innerHTML = window.event.screenX;
mySY.innerHTML = window.event.screenY;
mySH.innerHTML = myDiv.scrollHeight;
mySW.innerHTML = myDiv.scrollWidth;
}
```

```
function B1() {
mySL.innerHTML = myDiv.scrollLeft;
myST.innerHTML = myDiv.scrollTop;
}
</script>
<p><b>X Coordinate:</b> <span id="myX">0</span></p>
<p><b>Y Coordinate:</b> <span id="myY">0</span></p>
<p><b>Screen X:</b> <span id="mySX">0</span></p>
<p><b>Screen Y:</b> <span id="mySY">0</span></p>
<p><b>Scroll Height:</b> <span id="mySH">0</span></p>
<p><b>Scroll Width:</b> <span id="mySW">0</span></p>
<p><b>Scroll Left:</b> <span id="mySL">0</span></p>
<p><b>Scroll Top:</b> <span id="myST">0</span></p>
<div id="myDiv" onmousemove="C1();" onscroll="B1();" style="border:solid;
width:200; height:50; overflow:scroll;">
<img src="yourimage.gif"></div>
```

Applies to:

event

onLine

Compatibility: IE4, IE5, IE5.5, IE6

Read-only property. Returns a value that indicates whether or not the browser can only view pages, even those that are cached, while connected to the Internet. Values: true or false.

Syntax:

objectName.onLine

Example:

```
<script language="JavaScript">
function ol() {
  var m = navigator.onLine;
  alert("The onLine value is: \n"+m);
}
</script>
<input type="Button" value='Get the onLine value' onClick="ol();">
```

Applies to:

clientInformation, navigator

onOffBehavior

Compatibility: IE4, IE5, IE5.5, IE6

Read-only property. Returns a value indicating whether or not a Microsoft HTML+TIME Direct Animation behavior is running. However, this property is only compatible with HTML+TIME version 1. Version 2 no longer supports this property, and its use with Internet Explorer 6 and beyond is not supported.

Syntax:

```
objectName.onOffBehavior
```

Applies to:

```
currentStyle, <input type="button">, <input type="checkbox">, <input type="file">,
<input type="image">, <input type="password">, <input type="radio">, <input
type="reset">, <input type="submit">, <input type="text">, runtimeStyle, style
```

opener

Compatibility: NN4, NN6, NN7, IE4, IE5, IE5.5, IE6

Read and write property. Establishes the relationship between a window opened with the window.open() method and the parent window.

Syntax:

```
window.opener = value
```

It is possible to use the following syntax to reach deeper into the heritage of the window:

```
window.opener.opener...
```

To use a property of the parent window, you can use this syntax:

```
window.opener.document.getElementById("elementID").propertyName = value
```

Example:

```
<script language="JavaScript">
var newWin
function open1() {
newWin = window.open("subwindow.html", "subwindow", "width=400,
height=150, left=200, resizable, top=250")
}
function hi() {
if (!newWin.closed) {alert("The subwindow is closed");}}
</script>
<p style="text-decoration:underline; cursor:hand;" onClick="open1();">Click to open
new window</p>
```

Subwindow code:

```
<html>
<script language="JavaScript">
setTimeout("close1()", 3000);
function close1() {
self.close();
}
</script>
<body bgcolor="#FFFFFF" text="#000000" onUnload="window.opener.hi()">
<font color="#FF0000">This is a subwindow</font>
<p align="center">Will close in 3 seconds.</p>
</body></html>
```

Applies to:

```
window
```

outerHTML

Compatibility: IE4, IE5, IE5.5, IE6

Read and write property. Specifies all of the HTML content of the element node.
Syntax:

```
document.all.elementID.outerHTML = value
```

Example:

```
<button type="button" style="border-width:thin; color:red; border-color:#cccccc;
cursor:hand; background-color:white;" onClick="B1();">Button. Repeat</button>
<div id="myD"></div>
<script language="JavaScript">
function B1(){
var m = event.srcElement;
if(m.tagName != "p"){
alert("Repeating the following HTML element:\n" + m.outerHTML);
myD.innerHTML += m.outerHTML + "<br>";
}}
</script>
```

Applies to:

```
<a>, <acronym>, <address>, <applet>, <area>, <b>, <bdo>, <bgsound>, <big>,
<blockquote>, <br>, <button>, <caption>, <center>, <cite>, <code>, <col>,
<colgroup>, <custom>, <dd>, <del>, <dfn>, <dir>, <div>, <dl>, <dt>, <em>, <embed>,
<fieldset>, <font>, <form>, <frameset>, <hn>, <hr>, <html>, <i>, <iframe>, <img>,
<input type="button">, <input type="checkbox">, <input type="file">, <input
type="hidden">, <input type="image">, <input type="password">, <input
```

type="radio">, <input type="reset">, <input type="submit">, <input type="text">, <ins>, <kbd>, <label>, <legend>, <li>, <listing>, <map>, <marquee>, <menu>, <nobr>, <object>, <ol>, <p>, <plaintext>, <pre>, <q>, <rt>, <ruby>, <s>, <samp>, <select>, <small>, <span>, <strike>, <strong>, <sub>, <sup>, <table>, <tbody>, <td>, <textarea>, <tfoot>, <th>, <thead>, <tr>, <tt>, <u>, <ul>, <var>, <wbr>, <xmp>

outerText

Compatibility: IE4, IE5, IE5.5, IE6

Read and write property. Specifies all of the text of the element node.

Syntax:

```
document.all.elementID.outerText = value
```

Example:

```
<p id="par">The journey was an exercise in <b>discipline</b>. And discipline was
not foreign to <u>these drivers</u>.</p>
<button id="myButton" onclick="B1();">Make Text Above Plain</button>
<script language="javascript">
function B1(){
document.all.par.outerText = "The journey was an exercise in discipline. And
discipline was not foreign to these drivers."
myButton.disabled = true;}
</script>
```

Applies to:

```
<a>, <acronym>, <address>, <applet>, <area>, <b>, <bdo>, <bgsound>, <big>,
<blockquote>, <br>, <button>, <center>, <cite>, <code>, <comment>, <custom>, <dd>,
<del>, <dfn>, <dir>, <div>, <dl>, <dt>, <em>, <embed>, <fieldset>, <font>, <form>,
<hn>, <hr>, <html>, <i>, <iframe>, <img>, <input type="button">, <input
type="checkbox">, <input type="file">, <input type="hidden">, <input type="image">,
<input type="password">, <input type="radio">, <input type="reset">, <input
type="submit">, <input type="text">, <ins>, <kbd>, <label>, <legend>, <li>,
<listing>, <map>, <marquee>, <menu>, <nobr>, <object>, <ol>, <p>, <plaintext>,
<pre>, <q>, <rt>, <ruby>, <s>, <samp>, <select>, <small>, <span>, <strike>,
<strong>, <sub>, <sup>, <table>, <tbody>, <td>, <textarea>, <tfoot>, <th>, <thead>,
<tr>, <tt>, <u>, <ul>, <var>, <wbr>, <xmp>
```

ownerDocument

Compatibility: NN6, NN7, IE6

Read-only property. Returns a reference to the document object that contains the element.

Syntax:

```
document.getElementById("elementID").ownerDocument
document.all.elementID.ownerDocument // IE only
```

Example:

```
<div id="myD"><p id="myP">This is a sample text.</p></div><br>
<input type="button" value="ownerDocument" onclick="B1();">
<script language="JavaScript">
function B1() {alert(document.all.myP.ownerDocument);}
</script>
```

Applies to:

```
<a>, <acronym>, <address>, <applet>, <area>, attribute, <b>, <base>, <basefont>,
<bdo>, <big>, <blockquote>, <body>, <br>, <button>, <caption>, <center>, <cite>,
<code>, <col>, <colgroup>, <comment>, <dd>, <del>, <dfn>, <dir>, <div>, <dl>, <dt>,
<em>, <embed>, <fieldset>, <font>, <form>, <frame>, <frameset>, <head>, <hn>, <hr>,
<html>, <i>, <iframe>, <img>, <input type="button">, <input type="checkbox">,
<input type="file">, <input type="image">, <input type="password">, <input
type="radio">, <input type="reset">, <input type="submit">, <input type="text">,
<ins>, <isindex>, <kbd>, <label>, <legend>, <li>, <link>, <listing>, <map>,
<marquee>, <menu>, <meta>, <noframes>, <noscript>, <object>, <ol>, <optgroup>,
<option>, <p>, <param>, <pre>, <q>, <s>, <samp>, <script>, <select>, <small>,
<span>, <strike>, <strong>, <style>, <sub>, <sup>, <table>, <tbody>, <td>,
<textarea>, <tfoot>, <th>, <thead>, <title>, <tr>, <tt>, <u>, <ul>, <var>, <xmp>
```

owningElement

Compatibility: IE4, IE5, IE5.5, IE6

Read-only property. Returns a reference to the element in which the styleSheet is defined.

Syntax:

```
document.styleSheets[index].owningElement
```

Example:

```
<style id="myS">
#myP1 { color:red; font-family:verdana; font-size:16 }
#myP2 { color:green; font-family:times new roman; font-size:18 }
</style>
<p id="myP1">This is a sample text.</p>
<p id="myP2">This is a second sample text.</p>
<input type="button" value="owningElement" onclick="B1();">
<script language="JavaScript">
function B1() {
var m = document.styleSheets[0].owningElement.id;
alert(m);
}
</script>
```

Applies to:

styleSheet

pageX

Compatibility: NN6, NN7

Read-only property. Establishes the X coordinate in pixels of the cursor position relative to the page.

Syntax:

event.pageX
eventName.pageX

Example:

```
<script>
function B1(myEvent) {
    document.getElementById("myX").innerHTML = myEvent.pageX;
    document.getElementById("myY").innerHTML = myEvent.pageY;
}
document.onmousemove = B1;
</script>
<p><b>Page X Coordinate:</b> <span id="myX">0</span></p>
<p><b>Page Y Coordinate:</b> <span id="myY">0</span></p>
```

Applies to:

event

pageY

Compatibility: NN6, NN7

Read-only property. Establishes the Y coordinate in pixels of the cursor position relative to the page.

Syntax:

event.pageY
eventName.pageY

Example: See the pageY property example.
Applies to:

event

palette

Compatibility: IE4, IE5, IE5.5, IE6

Read-only property. Returns the palette used for the <embed> element.

Syntax:

```
document.all.embedID.palette
```

Example:

```
<embed id="myE" palette="foreground" src="Puzzle.swf" quality="high"
pluginspage="http://www.macromedia.com/shockwave/download/
index.cgi?P1_Prod_Version=ShockwaveFlash" type="application/x-shockwave-flash"
width="250" height="230"></embed>
<button onclick="B1();">Click Here</button>
<script language="JavaScript">
function B1() {
var m = document.all.myE.palette;
alert('"'+m+'"');
}
</script>
```

Applies to:

```
<embed>
```

parent

Compatibility: NN4, NN6, NN7, IE4, IE5, IE5.5, IE6

Read-only property. In a multiframe environment, returns a reference to the parent window of the current active window.

Syntax:

```
window.parent
```

Example:

```
<html>
<frameset rows="100,*" frameborder="yes" border="20px" framespacing="5" cols="*">
  <frame name="topFrame" scrolling="NO" noresize src="topframe1.html">
  <frameset cols="41%,*" border="15px" framespacing="0" rows="*">
    <frame name="topFrame" src="topframe2.htm">
    <frame name="mainFrame" src="mainframe.htm">
  </frameset>
</frameset>
</html>
```

Contents of topframe2.htm:

```
<html><head>
<script language="JavaScript">
function P1() {
alert(window.parent.mainFrame.document.all.CBP.innerText);}
</script></head>
<body style="background-color:white;">
<input type="button" value="View Content of CBP" onclick="P1();">
</body></html>
```

Contents of mainframe.htm:

```
<html>
<body bgcolor="white" text="#000000">
<p>MainFrame</p><pre id="CBP">Pre-element content</pre>
</body></html>
```

Applies to:

```
window
```

parentElement

Compatibility: IE4, IE5, IE5.5, IE6

Read-only property. Returns a reference to the element's parent element.
Syntax:

```
document.all.elementID.parentElement
```

Example:

```
<form id="myF"><input id="myB" type="button" value="The parent element of this
button" onclick="B1();"></form>
<script language="JavaScript">
function B1() {
var m = document.all.myB.parentElement.id;
alert("Parent element: <FORM>, ID = "+'"'+m+'"');
}
</script>
```

Applies to:

```
<a>, <acronym>, <address>, <applet>, <area>, <b>, <base>, <basefont>, <bdo>,
<bgsound>, <big>, <blockquote>, <body>, <br>, <button>, <caption>, <center>,
<cite>, <code>, <col>, <colgroup>, <comment>, <custom>, <dd>, <del>, <dfn>, <dir>,
<div>, <dl>, <dt>, <em>, <embed>, <fieldset>, <font>, <form>, <frame>, <frameset>,
<head>, <hn>, <hr>, <html>, <i>, <iframe>, <img>, <input type="button">, <input
type="checkbox">, <input type="file">, <input type="hidden">, <input type="image">,
```

`<input type="password">`, `<input type="radio">`, `<input type="reset">`, `<input type="submit">`, `<input type="text">`, `<ins>`, `<isindex>`, `<kbd>`, `<label>`, `<legend>`, `<li>`, `<link>`, `<listing>`, `<map>`, `<marquee>`, `<menu>`, `<nobr>`, `<noframes>`, `<noscript>`, `<object>`, `<ol>`, `<option>`, `<p>`, `<plaintext>`, `<pre>`, `<q>`, `<rt>`, `<ruby>`, `<s>`, `<samp>`, `<script>`, `<select>`, `<small>`, `<span>`, `<strike>`, `<strong>`, `<sub>`, `<sup>`, `<table>`, `<tbody>`, `<td>`, `<textarea>`, `<tfoot>`, `<th>`, `<thead>`, `<title>`, `<tr>`, `<tt>`, `<u>`, `<ul>`, `<var>`, `<wbr>`, `<xml>`, `<xmp>`

parentNode

Compatibility: NN6, NN7, IE5, IE5.5, IE6

Read-only property. Returns a reference to the node's parent node.

Syntax:

```
document.getElementById("elementID").parentNode
document.all.elementID.parentNode // IE only
```

Example:

```
<form id="myF"><input id="myB" type="button" value="The parent node of this button"
onclick="B1();"></form>
<script language="JavaScript">
function B1() {
var m = document.all.myB.parentNode.id;
alert("Parent node: <form>, id = "+'"'+m+'"');
}
</script>
```

Applies to:

`<a>`, `<acronym>`, `<address>`, `<applet>`, `<area>`, attribute, `<b>`, `<base>`, `<basefont>`, `<bdo>`, `<bgsound>`, `<big>`, `<blockquote>`, `<body>`, `<br>`, `<button>`, `<caption>`, `<center>`, `<cite>`, `<code>`, `<col>`, `<colgroup>`, `<comment>`, `<dd>`, `<del>`, `<dfn>`, `<dir>`, `<div>`, `<dl>`, `<dt>`, `<em>`, `<embed>`, `<fieldset>`, `<font>`, `<form>`, `<frame>`, `<frameset>`, `<head>`, `<hn>`, `<hr>`, `<html>`, `<i>`, `<iframe>`, `<img>`, `<input type="button">`, `<input type="checkbox">`, `<input type="file">`, `<input type="hidden">`, `<input type="image">`, `<input type="password">`, `<input type="radio">`, `<input type="reset">`, `<input type="submit">`, `<input type="text">`, `<ins>`, `<isindex>`, `<kbd>`, `<label>`, `<legend>`, `<li>`, `<link>`, `<listing>`, `<map>`, `<marquee>`, `<menu>`, `<meta>`, `<noframes>`, `<noscript>`, `<object>`, `<ol>`, `<optgroup>`, `<option>`, `<p>`, `<param>`, `<plaintext>`, `<pre>`, `<q>`, `<s>`, `<samp>`, `<script>`, `<select>`, `<small>`, `<span>`, `<strike>`, `<strong>`, `<style>`, `<sub>`, `<sup>`, `<table>`, `<tbody>`, `<td>`, `<textarea>`, textNode, `<tfoot>`, `<th>`, `<thead>`, `<title>`, `<tr>`, `<tt>`, `<u>`, `<ul>`, `<var>`, `<xmp>`

parentStyleSheet

Compatibility: NN6, NN7, IE4, IE5, IE5.5, IE6

Read-only property. Returns a reference to the styleSheet file that the current style sheet used in the document came from. If the styleSheet object is not imported via @import, the returned value is null.

Syntax:

```
document.styleSheets[index].parentStyleSheet
document.all.styleID.parentStyleSheet
```

Example:

```
<style id="myStyle" type="text/css">@import url("external.css");</style>
<p id="myP1">This is a sample text.</p>
<p id="myP2">This is a second sample text.</p>
<input type="button" value="The parent style sheet" onclick="B1();">
<script language="JavaScript">
function B1() {alert(document.styleSheets[0].imports[0].href);}
</script>
```

Contents of external.css:

```
#myP1 { color:red; font-family:verdana; font-size:16 }
#myP2 { color:green; font-family:times new roman; font-size:18 }
```

Applies to:

```
styleSheet
```

parentTextEdit

Compatibility: IE4, IE5, IE5.5, IE6

Read-only property. Returns a reference to the element's outermost container that is capable of creating a text range.

Syntax:

```
document.all.elementID.parentTextEdit
```

Example:

```
<script language="JavaScript">
function B1() {
    var choose, range;
    for (var i = 0; i < document.forms[0].choose.length; i++) {
        if (document.forms[0].choose[i].checked) {
            choose = document.forms[0].choose[i].value;
            break;
        }
    }
    var x = window.event.clientX;
    var y = window.event.clientY;
    if (window.event.srcElement.parentTextEdit) {
```

```
            range = window.event.srcElement.parentTextEdit.createTextRange()
            range.collapse();
            range.moveToPoint(x, y);
            range.expand(choose);
            range.select();
    }
}
</script>
<form>
<input type="radio" name="choose" value="character" checked>character
<input type="radio" name="choose" value="word">word
<input type="radio" name="choose" value="sentence">sentence
</form>
<p onClick="B1();"> Some text.</p>
```

Applies to:

```
<a>, <acronym>, <address>, <applet>, <area>, <b>, <base>, <basefont>, <bdo>,
<bgsound>, <big>, <blockquote>, <body>, <br>, <button>, <caption>, <center>,
<cite>, <code>, <col>, <colgroup>, <comment>, <custom>, <dd>, <del>, <dfn>, <dir>,
<div>, <dl>, <dt>, <em>, <embed>, <fieldset>, <font>, <form>, <frame>, <frameset>,
<head>, <hn>, <hr>, <html>, <i>, <iframe>, <img>, <input type="button">, <input
type="checkbox">, <input type="file">, <input type="hidden">, <input type="image">,
<input type="password">, <input type="radio">, <input type="reset">, <input
type="submit">, <input type="text">, <ins>, <kbd>, <label>, <legend>, <li>, <link>,
<listing>, <map>, <marquee>, <menu>, <meta>, <nobr>, <object>, <ol>, <option>, <p>,
<plaintext>, <pre>, <q>, <s>, <samp>, <script>, <select>, <small>, <span>,
<strike>, <strong>, <sub>, <sup>, <table>, <tbody>, <td>, <textarea>, <tfoot>,
<th>, <thead>, <title>, <tr>, <tt>, <u>, <ul>, <var>, <xmp>
```

parentWindow

Compatibility: IE4, IE5, IE5.5, IE6

Read-only property. Returns a reference to the window that contains the document.

Syntax:

```
document.parentWindow
```

Example:

```
<script language="JavaScript">
function B1() {alert(document.parentWindow.frames.length);}
</script>
<input type="button" value="How many frames in this window?" onclick="B1();">
```

Applies to:

```
document
```

pathname

Compatibility: NN4, NN6, NN7, IE4, IE5, IE5.5, IE6

Read and write property. Specifies the path name of the object.
    Syntax:

```
document.getElementById("elementID").pathName = value
document.all.elementID.pathName = value // IE only
location.pathName
```

    Example:

```
<script language="JavaScript">
function B1() {alert(document.getElementById("myA").pathname);}
</script>
<a id="myA" href="http://www.advocar.com/home.asp" target="_blank">Advocar home
page</a>
<input type="Button" id="myB" value="File and path to the page" onClick="B1();">
```

    Applies to:

```
<a>, <area>, location
```

PI

Compatibility: NN4, NN6, NN7, IE4, IE5, IE5.5, IE6

Read-only property. A mathematical constant that returns the value of pi.
    Syntax:

```
Math.PI
```

    Example:

```
<button onclick="alert(Math.PI);">Math.PI</button>
```

    Applies to:

```
Math
```

platform

Compatibility: NN6, NN7, IE4, IE5, IE5.5, IE6

Read-only property. Returns the name of the computer's operating system.
Values: HP-UX, Mac68K, SunOS, Win16, and Win32.
    Syntax:

```
objectName.platform
```

Example:

```
<script language="JavaScript">
function B1() {alert(navigator.platform);}
</script>
<input type="button" value="Platform" onclick="B1();">
```

Applies to:

```
clientInformation, navigator
```

pluginspage

Compatibility: IE4, IE5, IE5.5, IE6

Read-only property. Returns the URL of the plug-in referenced in the `<embed>` element.

Syntax:

```
document.all.embedID.pluginspage
```

Example:

```
<script language="JavaScript">
var m = document.all.myE.pluginspage;
alert(m);
</script>
<!—The inserted object is a Flash movie -->
<object classid="clsid:D27CDB6E-AE6D-11cf-96B8-444553540000" codebase="http://
download.macromedia.com/pub/shockwave/cabs/flash/swflash.cab#version=5,0,0,0"
width="243" height="194">
    <param name="movie" value="yourshockwavefile.swf">
    <param name="quality" value="high">
    <embed id="myE" src="yourFlashMovie.swf" quality="high" type="application/x-
shockwave-flash" width="243" height="194"></embed>
</object>
```

Applies to:

```
<embed>
```

port

Compatibility: NN4, NN6, NN7, IE4, IE5, IE5.5, IE6

Read and write property. Specifies the port number of the URL.

Syntax:

```
document.getElementById("elementID").port = value
document.all.elementID.port = value // IE only
location.port = value
```

Example:

```
<script language="JavaScript">
function B1() {alert(document.getElementById("myA").port);}
</script>
<a id="myA" href="http://.www.advocar.com" target="_blank">Advocar home page</a>
<input type="Button" value="Port Number" onClick="B1();">
```

Applies to:

`<a>`, `<area>`, location

POSITIVE_INFINITY

Compatibility: NN4, NN6, NN7, IE4, IE5, IE5.5, IE6

Read-only property. A mathematical constant that returns infinity.
  Syntax:

`Number.POSITIVE_INFINITY`

Example: See the MAX_VALUE property example.
Applies to:

Number

previousSibling

Compatibility: NN6, NN7, IE5, IE5.5, IE6

Read-only property. Returns a reference to the previous child element of the parent element.
  Syntax:

```
document.getElementById("elementID").previousSibling
document.all.elementID.previousSibling // IE only
```

Example: See the nextSibling property example.
Applies to:

`<a>`, `<acronym>`, `<address>`, `<applet>`, `<area>`, attribute, `<b>`, `<base>`, `<basefont>`, `<bdo>`, `<bgsound>`, `<big>`, `<blockquote>`, `<body>`, `<br>`, `<button>`, `<caption>`, `<center>`, `<cite>`, `<code>`, `<col>`, `<colgroup>`, `<comment>`, `<dd>`, `<del>`, `<dfn>`, `<dir>`, `<div>`, `<dl>`, `<dt>`, `<em>`, `<embed>`, `<fieldset>`, `<font>`, `<form>`, `<frame>`, `<frameset>`, `<head>`, `<hn>`, `<hr>`, `<html>`, `<i>`, `<iframe>`, `<img>`, `<input>`, `<input type="button">`, `<input type="checkbox">`, `<input type="file">`, `<input type="hidden">`, `<input type="image">`, `<input type="password">`, `<input type="radio">`, `<input type="reset">`, `<input type="submit">`, `<input type="text">`, `<ins>`, `<isindex>`, `<kbd>`, `<label>`, `<legend>`, `<li>`, `<link>`, `<listing>`, `<map>`, `<marquee>`, `<menu>`, `<meta>`, `<noframes>`, `<noscript>`,

`<object>, <ol>, <optgroup>, <option>, <p>, <param>, <plaintext>, <pre>, <q>, <s>, <samp>, <script>, <select>, <small>, <span>, <strike>, <strong>, <style>, <sub>, <sup>, <table>, <tbody>, <td>, <textarea>, TextNode, <tfoot>, <th>, <thead>, <title>, <tr>, <tt>, <u>, <ul>, <var>, <xmp>`

profile

Compatibility: NN6, NN7, IE6

Read and write property. Specifies the location (the Uniform Resource Identifier, or URI) of a `<meta>` data profile, which can be used by search engines.

Syntax:

```
document.getElementById("headID").profile = value
document.all.headID.profile = value // IE only
```

Example:

```
<html><head id="myH">
<script language="JavaScript">
function B1() {
alert('The following profile has been added:\n"http://www.acme.com/profiles/
core"');
document.all.myH.profile = "http://www.acme.com/profiles/core";
}
</script></head>
<body bgcolor="#FFFFFF" text="#000000">
<input type="button" value="Add profile" onClick="B1();">
</body></html>
```

Applies to:

```
<head>
```

propertyName

Compatibility: IE5, IE5.5, IE6

Read and write property. Specifies the name of the property whose value changes during the event.

Syntax:

```
window.event.propertyName = value
```

Example:

```
<script language="JavaScript">
function B1(){alert(event.propertyName);}
</script>
```

```
<button onclick="this.style.color='white'; this.style.backgroundColor='red';"
onpropertychange="B1();">propertyName</button>
```

Applies to:

```
event
```

protocol

Compatibility: NN4, NN6, NN7, IE4, IE5, IE5.5, IE6

Read and write property. Specifies the protocol part of the URL established by
the object (such as http:).

The protocolLong property, no longer supported, still works for IE5 and
returns a verbose rendition of the protocol (such as Hypertext Transfer Protocol
instead of http:).

Syntax:

```
document.getElementById("elementID").protocol = value
document.all.elementID.protocol = value // IE only
objectName.protocol
```

Example:

```
<script language="JavaScript">
function B1() {alert(document.getElementById("myA").protocol);}
</script>
<a id="myA" href="http://.www.cnn.com" target="_blank">CNN home page</a>
<input type="Button" id="myB" value="Protocol" onClick="B1();">
```

Applies to:

```
<a>, <area>, document, <img>, location
```

pseudoClass

Compatibility: IE5.5, IE6

Read and write property. Returns the name of the pseudo class to which an @page
rule has been applied. Values: first, left, and right.

Syntax:

```
document.all.elementID.pseudoClass = value
```

Example:

```
<html><head>
<style>@page:first { background-color: blue; }</style>
```

```
<script language="JavaScript">
function B1() {
var m = document.styleSheets[0].pages[0];
alert(m.pseudoClass);}</script></head>
<body><button onclick="B1();">First @page</button></body></html>
```

Applies to:

page

qualifier

Compatibility: IE5, IE5.5, IE6

Read-only property. Returns the name of the data member associated with a data source that receives the event.

Syntax:

window.event.qualifier

Example:

```
<script language="JavaScript">
function B1() {var m = window.event.qualifier; alert(m)}
</script>
<a datasrc="#myDT" datafld="column1" dataformatas="html" target="_blank">Late-breaking News from CNN</a>
<object id="myDT" classid="clsid:333C7BC4-460F-11D0-BC04-0080C7055A83">
    <param name="DataURL" value="yourDatafldDatasrc.txt">
    <param name="FieldDelim" value="\">
    <param name="RowDelim" value="\">
</object>
<input type="button" value="Get qualifier" onclick="B1();">
```

Applies to:

event

readOnly (1)

Compatibility: NN6, NN7, IE4, IE5, IE5.5, IE6

Read and write property. Specifies whether or not the element's content is read-only. Values: true or false (the default).

Syntax:

```
document.getElementById("elementID").readOnly = value
document.all.elementID.readOnly = value // IE only
```

Example:

```
<input type="text" id="rot" value="This text field is not editable" size="30">
<script language="JavaScript">
document.getElementById("rot").readOnly = true;
</script>
```

Applies to:

```
<input type="password">, <input type="text">, <textarea>
```

readOnly (2)

Compatibility: IE4, IE5, IE5.5, IE6

Read-only property. Indicates whether or not the rule or style sheet applied to the object is defined on the page. Values: true or false (the default).

Syntax:

```
document.collectionName[index].readOnly
```

Example:

```
<html>
<body bgcolor="#FFFFFF" text="#000000">
<style>
#myP1 { color:red; font-family:verdana; font-size:16 }
#myP2 { color:green; font-family:times new roman; font-size:18 }
</style>
<p id="myP1">This is a sample text.</p>
<p id="myP2">This is a second sample text.</p>
<input type="button" value="style sheet source" onclick="B1();">
<script language="JavaScript">
function B1() {
var m = document.styleSheets[0].readOnly;
if (m == true) {alert("The style sheet is defined on the page");
} else {alert("The style sheet is imported");}}
</script>
</body></html>
```

Applies to:

```
styleSheet, rule
```

readyState

Compatibility: IE4, IE5, IE5.5, IE6

Read-only property. Returns the current state of the element. Values: complete (object and data are fully loaded), interactive (user can interact with the object, even if data is not fully loaded), loaded (data is fully loaded), loading (data is loading), and uninitialized (object does not have data).

Syntax:

```
document.all.elementID.readyState
```

Example:

```
<script language="JavaScript">
function B1() {var m = document.all.myI.readyState; alert(m);}
</script>
<img id="myI" src="yourimage.jpg" alt="" width="300" height="225">
<input type="button" value="Get the state of the image object" onclick="B1();">
```

Applies to:

```
<a>, <acronym>, <address>, <applet>, <area>, <b>, <base>, <basefont>, <bdo>,
<bgsound>, <big>, <blockquote>, <body>, <br>, <button>, <caption>, <center>,
<cite>, <code>, <col>, <colgroup>, <comment>, <custom>, <dd>, <del>, <dfn>, <dir>,
<div>, <dl>, document, <dt>, <em>, <embed>, <fieldset>, <font>, <form>, <frame>,
<frameset>, <head>, <hn>, <hr>, <html>, <i>, <iframe>, <img>, <input
type="button">, <input type="checkbox">, <input type="file">, <input
type="hidden">, <input type="image">, <input type="password">, <input
type="radio">, <input type="reset">, <input type="submit">, <input type="text">,
<ins>, <isindex>, <kbd>, <label>, <legend>, <li>, <link>, <listing>, <map>,
<marquee>, <menu>, namespace, <nobr>, <noframes>, <noscript>, <object>, <ol>,
<option>, <p>, <plaintext>, <pre>, <q>, <rt>, <ruby>, <s>, <samp>, <script>,
<select>, <small>, <span>, <strike>, <strong>, <sub>, <sup>, <table>, <tbody>,
<td>, <textarea>, <tfoot>, <th>, <thead>, <title>, <tr>, <tt>, <u>, <ul>, <var>,
<xml>, <xmp>
```

reason

Compatibility: IE4, IE5, IE5.5, IE6

Read-only property. Returns the result of the data transfer. Values: 0 (data has been transfered successfully), 1 (data transfer was aborted), and 2 (data transfer produced an error).

Syntax:

```
window.event.reason
```

Example: See the dataFld (1) property example.
Applies to:

```
event
```

recordNumber

Compatibility: IE4, IE5, IE5.5, IE6

Read and write property. Returns the ordinal number of the record from the data set that generated the object.

Syntax:

```
document.all.elementID.recordNumber = value
```

Example: See the dataFld (1) property example.
Applies to:

```
<a>, <button>, <div>, <frame>, <iframe>, <img>, <input type="checkbox">, <input
type="hidden">, <input type="password">, <input type="radio">, <input type="text">,
<label>, <legend>, <marquee>, <select>, <span>, <textarea>
```

recordset

Compatibility: IE4, IE5, IE5.5, IE6

Read-only property. Returns a reference to the recordset.

Syntax:

```
window.event.recordset
document.all.elementID.recordset
```

Example: See the dataFld (1) property example.
Applies to:

```
event, <object>, <xml>
```

referrer

Compatibility: NN4, NN6, NN7, IE4, IE5, IE5.5, IE6

Read-only property. Returns the URL of the web page containing the link that brought the user to the current document. Returns an empty string if the page has no referrer.

Syntax:

```
document.referrer
```

Example:

```
<a href="pr_referrer_jump.html">Jump to another page</a>
```

Contents of pr_referrer_jump.html:

```
<script language="JavaScript">
function B1() {var m = document.referrer; alert(m);}
</script>
<input type="button" value="Get referrer" onclick="B1();">
```

Applies to:

```
document
```

rel

Compatibility: NN4, NN6, NN7, IE4, IE5, IE5.5, IE6

Read and write property. Establishes the relationship between the element and the destination of its href attribute. Values: Alternate (a substitute file), Appendix (an appendix page), Bookmark, Chapter (a chapter page), Contents (the table of contents), Copyright, Glossary, Help, Index (the index page), Next (the next page), Prev (the previous page), Section (a page that is a section of a group of pages), Shortcut Icon (the href to an icon), Start (the first page), Stylesheet, or Subsection (a subsection page). You can string together multiple space-delimited values.
Syntax:

```
document.getElementById("elementID").rel = value
document.all.elementID.rel = value // IE only
```

Example:

```
<a id="myL" href="examples.css" target="_blank">
The style sheet attached to this document</a>
<script language="JavaScript">
document.getElementById("myL").rel = "stylesheet";
</script>
```

Applies to:

```
<a>, <link>
```

repeat

Compatibility: IE5, IE5.5, IE6

Read-only property. Returns a value indicating whether or not the onKeyDown event is firing repeatedly. Values: true or false.
Syntax:

```
window.event.repeat
```

Example:

```
<script language="JavaScript">
function keyStatus() {x = event.repeat; if (x == true) {
alert("A key has been hold down");}}
</script>
<a id="myL" href="http://www.advocar.com/" target="_blank"
onKeyDown="keyStatus();">Advocar Network</a>
```

Applies to:

event

returnValue

Compatibility: IE4, IE5, IE5.5, IE6

Read and write property. For the event object, it specifies the return value of the event (if false, the action is canceled). For the window object, it specifies the value of a modal dialog window.

Syntax:

```
window.event.returnValue = value
window.returnValue = value
```

Example:

```
<script language="JavaScript">
function L1() {event.returnValue = false;}
</script>
<a id="L1" href="http://www.advocar.com" target="_blank" onClick="L1();">This link
opens the Advocar home page, but it will be canceled</a>
```

Applies to:

event, window

rev

Compatibility: NN6, NN7, IE4, IE5, IE5.5, IE6

Read and write property. Specifies the relationship between the destination of the element's href attribute and the element itself. This is like the rel property, but rev specifies the relationship from the opposite point of view (that is, from the point of view of the href destination). Values: Alternate (a substitute file), Appendix (an appendix page), Bookmark, Chapter (a chapter page), Contents (the table of contents), Copyright, Glossary, Help, Index (the index page), Next (the next page), Prev (the previous page), Section (a page that is a section of a group of pages), Shortcut Icon (the href to an icon), Start (the first page), Stylesheet, or Subsection (a subsection page). You can string together multiple space-delimited values.

Syntax:

```
document.getElementById("elementID").rev = value
document.all.elementID.rev = value // IE only
```

Example:

```
<a id="myL" href="examples.css" target="_self">
The relationship from this anchor to the style sheet attached to this document</a>
<script language="JavaScript">
document.getElementById("myL").rev = "stylesheet";
</script>
```

Applies to:

```
<a>, <link>
```

right

Compatibility: IE5, IE5.5, IE6

Read and write property. Establishes the right coordinate in pixels for the container rectangle object of a text element.

Syntax:

```
textRectangleName.right = value
```

Example: See the bottom property example.
Applies to:

```
TextRectangle
```

rightMargin

Compatibility: IE4, IE5, IE5.5, IE6

Read and write property. Specifies the right margin in pixels of the <body> element. Default value is 10.

Syntax:

```
document.all.bodyID.rightMargin = value
```

Example: See the bottomMargin property example.

Applies to:

<body>

rowIndex

Compatibility: NN6, NN7, IE4, IE5, IE5.5, IE6

Read-only property. Returns the row number of the specified row within the table.

Syntax:

```
document.getElementById("trID").rowIndex
document.all.trID.rowIndex // IE only
```

Example:

```
<script language="JavaScript">
function B1(elem) {var m = elem.rowIndex; alert("Row Index: "+m);}
</script>
<table width="100" border="3" cellspacing="2" cellpadding="2">
    <tr id="tr1" onclick="B1(this);"><td>Row 1</td></tr>
    <tr id="tr2" onclick="B1(this);"> <td>Row 2</td></tr>
    <tr id="tr3" onclick="B1(this);"> <td>Row 3</td></tr>
    <tr id="tr4" onclick="B1(this);"> <td>Row 4</td></tr>
</table>
```

Applies to:

<tr>

rows (1)

Compatibility: NN4, NN6, NN7, IE4, IE5, IE5.5, IE6

Read and write property. Specifies a comma-delimited list of the heights of the frames in the frameset. Values: A number of pixels, a percentage of the total height of the frameset, or a number followed by an asterisk (*), specifying frame height as a relative value. Once regions of the frameset's height are allocated to frames with heights specified in pixels and percentages, the remaining vertical space in the frameset is divided between frames with an asterisk.

Syntax:

```
document.getElementById("framesetID").rows = value
document.framesetID.rows = value // IE only
```

Example:

```
<html><head>
<script language="JavaScript">
document.getElementById("yourFrameset").rows = 600;
</script></head>
<frameset id="yourFrameset" frameborder="yes" border="20px" framespacing="5"
cols="*">
<frame id="topF" name="topFrame" scrolling="NO" noresize src="frameTop.htm">
<frame name="leftFrame" marginwidth="15" noresize scrolling="NO"
src="frameLeft.htm">
<frame name="mainFrame" src="frameMain.html">
</frameset>
</html>
```

Applies to:

```
<frameset>
```

rows (2)

Compatibility: NN4, NN6, NN7, IE4, IE5, IE5.5, IE6

Read and write property. Specifies the number of horizontal rows contained in the element.

Syntax:

```
document.getElementById("textareaID").rows = value
document.all.textareaID.rows = value // IE only
```

Example: See the cols (3) property example.

Applies to:

```
<textarea>
```

rowSpan

Compatibility: NN4, NN6, NN7, IE4, IE5, IE5.5, IE6

Read and write property. Specifies the number of table rows that the cell should span.

Syntax:

```
document.getElementById("elementID").rowSpan = value
document.all.elementID.rowSpan = value // IE only
```

Example:

```
<script language="JavaScript">
function B1() {document.getElementById("th1").rowSpan = 2;}
function B2() {location.reload();}
</script>
<table width="542" border="10" bordercolor="red" cellpadding="20">
    <tr><th id="th1">Cell 1</th><th>Cell 2</th><th id="th5">Cell 3</th></tr>
    <tr><th>Cell 4</th><th id="th2">Cell 5</th><th>Cell 6</th></tr>
    <tr><th>Cell 7</th><th>Cell 8</th><th>Cell 9</th></tr>
    <tr><th >Cell 10</th><th >Cell 11</th><th >Cell 12</th></tr>
</table>
<input type="button" value="Span(2) Cell 1" onClick="B1();">
<input type="button" value="Restore" onClick="B2();">
```

Applies to:

`<td>`, `<th>`

rules

Compatibility: NN6, NN7, IE4, IE5, IE5.5, IE6

Read and write property. Specifies the inner borders to be displayed in a table.
Values: all, cols, groups, none, or rows.

Syntax:

```
document.getElementById("tableID").rules = value
document.all.tableID.rules = value // IE only
```

Example:

```
<script language="JavaScript">
function B1() {document.getElementById("myT2").rules = "all";}
function B2() {document.getElementById("myT2").rules = "cols";}
function B3() {document.getElementById("myT2").rules = "groups";}
function B4() {document.getElementById("myT2").rules = "none";}
function B5() {document.getElementById("myT2").rules = "rows";}
</script>
<table id="myT2" border="" rules="">
<tr><td id="C1">Cell 1</td><td>Cell 2</td><td>Cell 3</td></tr>
<tr><td id="C1">Cell 4</td><td>Cell 5</td><td>Cell 6</td></tr>
</table>
<input type="button" value='rules = "all"' onClick="B1();">
<input type="button" value='rules = "cols"' onClick="B2();">
<input type="button" value='rules = "groups"' onClick="B3();">
<input type="button" value='rules = "none"' onClick="B4();">
<input type="button" value='rules = "rows"' onClick="B5();">
```

Applies to:

`<table>`

---

saveType

Compatibility: IE5.5, IE6

Read-only property. Returns the clipboard content format. This property requires that the onContentSave event be triggered, which fires just before the content of an element that is attached to an element behavior is saved or copied to the clipboard. Values: text or html.

Syntax:

```
window.event.saveType
```

Example:

```
<html xmlns:yourNs><head>
<style>
@media all { IE\:homePage {behavior:url(#default#homepage)}}
</style>
<script language="JavaScript">
function goHomePage(){
    HP.navigateHomePage();
    event.returnValue=false;
}
function B1() {var m = event.saveType; alert(m);}
</script></head>
<body bgcolor="#FFFFFF" text="#000000">
<yourNs:homepage id="HP"/>
<public:attach event="oncontentsave" onevent="cbCopy()" for = myA/>
<a id="secL" href="" onClick="goHomePage();">Navigate to your home page</a>
<input type="button" value="Content type" onclick="B1();">
</body></html>
```

Applies to:

---

event

---

scheme

Compatibility: NN6, NN7, IE6

Read and write property. Establishes a value that allows for better understanding of the content attribute of a `<meta>` element.

Syntax:

```
document.getElementById("metaID").scheme = value
document.all.metaID.scheme = value // IE only
```

Example:

```
<head>
<meta id="myM1" name="date" content="10-25-2003">
<meta id="myM2" name="date" content="25-10-2003">
<script language="JavaScript">
document.all.myM1.scheme = "USA";
document.all.myM2.scheme = "Europe";
</script></head>
```

Applies to:

```
<meta>
```

scope

Compatibility: NN6, NN7, IE6

Read and write property. Enables a cell to act as a header cell for other cells in the same row or column. Values: row, col, rowgroup, and colgroup.

Syntax:

```
document.getElementById("elementID").scope = value
document.all.elementID.scope = value // IE only
```

Example:

```
<table id="myT2"><tr>
<th id="th1">Row 1</th>
<td>Cell</td><td>Cell</td><td>Cell</td>
<td id="td1">Cell info 1</td><td>Cell</td>
</tr></table>
<script language="JavaScript">
document.all.th1.scope = "colgroup";
</script>
<button onclick="alert('This cell provides header information for its col.');">
Cell info 1</button>
```

Applies to:

```
<td>, <th>
```

scopeName

Compatibility: IE5, IE5.5, IE6

Read-only property. Associated with an XML island inserted within the HTML document. Returns the namespace defined for the element.

Syntax:

```
document.all.elementID.scopeName
```

Example:

```
<html id="myHtml" xmlns:yourNs>
<body bgcolor="#FFFFFF" text="#000000">
<button onclick="alert('The scopeName property value is
'+document.all.myHtml.scopeName)">Click here</button>
</body></html>
```

Applies to:

```
<a>, <acronym>, <address>, <applet>, <area>, <b>, <base>, <basefont>, <bdo>,
<bgsound>, <big>, <blockquote>, <body>, <br>, <button>, <caption>, <center>,
<cite>, <code>, <col>, <colgroup>, <comment>, <custom>, <dd>, <del>, <dfn>, <dir>,
<div>, <dl>, <dt>, <em>, <embed>, <fieldset>, <font>, <form>, <frame>, <frameset>,
<head>, <hn>, <hr>, <html>, <i>, <iframe>, <img>, <input type="button">, <input
type="checkbox">, <input type="file">, <input type="hidden">, <input type="image">,
<input type="password">, <input type="radio">, <input type="reset">, <input
type="submit">, <input type="text">, <ins>, <isindex>, <kbd>, <label>, <legend>,
<li>, <link>, <listing>, <map>, <marquee>, <menu>, <nobr>, <noframes>, <noscript>,
<object>, <ol>, <option>, <p>, <plaintext>, <pre>, <q>, <rt>, <ruby>, <s>, <samp>,
<script>, <select>, <small>, <span>, <strike>, <strong>, <sub>, <sup>, <table>,
<tbody>, <td>, <textarea>, <tfoot>, <th>, <thead>, <title>, <tr>, <tt>, <u>, <ul>,
<var>, <wbr>, <xml>, <xmp>
```

screenLeft, screenTop

Compatibility: IE5, IE5.5, IE6

Read-only properties. Return the coordinates in pixels of the top-left corner of the browser window position, relative to the screen.

Syntax:

```
window.screenLeft
window.screenTop
```

Example:

```
<script language="JavaScript">
function B1() {
    var m = ""
    m = "The left coordinate is: " + window.screenLeft + "\n";
```

```
    m += "The top coordinate is: " + window.screenTop + "\n";
    alert(m);
}
</script>
<body bgcolor="#FFFFFF" bottommargin="150">
<input type="button" value="Extract the coordinates" onclick="B1();">
```

Applies to:

window

screenX, screenY (1)

Compatibility: IE4, IE5, IE5.5, IE6

Read and write property. Return the coordinates in pixels of the mouse pointer position relative to the computer screen.

Syntax:

```
window.event.screenX = value
```

Example: See the offsetX, offsetY property example.
Applies to:

event

screenX, screenY (2)

Compatibility: NN6, NN7

Read-only property. Returns the position in pixels of the outer boundary of the browser's window. These values are not the same as screenX (1) and screenY (1) for Internet Explorer, because the browser window includes a four-pixel-wide bar all around. Thus, if you subtract 4 pixels from these values, you'll get the IE values.

Syntax:

```
window.screenX
window.screenY
```

Example: See the offsetX, offsetY property example.
Applies to:

window

scroll

Compatibility: IE4, IE5, IE5.5, IE6

Read and write property. Establishes whether or not both horizontal and vertical scroll bars should appear. Values: yes (scroll bars appear regardless of the size of the document), no (scroll bars do not appear), and auto (scroll bars appear when necessary).

Syntax:

```
document.all.elementID.scroll = value
```

Example:

```
<html>
<body id="myBody" bgcolor="white" text="#000000">
<button onclick="myBody.scroll='yes';">Scroll bars do appear</button>
<button onclick="myBody.scroll='no';">Scroll bars do not appear</button>
<button onclick="myBody.scroll='auto';">Scroll = auto</button>
</body></html>
```

Applies to:

```
<body>, <html> (IE6 only)
```

scrollAmount

Compatibility: IE4, IE5, IE5.5, IE6

Read and write property. Specifies the number of pixels the <marquee> text shifts each time it is redrawn. The default value is 6. The smaller the number, the smoother the scrolling.

Syntax:

```
document.all.marqueeID.scrollAmount = value
```

Example:

```
<script language="JavaScript">
function M3(){document.all.myM.scrollAmount = 2;}
</script>
<marquee id="myM" bgcolor="cyan">Check out our weekly specials.</marquee>
<input type="button" name="S2" value="scrollAmount = 2" onClick="M3();">
```

Applies to:

```
<marquee>
```

scrollDelay

Compatibility: IE4, IE5, IE5.5, IE6

Read and write property. Establishes the speed of the `<marquee>` scroll in milliseconds. The default value is 85. The smaller the number, the slower and smoother the scrolling.

Syntax:

```
document.all.marqueeID.scrollDelay = value
```

Example:

```
<script language="JavaScript">
function B1(){document.all.myM.scrolldelay = 20;}
</script>
<marquee id="myM" bgcolor="cyan">Sample Text</marquee>
<input type="button" value="truespeed" onClick="B1();">
```

Applies to:

```
<marquee>
```

scrollHeight, scrollWidth

Compatibility: NN6, NN7, IE4, IE5, IE5.5, IE6

Read-only properties. Return the total height and width of the element or object.

Syntax:

```
document.all.getElementById("elementID").scrollHeight
document.all.elementID.scrollHeight // IE only
document.all.getElementById("elementID").scrollWidth
document.all.elementID.scrollWidth // IE only
```

Example: See the `offsetX`, `offsetY` property example.

Applies to:

```
<a>, <acronym>, <address>, <applet>, <area>, <b>, <base>, <basefont>, <bdo>, <big>,
<blockquote>, <body>, <br>, <button>, <caption>, <center>, <cite>, <code>, <col>,
<colgroup>, <custom>, <dd>, <del>, <dfn>, <dir>, <div>, <dl>, <dt>, <em>, <embed>,
<fieldset>, <form>, <frame>, <frameset>, <head>, <hn>, <hr>, <html>, <i>, <iframe>,
<img>, <input>, <input type="button">, <input type="checkbox">, <input
type="file">, <input type="image">, <input type="password">, <input type="radio">,
<input type="reset">, <input type="submit">, <input type="text">, <ins>, <isindex>,
<kbd>, <label>, <legend>, <li>, <link>, <listing>, <map>, <marquee>, <menu>,
<meta>, <nobr>, <noframes>, <noscript>, <object>, <ol>, <optgroup>, <option>, <p>,
<param>, <plaintext>, <pre>, <q>, <s>, <samp>, <script>, <select>, <small>, <span>,
<strike>, <strong>, <style>, <sub>, <sup>, <table>, <tbody>, <td>, <textarea>,
<tfoot>, <th>, <thead>, <title>, <tr>, <tt>, <u>, <ul>, <var>, <xmp>
```

scrollLeft, scrollTop

Compatibility: NN6, NN7, IE4, IE5, IE5.5, IE6

Read-only properties. Return the width and height of the element's viewable area that will be exposed by scrolling to the left and to the top, respectively.
Syntax:

```
document.all.getElementById("elementID").scrollLeft
document.all.elementID.scrollLeft // IE only
document.all.getElementById("elementID").scrollTop
document.all.elementID.scrollTop // IE only
```

Example: See the offsetX, offsetY property example.
Applies to:

```
<a>, <acronym>, <address>, <applet>, <area>, <b>, <base>, <basefont>, <bdo>, <big>,
<blockquote>, <body>, <br>, <button>, <caption>, <center>, <cite>, <code>, <col>,
<colgroup>, <custom>, <dd>, <del>, <dfn>, <dir>, <div>, <dl>, <dt>, <em>, <embed>,
<fieldset>, <form>, <frame>, <frameset>, <head>, <hn>, <hr>, <html>, <i>, <iframe>,
<img>, <input>, <input type="button">, <input type="checkbox">, <input
type="file">, <input type="image">, <input type="password">, <input type="radio">,
<input type="reset">, <input type="submit">, <input type="text">, <ins>, <isindex>,
<kbd>, <label>, <legend>, <li>, <link>, <listing>, <map>, <marquee>, <menu>,
<meta>, <nobr>, <noframes>, <noscript>, <object>, <ol>, <optgroup>, <option>, <p>,
<param>, <plaintext>, <pre>, <q>, <s>, <samp>, <script>, <select>, <small>, <span>,
<strike>, <strong>, <style>, <sub>, <sup>, <table>, <tbody>, <td>, <textarea>,
<tfoot>, <th>, <thead>, <title>, <tr>, <tt>, <u>, <ul>, <var>, <xmp>
```

search

Compatibility: NN4, NN6, NN7, IE4, IE5, IE5.5, IE6

Read and write property. When a question mark (?) exists in a URL, this property specifies the string that follows the question mark.
Syntax:

```
document.getElementById("elementID").search = value
document.all.elementID.search = value // IE only
document.location.search = value
```

Example:

```
<script language="JavaScript">
function H1() {alert(document.getElementById("myA").search);}
</script>
<a id="myA" href="http://www.advocar.com?cuid=4"
target="_blank">Wescom Advocar Site</a>
<input type="Button" id="myB" value="Wescom Advocar" onClick="H1();">
```

Applies to:

```
<a>, <area>, location
```

Compatibility: NN6, NN7, IE4, IE5, IE5.5, IE6

Read-only property. Returns the position of the specified <tr> element among the rows of a <tbody>, <thead>, or <tfoot> element. If the specified row does not reside within a <tbody>, <thead>, or <tfoot> element, then this property returns the position of the row among all of the rows in the table.

Syntax:

```
document.getElementById("trID").sectionRowIndex
document.all.trID.sectionRowIndex // IE only
```

Example:

```
<script language="JavaScript">
function B1(elem) {
var m = elem.sectionRowIndex;
alert("The zero-based row index is: "+m);
}
</script>
<table width="100" border="3" cellspacing="2" cellpadding="2">
    <tr id="tr1" onclick="B1(this);"><td>Row 1</td></tr>
    <tr id="tr2" onclick="B1(this);"><td>Row 2</td></tr>
    <tr id="tr3" onclick="B1(this);"><td>Row 3</td></tr>
    <tr id="tr4" onclick="B1(this);"><td>Row 4</td></tr>
</table>
```

Applies to:

```
<tr>
```

selected

Compatibility: NN4, NN6, NN7, IE4, IE5, IE5.5, IE6

Read and write property. Specifies whether or not the <option> element inside a <select> list element is selected. Values: true or false.

Syntax:

```
document.getElementById("optionID").selected = value
document.all.optionID.selected = value // IE only
```

Example:

```
<html><head>
<script>
function B2(colors) {
var col = (colors.options[colors.selectedIndex].value);
```

```
document.all.myOpt.selected = true;
if (col) {document.bgColor = col;}}
</script></head>
<body id="myBody" bgcolor="#FFFFFF" text="#000000"
onUnload="document.forms[0].reset();">
<form method="post" action="">
<select name="colors" onChange="B2(this);">
    <option value="white">White</option>
    <option id="myOpt" value="cyan">Cyan</option>
    <option value="ivory">Ivory</option>
</select>
</form>
</body></html>
```

Applies to:

`<option>`

selectedIndex

Compatibility: NN4, NN6, NN7, IE4, IE5, IE5.5, IE6

Read and write property. Specifies the index of the selected `<option>` element in the `<select>` list element.

Syntax:

```
document.getElementById("selectID").selectedIndex = value
document.all.selectID.selectedIndex = value // IE only
```

Example:

```
<script>
function B2(colors) {
var col = (colors.options[colors.selectedIndex].value);
if (col) {
document.bgColor = col;
}
alert("SelectedIndex value = "+col);
}
</script>
<form method="post" action="">
<select name="colors" onChange="B2(this);">
    <option value="white" selected>White</option>
    <option value="cyan">Cyan</option>
    <option value="ivory">Ivory</option>
    <option id="myO" value="blue">Blue</option>
    <option value="red">Red</option>
    <option value="lightblue">Lightblue</option>
    <option value="beige">Beige</option>
```

```
</select>
</form>
```

Applies to:

```
<select>
```

selector

Compatibility: IE5.5, IE6

Read-only property. Returns the set of pages an @page rule applies to.
    Syntax:

```
document.styleSheets[index1].pages[index2].selector
```

Example:

```
<style>
@page:first { background-color: red }
@page:left { background-color: blue }
@page:right { background-color: orange }
</style>
<script language="JavaScript">
function B1() {
var m = document.styleSheets[0].pages[1];
var n = m.selector;
alert(n);
}
</script>
<input type="button" value="Click here" onclick="B1();">
```

Applies to:

```
page
```

selectorText

Compatibility: IE5, IE5.5, IE6

Read and write property. Specifies the selector portion of the style sheet rule.
The selector is either the element id or the element tag name to which the
style applies.
    Syntax:

```
document.styleSheets[index1].rules[index2].selectorText = value
```

Example:

```
<style>
#myP { font-family:verdana, arial; font-weight:bold; font-size:16px; }
</style>
<script language="JavaScript">
function B1() {alert(document.styleSheets[0].rules[0].selectorText);}
</script>
<p id="myP" onclick="B1()">Sample text.</p>
<input type="button" value="Selector Text" onclick="B1()">
```

Applies to:

page, rule

self

Compatibility: NN4, NN6, NN7, IE4, IE5, IE5.5, IE6

Read-only property. Returns a reference to the current active window or frame.
Syntax:

```
window.self
document.all.frameID.self // IE only
```

Example:

```
<body id="myB" bottommargin=150>
<script language="JavaScript">
function B1() {alert(window.self.myB.bottomMargin);}
</script>
<input type="button" value="Bottom Margin" onclick="B1();">
```

Applies to:

<frame>, window

shape

Compatibility: NN6, NN7, IE4, IE5, IE5.5, IE6

Read and write property. Specifies the shape of the element. Values: circ, circle, rect, rectangle, poly, and polygon.
Syntax:

```
document.getElementById("elementID").shape = value
document.all.elementID.shape = value // IE only
```

Example: See the coords property example.

Applies to:

```
<a> (NN6, NN7, IE6 only), <area>
```

shiftKey

Compatibility: IE4, IE5, IE5.5, IE6

Read-only property. Returns the a value that indicates whether or not the SHIFT key was pressed. Values: true or false.

Syntax:

```
window.event.shiftKey
```

Example:

```
<script language="JavaScript">
function B1() {
var x = event.shiftKey;
if (x == false) {y = "not pressed."} else {y = "pressed."}
alert("The status of the Shift key is "+y);
var y = event.shiftLeft;
if (y == false) {y = "not pressed."; } else {y = "pressed.";}
alert("The status of the left Shift key is "+y);
}
</script>
<a id="myL" title="The Advocar home page" href="http://www.advocar.com/"
target=_blank
onmouseover="B1()">Hover the mouse over this link to unveil the status of the Shift
key</a>
```

Applies to:

```
event
```

shiftLeft

Compatibility: IE5.5, IE6

Read-only property. Returns the a value that indicates whether or not the left SHIFT key was pressed. Values: true or false.

Syntax:

```
window.event.shiftLeft
```

Example: See the shiftKey property example.

Applies to:

event

size (1)

Compatibility: NN4, NN6, NN7, IE4, IE5, IE5.5, IE6

Read and write property. Specifies the font size. Value: Integer from 1 to 7.
Syntax:

```
document.getElementById("elementID").size = value
document.all.elementID.size = value // IE only
```

Example:

```
<font id="myFont" size="2">This is a Font size 2</font>
<button onclick="myFont.size = 4;">Make the Size 4</button>
```

Applies to:

`<basefont>`, `<font>`

size (2)

Compatibility: NN6, NN7, IE4, IE5, IE5.5, IE6

Read and write property. Specifies the height of the horizontal rule in pixels.
Syntax:

```
document.getElementById("hrID").size = value
document.all.hrID.size = value // IE only
```

Example:

```
<script language="JavaScript">
function B3() {document.getElementById("myR").size = "30";}
</script>
<hr id="myR" color="green">
<input type="button" value="Size=30" onClick="B3();">
```

Applies to:

`<hr>`

size (3)

Compatibility: NN6, NN7, IE4, IE5, IE5.5, IE6

Read and write property. Specifies the size, in characters, of the input element.
Syntax:

```
document.getElementById("inputID").size = value
document.all.inputID.size = value // IE only
```

Example:

```
<input id="yourPass" type="password">
<script language="JavaScript">
document.getElementById("yourPass").size = 8;
</script>
```

Applies to:

```
<input type="button">, <input type="checkbox">, <input type="file">, <input
type="image">, <input type="password">, <input type="radio">, <input type="reset">,
<input type="submit">, <input type="text">
```

size (4)

Compatibility: NN6, NN7, IE4, IE5, IE5.5, IE6

Read and write property. Specifies the number of rows in the <select> list element.
Syntax:

```
document.getElementById("selectID").size = value
document.all.selectID.size = value // IE only
```

Example:

```
<script>
function B1() {
var col = document.all.colors.size;
alert(col+" number of options")
}
</script>
<form method="post" action="">
<select id="colors" size="10">
    <option value="white" selected>White</option>
    <option value="cyan">Cyan</option>
    <option value="ivory">Ivory</option>
    <option value="blue">Blue</option>
    <option value="red">Red</option>
    <option value="lightblue">Lightblue</option>
    <option value="beige">Beige</option>
```

```
</select>
<input type="button" value="Number of options" onclick="B1();">
</form>
```

Applies to:

```
<select>
```

sourceIndex

Compatibility: IE4, IE5, IE5.5, IE6

Read-only property. Returns the position of the element within the all collection.

Syntax:

```
document.all.elementID.sourceIndex
```

Example:

```
<button onclick="alert(this.sourceIndex)">Source Index</button>
```

Applies to:

```
<a>, <acronym>, <address>, <applet>, <area>, <b>, <base>, <basefont>, <bdo>,
<bgsound>, <big>, <blockquote>, <body>, <br>, <button>, <caption>, <center>,
<cite>, <code>, <col>, <colgroup>, <comment>, <custom>, <dd>, <del>, <dfn>, <dir>,
<div>, <dl>, <dt>, <em>, <embed>, <fieldset>, <font>, <form>, <frame>, <frameset>,
<head>, <hn>, <hr>, <html>, <i>, <iframe>, <img>, <input type="button">, <input
type="checkbox">, <input type="file">, <input type="hidden">, <input type="image">,
<input type="password">, <input type="radio">, <input type="reset">, <input
type="submit">, <input type="text">, <ins>, <kbd>, <label>, <li>, <link>,
<listing>, <map>, <marquee>, <menu>, <nobr>, <object>, <ol>, <p>, <pre>, <q>, <s>,
<samp>, <script>, <select>, <small>, <span>, <strike>, <strong>, <sub>, <sup>,
<table>, <tbody>, <td>, <textarea>, <tfoot>, <th>, <thead>, <title>, <tr>, <tt>,
<u>, <ul>, <var>, <xmp>
```

span

Compatibility: NN6, NN7, IE4, IE5, IE5.5, IE6

Read and write property. Specifies the number of columns in the group, for the purpose of applying a single style to all columns in the group. This property does not change the rendering of the table.

Syntax:

```
document.getElementById("elementID").span = value
document.all.elementID.span = value // IE only
```

Example:

```
<table border="3" cellspacing="5" cellpadding="5">
  <colgroup>
    <col id="col_1">
    <col id="col_2">
    <col id="col_3">
    <tr><td>Column 1</td><td>Column 2</td><td>Column 3</td><td>Column 4</td>
<td>Column 5</td><td>Column 6</td></tr>
    <tr><td>Cell 1</td><td>Cell 2</td><td>Cell 3</td><td>Cell 4</td><td>Cell 5</td>
<td>Cell 6</td></tr>
</table>
<input type="button" value="Span" onClick="C2();">
<script language="JavaScript">
document.getElementById("col_1").span = 2;
document.getElementById("col_2").span = 3;
document.getElementById("col_3").span = 1;
function C2() {
document.getElementById("col_2").align = "center"
document.getElementById("col_2").style.color = "green";
}
</script>
```

Applies to:

```
<col>, <colgroup>
```

specified

Compatibility: IE5, IE5.5, IE6

Read-only property. Indicates whether or not the attribute has been explicitly specified in the code. Values: true or false.

Syntax:

```
document.all.elementID.attributes[index].specified
```

Example:

```
<button id="myButton" onclick="alert(this.attributes['id'].specified);">Specified
Attributes</button>
```

Applies to:

```
attribute
```

SQRT1_2

Compatibility: NN4, NN6, NN7, IE4, IE5, IE5.5, IE6

Read-only property. A mathematical constant that returns the square root of 1/2.
Syntax:

```
Math.SQRT1_2
```

Example:

```
<button onclick="alert(Math.SQRT1_2);">Math.Sqrt1_2</button>
```

Applies to:

```
Math
```

SQRT2

Compatibility: NN4, NN6, NN7, IE4, IE5, IE5.5, IE6

Read-only property. A mathematical constant that returns the square root of 2.
Syntax:

```
Math.SQRT2
```

Example:

```
<button onclick="alert(Math.SQRT2);">Math.Sqrt2</button>
```

Applies to:

```
Math
```

src

Compatibility: NN4, NN6, NN7, IE4, IE5, IE5.5, IE6

Read and write property. Specifies the URL of the source of the object.
Syntax:

```
document.getElementById("elementID").src = value
document.all.elementID.src = value // IE only
```

Example:

```
<img id="myImg" src="" alt="" onClick="B1();">
<button onclick="B1();">Click here to load image</button>
<script language="JavaScript">
function B1() {document.all.myImg.src = "yourimage.gif";}
</script>
```

Applies to:

```
<applet>, <bgsound> (IE4, IE5, IE5.5, IE6), <embed>, <frame>, <iframe>, <img>,
<input type="image">, <script>, <xml>
```

---

srcElement

Compatibility: IE4, IE5, IE5.5, IE6

Read and write property. Specifies the object that fires the event.
   Syntax:

```
window.event.srcElement = value
```

   Example:

```
<script language="JavaScript">
function B1() {alert(window.event.srcElement.id);}
</script>
<body id="myBody" onclick="B1();">
<button id="myButton1" onclick="B1();">Button One</button>
<button id="myButton2" onclick="B1();">Button Two</button>
</body>
```

   Applies to:

---

event

---

srcFilter

Compatibility: IE4, IE5, IE5.5, IE6

Read-only property. Specifies the name of the filter that fires the onFilterChange
event. Currently, the only supported value of this property is null.
   Syntax:

```
window.event.srcFilter
```

   Example:

```
<html><head>
<script language="JavaScript">
function B1() {
Layer1.filters[0].Apply();
if (Layer1.style.visibility == "visible") {
    Layer1.style.visibility = "hidden";
    Layer1.filters.revealTrans.transition = 2;
    } else {
```

```
        Layer1.style.visibility = "visible";
        Layer1.filters[0].revealTrans.transition = 3;
    }
    Layer1.filters[0].Play();
    var m = window.event.srcFilter;
    alert(m);
}
</script></head>
<body bgcolor="#FFFFFF" text="#000000" bottommargin="150">
<div id="Layer1" style="position:absolute; visibility:visible;
Filter:revealTrans(duration=2, transition=3); left:92px; top:257px; width:100px;
background-color:#FFFF99;">
<img src="yourimage.gif" width="99" height="75"></div>
<input type="button" id="myB1" onClick="B1();" value="Play Transition">
</body></html>
```

Applies to:

event

srcUrn

Compatibility: IE5, IE5.5, IE6

Read-only property. Returns the URN (Uniform Resource Name) of the
behavior that triggered the event. A URN specifies the identity of a resource
rather than its location.

Syntax:

```
window.event.srcUrn
```

Example:

```
<style>
@media all {IE\:homePage {behavior:url(#default#homepage)}}
</style>
<script language="JavaScript">
function goHomePage(){
    HP.navigateHomePage();
    event.returnValue=false;
}
</script>
<script language="JavaScript" for="myA" event="onmouseout">
var m = event.srcUrn;
alert("The value of property srcUrn is: "+m);
</script>
<yourNs:homepage id="HP"/>
<a id="myA" href="" onClick="goHomePage();">Navigate to your home page</a>
```

Applies to:

event

standBy

Compatibility: NN6, NN7, IE6

Read and write property. Specifies a string with the standby value.
Syntax:

```
document.getElementById("objectID").standBy
document.all.objectID.standBy = value // IE only
```

Example:

```
<object classid="clsid:D27CDB6E-AE6D-11cf-96B8-444553540000"
codebase="http://download.macromedia.com/pub/shockwave/cabs/flash/
swflash.cab#version=5,0,0,0"
width="250" height="230" id="myO">
    <param name="movie" value="Puzzle.swf">
    <param name="quality" value="high">
</object>
<script language="JavaScript">
document.all.myO.standby = "You can play this puzzle";
alert(document.all.myO.standby);
</script>
```

Applies to:

<object>

start (1)

Compatibility: IE4, IE5, IE5.5, IE6

Read and write property. Specifies when a video clip viewed through the <img>
element should begin playing. Values: fileopen (starts playing as soon as the file
finishes loading) or mouseover (starts playing when the user moves the mouse over
the object).
Syntax:

```
document.all.elementID.start = value
```

Example:

```
<img id="myI" dynsrc="yourvideofile.avi" alt="">
<script language="JavaScript">
```

```
document.all.myI.start = "mouseover";
</script>
```

Applies to:

```
<img>, <input>, <input type="image">
```

start (2)

Compatibility: NN6, NN7, IE4, IE5, IE5.5, IE6

Read and write property. Establishes the starting number for a <li> element in an <ol> element.
  Syntax:

```
document.getElementById("olID").start = value
document.all.olID.start = value // IE only
```

Example:

```
<ol id="myList"><li>Item One</li><li>Item Two</li>
<li>Item Three</li><li>Item Four</li><li>Item Five</li></ol>
<button onclick="document.all.myList.start=12;">Set Start</button>
```

Applies to:

```
<ol>
```

status (1)

Compatibility: NN4, NN6, NN7, IE4, IE5, IE5.5, IE6

Read and write property. Specifies the status of the control element. Values: true (element is selected), false (the default; element is not selected), or null (element is not initialized).
  Syntax:

```
document.getElementById("elementID").status = value
document.all.elementID.status = value // IE only
```

Example:

```
<html><head>
<script language="JavaScript">
function B2() {var m = document.all.myR.status; alert(m);}
function B3() {var m = document.all.myC.status; alert(m);}
</script></head>
<body bgcolor="#FFFFFF" text="#000000">
```

```
<input type="radio" id="myR" checked>Radio
<input type="button" value="Check Status" onclick="B2();">
<input type="checkbox" id="myC">Checkbox
<input type="button" value="Check Status" onclick="B3();">
</body></html>
```

Applies to:

```
<input type="checkbox">, <input type="radio">, <textarea>
```

status (2)

Compatibility: NN4, NN6, NN7, IE4, IE5, IE5.5, IE6

Read and write property. Specifies the message in the status bar of the window.
   Syntax:

```
window.status = value
```

Example:

```
<html><head>
<script language="JavaScript">
function B1() {window.status = "Welcome to my page";}
</script></head>
<body bgcolor="#FFFFFF" text="#000000">
<p onmouseover="B1();" style="cursor:hand">Move over this text to read the message
in the status bar of this window.</p>
</body></html>
```

Applies to:

```
window
```

suffixes

Compatibility: NN6, NN7

Read-only property. Specifies the valid file extension names for the MIME type.
   Syntax:

```
navigator.mimeTypes[index].suffixes
```

Example: See the description property example.
Applies to:

```
mimeType
```

Compatibility: NN6, NN7, IE6

Read and write property. Specifies the summary information about a table that browsers present through nonvisual means.

Syntax:

```
document.getElementById("tableID").summary = value
document.all.tableID.summary = value // IE only
```

Example:

```
<script language="JavaScript">
function B1() {
document.all.myTable.summary = "Table Contains 4 cells";}
</script>
<table id="myTable" width="542" border="3" cellspacing="5" cellpadding="5">
    <tr><th>Header 1 content</th><th>Header 2 content</th></tr>
    <tr><td>Cell 1 content</td><td>Cell 2 content</td></tr>
</table>
<button onclick="B1();">Add Summary</button>
<button onclick="alert(document.all.myTable.summary);">View Summary</button>
```

Applies to:

```
<table>
```

systemLanguage

Compatibility: IE4, IE5, IE5.5, IE6

Read-only property. Returns the system's default language.

Syntax:

```
objectName.systemLanguage
```

Example:

```
<input type="button" value="Check System Language"
onclick='alert("Your system language code is: \n"+navigator.systemLanguage);'>
```

Applies to:

```
clientInformation, navigator
```

tabIndex

Compatibility: NN6, NN7, IE4, IE5, IE5.5, IE6

Read and write property. Specifies the element's position in the tab order.
Syntax:

```
document.getElementById("elementID").tabIndex = value
document.all.elementID.tabIndex = value // IE only
```

Example:

```
<input type="text" value="Tab 1" tabindex="0"</input>
<input id="myText" type="text" value="Tab 2" tabindex="1"</input>
<button onclick="alert(myText.tabIndex);">Tab Index of second text box</button>
```

Applies to:

```
<a>, <acronym>, <address>, <applet>, <area>, <b>, <bdo>, <big>, <blockquote>,
<body>, <button>, <caption>, <center>, <cite>, <custom>, <dd>, <del>, <dfn>, <dir>,
<div>, <dl>, <dt>, <em>, <fieldset>, <font>, <form>, <frame>, <frameset>, <hn>,
<hr>, <i>, <iframe>, <img>, <input type="button">, <input type="checkbox">, <input
type="file">, <input type="image">, <input type="password">, <input type="radio">,
<input type="reset">, <input type="submit">, <input type="text">, <ins>, <isindex>,
<kbd>, <label>, <legend>, <li>, <listing>, <marquee>, <menu>, <object>, <ol>, <p>,
<plaintext>, <pre>, <q>, <rt>, <ruby>, <s>, <samp>, <select>, <small>, <span>,
<strike>, <strong>, <sub>, <sup>, <table>, <tbody>, <td>, <textarea>, <tfoot>,
<th>, <thead>, <tr>, <tt>, <u>, <ul>, <var>, <xmp>
```

tabStop

Compatibility: IE5.5, IE6

Read and write property. This property specifies whether the element participates in the tab order functionality.
Syntax:

```
defaults.tabStop = value
```

Example:

```
<html xmlns:yourNs>
<head><?import namespace="yourNs" implementation="yourHTC.htc"></head>
<body><yourNs:yourTagName></yourNs:yourTagName>
</body></html>
```

Contents of yourHTC.htc:

```
<public:component tagName="yourTagName">
<attach event="oncontentready" onevent=contentReady() />
</public:component>
<script language="JavaScript">
function contentReady(){
```

```
defaults.viewLink = document;
defaults.viewInheritStyle = false;
defaults.viewMasterTab = false;}
</script>
<body><button onclick="alert(defaults.tabStop);">tab stop</button></body>
```

Applies to:

defaults

tagName

Compatibility: NN6, NN7, IE4, IE5, IE5.5, IE6

Read-only property. Returns the tag name of the element.
Syntax:

```
document.getElementById("elementID").tagName
document.all.elementID.tagName // IE only
```

Example:

```
<button onclick="alert(this.tagName);">Tag Name</button>
```

Applies to:

```
<a>, <acronym>, <address>, <applet>, <area>, <b>, <base>, <basefont>, <bdo>,
<bgsound>, <big>, <blockquote>, <body>, <br>, <button>, <caption>, <center>,
<cite>, <code>, <col>, <colgroup>, <comment>, <custom>, <dd>, <del>, <dfn>, <dir>,
<div>, <dl>, <dt>, <em>, <embed>, <fieldset>, <font>, <form>, <frame>, <frameset>,
<head>, <hn>, <hr>, <html>, <i>, <iframe>, <img>, <input>, <input type="button">,
<input type="checkbox">, <input type="file">, <input type="hidden">, <input
type="image">, <input type="password">, <input type="radio">, <input type="reset">,
<input type="submit">, <input type="text">, <ins>, <isindex>, <kbd>, <label>,
<legend>, <li>, <link>, <listing>, <map>, <marquee>, <menu>, <meta>, <nobr>,
<noframes>, <noscript>, <object>, <ol>, <optgroup>, <option>, <p>, <param>,
<plaintext>, <pre>, <q>, <rt>, <ruby>, <s>, <samp>, <script>, <select>, <small>,
<span>, <strike>, <strong>, <style>, <sub>, <sup>, <table>, <tbody>, <td>,
<textarea>, <tfoot>, <th>, <thead>, <title>, <tr>, <tt>, <u>, <ul>, <var>, <xmp>
```

tagUrn

Compatibility: IE5, IE5.5, IE6

Read-only property. Returns the URN for the namespace of the element.
Syntax:

```
document.getElementById("elementID").tagUrn
document.all.elementID.tagUrn // IE only
```

Example:

```
<HTML XMLNS:Advocar='http://www.advocar.com'>
<button onclick="alert(myA.tagUrn);">Tag Urn</button>
<Advocar:HELLO ID='myA'>
```

Applies to:

```
<a>, <acronym>, <address>, <applet>, <area>, <b>, <base>, <basefont>, <bdo>,
<bgsound>, <big>, <blockquote>, <body>, <br>, <button>, <caption>, <center>,
<cite>, <code>, <col>, <colgroup>, <comment>, <custom>, <dd>, <del>, <dfn>, <dir>,
<div>, <dl>, <dt>, <em>, <embed>, <fieldset>, <font>, <form>, <frame>, <frameset>,
<head>, <hn>, <hr>, <html>, <i>, <iframe>, <img>, <input type="button">, <input
type="checkbox">, <input type="file">, <input type="hidden">, <input type="image">,
<input type="password">, <input type="radio">, <input type="reset">, <input
type="submit">, <input type="text">, <ins>, <isindex>, <kbd>, <label>, <legend>,
<li>, <link>, <listing>, <map>, <marquee>, <menu>, <nobr>, <noframes>, <noscript>,
<object>, <ol>, <option>, <p>, <plaintext>, <pre>, <q>, <rt>, <ruby>, <s>, <samp>,
<script>, <select>, <small>, <span>, <strike>, <strong>, <sub>, <sup>, <table>,
<tbody>, <td>, <textarea>, <tfoot>, <th>, <thead>, <title>, <tr>, <tt>, <u>, <ul>,
<var>, <wbr>, <xml>, <xmp>
```

target (1)

Compatibility: NN4, NN6, NN7, IE4, IE5, IE5.5, IE6

Read and write property. Specifies the window or frame target for the element's content. Values: _blank, _media, _parent, _search, _self (the default), or _top.

Syntax:

```
document.getElementById("elementID").target = value
document.all.elementID.target = value // IE only
```

Example:

```
<html><head>
<script language="JavaScript">
document.getElementById("yourAnchor").target = "_blank";
</script></head>
<body bgcolor="#FFFFFF" text="#000000">
<a id="yourAnchor" href="http://www.advocar.com">Advocar website</a>
</body></html>
```

Applies to:

```
<a>, <area>, <base>, <form>, <link>
```

target (2)

Compatibility: NN4, NN6, NN7

Read-only property. Returns the event target object name.
    Syntax:

```
event.target
eventName.target
```

    Example: See the `layerX` property example.
    Applies to:

```
event
```

text (1)

Compatibility: NN6, NN7, IE4, IE5, IE5.5, IE6

Read and write property. Specifies the foreground color. Value: Web color name or the hexadecimal value in #RRGGBB format.
    Syntax:

```
document.body.text = value
document.getElementById("bodyID").text = value
document.all.bodyID.text = value // IE only
```

    Example:

```
<html><head>
<script language="JavaScript">
function T1() {document.all.myBody.text = "blue";}
</script></head>
<body id="myBody">Some text
<input type="button" value="Change to blue" onClick="T1();">
</body></html>
```

    Applies to:

```
<body>
```

text (2)

Compatibility: NN6, NN7, IE4, IE5, IE5.5, IE6

Read and write property. Specifies the text string for the element.
    Syntax:

```
document.getElementById("elementID").text = value
document.all.elementID.text = value // IE only
```

Example:

```
<script language="JavaScript" id="myS">
function B1() {var m = document.all.myS.text; alert(m);}
</script>
<input type="button" value="View the script code for B1() function"
onclick="B1();">
```

Applies to:

`<a>`, `<comment>`, `<script>`, `<title>`

text (3)

Compatibility: NN6, NN7, IE4, IE5, IE5.5, IE6

Read and write property. Specifies the text string for the element.
Syntax:

```
document.getElementById("optionID").text = value
document.all.optionID.text = value // IE only
```

Example:

```
<script>
function B2(colors) {
var col = (colors.options[colors.selectedIndex].text);
colors.options[colors.selectedIndex].text = "New "+col;
}
</script>
<form method="post" action="">
<select name="colors" onChange="B2(this);">
    <option value="white" selected>White</option>
    <option value="cyan">Cyan</option>
    <option value="ivory">Ivory</option>
    <option id="myO" value="blue">Blue</option>
    <option value="red">Red</option>
    <option value="lightblue">Lightblue</option>
    <option value="beige">Beige</option>
</select>
</form>
```

Applies to:

`<option>`

text (4)

Compatibility: IE4, IE5, IE5.5, IE6

Read and write property. Specifies the text string contained in the textRange object.

Syntax:

```
textRangeName.text = value
```

Example:

```
<script language="javascript">
function B1(){
textRange = document.body.createTextRange();
textRange.text = 'This is a test';}
</script>
<button onclick="B1();">See Text in TextRange</button>
```

Applies to:

```
TextRange
```

tFoot

Compatibility: NN6, NN7, IE4, IE5, IE5.5, IE6

Read and write property. Specifies a reference to a <tfoot> element.

Syntax:

```
document.getElementById("tableID").tFoot = value
document.all.tableID.tFoot = value // IE only
```

Example:

```
<script language="JavaScript">
function T1() {document.all.myT.tHead.style.backgroundColor = "blue";}
function T2() {document.all.myT.tFoot.style.backgroundColor = "red";}
</script>
<table id="myT" border="1" width="500">
  <thead><tr><td>tHead, Cell 1</td></tr></thead>
  <tbody><tr><td>tBody, Cell 2</td></tr>
  <tr><td>tBody, Cell 3</td></tr>
  <tr><td>tBody, Cell 4</td></tr></tbody>
  <tfoot><tr><td>tFoot, Cell 5</td></tr></tfoot>
</table>
<button onclick="T1();">Turn Head Blue</button>
<button onclick="T2();">Turn Foot Red</button>
```

Applies to:

```
<table>
```

tHead

Compatibility: NN6, NN7, IE4, IE5, IE5.5, IE6

Read and write property. Specifies a reference to a <thead> element.
   Syntax:

```
document.getElementById("tableID").tHead = value
document.all.tableID.tHead = value // IE only
```

   Example: See the tFoot property example.
   Applies to:

```
<table>
```

title (1)

Compatibility: NN6, NN7, IE4, IE5, IE5.5, IE6

Read and write property. Establishes a tooltip for the element.
   Syntax:

```
document.getElementById("elementID").title = value
document.all.elementID.title = value // IE only
```

   Example:

```
<a id="myL" href="http://www.advocar.com/" target="_blank" title="Advocar
website">A website</a>
<button onclick="alert(myL.title);">Title</button>
```

   Applies to:

```
<a>, <acronym>, <address>, <applet>, <area>, <b>, <base>, <basefont>, <bdo>, <big>,
<blockquote>, <body>, <br>, <button>, <caption>, <cite>, <code>, <col>, <colgroup>,
<custom>, <dd>, <del>, <dfn>, <dir>, <div>, <dl>, <dt>, <em>, <embed>, <fieldset>,
<font>, <form>, <frame>, <frameset>, <head>, <hn>, <hr>, <html>, <i>, <iframe>,
<img>, <input>, <input type="button">, <input type="checkbox">, <input
type="file">, <input type="image">, <input type="password">, <input type="radio">,
<input type="reset">, <input type="submit">, <input type="text">, <ins>, <isindex>,
<kbd>, <label>, <legend>, <li>, <link>, <listing>, <map>, <marquee>, <menu>,
<meta>, <noframes>, <noscript>, <object>, <ol>, <optgroup>, <option>, <p>, <param>,
<pre>, <q>, <rt>, <ruby>, <s>, <samp>, <script>, <small>, <span>, <strike>,
<strong>, <sub>, <sup>, <table>, <tbody>, <td>, <textarea>, <tfoot>, <th>, <thead>,
<title>, <tr>, <tt>, <u>, <ul>, <var>, <xmp>
```

title (2)

Compatibility: NN4, NN6, NN7, IE4, IE5, IE5.5, IE6

Read-only property in NN4; read and write property in NN6+ and IE4+. Returns the string between the opening and closing tags of the <title> element.

Syntax:

```
document.title = value
```

Example:

```
<html><head>
<title>properties_title</title>
<script language="JavaScript">
function B1() {document.title = "This is the new title ";}
function B2() {var n = document.title; alert(n);}
</script></head>
<body bgcolor="#FFFFFF" text="#000000">
<button onclick="B1();">Click here to change the title of this page</button>
<button onclick="B2();">Click here to display the title of this page</button>
</body></html>
```

Applies to:

```
document
```

title (3)

Compatibility: IE4, IE5, IE5.5, IE6

Read and write property. Specifies the title of the style sheet.

Syntax:

```
document.styleSheets[index].title
document.all.styleID.title
```

Example:

```
<style id="yourStyleSheet">
.body { font-family:verdana; color:blue }
</style>
<script language="JavaScript">
document.getElementById("yourStyleSheet").title = "This is my internal style sheet";
alert(document.styleSheets[0].title);
</script>
```

Applies to:

```
stylesheet
```

Compatibility: IE4, IE5, IE5.5, IE6

Read-only property. When you move the mouse across a page, the onmousemove, onmouseover, and onmouseout events are triggered every time you enter the region of an element. This property returns an instance of the element that is directly underneath the mouse pointer when one of the aforementioned events fires.

Syntax:

```
window.event.toElement
```

Example:

```
<html><head><script>
function alertMe() {alert(event.toElement.innerText);}
</script></head>
<body>
<table border="1">
<tr><td onmouseover="alertMe();">CELL 1</td></tr>
<tr><td onmouseover="alertMe();">CELL 2</td></tr>
<tr><td onmouseover="alertMe();">CELL 3</td></tr>
</table>
</body></html>
```

Applies to:

```
event
```

top (1)

Compatibility: NN4, NN6, NN7, IE4, IE5, IE5.5, IE6

Read-only property. When a window contains frames, this property returns a reference to the parent window of all the frames.

Syntax:

```
window.top
```

Example:

```
<html><head>
<script language="JavaScript">
function B1() {
var m = window.top.document.getElementById("myP").tagName;     alert("Tag name:
<"+m+">");
}
</script></head>
<body>
```

```
<div id="myP" onClick="B1();" style="background-color:black; color:white">Click in
this text to check its tag name.</div>
</body></html>
```

Applies to:

window

top (2)

Compatibility: IE5, IE5.5, IE6

Read and write property. Establishes the value in pixels of the top coordinate of
the container rectangle surrounding the element's content.
Syntax:

```
textRectangleName.top = value
```

Example: See the bottom property example.
Applies to:

TextRectangle

topMargin

Compatibility: IE4, IE5, IE5.5, IE6

Read and write property. Specifies the top margin of the <body> element in pixels.
Default value is 15.
Syntax:

```
document.all.bodyID.topMargin = value
```

Example: See the bottomMargin property example.
Applies to:

<body>

trueSpeed

Compatibility: IE4, IE5, IE5.5, IE6

Read and write property. Specifies whether or not the speed of the <marquee>
can be faster than a scrollDelay value of 60. Values: true (sets the speed to the
scrollDelay value) or false (the default; sets the speed to 60).
Syntax:

```
document.all.marqueeID.trueSpeed = value
```

Example:

```
<script language="JavaScript">
function B1(){document.all.myM.trueSpeed = false;}
</script>
<marquee id="myM" bgcolor="cyan">Sample Text</marquee>
<input type="button" value="truespeed" onClick="B1();">
```

Applies to:

```
<marquee>
```

type (1)

Compatibility: NN6, NN7, IE6

Read and write property. Establishes the MIME type for the element.
    Syntax:

```
document.getElementById("elementID").type = value
document.all.elementID.type = value // IE only
```

Example:

```
<button onClick="alert(myL.type);">MIME type for link</button>
<a id="myL" href="yourvideo.avi" type="video/mpeg">The video sample</a>
```

Applies to:

```
<a>, <link>, <object>, <script>
```

type (2)

Compatibility: NN4, NN6, NN7, IE4, IE5, IE5.5, IE6

Read-only property. Returns the value of the type attribute of the `<button>`
element. Values: button (the default), reset , or submit.
    Syntax:

```
document.getElementById("buttonID").type
document.all.buttonID.type // IE only
```

Example:

```
<html>
<body bgcolor="#FFFFFF" text="#000000">
<input type="button" value='type = "button"'
```

```
onClick="alert('The value of type property for this element is:\
n&quot;'+this.type+'&quot;');">
<input type="reset" value='type = "reset"'
onClick="alert('The value of type property for this element is:\
n&quot;'+this.type+'&quot;');">
<input type="submit" value='type = "submit"'
onClick="alert('The value of type property for this element is:\
n&quot;'+this.type+'&quot;');">
</body></html>
```

Applies to:

```
<button>
```

type (3)

Compatibility: NN4, NN6, NN7, IE4, IE5, IE5.5, IE6

Read-only property. Specifies the name of the event.

Syntax:

```
eventName.type // NN only
window.event.type // IE only
```

Example:

```
<html><head>
<script language="JavaScript">
function B1(){var m = window.event.type; alert(m)}
</script></head>
<body bgcolor="#FFFFFF" text="#000000">
<input type="button" value='type = "button"'
onClick="B1();">
</body></html>
```

Applies to:

```
event
```

type (4)

Compatibility: NN6, NN7, IE4, IE5, IE5.5, IE6

Read and write property. Specifies the style of the <ol> or <ul> elements. Values: 1 (the default; numeric list), a (alphabetical lowercase), A (alphabetical uppercase), i (roman numerals lowercase), I (roman numerals uppercase), disc (show a filled circle), circle (show an empty circle), and square (show an empty box).

Syntax:

```
document.getElementById("elementID").type = value
document.all.elementID.type = value // IE only
```

Example:

```
<ol id="myOl"><li>Item One<li>Item Two<li>Item Three</ol>
<script language="JavaScript">
document.getElementById("myOl").type = "i"
</script>
</body></html>
```

Applies to:

```
<li>, <ol>, <ul>
```

type (5)

Compatibility: NN6, NN7, IE6

Read and write property. Specifies the content type of a `<param>` element's value attribute when its valueType attribute is set to ref.

Syntax:

```
document.getElementById("paramID").type = value
document.all.paramID.type = value // IE only
```

Example:

```
<html>
<body>
<object classid="clsid:D27CDB6E-AE6D-11cf-96B8-444553540000" codebase="http://
download.macromedia.com/pub/shockwave/cabs/flash/swflash.cab#version=5,0,0,0"
width="243" height="194">
<param id="myP1" name="movie" valuetype="ref">
<param id="myP2" name="quality">
<script language="JavaScript">
document.getElementById("myP1").type = "video/*";
</script>
<embed id="myE" src="yourFlashMovie.swf" quality="high" pluginspage="http://
www.macromedia.com/shockwave/download/index.cgi?P1_Prod_Version=ShockwaveFlash"
type="application/x-shockwave-flash" width="243" height="194">
</embed></object>
</body></html>
```

Applies to:

```
<param>
```

type (6)

Compatibility: NN4, NN6, NN7, IE4, IE5, IE5.5, IE6

Read-only property. Determines whether or not a <select> element can have multiple selections. This property is equivalent to using the multiple attribute. Values: select-multiple or select-one (the default).

Syntax:

```
document.getElementById("selectID").type
document.all.selectID.type // IE only
```

Example:

```
<select id="mySelect" size="5" multiple="select-multiple">
<option>Item 1</option><option>Item 2</option>
<option>Item 3</option><option>Item 4</option>
<option>Item 5</option>
</select>
<button onclick="alert(mySelect.multiple);">Multiple</button>
```

Applies to:

```
<select>
```

type (7)

Compatibility: IE4, IE5, IE5.5, IE6

Read-only property. Returns the type of the user's selection. Values: none (no selection), text (a text selection), or control (a control selection).

Syntax:

```
document.selection.type
```

Example:

```
<html>
<body onclick="alert(document.selection.type);">
<p>Select any element in the page</p>
<input type="text" value="Some text">
<input type="button" value="Some button">
</body></html>
```

Applies to:

```
selection
```

type (8)

Compatibility: NN6, NN7, IE4, IE5, IE5.5, IE6

Read and write property. Specifies the CSS language version used to create the style sheet. Values: CSS1, CSS2, or CSS-P.

Syntax:

```
document.getElementById("styleID").type = value
document.all.styleID.type = value // IE only
```

Example:

```
<style id="myS" type="CSS2"></style>
<button onclick="alert(document.all.myS.type);">style sheet</button>
```

Applies to:

```
<style>
```

type (9)

Compatibility: NN6, NN7, IE4, IE5, IE5.5, IE6

Read and write property. Specifies the value of the type attribute for a <style> or <link> element associated with an external style sheet. Value: text/css.

Syntax:

```
document.styleSheets[index].type = value
```

Example:

```
<link id="myStyle" rel="stylesheet" href="yourstyle.css" type="text/css">
<script language="JavaScript">
function B1() {alert(document.styleSheets[0].type);}
</script>
<input type="button" value="Click here" onClick="B1();">
```

Applies to:

```
stylesheet
```

type (10)

Compatibility: NN4, NN6, NN7, IE4, IE5, IE5.5, IE6

Read-only property. Returns the type of input element. Value: textarea.

Syntax:

```
document.getElementById("textareaID").type
document.all.textareaID.type // IE only
```

Example:

```
<html><head>
<script language="JavaScript">
function B1() {
alert("The 'myElem' element has a type value of:\n"+myElem.type);
}
</script></head>
<body bgcolor="#FFFFFF" text="#000000">
<textarea name="myElem" cols="20" rows="8"></textarea>
<input type="button" value="Click here" onClick="B1();">
</body></html>
```

Applies to:

```
<textarea>
```

type (11)

Compatibility: NN4, NN6, NN7, IE4, IE5, IE5.5, IE6

Read and write-once property, meaning that after the <input> element is created, its type property cannot be modified. If you wish to set the type value during run time, you must first create the element with the createElement() method and then change the property before the element is inserted in the document.

Syntax:

```
document.getElementById("inputID").type
document.all.inputID.type // IE only
```

Example:

```
<script language="JavaScript">
function B1(){
   var newN = document.createElement("input");
   newN.type = "text";
   myL.appendChild(newN);
   newN.innerText="Testing";}
</script>
<form id="myL">
<button onclick="B1();" type="button">Add Text Input</button>
</form>
```

Applies to:

`<input>`

---

type (12)

Compatibility: NN6, NN7

Read-only property. Specifies the type of a `mimetype` object.
Syntax:

`navigator.mimeTypes[index].type`

Example: See the `description` property example.
Applies to:

`mimeType`

---

typeDetail

Compatibility: IE5.5, IE6

Read-only property. Reserved for some future use, it returns the name of the selection type. Value: undefined.
Syntax:

`document.selection.typeDetail`

Example:

```
<p>Select a portion of the sample text here. Then click the button</p>
<input type="button" value="Click here"
onclick="alert(document.selection.typeDetail);">
```

Applies to:

`selection`

---

uniqueID

Compatibility: IE5, IE5.5, IE6

Read-only property. Returns the unique ID of the element within the page.
Syntax:

`document.all.elementID.uniqueID`

Example:

```
<button onclick="alert(this.uniqueID);">Unique ID</button>
```

Applies to:

```
<a>, <acronym>, <address>, <applet>, <area>, <b>, <base>, <basefont>, <bgsound>,
<big>, <blockquote>, <body>, <br>, <button>, <caption>, <center>, <cite>, <code>,
<col>, <colgroup>, <comment>, <dd>, <del>, <dfn>, <dir>, <div>, <dl>, document,
<dt>, <em>, <embed>, <fieldset>, <font>, <form>, <frame>, <frameset>, <head>, <hn>,
<hr>, <html>, <i>, <iframe>, <img>, <input type="button">, <input type="checkbox">,
<input type="file">, <input type="hidden">, <input type="image">, <input
type="password">, <input type="radio">, <input type="reset">, <input
type="submit">, <input type="text">, <ins>, <kbd>, <label>, <legend>, <li>, <link>,
<listing>, <map>, <marquee>, <menu>, <nobr>, <object>, <ol>, <option>, <p>,
<plaintext>, <pre>, <q>, <s>, <samp>, <script>, <select>, <small>, <span>,
<strike>, <strong>, <sub>, <sup>, <table>, <tbody>, <td>, <textarea>, <tfoot>,
<th>, <thead>, <title>, <tr>, <tt>, <u>, <ul>, <var>, <xmp>
```

units

Compatibility: IE4, IE5, IE5.5, IE6

Read-only property. Returns the units of measurement for the element's height and width. Values: px or em.

Syntax:

```
document.all.embedID.units
```

Example:

```
<embed id="myE" src="yourshockwavefile.swf" quality=high
pluginspage="http://www.macromedia.com/shockwave/download/
index.cgi?P1_Prod_Version=ShockwaveFlash"
type="application/x-shockwave-flash" width="243" height="194" units="px"></embed>
<button onclick="alert(myE.units);">Units</button>
```

Applies to:

```
<embed>
```

updateInterval

Compatibility: IE4, IE5, IE5.5, IE6

Read and write property. Specifies the number of milliseconds between screen updates. A value too small or too large can adversely affect the page rendering response. The default value is 0, which means that no interval is set.

Syntax:

```
screen.updateInterval = value
```

Example:

```
<button onclick="screen.updateInterval=2000; alert(screen.updateInterval);">Update
Interval</button>
```

Applies to:

```
screen
```

URL

Compatibility: NN4, NN6, NN7, IE4, IE5, IE5.5, IE6

Read-only property. Returns the URL of the document object.
Syntax:

```
document.URL
```

Example:

```
<button onclick="alert(document.URL);">URL</button>
<button onclick="alert(document.URLUnencoded);">URL Unencoded</button>
```

Applies to:

```
document
```

URLUnencoded

Compatibility: NN4, NN6, NN7, IE5.5, IE6

Read-only property. Returns the unencoded URL of the current document.
Syntax:

```
document.URLUnencoded
```

Example: See the URL property example.
Applies to:

```
document
```

urn

Compatibility: IE4, IE5, IE5.5, IE6

Read and write property. Specifies the URN (Uniform Resource Name) for a document that is the target of an <a> element or namespace object.

Syntax:

```
document.all.elementID.urn = value
namespace.urn = value
```

Example:

```
<script language="JavaScript">
function B1() {var m = document.all.myA.urn; alert(m);}
</script>
<input type="button" value="Get the urn" onclick="B1();">
<a id="myA" href=http://www.advocar.com/ urn="Advocar Website">Advocar</a>
```

Applies to:

```
<a>, namespace (IE5.5, IE6 only)
```

useMap

Compatibility: NN4 (<img> only), NN6, NN7, IE4, IE5, IE5.5, IE6

Read and write property. Specifies the URL to use as a client-side image map.

Syntax:

```
document.getElementById("elementID").useMap = value
document.all.elementID.useMap = value // IE only
```

Example: See the coords property example.

Applies to:

```
<img>, <input> (NN6, NN7, and IE6 only), <object> (IE6 only)
```

userAgent

Compatibility: NN4, NN6, NN7, IE4, IE5, IE5.5, IE6

Read-only property. Returns the name and version of the user agent, or browser.

Syntax:

```
objectName.userAgent
```

Example:

```
<button onclick="alert(navigator.userAgent);">User Agent</button>
```

Applies to:

clientInformation, navigator

userLanguage

Compatibility: IE4, IE5, IE5.5, IE6

Read-only property. Returns the system's language.
   Syntax:

objectName.userLanguage

   Example:

```
<button onclick="alert(navigator.userLanguage);">User Language</button>
```

   Applies to:

clientInformation, navigator

vAlign (1)

Compatibility: IE4, IE5, IE5.5, IE6

Read and write property. Specifies whether the <caption> element associated with a table appears above or under the table. Values: top (the default) or bottom.
   Syntax:

document.all.*captionID*.vAlign = *value*

   Example:

```
<table width="200" border="8" cellspacing="5" cellpadding="5" align="left">
   <caption id="myC" style="color:red;">Table 2-5. This is the caption for this
table.</caption>
<script language="JavaScript">
document.all.myC.vAlign = "bottom";
</script>
   <tr><td>Cell 1</td><td>Cell 2</td></tr>
   <tr><td>Cell 3</td><td>Cell 4</td></tr>
</table>
```

   Applies to:

<caption>

Compatibility: NN4, NN6, NN7, IE4, IE5, IE5.5, IE6

Read and write property. Specifies how the element's content is vertically aligned. Values: `middle` (the default), `baseline`, `bottom`, or `top`.

Syntax:

```
document.getElementById("elementID").vAlign = value
document.all.elementID.vAlign = value // IE only
```

Example:

```
<html>
<body bgcolor="#FFFFFF" text="#000000">
<table border="3" cellspacing="5" cellpadding="5" align="left">
<tr id="tr1">
<td>Cell 1. Aligned top.</td><td>Cell 2. Aligned top.</td>      <td><img
src="yourImage1.jpg" width="90" height="90"></td>
</tr>
<tr id="tr2">
<td>Cell 4. Aligned bottom.</td><td>Cell 5. Aligned bottom.</td>      <td><img
src="yourImage2.gif" width="96" height="96"></td>
</tr>
</table>
<script language="JavaScript">
document.getElementById("tr1").vAlign = "top";
document.getElementById("tr2").vAlign = "bottom";
</script>
</body></html>
```

Applies to:

```
<col>, <colgroup>, <tbody>, <td>, <tfoot>, <th>, <thead>, <tr>
```

value (1)

Compatibility: IE6

Read and write property. Specifies the value of the attribute object. The attribute object is accessible through the attributes collection.

Syntax:

```
document.all.elementID.attributes[index].value = value
```

Example:

```
<button id="myButton" onclick="alert(this.attributes('id').value);">ID of this
button</button>
```

Applies to:

attribute

value (2)

Compatibility: NN4, NN6, NN7, IE4, IE5, IE5.5, IE6

Read and write property. Specifies the value of the control element.
    Syntax:

```
document.getElementById("elementID").value = value
document.all.elementID.value = value // IE only
```

Example:

```html
<html>
<body bgcolor="#FFFFFF" text="#000000">
<form id="myForm"><table><tr>
<td><input id="E1" type="button" onClick="alert('This element value is:\
n'+this.value);"></td>
<td><input id="E2" type="reset" onClick="alert('This element value is:\
n'+this.value);"></td>
<td><input id="E3" type="submit" onClick="alert('This element value is:\
n'+this.value);"></td>
</tr></table></form>
<script language="JavaScript">
document.getElementById("E1").value = 'input type = "button"';
document.getElementById("E2").value='input type = "reset"';
document.getElementById("E3").value='input type = "submit"';
</script>
</body></html>
```

Applies to:

```
<button>, <input>, <input type="button">, <input type="checkbox">, <input
type="file">, <input type="hidden">, <input type="password">, <input type="radio">,
<input type="reset">, <input type="submit">, <input type="text">
```

value (3)

Compatibility: NN6, NN7, IE4, IE5, IE5.5, IE6

Read and write property. Specifies the value of the <li> element.
    Syntax:

```
document.getElementById("liID").value = value
document.all.liID.value = value // IE only
```

Example:

```
<ul style="border:solid; cursor:hand;">
    <li id="li1" style="background-color:blue;" onClick="alert(this.value);">Click Item 1
    <li id="li2" style="background-color:gold;" onClick="alert(this.value);">Click Item 2
    <li id="li3" style="background-color:blue;" onClick="alert(this.value);">Click Item 3
    <li id="li4" style="background-color:gold;" onClick="alert(this.value);">Click Item 4
    <li id="li5" style="background-color:blue;" onClick="alert(this.value);">Click Item 5
</ul>
<script language="JavaScript">
document.getElementById("li1").value = 1;
document.getElementById("li2").value = 2;
document.getElementById("li3").value = 3;
document.getElementById("li4").value = 4;
document.getElementById("li5").value = 5;
</script>
```

Applies to:

```
<li>
```

value (4)

Compatibility: NN4, NN6, NN7, IE4, IE5, IE5.5, IE6

Read and write property. Specifies the value of the element when the form is submitted to the server.

Syntax:

```
document.getElementById("elementID").value = value
document.all.elementID.value = value // IE only
```

Example:

```
<select onchange="alert(this.options[this.selectedIndex].value);">
<option value="March 6">Elizabeth</option>
<option value="April 4">Emily</option>
<option value="April 7">Lázaro</option>
<option value="June 10">Karen</option>
<option value="June 11">John</option>
</select>
```

Applies to:

```
<option>, <select>
```

value (5)

Compatibility: NN4, NN6, NN7, IE4, IE5, IE5.5, IE6

Read-only property. Retrieves the text in the element.
   Syntax:

```
document.getElementById("textareaID").value
document.all.textareaID.value // IE only
```

Example:

```
<html><head><script language="JavaScript">
function B1() {alert(myT.value); }
</script></head>
<body onload="B1();">
<textarea id="myT">textarea value</textarea>
</body></html>
```

Applies to:

```
<textarea>
```

value (6)

Compatibility: NN4, NN6, NN7, IE4, IE5, IE5.5, IE6

Read and write property. Specifies the value for the <param> element.
   Syntax:

```
document.getElementById("paramID").valueType = value
document.all.paramID.valueType = value // IE only
```

Example: See the valueType property example.
   Applies to:

```
<param>
```

valueType

Compatibility: NN6, NN7, IE6

Read and write property. Specifies the data type of the value attribute of the
<param> element. Values: data, ref (the value attribute is a URI), or object (the
value attribute is the name of an object).
   Syntax:

```
document.getElementById("paramID").valueType = value
document.all.paramID.valueType = value // IE only
```

Example:

```
<object classid="clsid:D27CDB6E-AE6D-11cf-96B8-444553540000"
codebase="http://download.macromedia.com/pub/shockwave/cabs/flash/
swflash.cab#version=5,0,0,0"
width="243" height="194">
    <param id="myP1" name="movie" value="yourshockwavefile.swf" valuetype="ref"
type="video/*">
    <param id="myP2" value="high" name="quality">
<script language="JavaScript">
document.getElementById("myP1").valueType = "ref";
</script>
</object>
```

Applies to:

```
<param>
```

vcard_name

Compatibility: IE5, IE5.5, IE6

Write-only property. Specifies the vCard values to use when autocomplete is turned on for the `<input type="password">` or `<input type="text">` element. Value: vcard. followed by Business.City, Business.Country, Business.Fax, Business.Phone, Business.State, Business.StreetAddress, Business.URL, Business.Zipcode, Cellular, Company, Department, DisplayName, Email, FirstName, Gender, Home.City, Home.Country, Home.Fax, Home.Phone, Home.State, Home.StreetAddress, Home.Zipcode, Homepage, JobTitle, LastName, MiddleName, Notes, Office, or Pager.

Syntax:

```
document.all.inputID.vCard_name = value
```

Example:

```
<input id="myText" type="text" name="firstName">
<script language="JavaScript">
document.all.myText.vcard_name = "vCard.FirstName";
</script>
```

Applies to:

```
<input type="password">, <input type="text">
```

version

Compatibility: NN6, NN7, IE6

Read and write property. Specifies the DTD version for the current document.
Syntax:

```
document.html.version = value
```

Example:

```
<script language="JavaScript">
var m = document.html.version; alert(m);
</script>
```

Applies to:

```
<html>
```

viewInheritStyle

Compatibility: IE5.5, IE6

Read and write property. Specifies whether or not a document fragment imported into the document inherits the styles set in the document's style sheet. Values: true or false.
Syntax:

```
document.defaults.viewInheritStyle = value
```

Example: See the tabStop property example.
Applies to:

```
defaults
```

viewLink

Compatibility: IE5.5, IE6

Read-only property. Retrieves the document object that originally contained an element in the current document.
Syntax:

```
document.defaults.viewLink
```

Example: See the tabStop property example.
Applies to:

```
defaults
```

viewMasterTab

Compatibility: IE5.5, IE6

Read and write property. Specifies whether or not the element affected by the viewLink property is included in the tab sequence of the current document. Values: true or false.

Syntax:

```
document.defaults.viewMasterTab = value
```

Example: See the tabStop property example.
Applies to:

```
defaults
```

vLink

Compatibility: NN6, NN7, IE4, IE5, IE5.5, IE6

Read and write property. Specifies the text color of all <a> elements that have already been visited. Value: Web color name or a hexadecimal value in #RRGGBB format.

Syntax:

```
document.body.vLink = value
document.getElementById("bodyID").vLink = value
document.all.bodyID.vLink = value // IE only
```

Example:

```
<body bgcolor="white" text="#000000">
<a href="http://www.advocar.com" target="_blank">Advocar Home Page</a>
<script language="JavaScript">
document.body.vLink = "gold";
</script>
</body>
```

Applies to:

```
<body>, defaults
```

vlinkColor

Compatibility: NN4, NN6, NN7, IE4, IE5, IE5.5, IE6

Read and write property. Specifies the text color of all `<a>` elements that have already been visited. This property is very similar to the vLink property, except that vlinkColor affects the document object rather than the `<body>` element. Value: Web color name or hexadecimal value in #RRGGBB format.

Syntax:

```
document.getElementById("elementID").vlinkColor = value
document.all.elementID.vlinkColor = value // IE only
```

Example:

```
<body bgcolor="white" text="#000000">
<a href="http://www.nostarch.com" target="_blank">No Starch Press Home Page</a>
<script language="JavaScript">document.vLinkColor = "orange";
</script>
</body>
```

Applies to:

```
document
```

volume

Compatibility: IE4, IE5, IE5.5, IE6

Read and write property. Establishes the volume for the `<bgsound>` element. Value: A number from -10,000 (lowest volume) to 0 (highest volume).

Syntax:

```
document.all.bgsoundID.volume = value
```

Example: See the balance property example.
Applies to:

```
<bgsound>
```

vspace

Compatibility: NN4, NN6 and NN7 (`<applet>`, `<object>` only), IE4, IE5, IE5.5, IE6

Read and write property. Establishes the number of pixels of space on the top and bottom sides of the element.

Syntax:

```
document.getElementById("elementID").vspace = value
document.all.elementID.vspace = value // IE only
```

Example: See hspace property example.

Applies to:

<applet>, <iframe>, <img>, <input>, <input type="image">, <marquee>, <object>

wheelDelta

Compatibility: IE5.5, IE6

Read-only property. Returns a value of 120 if the mouse wheel is rotated up and -120 if it is rotated down.

Syntax:

```
window.event.wheelDelta
```

Example:

```
<html><body>
<p>Move the pointer on top of the image and then move the mouse wheel up or down.</p>
<img id="yourimage" src="yourimage.gif" onmousewheel="alert('Wheel Delta: ' +
event.wheelDelta);">
</body></html>
```

Applies to:

event

width (1)

Compatibility: NN4, NN6, NN7, IE4, IE5, IE5.5, IE6

Read and write property. Establishes the width of the element. Value: An integer (specifying a number of pixels) or integer% (a percent of the width of the element's parent).

Syntax:

```
document.getElementById("elementID").width = value
document.all.elementID.width = value // IE only
```

Example:

```
<html><head><script language="JavaScript">
function W1() {document.getElementById("myT").width = "300";}
function W2() {document.getElementById("myT").width = "500";}
</script></head>
<body bgcolor="#ccffcc" text="#000000">
<table id="myT" cols="3" border="3" cellspacing="5" cellpadding="5">
<script language="JavaScript">
document.getElementById("myT").width = 500;
```

```
</script>
<tr><th>Column 1</th><th>Column 2</th><th>Column 3</th></tr>
<tr><td>Cell 1</td><td>Cell 2</td><td>Cell 3</td></tr>
</table>
<input type="button" value="Change table width to 300px" onClick="W1();">
<input type="button" value="Restore table width to 500px" onClick="W2();">
</body></html>
```

Applies to:

<applet>, <col>, <colgroup>, <embed>, <frame>, <frameset>, <iframe>, <marquee>, <object>, <table>, <td>, <th>, <tr>

width (2)

Compatibility: NN4, NN6, NN7, IE4, IE5, IE5.5, IE6

Read and write property. Establishes the width of the element.

Syntax:

```
document.getElementById("elementID").width = value
document.all.elementID.width = value // IE only
```

Example:

```
<script language="JavaScript">
function B1() {alert(document.getElementById("myI").width+"px");}
</script>
<img id="myI" src="yourimage.jpg" alt="" width="300" height="225">
<input type="button" value="Image width" onclick="B1();">
```

Applies to:

<img>, <input type="button">, <input type="checkbox">, <input type="file">, <input type="image">, <input type="password">, <input type="radio">, <input type="reset">, <input type="submit">, <input type="text">, <hr>

width (3)

Compatibility: NN6, NN7, IE6

Read and write property. Establishes the width of the element.

Syntax:

```
document.getElementById("preID").width = value
document.all.preID.width = value // IE only
```

Example:

```
<html><body bgcolor="#FFFFFF" text="#000000">
<pre id="myPre" style="font-size:14pt;">This text is embedded within pre tags.</pre>
<script language="JavaScript">
document.all.myPre.width = "300";
</script>
</body></html>
```

Applies to:

```
<pre>
```

width (4)

Compatibility: NN6, NN7, IE4, IE5, IE5.5, IE6

Read-only property. Returns the width of the object in pixels.
Syntax:

```
objectName.width
```

Example:

```
<button onclick="alert(screen.width);">Screen Width</button>
```

Applies to:

```
document (NN6 and NN7 only), event (NN6 and NN7 only), screen
```

wrap

Compatibility: IE4, IE5, IE5.5, IE6

Read and write property. Specifies how word wrapping should be handled in the element. Values: soft (the default; word wrapped without carriage returns and line feeds), hard (word wrapped with carriage returns and line feeds), or off (no word wrapping).
Syntax:

```
document.all.elementID.wrap = value
```

Example:

```
<textarea id="W1" rows="4"> . . . Long text . . . </textarea>
<textarea id="W2" rows="4"> . . . Long text . . . </textarea>
<textarea id="W3" rows="4"> . . . Long text . . . </textarea>
```

```
<script language="JavaScript">
document.all.W1.wrap = "soft";
document.all.W2.wrap = "hard";
document.all.W3.wrap = "off";
</script>
```

Applies to:

`<pre>` (IE5.5, IE6 only), `<textarea>`

x

Compatibility: IE4, IE5, IE5.5, IE6

Read and write property. Establishes the X coordinate in pixels of the cursor position.

Syntax:

```
window.event.x = value
```

Example:

```
<script language="JavaScript">
function C1() {
    myX.innerHTML = window.event.x;
    myY.innerHTML = window.event.y;
}
</script>
<p><b>X Coordinate:</b> <span id="myX">0</span></p>
<p><b>Y Coordinate:</b> <span id="myY">0</span></p>
<div id="myDiv" onmousemove="C1();" style="border:solid; width:500; height:200;"></div>
```

Applies to:

event

XMLDocument

Compatibility: IE5, IE5.5, IE6

Read and write property. Returns a reference to an XML document.

Syntax:

```
document.XMLDocument;
document.all.xmlID.XMLDocument;
```

Example:

```
<script>
function B1(){alert(myData.XMLDocument.hasChildNodes);}
</script>
<xml id="myData">
    <customer>
    <name>SoftSmart Systems</name>
    <address>3400 Success Way</address>
    <city>Los Angeles</city>
    </customer>
</xml>
<button onclick="B1();">XML Has Child Nodes</button>
```

Applies to:

document, <xml>

y

Compatibility: IE4, IE5, IE5.5, IE6

Read and write property. Establishes the Y coordinate in pixels of the cursor position.

Syntax:

```
window.event.y = value
```

Example: See the x property example.

Applies to:

event

12

JAVASCRIPT METHODS

JavaScript methods are the verbs of the JavaScript language. Each method in this chapter contains compatibility information, a brief description, syntax information, parameter values (where applicable), a functional example, and an applies-to list identifying all the HTML elements, JavaScript collections, and JavaScript objects that the method can be used with.

In order to distinguish the HTML elements, JavaScript collections, and JavaScript objects that appear in the applies-to lists, the following conventions have been used:

- Angle bracket tags (< and >) surround the names of HTML elements (for example, <html>).

- An asterisk follows the names of JavaScript collections (areas*).

- The names of JavaScript objects appear without adornment (window).

See Chapter 4 for an introduction to JavaScript methods.

abs()

Compatibility: NN4, NN6, NN7, IE4, IE5, IE5.5, IE6

This method returns the absolute value for the number specified.
Syntax:

```
Math.abs(param1)
```

param1 Required; the number to convert.

Example:

```
<button onclick="alert(Math.abs(-10));">ABS</button>
```

Applies to:

```
Math
```

acos()

Compatibility: NN4, NN6, NN7, IE4, IE5, IE5.5, IE6

This method returns the arccosine value for the number specified.
Syntax:

```
Math.acos(param1)
```

param1 Required; the number to convert.

Example:

```
<button onclick="alert(Math.acos(1));">ACOS</button>
```

Applies to:

```
Math
```

add() (1)

Compatibility: IE4, IE5, IE5.5, IE6

This method adds an element to the collection.
Syntax:

```
document.all.selectID.add(param1, param2)
collectionName.add(param1, param2)
```

param1   Required; the element to add.

param2   Optional; the index position for the added element.

Example:

```
<script language="JavaScript">
function B1() {
var newOption = document.createElement('<option value="TOYOTA">');
document.all.mySelect.options.add(newOption);
newOption.innerText = "Toyota";}
function B2() {document.all.mySelect.options.remove(0);}
</script>
<select id="mySelect">
<option value="HONDA">Honda</option>
<option value="ACURA">Acura</option>
<option value="LEXUS">Lexus</option>
</select>
<input type="button" value="Add" onclick="B1();">
<input type="button" value="Remove" onclick="B2();">
```

Applies to:

```
areas*, controlRange*, options*, <select>
```

add() (2)

Compatibility: IE5.5, IE6

This method adds a new namespace object to the namespaces collection.

Syntax:

```
namespaces.add(param1, param2, param3)
```

param1   Required; the name of the namespace to add.

param2   Required; the URN of the namespace.

param3   Optional; the URL of the behavior to be added to the namespace.

Example:

```
<html xmlns:firstNS>
<head>
<?import namespace="firstNS" implementation="someFile1.htc">
<script>
function addNS(){
namespaces.add(secondNS, someFile2.htc);
namespaces.add(thirdNS, someFile3.htc);
}
</script></head>
```

```
<body>
<button onclick="addNS();">Add namespace names</button>
</body></html>
```

Applies to:

namespaces*

addBehavior()

Compatibility: IE5, IE5.5, IE6

This method inserts a behavior into an HTML element.
Syntax:

```
document.all.elementID.addBehavior(param1)
```

param1 Required; the URL of the behavior.

Example:

```
<script language="JavaScript">
var behaviorID
function commandAdd() {behaviorID = document.all.myDiv.addBehavior('makered.htc');}
function commandRemove() {document.all.myDiv.removeBehavior(behaviorID);}
</script>
<button onclick="commandAdd();">Add behavior</button>
<button onclick="commandRemove();">Remove behavior</button>
<div id="myDiv" style="border:solid; width:500; height:200;">This is a div</div>
```

Contents of makeRed.htc:

```
<public:attach event="onmouseover" onevent="turnRed()" />
<public:attach event="onmouseout" onevent="turnNormal()" />
<public:property name="redColor" />
<public:method name="setRedColor" />
<script language="JavaScript">
var black
var redColor = "red"
function setRedColor(color) {
   redColor = color
}
function turnRed() {
    if (event.srcElement == element) {
        black = style.color
        runtimeStyle.color = redColor
    }
}
function turnNormal() {
```

```
    if (event.srcElement == element) {
        runtimeStyle.color = black
    }
}
</script>
```

Applies to:

```
<a>, <acronym>, <address>, <applet>, <area>, <b>, <base>, <basefont>, <bgsound>,
<big>, <blockquote>, <body>, <br>, <button>, <caption>, <center>, <cite>, <code>,
<col>, <colgroup>, <comment>, <custom>, <dd>, <del>, <dfn>, <dir>, <div>, <dl>,
<dt>, <em>, <embed>, <fieldset>, <font>, <form>, <frame>, <frameset>, <head>, <hn>,
<hr>, <html>, <i>, <iframe>, <img>, <input type="button">, <input type="checkbox">,
<input type="file">, <input type="hidden">, <input type="image">, <input
type="password">, <input type="radio">, <input type="reset">, <input
type="submit">, <input type="text">, <ins>, <isindex>, <kbd>, <label>, <legend>,
<li>, <link>, <listing>, <map>, <marquee>, <menu>, <nobr>, <noframes>, <noscript>,
<object>, <ol>, <option>, <p>, <plaintext>, <pre>, <q>, <rt>, <ruby>, <s>, <samp>,
<script>, <select>, <small>, <span>, <strike>, <strong>, <style>, <sub>, <sup>,
<table>, <tbody>, <td>, <textarea>, <tfoot>, <th>, <thead>, <title>, <tr>, <tt>,
<u>, <ul>, <var>, <wbr>, <xml>, <xmp>
```

AddChannel()

Compatibility: IE4, IE5, IE5.5, IE6

This method is part of Microsoft's Active Channel technology that allows web users to receive updated pages automatically. This method adds a channel on the user's system to allow future updates to be downloaded automatically.

Syntax:

```
window.external.AddChannel(param1)
```

param1   Required; the URL of the CDF file to be installed on the user's machine.

Example:

```
window.external.AddChannel("http://www.yoururl.com/cdffile.cdf");
```

NOTE   *The preceding example requires a .cdf file, which is created using C++. The use of this property requires that you have a thorough understanding of C++ and the Internet Explorer API.*

Applies to:

```
external
```

AddDesktopComponent()

Compatibility: IE4, IE5, IE5.5, IE6

This method inserts a web page or image into the active desktop.
Syntax:

```
window.external.AddDesktopComponent(param1, param2, param3, param4, param5, param6)
```

param1 Required; the URL of the file to add to the desktop.

param2 Required; image or website.

param3 Optional; the offset of the left border in pixels.

param4 Optional; the offset of the top border in pixels.

param5 Optional; the width in pixels.

param6 Optional; the height in pixels.

Example:

```
<html><head>
<script language="JavaScript">
function B1() {
window.external.AddDesktopComponent("yourimage.jpg",
"image", 150, 150, 95, 95);}
</script></head>
<body>
<button onclick="B1();">Click here to add the new active desktop component</button>
</body></html>
```

Applies to:

```
external
```

addElement()

Compatibility: IE5.5, IE6

This method adds an element to the controlRange collection.
Syntax:

```
controlRangeName.addElement(param1)
```

param1 Required; the element to add.

Example:

```
<html><head>
<script language="JavaScript">
function B1() {
    myRange = document.body.createControlRange();
    myDiv = document.createElement('div');
    document.body.insertBefore(myDiv);
    myDiv.style.position = 'absolute';
```

```
    myDiv.innerText = 'New div element has been created';
    myRange.addElement(myDiv);
}
</script></head>
<body>
<input id=myB type="button" value="Add element to the controlRange collection"
onclick="B1();">
</body></html>
```

Applies to:

controlRange*

AddFavorite()

Compatibility: IE4, IE5, IE5.5, IE6

This method opens the "Add Favorite" dialog window and provides the user with the ability to specify a description for the page that will be added to the list of favorites.

Syntax:

```
window.external.AddFavorite(param1, param2)
```

param1   Required; the URL of the favorite element.

param2   Optional; the user's description for the page being added.

Example:

```
<html><head>
<script language="JavaScript">
function B1() {window.external.AddFavorite('http://www.advocar.com');}
</script></head>
<body>
<button onclick="B1();">Click here to add Advocar's main page to your favorites
</button>
</body></html>
```

Applies to:

external

addImport()

Compatibility: IE4, IE5, IE5.5, IE6

This method adds a style sheet to the imported styleSheets collection and returns the index of the style sheet in the collection.

Syntax:

```
document.styleSheets[index].addImport(param1, param2)
```

> **param1**   Required; the location of the style sheet file.
>
> **param2**   Optional; the index of the style sheet being added. If an index is not specified, the style sheet is added to the end of the collection.

Example:

```
<html><head>
<script language="JavaScript">
document.styleSheets[0].addImport('yourstylesheet.css', 2);
</script></head>
<body>Body content</body>
</html>
```

Applies to:

---

styleSheet

---

addPageRule()

Compatibility: IE5.5, IE6

This method adds a new @page rule to a styleSheet object.

Syntax:

```
document.styleSheets[index].addPageRule(param1, param2, param3)
```

> **param1**   Required; the style selector.
>
> **param2**   Required; the style declaration.
>
> **param3**   Optional; the index of the @page rule in the collection. If the index is omitted, the @page rule is added to the end of the collection.

Example: Using this method in current browsers will not provide any results.

Applies to:

---

styleSheet

---

addReadRequest()

Compatibility: IE4, IE5, IE5.5, IE6

This method adds a vCard name to the read-requests queue in the userProfile object. The read-requests queue contains a list of requests to access and perform read actions on a user's profile information. The method returns true (successful) or false (failed).

Syntax:

```
navigator.userProfile.addReadRequest(param1)
window.clientInformation.userProfile.addReadRequest(param1)
```

param1   Required; one of the standard vCard_name property values. For a list of vCard_name property values, see Chapter 11.

Example:

```
<html><head>
<script language="JavaScript">
function B1() {
navigator.userProfile.addReadRequest("Business.phone");
var m = navigator.userProfile.addReadRequest("Business.phone");
alert(m);}
</script></head>
<body>
<button onclick="B1();">Add an entry to read request</button>
</body></html>
```

Applies to:

```
userProfile
```

addRule()

Compatibility: IE4, IE5, IE5.5, IE6

This method adds a new rule to a style sheet and always returns -1.
Syntax:

```
document.styleSheets[index].addRule(param1, param2, param3)
```

param1   Required; the selector.

param2   Required; the style declarations.

param3   Optional; the index of the rule in the collection. If the index is omitted, the rule is added to the end of the collection.

Example:

```
<html><head>
<style id="myS">.one { font-family:verdana; font-size:14pt }</style>
<script language="JavaScript">
function B1() {document.styleSheets[0].addRule("div", "color:white; background-
color:red;");}
</script></head>
<body><div>This is a sample text.</div>
<button onclick="B1()">Add new rule</button>
</body></html>
```

Applies to:

styleSheet

alert()

Compatibility: NN4, NN6, NN7, IE4, IE5, IE5.5, IE6

This method provides the user with an alert message in a dialog window.
Syntax:

window.alert(*param1*)

> **param1**   Optional; the text of the message.
>
> Example:

```
<input style="background-color:blue; color:white; font-family:verdana; font-weight:bold" type="button" onClick="alert('This is an alert window');" value="Click me">
```

> Applies to:

window

anchor()

Compatibility: NN4, NN6, NN7, IE4, IE5, IE5.5, IE6

This method creates an <a> element using the contents of the String object.
Syntax:

stringName.anchor(*param1*)

> **param1**   Required; the value of the <a> element's name attribute.
>
> Example:

```
<button onclick="var myS = new String('Sample String');
alert(myS.anchor('myAnchor'));">ANCHOR</button>
```

> Applies to:

String

appendChild()

Compatibility: NN6, NN7, IE5, IE5.5, IE6

This method appends a child element to the HTML element.

Syntax:

```
attributeName.appendChild(param1) // IE only
document.getElementById("elementID").appendChild(param1)
document.all.elementID.appendChild(param1) // IE only
```

param1 Required; the element to append.

Example:

```
<script language="javascript">
function B1(){
    var myElement = document.createElement('<div style="width:600; height:200;
background-color:blue;"></div>');
    document.all.myBody.appendChild(myElement);
}
</script>
<body id="myBody"><button onclick="B1();">Append child</button></body>
```

Applies to:

```
<a>, <acronym>, <address>, <applet>, <area>, attribute, <b>, <base>, <basefont>,
<bdo>, <big>, <blockquote>, <body>, <br>, <button>, <caption>, <center>, <cite>,
<code>, <col>, <colgroup>, <comment>, <dd>, <del>, <dfn>, <dir>, <div>, <dl>, <dt>,
<em>, <fieldset>, <font>, <form>, <frame>, <frameset>, <head>, <hn>, <hr>, <html>,
<i>, <iframe>, <img>, <input type="button">, <input type="checkbox">, <input
type="file">, <input type="image">, <input type="password">, <input type="radio">,
<input type="reset">, <input type="submit">, <input type="text">, <ins>, <isindex>,
<kbd>, <label>, <legend>, <li>, <link>, <listing>, <map>, <marquee>, <menu>,
<meta>, <noframes>, <noscript>, <object>, <ol>, <optgroup>, <option>, <p>, <param>,
<plaintext>, <pre>, <q>, <s>, <samp>, <script>, <select>, <small>, <span>,
<strike>, <strong>, <style>, <sub>, <sup>, <table>, <tbody>, <td>, <textarea>,
<tfoot>, <th>, <thead>, <title>, <tr>, <tt>, <u>, <ul>, <var>, <xmp>
```

appendData()

Compatibility: NN6 (<comment> only), NN7 (<comment> only), IE6

This method appends a character string to the end of the object.
Syntax:

```
textNodeName.appendData(param1) // IE only
document.getElementById("commentID").appendData(param1)
document.all.commentID.appendData(param1) // IE only
```

param1 Required; the new character string.

Example:

```
<p id="myP" class="explanations">Sample text.</p>
<script language="JavaScript">
```

```
function B1(){
var m = myP.firstChild.appendData(" This is the added string.");}
</script>
<input type="button" onClick="B1();" value="Append data">
```

Applies to:

```
<comment>, TextNode
```

applyElement()

Compatibility: IE5, IE5.5, IE6

This method adds a new element as either the parent or the child of the specified element.

Syntax:

```
document.all.elementID.applyElement(param1, param2)
```

param1   Required; the new element to insert.

param2   Optional; outside (the default; the element being applied is the parent of the specified element) or inside (the element being applied is the child of the specified element).

Example:

```
<script language="javascript">
function B1(){
    var myElement = document.createElement('<div style="width:600; height:200;
background-color:blue;"></div>');
    document.all.myBody.applyElement(myElement, 'inside');
}
</script>
<body id="myBody"><button onclick="B1();">Apply element</button></body>
```

Applies to:

```
<a>, <acronym>, <address>, <applet>, <area>, <b>, <base>, <basefont>, <bdo>,
<bgsound>, <big>, <blockquote>, <body>, <br>, <button>, <caption>, <center>,
<cite>, <code>, <col>, <colgroup>, <comment>, <custom>, <dd>, <del>, <dfn>, <dir>,
<div>, <dl>, <dt>, <em>, <embed>, <fieldset>, <font>, <form>, <frame>, <frameset>,
<head>, <hn>, <hr>, <html>, <i>, <iframe>, <img>, <input type="button">, <input
type="checkbox">, <input type="file">, <input type="hidden">, <input type="image">,
<input type="password">, <input type="radio">, <input type="reset">, <input
type="submit">, <input type="text">, <ins>, <kbd>, <label>, <legend>, <li>, <link>,
<listing>, <map>, <marquee>, <menu>, <object>, <ol>, <option>, <p>, <plaintext>,
<pre>, <q>, <s>, <samp>, <script>, <select>, <small>, <span>, <strike>, <strong>,
<sub>, <sup>, <table>, <tbody>, <td>, <textarea>, <tfoot>, <th>, <thead>, <title>,
<tr>, <tt>, <u>, <ul>, <var>, <xmp>
```

asin()

Compatibility: NN4, NN6, NN7, IE4, IE5, IE5.5, IE6

This method returns the arcsine value for the number specified.

Syntax:

```
Math.asin(param1)
```

param1   Required; the number to convert.

Example:

```
<button onclick="alert(Math.asin(1));">ASIN</button>
```

Applies to:

```
Math
```

assign()

Compatibility: NN4, NN6, NN7, IE4, IE5, IE5.5, IE6

This method causes the browser to load a new HTML document.

Syntax:

```
location.assign(param1)
```

param1   Required; the URL of the new document.

Example:

```
<script language="JavaScript">
function B1() {location.assign("http://www.advocar.com/");}
</script>
<input type="button" value="Load new page" onclick="B1();">
```

Applies to:

```
location
```

atan()

Compatibility: NN4, NN6, NN7, IE4, IE5, IE5.5, IE6

This method returns the arctangent value for the number specified.

Syntax:

```
Math.atan(param1)
```

param1 Required; the number to convert.

Example:

```
<button onclick="alert(Math.atan(1));">ATAN</button>
```

Applies to:

```
Math
```

atan2()

Compatibility: NN4, NN6, NN7, IE4, IE5, IE5.5, IE6

This method returns the arctangent value, which is a number between pi and negative pi, resulting from a point defined by its X and Y coordinates.

Syntax:

```
Math.atan2(param1, param2)
```

param1 Required; the Y coordinate of the point.

param2 Required; the X coordinate of the point.

Example:

```
<button onclick="alert(Math.atan2(1,1));">ATAN2</button>
```

Applies to:

```
Math
```

attachEvent()

Compatibility: IE5, IE5.5, IE6

This method causes the specified event handler to be bound to a specified function in the page. When the event fires, the specified function is executed. Returns true (successful) or false (failed).

Syntax:

```
window.attachEvent(param1, param2)
document.all.elementID.attachEvent(param1, param2)
```

param1 Required; the name of the event.

param2 Required; the name of the function.

Example:

```
<button id="myButton">Button</button>
<button onclick="B0();">Apply an event handler "Button"</button>
<button onclick="B2();">Detach</button>
```

```
<script language="JavaScript">
function B0() {document.all.myButton.attachEvent("onclick", B1)}
function B1() {document.bgColor = 'red';}
function B2() {document.bgColor = 'white';
document.all.myButton.detachEvent('onclick', B1);}
</script>
```

Applies to:

`<a>`, `<acronym>`, `<address>`, `<applet>`, `<area>`, `<b>`, `<base>`, `<basefont>`, `<bgsound>`, `<big>`, `<blockquote>`, `<body>`, `<br>`, `<button>`, `<caption>`, `<center>`, `<cite>`, `<code>`, `<col>`, `<colgroup>`, `<comment>`, `<custom>`, `<dd>`, `<del>`, `<dfn>`, `<dir>`, `<div>`, `<dl>`, document, `<dt>`, `<em>`, `<embed>`, `<fieldset>`, `<font>`, `<form>`, `<frame>`, `<frameset>`, `<head>`, `<hn>`, `<hr>`, `<html>`, `<i>`, `<iframe>`, `<img>`, `<input type="button">`, `<input type="checkbox">`, `<input type="file">`, `<input type="hidden">`, `<input type="image">`, `<input type="password">`, `<input type="radio">`, `<input type="reset">`, `<input type="submit">`, `<input type="text">`, `<ins>`, `<kbd>`, `<label>`, `<legend>`, `<li>`, `<link>`, `<listing>`, `<map>`, `<marquee>`, `<menu>`, namespace, `<nobr>`, `<object>`, `<ol>`, `<option>`, `<p>`, `<plaintext>`, `<pre>`, `<q>`, `<s>`, `<samp>`, `<script>`, `<select>`, `<small>`, `<span>`, `<strike>`, `<strong>`, `<sub>`, `<sup>`, `<table>`, `<tbody>`, `<td>`, `<textarea>`, `<tfoot>`, `<th>`, `<thead>`, `<title>`, `<tr>`, `<tt>`, `<u>`, `<ul>`, `<var>`, window, `<xmp>`

AutoCompleteSaveForm()

Compatibility: IE5, IE5.5, IE6

This method adds the specified form input to the autocomplete list.
   Syntax:

```
window.external.AutoCompleteSaveForm(param1)
```

param1   Required; the name of the form.

Example:

```
<form name="myForm">
First Name: <input type="text" name="firstName"><br>
Last Name: <input type="text" name="lastName" autocomplete="off">
</form>
<script language="JavaScript">
function B1(){
   window.external.AutoCompleteSaveForm(document.forms[0]);
   myForm.firstName.value="";
   myForm.lastName.value="";
}
</script>
<button onclick="B1();">Save</button>
```

Applies to:

external

AutoScan()

Compatibility: IE5, IE5.5, IE6

This method attempts to connect to a web server by passing a domain address that begins with www and ends with .com, .org, .net, or .edu.

Syntax:

```
window.external.AutoScan(param1, param2, param3)
```

param1   Required; the domain address without www. and the . extension.

param2   Required; the web page to connect to if param1 is invalid.

param3   Optional; a target window or frame.

```
<html><head>
<script language="JavaScript">
function B1() {
window.external.AutoScan("advocar", "home.asp");}
</script></head>
<body><button onclick="B1();">Open "Advocar" site</button>
</body></html>
```

Applies to:

```
external
```

back()

Compatibility: NN4, NN6, NN7, IE4, IE5, IE5.5, IE6

This method loads a URL that the browser has already visited. It simulates the clicking of the browser's back button.

Syntax:

```
objectName.back(param1)
```

param1   Optional; the number of URLs to go back.

Example:

```
<script language="JavaScript">
function B1(){history.back(1);}
</script>
<input type="button" value="Go back" onclick="B1();">
```

Applies to:

```
history, window (NN4 only)
```

big()

Compatibility: NN4, NN6, NN7, IE4, IE5, IE5.5, IE6

This method causes a string to be rendered in a font size that is one greater than the current font size in the document.

Syntax:

```
stringName.big()
```

Example:

```
<button onclick="var myS = new String('Sample String'); document.write('regular
string'+myS.big());">BIG</button>
```

Applies to:

```
String
```

blink()

Compatibility: NN4, NN6, NN7

This method causes a string to blink.

Syntax:

```
stringName.blink()
```

Example:

```
<button onclick="var myS = new String('Sample String');
document.write(myS.blink());">BLINK</button>
```

Applies to:

```
String
```

blur()

Compatibility: NN4, NN6, NN7, IE4, IE5, IE5.5, IE6

This method will cause an element to lose focus. The onBlur event is triggered as a result of calling this method.

Syntax:

```
window.blur()
document.getElementById("elementID").blur()
document.all.elementID.blur() // IE only
```

Example:

```
<script language="JavaScript">
function B1(){
  document.getElementById("myButton").blur();
  document.getElementById("myButton").innerText = "This button lost its focus";
  alert("The button lost its focus");
}
</script>
<input id="myButton" type="button" onclick="B1();" value="This button doesn't yet
have focus. Tab to put in focus." onFocus="this.innerText='In focus. Click me to
lose focus'">
```

Applies to:

`<a>`, `<acronym>`, `<address>`, `<applet>`, `<area>`, `<b>`, `<bdo>`, `<big>`, `<blockquote>`,
`<body>`, `<button>`, `<caption>`, `<center>`, `<cite>`, `<custom>`, `<dd>`, `<del>`, `<dfn>`, `<dir>`,
`<div>`, `<dl>`, `<dt>`, `<em>`, `<embed>`, `<fieldset>`, `<font>`, `<form>`, `<frame>`, `<frameset>`,
`<hn>`, `<hr>`, `<i>`, `<iframe>`, `<img>`, `<input type="button">`, `<input type="checkbox">`,
`<input type="file">`, `<input type="image">`, `<input type="password">`, `<input
type="radio">`, `<input type="reset">`, `<input type="submit">`, `<input type="text">`,
`<ins>`, `<isindex>`, `<kbd>`, `<label>`, `<legend>`, `<li>`, `<listing>`, `<marquee>`, `<menu>`,
`<object>`, `<ol>`, `<p>`, `<plaintext>`, `<pre>`, `<q>`, `<rt>`, `<ruby>`, `<s>`, `<samp>`, `<select>`,
`<small>`, `<span>`, `<strike>`, `<strong>`, `<sub>`, `<sup>`, `<table>`, `<tbody>`, `<td>`,
`<textarea>`, `<tfoot>`, `<th>`, `<thead>`, `<tr>`, `<tt>`, `<u>`, `<ul>`, `<var>`, window, `<xmp>`

bold()

Compatibility: NN4, NN6, NN7, IE4, IE5, IE5.5, IE6

This method causes a string to be rendered in bold.

Syntax:

```
stringName.bold()
```

Example:

```
<button onclick="var myS = new String('Sample String'); document.write('regular
string'+myS.bold());">BOLD</button>
```

Applies to:

String

ceil()

Compatibility: NN4, NN6, NN7, IE4, IE5, IE5.5, IE6

This method rounds the specified number up to the nearest integer.
Syntax:

```
Math.ceil(param1)
```

param1   Required; the number to convert.

Example:

```
<button onclick="alert(Math.ceil(1.1));">CEIL</button>
```

Applies to:

```
Math
```

charAt()

Compatibility: NN4, NN6, NN7, IE4, IE5, IE5.5, IE6

This method returns the character located at the specified index position of the string.
Syntax:

```
stringName.charAt(param1)
```

param1   Required; the index position of the character.

Example:

```
<button onclick="var myS = new String('Sample String');
alert(myS.charAt(3));">CHARAT</button>
```

Applies to:

```
String
```

charCodeAt()

Compatibility: NN4, NN6, NN7, IE4, IE5, IE5.5, IE6

This method returns the Unicode value of the character located at the specified index position of the string.
Syntax:

```
stringName.charCodeAt(param1)
```

param1   Required; the index position of the character.

Example:

```
<button onclick="var myS = new String('Sample String');
alert(myS.charCodeAt(3));">CHARCODEAT</button>
```

Applies to:

```
String
```

ChooseColorDlg()

Compatibility: IE6

This method allows the user to pick a color by calling the browser's color selection dialog window. The Dialog Helper object must be created by supplying a classid code.

Syntax:

document.all.*DialogHelperID*.ChooseColorDlg(*param1*)

> **param1**   Optional; the default color selected when the dialog window opens.

Example:

```
<script language="JavaScript">
function B1(){
    var myColor = dlgColor.ChooseColorDlg();
    alert(myColor);
}
</script>
<object id="dlgColor" classid="clsid:3050f819-98b5-11cf-bb82-00aa00bdce0b">
</object>
<button onclick="B1();">Choose color</button>
```

Applies to:

Dialog Helper

clear()

Compatibility: IE4, IE5, IE5.5, IE6

This method causes the contents of the selection to be deleted from the page.

Syntax:

document.selection.clear()

Example:

```
<head><script language="JavaScript">
function B1() {document.selection.clear();}
</script></head>
<body>
<p id="myP" contenteditable>This text is selectable. Select any part of it and
click the button below.</p>
<button onclick="B1();">Delete selection</button>
</body>
```

Applies to:

---

selection

---

clearAttributes()

Compatibility: IE5, IE5.5, IE6

This method removes all attributes, except name and id, from an element.
  Syntax:

---

document.all.*elementID*.clearAttributes()

Example:

```
<script language="JavaScript">
function B1() {
document.all.myP.clearAttributes();
}
</script>
<p id="myP" style="color:red">This text has the style and id attributes.</p>
<button onclick="B1();">Clear attributes()</button>
```

Applies to:

<a>, <acronym>, <address>, <applet>, <area>, <b>, <base>, <basefont>, <bdo>,
<bgsound>, <big>, <blockquote>, <body>, <br>, <button>, <caption>, <center>,
<cite>, <code>, <col>, <colgroup>, <comment>, <custom>, <dd>, <del>, <dfn>, <dir>,
<div>, <dl>, <dt>, <em>, <embed>, <fieldset>, <font>, <form>, <frame>, <frameset>,
<head>, <hn>, <hr>, <html>, <i>, <iframe>, <img>, <input type="button">, <input
type="checkbox">, <input type="file">, <input type="hidden">, <input type="image">,
<input type="password">, <input type="radio">, <input type="reset">, <input
type="submit">, <input type="text">, <ins>, <kbd>, <label>, <legend>, <li>, <link>,
<listing>, <map>, <marquee>, <menu>, <object>, <ol>, <option>, <p>, <plaintext>,
<pre>, <q>, <s>, <samp>, <script>, <select>, <small>, <span>, <strike>, <strong>,
<sub>, <sup>, <table>, <tbody>, <td>, <textarea>, <tfoot>, <th>, <thead>, <title>,
<tr>, <tt>, <u>, <ul>, <var>, <xmp>

---

clearData()

Compatibility: IE5, IE5.5, IE6

This method clears the clipboard of one or more data formats.
  Syntax:

---

event.*objectName*.clearData(*param1*)

---

param1   Optional; one or more of the following data formats: Text, URL, File,
HTML, and Image. Leave blank to clear all data formats.

Example:

```
<button onclick="clipboardData.setData('Text',
document.selection.createRange().text);">Copy</button>
<button onclick="myText.value = clipboardData.getData('Text');">Paste</button>
<button onclick="clipboardData.clearData('Text');">Clear clipboard</button>
<p>This is some sample text</p>
<textarea id="myText" style="width:600; height:100"></textarea>
```

Applies to:

clipboardData, dataTransfer

clearInterval()

Compatibility: NN4, NN6, NN7, IE4, IE5, IE5.5, IE6

This method removes an interval that was initialized using the setInterval() method. An interval allows a function to be called each time the interval time has elapsed.

Syntax:

window.clearInterval(*param1*)

param1   Required; the numeric interval ID previously returned by the window.setInterval() method.

Example:

```
<script language="javascript">
var intInterval = 0
function myInterval(){alert('Hello');}
</script>
<button onclick="intInterval=window.setInterval('myInterval()', 1000);">Start
interval</button>
<button onclick="intInterval=window.clearInterval(intInterval);">Stop interval</
button>
```

Applies to:

window

clearRequest()

Compatibility: IE4, IE5, IE5.5, IE6

This method clears the read-requests queue from the userProfile object. The read-requests queue contains a list of requests to access and perform read actions on a user's profile information.

Syntax:

```
navigator.userProfile.clearRequest()
window.clientInformation.userProfile.clearRequest()
```

Example:

```
<html><head>
<script language="JavaScript">
function B1() {navigator.userProfile.clearRequest();}
</script></head>
<body>
<button onclick="B1();">Clear the read-requests queue</button>
</body></html>
```

Applies to:

```
userProfile
```

clearTimeout()

Compatibility: NN4, NN6, NN7, IE4, IE5, IE5.5, IE6

This method removes a timeout that was initialized using the setTimeout() method. A timeout allows a function to be called once after the specified time has elapsed.

Syntax:

```
window.clearTimeout(param1)
```

param1   Required; the numeric timeout ID previously returned by the window.setTimeout() method.

Example:

```
<script language="javascript">
var intValue = 0
function myMethod(){alert('Hello');}
</script>
<button onclick="intValue=window.setTimeout('myMethod()', 1000);">Start timeout</
button>
<button onclick="intValue=window.clearTimeout(intValue);">Stop timeout</button>
```

Applies to:

```
window
```

click()

Compatibility: NN4, NN6, NN7, IE4, IE5, IE5.5, IE6

This method allows you to simulate the clicking of an element, triggering the onClick event.

Syntax:

```
document.getElementById("elementID").click()
document.all.elementID.click() // IE only
```

Example:

```
<script language="JavaScript">
function B1() {myCheckbox.focus(); myCheckbox.click();}
</script>
<input type="checkbox" id="myCheckbox" value="checkbox">
<button onclick="B1();">Click the checkbox</button>
```

Applies to:

```
<a>, <address>, <applet>, <area>, <b>, <big>, <blockquote>, <body>, <button>,
<caption>, <center>, <cite>, <code>, <custom>, <dd>, <dfn>, <dir>, <div>, <dl>,
<dt>, <em>, <embed>, <fieldset>, <font>, <form>, <hn>, <hr>, <i>, <img>, <input
type="button">, <input type="checkbox">, <input type="file">, <input type="image">,
<input type="password">, <input type="radio">, <input type="reset">, <input
type="submit">, <input type="text">, <kbd>, <label>, <legend>, <li>, <listing>,
<map>, <marquee>, <menu>, <nobr>, <object>, <ol>, <option>, <p>, <plaintext>,
<pre>, <s>, <samp>, <select>, <small>, <span>, <strike>, <strong>, <sub>, <sup>,
<table>, <tbody>, <td>, <textarea>, <tfoot>, <th>, <thead>, <tr>, <tt>, <u>, <ul>,
<var>, <xmp>
```

cloneNode()

Compatibility: NN6, NN7, IE5, IE5.5, IE6

This method creates a copy of the current node. After an element is cloned, referring to the id of that element returns a collection.

Syntax:

```
document.getElementById("elementID").cloneNode(param1)
document.all.elementID.cloneNode(param1) // IE only
```

param1 Optional; either true or false, indicating whether or not you want to clone child nodes as well.

Example:

```
<script language="JavaScript">
function B1(){
    var myNode = myButton.cloneNode(true);
```

```
    alert(myNode.innerHTML);
}
</script>
<button id="myButton" onclick="B1();">Clone node</button>
```

Applies to:

`<a>`, `<acronym>`, `<address>`, `<applet>`, `<area>`, attribute, `<b>`, `<base>`, `<basefont>`, `<bdo>`, `<bgsound>`, `<big>`, `<blockquote>`, `<body>`, `<br>`, `<button>`, `<caption>`, `<center>`, `<cite>`, `<code>`, `<col>`, `<colgroup>`, `<comment>`, `<dd>`, `<del>`, `<dfn>`, `<dir>`, `<div>`, `<dl>`, `<dt>`, `<em>`, `<embed>`, `<fieldset>`, `<font>`, `<form>`, `<frame>`, `<frameset>`, `<head>`, `<hn>`, `<hr>`, `<html>`, `<i>`, `<iframe>`, `<img>`, `<input type="button">`, `<input type="checkbox">`, `<input type="file">`, `<input type="hidden">`, `<input type="image">`, `<input type="password">`, `<input type="radio">`, `<input type="reset">`, `<input type="submit">`, `<input type="text">`, `<ins>`, `<isindex>`, `<kbd>`, `<label>`, `<legend>`, `<li>`, `<link>`, `<listing>`, `<map>`, `<marquee>`, `<menu>`, `<meta>`, `<noframes>`, `<noscript>`, `<object>`, `<ol>`, `<optgroup>`, `<option>`, `<p>`, `<param>`, `<plaintext>`, `<pre>`, `<q>`, `<s>`, `<samp>`, `<script>`, `<select>`, `<small>`, `<span>`, `<strike>`, `<strong>`, `<style>`, `<sub>`, `<sup>`, `<table>`, `<tbody>`, `<td>`, `<textarea>`, `<tfoot>`, `<th>`, `<thead>`, `<title>`, `<tr>`, `<tt>`, `<u>`, `<ul>`, `<var>`, `<xmp>`

close()

Compatibility: NN4, NN6, NN7, IE4, IE5, IE5.5, IE6

This method closes the current window or document. When executing this method, the user will be prompted to confirm that they wish close the browser window.

Syntax:

```
objectName.close()
```

Example:

```
<button onclick="window.close();">Close window</button>
```

Applies to:

```
document, window
```

collapse()

Compatibility: IE4, IE5, IE5.5, IE6

This method shrinks a text range down to a single insertion point.

Syntax:

```
textRangeName.collapse(param1)
```

param1   Optional; true (insertion point is placed at the start of the text) or false (insertion point is placed at the end of the text).

Example:

```
<script language="JavaScript">
function B1() {
  var choose, range
  for (var i = 0; i < document.forms[0].choose.length; i++) {
    if (document.forms[0].choose[i].checked) {
        choose = document.forms[0].choose[i].value
        break
    }
  }
  var x = window.event.clientX
  var y = window.event.clientY
  if (window.event.srcElement.parentTextEdit) {
    range = window.event.srcElement.parentTextEdit.createTextRange()
    range.collapse()
    range.moveToPoint(x, y)
    range.expand(choose)
    range.select()
  }
}
</script>
<form>
<input type="radio" value="character" checked name="choose">character
<input type="radio" value="word" name="choose">word
<input type="radio" value="sentence" name="choose">sentence
</form>
<p onClick="B1();" style="cursor:hand">Make a radio selection and then click here</p>
```

Applies to:

TextRange

compareEndPoints()

Compatibility: IE4, IE5, IE5.5, IE6

This method compares the position of the start and/or end points of two text ranges. Return value: -1 (the end or start point of the first range is after the end or start point of the second range), 0 (the end or start points of both ranges are at the same location), or 1 (the end or start point of the second range is after the end or start point of the first range).

Syntax:

textRangeName.compareEndPoints(*param1*, *param2*)

param1 Required; the type of comparison: StartToEnd, StartToStart, EndToStart, or EndToEnd.

param2 Required; the second text range.

Example:

```
<html><head>
<script language="JavaScript">
var myRange
function B1() {
    myRange = document.body.createTextRange();
    myRange.moveToElementText(myText1);
}
function B2() {
    var selectR = document.selection.createRange();
    alert(myRange.compareEndPoints("StartToEnd", selectR));
}
function B3() {
    var selectR = document.selection.createRange();
    alert(myRange.compareEndPoints("StartToStart", selectR));
}
function B4() {
    var selectR = document.selection.createRange();
    alert(myRange.compareEndPoints("EndToStart", selectR));
}
function B5() {
    var selectR = document.selection.createRange();
    alert(myRange.compareEndPoints("EndToEnd", selectR));
}
</script></head>
<body onLoad="B1();">
<p>This is some text before the text that is used for comparison.</p>
<p id="myText1" style="color:red;">This is a text stream that is used for the first
part of the comparison.</p>
<p>This is a text stream that is used for the second part of the comparison.
Highlight any part of this section with your mouse, then click one of the buttons
below.</p>
<input type="button" value="StartToEnd" onclick="B2();">
<input type="button" value="StartToStart" onclick="B3();">
<input type="button" value="EndToStart" onclick="B4();">
<input type="button" value="EndToEnd" onclick="B5();">
```

Applies to:

TextRange

componentFromPoint()

Compatibility: IE4, IE5, IE5.5, IE6

This method finds the object that is located at the specified coordinates on the page and returns a value describing its location. For a complete list of possible return values, go to: http://msdn.microsoft.com/workshop/author/dhtml/reference/methods/componentfrompoint.asp?frame=true.

Syntax:

```
document.all.elementID.componentFromPoint(param1, param2)
```

param1   Required; the X coordinate relative to the client area.

param2   Required; the Y coordinate relative to the client area.

Example:

```
<button onclick="alert(this.componentFromPoint(0, 0));">X coordinate</button>
```

Applies to:

```
<a>, <acronym>, <address>, <applet>, <area>, <b>, <base>, <basefont>, <bdo>,
<bgsound>, <big>, <blockquote>, <body>, <br>, <button>, <caption>, <center>,
<cite>, <code>, <col>, <colgroup>, <comment>, <custom>, <dd>, <del>, <dfn>, <dir>,
<div>, <dl>, <dt>, <em>, <embed>, <fieldset>, <font>, <form>, <frame>, <frameset>,
<head>, <hn>, <hr>, <html>, <i>, <iframe>, <img>, <input type="button">, <input
type="checkbox">, <input type="file">, <input type="hidden">, <input type="image">,
<input type="password">, <input type="radio">, <input type="reset">, <input
type="submit">, <input type="text">, <ins>, <isindex>, <kbd>, <label>, <legend>,
<li>, <link>, <listing>, <map>, <marquee>, <menu>, <nobr>, <noframes>, <noscript>,
<object>, <ol>, <option>, <p>, <plaintext>, <pre>, <q>, <rt>, <ruby>, <s>, <samp>,
<script>, <select>, <small>, <span>, <strike>, <strong>, <sub>, <sup>, <table>,
<tbody>, <td>, <textarea>, <tfoot>, <th>, <thead>, <title>, <tr>, <tt>, <u>, <ul>,
<var>, <wbr>, <xml>, <xmp>
```

concat() (1)

Compatibility: NN4, NN6, NN7, IE4, IE5, IE5.5, IE6

This method merges two or more arrays together.

Syntax:

```
arrayName.concat(paramN, . . . ,paramN)
```

paramN   Required; an array object.

Example:

```
<button onclick="var myA = new Array(10,11,12);
alert(myA.concat(13,14,15));">CONCAT</button>
```

Applies to:

```
Array
```

concat() (2)

Compatibility: NN4, NN6, NN7, IE4, IE5, IE5.5, IE6

This method merges multiple strings together to form a new string, which is the return value.

Syntax:

```
stringName.concat(paramN, . . . ,paramN)
```

paramN   Required; a string or String object.

Example:

```
<button onclick="var myS = new String('Sample String'); alert(myS.concat('Sample
String 2'));">CONCAT</button>
```

Applies to:

```
String
```

confirm()

Compatibility: NN4, NN6, NN7, IE4, IE5, IE5.5, IE6

This method opens a confirmation dialog window that has OK and Cancel buttons. Returns true (OK button was clicked) or false (Cancel button was clicked).

Syntax:

```
window.confirm(param1)
```

param1   Optional; the message displayed in the confirmation dialog window.

Example:

```
<script language="JavaScript">
function B1() {window.confirm("Confirmation window");}
</script>
<input type="button" value="Click to bring up a confirm window" onclick="B1();">
```

Applies to:

```
window
```

contains()

Compatibility: IE4, IE5, IE5.5, IE6

This method indicates whether or not the element specified by the parameter is inside the element to which this method is applied. Returns true or false.

Syntax:

```
document.all.elementID.contains(param1)
```

---

param1   Required; the element to check.

Example:

```
<script language="JavaScript">
function B1() {
var m = document.all.myDiv.contains(myB);
if (m == true){ m = "YES"} else {m = "NO"}
alert(m)}
</script>
<div id="myDiv" style="width:300; height:100; border:solid; 1px blue">div
element<br>
<input id="myB" type="button" value="Is this button contained within the div
element?" onclick="B1();">
</div>
```

Applies to:

```
<a>, <address>, <applet>, <area>, <b>, <base>, <basefont>, <big>, <blockquote>,
<body>, <button>, <caption>, <center>, <cite>, <code>, <col>, <colgroup>, <custom>,
<dd>, <dfn>, <dir>, <div>, <dl>, <dt>, <em>, <embed>, <fieldset>, <font>, <form>,
<frame>, <frameset>, <head>, <hn>, <hr>, <html>, <i>, <iframe>, <img>, <input
type="button">, <input type="checkbox">, <input type="file">, <input type="image">,
<input type="password">, <input type="radio">, <input type="reset">, <input
type="submit">, <input type="text">, <kbd>, <label>, <legend>, <li>, <link>,
<listing>, <map>, <marquee>, <menu>, <meta>, <nobr>, <ol>, <option>, <p>,
<plaintext>, <pre>, <s>, <samp>, <script>, <select>, <small>, <span>, <strike>,
<strong>, <sub>, <sup>, <table>, <tbody>, <td>, <textarea>, <tfoot>, <th>, <thead>,
<title>, <tr>, <tt>, <u>, <ul>, <var>, <xmp>
```

---

cos()

Compatibility: NN4, NN6, NN7, IE4, IE5, IE5.5, IE6

This method returns the cosine of the specified number.

Syntax:

```
Math.cos(param1)
```

---

param1   Required; the number to convert.

Example:

```
<button onclick="alert(Math.cos(1));">COS</button>
```

Applies to:

```
Math
```

---

createAttribute()

Compatibility: NN6, NN7, IE6

This method creates an attribute node. It also works with user-defined XML elements, allowing for the creation of custom attributes.

Syntax:

```
document.createAttribute(param1)
```

param1   Required; the name of the attribute.

Example:

```
<script language="JavaScript">
function B1() {
var newAttr = document.createAttribute("width");
newAttr.nodeValue = "400px"
document.getElementById("myB").setAttributeNode(newAttr);
}
</script>
<table id="myB" border=3 cellpadding="5" style="border-color:blue">
<tr><th>Expand this table</th><th>This is another cell</th><tr>
</table>
<input id="myB" type="button" value="Add attribute to the table" onclick="B1();">
```

Applies to:

```
document
```

createCaption()

Compatibility: NN6, NN7, IE4, IE5, IE5.5, IE6

This method creates a <caption> element associated with the specified table. The contents of the <caption> must also be set at run time.

Syntax:

```
document.getElementById("tableID").createCaption()
document.all.tableID.createCaption() // IE only
```

Example:

```
<script language="JavaScript">
function B1() {
var myC = document.getElementById("myT").createCaption();
myC.innerText = "This is the new caption text"
}
</script>
<table id="myT" border="3" cellpadding="5" style="border-color:blue">
```

```
<tr><th>This table has no caption</th></tr>
</table>
<input id="myT" type="button" value="Add caption" onclick="B1();">
```

Applies to:

```
<table>
```

createComment()

Compatibility: IE6

This method creates a `<comment>` element.

    Syntax:

```
document.createComment(param1)
```

    param1   Required; the text of the comment.

    Example:

```
<html>
<body>Body content.
<script language="JavaScript">
document.createComment("This is the comment text");
</script>
</body></html>
```

    Applies to:

```
document
```

createControlRange()

Compatibility: IE5, IE5.5, IE6

This method creates a `controlRange` collection. See Chapter 13 for more information on the `controlRange` collection.

    Syntax:

```
document.body.createControlRange()
```

    Example:

```
<script language="JavaScript">
function B1() {
var myControlR = document.body.createControlRange();
myControlR.add(myT);
var m = myControlR.length;
alert("There are "+ m +" elements in the controlRange collection")
```

```
}
</script>
<input id="myT" type="button" value="Click me" onclick="B1();">
```

Applies to:

```
<body>
```

createDocumentFragment()

Compatibility: IE5, IE5.5, IE6

This method creates a new document object.

Syntax:

```
document.createDocumentFragment()
```

Example:

```
<script language="JavaScript">
function B1() {
    var newDoc = document.createDocumentFragment();
    newDoc.innerHTML = "<p>Body Content</p>";
    alert(newDoc.innerHTML);
}
</script>
<input id="myT" type="button" value="Click me" onclick="B1();">
```

Applies to:

```
document
```

createElement()

Compatibility: NN6, NN7, IE4, IE5, IE5.5, IE6

This method creates a new element.

Syntax:

```
document.createElement(param1)
```

param1   Required; the tag name of the new element.

Example:

```
<script language="javascript">
function B1(){
    var myElement = document.createElement('<hr>');
    myBody.appendChild(myElement);}
</script>
```

```
<body id="myBody">
<button onClick="B1();">Put horizontal rule</button>
</body>
```

Applies to:

document

createEventObject()

Compatibility: IE5.5, IE6

This method creates an event object, which can then be passed as a parameter to the fireEvent() method of any element.

Syntax:

```
document.createEventObject(param1)
```

param1   Optional; the name of an existing event object to clone.

Example:

```
<script language="JavaScript">
function B1() {
    var myEvent = document.createEventObject();
    parent.document.all.myButton.fireEvent("onclick", myEvent);
    event.cancelBubble = true;
}
function B2() {alert('hello');}
</script>
<button onclick="B1();">Click to see alert from ---></button>
<button id="myButton" onclick="B2();">Click here to see alert</button>
```

Applies to:

document

createPopup()

Compatibility: IE5.5, IE6

This method creates a pop-up window. When first created, the pop-up window is empty and is not displayed. To make it visible and populate it with content, you must use the reference returned by this method.

Syntax:

```
window.createPopup()
```

Example:

```
<script language="JavaScript">
var popup = window.createPopup();
popup.document.body.innerHTML = 'This will navigate to another site!';
popup.document.body.style.backgroundColor = 'yellow';
</script>
<input type="button" onClick="location.href='http://www.advocar.com';"
onmouseover="popup.show(100, 100, 200, 100, document.body);"
onmouseout="popup.hide();" value="Navigate to Another Site">
```

Applies to:

window

createRange()

Compatibility: IE4, IE5, IE5.5, IE6

This method creates a `TextRange` object with the text inside the selection object.
Syntax:

```
document.selection.createRange()
```

Example: See the `compareEndPoints()` method example.
Applies to:

selection

createStyleSheet()

Compatibility: IE4, IE5, IE5.5, IE6

This method creates a style sheet that is applied to the current document.
Syntax:

```
document.createStyleSheet(param1, param2)
```

param1 Optional; specifies whether the newly created style sheet should be added as a `<link>` element (by supplying the style sheet's URL) or as a `<style>` element (by supplying the style sheet's rules).

param2 Optional; the index of the newly created style sheet within the `styleSheets` collection.

Example:

```
<script language="JavaScript">
function B1() {document.createStyleSheet("yourstylesheet.css")}
</script>
```

```
Hello world!<br>
<input type="button" value="Create style sheet" onclick="B1();">
```

Applies to:

document

createTextNode()

Compatibility: NN6, NN7, IE5, IE5.5, IE6

This method creates a new text node.
    Syntax:

```
document.createTextNode(param1)
```

param1   Optional; the nodeValue property value. See Chapter 11 for more
information on the nodeValue property.

Example:

```
<script language="JavaScript">
function B11() {
    var myNode = document.createTextNode("New Text Node");
    document.body.appendChild(myNode);
}
</script>
<button onclick="B11();">Create text node</button>
```

Applies to:

document

createTextRange()

Compatibility: IE4, IE5, IE5.5, IE6

This method creates a new TextRange object with the text contained by the
element.
    Syntax:

```
document.all.elementID.createTextRange()
```

Example:

```
<script language="JavaScript">
function B1() {
    var myNode = document.body.createTextRange();
    myNode.text = 'This is the new text';
}
```

```
</script>
<button onclick="B1();">Create text range</button>
```

Applies to:

```
<body>, <button>, <input type="button">, <input type="hidden">, <input
type="password">, <input type="reset">, <input type="submit">, <input type="text">,
<textarea>
```

createTFoot(), createTHead()

Compatibility: NN6, NN7, IE4, IE5, IE5.5, IE6

These methods create empty `<tfoot>` and `<thead>` rows for the table.
  Syntax:

```
document.getElementById("tableID").createTFoot()
document.all.tableID.createTFoot() // IE only
document.getElementById("tableID").createTHead()
document.all.tableID.createTHead() // IE only
```

Example:

```
<script language="JavaScript">
function B1() {
   var m = document.all.myT.createTFoot();
   m.bgColor = 'red';
}
function B2() {
   var n = document.all.myT.createTHead();
   n.bgColor = 'yellow';
}
</script>
<table id="myT">
<thead id="th"><tr><th>Cell 1</th><th>Cell 2</th></tr>
<tfoot id="tf"><tr><td>Cell 3</td><td>Cell 4</td></tr>
</table>
<input type="button" value="Create tfoot" onclick="B1();">
<input type="button" value="Create thead" onclick="B2();">
```

Applies to:

```
<table>
```

deleteCaption()

Compatibility: NN6, NN7, IE4, IE5, IE5.5, IE6

This method removes the `<caption>` element from a table.

Syntax:

```
document.getElementById("tableID").deleteCaption()
document.all.tableID.deleteCaption() // IE only
```

Example:

```
<script language="JavaScript">
function B1() {
document.all.myT.deleteCaption();
}
</script>
<table id="myT">
<caption id = myC style="color:red">This is the caption element</caption>
<tr><th>Cell 1</th><th>Cell 2</th></tr>
</table>
<input type="button" value="Remove caption" onclick="B1();">
```

Applies to:

```
<table>
```

deleteCell()

Compatibility: NN6, NN7, IE4, IE5, IE5.5, IE6

This method removes a cell from a table row.

Syntax:

```
document.getElementById("trID").deleteCell(param1)
document.all.trID.deleteCell(param1) // IE only
```

param1   Optional; the index of the cell's position in the row. If omitted, the last cell in the row will be removed.

Example:

```
<script language="JavaScript">
function B1() {document.all.myTr.deleteCell(2);}
</script>
<table><tr id="myTr"><td>Cell 1</td><td>Cell 2</td><td>Cell 3</td><td>Cell 4</td></tr></table>
<input type="button" value="Remove Cell 3" onclick="B1();">
```

Applies to:

```
<tr>
```

deleteData()

Compatibility: NN6 (<comment> only), NN7 (<comment> only), IE6

This method deletes a character string from the object.
    Syntax:

```
textNodeName.deleteData(param1, param2) // IE only
document.getElementById("commentID").deleteData(param1, param2)
document.all.commentID.deleteData(param1, param2) // IE only
```

param1   Required; the first character in the string to remove.

param2   Required; the number of characters to remove.

Example:

```
<script language="JavaScript">
function B1() {
   var m = document.createTextNode("This is the text from which you can delete
data.");
   var n = myP.firstChild.replaceNode(m);
   m.deleteData(5, 10);
}
</script>
<p id="myP">Sample text.</p>
<input type="button" value="Remove data" onclick="B1();">
```

    Applies to:

```
<comment>, TextNode
```

deleteRow()

Compatibility: NN6, NN7, IE4, IE5, IE5.5, IE6

This method deletes a row from the rows collection, or from a <table>, <tbody>, <tfoot>, or <thead> element.
    Syntax:

```
document.all.tableID.rows[index].deleteRow(param1)
document.getElementById("elementID").deleteRow(param1)
document.all.elementID.deleteRow(param1) // IE only
```

param1   Optional; the index of the row's position in the rows collection. If omitted, the last row will be removed.

Example:

```
<script language="JavaScript">
function B1() {document.all.myT.deleteRow(2);}
```

```
</script>
<table id="myT" width="25%" border="1">
<tr><td>Row 1</td><td>Cell 1</td></tr>
<tr><td>Row 2</td><td>Cell 2</td></tr>
<tr><td>Row 3</td><td>Cell 3</td></tr>
<tr><td>Row 4</td><td>Cell 4</td></tr>
</table>
<input type="button" value="Remove Row 3" onclick="B1();">
```

Applies to:

rows*, <table>, <tbody>, <tfoot>, <thead>

deleteTFoot(), deleteTHead()

Compatibility: NN6, NN7, IE4, IE5, IE5.5, IE6

These methods delete a <tfoot> or <thead> element from its parent element.
   Syntax:

```
document.getElementById("elementID").deleteTFoot()
document.all.elementID.deleteTFoot() // IE only
document.getElementById("elementID").deleteTHead()
document.all.elementID.deleteTHead() // IE only
```

Example:

```
<script language="JavaScript">
function B1() {document.all.myT.deleteTFoot();}
</script>
<table id="myT" width="25%" border="1">
<tr><td>Row 1</td><td>Cell 1</td></tr>
<tr><td>Row 2</td><td>Cell 2</td></tr>
<tr><td>Row 3</td><td>Cell 3</td></tr>
<tfoot><tr><td>TFOOT</td><td>Cell 4</td></tr></tfoot>
</table>
<input type="button" value="Remove TFOOT" onclick="B1();">
```

Applies to:

<table>, <tbody>

detachEvent()

Compatibility: IE5, IE5.5, IE6

This method causes a previously attached event handler function to be detached from its event. This is the opposite of the attachEvent() method.

Syntax:

```
window.detachEvent(param1, param2)
document.all.elementID.detachEvent(param1, param2)
```

param1   Required; the name of the event.

param2   Required; the name of the function.

Example: See the attachEvent() method example.

Applies to:

```
<a>, <acronym>, <address>, <applet>, <area>, <b>, <base>, <basefont>, <bgsound>,
<big>, <blockquote>, <body>, <br>, <button>, <caption>, <center>, <cite>, <code>,
<col>, <colgroup>, <comment>, <custom>, <dd>, <del>, <dfn>, <dir>, <div>, <dl>,
document, <dt>, <em>, <embed>, <fieldset>, <font>, <form>, <frame>, <frameset>,
<head>, <hn>, <hr>, <html>, <i>, <iframe>, <img>, <input type="button">, <input
type="checkbox">, <input type="file">, <input type="hidden">, <input type="image">,
<input type="password">, <input type="radio">, <input type="reset">, <input
type="submit">, <input type="text">, <ins>, <kbd>, <label>, <legend>, <li>, <link>,
<listing>, <map>, <marquee>, <menu>, namespace, <nobr>, <object>, <ol>, <option>,
<p>, <plaintext>, <pre>, <q>, <s>, <samp>, <script>, <select>, <small>, <span>,
<strike>, <strong>, <sub>, <sup>, <table>, <tbody>, <td>, <textarea>, <tfoot>,
<th>, <thead>, <title>, <tr>, <tt>, <u>, <ul>, <var>, window, <xmp>
```

doImport()

Compatibility: IE5.5, IE6

This method imports an element behavior into the namespace object. This method differs from the add() (2) method in that the add() (2) method adds a new namespace object to the namespaces collection.

Syntax:

```
document.namespaces[index].doImport(param1)
```

param1   Required; the URL of the element behavior.

Example:

```
<html xmlns:namespace1>
<button onclick="document.namespaces(0).doImport('yourfile.htc');">
Import HTC file</button>
```

Applies to:

```
namespace
```

doReadRequest()

Compatibility: IE4, IE5, IE5.5, IE6

This method executes all requests of the read-requests queue. The read-requests queue contains a list of requests to access and perform read actions on a user's profile information.

Syntax:

```
userProfile.doReadRequest(param1, param2, param3, param4, param5)
```

param1 Required; a code from 0 to 12. For a complete list and description of the codes, go to http://msdn.microsoft.com/workshop/author/dhtml/reference/methods/doreadrequest.asp?frame=true.

param2 Optional; the name of the requesting party.

param3 Optional; the pages the user's choice applies to in the future.

param4 Optional; the path to the server requesting access.

param5 Optional; the amount of time.

Example:

```
<html><head>
<script language="JavaScript">
function B1() {
userProfile.doReadRequest(5, 'Microsoft');
alert('done');
}
</script></head>
<body>
<button onclick="B1();">Perform all requests located in the read-requests queue</button>
</body></html>
```

Applies to:

```
userProfile
```

doScroll()

Compatibility: IE5, IE5.5, IE6

This method simulates a user action on a scroll bar component.

Syntax:

```
document.all.elementID.doScroll(param1)
```

param1 Optional; the scrolling action. For a complete list of possible values, go to http://msdn.microsoft.com/workshop/author/dhtml/reference/methods/doscroll.asp?frame=true.

Example:

```
<body id="myBody"><button
onclick="document.all.myBody.doScroll('scrollbarPageDown');">Page Down</button>
<button onclick="document.all.myBody.doScroll('scrollbarPageUp');">Page Up</button>
```

```
<div style="height:5000; width:500; background-color:blue;">Very large div
element</div></body>
```

Applies to:

```
<body>, <custom>, <div>, <span>, <textarea>
```

dragDrop()

Compatibility: IE5.5, IE6

This method starts a drag-and-drop operation. Returns true (successful) or
false (failed).

Syntax:

```
document.all.elementID.dragDrop()
```

Example:

```
<script language="JavaScript">
function B1() {
document.all.sourceObject.dragDrop()
var m = document.all.sourceObject.dragDrop()
alert(m+".\nDrag operation is not yet completed")
}
</script>
<div onmouseup="B1();">
<input id="sourceObject" size=50 value="The (whole or part) text to drag">
<p>Drop selected text into the following text field.</p>
<input id="targetObject" size=50 value="Drag destination element">
</div>
```

Applies to:

```
<a>, <area>, <basefont>, <bgsound>, <body>, <br>, <button>, <caption>, <col>,
<comment>, <dd>, <div>, <dt>, <embed>, <font>, <form>, <frame>, <head>, <hr>,
<html>, <iframe>, <img>, <input type="button">, <input type="checkbox">, <input
type="file">, <input type="image">, <input type="password">, <input type="radio">,
<input type="reset">, <input type="submit">, <input type="text">, <isindex>,
<label>, <legend>, <li>, <map>, <marquee>, <meta>, <object>, <ol>, <option>, <p>,
<script>, <select>, <span>, <style>, <table>, <td>, <textarea>, <title>, <tr>, <ul>
```

duplicate()

Compatibility: IE4, IE5, IE5.5, IE6

This method creates a duplicate of the specified TextRange object.

Syntax:

```
textRangeName.duplicate()
```

Example:

```
<script language="JavaScript">
function B1() {
var myText = myButton.createTextRange();
alert(myText.duplicate().text);
}
</script>
<button id="myButton" onclick="B1();">Click this button</button>
```

Applies to:

TextRange

elementFromPoint()

Compatibility: IE4, IE5, IE5.5, IE6

This method returns the element located at the specified point.
Syntax:

```
document.elementFromPoint(param1, param2)
```

param1   Required; the X coordinate of the specified point.

param2   Required; the Y coordinate of the specified point.

Example:

```
<script language="JavaScript">
function B1() {
var m = document.elementFromPoint(150, 150);
var n = m.tagName;
alert("The element located at point (150, 150) is "+n);
}
</script>
<button onclick="B1();">Click to reveal element</button>
```

Applies to:

document

empty()

Compatibility: IE4, IE5, IE5.5, IE6

This method clears the content of the selection object.
Syntax:

```
document.selection.empty()
```

Example:

```
<script language="JavaScript">
function B1() {document.selection.empty();}
</script>
<p onMouseUp="B1();">You can't select text in this paragraph because empty() is
being applied to it as soon as you release the mouse.</p>
<p>You can select text in this paragraph in various places because empty() is not
being applied to it.</p>
```

Applies to:

selection

escape()

Compatibility: NN4, NN6, NN7, IE4, IE5, IE5.5, IE6

This method URL-encodes the specified string.

Syntax:

escape(*param1*)

> **param1**   Required; the string to URL-encode.

Example:

```
<button onclick="alert(escape('Hello World!'));">Escape function</button>
<button onclick="alert(unescape('Hello%20World%21'));">Unescape function</button>
```

Applies to: n/a.

eval()

Compatibility: NN4, NN6, NN7, IE4, IE5, IE5.5, IE6

This method evaluates the specified string as if it were JavaScript code.

Syntax:

eval(*param1*)

> **param1**   Required; the string to be evaluated.

Example:

```
<script language="javascript">
function B1(){
    var fullName = 'Gidon Shuly';
    var mySentence = eval('"My name is " + fullName;');
    alert(mySentence);
}
```

```
</script>
<button onclick="B1();">Eval function</button>
```

Applies to: n/a.

execCommand()

Compatibility: IE4, IE5, IE5.5, IE6

This method executes one of the several commands that Internet Explorer supports outside the regular methods defined for HTML elements. Returns true (successful) or false (failed).

Syntax:

```
controlRangeName.execCommand(param1, param2, param3)
objectName.execCommand(param1, param2, param3)
```

param1   Required; the name of the command. For a complete list of available commands, go to http://msdn.microsoft.com/workshop/author/ dhtml/reference/commandids.asp.

param2   Optional; true or false, indicating whether or not to display a user interface if the command supports one.

param3   Optional; only applies to some of the commands.

Example:

```
<script language="JavaScript">
function B1() {document.execCommand("Refresh", "false", "false");}
</script>
<button onclick="B1();">Refresh page</button>
```

Applies to:

```
controlRange*, document, TextRange
```

execScript()

Compatibility: IE4, IE5, IE5.5, IE6

This method executes a script. Always returns undefined.

Syntax:

```
window.execScript(param1, param2)
```

param1   Required; the code to execute.

param2   Required; the code's script language. Values: vbscript and javascript (the default).

Example:

```
<script language="JavaScript">
function B1() {
var m = window.execScript("alert('test');", "JavaScript");
alert("The method returns always "+'"'+m+'"'");
}
</script>
<input type="button" value="Click to execute the script" onclick="B1();">
```

Applies to:

```
window
```

exp()

Compatibility: NN4, NN6, NN7, IE4, IE5, IE5.5, IE6

This method returns the base of the natural logarithm raised to the power of the specified number.

Syntax:

```
Math.exp(param1)
```

param1   Required; the exponent to use.

Example:

```
<button onclick="alert(Math.exp(1));">EXP</button>
```

Applies to:

```
Math
```

expand()

Compatibility: IE4, IE5, IE5.5, IE6

This method expands the text range (collapsed or not) to include the character, word, or sentence that contains the selected text. Returns true (successful) or false (failed).

Syntax:

```
textRangeName.expand(param1)
```

param1   Required; the member to expand. Values: character, word, sentence, or textedit (expands to enclose the entire range).

Example:

```
<script language="JavaScript">
function B1() {
    var m = document.selection.createRange();
    m.expand("sentence");
    alert(m.text);
}
</script>
<p onmouseup="B1();" style="color:blue">Selection extended to sentence</p>
```

Applies to:

TextRange

findText()

Compatibility: IE4, IE5, IE5.5, IE6

This method searches a TextRange object for the specified string and highlights it if found.

Syntax:

```
textRangeName.findText(param1, param2, param3)
```

param1 Required; the text to find.

param2 Optional; the number of characters of the text range to search through. A positive value indicates a forward count; a negative one indicates a backward count.

param3 Optional; the type of search. Values: 0 (the default; allow partial words to be matched), 1 (search backwards), 2 (match whole words only), 4 (make search case sensitive), 131072 (search for byte values), 536870912 (match special marks), 1073741824 (match Far East characters), or 2147483648 (match Hebrew/Arabic characters).

Example:

```
<script language="JavaScript">
function B1() {
    var m = document.body.createTextRange();
    m.findText('"test"');
    m.select();
}
</script>
<p>Search the "test" word in this paragraph</p>
<button onclick="B1();">Find test</button>
```

Applies to:

TextRange

fireEvent()

Compatibility: IE5.5, IE6

This method causes the specified event to fire on the element. Returns true (successful) or false (failed).

Syntax:

```
document.styleSheets[index].fireEvent(param1, param2)
document.all.elementID.fireEvent(param1, param2)
```

param1 Required; the name of the event.

param2 Optional; an existing event object to clone.

Example:

```
<button onmouseover="this.fireEvent('onclick')" onclick="alert('Hello');">Fire
onclick event</button>
```

Applies to:

```
<a>, <acronym>, <address>, <applet>, <area>, <b>, <base>, <basefont>, <bdo>,
<bgsound>, <big>, <blockquote>, <body>, <br>, <button>, <caption>, <center>,
<cite>, <code>, <col>, <colgroup>, <comment>, <custom>, <dd>, <del>, <dfn>, <dir>,
<div>, <dl>, <dt>, <em>, <embed>, <fieldset>, <font>, <form>, <frame>, <frameset>,
<head>, <hn>, <hr>, <html>, <i>, <iframe>, <img>, <input type="button">, <input
type="checkbox">, <input type="file">, <input type="hidden">, <input type="image">,
<input type="password">, <input type="radio">, <input type="reset">, <input
type="submit">, <input type="text">, <ins>, <isindex>, <kbd>, <label>, <legend>,
<li>, <link>, <listing>, <map>, <marquee>, <menu>, <nobr>, <noframes>, <noscript>,
<object>, <ol>, <option>, <p>, <plaintext>, <pre>, <q>, <rt>, <ruby>, <s>, <samp>,
<script>, <select>, <small>, <span>, <strike>, <strong>, styleSheet, <sub>, <sup>,
<table>, <tbody>, <td>, <textarea>, <tfoot>, <th>, <thead>, <title>, <tr>, <tt>,
<u>, <ul>, <var>, <wbr>, <xml>, <xmp>
```

firstPage()

Compatibility: IE5, IE5.5, IE6

This method displays the first page of external data to which a table is bound.

Syntax:

```
document.all.tableID.firstPage()
```

Example:

```
<html><head><script language="javascript">
function goFirst(){
    document.all.myTable.dataPageSize = 2;
    myTable.firstPage();
}
function goPrevious(){
```

```
        document.all.myTable.dataPageSize = 2;
        myTable.previousPage();
    }
    function goNext(){
        document.all.myTable.dataPageSize = 2;
        myTable.nextPage();
    }
    function goLast(){
        document.all.myTable.dataPageSize = 2;
        myTable.lastPage();
    }
</script>
<body>
<button onclick="goFirst();">First Page</button>
<button onclick="goPrevious();">Previous Page</button>
<button onclick="goNext();">Next Page</button>
<button onclick="goLast();">Last Page</button>
<button onclick="alert(document.all.myData.namedRecordset(''));">Named recordset</
button>
<object classid="clsid:333C7BC4-460F-11D0-BC04-0080C7055A83" id="myData">
    <param name="DataURL" value="mydata.csv">
    <param name="UseHeader" value="True">
    <param name="TextQualifier" value="'">
</object>
<table id="myTable" datasrc="#myData">
<thead>
<tr style="font-weight:bold"><td>First</td><td>Last</td><td>Age</td></tr></thead>
<tbody>
<tr id="tableList">
    <td><span datafld="firstname"></span></td>
    <td><span datafld="lastname"></span></td>
    <td><span datafld="age"></span></td>
</tr>
</tbody>
</table>
</body></html>
```

Contents of mydata.csv:

```
firstname:STRING,lastname:STRING,age:INT
Candy,Shuly,23
Silvana,Shuly,1
Troy,Shuly,3
Gidon,Shuly,30
Barak,Shuly,25
Mike,Belwitch,32
```

Applies to:

```
<table>
```

fixed()

Compatibility: NN4, NN6, NN7, IE4, IE5, IE5.5, IE6

This method returns a string that is displayed in a fixed-width font format.
Syntax:

```
stringName.fixed()
```

Example:

```
<button onclick="var myS = new String('Sample String'); document.write('regular
string'+myS.fixed());">FIXED</button>
```

Applies to:

```
String
```

floor()

Compatibility: NN4, NN6, NN7, IE4, IE5, IE5.5, IE6

This method rounds the specified number down to the nearest integer.
Syntax:

```
Math.floor(param1)
```

param1   Required; the number to convert.

Example:

```
<button onclick="alert(Math.floor(1.1));">FLOOR</button>
```

Applies to:

```
Math
```

focus()

Compatibility: NN4, NN6, NN7, IE4, IE5, IE5.5, IE6

This method gives focus to an element and fires the onFocus event handler.
Syntax:

```
document.getElementById("elementID").focus()
document.all.elementID.focus() // IE only
```

Example:

```
<script language="JavaScript">
function B1() {document.all.myElement.focus();}
```

```
function B2() {alert("onFocus event has been fired");}
</script>
<input id="myElement" type="text" value="" onfocus="B2();">
<input type="button" value="Give focus to the text input element and fire the
event" onclick="B1();">
```

Applies to:

```
<a>, <acronym>, <address>, <applet>, <area>, <b>, <bdo>, <big>, <blockquote>,
<body>, <button>, <caption>, <center>, <cite>, <custom>, <dd>, <del>, <dfn>, <dir>,
<dl>, document, <dt>, <em>, <embed>, <fieldset>, <font>, <form>, <frame>,
<frameset>, <hn>, <hr>, <i>, <iframe>, <img>, <input type="button">, <input
type="checkbox">, <input type="file">, <input type="image">, <input
type="password">, <input type="radio">, <input type="reset">, <input
type="submit">, <input type="text">, <ins>, <isindex>, <kbd>, <label>, <legend>,
<li>, <listing>, <marquee>, <menu>, <object>, <ol>, <p>, <plaintext>, <pre>, <q>,
<rt>, <ruby>, <s>, <samp>, <select>, <small>, <span>, <strike>, <strong>, <sub>,
<sup>, <table>, <tbody>, <td>, <textarea>, <tfoot>, <th>, <thead>, <tr>, <tt>, <u>,
<ul>, <var>, window, <xmp>
```

fontColor()

Compatibility: NN4, NN6, NN7, IE4, IE5, IE5.5, IE6

This method returns a string that is displayed in the specified color.
Syntax:

```
stringName.fontColor(param1)
```

param1   Required; web color name or hexadecimal value in #RRGGBB
format.

Example:

```
<button onclick="var myS = new String('Sample String'); document.write('regular
string'+myS.fontcolor('blue'));">FONTCOLOR</button>
```

Applies to:

```
String
```

fontSize()

Compatibility: NN4, NN6, NN7, IE4, IE5, IE5.5, IE6

This method returns a string that is displayed in the specified font size.
Syntax:

```
stringName.fontSize(param1)
```

param1   Required; a number between 1 and 7.

Example:

```
<button onclick="var myS = new String('Sample String'); document.write('regular
string'+myS.fontsize(7));">FONTSIZE</button>
```

Applies to:

String

forward()

Compatibility: NN4, NN6, NN7, IE4, IE5, IE5.5, IE6

This method loads a URL that the browser has already visited. It simulates the clicking of the browser's forward button.

Syntax:

```
objectName.forward()
```

Example:

```
<script language="JavaScript">
function B1() {history.forward();}
</script>
<a href="somePage.html">Open a new document to build the history object</a>
<input type="button" value="Go forward" onclick="B1();">
```

Applies to:

```
history, window (NN4 only)
```

fromCharCode()

Compatibility: NN4, NN6, NN7, IE4, IE5, IE5.5, IE6

This method returns a string that is created by combining the characters that correspond to the specified Unicode values.

Syntax:

```
stringName.fromCharCode(paramN, . . . paramN)
```

paramN   Required; a Unicode value.

Example:

```
<button onclick="alert(String.fromCharCode(79,80));">FROMCHARCODE</button>
```

Applies to:

String

getAdjacentText()

Compatibility: IE5, IE5.5, IE6

This method returns the text that is located in the specified position relative to the element.

Syntax:

```
document.all.elementID.getAdjacentText(param1)
```

param1 Required; Values: beforeBegin (just before the beginning of the element), afterBegin (just after the beginning of the element), beforeEnd (just before the end of the element), or afterEnd (just after the end of the element).

Example:

```
<p>This is some <b id="myBold">Adjacent Text</b> example</p>
<input type="button" value="Find text"
onclick="alert(myBold.getAdjacentText('beforeBegin'));">
```

Applies to:

```
<a>, <acronym>, <address>, <applet>, <area>, <b>, <base>, <basefont>, <bdo>, <big>,
<blockquote>, <body>, <br>, <button>, <caption>, <center>, <cite>, <code>, <col>,
<colgroup>, <comment>, <custom>, <dd>, <del>, <dfn>, <dir>, <div>, <dl>, <dt>,
<em>, <embed>, <fieldset>, <font>, <form>, <frame>, <frameset>, <head>, <hn>, <hr>,
<html>, <i>, <iframe>, <img>, <input type="button">, <input type="checkbox">,
<input type="file">, <input type="hidden">, <input type="image">, <input
type="password">, <input type="radio">, <input type="reset">, <input
type="submit">, <input type="text">, <ins>, <kbd>, <label>, <legend>, <li>, <link>,
<listing>, <map>, <marquee>, <menu>, <object>, <ol>, <option>, <p>, <plaintext>,
<pre>, <q>, <s>, <samp>, <script>, <select>, <small>, <span>, <strike>, <strong>,
<sub>, <sup>, <table>, <tbody>, <td>, <textarea>, <tfoot>, <th>, <thead>, <title>,
<tr>, <tt>, <u>, <ul>, <var>, <xmp>
```

getAttribute()

Compatibility: NN6, NN7, IE4, IE5, IE5.5, IE6

This method returns the value of the specified attribute.

Syntax:

```
objectName.getAttribute(param1, param2)
document.getElementById("elementID").getAttribute(param1, param2)
document.all.elementID.getAttribute(param1, param2) // IE only
```

param1 Required; the attribute's name.

param2 Optional; Values: 0 (the default; performs a search that is not case sensitive) or 1 (performs a case-sensitive search).

Example:

```
<script language="JavaScript">
function B1(){
var m = document.getElementById("myDiv").getAttribute("id");
alert(m);}
</script>
<div id="myDiv">This is a div element</div>
<input type="button" value="Get id attribute value" onclick="B1();">
```

Applies to:

```
<a>, <acronym>, <address>, <applet>, <area>, <b>, <base>, <basefont>, <bdo>,
<bgsound>, <big>, <blockquote>, <body>, <br>, <button>, <caption>, <center>,
<cite>, <code>, <col>, <colgroup>, <comment>, currentStyle, <custom>, <dd>, <del>,
<dfn>, <dir>, <div>, <dl>, <dt>, <em>, <embed>, <fieldset>, <font>, <form>,
<frame>, <frameset>, <head>, <hn>, <hr>, <html>, <i>, <iframe>, <img>, <input
type="button">, <input type="checkbox">, <input type="file">, <input
type="hidden">, <input type="image">, <input type="password">, <input
type="radio">, <input type="reset">, <input type="submit">, <input type="text">,
<ins>, <isindex>, <kbd>, <label>, <legend>, <li>, <link>, <listing>, <map>,
<marquee>, <menu>, <meta>, <nobr>, <noframes>, <noscript>, <object>, <ol>,
<optgroup>, <option>, <p>, <param>, <plaintext>, <pre>, <q>, runtimeStyle, <s>,
<samp>, <script>, <select>, <small>, <span>, <strike>, <strong>, style, <style>,
<sub>, <sup>, <table>, <tbody>, <td>, <textarea>, <tfoot>, <th>, <thead>, <title>,
<tr>, <tt>, <u>, <ul>, userProfile, <var>, <wbr>, <xmp>
```

getAttributeNode()

Compatibility: NN6, NN7, IE6

This method returns an instance of the attribute object that belongs to the specified element.

Syntax:

```
document.getElementById("elementID").getAttributeNode(param1)
document.all.elementID.getAttributeNode(param1) // IE only
```

param1   Required; the name of the attribute.

Example:

```
<script language="JavaScript">
function B1(){
var m = document.getElementById("myDiv").getAttributeNode("id");
var n = m.value;
alert(n);
}
</script>
<div id="myDiv">This is a div element</div>
<input type="button" value="Get id attribute node value" onclick="B1();">
```

Applies to:

`<a>`, `<acronym>`, `<address>`, `<applet>`, `<area>`, `<b>`, `<base>`, `<basefont>`, `<bdo>`, `<bgsound>`, `<big>`, `<blockquote>`, `<body>`, `<br>`, `<button>`, `<caption>`, `<center>`, `<cite>`, `<code>`, `<col>`, `<colgroup>`, `<comment>`, `<custom>`, `<dd>`, `<del>`, `<dfn>`, `<dir>`, `<div>`, `<dl>`, `<dt>`, `<em>`, `<embed>`, `<fieldset>`, `<font>`, `<form>`, `<frame>`, `<frameset>`, `<head>`, `<hn>`, `<hr>`, `<html>`, `<i>`, `<iframe>`, `<img>`, `<input type="button">`, `<input type="checkbox">`, `<input type="file">`, `<input type="hidden">`, `<input type="image">`, `<input type="password">`, `<input type="radio">`, `<input type="reset">`, `<input type="submit">`, `<input type="text">`, `<ins>`, `<isindex>`, `<kbd>`, `<label>`, `<legend>`, `<li>`, `<link>`, `<listing>`, `<map>`, `<marquee>`, `<menu>`, `<meta>`, `<nobr>`, `<noframes>`, `<noscript>`, `<object>`, `<ol>`, `<optgroup>`, `<option>`, `<p>`, `<param>`, `<plaintext>`, `<pre>`, `<q>`, `<rt>`, `<ruby>`, `<s>`, `<samp>`, `<script>`, `<select>`, `<small>`, `<span>`, `<strike>`, `<strong>`, `<style>`, style, `<sub>`, `<sup>`, `<table>`, `<tbody>`, `<td>`, `<textarea>`, `<tfoot>`, `<th>`, `<thead>`, `<title>`, `<tr>`, `<tt>`, `<u>`, `<ul>`, `<var>`, `<wbr>`, `<xml>`, `<xmp>`

getBookmark()

Compatibility: IE4, IE5, IE5.5, IE6

This method can be used to create a bookmark for the referenced `TextRange` object, and it allows you to locate a particular text string within the object. If the desired text is not found, this method returns a `null` value.

Syntax:

```
textRangeName.getBookmark()
```

Example:

```
<script language="JavaScript">
function B1() {
    var m = document.body.createTextRange();
    var n = m.getBookmark();
    m.moveToBookmark(n);
    m.findText("samp");
    m.select();
}
</script>
<p>This is some sample text.</p>
<input type="button" value="Select samp" onclick="B1();">
```

Applies to:

TextRange

getBoundingClientRect()

Compatibility: IE5, IE5.5, IE6

This method returns a TextRectangle object, specifying its four coordinates (top, left, right, and bottom) in pixels. The client area is 2.2 pixels wider than the window area.

Syntax:

```
textRangeName.getBoundingClientRect()
document.all.elementID.getBoundingClientRect()
```

Example:

```
<button onclick="alert(this.getBoundingClientRect().left);">
GetBoundingClientRect</button>
```

Applies to:

```
<a>, <acronym>, <address>, <applet>, <area>, <b>, <base>, <basefont>, <big>,
<blockquote>, <body>, <button>, <caption>, <center>, <cite>, <code>, <col>,
<colgroup>, <comment>, <custom>, <dd>, <del>, <dfn>, <dir>, <div>, <dl>, <dt>,
<em>, <embed>, <fieldset>, <font>, <form>, <hn>, <i>, <img>, <input type="button">,
<input type="checkbox">, <input type="file">, <input type="image">, <input
type="password">, <input type="radio">, <input type="reset">, <input
type="submit">, <input type="text">, <ins>, <isindex>, <kbd>, <label>, <legend>,
<li>, <link>, <listing>, <map>, <marquee>, <menu>, <nobr>, <object>, <ol>,
<option>, <p>, <pre>, <q>, <s>, <samp>, <select>, <small>, <span>, <strike>,
<strong>, <sub>, <sup>, <table>, <tbody>, <td>, <textarea>, TextRange, <tfoot>,
<th>, <thead>, <tr>, <tt>, <u>, <ul>, <var>, <xmp>
```

getCharset()

Compatibility: IE6

This method returns the character set of the specified font. For a complete list of return values, go to http://msdn.microsoft.com/workshop/author/dhtml/reference/constants/dlgsafehelper_charset.asp.

Syntax:

```
document.all.DialogHelperID.getCharset(param1)
```

param1 Required; the font name.

Example:

```
<script language="JavaScript">
function B1() {alert(myDiaHelp.getCharset("Verdana"));}
</script>
<input type="button" value="GetCharSet" onclick="B1();">
<object id="myDiaHelp" classid="clsid:3050f819-98b5-11cf-bb82-00aa00bdce0b"
width="0px" height="0px"></object>
```

Applies to:

Dialog Helper

getClientRects()

Compatibility: IE5, IE5.5, IE6

This method returns a TextRectangle object that contains the boundaries of the element's content.

Syntax:

```
textRangeName.getClientRects()
document.all.elementID.getClientRects()
```

Example:

```
<button onclick="alert(this.getClientRects().length);">ClientRect</button>
```

Applies to:

```
<a>, <acronym>, <address>, <applet>, <area>, <b>, <base>, <basefont>, <big>,
<blockquote>, <body>, <button>, <caption>, <center>, <cite>, <code>, <col>,
<colgroup>, <comment>, <custom>, <dd>, <del>, <dfn>, <dir>, <div>, <dl>, <dt>,
<em>, <embed>, <fieldset>, <font>, <form>, <hn>, <i>, <img>, <input type="button">,
<input type="checkbox">, <input type="file">, <input type="image">, <input
type="password">, <input type="radio">, <input type="reset">, <input
type="submit">, <input type="text">, <ins>, <isindex>, <kbd>, <label>, <legend>,
<li>, <link>, <listing>, <map>, <marquee>, <menu>, <nobr>, <object>, <ol>,
<option>, <p>, <pre>, <q>, <s>, <samp>, <select>, <small>, <span>, <strike>,
<strong>, <sub>, <sup>, <table>, <tbody>, <td>, <textarea>, TextRange, <tfoot>,
<th>, <thead>, <tr>, <tt>, <u>, <ul>, <var>, <xmp>
```

getData()

Compatibility: IE5, IE5.5, IE6

This method retrieves the specified type of data from the clipboard.

Syntax:

```
event.objectName.getData(param1)
```

param1   Required; text or URL.

Example: See the clearData() method example.

Applies to:

clipboardData, dataTransfer

getDate()

Compatibility: NN4, NN6, NN7, IE4, IE5, IE5.5, IE6

This method returns the Date object's numeric day of the month.
Syntax:

```
dateName.getDate()
```

Example:

```
<button onclick="var myDate = new Date(); alert(myDate.getDate());">GETDATE</button>
```

Applies to:

```
Date
```

getDay()

Compatibility: NN4, NN6, NN7, IE4, IE5, IE5.5, IE6

This method returns the Date object's numeric day of the week. Return values: 0 to 6, with 0 representing Sunday and 6 representing Saturday.
Syntax:

```
dateName.getDay()
```

Example:

```
<button onclick="var myDate = new Date(); alert(myDate.getDay());">GETDAY</button>
```

Applies to:

```
Date
```

getElementById()

Compatibility: NN6, NN7, IE5, IE5.5, IE6

This method returns the element whose id attribute value matches the specified one.
Syntax:

```
document.getElementById(param1)
```

param1   Required; the element's id value.

Example:

```
<script language="JavaScript">
function B1() {
   var m = document.getElementById("myA");
   alert(m.innerText);
}
</script>
<p>Click in the following element:</p>
<a id="myA" href="http://www.advocar.com" onclick="return(false);"
onmouseup="B1();">This is a link</a>
```

Applies to:

document

getElementsByName()

Compatibility: NN6, NN7, IE5, IE5.5, IE6

This method returns a collection of all the elements that have either an id or name attribute that matches the specified value.

Syntax:

document.getElementsByName(*param1*)

param1   Required; the element's name or id attribute value.

Example:

```
<script language="JavaScript">
function B1() {
   var m = document.getElementsByName("myE");
   alert(m.length);
}
</script>
<a id="myE" href="http://www.advocar.com" onclick="return(false);">This is a link</a>
<div id="myE">This is a div element</div>
<p id="myE" style="cursor:hand">This is a p element</p>
<input type="button" value="Get the number of elements that have the same name"
onClick="B1();">
```

Applies to:

document

getElementsByTagName()

Compatibility: NN6, NN7, IE5, IE5.5, IE6

This method returns a collection of all the elements that have the specified tag name.

Syntax:

```
document.getElementsByTagName(param1)
document.all.elementID.getElementsByTagName(param1) // IE only
```

param1   Required; the tag name.

Example:

```
<script language="JavaScript">
function B1() {
    var m = document.getElementsByTagName("P");
    alert(m.length);
}
</script>
<input type="button" value="Get the number of p elements in this page"
onClick="B1();">
```

Applies to:

```
<a>, <acronym>, <address>, <applet>, <area>, <b>, <base>, <basefont>, <bdo>,
<bgsound>, <big>, <blockquote>, <body>, <br>, <button>, <caption>, <center>,
<cite>, <code>, <col>, <colgroup>, <custom>, <dd>, <del>, <dfn>, <dir>, <div>,
<dl>, document, <dt>, <em>, <embed>, <fieldset>, <font>, <form>, <frame>,
<frameset>, <head>, <hn>, <hr>, <html>, <i>, <iframe>, <img>, <ins>, <isindex>,
<kbd>, <label>, <legend>, <li>, <link>, <listing>, <map>, <marquee>, <menu>,
<meta>, <noframes>, <noscript>, <object>, <ol>, <optgroup>, <option>, <p>, <param>,
<plaintext>, <pre>, <q>, <s>, <samp>, <script>, <select>, <small>, <span>,
<strike>, <strong>, <style>, <sub>, <sup>, <table>, <tbody>, <td>, <textarea>,
<tfoot>, <th>, <thead>, <title>, <tr>, <tt>, <u>, <ul>, <var>, <xmp>
```

getExpression()

Compatibility: IE5, IE5.5, IE6

This method returns the expression of the specified dynamic property. To use this method, you must first have used the setExpression() method.

Syntax:

```
objectName.getExpression(param1)
document.all.elementID.getExpression(param1)
```

param1   Required; the name of the property.

Example:

```
<script language="JScript">
function B1() {
    myDiv.style.setExpression("height","eval(myDiv.innerHTML)");
```

```
}
function B2() {alert(myDiv.style.getExpression("height"));}
function B3() {alert(myDiv.style.removeExpression("height"));}
function B4() {myDiv.innerHTML = 100; document.recalc();}
</script>
<button onclick="B1();">Set expression</button>
<button onclick="B2();">Get expression</button>
<button onclick="B3();">Remove expression</button>
<button onclick="B4();">Recalc</button>
<div id="myDiv" style="height:300; width:200; border:solid 1px black">20</div>
```

Applies to:

\<a>, \<acronym>, \<address>, \<area>, \<b>, \<bdo>, \<big>, \<blockquote>, \<body>, \
,
\<button>, \<caption>, \<center>, \<cite>, \<code>, \<col>, \<colgroup>, currentStyle,
\<custom>, \<dd>, \<del>, \<dfn>, \<dir>, \<div>, \<dl>, \<dt>, \<em>, \<fieldset>, \<font>,
\<form>, \<hn>, \<hr>, \<i>, \<iframe>, \<img>, \<input type="button">, \<input
type="checkbox">, \<input type="file">, \<input type="hidden">, \<input type="image">,
\<input type="password">, \<input type="radio">, \<input type="reset">, \<input
type="submit">, \<input type="text">, \<ins>, \<kbd>, \<label>, \<legend>, \<li>,
\<listing>, \<marquee>, \<menu>, \<nobr>, \<object>, \<ol>, \<option>, \<p>, \<pre>, \<q>,
\<rt>, \<ruby>, runtimeStyle, \<s>, \<samp>, \<select>, \<small>, \<span>, \<strike>,
\<strong>, style, \<sub>, \<sup>, \<table>, \<tbody>, \<td>, \<textarea>, \<tfoot>, \<th>,
\<thead>, \<tr>, \<tt>, \<u>, \<ul>, \<var>

---

getFullYear()

Compatibility: NN4, NN6, NN7, IE4, IE5, IE5.5, IE6

This method returns the Date object's four-digit year.
   Syntax:

---

dateName.getFullYear()

   Example:

```
<button onclick="var myDate = new Date();
alert(myDate.getFullYear());">GETFULLYEAR</button>
```

   Applies to:

Date

---

getHours()

Compatibility: NN4, NN6, NN7, IE4, IE5, IE5.5, IE6

This method returns the Date object's hour of the day. Return value: 0 to 23.
   Syntax:

---

dateName.getHours()

Example:

```
<button onclick="var myDate = new Date(); alert(myDate.getHours());">GETHOURS</
button>
```

Applies to:

Date

getMilliseconds()

Compatibility: NN4, NN6, NN7, IE4, IE5, IE5.5, IE6

This method returns the Date object's number of milliseconds that have elapsed
during its current second. Return value: 0 to 999.

Syntax:

dateName.getMilliseconds()

Example:

```
<button onclick="var myDate = new Date();
alert(myDate.getMilliseconds());">GETMILLISECONDS</button>
```

Applies to:

Date

getMinutes()

Compatibility: NN4, NN6, NN7, IE4, IE5, IE5.5, IE6

This method returns the Date object's number of minutes. Return value: 0 to 59.

Syntax:

dateName.getMinutes()

Example:

```
<button onclick="var myDate = new Date(); alert(myDate.getMinutes());">GETMINUTES</
button>
```

Applies to:

Date

getMonth()

Compatibility: NN4, NN6, NN7, IE4, IE5, IE5.5, IE6

This method returns the Date object's month. Return value: 0 to 11, with 0 representing January and 11 representing December.

Syntax:

`dateName.getMonth()`

Example:

```
<button onclick="var myDate = new Date(); alert(myDate.getMonth());">GETMONTH</button>
```

Applies to:

Date

getNamedItem()

Compatibility: IE6

This method returns the value of the specified attribute, provided that it has been explicitly defined in the element.

Syntax:

`document.all.elementID.attributes.getNamedItem(param1)`

param1 Required; the name of the attribute.

Example:

```
<button
onclick="alert(this.attributes.getNamedItem('onclick').value);">getNamedItem</
button>
```

Applies to:

attributes*

getSeconds()

Compatibility: NN4, NN6, NN7, IE4, IE5, IE5.5, IE6

This method returns the Date object's number of seconds. Return value: 0 to 59.

Syntax:

`dateName.getSeconds()`

Example:

```
<button onclick="var myDate = new Date(); alert(myDate.getSeconds());">GETSECONDS</
button>
```

Applies to:

Date

getTime()

Compatibility: NN4, NN6, NN7, IE4, IE5, IE5.5, IE6

This method returns the total number of milliseconds that have elapsed since January 1, 1970.
Syntax:

dateName.getTime()

Example:

```
<button onclick="var myDate = new Date(); alert(myDate.getTime());">GETTIME</
button>
```

Applies to:

Date

getTimezoneOffset()

Compatibility: NN4, NN6, NN7, IE4, IE5, IE5.5, IE6

This method returns the difference in minutes between Greenwich Mean Time (GMT) and the local system's time.
Syntax:

dateName.getTimezoneOffset()

Example:

```
<button onclick="var myDate = new Date();
alert(myDate.getTimezoneOffset());">GETTIMEZONEOFFSET</button>
```

Applies to:

Date

getUTCDate()

Compatibility: NN4, NN6, NN7, IE4, IE5, IE5.5, IE6

This method returns the Date object's day of the month based on UTC time.

Syntax:

---

dateName.getUTCDate()

Example:

```
<button onclick="var myDate = new Date(); alert(myDate.getUTCDate());">GETUTCDATE</button>
```

Applies to:

Date

---

getUTCDay()

Compatibility: NN4, NN6, NN7, IE4, IE5, IE5.5, IE6

This method returns the Date object's day of the week based on UTC time. Return values: 0 to 6, with 0 representing Sunday and 6 representing Saturday.

Syntax:

---

dateName.getUTCDay()

Example:

```
<button onclick="var myDate = new Date(); alert(myDate.getUTCDay());">GETUTCDAY</button>
```

Applies to:

Date

---

getUTCFullYear()

Compatibility: NN4, NN6, NN7, IE4, IE5, IE5.5, IE6

This method returns the Date object's four-digit year based on UTC time.

Syntax:

---

dateName.getUTCFullYear()

Example:

```
<button onclick="var myDate = new Date();
alert(myDate.getUTCFullYear());">GETUTCFULLYEAR</button>
```

Applies to:

Date

---

getUTCHours()

Compatibility: NN4, NN6, NN7, IE4, IE5, IE5.5, IE6

This method returns the Date object's hour based on UTC time. Return value: 0 to 23.

Syntax:

```
dateName.getUTCHours()
```

Example:

```
<button onclick="var myDate = new Date();
alert(myDate.getUTCHours());">GETUTCHOURS</button>
```

Applies to:

```
Date
```

getUTCMilliseconds()

Compatibility: NN4, NN6, NN7, IE4, IE5, IE5.5, IE6

This method returns the Date object's number of milliseconds that have elapsed during its current second based on UTC time. Return value: 0 to 999.

Syntax:

```
dateName.getUTCMilliseconds()
```

Example:

```
<button onclick="var myDate = new Date();
alert(myDate.getUTCMilliseconds());">GETUTCMILLISECONDS</button>
```

Applies to:

```
Date
```

getUTCMinutes()

Compatibility: NN4, NN6, NN7, IE4, IE5, IE5.5, IE6

This method returns the Date object's minute based on UTC time. Return value: 0 to 59.

Syntax:

```
dateName.getUTCMinutes()
```

Example:

```
<button onclick="var myDate = new Date();
alert(myDate.getUTCMinutes());">GETUTCMINUTES</button>
```

Applies to:

```
Date
```

getUTCMonth()

Compatibility: NN4, NN6, NN7, IE4, IE5, IE5.5, IE6

This method returns the Date object's month based on UTC time. Return value: 0 to 11, with 0 representing January and 11 representing December.
   Syntax:

```
dateName.getUTCMonth()
```

Example:

```
<button onclick="var myDate = new Date();
alert(myDate.getUTCMonth());">GETUTCMONTH</button>
```

Applies to:

```
Date
```

getUTCSeconds()

Compatibility: NN4, NN6, NN7, IE4, IE5, IE5.5, IE6

This method returns the Date object's seconds based on UTC time. Return value: 0 to 59.
   Syntax:

```
dateName.getUTCSeconds()
```

Example:

```
<button onclick="var myDate = new Date();
alert(myDate.getUTCSeconds());">GETUTCSECONDS</button>
```

Applies to:

```
Date
```

getYear()

Compatibility: NN4, NN6, NN7, IE4, IE5, IE5.5, IE6

This method returns the Date object's year. When the year is before 2000, the return value is the year minus 1900. When the year is 2000 or after, the return value is the four-digit year.

Syntax:

```
dateName.getYear()
```

Example:

```
<button onclick="var myDate = new Date(); alert(myDate.getYear());">GETYEAR</button>
```

Applies to:

```
Date
```

go()

Compatibility: NN4, NN6, NN7, IE4, IE5, IE5.5, IE6

This method loads a document from the history list.

Syntax:

```
history.go(param1)
```

param1   Optional; either a URL in the history list or the number of URLs to go forward or back in the history list (a positive number will go forward, and a negative number will go back).

Example:

```
<script language="JavaScript">
function B1() {history.go(1);}
</script>
<a href="yourfile.htm">Open another page first</a>
<input type="button" value="GO" onclick="B1();">
```

Applies to:

```
history
```

hasChildNodes()

Compatibility: NN6, NN7, IE5, IE5.5, IE6

This method indicates whether or not the element has child nodes. Returns true or false.

Syntax:

```
document.getElementById("elementID").hasChildNodes()
document.all.elementID.hasChildNodes() // IE only
```

Example:

```
<script language="JavaScript">
function B1() { alert(document.getElementById("myText").hasChildNodes());}
</script>
<p id="myText">This sample <b>text</b> has child nodes.</p>
<button onclick="B1();">HasChildNodes</button>
```

Applies to:

```
<a>, <acronym>, <address>, <applet>, <area>, attribute, <b>, <base>, <basefont>,
<bdo>, <big>, <blockquote>, <body>, <br>, <button>, <caption>, <center>, <cite>,
<code>, <col>, <colgroup>, <comment>, <dd>, <del>, <dfn>, <dir>, <div>, <dl>, <dt>,
<em>, <embed>, <fieldset>, <font>, <form>, <frame>, <frameset>, <head>, <hn>, <hr>,
<html>, <i>, <iframe>, <img>, <input type="button">, <input type="checkbox">,
<input type="file">, <input type="image">, <input type="password">, <input
type="radio">, <input type="reset">, <input type="submit">, <input type="text">,
<ins>, <isindex>, <kbd>, <label>, <legend>, <li>, <link>, <listing>, <map>,
<marquee>, <menu>, <meta>, <noframes>, <noscript>, <object>, <ol>, <optgroup>,
<option>, <p>, <param>, <plaintext>, <pre>, <q>, <s>, <samp>, <script>, <select>,
<small>, <span>, <strike>, <strong>, <style>, <sub>, <sup>, <table>, <tbody>, <td>,
<textarea>, <tfoot>, <th>, <thead>, <title>, <tr>, <tt>, <u>, <ul>, <var>, <xmp>
```

hasFeature()

Compatibility: IE6

This method indicates whether or not a document uses the specified DOM standard. Returns true or false.

Syntax:

```
document.implementation.hasFeature(param1, param2)
```

param1   Required; the standard: HTML or XML.

param2   Optional; the standard's version number.

Example:

```
<script language="JavaScript">
function B1() {alert(document.implementation.hasFeature("HTML"));}
</script>
<input type="button" value="HasFeature" onclick="B1();">
```

Applies to:

---
implementation
---

hasFocus()

Compatibility: IE4, IE5, IE5.5, IE6

This method indicates whether or not the document has focus. Returns true or false.

Syntax:

```
document.hasFocus()
```

Example:

```
<button onclick="alert(document.hasFocus());">HasFocus</button>
```

Applies to:

---
document
---

hasOwnProperty()

Compatibility: IE5, IE5.5, IE6

This method indicates whether or not the Object object contains the specified property. Returns true or false.

Syntax:

```
objectName.hasOwnProperty(param1)
```
---

param1   Required; the property name.

Example:

```
<script language="javascript">
function Object(firstName, lastName){
    this.firstName = firstName;
    this.lastName = lastName;
}
function B1(){
    myObject.age = B3;
    alert(myObject.age());
}
function B2(){
    myObject.favoriteColor = 'Blue';
```

```
        alert(myObject.favoriteColor);
}
function B3(){return 34;}
var myObject = new Object('John', 'Smith');
</script>
<button onclick="B2();">Add property</button>
<button onclick="B1();">Add method</button>
<button onclick="alert(myObject.constructor);">Constructor</button>
<button onclick="alert(myObject.isPrototypeOf(myObject));">PrototypeOf</button>
<button onclick="alert(myObject.hasOwnProperty('lastName'));">HasProperty</button>
```

Applies to:

```
Object
```

hide()

Compatibility: IE5.5, IE6

This method hides a pop-up window. To show it again, you must use the show() method.

    Syntax:

```
popupName.hide()
```

    Example:

```
<script language="JavaScript">
var myPopup
function B1() {
    myPopup = window.createPopup();
    myPopup.document.body.style.backgroundColor = 'yellow';
    myPopup.show(100,100,100,200,document.body);
}
</script>
<input type="button" value="Show popup window" onclick="B1();">
<input type="button" value="Hide popup window" onclick="myPopup.hide();">
```

Applies to:

```
popup
```

ImportExportFavorites()

Compatibility: IE4, IE5, IE5.5, IE6

This method controls the import and export of the browser's favorites list.

    Syntax:

```
window.external.ImportExportFavorites(param1, param2)
```

param1 Required; true (import) or false (export).

param2 Required; the URL to export or import. If param2 is an empty string (""), the method opens the file dialog box to find the local page to import.

Example:

```
<script language="JavaScript">
function B1() {window.external.ImportExportFavorites(true, "");}
</script>
<button onclick="B1();">Show dialog</button>
```

Applies to:

```
external
```

indexOf()

Compatibility: NN4, NN6, NN7, IE4, IE5, IE5.5, IE6

This method performs a search for the specified string and returns the character number in the string at which the match starts. If no match is found, it returns -1.
Syntax:

```
stringName.indexOf(param1, param2)
```

param1 Required; the string to search for.

param2 Optional; the character number in the string at which to start the search.

Example:

```
<button onclick="var myS = new String('Sample String');
alert(myS.indexOf('String'));">INDEXOF</button>
```

Applies to:

```
String
```

inRange()

Compatibility: IE4, IE5, IE5.5, IE6

This method indicates whether or not the specified range is inside another range. Returns true or false.
Syntax:

```
textRangeName.inRange(param1)
```

param1   Required; the text range that may or may not be contained within *textRangeName*.

Example:

```
<script language="JavaScript">
function B1() {
    var myText = document.body.createTextRange();
    var myText2 = document.all.myText.createTextRange();
    alert(myText.inRange(myText2));
}
</script>
<textarea id="myText" style="width:600; height:100;">Sample textarea text</textarea>
<button onclick="B1();">InRange</button>
```

Applies to:

TextRange

insertAdjacentElement()

Compatibility: IE5, IE5.5, IE6

This method inserts an element in the specified position relative to the location of another element.

Syntax:

```
document.all.elementID.insertAdjacentElement(param1, param2)
```

param1   Required; Values: beforeBegin (just before the beginning of the element), afterBegin (just after the beginning of the element), beforeEnd (just before the end of the element), or afterEnd (just after the end of the element).

param2   Required; the element to be inserted.

Example:

```
<script language="JavaScript">
function B1() {
    var myElement = document.createElement('<div style="width:300; height:200;
border:solid black 1px;"></div>');
    document.all.myButton.insertAdjacentElement('afterEnd', myElement);
}
</script>
<button id="myButton" onclick="B1();">Insert element</button>
```

Applies to:

<a>, <acronym>, <address>, <applet>, <area>, <b>, <base>, <basefont>, <bdo>, <bgsound>, <big>, <blockquote>, <body>, <br>, <button>, <caption>, <center>,

<cite>, <code>, <col>, <colgroup>, <comment>, <dd>, <del>, <dfn>, <dir>, <div>, <dl>, <dt>, <em>, <embed>, <fieldset>, <font>, <form>, <frame>, <frameset>, <head>, <hn>, <hr>, <html>, <i>, <iframe>, <img>, <input type="button">, <input type="checkbox">, <input type="file">, <input type="hidden">, <input type="image">, <input type="password">, <input type="radio">, <input type="reset">, <input type="submit">, <input type="text">, <ins>, <kbd>, <label>, <legend>, <li>, <link>, <listing>, <map>, <marquee>, <menu>, <object>, <ol>, <option>, <p>, <plaintext>, <pre>, <q>, <s>, <samp>, <script>, <select>, <small>, <span>, <strike>, <strong>, <sub>, <sup>, <table>, <tbody>, <td>, <textarea>, <tfoot>, <th>, <thead>, <title>, <tr>, <tt>, <u>, <ul>, <var>, <xmp>

insertAdjacentHTML()

Compatibility: IE4, IE5, IE5.5, IE6

This method inserts HTML content in the specified position relative to the location of an existing element.

Syntax:

```
document.all.elementID.insertAdjacentHTML(param1, param2)
```

param1   Required; Values: beforeBegin (just before the beginning of the element), afterBegin (just after the beginning of the element), beforeEnd (just before the end of the element), or afterEnd (just after the end of the element).

param2   Required; the HTML to be inserted.

Example:

```
<script language="JavaScript">
function B1() {
    var myElement = '<div style="width:300; height:200; border:solid black
1px;"></div>';
    document.all.myButton.insertAdjacentHTML('afterEnd', myElement);
}
</script>
<button id="myButton" onclick="B1();">Insert HTML</button>
```

Applies to:

<a>, <address>, <area>, <b>, <basefont>, <big>, <blockquote>, <body>, <button>, <caption>, <center>, <cite>, <code>, <comment>, <custom>, <dd>, <dfn>, <dir>, <div>, <dl>, <dt>, <em>, <fieldset>, <font>, <form>, <frameset>, <hn>, <hr>, <i>, <iframe>, <img>, <input type="button">, <input type="checkbox">, <input type="file">, <input type="hidden">, <input type="image">, <input type="password">, <input type="radio">, <input type="reset">, <input type="submit">, <input type="text">, <kbd>, <label>, <legend>, <li>, <listing>, <map>, <marquee>, <menu>, <nobr>, <ol>, <option>, <p>, <plaintext>, <pre>, <s>, <samp>, <select>, <small>, <span>, <strike>, <strong>, <sub>, <sup>, <td>, <textarea>, <th>, <tt>, <u>, <ul>, <var>, <xmp>

insertAdjacentText()

Compatibility: IE4, IE5, IE5.5, IE6

This method inserts text into the specified position relative to the location of an existing element.

Syntax:

```
document.all.elementID.insertAdjacentText(param1, param2)
```

param1 Required; Values: beforeBegin (just before the beginning of the element), afterBegin (just after the beginning of the element), beforeEnd (just before the end of the element), or afterEnd (just after the end of the element).

param2 Required; the text to be inserted.

Example:

```
<script language="JavaScript">
function B1() {
    var myText = 'Some Sample Text';
    document.all.myDiv.insertAdjacentText('afterBegin', myText);
}
</script>
<button onclick="B1();">Insert element</button>
<div id="myDiv" style="width:300; height:200; border:solid black 1px;"></div>
```

Applies to:

```
<a>, <address>, <area>, <b>, <basefont>, <big>, <blockquote>, <body>, <button>,
<caption>, <center>, <cite>, <code>, <comment>, <custom>, <dd>, <dfn>, <dir>,
<div>, <dl>, <dt>, <em>, <fieldset>, <font>, <form>, <frameset>, <hn>, <hr>, <i>,
<iframe>, <img>, <input type="button">, <input type="checkbox">, <input
type="file">, <input type="hidden">, <input type="image">, <input type="password">,
<input type="radio">, <input type="reset">, <input type="submit">, <input
type="text">, <kbd>, <label>, <legend>, <li>, <listing>, <map>, <marquee>, <menu>,
<nobr>, <ol>, <option>, <p>, <pre>, <s>, <samp>, <select>, <small>, <span>,
<strike>, <strong>, <sub>, <sup>, <td>, <textarea>, <th>, <tt>, <u>, <ul>, <var>
```

insertBefore()

Compatibility: NN6, NN7, IE5, IE5.5, IE6

This method inserts an element either at the end of the document or after the specified element.

Syntax:

```
document.getElementById("elementID").insertBefore(param1, param2)
document.all.elementID.insertBefore(param1, param2) // IE only
```

param1   Required; the new element to be inserted.

param2   Optional; the element after which to insert the new element.
If omitted, the new element is inserted at the end of the document.

Example:

```
<script language="JavaScript">
function B1() {
    var myElement = document.createElement('<div style="width:300; height:200;
background-color:blue;"></div>');
    document.all.myDiv.insertBefore(myElement);
}
</script>
<button id="myButton" onclick="B1();">Insert element</button>
<div id="myDiv" style="width:300; height:200; border:solid black 1px;"></div>
```

Applies to:

```
<a>, <acronym>, <address>, <applet>, <area>, attribute, <b>, <base>, <basefont>,
<bdo>, <big>, <blockquote>, <body>, <br>, <button>, <caption>, <center>, <cite>,
<code>, <col>, <colgroup>, <comment>, <dd>, <del>, <dfn>, <dir>, <div>, <dl>, <dt>,
<em>, <fieldset>, <font>, <form>, <frame>, <frameset>, <head>, <hn>, <hr>, <html>,
<i>, <iframe>, <img>, <input type="button">, <input type="checkbox">, <input
type="file">, <input type="image">, <input type="password">, <input type="radio">,
<input type="reset">, <input type="submit">, <input type="text">, <ins>, <isindex>,
<kbd>, <label>, <legend>, <li>, <link>, <listing>, <map>, <marquee>, <menu>,
<meta>, <noframes>, <noscript>, <object>, <ol>, <optgroup>, <option>, <p>, <param>,
<plaintext>, <pre>, <q>, <s>, <samp>, <script>, <select>, <small>, <span>,
<strike>, <strong>, <style>, <sub>, <sup>, <table>, <tbody>, <td>, <textarea>,
<tfoot>, <th>, <thead>, <title>, <tr>, <tt>, <u>, <ul>, <var>, <xmp>
```

insertCell()

Compatibility: NN6, NN7, IE4, IE5, IE5.5, IE6

This method adds a cell to the specified table row.
Syntax:

```
document.getElementById("trID").insertCell(param1)
document.all.trID.insertCell(param1) // IE only
```

param1   Optional; the index of the new cell's position in the cells
collection. The default value is -1, which appends the cell to the end
of the collection.

Example:

```
<script language="JavaScript">
function B1() {
    var myRow = document.all.myTable.insertRow();
```

```
        var myCell = myRow.insertCell();
        myCell.innerText = "The added cell";
}
</script>
<table id="myTable" border="1" cellspacing="5" cellpadding="5">
  <tr><td width="100"> </td><td width="100"> </td></tr>
  <tr><td> </td><td> </td></tr>
</table>
<button onclick="B1();">Add a cell</button>
```

Applies to:

`<tr>`

insertData()

Compatibility: NN6 (`<comment>` only), NN7 (`<comment>` only), IE6

This method adds a string inside the element.

Syntax:

```
textNodeName.insertData(param1, param2) // IE only
document.getElementById("commentID").insertData(param1, param2)
document.all.commentID.insertData(param1, param2) // IE only
```

param1 Required; the character position at which to begin the insertion.

param2 Required; the string to be inserted.

Example:

```
<script language="JavaScript">
function B1() {
    var m = document.getElementById("myP").firstChild;
    m.insertData(10, 'INSERTED TEXT')}
</script>
<p id="myP">Sample text paragraph</p>
<input type="button" value="InsertData" onclick="B1();">
```

Applies to:

`<comment>`, TextNode

insertRow()

Compatibility: NN6, NN7, IE4, IE5, IE5.5, IE6

This method adds a row to the specified element.

Syntax:

```
document.elementID.rows.insertRow(param1)
document.getElementById("elementID").insertRow(param1)
document.all.elementID.insertRow(param1) // IE only
```

param1   Optional; the index of the new row's position in the rows collection. The default value is -1, which appends the new row to the end of the collection.

Example: See the insertCell() method example.
Applies to:

rows*, <table>, <tbody>, <tfoot>, <thead>

isEqual()

Compatibility: IE4, IE5, IE5.5, IE6

This method indicates whether or not a given range is equal to a second range. Returns true or false.

Syntax:

```
textRangeName.isEqual(param1)
```

param1   Required; a second text range.

Example:

```
<script language="JavaScript">
function B1(){
   var myRange1 = document.body.createTextRange();
   var myRange2 = myRange1.duplicate();
   alert(myRange1.isEqual(myRange2));
}
</script>
<p>This is some sample range used in comparison</p>
<button onclick="B1();">IsEqual</button>
```

Applies to:

TextRange

isNaN()

Compatibility: NN4, NN6, NN7, IE4, IE5, IE5.5, IE6

This method indicates whether or not the specified string is not numeric. Returns true or false.

Syntax:

---

isNaN(*param1*)

---

param1   Required; the string to be evaluated.

Example:

```
<button onclick="alert(isNaN('12.34'));">isNaN True</button>
<button onclick="alert(isNaN('Hello'));">isNaN False</button>
```

Applies to: n/a.

isPrototypeOf()

Compatibility: IE5, IE5.5, IE6

This method indicates whether or not the specified object is an instance of the Object object. Returns true or false.

Syntax:

---

objectName.isPrototypeOf(*param1*)

---

param1   Required; the object to check.

Example: See the hasOwnProperty() method example.
Applies to:

Object

IsSubscribed()

Compatibility: IE4, IE5, IE5.5, IE6

This method indicates whether or not the browser is subscribed to the specified channel (a hosting application other than Internet Explorer). This method is not supported in HTAs (HTML applications). Returns true or false.

Syntax:

---

window.external.IsSubscribed(*param1*)

---

param1   Required; the URL of a .cdf file.

Example:

```
window.external.IsSubscribed("http://yourdomain/yourcdffile.cdf");
```

NOTE   *The preceding example requires a .cdf file, which is created using C++. The use of this property requires that you have a thorough understanding of C++ and the Internet Explorer API.*

Applies to:

external

italics()

Compatibility: NN4, NN6, NN7, IE4, IE5, IE5.5, IE6

This method returns a string that is displayed in italics.
Syntax:

stringName.italics()

Example:

```
<button onclick="var myS = new String('Sample String'); document.write('regular
string'+myS.italics());">ITALICS</button>
```

Applies to:

String

item()

Compatibility: NN6, NN7, IE4, IE5, IE5.5, IE6

This method returns either the item at the specified index in the collection or
the `<input>` element at the specified position of a `<form>` element.
Syntax:

```
collectionName.item(param1, param2)
document.formID.item(param1, param2)
document.all.formID.item(param1, param2) // IE only
```

param1   Required; either the zero-based index of the desired member of
the collection or the value of the desired member's `id` or `name` attribute.

param2   Optional; the zero-based index of the desired member of the
collection returned when param1 matches the `id` or `name` attribute value of
more than one element.

Example:

```
<input type="button" id="button" value="See the value of this button"
onclick="alert(document.all.item('button').value);">
```

Applies to:

all*, anchors*, applets*, areas*, attributes*, behaviorUrns*, blockFormats*,
boundElements*, cells*, childNodes*, children*, controlRange*, elements*, embeds*,
filters*, fonts*, <form>, forms*, frames*, images*, imports*, links*, mimeTypes*,
namespaces*, options*, pages*, plugins*, rows*, rules*, scripts*, styleSheets*, tBodies*

javaEnabled()

Compatibility: NN4, NN6, NN7, IE4, IE5, IE5.5, IE6

This method indicates whether or not Java is enabled. Returns true or false.
Syntax:

```
objectName.javaEnabled()
```

Example:

```
<button onclick="alert(clientInformation.javaEnabled());">
JavaEnabled</button>
```

Applies to:

```
clientInformation, navigator
```

join()

Compatibility: NN4, NN6, NN7, IE4, IE5, IE5.5, IE6

This method joins all elements of an array into a single string, with the individual elements separated by the specified delimiter.
Syntax:

```
arrayName.join(param1)
```

param1   Required; the delimiter to use.

Example:

```
<button onclick="var myA = new Array(10,11,12); alert(myA.join('---'));">JOIN</button>
```

Applies to:

```
Array
```

lastIndexOf()

Compatibility: NN4, NN6, NN7, IE4, IE5, IE5.5, IE6

This method performs a search for the specified string, and it returns the final character position at which a match appears. If no match is found, it returns -1.
Syntax:

```
stringName.lastIndexOf(param1, param2)
```

param1 Required; the string to search for.

param2 Optional; the character position at which to start the search.

Example:

```
<button onclick="var myS = new String('Sample String String');
alert(myS.lastIndexOf('String'));">LASTINDEXOF</button>
```

Applies to:

```
String
```

lastPage()

Compatibility: IE5, IE5.5, IE6

This method displays the last page of external data to which a table is bound.
Syntax:

```
document.all.tableID.lastPage()
```

Example: See the `firstPage()` method example.
Applies to:

```
<table>
```

link()

Compatibility: NN4, NN6, NN7, IE4, IE5, IE5.5, IE6

This method creates an `<a>` element with the `String` object's value located between its opening and closing tags, and an `href` attribute value equal to the specified parameter.
Syntax:

```
stringName.link(param1)
```

param1 Required; the URL.

Example:

```
<button onclick="var myS = new String('Advocar Home Page'); alert(myS.link('http://
www.advocar.com/'));">LINK</button>
```

Applies to:

```
String
```

localeCompare()

Compatibility: IE5.5, IE6

This method compares the String object's value to the parameter value and indicates whether or not they match according to the system's locale settings. Returns 0 (match), -1 (no match, and the parameter value comes before the String object's value in the locale sort order), or 1 (no match, and the parameter value comes after the String object's value in the locale sort order).

Syntax:

```
stringName.localeCompare(param1)
```

param1 Required; the string to search for inside the object.

Example:

```
<button onclick="var myS = new String('Sample String');
alert(myS.localeCompare('Sample String'));">LOCALECOMPARE</button>
```

Applies to:

```
String
```

log()

Compatibility: NN4, NN6, NN7, IE4, IE5, IE5.5, IE6

This method returns the natural logarithm of a number.

Syntax:

```
Math.log(param1)
```

param1 Required; the number to convert.

Example:

```
<button onclick="alert(Math.log(1));">LOG</button>
```

Applies to:

```
Math
```

match()

Compatibility: NN4, NN6, NN7, IE4, IE5, IE5.5, IE6

This method searches the String object using a regular expression.

Syntax:

```
stringName.match(param1)
```

param1   Required; the regular expression.

Example:

```
<button onclick="var myS = new String('Sample String'); alert(myS.match(/sam/
i));">MATCH</button>
```

Applies to:

```
String
```

max()

Compatibility: NN4, NN6, NN7, IE4, IE5, IE5.5, IE6

This method evaluates two numbers and returns the larger one.
Syntax:

```
Math.max(param1, param2)
```

param1   Required; the first number.

param2   Required; the second number.

Example:

```
<button onclick="alert(Math.max(1, 2));">MAX</button>
```

Applies to:

```
Math
```

mergeAttributes()

Compatibility: IE5, IE5.5, IE6

This method copies all attributes (except id and name) from one element to
another.
Syntax:

```
document.all.elementID.mergeAttributes(param1, param2)
```

param1   Required; the element from which the attributes are to be copied.

param2   Optional (not used in IE5); true or false, indicating whether or
not the id of the element with which the attributes are being merged is to be
preserved.

Example:

```
<script language="JavaScript">
function B1(){myDiv2.mergeAttributes(myDiv1);}
</script>
<div id="myDiv1" style="border:solid blue 2px; width:600; height:200;"></div>
<div id="myDiv2"></div>
<button onclick="B1();">Merge attributes</button>
```

Applies to:

```
<a>, <acronym>, <address>, <applet>, <area>, <b>, <base>, <basefont>, <bdo>,
<bgsound>, <big>, <blockquote>, <body>, <br>, <button>, <caption>, <center>,
<cite>, <code>, <col>, <colgroup>, <comment>, <custom>, <dd>, <del>, <dfn>, <dir>,
<div>, <dl>, <dt>, <em>, <embed>, <fieldset>, <font>, <form>, <frame>, <frameset>,
<head>, <hn>, <hr>, <html>, <i>, <iframe>, <img>, <input type="button">, <input
type="checkbox">, <input type="file">, <input type="hidden">, <input type="image">,
<input type="password">, <input type="radio">, <input type="reset">, <input
type="submit">, <input type="text">, <ins>, <kbd>, <label>, <legend>, <li>, <link>,
<listing>, <map>, <marquee>, <menu>, <object>, <ol>, <option>, <p>, <plaintext>,
<pre>, <q>, <s>, <samp>, <script>, <select>, <small>, <span>, <strike>, <strong>,
<sub>, <sup>, <table>, <tbody>, <td>, <textarea>, <tfoot>, <th>, <thead>, <title>,
<tr>, <tt>, <u>, <ul>, <var>, <xmp>
```

min()

Compatibility: NN4, NN6, NN7, IE4, IE5, IE5.5, IE6

This method evaluates two numbers and returns the smaller one.

Syntax:

```
Math.min(param1, param2)
```

param1   Required; the first number.

param2   Required; the second number.

Example:

```
<button onclick="alert(Math.min(1, 2));">MIN</button>
```

Applies to:

```
Math
```

move()

Compatibility: IE4, IE5, IE5.5, IE6

This method performs two operations simultaneously. First, it compacts the text range by eliminating extra spaces. Second, it moves the insertion point of a text range to a new location, and returns the number of units moved.

Syntax:

`textRangeName.move(param1, param2)`

---

param1 Required; the type of units to move. Values: `character`, `word`, sentence, or textedit (start or end of the text range).

param2 Optional; the number of units to move.

Example:

```
<script language="JavaScript">
var range;
function B1(elem) {
    range = elem.createTextRange()
    var m = range.move("word", 2)
    range.select()
}
</script>
<input id="myT" type="text" value="Some sample text">
<input type="button" value="Move cursor" onclick="B1(myT);">
```

Applies to:

TextRange

moveBy()

Compatibility: NN4, NN6, NN7, IE4, IE5, IE5.5, IE6

This method moves the window by the specified horizontal and vertical offsets.
Syntax:

`window.moveBy(param1, param2)`

---

param1 Required; the horizontal offset in pixels.

param2 Required; the vertical offset in pixels.

Example:

```
<script language="JavaScript">
function B1() {window.moveBy(100,100);}
</script>
<input type="button" value="Move the window 100 pixels to the left and 100 pixels
from the top of the current location" onclick="B1();">
```

Applies to:

---

window

---

moveEnd()

Compatibility: IE4, IE5, IE5.5, IE6

This method moves the end position of a text range to a new location and returns the number of units moved.

Syntax:

```
textRangeName.moveEnd(param1, param2)
```

param1   Required; the type of units to move. Values: character, word, sentence, or textedit (start or end of the text range).

param2   Optional; the number of units to move.

Example:

```
<script language="JavaScript">
var range;
function B1() {
    range = myT.createTextRange();
    var m = range.moveEnd("textedit");
    range.select();
}
</script>
<input id="myT" type="text" value="Some sample text. This text is editable"
size="50">
<input type="button" value="Select the text inside the textbox" onclick="B1();">
```

Applies to:

TextRange

moveRow()

Compatibility: IE5, IE5.5, IE6

This method moves the specified row to a new position in the element.

Syntax:

```
document.all.elementID.moveRow(param1, param2)
```

param1   Required; the index of the row to move.

param2   Required; the index of the new position.

Example:

```
<script language="JavaScript">
function B1() {document.all.myT.moveRow(-1, 2);}
</script>
```

```
<table id="myT" border="1" cellspacing="5" cellpadding="5">
<tr><td>First Row</td><td> </td></tr>
<tr><td>Second Row</td><td> </td></tr>
<tr><td style="background-color:blue">Third Row</td><td> </td></tr>
<tr><td style="background-color:red">Fourth Row</td><td> </td></tr>
</table>
<button onclick="B1();">Move Row</button>
```

Applies to:

`<table>`, `<tbody>`, `<tfoot>`, `<thead>`

moveStart()

Compatibility: IE4, IE5, IE5.5, IE6

This method moves the start position of the text range to a new location and returns the number of units moved.

Syntax:

```
textRangeName.moveStart(param1, param2)
```

> **param1** Required; the type of units to move. Values: `character`, `word`, `sentence`, or `textedit` (start or end of the text range).
>
> **param2** Optional; the number of units to move.

Example:

```
<script language="JavaScript">
var range;
function B1(elem) {
    range = elem.createTextRange();
    var m = range.moveStart("textedit");
    range.select();
}
</script>
<input id="myT" type="text" value="Some sample text. This text is editable"
size="50">
<input type="button" value="Move the start position to the end" onclick="B1(myT);">
```

Applies to:

TextRange

moveTo()

Compatibility: NN4, NN6, NN7, IE4, IE5, IE5.5, IE6

This method moves the current window to the specified coordinates.

Syntax:

```
window.moveTo(param1, param2)
```

param1 Required; the X coordinate of the new position.

param2 Required; the Y coordinate of the new position.

Example:

```
<script language="JavaScript">
function B1() {window.moveTo(100,300);}
</script>
<input type="button" value="Move window" onclick="B1();">
```

Applies to:

```
window
```

moveToBookmark()

Compatibility: IE4, IE5, IE5.5, IE6

This method moves the referenced TextRange object to a bookmark that was previously defined using the getBookmark() method. Returns true (successful) or false (failed).

Syntax:

```
textRangeName.moveToBookmark(param1)
```

param1 Required; the name of the bookmark.

Example:

```
<script language="JavaScript">
function B1() {
    var m = document.body.createTextRange();
    var n = m.getBookmark();
    m.findText("sample", 6, 2);
    m.select();
    m.moveToBookmark(n);
    m.findText("sample");
    m.select();
}
</script>
<p>This is some sample text<p>
<input type="button" value="MoveToBookmark" onclick="B1();">
```

Applies to:

```
TextRange
```

moveToElementText()

Compatibility: IE5, IE5.5, IE6

This method moves a text range to encompass the contents of the specified element.

Syntax:

```
textRangeName.moveToElementText(param1)
```

param1   Required; the element to which the text range will be moved.

Example:

```
<script language="JavaScript">
function B1(){
    var myRange1 = document.body.createTextRange();
    myRange1.moveToElementText(myDiv1);
    myRange1.findText('test');
    myRange1.select();
}
</script>
<div id="myDiv1" style="background-color:blue; width:250; height:200;">Testing</div>
<input type="button" value="MoveToElementText" onclick="B1();">
```

Applies to:

TextRange

moveToPoint()

Compatibility: IE4, IE5, IE5.5, IE6

This method performs two operations simultaneously. First, it compacts the current text range by eliminating extra spaces. Second, it moves the empty text range to the specified point.

Syntax:

```
textRangeName.moveToPoint(param1, param2)
```

param1   Required; the X coordinate of the point.
param2   Required; the Y coordinate of the point.

Example:

```
<script language="JavaScript">
function B1(){
    var range = document.body.createTextRange();
    var myX = window.event.clientX;
    var myY = window.event.clientY;
```

```
        range.moveToPoint(myX, myY);
        range.expand("sentence");
        range.select();}
</script>
<body onclick="B1();">Sample text range, click here</body>
```

Applies to:

TextRange

namedItem()

Compatibility: NN6, NN7, IE6

This method returns the named element from the collection or the named item from a <form> or <select> element.

   Syntax:

```
collectionName.namedItem(param1)
document.getElementById("elementID").namedItem(param1)
document.all.elementID.namedItem(param1) // IE only
```

   param1   Required; the name or id of the element.

   Example:

```
<script language="JavaScript">
function B1() {
document.all.namedItem("myDiv1").innerText = "Named Item";
}
</script>
<div id="myDiv1" style="width:600; height:200; background-color:blue;">Click button
to change me</div>
<button onclick="B1();">Named item</button>
```

   Applies to:

all*, anchors*, applets*, areas*, boundElements*, cells*, elements*, embeds*,
filters*, <form>, forms*, frames*, images*, imports*, links*, options*, plugins*,
rows*, <select>, scripts*, styleSheets*, tBodies*

namedRecordset()

Compatibility: IE5, IE5.5, IE6

This method returns the recordset corresponding to the specified data member of a data source object.

   Syntax:

```
document.all.elementID.namedRecordset(param1, param2)
```

param1   Required; the name of the data member. An empty string indicates the default data member.

param2   Optional; the path to the data set.

Example: See the `firstPage()` method example.
Applies to:

`<applet>, <object>, <xml>`

---

navigate()

Compatibility: IE4, IE5, IE5.5, IE6

This method loads a new document into the current window.
    Syntax:

`window.navigate(param1)`

---

param1   Required; the URL of the document.

Example:

```
<script language="JavaScript">
function B1() {window.navigate("http://www.nostarch.com");}
</script>
<input id=myB type="button" value="Navigate to No Starch Press home page"
onclick="B1();">
```

Applies to:

`window`

NavigateAndFind()

Compatibility: IE4, IE5, IE5.5, IE6

This method loads a new document into the current window and selects the specified text if it exists in the new document.
    Syntax:

`window.external.NavigateAndFind(param1, param2, param3)`

---

param1   Required; the URL of a web page.

param2   Required; the text to select.

param3   Required; the name of the target frame.

Example:

```
<script language="JavaScript">
function B1() {
```

```
window.external.NavigateAndFind('file://c:/test.htm', 'word', '');
}
</script>
<body>
<input id=myB type="button" value="Navigate and Find" onclick="B1();">
When you click the Navigate and Find button, this "document" will be reloaded as a
file and this "word" will be highlighted. Make sure you copy this code to a file
with the name "test.htm" and put it in your c:\ drive.</body>
```

Applies to:

external

nextPage()

Compatibility: IE4, IE5, IE5.5, IE6

This method displays the next page of external data to which a table is bound.
Syntax:

```
document.all.tableID.nextPage()
```

Example: See the firstPage() method example.
Applies to:

<table>

normalize()

Compatibility: NN6, NN7, IE6

This method merges two adjacent text nodes into a single text node. In the
syntax below, elementID refers to either of two adjacent text nodes.
Syntax:

```
document.getElementById("elementID").normalize()
document.all.elementID.normalize() // IE only
```

Example:

```
<script language="JavaScript">
function B1() {
document.all.myP.normalize();
alert("The second paragraph has been normalized");
}
</script>
<p>First paragraph.</p><p id="myP">Second paragraph.</p>
<input id="myB" type="button" value="Normalize second paragraph" onclick="B1();">
```

Applies to:

`<a>`, `<acronym>`, `<address>`, `<applet>`, `<area>`, `<b>`, `<base>`, `<basefont>`, `<bdo>`, `<bgsound>`, `<big>`, `<blockquote>`, `<body>`, `<br>`, `<button>`, `<caption>`, `<center>`, `<cite>`, `<code>`, `<col>`, `<colgroup>`, `<comment>`, `<custom>`, `<dd>`, `<del>`, `<dfn>`, `<dir>`, `<div>`, `<dl>`, `<dt>`, `<em>`, `<embed>`, `<fieldset>`, `<font>`, `<form>`, `<frame>`, `<frameset>`, `<head>`, `<hn>`, `<hr>`, `<html>`, `<i>`, `<iframe>`, `<img>`, `<input type="button">`, `<input type="checkbox">`, `<input type="file">`, `<input type="hidden">`, `<input type="image">`, `<input type="password">`, `<input type="radio">`, `<input type="reset">`, `<input type="submit">`, `<input type="text">`, `<ins>`, `<isindex>`, `<kbd>`, `<label>`, `<legend>`, `<li>`, `<link>`, `<listing>`, `<map>`, `<marquee>`, `<menu>`, `<meta>`, `<nobr>`, `<noframes>`, `<noscript>`, `<object>`, `<ol>`, `<optgroup>`, `<option>`, `<p>`, `<param>`, `<plaintext>`, `<pre>`, `<q>`, `<rt>`, `<ruby>`, `<s>`, `<samp>`, `<script>`, `<select>`, `<small>`, `<span>`, `<strike>`, `<strong>`, style, `<sub>`, `<sup>`, `<table>`, `<tbody>`, `<td>`, `<textarea>`, `<tfoot>`, `<th>`, `<thead>`, `<title>`, `<tr>`, `<tt>`, `<u>`, `<ul>`, `<var>`, `<wbr>`, `<xml>`, `<xmp>`

---

open()

Compatibility: NN4, NN6, NN7, IE4, IE5, IE5.5, IE6

This method opens a new window.

Syntax:

`objectName.open(param1, param2, param3, param4)`

---

param1 Optional; the URL of the document to display. If omitted, a blank window is opened.

param2 Optional; the name of the window. Values: _blank, _media, _parent, _search, _self, _top, or any string.

param3 Optional; the attributes for the new window. Where applicable, each attribute must be accompanied by its corresponding value, and each attribute-value pair must be separated by a comma. For a complete list of options, go to: http://msdn.microsoft.com/workshop/author/dhtml/reference/methods/open_0.asp.

param4 Optional; true or false, indicating whether to replace the current document in the history list or to create a new entry for the new document.

Example:

```
<input type="button" value="Open a new window" onClick="window.open('test.htm',
'_blank')">
<input type="button" value="Open a blank document"
onClick="document.open('test.htm', '_blank')">
```

Applies to:

---

document, window

---

parentElement()

Compatibility: IE4, IE5, IE5.5, IE6

This method returns a reference to the parent node of the text range.
Syntax:

```
textRangeName.parentElement()
```

Example:

```
<script language="JavaScript">
function B1() {
var myRange = document.selection.createRange();
var m = myRange.parentElement();
m.innerText = 'ParentElement';
}
</script>
<input id="myB" type="button" value="Click me" onclick="B1();">
```

Applies to:

TextRange

parse()

Compatibility: NN4, NN6, NN7, IE4, IE5, IE5.5, IE6

This method returns the total number of milliseconds that have elapsed between the specified date and January 1, 1970.
Syntax:

```
dateName.parse(param1)
```

param1   Required; the ending date of the calculation.

Example:

```
<button onclick="var myDate = new Date(); alert(Date.parse(myDate));">PARSE</button>
```

Applies to:

Date

parseFloat()

Compatibility: NN4, NN6, NN7, IE4, IE5, IE5.5, IE6

This method converts the specified string to a floating-point number. Returns a floating-point number if value supplied is numeric, or NaN if value supplied is not numeric.
Syntax:

```
parseFloat(param1)
```

param1   Required; the string to be evaluated.

Example:

```
<button onclick="alert(parseFloat('12.34'));">Number</button>
<button onclick="alert(parseFloat('Hello'));">NaN</button>
```

Applies to: n/a.

parseInt()

Compatibility: NN4, NN6, NN7, IE4, IE5, IE5.5, IE6

This method converts the specified string to an integer. Returns an integer if value supplied is numeric or NaN if value supplied is not numeric.

Syntax:

```
parseInt(param1)
```

param1   Required; the string to be evaluated.

Example:

```
<button onclick="alert(parseInt('12.34'));">Number</button>
<button onclick="alert(parseInt('Hello'));">NaN</button>
```

Applies to: n/a.

pasteHTML()

Compatibility: IE4, IE5, IE5.5, IE6

This method replaces the content of a text range with HTML.

Syntax:

```
textRangeName.pasteHTML(param1)
```

param1   Required; the HTML text to paste.

Example:

```
<script language="JavaScript">
function B1() {
var myRange = document.selection.createRange();
var m = myRange.pasteHTML('<p>Hello World</p>');
}
</script>
<p>Highlight a part of this text, then click button below</p>
<input id="myB" type="button" value="Click me" onclick="B1();">
```

Applies to:

TextRange

pop()

Compatibility: NN4, NN6, NN7, IE4, IE5, IE5.5, IE6

This method removes the last element in an array. Returns the last element of the array.

Syntax:

arrayName.pop()

Example:

```
<button onclick="var myA = new Array(10,11,12); myA.pop(); alert(myA);">POP</button>
```

Applies to:

Array

pow()

Compatibility: NN4, NN6, NN7, IE4, IE5, IE5.5, IE6

This method evaluates two numbers, using one as the base number and one as the exponent.

Syntax:

Math.pow(*param1*, *param2*)

param1   Required; the number to use as the base.

param2   Required; the number to use as the exponent.

Example:

```
<button onclick="alert(Math.pow(2,2));">POW</button>
```

Applies to:

Math

previousPage()

Compatibility: IE4, IE5, IE5.5, IE6

This method displays the previous page of external data to which a table is bound.

Syntax:

```
document.all.tableID.previousPage()
```

Example: See the firstPage() method example.
Applies to:

```
<table>
```

print()

Compatibility: NN4, NN6, NN7, IE4, IE5, IE5.5, IE6

This method prints the current window's document.
Syntax:

```
window.print()
```

Example:

```
<script language="JavaScript">
function B1() {window.print();}
</script>
<input type="button" value="Print this window" onclick="B1();">
```

Applies to:

```
window
```

prompt()

Compatibility: NN4, NN6, NN7, IE4, IE5, IE5.5, IE6

This method opens a prompt window. Returns the string typed in by the user.
Syntax:

```
window.prompt(param1, param2)
```

param1 Optional; the message to display in the prompt window.

param2 Optional; a default value for the input field.

Example:

```
<script language="JavaScript">
function B1() {
window.prompt("Please, enter your full name", "Yes, here");
}
</script>
<input type="button" value="Open a prompt window" onclick="B1();">
```

Applies to:

```
window
```

push()

Compatibility: NN4, NN6, NN7, IE4, IE5, IE5.5, IE6

This method adds one or more elements to the end of an array and returns the array's length.

Syntax:

```
arrayName.push(paramN, . . . ,paramN)
```

> **paramN**   Required; the elements to add to the array.

Example:

```
<button onclick="var myA = new Array(10,11,12); myA.push(13,14,15);
alert(myA);">PUSH</button>
```

Applies to:

```
Array
```

queryCommandEnabled()

Compatibility: IE4, IE5, IE5.5, IE6

This method indicates whether or not the specified command can be successfully executed. Query commands are useful because the execCommand() method cannot be invoked before the page is fully loaded. Returns true or false.

Syntax:

```
controlRangeName.queryCommandEnabled(param1)
objectName.queryCommandEnabled(param1)
```

> **param1**   Required; the name of the command. For a complete list of commands, go to http://msdn.microsoft.com/workshop/author/dhtml/ reference/commandids.asp.

Example:

```
<script language="JavaScript">
function B1() {
    var myText = document.selection.createRange();
    if (myText.queryCommandEnabled("Delete") == true) {
        document.execCommand("Delete");
    }
```

```
}
</script>
<p id="myText">Sample text to be selected and deleted.</p>
<input type="button" value="Delete selection" onclick="B1();">
```

Applies to:

controlRange*, document, TextRange

queryCommandIndeterm()

Compatibility: IE4, IE5, IE5.5, IE6

This method indicates whether or not the specified command is indeterminate (meaning it cannot be accessed). Returns true or false.
   Syntax:

```
controlRangeName.queryCommandIndeterm(param1)
objectName.queryCommandIndeterm(param1)
```

> **param1**   Required; the name of the command. For a complete list of commands, go to http://msdn.microsoft.com/workshop/author/dhtml/reference/commandids.asp.
>
> Example:

```
<script language="JavaScript">
function B2() {
    var myText = document.body.createTextRange();
    var m = myText.queryCommandIndeterm("delete");
    if (m == false) {
    alert("Command is NOT indeterminate");
    }
}
</script>
<input type="button" value="Click to check the Delete command status"
onclick="B2();">
```

Applies to:

controlRange*, document, TextRange

queryCommandState()

Compatibility: IE4, IE5, IE5.5, IE6

This method indicates whether or not the command has already been executed. Returns true or false.

Syntax:

```
controlRangeName.queryCommandState(param1)
objectName.queryCommandState(param1)
```

param1 Required; the name of the command. For a complete list of commands, go to http://msdn.microsoft.com/workshop/author/dhtml/ reference/commandids.asp.

Example:

```
<script language="JavaScript">
function B1() {
    var myText = document.selection.createRange();
    if (!myText==""){
    if (myText.queryCommandEnabled("Delete") == true) {
        document.execCommand("Delete");
    }}
    var m = myText.queryCommandState("Delete");
    if (m == false) {
        alert("Delete command has not been executed");
    }
}
</script>
<p id="myText">First, select text in this paragraph, and then click the following
button to apply the method.</p>
<input type="button" value="Click to delete selection and verify command state"
onclick="B1();">
```

Applies to:

```
controlRange*, document, TextRange
```

queryCommandSupported()

Compatibility: IE4, IE5, IE5.5, IE6

This method indicates whether or not the specified command is supported. Returns true or false.

Syntax:

```
controlRangeName.queryCommandSupported(param1)
objectName.queryCommandSupported(param1)
```

param1 Required; the name of the command. For a complete list of commands, go to http://msdn.microsoft.com/workshop/author/dhtml/ reference/commandids.asp.

Example:

```
<script language="JavaScript">
function B1() {
    var myText = document.selection.createRange();
    if (!myText==""){
    if (myText.queryCommandSupported("Delete") == true) {
        document.execCommand("Delete");
    }}
    var m = myText.queryCommandSupported("delete");
    if (m == true) {
        alert("The Delete command is supported");
    }
}
</script>
<p id="myText">First, select text in this paragraph, and then click the following
button to apply the method.</p>
<input type="button" value="Click to delete selection" onclick="B1();">
```

Applies to:

controlRange*, document, TextRange

queryCommandValue()

Compatibility: IE4, IE5, IE5.5, IE6

This method returns the value of the specified command.

Syntax:

```
controlRangeName.queryCommandValue(param1)
objectName.queryCommandValue(param1)
```

param1   Required; the name of the command. For a complete list of commands, go to: http://msdn.microsoft.com/workshop/author/dhtml/reference/commandids.asp.

Example:

```
<script language="JavaScript">
function B1() {
    var myText = document.body.createTextRange();
    var m = myText.queryCommandValue("delete");
    alert("The command value for this object is: "+'"'+m+'"');
}
</script>
<input type="button" value="Delete Command Value" onclick="B1();">
```

Applies to:

controlRange*, document, TextRange

random()

Compatibility: NN4, NN6, NN7, IE4, IE5, IE5.5, IE6

This method returns a random number between 0 and 1.
Syntax:

Math.random()

Example:

```
<button onclick="alert(Math.random());">RANDOM</button>
```

Applies to:

Math

recalc()

Compatibility: IE5, IE5.5, IE6

This method refreshes all properties that can be dynamically set using the
setExpression() method.
Syntax:

document.recalc(*param1*)

> **param1**   Optional; true or false, indicating whether to recalculate all
> expressions or only the expressions that have changed since the last recalc()
> operation.
>
> Example: See the getExpression() method example.
> Applies to:

document

refresh() (1)

Compatibility: IE4, IE5, IE5.5, IE6

This method causes the contents of the table to be redrawn.
Syntax:

document.all.*tableID*.refresh()

Example:

```
<script language="JavaScript">
function B1() {
document.all.myT.style.fontFamily = "Times";
document.all.myT.style.fontWeight = "bold";
document.all.myT.refresh();
}
function B2() {location.reload();}
</script>
<table id="myT" width="25%" border="1">
 <tr><td>Row 1</td><td>Cell 1</td></tr>
 <tr><td>Row 2</td><td>Cell 2</td></tr>
 <tr><td>Row 3</td><td>Cell 3</td></tr>
 <tr><td>Row 4</td><td>Cell 4</td></tr>
</table>
<input type="button" value="Replace font and weight" onclick="B1();">
<input type="button" value="Restore" onclick="B2();">
```

Applies to:

```
<table>
```

refresh() (2)

Compatibility: NN4, NN6, NN7

This method refreshes the browser's plug-ins list without quitting and re-launching the browser, as is usually required when a new plug-in is added.

Syntax:

```
navigator.plugins.refresh()
```

Example:

```
<head><script>
function B1() {
window.location.href = "http://www.macromedia.com/shockwave/download/"
navigator.plugins.refresh();
}
</script></head>
<body><button onclick="B1();">Add new plug-in</button></body>
```

Applies to:

```
plugins*
```

releaseCapture()

Compatibility: IE5, IE5.5, IE6

This method causes mouse capture, set with the setCapture() method, to terminate.

Syntax:

```
document.all.elementID.releaseCapture()
```

Example:

```
<script language="JavaScript">
function C1() {
    myX.innerHTML = window.event.offsetX;
    myY.innerHTML = window.event.offsetY;
}
function B1() {myDiv.setCapture();}
function B2() {myDiv.releaseCapture();}
</script>
<p><b>X Coordinate:</b> <span id="myX">0</span></p>
<p><b>Y Coordinate:</b> <span id="myY">0</span></p>
<div id="myDiv" onmousemove="C1();" onclick="B2();" style="border:solid; width:500;
height:200;">Click inside the box to disable mouse capture outside the box</div>
<button onclick="B1()">Set capture</button>
```

Applies to:

```
<a>, <address>, <applet>, <area>, <b>, <big>, <blockquote>, <body>, <br>, <button>,
<caption>, <center>, <cite>, <code>, <custom>, <dd>, <dfn>, <dir>, <div>, <dl>,
document, <dt>, <em>, <embed>, <fieldset>, <font>, <form>, <hn>, <hr>, <i>, <img>,
<input type="button">, <input type="checkbox">, <input type="file">, <input
type="hidden">, <input type="image">, <input type="password">, <input
type="radio">, <input type="reset">, <input type="submit">, <input type="text">,
<kbd>, <label>, <legend>, <li>, <listing>, <map>, <marquee>, <menu>, <nobr>,
<object>, <ol>, <option>, <p>, <plaintext>, <pre>, <s>, <samp>, <select>, <small>,
<span>, <strike>, <strong>, <sub>, <sup>, <table>, <tbody>, <td>, <textarea>,
<tfoot>, <th>, <thead>, <tr>, <tt>, <u>, <ul>, <var>, <xmp>
```

reload()

Compatibility: NN4, NN6, NN7, IE4, IE5, IE5.5, IE6

This method reloads the current document.

Syntax:

```
location.reload(param1)
```

param1 Optional; true or false, indicating whether or not to reload the document from the browser's cache.

Example:

```
<html><head>
<script language="JavaScript">
function B1() {window.location.reload(true);}
function B2() {window.location.reload(false);}
</script></head>
<body>
<button onclick="B1();">Memory reload</button>
<button onclick="B2();">Server reload</button>
</body></html>
```

Applies to:

```
location
```

remove()

Compatibility: IE4, IE5, IE5.5, IE6

This method removes the specified element from a collection or <select> element.
Syntax:

```
document.all.selectID.remove(param1)
collectionName.remove(param1)
```

param1   Required; the index of the element to remove.

Example: See the add() method example.
Applies to:

```
areas*, controlRange* (IE5, IE5.5, IE6), options*, <select>
```

removeAttribute()

Compatibility: NN6, NN7, IE4, IE5, IE5.5, IE6

This method removes the specified attribute value from the element. Returns true (successful) or false (failed).
Syntax:

```
document.getElementById("elementID").removeAttribute(param1, param2)
document.all.elementID.removeAttribute(param1, param2) // IE only
```

param1   Required; the name of the attribute.

param2   Optional; the type of search. Values: 1 (the default) for a case-sensitive search and any other value for a non–case-sensitive search.

Example:

```
<script language="JavaScript">
function B1(){
var m = document.getElementById("myDiv").removeAttribute("id");
document.all.myB.innerText = "Click again";
if (m == true) {
alert("Attribute removed\nVerify by clicking again to produce error");
}}
</script>
<div id="myDiv">This is a div element</div>
<input id="myB" type="button" value="Remove id attribute" onclick="B1();">
```

Applies to:

```
<a>, <acronym>, <address>, <applet>, <area>, <b>, <base>, <basefont>, <bdo>,
<bgsound>, <big>, <blockquote>, <body>, <br>, <button>, <caption>, <center>, <cite>,
<code>, <col>, <colgroup>, <comment>, <custom>, <dd>, <del>, <dfn>, <dir>, <div>,
<dl>, <dt>, <em>, <embed>, <fieldset>, <font>, <form>, <frame>, <frameset>, <head>,
<hn>, <hr>, <html>, <i>, <iframe>, <img>, <input>, <input type="button">, <input
type="checkbox">, <input type="file">, <input type="hidden">, <input type="image">,
<input type="password">, <input type="radio">, <input type="reset">, <input
type="submit">, <input type="text">, <ins>, <isindex>, <kbd>, <label>, <legend>,
<li>, <link>, <listing>, <map>, <marquee>, <menu>, <meta>, <nobr>, <noframes>,
<noscript>, <object>, <ol>, <optgroup>, <option>, <p>, <param>, <plaintext>, <pre>,
<q>, runtimeStyle, <s>, <samp>, <script>, <select>, <small>, <span>, <strike>,
<strong>, style, <sub>, <sup>, <table>, <tbody>, <td>, <textarea>, <tfoot>, <th>,
<thead>, <title>, <tr>, <tt>, <u>, <ul>, <var>, <wbr>, <xmp>
```

removeAttributeNode()

Compatibility: NN6, NN7, IE6

This method removes the given attribute node from the element.
Syntax:

```
document.getElementById("elementID").removeAttributeNode(param1)
document.all.elementID.removeAttributeNode(param1) // IE only
```

param1   Required; the name of the attribute to be removed.

Example:

```
<script language="JavaScript">
function B1(){
var m = document.getElementById("myDiv").getAttributeNode("id");
alert("The value of the attributeNode is: "+'"'+m.value+'"');
var n = document.all.myDiv.removeAttributeNode(m);
alert("The attribute node has been removed\nClick again to verify by producing
error");
}
```

```
</script>
<div id="myDiv">This is a div element</div>
<input type="button" value="Get id attribute node value" onclick="B1();">
```

Applies to:

`<a>`, `<acronym>`, `<address>`, `<applet>`, `<area>`, `<b>`, `<base>`, `<basefont>`, `<bdo>`, `<bgsound>`, `<big>`, `<blockquote>`, `<body>`, `<br>`, `<button>`, `<caption>`, `<center>`, `<cite>`, `<code>`, `<col>`, `<colgroup>`, `<comment>`, `<custom>`, `<dd>`, `<del>`, `<dfn>`, `<dir>`, `<div>`, `<dl>`, `<dt>`, `<em>`, `<embed>`, `<fieldset>`, `<font>`, `<form>`, `<frame>`, `<frameset>`, `<head>`, `<hn>`, `<hr>`, `<html>`, `<i>`, `<iframe>`, `<img>`, `<input>`, `<input type="button">`, `<input type="checkbox">`, `<input type="file">`, `<input type="hidden">`, `<input type="image">`, `<input type="password">`, `<input type="radio">`, `<input type="reset">`, `<input type="submit">`, `<input type="text">`, `<ins>`, `<isindex>`, `<kbd>`, `<label>`, `<legend>`, `<li>`, `<link>`, `<listing>`, `<map>`, `<marquee>`, `<menu>`, `<meta>`, `<nobr>`, `<noframes>`, `<noscript>`, `<object>`, `<ol>`, `<optgroup>`, `<option>`, `<p>`, `<param>`, `<plaintext>`, `<pre>`, `<q>`, `<rt>`, `<ruby>`, `<s>`, `<samp>`, `<script>`, `<select>`, `<small>`, `<span>`, `<strike>`, `<strong>`, style, `<sub>`, `<sup>`, `<table>`, `<tbody>`, `<td>`, `<textarea>`, `<tfoot>`, `<th>`, `<thead>`, `<title>`, `<tr>`, `<tt>`, `<u>`, `<ul>`, `<var>`, `<wbr>`, `<xml>`, `<xmp>`

removeBehavior()

Compatibility: IE5, IE5.5, IE6

This method removes a behavior from the element. Returns true (successful) or false (failed).

Syntax:

`document.all.`*elementID*`.removeBehavior(`*param1*`)`

param1 Required; the behavior identifier.

Example: See the `addBehavior()` method example.
Applies to:

`<a>`, `<acronym>`, `<address>`, `<applet>`, `<area>`, `<b>`, `<base>`, `<basefont>`, `<bgsound>`, `<big>`, `<blockquote>`, `<body>`, `<br>`, `<button>`, `<caption>`, `<center>`, `<cite>`, `<code>`, `<col>`, `<colgroup>`, `<comment>`, `<custom>`, `<dd>`, `<del>`, `<dfn>`, `<dir>`, `<div>`, `<dl>`, `<dt>`, `<em>`, `<embed>`, `<fieldset>`, `<font>`, `<form>`, `<frame>`, `<frameset>`, `<head>`, `<hn>`, `<hr>`, `<html>`, `<i>`, `<iframe>`, `<img>`, `<input type="button">`, `<input type="checkbox">`, `<input type="file">`, `<input type="hidden">`, `<input type="image">`, `<input type="password">`, `<input type="radio">`, `<input type="reset">`, `<input type="submit">`, `<input type="text">`, `<ins>`, `<isindex>`, `<kbd>`, `<label>`, `<legend>`, `<li>`, `<link>`, `<listing>`, `<map>`, `<marquee>`, `<menu>`, `<nobr>`, `<noframes>`, `<noscript>`, `<object>`, `<ol>`, `<option>`, `<p>`, `<plaintext>`, `<pre>`, `<q>`, `<rt>`, `<ruby>`, `<s>`, `<samp>`, `<script>`, `<select>`, `<small>`, `<span>`, `<strike>`, `<strong>`, `<style>`, `<sub>`, `<sup>`, `<table>`, `<tbody>`, `<td>`, `<textarea>`, `<tfoot>`, `<th>`, `<thead>`, `<title>`, `<tr>`, `<tt>`, `<u>`, `<ul>`, `<var>`, `<wbr>`, `<xml>`, `<xmp>`

removeChild()

Compatibility: NN6, NN7, IE5, IE5.5, IE6

This method removes a child node from the element. The child node to be removed must have been created by the createTextNode() method.

Syntax:

```
document.getElementById("elementID").removeChild(param1)
document.all.elementID.removeChild(param1) // IE only
```

param1   Required; the name of the element to be removed.

Example:

```
<script language="JavaScript">
function B2() {
    var m = "New Element";
    var n = document.createElement("li");
    n.appendChild(document.createTextNode(m));
    document.getElementById("myList").appendChild(n);
}
function B3() {myList.removeChild(myList.lastChild);}
</script>
<ul id="myList"><li>First list element<li>Second list element</ul>
<input type="button" value="Add list item" onClick="B2();">
<input type="button" value="Remove added items" onClick="B3();">
```

Applies to:

```
<a>, <acronym>, <address>, <applet>, <area>, attribute, <b>, <base>, <basefont>,
<bdo>, <big>, <blockquote>, <body>, <br>, <button>, <caption>, <center>, <cite>,
<code>, <col>, <colgroup>, <comment>, <dd>, <del>, <dfn>, <dir>, <div>, <dl>, <dt>,
<em>, <fieldset>, <font>, <form>, <frame>, <frameset>, <head>, <hn>, <hr>, <html>,
<i>, <iframe>, <img>, <input>, <input type="button">, <input type="checkbox">,
<input type="file">, <input type="hidden">, <input type="image">, <input
type="password">, <input type="radio">, <input type="reset">, <input
type="submit">, <input type="text">, <ins>, <isindex>, <kbd>, <label>, <legend>,
<li>, <link>, <listing>, <map>, <marquee>, <menu>, <meta>, <noframes>, <noscript>,
<object>, <ol>, <optgroup>, <option>, <p>, <param>, <plaintext>, <pre>, <q>, <s>,
<samp>, <script>, <select>, <small>, <span>, <strike>, <strong>, <style>, <sub>,
<sup>, <table>, <tbody>, <td>, <textarea>, <tfoot>, <th>, <thead>, <title>, <tr>,
<tt>, <u>, <ul>, <var>, <xmp>
```

removeExpression()

Compatibility: IE5, IE5.5, IE6

This method removes the expression from a dynamic property. Returns true (successful) or false (failed).

Syntax:

```
objectName.removeExpression(param1)
document.all.elementID.removeExpression(param1)
```

param1 Required; the name of the property.

Example: See the getExpression() method example.
Applies to:

```
<a>, <acronym>, <address>, <applet>, <area>, <b>, <bdo>, <big>, <blockquote>,
<body>, <br>, <button>, <caption>, <center>, <cite>, <code>, <col>, <colgroup>,
<custom>, <dd>, <del>, <dfn>, <dir>, <div>, <dl>, <dt>, <em>, <embed>, <fieldset>,
<font>, <form>, <hn>, <hr>, <i>, <iframe>, <img>, <input type="button">, <input
type="checkbox">, <input type="file">, <input type="hidden">, <input type="image">,
<input type="password">, <input type="radio">, <input type="reset">, <input
type="submit">, <input type="text">, <ins>, <kbd>, <label>, <legend>, <li>,
<listing>, <marquee>, <menu>, <nobr>, <object>, <ol>, <option>, <p>, <pre>, <q>,
<rt>, <ruby>, runtimeStyle, <s>, <samp>, <select>, <small>, <span>, <strike>,
<strong>, style, <sub>, <sup>, <table>, <tbody>, <td>, <textarea>, <tfoot>, <th>,
<thead>, <tr>, <tt>, <u>, <ul>, <var>
```

---

removeNamedItem()

Compatibility: IE6

This method removes a named item from the attributes collection and returns an instance of the removed attribute.

Syntax:

```
document.all.elementID.attributes.removeNamedItem(param1)
```

---

param1 Required; the name of the attribute.

Example:

```
<script language="JavaScript">
function B1() {
    alert(document.all.myButton.name);
    var myA = document.all.myButton.attributes;
    var m = myA.removeNamedItem("name");
}
</script>
<button id=3"myButton" onclick="B1();" name="Hello">Click me twice</button>
```

Applies to:

---

attributes*

---

removeNode()

Compatibility: IE5, IE5.5, IE6

This method removes the specified node from the document's hierarchy.

Syntax:

```
document.all.elementID.removeNode(param1)
```

---

param1 Required; true or false, indicating whether or not to remove the child nodes of the node marked for removal.

Example:

```
<script language="JavaScript">
function B1() {document.all.myB.removeNode(true);}
</script>
<button id="myB" onclick="B1();">Remove me</button>
```

Applies to:

```
<a>, <acronym>, <address>, <b>, <bdo>, <big>, <blockquote>, <body>, <button>,
<caption>, <center>, <cite>, <code>, <col>, <colgroup>, <comment>, <dd>, <del>,
<dfn>, <dir>, <div>, <dl>, <dt>, <em>, <fieldset>, <font>, <form>, <frameset>,
<head>, <hn>, <html>, <i>, <iframe>, <input type="button">, <input type="checkbox">,
<input type="file">, <input type="image">, <input type="password">, <input
type="radio">, <input type="reset">, <input type="submit">, <input type="text">,
<ins>, <kbd>, <label>, <legend>, <li>, <listing>, <map>, <marquee>, <menu>,
<object>, <ol>, <option>, <p>, <plaintext>, <pre>, <q>, <s>, <samp>, <select>,
<small>, <span>, <strike>, <strong>, <style>, <sub>, <sup>, <table>, <tbody>, <td>,
<textarea>, <tfoot>, <th>, <thead>, <tr>, <tt>, <u>, <ul>, <var>, <xmp>
```

removeRule()

Compatibility: IE4, IE5, IE5.5, IE6

This method removes a rule from the specified style sheet.

Syntax:

```
document.styleSheets[index].removeRule(param1)
```

param1 Optional; the index of the rule within the rules collection.

Example:

```
<style>.myClass {background-color:red; font-decoration:bold;}</style>
<script language="JavaScript">
function B1() {document.styleSheets[0].removeRule(0);}
</script>
<button id="myB" onclick="B1();" class="myClass">Remove rule</button>
```

Applies to:

```
styleSheet
```

replace() (1)

Compatibility: NN4, NN6, NN7, IE4, IE5, IE5.5, IE6

This method causes a new document to be loaded and the current document to be removed from the history list.

Syntax:

```
location.replace(param1)
```

param1   Required; the URL of the new document.

Example:

```
<script language="JavaScript">
function B1() {location.replace("http://www.nostarch.com");}
</script>
<input id="myB" type="button" value="Replace" onClick="B1();">
```

Applies to:

```
location
```

replace() (2)

Compatibility: NN4, NN6, NN7, IE4, IE5, IE5.5, IE6

This method searches the String object using a regular expression and replaces any matching content with the specified string.

Syntax:

```
stringName.replace(param1, param2)
```

param1   Required; the regular expression.
param2   Required; the string with which to replace matching content.

Example:

```
<button onclick="var myS = new String('Sample String'); alert(myS.replace(/sam/i, 'Text'));">REPLACE</button>
```

Applies to:

```
String
```

replaceAdjacentText()

Compatibility: IE5, IE5.5, IE6

This method replaces the text that is located in the specified position relative to the element.

Syntax:

```
document.all.elementID.replaceAdjacentText(param1, param2)
```

---

param1   Required; Values: beforeBegin (just before the beginning of the element), afterBegin (just after the beginning of the element), beforeEnd (just before the end of the element), or afterEnd (just after the end of the element).

param2   Required; the text that will replace the adjacent text.

Example:

```
<script language="JavaScript">
function B1() {
    var myText = 'Some Sample Text';
    document.all.myDiv.replaceAdjacentText('beforeEnd', myText);
}
</script>
<button onclick="B1();">Replace text</button>
<div id="myDiv" style="width:300; height:200; border:solid black 1px;">Sample
text</div>
```

Applies to:

```
<a>, <acronym>, <address>, <applet>, <area>, <b>, <base>, <basefont>, <bdo>, <big>,
<blockquote>, <body>, <br>, <button>, <caption>, <center>, <cite>, <code>, <col>,
<colgroup>, <comment>, <custom>, <dd>, <del>, <dfn>, <dir>, <div>, <dl>, <dt>,
<em>, <embed>, <fieldset>, <font>, <form>, <frame>, <frameset>, <head>, <hn>, <hr>,
<html>, <i>, <iframe>, <img>, <input type="button">, <input type="checkbox">,
<input type="file">, <input type="hidden">, <input type="image">, <input
type="password">, <input type="radio">, <input type="reset">, <input
type="submit">, <input type="text">, <ins>, <kbd>, <label>, <legend>, <li>, <link>,
<listing>, <map>, <marquee>, <menu>, <object>, <ol>, <option>, <p>, <plaintext>,
<pre>, <q>, <s>, <samp>, <script>, <select>, <small>, <span>, <strike>, <strong>,
<sub>, <sup>, <table>, <tbody>, <td>, <textarea>, <tfoot>, <th>, <thead>, <title>,
<tr>, <tt>, <u>, <ul>, <var>, <xmp>
```

---

replaceChild()

Compatibility: NN6, NN7, IE5, IE5.5, IE6

This method replaces one element node with another.

Syntax:

```
document.getElementById("elementID").replaceChild(param1, param2)
document.all.elementID.replaceChild(param1, param2) // IE only
```

---

param1   Required; the replacement element node.

param2   Required; the element node to be replaced.

Example:

```
<script language="JavaScript">
function B1() {
    var newElement = document.createElement('u');
    newElement.innerHTML = 'Text';
    var oldElement = document.all.myBold;
    document.all.myDiv.replaceChild(newElement, oldElement);
}
</script>
<button onclick="B1();">Replace text</button>
<div id="myDiv" style="width:300; height:200; border:solid black 1px;">Sample <b
id="myBold">text</b></div>
```

Applies to:

`<a>`, `<acronym>`, `<address>`, `<applet>`, `<area>`, attribute, `<b>`, `<base>`, `<basefont>`,
`<bdo>`, `<big>`, `<blockquote>`, `<body>`, `<br>`, `<button>`, `<caption>`, `<center>`, `<cite>`,
`<code>`, `<col>`, `<colgroup>`, `<comment>`, `<dd>`, `<del>`, `<dfn>`, `<dir>`, `<div>`, `<dl>`, `<dt>`,
`<em>`, `<fieldset>`, `<font>`, `<form>`, `<frame>`, `<frameset>`, `<head>`, `<hn>`, `<hr>`, `<html>`,
`<i>`, `<iframe>`, `<img>`, `<input>`, `<input type="button">`, `<input type="checkbox">`,
`<input type="file">`, `<input type="hidden">`, `<input type="image">`, `<input
type="password">`, `<input type="radio">`, `<input type="reset">`, `<input
type="submit">`, `<input type="text">`, `<ins>`, `<isindex>`, `<kbd>`, `<label>`, `<legend>`,
`<li>`, `<link>`, `<listing>`, `<map>`, `<marquee>`, `<menu>`, `<meta>`, `<noframes>`, `<noscript>`,
`<object>`, `<ol>`, `<optgroup>`, `<option>`, `<p>`, `<param>`, `<plaintext>`, `<pre>`, `<q>`, `<s>`,
`<samp>`, `<script>`, `<select>`, `<small>`, `<span>`, `<strike>`, `<strong>`, `<style>`, `<sub>`,
`<sup>`, `<table>`, `<tbody>`, `<td>`, `<textarea>`, `<tfoot>`, `<th>`, `<thead>`, `<title>`, `<tr>`,
`<tt>`, `<u>`, `<ul>`, `<var>`, `<xmp>`

replaceData()

Compatibility: NN6 (`<comment>` only), NN7 (`<comment>` only), IE6

This method replaces one string in the object with a new string.

Syntax:

```
textNodeName.replaceData(param1, param2, param3) // IE only
document.getElementById("commentID").replaceData(param1, param2, param3)
document.all.commentID.replaceData(param1, param2, param3) // IE only
```

param1   Required; the first character in the string to replace.

param2   Required; the number of characters to replace.

param3   Required; the replacement string.

Example:

```
<script language="JavaScript">
function B1() {
    var m = document.getElementById("myP").firstChild;
```

```
        var myText = " (........ The replacement text .........) ";
        m.replaceData(12, 9, myText);
}
</script>
<p id="myP">This is the reference text node.</p>
<input type = "button" value = 'Replace the word "reference"' onclick="B1();">
```

Applies to:

`<comment>`, TextNode

replaceNode()

Compatibility: IE5, IE5.5, IE6

This method replaces an element node with a new node.

Syntax:

`document.all.elementID.replaceNode(param1)`

param1   Required; the replacement node.

Example:

```
<script language="JavaScript">
function B1() {
    var newElement = document.createElement('u');
    newElement.innerHTML = 'Text';
    var oldElement = document.all.myBold;
    document.all.myBold.replaceNode(newElement);
}
</script>
<button onclick="B1();">Replace text</button>
<div id="myDiv" style="width:300; height:200; border:solid black 1px;">Sample <b
id="myBold">text</b></div>
```

Applies to:

`<a>`, `<acronym>`, `<address>`, `<b>`, `<bdo>`, `<big>`, `<blockquote>`, `<body>`, `<button>`, `<caption>`, `<center>`, `<cite>`, `<code>`, `<col>`, `<colgroup>`, `<comment>`, `<dd>`, `<del>`, `<dfn>`, `<dir>`, `<div>`, `<dl>`, `<dt>`, `<em>`, `<fieldset>`, `<font>`, `<form>`, `<frameset>`, `<head>`, `<hn>`, `<html>`, `<i>`, `<iframe>`, `<input type="button">`, `<input type="checkbox">`, `<input type="file">`, `<input type="image">`, `<input type="password">`, `<input type="radio">`, `<input type="reset">`, `<input type="submit">`, `<input type="text">`, `<ins>`, `<kbd>`, `<label>`, `<legend>`, `<li>`, `<listing>`, `<map>`, `<marquee>`, `<menu>`, `<object>`, `<ol>`, `<option>`, `<p>`, `<plaintext>`, `<pre>`, `<q>`, `<s>`, `<samp>`, `<select>`, `<small>`, `<span>`, `<strike>`, `<strong>`, `<sub>`, `<sup>`, `<table>`, `<tbody>`, `<td>`, `<textarea>`, `<tfoot>`, `<th>`, `<thead>`, `<tr>`, `<tt>`, `<u>`, `<ul>`, `<var>`, `<xmp>`

reset()

Compatibility: NN4, NN6, NN7, IE4, IE5, IE5.5, IE6

This method restores all form elements to their default values.

Syntax:

```
document.formID.reset()
document.all.formID.reset() // IE only
```

Example:

```
<script language="JavaScript">
function B1(){document.all.myForm.reset();}
</script>
<form name="myForm" method="post" action="">
<input type="text" size="50" value="Type something here">
<input type="button" value="reset" onClick="B1();">
</form>
```

Applies to:

```
<form>
```

resizeBy()

Compatibility: NN4, NN6, NN7, IE4, IE5, IE5.5, IE6

This method resizes the window by the specified values, preserving the window's left and top positions.

Syntax:

```
window.resizeBy(param1, param2)
```

param1   Required; the number of pixels by which to resize the width.

param2   Required; the number of pixels by which to resize the height.

Example:

```
<script language="JavaScript">
function B1(){window.resizeBy(-100,-100);}
</script>
<input type="button" value="Resize this window by (-100,-100)" onClick="B1();">
```

Applies to:

```
window
```

resizeTo()

Compatibility: NN4, NN6, NN7, IE4, IE5, IE5.5, IE6

This method resizes the window to the specified width and height.
    Syntax:

```
window.resizeTo(param1, param2)
```

    param1   Required; the new width of the window in pixels.

    param2   Required; the new height of the window in pixels.

    Example:

```
<script language="JavaScript">
function B1(){window.resizeTo(400,300);}
</script>
<input type="button" value="Resize this window to (400,300)" onClick="B1();">
```

    Applies to:

```
window
```

reverse()

Compatibility: NN4, NN6, NN7, IE4, IE5, IE5.5, IE6

This method reverses the order of the elements in an array.
    Syntax:

```
arrayName.reverse()
```

    Example:

```
<button onclick="var myA = new Array(10,11,12); myA.reverse();
alert(myA);">REVERSE</button>
```

    Applies to:

```
Array
```

round()

Compatibility: NN4, NN6, NN7, IE4, IE5, IE5.5, IE6

This method rounds the specified number to the nearest integer value.
    Syntax:

```
Math.round(param1)
```

param1   Required; the number to convert.

Example:

```
<button onclick="alert(Math.round(1.33));">ROUND</button>
```

Applies to:

```
Math
```

scroll()

Compatibility: NN4, NN6, NN7, IE4, IE5, IE5.5, IE6

This method scrolls the window to the specified values.
Syntax:

```
window.scroll(param1, param2)
```

param1   Required; the horizontal scroll amount in pixels.

param2   Required; the vertical scroll amount in pixels.

Example: See the scrollTo() method example.
Applies to:

```
window
```

scrollBy()

Compatibility: NN4, NN6, NN7, IE4, IE5, IE5.5, IE6

This method scrolls the window by the specified values.
Syntax:

```
window.scrollBy(param1, param2)
```

param1   Required; the horizontal scroll amount in pixels.

param2   Required; the vertical scroll amount in pixels.

Example:

```
<script language="JavaScript">
function B1(){window.scrollBy(200,200);}
</script>
<input type="button" value="Scroll by (200,200)" onClick="B1();">
<div style="height:1000px;width:1400;background-color:blue"></div>
```

Applies to:

```
window
```

scrollIntoView()

Compatibility: IE4, IE5, IE5.5, IE6

This method scrolls the window until the element is visible.

Syntax:

```
document.all.elementID.scrollIntoView(param1)
```

param1   Optional; true or false, indicating whether the top of the element is scrolled to the top of the window or the bottom of the element is scrolled to the bottom of the window.

Example:

```
<script language="JavaScript">
function B1(){document.all.myDiv.scrollIntoView(true)}
function B2(){window.scrollTo(0,0)}
</script>
<input type="button" value=" Scroll to the myDiv" onClick="B1();">
<div style="height:1000;background-color:blue;"></div>
<div id=myDiv onclick="B2();">This is the element scrolled into view. Click here to
go to top.</div>
```

Applies to:

```
<a>, <address>, <applet>, <area>, <b>, <big>, <blockquote>, <br>, <button>,
<caption>, <center>, <cite>, <code>, <col>, <colgroup>, <comment>, controlRange*,
<custom>, <dd>, <dfn>, <dir>, <div>, <dl>, <dt>, <em>, <embed>, <fieldset>, <font>,
<form>, <hn>, <hr>, <i>, <iframe>, <img>, <input type="button">, <input
type="checkbox">, <input type="file">, <input type="image">, <input type="password">,
<input type="radio">, <input type="reset">, <input type="submit">, <input
type="text">, <kbd>, <label>, <legend>, <li>, <listing>, <map>, <marquee>, <menu>,
<nobr>, <object>, <ol>, <p>, <plaintext>, <pre>, <s>, <samp>, <select>, <small>,
<span>, <strike>, <strong>, <sub>, <sup>, <table>, <tbody>, <td>, <textarea>,
TextRange, <tfoot>, <th>, <thead>, <tr>, <tt>, <u>, <ul>, <var>, <wbr>, <xmp>
```

scrollTo()

Compatibility: NN4, NN6, NN7, IE4, IE5, IE5.5, IE6

This method scrolls the window to the specified values. This method is a new version of the scroll() method.

Syntax:

```
window.scrollTo(param1, param2)
```

param1   Required; the horizontal scroll amount in pixels.

param2   Required; the vertical scroll amount in pixels.

Example:

```
<script language="JavaScript">
function B1(){window.scrollTo(200,200);}
function B2(){window.scroll(200,200);}
</script>
<input type="button" value="Scroll to (200,200)" onClick="B1();">
<input type="button" value="Scroll(200,200)" onClick="B2();">
<div style="height:1000;width:1500;background-color:blue;"></div>
```

Applies to:

```
window
```

search()

Compatibility: NN4, NN6, NN7, IE4, IE5, IE5.5, IE6

This method searches the String object using a regular expression.
Syntax:

```
stringName.search(param1)
```

param1   Required; the regular expression.

Example:

```
<button onclick="var myS = new String('Sample String');
alert(myS.search('String'));">SEARCH</button>
```

Applies to:

```
String
```

select() (1)

Compatibility: IE4, IE5, IE5.5, IE6

This method causes the specified object to be highlighted.
Syntax:

```
controlRangeName.select()
textRangeName.select()
```

Example: See the findText() method example.
Applies to:

```
controlRange*, TextRange
```

Compatibility: NN4, NN6, NN7, IE4, IE5, IE5.5, IE6

This method highlights all the text within an element.

Syntax:

```
document.getElementById("elementID").select()
document.all.elementID.select()
```

Example:

```
<script language="JavaScript">
function B2() {document.all.myT.select();}
</script>
<textarea id=myT>Some text</textarea>
<input type="button" value='Select the textarea' onclick="B2()">
```

Applies to:

```
<input type="button">, <input type="checkbox">, <input type="file">, <input
type="image">, <input type="password">, <input type="radio">, <input type="reset">,
<input type="submit">, <input type="text">, <textarea>
```

setActive()

Compatibility: IE5.5, IE6

This method changes an element's status to active, giving it the focus.

Syntax:

```
document.all.elementID.setActive()
```

Example:

```
<script language="JavaScript">
function B1() {document.all.myT.setActive();}
</script>
<textarea id="myT">Some text</textarea>
<input type="button" value='Insert the cursor inside the textarea' onclick="B1();">
```

Applies to:

```
<a>, <acronym>, <address>, <applet>, <area>, <b>, <bdo>, <big>, <blockquote>,
<body>, <button>, <caption>, <center>, <cite>, <custom>, <dd>, <dfn>, <dir>, <div>,
<dl>, document, <dt>, <em>, <embed>, <fieldset>, <font>, <form>, <frame>,
<frameset>, <hn>, <hr>, <i>, <iframe>, <img>, <input type="button">, <input
type="checkbox">, <input type="file">, <input type="hidden">, <input type="image">,
<input type="password">, <input type="radio">, <input type="reset">, <input
```

type="submit">, <input type="text">, <ins>, <isindex>, <kbd>, <label>, <legend>, <li>, <listing>, <marquee>, <menu>, <object>, <ol>, <p>, <plaintext>, <pre>, <q>, <rt>, <ruby>, <s>, <samp>, <select>, <small>, <span>, <strike>, <strong>, <sub>, <sup>, <table>, <tbody>, <td>, <textarea>, <tfoot>, <th>, <thead>, <tr>, <tt>, <u>, <ul>, <var>, window, <xmp>

setAttribute()

Compatibility: NN6, NN7, IE4, IE5, IE5.5, IE6

This method assigns the specified value to the specified attribute.
   Syntax:

```
document.getElementById("elementID").setAttribute(param1, param2, param3)
document.all.elementID.setAttribute(param1, param2, param3) // IE only
```

param1   Required; the attribute's name.

param2   Required; the value assigned to the attribute.

param3   Optional; Values: 0 (not case sensitive) or 1 (the default; case sensitive).

   Example:

```
<script language="JavaScript">
function B1() {document.all.myP.setAttribute("align", "center");}
</script>
<p id="myP" align="left">This is a sample text.</p>
<input type="button" value='Align center the text above' onclick="B1();">
```

   Applies to:

<a>, <acronym>, <address>, <applet>, <area>, <b>, <base>, <basefont>, <bdo>, <bgsound>, <big>, <blockquote>, <body>, <br>, <button>, <caption>, <center>, <cite>, <code>, <col>, <colgroup>, <comment>, currentStyle, <custom>, <dd>, <del>, <dfn>, <dir>, <div>, <dl>, <dt>, <em>, <embed>, <fieldset>, <font>, <form>, <frame>, <frameset>, <head>, <hn>, <hr>, <html>, <i>, <iframe>, <img>, <input>, <input type="button">, <input type="checkbox">, <input type="file">, <input type="hidden">, <input type="image">, <input type="password">, <input type="radio">, <input type="reset">, <input type="submit">, <input type="text">, <ins>, <isindex>, <kbd>, <label>, <legend>, <li>, <link>, <listing>, <map>, <marquee>, <menu>, <meta>, <nobr>, <noframes>, <noscript>, <object>, <ol>, <optgroup>, <option>, <p>, <param>, <plaintext>, <pre>, <q>, runtimeStyle, <s>, <samp>, <script>, <select>, <small>, <span>, <strike>, <strong>, <style>, style, <sub>, <sup>, <table>, <tbody>, <td>, <textarea>, <tfoot>, <th>, <thead>, <title>, <tr>, <tt>, <u>, <ul>, userProfile, <var>, <wbr>, <xmp>

setAttributeNode()

Compatibility: NN6, NN7, IE6

This method adds an attribute node to the element.

Syntax:

```
document.getElementById("elementID").setAttributeNode(param1)
document.all.elementID.setAttributeNode(param1) // IE only
```

param1   Required; the name of the attribute to be added.

Example: See the createAttribute() method example.
Applies to:

`<a>`, `<acronym>`, `<address>`, `<applet>`, `<area>`, `<b>`, `<base>`, `<basefont>`, `<bdo>`, `<bgsound>`, `<big>`, `<blockquote>`, `<body>`, `<br>`, `<button>`, `<caption>`, `<center>`, `<cite>`, `<code>`, `<col>`, `<colgroup>`, `<comment>`, `<custom>`, `<dd>`, `<del>`, `<dfn>`, `<dir>`, `<div>`, `<dl>`, `<dt>`, `<em>`, `<embed>`, `<fieldset>`, `<font>`, `<form>`, `<frame>`, `<frameset>`, `<head>`, `<hn>`, `<hr>`, `<html>`, `<i>`, `<iframe>`, `<img>`, `<input>`, `<input type="button">`, `<input type="checkbox">`, `<input type="file">`, `<input type="hidden">`, `<input type="image">`, `<input type="password">`, `<input type="radio">`, `<input type="reset">`, `<input type="submit">`, `<input type="text">`, `<ins>`, `<isindex>`, `<kbd>`, `<label>`, `<legend>`, `<li>`, `<link>`, `<listing>`, `<map>`, `<marquee>`, `<menu>`, `<meta>`, `<nobr>`, `<noframes>`, `<noscript>`, `<object>`, `<ol>`, `<optgroup>`, `<option>`, `<p>`, `<param>`, `<plaintext>`, `<pre>`, `<q>`, `<rt>`, `<ruby>`, `<s>`, `<samp>`, `<script>`, `<select>`, `<small>`, `<span>`, `<strike>`, `<strong>`, `<style>`, style, `<sub>`, `<sup>`, `<table>`, `<tbody>`, `<td>`, `<textarea>`, `<tfoot>`, `<th>`, `<thead>`, `<title>`, `<tr>`, `<tt>`, `<u>`, `<ul>`, `<var>`, `<wbr>`, `<xml>`, `<xmp>`

setCapture()

Compatibility: IE5, IE5.5, IE6

This method turns mouse capture on for the specified element. When mouse capture is set to an element, that element will fire all mouse-related events.
Syntax:

```
document.all.elementID.setCapture(param1)
```

param1   Optional; true or false, indicating whether or not the mouse capture affects the element's parent.

Example: See the releaseCapture() method example.
Applies to:

`<a>`, `<address>`, `<applet>`, `<area>`, `<b>`, `<big>`, `<blockquote>`, `<body>`, `<br>`, `<button>`, `<caption>`, `<center>`, `<cite>`, `<code>`, `<custom>`, `<dd>`, `<dfn>`, `<dir>`, `<div>`, `<dl>`, `<dt>`, `<em>`, `<embed>`, `<fieldset>`, `<font>`, `<form>`, `<hn>`, `<hr>`, `<i>`, `<img>`, `<input type="button">`, `<input type="checkbox">`, `<input type="file">`, `<input type="hidden">`, `<input type="image">`, `<input type="password">`, `<input type="radio">`, `<input type="reset">`, `<input type="submit">`, `<input type="text">`, `<kbd>`, `<label>`, `<legend>`, `<li>`, `<listing>`, `<map>`, `<marquee>`, `<menu>`, `<nobr>`, `<object>`, `<ol>`, `<option>`, `<p>`, `<plaintext>`, `<pre>`, `<s>`, `<samp>`, `<select>`, `<small>`, `<span>`, `<strike>`, `<strong>`, `<sub>`, `<sup>`, `<table>`, `<tbody>`, `<td>`, `<textarea>`, `<tfoot>`, `<th>`, `<thead>`, `<tr>`, `<tt>`, `<u>`, `<ul>`, `<var>`, `<xmp>`

setData()

Compatibility: IE5, IE5.5, IE6

This method assigns data to the object in the specified format. Returns true (successful) or false (failed).

Syntax:

```
event.objectName.setData(param1, param2)
```

> **param1**   Required; the data format: text or URL.
>
> **param2**   Required; the data supplied.

Example: See the clearData() method example.
Applies to:

```
clipboardData, dataTransfer
```

setDate()

Compatibility: NN4, NN6, NN7, IE4, IE5, IE5.5, IE6

This method sets the Date object's day of the month.

Syntax:

```
dateName.setDate(param1)
```

> **param1**   Required; the day of the month. Value: 1 to 31.

Example:

```
<button onclick="var myDate = new Date(); myDate.setDate(20);
alert(myDate);">SETDATE</button>
```

Applies to:

```
Date
```

setEndPoint()

Compatibility: IE4, IE5, IE5.5, IE6

This method adjusts the start or end point of the text range with respect to the start or end point of the text range specified by param2.

Syntax:

```
textRangeName.setEndPoint(param1, param2)
```

param1   Required; the type of adjustment: StartToEnd, StartToStart, EndToStart, EndToEnd.

param2   Required; the base text range.

Example:

```
<script language="JavaScript">
function B1() {
    var range1 = document.body.createTextRange();
    alert(range1.text);
    var range2 = document.selection.createRange();
    range1.setEndPoint("StartToEnd", range2);
    alert(range1.text);
}
</script>
<body>
Highlight any section of the text, and then click the button and the start of the
range will be reset to the point from which you made the selection.<br>
<input type="button" value='Adjust end points' onclick="B1()">
</body>
```

Applies to:

TextRange

setExpression()

Compatibility: IE5, IE5.5, IE6

This method makes the specified property a dynamic property.
Syntax:

```
objectName.setExpression(param1, param2, param3)
document.all.elementID.setExpression(param1, param2, param3)
```

param1   Required; the name of the property.

param2   Required; the script statement without any quotations or semicolons. References to arrays and collections are not allowed in this script.

param3   Optional; the script language used with the script. Values: JScript (the default), VBScript, or JavaScript.

Example: See the getExpression() method example.
Applies to:

<a>, <acronym>, <address>, <applet>, <area>, <b>, <bdo>, <big>, <blockquote>, <body>, <br>, <button>, <caption>, <center>, <cite>, <code>, <col>, <colgroup>, currentStyle, <custom>, <dd>, <del>, <dfn>, <dir>, <div>, <dl>, <dt>, <em>, <embed>, <fieldset>, <font>, <form>, <hn>, <hr>, <i>, <iframe>, <img>, <input type="button">, <input type="checkbox">, <input type="file">, <input

type="hidden">, <input type="image">, <input type="password">, <input
type="radio">, <input type="reset">, <input type="submit">, <input type="text">,
<ins>, <kbd>, <label>, <legend>, <li>, <listing>, <marquee>, <menu>, <nobr>,
<object>, <ol>, <option>, <p>, <pre>, <q>, <rt>, <ruby>, runtimeStyle, <s>, <samp>,
<select>, <small>, <span>, <strike>, <strong>, style, <sub>, <sup>, <table>,
<tbody>, <td>, <textarea>, <tfoot>, <th>, <thead>, <tr>, <tt>, <u>, <ul>, <var>

setFullYear()

Compatibility: NN4, NN6, NN7, IE4, IE5, IE5.5, IE6

This method sets the Date object's year. By supplying the optional parameters,
you can also set the object's month and day.

Syntax:

dateName.setFullYear(*param1*, *param2*, *param3*)

> **param1**   Required; the four-digit year.
>
> **param2**   Optional; the month. Value: 0 to 11.
>
> **param3**   Optional; the day of the month. Value: 1 to 31.

Example:

```
<button onclick="var myDate = new Date(); myDate.setFullYear(2000);
alert(myDate);">SETFULLYEAR</button>
```

Applies to:

Date

setHours()

Compatibility: NN4, NN6, NN7, IE4, IE5, IE5.5, IE6

This method sets the Date object's hour.

Syntax:

dateName.setHours(*param1*, *param2*, *param3*, *param4*)

> **param1**   Required; the hour. Value: 0 to 23.
>
> **param2**   Optional; the minute. Value: 0 to 59.
>
> **param3**   Optional; the seconds. Value: 0 to 59.
>
> **param4**   Optional; the milliseconds that have elapsed during the current
> second. Value: 0 to 999.

Example:

```
<button onclick="var myDate = new Date(); myDate.setHours(12);
alert(myDate);">SETHOURS</button>
```

Applies to:

Date

---

setInterval()

Compatibility: NN4, NN6, NN7, IE4, IE5, IE5.5, IE6

This method establishes a timed loop that will evaluate an expression at regular intervals. Returns an integer that can be used by the clearInterval() method to cancel the timer.

Syntax:

---

window.setInterval(*param1*, *param2*, *param3*)

---

param1   Required; a function name or string of code that will execute at the end of each cycle.

param2   Required; the number of milliseconds in the interval.

param3   Optional; param1's script language. Values: JScript, vbscript, vbs, javascript, or XML.

Example: See the clearInterval() method example.

Applies to:

---

window

---

setMilliseconds()

Compatibility: NN4, NN6, NN7, IE4, IE5, IE5.5, IE6

This method sets the number of milliseconds that have elapsed during the Date object's current second.

Syntax:

---

dateName.setMilliseconds(*param1*)

---

param1   Optional; the milliseconds. Value: 0 to 999.

Example:

```
<button onclick="var myDate = new Date(); myDate.setMilliseconds(845);
alert(myDate);">SETMILLISECONDS</button>
```

Applies to:

Date

---

setMinutes()

Compatibility: NN4, NN6, NN7, IE4, IE5, IE5.5, IE6

This method sets the Date object's minutes.
Syntax:

---

dateName.setMinutes(*param1, param2, param3*)

> **param1**   Required; the minutes. Value: 0 to 59.
>
> **param2**   Optional; the seconds. Value: 0 to 59.
>
> **param3**   Optional; the number of milliseconds that have elapsed during the current second. Value: 0 to 999.
>
> Example:

```
<button onclick="var myDate = new Date(); myDate.setMinutes(2);
alert(myDate);">SETMINUTES</button>
```

> Applies to:

Date

---

setMonth()

Compatibility: NN4, NN6, NN7, IE4, IE5, IE5.5, IE6

This method sets the Date object's month.
Syntax:

---

dateName.setMonth(*param1, param2*)

> **param1**   Required; the month. Value: 0 to 11.
>
> **param2**   Optional; the day of the month. Value: 1 to 31.
>
> Example:

```
<button onclick="var myDate = new Date(); myDate.setMonth(5);
alert(myDate);">SETMONTH</button>
```

> Applies to:

Date

---

setNamedItem()

Compatibility: IE6

This method adds an attribute to the attributes collection. If the new attribute shares its name with a previously existing attribute, this method returns a reference to the previously existing attribute.

Syntax:

```
document.all.elementID.attributes.setNamedItem(param1)
```

param1   Required; the name of the attribute.

Example:

```
<script language="JavaScript">
function B1() {
    var myAttrib = document.createAttribute("ID");
    myAttrib.value = 'myDiv2';
    document.all.myB.attributes.setNamedItem(myAttrib);
    alert(myAttrib.value);
}
</script>
<input id="myB" type="button" value="Click me twice" onClick="B1();">
```

Applies to:

```
attributes*
```

setSeconds()

Compatibility: NN4, NN6, NN7, IE4, IE5, IE5.5, IE6

This method sets the Date object's seconds.

Syntax:

```
dateName.setSeconds(param1, param2)
```

param1   Required; the seconds. Value: 0 to 59.

param2   Optional; the number of milliseconds that have elapsed for during the current second. Value: 0 to 999.

Example:

```
<button onclick="var myDate = new Date(); myDate.setSeconds(20);
alert(myDate);">SETSECONDS</button>
```

Applies to:

```
Date
```

setTime()

Compatibility: NN4, NN6, NN7, IE4, IE5, IE5.5, IE6

This method sets the Date object's time by supplying total the number of milliseconds that have elapsed since January 1, 1970.

Syntax:

```
dateName.setTime(param1)
```

param1   Required; the number of milliseconds.

Example:

```
<button onclick="var myDate = new Date(); myDate.setTime(myDate.getTime());
alert(myDate);">SETTIME</button>
```

Applies to:

```
Date
```

setTimeout()

Compatibility: NN4, NN6, NN7, IE4, IE5, IE5.5, IE6

This method establishes the amount of time that should elapse before the specified expression is executed and returns an integer that can be used by the clearTimeout() method to cancel the timer.

Syntax:

```
window.setTimeout(param1, param2, param3)
```

param1   Required; a function name or string of code that will execute when the timeout has elapsed.

param2   Required; the length of the timeout in milliseconds.

param3   Optional; param1's script language. Values: JScript, vbscript, vbs, javascript, or XML.

Example: See the clearTimeout() method example.
Applies to:

```
window
```

setUTCDate()

Compatibility: NN4, NN6, NN7, IE4, IE5, IE5.5, IE6

This method uses UTC time to set the Date object's day of the month.

Syntax:

---

dateName.setUTCDate(*param1*)

---

param1   Required; the day of the month. Value: 1 to 31.

Example:

```
<button onclick="var myDate = new Date(); myDate.setUTCDate(20);
alert(myDate);">SETUTCDATE</button>
```

Applies to:

Date

---

setUTCFullYear()

Compatibility: NN4, NN6, NN7, IE4, IE5, IE5.5, IE6

This method uses UTC time to set the Date object's year.
   Syntax:

---

dateName.setUTCFullYear(*param1, param2, param3*)

---

param1   Required; the year.

param2   Optional; the month. Value: 0 to 11.

param3   Optional; the day of the month. Value: 1 to 31.

Example:

```
<button onclick="var myDate = new Date(); myDate.setUTCFullYear(2030);
alert(myDate);">SETUTCFULLYEAR</button>
```

Applies to:

Date

---

setUTCHours()

Compatibility: NN4, NN6, NN7, IE4, IE5, IE5.5, IE6

This method uses UTC time to set the Date object's hour.
   Syntax:

---

dateName.setUTCHours(*param1, param2, param3, param4*)

---

param1   Required; the hour. Value: 0 to 23.

param2   Optional; the minute. Value: 0 to 59.

param3   Optional; the seconds. Value: 0 to 59.

param4   Optional; the milliseconds that have elapsed during the current second. Value: 0 to 999.

Example:

```
<button onclick="var myDate = new Date(); myDate.setUTCHours(11);
alert(myDate);">SETUTCHOURS</button>
```

Applies to:

Date

setUTCMilliseconds()

Compatibility: NN4, NN6, NN7, IE4, IE5, IE5.5, IE6

This method uses UTC time to set the number of milliseconds that have elapsed during the Date object's current second.

Syntax:

dateName.setUTCMilliseconds(*param1*)

param1   Required; the number of milliseconds. Value: 0 to 999.

Example:

```
<button onclick="var myDate = new Date(); myDate.setUTCMilliseconds(20);
alert(myDate);">SETUTCMILLISECONDS</button>
```

Applies to:

Date

setUTCMinutes()

Compatibility: NN4, NN6, NN7, IE4, IE5, IE5.5, IE6

This method uses UTC time to set the Date object's minutes.

Syntax:

dateName.setUTCMinutes(*param1, param2, param3*)

param1   Required; the minutes. Value: 0 to 59.

param2   Optional; the seconds. Value: 0 to 59.

param3   Optional; the milliseconds that have elapsed during the current second. Value: 0 to 999.

Example:

```
<button onclick="var myDate = new Date(); myDate.setUTCMinutes(22);
alert(myDate);">SETUTCMINUTES</button>
```

Applies to:

Date

setUTCMonth()

Compatibility: NN4, NN6, NN7, IE4, IE5, IE5.5, IE6

This method uses UTC time to set the Date object's month.
Syntax:

```
dateName.setUTCMonth(param1, param2)
```

param1 Required; the month. Value: 0 to 11.

param2 Optional; the day of the month. Value: 1 to 31.

Example:

```
<button onclick="var myDate = new Date(); myDate.setUTCMonth(2);
alert(myDate);">SETUTCMONTH</button>
```

Applies to:

Date

setUTCSeconds()

Compatibility: NN4, NN6, NN7, IE4, IE5, IE5.5, IE6

This method uses UTC time to set the Date object's seconds.
Syntax:

```
dateName.setUTCSeconds(param1, param2)
```

param1 Required; the seconds. Value: 0 to 59.

param2 Optional; the milliseconds that have elapsed during the current second. Value: 0 to 999.

Example:

```
<button onclick="var myDate = new Date(); myDate.setUTCSeconds(12);
alert(myDate);">SETUTCSECONDS</button>
```

Applies to:

Date

setYear()

Compatibility: NN4, NN6, NN7, IE4, IE5, IE5.5, IE6

This method sets the Date object's year.
Syntax:

dateName.setYear(*param1*)

param1   Required; the year using either two or four digits. If two digits are specified, the year will be 1900 plus the two-digit number.

Example:

```
<button onclick="var myDate = new Date(); myDate.setYear(2000);
alert(myDate);">SETYEAR</button>
```

Applies to:

Date

shift()

Compatibility: NN4, NN6, NN7, IE4, IE5, IE5.5, IE6

This method removes the first element in an array. Returns the element being removed.
Syntax:

arrayName.shift()

Example:

```
<button onclick="var myA = new Array(10,11,12); myA.shift(); alert(myA);">SHIFT</button>
```

Applies to:

Array

show()

Compatibility: IE5.5, IE6

This method causes a pop-up window to be displayed.

Syntax:

`popupName.show(param1, param2, param3, param4, param5)`

---

param1 Required; the X coordinate of the pop-up window in pixels.

param2 Required; the Y coordinate of the pop-up window in pixels.

param3 Required; the width of the pop-up window in pixels.

param4 Required; the height of the pop-up window in pixels.

param5 Optional; the name of the object relative to which param1 and param2 are calculated. If param5 is omitted, param1 and param2 are calculated relative to the screen.

Example: See the `hide()` method example.
Applies to:

`popup`

ShowBrowserUI()

Compatibility: IE5, IE5.5, IE6

This method opens the specified dialog window.
Syntax:

`window.external.ShowBrowserUI(param1, param2)`

---

param1 Required; the type of dialog window to open. Values: `LanguageDialog`, `OrganizeFavorites`, or `PrivacySettings`.

param2 Required; only `null` value is presently accepted.

Example:

```
<script language="JavaScript">
function B1() {window.external.ShowBrowserUI('LanguageDialog', null);}
function B2() {window.external.ShowBrowserUI('OrganizeFavorites', null);}
function B3() {window.external.ShowBrowserUI('PrivacySettings', null);}
</script>
<input type="button" value="Open the Language Preferences dialog box."
onclick="B1();">
<input type="button" value="Open the Organize Favorites dialog box."
onclick="B2();">
<input type="button" value="Open the Privacy Preferences dialog box."
onclick="B3();">
```

Applies to:

`external`

---

showHelp()

Compatibility: IE4, IE5, IE5.5, IE6

This method opens a help window with the specific help file.

Syntax:

```
window.showHelp(param1, param2)
```

param1   Required; the URL of the help file, ending with the .hlp extension.

param2   Optional; a context identifier in the help file that will cause a particular section of the help file to be displayed.

Example:

```
<script language="JavaScript">
function B1() {window.showHelp('http://www.nostarch.com');}
</script>
<input type="button" value="Open the help document" onclick="B1();">
```

Applies to:

```
window
```

showModalDialog()

Compatibility: IE4, IE5, IE5.5, IE6

This method opens a dialog window and prevents access to other windows until the dialog window is closed.

Syntax:

```
window.showModalDialog(param1, param2, param3)
```

param1   Required; the URL of the document to display.

param2   Optional; an object with added properties. The modal window will receive this object using its `dialogArguments` property.

param3   Optional; a semicolon-delimited list of one or more of the style attributes listed at http://msdn.microsoft.com/workshop/author/dhtml/reference/methods/showmodaldialog.asp.

Example:

```
<script language="JavaScript">
function openWindow() {
    var myArguments = new Object();
    myArguments.param1 = document.all.myColor.value;
    window.showModalDialog("dw.htm", myArguments, '');
```

```
}
</script>
<select id="myColor">
<option value="red">Red</option><option value="green">Green</option>
<option value="blue">Blue</option><option value="yellow">Yellow</option>
</select>
<button onclick="openWindow();">Open window</button>
```

Contents of dw.htm:

```
<script language="JavaScript">
function loadForm(){
    myBody.style.backgroundColor = window.dialogArguments.param1;
    myBody.style.color = 'black';
    myBody.style.fontSize = '14pt';
    window.dialogHeight = '300px';
    window.dialogLeft = '500px';
    window.dialogTop = '300px';
    window.dialogWidth = '500px';
}
</script>
<body id="myBody" onload="loadForm();"><br>
This window has the color specified in the previous window<br><br>
<button onclick="window.close();">Close this window</button>
</body>
```

Applies to:

```
window
```

showModelessDialog()

Compatibility: IE5, IE5.5, IE6

This method opens a modeless dialog window pointing to the specified URL. The user can switch windows even when the modeless dialog box is displayed.
Syntax:

```
window.showModelessDialog(param1, param2, param3)
```

param1   Required; the URL of the document to display.

param2   Optional; an object with added properties. The modeless window will receive this object using its dialogArguments property.

param3   Optional; a semicolon-delimited list of one or more of the style attributes listed at http://msdn.microsoft.com/workshop/author/dhtml/reference/methods/showmodaldialog.asp.

Example: See the `showModalDialog()` method example and replace
`showModalDialog()` with `showModelessDialog()`.
Applies to:

```
window
```

sin()

Compatibility: NN4, NN6, NN7, IE4, IE5, IE5.5, IE6

This method returns the sine of the specified number.
Syntax:

```
Math.sin(param1)
```

param1 Required; the number to convert.

Example:

```
<button onclick="alert(Math.sin(1));">SIN</button>
```

Applies to:

```
Math
```

slice()

Compatibility: NN4, NN6, NN7, IE4, IE5, IE5.5, IE6

This method returns a part of an `Array` or `String` object.
Syntax:

```
objectName.slice(param1, param2)
```

param1 Required; starting character of a string or starting element of an array.

param2 Required; ending character of a string or ending element of an array.

Example:

```
<button onclick="var myS = new String('Sample String');
alert(myS.slice(4,7));">SLICE STRING</button>
<button onclick="var myA = new Array(10,11,12,13,14,15);
alert(myA.slice(1,3));">SLICE ARRAY</button>
```

Applies to:

```
Array, String
```

small()

Compatibility: NN4, NN6, NN7, IE4, IE5, IE5.5, IE6

This method causes a string to be rendered in a font size that is one smaller than the current font size in the document.

Syntax:

```
stringName.small()
```

Example:

```
<button onclick="var myS = new String('Sample String'); document.write('regular
string'+myS.small());">SMALL</button>
```

Applies to:

```
String
```

sort()

Compatibility: NN4, NN6, NN7, IE4, IE5, IE5.5, IE6

This method sorts the elements in the array alphabetically.

Syntax:

```
arrayName.sort()
```

Example:

```
<button onclick="var myA = new Array(10,15,13,11,12,14,16); myA.sort();
alert(myA);">SORT</button>
```

Applies to:

```
Array
```

splice()

Compatibility: NN4, NN6, NN7, IE4, IE5, IE5.5, IE6

This method removes elements from the array and adds new elements in their place.

Syntax:

```
arrayName.splice(param1, param2, paramN, . . . ,paramN)
```

param1   Required; the index of the first element to remove.

param2   Required; the index of the last element to remove.

paramN   Required; elements to be added to the array.

Example:

```
<button onclick="var myA = new Array(10,11,12,13,14,15);
alert(myA.splice(1,3));">SPLICE</button>
```

Applies to:

```
Array
```

split()

Compatibility: NN4, NN6, NN7, IE4, IE5, IE5.5, IE6

This method uses the specified delimiter to split the String object into an array of String objects.

Syntax:

```
stringName.split(param1, param2)
```

param1   Required; the delimiter to use.

param2   Optional; the maximum number of elements to return in the array.

Example:

```
<script language="javascript">
function B1(){
    var myString = 'Sample String';
    var myArray = myString.split(' ');
    alert(myArray.length);
}</script>
<button onclick="B1();">SPLIT</button>
```

Applies to:

```
String
```

splitText()

Compatibility: IE5, IE5.5, IE6

This method splits a text node at a specified point.

Syntax:

```
textNodeName.splitText(param1)
```

param1   Optional; the character number at which to split the node.

Example:

```
<script language="JavaScript">
function B1() {
    var myNode = document.all.myParagraph.childNodes(0);
    var myNew = myNode.splitText(5);
    alert(myNew.nodeValue);
}
</script>
<p id="myParagraph">This is some <b>sample</b> text</p>
<input type="button" value="Click here to split" onClick="B1();">
```

Applies to:

TextNode

sqrt()

Compatibility: NN4, NN6, NN7, IE4, IE5, IE5.5, IE6

This method returns the square root of the specified number.

Syntax:

```
Math.sqrt(param1)
```

param1   Required; the number to convert.

Example:

```
<button onclick="alert(Math.sqrt(2));">SQRT</button>
```

Applies to:

Math

start()

Compatibility: IE4, IE5, IE5.5, IE6

This method starts playing the <marquee> element without firing the onStart event handler.

Syntax:

```
document.all.marqueeID.start()
```

Example:

```
<script language="JavaScript">
function B1(){document.all.myMarquee.stop();}
```

```
function B2(){document.all.myMarquee.start();}
</script>
<marquee align="left" id="myMarquee" bgcolor="red"  width="300">
Sample Text</marquee>
<input type="button" value="Start" onClick="B2();">
<input type="button" value="Stop" onClick="B1();">
```

Applies to:

```
<marquee>
```

stop()

Compatibility: IE4, IE5, IE5.5, IE6

This method stops playing the <marquee> element.
Syntax:

```
document.all.marqueeID.stop()
```

Example: See the start() method example.
Applies to:

```
<marquee>
```

strike()

Compatibility: NN4, NN6, NN7, IE4, IE5, IE5.5, IE6

This method causes a string to appear as if it has been crossed out.
Syntax:

```
stringName.strike()
```

Example:

```
<button onclick="var myS = new String('Sample String'); document.write('regular
string'+myS.strike());">STRIKE</button>
```

Applies to:

```
String
```

sub()

Compatibility: NN4, NN6, NN7, IE4, IE5, IE5.5, IE6

This method causes a string to be displayed as subscript text.

Syntax:

```
stringName.sub()
```

Example:

```
<button onclick="var myS = new String('Sample String'); document.write('regular
string'+myS.sub());">SUB</button>
```

Applies to:

```
String
```

submit()

Compatibility: NN4, NN6, NN7, IE4, IE5, IE5.5, IE6

This method sends a form's data to the server.

Syntax:

```
document.getElementById("formID").submit()
document.all.formID.submit() // IE only
```

Example:

```
<script language="JavaScript">
function B1(){document.all.myF.submit();}
</script>
<form id="myF" class="explanations" method="post" action="yourserverfilename.asp">
Enter your first name: <input type="text"></form>
<input type="button" value="Send the form" onClick="B1();">
```

Applies to:

```
<form>
```

substr()

Compatibility: NN4, NN6, NN7, IE4, IE5, IE5.5, IE6

This method returns part of a String object.

Syntax:

```
stringName.substr(param1, param2)
```

param1 Required; the character number that is to be the first character of the subset string.

param2 Required; the length of the subset string.

Example:

```
<button onclick="var myS = new String('Sample String');
alert(myS.substr(4,7));">SUBSTR</button>
```

Applies to:

String

substring()

Compatibility: NN4, NN6, NN7, IE4, IE5, IE5.5, IE6

This method returns part of a String object.

Syntax:

```
stringName.substring(param1, param2)
```

param1 Required; the character number that is to be the first character of the subset string.

param2 Required; the character number that is to be the last character of the subset string.

Example:

```
<button onclick="var myS = new String('Sample String');
alert(myS.substring(4,7));">SUBSTRING</button>
```

Applies to:

String

substringData()

Compatibility: NN6 (<comment> only), NN7 (<comment> only), IE6

This method returns a string from the text object.

Syntax:

```
textNodeName.subStringData(param1, param2) // IE only
document.getElementById("commentID").subStringData(param1, param2)
document.all.commentID.subStringData(param1, param2) // IE only
```

param1 Required; the character number that is to be the first character of the subset string.

param2 Required; the length of the subset string. The sum of param1 and param2 may not be greater than the length of the original object.

Example:

```
<script language="JavaScript">
function B1() {
    var range = document.all.myP1.firstChild;
    var m = range.substringData(5, 10);
    alert(m);
}
</script>
<p id="myP1">This is a sample text.</p>
<input type="button" value='Extract data from 5 to 10' onclick="B1();">
```

Applies to:

```
<comment>, TextNode
```

sup()

Compatibility: NN4, NN6, NN7, IE4, IE5, IE5.5, IE6

This method causes a string to be displayed as superscript text.
Syntax:

```
stringName.sup()
```

Example:

```
<button onclick="var myS = new String('Sample String'); document.write('regular string'+myS.sup());">SUP</button>
```

Applies to:

```
String
```

swapNode()

Compatibility: IE5, IE5.5, IE6

This method swaps the location of two nodes.
Syntax:

```
textNodeName.swapNode(param1)
```

param1   Required; one of the two nodes to exchange positions.

Example:

```
<script language="JavaScript">
function B1() {
```

```
if (document.all) {
    var myNew = document.createElement("div");
    myNew.innerText = "This is a swapped element"
    myNew.style.color = "red"
    myDiv.swapNode(myNew);
    }
}
</script>
<div id="myDiv">This is a div element</div>
<input type="button" value="SwapNode" onClick="B1();">
```

Applies to:

`<a>`, `<acronym>`, `<address>`, `<applet>`, `<area>`, `<b>`, `<base>`, `<basefont>`, `<bdo>`, `<bgsound>`, `<big>`, `<blockquote>`, `<body>`, `<br>`, `<button>`, `<caption>`, `<center>`, `<cite>`, `<code>`, `<col>`, `<colgroup>`, `<comment>`, `<dd>`, `<del>`, `<dfn>`, `<dir>`, `<div>`, `<dl>`, `<dt>`, `<em>`, `<embed>`, `<fieldset>`, `<font>`, `<form>`, `<frame>`, `<frameset>`, `<head>`, `<hn>`, `<hr>`, `<html>`, `<i>`, `<iframe>`, `<img>`, `<input type="button">`, `<input type="checkbox">`, `<input type="file">`, `<input type="hidden">`, `<input type="image">`, `<input type="password">`, `<input type="radio">`, `<input type="reset">`, `<input type="submit">`, `<input type="text">`, `<ins>`, `<kbd>`, `<label>`, `<legend>`, `<li>`, `<link>`, `<listing>`, `<map>`, `<marquee>`, `<menu>`, `<object>`, `<ol>`, `<option>`, `<p>`, `<plaintext>`, `<pre>`, `<q>`, `<s>`, `<samp>`, `<script>`, `<select>`, `<small>`, `<span>`, `<strike>`, `<strong>`, `<sub>`, `<sup>`, `<table>`, `<tbody>`, `<td>`, `<textarea>`, `<tfoot>`, `<th>`, `<thead>`, `<title>`, `<tr>`, `<tt>`, `<u>`, `<ul>`, `<var>`, `<xmp>`

tags()

Compatibility: IE4, IE5, IE5.5, IE6

This method returns a collection containing all the elements that have the specified tag name. Returns null if no match is found.

Syntax:

collectionName.tags(*param1*)

param1 Required; the tag's name.

Example:

```
<script language="JavaScript">
function B1() {alert(document.all.tags("p").length);}
</script>
<p>This is a sample text.</p><p>This is another sample text.</p>
<input type="button" value="Number of p elements" onClick="B1();">
```

Applies to:

all*, anchors*, applets*, areas*, boundElements*, cells*, children*, elements*, embeds*, forms*, images*, links*, options*, plugins*, rows*, scripts*, tBodies*

taintEnabled()

Compatibility: NN6, NN7, IE4, IE5, IE5.5, IE6

This method indicates whether or not data tainting is enabled. Disabling data tainting is a browser security method that prevents a script from accessing functionality on the web server. Returns true or false.

Syntax:

```
objectName.taintEnabled()
```

Example:

```
<script language="JavaScript">
function B1() {
    var m = navigator.taintEnabled();
    if (m == true) {alert("YES");} else {alert("NO");}
}
</script>
<input type="button" value="Is data tainting in my browser enabled?"
onClick="B1();">
```

Applies to:

```
clientInformation, navigator
```

tan()

Compatibility: NN4, NN6, NN7, IE4, IE5, IE5.5, IE6

This method returns the tangent value for the number specified.
Syntax:

```
Math.tan(param1)
```

param1   Required; the number to convert.

Example:

```
<button onclick="alert(Math.tan(1));">TAN</button>
```

Applies to:

```
Math
```

toExponential()

Compatibility: IE5.5, IE6

This method converts the value of a Number object into exponential notation.

Syntax:

```
numberName.toExponential(param1)
```

param1   Required; number of decimal places in the exponential notation.

Example:

```
<button onclick="var myNum = new Number(100);
alert(myNum.toExponential(1));">TOEXPONENTIAL</button>
```

Applies to:

Number

toFixed()

Compatibility: IE5.5, IE6

This method rounds the Number object's value to the specified number of decimal places.

Syntax:

```
numberName.toFixed(param1)
```

param1   Required; the number of decimal places.

Example:

```
<button onclick="var myNum = new Number(100.22);
alert(myNum.toFixed(1));">TOFIXED</button>
```

Applies to:

Number

toGMTString()

Compatibility: NN4, NN6, NN7, IE4, IE5, IE5.5, IE6

This method uses the difference between local time and Greenwich Mean Time (GMT) to convert the date to a format that is locale specific.

Syntax:

```
dateName.toGMTString()
```

Example:

```
<button onclick="var myDate = new Date();
alert(myDate.toGMTString());">TOGMTSTRING</button>
```

Applies to:

Date

toLocaleLowerCase()

Compatibility: IE5.5, IE6

This method uses the system's locale settings to convert a String object's value to lowercase.

Syntax:

```
stringName.toLocaleLowerCase()
```

Example:

```
<button onclick="var myS = new String('Sample String');
alert(myS.toLocaleLowerCase());">TOLOCALELOWERCASE</button>
```

Applies to:

String

toLocaleString()

Compatibility: NN6, NN7, IE5.5, IE6

This method converts the object to a format that is locale specific.

Syntax:

```
objectName.toLocaleString()
```

Example:

```
<button onclick="var myDate = new Date();
alert(myDate.toLocaleString());">TOLOCALESTRING</button>
```

Applies to:

Date, Number (IE5.5 and IE6 only), Object

toLocaleUpperCase()

Compatibility: IE5.5, IE6

This method uses the system's locale settings to convert a String object's value to lowercase.

Syntax:

```
stringName.toLocaleUpperCase()
```

Example:

```
<button onclick="var myS = new String('Sample String');
alert(myS.toLocaleUpperCase());">TOLOCALEUPPERCASE</button>
```

Applies to:

String

toLowerCase()

Compatibility: NN4, NN6, NN7, IE4, IE5, IE5.5, IE6

This method converts the String object's value to lowercase.
    Syntax:

```
stringName.toLowerCase()
```

Example:

```
<button onclick="var myS = new String('Sample String');
alert(myS.toLowerCase());">TOLOWERCASE</button>
```

Applies to:

String

toPrecision()

Compatibility: IE5.5, IE6

This method is very similar to the toExponential() method, which converts a number to exponential notation. However, the toPrecision() method only converts a number to exponential notation if it contains more digits than are specified by the parameter.
    Syntax:

```
numberName.toPrecision(param1)
```

param1   Required; minimum number of digits to convert to exponential notation.

Example:

```
<button onclick="var myNum = new Number(100);
alert(myNum.toPrecision(1));">TOPRECISION</button>
```

Applies to:

Number

toSource()

Compatibility: NN4, NN6, NN7

This method returns the string that was used to create the object.

Syntax:

```
objectName.toSource()
```

Example:

```
<button onclick="var myA = new Array(10,11,12,13,14,15);
alert(myA.toSource());">TOSOURCE</button>
<button onclick="var myDate = new Date(); alert(myDate.toSource());">TOSOURCE</button>
```

Applies to:

```
Array, Date, Number, Object, String
```

toString()

Compatibility: NN4, NN6, NN7, IE4, IE5, IE5.5, IE6

This method converts the object's value to a string.

Syntax:

```
objectName.toString()
```

Example:

```
<button onclick="var myA = new Array(10,11,12,13,14,15);
alert(myA.toString());">TOSTRING</button>
<button onclick="var myDate = new Date(); alert(myDate.toString());">TOSTRING</button>
```

Applies to:

```
Array, Date, Number, Object
```

toUpperCase()

Compatibility: NN4, NN6, NN7, IE4, IE5, IE5.5, IE6

This method converts the String object's value to uppercase.

Syntax:

```
stringName.toUpperCase()
```

Example:

```
<button onclick="var myS = new String('Sample String');
alert(myS.toUpperCase());">TOUPPERCASE</button>
```

Applies to:

String

toUTCString()

Compatibility: NN4, NN6, NN7, IE4, IE5, IE5.5, IE6

This method uses UTC time to convert the Date object's value to a locale-specific format.

Syntax:

```
dateName.toUTCString()
```

Example:

```
<button onclick="var myDate = new Date();
alert(myDate.toUTCString());">TOUTCSTRING</button>
```

Applies to:

Date

unescape()

Compatibility: NN4, NN6, NN7, IE4, IE5, IE5.5, IE6

This method converts URL encoded text back to normal text.

Syntax:

```
unescape(param1)
```

param1   Required; a URL encoded string.

Example:

```
<button onclick="alert(escape('Hello World!'));">Escape function</button>
<button onclick="alert(unescape('Hello%20World%21'));">Unescape function</button>
```

Applies to: n/a.

unshift()

Compatibility: NN4, NN6, NN7, IE4, IE5, IE5.5, IE6

This method adds elements to the beginning of an Array object and returns the enlarged array.

Syntax:

```
arrayName.unshift(paramN, . . . ,paramN)
```

paramN   Required; the elements to be added.

Example:

```
<button onclick="var myA = new Array(10,11,12); myA.unshift(14);
alert(myA);">UNSHIFT</button>
```

Applies to:

```
Array
```

urns()

Compatibility: IE5, IE5.5, IE6

This method returns a collection containing all the elements that have the specified behavior attached. Returns null if no behavior has been found.

Syntax:

```
document.all.elementID.urns(param1)
collectionName.urns(param1)
```

param1   Required; the behavior's name.

Example:

```
<script language="JavaScript">
function B1() {
    var m = document.all.urns("clientCaps");
    if (m) {alert('YES');} else {alert("NO");}
}
</script>
<input type="button" value="Is there any 'clientCaps' behavior attached to this
page?" onClick="B1();">
```

Applies to:

```
all*, anchors*, applets*, areas*, boundElements*, cells*, childNodes*, children*,
elements*, embeds*, <form>, forms*, images*, links*, options*, rows*, scripts*,
<select>, styleSheets*, tBodies*
```

UTC()

Compatibility: NN7

This method uses UTC time to return the total number of milliseconds that have elapsed between January 1, 1970 and the specified date.

Syntax:

```
dateName.UTC(param1, param2, param3, param4, param5, param6, param7)
```

param1 Required; the four-digit year.

param2 Optional; the month. Value: 0 to 11.

param3 Optional; the day of the month. Value: 1 to 31.

param4 Optional; the hour. Value: 0 to 23.

param5 Optional; the minutes. Value: 0 to 59.

param6 Optional; the seconds. Value: 0 to 59.

param7 Optional; the number of milliseconds that have elapsed during the current second. Value: 0 to 999.

Example:

```
<button onclick="var myDate = new Date(); alert(Date.UTC(myDate));">UTC</button>
```

Applies to:

```
Date
```

valueOf()

Compatibility: NN4, NN6, NN7, IE4, IE5, IE5.5, IE6

This method converts the object's value to a string. There is virtually no difference between this method and the toString() method.
Syntax:

```
objectName.valueOf()
```

Example:

```
<button onclick="var myDate = new Date(); alert(myDate.valueOf());">VALUEOF</button>
```

Applies to:

```
Array, Date, Number, Object, String
```

write()

Compatibility: NN4, NN6, NN7, IE4, IE5, IE5.5, IE6

This method writes HTML document content.
Syntax:

```
document.write(param1)
```

param1 Required; the text and HTML tags to write.

Example:

```
<script language="JavaScript">
function B1() {
    var m = "<p style='color:red'>This is a sample text. First paragraph.</p>";
    m += "<p style='color:blue'>This is the second paragraph.</p>"
    document.write(m);
}
</script>
<input type="button" value="Add some HTML content to this page" onClick="B1();">
```

Applies to:

document

writeln()

Compatibility: NN4, NN6, NN7, IE4, IE5, IE5.5, IE6

This method writes HTML document content, followed by a carriage return.

Syntax:

```
document.writeln(param1)
```

param1 Required; the text and HTML tags to write.

Example:

```
<script language="JavaScript">
function B1() {
    var m = "<p style='color:red'>This is a sample text. First paragraph.</p>";
    m += "<p style='color:blue'>This is the second paragraph.</p>"
    document.writeln(m);
}
</script>
<input type="button" value="Add some HTML content to this page" onClick="B1();">
```

Applies to:

document

13

JAVASCRIPT COLLECTIONS

The collections listed in this chapter are those that JavaScript has predefined, and each is a read-only property of the HTML and other objects that contain them.

For each collection compatibility information is provided, along with a brief description, syntax information, parameter values (where applicable), a functional example, and an applies-to list identifying all of the HTML elements and JavaScript objects that the collection can be used with.

In order to distinguish between the HTML elements and JavaScript objects that appear in the applies-to lists, the following conventions have been used:

- Angle bracket tags (< and >) surround the names of HTML elements (for example, <html>).

- The names of JavaScript objects appear without adornment (window).

Each collection in this chapter also has a list of properties and methods that can be used with the collection. These properties and methods appear in lists that follow the collection headings, and each list heading has numbers inside parentheses that correspond to the chapters in which the properties and methods are covered in greater depth. The properties are listed by name (such as length), and the methods are listed by name followed by parentheses (such as example()). See Chapter 11 for more information on how to use the properties, and see Chapter 12 for more information on how to use the methods.

all

Compatibility: IE4, IE5, IE5.5, IE6

This collection returns an array of all the elements in the object.
   Syntax:

```
objectName.all // returns all elements
objectName.all(param1, param2) // returns an individual element
```

param1   Required; either the zero-based index of the desired member of the collection or the value of the desired member's id or name attribute.

param2   Optional; the zero-based index of the desired member of the collection returned when param1 matches the id or name value of more than one element.

Example:

```
<input type="button" id="button" value="See the value of this button"
onclick="alert(document.all('button').value);">
```

   Applies to:

```
<a>, <acronym>, <address>, <applet>, <area>, <b>, <base>, <basefont>, <bdo>,
<bgsound>, <big>, <blockquote>, <body>, <button>, <caption>, <center>, <cite>,
<code>, <col>, <colgroup>, <custom>, <dd>, <del>, <dfn>, <dir>, <div>, <dl>,
document, <dt>, <em>, <embed>, <fieldset>, <font>, <form>, <frame>, <frameset>,
<head>, <hn>, <hr>, <html>, <i>, <iframe>, <img>, <ins>, <kbd>, <label>, <legend>,
<li>, <link>, <listing>, <map>, <marquee>, <menu>, <object>, <ol>, <option>, <p>,
<pre>, <q>, <s>, <samp>, <script>, <select>, <small>, <span>, <strike>, <strong>,
<sub>, <sup>, <table>, <tbody>, <td>, <textarea>, <tfoot>, <th>, <thead>, <title>,
<tr>, <tt>, <u>, <ul>, <var>, <xmp>
```

   JavaScript properties (11) and JavaScript methods (12):

```
item(), length, namedItem(), tags(), urns()
```

anchors

Compatibility: NN4, NN6, NN7, IE4, IE5, IE5.5, IE6

This collection returns an array of all <a> elements in the document.

Syntax:

```
document.anchors // returns all anchors
document.anchors(param1, param2) // returns an individual anchor
```

param1 Required; either the zero-based index of the desired member of the collection or the value of the desired member's id or name attribute.

param2 Optional; the zero-based index of the desired member of the collection returned when param1 matches the id or name value of more than one element.

Example:

```
<a href="http://www.advocar.com/" id="advocar">Advocar</a>
<input type="button" value="Retrieve the number of anchors in this document"
onclick="alert(document.anchors.length);">
```

Applies to:

```
document
```

JavaScript properties (11) and JavaScript methods (12):

```
item(), length, namedItem(), tags(), urns()
```

applets

Compatibility: NN4, NN6, NN7, IE4, IE5, IE5.5, IE6

This collection returns an array of all <applet> elements in the document.
Syntax:

```
document.applets // returns all applets
document.applets(param1, param2) // returns an individual applet
```

param1 Required; either the zero-based index of the desired member of the collection or the value of the desired member's id or name attribute.

param2 Optional; the zero-based index of the desired member of the collection returned when param1 matches the id or name value of more than one element.

Example:

```
<!-- Body content with some applets -->
<input type="button" value="Retrieve the number of applets in this document"
onclick="alert(document.applets.length);"><br>
```

Applies to:

document

JavaScript properties (11) and JavaScript methods (12):

item(), length, namedItem(), tags(), urns()

areas

Compatibility: NN6, NN7, IE4, IE5, IE5.5, IE6

This collection returns an array of all <area> elements contained in a <map> element.

Syntax:

```
document.getElementById("mapID").areas // returns all areas
document.getElementById("mapID").areas(param1, param2) // returns an individual area
document.all.mapID.areas // IE only
document.all.mapID.areas(param1, param2) // IE only
```

param1   Required; either the zero-based index of the desired member of the collection or the value of the desired member's id or name attribute.

param2   Optional; the zero-based index of the desired member of the collection returned when param1 matches the id or name value of more than one element.

Example:

```
<html><head>
<script language="JavaScript">
function B1() {
var m = document.all.myMap2.areas.length;
alert("There are "+m+' areas within the map "myMap2"');
}
</script></head>
<body bgcolor="#FFFFFF" text="#000000" onload="B1();">
<p><img src="yourImage.gif" alt="" width="200" height="100" usemap="#myMap2">
<map name="myMap2">
<area id="area1" shape="rect" coords="0, 0, 100, 50" href="..." onClick="return
false">
<area id="area2" shape="rect" coords = "100, 0, 200, 50" href="..." onClick="return
false">
<area id="area3" shape="rect" coords =  "0, 50, 100, 100" href="..."
onClick="return false">
<area id="area4" shape="rect" coords = "0, 0, 0, 0" href="..." onClick="return
false">
</map></p>
</body></html>
```

Applies to:

`<map>`

JavaScript properties (11) and JavaScript methods (12):

`add()`, `item()`, `length`, `namedItem()`, `remove()`, `tags()`, `urns()`

---

attributes

Compatibility: NN6, NN7, IE5, IE5.5, IE6

This collection returns an array of all specified and unspecified attributes of an element.

Syntax:

```
document.getElementById("elementID").attributes // returns all attributes
document.getElementById("elementID").attributes(param1) // returns an individual
attribute
document.all.elementID.attributes // IE only
document.all.elementID.attributes(param1) // IE only
```

---

param1 Required; the zero-based index of the desired member of the collection.

Example:

```
<input type="button" value="Get the value of this button"
onclick="alert(this.attributes('value').value);">
```

Applies to:

`<a>`, `<acronym>`, `<address>`, `<applet>`, `<area>`, `<b>`, `<base>`, `<basefont>`, `<bdo>`, `<bgsound>`, `<big>`, `<blockquote>`, `<body>`, `<br>`, `<button>`, `<caption>`, `<center>`, `<cite>`, `<code>`, `<col>`, `<colgroup>`, `<comment>`, `<dd>`, `<del>`, `<dfn>`, `<dir>`, `<div>`, `<dl>`, `<dt>`, `<em>`, `<embed>`, `<fieldset>`, `<font>`, `<form>`, `<frame>`, `<frameset>`, `<head>`, `<hn>`, `<hr>`, `<html>`, `<i>`, `<iframe>`, `<img>`, `<input type="button">`, `<input type="checkbox">`, `<input type="file">`, `<input type="hidden">`, `<input type="image">`, `<input type="password">`, `<input type="radio">`, `<input type="reset">`, `<input type="submit">`, `<input type="text">`, `<ins>`, `<isindex>`, `<kbd>`, `<label>`, `<legend>`, `<li>`, `<link>`, `<listing>`, `<map>`, `<marquee>`, `<menu>`, `<meta>`, `<noframes>`, `<noscript>`, `<object>`, `<ol>`, `<optgroup>`, `<option>`, `<p>`, `<param>`, `<pre>`, `<q>`, `<s>`, `<samp>`, `<script>`, `<select>`, `<small>`, `<span>`, `<strike>`, `<strong>`, `<style>`, `<sub>`, `<sup>`, `<table>`, `<tbody>`, `<td>`, `<textarea>`, `<tfoot>`, `<th>`, `<thead>`, `<title>`, `<tr>`, `<tt>`, `<u>`, `<ul>`, `<var>`, `<xmp>`

JavaScript properties (11) and JavaScript methods (12):

`item()`, `length`, `getNamedItem()`, `removeNamedItem()`, `setNamedItem()`

---

behaviorUrns

Compatibility: IE5, IE5.5, IE6

This collection returns an array of all behaviors attached to the element.
Syntax:

```
document.all.elementID.behaviorUrns // returns all behaviors
document.all.elementID.behaviorUrns(param1) // returns an individual behavior
```

param1   Required; the zero-based index of the desired member of the collection.

Example:

```
<!-- Body content with some behaviors added to the page -->
<input type="button" value="Retrieve the number of behaviors in this document"
onclick="alert(this.behaviorUrns.length);">
```

Applies to:

```
<a>, <acronym>, <address>, <applet>, <area>, <b>, <base>, <basefont>, <bdo>,
<bgsound>, <big>, <blockquote>, <body>, <br>, <button>, <caption>, <center>,
<cite>, <code>, <col>, <colgroup>, <comment>, <custom>, <dd>, <del>, <dfn>, <dir>,
<div>, <dl>, <dt>, <em>, <embed>, <fieldset>, <font>, <form>, <frame>, <frameset>,
<head>, <hn>, <hr>, <html>, <i>, <iframe>, <img>, <input type="button">, <input
type="checkbox">, <input type="file">, <input type="hidden">, <input type="image">,
<input type="password">, <input type="radio">, <input type="reset">, <input
type="submit">, <input type="text">, <ins>, <isindex>, <kbd>, <label>, <legend>,
<li>, <link>, <listing>, <map>, <marquee>, <menu>, <nobr>, <noframes>, <noscript>,
<object>, <ol>, <option>, <p>, <pre>, <q>, <rt>, <ruby>, <s>, <samp>, <script>,
<select>, <small>, <span>, <strike>, <strong>, <style>, <sub>, <sup>, <table>,
<tbody>, <td>, <textarea>, <tfoot>, <th>, <thead>, <title>, <tr>, <tt>, <u>, <ul>,
<var>, <wbr>, <xml>, <xmp>
```

JavaScript properties (11) and JavaScript methods (12):

```
item(), length
```

blockFormats

Compatibility: IE5, IE5.5, IE6

This collection returns an array of all block formats available in the Dialog Helper object.

NOTE   *The* blockFormats *collection has the* Count *property instead of the common* length *property.*
The Count *property returns the number of available block format tags within the array.*
Its syntax is document.all.dialogHelperID.blockFormats.Count = *integer.*

Syntax:

```
dialogHelperName.blockFormats // returns all block formats
dialogHelperName.blockFormats(param1) // returns an individual block format
```

param1   Required; the zero-based index of the desired member of the collection.

Example:

```
<script language="JavaScript">
function B1(){
    alert('Number of blockformats: '+ myDhelper.blockFormats.count);
    var element = '';
    for (i = 1;i < myDhelper.blockFormats.Count;i++) {
        element = element + ', ' + myDhelper.blockFormats(i);
    }
    alert('The names are:\n' + element);
}
</script>
<object id="myDhelper" classid="clsid:3050f819-98b5-11cf-bb82-00aa00bdce0b"
width="0px" height="0px"></object>
<input type="button" value="Retrieve blockFormats" onclick="B1();">
```

Applies to:

```
Dialog Helper
```

JavaScript properties (11) and JavaScript methods (12):

```
Count, item()
```

boundElements

Compatibility: IE5, IE5.5, IE6

This collection returns an array of all elements bound to a data set. Only the following data-related events are affected: onAfterUpdate, onBeforeUpdate, onCellChange, onDataAvailable, onDatasetChanged, onDatasetComplete, onErrorUpdate, onRowEnter, onRowExit, onRowsDelete, and onRowsInserted.

Syntax:

```
event.boundElements // returns all bound elements
event.boundElements(param1, param2) // returns an individual bound element
```

param1   Required; either the zero-based index of the desired member of the collection or the value of the desired member's id or name attribute.

param2 Optional; the zero-based index of the desired member of the collection returned when param1 matches the id or name value of more than one element.

Example:

```
<html>
<head><title>Recordset Events</title>
<script language="javascript">
function rowEnter(){
myTable.rows[myData.recordset.AbsolutePosition].style.backgroundColor = 'yellow';}
function add(){myData.recordset.AddNew();}
function del(){if (myData.recordset.RecordCount > 0) myData.recordset.Delete();}
</script>
<script for="myTable" event="onreadystatechange">
    if (this.readyState == 'complete')
    {
    this.rows(myData.recordset.AbsolutePosition).style.backgroundColor = 'yellow';
    myData.onrowenter = rowEnter;
    }
</script>
<script for="myData" event="onrowexit">
    for (var i = 1; i <= myData.recordset.RecordCount; i++) {
        myTable.rows[i].style.backgroundColor = '';
    }
</script>
<script for="tableList" event="onclick">
    myData.recordset.AbsolutePosition = this.recordNumber;
    window.event.cancelBubble = true;
</script>
<script for="myData" event="oncellchange">alert(event.boundElements(0, 0).value);</
script>
</head>
<body>
<input id=cmdAdd type="button" value="ADD RECORD" onclick="add();">
<input id=cmdDelete type="BUTTON" value="DELETE" onclick="del();">
<object classid="clsid:333C7BC4-460F-11D0-BC04-0080C7055A83" id="myData">
    <param name ="DataURL" value="relatives.csv">
    <param name="UseHeader" value="True">
    <param name="TextQualifier" value="'">
</object>
<table>
<tr><td>First Name</td><tr><input id="firstname" type="text" datasrc="#myData"
datafld="firstname"></td></tr>
<tr><td>Last Name</td><td><input id="lastname" type="text" datasrc="#myData"
datafld="lastname"></td></td>
<tr><td>Year Born</td><td><input id="birth" type="text" datasrc=#myData
datafld="birth"></td></tr>
```

```
</table>
<table id="myTable" datasrc="#myData">
<thead><tr style="font-weight:bold"><td>First</td><td>Last</td><td>Age</td></tr>
</thead>
<tbody>
<tr id="tableList">
    <td><span datafld="firstname"></span></td>
    <td><span datafld="lastname"></span></td>
    <td><span datafld="birth"></span></td>
</tr>
</tbody>
</table>
</body>
</html>
```

Contents of relatives.csv:

```
firstname:string,lastname:string,birth:int
John,Smith,2003
Manny,Ramirez,1956
Troy,Belling,1956
```

Applies to:

event

JavaScript properties (11) and JavaScript methods (12):

item(), length, namedItem(), tags(), urns()

cells

Compatibility: IE4, IE5, IE5.5, IE6

This collection returns an array of all cells in a ‹table› or ‹tr› element.
Syntax:

```
document.all.elementID.cells // returns all cells
document.all.elementID.cells(param1, param2) // returns an individual cell
```

param1 Required; either the zero-based index of the desired member of
the collection or the value of the desired member's id or name attribute.

param2 Optional; the zero-based index of the desired member of the collection returned when param1 matches the id or name value of more than
one element.

Example:

```
<table id="myTable" border="1">
<tr id="myRow"><td>Cell 1</td><td>Cell 2</td></tr>
<tr><td>Cell 3</td><td>Cell 4</td></tr>
</table>
<button onclick="alert(myTable.cells.length);">Length of table</button>
<button onclick="alert(myRow.cells.length);">Length of row</button>
```

Applies to:

```
<table> (not IE4), <tr>
```

JavaScript properties (11) and JavaScript methods (12):

```
item(), length, namedItem(), tags(), urns()
```

childNodes

Compatibility: NN6, NN7, IE5, IE5.5, IE6

This collection returns an array of all first-generation nodes, including text nodes, of the object.

Syntax:

```
document.getElementById("elementID").childNodes // returns all child nodes
document.getElementById("elementID").childNodes(param1) // returns an individual
child node
document.all.elementID.childNodes // IE only
document.all.elementID.childNodes(param1) // IE only
```

param1   Required; the zero-based index of the desired member of the collection.

Example:

```
<html><head>
<script language="JavaScript">
function B1() {
    var m = document.all.myBody.childNodes;
    alert(m.length)
}
</script></head>
<body bgcolor="#FFFFFF" text="#000000" id="myBody">
<input id=myB type="button" value="How many child nodes have this body element?"
onclick="B1()">
</body></html>
```

Applies to:

<a>, attribute, <acronym>, <address>, <applet>, <area>, <b>, <base>, <basefont>,
<bdo>, <big>, <blockquote>, <body>, <br>, <button>, <caption>, <center>, <cite>,
<code>, <col>, <colgroup>, <comment>, <dd>, <del>, <dfn>, <dir>, <div>, <dl>,
document, <dt>, <em>, <embed>, <fieldset>, <font>, <form>, <frame>, <frameset>,
<head>, <hn>, <hr>, <html>, <i>, <iframe>, <img>, <ins>, <isindex>, <kbd>, <label>,
<legend>, <li>, <link>, <listing>, <map>, <marquee>, <menu>, <meta>, <noframes>,
<noscript>, <object>, <ol>, <optgroup>, <option>, <p>, <param>, <pre>, <q>, <s>,
<samp>, <script>, <select>, <small>, <span>, <strike>, <strong>, <style>, <sub>,
<sup>, <table>, <tbody>, <td>, <textarea>, <tfoot>, <th>, <thead>, <title>, <tr>,
<tt>, <u>, <ul>, <var>, <xmp>

JavaScript properties (11) and JavaScript methods (12):

item(), length, urns()

children

Compatibility: IE4, IE5, IE5.5, IE6

This collection returns an array of all first-generation elements of the element.
Syntax:

```
document.all.elementID.children // returns all child elements
document.all.elementID.children(param1, param2) // returns an individual child
element
```

param1   Required; either the zero-based index of the desired member of
the collection or the value of the desired member's id or name attribute.

param2   Optional; the zero-based index of the desired member of the col-
lection returned when param1 matches the id or name value of more than
one element.

Example:

```
<html><head>
<script language="JavaScript">
function B1() {
    var m = document.all.myBody.children;
    for (i=0; i<m.length; i++)
    alert(m.item(i).tagName);
}
</script></head>
<body id="myBody">
<input id=myB type="button" value="Direct descendants of this body element"
onclick="B1();">
</body></html>
```

Applies to:

`<a>`, `<acronym>`, `<address>`, `<applet>`, `<area>`, `<b>`, `<base>`, `<basefont>`, `<bdo>`, `<big>`, `<blockquote>`, `<body>`, `<button>`, `<caption>`, `<center>`, `<cite>`, `<code>`, `<col>`, `<colgroup>`, `<custom>`, `<dd>`, `<del>`, `<dfn>`, `<dir>`, `<div>`, `<dl>`, `<dt>`, `<em>`, `<embed>`, `<fieldset>`, `<font>`, `<form>`, `<frame>`, `<frameset>`, `<head>`, `<hn>`, `<hr>`, `<html>`, `<i>`, `<iframe>`, `<img>`, `<ins>`, `<kbd>`, `<label>`, `<legend>`, `<li>`, `<link>`, `<listing>`, `<map>`, `<marquee>`, `<menu>`, `<ol>`, `<option>`, `<p>`, `<pre>`, `<q>`, `<rt>`, `<ruby>`, `<s>`, `<samp>`, `<script>`, `<select>`, `<small>`, `<span>`, `<strike>`, `<strong>`, `<sub>`, `<sup>`, `<table>`, `<tbody>`, `<td>`, `<textarea>`, `<tfoot>`, `<thead>`, `<title>`, `<tr>`, `<tt>`, `<u>`, `<ul>`, `<var>`, `<xmp>`

JavaScript properties (11) and JavaScript methods (12):

`item()`, `length`, `tags()`, `urns()`

---

controlRange

Compatibility: IE5, IE5.5, IE6

This collection is an array of elements that can only be created in JavaScript using the `createControlRange()` and `createRange()` methods.

Syntax:

```
controlRangeName = document.body.createControlRange()
controlRangeName.memberName
```

Example:

```
<script>
function loadform(){
    var elem = document.createElement('<input id="test" type="text"
value="testing">')
    document.body.insertBefore(elem);
    var range = document.body.createControlRange();
    range.add(document.all.test);
    alert(range.item(0).value);
}
</script>
<body>
<button onclick="loadform();">Load Control Range on the page</button>
</body>
```

Applies to: n/a.

JavaScript properties (11) and JavaScript methods (12):

`add()`, `addElement()`, `execCommand()`, `item()`, `length`, `queryCommandEnabled()`, `queryCommandIndeterm()`, `queryCommandState()`, `queryCommandSupported()`, `queryCommandValue()`, `remove()`, `scrollIntoView()`, `select()`

---

elements

Compatibility: NN4, NN6, NN7, IE4, IE5, IE5.5, IE6

This collection returns an array of all <input> and <textarea> elements that are within the opening and closing tags of a <form> element. This collection does not includes <input> elements whose type attribute equals image.

Syntax:

```
document.getElementById("formID").elements // returns all form elements
document.getElementById("formID").elements(param1, param2) // returns an individual
form element
document.all.formID.elements // IE only
document.all.formID.elements(param1, param2) // IE only
```

param1 Required; either the zero-based index of the desired member of the collection or the value of the desired member's id or name attribute.

param2 Optional; the zero-based index of the desired member of the collection returned when param1 matches the id or name value of more than one element.

Example:

```
<script language="JavaScript">
function B1() {
    var m = document.all.myForm.elements(2);
    alert("It is a "+'"'+m.type+'"'+" element");
}
</script>
<form id="myForm" method="post" action="">
<input type="text">
<textarea></textarea>
<input type="checkbox" value="checkbox">
<select></select>
<input id="myB" type="button" value="What is the third element in the above form?"
onclick="B1();">
</form>
```

Applies to:

```
<form>
```

JavaScript properties (11) and JavaScript methods (12):

```
item(), length, namedItem(), tags(), urns()
```

embeds

Compatibility: NN4, NN6, NN7, IE4, IE5, IE5.5, IE6

This collection returns an array of all <embed> elements in a document.
Syntax:

```
document.embeds // returns all embed elements
document.embeds(param1, param2) // returns an individual embed element
```

param1   Required; either the zero-based index of the desired member of the collection or the value of the desired member's id or name attribute.

param2   Optional; the zero-based index of the desired member of the collection returned when param1 matches the id or name value of more than one element.

Example:

```
<!-- Body content with some embed objects -->
<input type="button" value="Retrieve the number of embeds in this document"
onclick="alert(document.embeds.length);">
```

Applies to:

```
document
```

JavaScript properties (11) and JavaScript methods (12):

```
item(), length, namedItem(), tags(), urns()
```

filters

Compatibility: IE4, IE5, IE5.5, IE6

This collection returns an array of all filters that have been added to the element.
Syntax:

```
document.all.elementID.filters // returns all filters
document.all.elementID.filters(param1) // returns an individual filter
```

param1   Required; either the zero-based index of the desired filter or the name of the filter being used.

Example:

```
<html><head>
<script language="JavaScript">
function applyFilter(){
myDiv.style.filter = "progid:DXImageTransform.Microsoft.shadow()
progid:DXImageTransform.Microsoft.motionblur();"
myDiv.filters.item('DXImageTransform.Microsoft.shadow').direction=4
myDiv.filters.item('DXImageTransform.Microsoft.shadow').color='red';
myDiv.filters.item('DXImageTransform.Microsoft.shadow').enabled=true;
```

```
myDiv.filters.item('DXImageTransform.Microsoft.motionblur').strength=12;
myDiv.filters.item('DXImageTransform.Microsoft.motionblur').enabled=true;
alert(document.all.myDiv.filters.length);
}
</script></head>
<body>
<img id="myDiv" src="yourimage.gif"><br><br><br><br>
<button onclick="applyFilter();">Apply Filter</button>
</body></html>
```

Applies to:

`<bdo>`, `<body>`, `<button>`, `<custom>`, `<div>`, `<fieldset>`, `<img>`, `<input type="button">`, `<input type="checkbox">`, `<input type="file">`, `<input type="image">`, `<input type="password">`, `<input type="radio">`, `<input type="reset">`, `<input type="submit">`, `<input type="text">`, `<marquee>`, `<rt>`, `<ruby>`, `<span>`, `<table>`, `<td>`, `<textarea>`, `<th>`

JavaScript properties (11) and JavaScript methods (12):

`item()`, `length`, `namedItem()`

fonts

Compatibility: IE5, IE5.5, IE6

This collection returns an array of system-supported fonts in the `Dialog Helper` object.

NOTE   *The* fonts *collection has the* Count *property instead of the common* length *property. The* Count *property returns the number of available fonts within the array. Its syntax is* document.all.*dialogHelperID*.fonts.Count = *integer*.

Syntax:

```
dialogHelperName.fonts // returns all fonts
dialogHelperName.fonts(param1) // returns an individual font
```

param1   Required; the zero-based index of the desired member of the collection.

Example:

```
<object id="myHelper" classid="clsid:3050f819-98b5-11cf-bb82-00aa00bdce0b"
width="0px" height="0px"></object>
<button onclick="alert(myHelper.fonts.Count);">Number of fonts in the system</button>
```

Applies to:

`Dialog Helper`

JavaScript properties (11) and JavaScript methods (12):

Count, item()

forms

Compatibility: NN4, NN6, NN7, IE4, IE5, IE5.5, IE6

This collection returns an array of all <form> elements in the document.
Syntax:

```
document.forms // returns all forms
document.forms(param1, param2) // returns an individual form
```

> **param1**   Required; either the zero-based index of the desired member of
> the collection or the value of the desired member's id or name attribute.
>
> **param2**   Optional; the zero-based index of the desired member of the col-
> lection returned when param1 matches the id or name value of more than
> one element.
>
> Example:

```
<html><body>
<form name="form1" method="post" action=""><textarea></textarea></form>
<form name="form2" method="post" action=""><p><input type="text"></p></form>
<form name="form3" method="post" action=""><input type="radio"><input
type="checkbox"></form>
<button onclick="alert(document.forms.length);">Number of forms in the page</button>
</body></html>
```

> Applies to:

document

> JavaScript properties (11) and JavaScript methods (12):

item(), length, namedItem(), tags(), urns()

frames

Compatibility: NN4, NN6, NN7, IE4, IE5, IE5.5, IE6

This collection returns an array of all <frame> elements in the object.
Syntax:

```
objectName.frames // returns all frames
objectName.frames(param1, param2) // returns an individual frame
```

param1 Required; either the zero-based index of the desired member of the collection or the value of the desired member's id or name attribute.

param2 Optional; the zero-based index of the desired member of the collection returned when param1 matches the id or name value of more than one element.

Example:

```
<html>
<frameset rows="*" cols="125,*" frameborder="yes" border="20px" framespacing="5">
    <frame name="leftFrame" scrolling="NO" noresize src="frame1.html">
  <frameset rows="200,*" border="15px" framespacing="0">
    <frame name="topFrame" noresize scrolling="NO" src="frame2.html">
    <frame name="mainFrame" src="frame3.html">
  </frameset>
</frameset>
</html>
```

Contents of frame2.html:

```
<html>
<script language="JavaScript">
var m = window.parent.frames.length;
alert(m);
</script>
<body bgcolor="white">
<h2>Frame 3</h2>
</body></html>
```

Applies to:

```
document, window
```

JavaScript properties (11) and JavaScript methods (12):

```
item(), length, namedItem()
```

images

Compatibility: NN4, NN6, NN7, IE4, IE5, IE5.5, IE6

This collection returns an array of all <img> elements in the document.
Syntax:

```
document.images // returns all images
document.images(param1, param2) // returns an individual image
```

param1   Required; either the zero-based index of the desired member of the collection or the value of the desired member's id or name attribute.

param2   Optional; the zero-based index of the desired member of the collection returned when param1 matches the id or name value of more than one element.

Example:

```
<img src="image1.jpg" width="100" height="100">
<img src="image2.jpg" width="100" height="100">
<img src="image3.jpg" width="100" height="100">
<button onclick="alert(document.images.length);">Number of images in the document</button>
```

Applies to:

```
document
```

JavaScript properties (11) and JavaScript methods (12):

```
item(), length, namedItem(), tags(), urns()
```

imports

Compatibility: IE4, IE5, IE5.5, IE6

This collection returns an array of all style sheets that have been linked to the page using the @import rule (see Chapter 8).

Syntax:

```
document.styleSheets(index).imports // returns all style sheets
document.styleSheets(index).imports(param1) // returns an individual style sheet
```

param1   Required; the zero-based index of the desired member of the collection.

Example:

```
<html>
<head><style type="text/css" id="myStyle">
@import "external.css";
@import "examples.css";
@import "heading.css";
</style></head>
<body bgcolor="#FFFFFF" text="#000000"><p>Body content.</p>
<script language="JavaScript">
alert(document.styleSheets(0).imports.length);
</script>
</body></html>
```

Applies to:

styleSheet

JavaScript properties (11) and JavaScript methods (12):

item(), length, namedItem()

links

Compatibility: NN4, NN6, NN7, IE4, IE5, IE5.5, IE6

This collection returns an array of all links in both the <a> and <area> elements in a document.

Syntax:

```
document.links // returns all links
document.links(param1) // returns an individual link
```

param1 Required; the zero-based index of the desired member of the collection.

Example:

```
<a href="http://www.advocar.com">Advocar.com website</a>
<button onclick="alert(document.links.length);">No. of links on page</button>
```

Applies to:

document

JavaScript properties (11) and JavaScript methods (12):

item(), length, namedItem(), tags(), urns()

mimeTypes

Compatibility: NN6, NN7

This collection returns an array of all mimeType objects.

Syntax:

```
navigator.mimeTypes  // returns all mimeTypes
navigator.mimeTypes[param1] // returns an individual mimeType
```

param1 Required; the zero-based index of the desired member of the collection.

Example:

```
<button onclick="alert(navigator.mimeTypes.length);">length</button>
```

Applies to:

```
navigator
```

JavaScript properties (11) and JavaScript methods (12):

```
item(), length
```

namespaces

Compatibility: IE5.5, IE6

This collection returns an array of all the `namespace` objects in the document.
  Syntax:

```
document.namespaces // returns all namespaces
document.namespaces(param1) // returns an individual namespace
```

param1 Required; the zero-based index of the desired member of the collection.

Example:

```
<html xmlns:namespace1 xmlns:namespace2>
<button onclick="alert(document.namespaces.length);">Number of namespaces on the
page</button>
```

Applies to:

```
document
```

JavaScript properties (11) and JavaScript methods (12):

```
add(), item(), length
```

options

Compatibility: NN4, NN6, NN7, IE4, IE5, IE5.5, IE6

This collection returns an array of all the `<option>` elements listed inside a `<select>`
element's opening and closing tags.

```
document.getElementById("selectID").options // returns all options
document.getElementById("selectID").options(param1, param2) // returns an
individual option
```

```
document.all.selectID.options // IE only
document.all.selectID.options(param1, param2) // IE only
```

param1 Required; either the zero-based index of the desired member of the collection or the value of the desired member's id or name attribute.

param2 Optional; the zero-based index of the desired member of the collection returned when param1 matches the id or name value of more than one element.

Example:

```
<select id="mySelect">
    <option>List Item 1</option>
    <option>List Item 2</option>
    <option>List Item 3</option>
</select>
<button onclick="alert(mySelect.options.length);">Number of options in the select
list</button>
```

Applies to:

```
<select>
```

JavaScript properties (11) and JavaScript methods (12):

```
add(), item(), length, namedItem(), remove(), tags(), urns()
```

pages

Compatibility: IE5.5, IE6

This collection returns an array of all style sheets that make use of the @page rule (see Chapter 8).

Syntax:

```
document.styleSheets(index).pages // returns all @page rules
document.styleSheets(index).pages(param1) // returns an individual @page rule
```

param1 Required; the zero-based index of the desired member of the collection.

Example:

```
<html>
<head><style type="text/css" id="myStyle">
@page:first {font-family:Times New Roman; font-size:18pt; color:blue;}
@page:left {font-family: Verdana; font-size: 14pt;}
@page:right {font-family: Verdana; font-size: 14pt;}
</style></head>
```

```
<body>Body content.
<script language="JavaScript">
var m = document.styleSheets(0).pages.length; alert(m);
</script>
</body></html>
```

Applies to:

```
styleSheet
```

JavaScript properties (11) and JavaScript methods (12):

```
item(), length
```

plugins (1)

Compatibility: NN4, NN6, NN7, IE4, IE5, IE5.5, IE6

This collection returns an array of all `<embed>` elements in a page. The `plugins` and embeds collections return the exact same elements.

Syntax:

```
objectName.plugins // returns all embed elements
objectName.plugins(param1) // returns an individual embed element
```

param1   Required; the zero-based index of the desired member of the collection.

Example: See the embeds collection example, and replace `embeds` with `plugins`. Applies to:

```
document (NN4, NN6, NN7), clientInformation, navigator (IE4, IE5, IE5.5, IE6)
```

JavaScript properties (11) and JavaScript methods (12):

```
item(), length, namedItem(), refresh(), tags()
```

plugins (2)

Compatibility: NN4, NN6, NN7

This collection returns an array of all `plugin` objects available to the navigator object.

Syntax:

```
navigator.plugins // returns all plugins
navigator.plugins[param1] // returns an individual plugin
```

param1   Required; the zero-based index of the desired member of the collection.

Example:

```
<button onclick="alert(navigator.plugins.length);">length</button>
<button onclick="alert(navigator.plugins[0].description);">mimetype</button>
<button onclick="alert(navigator. plugins[0].filename);">suffixes</button>
<button onclick="alert(navigator.plugins[0].name);">type</button>
```

Applies to:

```
navigator
```

JavaScript properties (11) and JavaScript methods (12):

```
item(), length
```

rows

Compatibility: NN6, NN7, IE4, IE5, IE5.5, IE6

This collection returns an array of all the rows in a `<table>` element.
Syntax:

```
document.getElementById("elementID").rows // returns all rows
document.getElementById("elementID").rows(param1, param2) // returns an individual row
document.all.elementID.rows // IE only
document.all.elementID.rows(param1, param2) // IE only
```

param1   Required; either the zero-based index of the desired member of the collection or the value of the desired member's `id` or `name` attribute.

param2   Optional; the zero-based index of the desired member of the collection returned when param1 matches the `id` or `name` value of more than one element.

Example:

```
<html><body>
<table id=myT width="16%" border="1">
<tr><td>Row 1</td></tr>
<tr><td>Row 2</td></tr>
<tr><td>Row 3</td></tr>
</table>
<script language="JavaScript">
var m = document.getElementById("myT").rows.length;
alert(m);
</script>
</body></html>
```

Applies to:

```
<table>, <tbody>, <tfoot>, <thead>
```

JavaScript properties (11) and JavaScript methods (12):

```
deleteRow(), item(), insertRow(), length, namedItem(), tags(), urns()
```

rules

Compatibility: IE4, IE5, IE5.5, IE6

This collection returns an array of all style sheets that make use of the @rule rule (see Chapter 8).

Syntax:

```
document.styleSheets(index).rules // returns all rules
document.styleSheets(index).rules(param1) // returns an individual rule
```

param1 Required; the zero-based index of the desired member of the collection.

Example:

```
<html><head>
<style type="text/css" id="myStyle">
.rule1 { font-family:Times New Roman; font-size:18pt; color:blue; }
.rule2 { font-family:Verdana; color:red; }
</style></head>
<body>
<button onclick="alert(document.styleSheets(0).rules.length);">Get number of
rules</button>
```

Applies to:

```
styleSheet
```

JavaScript properties (11) and JavaScript methods (12):

```
item(), length
```

scripts

Compatibility: IE4, IE5, IE5.5, IE6

This collection returns an array of all <script> elements in a document.

Syntax:

```
document.scripts // returns all scripts
document.scripts(param1, param2) // returns an individual script
```

param1   Required; either the zero-based index of the desired member of the collection or the value of the desired member's id or name attribute.

param2   Optional; the zero-based index of the desired member of the collection returned when param1 matches the id or name value of more than one element.

Example:

```
<button onclick="getTotal();">Get total script tags</button>
<script language="JavaScript">
function getTotal() {var m = document.scripts.length; alert(m);}
</script>
<script language="JavaScript"></script>
```

Applies to:

```
document
```

JavaScript properties (11) and JavaScript methods (12):

```
item(), length, namedItem(), tags(), urns()
```

styleSheets

Compatibility: NN6, NN7, IE4, IE5, IE5.5, IE6

This collection returns an array of all the style sheets that have been created in the document using the <link> and <style> elements.
    Syntax:

```
document.styleSheets // returns all style sheets
document.styleSheets(param1, param2) // returns an individual style sheet
```

param1   Required; either the zero-based index of the desired member of the collection or the value of the desired member's id or name attribute.

param2   Optional; the zero-based index of the desired member of the collection returned when param1 matches the id or name value of more than one element.

Example:

```
<html><head>
<style type="text/css">
.rule1 { font-family:Times New Roman; font-size:18pt; color:blue; }
</style>
<style type="text/css">
.rule2 { font-family:Verdana; color:red; }
</style></head>
```

```
<body>
<button onclick="fn1();">Get total style sheets in this document.</button>
<script language="JavaScript">
function fn1() {var m = document.styleSheets.length; alert(m);}
</script>
</body></html>
```

Applies to:

document

JavaScript properties (11) and JavaScript methods (12):

item(), length, namedItem(), urns()

tBodies

Compatibility: NN6, NN7, IE4, IE5, IE5.5, IE6

This collection returns an array of all <tbody> elements in a table, both specified and implied.

Syntax:

```
document.getElementById("tableID").tBodies // returns all tbodies
document.getElementById("tableID").tBodies(param1, param2) // returns an individual
tbody
document.all.tableID.tbodies // IE only
document.all.tableID.tbodies(param1, param2) // IE only
```

param1 Required; either the zero-based index of the desired member of the collection or the value of the desired member's id or name attribute.

param2 Optional; the zero-based index of the desired member of the collection returned when param1 matches the id or name value of more than one element.

Example:

```
<html><body>
<table id="myT" width="16%" border="1">
<tbody>
<tr><td>Row 1</td></tr>
<tr><td>Row 2</td></tr>
<tr><td>Row 3</td></tr>
</tbody>
<tbody>
<tr><td>Row 4</td></tr>
<tr><td>Row 5</td></tr>
<tr><td>Row 6</td></tr>
</tbody>
```

```
</table>
<button onclick="fn();">Get total number of tbody elements</button>
<script language="JavaScript">
function fn() {
var m = document.getElementById("myT").tBodies.length; alert(m);
}
</script>
</body></html>
```

Applies to:

`<table>`

JavaScript properties (11) and JavaScript methods (12):

`item(), length, namedItem(), tags(), urns()`

14

JAVASCRIPT OBJECTS

The objects described in this chapter are not HTML elements and do not pertain to the HTML hierarchy tree. For each object listed in this chapter, compatibility information is provided, along with a brief description, syntax information, a functional example, and an applies-to list identifying all of the HTML elements, JavaScript collections, and JavaScript objects that the object can be used with.

In order to distinguish between the HTML elements, JavaScript collections, and JavaScript objects that appear in the applies-to lists, the following conventions have been used:

- Angle bracket tags (< and >) surround the names of HTML elements (for example, <html>).
- An asterisk follows the names of JavaScript collections (areas*).
- The names of JavaScript objects appear without adornment (window).

In addition, many of the objects in this chapter have events, styles, filters, properties, methods, collections, and objects of their own. These different categories of object members appear in lists that follow the object headings, and each list has a number inside parentheses that corresponds to the chapter in which the object members are covered in greater depth. For more information on any particular object member, look up the member of interest in the relevant chapter. See Chapter 7 for events, Chapter 8 for CSS attributes and JavaScript style properties, Chapter 10 for filters, Chapter 11 for JavaScript properties, Chapter 12 for JavaScript methods, and Chapter 13 for JavaScript collections.

There are two other details related to the content of this chapter that you should be aware of. First, not every object has events, styles, filters, properties, methods, and collections of its own. When one of these categories does not pertain to an object, no list for that category will appear under the object's heading. For example, the Array object does not have any collections, so there is no collections list in the Array object section.

Second, it is important to note that the CSS attribute and JavaScript style property lists contain property names that are written using CSS syntax. To convert CSS syntax (which is not case sensitive) to JavaScript syntax (which is case sensitive), simply remove the dashes and capitalize the first letter of all words other than the first word. For example, the CSS style property text-underline-position would be written in JavaScript as textUnderlinePosition.

Array

Compatibility: NN4, NN6, NN7, IE4, IE5, IE5.5, IE6

This object allows you to create and store information into an array.

Syntax:

```
var arrayName = new Array()
arrayName.memberName
```

Example:

```
<script language="javascript">
function myFunction(){
    var array = new Array();
    array[0] = 'Testing 1';
    array[1] = 'Testing 2';
    alert(array.length);
}
</script>
<button onclick="myFunction();">Array length</button>
```

Applies to: n/a.

JavaScript properties (11):

---

constructor, length

JavaScript methods (12):

---

concat, join, pop, push, reverse, shift, slice, sort, splice, toSource, toString, unshift, valueOf

---

attribute

Compatibility: NN6, NN7, IE5, IE5.5, IE6

This object contains information about an attribute of an element. You can only access the attribute object by referencing the desired index in the attributes collection.

Syntax:

---

document.all.*elementID*.attributes(*index*).*memberName*

Example:

```
<input type="button" value="Get the value of this button"
onclick="alert(this.attributes('value').value);">
```

Applies to:

---

attributes*

JavaScript properties (11):

---

expando, firstChild, lastChild, name, nextSibling, nodeName, nodeType, nodeValue, ownerDocument, parentNode, previousSibling, specified, value

---

JavaScript methods (12):

---

appendChild, cloneNode, hasChildNodes, insertBefore, removeChild, replaceChild

---

JavaScript collections (13):

---

childNodes

Boolean

Compatibility: NN4, NN6, NN7, IE4, IE5, IE5.5, IE6

This object is equivalent to a Boolean type variable.

Syntax:

```
var booleanName = new Boolean(value) // value is true or false
booleanName.memberName
```

Example:

```
<script language="javascript">
function myFunction(){var bool = new Boolean(true); alert(bool);}
</script>
<button onclick="myFunction();">True or false</button>
```

Applies to: n/a.
JavaScript properties (11):

```
constructor
```

clientInformation

Compatibility: IE4, IE5, IE5.5, IE6

This object has a set of properties that provide information about the user's browser, computer, and operating system.
Syntax:

```
window.clientInformation.memberName
```

Example:

```
<button onclick="alert(window.clientInformation.appName);">Browser name</button>
<button onclick="alert(window.clientInformation.appVersion);">Browser version</button>
```

Applies to:

```
window
```

JavaScript properties (11):

```
appCodeName, appMinorVersion, appName, appVersion, browserLanguage, cookieEnabled,
cpuClass, onLine, platform, systemLanguage, userAgent, userLanguage
```

JavaScript methods (12):

```
javaEnabled, taintEnabled
```

JavaScript collections (13):

```
plugins
```

JavaScript objects (14):

userProfile

clipboardData

Compatibility: IE5, IE5.5, IE6

This object allows data to be transferred to and from the clipboard. Its methods, clearData(), getData(), and setData(), perform the actions cut, copy, and paste, respectively.

Syntax:

window.clipboardData.*memberName*

Example:

```
<button onclick="window.clipboardData.setData('text', 'This is sample text');">Copy
sample text to clipboard</button>
<button onclick="alert(window.clipboardData.getData('text'));">Display data copied
to clipboard</button>
```

Applies to:

window

JavaScript methods (12):

clearData, getData, setData

currentStyle

Compatibility: IE5, IE5.5, IE6

This object returns all the styles applied to an element. It differs from the style object in that the style object only returns the styles that have been applied to the element inline.

Syntax:

document.all.*elementID*.currentStyle.*memberName*

Example:

```
<html>
<head><style>
td {background-color:red; font-family:verdana; font-size:12pt; font-weight:bold;
color:white; width:100%}
</style></head>
<body>
```

```
<table><tr><td width="1100" id="myCell">content</td></tr></table>
<button onclick="alert(myCell.currentStyle.width);">Width of the table</button>
</body></html>
```

Applies to:

`<a>`, `<acronym>`, `<address>`, `<applet>`, `<b>`, `<bdo>`, `<big>`, `<blockquote>`, `<body>`, `<br>`, `<button>`, `<caption>`, `<center>`, `<cite>`, `<code>`, `<col>`, `<colgroup>`, `<custom>`, `<dd>`, `<del>`, `<dfn>`, `<dir>`, `<div>`, `<dl>`, `<dt>`, `<em>`, `<embed>`, `<fieldset>`, `<font>`, `<form>`, `<hn>`, `<hr>`, `<html>`, `<i>`, `<img>`, `<input type="button">`, `<input type="checkbox">`, `<input type="file">`, `<input type="image">`, `<input type="password">`, `<input type="radio">`, `<input type="reset">`, `<input type="submit">`, `<input type="text">`, `<ins>`, `<isindex>`, `<kbd>`, `<label>`, `<legend>`, `<li>`, `<listing>`, `<marquee>`, `<menu>`, `<nobr>`, `<object>`, `<ol>`, `<option>`, `<p>`, `<pre>`, `<q>`, `<s>`, `<samp>`, `<select>`, `<small>`, `<span>`, `<strike>`, `<strong>`, `<sub>`, `<sup>`, `<table>`, `<tbody>`, `<td>`, `<textarea>`, `<tfoot>`, `<th>`, `<thead>`, `<tr>`, `<tt>`, `<u>`, `<ul>`, `<var>`, `<wbr>`, `<xmp>`

CSS attributes and JavaScript style properties (8):

NOTE *The names are in CSS syntax. See the introduction to this chapter for the JavaScript syntax rules. Names noted with an asterisk (*) are JavaScript properties only.*

accelerator, background, background-attachment, background-color, background-image, background-position, background-position-x, background-position-y, background-repeat, behavior, border, border-bottom, border-bottom-color, border-bottom-style, border-bottom-width, border-color, border-left, border-left-color, border-left-style, border-left-width, border-right, border-right-color, border-right-style, border-right-width, border-style, border-top, border-top-color, border-top-style, border-top-width, border-width, color, cursor, direction, display, filter, font, font-family, font-size, font-style, font-variant, font-weight, hasLayout(*), layout-grid, layout-grid-char, layout-grid-line, layout-grid-mode, layout-grid-type, letter-spacing, line-break, line-height, margin, margin-bottom, margin-left, margin-right, margin-top, overflow, overflow-x, overflow-y, padding, padding-bottom, padding-left, padding-right, padding-top, page-break-after, page-break-before, pixelBottom(*), pixelHeight(*), pixelLeft(*), pixelRight(*), pixelTop(*), pixelWidth(*), posBottom(*), posHeight(*), posLeft(*), posRight(*), posTop(*), posWidth(*), scrollbar-3dlight-color, scrollbar-arrow-color, scrollbar-base-color, scrollbar-darkshadow-color, scrollbar-face-color, scrollbar-highlight-color, scrollbar-shadow-color, scrollbar-track-color, text-align, text-align-last, text-autospace, text-decoration, text-indent, text-justify, text-kashida-space, text-overflow, text-transform, text-underline-position, textDecorationBlink(*), textDecorationLineThrough(*), textDecorationNone(*), textDecorationOverline(*), textDecorationUnderline(*), unicode-bidi, visibility, white-space, word-break, word-spacing, word-wrap, zoom

JavaScript properties (11):

blockDirection, clipBottom, clipLeft, clipRight, clipTop, hasLayout, onOffBehavior

JavaScript methods (12):

getAttribute, getExpression, setAttribute, setExpression

dataTransfer

Compatibility: IE5, IE5.5, IE6

This object provides access to clipboard data formats. It is used in drag-and-drop operations.

Syntax:

```
event.dataTransfer.memberName
```

Example:

```
<html><head>
<script language="JavaScript">
function transferDrop() {
    window.event.srcElement.innerText = window.event.dataTransfer.getData("text");
    window.event.returnValue = false;
}
function transferDrag() {
    window.event.dataTransfer.dropEffect = 'move';
    window.event.returnValue = false;
}
</script></head>
<body bgcolor="#FFFFFF" text="#000000" bottommargin="150">
<p id="mySource" ondragstart="window.event.dataTransfer.effectAllowed =
'move';">Highlight text in this paragraph and drag it to the text area below</p>
<textarea id="myTarget" ondrop="transferDrop();"
ondragover="window.event.returnValue = false;" ondragenter="transferDrag();">
</textarea>
</body></html>
```

Applies to:

```
event
```

JavaScript properties (11):

```
dropEffect, effectAllowed
```

JavaScript methods (12):

```
clearData, getData, setData
```

Date

Compatibility: NN4, NN6, NN7, IE4, IE5, IE5.5, IE6

This object allows you to perform date computations.

Syntax:

```
var dateName = new Date(value) // value is empty or a date string
dateName.memberName
```

Example:

```
<script language="javascript">
function myFunction(){var date = new Date(); alert(date.toString());}
</script>
<button onclick="myFunction();">Today's date</button>
```

Applies to: n/a.
JavaScript properties (11):

```
constructor
```

JavaScript methods (12):

```
getDate, getDay, getFullYear, getHours, getMilliseconds, getMinutes, getMonth,
getSeconds, getTime, getTimezoneOffset, getUTCDate, getUTCDay, getUTCFullYear,
getUTCHours, getUTCMilliseconds, getUTCMinutes, getUTCMonth, getUTCSeconds,
getYear, parse, setDate, setFullYear, setHours, setMilliseconds, setMinutes,
setMonth, setSeconds, setTime, setUTCDate, setUTCFullYear, setUTCHour,
setUTCMilliseconds, setUTCMinutes, setUTCMonth, setUTCSeconds, setYear,
toGMTString, toLocaleString, toSource, toString, valueOf
```

defaults

Compatibility: IE5.5, IE6

This object establishes the default properties of an element's behavior. To set default properties for an element, you must use an HTML component (HTC).
Syntax:

```
defaults.memberName
```

Example:

```
<html xmlns:yourNs>
<head><?import namespace="yourNs" implementation="yourHTC.htc"></head>
<body><div style= "color:red; font-size:20pt; font-Style:italic; border:2px solid blue">
<br>Sample text in the main document<br>
<yourNs:yourTagName></yourNs:yourTagName>
</div>
</body></html>
```

Contents of yourHTC.htc:

```
<public:component tagName="yourTagName">
<attach event="oncontentready" onevent=contentReady() />
</public:component>
<script language="JavaScript">
function contentReady(){
defaults.viewLink = document;
defaults.viewInheritStyle = false;
defaults.viewMasterTab = false;
}
function inheritStyle() {
boolInherit = defaults.viewInheritStyle;
defaults.viewInheritStyle = true;
}
</script>
<body>
<div id="extDiv" style="font-size:20pt; font-weight:bold; border:3px solid
green">Imported Document Text</div><br>
<button onclick="inheritStyle();">Set Inheritance to True</button>
</body>
```

Applies to: n/a.
Event handlers (7):

---

onBeforeEditFocus

CSS attributes and JavaScript style properties (8):

NOTE *The names are in CSS syntax. See the introduction to this chapter for the JavaScript syntax rules. Names noted with an asterisk (*) are JavaScript properties only.*

---

accelerator, background, background-attachment, background-color, background-image, background-position, background-position-x, background-position-y, background-repeat, behavior, border, border-bottom, border-bottom-color, border-bottom-style, border-bottom-width, border-color, border-left, border-left-color, border-left-style, border-left-width, border-right, border-right-color, border-right-style, border-right-width, border-style, border-top, border-top-color, border-top-style, border-top-width, border-width, color, cursor, direction, display, filter, font, font-family, font-size, font-style, font-variant, font-weight, hasLayout(*), layout-grid, layout-grid-char, layout-grid-line, layout-grid-mode, layout-grid-type, letter-spacing, line-break, line-height, margin, margin-bottom, margin-left, margin-right, margin-top, overflow, overflow-x, overflow-y, padding, padding-bottom, padding-left, padding-right, padding-top, page-break-after, page-break-before, pixelBottom(*), pixelHeight(*), pixelLeft(*), pixelRight(*), pixelTop(*), pixelWidth(*), posBottom(*), posHeight(*), posLeft(*), posRight(*), posTop(*), posWidth(*), scrollbar-3dlight-color, scrollbar-arrow-color, scrollbar-base-color, scrollbar-darkshadow-color, scrollbar-face-color, scrollbar-highlight-color, scrollbar-shadow-color, scrollbar-track-color, text-align, text-align-last, text-autospace, text-decoration, text-indent, text-justify, text-kashida-space, text-

---

overflow, text-transform, text-underline-position, textDecorationBlink(*), textDecorationLineThrough(*), textDecorationNone(*), textDecorationOverline(*), textDecorationUnderline(*), unicode-bidi, visibility, white-space, word-break, word-spacing, word-wrap, zoom

JavaScript properties (11):

blockDirection, canHaveHTML, contentEditable, disabled, isMultiline, tabStop, viewInheritStyle, viewLink, viewMasterTab, vLink

JavaScript objects (14):

style

Dialog Helper

Compatibility: IE5.5, IE6

This object provides access to the color dialog box. You can create this object using the ‹object› element, and you can reference it in JavaScript through its id attribute value.

Syntax:

document.all.*dialogHelperID*.*memberName*

Example:

```
<object id="myDhelper" classid="clsid:3050f819-98b5-11cf-bb82-00aa00bdce0b"></object>
<button onclick="myDhelper.chooseColorDlg();">Show color dialog</button>
```

Applies to: n/a.
JavaScript methods (12):

chooseColorDlg, getCharset

JavaScript collections (13):

blockFormats, fonts

document

Compatibility: NN4, NN6, NN7, IE4, IE5, IE5.5, IE6

This object provides access to all the objects in a page.

Syntax:

objectName.document.*memberName*

Example:

```
<title>document object example</title>
<button onclick="alert(document.title);">Document title</button>
```

Applies to:

`<custom>`, popup, window

Event handlers (7):

onActivate, onBeforeActivate, onBeforeCut, onBeforeDeactivate, onBeforeEditFocus, onBeforePaste, onClick, onContextMenu, onControlSelect, onCut, onDblClick, onDeactivate, onDrag, onDragEnd, onDragEnter, onDragLeave, onDragOver, onDragStart, onDrop, onFocusIn, onFocusOut, onHelp, onKeyDown, onKeyPress, onKeyUp, onMouseDown, onMouseMove, onMouseOut, onMouseOver, onMouseUp, onMouseWheel, onMove, onMoveEnd, onMoveStart, onPaste, onPropertyChange, onReadyStateChange, onResizeEnd, onResizeStart, onSelectionChange, onStop

JavaScript properties (11):

activeElement, alinkColor, bgColor, charset, compatMode, cookie, defaultCharset, designMode, dir, doctype, documentElement, domain, encoding, expando, fgColor, fileCreatedDate, fileModifiedDate, fileSize, height, lastModified, linkColor, parentWindow, protocol, readyState, referrer, title, uniqueID, URL, URLUnencoded, vlinkColor, width, XMLDocument

JavaScript methods (12):

attachEvent, close, createAttribute, createComment, createDocumentFragment, createElement, createEventObject, createStyleSheet, createTextNode, detachEvent, elementFromPoint, execCommand, focus, getElementById, getElementsByName, getElementsByTagName, hasFocus, open, queryCommandEnabled, queryCommandIndeterm, queryCommandState, queryCommandSupported, queryCommandValue, recalc, releaseCapture, setActive, write, writeln

JavaScript collections (13):

all, anchors, applets, childNodes, embeds, forms, frames, images, links, namespaces, plugins, scripts, styleSheets

JavaScript objects (14):

`<body>`, implementation, location, selection, `<title>`

event

Compatibility: NN4, NN6, NN7, IE4, IE5, IE5.5, IE6

This object is created each time an event is fired with a set of properties that correspond to the fired event.

Syntax:

```
window.event.memberName
```

Example:

```
<button style="position:absolute; left:10; top:10;" onclick="alert(event.x);">The x
coordinate of your pointer when you click this button is!</button>
```

Applies to:

```
window
```

JavaScript properties (11):

```
altKey, altLeft, button, cancelBubble, clientX, clientY, contentOverflow, ctrlKey,
ctrlLeft, dataFld, fromElement, height, keyCode, layerX, layerY, nextPage, offsetX,
offsetY, pageX, pageY, propertyName, qualifier, reason, recordset, repeat,
returnValue, saveType, screenX, screenY, shiftKey, shiftLeft, srcElement,
srcFilter, srcUrn, target, toElement, type, wheelDelta, width, x, y
```

JavaScript collections (13):

```
boundElements
```

JavaScript objects (14):

```
dataTransfer
```

---

external

Compatibility: IE4, IE5, IE5.5, IE6

This object provides access to the browser components when the browser window
is a component in another application.

Syntax:

```
window.external.memberName
```

Example:

```
<script language = "JavaScript">
var yourWindow = window.external.menuArguments;
var theDocument = yourWindow.document;
</script>
```

NOTE *The preceding example requires that you place the browser as a component in your VB or
C++ application.*

Applies to:

```
window
```

JavaScript properties (11):

```
menuArguments
```

JavaScript methods (12):

```
addChannel, addDesktopComponent, addFavorite, autoCompleteSaveForm, autoScan,
importExportFavorites, isSubscribed, navigateAndFind, showBrowserUI
```

history

Compatibility: NN4, NN6, NN7, IE4, IE5, IE5.5, IE6

This object allows you to navigate through web pages that have previously been visited.

Syntax:

```
window.history.memberName
```

Example:

```
<html><head>
<script language="JavaScript">
function B1(){history.back(1);}
</script></head>
<body><input id="myButton" type="button" onclick="B1();" value="Go back 1 step in
the history list">
</body></html>
```

Applies to:

```
window
```

JavaScript properties (11):

```
length
```

JavaScript methods (12):

```
back, forward, go
```

implementation

Compatibility: IE6

This object contains a method that reveals information about the DOM features that are implemented by the document object.

Syntax:

```
document.implementation.memberName
```

Example:

```
<html><head>
<script language="JavaScript">
function b1() {
  var m = document.implementation.hasFeature("HTML");
  alert("Implementation value: "+m);
}
</script></head>
<body bgcolor="#FFFFFF" text="#000000">
<input type="button" value="Click here" onClick="b1();">
</body></html>
```

Applies to:

```
document
```

JavaScript methods (12):

```
hasFeature
```

location

Compatibility: NN4, NN6, NN7, IE4, IE5, IE5.5, IE6

This object contains a set of properties that reveal basic information about the current site being visited in the browser.

Syntax:

```
objectName.location.memberName
```

Example:

```
<table id="myT"><tr><td>Row 1</td></tr><tr><td>Row 2</td></tr><tr><td>Row 3</td>
</tr></table>
<button onclick="myT.style.fontWeight = 'bold';">Bold</button>
<button onclick="location.reload();">Reload page</button>
```

Applies to:

```
document, window
```

JavaScript properties (11):

hash, host, hostname, href, pathname, port, protocol, search

JavaScript methods (12):

assign, reload, replace

Math

Compatibility: NN4, NN6, NN7, IE4, IE5, IE5.5, IE6

This object allows you to perform mathematical operations.
Syntax:

Math.*memberName*

Example:

```
<script language="javascript">
function myFunction(){alert(Math.max(2, 4));}
</script>
<button onclick="myFunction();">Math function returns greater of 2 numbers (2 or
4)</button>
```

Applies to: n/a.
JavaScript properties (11):

constructor, E, LN10, LN2, lOG10E, lOG2E, PI, SQRT1_2, SQRT2

JavaScript methods (12):

abs, acos, asin, atan, atan2, ceil, cos, exp, floor, log, max, min, pow, random,
round, sin, sqrt, tan

mimeType

Compatibility: NN4, NN6, NN7

This object contains a set of properties that provide information about the MIME
type in the navigator object's mimeTypes array.
Syntax:

navigator.mimeTypes[*index*].*memberName*

Example:

```
<button onclick="alert(navigator.mimeTypes[0].description);">mimetype</button>
<button onclick="alert(navigator.mimeTypes[0].suffixes);">suffixes</button>
<button onclick="alert(navigator.mimeTypes[0].type);">type</button>
```

Applies to:

```
mimeTypes*
```

JavaScript properties (11):

```
description, suffixes, type
```

namespace

Compatibility: IE5.5, IE6

This object allows you to embed an element's behavior into the document. You can only access the namespace object by referencing the desired index in the namespaces collection.

Syntax:

```
document.namespaces(index).memberName
```

Example:

```
<html xmlns:namespace1 xmlns:namespace2>
<button onclick="alert(document.namespaces(0).name);">Name of first namespace on
the page</button>
```

Applies to:

```
namespaces*
```

Event handlers (7):

```
onReadyStateChange
```

JavaScript properties (11):

```
name, readyState, urn
```

JavaScript methods (12):

```
attachEvent, detachEvent, doImport
```

navigator

Compatibility: NN4, NN6, NN7, IE4, IE5, IE5.5, IE6

This object contains properties and methods that provide information about the browser and the system.

Syntax:

```
window.navigator.memberName
```

Example:

```
<html><head>
<script language="JavaScript">
function B1() {
var m = navigator.appName;
alert("The name of your browser is "+'"'+m+'"');}
</script></head>
<body bgcolor="#FFFFFF" text="#000000">
<input type="button" value="Click here" onClick="B1();">
</body></html>
```

Applies to:

```
window
```

JavaScript properties (11):

```
appCodeName, appMinorVersion, appName, appVersion, browserLanguage, cookieEnabled,
cpuClass, language, onLine, platform, systemLanguage, userAgent, userLanguage
```

JavaScript methods (12):

```
javaEnabled, taintEnabled
```

JavaScript collections (13):

```
mimeTypes, plugins
```

JavaScript objects (14):

```
userProfile
```

Number

Compatibility: NN4, NN6, NN7, IE4, IE5, IE5.5, IE6

This object allows you to perform numerical operations.

Syntax:

```
var numberName = new Number(value) // value is any number
numberName.memberName
```

Example:

```
<script language="javascript">
function myFunction(){
    var number = new Number(23003.340304);
    alert(number.toFixed(2));
}
</script>
<button onclick="myFunction();">Round the number</button>
```

Applies to: n/a.
JavaScript properties (11):

```
constructor, MAX_VALUE, MIN_VALUE, NEGATIVE_INFINITE, POSITIVE_INFINITE
```

JavaScript methods (12):

```
toExponential, toFixed, toLocaleString, toPrecision, toString, toSource, valueOf
```

Object

Compatibility: NN4, NN6, NN7, IE4, IE5, IE5.5, IE6

This object provides the basic building blocks for creating customized objects. To create a custom object, use the following steps:

1. Using the new keyword, instantiate the object into a variable.

```
var myObject = new Object();
```

2. Add each property to the object by choosing a property name and assigning a value to it.

```
myObject.firstName = 'John'
```

3. Add each method to the object by choosing a method name and assigning a function to it.

```
myObject.age = B1;
```

Syntax:

```
var objectName = new Object()
objectName.memberName
```

Example:

```
<script language="javascript">
function Object(firstName, lastName){
```

```
     this.firstName = firstName;
     this.lastName = lastName;
}
function B1(){
     myObject.age = B3;
     alert(myObject.age());
}
function B2(){
     myObject.favoriteColor = 'Blue';
     alert(myObject.favoriteColor);
}
function B3(){return 34;}
var myObject = new Object('John', 'Smith');
</script>
<button onclick="B2();">Add Property</button>
<button onclick="B1();">Add Method</button>
<button onclick="alert(myObject.constructor);">Constructor</button>
<button onclick="alert(myObject.isPrototypeOf(myObject));">PrototypeOf</button>
<button onclick="alert(myObject.hasOwnProperty('lastName'));">HasProperty</button>
```

Applies to: n/a.

JavaScript properties (11):

constructor

JavaScript methods (12):

isPrototypeOf, hasOwnProperty, toLocaleString, toSource, toString, valueOf

page

Compatibility: IE5.5, IE6

This object provides access to an @page rule. You can access the page object only by referencing the desired index in the pages collection.

Syntax:

document.styleSheets(*index1*).pages(*index2*).*memberName*

Example:

```
<html><head>
<style>@page:first { background-color: blue; }</style>
<script language="JavaScript">
function B1() {
var m = document.styleSheets(0).pages(0);
var n = m.pseudoClass;
alert(n);}
</script></head>
```

```
<body bgcolor="#FFFFFF" text="#000000">
<input type="button" value="Click here for the name of the first @page rule"
onclick="B1();">
</body></html>
```

Applies to:

pages*

JavaScript properties (11):

pseudoClass, readOnly, selector, selectorText

plugin

Compatibility: NN4, NN6, NN7

This object contains a set of properties that provide information about the
plugins installed in the browser.

Syntax:

navigator.plugins[*index*].*memberName*

Example:

```
<button onclick="alert(navigator.plugins[0].description);">mimetype</button>
<button onclick="alert(navigator. plugins[0].filename);">suffixes</button>
<button onclick="alert(navigator.plugins[0].name);">type</button>
```

Applies to:

plugins*

JavaScript properties (11):

description, filename, name

popup

Compatibility: IE5.5, IE6

This object provides you with the ability to display customized HTML code in a
tooltip or pop-up area on the page.

Syntax:

popup.*memberName*

Example:

```
<script language="JavaScript">
var popup = window.createPopup();
popup.document.body.innerHTML = 'This button will navigate to another site!';
popup.document.body.style.backgroundColor = 'yellow';
</script>
<input type="button" onClick="location.href='http://www.advocar.com/';"
onmouseover="popup.show(100, 100, 200, 100, document.body);"
onmouseout="popup.hide();" value="Navigate to another site">
```

Applies to: n/a.
JavaScript properties (11):

isOpen

JavaScript methods (12):

hide, show

JavaScript objects (14):

document

rule

Compatibility: IE4, IE5, IE5.5, IE6

This object contains a set of properties and methods that affect a specific rule in a style sheet. You can only access the rule object by referencing the desired index in the rules collection.

Syntax:

```
document.styleSheets(index1).rules(index2).memberName
```

Example:

```
<html><head>
<style>
#myP { font-family:verdana, arial; font-weight:bold; font-size:16px; }
</style>
<script language="JavaScript">
function B1() {
var myRule = document.styleSheets(0).rules(0);
var n = myRule.selectorText;
alert(n);
}
</script></head>
```

```
<body bgcolor="#FFFFFF" text="#000000">
<p id="myP">This is the text with a specific style rule applied.</p>
<input type="button" value="Click here to view the styleSheet selector"
onclick="B1();">
</body></html>
```

Applies to:

rules*

JavaScript properties (11):

readOnly, selectorText

JavaScript objects (14):

style

runtimeStyle

Compatibility: IE5, IE5.5, IE6

This object allows you to specify a style that will override any other style defined for the specified element.

Syntax:

document.all.*elementID*.runtimeStyle.*memberName*

Example:

```
<div id="myDiv" style="width:100; height:100;"></div>
<button onclick="myDiv.runtimeStyle.backgroundColor = 'blue';">Change div color</
button>
```

Applies to:

```
<a>, <acronym>, <address>, <applet>, <b>, <big>, <blockquote>, <body>, <br>,
<button>, <caption>, <center>, <cite>, <code>, <col>, <colgroup>, <custom>, <dd>,
<del>, <dfn>, <dir>, <div>, <dl>, <dt>, <em>, <embed>, <fieldset>, <font>, <form>,
<frame>, <frameset>, <hn>, <hr>, <html>, <i>, <iframe>, <img>, <input
type="button">, <input type="checkbox">, <input type="file">, <input
type="hidden">, <input type="image">, <input type="password">, <input
type="radio">, <input type="reset">, <input type="submit">, <input type="text">,
<ins>, <kbd>, <label>, <legend>, <li>, <listing>, <marquee>, <menu>, <nobr>,
<object>, <ol>, <option>, <p>, <pre>, <q>, <s>, <samp>, <select>, <small>, <span>,
<strike>, <strong>, <sub>, <sup>, <table>, <tbody>, <td>, <textarea>, <tfoot>,
<th>, <thead>, <tr>, <tt>, <u>, <ul>, <var>, <xmp>
```

CSS attributes and JavaScript style properties (8):

NOTE *The names are in CSS syntax. See the introduction to this chapter for the JavaScript syntax rules. Names noted with an asterisk (*) are JavaScript properties only.*

accelerator, background, background-attachment, background-color, background-image, background-position, background-position-x, background-position-y, background-repeat, behavior, border, border-bottom, border-bottom-color, border-bottom-style, border-bottom-width, border-color, border-left, border-left-color, border-left-style, border-left-width, border-right, border-right-color, border-right-style, border-right-width, border-style, border-top, border-top-color, border-top-style, border-top-width, border-width, color, cursor, direction, display, filter, font, font-family, font-size, font-style, font-variant, font-weight, hasLayout(*), layout-grid, layout-grid-char, layout-grid-line, layout-grid-mode, layout-grid-type, letter-spacing, line-break, line-height, margin, margin-bottom, margin-left, margin-right, margin-top, overflow, overflow-x, overflow-y, padding, padding-bottom, padding-left, padding-right, padding-top, page-break-after, page-break-before, pixelBottom(*), pixelHeight(*), pixelLeft(*), pixelRight(*), pixelTop(*), pixelWidth(*), posBottom(*), posHeight(*), posLeft(*), posRight(*), posTop(*), posWidth(*), scrollbar-3dlight-color, scrollbar-arrow-color, scrollbar-base-color, scrollbar-darkshadow-color, scrollbar-face-color, scrollbar-highlight-color, scrollbar-shadow-color, scrollbar-track-color, text-align, text-align-last, text-autospace, text-decoration, text-indent, text-justify, text-kashida-space, text-overflow, text-transform, text-underline-position, textDecorationBlink(*), textDecorationLineThrough(*), textDecorationNone(*), textDecorationOverline(*), textDecorationUnderline(*), unicode-bidi, visibility, white-space, word-break, word-spacing, word-wrap, zoom

Microsoft filters (10):

Alpha, Barn, BasicImage, BlendTrans, Blinds, Blur, CheckerBoard, Chroma, Compositor, DropShadow, Emboss, Engrave, Fade, FlipH, FlipV, Glow, GradientWipe, Gray, ICMFilter, Inset, Invert, Iris, Light, MaskFilter, Matrix, MotionBlur, Pixelate, RadialWipe, RandomBars, RandomDissolve, RevealTrans, Shadow, Slide, Spiral, Stretch, Strips, Wave, Wheel, Xray, Zigzag

JavaScript properties (11):

cssText, onOffBehavior

JavaScript methods (12):

getAttribute, getExpression, removeAttribute, removeExpression, setAttribute, setExpression

screen

Compatibility: NN4, NN6, NN7, IE4, IE5, IE5.5, IE6

This object contains a set of properties that will provide you with information regarding the computer screen.

Syntax:

```
window.screen.memberName
```

Example:

```
<button onclick="alert(screen.width + 'x' + screen.height);">Screen resolution</
button>
```

Applies to:

```
window
```

JavaScript properties (11):

```
availHeight, availLeft, availTop, availWidth, bufferDepth, colorDepth, deviceXDPI,
deviceYDPI, fontSmoothingEnabled, height, logicalXDPI, logicalYDPI, updateInterval,
width
```

selection

Compatibility: IE4, IE5, IE5.5, IE6

This object represents an area in the document that has been highlighted by the user.

Syntax:

```
document.selection.memberName
```

Example:

```
<body onclick="alert(document.selection.type);">
<p>Select this text</p></body>
```

Applies to:

```
document
```

Event handlers (7):

```
onTimeError
```

JavaScript properties (11):

```
type, typeDetail
```

JavaScript methods (12):

```
clear, createRange, empty
```

String

Compatibility: NN4, NN6, NN7, IE4, IE5, IE5.5, IE6

This object allows you to manipulate a string.

Syntax:

```
var stringName = new String('value') // value is any string
stringName.memberName
```

Example:

```
<div id="myDiv" style="width:100; height:100;">This is some sample text</div>
<script language="javascript">
function myFunction(){
    var temp = new String(); temp = myDiv.innerText; alert(temp);
}
</script>
<button onclick="myFunction();">String function</button>
```

Applies to: n/a.
JavaScript properties (11):

```
constructor, length
```

JavaScript methods (12):

```
anchor, big, blink, bold, charAt, charCodeAt, concat, fixed, fontColor, fontSize,
fromCharCode, indexOf, italics, lastIndexOf, link, localeCompare, match, replace,
search, slice, small, split, strike, sub, substr, substring, sup,
toLocaleLowerCase, toLocaleUpperCase, toLowerCase, toSource, toUpperCase, valueOf
```

style

Compatibility: NN4, NN6, NN7, IE4, IE5, IE5.5, IE6

This object represents the current style sheet settings for a given element.
Syntax:

```
document.all.elementID.style.memberName
```

Example:

```
<div id="myDiv" style="width:100; height:100;"></div>
<button onclick="myDiv.style.backgroundColor = 'blue';">Change color</button>
```

Applies to:

```
<a>, <acronym>, <address>, <applet>, <b>, <big>, <blockquote>, <body>, <br>,
<button>, <caption>, <center>, <cite>, <code>, <col>, <colgroup>, <custom>, <dd>,
defaults, <del>, <dfn>, <dir>, <div>, <dl>, <dt>, <em>, <embed>, <fieldset>,
```

`<font>`, `<form>`, `<frame>`, `<frameset>`, `<hn>`, `<hr>`, `<html>`, `<i>`, `<iframe>`, `<img>`, `<input type="button">`, `<input type="checkbox">`, `<input type="file">`, `<input type="hidden">`, `<input type="image">`, `<input type="password">`, `<input type="radio">`, `<input type="reset">`, `<input type="submit">`, `<input type="text">`, `<ins>`, `<kbd>`, `<label>`, `<legend>`, `<li>`, `<listing>`, `<marquee>`, `<menu>`, `<nobr>`, `<object>`, `<ol>`, `<option>`, `<p>`, `<pre>`, `<q>`, rule, `<s>`, `<samp>`, `<select>`, `<small>`, `<span>`, `<strike>`, `<strong>`, `<sub>`, `<sup>`, `<table>`, `<tbody>`, `<td>`, `<textarea>`, `<tfoot>`, `<th>`, `<thead>`, `<tr>`, `<tt>`, `<u>`, `<ul>`, `<var>`, `<xmp>`

CSS attributes and JavaScript style properties (8):

NOTE *The names are in CSS syntax. See the introduction to this chapter for the JavaScript syntax rules. Names noted with an asterisk (*) are JavaScript properties only.*

accelerator, background, background-attachment, background-color, background-image, background-position, background-position-x, background-position-y, background-repeat, behavior, border, border-bottom, border-bottom-color, border-bottom-style, border-bottom-width, border-color, border-left, border-left-color, border-left-style, border-left-width, border-right, border-right-color, border-right-style, border-right-width, border-style, border-top, border-top-color, border-top-style, border-top-width, border-width, color, cursor, direction, display, filter, font, font-family, font-size, font-style, font-variant, font-weight, hasLayout(*), layout-grid, layout-grid-char, layout-grid-line, layout-grid-mode, layout-grid-type, letter-spacing, line-break, line-height, margin, margin-bottom, margin-left, margin-right, margin-top, overflow, overflow-x, overflow-y, padding, padding-bottom, padding-left, padding-right, padding-top, page-break-after, page-break-before, pixelBottom(*), pixelHeight(*), pixelLeft(*), pixelRight(*), pixelTop(*), pixelWidth(*), posBottom(*), posHeight(*), posLeft(*), posRight(*), posTop(*), posWidth(*), scrollbar-3dlight-color, scrollbar-arrow-color, scrollbar-base-color, scrollbar-darkshadow-color, scrollbar-face-color, scrollbar-highlight-color, scrollbar-shadow-color, scrollbar-track-color, text-align, text-align-last, text-autospace, text-decoration, text-indent, text-justify, text-kashida-space, text-overflow, text-transform, text-underline-position, textDecorationBlink(*), textDecorationLineThrough(*), textDecorationNone(*), textDecorationOverline(*), textDecorationUnderline(*), unicode-bidi, visibility, white-space, word-break, word-spacing, word-wrap, zoom

Microsoft filters (10):

Alpha, Barn, BasicImage, BlendTrans, Blinds, Blur, CheckerBoard, Chroma, Compositor, DropShadow, Emboss, Engrave, Fade, FlipH, FlipV, Glow, GradientWipe, Gray, ICMFilter, Inset, Invert, Iris, Light, MaskFilter, Matrix, MotionBlur, Pixelate, RadialWipe, RandomBars, RandomDissolve, RevealTrans, Shadow, Slide, Spiral, Stretch, Strips, Wave, Wheel, Xray, Zigzag

JavaScript properties (11):

cssText, onOffBehavior

JavaScript methods (12):

getAttribute, getAttributeNode, getExpression, normalize, removeAttribute, removeAttributeNode, removeExpression, setAttribute, setAttributeNode, setExpression

styleSheet

Compatibility: IE4, IE5, IE5.5, IE6

This object represents a single style sheet declaration in the document, and it is only accessible through the styleSheets collection.

Syntax:

```
document.styleSheets(index).memberName
```

Example:

```
<style>body {background-color: white;}</style>
<button onclick="document.styleSheets(0).rules(0).style.backgroundColor =
'blue';">Change color</button>
```

Applies to:

```
styleSheets*
```

CSS attributes and JavaScript style properties (8):

NOTE *The names are in CSS syntax. See the introduction to this chapter for the JavaScript syntax rules.*

```
text-autospace
```

JavaScript properties (11):

```
canHaveHTML, cssRules, cssText, disabled, href, id, isContentEditable, isDisabled,
isMultiline, media, owningElement, parentStyleSheet, readOnly, title, type
```

JavaScript methods (12):

```
addImport, addPageRule, addRule, fireEvent, removeRule
```

JavaScript collections (13):

```
imports, pages, rules
```

TextNode

Compatibility: IE5, IE5.5, IE6

This object provides access to a text node in the document that is created using the createTextNode() method.

Syntax:

```
textNodeName = document.createTextNode("value")
textNodeName.memberName
```

Example:

```
<html><head>
<script>
function replaceText(){
    var myTextNode = document.createTextNode("Text was replaced");
    var newTN = replaceMe.firstChild.replaceNode(myTextNode);
}
</script></head>
<p id="replaceMe">This is some text that will be replaced</p>
<button onclick="replaceText();">Replace text</button>
</body></html>
```

Applies to: n/a.
JavaScript properties (11):

```
data, length, nextSibling, nodeName, nodeType, nodeValue, parentNode, previousSibling
```

JavaScript methods (12):

```
appendData, deleteData, insertData, replaceData, splitText, substringData
```

TextRange

Compatibility: IE4, IE5, IE5.5, IE6

This object provides access to a chunk of text that is created using the createRange() and createTextRange() methods.

Syntax:

```
textRangeName = document.all.elementID.createTextRange()
textRangeName = document.selection.createRange()
textNameRange.memberName
```

Example:

```
<html><head>
<script language="javascript">
function displayText(){
    textRange = document.all.myBody.createTextRange();
    textRange.moveToElementText(myP);
    var m = textRange.text;
    alert(m);
}
</script></head>
<body id="myBody">
<p id="myP">This is some text in the document inside a p element</p>
<button onclick="displayText();">Display the text range</button>
</body></html>
```

Applies to: n/a.
JavaScript properties (11):

---

boundingHeight, boundingLeft, boundingTop, boundingWidth, htmlText, offsetLeft,
offsetTop, text

JavaScript methods (12):

---

collapse, compareEndPoints, duplicate, execCommand, expand, findText, getBookmark,
getBoundingClientRect, getClientRects, inRange, isEqual, move, moveEnd, moveStart,
moveToBookmark, moveToElementText, moveToPoint, parentElement, pasteHTML,
queryCommandEnabled, queryCommandIndeterm, queryCommandState,
queryCommandSupported, queryCommandValue, scrollIntoView, select, setEndPoint

---

TextRectangle

Compatibility: IE5, IE5.5, IE6

This object provides access to the container rectangle of the text in any
document element. To create this object, you must use the getClientRects()
or getBoundingClientRect() method.
  Syntax:

```
textRectangleName = document.all.elementID.getClientRects()
textRectangleName = document.all.elementID.getBoundingClientRect()
textRectangleName.memberName
```

Example:

```
<html><head>
<script language="JavaScript">
function B1(elem) {
var m = elem.getBoundingClientRect();
alert('Left: '+ m.left +'\nRight: '+ m.right +'\nTop: '+m.top+'\nBottom:
'+m.bottom);
}
</script></head>
<body><div onClick="B1(this);" style="background-color:black; color:white;
width:300; height:100;">Click here to display the TextRectangle properties</div>
</body></html>
```

Applies to: n/a.
JavaScript properties (11):

---

bottom, left, right, top

---

userProfile

Compatibility: IE4, IE5, IE5.5, IE6

This object provides access to information in the user's profile. However, access to the user profile is difficult to obtain because of system permissions and Internet connection settings.

Syntax:

```
navigator.userProfile.memberName
```

Example:

```
<html><head>
<script language="JavaScript">
function B1() {
navigator.userProfile.addReadRequest("vCard.DisplayName");
navigator.userProfile.doReadRequest(1, "Desk Reference");
alert(navigator.userProfile.getAttribute("vcard.DisplayName"));
navigator.userProfile.clearRequest();
}
</script></head>
<body><button onclick="B1();">Click here</button>
</body></html>
```

Applies to:

```
navigator, clientInformation
```

JavaScript methods (12):

```
addReadRequest, clearRequest, doReadRequest, getAttribute, setAttribute
```

window

Compatibility: NN4, NN6, NN7, IE4, IE5, IE5.5, IE6

This object provides access to a browser window. If a web page contains frames, then each frame will correspond to its own window object.

Syntax:

```
window.memberName
```

Example:

```
<button onclick="window.navigate('http://www.advocar.com');">Go to Advocar page</button>
```

Applies to: n/a.
Event handlers (7):

```
onActivate, onAfterPrint, onBeforeDeactivate, onBeforePrint, onBeforeUnload,
onBlur, onControlSelect, onDeactivate, onError, onFocus, onHelp, onLoad, onMove,
onMoveEnd, onMoveStart, onResize, onResizeEnd, onResizeStart, onScroll, onUnload
```

JavaScript properties (11):

---

closed, defaultStatus, dialogArguments, dialogHeight, dialogLeft, dialogTop, dialogWidth, frameElement, length, name, offscreenBuffering, opener, parent, returnValue, screenLeft, screenTop, self, status, top

---

JavaScript methods (12):

---

alert, attachEvent, back, blur, clearInterval, clearTimeout, close, confirm, createPopup, detachEvent, execScript, focus, forward, moveBy, moveTo, navigate, open, print, prompt, resizeBy, resizeTo, scroll, scrollBy, scrollTo, setActive, setInterval, setTimeout, showHelp, showModalDialog, showModelessDialog

---

JavaScript collections (13):

---

frames

JavaScript objects (14):

---

clientInformation, clipboardData, document, event, external, history, location, navigator, screen

---

15

HTML+TIME MICROSOFT TECHNOLOGY

The HTML+TIME (Timed Interactive Multimedia Extensions) Microsoft technology was first introduced in Internet Explorer 5.0, and it is not compatible with any browsers other than Internet Explorer. When other browsers encounter an HTML element with an attached HTML+TIME behavior, they ignore the behavior and render the element normally.

HTML+TIME is essentially a Microsoft behavior. In Internet Explorer versions 5.0 and later, HTML+TIME adds timing and media synchronization support to HTML pages, meaning that you can now use HTML to quickly and easily create multimedia-rich interactive presentations with little or no scripting. There are two versions of this technology:

HTML+TIME 1.0 The first version was only made available through XML documents, while HTML and DHTML document implementation was not supported. The first version was compatible with Internet Explorer 5.0, and it was accessed using the time behavior.

HTML+TIME 2.0 This version was made available not only to XML documents, but to HTML and DHTML documents as well. Version 2.0 is compatible with Internet Explorer 5.5 and later, and it is accessed using the time2 behavior. The syntax throughout this chapter is based on the time2 behavior.

With special HTML+TIME HTML elements and attributes, you can specify when an element appears on a page, how long it remains displayed, and how the surrounding HTML elements are affected. For example, you can specify if and when a sound file should start playing, when it should stop, and how many times it should repeat.

Using this Microsoft technology, HTML elements can also be grouped together, allowing a single timing effect to act on all the elements in the group, either simultaneously or sequentially.

The following steps will allow you to add an HTML+TIME behavior to an HTML page:

1. Create the XML namespace :t by declaring it inside the HTML tag, as follows:

```
<html xmlns:t="urn:schemas-microsoft-com:time">
```

2. Introduce the HTML+TIME behavior of interest in one of two ways. Either introduce it as an inline style attribute of the element that is to be affected by the behavior, as follows:

```
<element style="behavior:url(#default#time2)">
```

Or introduce the behavior in a style sheet and then reference the class in the class attribute of the element that is to be affected by the behavior, as follows:

```
<style>.time{behavior:url(#default#time2);}</style>
<element class="time">
```

3. Establish t: as the namespace, and import the time2 behavior into the namespace as follows:

```
<?import namespace="t" implementation="#default#time2">
```

4. Specify the beginning and ending times for the behavior. This is accomplished by specifying the begin and end attributes in the affected element.

5. (Optional.) Specify an action to take while the element is active on the timeline by adding the desired attribute.

6. (Optional.) If you want to be able to access the created HTML+TIME element in JavaScript, you must expose the element by setting its id attribute using the following syntax:

```
<t:element id="stringID"/>
```

Organization of This Chapter

As stated in the introduction to Part II of this book, this chapter contains all of the information related to the HTML+TIME technology. Rather than distributing all of the HTML+TIME-related HTML elements, HTML attributes, events, JavaScript properties, JavaScript methods, JavaScript collections, and JavaScript objects throughout Chapters 5, 6, 7, 11, 12, 13, and 14, respectively, all of this information is organized here in one place.

However, in the interest of consistency, the sections in this chapter are organized in the same order as the reference chapters listed above. Therefore, you will encounter HTML+TIME-compatible HTML elements first, followed by the compatible HTML attributes (and JavaScript properties, because they are related), events, JavaScript methods, JavaScript collections, and JavaScript objects.

HTML Elements

All of the HTML+TIME HTML elements are listed here in the same manner that the non-HTML+TIME HTML elements are listed in Chapter 5. For each element, you will find a compatibility listing, a description, a syntax listing, and an example, followed by lists of the compatible HTML+TIME HTML attributes, events, JavaScript properties, JavaScript methods, JavaScript collections, and JavaScript objects.

<t:animate/>

Compatibility: IE5.5, IE6

This element animates the attribute specified by attributeName of the element specified by targetElement. The animated attribute must have an initial value when the <t:animate/> element is loaded.

Syntax:

```
<t:animate attributes events/>
```

Example:

```
<html xmlns:t="urn:schemas-microsoft-com:time">
<head><?import namespace="t" implementation="#default#time2"></head>
<body><div id="myDiv" style="position:absolute; top:50px; left:100px; width:200px;
height:100px; background-color:blue"></div>
```

```
<t:animate targetElement="myDiv" attributeName="top" by="200" begin="2" dur="5"
accelerate="1.0"/>
</body></html>
```

HTML attributes:

accelerate, accumulate, additive, attributename, autoreverse, begin, by, calcmode,
decelerate, dur, end, fill, from, keysplines, keytimes, repeatcount, repeatdur,
restart, speed, systembitrate, systemcaptions, systemlanguage,
systemoverduborsubtitle, targetelement, timecontainer, to, values

Event handlers:

onBegin, onEnd, onPause, onRepeat, onReset, onResume, onReverse

JavaScript properties:

accelerate, accumulate, additive, attributeName, autoReverse, begin, by, calcMode,
decelerate, dur, end, fill, from, hasMedia, keySplines, keyTimes, repeatCount,
repeatDur, restart, speed, targetElement, timeContainer, timeParent, to, values

JavaScript methods:

activeTimeToParentTime, activeTimeToSegmentTime, beginElement, beginElementAt,
documentTimeToParentTime, endElement, endElementAt, parentTimeToActiveTime,
parentTimeToDocumentTime, pauseElement, resetElement, resumeElement,
seekActiveTime, seekSegmentTime, seekTo, seekToFrame, segmentTimeToActiveTime,
segmentTimeToSimpleTime, simpleTimeToSegmentTime

JavaScript objects:

currTimeState

<t:animatecolor/>

Compatibility: IE5.5, IE6

This element animates the color of the attribute specified by attributeName of the
element specified by targetElement. The animated color attribute must have an
initial value when the <t:animatecolor/> element is loaded.

Syntax:

```
<t:animatecolor attributes events/>
```

Example:

```
<html xmlns:t="urn:schemas-microsoft-com:time">
<head><?import namespace="t" implementation="#default#time2"></head>
<body><div id="myDiv" style="width:200px; height:100px; background-color:blue;"></div>
<t:animatecolor targetElement="myDiv" attributeName="backgroundColor"
```

```
to="tan" begin="1" dur="3" fill="hold"/>
</body></html>
```

HTML attributes:

accelerate, accumulate, additive, attributename, autoreverse, begin, by, calcmode, decelerate, dur, end, fill, from, keysplines, keytimes, repeatcount, repeatdur, restart, speed, systembitrate, systemcaptions, systemlanguage, systemoverduborsubtitle, targetelement, timecontainer, to, values

Event handlers:

onBegin, onEnd, onPause, onRepeat, onReset, onResume, onReverse

JavaScript properties:

accelerate, accumulate, additive, attributeName, autoReverse, begin, by, calcMode, decelerate, dur, end, fill, from, hasMedia, keySplines, keyTimes, repeatCount, repeatDur, restart, speed, targetElement, timeContainer, timeParent, to, values

JavaScript methods:

activeTimeToParentTime, activeTimeToSegmentTime, beginElement, beginElementAt, documentTimeToParentTime, endElement, endElementAt, parentTimeToActiveTime, parentTimeToDocumentTime, pauseElement, resetElement, resumeElement, seekActiveTime, seekSegmentTime, seekTo, seekToFrame, segmentTimeToActiveTime, segmentTimeToSimpleTime, simpleTimeToSegmentTime

JavaScript objects:

currTimeState

<t:animatemotion/>

Compatibility: IE5.5, IE6

This element animates the position of the element specified by targetElement.

Syntax:

```
<t:animatemotion attributes events/>
```

Example:

```
<html xmlns:t="urn:schemas-microsoft-com:time">
<head><?import namespace="t" implementation="#default#time2"></head>
<body><div id="myDiv" style="position:absolute; top:100px; left:100px; width:200px;
height:50px; background-color:red"></div>
<t:animatemotion targetElement="myDiv" to="150,200" begin="3" dur="5" fill="hold"
calcMode="linear"/>
</body></html>
```

HTML attributes:

accelerate, accumulate, additive, autoreverse, begin, by, calcmode, decelerate,
dur, end, fill, from, keysplines, keytimes, origin, path, repeatcount, repeatdur,
restart, speed, systembitrate, systemcaptions, systemlanguage,
systemoverduborsubtitle, targetelement, timecontainer, to, values

Event handlers:

onBegin, onEnd, onPause, onRepeat, onReset, onResume, onReverse

JavaScript properties:

accelerate, accumulate, additive, autoReverse, begin, by, calcMode, decelerate,
dur, end, fill, from, hasMedia, keySplines, keyTimes, origin, path, repeatCount,
repeatDur, restart, speed, targetElement, timeContainer, timeParent, to, values

JavaScript methods:

activeTimeToParentTime, activeTimeToSegmentTime, beginElement, beginElementAt,
documentTimeToParentTime, endElement, endElementAt, parentTimeToActiveTime,
parentTimeToDocumentTime, pauseElement, resetElement, resumeElement,
seekActiveTime, seekSegmentTime, seekTo, seekToFrame, segmentTimeToActiveTime,
segmentTimeToSimpleTime, simpleTimeToSegmentTime

JavaScript objects:

currTimeState

<t:animation> . . . </t:animation>

Compatibility: IE5.5, IE6

This element provides better control over the playback of animated GIF images.
Syntax:

<t:animation *attributes events*> . . . </t:animation>

Example:

```
<html xmlns:t="urn:schemas-microsoft-com:time">
<head><?import namespace="t" implementation="#default#time2"></head>
<body>
<t:animation targetElement="myImg" begin="3" dur="5" autoreverse="true"
fill="hold"><img id="myImg" src="youranimatedgif.gif"></t:animation>
</body></html>
```

HTML attributes:

accelerate, autoreverse, begin, boundary, clipbegin, clipend, decelerate, dur, end, fill, immediateend, longtransition, modulate, motifname, mute, player, repeatcount, repeatdur, restart, segmenttype, speed, src, syncbehavior, syncmaster, systembitrate, systemcaptions, systemlanguage, systemoverduborsubtitle, timeaction, timecontainer, type, updatemode, volume

Event handlers:

onBegin, onEnd, onMediaComplete, onMediaError, onOutOfSync, onPause, onRepeat, onReset, onResume, onReverse, onSeek, onSyncRestored

JavaScript properties:

abstract, accelerate, author, autoReverse, begin, bufferingProgress, canPause, canSeek, clipBegin, clipEnd, copyright, currentFrame, decelerate, downloadCurrent, downloadTotal, dur, end, fill, hasAudio, hasDownloadProgress, hasMedia, hasVisual, isStreamed, latestMediaTime, mediaDur, mediaHeight, mediaWidth, mimeType, mute, player, playerObject, rating, repeatCount, repeatDur, restart, speed, src, syncBehavior, syncMaster, syncTolerance, timeAction, timeContainer, timeParent, title, type, updateMode, volume

JavaScript methods:

activeTimeToParentTime, activeTimeToSegmentTime, beginElement, beginElementAt, documentTimeToParentTime, endElement, endElementAt, parentTimeToActiveTime, parentTimeToDocumentTime, pauseElement, resetElement, resumeElement, seekActiveTime, seekSegmentTime, seekTo, seekToFrame, segmentTimeToActiveTime, segmentTimeToSimpleTime, simpleTimeToSegmentTime

<t:audio/>

Compatibility: IE5.5, IE6

This element provides better control over the playback of audio files.
   Syntax:

```
<t:audio attributes events/>
```

Example:

```
<html xmlns:t="urn:schemas-microsoft-com:time">
<head><?import namespace="t" implementation="#default#time2">
<bgsound id="mySound" src="sound.mp3"></head>
<body><t:audio targetElement="mySound" begin="0" dur="10" motifname=""
repeatcount="indefinite"/>
</body></html>
```

HTML attributes:

accelerate, autoreverse, begin, boundary, clipbegin, clipend, decelerate, dur, end, fill, immediateend, longtransition, modulate, motifname, mute, player, repeatcount, repeatdur, restart, segmenttype, speed, src, syncbehavior, syncmaster, systembitrate, systemcaptions, systemlanguage, systemoverduborsubtitle, timeaction, timecontainer, transitiontype, type, updatemode, volume

Event handlers:

onBegin, onEnd, onMediaComplete, onMediaError, onOutOfSync, onPause, onRepeat, onReset, onResume, onReverse, onSeek, onSyncRestored, onTrackChange

JavaScript properties:

abstract, accelerate, author, autoReverse, begin, bufferingProgress, canPause, canSeek, clipBegin, clipEnd, copyright, currentFrame, decelerate, downloadCurrent, downloadTotal, dur, end, fill, hasAudio, hasDownloadProgress, hasMedia, hasPlayList, hasVisual, isStreamed, latestMediaTime, mediaDur, mediaHeight, mediaWidth, mimeType, mute, player, playerObject, rating, repeatCount, repeatDur, restart, speed, src, syncBehavior, syncMaster, syncTolerance, timeAction, timeContainer, timeParent, title, type, updateMode, volume

JavaScript methods:

activeTimeToParentTime, activeTimeToSegmentTime, beginElement, beginElementAt, documentTimeToParentTime, endElement, endElementAt, parentTimeToActiveTime, parentTimeToDocumentTime, pauseElement, resetElement, resumeElement, seekActiveTime, seekSegmentTime, seekTo, seekToFrame, segmentTimeToActiveTime, segmentTimeToSimpleTime, simpleTimeToSegmentTime

JavaScript collections:

playList

JavaScript objects:

currTimeState

<t:excl> ... </t:excl>

Compatibility: IE5.5, IE6

This element adds all elements appearing between its opening and closing tags to the animation. When rendering the animation, only one child element will be displayed at a time.

Syntax:

<t:excl attributes events> . . . </t:excl>

Example:

```
<html xmlns:t="urn:schemas-microsoft-com:time">
<head><?import namespace="t" implementation="#default#time2">
<style>.time{behavior:url(#default#time2);}</style></head>
<body><t:excl>
<div id="myDiv1" class="time" begin="0" dur="4" style="background-color:red;
width:100px; height:50px"></div>
<div id="myDiv2" class="time" begin="1" dur="4" style="background-color:blue;
width:100px; height:50px"></div>
<div id="myDiv3" class="time" begin="2" dur="4" style="background-color:green;
width:100px; height:50px"></div>
<div id="myDiv4" class="time" begin="6" dur="indefinite" style="background-
color:yellow; width:100px; height:50px"></div>
</t:excl>
</body></html>
```

HTML attributes:

accelerate, autoreverse, decelerate, dur, endsync, repeatdur, syncbehavior

Event handlers:

onEnd, onMediaError, onRepeat, onReset, onReverse, onSeek

JavaScript properties:

accelerate, autoReverse, decelerate, downloadCurrent, downloadTotal, dur, endSync,
repeatDur, syncBehavior, syncTolerance

JavaScript methods:

activeTimeToParentTime, activeTimeToSegmentTime, beginElement,
documentTimeToParentTime, endElement, parentTimeToActiveTime,
parentTimeToDocumentTime, resetElement, seekTo, seekToFrame,
segmentTimeToActiveTime, segmentTimeToSimpleTime, simpleTimeToSegmentTime

JavaScript collections:

activeElements, timeAll, timeChildren

<t:img> ... </t:img>

Compatibility: IE5.5, IE6

This element animates a series of image elements.

Syntax:

```
<t:img attributes events> . . . </t:img>
```

Example:

```
<html xmlns:t="urn:schemas-microsoft-com:time">
<head><?import namespace="t" implementation="#default#time2">
<style>.time{behavior:url(#default#time2);}</style></head>
<body><t:img>
<img src="yourimage1.gif" class="time" begin="0" dur="4">
<img src="yourimage2.gif" class="time" begin="2" dur="4">
<img src="yourimage3.gif" class="time" begin="4" dur="4">
</t:img>
</body></html>
```

HTML attributes:

accelerate, autoreverse, begin, boundary, clipbegin, clipend, decelerate, dur, end, fill, immediateend, longtransition, modulate, motifname, mute, player, repeatcount, repeatdur, restart, segmenttype, speed, src, syncbehavior, syncmaster, systembitrate, systemcaptions, systemlanguage, systemoverduborsubtitle, timeaction, timecontainer, transitiontype, type, updatemode, volume

Event handlers:

onBegin, onEnd, onMediaComplete, onMediaError, onOutOfSync, onPause, onRepeat, onReset, onResume, onReverse, onSeek, onSyncRestored

JavaScript properties:

abstract, accelerate, author, autoReverse, begin, bufferingProgress, canPause, canSeek, clipBegin, clipEnd, copyright, currentFrame, decelerate, downloadCurrent, downloadTotal, dur, end, fill, hasAudio, hasDownloadProgress, hasMedia, hasVisual, isStreamed, latestMediaTime, mediaDur, mediaHeight, mediaWidth, mimeType, mute, player, playerObject, rating, repeatCount, repeatDur, restart, speed, src, syncBehavior, syncMaster, syncTolerance, timeAction, timeContainer, timeParent, title, type, updateMode, volume

JavaScript methods:

activeTimeToParentTime, activeTimeToSegmentTime, beginElement, beginElementAt, documentTimeToParentTime, endElement, endElementAt, parentTimeToActiveTime, parentTimeToDocumentTime, pauseElement, resetElement, resumeElement, seekActiveTime, seekSegmentTime, seekTo, seekToFrame, segmentTimeToActiveTime, segmentTimeToSimpleTime, simpleTimeToSegmentTime

JavaScript objects:

currTimeState

<t:media> . . . </t:media>

Compatibility: IE5.5, IE6

This element provides better control over the playback of audio and video media files.

Syntax:

```
<t:media attributes events> . . . </t:media>
```

Example:

```
<html xmlns:t="urn:schemas-microsoft-com:time">
<head><?import namespace="t" implementation="#default#time2"></head>
<body><t:media><img id="myMedia" src="yourimage.gif" begin="3" dur="5"
repeatcount="5"/></t:media>
</body></html>
```

HTML attributes:

accelerate, autoreverse, begin, boundary, clipbegin, clipend, decelerate, dur, end, fill, immediateend, longtransition, modulate, motifname, mute, player, repeatcount, repeatdur, restart, segmenttype, speed, src, syncbehavior, syncmaster, systembitrate, systemcaptions, systemlanguage, systemoverduborsubtitle, timeaction, timecontainer, transitiontype, type, updatemode, volume

Event handlers:

onBegin, onEnd, onMediaComplete, onMediaError, onOutOfSync, onPause, onRepeat, onReset, onResume, onReverse, onSeek, onSyncRestored, onTrackChange

JavaScript properties:

abstract, accelerate, author, autoReverse, begin, bufferingProgress, canPause, canSeek, clipBegin, clipEnd, copyright, currentFrame, decelerate, downloadCurrent, downloadTotal, dur, end, fill, hasAudio, hasDownloadProgress, hasMedia, hasPlayList, hasVisual, isStreamed, latestMediaTime, mediaDur, mediaHeight, mediaWidth, mimeType, mute, player, playerObject, rating, repeatCount, repeatDur, restart, speed, src, syncBehavior, syncMaster, syncTolerance, timeAction, timeContainer, timeParent, title, type, updateMode, volume

JavaScript methods:

activeTimeToParentTime, activeTimeToSegmentTime, beginElement, beginElementAt, documentTimeToParentTime, endElement, endElementAt, nextTrack, parentTimeToActiveTime, parentTimeToDocumentTime, pauseElement, prevTrack, resetElement, resumeElement, seekActiveTime, seekSegmentTime, seekTo, seekToFrame, segmentTimeToActiveTime, segmentTimeToSimpleTime, simpleTimeToSegmentTime

JavaScript collections:

playList

JavaScript objects:

---

currTimeState

<t:par> . . . </t:par>

Compatibility: IE5.5, IE6

This element adds all elements appearing between its opening and closing tags to the animation. This element is very similar to <t:excl>, differing only in that it lets you display multiple elements simultaneously.

Syntax:

<t:par *attributes events*> . . . </t:par>

Example:

```
<html xmlns:t="urn:schemas-microsoft-com:time">
<head><style>.time{behavior:url(#default#time2);}</style>
<?import namespace="t" implementation="#default#time2"></head>
<body><t:par begin="0" dur="15" timeaction="display">
<img src="yourimage1.gif" width="79" height="99">
<div class=time begin="5"><img src="yourimage2.gif" width="99" height="76"></div>
</t:par>
</body></html>
```

HTML attributes:

---

accelerate, autoreverse, decelerate, dur, endsync, fill, mute, repeatcount, repeatdur, restart, speed, syncbehavior, timeaction, volume

---

Event handlers:

---

onBegin, onEnd, onMediaComplete, onMediaError, onOutOfSync, onPause, onRepeat, onReset, onResume, onReverse, onSeek, onSyncRestored

---

JavaScript properties:

---

accelerate, autoReverse, decelerate, dur, endSync, fill, mediaDur, mediaHeight, mediaWidth, mute, repeatCount, repeatDur, restart, speed, syncBehavior, syncTolerance, timeAction, timeParent, volume

---

JavaScript methods:

---

activeTimeToParentTime, activeTimeToSegmentTime, beginElement, beginElementAt, documentTimeToParentTime, endElement, endElementAt, nextTrack, parentTimeToActiveTime, parentTimeToDocumentTime, pauseElement, prevTrack, resetElement, resumeElement, seekActiveTime, seekSegmentTime, seekTo, seekToFrame, segmentTimeToActiveTime, segmentTimeToSimpleTime, simpleTimeToSegmentTime

---

JavaScript collections:

---

activeElements, timeAll, timeChildren

JavaScript objects:

---

currTimeState

<t:priorityclass> . . . </t:priorityclass>

Compatibility: IE5.5, IE6

This element appears between the `<t:excl>` element's opening and closing tags and controls the display of elements with conflicting timelines.

Syntax:

```
<t:priorityclass attributes events> . . . </t:priorityclass>
```

Example:

```
<html xmlns:t="urn:schemas-microsoft-com:time">
<head><?import namespace="t" implementation="#default#time2">
<style>.time{behavior:url(#default#time2);}</style></head>
<body><t:excl id="myExcl" begin="0">
<t:priorityclass><div id="myDiv1" class="time" begin="5" dur="4" style="background-
color:red; width:100px; height:50px">Higher Priority</div></t:priorityclass>
<t:priorityclass id="myPriority" higher="pause" lower="defer">
<div id="myDiv2" class="time" begin="0" dur="12" style="background-color:blue;
width:100px; height:50px">Lower priority</div></t:priorityclass>
</t:excl>
<button onclick="alert(myPriority.higher);">higher</button>
<button onclick="alert(myPriority.lower);">lower</button>
</body></html>
```

HTML attributes:

---

higher, lower, peers

JavaScript properties:

---

higher, lower, peers

<t:ref> . . . </t:ref>

Compatibility: IE5.5, IE6

This element adds all elements appearing between its opening and closing tags to the animation. It is virtually identical to `<t:par>`.

Syntax:

```
<t:ref attributes events> . . . </t:ref>
```

Example:

```
<html xmlns:t="urn:schemas-microsoft-com:time">
<head><style>.time{behavior:url(#default#time2);}</style>
<?import namespace="t" implementation="#default#time2"></head>
<body><t:ref begin="2" timeaction="display"><img src="yourimage.gif">
<span class="time" begin="7"><img src="yourimage.gif"></span></t:ref>
</body></html>
```

HTML attributes:

```
accelerate, autoreverse, begin, boundary, clipbegin, clipend, decelerate, dur, end,
fill, immediateend, longtransition, modulate, motifname, mute, player, repeatcount,
repeatdur, restart, segmenttype, speed, src, syncbehavior, syncmaster,
systembitrate, systemcaptions, systemlanguage, systemoverduborsubtitle, timeaction,
timecontainer, transitiontype, type, updatemode, volume
```

Event handlers:

```
onBegin, onEnd, onMediaComplete, onMediaError, onOutOfSync, onPause, onRepeat,
onReset, onResume, onReverse, onSeek, onSyncRestored, onTrackChange
```

JavaScript properties:

```
abstract, accelerate, author, autoReverse, begin, bufferingProgress, canPause,
canSeek, clipBegin, clipEnd, copyright, currentFrame, decelerate, downloadCurrent,
downloadTotal, dur, end, fill, hasAudio, hasDownloadProgress, hasMedia,
hasPlayList, hasVisual, isStreamed, latestMediaTime, mediaDur, mediaHeight,
mediaWidth, mimeType, mute, player, playerObject, rating, repeatCount, repeatDur,
restart, speed, src, syncBehavior, syncMaster, syncTolerance, timeAction,
timeContainer, timeParent, title, type, updateMode, volume
```

JavaScript methods:

```
activeTimeToParentTime, activeTimeToSegmentTime, beginElement, beginElementAt,
documentTimeToParentTime, endElement, endElementAt, nextTrack,
parentTimeToActiveTime, parentTimeToDocumentTime, pauseElement, prevTrack,
resetElement, resumeElement, seekActiveTime, seekSegmentTime, seekTo, seekToFrame,
segmentTimeToActiveTime, segmentTimeToSimpleTime, simpleTimeToSegmentTime
```

JavaScript collections:

```
playList
```

JavaScript objects:

```
currTimeState
```

<t:seq> ... </t:seq>

Compatibility: IE5.5, IE6

This element allows you to display multiple elements in an animation. Only one element is displayed at a time.

Syntax:

```
<t:seq attributes events> . . . </t:seq>
```

Example:

```
<html xmlns:t="urn:schemas-microsoft-com:time">
<head><?import namespace="t" implementation="#default#time2">
<style>.time{behavior:url(#default#time2);}</style></head>
<body><t:seq begin="5">
<img src="yourimage1.gif" class="time" dur="2">
<img src="yourimage2.gif" class="time" dur="3">
<img src="yourimage3.gif" class="time" dur="4">
<div id="myDiv" class="time" dur="indefinite" style="background-color:yellow;
width:100px; height:50px">END</div>
</t:seq>
</body></html>
```

HTML attributes:

accelerate, autoreverse, begin, decelerate, dur, end, fill, mute, repeatcount, repeatdur, restart, speed, syncbehavior, systembitrate, systemcaptions, systemlanguage, systemoverduborsubtitle, timeaction, timecontainer, volume

Event handlers:

onBegin, onEnd, onMediaComplete, onMediaError, onOutOfSync, onPause, onRepeat, onReset, onResume, onReverse, onSeek, onSyncRestored

JavaScript properties:

accelerate, autoReverse, begin, decelerate, dur, end, fill, hasMedia, mediaDur, mediaHeight, mediaWidth, mute, repeatCount, repeatDur, restart, speed, syncBehavior, syncTolerance, timeAction, timeContainer, timeParent, volume

JavaScript methods:

activeTimeToParentTime, activeTimeToSegmentTime, beginElement, beginElementAt, documentTimeToParentTime, endElement, endElementAt, nextElement, nextTrack, parentTimeToActiveTime, parentTimeToDocumentTime, pauseElement, prevElement, prevTrack, resetElement, resumeElement, seekActiveTime, seekSegmentTime, seekTo, seekToFrame, segmentTimeToActiveTime, segmentTimeToSimpleTime, simpleTimeToSegmentTime

JavaScript collections:

---

activeElements, timeAll, timeChildren

JavaScript objects:

---

currTimeState

<t:set/>

Compatibility: IE5.5, IE6

This element animates the attribute specified by attributeName of the element specified by targetElement. This element is very similar to <t:animate/>, differing only in that <t:set/> does not require the animated attribute to have an initial value.

Syntax:

<t:set *attributes events*/>

Example:

```html
<html xmlns:t="urn:schemas-microsoft-com:time">
<head><?import namespace="t" implementation="#default#time2"></head>
<body><div id="myDiv" style="width:200px; height:150px; background-color:red;"></div>
<t:set attributeName="visibility" begin="1" to="hidden" dur="5"
targetElement="myDiv"/>
</body></html>
```

HTML attributes:

---

attributename, autoreverse, begin, dur, end, fill, repeatdur, restart, systembitrate, systemcaptions, systemlanguage, systemoverduborsubtitle, targetelement, timecontainer, to

---

Event handlers:

---

onBegin, onEnd, onPause, onRepeat, onReset, onResume, onReverse

---

JavaScript properties:

---

attributeName, autoReverse, begin, dur, end, fill, hasMedia, repeatDur, restart, targetElement, timeContainer, timeParent, to

---

JavaScript methods:

---

activeTimeToParentTime, activeTimeToSegmentTime, beginElement, beginElementAt, documentTimeToParentTime, endElement, endElementAt, parentTimeToActiveTime, parentTimeToDocumentTime, pauseElement, resetElement, resumeElement,

---

seekActiveTime, seekSegmentTime, seekTo, seekToFrame, segmentTimeToActiveTime, segmentTimeToSimpleTime, simpleTimeToSegmentTime

JavaScript objects:

currTimeState

<t:switch> ... </t:switch>

Compatibility: IE5.5, IE6

This element displays the first element between its opening and closing tags whose systembitrate, systemcaption, systemlanguage, or systemoverduborsubtitle attribute value evaluates to true.

NOTE *You must enclose all HTML comments within another element (such as <div> or <span>) if you don't want them to affect the <t:switch> operation.*

Syntax:

<t:switch *attributes events*> . . . </t:switch>

Example:

```
<html xmlns:t="urn:schemas-microsoft-com:time">
<head><?import namespace="t" implementation="#default#time2"></head>
<body><t:switch>
<span class="time" systemLanguage="es">ESPANOL</span>
<span class="time" systemLanguage="en">ENGLISH</span></t:switch>
</body></html>
```

HTML attributes:

systembitrate, systemcaptions, systemlanguage, systemoverduborsubtitle

JavaScript properties:

hasMedia

<t:transitionfilter />

Compatibility: IE6

This element gradually renders the element specified by the targetElement attribute using the animation specified by the type attribute.
Syntax:

<t:transitionfilter *attributes events*/>

Example:

```
<html xmlns:t="urn:schemas-microsoft-com:time">
<head><?import namespace="t" implementation="#default#time2"></head>
<body><div id="myDiv" style="position:absolute; top:150px; left:100px; width:300px;
height:200px; background-color:red;"></div>
<t:transitionfilter id="myTrans" type="fade" begin="0" dur="5" mode="in"
targetelement="myDiv"/>
<button onclick="alert(myTrans.mode);">Mode</button>
</body></html>
```

HTML attributes:

accelerate, accumulate, additive, autoreverse, begin, by, calcmode, decelerate,
dur, end, from, keysplines, keytimes, mode, repeatcount, repeatdur, restart, speed,
subtype, targetelement, to, type, values

Event handlers:

onBegin, onEnd, onPause, onRepeat, onResume, onReverse, onSeek

JavaScript properties:

accelerate, accumulate, additive, autoReverse, begin, by, calcMode, decelerate,
dur, end, from, keySplines, keyTimes, mode, repeatCount, repeatDur, restart, speed,
subtype, targetElement, to, type, values

JavaScript methods:

activeTimeToParentTime, activeTimeToSegmentTime, beginElement, beginElementAt,
documentTimeToParentTime, endElement, endElementAt, parentTimeToActiveTime,
parentTimeToDocumentTime, pauseElement, resumeElement, seekActiveTime,
seekSegmentTime, seekTo, segmentTimeToActiveTime, segmentTimeToSimpleTime,
simpleTimeToSegmentTime

JavaScript objects:

currTimeState

<t:video/>

Compatibility: IE5.5, IE6

This element provides better control over the animation of video clips.
Syntax:

```
<t:video attributes events/>
```

Example:

```
<html xmlns:t="urn:schemas-microsoft-com:time">
<head><?import namespace="t" implementation="#default#time2"></head>
```

```
<body><t:video begin="3" dur="5" src="yourvideo.avi" end="indefinite"/>
</body></html>
```

HTML attributes:

accelerate, autoreverse, begin, boundary, clipbegin, clipend, decelerate, dur, end,
fill, immediateend, longtransition, modulate, motifname, mute, player, repeatcount,
repeatdur, restart, segmenttype, speed, src, syncbehavior, syncmaster,
systembitrate, systemcaptions, systemlanguage, systemoverduborsubtitle, timeaction,
timecontainer, transitiontype, type, updatemode, volume

Event handlers:

onBegin, onEnd, onMediaComplete, onMediaError, onOutOfSync, onPause, onRepeat,
onReset, onResume, onReverse, onSeek, onSyncRestored, onTrackChange

JavaScript properties:

abstract, accelerate, author, autoReverse, begin, bufferingProgress, canPause,
canSeek, clipBegin, clipEnd, copyright, currentFrame, decelerate, downloadCurrent,
downloadTotal, dur, end, fill, hasAudio, hasDownloadProgress, hasMedia,
hasPlayList, hasVisual, isStreamed, latestMediaTime, mediaDur, mediaHeight,
mediaWidth, mimeType, mute, player, playerObject, rating, repeatCount, repeatDur,
restart, speed, src, syncBehavior, syncMaster, syncTolerance, timeAction,
timeContainer, timeParent, title, type, updateMode, volume

JavaScript methods:

activeTimeToParentTime, activeTimeToSegmentTime, beginElement, beginElementAt,
documentTimeToParentTime, endElement, endElementAt, parentTimeToActiveTime,
parentTimeToDocumentTime, pauseElement, resetElement, resumeElement,
seekActiveTime, seekSegmentTime, seekTo, seekToFrame, segmentTimeToActiveTime,
segmentTimeToSimpleTime, simpleTimeToSegmentTime

JavaScript collections:

playList

JavaScript objects:

currTimeState

HTML Attributes and JavaScript Properties

This section of the chapter contains all the HTML attributes and JavaScript properties that apply to HTML+TIME HTML elements. The HTML attributes and
JavaScript properties are grouped together here because they represent two
different ways to access the same HTML object information.

In the applies-to lists, you will see items of three kinds: HTML elements,
JavaScript collections, and JavaScript objects. In order to distinguish between
these items in the applies-to lists, the following conventions have been used:

- < and > angle bracket tags surround the names of HTML elements (for example, <t:animation>).

- An asterisk follows the names of JavaScript collections (for example, activeElements*).

- The names of JavaScript objects appear without adornment (for example, playItem).

abstract

Compatibility: IE5.5, IE6

Read-only JavaScript property. Retrieves the contents of the tag inside an ASX file, which is an XML type of document that contains all the information that Windows Media Player needs to play a sequence of sound or video media files.

Syntax:

```
elementID.abstract
elementID.playList(index).abstract
```

Example:

```
<html xmlns:t="urn:schemas-microsoft-com:time">
<head><?import namespace="t" implementation="#default#time2"></head>
<body>
<t:video id="myVideo" begin="0" src="myasx.asx" end="indefinite"
ontrackchange="alert(event.MoreInfo);" type="avi"/><br><br>
<button onclick="alert(myVideo.abstract);">Abstract</button>
<button onclick="alert(myVideo.author);">Author</button>
<button onclick="alert(myVideo.playList(0).Banner);">Banner</button>
<button onclick="alert(myVideo.playList(0).BannerAbstract);">BannerAbstract</button>
<button onclick="alert(myVideo.playList(0).BannerMoreInfo);">BannerMoreInfo</button>
<button onclick="alert(myVideo.playList(0).copyright);">Copyright</button>
<button onclick="alert(myVideo.playList(0).title);">Title</button><br>
</body></html>
```

Contents of myasx.asx:

```
<asx version="3.0">
   <entry>
      <abstract>Your Media 1</abstract>
      <title>Title 1</title>
      <author>Author 1</author>
      <banner href="yourvideo.avi">
         <moreinfo href="yourvideo.avi"/>
         <abstract>Banner 1</abstract>
      </banner>
      <copyright>copyright 1</copyright>
```

```
        <ref href="yourvideo.avi"/>
    </entry>
    <entry>
        <abstract>Your Media 2</abstract>
        <title>Title 2</title>
        <author>Author 2</author>
        <banner href="sound.mp3">
            <moreinfo href="sound.mp3"/>
            <abstract>Banner 2</abstract>
        </banner>
        <copyright>copyright 2</copyright>
        <ref href="sound.mp3"/>
    </entry>
</asx>
```

Applies to:

```
playItem, <t:animation>, <t:audio/>, <t:img>, <t:media>, <t:ref>, <t:video/>
```

accelerate

Compatibility: IE5.5, IE6

Read and write JavaScript property and HTML attribute. Defines the acceleration of a timed element. Value: A floating-point number from 0 (the default; no acceleration) to 1 (maximum acceleration).

Syntax:

```
<t:element accelerate = "value"/>
elementID.accelerate = value
```

Example:

```
<html xmlns:t="urn:schemas-microsoft-com:time">
<head><?import namespace="t" implementation="#default#time2"></head>
<body><div id="myDiv" style="position:absolute; top:50px; left:100px; width:200px;
height:100px; background-color:blue"></div>
<t:animate targetElement="myDiv" attributeName="top" by="200" begin="2" dur="5"
accelerate="1.0"/>
<t:animate targetElement="myDiv" attributeName="top" by="200" begin="8" dur="5"
decelerate="1.0"/>
</body></html>
```

Applies to:

```
<t:animate/>, <t:animatecolor/>, <t:animatemotion/>, <t:animation>, <t:audio/>,
<t:excl>, <t:img>, <t:media>, <t:par>, <t:ref>, <t:seq>, <t:transitionfilter/>,
<t:video/>
```

accumulate

Compatibility: IE5.5, IE6

Read and write JavaScript property and HTML attribute. Determines whether or not each iteration of the animation builds upon the value of the previous iteration. Values: none (the default; not cumulative) and sum (cumulative).

Syntax:

```
<t:element accumulate = "value"/>
elementID.accumulate = value
```

Example:

```
<html xmlns:t="urn:schemas-microsoft-com:time">
<head><?import namespace="t" implementation="#default#time2"></head>
<body><div id="myDiv" style="position:absolute; top:50px; left:100px; width:200px;
height:100px; background-color:orange"></div>
<t:animate id="myTime" targetElement="myDiv" attributeName="top" by="200" begin="2"
end="indetermine" dur="5" accumulate="sum"/>
<button onclick="alert(myTime.accumulate);">Accumulate</button>
</body></html>
```

Applies to:

```
<t:animate/>, <t:animatecolor/>, <t:animatemotion/>, <t:transitionfilter/>
```

activeDur

Compatibility: IE5.5, IE6

Read-only JavaScript property. Retrieves the total duration of the animation in seconds.

Syntax:

```
elementID.currTimeState.activeDur
```

Example:

```
<html xmlns:t="urn:schemas-microsoft-com:time">
<head><?import namespace="t" implementation="#default#time2">
<style>.time{behavior:url(#default#time2) }</style></head>
<body><t:excl id="myAnim" dur="3" repeatcount="3">
<div id="div1" class="time" begin="0" dur="3" style="background-color:yellow;
width:150;"></div>
<div id="div2" class="time" begin="1" dur="2" style="background-color:beige;
width:150;"></div>
<div id="div3" class="time" begin="2" dur="1" style="background-color:lavender;
width:150;"></div>
</t:excl>
```

```
<button onclick="alert(myAnim.currTimeState.activeDur);">ActiveDur</button>
<button onclick="alert(myAnim.currTimeState.activeTime);">ActiveTime</button>
</body></html>
```

Applies to:

currTimeState

activeTime

Compatibility: IE5.5, IE6

Read-only JavaScript property. Retrieves the amount of time in seconds that has elapsed since the beginning of the animation.

Syntax:

elementID.currTimeState.activeTime

Example: See the activeDur property example.

Applies to:

currTimeState

activeTrack

Compatibility: IE5.5, IE6

Read-only JavaScript property. Returns the playItem object that is currently active in the playList collection.

Syntax:

elementID.playList.activeTrack

Example (use the ASX file listed in the abstract property example):

```
<html xmlns:t="urn:schemas-microsoft-com:time">
<head><?import namespace="t" implementation="#default#time2">
<style>.time{behavior:url(#default#time2);}</style>
<script language="JavaScript">
function B1() {
myPlayList.beginElement();
alert(myPlayList.playList.activeTrack.title);}
</script></head>
<body><div><t:media id="myPlayList"
src="myasx.asx" begin="indefinite" timeAction="visibility"/>
<button onclick="B1();">Start</button>
<button onclick="myPlayList.endElement();">Stop</button>
</div>
</body></html>
```

Applies to:

playList*

additive

Compatibility: IE5.5, IE6

Read and write JavaScript property and HTML attribute. Defines how an animation is combined with other animations. Values: sum and replace (the default).
Syntax:

```
<t:element additive = "value"/>
elementID.additive = value
```

Example:

```
<html xmlns:t="urn:schemas-microsoft-com:time">
<head><?import namespace="t" implementation="#default#time2"></head>
<body bgcolor="#FFFFFF" text="#000000">
<div id="myObject" class="time" style="position:absolute; top:300px; left:50px;
width:200px; height:100px; background-color:lightblue;"></div>
<div id="myObject2" style="position:absolute; top:480px; left:50px; width:200px;
height:100px; background-color:red;"></div>
<t:animatecolor targetElement="myObject" attributeName="backgroundColor"
to="yellow" start="1" dur="5" fill="hold">
<t:animatemotion targetElement="myObject2" to="0,-180" dur="5" fill="hold"
origin="default">
<t:animatecolor id="myA" targetElement="myObject2" attributeName="backgroundColor"
to="cyan" start="1" dur="5" fill="hold">
<t:animatemotion id="myAnim" targetElement="myObject" to="400,0" dur="5"
fill="hold" additive="sum" origin="element">
<button onclick="alert(myAnim.additive);">Additive</button>
<button onclick="alert(myAnim.origin);">Origin</button>
</body></html>
```

Applies to:

```
<t:animate/>, <t:animatecolor/>, <t:animatemotion/>, <t:transitionfilter/>
```

attributeName

Compatibility: IE5.5, IE6

Read and write JavaScript property and HTML attribute. Specifies the attribute to animate of the element specified by targetElement.
Syntax:

```
<t:element attributename = "value"/>
elementID.attributeName = value
```

Example:

```
<html xmlns:t="urn:schemas-microsoft-com:time">
<head><?import namespace="t" implementation="#default#time2"></head>
<body><div id="myDiv" style="position:absolute; top:150px; left:100px; width:200px;
height:150px; background-color:red;"></div>
<t:animate targetElement="myDiv" attributeName="left" by="150" begin="3" dur="5"
fill="hold"/>
</body></html>
```

Applies to:

```
<t:animate/>, <t:animatecolor/>, <t:set/>
```

author

Compatibility: IE5.5, IE6

Read-only JavaScript property. Retrieves the contents of the <author> tag inside an ASX file, which is an XML type of document that contains all the information that Windows Media Player needs to play a sequence of sound or video media files.

Syntax:

```
elementID.author
elementID.playList[index].author
```

Example: See the abstract property example.
Applies to:

```
playItem, <t:animation>, <t:audio/>, <t:img>, <t:media>, <t:ref>, <t:video/>
```

autoReverse

Compatibility: IE5.5, IE6

Read and write JavaScript property and HTML attribute. Establishes whether or not the element should begin playing in reverse once the forward animation completes. If the autoReverse property is set to true, many other properties whose values normally increment as a timeline progresses will instead decrement. Values: true and false.

Syntax:

```
<t:element autoreverse = "value"/>
elementID.autoReverse = value
```

Example:

```
<html xmlns:t="urn:schemas-microsoft-com:time">
<head><?import namespace="t" implementation="#default#time2"></head>
```

```
<body>
<div id="myDiv" style="position:absolute; top:50px; left:100px; width:200px;
height:100px; background-color:blue"></div>
<t:animate id="myTime" targetElement="myDiv" attributeName="top" by="200" begin="2"
end="indetermine" dur="5" accumulate="sum" autoreverse="true"/>
<button onclick="alert(myTime.autoReverse);">Autoreverse</button>
</body></html>
```

Applies to:

```
<t:animate/>, <t:animatecolor/>, <t:animatemotion/>, <t:animation>, <t:audio/>,
<t:excl>, <t:img>, <t:media>, <t:par>, <t:ref>, <t:seq>, <t:set/>,
<t:transitionfilter/>, <t:video/>
```

Banner

Compatibility: IE6

Read-only JavaScript property. Retrieves the contents of the <banner> tag inside
an ASX file, which is an XML type of document that contains all the information
that Windows Media Player needs to play a sequence of sound or video media
files.

Syntax:

```
elementID.playList(index).Banner
```

Example: See the abstract property example.
Applies to:

```
playItem
```

BannerAbstract

Compatibility: IE6

Read-only JavaScript property. Retrieves the contents of the tag inside
the <banner> tag inside an ASX file. An ASX file is an XML type of document that
contains all the information that Windows Media Player needs to play a sequence
of sound or video media files.

Syntax:

```
elementID.playList(index).BannerAbstract
```

Example: See the abstract property example.
Applies to:

```
playItem
```

Compatibility: IE6

Read-only JavaScript property. Retrieves the contents of the <moreinfo> tag inside the <banner> tag inside an ASX file. An ASX file is an XML type of document that contains all the information that Windows Media Player needs to play a sequence of sound or video media files.

Syntax:

```
elementID.playList(index).BannerMoreInfo
```

Example: See the abstract property example.

Applies to:

```
playItem
```

begin

Compatibility: IE5.5, IE6

Read and write JavaScript property and HTML attribute. Establishes the amount of time between the loading of the page and the beginning of the timeline.

Syntax:

```
<t:element begin = "value"/>
elementID.begin = value
elementID.playList[index].begin
```

Values:

indefinite	The animation is started by a call to beginElement().
time value	A number followed by a units designator (h for hours, min for minutes, s for seconds, and ms for milliseconds), or a clock value in the h:min:s.ms format.
elementID. eventName [+time value]	The animation starts relative to the firing of the specified event. An additional time value delay is optional, and takes either of the two time value formats outlined above.

Example:

```
<html xmlns:t="urn:schemas-microsoft-com:time">
<head><?import namespace="t" implementation="#default#time2"></head>
<body><div id="myDiv" style="position:absolute; top:150px; left:100px; width:200px;
height:150px; background-color:red;"></div>
<t:animatemotion targetElement="myDiv" begin="0" dur="500ms" to="50,50"/>
</body></html>
```

Applies to:

`<a>`, `<acronym>`, `<address>`, `<area>`, `<b>`, `<big>`, `<blockquote>`, `<button>`, `<caption>`, `<center>`, `<cite>`, `<code>`, `<dd>`, `<del>`, `<dir>`, `<div>`, `<dl>`, `<dt>`, `<em>`, `<fieldset>`, `<font>`, `<form>`, `<hn>`, `<hr>`, `<i>`, `<iframe>`, `<img>`, `<input type="button">`, `<input type="checkbox">`, `<input type="file">`, `<input type="hidden">`, `<input type="image">`, `<input type="password">`, `<input type="radio">`, `<input type="reset">`, `<input type="submit">`, `<input type="text">`, `<ins>`, `<kbd>`, `<legend>`, `<li>`, `<listing>`, `<marquee>`, `<menu>`, `<ol>`, `<option>`, `<p>`, `<plaintext>`, playItem, `<pre>`, `<q>`, `<s>`, `<samp>`, `<small>`, `<span>`, `<strike>`, `<strong>`, `<sub>`, `<sup>`, `<t:animate/>`, `<t:animatecolor/>`, `<t:animatemotion/>`, `<t:animation>`, `<t:audio/>`, `<t:img>`, `<t:media>`, `<t:ref>`, `<t:seq>`, `<t:set/>`, `<t:transitionfilter/>`, `<t:video/>`, `<table>`, `<tbody>`, `<td>`, `<textarea>`, `<tfoot>`, `<th>`, `<thead>`, `<tr>`, `<tt>`, `<u>`, `<ul>`, `<var>`, `<xmp>`

---

boundary

Compatibility: IE5.5, IE6

Read and write HTML attribute. Specifies when the Microsoft DirectMusic player will begin to play. This attribute is only applicable when the player attribute has a value of DMusic. Values: default, beat, grid, immediate, and measure. For more information on DirectMusic, see http://msdn.microsoft.com/workshop/author/behaviors/reference/time2/time_dmusic_ovw.asp.

Syntax:

```
<t:element boundary = "value"/>
```

Example:

```
<html xmlns:t="urn:schemas-microsoft-com:time">
<head><?import namespace="t" implementation="#default#time2"></head>
<body>
<t:media><bgsound id="myMedia" src="sound.mp3" player="DMusic" boundary="beat"
begin="3" dur="5" repeatcount="5" transitiontype="fill"/></t:media>
</body></html>
```

Applies to:

`<t:animation>`, `<t:audio/>`, `<t:img>`, `<t:media>`, `<t:ref>`, `<t:video/>`

---

bufferingProgress

Compatibility: IE6

Read-only JavaScript property. Retrieves the percentage of the media file that the browser has received. Buffering is only allowed when the file being downloaded allows streaming content.

Syntax:

```
elementID.bufferingProgress
```

Example (use the ASX file listed in the abstract property example):

```
<html xmlns:t="urn:schemas-microsoft-com:time">
<head><?import namespace="t" implementation="#default#time2">
<style>.time{behavior:url(#default#time2)}</style></head>
<body>
<t:media id="myMedia" src="myasx.asx" timeAction="display"/>
<p>Buffering Progress: <span class="time" dur="0.1" repeatCount="indefinite"
onrepeat="innerText=myMedia.bufferingProgress;">0</span></p>
</body></html>
```

Applies to:

```
<t:animation>, <t:audio/>, <t:img>, <t:media>, <t:ref>, <t:video/>
```

by (1)

Compatibility: IE5.5, IE6

Read and write JavaScript property and HTML attribute. Specifies the distance that the animated element moves.

NOTE *The* to, values, *and* path *properties have precedence over the* by *property.*

Syntax:

```
<t:element by = "value"/>
elementID.by = value
elementID.by(value)
```

Example:

```
<html xmlns:t="urn:schemas-microsoft-com:time">
<head><?import namespace="t" implementation="#default#time2"></head>
<body><button onclick="alert(myTime.by);">By</button>
<div id="myDiv" style="position:absolute; top:50px; left:100px; width:200px;
height:100px; background-color:blue"></div>
<t:animate id="myTime" targetElement="myDiv" attributeName="top" by="200" begin="2"
by="200px" end="indetermine" dur="5" accumulate="sum"/>
</body></html>
```

Applies to:

```
<t:animate/>, <t:animatemotion/>
```

by (2)

Compatibility: IE5.5, IE6

Read and write JavaScript property and HTML attribute. Specifies the color that will be blended with the animated element's color to produce a third color.

Syntax:

```
<t:animatecolor by = "value"/>
animatecolorID.by = value
animatecolorID.by(value)
```

Example:

```
<html xmlns:t="urn:schemas-microsoft-com:time">
<head><?import namespace="t" implementation="#default#time2"></head>
<div id="myDiv" style="position:absolute; height:200px; width:300px; background-
color:green"></div>
<t:animatecolor targetElement="myDiv" attributeName="background-color" by="red"
begin="0" dur="7"/>
</body></html>
```

Applies to:

```
<t:animatecolor/>
```

by (3)

Compatibility: IE6

Read and write JavaScript property and HTML attribute. Specifies the percentage of the transition filter's animation that will be rendered. Value: A floating-point number from 0 to 1 (the default).

Syntax:

```
<t:transitionfilter by = "value"/>
transitionfilterID.by = value
transitionfilterID.by(value)
```

Example:

```
<html xmlns:t="urn:schemas-microsoft-com:time">
<head><?import namespace="t" implementation="#default#time2"/>
<style>.time{behavior:url(#default#time2);}</style></head>
<body><t:transitionfilter from="0.3" by="0.4" type="irisWipe" dur="3"
targetelement="myDiv"/>
<div class="time" id="myDiv" style="width:420px; height:200px; background-
color:blue;"></div>
</body></html>
```

Applies to:

```
<t:transitionfilter/>
```

calcMode

Compatibility: IE5.5, IE6

Read and write JavaScript property and HTML attribute. Establishes the type of transition between frames in the animation.

If you want to take full advantage of calcMode, it is important that you understand the concept of interpolation. Every animation consists of many still shots (or frames) that create the appearance of continuous motion when displayed one after another. Interpolation is the process used to fill the gaps between frames, making the gaps invisible to the naked eye.

Syntax:

```
<t:element calcmode = "value"/>
elementID.calcMode = value
elementID.calcMode(value)
```

Values:

discrete	The animation moves from one frame to the next without any interpolation. If there are only two values in the animation, from and to, the animation will jump from the initial frame to the end frame.
linear	The default; the interpolation is calculated by filling the gaps between frames with straight lines.
paced	The interpolation is defined by several equidistant points between each pair of frames. This method of interpolation is used in Flash movies.
spline	The interpolation calculates the best points between the frames using an algorithm that incorporates the values assigned to the keySplines property.

Example:

```
<html xmlns:t="urn:schemas-microsoft-com:time">
<head><?import namespace="t" implementation="#default#time2">
<style>.time{behavior:url(#default#time2);}</style></head>
<body><div id="myDiv" style="position:absolute; top:50px; left:50px; height:75px;
width:100px; background-color:yellow;"></div>
<t:animate begin="1" dur="5" calcMode="spline" keySplines="0 0 1 1" keyTimes="0; 1"
values="200;500" attributeName="left" targetElement="myDiv" fill="hold"/>
</body></html>
```

Applies to:

```
<t:animate/>, <t:animatecolor/>, <t:animatemotion/>, <t:transitionfilter/>
```

canPause

Compatibility: IE5.5, IE6

Read-only JavaScript property. Indicates whether or not the media file can be paused. Values: true and false.

Syntax:

```
elementID.canPause
```

Example:

```
<html xmlns:t="urn:schemas-microsoft-com:time">
<head><?import namespace="t" implementation="#default#time2">
</head>
<body><t:video id="vt" begin="0" dur="5" src="yourvideo.avi"
onbegin="alert(vt.canSeek); alert(vt.canPause);" end="indefinite"/>
</body></html>
```

Applies to:

```
<t:animation>, <t:audio/>, <t:img>, <t:media>, <t:ref>, <t:video/>
```

canSeek

Compatibility: IE5.5, IE6

Read-only JavaScript property. Indicates whether or not the media file can be fast-forwarded to a specific point. Values: true and false.

Syntax:

```
elementID.canSeek
```

Example: See the canPause property example.
Applies to:

```
<t:animation>, <t:audio/>, <t:img>, <t:media>, <t:ref>, <t:video/>
```

clipBegin

Compatibility: IE5.5, IE6

Read and write JavaScript property and HTML attribute. Establishes the amount of time to wait after the animation starts before beginning to show it. Value: A time value consisting of a number followed by a units designator (h for hours, min for minutes, s for seconds, and ms for milliseconds), or a clock value in the h:min:s.ms format.

Syntax:

```
<t:element clipbegin = "value"/>
elementID.clipBegin = value
```

Example:

```
<html xmlns:t="urn:schemas-microsoft-com:time">
<head><?import namespace="t" implementation="#default#time2">
```

```
</head>
<body><t:video id="myVideo" begin="3" dur="5" src="yourvideo.avi"
onbegin="alert(myVideo.clipBegin); alert(myVideo.clipEnd);" end="indefinite"
clipBegin="2s" clipEnd="3s"/>
</body></html>
```

Applies to:

```
<t:animation>, <t:audio/>, <t:img>, <t:media>, <t:ref>, <t:video/>
```

clipEnd

Compatibility: IE5.5, IE6

Read and write JavaScript property and HTML attribute. Establishes the amount of time to wait after the animation starts before stopping to show it. Value: A time value consisting of a number followed by a units designator (h for hours, min for minutes, s for seconds, and ms for milliseconds), or a clock value in the h:min:s.ms format.

Syntax:

```
<t:element clipend = "value"/>
elementID.clipEnd = value
```

Example: See the clipBegin property example.
Applies to:

```
t:animation>, <t:audio/>, <t:img>, <t:media>, <t:ref>, <t:video/>
```

copyright

Compatibility: IE5.5, IE6

Read-only JavaScript property. Retrieves the contents of the <copyright> tag inside an ASX file, which is an XML type of document that contains all the information that Windows Media Player needs to play a sequence of sound or video media files.

Syntax:

```
elementID.copyright
elementID.playList[index].copyright
```

Example: See the abstract property example.
Applies to:

```
playItem, <t:animation>, <t:audio/>, <t:img>, <t:media>, <t:ref>, <t:video/>
```

currentFrame

Compatibility: IE5.5, IE6

Read-only JavaScript property. Retrieves the current frame number of the animation. To display this information, use the parseInt() JavaScript method.

Syntax:

```
elementID.currentFrame
```

Example:

```
<html xmlns:t="urn:schemas-microsoft-com:time">
<head><?import namespace="t" implementation="#default#time2"></head>
<body><t:video id="vt" begin="3" dur="5" src="yourvideo.avi" end="indefinite"/>
<button onclick="alert(parseInt(vt.currentFrame));">Current frame</button>
</body></html>
```

Applies to:

```
<t:animation>, <t:audio/>, <t:img>, <t:media>, <t:ref>, <t:video/>
```

decelerate

Compatibility: IE5.5, IE6

Read and write JavaScript property and HTML attribute. Establishes the deceleration of a timed element. Value: A floating-point number from 0 (the default; no deceleration) to 1 (maximum deceleration).

Syntax:

```
<t:element decelerate = "value"/>
elementID.decelerate = value
```

Example:

```
<html xmlns:t="urn:schemas-microsoft-com:time">
<head><?import namespace="t" implementation="#default#time2">
</head>
<body><t:video id="vt" begin="3" dur="5" src="yourvideo.avi" end="indefinite"
decelerate=".2"/>
<button onclick="alert(vt.decelerate);">Decelerate</button>
</body></html>
```

Applies to:

```
<t:animate/>, <t:animatecolor/>, <t:animatemotion/>, <t:animation>, <t:audio/>,
<t:excl>, <t:img>, <t:media>, <t:par>, <t:ref>, <t:seq>, <t:transitionfilter/>,
<t:video/>
```

downloadCurrent

Compatibility: IE6

Read-only JavaScript property. Retrieves the amount of data, in bytes, being downstreamed from the server to the client.
Syntax:

```
elementID.downloadCurrent
```

Example (use the ASX file listed in the abstract property example):

```
<html xmlns:t="urn:schemas-microsoft-com:time">
<head><?import namespace="t" implementation="#default#time2">
<style>.time{behavior:url(#default#time2)}</style>
</head>
<body><t:media id="myMedia" src="myasx.asx" syncBehavior="locked"
timeAction="display"/>
<button onclick="alert(myMedia.downloadCurrent);">DownloadCurrent</button>
<button onclick="alert(myMedia.downloadTotal);">DownloadTotal</button>
</body></html>
```

Applies to:

```
<t:animation>, <t:audio/>, <t:excl>, <t:img>, <t:media>, <t:ref>, <t:video/>
```

downloadTotal

Compatibility: IE6

Read-only JavaScript property. Retrieves the size of the file being downstreamed.
Syntax:

```
elementID.downloadTotal
```

Example: See the downloadCurrent property example.
Applies to:

```
<t:animation>, <t:audio/>, <t:excl>, <t:img>, <t:media>, <t:ref>, <t:video/>
```

dur

Compatibility: IE5.5, IE6

Read and write JavaScript property and HTML attribute. Defines the duration of the animation.
Syntax:

```
<t:element dur = "value"/>
elementID.dur = value
elementID.playList[index].dur = value
elementID.playList.dur = value
```

Values:

indefinite	The animation remains active indefinitely.
time value	A number followed by a units designator (h for hours, min for minutes, s for seconds, and ms for milliseconds), or a clock value in the h:min:s.ms format.

Example:

```
<html xmlns:t="urn:schemas-microsoft-com:time">
<head><?import namespace="t" implementation="#default#time2"></head>
<body><div id="myDiv" style="position:absolute; top:50px; left:100px; width:200px;
height:100px; background-color:blue"></div>
<t:animate targetElement="myDiv" attributeName="top" by="200" begin="2" dur="5">
</body></html>
```

Applies to:

```
playItem, playList*, <t:animate/>, <t:animatecolor/>, <t:animatemotion/>,
<t:animation>, <t:audio/>, <t:excl>, <t:img>, <t:media>, <t:par>, <t:ref>, <t:seq>,
<t:set/>, <t:transitionfilter/>, <t:video/>
```

end

Compatibility: IE5.5, IE6

Read and write JavaScript property and HTML attribute. Establishes the amount of time between the loading of the page and the ending of the timeline.

Syntax:

```
<t:element end = "value"/>
elementID.end = value
elementID.playList[index].end = value
```

Values:

indefinite	The animation is ended by a call to endElement().
time value	A number followed by a units designator (h for hours, min for minutes, s for seconds, and ms for milliseconds), or a clock value in the h:min:s.ms format.
elementID.**begin** [+*time value*]	The animation ends relative to the begin time of another element. An additional time value delay is optional, and it takes either of the two time value formats outlined above.
elementID.**end** [+*time value*]	The animation ends relative to the end time of another element. An additional time value delay is optional, and it takes either of the first two time value formats outlined above.

Example:

```
<html xmlns:t="urn:schemas-microsoft-com:time"><head>
<?import namespace="t" implementation="#default#time2"></head>
```

```
<body><div id="myDiv" style="width:200px; height:100px; background-color:blue;"></div>
<t:animatecolor targetElement="myDiv" attributeName="backgroundColor" to="red"
begin="1" dur="9" end="5"/>
</body></html>
```

Applies to:

`<a>`, `<acronym>`, `<address>`, `<area>`, `<b>`, `<big>`, `<blockquote>`, `<button>`, `<caption>`, `<center>`, `<cite>`, `<code>`, `<dd>`, `<del>`, `<dir>`, `<div>`, `<dl>`, `<dt>`, `<em>`, `<fieldset>`, `<font>`, `<form>`, `<hn>`, `<hr>`, `<i>`, `<iframe>`, `<img>`, `<input type="button">`, `<input type="checkbox">`, `<input type="file">`, `<input type="hidden">`, `<input type="image">`, `<input type="password">`, `<input type="radio">`, `<input type="reset">`, `<input type="submit">`, `<input type="text">`, `<ins>`, `<kbd>`, `<legend>`, `<li>`, `<listing>`, `<marquee>`, `<menu>`, `<ol>`, `<option>`, `<p>`, `<plaintext>`, playItem, `<pre>`, `<q>`, `<s>`, `<samp>`, `<small>`, `<span>`, `<strike>`, `<strong>`, `<sub>`, `<sup>`, `<t:animate/>`, `<t:animatecolor/>`, `<t:animatemotion/>`, `<t:animation>`, `<t:audio/>`, `<t:img>`, `<t:media>`, `<t:ref>`, `<t:seq>`, `<t:set/>`, `<t:transitionfilter/>`, `<t:video/>`, `<table>`, `<tbody>`, `<td>`, `<textarea>`, `<tfoot>`, `<th>`, `<thead>`, `<tr>`, `<tt>`, `<u>`, `<ul>`, `<var>`, `<xmp>`

endSync

Compatibility: IE5.5, IE6

Read and write JavaScript property and HTML attribute. Affects the synchronization between a parent timeline element and its timed child elements.

Syntax:

```
<t:element endsync = "value"/>
elementID.endSync = value
```

Values:

all	Parent ends when all of the child elements have ended their animations.
first	Parent ends when the first of the child elements ends.
childID	Parent ends when the specified child element ends.
last	The default; parent ends when the last of the child elements ends.
none	Parent ends according to the value of its dur or end property.

Example:

```
<html xmlns:t="urn:schemas-microsoft-com:time">
<head><style>.time{behavior:url(#default#time2);}</style>
<?import namespace="t" implementation="#default#time2"></head>
<body>
<p>The parent element has three child elements, but its timeline will end when the
second child element has ended</p>
<div style="background-color:lightblue; width:250; padding:25">
<t:excl id="parent" endsync="div2">
```

```
<div id="div1" class="time" begin="0" dur="2" style="background-color:yellow;
width:150; height:75;"></div>
<div id="div2" class="time" begin="2" dur="3" style="background-color:yellow;
width:150; height:75;"></div>
<div id="div3" class="time" begin="4" dur="4"></div></t:excl></div>
</body></html>
```

Applies to:

`<t:excl>`, `<t:par>`

fill

Compatibility: IE5.5, IE6

Read and write JavaScript property and HTML attribute. Establishes what a child element will do when it ends before its parent element.

Syntax:

```
<t:element fill = "value"/>
elementID.fill = value
```

Values:

freeze	Depending on the parent element, the child element will remain at the end of its animation until either another child of the parent with precedence takes over or the parent animation ends.
hold	The child element will remain at the end of its animation until the parent element ends, at which point the child element will also end.
remove	The child element will be removed at the end of its animation, regardless of where the parent element is.
transition	The child element will remain at the end of its animation until the parent ends. This only applies when the parent element is a `<t:transitionfilter/>` element.

Example:

```
<html xmlns:t="urn:schemas-microsoft-com:time">
<head><?import namespace="t" implementation="#default#time2">
<style>.time{behavior:url(#default#time2);}</style></head>
<body>
<t:par id="myPar" begin="0" dur="15">
<div>This div will remain</div>
<div id="myDiv" class="time" begin="0" dur="3" fill="freeze" style="background-
color:beige; width:300">This div will disappear</div></t:par>
<button onclick="alert(myDiv.fill);">Fill property value</button>
</body></html>
```

Applies to:

<t:animate/>, <t:animatecolor/>, <t:animatemotion/>, <t:animation>, <t:audio/>, <t:img>, <t:media>, <t:par>, <t:ref>, <t:seq>, <t:set/>, <t:video/>

from (1)

Compatibility: IE5.5, IE6

Read and write JavaScript property and HTML attribute. Establishes the starting position of the animation.

NOTE *The* values *and* path *properties have precedence over the* from *property.*

Syntax:

```
<t:element from = "value"/>
elementID.from = value
elementID.from(value)
```

Example:

```
<html xmlns:t="urn:schemas-microsoft-com:time">
<head><?import namespace="t" implementation="#default#time2">
<style>.time{behavior:url(#default#time2);}</style></head>
<body>
<t:animate id="myAnim" autoreverse="true" begin="3" from="200px"
targetElement="myDiv" attributeName="left" dur="5" to="400px" fill="hold"/>
<div id="myDiv" class="time" style="position:absolute; left:0px; top:100px;
background-color:beige;"></div>
<button onclick="alert(myAnim.from);">FROM value</button>
</body></html>
```

Applies to:

<t:animate/>, <t:animatemotion/>

from (2)

Compatibility: IE5.5, IE6

Read and write JavaScript property and HTML attribute. Establishes the starting color of the animation. Value: A web color name or the hexadecimal value in #RRGGBB format.

Syntax:

```
<t:animatecolor from = "value"/>
animatecolorID.from = value
animatecolorID.from(value)
```

Example:

```
<html xmlns:t="urn:schemas-microsoft-com:time">
<head><style>.time{behavior:url(#default#time2);}</style>
<?import namespace="t" implementation="#default#time2"></head>
<body>
<t:par begin="0" dur="15" fill="hold">
<t:animatecolor attributeName="background-color" targetElement="myDiv1" from="blue"
to="red" begin="0" dur="5" fill="hold"/>
<t:animatecolor attributeName="background-color" targetElement="myDiv2" from="red"
to="blue" begin="0" dur="5" fill="hold"/>
</t:par>
<div id="myDiv1" class="time" style="left:100px; width:350px; position:absolute;
top:50px; height:220px; background-color:blue;"></div>
<div id="myDiv2" class="time" style="left:300px; width:200px; position:absolute;
top:110px; height:100px; background-color:red;"></div>
</body></html>
```

Applies to:

```
<t:animatecolor/>
```

from (3)

Compatibility: IE6

Read and write JavaScript property and HTML attribute. Specifies the percentage of the transition filter's timeline that will be skipped before play begins. Value: A floating-point number from 0 (the default) to 1.

Syntax:

```
<t:transitionfilter from = "value"/>
transitionfilterID.from = value
transitionfilterID.from(value)
```

Example:

```
<html xmlns:t="urn:schemas-microsoft-com:time">
<head><?import namespace="t" implementation="#default#time2"></head>
<body>
<div id="myDiv" style="position:absolute; top:150px; left:200px; width:300px;
height:200px; background-color:red;"></div>
<t:transitionfilter type="fanWipe" begin="0" dur="5" from=".2" to=".6"/>
</body></html>
```

Applies to:

```
<t:transitionfilter/>
```

hasAudio

Compatibility: IE5.5, IE6

Read-only JavaScript property. Indicates whether or not the media file has audio content. Values: true and false.

Syntax:

```
elementID.hasAudio
```

Example (use the ASX file listed in the abstract property example):

```
<html xmlns:t="urn:schemas-microsoft-com:time">
<head><?import namespace="t" implementation="#default#time2"></head>
<body>
<t:video id="myVideo" begin="0" dur="5" src="myasx.asx" end="indefinite"/>
<button onclick="alert(myVideo.hasAudio);">Has audio</button>
<button onclick="alert(myVideo.hasMedia);">Has media</button>
<button onclick="alert(myVideo.hasPlayList);">Has play list</button>
<button onclick="alert(myVideo.hasVisual);">Has visual</button>
<button onclick="alert(myVideo.hasDownloadProgress);">Has download progress</button>
</body></html>
```

Applies to:

```
<t:animation>, <t:audio/>, <t:img>, <t:media>, <t:ref>, <t:video/>
```

hasDownloadProgress

Compatibility: IE6

Read-only JavaScript property. Indicates whether or not the media file has begun downloading to the browser. Values: true and false.

Syntax:

```
elementID.hasDownloadProgress
```

Example: See the hasAudio property example.

Applies to:

```
<t:animation>, <t:audio/>, <t:img>, <t:media>, <t:ref>, <t:video/>
```

hasMedia

Compatibility: IE5.5, IE6

Read-only JavaScript property. Indicates whether or not the element has media content. Values: true and false.

Syntax:

---

elementID.hasMedia

Example: See the hasAudio property example.
Applies to:

<t:animate/>, <t:animatecolor/>, <t:animatemotion/>, <t:animation>, <t:audio/>,
<t:img>, <t:media>, <t:ref>, <t:seq>, <t:set/>, <t:switch>, <t:video/>

---

hasPlayList

Compatibility: IE5.5, IE6

Read-only JavaScript property. Indicates whether or not the element contains a
playList collection. Values: true and false.
Syntax:

---

elementID.hasPlayList

Example: See the hasAudio property example.
Applies to:

<t:audio/>, <t:media>, <t:ref>, <t:video/>

---

hasVisual

Compatibility: IE5.5, IE6

Read-only JavaScript property. Indicates whether or not the element is visible.
Values: true and false.
Syntax:

---

elementID.hasVisual

Example: See the hasAudio property example.
Applies to:

<t:animation>, <t:audio/>, <t:img>, <t:media>, <t:ref>, <t:video/>

---

higher

Compatibility: IE5.5, IE6

Read and write JavaScript property and HTML attribute. Establishes how a
child element of the <t:priorityClass> element will affect other children of
<t:priorityClass> elements that have a lower priority (those that appear lower
in the <t:priorityClass> list) when its animation begins.

Syntax:

```
<t:priorityclass higher = "value"/>
priorityclassID.higher = value
```

Values:

pause	The default; any child element that is active is paused and set aside for execution when the higher priority element ends its animation.
stop	Any child element that is active or paused is stopped.

Example: See the <t:priorityclass> element example.
Applies to:

```
<t:priorityclass>
```

immediateend

Compatibility: IE5.5, IE6

Read and write HTML attribute. Establishes whether or not the Microsoft DirectMusic player plays a transition before ending a segment. Values: true and false.
Syntax:

```
<t:element immediateend = "value"/>
```

Example (use the ASX file listed in the abstract property example):

```
<html xmlns:t="urn:schemas-microsoft-com:time">
<head><?import namespace="t" implementation="#default#time2">
<style>.time{behavior:url(#default#time2);}</style></head>
<body><t:video id="myVideo" immediateend="false" src="myasx.asx"/>
</body></html>
```

Applies to:

```
<t:animation>, <t:audio/>, <t:img>, <t:media>, <t:ref>, <t:video/>
```

index

Compatibility: IE5.5, IE6

Read-only JavaScript property. Retrieves the index value of a playItem object within the playList collection.
Syntax:

```
elementID.playList[index].index
```

Example (use the ASX file listed in the abstract property example):

```
<html xmlns:t="urn:schemas-microsoft-com:time">
<head><?import namespace="t" implementation="#default#time2"></head>
<body><t:video id="myVideo" begin="0" src="myasx.asx" end="indefinite"
ontrackchange="alert(event.MoreInfo);" type="avi"/><br><br>
<button onclick="alert(myVideo.playList(0).index);">Index</button>
<br>
</body></html>
```

Applies to:

playItem

isActive

Compatibility: IE5.5, IE6

Read-only JavaScript property. Indicates whether or not the element is currently active. Values: true and false.

Syntax:

elementID.currTimeState.isActive

Example (use the ASX file listed in the abstract property example):

```
<html xmlns:t="urn:schemas-microsoft-com:time">
<head><?import namespace="t" implementation="#default#time2">
<style>.time{behavior:url(#default#time2);}</style></head>
<body><t:video id="myMedia" begin="0" src="myasx.asx" fill="remove"/>
<br><br><button onclick="myMedia.mute='false'; myMedia.volume=100;">Unmute</button>
<button onclick="myMedia.mute='true';">Mute</button>
<button onclick="myMedia.pauseElement();">Pause</button>
<button onclick="myMedia.resumeElement();">Resume</button>
<br>
<button onclick="alert(myMedia.currTimeState.isOn);">Is on</button>
<button onclick="alert(myMedia.currTimeState.isActive);">Is active</button>
<button onclick="alert(myMedia.currTimeState.isMuted);">Is muted</button>
<button onclick="alert(myMedia.isStreamed);">Is streamed</button>
<button onclick="alert(myMedia.currTimeState.isPaused);">Is paused</button>
</body></html>
```

Applies to:

currTimeState

isMuted

Compatibility: IE5.5, IE6

Read-only JavaScript property. Indicates whether or not the element is muted. Values: true and false.

Syntax:

```
elementID.currTimeState.isMuted
```

Example: See the isActive property example.
Applies to:

```
currTimeState
```

isOn

Compatibility: IE5.5, IE6

Read-only JavaScript property. Indicates whether or not the element is either 1) active or 2) has finished its animation and is waiting for its parent timeline to end. Values: true and false.

Syntax:

```
elementID.currTimeState.isOn
```

Example: See the isActive property example.
Applies to:

```
currTimeState
```

isPaused

Compatibility: IE5.5, IE6

Read-only JavaScript property. Indicates whether or not the element is paused. Values: true and false.

Syntax:

```
elementID.currTimeState.isPaused
```

Example: See the isActive property example.
Applies to:

```
currTimeState
```

isStreamed

Compatibility: IE6

Read-only JavaScript property. Indicates whether or not the element's content is streamed. Values: true and false.

Syntax:

```
elementID.isStreamed
```

Example: See the isActive property example.
Applies to:

```
<t:animation>, <t:audio/>, <t:img>, <t:media>, <t:ref>, <t:video/>
```

keySplines

Compatibility: IE5.5, IE6

Read and write JavaScript property and HTML attribute. Establishes interval points between frames to manage the pacing of an animation. To use this property, calcMode must be set to spline.

Value: A space-delimited set of four floating-point values between 0 and 1 that define each interval point between frames; these values are X1, Y1, X2, and Y2. Each set of interval points must be separated by a semicolon.

Syntax:

```
<t:element keysplines = "value"/>
elementID.keySplines = value
elementID.keySplines(value)
```

Example: See the calcMode property example.
Applies to:

```
<t:animate/>, <t:animatecolor/>, <t:animatemotion/>, <t:transitionfilter/>
```

keyTimes

Compatibility: IE5.5, IE6

Read and write JavaScript property and HTML attribute. Establishes a semicolon-delimited list of time values that control when in a timeline's duration particular actions happen. The actions that happen are defined in the values property list, and each member of the keyTimes property list corresponds to a member of the values property list (meaning that both lists must have the same number of values).

To use keyTimes, calcmode must be set to linear, spline, or discrete. Furthermore, each value in the keyTimes list must be equal to or greater than the preceding one. When calcmode is linear or spline, the keyTimes values list must start with a value of 0 and end with 1. When the calcmode value is discrete, the keyTimes values list must start with a value of 0, but does not need to end with a value of 1.

Syntax:

```
<t:element keytimes = "value"/>
elementID.keyTimes = value
elementID.keyTimes(value)
```

Example: See the `calcMode` property example.
Applies to:

```
<t:animate/>, <t:animatecolor/>, <t:animatemotion/>, <t:transitionfilter/>
```

latestMediaTime

Compatibility: IE6

Read-only JavaScript property. Indicates the amount of time it takes for the animation to start playing. This property does not apply to streaming content.
Syntax:

```
elementID.latestMediaTime
```

Example (use the ASX file listed in the abstract property example):

```
<html xmlns:t="urn:schemas-microsoft-com:time">
<head><?import namespace="t" implementation="#default#time2"></head>
<body>
<t:video id="myVideo" begin="0" src="myasx.asx" end="indefinite"/>
<button onclick="alert(myVideo.latestMediaTime);">Latest media time</button>
</body></html>
```

Applies to:

```
<t:animation>, <t:audio/>, <t:img>, <t:media>, <t:ref>, <t:video/>
```

length

Compatibility: IE5.5, IE6

Read-only JavaScript property. Retrieves the number of elements in an array.
Syntax:

```
collectionName.length
```

Example (use the ASX file listed in the abstract property example):

```
<html xmlns:t="urn:schemas-microsoft-com:time">
<head><?import namespace="t" implementation="#default#time2"></head>
<body>
```

```
<t:video id="myVideo" begin="0" src="myasx.asx" end="indefinite"/>
<button onclick="alert(myVideo.playList.length);">Length</button><br>
</body></html>
```

Applies to:

```
activeElements*, playList*, timeAll*, timeChildren*
```

longtransition

Compatibility: IE5.5, IE6

Read and write HTML attribute. Establishes whether or not the Microsoft DirectMusic player can play introduction and ending transitions that are longer than one measure for a music segment. Values: true and false. For more information on DirectMusic, see http://msdn.microsoft.com/workshop/author/behaviors/reference/time2/time_dmusic_ovw.asp.

   Syntax:

```
<t:element longtransition = "value"/>
```

   Example:

```
<html xmlns:t="urn:schemas-microsoft-com:time">
<head><?import namespace="t" implementation="#default#time2"></head>
<body><t:audio id="myAudio" begin="0" src="sound.mp3" end="indefinite"
modulate="true" longtransition="true" motifname="" player="DMusic"/>
</body></html>
```

   Applies to:

```
<t:animation>, <t:audio/>, <t:img>, <t:media>, <t:ref>, <t:video/>
```

lower

Compatibility: IE5.5, IE6

Read and write JavaScript property and HTML attribute. Establishes how a child element of the <t:priorityClass> element will respond when other children of <t:priorityClass> elements that have a higher priority (those that appear higher in the <t:priorityClass> list) are active when its animation begins.

   Syntax:

```
<t:priorityclass lower = "value"/>
priorityclassID.lower = value
```

Values:

defer	The default; the lower-priority element is paused until the higher-priority active element completes its animation.
never	The lower-priority element does not play at all.

Example: See the `<t:priorityclass>` element example.
Applies to:

`<t:priorityclass>`

mediaDur

Compatibility: IE5.5, IE6

Read-only JavaScript property. Retrieves the duration in seconds of the media file.

Syntax:

elementID.mediaDur

Example:

```
<html xmlns:t="urn:schemas-microsoft-com:time">
<head><?import namespace="t" implementation="#default#time2">
<style>.time{behavior:url(#default#time2);}</style></head>
<body>
<t:video id="myVideo" modulate="true" src="yourvideo.avi"/><br><br>
<button onclick="alert(myVideo.mediaDur);">Media duration</button>
<button onclick="alert(myVideo.mediaHeight);">Height</button>
<button onclick="alert(myVideo.mediaWidth);">Width</button>
<button onclick="alert(myMedia.mimeType);">MimeType</button>
</body></html>
```

Applies to:

`<t:animation>`, `<t:audio/>`, `<t:img>`, `<t:media>`, `<t:par>`, `<t:ref>`, `<t:seq>`, `<t:video/>`

mediaHeight

Compatibility: IE5.5, IE6

Read-only JavaScript property. Retrieves the height in pixels of the element containing the media file.

Syntax:

elementID.mediaHeight

Example: See the `mediaDur` property example.
Applies to:

`<t:animation>, <t:audio/>, <t:img>, <t:media>, <t:par>, <t:ref>, <t:seq>, <t:video/>`

---

mediaWidth

Compatibility: IE5.5, IE6

Read-only JavaScript property. Retrieves the width in pixels of the element containing the media file.
Syntax:

---

elementID`.mediaWidth`

Example: See the `mediaDur` property example.
Applies to:

`<t:animation>, <t:audio/>, <t:img>, <t:media>, <t:par>, <t:ref>, <t:seq>, <t:video/>`

---

mimeType

Compatibility: IE6

Read-only JavaScript property. Retrieves the MIME content type of the media element.
Syntax:

---

elementID`.mimeType`

Example: See the `mediaDur` property example.
Applies to:

`<t:animation>, <t:audio/>, <t:img>, <t:media>, <t:ref>, <t:video/>`

---

mode

Compatibility: IE6

Read and write JavaScript property and HTML attribute. Establishes whether the effect specified in the type property transitions in or out. Values: in and out.
Syntax:

```
<t:transitionfilter mode = "value"/>
transitionfilterID.mode = value
```

Example: See the `<t:transitionfilter/>` element example.

Applies to:

<t:transitionfilter/>

modulate

Compatibility: IE5.5, IE6

Read and write HTML attribute. Defines whether or not to modulate when the Microsoft DirectMusic player plays a transition between music segments. Values: true and false (the default). For more information on DirectMusic, see http://msdn.microsoft.com/workshop/author/behaviors/reference/time2/time_dmusic_ovw.asp.

Syntax:

<t:*element* modulate = "*value*"/>

Example: See the longtransition property example.
Applies to:

<t:animation>, <t:audio/>, <t:img>, <t:media>, <t:ref>, <t:video/>

MoreInfo

Compatibility: IE6

Read-only JavaScript property. Retrieves the contents of the <moreinfo> tag inside the <banner> tag inside an ASX file. An ASX file is an XML type of document that contains all the information that Windows Media Player needs to play a sequence of sound or video media files. This property is identical to BannerMoreInfo, but it is applicable to the event object only.

Syntax:

event.MoreInfo

Example: See the abstract property example.
Applies to:

event

motifname

Compatibility: IE5.5, IE6

Read and write HTML attribute. Defines the name of a motif to play instead of the file specified by src. This is only available when the player property is set to DMusic, and the music file is compatible with the Microsoft DirectMusic player. For more information on DirectMusic, see http://msdn.microsoft.com/workshop/author/behaviors/reference/time2/time_dmusic_ovw.asp.

Syntax:

```
<t:element motifname = "value"/>
```

Example: See the longtransition property example.
Applies to:

```
<t:animation>, <t:audio/>, <t:img>, <t:media>, <t:ref>, <t:video/>
```

mute

Compatibility: IE5.5, IE6

Read and write JavaScript property and HTML attribute. Establishes whether or not the element is muted. Values: true and false.
Syntax:

```
<t:element mute = "value"/>
elementID.mute = value
```

Example: See the isActive property example.
Applies to:

```
<t:animation>, <t:audio/>, <t:img>, <t:media>, <t:par>, <t:ref>, <t:seq>, <t:video/>
```

origin

Compatibility: IE5.5, IE6

Read and write JavaScript property and HTML attribute. Establishes the point of origin for the animation.
Syntax:

```
<t:animatemotion origin = "value"/>
animatemotionID.origin = value
```

Values:

parent	The parent element's origin value.
element	The upper-left corner of the element.
default	Same as element.

Example:

```
<html xmlns:t="urn:schemas-microsoft-com:time">
<head><?import namespace="t" implementation="#default#time2"></head>
<body><div id="myObject" class="time" style="position:absolute; top:300px;
left:50px; width:200px; height:100px; background-color:lightblue;"></div>
```

```
<div id="myObject2" style="position:absolute; top:480px; left:50px; width:200px;
height:100px; background-color:red;"></div>
<t:animatecolor targetElement="myObject" attributeName="backgroundColor"
to="yellow" start="1" dur="5" fill="hold">
<t:animatemotion targetElement="myObject2" to="0,-180" dur="5" fill="hold"
origin="default">
<t:animatecolor id="myA" targetElement="myObject2" attributeName="backgroundColor"
to="cyan" start="1" dur="5" fill="hold">
<t:animatemotion id="myAnim" targetElement="myObject" to="400,0" dur="5"
fill="hold" additive="sum" origin="element">
<button onclick="alert(myAnim.origin);">Origin</button>
</body></html>
```

Applies to:

```
<t:animatemotion/>
```

parentTimeBegin

Compatibility: IE5.5, IE6

Read-only JavaScript property. Retrieves the difference in seconds between the element's begin time and the parent's begin time.

Syntax:

```
elementID.currTimeState.parentTimeBegin
```

Example:

```
<html xmlns:t="urn:schemas-microsoft-com:time">
<head><?import namespace="t" implementation="#default#time2">
<style>.time{behavior:url(#default#time2) }</style>
</head>
<body>
<t:excl id="myAnim">
<div id="myDiv" class="time" begin="2" dur="7" style="width:500px; height:70px;
background-color:red;"></div></t:excl>
<button onclick="alert(myDiv.currTimeState.parentTimeBegin);">ParentTimeBegin</button>
<button onclick="alert(myDiv.currTimeState.parentTimeEnd);">ParentTimeEnd</button>
</body></html>
```

Applies to:

```
currTimeState
```

parentTimeEnd

Compatibility: IE5.5, IE6

Read-only JavaScript property. Retrieves the difference in seconds between the element's end time and the parent's begin time.

Syntax:

```
elementID.currTimeState.parentTimeEnd
```

Example: See the parentTimeBegin property example.

Applies to:

```
currTimeState
```

path

Compatibility: IE5.5, IE6

Read and write JavaScript property and HTML attribute. Establishes the "path" the element follows during its animation.

NOTE   *The* path *property has precedence over the* by, from, to, *and* values *properties.*

Syntax:

```
<t:animatemotion path = "value"/>
animatemotionID.path = value
animatemotionID.path(value)
```

Values:

(Relative commands are shown in lowercase, and absolute commands are shown in uppercase; relative commands specify values as offsets from an element's current value, and absolute commands specify values as coordinates in the screen.)

m/M	Moves the element to the specified coordinates.
l/L	Moves the element to new coordinates after the element has already moved using an m/M value.
h/H	Moves the element horizontally by the specified number of pixels.
v/V	Moves the element vertically by the specified number of pixels.
z/Z	Moves the element from its current position to its original starting position, closing the path.
c/C	Moves the element along a Bezier curve using three points: one for the element's origin (x, y), one for the start of the curve (x1, y1), and one for the end of the curve (x2, y2).

Example:

```
<html xmlns:t="urn:schemas-microsoft-com:time">
<head><?import namespace="t" implementation="#default#time2">
<style>.time{behavior:url(#default#time2);}</style></head>
<body>
```

```
<div id="myDiv1" class="time" style="position:absolute; top:200; width:200;
height;100; background-color:blue;"></div>
<div id="myDiv2" class="time" style="position:absolute; top:200; width:200;
height;100; background-color:red;"></div>
<t:animatemotion targetElement="myDiv1" begin="myButton.click" path="M 30 30 L 350
30 v 100 h -100 V 30" dur="3"/>
<t:animatemotion targetElement="myDiv2" begin="myButton.click" path="M 30 30 C 350
30 10 450 170 450" dur="5"/>
<button id="myButton" style="position:absolute">Start path</button>
</body></html>
```

Applies to:

```
<t:animatemotion/>
```

peers

Compatibility: IE5.5, IE6

Read and write JavaScript property and HTML attribute. Establishes how the
elements in a <t:priorityClass> list will affect and respond to one another. This
property is similar to the higher and lower properties, but unlike those properties
it isn't affected by priority order in the <t:priorityClass> list.

Syntax:

```
<t:priorityclass peers = "value"/>
priorityclassID.peers = value
```

Values:

stop	The default; when an element begins, all other active elements stop.
defer	An element will begin only when all other active elements have completed their animation.
never	An element will not play if another element is active when its begin time occurs.
pause	When an element begins, it causes all other active elements to pause.

Example:

```
<html xmlns:t="urn:schemas-microsoft-com:time">
<head><?import namespace="t" implementation="#default#time2">
<style>.time{behavior:url(#default#time2);}</style></head>
<body><t:excl id="myAnim">
<t:priorityclass id="myPriority" peers="pause">
<div id="myDiv1" class="time" begin="0" dur="12"><div style="background-color:red;
width:400; height:50;"></div></div>
<div id="myDiv2" class="time" begin="5" dur="5"><div style="background-
color:yellow; width:400; height:50;"></div></div>
<t:audio src="sound.mp3" begin="12" dur="10" player="DMusic"
segmenttype="secondary" id="myAudio">
```

```
</t:priorityclass></t:excl>
<button onclick="alert(myDiv1.currTimeState.segmentDur);">SegmentDur Div1</button>
<button onclick="alert(myDiv1.currTimeState.segmentTime);">SegmentTime Div1</button>
<button onclick="alert(myPriority.peers);">Peer</button>
</body></html>
```

Applies to:

```
<t:priorityclass>
```

player

Compatibility: IE5.5, IE6

Read and write JavaScript property and HTML attribute. Establishes the component to use to render the media file. The component must support HTML+TIME.

Syntax:

```
<t:element player = "value"/>
elementID.player = value
```

Values:

class identifier	The class identifier of the component in the following format: {XXXXXXXX-XXXX-XXXX-XXXX-XXXXXXXXXXXX}.
DMusic	The Microsoft DirectMusic player.
DVD	The digital video disc (DVD) movie player.

Example:

```
<html xmlns:t="urn:schemas-microsoft-com:time">
<head><?import namespace="t" implementation="#default#time2"></head>
<body><t:video id="myVideo" begin="3" dur="5" src="yoursound.wma" end="indefinite"
player="DMusic"/>
<button onclick="alert(myVideo.player);">Player</button>
<button onclick="alert(myVideo.playerObject);">Player object</button>
</body></html>
```

Applies to:

```
<t:animation>, <t:audio/>, <t:img>, <t:media>, <t:ref>, <t:video/>
```

playerObject

Compatibility: IE5.5, IE6

Read-only JavaScript property. Retrieves the component that was specified by player. This property returns a reference to the component object, and therefore allows the component's properties and methods to be exposed.

Syntax:

```
elementID.playerObject
```

Example: See the player property example.
Applies to:

```
<t:animation>, <t:audio/>, <t:img>, <t:media>, <t:ref>, <t:video/>
```

progress

Compatibility: IE5.5, IE6

Read-only JavaScript property. Retrieves the progress of the animation as a percentage of its total duration. Value: A floating-point number from 0 to 1.

Syntax:

```
elementID.currTimeState.progress
```

Example:

```
<html xmlns:t="urn:schemas-microsoft-com:time">
<head><?import namespace="t" implementation="#default#time2">
<style>.time{behavior:url(#default#time2);}</style>
<script language="JavaScript">
function B1() {mySpan.innerText = myVideo.currTimeState.progress;}
</script></head>
<body><t:video class="time" id="myVideo" src="yourvideo.avi"/>
<span id="timer" class="time" begin="myVideo.begin" dur=".25"
repeatcount="indefinite" onrepeat="B1();"></span><br><br>
<span style="background-color:blue; color:white;" id="mySpan">0</span>
</body></html>
```

Applies to:

```
currTimeState
```

rating

Compatibility: IE5.5, IE6

Read-only JavaScript property. Retrieves the rating of the media file, if available. This rating is similar to the rating given to movies.

Syntax:

```
elementID.rating
elementID.playList[index].rating
```

Example:

```
<html xmlns:t="urn:schemas-microsoft-com:time"><head>
<?import namespace="t" implementation="#default#time2">
<style>.time{behavior:url(#default#time2);}</style></head>
<body><t:video id="myVideo" src="yourvideo.avi"/>
<button onclick="alert(myVideo.rating);">Rating</button>
</body></html>
```

Applies to:

```
playItem, <t:animation>, <t:audio/>, <t:img>, <t:media>, <t:ref>, <t:video/>
```

repeatCount

Compatibility: IE5.5, IE6

Read and write JavaScript property and HTML attribute. Specifies the number of times a timeline repeats. For the currTimeState object, it returns the number of times the animation has been played.

Syntax:

```
<t:element repeatcount = "value"/>
elementID.repeatCount = value
elementID.currTimeState.repeatCount
```

Values:

number	A floating-point number (the default is 1) specifying the number of times the animation repeats.
indefinite	The animation repeats indefinitely.

Example:

```
<html xmlns:t="urn:schemas-microsoft-com:time">
<head><?import namespace="t" implementation="#default#time2">
<style>.time{behavior:url(#default#time2);}</style></head>
<body>
<button onclick="alert(myAnim.repeatCount);">RepeatCount</button>
<button onclick="alert(myAnim.repeatDur);">RepeatDur</button>
<button onclick="alert(myAnim.restart);">Restart</button>
<div id="myDiv" class="time" style="position:relative; top:10; left:10; height:100;
width:200; background-color:red;"></div>
<t:animatemotion id="myAnim" targetElement="myDiv" to="320,200" begin="0" dur="5"
autoreverse="true" repeatcount="indefinite" restart="never"/>
</body></html>
```

Applies to:

currTimeState, <t:animate/>, <t:animatecolor/>, <t:animatemotion/>, <t:animation>, <t:audio/>, <t:img>, <t:media>, <t:par>, <t:ref>, <t:seq>, <t:transitionfilter/>, <t:video/>

repeatDur

Compatibility: IE5.5, IE6

Read and write JavaScript property and HTML attribute. Specifies the number of seconds during which an animation repeats. This property can only be used when repeatCount is set to indefinite or to a numeric value greater than 1.

Syntax:

```
<t:element repeatdur = "value"/>
elementID.repeatDur = value
```

Values:

indefinite	The animation remains active indefinitely.
time value	A number followed by a units designator (h for hours, min for minutes, s for seconds, and ms for milliseconds), or a clock value in the h:min:s.ms format.

Example: See the repeatCount property example.

Applies to:

<t:animate/>, <t:animatecolor/>, <t:animatemotion/>, <t:animation>, <t:audio/>, <t:excl>, <t:img>, <t:media>, <t:par>, <t:ref>, <t:seq>, <t:set/>, <t:transitionfilter/>, <t:video/>

restart

Compatibility: IE5.5, IE6

Read and write JavaScript property and HTML attribute. Specifies when an element's timeline can be restarted.

Syntax:

```
<t:element restart = "value"/>
elementID.restart = value
elementID.restart(value)
```

Values:

always	The default; you can restart the animation at any time.
never	Animation cannot be restarted until the parent's timeline ends.
whenNotActive	Animation can only be restarted when it is not active.

Example: See the repeatCount property example.
Applies to:

`<t:animate/>`, `<t:animatecolor/>`, `<t:animatemotion/>`, `<t:animation>`, `<t:audio/>`, `<t:img>`, `<t:media>`, `<t:par>`, `<t:ref>`, `<t:seq>`, `<t:set/>`, `<t:transitionfilter/>`, `<t:video/>`

---

segmentDur

Compatibility: IE5.5, IE6

Read-only JavaScript property. Retrieves the duration in seconds of the current iteration in an animation. If the autoReverse property is set to true, segmentDur counts the autoReverse time as well.

Syntax:

---

elementID.currTimeState.segmentDur

Example:

```html
<html xmlns:t="urn:schemas-microsoft-com:time">
<head><?import namespace="t" implementation="#default#time2">
<style>.time{behavior:url(#default#time2);}</style></head>
<body><t:excl id="myAnim">
<t:priorityclass id="myPriority" peers="pause">
<div id="myDiv1" class="time" begin="0" dur="12"><div style="background-color:red; width:400; height:50;"></div></div>
<div id="myDiv2" class="time" begin="5" dur="5"><div style="background-color:yellow; width:400; height:50;"></div></div>
</t:priorityclass></t:excl>
<button onclick="alert(myDiv1.currTimeState.segmentDur);">SegmentDur myDiv1</button>
<button onclick="alert(myDiv1.currTimeState.segmentTime);">SegmentTime myDiv1</button>
</body></html>
```

Applies to:

---

currTimeState

---

segmentTime

Compatibility: IE5.5, IE6

Read-only JavaScript property. Retrieves the amount of time in seconds that has elapsed since the beginning of the current iteration in an animation. If the autoReverse property is set to true, segmentTime counts up during the autoReverse time.

Syntax:

---

elementID.currTimeState.segmentTime

Example: See the `segmentDur` property example.

Applies to:

---

currTimeState

---

segmenttype

Compatibility: IE5.5, IE6

Read and write HTML attribute. Specifies the type of segment that the Microsoft DirectMusic player will play. Values: primary (the default), control, and secondary. The control segment establishes properties that also affect the primary and secondary segments. For more information on DirectMusic, see http://msdn.microsoft.com/workshop/author/behaviors/reference/time2/time_dmusic_ovw.asp.

Syntax:

```
<t:element segmenttype = "value"/>
```

Example:

```
<html xmlns:t="urn:schemas-microsoft-com:time">
<head><?import namespace="t" implementation="#default#time2">
<style>.time{behavior:url(#default#time2);}</style></head>
<body><t:audio src="sound.mp3" begin="12" dur="10" player="DMusic"
segmenttype="secondary" id="myAudio">
</body></html>
```

Applies to:

`<t:animation>`, `<t:audio/>`, `<t:img>`, `<t:media>`, `<t:ref>`, `<t:video/>`

---

simpleDur

Compatibility: IE5.5, IE6

Read-only JavaScript property. Retrieves the duration in seconds of each iteration in an animation. If the `autoReverse` property is set to true, `simpleDur` counts the `autoReverse` time as well.

Syntax:

```
elementID.currTimeState.simpleDur
```

Example:

```
<html xmlns:t="urn:schemas-microsoft-com:time">
<head><?import namespace="t" implementation="#default#time2">
<style>.time{behavior:url(#default#time2) }</style></head>
<body><t:excl id="myAnim" dur="3" repeatcount="3">
```

```
<div id="div1" class="time" begin="0" dur="3" style="background-color:yellow;
width:150;"></div>
<div id="div2" class="time" begin="1" dur="2" style="background-color:beige;
width:150;"></div>
<div id="div3" class="time" begin="2" dur="1" style="background-color:lavender;
width:150;"></div></t:excl>
<button onclick="alert(myAnim.currTimeState.simpleDur);">SimpleDur</button>
<button onclick="alert(myAnim.currTimeState.simpleTime);">SimpleTime</button>
</body></html>
```

Applies to:

currTimeState

simpleTime

Compatibility: IE5.5, IE6

Read-only JavaScript property. Retrieves the number of seconds that have elapsed since the beginning of the current iteration in an animation. If the autoReverse property is set to true, simpleTime counts down during the autoReverse time.

Syntax:

```
elementID.currTimeState.simpleTime
```

Example: See the simpleDur property example.
Applies to:

currTimeState

speed

Compatibility: IE5.5, IE6

Read and write JavaScript property and HTML attribute. Establishes the playback speed of an element relative to its parent's playback speed. The child element's playback speed is determined by multiplying its speed value by the speed value of its parent. Value: A floating-point number from 0 to 1 (the default).

Syntax:

```
<t:element speed = "value"/>
elementID.speed = value
elementID.speed(value)
elementID.currTimeState.speed
```

Example:

```
<html xmlns:t="urn:schemas-microsoft-com:time">
<head><?import namespace="t" implementation="#default#time2">
```

```
<style>.time{behavior:url(#default#time2);}</style></head>
<body><t:excl id="t1" begin="0" dur="5" speed="0.5">
<div id="myDiv" class="time" begin="1" dur="1" speed="0.5" style="color:blue; font-size:1in">Sample Text</div></t:excl>
<button onclick="alert(myDiv.speed);">Speed</button>
</body></html>
```

Applies to:

currTimeState, <t:animate/>, <t:animatecolor/>, <t:animatemotion/>, <t:animation>, <t:audio/>, <t:img>, <t:media>, <t:par>, <t:ref>, <t:seq>, <t:transitionfilter/>, <t:video/>

src

Compatibility: IE5.5, IE6

Read and write JavaScript property and HTML attribute. Establishes the URL of the media file.

Syntax:

```
<t:element src = "value"/>
elementID.src = value
elementID.playList(index).src
```

Example:

```
<html xmlns:t="urn:schemas-microsoft-com:time">
<head><?import namespace="t" implementation="#default#time2"></head>
<body><t:media><img id="myMedia" src="yourimage.gif" begin="3" dur="5" repeatcount="5"/></t:media>
<button onclick="alert(myMedia.src);">SRC</button>
</body></html>
```

Applies to:

playItem, <t:animation>, <t:audio/>, <t:img>, <t:media>, <t:ref>, <t:video/>

state

Compatibility: IE5.5, IE6

Read-only JavaScript property. Retrieves a number that represents the current state of the element's animation. Values: 0 (inactive), 1 (active), 2 (media file is being queued), 3 (fast-forwarding to a specific point in the media file), and 4 (finished and is waiting until its parent element completes animation).

Syntax:

```
elementID.currTimeState.state
```

Example:

```
<html xmlns:t="urn:schemas-microsoft-com:time">
<head><?import namespace="t" implementation="#default#time2">
<style>.time{behavior:url(#default#time2);}</style></head>
<body><t:video class="time" id="myAnim" begin="0" src="yourvideo.avi"
fill="remove"/>
<button onclick="alert(myAnim.currTimeState.state);">Current state value</button>
<button onclick="alert(myAnim.currTimeState.stateString);">Current state string</
button>
```

Applies to:

```
currTimeState
```

stateString

Compatibility: IE5.5, IE6

Read-only JavaScript property. Retrieves a string corresponding to one of the five numeric values listed for the state property. Values: inactive, active, cueing, unknown, and holding.

Syntax:

```
elementID.currTimeState.stateString
```

Example: See the state property example.

Applies to:

```
currTimeState
```

subtype

Compatibility: IE6

Read and write JavaScript property and HTML attribute. Establishes the subtype of the transition specified by the type property of the `<t:transitionfilter/>` element.

Depending on the value of the type property, subtype can be assigned different values. For a list of the possibilities, see http://msdn.microsoft.com/workshop/author/behaviors/reference/time2/properties/subtype.asp?frame=true.

Syntax:

```
<t:transitionfilter subtype = "value"/>
transitionfilterID.subtype = value
```

Example:

```
<html xmlns:t="urn:schemas-microsoft-com:time">
<head><?import namespace="t" implementation="#default#time2"></head>
```

```
<body>
<div id="myDiv" style="position:absolute; top:150px; left:100px; width:300px;
height:200px; background-color:red;"></div>
<t:transitionfilter id="myTrans" type="irisWipe" subtype="diamond" begin="0"
dur="5" mode="in" targetelement="myDiv"/>
<button onclick="alert(myTrans.type);">Type</button>
<button onclick="alert(myTrans.subtype);">SubType</button>
</body></html>
```

Applies to:

```
<t:transitionfilter/>
```

syncBehavior

Compatibility: IE5.5, IE6

Read and write JavaScript property and HTML attribute. Establishes the type of
synchronization between the element's animation and its parent's animation.

Syntax:

```
<t:element syncbehavior = "value"/>
elementID.syncBehavior = value
```

Values:

canSlip	Child element is not synchronized with its parent.
locked	Child element is synchronized with its parent, which means, for example, that if the child is downloading a large file, the parent will be put on hold until the whole file is loaded.

Example:

```
<html xmlns:t="urn:schemas-microsoft-com:time">
<head><?import namespace="t" implementation="#default#time2"></head>
<body><t:media id="myMedia" begin="0" dur="25" timeAction="display"
syncMaster="true" syncBehavior="locked" onmediacomplete="alert('MediaComplete');"
src="yourvideo.avi"/>
<button onclick="alert(myMedia.syncMaster);">SyncMaster</button>
<button onclick="alert(myMedia.syncBehavior);">SyncBehavior</button>
<button onclick="alert(myMedia.syncTolerance);">SyncTolerance</button>
</body></html>
```

Applies to:

```
<t:animation>, <t:audio/>, <t:excl>, <t:img>, <t:media>, <t:par>, <t:ref>, <t:seq>,
<t:video/>
```

syncMaster

Compatibility: IE5.5, IE6

Read and write JavaScript property and HTML attribute. Establishes whether or not the element must synchronize playback with its parent. Values: true and false (the default).

Syntax:

```
<t:element syncmaster = "value"/>
elementID.syncMaster = value
```

Example: See the syncBehavior property example.

Applies to:

```
<a>, <acronym>, <address>, <area>, <b>, <big>, <blockquote>, <button>, <caption>,
<center>, <cite>, <code>, <dd>, <del>, <dir>, <div>, <dl>, <dt>, <em>, <fieldset>,
<font>, <form>, <hn>, <hr>, <i>, <iframe>, <img>, <input type="button">, <input
type="checkbox">, <input type="file">, <input type="hidden">, <input type="image">,
<input type="password">, <input type="radio">, <input type="reset">, <input
type="submit">, <input type="text">, <ins>, <kbd>, <legend>, <li>, <listing>,
<marquee>, <menu>, <ol>, <option>, <p>, <plaintext>, <pre>, <q>, <s>, <samp>,
<small>, <span>, <strike>, <strong>, <sub>, <sup>, <t:animation>, <t:audio/>,
<t:img>, <t:media>, <t:ref>, <t:video/>, <table>, <tbody>, <td>, <textarea>,
<tfoot>, <th>, <thead>, <tr>, <tt>, <u>, <ul>, <var>, <xmp>
```

syncTolerance

Compatibility: IE5.5, IE6

Read and write JavaScript property. Establishes the maximum asynchronization in seconds allowed between an element and its parent. This property applies only to elements that have their syncBehavior property set to locked.

Syntax:

```
elementID.syncTolerance = value
```

Example: See the syncBehavior property example.

Applies to:

```
<t:animation>, <t:audio/>, <t:excl>, <t:img>, <t:media>, <t:par>, <t:ref>, <t:seq>,
<t:video/>
```

systembitrate

Compatibility: IE5.5, IE6

Read-only HTML attribute. Determines whether or not the system's bandwidth is greater than or equal to the specified number of bits per second. This attribute is effective only when used with an element that is located between the opening and closing tags of a <t:switch> element.

Syntax:

```
<t:element systembitrate = "value">
```

Example:

```
<html xmlns:t="urn:schemas-microsoft-com:time">
<head><?import namespace="t" implementation="#default#time2"></head>
<body><t:par><t:switch>
<t:audio id="myAudio1" src="sound.mp3" systembitrate="10" dur="5"/>
<t:audio id="myAudio2" src="sound.mp3" systembitrate="20" dur="5"/>
</t:switch></t:par>
</body></html>
```

Applies to:

<a>, <acronym>, <address>, <area>, <b>, <big>, <blockquote>, <button>, <caption>, <center>, <cite>, <code>, <dd>, <del>, <dir>, <div>, <dl>, <dt>, <em>, <fieldset>, <font>, <form>, <hn>, <hr>, <i>, <iframe>, <img>, <input type="button">, <input type="checkbox">, <input type="file">, <input type="hidden">, <input type="image">, <input type="password">, <input type="radio">, <input type="reset">, <input type="submit">, <input type="text">, <ins>, <kbd>, <legend>, <li>, <listing>, <marquee>, <menu>, <ol>, <option>, <p>, <plaintext>, <pre>, <q>, <s>, <samp>, <small>, <span>, <strike>, <strong>, <sub>, <sup>, <t:animate/>, <t:animatecolor/>, <t:animatemotion/>, <t:animation>, <t:audio/>, <t:img>, <t:media>, <t:ref>, <t:seq>, <t:set/>, <t:switch>, <t:video/>, <table>, <tbody>, <td>, <textarea>, <tfoot>, <th>, <thead>, <tr>, <tt>, <u>, <ul>, <var>, <xmp>

systemcaptions

Compatibility: IE5.5, IE6

Read-only HTML attribute. Determines whether or not the system can display captions instead of the audio in media files. This attribute is effective only when used with an element that is located between the opening and closing tags of a <t:switch> element. Values: on and off.

Syntax:

```
<t:element systemcaptions="value">
```

Example:

```
<html xmlns:t="urn:schemas-microsoft-com:time">
<head><?import namespace="t" implementation="#default#time2"></head>
<body><t:par><t:switch>
<t:audio id="myAudio1" src="sound.mp3" systemcaptions="on"/>
<t:audio id="myAudio2" src="sound.mp3" systemcaptions="off"/>
</t:switch></t:par>
</body></html>
```

Applies to:

<a>, <acronym>, <address>, <area>, <b>, <big>, <blockquote>, <button>, <caption>, <center>, <cite>, <code>, <dd>, <del>, <dir>, <div>, <dl>, <dt>, <em>, <fieldset>, <font>, <form>, <hn>, <hr>, <i>, <iframe>, <img>, <input type="button">, <input

```
type="checkbox">, <input type="file">, <input type="hidden">, <input type="image">,
<input type="password">, <input type="radio">, <input type="reset">, <input
type="submit">, <input type="text">, <ins>, <kbd>, <legend>, <li>, <listing>,
<marquee>, <menu>, <ol>, <option>, <p>, <plaintext>, <pre>, <q>, <s>, <samp>,
<small>, <span>, <strike>, <strong>, <sub>, <sup>, <t:animate/>, <t:animatecolor/>,
<t:animatemotion/>, <t:animation>, <t:audio/>, <t:img>, <t:media>, <t:ref>,
<t:seq>, <t:set/>, <t:switch>, <t:video/>, <table>, <tbody>, <td>, <textarea>,
<tfoot>, <th>, <thead>, <tr>, <tt>, <u>, <ul>, <var>, <xmp>
```

systemlanguage

Compatibility: IE5.5, IE6

Read-only HTML attribute. Determines whether or not the system's language
preference supports one of the specified languages. This attribute is effective
only when used with an element that is located between the opening and closing
tags of a <t:switch> element. Value: A comma-delimited list of language names.

Syntax:

```
<t:element systemlanguage="value">
```

Example:

```
<html xmlns:t="urn:schemas-microsoft-com:time">
<head><?import namespace="t" implementation="#default#time2"></head>
<body><t:par><t:switch>
<t:audio id="myAudio1" src="sound.mp3" systemlanguage="en"/>
<t:audio id="myAudio2" src="sound.mp3" systemlanguage="es"/>
</t:switch></t:par>
</body></html>
```

Applies to:

```
<a>, <acronym>, <address>, <area>, <b>, <big>, <blockquote>, <button>, <caption>,
<center>, <cite>, <code>, <dd>, <del>, <dir>, <div>, <dl>, <dt>, <em>, <fieldset>,
<font>, <form>, <hn>, <hr>, <i>, <iframe>, <img>, <input type="button">, <input
type="checkbox">, <input type="file">, <input type="hidden">, <input type="image">,
<input type="password">, <input type="radio">, <input type="reset">, <input
type="submit">, <input type="text">, <ins>, <kbd>, <legend>, <li>, <listing>,
<marquee>, <menu>, <ol>, <option>, <p>, <plaintext>, <pre>, <q>, <s>, <samp>,
<small>, <span>, <strike>, <strong>, <sub>, <sup>, <t:animate/>, <t:animatecolor/>,
<t:animatemotion/>, <t:animation>, <t:audio/>, <t:img>, <t:media>, <t:ref>,
<t:seq>, <t:set/>, <t:switch>, <t:video/>, <table>, <tbody>, <td>, <textarea>,
<tfoot>, <th>, <thead>, <tr>, <tt>, <u>, <ul>, <var>, <xmp>
```

systemoverduborsubtitle

Compatibility: IE5.5, IE6

Read-only HTML attribute. Determines whether or not the system can overdub
or add subtitles to an animation. This attribute is effective only when used with
an element that is located between the opening and closing tags of a <t:switch>
element. Values: overdub and subtitle.

Syntax:

```
<t:element systemoverduborsubtitle="value">
```

Example:

```
<html xmlns:t="urn:schemas-microsoft-com:time">
<head><?import namespace="t" implementation="#default#time2"></head>
<body><t:par><t:switch>
<t:audio id="myAudio1" src="sound.mp3" systemoverduborsubtitle="subtitle"/>
<t:audio id="myAudio2" src="sound.mp3" systemoverduborsubtitle="overdub"/>
</t:switch></t:par>
</body></html>
```

Applies to:

```
<a>, <acronym>, <address>, <area>, <b>, <big>, <blockquote>, <button>, <caption>,
<center>, <cite>, <code>, <dd>, <del>, <dir>, <div>, <dl>, <dt>, <em>, <fieldset>,
<font>, <form>, <hn>, <hr>, <i>, <iframe>, <img>, <input type="button">, <input
type="checkbox">, <input type="file">, <input type="hidden">, <input type="image">,
<input type="password">, <input type="radio">, <input type="reset">, <input
type="submit">, <input type="text">, <ins>, <kbd>, <legend>, <li>, <listing>,
<marquee>, <menu>, <ol>, <option>, <p>, <plaintext>, <pre>, <q>, <s>, <samp>,
<small>, <span>, <strike>, <strong>, <sub>, <sup>, <t:animate/>, <t:animatecolor/>,
<t:animatemotion/>, <t:animation>, <t:audio/>, <t:img>, <t:media>, <t:ref>,
<t:seq>, <t:set/>, <t:switch>, <t:video/>, <table>, <tbody>, <td>, <textarea>,
<tfoot>, <th>, <thead>, <tr>, <tt>, <u>, <ul>, <var>, <xmp>
```

targetElement

Compatibility: IE5.5, IE6

Read and write JavaScript property and HTML attribute. Establishes the id of the element to be animated.

Syntax:

```
<t:element targetelement = "value"/>
elementID.targetElement = value
```

Example:

```
<html xmlns:t="urn:schemas-microsoft-com:time">
<head><?import namespace="t" implementation="#default#time2"></head>
<body><div id="myDiv" style="width:200px; height:100px; background-color:blue;"></div>
<t:animatecolor targetElement="myDiv" attributeName="backgroundColor"
to="tan" begin="1" dur="3" fill="hold"/>
</body></html>
```

Applies to:

```
<t:animate/>, <t:animatecolor/>, <t:animatemotion/>, <t:set/>, <t:transitionfilter/>
```

Compatibility: IE5.5, IE6

Read and write JavaScript property and HTML attribute. Establishes what the animation will do while it is being applied to the element.

Syntax:

```
<t:element timeaction = "value"/>
elementID.timeAction = value
```

Values:

class:*class1* [*class2 . . .*]	A list of class styles to apply.
display	The element disappears when its timeline ends, and the other elements on the page fill the void.
style	The style that was defined for the element will be applied only during the animation.
visibility	The element disappears when its timeline ends, but the other elements on the page do not fill the void.

Example:

```
<html xmlns:t="urn:schemas-microsoft-com:time">
<head><?import namespace="t" implementation="#default#time2">
<style>.time{behavior:url(#default#time2);}</style></head>
<body><t:animation targetElement="myDiv" fill="hold" timeaction="style"/>
<div id="myDiv" style="width:200; height:100; background-color:red;" class="time"
begin="3" dur="5"></div>
</t:animation>
</body></html>
```

Applies to:

```
<t:animation>, <t:audio/>, <t:img>, <t:media>, <t:par>, <t:ref>, <t:seq>, <t:video/>
```

timeContainer

Compatibility: IE5.5, IE6

Read and write JavaScript property and HTML attribute. Establishes a parent element that controls the synchronization of all its child elements.

Syntax:

```
<t:element timecontainer="value"/>
elementID.timeContainer = value
elementID.playList(index).timeContainer
```

Values:

none	The default; no action is taken on the child elements.
excl	Only one child element can play at a time.
par	The child elements have independent timing.
seq	The child elements are rendered in sequence.

Example:

```
<html xmlns:t="urn:schemas-microsoft-com:time">
<head><style>.time{behavior:url(#default#time2);}</style>
<?import namespace="t" implementation="#default#time2"></head>
<body>
<div class="time" timecontainer="seq" repeatcount="indefinite">
<div id="myDiv" class="time" dur="3" style="width:200; height:100; background-
color:red;"></div>
<div class="time" dur="3" style="width:200; height:100; background-color:green;">
</div></div>
</body></html>
```

Applies to:

```
<a>, <acronym>, <address>, <area>, <b>, <big>, <blockquote>, <button>, <caption>,
<center>, <cite>, <code>, <dd>, <del>, <dir>, <div>, <dl>, <dt>, <em>, <fieldset>,
<font>, <form>, <hn>, <hr>, <i>, <iframe>, <img>, <input type="button">, <input
type="checkbox">, <input type="file">, <input type="hidden">, <input type="image">,
<input type="password">, <input type="radio">, <input type="reset">, <input
type="submit">, <input type="text">, <ins>, <kbd>, <legend>, <li>, <listing>,
<marquee>, <menu>, <ol>, <option>, <p>, <plaintext>, playItem, <pre>, <q>, <s>,
<samp>, <small>, <span>, <strike>, <strong>, <sub>, <sup>, <t:animate/>,
<t:animatecolor/>, <t:animatemotion/>, <t:animation>, <t:audio/>, <t:img>,
<t:media>, <t:ref>, <t:seq>, <t:set/>, <t:video/>, <table>, <tbody>, <td>,
<textarea>, <tfoot>, <th>, <thead>, <tr>, <tt>, <u>, <ul>, <var>, <xmp>
```

timeParent

Compatibility: IE5.5, IE6

Read-only JavaScript property. Retrieves a reference to the element's parent element.

Syntax:

```
elementID.timeParent
```

Example:

```
<html xmlns:t="urn:schemas-microsoft-com:time">
<head><?import namespace="t" implementation="#default#time2">
<style>.time{behavior:url(#default#time2);}</style></head>
```

```
<body><t:excl id="myExcl" begin="0">
<t:priorityclass><div id="myDiv1" class="time" begin="5" dur="4" style="background-
color:red; width:100px; height:50px"></div></t:priorityclass>
<t:priorityclass>
<div id="myDiv2" class="time" begin="0" dur="12" style="background-color:blue;
width:100px; height:50px"></div></t:priorityclass></t:excl>
<button onclick="alert(myDiv1.timeParent.dur);">Parent dur</button>
</body></html>
```

Applies to:

```
<t:animate/>, <t:animatecolor/>, <t:animatemotion/>, <t:animation>, <t:audio/>,
<t:img>, <t:media>, <t:par>, <t:ref>, <t:seq>, <t:set/>, <t:video/>
```

title

Compatibility: IE5.5, IE6

Read-only JavaScript property. Retrieves the contents of the <title> tag inside an
ASX file. An ASX file is an XML type of document that contains all the information that Windows Media Player needs to play a sequence of sound or video
media files.

Syntax:

```
elementID.title
elementID.playList(index).title
```

Example: See the abstract property example.
Applies to:

```
playItem, <t:animation>, <t:audio/>, <t:img>, <t:media>, <t:ref>, <t:video/>
```

to (1)

Compatibility: IE5.5, IE6

Read and write JavaScript property and HTML attribute. Establishes the ending
position of the animation.

NOTE *The* to *property has precedence over the* by *property, but the* values *and* path *properties have
precedence over the* to *property.*

Syntax:

```
<t:element to = "value">
elementID.to = value
elementID.to(value)
```

Example: See the from (1) property example.

Applies to:

```
<t:animate/>, <t:animatemotion/>, <t:set/>
```

to (2)

Compatibility: IE5.5, IE6

Read and write JavaScript property and HTML attribute. Establishes the ending color of the animation. Value: A web color name or the hexadecimal value in #RRGGBB format.

Syntax:

```
<t:animatecolor to = "value"/>
animatecolorID.to = value
animatecolorID.to(value)
```

Example: See the from (2) property example.
Applies to:

```
<t:animatecolor/>
```

to (3)

Compatibility: IE6

Read and write JavaScript property and HTML attribute. Specifies the percentage of the transition filter's timeline at which play will end. Value: A floating-point number from 0 to 1 (the default).

Syntax:

```
<t:transitionfilter to = "value">
transitionfilterID.to = value
transitionfilterID.to(value)
```

Example: See the from (3) property example.
Applies to:

```
<t:transitionfilter/>
```

transitiontype

Compatibility: IE5.5, IE6

Read and write HTML attribute. Establishes the type of transition the Microsoft DirectMusic player will play between segments. Values: EndAndIntro, Break, End, Fill, Intro, None, and Regular.

Syntax:

```
<t:element transitiontype = "value"/>
```

Example: See the boundary property example.
Applies to:

```
<t:audio/>, <t:img>, <t:media>, <t:ref>, <t:video/>
```

type (1)

Compatibility: IE5.5, IE6

Read and write JavaScript property and HTML attribute. Specifies the MIME type of the media file.

Syntax:

```
<t:element type = "value">
elementID.type = value
elementID.playList(index).type
```

Example:

```
<html xmlns:t="urn:schemas-microsoft-com:time">
<head><?import namespace="t" implementation="#default#time2">
<style>.time{behavior:url(#default#time2);}</style></head>
<body><t:video id="myVideo" modulate="true" src="yourvideo.avi" type="avi"/>
<button onclick="alert(myVideo.type);">MIME Type</button>
</body></html>
```

Applies to:

```
playItem, <t:animation>, <t:audio/>, <t:img>, <t:media>, <t:ref>, <t:video/>
```

type (2)

Compatibility: IE6

Read and write JavaScript property and HTML attribute. Specifies the type of transition filter to apply. Values: starWipe, barWipe, barnDoorWipe, irisWipe, ellipseWipe, clockWipe, fanWipe, snakeWipe, spiralWipe, pushWipe, slideWipe, and fade.

Syntax:

```
<t:transitionfilter type = "value"/>
transitionfilterID.type = value
```

Example: See the subtype property example.
Applies to:

```
<t:transitionfilter/>
```

Compatibility: IE6

Read and write JavaScript property and HTML attribute. Specifies how and when the following properties are updated: dur, repeatCount, repeatDur, autoReverse, speed, end, begin, restart, and fill. Values: auto (updates the property settings while the animation is running) and reset (the default; restarts the animation and applies the updated settings).

Syntax:

```
<t:element updatemode = "value"/>
elementID.updateMode = value
```

Example:

```
<html xmlns:t="urn:schemas-microsoft-com:time"><head><?import namespace="t"
implementation="#default#time2">
<style>.time{behavior:url(#default#time2)}</style></head>
<body>
<t:video updateMode="reset" begin="bt1.click" style="width:175px; height:150px;"
src="yourvideo.avi" onbegin="alert(this.updateMode)"/>
<button id="bt1">Start video</button> 
<button onClick="document.body.beginElement()">Restart</button>
</body></html>
```

Applies to:

```
<t:animation>, <t:audio/>, <t:img>, <t:media>, <t:ref>, <t:video/>
```

values (1)

Compatibility: IE5.5, IE6

Read and write JavaScript property and HTML attribute. Determines the motion of an element with a semicolon-delimited list of numeric values.

NOTE *The* values *property has precedence over the* from, to, *and* by *properties, but the* path *property has precedence over the* values *property.*

Syntax:

```
<t:element values = "value">
elementID.values = value
elementID.values(value)
```

Example:

```
<html xmlns:t="urn:schemas-microsoft-com:time">
<head><style>.time{behavior:url(#default#time2)}</style>
<?import namespace="t" implementation="#default#time2"></head>
```

```
<body>
<t:animate id="myAnim" targetElement="myDiv" attributeName="left" values="50;350"
begin="0" dur="5" fill="hold"/>
<div id="myDiv" class="time" style="left:0px; width:200px; position:absolute;
top:100px; height:100px; background-color:blue;"></div>
</body></html>
```

Applies to:

```
<t:animate/>, <t:animatemotion/>
```

values (2)

Compatibility: IE5.5, IE6

Read and write JavaScript property and HTML attribute. Determines the color transformation of an element with a semicolon-delimited list of web color names or hexadecimal values in #RRGGBB format.

Syntax:

```
<t:animatecolor values = "value">
animatecolorID.values = value
animatecolorID.values(value)
```

Example:

```
<html xmlns:t="urn:schemas-microsoft-com:time">
<head><style>.time{behavior:url(#default#time2)}</style>
<?import namespace="t" implementation="#default#time2"></head>
<body><t:animatecolor id="myAnim" targetElement="myDiv" attributeName="background-
color" values="blue;cyan" begin="0" dur="5" fill="hold"/>
<div id="myDiv" class="time" style="left:50px; width:200px; position:absolute;
top:100px; height:100px; background-color:red;"></div>
</body></html>
```

Applies to:

```
<t:animatecolor/>
```

values (3)

Compatibility: IE6

Read and write JavaScript property and HTML attribute. Determines the percent progress of a transition with a semicolon-delimited list of floating-point values between 0 and 1.

Syntax:

```
<t:transitionfilter values = "value">
transitionfilterID.values = value
transitionfilterID.values(value)
```

Example:

```
<html xmlns:t="urn:schemas-microsoft-com:time">
<head><style>.time{behavior:url(#default#time2);}</style>
<?import namespace="t" implementation="#default#time2"/></head>
<body><t:transitionfilter begin="myDiv.begin" type="starWipe" subtype="fivePoint"
dur="5" targetelement="myDiv" values="0;.1;.2;.3;.4;.5;.6;.7;.8;.9;1.0"
calcmode="linear"/>
<div class="time" begin="0" id="myDiv" dur="indefinite"  style="position:relative;
left:20px; width:270px; height:181px; background-color:red;"></div>
</body></html>
```

Applies to:

```
<t:transitionfilter/>
```

volume

Compatibility: IE5.5, IE6

Read and write JavaScript property and HTML attribute. Specifies the element's
sound volume. Value: An integer from 0 (audio turned off) to 100 (full volume).

Syntax:

```
<t:element volume = "value">
elementID.volume = value
elementID.currTimeState.volume
```

Example:

```
<html xmlns:t="urn:schemas-microsoft-com:time">
<head><?import namespace="t" implementation="#default#time2"></head>
<body><t:audio id="mySound" src="sound.mp3" begin="0" dur="10" motifname=""
repeatcount="indefinite"/>
<button onclick="alert(mySound.volume);">Volume</button>
</body></html>
```

Applies to:

```
currTimeState, <t:animation>, <t:audio/>, <t:img>, <t:media>, <t:par>, <t:ref>,
<t:seq>, <t:video/>
```

Events and Event Handlers

The HTML+TIME specific events and event handlers use the same syntax as all other events and event handlers. For more information on event and event handler syntax, see Chapter 3.

Before moving on to the list of HTML+TIME-related events and event handlers, you should be familiar with two event object properties that are common to *all* of these events *except* the onTrackChange event. These two common properties are srcElement and type, and both are compatible with IE version 4 and all later versions.

The srcElement and type properties are read and write properties that retrieve the element that fired the event and the name of the event that was triggered, respectively. Their syntax is:

```
eventName.srcElement = value
event.type = value
```

onBegin

Compatibility: IE5.5, IE6

This event fires when an element's timeline begins.
Example:

```
<html xmlns:t="urn:schemas-microsoft-com:time">
<head><?import namespace="t" implementation="#default#time2">
<style>.time{behavior:url(#default#time2);}</style></head>
<body>
<button id="b1">Start</button>
<button onclick="a1.endElement()">Stop</button>
<button onclick="a1.resetElement()">Reset</button><br><br>
<t:animatemotion id="a1" targetElement="myDiv" begin="b1.click" dur="5"
repeatCount="5" to="350,0" onbegin="alert('begun');" onend="alert('ended');"
onreset="alert('reset');"/>
<div id="myDiv" class="time" style="position:relative; top:15px; left:25px;
height:75px; width:250px; background-color:yellow;"></div>
</body></html>
```

Applies to:

```
<t:animate/>, <t:animatecolor/>, <t:animatemotion/>, <t:animation>, <t:audio/>,
<t:img>, <t:media>, <t:par>, <t:ref>, <t:seq>, <t:set/>, <t:transitionfilter/>,
<t:video/>
```

onEnd

Compatibility: IE5.5, IE6

This event fires when an element's timeline ends.

Example: See the onBegin event example.
Applies to:

```
<t:animate/>, <t:animatecolor/>, <t:animatemotion/>, <t:animation>, <t:audio/>,
<t:excl>, <t:img>, <t:media>, <t:par>, <t:ref>, <t:seq>, <t:set/>,
<t:transitionfilter/>, <t:video/>
```

onMediaComplete

Compatibility: IE5.5, IE6

This event fires when a media file finishes loading.
Example (use the ASX file listed in the abstract property example):

```
<html xmlns:t="urn:schemas-microsoft-com:time">
<head><?import namespace="t" implementation="#default#time2">
<style>.time{behavior:url(#default#time2);}</style></head>
<body><t:video src=myasx.asx onmediacomplete="alert('Media Loaded');"/>
</body></html>
```

Applies to:

```
<t:animation>, <t:audio/>, <t:img>, <t:media>, <t:par>, <t:ref>, <t:seq>, <t:video/>
```

onMediaError

Compatibility: IE5.5, IE6

This event fires when a media file does not load correctly.
Example:

```
<html xmlns:t="urn:schemas-microsoft-com:time">
<head><?import namespace="t" implementation="#default#time2">
<style>.time{behavior:url(#default#time2);}</style></head>
<body><t:img id="img1" src="wrongImage.gif" begin="0" dur="1"
onmediaerror="alert('Media Error--Invalid path to image source file!')"/>
<span id="s1">An image is downloading</span>
</body></html>
```

Applies to:

```
<t:animation>, <t:audio/>, <t:excl>, <t:img>, <t:media>, <t:par>, <t:ref>, <t:seq>,
<t:video/>
```

onOutOfSync

Compatibility: IE5.5, IE6

This event fires when an element loses synchronization with the media source.

Example:

```
<html xmlns:t="urn:schemas-microsoft-com:time">
<head><?import namespace="t" implementation="#default#time2">
<style>.time{behavior:url(#default#time2);}</style></head>
<body><t:video src="yourVideoOnAServer.avi" onoutofsync="alert('The media sync is
interrupted');" onsyncrestored="alert('Synchronization has been restored');"/>
</body></html>
```

Applies to:

`<t:animation>`, `<t:audio/>`, `<t:img>`, `<t:media>`, `<t:par>`, `<t:ref>`, `<t:seq>`, `<t:video/>`

onPause

Compatibility: IE5.5, IE6

This event fires when an element's timeline pauses.

Example:

```
<html xmlns:t="urn:schemas-microsoft-com:time">
<head><?import namespace="t" implementation="#default#time2">
<style>.time{behavior:url(#default#time2);}</style></head>
<body>
<button id="b1">Start</button>
<button onclick="a1.pauseElement()">Pause</button>
<button onclick="a1.resumeElement()">Resume</button><br><br>
<t:animatemotion id="a1" targetElement="myDiv" begin="b1.click" dur="5"
repeatCount="5" to="350,0" onpause="alert('paused');" onresume="alert('resumed');"/>
<div id="myDiv" class="time" style="position:relative; top:15px; left:25px;
height:75px; width:250px; background-color:yellow;"></div>
</body></html>
```

Applies to:

`<t:animate/>`, `<t:animatecolor/>`, `<t:animatemotion/>`, `<t:animation>`, `<t:audio/>`,
`<t:img>`, `<t:media>`, `<t:par>`, `<t:ref>`, `<t:seq>`, `<t:set/>`, `<t:transitionfilter/>`,
`<t:video/>`

onRepeat

Compatibility: IE5.5, IE6

This event fires when an element's timeline repeats.

Example:

```
<html xmlns:t="urn:schemas-microsoft-com:time">
<head><?import namespace="t" implementation="#default#time2">
<style>.time{behavior:url(#default#time2);}</style></head>
```

```
<body><div id="myDiv" class="time" style="position:relative; top:15px; left:25px;
height:75px; width:250px; background-color:yellow;"></div>
<t:animatemotion targetElement="myDiv" begin="0" dur="5" repeatCount="5" to="350,0"
autoReverse="true" onreverse="alert('reverse');" onrepeat="alert('repeat');"/>
</body></html>
```

Applies to:

```
<t:animate/>, <t:animatecolor/>, <t:animatemotion/>, <t:animation>, <t:audio/>,
<t:excl>, <t:img>, <t:media>, <t:par>, <t:ref>, <t:seq>, <t:set/>,
<t:transitionfilter/>, <t:video/>
```

onReset

Compatibility: IE5.5, IE6

This event fires when the element's timeline is reset to its beginning.

Example: See the onBegin event example.

Applies to:

```
<t:animate/>, <t:animatecolor/>, <t:animatemotion/>, <t:animation>, <t:audio/>,
<t:excl>, <t:img>, <t:media>, <t:par>, <t:ref>, <t:seq>, <t:set/>, <t:video/>
```

onResume

Compatibility: IE5.5, IE6

This event fires when an element's timeline is resumed after being paused.

Example: See the onPause event example.

Applies to:

```
<t:animate/>, <t:animatecolor/>, <t:animatemotion/>, <t:animation>, <t:audio/>,
<t:img>, <t:media>, <t:par>, <t:ref>, <t:seq>, <t:set/>, <t:transitionfilter/>,
<t:video/>
```

onReverse

Compatibility: IE5.5, IE6

This event fires when an element's timeline begins to play in reverse.

Example: See the onRepeat event example.

Applies to:

```
<t:animate/>, <t:animatecolor/>, <t:animatemotion/>, <t:animation>, <t:audio/>,
<t:excl>, <t:img>, <t:media>, <t:par>, <t:ref>, <t:seq>, <t:set/>,
<t:transitionfilter/>, <t:video/>
```

onSeek

Compatibility: IE5.5, IE6

This event fires when the seekTo(), seekToFrame(), or seekActiveTime() method is called for a media file.

Example:

```
<html xmlns:t="urn:schemas-microsoft-com:time">
<head><?import namespace="t" implementation="#default#time2">
<style>.time{behavior:url(#default#time2)}</style></head>
<body><t:video onseek="alert('Seeking')" style="width:175px; height:150px;"
id="myVideo" src="yourvideo.avi"/><br><br>
<button onclick="myVideo.seekTo(1, 3);">Seek</button>
</body></html>
```

Applies to:

```
<t:animation>, <t:audio/>, <t:excl>, <t:img>, <t:media>, <t:par>, <t:ref>, <t:seq>,
<t:transitionfilter/>, <t:video/>
```

onSyncRestored

Compatibility: IE5.5, IE6

This event fires when an element's synchronization is restored to an element that lost it.

Example: See the onOutOfSync event example.

Applies to:

```
<t:animation>, <t:audio/>, <t:img>, <t:media>, <t:par>, <t:ref>, <t:seq>, <t:video/>
```

onTimeError

Compatibility: IE5.5, IE6

This event fires whenever an HTML+TIME-related error occurs. However, it is only compatible with non-HTML+TIME elements. See Chapter 7 for an example and its applicable HTML elements.

onTrackChange

Compatibility: IE6

This event fires when a new playItem object in a playList collection begins. The playList is defined in an ASX file.

Example (use the ASX file listed in the abstract property example):

```
<html xmlns:t="urn:schemas-microsoft-com:time">
<head><?import namespace="t" implementation="#default#time2"></head>
<body><t:video id="myVideo" begin="0" src="myasx.asx" end="indefinite"
ontrackchange="alert(event.MoreInfo);" type="avi"/>
</body></html>
```

Applies to:

<t:audio/>, <t:media>, <t:ref>, <t:video/>

JavaScript Methods

In the applies-to lists of the JavaScript methods in this section, you will see items of three kinds: HTML elements, JavaScript collections, and JavaScript objects. In order to distinguish between these items, the following conventions have been used in the applies-to lists:

- < and > angle bracket tags surround the names of HTML elements (for example, <t:animation>).
- An asterisk follows the names of JavaScript collections (for example, activeElements*).
- The names of JavaScript objects appear without adornment (for example, playItem).

activeTimeToParentTime()

Compatibility: IE5.5, IE6

This method returns the activeTime property value of the parent element that corresponds to the specified activeTime property value of the child element.

Syntax:

elementID.activeTimeToParentTime(*param1*)

param1   Required; an integer between 0 and the child element's activeDur property value.

Example:

```
<html xmlns:t="urn:schemas-microsoft-com:time">
<head><?import namespace="t" implementation="#default#time2">
<style>.time{behavior:url(#default#time2);}</style>
<script language="JavaScript">
function B1(myElement) {
var m = myAnim.activeTimeToParentTime(myDiv.currTimeState.activeTime);
myElement.innerText = m;}
function B2(myElement) {
var m = myDiv.parentTimeToActiveTime(myAnim.currTimeState.activeTime);
myElement.innerText = m;}
function B3(myElement) {
var m = myAnim.currTimeState.segmentTime; myElement.innerText = m;}
function B4(myElement) {
var m = myAnim.currTimeState.activeTime; myElement.innerText = m;}
</script></head>
```

```
<body>
<p>SegmentTime:<span class="time" dur=".5" repeatCount="indefinite"
onrepeat="B3(this);">0</span></p>
<p>ActiveTime:<span class="time" dur=".5" repeatCount="indefinite"
onrepeat="B4(this);">0</span></p>
<p>ActiveTimeToParentTime:<span class="time" dur=".5" repeatCount="indefinite"
onrepeat="B1(this);">0</span></p>
<p>ParentTimeToActiveTime:<span class="time" dur=".5" repeatCount="indefinite"
onrepeat="B2(this);">0</span></p>
<div id="myDiv" class="time" style="position:relative; top:10; left:10; height:100;
width:200; background-color:red;"></div>
<t:animatemotion id="myAnim" targetElement="myDiv" to="320,200" begin="2" dur="5"
autoreverse="true" repeatcount="indefinite"/>
</body></html>
```

Applies to:

```
<t:animate/>, <t:animatecolor/>, <t:animatemotion/>, <t:animation>, <t:audio/>,
<t:excl>, <t:img>, <t:media>, <t:par>, <t:ref>, <t:seq>, <t:set/>,
<t:transitionfilter/>, <t:video/>
```

activeTimeToSegmentTime()

Compatibility: IE5.5, IE6

This method returns the element's segmentTime property value that corresponds to the specified activeTime property value.

Syntax:

```
elementID.activeTimeToSegmentTime(param1)
```

param1   Required; an integer between 0 and the element's activeDur property value.

Example:

```
<html xmlns:t="urn:schemas-microsoft-com:time">
<head><?import namespace="t" implementation="#default#time2">
<style>.time{behavior:url(#default#time2);}</style>
<script language="JavaScript">
function B1(myElement) {
var m = myAnim.currTimeState.segmentTime; myElement.innerText = m;}
function B2(myElement) {
var m = myAnim.currTimeState.activeTime; myElement.innerText = m;}
function B3(myElement) {
var m =myAnim.activeTimeToSegmentTime(myDiv.currTimeState.activeTime);
myElement.innerText = m;}
function B4(myElement) {
var m =myAnim.segmentTimeToActivetime(myDiv.currTimeState.activeTime);
myElement.innerText = m;}
```

```
</script></head>
<body>
<p>SegmentTime:<span class="time" dur=".5" repeatCount="indefinite"
onrepeat="B1(this);">0</span></p>
<p>ActiveTime:<span class="time" dur=".5" repeatCount="indefinite"
onrepeat="B2(this);">0</span></p>
<p>ActiveTimeToSegmentTime:<span class="time" dur=".5" repeatCount="indefinite"
onrepeat="B3(this);">0</span></p>
<p>SegmentTimeToActiveTime:<span class="time" dur=".5" repeatCount="indefinite"
onrepeat="B4(this);">0</span></p>
<div id="myDiv" class="time" style="position:relative; top:10; left:10; height:100;
width:200; background-color:red"></div>
<t:animatemotion id="myAnim" targetElement="myDiv" to="320,200" begin="2" dur="5"
autoreverse="true" repeatcount="indefinite"/>
</body></html>
```

Applies to:

<t:animate/>, <t:animatecolor/>, <t:animatemotion/>, <t:animation>, <t:audio/>,
<t:excl>, <t:img>, <t:media>, <t:par>, <t:ref>, <t:seq>, <t:set/>,
<t:transitionfilter/>, <t:video/>

beginElement()

Compatibility: IE5.5, IE6

This method starts the element's animation.

Syntax:

```
elementID.beginElement()
```

Example:

```
<html xmlns:t="urn:schemas-microsoft-com:time">
<head><?import namespace="t" implementation="#default#time2">
<style>.time{behavior:url(#default#time2);}</style></head>
<body>
<button onclick="myAnim.beginElement();">Begin</button>
<button onclick="myAnim.beginElementAt(2);">Begin at 2</button>
<div id="myDiv" class="time" style="position:relative; top:10; left:10; height:100;
width:200; background-color:red"></div>
<t:animatemotion id="myAnim" targetElement="myDiv" to="320,200" dur="5"
begin="1000" autoreverse="true" repeatcount="indefinite"/>
</body></html>
```

Applies to:

<t:animate/>, <t:animatecolor/>, <t:animatemotion/>, <t:animation>, <t:audio/>,
<t:excl>, <t:img>, <t:media>, <t:par>, <t:ref>, <t:seq>, <t:set/>,
<t:transitionfilter/>, <t:video/>

beginElementAt()

Compatibility: IE5.5, IE6

This method starts the element's animation at the specified point in the document timeline.

Syntax:

```
elementID.beginElementAt(param1)
```

param1   Required; the offset in seconds.

Example: See the beginElement() method example.
Applies to:

```
<t:animate/>, <t:animatecolor/>, <t:animatemotion/>, <t:animation>, <t:audio/>,
<t:img>, <t:media>, <t:par>, <t:ref>, <t:seq>, <t:set/>, <t:transitionfilter/>,
<t:video/>
```

documentTimeToParentTime()

Compatibility: IE5.5, IE6

This method returns the activeTime property value of the parent element that corresponds to the specified amount of time since the document has been loaded.

Syntax:

```
elementID.documentTimeToParentTime(param1)
```

param1   Required; an integer between 0 and the number of seconds elapsed since the document was loaded.

Example:

```
<html xmlns:t="urn:schemas-microsoft-com:time">
<head><?import namespace="t" implementation="#default#time2">
<style>.time{behavior:url(#default#time2);}</style>
<script language="JavaScript">
function B1(myElement) {
var m = myAnim.currTimeState.segmentTime; myElement.innerText = m;}
function B2(myElement) {
var m = myAnim.currTimeState.activeTime; myElement.innerText = m;}
function B3(myElement) {
var m=myAnim.documentTimeToParentTime(myDiv.currTimeState.activeTime);
myElement.innerText = m;}
function B4(myElement) {
var m=myDiv.parentTimeToDocumentTime(myAnim.currTimeState.activeTime);
myElement.innerText = m;}
</script></head>
<body>
<p>SegmentTime:<span class="time" dur=".5" repeatCount="indefinite"
```

```
onrepeat="B1(this);">0</span></p>
<p>ActiveTime:<span class="time" dur=".5" repeatCount="indefinite"
onrepeat="B2(this);">0</span></p>
<p>DocumentTimeToParentTime:<span class="time" dur=".5" repeatCount="indefinite"
onrepeat="B3(this);">0</span></p>
<p>ParentTimeToDocumentTime:<span class="time" dur=".5" repeatCount="indefinite"
onrepeat="B4(this);">0</span></p>
<div id="myDiv" class="time" style="position:relative; top:10; left:10; height:100;
width:200; background-color:red;"></div>
<t:animatemotion id="myAnim" targetElement="myDiv" to="320,200" begin="2" dur="5"
autoreverse="true" repeatcount="indefinite"/>
</body></html>
```

Applies to:

```
<t:animate/>, <t:animatecolor/>, <t:animatemotion/>, <t:animation>, <t:audio/>,
<t:excl>, <t:img>, <t:media>, <t:par>, <t:ref>, <t:seq>, <t:set/>,
<t:transitionfilter/>, <t:video/>
```

endElement()

Compatibility: IE5.5, IE6

This method ends the element's animation.

Syntax:

```
elementID.endElement()
```

Example:

```
<html xmlns:t="urn:schemas-microsoft-com:time">
<head><?import namespace="t" implementation="#default#time2">
<style>.time{behavior:url(#default#time2);}</style></head>
<body>
<button onclick="myAnim.beginElement();">Begin Element</button>
<button onclick="myAnim.resetElement();">Reset</button>
<button onclick="myAnim.endElement();">End</button>
<button onclick="myAnim.endElementAt(myDiv.currTimeState.segmentTime+2);">End at
2</button>
<div id="myDiv" class="time" style="position:relative; top:10; left:10; height:100;
width:200; background-color:red"></div>
<t:animatemotion id="myAnim" targetElement="myDiv" to="320,200" dur="5"
begin="1000" autoreverse="true" repeatcount="indefinite"/>
</body></html>
```

Applies to:

```
<t:animate/>, <t:animatecolor/>, <t:animatemotion/>, <t:animation>, <t:audio/>,
<t:excl>, <t:img>, <t:media>, <t:par>, <t:ref>, <t:seq>, <t:set/>,
<t:transitionfilter/>, <t:video/>
```

endElementAt()

Compatibility: IE5.5, IE6

This method ends the element's animation at the specified point in the document timeline.

Syntax:

```
elementID.endElementAt(param1)
```

param1   Required; the offset in seconds.

Example: See the endElement() method example.
Applies to:

```
<t:animate/>, <t:animatecolor/>, <t:animatemotion/>, <t:animation>, <t:audio/>,
<t:img>, <t:media>, <t:par>, <t:ref>, <t:seq>, <t:set/>, <t:transitionfilter/>,
<t:video/>
```

item()

Compatibility: IE5.5, IE6

This method returns the item located at the zero-based index of the specified collection.

Syntax:

```
collectionName.item(param1)
```

param1   Optional; the collection index. If omitted, the item located at index 0 is returned.

Example (use the ASX file listed in the abstract property example):

```
<html xmlns:t="urn:schemas-microsoft-com:time">
<head><?import namespace="t" implementation="#default#time2">
<style>.time{behavior:url(#default#time2);}</style>
<script language="JavaScript">
function B1(){
    myTrack = myMedia.playList.activeTrack.index;
    alert(myMedia.playList.item(myTrack).title);}
</script></head>
<body><t:media id="myMedia" begin="0" src="myasx.asx"/>
<button onclick="B1();">Item.Track</button>
</body></html>
```

Applies to:

```
activeElements*, playList*, timeAll*, timeChildren*
```

nextElement()

Compatibility: IE5.5, IE6

This method starts the animation of the next element in the <t:seq> element sequence.

Syntax:

```
seqID.nextElement()
```

Example:

```
<html xmlns:t="urn:schemas-microsoft-com:time">
<head><?import namespace="t" implementation="#default#time2">
<style>.time{behavior:url(#default#time2);}</style></head>
<body>
<button onclick="myAnim.nextElement();">Next Element</button>
<button onclick="myAnim.prevElement();">Prev Element</button>
<t:seq id="myAnim" begin="0">
<div class="time" dur="3" style="position:relative; top:10; left:10; height:100;
width:200; background-color:red;"></div>
<div class="time" dur="3" style="position:relative; top:10; left:10; height:100;
width:200; background-color:blue;"></div>
<div class="time" dur="3" style="position:relative; top:10; left:10; height:100;
width:200; background-color:yellow;"></div>
<div class="time" dur="3" style="position:relative; top:10; left:10; height:100;
width:200; background-color:green;"></div>
</t:seq>
</body></html>
```

Applies to:

```
<t:seq>
```

nextTrack()

Compatibility: IE5.5, IE6

This method starts playing the next track in the media file or the next playItem object in the playList collection.

Syntax:

```
elementID.nextTrack()
elementID.playList.nextTrack()
```

Example (use the ASX file listed in the abstract property example):

```
<html xmlns:t="urn:schemas-microsoft-com:time">
<head><?import namespace="t" implementation="#default#time2">
<style>.time{behavior:url(#default#time2);}</style></head>
```

```
<body><t:media id="myMedia" begin="0" src="myasx.asx"/>
<button onclick="myMedia.playList.nextTrack();">Next track</button>
<button onclick="myMedia.playList.PrevTrack();">Previous track</button>
</body></html>
```

Applies to:

playList*, <t:media>, <t:par>, <t:ref>, <t:seq>

parentTimeToActiveTime()

Compatibility: IE5.5, IE6

This method returns the activeTime property value of the child element that corresponds to the specified activeTime property value of the parent element.
Syntax:

elementID.parentTimeToActiveTime(*param1*)

param1   Required; an integer between 0 and the parent element's activeDur property value.

Example: See the activeTimeToParentTime() method example.
Applies to:

<t:animate/>, <t:animatecolor/>, <t:animatemotion/>, <t:animation>, <t:audio/>, <t:excl>, <t:img>, <t:media>, <t:par>, <t:ref>, <t:seq>, <t:set/>, <t:transitionfilter/>, <t:video/>

parentTimeToDocumentTime()

Compatibility: IE5.5, IE6

This method returns the amount of time elapsed since the document was loaded that corresponds to the specified activeTime property value of the parent element.
Syntax:

elementID.parentTimeToDocumentTime(*param1*)

param1   Required; an integer between 0 and the parent element's activeDur property value.

Example: See the documentTimeToParentTime() method example.
Applies to:

<t:animate/>, <t:animatecolor/>, <t:animatemotion/>, <t:animation>, <t:audio/>, <t:excl>, <t:img>, <t:media>, <t:par>, <t:ref>, <t:seq>, <t:set/>, <t:transitionfilter/>, <t:video/>

pauseElement()

Compatibility: IE5.5, IE6

This method pauses the element's animation.

Syntax:

elementID.pauseElement()

Example:

```
<html xmlns:t="urn:schemas-microsoft-com:time">
<head><?import namespace="t" implementation="#default#time2">
<style>.time{behavior:url(#default#time2);}</style></head>
<body>
<button id="b1">Start</button>
<button onclick="a1.pauseElement()">Pause</button>
<button onclick="a1.resumeElement()">Resume</button><br><br>
<t:animatemotion id="a1" targetElement="myDiv" begin="b1.click" dur="5"
repeatCount="5" to="350,0"/>
<div id="myDiv" class="time" style="position:relative; top:15px; left:25px;
height:75px; width:250px; background-color:yellow;"></div>
</body></html>
```

Applies to:

```
<t:animate/>, <t:animatecolor/>, <t:animatemotion/>, <t:animation>, <t:audio/>,
<t:img>, <t:media>, <t:par>, <t:ref>, <t:seq>, <t:set/>, <t:transitionfilter/>,
<t:video/>
```

prevElement()

Compatibility: IE5.5, IE6

This method starts the animation of the previous element in the <t:seq> element sequence.

Syntax:

seqID.prevElement()

Example: See the nextElement() method example.
Applies to:

```
<t:seq>
```

prevTrack()

Compatibility: IE5.5, IE6

This method starts playing the previous track in the media file or the previous playItem object in the playList collection.

Syntax:

```
elementID.prevTrack()
elementID.playList.prevTrack()
```

Example: See the nextTrack() method example.
Applies to:

```
playList*, <t:media>, <t:par>, <t:ref>, <t:seq>
```

resetElement()

Compatibility: IE5.5, IE6

This method reinitializes the element. It has the same effect as reloading the page, but in this case only the element is reloaded.

Syntax:

```
elementID.resetElement()
```

Example: See the endElement() method example.
Applies to:

```
<t:animate/>, <t:animatecolor/>, <t:animatemotion/>, <t:animation>, <t:audio/>,
<t:excl>, <t:img>, <t:media>, <t:par>, <t:ref>, <t:seq>, <t:set/>, <t:video/>
```

resumeElement()

Compatibility: IE5.5, IE6

This method causes a paused element to resume its animation.

Syntax:

```
elementID.resumeElement()
```

Example: See the pauseElement() method example.
Applies to:

```
<t:animate/>, <t:animatecolor/>, <t:animatemotion/>, <t:animation>, <t:audio/>,
<t:img>, <t:media>, <t:par>, <t:ref>, <t:seq>, <t:set/>, <t:transitionfilter/>,
<t:video/>
```

seekActiveTime()

Compatibility: IE5.5, IE6

This method starts playing the animation at the point in its timeline that corresponds to the specified activeTime property value.

Syntax:

---

elementID.seekActiveTime(*param1*)

---

param1   Required; an integer between 0 and the element's activeDur property value.

Example:

```
<html xmlns:t="urn:schemas-microsoft-com:time">
<head><?import namespace="t" implementation="#default#time2">
<style>.time{behavior:url(#default#time2)}</style></head>
<body><button onclick="myVideo.seekActiveTime(5);">SeekActiveTime(5)</button>
<button onclick="myVideo.seekTo(1, 5);">SeekTo(1, 5)</button>
<button onclick="myVideo.seekToFrame(5);">SeekToFrame(5)</button>
<button onclick="myVideo.seekSegmentTime(5);">SeekSegmentTime(5)</button>
<t:video id="myVideo" src="yourvideo.avi"/>
</body></html>
```

Applies to:

<t:animate/>, <t:animatecolor/>, <t:animatemotion/>, <t:animation>, <t:audio/>,
<t:img>, <t:media>, <t:par>, <t:ref>, <t:seq>, <t:set/>, <t:transitionfilter/>,
<t:video/>

---

seekSegmentTime()

Compatibility: IE5.5, IE6

This method starts playing the animation at the point in its timeline that corresponds to the specified segmentTime property value.

Syntax:

---

elementID.seekSegmentTime(*param1*)

---

param1   Required; an integer between 0 and the element's segmentDur property value.

Example: See the seekActiveTime() method example.
Applies to:

<t:animate/>, <t:animatecolor/>, <t:animatemotion/>, <t:animation>, <t:audio/>,
<t:img>, <t:media>, <t:par>, <t:ref>, <t:seq>, <t:set/>, <t:transitionfilter/>,
<t:video/>

---

seekTo()

Compatibility: IE5.5, IE6

This method starts playing the animation at the point in its timeline that corresponds to the specified iteration number and the specified segmentTime property value.

Syntax:

```
elementID.seekTo(param1, param2)
```

param1   Required; the iteration number.

param2   Required; an integer between 0 and the element's segmentDur property value.

Example: See the seekActiveTime() method example.
Applies to:

```
<t:animate/>, <t:animatecolor/>, <t:animatemotion/>, <t:animation>, <t:audio/>,
<t:excl>, <t:img>, <t:media>, <t:par>, <t:ref>, <t:seq>, <t:set/>,
<t:transitionfilter/>, <t:video/>
```

seekToFrame()

Compatibility: IE5.5, IE6

This method starts playing the animation at the point in its timeline that corresponds to the specified frame.
Syntax:

```
elementID.seektoFrame(param1)
```

param1   Required; the starting frame number.

Example: See the seekActiveTime() method example.
Applies to:

```
<t:animate/>, <t:animatecolor/>, <t:animatemotion/>, <t:animation>, <t:audio/>,
<t:excl>, <t:img>, <t:media>, <t:par>, <t:ref>, <t:seq>, <t:set/>, <t:video/>
```

segmentTimeToActiveTime()

Compatibility: IE5.5, IE6

This method returns the element's activeTime property value that corresponds to the specified segmentTime property value.
Syntax:

```
elementID.segmentTimeToActiveTime(param1)
```

param1   Required; an integer between 0 and the element's segmentDur property value.

Example: See the activeTimeToSegmentTime() method example.
Applies to:

```
<t:animate/>, <t:animatecolor/>, <t:animatemotion/>, <t:animation>, <t:audio/>,
<t:excl>, <t:img>, <t:media>, <t:par>, <t:ref>, <t:seq>, <t:set/>,
<t:transitionfilter/>, <t:video/>
```

Compatibility: IE5.5, IE6

This method returns the element's simpleTime property value that corresponds to the specified segmentTime property value.

Syntax:

elementID.segmentTimeToSimpleTime(*param1*)

param1   Required; an integer between 0 and the element's segmentDur property value.

Example:

```
<html xmlns:t="urn:schemas-microsoft-com:time">
<head><?import namespace="t" implementation="#default#time2">
<style>.time{behavior:url(#default#time2);}</style>
<script language="JavaScript">
function B1(myElement) {
var m = myAnim.currTimeState.segmentTime; myElement.innerText = m;}
function B2(myElement) {
var m = myAnim.currTimeState.activeTime; myElement.innerText = m;}
function B3(myElement) {
var m=myAnim.segmentTimeToSimpleTime(myDiv.currTimeState.activeTime);
myElement.innerText = m;}
function B4(myElement) {
var m=myAnim.simpleTimeToSegmentTime(myDiv.currTimeState.activeTime);
myElement.innerText = m;}
</script></head>
<body>
<p>SegmentTime:<span class="time" dur=".5" repeatCount="indefinite"
onrepeat="B1(this);">0</span></p>
<p>ActiveTime:<span class="time" dur=".5" repeatCount="indefinite"
onrepeat="B2(this);">0</span></p>
<p>SegmentTimeToActiveTime:<span class="time" dur=".5" repeatCount="indefinite"
onrepeat="B3(this);">0</span></p>
<p>SegmentTimeToSimpleTime:<span class="time" dur=".5" repeatCount="indefinite"
onrepeat="B4(this);">0</span></p>
<div id="myDiv" class="time" style="position:relative; top:10; left:10; height:100;
width:200; background-color:red;"></div>
<t:animatemotion id="myAnim" targetElement="myDiv" to="320,200" begin="2" dur="5"
autoreverse="true" repeatcount="indefinite"/>
</body></html>
```

Applies to:

<t:animate/>, <t:animatecolor/>, <t:animatemotion/>, <t:animation>, <t:audio/>, <t:excl>, <t:img>, <t:media>, <t:par>, <t:ref>, <t:seq>, <t:set/>, <t:transitionfilter/>, <t:video/>

setActive()

Compatibility: IE5.5, IE6

This method sets the active item in the `playList` collection to the specified `playItem` object.

Syntax:

```
elementID.playList[index].setActive()
```

Example (use the ASX file listed in the abstract property example):

```html
<html xmlns:t="urn:schemas-microsoft-com:time">
<head><?import namespace="t" implementation="#default#time2">
<style>.time{behavior:url(#default#time2);}</style></head>
<body><t:media id="myMedia" begin="0" src="myasx.asx"/>
<button onclick="myMedia.playList.item(1).setActive();">Start track 2</button>
</body></html>
```

Applies to:

```
playItem
```

simpleTimeToSegmentTime()

Compatibility: IE5.5, IE6

This method returns the element's `segmentTime` property value that corresponds to the specified `simpleTime` property value.

Syntax:

```
elementID.simpleTimeToSegmentTime(param1)
```

param1   Required; an integer between 0 and the element's `simpleDur` property value.

Example: See the `segmentTimeToSimpleTime()` method example.
Applies to:

```
<t:animate/>, <t:animatecolor/>, <t:animatemotion/>, <t:animation>, <t:audio/>,
<t:excl>, <t:img>, <t:media>, <t:par>, <t:ref>, <t:seq>, <t:set/>,
<t:transitionfilter/>, <t:video/>
```

JavaScript Collections

This section of the chapter contains all HTML+TIME-related JavaScript collections. Each collection has a list of properties and methods that can be used with the collection. The properties are listed by name (for example, `length`), and the methods are listed by name followed by parentheses (for example, `item()`).

activeElements

Compatibility: IE5.5, IE6

This collection returns either a zero-based array of all animation elements that are currently active or the particular active element specified by the index parameter.

Syntax:

```
elementID.activeElements
elementID.activeElements(index)
```

Example:

```
<html xmlns:t="urn:schemas-microsoft-com:time">
<head><?import namespace="t" implementation="#default#time2">
<style>.time{behavior:url(#default#time2);}</style></head>
<body>
<button onclick="alert(myAnim.activeElements.length);">ActiveElements</button>
<button onclick="alert(document.body.timeAll.length);">TimeAll</button>
<button onclick="alert(myAnim.timeChildren.length);">TimeChildren</button>
<t:seq id="myAnim" begin="0">
<div class="time" dur="3" style="position:relative; top:10; left:10; height:100;
width:200; background-color:red;"></div>
<div class="time" dur="3" style="position:relative; top:10; left:10; height:100;
width:200; background-color:blue;"></div>
<div class="time" dur="3" style="position:relative; top:10; left:10; height:100;
width:200; background-color:yellow;"></div>
<div class="time" dur="3" style="position:relative; top:10; left:10; height:100;
width:200; background-color:green;"></div>
</t:seq></body></html>
```

Applies to:

```
<t:excl>, <t:par>, <t:seq>
```

Properties and methods:

```
length, item()
```

playList

Compatibility: IE5.5, IE6

This collection returns either a zero-based array of all playItem objects in playList, or the particular playItem object specified by the index parameter. This collection is only available while the parent element is active.

Syntax:

```
elementID.playList
elementID.playList(index)
```

Example (use the ASX file listed in the abstract property example):

```
<html xmlns:t="urn:schemas-microsoft-com:time">
<head><?import namespace="t" implementation="#default#time2"></head>
<body>
<t:video id="myVideo" begin="0" src="myasx.asx" end="indefinite"/>
<button onclick="alert(myVideo.playList.length);">Length</button><br>
</body></html>
```

Applies to:

`<t:audio/>`, `<t:media>`, `<t:ref>`, `<t:video/>`

Properties and methods:

`activeTrack, dur, item(), length, nextTrack(), prevTrack()`

timeAll

Compatibility: IE5.5, IE6

This collection returns either a zero-based array of all active and inactive timed elements, or the particular timed element specified by the index parameter.
Syntax:

```
elementID.timeAll
elementID.timeAll(index)
```

Example: See the activeElements collection example.
Applies to:

`<body>`, `<t:excl>`, `<t:par>`, `<t:seq>`

Properties and methods:

`item(), length`

timeChildren

Compatibility: IE5.5, IE6

This collection returns either a zero-based array of all active and inactive timed first-generation child elements or the particular timed first-generation child element specified by the index parameter.
Syntax:

```
elementID.timeChildren
elementID.timeChildren(index)
```

Example: See the activeElements collection example.

Applies to:

```
<body>, <t:excl>, <t:par>, <t:seq>
```

Properties and methods:

```
item(), length
```

JavaScript Objects

This section of the chapter contains all HTML+TIME-related JavaScript objects. Any properties and methods that belong to these objects are listed here as well.

currTimeState

Compatibility: IE5.5, IE6

This object contains information about the current animation.

Syntax:

```
elementID.currTimeState.propertyName
```

Example:

```
<html xmlns:t="urn:schemas-microsoft-com:time">
<head><?import namespace="t" implementation="#default#time2">
<style>.time{behavior:url(#default#time2);}</style></head>
<body><button onclick="alert(myDiv.currTimeState.activeTime);">Active time</button>
<div id="myDiv" class="time" style="position:relative; top:10; left:10; height:100;
width:200; background-color:red;"></div>
<t:animatemotion id="myAnim" targetElement="myDiv" to="320,200" begin="2" dur="5"
autoreverse="true" repeatcount="indefinite"/>
</body></html>
```

Applies to:

```
<t:animate/>, <t:animatecolor/>, <t:animatemotion/>, <t:audio/>, <t:img>,
<t:media>, <t:par>, <t:ref>, <t:seq>, <t:set/>, <t:transitionfilter/>, <t:video/>
```

JavaScript properties:

```
activeDur, activeTime, isActive, isMuted, isOn, isPaused, parentTimeBegin,
parentTimeEnd, progress, repeatCount, segmentDur, segmentTime, simpleDur,
simpleTime, speed, state, stateString, volume
```

playItem

Compatibility: IE5.5, IE6

This object contains information about a single track in a playList collection.

Syntax:

```
elementID.playList(index).memberName
elementID.playList.activeTrack.memberName
```

Example (use the ASX file listed in the abstract property example):

```
<html xmlns:t="urn:schemas-microsoft-com:time">
<head><?import namespace="t" implementation="#default#time2"></head>
<body>
<t:video id="myVideo" begin="0" src="myasx.asx" end="indefinite"/>
<button onclick="alert(myVideo.playList.activeTrack.Banner);">Banner</button>
<button onclick="alert(myVideo.playList(1).BannerAbstract);">BannerAbstract</button>
</body></html>
```

Applies to:

```
playList*
```

JavaScript properties:

```
abstract, author, Banner, BannerAbstract, BannerMoreInfo, begin, copyright, dur,
end, index, rating, src, timeContainer, title, type
```

JavaScript methods:

```
setActive()
```

INDEX OF HTML, CSS, AND JAVASCRIPT LISTINGS

O

THE BOOK OF JAVASCRIPT
A Practical Guide to Interactive Web Pages

by THAU!

NOVEMBER 2000, 400 PP. W/CD, $29.95 ($46.50 CDN)
ISBN 1-886411-36-0

"*The Book of JavaScript* shines. [It's] an outstanding model for teaching language by example." — *Web Techniques*

This tutorial/reference teaches JavaScript with real-world examples so you can learn how to work with image swaps, functions, frames, cookies, alarms, and more. Bestseller.

THE ART OF INTERACTIVE DESIGN
A Euphonious and Illuminating Guide to Building Successful Software

by CHRIS CRAWFORD

JANUARY 2003, 408 PP., $29.95 ($44.95 CDN)
ISBN 1-886411-84-0

An understanding of what makes things interactive is key to the successful creation of websites, computer games, and software. In *The Art of Interactive Design*, Chris Crawford explains what interactivity is, how it works, why it's important, and how to design good software applications and websites that are truly interactive.

STEAL THIS COMPUTER BOOK 3
What They Won't Tell You About the Internet

by WALLACE WANG

MAY 2003, 384 PP., $24.95 ($37.95 CDN)
ISBN 1-59327-000-3

This offbeat, non-technical book looks at what hackers do, how they do it, and how you can protect yourself. The third edition of this bestseller (over 150,000 copies sold) is updated to cover rootkits, spyware, web bugs, identity theft, hacktivism, wireless hacking (wardriving), biometrics, and firewalls.

HACKING THE XBOX
An Introduction to Reverse Engineering

by ANDREW "BUNNIE" HUANG

JULY 2003, 288 PP., $24.99 ($37.99 CDN)
ISBN 1-59327-029-1

"*Hacking the Xbox* (No Starch Press) is fast becoming the bible of a controversial geek movement called mod-chipping." — *Rolling Stone*

A hands-on guide to hardware hacking and reverse engineering using Microsoft's Xbox video game console. Covers basic hacking techniques such as reverse engineering and debugging, as well as Xbox security mechanisms and other advanced hacking topics. Includes a chapter written by the Electronic Frontier Foundation (EFF) about the rights and responsibilities of hackers.

HACKING
The Art of Exploitation

by JON ERICKSON

NOVEMBER 2003, 264 PP., $39.95 ($59.95 CDN)
ISBN 1-59327-007-0

A comprehensive introduction to the exploitation techniques and creative problem-solving methods known as "hacking." Explains technical aspects of hacking such as stack based overflows, heap based overflows, string exploits, return-into-libc, shellcode, and cryptographic attacks on 802.11b.

PHONE:
1 (800) 420-7240 OR
(415) 863-9900
MONDAY THROUGH FRIDAY,
9 A.M. TO 5 P.M. (PST)

FAX:
(415) 863-9950
24 HOURS A DAY,
7 DAYS A WEEK

EMAIL:
SALES@NOSTARCH.COM

WEB:
HTTP://WWW.NOSTARCH.COM

MAIL:
NO STARCH PRESS
555 DE HARO ST, SUITE 250
SAN FRANCISCO, CA 94107
USA

UPDATES

Visit **http://www.nostarch.com/wpdr.htm** for updates, errata, and other information.